September 23-26, 2014
Toronto, ON, Canada

Association for
Computing Machinery

Advancing Computing as a Science & Profession

MobileHCI'14

Proceedings of the 16th ACM International Conference on Human-Computer Interaction with Mobile Devices and Services

Sponsored by:

ACM SIGCHI

Contributors:

GRAND, MEIC, Flybits, Wavefront, iCanada Alliance, MaRS Innovation, Ryerson University, OCAD University, and George Brown College

Association for
Computing Machinery

Advancing Computing as a Science & Profession

The Association for Computing Machinery
2 Penn Plaza, Suite 701
New York, New York 10121-0701

ISBN: 978-1-4503-3004-6 (Digital)

ISBN: 978-1-4503-3368-9 (Print)

Additional copies may be ordered prepaid from:

ACM Order Department
PO Box 30777
New York, NY 10087-0777, USA

Phone: 1-800-342-6626 (USA and Canada)
+1-212-626-0500 (Global)
Fax: +1-212-944-1318
E-mail: acmhelp@acm.org
Hours of Operation: 8:30 am – 4:30 pm ET

Printed in the USA

MobileHCI 2014 Chairs' Welcome

On behalf of the organising and program committees for MobileHCI'14 we welcome you to Toronto, Canada, for the 16th International Conference on Human-Computer Interaction with Mobile Devices and Services. This year is particularly exciting given Toronto hosted CHI here earlier this year and now we return for this conference, the premier forum for innovations in mobile, portable and personal devices and with the services to which they enable access.

MobileHCI brings together people from diverse areas, which provides a multidisciplinary forum for academics, hardware and software developers, designers and practitioners to discuss the challenges and potential solutions for effective interaction with and through mobile devices, applications, and services.

The research community maintains a strong interest and commitment to the field with 211 paper submissions (134 full and 77 short). In the other submission categories we received 41 poster submissions, 11 demonstrations and mobile experience submissions, 8 doctoral consortium submissions, 16 industrial case study submissions, and 10 workshop submissions. This represents a doubling of industrial case study papers and a 5% increase in full paper submissions on 2013.

Our 26-member international program committee completed a peer review process involving a broad reach into the research community, with over 390 experts asked to provide reviews. Three external reviewers first reviewed each anonymous submission, and a meta-review was provided by a program committee member along with a further review by a second program committee member. The program committee met in person in Toronto, Canada, on Sunday, April 27th, to select the papers for the conference. This face-to-face committee meeting provided the opportunity to discuss the papers, expert reviews, and discussions and to reach a final consensus. In addition it allowed us to clarify papers to be shepherded, improvements to be made and to form the initial sessions for the conference. Submissions were finally accepted only after the authors provided a final revision addressing the committee's comments.

After this review process, the program committee accepted 45 papers (35 full papers and 10 short papers). The topics in the paper program, which are clustered into their respective sessions, include social networks, input and interaction, devices and interaction design, context awareness, 3D, e-learning, gesture interaction, user centered design, gesture and text entry, recommender systems and CSCW.

This year the program committee gave best paper awards to the authors of two papers, "An In-Situ Study of Mobile Phone Notifications" and "ProactiveTasks: the Short of Mobile Device Use Sessions" along with five further honorable mentions. These awards and honorable mentions represent a special recognition of excellence and come from the entire program committee that were guided by nominations from the external experts and committee.

In addition to our 45 papers it is our great pleasure to introduce the rest of this year's program which includes, 5 workshops on mapping, self-reflection, socio-technical practices, older adults and mobile healthcare, 4 tutorials on tangible interaction, mobile health, wearable computing and speech, 20 posters, 9 demonstrations and mobile experiences, 8 doctoral consortium papers, 5 industrial case studies, 7 design competition and future innovations along with a panel on mobile health in Canada. Our dedicated demonstrations and poster reception will allow you to see many of these parts of the program in more detail.

In addition we are pleased to have two keynotes this year:

- *Collective Mobile Interaction in Urban Spaces by Amahl Hazelton, Producer, Urban Spaces 2.0, Moment Factory*
- *Spaces of Innovation in Complex UX Design, Mark Vanderbeeken, CEO, Experientia*

Amahl Hazelton works at the convergence of art, event entertainment, architecture, urban design and digital technology. With a Masters degree in Urban Planning from McGill University, he is interested in new kinds of urban place making defined as much by digital technology and experience as by physical form. Inspiring urban gatherings, the technology /city interfaces that he directs cross technical boundaries, integrating massive urban projections with smart handset based control systems. X-Agora by Moment Factory is a scalable, connected, real time media management and playback system that can integrate motion sensors, video screens, and projectors with smartphone sensors, multi-media tools and data sources.

Mark Vanderbeeken will describe Spaces of Innovation in Complex UX Design. Leading practice in mobile user experience design presents complex opportunities and challenges not always fully revealed in academic exploration and research. Addressing users with cultural and behavioral differences; understanding economic imbalances and wide demographic ranges amongst individuals and networks; including ethical considerations such as right to privacy and confidentiality, authorship, and transparency; perception and cognition; larger sustainability concerns; and understanding often ignored biases within the client group - these many factors define the contemporary user experience design landscape. How can we create a space for innovation that takes these constraints and people's context and aspirations into account? Mark will illustrate these challenges with examples from Experientia's practice, particularly through a project they recently conducted with Intel.

Finally, a conference such as MobileHCI relies on the efforts of a large group of people willing to help, so we would like to firstly thank our volunteers, external expert reviewers, program committee and our entire organising committee of chairs for their tireless efforts over the past year. We thank all of our sponsors and donors for their financial and logistical support and the ACM without which we could not put this conference together.

Everyone attending and presenting at this conference should be justifiably excited and intrigued by the directions where MobileHCI is taking us. As Bill Buxton recently tweeted “Unless we think of “mobile” as an adverb (applied to human activity), rather than a noun (a thing), we will get the technology wrong”. We hope you enjoy all aspects of the MobileHCI 2014 program, and that you get to enjoy your time in Toronto seeing a city, which embraces the mobile experience.

Aaron Quigley
MobileHCI'14 General Chair
University of St Andrews, UK

Sara Diamond
MobileHCI'14 General Chair
OCAD, Toronto, Canada

Pourang Irani
MobileHCI'14 Papers Chair
University of Manitoba, Canada

Sriram Subramanian
MobileHCI'14 Papers Chair
University of Bristol, UK

Table of Contents

User-Centered Design

Session Chair: Per Ola Kristensson *(St. Andrews University)*

Input and Interaction

Session Chair: Stephen Brewster *(University of Glasgow)*

Gesture & Text-Entry

Session Chair: Michael Rohs *(Leibniz Universitat Hannover)*

Recommender Systems and CSCW

Session Chair: Rodrigo de Oliveira *(Google)*

Doctoral Consortium

Session Chairs: Stephen Brewster *(University of Glasgow)* & Keith Cheverst *(University of Lancaster)*

Demonstrations

Session Chairs: Markus Rittenbruch *(Queensland University of Technology)* & Jason Alexander *(Lancaster University)*

Poster Presentations

Session Chairs: Enrico Rukzio *(Hasselt University)* & Johannes Schöning *(University of Ulm)*

Tutorials

Session Chairs: Andrés Lucero *(University of Southern Denmark* & Karen Church *(Yahoo! Research)*

Workshop Summaries

Session Chairs: Sven Kratz *(FX Palo Alto Laboratory)* & Jürgen Steimle *(Max Planck Institute for Informatics)*

Design Competition & Future Innovations

Session Chairs: Geoffrey Shea *(OCAD University)* & Teri Rueb *(University at Buffalo)*

Industrial Case Studies

Session Chairs: Rodrigo de Oliveira *(Google)* & Jeffrey Nichols *(IBM Research Almaden)*

MobileHCI 2014 Conference Organization

Conference Chairs: Aaron Quigley *(University of St. Andrews, UK)*
Sara Diamond *(OCAD University, Canada)*

Papers Chairs: Pourang Irani *(University of Manitoba, Canada)*
Sriram Subramanian *(University of Bristol, UK)*

Local Arrangements Chair: Helmut Reichenbächer *(OCAD University, Canada)*

Workshop Chairs: Sven Kratz *(FX Palo Alto Laboratory, USA)*
Jürgen Steimle *(Max Planck Institute for Informatics, Germany)*

Demonstrations and Mobile Experience Chairs: Markus Rittenbruch *(Queensland University of Technology, Australia)*
Jason Alexander *(Lancaster University, UK)*

Design Competition and Future Innovations Chairs: Geoffrey Shea *(OCAD University, Canada)*
Teri Rueb *(University at Buffalo, USA)*

Interactive Tutorial Chairs: Andrés Lucero *(University of Southern Denmark, Denmark)*
Karen Church *(Yahoo Research, USA)*

Posters Chairs: Enrico Rukzio *(University of Ulm, Germany)*
Johannes Schöning *(Hasselt University, Belgium)*

Industrial Case Studies and Exhibit Chairs: Rodrigo de Oliveira *(Google, USA)*
Jeffrey Nichols *(IBM Research Almaden, USA)*

Doctoral Consortium Chairs: Stephen Brewster *(University of Glasgow, UK)*
Keith Cheverst *(University of Lancaster, UK)*

Doctoral Consortium Panelists: Parisa Eslambolchilar *(University of Swansea, UK)*
Antonio Kruger *(DFKI, Germany)*
Pourang Irani *(University of Manitoba, Canada)*
Simon Robinson *(University of Swansea, UK)*

Sponsorship Chair: Hossein Rahnama *(Ryerson Digital Media Zone, Canada)*

Keynote Chair: Herbert Enns *(University of Manitoba, Canada)*

Publicity Chair: Cosmin Munteanu *(National Research Council - Institute for Information Technology, Canada)*

E-Publication Chair: Deborah Fels *(Ryerson University, Canada)*

Volunteer Chairs: Martha Ladly *(OCAD University, Canada)*
Ross McLachlan *(University of Glasgow, UK)*

Web Chair: Khalad Hasan *(University of Manitoba, Canada)*

Registration Chair: Daniel Rough *(University of St Andrews, UK)*

Steering Committee Chair: Michael Rohs *(Leibniz Universität Hannover, Germany)*

Program Committee: Jason Alexander *(Lancaster University, UK)*
Elizabeth Bales *(University of California San Diego, USA)*
Sebastian Boring *(University of Copenhagen, Denmark)*
Karen Church *(Yahoo! Labs, USA)*
Edward Cutrell *(Microsoft ,USA)*
Alexander De Luca *(University of Munich, Germany)*
Audrey Girouard *(Carleton University, Canada)*
Juan David Hincapié-Ramos *(University of Manitoba, Canada)*
Johan Kildal *(Nokia Research, Finland)*
David Kirk *(Newcastle University, UK)*
Antonio Krüger *(DFKI/Saarland University, Germany)*
Yang Li *(Google Research, USA)*
Karon MacLean *(University of British Columbia, Canada)*
David McGookin *(Heriot-Watt University, UK)*
Antti Oulasvirta *(Max Planck Institute for Informatics, Germany)*
Jeffrey Pierce *(Samsung, USA)*
Derek Reilly *(Dalhousie University, Canada)*
Enrico Rukzio *(Ulm University, Germany)*
Alireza Sahami Shirazi *(University of Stuttgart, Germany)*
Dominik Schmidt *(Hasso Plattner Institute, Germany)*
Johannes Schöning *(Hasselt University, Belgium)*
Marcos Serrano *(University of Toulouse, France)*
Daniel Spelmezan *(University of Bristol, UK)*
Keith Vertanen *(Montana Tech, USA)*
Graham Wilson *(University of Glasgow, UK)*
Xing-Dong Yang *(University of Alberta, Canada)*

On-site Management and Planning: Ann Corbitt *(OCAD University, Canada)*
Pineda, Christine *(OCAD University, Canada)*

MobileHCI 2014 Additional Reviewers

Rachel Adler *(Northeastern Illinois University, USA)*
Ana Afonso *(Universidade de Lisboa, Portugal)*
David Ahlström *(Alpen-Adria University of Klagenfurt, Austria)*
Teemu Ahmaniemi *(Nokia Research Center, Finland)*
Florian Alt *(University of Munich, Germany)*
Fraser Anderson *(University of Alberta, Canada)*
Paul Andra *(Facebook, USA)*
Adrienne Andrew *(University of Washington, USA)*
Michelle Annett *(University of Alberta, Canada)*
Antti Oulasvira *(Max-Planck-Institut für Informatik, Germany)*
Caroline Appert *(Univ Paris-Sud, France)*
Ahmed Arif *(Ryerson University, Canada)*
Rosa Arriaga *(Georgia Institute of Technology, USA)*
Bhuvaneswari Arunachalan *(OCAD University, Canada)*
Amna Asif *(University of Oldenburg, Germany)*
Kumaripaba Athukorala *(Helsinki Institute for Information Technology HIIT, Finland)*
Matthew Aylett *(CereProc Ltd., UK)*
Shiri Azenkot *(University of Washington, USA)*
Gilles Bailly *(CNRS, France)*
Ravin Balakrishnan *(University of Toronto, Canada)*
Shumeet Baluja *(Google, USA)*
Nikola Banovic *(Carnegie Mellon University, USA)*
Xuan Bao *(Duke University, USA)*
Louise Barkhuus *(Stockholm University, Sweden)*
Ralph Barthel *(Centre for Advanced Spatial Analysis, UK)*
Tom Bartindale *(Newcastle University, UK)*
Agathe Battestini *(Nokia Research Center, USA)*
Kathy Baxter *(Google.com, USA)*
Ben Bedwell *(University of Nottingham, UK)*
Jessica Beltran *(Centro de Investigación Científica y Educación Superior, Mexico)*
Arne Berger *(Chemnitz University of Technology, Germany)*
Xiaojun Bi *(Google, California)*
Andrea Bianchi *(Korean Advanced Institute of Science and Technology, Korea)*
Gerald Bieber *(Fraunhofer IGD, Germany)*
Jon Bird *(City University London, UK)*
Jan Blom *(Nokia Research Center, Switzerland)*
Matthias Böhmer *(German Research Center for Artificial Intelligence (DFKI), Germany)*
Susanne Boll *(University of Oldenburg, Germany)*
David Bonnet *(Univ Paris-Sud, France)*
Anders Bouwer *(University of Amsterdam, The Netherlands)*
Cristian Bravo-Lillo *(Carnegie Mellon University, USA)*
Stephen Brewster *(University of Glasgow, UK)*
Anke Brock *(IRIT, France)*
Gregor Broll *(DOCOMO Euro-Labs, Germany)*
Barry Brown *(University of California San Diego, USA)*
Gerd Bruder *(University of Würzburg, Germany)*
Duncan Brumby *(University College London, UK)*
George Buchanan *(City University London, UK)*
Andrea Bunt *(University of Manitoba, Canada)*
Stefano Burigat *(University of Udine, Italy)*
Gary Burnett *(University of Nottingham, UK)*
Daniel Buschek *(University of Munich (LMU), Germany)*
Xiang Cao *(Lenovo Research & Technology, China)*
Scott Carter *(FXPAL, USA)*
Steven Castellucci *(York University, Canada)*
Jessica Cauchard *(Cornell Tech, USA)*
Alan Chamberlain *(The University of Nottingham, UK)*
Olivier Chapuis *(Univ Paris-Sud, France)*
David Chatting *(Newcastle University, UK)*
Alex Qiang Chen *(Nanyang Technological University, Singapore)*
Xiang 'Anthony' Chen *(Carnegie Mellon University, USA)*
Fanny Chevalier *(University of Toronto, Canada)*
Keith Cheverst *(Lancaster University, UK)*
Mark Chignell *(University of Toronto, Canada)*
Parmit Chilana *(University of Waterloo, Canada)*

Ming Ki Chong *(Lancaster University, UK)*
Delphine Christin *(Technische University of Darmstadt, Germany)*
Yu Shan Chuang *(eBay Inc., USA)*
James J. Clark *(McGill University, Canada)*
Graeme Coleman *(University of Dundee, UK)*
Ashley Colley *(University of Oulu, Finland)*
Christian Corsten *(RWTH Aachen University, Germany)*
Paul Coulton *(Lancaster University, UK)*
Celine Coutrix *(Helsinki Institute for Information Technology (HIIT), Finland)*
Lisa Cowan *(University of California, USA)*
Anna Cox *(University College London, UK)*
Henriette Cramer *(Yahoo Labs, USA)*
Paolo Cremonesi *(Politecnico di Milano)*
Andrew Crossan *(University of Glasgow, UK)*
Yanqing Cui *(Nokia Research Center, Finland)*
Mary Czerwinski *(Microsoft Research, USA)*
Florian Daiber *(DFKI GmbH, Germany)*
Nicola Dell *(University of Washington, USA)*
Carrie Demmans Epp *(University of Toronto, Canada)*
Brian DeRenzi *(University of Washington, USA)*
Anind Dey *(Carnegie Mellon University, USA)*
Christina Dicke *(Technical University Berlin, Germany)*
Sarah Diefenbach *(Folkwang University of the Arts, Germany)*
Tawanna Dillahunt *(University of Michigan, USA)*
Xianghua Ding *(Fudan University, China)*
Tilman Dingler *(University of Stuttgart, Germany)*
Anke Dittmar *(University of Rostock, Germany)*
Afsaneh Doryab *(Carnegie Mellon University, USA)*
Jakub Dostal *(University of St Andrews, UK)*
Andre Doucette *(University of Saskatchewan, Canada)*
John Dowell *(University College London, UK)*
Bruno Dumas *(Vrije Universiteit Brussel, Belgium)*
Mark Dunlop *(University of Strathclyde, UK)*
Paul Dunphy *(Newcastle University, UK)*
Abigail Durrant *(Newcastle University, UK)*
Florian Echtler *(Siemens Corporate Technology, Germany)*
Darren Edge *(Microsoft Research Asia, China)*
Keith Edwards *(Georgia Institute of Technology, USA)*
Chris Elsden *(Newcastle University, UK)*
Arvid Engström *(Mobile Life at Interactive Institute, Sweden)*
Barrett Ens *(University of Manitoba, Canada)*
Daniel Epstein *(University of Washington, USA)*
Georg Essl *(University of Michigan, USA)*
Siamak Faridani *(UC Berkeley, USA)*
Shelly Farnham *(Microsoft Research, USA)*
Pedro Ferreira *(Mobile Life @ KTH, Sweden)*
Bruce Ferwerda *(Johannes Kepler University, Austria)*
Andrea Finke *(Bielefeld University, Germany)*
Joel Fischer *(The University of Nottingham, UK)*
George Fitzmaurice *(Autodesk, Canada)*
Rowanne Fleck *(University College London, UK)*
Eelke Folmer *(University of Nevada, Nevada)*
Jutta Fortmann *(University of Oldenburg, Germany)*
Mike Fraser *(University of Bristol, UK)*
Dustin Freeman *(University of Toronto, Canada)*
Euan Freeman *(University of Glasgow, UK)*
Andre Freire *(Federal University of Lavras, Brazil)*
Jon Froehlich *(University of Washington, USA)*
Mads Frost *(IT University of Copenhagen, Denmark)*
Krzysztof Gajos *(Harvard University, USA)*
Sven Gehring *(German Research Center for Artificial Intelligence, Germany)*
Hans Gellersen *(Lancaster University, UK)*
Darren Gergle *(Northwestern University, USA)*
Mayank Goel *(University of Washington, USA)*
Mikhail Goubko *(Institute of Control Sciences, Russia)*
Sandy Gould *(University College London, UK)*
Tiago Guerreiro *(IST/UTL Technical Superior Institute/ Technical University of Lisboa, Portugal)*
Serafima Gurevich *(Hasso Plattner Institute, Germany)*
Penny Hagen *(University of Technology, Australia)*
Jonna Häkkilä *(University of Oulu, Finland)*
Martin Halvey *(University of Strathclyde, UK)*
Tracy Hammond *(Texas A&M University, USA)*
Mark Hancock *(University of Waterloo, Canada)*
Mark Handel *(The Boeing Company, USA)*
Alina Hang *(University of Munich (LMU), Germany)*
Marian Harbach *(Leibniz University Hannover, Germany)*

John Hardy *(Lancaster University, UK)*
Chris Harrison *(Carnegie Mellon University, USA)*
Khalad Hasan *(University of Manitoba, Canada)*
Kirstie Hawkey *(Dalhousie University, Canada)*
Eiji Hayashi *(Carnegie Mellon University, USA)*
Eric Hekler *(Arizona State University, USA)*
Alexis Heloir *(DFKI, Germany)*
Niels Henze *(University of Stuttgart, Germany)*
Teruo Higashino *(Osaka University, Japan)*
Serena Hillman *(Simon Fraser University, Canada)*
Cristy Ho *(The University of Hong Kong, Hong Kong)*
Eve Hoggan *(Aalto University, Finland)*
Paul Holleis *(DOCOMO Euro-Labs, Germany)*
David Holman *(Queen's University, Ontario)*
Christian Holz *(Yahoo Labs, USA)*
Jason Hong *(Carnegie Mellon University, USA)*
Steven Houben *(IT University of Copenhagen, Denmark)*
Gary Hsieh *(University of Washington, USA)*
Sungjae Hwang *(Korea Advanced Institute of Science and Technology, Korea)*
Selim Ickin *(Blekinge Institute of Technology, Sweden)*
Petra Isenberg *(INRIA, France)*
Poika Isokoski *(University of Tampere, Finland)*
Giulio Jacucci *(Aalto University, Finland)*
Ashis Jalote-Parmar *(Delft University of Technology, The Netherlands)*
Daniel Jamieson *(Newcastle University, UK)*
Myounghoon Jeon *(Michigan Technological University, USA)*
Yingying Jiang *(Chinese Academy of Sciences, China)*
Priscilla Jimenez Pazmino *(University of Illinois at Chicago, USA)*
Lynette Jones *(Massachusetts Institute of Technology, USA)*
Matt Jones *(Swansea University, UK)*
Anirudha Joshi *(Indian Institute of Technology, Maharashtra)*
Oskar Juhlin *(Stockholm University)*
Marko Jurmu *(University of Oulu, Finland)*
Sanjay Kairam *(Stanford University, USA)*
Santosh Kalwar *(Lappeenranta University of Technology, Finland)*
Matthew Kam *(American Institutes for Research, USA)*
Ankit Kamal *(University of Waterloo, Canada)*
Dietrich Kammer *(Technische University of Dresden, Germany)*
Shaun Kane *(University of Maryland Baltimore County, USA)*
Gopinaath Kannabiran *(Indiana University Bloomington, USA)*
Amy Karlson *(University of Maryland, USA)*
Abhijit Karnik *(University of Bristol, UK)*
Thorsten Karrer *(RWTH Aachen University, Germany)*
Daniel Keefe *(University of Minnesota, USA)*
Frederic Kerber *(German Research Center for Artificial Intelligence (DFKI), Germany)*
Dagmar Kern *(Bertrandt Ingenieurbuero GmbH, Germany)*
Wolf Kienzle *(Microsoft Research, USA)*
Juho Kim *(Massachusetts Institute of Technology, USA)*
Sunyoung Kim *(Carnegie Mellon University, USA)*
Kenrick Kin *(University of California, California)*
Jesper Kjeldskov *(Aalborg University, Denmark)*
Christian Koehler *(Carnegie Mellon University, USA)*
Lisa Koeman *(University College London, UK)*
Ilpo Koskinen *(University of Art and Design Helsinki, Finland)*
Matthias Kranz *(University of Passau, Germany)*
Sven Kratz *(FX Palo Alto Laboratory, USA)*
Per Ola Kristensson *(University of St Andrews, UK)*
Jens Kruger *(University Duisburg-Essen, Germany)*
Katherine Kuchenbecker *(University of Pennsylvania, USA)*
Hannu Kukka *(University of Oulu, Finland)*
Anuj Kumar *(Carnegie Mellon University, USA)*
Neha Kumar *(University of California, California)*
Kai Kunze *(Osaka Prefecture University, Japan)*
Stacey Kuznetsov *(Carnegie Mellon University, USA)*
Diana Laffler *(University of Würzburg, Germany)*
Bireswar Laha *(Virginia Polytechnic Institute and State University, USA)*
Shyong Lam *(Google, USA)*

James Michael Lampinen *(University of Arkansas, USA)*
Christian Lander *(German Research Center for Artificial Intelligence (DFKI), Germany)*
Nicholas Lane *(Microsoft, USA)*
Vuokko Lantz *(Nokia Research Center, Finland)*
Mark LaRosa *(University of Michigan, USA)*
Kevin Larson *(Microsoft Research, USA)*
Walter Lasecki *(University of Rochester, USA)*
Effie Law *(ETH Zurich, Switzerland)*
David Ledo *(University of Calgary, Canada)*
Geehyuk Lee *(Korea Advanced Institute of Science and Technology, Korea)*
Sang-su Lee *(Korea Advanced Institute of Science and Technology, Korea)*
Seungyon "Claire" Lee *(Google, USA)*
Luis A. Leiva *(Universitat Politècnica de València, Spain)*
Pascal Lessel *(Saarbruecken Graduate School of Computer Science, Germany)*
Kevin Li *(AT&T Labs - Research, USA)*
Hai-Ning Liang *(Xi'an Jiaotong-Liverpool University, China)*
Lassi Liikkanen *(Helsinki Institute for Information Technology HIIT, Finland)*
Brian Lim *(Fraunhofer Center for Sustainable Energy Systems, USA)*
David Lindlbauer *(Technical University Berlin, Germany)*
Siân Lindley *(Microsoft Research, UK)*
Li Liu *(Utah Valley University, USA)*
Markus Löchtefeld *(Lancaster University, UK)*
Diana Löffler *(University of Würzburg, Germany)*
Hao Lu *(Google, USA)*
Andrés Lucero *(Nokia Research Center, Finland)*
Kris Luyten *(Hasselt University - tUL - iMinds, Belgium)*
Bonnie MacKay *(Dalhousie University, Canada)*
Scott MacKenzie *(York University, Canada)*
Charlotte Magnusson *(Certec, Lund University, Sweden)*
Julie Maitland *(Populus Global Solutions Inc., Canada)*
Sylvain Malacria *(University College London, UK)*
Heiko Maller *(OFFIS - Institute for Information Technology, Germany)*
Anders Markussen *(University of Copenhagen, Denmark)*
Diogo Marques *(University of Lisbon, Portugal)*
Elena Marquez Segura *(Uppsala University, Sweden)*
Kevin Marshall *(Newcastle University, UK)*
Mark Marshall *(Sheffield Hallam University, UK)*
Paul Marshall *(University of Warwick, UK)*
Benoit Martin *(University de Lorraine, France)*
Rene Mayrhofer *(Lancaster University, UK)*
Marilyn McGee-Lennon *(University of Glasgow, UK)*
Mark McGill *(University of Glasgow, UK)*
William McGrath *(Stanford University, USA)*
Joanna McGrenere *(University of British Columbia, Canada)*
Ross McLachlan *(University of Glasgow, UK)*
Amir Meghdadi *(University of Manitoba, Canada)*
Florian Michahelles *(PCCV, Switzerland)*
Manas Mittal *(UC Berkeley EECS, USA)*
Andreas Moeller *(Technische University of Munich, Germany)*
Karyn Moffatt *(McGill University, Canada)*
Andrew Molineux *(Lancaster University, UK)*
Tomer Moscovich *(INRIA, France)*
Martin Murer *(University of Salzburg, Austria)*
Matei Negulescu *(University of Waterloo, Canada)*
Carman Neustaedter *(Simon Fraser University, Canada)*
Alexander Ng *(University of Glasgow, UK)*
Chuong Nguyen *(MPI Informatik, Germany)*
Jeffrey Nichols *(IBM Research - Almaden, USA)*
Hugo Nicolau *(University of Dundee, UK)*
Oded Nov *(Polytechnic University, USA)*
Petteri Nurmi *(Helsinki Institute for Information Technology, Sweden)*
Stina Nylander *(Swedish Institute of Computer Science, Sweden)*
Marita O'Brien *(University of Alabama-Huntsville, USA)*
Marianna Obrist *(University of Sussex, UK)*
Nuria Oliver *(Telefonica R&D, Spain)*
Stephen Oney *(Carnegie Mellon University, USA)*

Ant Ozok *(University of Maryland, Baltimore County, USA)*
Sabrina Panëels *(McGill University, Canada)*
Denise Paradowski *(German Research Center for Artificial Intelligence, Germany)*
Tapan Parikh *(UC Berkeley, USA)*
Eunil Park *(Sungkyunkwan University, Korea)*
Andrea Parker *(Northeastern University, USA)*
David Parsons *(Massey University, New Zealand)*
Kurt Partridge *(Google, California)*
Fabio Praternã *(CNR-ISTI, Italy)*
Jennifer Pearson *(Swansea University, UK)*
Simon Perrault *(National University of Singapore, Singapore)*
Mark Perry *(Brunel University, UK)*
Max Pfeiffer *(Leibniz University Hannover, Germany)*
Ken Pfeuffer *(Lancaster University, UK)*
Bastian Pfleging *(University of Stuttgart, Germany)*
Martin Pielot *(Telefonica Research, Spain)*
Thomas Pietrzak *(Université Lille 1, France)*
Beryl Plimmer *(The University of Auckland, New Zealand)*
Henning Pohl *(University of Hannover, Germany)*
Benjamin Poppinga *(OFFIS - Institute for Information Technology, Germany)*
Andy Pruett *(Georgia Institute of Technology)*
Philip Quinn *(University of Canterbury, New Zealand)*
Mashfiqui Rabbi *(Cornell University, USA)*
Raf Ramakers *(Hasselt University - tUL - iMinds, Belgium)*
Bhaskaran Raman *(Indian Institute of Technology Bombay, India)*
Gonzalo Ramos *(Microsoft Corporation, USA)*
Jussi Rantala *(University of Tampere, Finland)*
Umar Rashid *(University of Kent, UK)*
Mathieu Raynal *(University of Toulouse, France)*
Janet Read *(University of Central Lanncashire)*
Philippe Renevier Gonin *(Université Nice Sophia Antipolis, France)*
Andreas Riener *(Johannes Kepler University Linz, Austria)*
Simon Robinson *(Swansea University, UK)*
Yvonne Rogers *(University College London, UK)*
Michael Rohs *(University of Hannover, Germany)*
Christine Rosakranse *(Stanford University, USA)*
Stephanie Rosenthal *(Carnegie Mellon University, USA)*
Anne Roudaut *(University of Bristol, UK)*
Duncan Rowland *(University of Lincoln, UK)*
Jaime Ruiz *(Colorado State University, USA)*
Mohamad Salimian *(Research assistant at Dalhousie University, Canada)*
Antti Salovaara *(Aalto University, Finland)*
Corina Sas *(Lancaster University, UK)*
Martina Angela Sasse *(University College London, UK)*
Florian Schaub *(Carnegie Mellon University, USA)*
Falko Schmid *(University of Bremen, Germany)*
Stefan Schneegass *(University of Stuttgart, Germany)*
Oliver Schoenleben *(Max Planck Institut for Informatik, Germany)*
m.c. schraefel *(University of Southampton, UK)*
Johann Schrammel *(CURE - Center for Usability Research & Engineering, Austria)*
Julia Schwarz *(University of Washington, USA)*
Marcello Paolo Scipioni *(University of Lugano, Switzerland)*
Stacey Scott *(University of Waterloo, Canada)*
Julian Seifert *(Ulm University, Germany)*
Dvijesh Shastri *(University of Houston - Downtown, USA)*
Yuanchun Shi *(Tsinghua University, China)*
Buntarou Shizuki *(University of Tsukuba, Japan)*
Adalberto Simeone *(Lancaster University, UK)*
Rainer Simon *(Austrian Institute of Technology, Austria)*
Thomas Smyth *(Simon Fraser University, Canada)*
Hyunyoung Song *(University of Maryland, USA)*
Kevin Stanley *(University of Saskatchewan, Canada)*
Danae Stanton Fraser *(University of Bath, UK)*
Katarzyna Stawarz *(University College London, UK)*
Sophie Stellmach *(Technische Universitet Dresden, Germany)*
Steve Szigeti *(OCAD University, Canada)*
Aurélien Tabard *(University of Munich (LMU), Germany)*

Faisal Taher *(Lancaster University, UK)*
Federico Tajariol *(Université de Franche-Comté, France)*
Anthony Tang *(University of Calgary, Canada)*
Craig Tashman *(Georgia Institute of Technology, USA)*
Nick Taylor *(University of Dundee, UK)*
Smyth Thomas (*Georgia Institute of Technology, USA*)
Janko Timmermann *(OFFIS - Institute for Information Technology, Germany)*
Kashyap Todi *(Hasselt University - tUL - iMinds, Belgium)*
Chad Tossell *(Rice University, USA)*
Matthieu Trudeau *(University of Calgary, Canada)*
Philippe Truillet *(IRIT CNRS, France)*
Manfred Tscheligi *(University of Salzburg, Austria)*
Edward Tse *(SMART Technologies, Canada)*
Nikolaos Tselios *(University of Patras, Brazil)*
Brygg Ullmer *(Louisiana State University, USA)*
Heli Väätäjä *(Tampere University of Technology, Finland)*
Rajan Vaish *(University of California, USA)*
Dimitar Valkov *(University of Muenster, Germany)*
Radu-Daniel Vatavu *(University Stefan cel Mare of Suceava, Romania)*
Yolanda Vazquez-Alvarez *(University of Glasgow, UK)*
Eduardo Velloso *(Lancaster University, UK)*
Nervo Verdezoto *(Aarhus University, Denmark)*
Himanshu Verma *(EPFL, Switzerland)*
Jo Vermeulen *(Hasselt University - tUL - iMinds, Belgium)*
Akos Vetek *(Nokia Research Center, Finland)*
Chi Vi *(University of Bristol, UK)*
Jane Vincent *(University of Surrey, UK)*
Dong-Bach Vo *(Telecom Paristech, France)*
Juergen Vogel *(Bern University of Applied Sciences, Switzerland)*
Amy Voida *(Indiana University, Indiana)*
Stephen Voida *(Indiana University, USA)*
Emanuel von Zezschwitz *(University of Munich, Germany)*
Chat Wacharamanotham *(RWTH Aachen University, Germany)*
Julie Wagner *(INRIA, France)*
James Wallace *(University of Waterloo, Canada)*
Robert Walter *(Telekom Innovation Laboratories, Germany)*
Marion Walton *(University of Cape Town, South Africa)*
Xiying Wang *(Cornell University, USA)*
Peter Wardrip *(University of Pittsburgh, USA)*
Carolyn Wei *(Facebook, USA)*
Alexandra Weilenmann *(IT-University of Göteborg, Sweden)*
Danielle Wilde *(RMIT University, Australia)*
Kim Willems *(Vrije Universiteit Brussel, Belgium)*
Kaiton Williams *(Cornell University, USA)*
John Williamson *(University of Glasgow, UK)*
Max Wilson *(Swansea University, UK)*
Christian Winkler *(Ulm University, Germany)*
Katrin Wolf *(University of Stuttgart, Germany)*
Gavin Wood *(Newcastle University, UK)*
Andy Wu *(Georgia Institute of Technology, USA)*
Susan Wyche *(Michigan State University, USA)*
Robert Xiao *(Carnegie Mellon University, USA)*
Koji Yatani *(Microsoft Research Asia, China)*
Tom Yeh *(University of Colorado, USA)*
Chuang-wen You *(Academia Sinica, Taiwan)*
Massimo Zancanaro *(FBK-irst, Italy)*
Jian Zhao *(University of Toronto, Canada)*
Shengdong Zhao *(National University of Singapore, Singapore)*

MobileHCI 2014 Sponsor & Supporters

Sponsor: SIGCHI

Supporters: GRAND (Graphisme, animation et nouveaux médias / Graphics, Animation and New Media), MEIC, Flybits (inspiring mobility™), wavefront (accelerating wireless innovation & commercialization for Canada), i-CANADA ALLIANCE, MaRS Innovation

Institutional donor/supporters: Ryerson University (Everyone Makes a Mark), OCAD U, George Brown College

Collective Mobile Interaction for Urban Spaces

Amahl Hazelton
Producer, Urban Spaces 2.0
Moment Factory
Montreal, Quebec, Canada
amahl@momentfactory.com
http://www.momentfactory.com
http://xagora.ca/

Author Keywords
Urban Design and Digital Technology; Smart Handset interaction with Urban Screens; Multi-Media Environments

ACM Classification: H.5.m

MobileHCI 2014, September 23–26, 2014, Toronto, ON, Canada.
ACM 978-1-4503-3004-6/14/09.
http://dx.doi.org/10.1145/2628363.2634235

Abstract
Amahl Hazelton works at the convergence of art, event entertainment, architecture, urban design and digital technology. With a Masters degree in Urban Planning from McGill University, he is interested in new kinds of urban place-making defined as much by digital technology and experience as by physical form. Inspiring urban gatherings, the technology / city interfaces that he directs cross technical boundaries, integrating massive urban projections with smart handset based control systems. X-Agora by Moment Factory is a scalable, connected, real time media management and playback system that can integrate motion sensors, video screens, and projectors with smartphone sensors, multi media tools and data sources.

Related Work
Moment Factory has created urban sound and light spectacles around the world, including Barcelona, Dubai, Los Angeles, Montreal, New York, Ottawa, Rome, Rotterdam, Shanghai, Vancouver, and Valencia, and stage shows for Madonna, Arcade Fire, and Bon Jovi. Their fully interactive stage design for NineInchNails and Chris Milk was recognized by LiveDesign as one of the top-10 concert experiences in the history of rock music.

Speaker's Bio

Amahl Hazelton is a producer at Moment Factory specializing in the conception and production of multimedia environments combining video, lighting, architecture, sound and special effects to create remarkable experiences. Additional background information:

Current: Owner at Bridgenorth Group, Producer, Urban Spaces 2.0 at Moment Factory, Director, Project Development at Nordpont Management Past:Vice President, Conseil d'administration at Fondation de la Cinémathèque Québécoise, Vice-President, Board of Directors at Fondation de la Cinéma... Education: McGill University, McGill University, Cairine Wilson Secondary School.

Identity, Identification and Identifiability: The Language of Self-Presentation on a Location-Based Mobile Dating App

Jeremy Birnholtz
Department of Communication Studies
Northwestern University
Evanston, IL 60208
jeremyb@northwestern.edu

Colin Fitzpatrick
Technology & Social Behavior Program
Northwestern University
Evanston, IL 60208
fitzcn@u.northwestern.edu

Mark Handel
The Boeing Company
handel@gmail.com

Jed R. Brubaker
Dept. of Informatics
University of California - Irvine
Irvine, CA 92697
jed.brubaker@uci.edu

ABSTRACT
Location-aware mobile applications have become extremely common, with a recent wave of mobile dating applications that provide relatively sparse profiles to connect nearby individuals who may not know each other for immediate social or sexual encounters. These applications have become particularly popular among men who have sex with men (MSM) and raise a range of questions about self-presentation, visibility to others, and impression formation, as traditional geographic boundaries and social circles are crossed. In this paper we address two key questions around how people manage potentially stigmatized identities in using these apps and what types of information they use to self-present in the absence of a detailed profile or rich social cues. To do so, we draw on profile data observed in twelve locations on Grindr, a location-aware social application for MSM. Results suggest clear use of language to manage stigma associated with casual sex, and that users draw regularly on location information and other descriptive language to present concisely to others nearby.

Author Keywords
Online dating; self-presentation; sex; MSM; impression formation

ACM Classification Keywords
H.4.3. Communications Applications

INTRODUCTION
Location-aware mobile devices have become ubiquitous in recent years and are a common mechanism for initiating social interactions with both known contacts [22] and nearby strangers with similar interests [30] or who are involved in shared activities [21] .

In particular, dating sites and applications have become extremely popular in recent years, with 30% of opposite-sex and 70% of same-sex couples reporting having met online in a recent survey [27]. One type of mobile application that has gained recent traction is what Handel and Shklovski [13] refer to as the location-based real-time dating (LBRTD) app. These apps are used to locate and interact with nearby strangers who are interested in meeting, often soon, for a date or sexual encounter.

They typically work by displaying photos of nearby users, which can be clicked to reveal a more detailed profile and initiate immediate interaction via text chat. These applications stand in contrast to traditional dating sites which are typically PC/browser-based and where people might engage in weeks or months of online interaction prior to meeting face-to-face [24].

A key challenge in using mobile apps for meeting others is self-presentation. In contrast to traditional dating applications, where users can craft a richer presentation of self through their profiles and online interactions (e.g., [5]), mobile LBRTD apps rely heavily on images and comparatively simple profiles with limited opportunities for expression and self-presentation [1, 11].

While some LBRTD apps (e.g., Tinder) have recently become popular for people seeking opposite-sex partners, there is a longer history of these types of apps (e.g., Jack'd, Scruff, Mister and Grindr) being used by men who have sex with men (MSM) [1, 11, 26, 35]. This prior work notes that, in part, this history stems from two attributes of MSM. First, interest in sex with other men is not a visible trait, so LBRTD apps can help MSM identify each other. Second, interest in sex with men is a trait individuals choose to reveal to others. Self-presentation can then be an important strategy in avoiding stigma or unwanted attention.

These attributes, moreover, can be important in the formative stages of developing identity, exploring sexuality and "coming out" [29]. These might also be important for people engaged in behavior, such as seeking casual sex, that might be normatively acceptable among MSM LBRTD app users (e.g., [26]) but stigmatized by others [3].

Although the majority of the North American users of these systems would self-identify as "gay," a significant minority still do not use that label. Traditionally, the public health literature has used the term MSM to encompass both groups. We adopt that convention in this work as well.

MobileHCI 2014, September 23–26, 2014, Toronto, ON, Canada.

http://dx.doi.org/10.1145/2628363.2628406

In the paper that follows, we present an analysis of the language used in self-presentation profiles on Grindr, an LBRTD app for MSM. By examining structured and free text elements of user profiles, we seek to better understand how users draw on language and other resources to present themselves in a novel reduced-cue environment.

BACKGROUND

There have been numerous studies of self-presentation tactics on social networks (e.g., [19]) and online dating sites [5, 15, 24, 31]. In general these have found that people carefully select content to share with others to evoke a positive response either from friends (in the network case) or others (in the dating case). They may also embellish slightly, but within warranting constraints [34] and the possibility of a face-to-face meeting or trusting relationship [5]. There has been more limited study of people's language for presenting themselves on these sites and apps, focusing in particular on deception [31] and whether profiles contain words related to health issues or drug use [13].

From a self-presentation standpoint, mobile LBRTD apps raise multiple challenges. Given the physical constraints of a mobile device (e.g., screen size, etc.), people must present information very concisely. This is similar to the reduced cues environment of online chat rooms in Jones [17], where users move from abstract textual representations to more realized photographs, videos, and, at times, face-to-face interactions. LBRTD apps raise three unique questions around impression management where users may quickly from the abstract to the real or concrete. For each question, we draw on data from both large urban environments with diverse populations, and college or university towns where many people may see each other regularly and may also be exploring their sexuality or identity.

Appearing Attractive: Sharing Structured Information

Physical attractiveness has been shown to be a key trait in the success of online dating profiles [15]. On mobile LBRTD apps, attractiveness is typically conveyed via one's photograph and physical attributes entered into the structured elements of the profile [1]. Drawing on Goffman's [8] framework for self-presentation, these attributes in a mobile LBRTD become "given" aspects of impression in the decision to share them online, rather than "given off" in an in-person meeting. Though they are indicators of one's physical appearance (which is not typically malleable when it comes to matters of height and weight), they can be selectively or deceptively disclosed because of constrained cues of the online environment [17, 33].

These elements of the profile are important in mobile LBRTD apps for two reasons. First, they provide a concise summary of one's attributes and, ideally, an impression of attractiveness. Second, if one wishes to meet others face-to-face, the attributes must be reasonably accurate [32]. At the same time, they must also present the user in a positive light if they are to be effective. We therefore first asked:

RQ1: What types of information do mobile LBRTD app users share in the structured elements of the profile and what does this information communicate about them?

Language of Identification

In addition to structured parameters described above, people also have the opportunity to craft short text fragments that are part of their profiles in most LBRTD apps. Beyond creating the appearance of physical attractiveness, these can be used to craft a more detailed presentation. There are several ways in which we might expect this to occur. First, Goffman [8] suggests that setting plays an important part in impression formation. People may wish to identify themselves with their geographic location, such as a neighborhood, city or institution, an act that Jones terms social attraction, or relating oneself to a known group or entity [CITE]. This can serve to establish that they are nearby, and may also convey cues about socio-economic status, race, and other factors that can vary across geographic and institutional boundaries [16].

Identification with specific neighborhoods becomes problematic in many LBRTD apps, however, these apps do not reveal the actual location of others but instead reveal only the linear distance between the user and others signed in. That is, one can see who is nearby and one's distance from these users (in feet, meters, miles etc.), but cannot see their specific location or its name [1]. This differs from several prior location-aware technologies in which location names play a key role in both identifying the location of others for coordination and in self-presentation [12, 22].

In traditional dating sites, for example, people may identify with an explicit metropolitan area or geographic region. On social network sites people often identify with specific institutions (e.g., universities or employers) or cities and other places [19]. Check-in sites like Foursquare also allow people to identify with locations by checking in; and concerns about self-presentation have been shown to affect how people decide where to check in and how they form impressions of other users [12].

When identification cues are taken away, it is worthwhile for researchers and designers to explore how people respond. On the one hand, people might appreciate features that obfuscate location details and opt not to share these due to privacy or other concerns. On the other hand, they might seek strategies to re-insert this information for self-presentation, social attraction, or other goals. We asked:

RQ2: In the absence of overt location identifiers or descriptions, how do mobile LBRTD apps use language to craft identity around setting or other elements of self-presentation?

Seeking Sex? The Language of Stigma

Continuing to draw on Goffman's framework, cues related to sex and sexuality can be complicated in the case of mobile LBRTD apps for MSM. Drawing on Litt's [23] notion of the "imagined audience," we may consider that people exercise caution in self-presentation on LBRTDs because their ideal imagined audience of potential sex or dating partners may not correlate with the actual audience. This tension is likely to play out in several ways.

First, the notion of an MSM identity itself may be problematic for some in that it violates the norms or expectations of their social communities, in the sense described by Goffman's [9] notion of "stigma." These individuals, such as those on the "down low" described by King [18] or those who are exploring their identity [10, 29], may wish to avoid what Woo [36] refers to as "identifiability" on these apps. That is, they do not wish for their profile information to be easily traced back to their offline identity by others who may log into the app. Some may also wish to connect with others who are similarly concerned about discretion [18, 36].

Second, even for those who do not feel stigmatized, there is often concern about "slut shaming" or being perceived as one who frequently engages in casual sex [1, 3]. Thus, some users may be comfortable with the idea of appearing on an LBRTD app for MSM, but may seek to self-present in a way that distances them from seeking sex.

Third, despite the caveats above, users who are seeking sexual encounters may wish to present specific information about sexual preferences or characteristics specific to themselves [13]. Jones would describe this process as moving interactions from the abstract to the realized, and from social attraction to personal attraction. How they do so while balancing concerns around stigmatized identity, however, is an open question. We therefore asked:

RQ3: Is there evidence of stigma around sexuality for mobile LBRTD app users, and how do they manage it?

METHOD

About the App

Grindr, the LBRTD app we chose to study is one of the more popular MSM-oriented apps. These apps generally have a similar user interface, opening with a grid or list of a certain number of nearby users consisting of a thumbnail image, a username and very brief demographic information (e.g. age and height/weight, at most) for each. They allow the user to tap on a thumbnail to see a larger picture and more detailed description (see e.g., [1, 26] for more detail).

On Grindr, profile information consists of a user-chosen username (which can be omitted if desired); demographic details including age, height, weight, and ethnicity (Asian, black, Latino, Middle Eastern, Mixed, Native American, white, South Asian and other). The user can hide some or all of these attributes. In addition, there is a field called "Looking for," which includes a range of relationship types (from "chat" and "dates" to "friends" with multiple selections possible), and current relationship status (eight options, including "single," "dating," "married," and "open relationship;" this range is typical of MSM-oriented apps.) Both of these fields could also be set to "Do Not Show." Finally, there was an 80-character "headline," a 255-character "About me" section, and the full image of the thumbnail. App policy requires that users avoid explicit sexual images or text in their profile content.

Data Collection

Our data consist of observations gathered between January 13th and February 13th 2012 from Grindr. We were aware of ethical concerns raised in the past around the use of quasi-public profile data from social networking [37]. We believe it is reasonable to consider these data quasi-public as they are visible to anybody who downloads the free application, and users are instructed by Grindr's privacy policy to share no information that they do not consider to be or wish to be public.

At the same time, we do not wish to further share potentially sensitive information or in any way threaten the privacy of users or the integrity of the user community for the application we studied. In consultation with our Institutional Review Board, which approved this project, we do not report any profile details at the individual level that could in any way be identifying, relying instead on aggregate analyses or substituting similar terms where specific terms or details might be construed as identifying.

To gather data we used a custom-written Java application that emulated the Grindr client app. This application would log in every ten minutes, at a pre-determined, "pinned" location and gather information about all users visible from the pin location. Because of restrictions of the Grindr service, this would max out between 75-125 individuals. The information gathered included a unique user ID, distance from the application's location "pin," as well as their profile information. The profile information was collected anew at each ten-minute interval. We selected 12 locations, dividing these equally between large urban centers in North America, as well as cities and towns identified with large universities in the United States.

Because Grindr limits the number of users it displays, this in the large urban cities the "last" person on the list would often be less than 1km away from the pin, compared to 10-20km away from the pin in college towns. These locations were chosen to enable us to compare differences between urban and college town use of the app.

Analyses

Our data collection method allowed us to have several different units of analysis. For the population demographics, our unit of analysis is the unique user; regardless of the number of times the user was online, only the first observation was used.

We also did several textual analyses to learn about the content of the free text written by users. In these cases, our unit of analysis is the *distinct profile text*. Any change in the profile text (made up of the username, the headline and "about me" text) would generate a new distinct profile observation. So, this is more observations than unique users, but fewer than every incidence in the entire database. In general, profiles were not changed very often; across the entire set of urban and college town users, we saw about 15% of users change their profile at least once. However, the changes were often substantial. For instance, in one case the first profile included "*easy going and open minded,*" while the update was "*Not into hook-ups,*" showing a possible change in intentions in using the application. By capturing all variants of profiles, we can better understand the range of presentation styles. We explain details of each text analysis in the sections below.

RESULTS

Demographic statistics reported here are based on observations of 69,950 unique individual profiles observed in six college towns (23,530 profiles) around the midwest and southeast United States and six major urban areas (46,420 profiles) in the United States and Canada.

Structured Self-Presentation

We were first interested in what structured data people chose present, and how this varied across the two types of locations. Results can be seen in Table 1. We first look at general demographic traits overall, and for the specific locations. We note that – because people chose not to share certain traits – this is necessarily not an examination of the user base of this application, but rather an examination of the traits that people chose to share.

	College Town (N = 23591)			Urban (N = 47335)		
	Share	Mean	SD	Share	Mean	SD
Age	78.3%	28.7	8.9	76.5%	31.0	8.4
Height	82.1%	179.5	7.1	83.9%	178.9	6.9
Weight	71.2%	78.0	14.4	74.8%	75.8	12.0

Table 1. Age (in years), height (cm), weight (kg) and the fraction of users sharing each trait, by location type.

We first looked at general traits that people shared (see Table 1). A significant majority of people shared their age (77.0% overall), with similar fractions in both college towns (78.3%) and urban areas (76.5%). Not surprisingly the average age was lower for college towns (28.7 years) than for urban areas (31.0 years), but only by about 2 years.

Interestingly, when it came to physical attributes such as height and weight, both were shared by the majority of users but more people shared height (82.1% college towns; 83.9% urban) than shared weight (71.2% in college towns; 74.8% in urban). This likely reflects the importance of weight in assessing attractiveness of others. It is interesting, however, in that weight is a theoretically mutable trait that was frequently reported to be deceptive in prior studies of dating. Participants here may have found it more useful to simply exclude weight than to exaggerate or otherwise deceive others. As partial support for this argument, we note that the average weight reported by users (76.86 kg) is substantially less than the average for American men over 20 (88.3 kg, [25]). This stands in contrast to height, where the average height reported by users (178.8 cm) is nearly equal to the national average (176.3 cm).

As Table 2 shows, we looked at whether people shared ethnicity information. In both college towns (73.8%) and urban areas (72.7%), most users chose to share ethnicity or race. The vast majority of those who displayed ethnicity identified as white, though this fraction was higher in college towns (65.6%) than in urban areas (59.0%). The next most common reported ethnicity was "black" with 11.9% in college towns and 4.7% in urban areas.

	College town (N = 23591)	Urban (N = 47335)
Share ethnicity	73.8%	72.7%
Asian	2.4%	8.6%
Black	11.9%	4.7%
Latino	10.9%	14.7%
Middle Eastern	.41%	1.42%
Mixed	6.7%	9.1%
Native American	.4%	.2%
Other	1.5%	1.8%
South Asian	.2%	.4%
White	65.6%	59.0%
Share relationship status	61.5%	58.6%
Dating	2.3%	1.9%
Engaged	.3%	.2%
Exclusive	.9%	.6%
Married	1.4%	.9%
Open	2.5%	3.8%
Partnered	6.0%	5.9%
Single	85.1%	85.9%
Share relationship goals	61.%	54.6%
Friends	56.1%	47.5%
Chat	48.4%	38.5%
Dates	38.2%	38.2%
Networking	29.8%	26.7%
Relationship	27.4%	25.7%

Table 2. Profile attributes and fraction of users sharing each.

We next looked at whether people shared their relationship status. Again, this is an indicator of how people might wish to be perceived. For example, those seeking a relationship may be more likely to identify as "single," whereas those in relationships seeking extra-dyadic encounters (which are stigmatized by some) may be more likely to obfuscate by not sharing a relationship status. Overall, the proportion of users who shared any relationship status was slightly different between college towns (64.3%) and urban areas (58.4%).

Users generally reported being single in both college towns (85.1%) and urban areas (85.9%). The "open" option was not used frequently, but interestingly was used slightly more in urban (3.9%) than college town (2.5%) settings.

We next examined what relationship goals people expressed in using the app. Multiple goals can be expressed in the same profile via checkboxes. We view this as one indicator of how people wished to be seen as users of the app, and what sort of others they might be trying to attract.

As can be seen in Table 2, most users expressed at least one goal, with the fraction reporting being higher in college towns (61.6%) than in urban areas (54.6%). The distribution of goals varied somewhat according to the type of location being examined. While the distribution in both settings is skewed toward friends, it is more even across the different categories in urban environments.

To begin to address the issues in the next section on categorical self-impression using location words, we first wondered whether people allowed others to see their relative position (i.e., distance away). A significant majority of users shared relative position in both college towns (81.2%) and urban environments (83.4%), with similar proportions in both.

Language of Identification

To explore language use in profiles, we searched for any occurrence of words on several categorical lists (categories detailed below), for both the set of all college town (N=32,467) and urban (N=56,273) profiles containing free text. Each instance of a word was tracked, along with the total number of profiles containing at least one of the words in a category. One thing that became immediately clear in our analyses is that there was no apparently dominant strategy in linguistic self-presentation. All of the category analyses described below identified only 10-20% of profiles as using a particular approach. We describe the many approaches we observed.

	College Town (N=3795)	Urban (N=6493)
Neighborhood	22.4%	35.9%
Cities	29.2%	46.3%
States/provinces	28.0%	9.7%
Institutions	20.4%	8.1%

Table 3. Frequency of location and institution word usage.

Locative Language

We were interested in how users drew on language of places and locations to identify themselves in ways that identified them with these locations. To explore this question we first manually examined the text of the profiles in our data set as well as others visible to us through our own use of the app. Through this informal examination, found that users tended to identify with neighborhoods within cities, with cities or states (particularly when they were from elsewhere), and with institutions – particularly universities – in or around their location. We therefore created word lists at each of these levels of analysis. As Table 3 shows, we found that 3795 (11.7%) college town and 6493 (11.3%) urban profiles used location words.

Our list of 1565 neighborhoods was compiled by aggregating lists of neighborhoods from the Wikipedia page for each of the cities where data were collected. As Table 3 shows, of the profiles using at least one location word, 22.4% of college town and 35.9% of urban profiles used neighborhood words. Our list of cities included the 12 cities where we collected data (including common abbreviations and colloquialisms) plus cities in the vicinity of the college towns identified via maps and our own knowledge of the areas. Of the profiles using at least one location word, 36.4% of college town and 47.3% of urban profiles used city words. For states and provinces, we used a list of the 50 US states and all Canadian provinces and 2-letter postal abbreviations. We found that 28% of college town and 9.7% of urban profiles contained these terms.

Finally, we included institutions as locations because they are landmarks with which we found in our informal observations that people frequently seek to identify with. This could be particularly important from a self-presentation standpoint in college towns, where affiliation with a university can be a signal of socio-economic or educational status and where students may wish to meet only other students. We assembled a list of 33 educational institution names, abbreviations, and slang in and around the data gathering sites.Surprisingly, however, a relatively small fraction of college town profiles that used location words explicitly mentioned institutions (25.4%). This occurred much less frequently in urban profiles (8.2%).

From these data, there are two key observations. The first is intuitive in that neighborhoods seem to be used more for identification in larger cities than in smaller ones. From a location-awareness standpoint, this makes sense in that one may wish to signal to others that one is in or is from a particular neighborhood when seeking others or moving about a large urban area where displayed users may change more often given population density. Similarly, institutional identifiers were used much more often in college town profiles than in urban profiles, despite the presence of many universities in the cities where we gathered data. These could potentially be serving a locative function, but are more likely a way for students to identify each other and separate themselves from others in the area.

The second observation is less intuitive. Despite city words presumably being less useful as locative identifiers within cities themselves (i.e., when one is in Chicago, presumably everybody nearby is also in Chicago), they are actually used more frequently in urban environments than in college towns. This suggests that people are using city names for self-presentation, either within their city or when traveling.

To explore this possibility, we then looked for a set of 6 words related to travel and transience (i.e., "visiting," "in town," etc.). We found that 2.4% of college town (773) and 3.1% of urban (1762) profiles contained at least one of these terms. Of those profiles, "visiting" was by far the most common. It accounted for 86.2% and 89.5% of college and urban profiles respectively. We also looked for the co-occurrence of words related to transience along with the name of at least one city. These co-occurred in 13.3% (college town) and 17.7% (urban) of all city word uses.

	College Town (N=510)	Urban (N=1104)
Twink	11.0%	10.4%
Otter	8.8%	7.4%
Cub	3.7%	2.8%
Bear	14.9%	8.7%
Pup	1.0%	0.8%
Gym Bunny	0.2%	0.4%
Chub	1.2%	0.9%
Daddy	15.9%	15.5%
Gym Rat	2.7%	1.5%
Muscle	18.4%	42.0%
Wolf	3.3%	4.7%
Chaser	2.2%	2.0%
Bull	1.2%	0.5%
Average	21.8%	11.6%

Table 4. Frequency of body descriptor terms.

Personal Descriptors

Our informal observations suggested that people also used certain terms to describe themselves, in ways that were both physically descriptive or indicators of professional status.

For physical description, we compiled a list of words related to body type "cliques" (see Table 4). This list was assembled from the online Gay Cliques Census[1], which reflects historical, informal labels used among MSM (e.g., [20]). Again, a relatively small fraction of overall profiles contained at least one of these terms (3.0% college town; 4.1% urban). Of those who did include clique words, "muscle," occurred less often in college town (18.0%) than in urban settings (42.0%). In contrast to this, "average" (a body type not typically associated with substantial muscles) occurred more often in college towns (21.8%) than in urban settings (11.6%). Of other body type words, most others occurred at relatively similar frequencies with the exception of "bear," which occurred more frequently in college towns (14.9% vs. 8.7%). The key point here is that these category descriptors appear to be relatively universal in their usage in these locations, and that people clearly used these to self-present concisely.

In addition to physical descriptors, we also looked at categorical descriptors related to professional identity or educational status (see Table 5). We found that 6.0% of college town and 3.4% of urban profiles included at least one of these words. Not surprisingly, the words "college" and "student" occurred more often in college town profiles (57.1% "student"; 30.6% "college") than in urban profiles (30.6% "student"; 8.9% "college"). The opposite was true for the term "professional" (or "prof") and educated. Educated occurred in 11.6% of college town profiles and 22.3% of urban profiles; while "professional" occurred in 18.7% of college town profiles and 48.7% of urban profiles.

[1] http://www.studiomoh.com/fun/census/results.php

	College Town (N=1956)	Urban (N=1927)
College	21.5%	8.9%
Student	57.1%	30.6%
Professional	18.7%	48.7%
Educated	11.6%	22.3%

Table 5. Frequency of status words by location type.

What is interesting here is that the dominant terms both likely convey cues about status to the desired audience. Both students and professionals likely wish to meet others like themselves; these terms allow them to do so.

Language and Stigma

While we noted earlier that people used a wide range of linguistic strategies in self-presentation, we noticed that the most frequently occurring word across all profiles was "looking" (3951 appearances). This word likely occurs frequently because it has several meanings in this context, which were evident in our manual examination of profile text, experience with LBRTD apps, and in literature cited above. Specifically, "looking" can be used on it's own to indicate or verify that one is seeking an immediate sexual encounter (e.g., "looking now"), can be used to indicate what one seeks on the app (e.g., "looking for fun"), or can be used in the negative to indicate what one is *not* looking for on the app (e.g., "not looking for fun"). Given these potential meanings and relationships to adjacent words, we used a more detailed analytic approach.

Looking For "Looking For"

We ran a regular expression script to extract all words following the phrases "looking for" and "not looking for." We then used the frequencies of extracted words to generate an additional list of words for further analysis.

What is most striking in these results (see Figure 1) is the way in which people seem to manage potential stigma around seeking casual sex. Those who are seeking casual sex partners tend to use euphemistic terms (e.g., "fun") or abbreviations (e.g., "nsa," meaning "no strings attached"). Combined, these two terms occurred in 10.4% of college town and 14.1% of urban profiles that included a "looking" clause. The term "hookup" (and variants) was rarely (0.6% college town; 0.7% urban) used in a "looking" clause.

In contrast, people explicitly not seeking casual sex partners very rarely used euphemistic terms or abbreviations. "Fun" and "nsa" are used in a combined 0.0% of college town and 0.5% of urban profiles containing a "not looking for clause." Instead, these users tended to use the term "hookup" much more frequently, in 41.7% of college town and 25.2% of urban profiles containing a "not looking for"

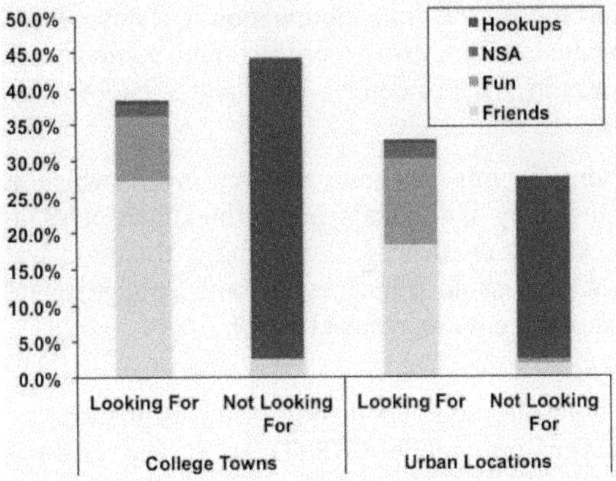

Figure 1. Terms in "looking for" and "not looking for" clauses, by location type.

clause. This is particularly interesting for college towns, where popular press reports suggest that slut shaming or other stigma related to sex might be a greater concern. Thus, people – and particularly those in college towns – seem to be carefully presenting themselves as not looking for casual sex to avoid potential stigma.

Another ambiguous term commonly used in "looking for" or "not looking for" clauses is "friends." Those looking for friends may be seeking genuine friendship, but may also be using the term euphemistically to refer to friendship with a sexual component (e.g., "friends with benefits;" see analysis below). Thus, as with other euphemistic terms potentially related to sex, we would expect to see a large number of people "looking for" friends and a small number of people who explicitly state that they are "not looking for" friends. Indeed, Figure 1 again reveals that this was the case, with 27.3% of college town and 18.2% of urban "looking for" clauses including friends, in contrast to only 2.6% and 1.8% of "not looking for" clauses, respectively.

No Means "No"

We were also interested in how people used the word "no." Again, this can be used in different ways. We found that 2637 college town (8%) and 5903 urban profiles (10.5%) had "no" clauses. The most common way to use a "no" clause was to specify an expectation that others have a face picture (or "pic") available if those others wished to chat or receive a reply. This is evident in that, of those profiles with "no" clauses, 7.5% (college town) and 12.2% (urban) contain "face;" 11.9% (college town) and 10.3% (urban) contain "pic(tures)" or "facepic;" 10.5% (college town) and 12.1% (urban) contain "chat;" and 5.5% (college town) and 5.2% contain "response." These are by far the most common words that occurred in "no" clauses.

The next most common use of "no" clauses was similar to the use of "not looking for" clauses (see above) to define oneself in opposition to certain traits or practices. Examples of terms in this category included "hookups" (10.6% college town; 6% urban) and "drugs" (0.6% college town; 1.6% urban. These terms serve to distance the user (and others' impressions, presumably) from stigmatized behaviors such as sex or drugs. Relatedly, some others used a "no" clause to mitigate or soften others' impressions of what they were looking for or how actively they were using the app. For example, several people said they had no "agenda" (2.6% college town; 1.5% urban) or "expectations" (1.9% college town; 2.2% urban).

Another common use for "no" clauses was to attempt pre-emptively to avoid interaction with certain others. While no single term was dominant in this regard, people used a wide range of terms. A few examples included: old(ies) (0.7% college town; 0.2% urban), fems/feminine/girly/flamers, referring to stereotypically feminine bodily presentation (1.5% college town; 0.7% urban), fat/chubs (0.4% college town; 0.2% urban), skinny (0.1% college town; 0% urban), married/partnered/couples (0.4% college town; 0.7% urban), smoking/smokers (0.2% college town; 0.4% urban), asians, (0.6% college town; 0% urban), and republicans (0.7% college town; 0.3% urban). These "no" clauses serve an interesting dual purpose from an impression management standpoint. On the one hand, it is may be okay if the categories of people named in the "no" clause form a negative impression of a user, because the user has no interest in them in the first place. On the other hand, the use of certain words in "no" clauses (particularly around sensitive categories such as race or body weight) may cause a negative impression to be formed even by desired others.

Finally, we saw people use "no" clauses to characterize the experience they sought via terms like attitude, bs, strings, games, and drama. Together, these occurred in 8.0% of college town and 4.7% of urban profiles with no clauses.

Discretion and Sex

Having established that many users sought to self-present using terms that referred to sex euphemistically or defined themselves in opposition to sex, many also did use language that indicated sexual preferences more explicitly. Using our initial examination of profiles and our experience as a guide, we aggregated a set of 18 common terms related to sex acts, preferences, and sexually-transmitted infections and HIV status. Of all the profiles we examined, 2227 (6.9%) of college town and 5643 (10.0%) contained at least one sex-related term. This difference likely reflects the concerns around slut shaming and community that are likely more prevalent in college environments or smaller communities, as discussed earlier.

Of those profiles that do contain sex-related terms, the most common terms are those related to preferred roles in sexual intercourse. These roles ("top" or "bottom") describe whether one plays a primarily penetrative (top) or primarily receptive (bottom) role. These terms (including variants e.g. "btm" or "bttm") combined were included in 89.4% of college town and 89.1% of urban profiles that contained sex words. There were substantially more profiles using "top" (55.3% college town; 52.7% urban) than "bottom" (34.4% college town; 36.4% urban).

	College Town (N=2227)	Urban (N=5643)
Making out/kissing	0.7%	1.7%
Positive	1.2%	0.5%
Bottom	34.4%	36.4%
Snuggle	8.1%	9.2%
FB	1.2%	1.0%
Oral	2.9%	1.5%
Negative	3.9%	9.0%
PNP	0.4%	2.1%
FWB	5.8%	2.6%
DDF	5.5%	4.4%
Top	55.3%	52.7%
Pitcher	0.5%	0.6%
Catcher	0.3%	0.8%

Table 6. Frequency of sex-related terms.

Other words related to sexual activities included cuddling/snuggling (8.1% college town; 9.2% urban) and oral (2.9% college; 1.5% urban). Another activity-related term was "pnp" (party n' play; a euphemistic term for drug use and sex together [7]), which occurred more often in urban profiles (2.1%) than in college town profiles (0.4%), though it did not occur frequently in either context.

There were a small number of profiles that mentioned disease or status. The most common of these was "ddf" ("drug and disease free"), which occurred in 5.5% of college town and 4.4% of urban profiles. Negative HIV status occurred in 3.9% of college town and 9.0% of urban profiles using sex terms, and positive status was mentioned in 1.2% of college town and 0.5% of urban profiles. Note that the Grindr app does not support an explicit field for drug use or HIV status, unlike some others.

	College Town (N=836)	Urban (N=743)
Closet	4.9%	2.8%
Not out	11.7%	3.8%
Discreet	67.2%	73.1%
DL	5.1%	5.7%
Curious	20.1%	19.1%

Table 7. Frequency of discretion and exploration words.

Finally, given the stigma associated with MSM identity and the exploratory nature of some sexual behavior, we aggregated terms related to exploration or discretion. As Table 7 shows, 2.6% of college town and 1.3% of urban profiles contained at least one of these terms. Of those profiles, a majority used terms related to discretion. The most common was "discreet" (often misspelled "discrete," but aggregated), which was used in 67.2% of college town and 73.1% of urban profiles. Interestingly, the terms "not out" (11.7% college town; 3.8% urban) and "closet" (4.9% college town; 2.8% urban) were used more often in college towns, likely suggesting that those in college towns may still be negotiating identity and coming out. The final term related to discretion, "dl," (an abbreviation for "down low," often associated with Afro-Americans and Latinos, see King[18]) was in 5.1% of college town and 5.7% of urban profiles.

The final term in this category was "curious," which is commonly used by individuals portraying themselves as exploring sexuality or identity. Surprisingly, this term was used at about the same frequency in both college towns (20.1%) and urban environments (19.1%).

DISCUSSION

We began with questions about impression formation and self-presentation on mobile LBRTD apps. Our findings have several implications for theories of social engagement using mobile devices and for designing novel mobile apps.

Implications for Theory

Grindr has provided us with an opportunity to explore behavior and assumptions around using mobile applications to meet others in an environment where some users are engaging in stigmatized behaviors or the application itself may be stigmatized in some ways. In using Grindr and apps like it, MSM manage disclosure and risk on several fronts.

Attractiveness and Rejection

The first is the risk of rejection by others. In disclosing information in their profiles that is likely to make the user seem attractive to others, and users arguably aim to make it more likely that their interactions will persist, and that they will transition from an online to face-to-face context when this is desirable. In contrast to the chat rooms observed by Jones [17], however, where most information was revealed progressively over the course of conversation, user profiles on Grindr can reveal substantial information about the user before conversation even begins.

For example, we saw users demarcate ties to particular subgroups that convey aspects of physical appearance (e.g., "muscle", "otter") but that retain anonymity around other aspects of identity. At the same time, we also saw users identify ties to groups or institutions that could be more revealing (e.g., "senior at *University X*").

Identifiability and Stigma

The second type of risk is that of identifiability [36] by others nearby, to whom users may not wish to disclose their interest in sex with men or that they are seeking casual sex partners [1]. This risk is related to notions of privacy on mobile devices in that it concerns the disclosure of personal or identifying information. What is distinct about identifiability, however, is that users in prior work were concerned not primarily by sharing the information with strangers, but rather by sharing it with those who might identify them.

Our results further support this idea in that we saw some users present profiles in a way that publicly distances themselves from stigmatized behaviors (e.g., hookups, homosexuality) for a broad and unknown audience, but may also provide enough detail to signal their actual intent to others (in ways analogous to social steganography [2]). When they find a potential partner, they can then gauge when it is appropriate to share additional details through more private channels.

There was a clear tension for people around sex and sexuality, particularly with regard to potentially stigmatized behavior such as casual sex or "hooking up." The results for "looking," "not looking" and "no" clauses are particularly telling here. Of those who used "not looking" clauses, the most popular term by far was "hookups," and these occurred frequently in "no" clauses as well. Very few participants, on the other hand, identified themselves as overtly looking for "hookups," using euphemisms such as "fun," "nsa," and "friends" instead.

These results suggest that, in theorizing about how people use mobile applications, we should consider the possibility of stigmatized behaviors or practices. When we consider dating applications, for example, the predominant focus has been on honesty or deception about physical traits or characteristics (e.g., [5, 31]). These settings, however, are importantly distinct from the case we studied here. With Grindr, people appear to be using euphemism as a strategy for negotiating the tension between what Litt [23] refers to as the imagined and actual audiences, or for separating facets of their online lives [6]. This tension is arguably particularly acute in a location-aware application that enables stigmatized behaviors, because one could be visible to neighbors or others who happen to be nearby.

Disclosing Location Information

There is also, of course, some potential risk from sharing location information, which has been identified in past work (e.g., [28])) as a significant user concern even when sharing location with known contacts. We note, however, that this concern has largely not arisen in studies of how MSM use location-aware technologies [1, 11, 26], and does not seem to have hindered widespread adoption of Grindr and related apps.

Contrary to concerns expressed in prior studies about location privacy, in fact, we actually saw our participants re-insert elements of location details that were blurred by Grindr's sharing of only distance information. They did this by using neighborhoods, city names and institutions to identify with these and send signals that would otherwise be obscured by the way Grindr handles location information.

The behavior we observed, in light of past location privacy concerns, suggests that, as we think about the ways that location information is used by mobile apps, it is important to distinguish between notions of knowing that somebody is nearby (as in Grindr), knowing where somebody is in the sense of their geographic coordinates, and knowing the socially defined space that somebody currently identifies with [14]. In some ways, this revives old questions about places and spaces by providing new technological ways of understanding proximity and location. It also raises questions about how people identify location to others in systems that represent location in different ways [4].

Limitations & Future Work

There are several limitations to consider when interpreting these results. One clear limitation is that analysis of profile text does not allow us to verify that app users had particular intentions. Our results are consistent with initial qualitative explorations of apps for MSM in work cited above, but additional qualitative work is needed to understand people's self-presentation tactics. In addition, usage patterns in our data set could be used to understand if self presentation varies by time: would users on a break at work present differently than a user coming home from a bar or club.

In addition, we used relatively simple analysis techniques in understanding the profile data. We attempted automated classification of profiles for more sophisticated analysis, but had some difficulties. We used emergent text categorization algorithms, Latent Dirichlet Allocation and the Correlated Topic Model algorithms. Results were not stable but were indicative of several categories. Based on an analysis of these suggestions, we created a set of six categories, and attempted to hand code. However, two coders were unable to achieve good agreement. Preliminary analysis suggested that the profiles often had aspects of multiple categories. We encourage more sophisticated analysis of self-presentation tactics in these apps, however, to understand how language is used to create different impressions. A first step in this direction may be to examine the features implemented across the different apps available and compare and contrast how they may affect impression formation and management.

ACKNOWLEDGEMENTS

This work was supported in part by a grant from the Sexualities Project at Northwestern.

REFERENCES

1. Blackwell, C., Birnholtz, J. and Abbott, C. Seeing and being seen: co-situation and impression formation in a location-aware gay dating app. *New Media and Society* (in press).
2. boyd, d. and Marwick, A. Social Steganography: Privacy in Networked Publics. Paper presented at the . *International Communication Association* 2011.
3. Conley, T. D. Perceived proposer personality characteristics and gender differences in acceptance of casual sex offers. *Journal of Personality and Social Psychology*, 100(2011), 309-329.
4. Cramer, H., Rost, M. and Holmquist, L. Performing a check-in: emerging practices, norms and 'conflicts' in location-sharing using foursquare. In *Proc. Mobile HCI* (2011), 57-66.
5. Ellison, N. B., Hancock, J. T. and Toma, C. Profile as Promise: A Framework for Conceptualizing Veracity in Online Dating Self-Presentations. *New Media and Society*, 14, 1 (2012), 45-62.

6. Farnham, S. D. and Churchill, E. Faceted identity, faceted lives: social and technical issues with being yourself online. In *Proc. ACM CSCW* (2011), 359-368.

7. Frederick, B. *Partying with a purpose: Finding meaning in an online "party n' play" subculture*. Thesis. California State University, Long Beach, Long Beach, CA, 2012.

8. Goffman, E. *The presentation of self in everyday life*. Anchor Books, New York, 1959.

9. Goffman, E. *Stigma: notes on the management of spoiled identity*. Prentice-Hall, Englewood Cliffs, N.J. , 1963.

10. Gray, M. L. *Out in the country: youth, media, and queer visibility in rural America*. NYU Press, New York, 2009.

11. Gudelunas, D. There's an app for that: The uses and gratifications of online social networks for gay men. *Sexuality and Culture*, 16(2012), 346-365.

12. Guha, S. and Birnholtz, J. Can you see me now? Location, visibility and the management of impressions on foursquare. In *Proc. Mobile HCI* (2013), 183-192.

13. Handel, M. and Shklovski, I. Disclosure, ambiguity & risk reduction in real-time dating sites. In *Proc. ACM GROUP* (2012), 175-178.

14. Harrison, S. and Dourish, P. Re-place-ing space: the roles of place and space in collaborative systems. In *Proc. ACM CSCW* (1996), 67-76.

15. Hitsch, G., Hortacsu, A. and Ariely, D. What makes you click? Mate preferences in online dating. *Quantitative Marketing Economics*, 8(2010), 393-427.

16. Johnston, L. and Longhurst, R. *Space, place and sex*. Rowman & Littlefield, Lanham, MD, 2010.

17. Jones, R. H. 'You show me yours, I'll show you mine': the negotiation of shifts from textual to visual modes in computer-mediated interaction among gay men. *Visual Communication*, 4, 1 (2005), 69-92.

18. King, J. L. *On the down low: a journey into the lives of 'straight' black men who sleep with men*. Three Rivers Press, New York, 2005.

19. Lampe, C., Ellison, N. and Steinfield, C. A familiar face(book): profile elements as signals in an online social network. In *Proc. ACM CHI* (2007), 435-444.

20. Levesque, M. and Vichesky, D. Raising the bar on the body beautiful: An analysis of the body image concerns of homosexual men. *Body Image*, 3, 1 (2006), 45-55.

21. Licoppe, C. and Inada, Y. Geolocalized technologies, location aware communities and personal territories: The Mogi case. *Journal of Urban Technology*, 15, 3 (2008), 5-24.

22. Lindqvist, J., Cranshaw, J., Wiese, J., Hong, J. and Zimmerman, J. I'm the mayor of my house: examining why people use foursquare - a social-driven location sharing application. In *Proc. ACM CHI* (2011), 2409-2418.

23. Litt, E. Knock, Knock. Who's There? The Imagined Audience. *Journal of Broadcasting & Electronic Media*, 56, 3 (2012), 330-345.

24. Mascaro, C., Magee, R. and Goggins, S. Not just a wink and smile: an analysis of user-defined success in online dating. In *Proc. iConference 2012* (2012), 200-206.

25. McDowell, M., Fryar, C., Ogden, C. and Flegal, K. *Anthropometric Reference Data for Children and Adults: United States, 2003–2006* Centers for Disease Control and Prevention National Center for Health Statistics, 2008.

26. Mowlabocus, S. *Gaydar culture: gay men, technology and embodiment in the digital age*. Ashgate, Burlington, VT, 2010.

27. Rosenfeld, M. J. and Thomas, R. J. Searching for a mate: the rise of the Internet as a social intermediary. *American Sociological Review*, 77, 4 (2012), 523-547.

28. Sadeh, N., Hong, J., Cranor, L. F., Fette, I., Kelley, P., Prabaker, M. and Rao, J. Understanding and capturing people's privacy policies in a mobile social networking application. *Personal and Ubiquitous Computing*, 13, 6 (2009), 401-412.

29. Savin-Williams, R. C. *The new gay teenager*. Harvard University Press, Cambridge, Mass., 2005.

30. Sutko, D. M. and de Souza e Silva, A. Location aware mobile media and urban sociability. *New Media and Society*, 13, 5 (2011), 807-823.

31. Toma, C. and Hancock, J. T. What lies beneath: The linguistic traces of deception in online dating profiles. *Journal of Communication*, 62, 1 (2012), 78-97.

32. Toma, C., Hancock, J. T. and Ellison, N. Separating fact from fiction: an examination of deceptive self-presentation in online dating profiles. *Personality and Social Psychology Bulletin*, 34(2008), 1023-1036.

33. Turkle, S. *Life on the screen: identity in the age of the Internet*. Simon & Schuster, New York, 1995.

34. Walther, J. and Parks, M. Cues filtered out, cues filtered in: Computer-mediated communication and relationships. In M. L. Knapp and J. A. Daly, ed. *Handbook of Interpersonal Communication*. Sage, Thousand Oaks, CA, 2002.

35. Woo, D. *Meet Grindr: How one app changed the way we connect*. Amazon Digital Services, 2013.

36. Woo, J. The right not to be identified: privacy and anonymity in the interactive media environment. *New Media & Society*, 8, 7 (2006), 949-967.

37. Zimmer, M. "But the data is already public": on the ethics of research in Facebook. *Ethics and Information Technology*, 12, 4 (2010), 313-325.

Understanding Localness of Knowledge Sharing: A Study of Naver KiN "Here"

Sangkeun Park, Yongsung Kim, Uichin Lee, Mark S. Ackerman[†]
Department of Knowledge Service Engineering, KAIST
[†]School of Information and Department of Computer Science and Engineering, University of Michigan
sk.park@kaist.ac.kr, yongsung7@gmail.com, uclee@kaist.ac.kr
[†]ackerm@umich.edu

ABSTRACT
In location-based social Q&A, the questions related to a local community (e.g. local services and places) are typically answered by local residents (i.e. who have the local knowledge). In this work, we wanted to deepen our understanding of the localness of knowledge sharing through investigating the topical and typological patterns related to the geographic characteristics, geographic locality of user activities, and motivations of local knowledge sharing. To this end, we analyzed a 12-month period Q&A dataset from Naver KiN "Here" and a supplementary survey dataset from 285 mobile users. Our results revealed several unique characteristics of location-based social Q&A. When compared with conventional social Q&A sites, Naver KiN "Here" had very different topical/typological patterns. Naver KiN "Here" exhibited a strong spatial locality where the answerers mostly had 1-3 spatial clusters of contributions, the topical distributions varied widely across different districts, and a typical cluster spanned a few neighboring districts. In addition, we uncovered unique motivators, e.g. ownership of local knowledge and sense of local community. The findings reported in the paper have significant implications for the design of Q&A systems, especially location-based social Q&A systems.

Author Keywords
Location-based Social Q&A; Localness of Knowledge Sharing

ACM Classification Keywords
H.5.m. Information Interfaces and Presentation (e.g. HCI): Miscellaneous

INTRODUCTION
Location-based social Q&A allows users to directly tap into the knowledge of local people to obtain information related to a particular geographic location or area (e.g. insider tips about the best places to go). When compared with the traditional social Q&A services such as Yahoo! Answers and Naver KiN, one significant distinction of location-based social Q&A is the localness of knowledge sharing: the questions that are related to a local community (i.e. primarily about local places and services) are answered by those who have the local knowledge (e.g. current local residents). As will be seen from our findings, this leads to very different usage and distinct design implications compared to traditional social Q&A services.

Researchers have strived to build location-based online social platforms that facilitate social interaction and local knowledge sharing; e.g. SocialSearchBrowser [10] and MicroBlog [15]. Also, recently commercial platforms have been designed for location-based social Q&A, such as Locql [4], LocalMind [2], LocalUncle [3], and Naver KiN "Here" [5]. Understanding the localness of knowledge sharing is critical when designing the key features of location-based social Q&A; e.g. categorizing questions/answers, retrieving relevant answers, routing questions, and motivating user contributions. However, our understanding of the localness of knowledge sharing remains limited because prior studies have primarily focused on evaluating prototype systems and drawing design implications with small-scale user studies [10, 11, 15].

In this paper, we deepen the understanding of the localness of knowledge sharing through analyzing a large-scale, longitudinal dataset and surveying current users from Naver KiN "Here", a mobile app for location-based social Q&A in Korea. We consider the following research questions to investigate the key aspects on localness:

- First, are topical/typological patterns related to geographic characteristics, and how?
- Second, how are users geographically focused in their asking/answering activities?
- Third, what are the answer motivations that are unique in location-based social Q&A?

To the best of our knowledge, our work is the first of its kind to investigate the localness of knowledge sharing through analyzing a large-scale real-world dataset.

To answer the research questions, we crawled a 12-month period Q&A dataset from Naver KiN "Here", and we performed supplementary surveys with 285 Naver KiN "Here" users. Using these datasets, we first performed topic analyses using

MobileHCI '14, September 23 - 26 2014, Toronto, ON, Canada

http://dx.doi.org/10.1145/2628363.2628407

different geographic scales (e.g. district/city) and evaluated how the geographic characteristics were reflected in the Q&A activities. We analyzed the district/city-level activity patterns of users in order to gain insights into their geographic focus, and performed spatial clustering analyses to quantify the geographic locality of user contributions. In addition, we performed content analysis of the user survey results to identify the user motives of local knowledge sharing that are unique to location-based social Q&A.

Our primary findings are summarized as follows. First, Naver KiN "Here" had very different typical/typological patterns when compared with traditional social Q&A sites. The factual information seeking was surprisingly high (72.2%), followed by recommendations (17.9%). The overall topic distribution had a significantly higher level of travel and lifestyle information seeking topics, which are often localized in nature. We found that topical distributions varied widely across different districts, as were appropriate for the areas in question. Second, there was strong spatial locality of user contributions where answerers primarily focused on 1-3 spatial clusters. These clusters were closely related to the users' life experiences (e.g. current/former home as well as work and school); many questions required very specific local knowledge that is difficult to answer without local experience. A typical cluster spanned only a few neighboring districts; and its geographic size was much smaller than that found in analyses of Wikipedia knowledge sharing [16, 24]. Third, we found unique motivators for local knowledge sharing, i.e. ownership of local knowledge (competence about local knowledge learned over many years) and sense of community (membership and fulfillment of needs). These are all different from those reported for "normal" social Q&A systems. Finally, we discuss several practical system design implications, such as geographic information retrieval, question routing, and user contribution encouragement.

BACKGROUND AND RELATED WORK

Conventional Social Q&A

Characteristics of social Q&A in general have been heavily studied. For example, Kim et al. [19] classified questions as soliciting facts, opinions, and suggestions. As another example, in their analysis of Yahoo! Answers, Adamic et al. [7] found that user participation varied widely depending on the topic (and are skewed), and that knowledge sharing patterns across different topic categories existed (e.g. experts in different domains that help one another). Similarly, Nam et al. [28] demonstrated that Naver KiN users' level of participation is highly skewed, intermittent, and that the expected level of their expertise is lower than that found in online help forums. Our work differs from the prior studies in that we investigate the localness of knowledge sharing by analyzing the topical/typological patterns related to geographic characteristics, and geographic locality of user activities.

The motivation behind answering questions is largely dependent on a mixture of intrinsic factors (e.g. enjoyment, and feelings of gratitude and respect) and extrinsic factors (e.g. monetary rewards, reputation systems, etc.) [30]. Nam et al. [28] demonstrated that the motivation for answering in Naver KiN results from both intrinsic and extrinsic factors, i.e. altruism is the leading factor, followed by business motives, learning, hobbies, and earning points. In pay-for-answer Q&A sites, researchers have reported that financial incentives and social factors are the key motivators [13, 31, 32, 23]. In this work, we extend the prior studies by identifying unique motivators for local knowledge sharing.

Service	Message Access	Question Delivery	Message Content	Delivery Target	Filtering
GeoNote[14]	Remote *In-situ*	Pull Push (geocast)	Text/MM /Map	Area/ Thing	Topic/ Proximity
SocialSearch Browser[10]	*In-situ*	Pull	Text/Map	Area	Topic/ Proximity
Micro-Blog[15]	Remote *In-situ*	Pull Push (geocast)	Text/MM /Map	Area	Topic/ Proximity
CityFlocks[9]	Remote *In-situ*	Pull Push (unicast)	Text/Map	Area/ Person	Proximity
LocalUncle[3]	Remote *In-situ*	Pull Push (multicast)	Text/Map	POI/City	N/A
Twitter[29] **(TSA Tracker)**	Remote *In-situ*	Pull Push (multicast)	Text/Map	Area/ Person	N/A
Locql[4]	Remote	Pull	Text/Map	POI/City	Interest Areas
Yahoo! Answers[6]	Remote	Pull	Text/Map	City	Topic
Naver KiN "Here"[5]	Remote *In-situ*	Pull Push (geocast)	Text/Map /Map	Area	Interest Areas

Table 1: Classification of location-based social Q&A

Mobile Information Seeking and Local Searches

Recently, mobile information seeking has received significant attention. In their diary study, Sohn et al. found that approximately 38% of mobile information needs have local intent and 72% were prompted by explicit contextual factors, including activity, location, time, and conversation [33]. Similarly, Church et al. demonstrated that over 40% of entries were location-based and 67% of entries were generated when users were away from their familiar contexts [12]. Henrich and Ludecke analyzed the key properties of geographic information needs from the perspective of geographic information retrieval [17], and they found the intention of a geo reference (e.g. to perform activities and obtain facts in a given location), geo-coverage of relevant documents, the shape of geo information needs (point/region, near/within), and the current location of a user.

Search engines are frequently used as information channels for mobile information seeking; this usage is called *local searches*. Researchers have analyzed the search engine log data in order to understand the usage of local search. Gan et al. used an extended version of web query classifications and demonstrated that 12.9% of the overall traffic in an AOL 2006 dataset had local intent. In recent years, the overall portion of geo queries has increased sharply (possibly due to increased smartphone use); Google and Bing reported that geo queries comprise 50% (2012) and 53% (2010), respectively, of their mobile search traffic [34]. Furthermore, Jones et al. [18] analyzed Yahoo! query logs and reported the characteristics of their geo queries: the distance between the home location and queried location (30% were within 100 km), and query reformulation patterns. Teevan et al. [36] conducted a survey of local search usage and found that local searches tended to be highly contextual in that current location and that time constraints and social factors had a significant impact on usage behavior. In this work, we complement earlier studies on

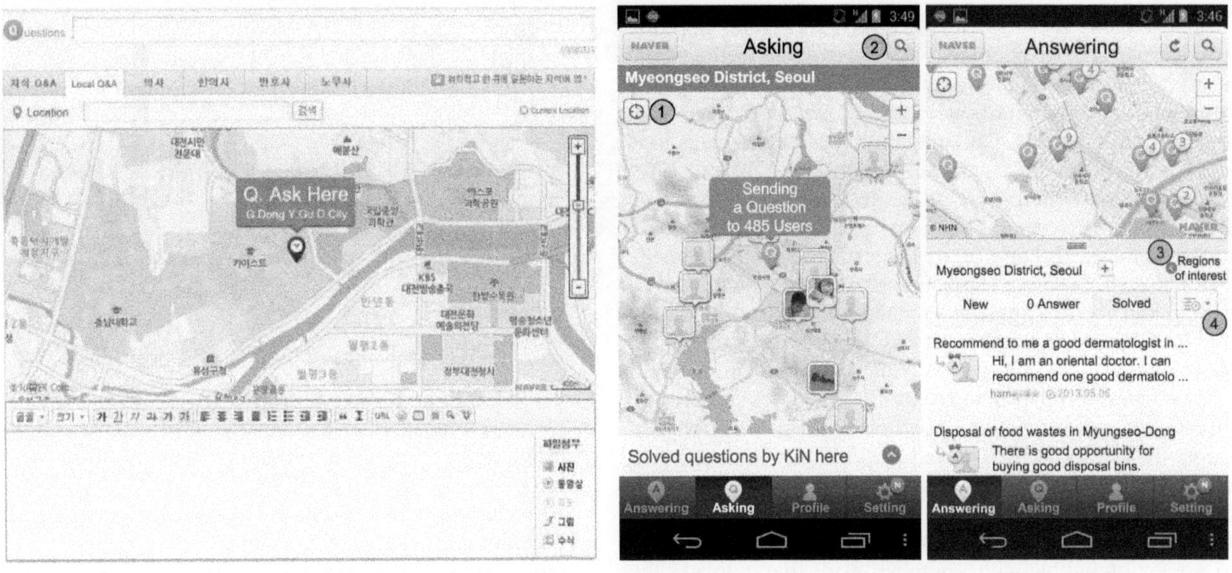

(a) Web (b) App

Figure 1: Naver Local Q&A interface. (Web App). In the case of App, the numbered labels are (1) GPS, (2) search, (3) region of interest, and (4) sort by distance/time. The original text was translated into English for the easier of illustration.

geographic information needs [10, 11, 17, 33] using a real-world dataset; the existing studies examined limited datasets such as web search logs [17] and small-scale user data (e.g. diaries, user study) [10, 11, 33].

Location-based Social Q&A

In Table 1, we summarize the existing location-based social Q&A systems based on their design features, i.e. message access (remote, *in situ*), delivery (push, pull), message content (text, multimedia: MM), user interface (text, map), message destination (location, thing, Point of Interest (POI), city), and message filtering (topic/area subscription, proximity). In the existing systems, message access modes are the key differentiating factor. Remote access means that a user can post and retrieve messages in a remote location; *in situ* access means that a user can retrieve relevant messages only when the user approaches the area of interest. *In situ* access is suitable for facilitating information sharing among local residents, such as in SocialSearchBrowser. Questions can be delivered to target users in various ways: pushing questions to people in a regional area as in Naver KiN "Here" and MicroBlog (geocast), sending questions to subscribed people as in LocalUncle (multicast), and sending questions directly to a person as in CityFlock (unicast). For location-based social Q&A services, text and interactive maps can be used for question/answer navigation [11]. The existing systems support various filtering mechanisms ranging from place/area/topic subscription to proximity sensitive filtering. In this paper, we study localness of local knowledge sharing by studying Naver KiN "Here", which has representative design features.

Localness of Information Sharing Behavior

Prior studies have explored the localness of information sharing such as influence of regional characters on social media usage [21], and user contribution behavior of local content in online social systems [16, 24, 38]. Kulshrestha et al. demonstrated that shared national, linguistic, and cultural backgrounds had a significant impact on Twitter usage (e.g. social links and information exchanges) [21]. Yardi and Boyd investigated how local community members used Twitter to share and exchange information about local events [38]. A large percentage of Wikipedia users only edit a few geo-pages (e.g. city, school), and the geo-locations of the edited geo-pages tended to be localized within a 100 km radius [24]. Hecht and Gergle compared the mean contribution distance of Flicker posts and Wikipedia edits (geo-pages) and demonstrated that the Wikipedia edits had a longer contribution distance than Flickr posts [16]. Prior studies have provided a valuable insight into the localness of knowledge sharing. However, knowledge sharing in location-based social Q&A differs significantly from that in Twitter and Wikipedia because it is designed to resolve everyday life geographic information needs with the help of local experts. Our goal is to study the localness of location-based social Q&A through conducting topic analyses and spatial clustering analyses of a large-scale real-world Q&A dataset.

INTERACTION IN LOCAL Q&A

We investigate Naver KiN "Here", which is a location-based social Q&A that was released in December 3, 2012. Naver KiN "Here" extends its existing service called Naver KiN Local to mobile services. For the location-based Q&A, the registered users can interact with the content on either the mobile app or webpages. Both interfaces allow the use of an interactive map to represent the location/region of interest, and the questions are categorized by region names (based on administrative divisions) instead of content topic categories.

The question asking is similar to conventional social Q&A sites such as Yahoo! Answers and Naver KiN. The key difference is that instead of choosing the content topic, users are asked to select the regions using an interactive map in order to categorize the question. In the Naver KiN "Here" app, the user also interacts with a map, which also displays the active app users who have answered more than five questions in a given area. A posted question will be shown on the webpage and app simultaneously. Unlike the web access, the questions posted using the mobile app are pushed to users whose regions of interest match those of the questions. The app users can switch off the push notifications. The registered users can post answers via the app or web interfaces. The front page of the Naver KiN "Here" app (Figure 1) presents an interactive map and a list of questions related to the current location based on GPS; however, the app and web interfaces differ for answering questions. On the web, the questions are ordered based on recency rather than proximity, and users can browse all questions and filter them based on regional hierarchy. In the app, the questions are ordered by proximity to the current location by default. When a user pans or zooms with the map, the list is automatically updated. Depending on the zooming level, the questions in a close geographic area are aggregated into a question bubble with a number inside that indicates the number of questions. Both web and app users can subscribe to the regions of interest for question filtering. For app users, the system automatically pushes new questions based on the subscription information. Naver KiN "Here" users receive points for asking and answering activities. Furthermore, the mobile app users can acquire various types of badges, ranging from app installation and continued use to expert answerer status, which can be obtained through providing fast responses and accurate answers.

Before detailing our results, an illustration of the administrative divisions in Korea is important because it differs to other countries. The administrative divisions have four levels: province ("Do"; there are nine provinces in Korea), city ("Si"; typical size of 100-1000 km^2), sub-city ("Gu"; typical size of 10-100 km^2), and district ("Dong", typical size of 1-10 km^2). The levels are more fine-grained than those of western countries, e.g. the USA, which are typically composed of three levels: state, county/shire, and city/town/village. People typically refer to city/sub-city/district names when searching for or speaking about places in Korea.

METHODOLOGY

Our data collection method was comprised of two complementary parts: automated crawling of publicly accessible local question-answer pairs on Naver KiN "Here" local Q&A and a web-based survey. The data were obtained for the period from December 17, 2012 to December 31, 2013; a total of 508,334 questions and 567,156 answers were obtained. The crawled data enabled comprehensive statistics on user behavior, while the web-based survey aided in obtaining an in-depth understanding of the observed usage behavior.

We supplemented the question and answer data with the web-based surveys of Naver KiN "Here" local Q&A users. In August 2013, we sent a questionnaire link via Naver email to 4,557 users who had asked/answered at least one question via the Naver KiN "Here" app. The link lasted for a week, and the total number of participants was 285 after removing duplicate and erroneous responses. The low response rate may have been caused by the fact that Naver emails may not be users' primary email accounts. At the end of the survey, we randomly selected 50 participants and rewarded an online gift voucher worth $10. The survey questions asked about demographics (e.g. age, gender, occupation), app settings, and user motivations. The survey data demonstrated that 59.7% of participants were males and 40.3% were females. Participants were predominantly in their teens (10-19 years; 30%) and in their 20s (43%); the remainder were in their 30s (14.4%), 40s (10.8%), and 50s (1.8%). The occupations were quite diverse: middle/high school students (29.8%), college/graduate students (23.3%), financial/service workers (12.1%), lawyers (0.3%), designers/artists (3%), homemakers (2.3%), architects (2.3%), engineers (7.2%), miscellaneous area workers (11.8%), and unemployed (6.2%).

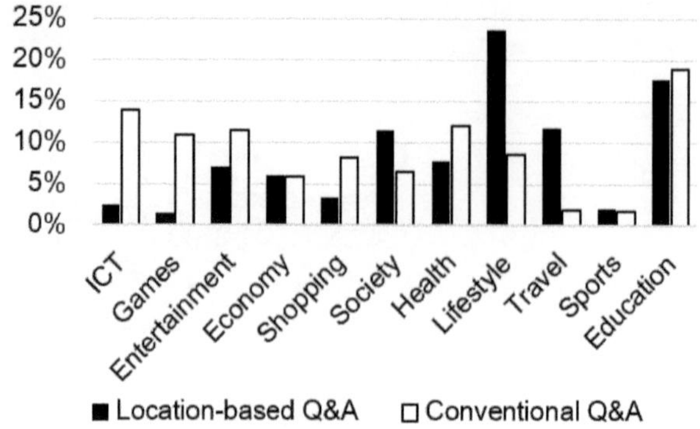

Figure 2: Topic distribution

TOPICAL LOCALITY IN KNOWLEDGE SHARING

We performed content analyses in order to characterize the topical patterns (overall distributions and geographic/typological differences). We used the topic categories from Naver KiN: information and communication technology (ICT), games, entertainment/art (e.g. TV, radio, movies), economy (e.g. banking, tax, real estate), shopping, society (e.g. laws, politics, culture, governments), health, lifestyle (e.g. food, pets, cars), travel/transportation, sports, and education. Unlike traditional social Q&A, Naver KiN "Here" does not have a topic field as questions are categorized based on location. We automatically classified the topic categories as follows: for a given question we extracted the key words using a Korean parser called KKMA (Kokoma Korean Morpheme Analysis) [1]. Then, we searched the extracted keywords using Naver KiN in which the question askers manually select the relevant topics when posting questions. From the top 100 search results, the most frequent topic category was selected as the topic category for the question. In order to confirm whether the automatic classification provided accurate results, we manually coded the topics of 100 randomly selected questions, and we measured the inter-rater agreement (between automatic and manual classifications) using Cohen's Kappa statistic. The measured value for the topic classification was $k = 0.87$, which indicates substantial agreement.

In Figure 2, we present the topic distributions of the location-based social Q&A (Naver KiN "Here") as well as conventional social Q&A (Naver KiN). Key differences were found in the ICT, games, lifestyle, and travel/transportation

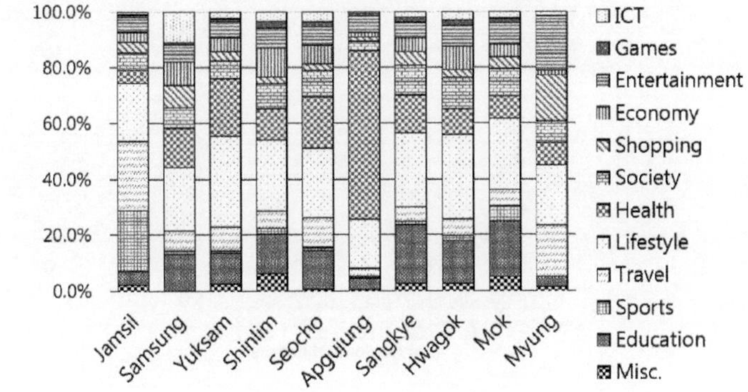

Figure 3: Topic distribution of top 10 districts

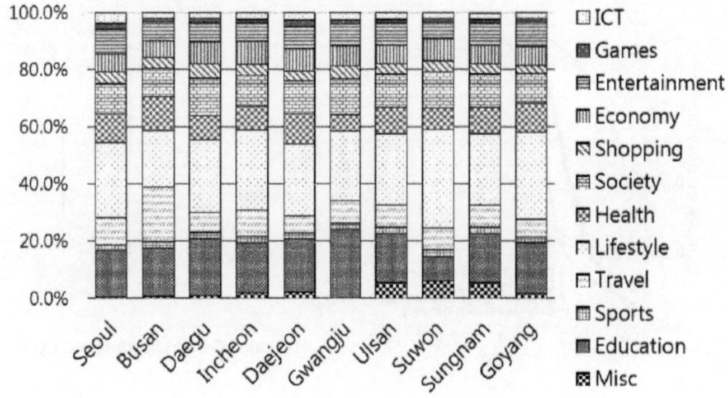

Figure 4: Topic distribution of top 10 cities

topic categories. In the location-based social Q&A, lifestyle (23.7%) and travel (11.7%) were dominant, whereas ICT (2.5%) and games (1.5%) were minimal. Our results confirm that there is a significant difference in the topical distributions between location-based social Q&A and conventional social Q&A.

Next, we investigated whether the characteristics of a region were reflected in the Q&A usage. Identifying such characteristics is beneficial when building geographic information retrieval systems. We found that, in general, the geographic characteristics were well reflected and that some patterns of topical locality existed. In addition, the topical distributions were largely dependent on the size and functional complexity of the region.

In order to understand how regional characters are reflected in the Q&A usage, we first analyzed the topic distributions of the top 10 districts in Seoul (Figure 3). Overall, the regional characteristics were well reflected in the district level questions. For example, the Jamsil district, which is well known for its sports stadium, had a large percentage of sports questions (22.2%). The Apgujeong district had a high percentage of health questions (60.4%) because it is famous for its medical area that is densely populated with plastic surgery clinics. Therefore, we hypothesized that such observations were partly related to the concept of zoning in urban planning; zoning is a method of urban planning that prevents new developments from interfering with the existing residents or businesses and preserves the "character" of a community [8]. This type of planning is widely adopted in most developed nations, and local municipalities in Korea also abide by the national zoning guidelines.

Furthermore, we examined whether there were significant differences in the topical distributions in different geographic scales. In Figure 4, we plotted the topic distributions of the top 10 cities ranked in terms of the number of questions. Unlike the questions in the districts, there were only minor variations in categories across the different cities. Note that there were a few cities that have significant tourist attractions and therefore have distinctive topic distributions with higher percentages of shopping, entertainment, and travel categories, e.g. Jeju Island, which was voted as one of the New7Wonders of Nature in 2011, had significantly high number of questions/answers related to travel.

We also classified the types of questions using previously studied categories [19, 22] where questions were classified into information, suggestion, and opinion questions. Information questions are used to find specific facts; suggestion questions are used to seek recommendations; opinion questions are used to survey other people's thoughts or preferences. In order to analyze these question types, we randomly selected 1000 questions and coded the questions using two external raters. They first coded 200 questions together, and then separately coded the remaining 800 questions (i.e. 400 questions each). These common questions were used to measure the inter-rater agreement using Cohen's Kappa statistic. The measured value for the type classification was $k = 0.84$, which indicates substantial agreement. We found that the information and suggestion question types were dominant, and they comprised 72.2% and 17.9% of the questions, respectively, followed by opinion questions (6.4%) and miscellaneous questions (3.5%). This type distribution differs significantly from other social Q&A sites [19, 22, 27]. In mobile social Q&A, information questions comprised 51.1% of all questions, followed by suggestion (23.4%) and opinion (18.8%) questions [22]. Thus, location-based social Q&A has a significantly higher percentage of information questions and a lower percentage of opinion questions when compared with the conventional social Q&A. Considering the high percentage of factual questions, it would be beneficial to archive them for local searches.

SPATIAL LOCALITY OF USER ACTIVITIES

City/District-level User Activities

We analyzed the dataset in order to understand the geographic focus of the users' activities (asking/answering). In order to capture the degree of geographic focus by an asker/answerer, we used an entropy measure, i.e. the lower the entropy, the higher the level of focus on certain regions. Considering an answerer i who made p_k percentage of answers for region k, the answerer's entropy is given as $-\sum_k p_k \log_2 p_k$. If a user only answered for a single region, e.g. region j (i.e., $p_j = 1$ and $p_i = 0$ for all i other than j), the entropy value is zero. The entropy is maximized when any region is equally likely to be asked by a user (i.e. a uniform distribution). We only considered users who asked/answered more than ten questions/answers for the entropy calculation. In addition, we used the two different region levels of district and city. Note that due to privacy concerns, Naver only revealed three characters

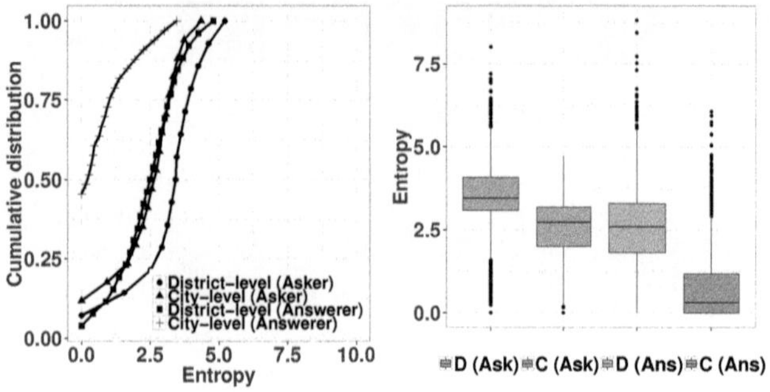

Figure 5: CDF and Boxplot of entropy (C:City, D:District)

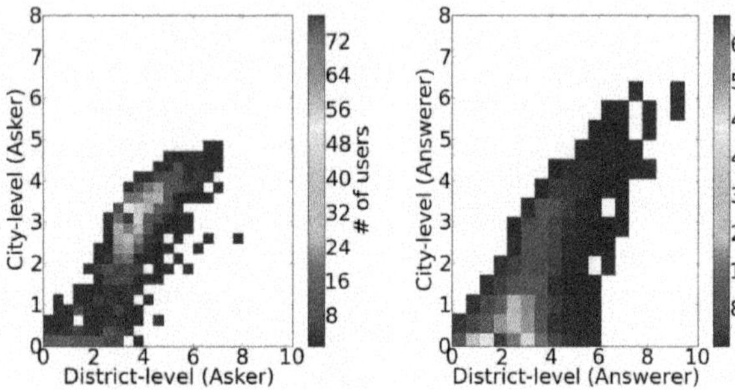

Figure 6: Heat map of entropy

of the asker's ID. Nonetheless, we could uniquely identify a user because the ID was accompanied with two other statistics, the question closing rate and answer acceptance rate. Those who answered more than ten questions tended to have diverse numbers.

In Figure 5, we present the cumulative distributions and corresponding boxplots in parallel. The results demonstrated that, in general, the asking activities had higher entropy values than the answering activities: asking at the district/city levels had means of 3.5/2.5 and answering at the district/city levels had means of 2.6/0.8. In order to better understand the geographic containment (e.g. many districts but in the same city) for each user, we arranged a pair of entropy values, i.e. (district, city), and drew a heat map for both activities as seen in Figure 6. This heat map allows better visualization of the geographic focus and containment. For the asking activities, the figure demonstrates that the center area has bright colors. This shape indicates that the askers' activities typically span multiple districts and cities. Furthermore, the core of the shape had an entropy value of 3 at the city level, which represents eight cities, if a uniform distribution is assumed. In practice, the distribution was usually skewed, and the actual number was significantly larger. For the answering activities, we found that the overall shape and color differed significantly from that of the asking activities. In particular, the cores were located at the bottom in the city level, whereas the district levels were widely scattered, which indicates the localness of answering activities.

In order to understand localness, we asked the survey participants to report 1) the number of their selected regions of interests in the app, and 2) a list of those names as well as the reason for each choice. The number of selected regions of interests is presented in Figure 7. The mean number of

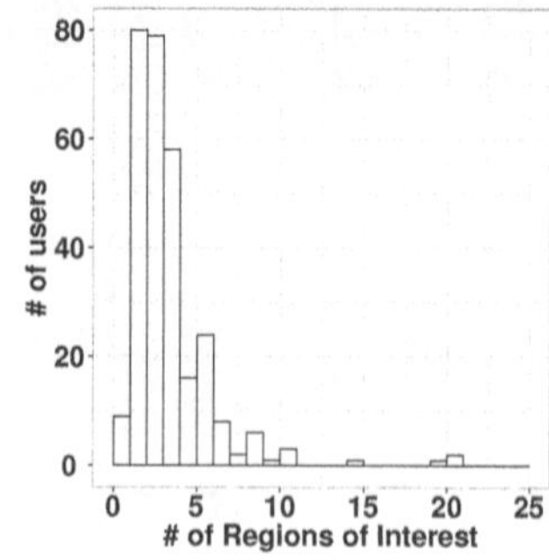

Figure 7: Number of regions of interest per user

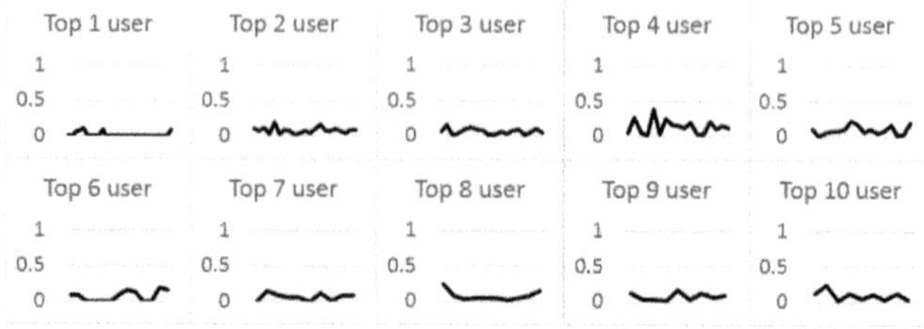

Figure 8: City-level entropy changes of top 10 answerers

districts was 2.9 (SD = 3.2) and the maximum number was 35. Regarding the second part, there were 142 valid answers with a detailed list of interest regions and the reasons for their choices, and this led to 317 annotated regions of interest. The major categories of areas included home, work/school, and downtown areas. The manual classification results indicated the following: home (93.7%), nearby home (16.2%), previous home (14.8%), school (23.9%), nearby school (0.7%), previous school (0.7%), work (28.9%), nearby work (2.1%), previous work (3.5%), and downtown (24.6%). When those who had their home/work in the same region, they were counted twice. Miscellaneous regions of interest (25 regions) included churches, hobby places, parents' houses, relatives' houses, and tutoring institutes. The results aided in understanding the relationship between a user's local connection and knowledge. However, despite local familiarity (home, work, school), the survey participants reported that perceived percentage of answerable questions was 37% on average (SD = 24%). As shown later, many of the questions required very specific knowledge based on local experiences, e.g. *"In Daejeon, are there any places that I can buy big dumplings after midnight?"* and *"In Wonju, please let me know where I can buy less expensive medium and large size vases."*

In Figure 8, we plotted the city-level entropy changes of the top 10 answerers. For a series of answers by a user, we calculated the entropy in each block of 50 consecutive questions. Then, we plotted the magnitude of the entropy differences between two consecutive blocks. The figures clearly demonstrate that the changes in the entropy values were quite small. This indicates that the city selection strategies did not significantly change over time: those who had low/high entropy values would continue to have low/high values.

We divided the users into two groups based on the city-level entropy values. If the city-level entropy was greater than 2, we assumed that the user's activities were geographically scat-

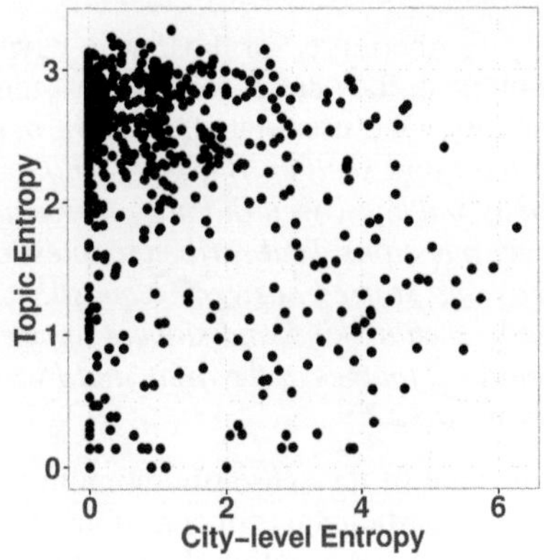

Figure 9: City-level entropy vs. topic entropy of a user

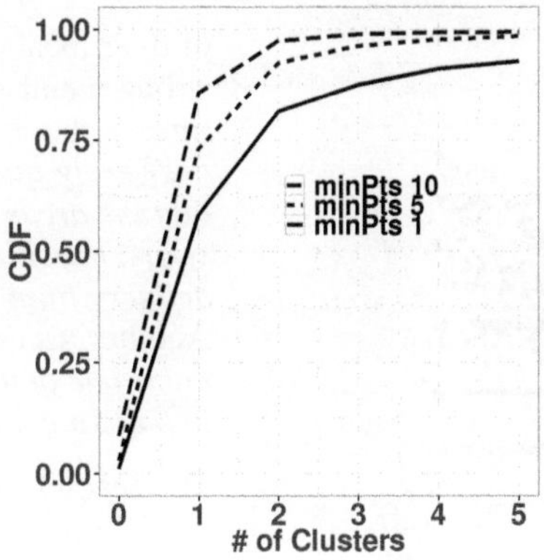

Figure 10: Number of clusters per user

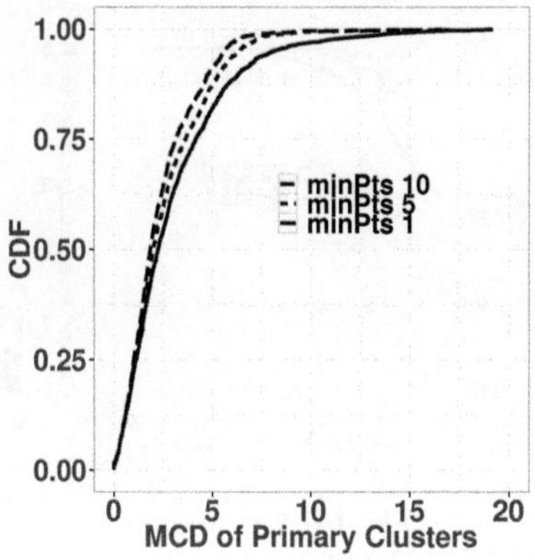

Figure 11: Distribution of MCD values

tered (GS group); otherwise, we assumed that the user's activities were geographically focused (GF group). From this categorization, 81% of heavy users had city-level entropy values of less than two (mean = 0.48), and the actual number of contributed cities was typically less than four.

However, the remaining 19% of the heavy users had activities that were scattered. The GS group's city-level entropy (mean = 3.67, SD = 1.11) was significantly higher than the GF group's (mean = 0.57, SD = 0.57). In Figure 9, we present a scatter plot: each dot represents a user's city-level entropy and topic entropy. We manually investigated the answerers in the GS group in order to understand what types of local knowledge they were providing. Those who had high topic entropy values were mostly top-ranked answerers in Naver KiN. The manual investigations revealed two types of answerers: active web searchers and province-level local experts. The active web searchers typically provided local answers that were easily searchable on the web (mostly factual) such as transportation costs, traffic status, and local facilities. The province-level experts were actively contributing to a number of cities within a province; however, detailed local answers were more skewed to a few familiar cities. Interestingly, those who had low topic entropy values mostly promoted their business (e.g. clinics, lawyers, online shopping malls) or online communities (e.g. volunteering). It appears that these users tended to copy and paste similar, but lengthy, general answers about specific topics. For example, a medical doctor answered local questions about recommending local clinics for a specific cosmetic surgery, but the lengthy answers only provided general information about that surgery.

Spatial Cluster Analysis

The city/district-level analyses assisted in gaining a good insight into spatial locality, but they had several limitations: only coarse-grained spatial locality could be found and they did not provide a user's locus of contributions. Therefore, we extended our locality analyses through performing spatial cluster analyses. We ran a density-based clustering algorithm (called DBSCAN) where the radius (known as eps) was set to 10 km in order to merge nearby districts, and clusters were repeatedly expanded as long as the number of minimum points (minPts) is greater than thresholds (e.g. minPts = 1, 5, 10). When we gave minPts threshold of 1, we repeatedly expanded a cluster whenever there are at least two questions within 10 km radius. Due to the requirements of the minimum points for the spatial cluster analysis, we only considered heavy users whose number of answers was equal to or greater than 30; this resulted in 1492 users. Note that the city/district-level entropy distributions with these users were consistent with the earlier results.

Figure 10 presents a Cumulative Distribution Function (CDF) of the number of clusters with different minPts thresholds. A majority of users had a single cluster; in particular when minPts = 1, more than 50% of users had a single cluster, and more than 75% of users had less than two clusters. The mean values of the minPts = 1, 5, and 10 were 2.3, 1.5, and 1.2, respectively. The maximum values of the minPts = 1, 5, and 10 were 101, 61, and 40, respectively; indeed, there were some users whose contributions were widely scattered across many cities.

We used the mean contribution distance (MCD) to measure the localness of the user contributions in each cluster [16]. For a given cluster of a user, the cluster's MCD was defined as $\sum_{i=1}^{n} d(C, c_i)/n$, where C is the centroid of the cluster, c_i is the location of an answered question, $d(C, c_i)$ is the Euclidean distance between two points (C and c_i), and n is the total number of answers in a cluster. In Figure 11, we plot the CDF of the MCD values from the users' primary clusters (i.e. the cluster with the largest number of answers). The mean MCD values for minPts = 1, 5, and 10 were 3.1, 2.6, and 2.3 km, respectively. This indicates that the primary clusters' MCD values covered a few nearby districts, e.g. home and nearby home, and work and nearby work.

In Figure 12, we plot the cluster-level entropy values. Because the number of clusters was very small, a majority of users had a zero entropy value. Then, we compared the city-level entropy and cluster-level entropy values; Figure 13 presents the scatter plots with minPts = 1. The figure demonstrates that there is a linear relationship between these two variables. The cluster-level entropy is smaller than the city-level entropy because the DBSCAN removed the noisy clusters that had points less than or equal to the minPts. Interestingly, those users whose cluster entropy values were zero, but had high city-level entropy values, were mostly business promoters.

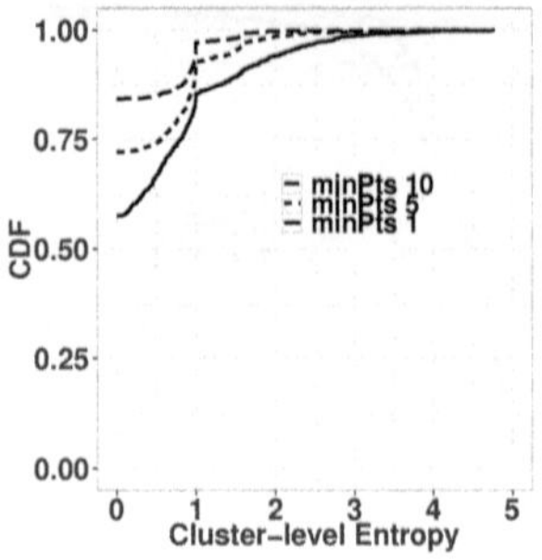

Figure 12: CDF of cluster-level entropy values

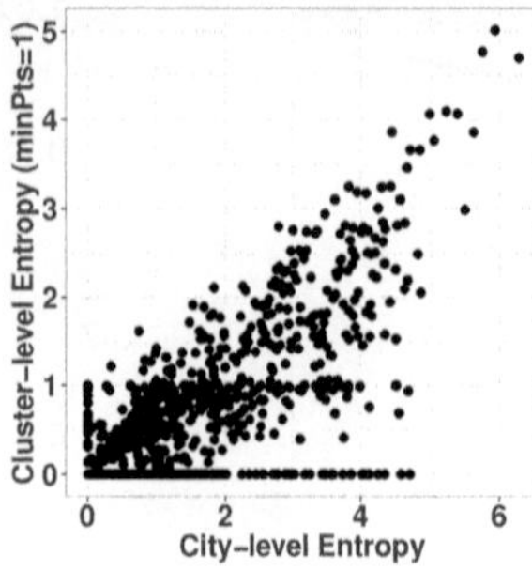

Figure 13: City-and cluster-level entropy (minPts=1)

ANSWER MOTIVATIONS

In order to understand the answer motivation, we asked the participants to write in detail why they answered questions posted in Naver KiN's Local Q&A using an open-ended question. From the answers, we extracted all motivators and performed affinity diagramming. The following major themes were derived: knowledge exchange (24.9%), altruism (18.2%), ownership of local knowledge (10.1%), points (9.8%), pastime (9.2%), and sense of community (7.0%). Miscellaneous themes included business promotion and learning. Unlike the existing results on social Q&A that reported intrinsic (altruism, enjoyment), external (points), and social (knowledge exchange) motivators [28, 30], we found two unique motivators in the location-based social Q&A: ownership of local knowledge (competence about local knowledge learned over many years) and sense of community (serving the information needs of other community members).

Researchers have demonstrated that when people believed they owned information, they were more likely to engage in knowledge sharing [37]. This result can be attributed to individuals' internal satisfaction derived from sharing their knowledge with others. As they have lived in that location for a long time, we expected that the local residents gained a strong ownership of local knowledge, ranging from specific goods/services to distinctions between places and place popularity [25]. In our survey, the ownership of local knowledge was clearly noted as follows. One user stated, *"Because I know everything about my town as I have lived in my town for a long time"*; another user stated his experience by saying, *"I have been living here for 20 years and went to schools in this region. With this knowledge, I'm sure I can help answer other people's questions. That's why I started answering here."*

Another theme was the sense of community. McMillan and Chavis [26] defined the sense of community as "a feeling that members have of belonging, a feeling that members matter to one another and to the group, and a shared faith that members' needs will be met through their commitment to be together". Some key factors in the sense of community include *membership* and *fulfillment* of needs. Note that the sense of community in location-based Q&A differs significantly from that in social network services (and the Q&A therein) because the interpersonal relationships among answerers are weak. In our survey, we found that many users stated "my regions", which is a good indicator that they regard themselves as members of their local community. Furthermore, for those who have a strong membership attachment, they are eager to invest their time in the local community. One user stated, *"I have been answering questions in the Laws section. But after I noticed that the areas that I live in and know well did not receive answers, I decided to answer questions. I subscribed to question delivery from those areas and started answering questions."* Another user commented, *"I think kind and sincere answering is one of the representative images of the area, and I want to build a good image of my area."*

The second important element of the sense of community is the fulfillment of needs. Our participants concurred that they wanted to serve the information needs within their communities (for both members and visitors). A user expressed their feeling as follows: *"Knowing that I can help other local community members makes me feel really great."* In addition, responsibility as a community member was expressed: *"I was born here, and I know [this region] very well. I feel fresh because people from other areas often ask questions. I feel like I should take care of them just like taking care of a baby."* Some users fulfilled the needs in the expectation of receiving useful help in return later, e.g. *"By exchanging questions, I can receive help from other people when I visit other areas; I can also give help to other people when they visit ours."*

DISCUSSION

We present practical design implications based on our findings and discuss the limitations of this work.

Leveraging Topical/Typological Patterns

Our topical and typological analyses results provide insights into the design dimensions of location-based social Q&A, e.g. category refinement, question routing, and related answer searches. When compared with conventional social Q&A sites [7, 23], the overall topic distribution of location-based social Q&A had a higher level of travel and lifestyle information seeking, but a lower level of computer related questions. Our manual investigation of sample questions revealed that local questions were primarily related to local services (e.g. housing, entertainment, shopping, eating/drinking, education, transportation) and local attributes (e.g. culture, history, geography).

Recall that KiN "Here" users are asked to subscribe to regions of interest. The users will be automatically notified of questions sent to these regions via push messages. Because our participants reported that 37% of the questions were answerable on average, it would be beneficial to include an additional option for selecting topical categories that are customized for location-based social Q&A. This will assist in filtering the push notifications based on topics of interest to lower interruption overhead.

Our typological analyses demonstrated that factual information seeking was high (72.2%), followed by recommendations (17.9%); it also demonstrated that the topic distributions varied widely across different districts. This observation implies that a location-based social Q&A dataset could be effectively archived for local searches. For some areas, similar questions were posted repeatedly; the localized content analyses and ranking may aid in improving the quality of the retrieved answers. Furthermore, topic clustering algorithms could be applied such that the regional topic characteristics could automatically be extracted and utilized for local search optimization. In some cases, a user would prefer to post a local question via traditional social Q&A services; in this case, it would be beneficial to recognize that it is a local question, and the system could automatically recommend a candidate place for the question routing.

Leveraging the Spatio-Temporal Activity Analyses

Our spatial locality analyses revealed that there was strong spatial locality of user contributions. The answerers primarily focused on 1-3 spatial clusters that were closely related to their life experiences (e.g. current/former home, work, and school), and a cluster typically spanned a few neighboring districts. The mean contribution distance in Naver KiN "Here" was approximately 2-3 kilometers on average, whereas those in Wikipedia were much greater in scale (hundreds of kilometers) [16, 24]—most Wikipedia geo-pages contain "general" information about regions and famous POIs. Our results imply that while a user's subscribed districts are currently considered for push notifications, the radius of question geocasting could be extended slightly to a few neighboring districts. Another implication is that whenever a user subscribes to a new district, we could recommend that the user also subscribe to neighboring districts. Alternatively, during the service subscription process, users could be asked to enter district and city names related to familiar places and to automatically recommend corresponding districts for subscription.

We found that many questions required very specific local knowledge, which were difficult to answer without local experience. Most heavy users were geographically focused. Our spatial-topical entropy analyses revealed that some heavy users who showed high topical diversity were the web searchers (who heavily used geographic information systems such as transportation schedule/status pages), province-level experts (covering nearby local cities), and business promoters (who tended to copy and paste similar content). Providing local search tools that are specialized for popular topics of geographic information seeking will help improve user participation and answer quality. Furthermore, it is possible to identify local business promoters by applying machine learning techniques; several useful features would be the cluster and city-level entropy values, content similarity of posted answers, and the best answer selection rates.

Motivating User Contributions

We found additional motivators that are unique in location-based social Q&A, i.e. ownership of local knowledge and sense of community. These motivators could be leveraged to encourage user contributions and increase user commitment. One immediate method is to use community-level symbols. A key element of membership in a sense of community [26] is a common symbol system. Considering that the existing location-based services often employ badges, we could create community badges and award them to those who are actively participating in that community, which could reinforce their motivation [20].

We could use to leverage local membership and attachment. First, when a question is pushed, framing the request in a way that aligns with the motivators of ownership of local knowledge and sense of community could increase contributions. Second, sending out hyperlocal news about recent regional activities could increase regional members' awareness of the service and may encourage contributions. In addition, visualizing popular/trending topics in location-based social Q&A would help people understand local characteristics (e.g. knowing "hot topics" in my area). This would not only provide significant insights for the local residents about their regions, but it would also assist in people from other regions to understand topical characteristics of the region. Third, introducing regional competition could elicit more contributions; for example, the system could display scoreboards (e.g. answer and selection rates of nearby regions) at different geographic scales (e.g. district- and city-level). Fourth, when a new user starts contributing to the location-based social Q&A, we can automatically classify the user's topical interests and the level of expertise on that topics as in conventional social Q&A [35], and this along with location information can be leveraged to encourage user participation.

Limitations

As with any qualitative or single-site work, the generalizability of this work is limited such that additional work on similar location-based social Q&A services, such as Locql, LocalUncle, and Yahoo! Answers' Local Business, is necessary, which will be part of our future work. In addition, because social networking services can be used to ask questions [26], it would be interesting to see if existing location-based social Q&A services such as Foursquare are used for social Q&A activities.

CONCLUSION

We investigated the localness of knowledge sharing through analyzing the topical and typological patterns related to geographic characteristics, geographic locality of user activities, and motivations of local knowledge sharing. We collected a large-scale real-world dataset from Naver KiN "Here" and conducted a complementary survey of 285 mobile app users. From the analyses, we found that, compared with conventional social Q&A sites, the location-based social Q&A has unique topical and typological patterns that vary widely across different districts. A strong spatial locality of contributions exists around a few spatial clusters related to users' life experiences, which span a few neighboring districts. Localness is well reflected in the motives for local knowledge sharing, i.e. ownership of local knowledge and a sense of community. Finally, we discussed several practical system design implications such as leveraging topical and spatio-temporal activity patterns (e.g. question routing, local searches) and motivating user contributions (e.g. badges, request framing, hyperlocal news).

ACKNOWLEDGMENTS

This research was supported by Basic Science Research Program through the National Research Foundation of Korea (NRF) funded by the Ministry of Science, ICT & Future Planning (NRF-2012R1A1A1008858).

REFERENCES

1. KKMA. http://kkma.snu.ac.kr.
2. Localmind. http://www.localmind.com.
3. Localuncle. http://www.localuncle.com.
4. LOCQL. http://www.locql.com.
5. Naver Local Q&A. http://kin.naver.com/qna/list.nhn?dirId=12.
6. Yahoo! Answers. https://answers.yahoo.com/.
7. Adamic, L. A., Zhang, J., Bakshy, E., and Ackerman, M. S. Knowledge Sharing and Yahoo Answers: Everyone Knows Something. In *WWW* (2008).
8. Berke, P., and Kaiser, E. J. *Urban Land Use Planning*. University of Illinois Press, 2006.
9. Bilandzic, M., Foth, M., and De Luca, A. CityFlocks: Designing Social Navigation for Urban Mobile Information Systems. In *DIS* (2008).
10. Church, K., Neumann, J., Cherubini, M., and Oliver, N. SocialSearchBrowser: A Novel Mobile Search and Information Discovery Tool. In *IUI* (2010).
11. Church, K., Neumann, J., Cherubini, M., and Oliver, N. The "Map Trap"?: An Evaluation of Map Versus Text-based Interfaces for Location-based Mobile Search Services. In *WWW* (2010).
12. Church, K., and Smyth, B. Understanding the Intent Behind Mobile Information Needs. In *IUI* (2009).
13. Edelman, B. Earnings and Ratings at Google Answers. *Economic Inquiry* (2012).
14. Espinoza, F., Persson, P., Sandin, A., Nyström, H., Cacciatore, E., and Bylund, M. Geonotes: Social and Navigational Aspects of Location-Based Information Systems. In *Ubicomp* (2001).
15. Gaonkar, S., Li, J., Choudhury, R. R., Cox, L., and Schmidt, A. Micro-Blog: Sharing and Querying Content Through Mobile Phones and Social Participation. In *MobiSys* (2008).
16. Hecht, B. J., and Gergle, D. On the "Localness" of User-generated Content. In *CSCW* (2010).
17. Henrich, A., and Luedecke, V. Characteristics of Geographic Information Needs. In *GIR* (2007).
18. Jones, R., Zhang, W. V., Rey, B., Jhala, P., and Stipp, E. Geographic Intention and Modification in Web Search. *International Journal of Geographical Information Science* (2008).
19. Kim, S., Oh, J. S., and Oh, S. Best-Answer Selection Criteria in a Social Q&A Site from the User-Oriented Relevance Perspective. *Proceedings of the American Society for Information Science and Technology* (2007).
20. Kraut, R. E., and Resnick, P. Encouraging Contribution to Online Communities. *Building Successful Online Communities: Evidence-based Social Design* (2011).
21. Kulshrestha, J., Kooti, F., Nikravesh, A., and Gummadi, P. K. Geographic Dissection of the Twitter Network. In *ICWSM* (2012).
22. Lee, U., Kang, H., Yi, E., Yi, M., and Kantola, J. Understanding Mobile Q&A Usage: An Exploratory Study. In *CHI* (2012).
23. Lee, U., Kim, J., Yi, E., Sung, J., and Gerla, M. Analyzing Crowd Workers in Mobile Pay-for-Answer Q&A. In *CHI* (2013).
24. Lieberman, M. D., and Lin, J. You Are Where You Edit: Locating Wikipedia Contributors through Edit Histories. In *ICWSM* (2009).
25. Ludford, P. J., Priedhorsky, R., Reily, K., and Terveen, L. Capturing, Sharing, and Using Local Place Information. In *CHI* (2007).
26. McMillan, D. W., and Chavis, D. M. Sense of Community: A Definition and Theory. *Journal of community psychology* (1986).
27. Morris, M. R., Teevan, J., and Panovich, K. What Do People Ask Their Social Networks, and Why?: A Survey Study of Status Message Q&a Behavior. In *CHI* (2010).
28. Nam, K. K., Ackerman, M. S., and Adamic, L. A. Questions in, Knowledge in?: A Study of Naver's Question Answering Community. In *CHI* (2009).
29. Nichols, J., and Kang, J.-H. Asking Questions of Targeted Strangers on Social Networks. In *CSCW* (2012).
30. Raban, D., and Harper, F. Motivations for Answering Questions Online. *New media and innovative technologies* (2008).
31. Raban, D. R. The Incentive Structure in an Online Information Market. *Journal of the American Society for Information Science and Technology* (2008).
32. Shah, C., Oh, J. S., and Oh, S. Exploring Characteristics and Effects of User Participation in Online Social Q&A Sites. *First Monday* (2008).
33. Sohn, T., Li, K. A., Griswold, W. G., and Hollan, J. D. A Diary Study of Mobile Information Needs. In *CHI* (2008).
34. Sterling, G. Study: 43 Percent Of Total Google Search Queries Are Local. Search Engine Land, 2012.
35. Sung, J., Lee, J.-G., and Lee, U. Booming Up the Long Tails: Discovering Potentially Contributive Users in Community-based Question Answering Services. In *ICWSM* (2013).
36. Teevan, J., Karlson, A., Amini, S., Brush, A. J. B., and Krumm, J. Understanding the Importance of Location, Time, and People in Mobile Local Search Behavior. In *MobileHCI* (2011).
37. Wang, S., and Noe, R. A. Knowledge Sharing: A Review and Directions for Future Research. *Human Resource Management Review* (2010).
38. Yardi, S., and Boyd, D. Tweeting from the Town Square: Measuring Geographic Local Networks. In *ICWSM* (2010).

Comparing Evaluation Methods for Encumbrance and Walking on Interaction with Touchscreen Mobile Devices

Alexander Ng, John Williamson and Stephen Brewster
Glasgow Interactive Systems Group
School of Computing Science, University of Glasgow
a.ng.1@research.gla.ac.uk, jhw@dcs.gla.ac.uk, stephen.brewster@glasgow.ac.uk

ABSTRACT
In this paper, two walking evaluation methods were compared to evaluate the effects of encumbrance while the preferred walking speed (PWS) is controlled. Users frequently carry cumbersome objects (e.g. shopping bags) and use mobile devices at the same time which can cause interaction difficulties and erroneous input. The two methods used to control the PWS were: walking on a treadmill and walking around a predefined route on the ground while following a pacesetter. The results from our target acquisition experiment showed that for ground walking at 100% of PWS, accuracy dropped to 36% when carrying a bag in the dominant hand while accuracy reduced to 34% for holding a box under the dominant arm. We also discuss the advantages and limitations of each evaluation method when examining encumbrance and suggest treadmill walking is not the most suitable approach to use if walking speed is an important factor in future mobile studies.

Author Keywords
Encumbrance; Preferred walking speed; Target acquisition; Mobile interactions.

ACM Classification Keywords
H.5.2. User Interfaces: *Input devices and strategies*

INTRODUCTION
The continuous development of touchscreen mobile devices and apps provide users with a variety of functionality while on the move. As a result, handheld devices are being used in a diverse range of mobile contexts. One important area that deserves more focus from researchers is the effect of encumbrance: for example, interacting while carrying objects such as bags and boxes or using an umbrella when it is raining. People often carry these types of objects in their day-to-day activities and are therefore likely to experience usability problems when their hands are full and attention from the mobile device is required. Users may struggle to input accurately or in an effective manner when their hands are physically hampered by holding objects at the same time which can cause interaction to become frustrating and prone to errors. As a result, it is important to assess the impact of encumbrance, especially when the user is also on the move, a situation already known to cause interaction problems [21,22]. A greater understanding of the issues caused by encumbrance while walking would mean better interaction techniques and more efficient interfaces can be developed to assist the user in these physically awkward and mentally demanding situations.

To examine the effects of encumbrance and mobility in a controlled study, several experimental design issues need to be addressed. Firstly, what objects should be used to replicate realistic encumbrance scenarios? There are many possible objects that a user may carry during interaction and many ways in which the objects may be carried. Ng *et al.* [21] conducted an observational study to assess the typical objects that users carried when using mobile devices in the public and reported that different types of bags and boxes were the most common objects that users held. In the user study presented in this paper, we used a similar approach and selected a typical shopping bag and a packaging box as the encumbrance objects. Both objects are frequently handled during interaction and present users with physical challenges due to each object's size, weight and cumbersome nature.

Secondly, which mobile evaluation method should be used to assess the effects of walking *and encumbrance* on interaction? In previous studies, two broad methods have been used to examine the effects of mobility on input performance with handheld devices: 1) walking on a treadmill [3,4] and 2) walking around a predefined route [3,13,25]. Barnard *et al.* [3] compared both methods and reported the advantages and limitations of each to examine the impact of walking on interactions with mobile devices. However, it is unclear if the two approaches are still appropriate to examine the effects of encumbrance while the user is on the move. Therefore, an experiment was conducted to compare the two walking evaluation techniques to assess their effectiveness.

Thirdly, should the user's preferred walking speed (PWS) be controlled during an encumbered experiment? A potential confounding issue with not controlling the PWS in walking studies is that input performance can be traded with walking speed. For example, the user could walk significantly slower to select onscreen targets more accurately. It is then difficult to measure the true cost of mobility on

MobileHCI '14, September 23 - 26 2014, Toronto, ON, Canada

http://dx.doi.org/10.1145/2628363.2628382

interaction in a controlled experiment. This problem is likely to be further compounded when examining encumbrance while walking as the PWS may be further reduced when input becomes too physically and mentally difficult to interact in an efficient manner. As a result, it is problematic to examine the effects of encumbrance as it is mixed up with walking speed. Therefore, to separate the two physical factors (encumbrance and walking), the users in the experiment presented in this paper maintained PWS during input.

The question then arises as to how to control the PWS for each walking evaluation technique. The treadmill method is straightforward once the user adjusts the speed of the treadmill to the pace at which he/she would normally walk. No extra effort is required to control the PWS. The treadmill guides the user to walk at a constant pace without having to divide attentional resources between interaction, navigation and avoiding nearby obstacles. For walking around a predefined route, we used the method of Ng *et al.* [22] to control the user's PWS by using a human pacesetter. An experimenter who acted as the pacesetter walked at each user's PWS (which was measured at the beginning of the study). The methods we chose to control the PWS allowed us to directly compare walking speed and input performance while encumbered between the two mobile evaluation methods.

BACKGROUND

The Effects of Encumbrance

In one of the few studies that has examined the effects of encumbrance, Ng *et al.* [20] extended the work of Crossan *et al.* [7] by investigating wrist rotation gestures as an alternative form of input with mobile devices when the user was encumbered. The users were walking and either carrying a bag in the dominant hand or clutching a box under the preferred arm while performing the gestures to select targets on a mobile phone. The results from their mobile Fitts' Law pointing experiment showed that input performance when carrying the box under the arm was very similar to unencumbered as users were able to stabilize their forearms against the box which helped to successfully perform the wrist-based gestures. In contrast, accuracy significantly decreased when holding the bag as the swinging motion of the user's arm when walking made it physically difficult to create a steady arm posture to input. This shows that encumbrance can have unpredictable effects on mobile interactions.

Ng *et al.* [21] conducted an observational study across three different types of locations in a major city to identify the objects that users frequently held during interaction. The observations showed that users carried different types of handheld bags the most often (46% of 878 objects). Mainwaring *et al.* [17] and Jain [11] both reported similar findings. Based on this, they then examined the impact of encumbrance while walking by measuring targeting performance on a touchscreen mobile phone. The results showed that the users where significantly less accurate when encumbered compared to holding no objects. Motion capture cameras were used to track body movements during input and showed a significant increase in hand instability when the dominant hand or arm (which was also doing the target selection) was encumbered.

More recently, Ng *et al.* [22] assessed the impact of encumbrance on one- and two- handed interactions. Users performed a target acquisition task in three common input postures (two-handed index finger, one-handed preferred thumb and two-handed both thumbs) while walking and carrying multiple objects (a bag in each hand). The results showed that encumbrance caused target accuracy to decrease while selection time took significantly longer than interaction alone. Interestingly, target accuracy using both thumbs was not significantly better than single thumb or single index finger input when both hands were encumbered. The index finger was significantly quicker at selecting the targets than both thumb-based input postures. The advantage of having an extra finger to input is likely to diminish when both hands are busy carrying cumbersome objects during interaction.

Oulasvirta and Bergstrom-Lehtovirta [23] evaluated the user's physical ability to multitask when interacting with different types of computing devices. The physical tasks covered a range of hand postures and holding differently sized objects, ranging from small items such as a ballpoint pen to larger things like a basketball, while either performing a pointing task on a laptop or text entry on a mobile device. Their findings showed that mouse input on a laptop was affected more than using a trackpad and trackpoint when holding small and medium sized objects at the same time. Furthermore, switching from two-handed to one-handed typing on a mobile device while multitasking caused a decrease in text entry performance. Users performed the tasks while stationary therefore mobility was not examined.

The Effects of Mobility

Many previous studies have examined the impact of walking when using mobile devices. One common method to evaluate the impact of mobility is to use a treadmill [3,4,13]. The user sets the preferred pace on the treadmill by estimating PWS. The recorded walking speed is then used for each trial during the experiment. No additional effort is required to control the PWS as the user walks at a constant pace. However, walking on a treadmill might not be adequate to assess mobility since studies such as [1,19] have found that people's physical movements are different to normal walking on the ground.

In addition, walking on a treadmill is cognitively less demanding than walking in realistic outdoor settings due to the loss of environmental distractions. Consequently, the recorded PWS on the treadmill may not be an accurate representation of the user's real world walking pace as interferences such as avoiding nearby obstacles and keeping a personal distance from others increase mental workload. Oulasvirta *et al.* [24] found that in everyday situations, interaction with mobile devices was fragmented into periods between four to eight seconds as interruptions constantly competed for the user's attention. Users are also exposed to constantly changing surfaces and other outdoor features that are difficult to replicate on the treadmill which could have an adverse impact on PWS and the user's ability to input accurately. Hyman *et al.* [10] reported that users walked slower and were more unaware to nearby events when using mobile phones. Users could be further affected if they also had to carry bulky objects during interaction, as shown by [21,22].

Mobile studies in the real world present their own challenges. For example, it is difficult to control outdoor elements (weather, lighting, number of surrounding people etc.) to keep the experimental conditions consistent and not introduce noise in the results. As an alternative, researchers have replicated real world settings by creating walking routes indoors [3,14,25] and outdoors [5,12,13] for users to navigate. Some studies [3,14,15] have also added obstacles to the walking path to increase the user's cognitive workload. Barnard *et al.* [3] varied room illumination to simulate realistic lighting changes to reproduce "an actual user experience" when comparing treadmill and ground walking. In the mobile study by Mackay *et al.* [16], users were instructed to stop walking and stand still at random intervals to replicate scenarios where the user is suddenly interrupted.

The majority of studies that use the predefined route evaluation method have not controlled the user's walking speed since the purpose of this experimental setup is to replicate walking in the real world. As mentioned earlier, the user can then trade walking speed to improve input accuracy by walking slower. Bergstrom-Lehtovirta *et al.* [4] showed that reducing PWS by 20% (on the treadmill at least) caused targeting performance on a touchscreen device to begin to level off. If walking speed is controlled during input, then the results will give a more accurate reflection of the user's targeting performance while walking without introducing confounding factors. An 'ideal' device would also not slow users down when using it on the move. A human pacesetter is typically used to regulate the user's walking speed when navigating around a predefined route [8,12]. In the outdoor mobile study by Kane *et al.* [12], all users walked at the same pre-set pace by following a experimenter and kept within a certain distance. We used a similar method to Ng *et al.* [22] to control walking speed in our experiment as users walked at their own measured PWS.

Previous research has shown the impact of using mobile devices on the user's walking speed. In the treadmill study by Bergstrom-Lehtovirta *et al.* [4], the mean PWS decreased by 24% to 2.97km/h when targeting on a touchscreen mobile phone compared to walking alone. Similarly, Lin *et al.* [15] stated that users were able to maintain 90% accuracy at the expense of dropping 36% of their walking speed when users walked around a predefined route. Lim and Feria [14] reported a decrease in walking speed of 22% when conducting a visual searching experiment on a handheld device. Mizobuchi *et al.* [18] recorded a low average walking speed of 1.77 km/h when examining different button dimensions to identify the optimal size for text entry via stylus input. The encumbrance and mobile targeting experiment by Ng *et al.* [21] reported a mean PWS of 2.3 km/h during input (unencumbered) which resulted in a mean target accuracy of 42%. When users were carrying a broad box under the non-dominant arm, PWS decreased to 1.6 km/h (a difference of 41% compared to normal walking speed) which caused a mean target accuracy of 37%. The cited mobile studies have all reported the cost of interaction on mobility and found users to reduce walking speed as a compromise to improve input performance.

EXPERIMENT

A mobile target acquisition experiment was carried out to examine the effects of encumbrance while PWS was controlled. Two established methods used in the current literature to evaluate the effects of mobility were compared: walking on a treadmill and walking around a predefined route on the ground. In previous encumbrance studies [20,21,22], the predefined route method was used therefore no studies have yet to use a treadmill to evaluate the impact of walking while encumbered. The participants were given a target selection task on a touchscreen mobile phone while walking and carrying typical everyday objects. We also measured targeting performance at various levels of PWS to simulate situations where the user is walking slower (the user is being held up) and faster (the user is in a rush) than the preferred pace.

Measuring and Controlling PWS

A calibrated Woodway Bari-Mill treadmill with handrail support (see bottom images of Figure 1) was used for the treadmill walking conditions. Each participant's PWS on the treadmill was recorded before the experiment began and was measured by increasing the speed of the treadmill at 0.1 km/h increments up to the speed the user would normally walk. Like Barnard *et al.* [3] and Bergstrom *et al.* [4], participants were asked to think about the speed he/she would usually walk while not in a hurry when estimating the PWS. Once the PWS was recorded, the experimenter adjusted the pace accordingly for all the treadmill conditions for each participant.

For the ground walking conditions, an oval-shaped path was marked out using small plastic cones in a spacious and quiet room. The total length of the route was 20 meters long by 1.5 meters wide, as shown in the top image of Figure 1. The distance between each outer cone (red) was two meters to assist the pacesetter to walk at each participant's PWS. The PWS on the ground was measured by asking each participant to walk the route for six laps. The total time from lap two to lap six was recorded and since the distance was known, the average walking speed was calculated to determine the PWS. The duration of the first lap was not included in the calculation to allow the participants to build up to their normal walking speeds.

To control the PWS for the ground walking conditions, the participants walked side-by-side with an experimenter who acted as a pacesetter. A metronome application was developed in Android 4.1 and ran on a HTC One X mobile phone. The pacesetter used this to tune the metronome speed for each participant once the PWS was calculated. Audio feedback from the application kept the pacesetter at the appropriate walking speed for each participant. Noise levels from the application were kept to a minimum to avoid distracting the participants. Vibrotactile feedback was considered but during initial testing, the experimenter had difficulties walking at the desired pace thus auditory feedback was used. For each experimental condition, the pacesetter and the participant started walking and once the participant was satisfied with the pace and was comfortable with carrying the objects, he/she began a targeting task on a touchscreen mobile phone. Participants were instructed to avoid drifting out of the boundaries of the path during the experiment. Participants were also told to keep up or slow down if they failed to keep pace with the experimenter.

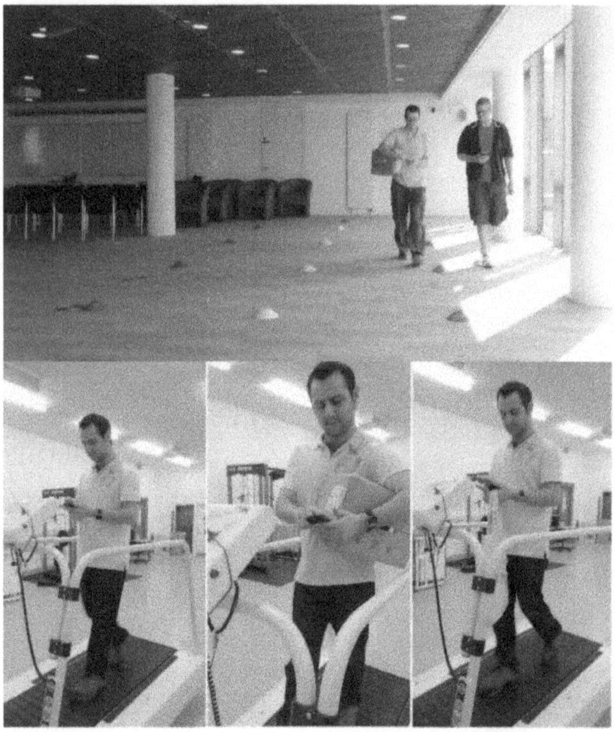

Figure 1. Top image illustrates part of the predefined oval route used in the ground walking conditions. The route was marked with plastic cones. The participant (inside) maintained PWS by walking alongside a pacesetter (outside). The bottom images show a participant performing the task while encumbered and walking on the treadmill.

We also measured targeting performance at various levels of PWS to simulate situations where the user walks slower (for example, when using a mobile device and keeping personal distance from other people) and faster (for instance, the user is in a hurry to get to a meeting). This allowed us to see if the two evaluation methods were practical at controlling different levels of walking speed and to see what effects these different speeds would have on input performance. Based on the findings from Bergstrom-Lehtovirta *et al.* [4], who reported that targeting performance began to level-off when the normal walking speed was decreased by 20%, the PWS was reduced to 80% in our experiment for the slow walking conditions. The walking speed was increased to 120% of the PWS for the fast walking conditions.

Encumbrance Scenarios

Based on the observational study by Ng *et al.* [21], a standard supermarket carrier bag and a packaging box were selected as the encumbrance objects. The dimensions (width x height x depth) of the bag were 45 x 55 x 25 cm, while the measurement of the box were 39 x 30 x 29 cm. Similar to [21,22], the bag and box both weighed 3kg to simulate the physical effects of carrying realistic objects yet reduce the amount of fatigue and tiredness on the participants. The bag was held in the hand while the box was held underarm as these are common ways to hold the objects. Each object was either held in the non-dominant (*ND*) hand/arm or the dominant (*D*) hand/arm during input. Figure 2 shows the bag and box that we used and the ways the objects were held.

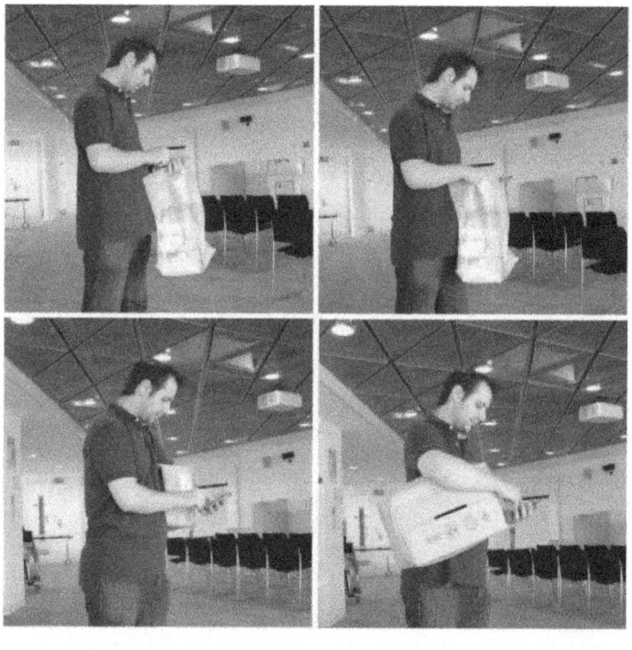

Figure 2. The encumbrance scenarios that were evaluated in the experiment: holding the bag in ND hand (top left), holding the bag in the D hand (top right), carrying the box under the ND arm (bottom left), and carrying the box under the D arm (bottom right). ND = non-dominant and D = dominant.

Experimental Task

The participants selected a series of targets on a touchscreen mobile phone as quickly and as accurately as possible. This type of tapping task has been used in previous studies [4,6,21,22] to measure general targeting performance on a mobile device. There were nine target positions located in a 3 x 3 grid: one centre and eight outer targets. Each outer target was selected ten times in a random order and every second selection was the centre target. As a result, there were 160 target selections per condition for each participant. Like Crossan *et al.* [6], a random interval ranging from 0.5 and 1.5 seconds was placed in between each target selection to reduce any rhythm created between the participant's walking and input. A Samsung Galaxy S3 smartphone with a touchscreen resolution of 720 x 1280 pixels (~12 pixels/mm) was used. Each target was 60 pixels (5mm) wide and 96 pixels (8mm) long with a central crosshair measuring 30 pixels (2.5mm) in both directions (the same size as a key on the standard onscreen Android keyboard for the S3). The device was held in the non-dominant hand while the index finger of the dominant hand was used for input. We chose this type of two-handed input because it is a familiar interaction posture [2,9,22] and to remove the problem of selecting targets that are difficult to reach (in the one-handed preferred thumb posture, for example). The target selection task and input posture are shown in Figure 3.

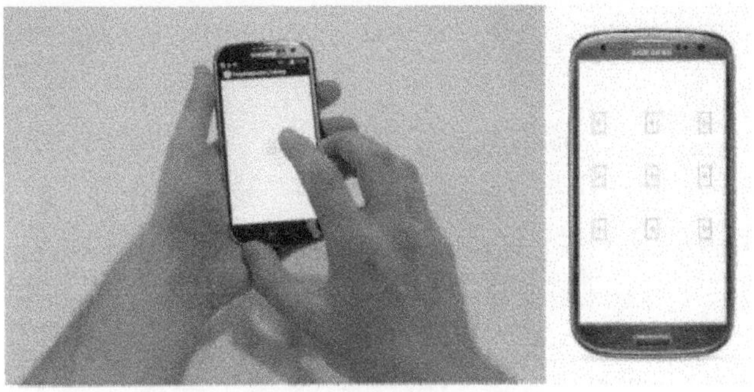

Figure 3. The two-handed index finger input posture used to select onscreen targets (left). The nine target positions on a Samsung Galaxy S3 mobile phone (right).

Experimental Design

A within-subjects design was used for the experiment. Twenty right-handed students (10 male, 10 female) aged between 18 – 41 years (mean = 22.4, SD = 5.3) were recruited from the university. The experiment was split into two sessions and took place on different days as we were concerned with the participants' fatigue and wellbeing. The participants were also given a sufficient resting period between each condition. All the treadmill conditions were completed in one session while all the ground walking conditions were done in the other session. Half of the participants (randomly chosen) completed the treadmill walking conditions first while the other half of the participants began with the ground walking conditions. Each session lasted an approximately one hour (*introduction + training + performing the task + debriefing*) and participants were paid £12 upon completing both sessions.

The Independent Variables were *type of encumbrance* (5 levels - unencumbered, holding the bag either in the *ND* or *D* hand, and holding the box either under the *ND* or *D* arm), *walking method* (2 levels – walking on the treadmill and walking around the predefined route on the ground) and *walking speed* (3 levels - walking at 80%, 100% and 120% of PWS). As a result, there were 30 conditions in total (15 for each session). The conditions in each session were randomised for each participant to reduce learning effects and bias in the results.

The Dependent Variables were target accuracy, target error and selection time. A target was accurately selected if the recorded touch up position was within the target borders. Target error (in millimetres) was the absolute distance from the centre of the target crosshair to the recorded finger touch up position on the screen. Selection time (in milliseconds) was the duration from the display of the current target to the instant that a press up event was logged.

The hypotheses were:

H1: Both error and selection time will be significantly increased while accuracy will be significantly decreased when encumbered compared to unencumbered;

H2: Holding the bag/box in the dominant hand/arm will cause accuracy to decrease significantly and selection time to increase significantly more than holding the objects in the non-dominant side.

H3: Target accuracy will be significantly higher and selection time will be significantly faster when walking at 80% of PWS compared to walking at 100% of PWS;

H4: Target accuracy will be significantly reduced and selection time will be significantly slower when walking at 120% of PWS compared to walking at 100% of PWS;

H5: Target accuracy will be significantly decreased while both error and selection time will be significantly increased for walking on the ground when compared to walking on the treadmill;

H6: The PWS will be significantly faster for walking on the treadmill than walking around the predefined route on the ground.

RESULTS

There were 160 target selections per condition therefore 4800 targets per participant (30 conditions). Twenty participants resulted in a total of 96000 targets for the whole experiment. To filter out unintentional screen taps, targets that took less than 100ms to select were removed from the data set. As a result, 21 targets were eliminated from the analysis. Three factor (type of encumbrance, walking method and walking speed) repeated-measures ANOVAs were conducted to analyse target accuracy, target error and selection time.

Target Accuracy

The mean target accuracy for each walking condition is shown in Figure 4. The ANOVA for accuracy showed a significant main effect for walking method, $F(1, 19) = 10.906$, $p < 0.01$. Target selection was significantly more accurate for walking on the treadmill than walking on the ground (mean difference = 4.85%). A significant main effect was observed for walking at the different levels of PWS, $F(2, 38) = 49.106$, $p < 0.001$. *Post hoc* pairwise comparisons with Bonferroni corrections showed that target accuracy was significantly higher when walking at 80% of PWS than 100% of PWS (mean difference = 3.55%). The participants were significantly less accurate at targeting when walking at 120% of PWS than walking at 100% of PWS (mean difference = 2.63%). A significant main effect was also found for type of encumbrance, $F(4, 76) = 60.933$

, $p < 0.001$. *Post hoc* pairwise comparisons with Bonferroni corrections showed that accuracy was significantly higher when unencumbered compared to holding the objects during input. Target accuracy while carrying the bag in the *D* hand was significantly lower than the *ND* hand. There was no significant difference for accuracy between the *D* and *ND* sides when holding the box underarm. All type of encumbrance pairwise comparisons for accuracy are shown in Table 1. No significant interaction was observed between the factors ($p > 0.05$).

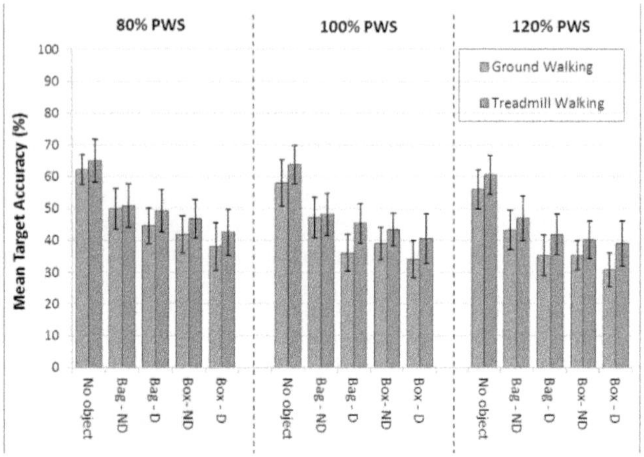

Figure 4. The mean target accuracy (%) for each walking condition, grouped by the % of PWS. The blue and red bars represent the ground and treadmill walking conditions respectively. Error bars denote 95% CI.

Comparison		Mean Difference (%)	Sig*
No object	Bag ND	13.19	0.000
No object	Bag D	18.82	0.000
No object	Box ND	19.79	0.000
No object	Box D	23.39	0.000
Bag ND	Bag D	5.64	0.007
Bag ND	Box ND	6.61	0.002
Bag ND	Box D	10.20	0.000
Bag D	***Box ND***	***0.97***	***1.000***
Bag D	***Box D***	***4.56***	***0.423***
Box ND	***Box D***	***3.60***	***0.253***

Table 1. The pairwise comparisons of type of encumbrance for target accuracy (%). The mean difference that are non-significant are italicised and highlighted in bold. *Adjustment for multiple comparisons: Bonferroni.

Target Error

The mean target error for each walking condition is shown in Figure 5. The ANOVA for target error showed a significant main effect for walking method, $F(1, 19) = 5.198$, $p < 0.05$. Target error was significantly higher when walking on the ground than walking on the treadmill (mean difference = 0.4mm). A significant main effect was also observed for walking speed, $F(2, 38) = 24.286$, $p < 0.001$. *Post hoc* pairwise comparisons with Bonferroni corrections showed that error was significantly higher for walking at 100% of PWS compared to 80% (mean difference = 0.3mm). On the other hand, error at 100% of PWS was significantly lower than walking at 120% of PWS (mean difference = 0.3mm). A main effect was found for type of encumbrance, $F(4, 76) = 32.595$, $p < 0.001$). *Post hoc* pairwise comparisons with Bonferroni corrections (Table 2) showed that error was significantly higher when holding the objects than unencumbered interaction. Target error was significantly higher when the bag was held in the *D* hand than the *ND* hand. Likewise, holding the box under the *D* arm resulted in a significant increase in error compared to the *ND* arm. No significant interaction was found between the factors ($p > 0.05$).

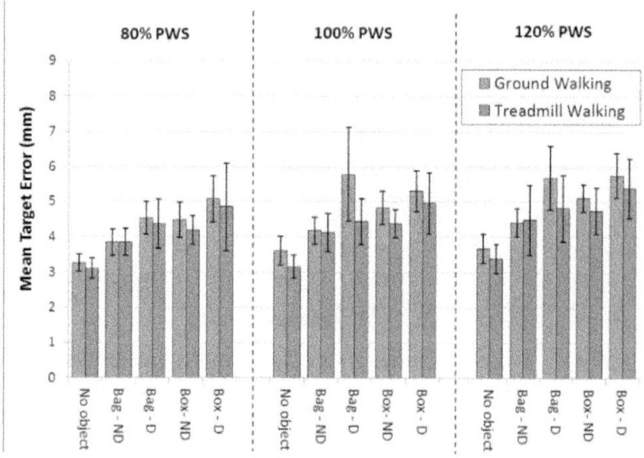

Figure 5. The mean target error (mm) for each walking condition. Error bars denote 95% CI.

Comparison		Mean Difference (mm)	Sig*
No object	Bag ND	-0.8	0.000
No object	Bag D	-1.6	0.000
No object	Box ND	-1.3	0.000
No object	Box D	-1.9	0.000
Bag ND	Bag D	-0.8	0.004
Bag ND	Box ND	-0.5	0.003
Bag ND	Box D	-1.1	0.000
Bag D	***Box ND***	***0.3***	***1.000***
Bag D	***Box D***	***-0.3***	***0.605***
Box ND	Box D	-0.6	0.05

Table 2. The pairwise comparisons of type of encumbrance for target error (mm).

Selection time

Figure 6 shows the mean selection time for each walking condition. The ANOVA for selection time showed a significant main effect for walking method, $F(1, 19) = 23.320$, $p < 0.001$. Selection time was significantly quicker for walking on the treadmill than walking on the ground (mean difference = 26.1ms). A significant main effect was observed for walking at the three different levels of PWS, $F(2, 38) = 7.543$, $p < 0.05$. *Post hoc* pairwise comparisons with Bonferroni corrections showed that selection time was not significantly quicker for walking at 80% of PWS than 100% of PWS. There was also no significant difference for selection time between walking at 100% and 120% of PWS. However, selection time was significantly quicker when walking at 120% of PWS than 80% of PWS, a mean difference of 14.3ms. A significant main effect was found for type of encumbrance, $F(4, 76) = 27.198$, $p < 0.001$. *Post hoc* pairwise comparisons (Table 3) showed that target selections were significantly quicker when unencumbered compared to carrying the objects, except for holding the bag in the *ND* hand. The participants were significantly quicker at selecting the targets when the bag/box was held in the *ND* hand/arm than holding the objects in the *D* side. There was no significant interaction between the factors.

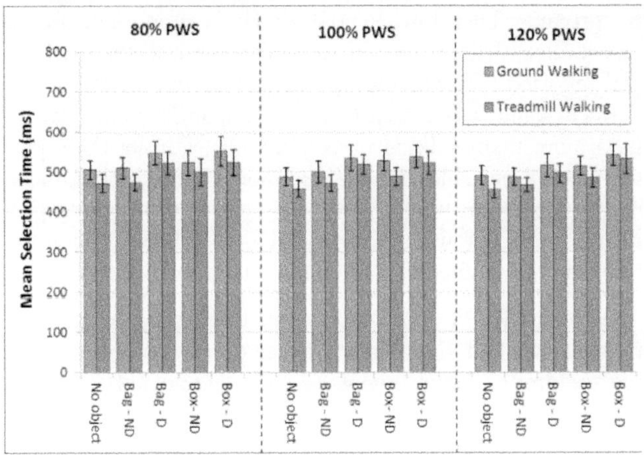

Figure 6. The mean selection time (ms) for each walking condition. Error bars denote 95% CI.

Comparison		Mean Difference (ms)	Sig*
No object	***Bag ND***	***-6.7***	***0.865***
No object	Bag D	-44.0	0.000
No object	Box ND	-28.1	0.000
No object	Box D	-56.7	0.000
Bag ND	Bag D	-37.3	0.000
Bag ND	Box ND	-21.4	0.012
Bag ND	Box D	-50.0	0.000
Bag D	***Box ND***	***15.9***	***0.252***
Bag D	***Box D***	***-12.7***	***1.000***
Box ND	Box D	-28.6	0.009

Table 3. The pairwise comparisons of type of encumbrance for selection time (ms).

PWS, Distance Walked and Experiment Completion Time for Treadmill and Ground Walking

A paired t-test was conducted to compare the measured PWS between the two walking methods. There was a significant difference in walking speed (km/h) for ground walking (mean = 4.88, SD = 0.70) and treadmill walking (mean = 3.57, SD = 1.03); $t(19) = 6.556$, $p < 0.05$. The participants walked significantly faster on the ground than on the treadmill (a drop in walking speed of 26.8%). Furthermore, each participant's PWS on the treadmill was slower than walking on the ground. In the encumbrance and ground walking study by Ng *et al.* [22], who used the same method to control the user's walking speed, a similar mean PWS of 4.9km/h was reported.

Table 4 shows the approximate mean distance walked and total interaction time to complete all 15 conditions for each walking method. Please note, the interaction times do not include any resting periods or the time required to switch between conditions in each session. For comparison, Ng *et al.* [22] reported a mean distance of 1.480km and a total interaction time of 18.3mins to complete their ground walking encumbered study.

	Ground Walking	**Treadmill Walking**
Mean distance walked (km)	1.722 (SD = 0.166)	1.193 (SD = 0.108)
Mean interaction time (mins)	21.17 (SD = 2.04)	20.05 (SD = 1.82)

Table 4. The approximate mean walking distance and total interaction time for each walking method.

DISCUSSION

The results for encumbrance showed that target selections while carrying the bag or box caused accuracy to decrease while error increased when compared to unencumbered. However, there was no significant difference in terms of selection time between unencumbered and carrying the bag in the *ND* hand, despite a significant difference observed for all other pair comparisons. Therefore, hypothesis H1 can only be partially supported.

The results also revealed that holding the bag or the box in the *D* hand or arm caused selection times to significantly increase when compared to holding the objects in the *ND* side. However, it is worth noting that the difference is minimal (28.6ms for the box and 37.3ms for the bag). There was no significant difference for target accuracy between the *D* and *ND* arms when carrying the box thus, hypothesis H2 can only be partially supported. We anticipated significant results since Ng *et al.* [21] found that users experienced more hand movements when the *D* hand or arm was physically hampered which caused accuracy to significantly decrease when compared to the *ND* side.

As previous walking studies have shown, there is always a cost to performance when the user is on the move as target accuracy dropped to 58.0% and 63.8% for ground and treadmill walking respectively (when walking at 100% of PWS). Once the users were also encumbered while maintaining 100% of PWS on the ground, target accuracy decreased to 34.1% for carrying the box under the *D* arm. For comparison, target accuracy for the same walking condition was 36.1% when the bag was held in the *D* hand. For treadmill walking at 100% of PWS, target accuracy was 40.6% and 43.4% for carrying the box under the *D* and *ND* arm respectively. While walking on the treadmill at 100% of PWS, the bag caused target accuracy to drop to 45.4% and 48.1% for the *D* and *ND* hand respectively. From our observations and comments from the participants, the size of the box made it awkward and physically challenging to input accurately, while the participants felt that the weight of the bag caused them more problems in aiming at the touchscreen to input precisely despite both objects weighing the same.

In terms of the impact encumbrance had on selection time, the box (held under either arm) caused significantly longer target selections than unencumbered input. The bag also resulted in significantly slower selection times when it was held in the *D* hand compared to unencumbered interaction. Again, the significant selection times were marginal. The longest mean selection times while walking on the ground at 100% of PWS was 534ms and 537ms for carrying the bag (*D* hand) and the box (*D* arm) respectively. For comparison, treadmill walking at 100% of PWS resulted in mean selection times of 518ms and 521ms for the same encumbrances. While selection times were similar, a greater difference was shown for target accuracy between unencumbered and holding the objects, so the participants might have traded input speed for accuracy.

We measured targeting performance at different levels of the PWS to simulate situations where the user was walking slower and faster than normal. No previous studies have examined the effects of carrying cumbersome objects during interaction while varying walking speed. The results showed that reducing PWS by 20% significantly improved target accuracy and decreased targeting error. However, walking slower at 80% of PWS did not cause significantly quicker selection time than walking at 100% of PWS therefore hypothesis H3 is partial supported. Despite a significant effect being found for target accuracy, the mean accuracy rate only improved by 3.55% when walking at 80% of PWS. Similarly, the difference in mean targeting error between 80% and 100% of PWS was also small at 0.3mm. This suggests that the user would need to reduce walking speed further in order to gain better input accuracy. In the unencumbered treadmill study by Bergstrom *et al.*[4], an ideal trade-off was reported between targeting performance and walking at 40-80% PWS.

The results for walking faster at 120% of PWS showed that target accuracy significantly decreased when compared to 100% of PWS. However, selection time did not take significantly longer than 100% PWS, hence hypothesis H4 is partially supported. Similar to walking slower, the difference in mean target accuracy between 100% and 120% of PWS was small at 2.63%. The highest mean targeting error of 5.8mm was caused by holding the bag in the *D* hand while walking at 100% of PWS on the ground, which was near identical to walking at 120% of PWS (5.7mm). One surprising result from the experiment was that the mean selection time significantly decreased as the PWS increased. In other words, the faster the user walked, the faster the input. We expected the user would need more time to aim accurately at the screen when carrying the cumbersome objects and walking faster than normal. A random delay was placed between each target selection to negate any rhythm between targeting and the user's gait. However, we can only assume that when walking faster, users felt more rushed to input, perhaps to keep up with the body movements when walking.

The comparison between the two evaluation methods showed that target accuracy significantly decreased for ground walking when compared to walking on the treadmill. The mean target accuracy for each ground walking condition was lower than the equivalent treadmill one. Target error was significantly higher for walking on the ground than on the treadmill. As predicted, selection time was shorter for walking on the treadmill than walking on the ground. Therefore, hypothesis H5 is supported. Previous studies [3,13] have compared the two walking methods and reported that walking on the ground and around a predefined route will increase the participant's mental workload more than walking on a treadmill. Furthermore, participants in our study maintained their PWS which reduced the possibility of trading walking speed with targeting performance. Therefore, input is likely to differ between the two walking methods, as shown in our study.

The mean PWS for both walking methods showed that participants walked significantly faster on the ground than on the treadmill. Thus, hypothesis H6 is rejected. We expected the PWS for walking on the ground to be slower than on the treadmill because the participants had to navigate and keep within the path. However, further data analysis showed that all participants walked slower on the treadmill than on the ground. Seven out of twenty participants reduced their PWS on the treadmill by more than 25% when compared to walking on the ground. One particular participant dropped PWS by 71%. The difference in PWS between the two walking methods could have been one reason why targeting performance was significantly better for walking on the treadmill than on the ground.

At the end of the experiment, we asked each participant to walk at the PWS (measured for ground walking) on the treadmill. A majority of the participants were surprised by the difference in walking speed and commented that it was difficult to judge the pace that he/she would normally walk on the treadmill because there was no point of reference. Comments also suggested that the participants walked at a more conservative pace to prevent them from getting close to the edge of the treadmill. This implies that there are possible confounding psychological factors as well as physical factors [1,19] associated with treadmill-based evaluations that cause participants to walk differently from their normal walking speed. Our results and observations showed that the treadmill method should be used cautiously for assessing interactions on the move. The ground walking method is better at measuring the user's PWS more accurately than using a treadmill and should be used if natural walking speed is an important factor in future mobile studies.

Despite the disparity in PWS between the two evaluation techniques, both methods are appropriate to examine the effects of walking while encumbered if extra care is taken when planning a mobile experiment. From our observations, we make the following recommendations and discuss the limitations of each walking method.

The treadmill method is suitable if limited space is available to setup a walking route indoors. Also, it is simpler to arrange than the ground walking method and no additional effort is required from an experimenter to control the PWS once the user estimates his/her walking speed on the treadmill. The user walks at a consistent pace during the experiment without variation in walking speed. On the other hand, the ground walking method requires more initial work to map out and measure the walking route. A human pacesetter is needed to control each participant's PWS. It is a challenging task for the pacesetter to walk at the required walking speed consistently for each participant across all the conditions. Training is required for the pacesetter to walk consistently across a wide range of walking speeds and we advise taking regular resting periods during the experiment to reduce tiredness. Another issue with the ground walking method is that the participants might struggle to keep pace with the pacesetter especially when encumbered. As a result, a difference in walking speed between the user and the pacesetter may occur during input. In our study, the participants were asked to speed up or slow down if they failed to walk at the correct speed with the pacesetter. From our observations, all the participants were able to maintain walking speed with the pacesetter with the exception of a few minor instances where the participant struggled to walk at the correct pace.

In terms of using the evaluation methods to examine the impact of encumbrance while walking, a potential issue with the treadmill is the limited space due to the safety sidebars. In our study, we ensured that carrying the bag and the box on the treadmill would not cause the user any input problems. One constraint of the treadmill method is that it restricts the types of encumbrance scenarios that can be assessed. For example, it is likely to be difficult to evaluate the effects of carrying multiple cumbersome objects [22] and new encumbrance scenarios that require more complex movements such as pushing objects (e.g. a pram) [21,23]. There is no such problem with the ground walking method as the user is not restricted in upper body movements and has more physical space to carrying the objects and input at the same time.

One of the main goals of our experiment was to compare two evaluation methods to examine the effects of walking while encumbered. The other was to widen our understanding of the effects of encumbrance on mobile interactions and make researchers more aware of the usability problems in these contexts. Touchscreen mobile devices such as smartphones present developers with design challenges due to the limited screen space. Interface components such as buttons and icons are small in size which makes them difficult to select accurately when the user is walking and encumbered. A possible solution is to make touchable elements larger to give users bigger target areas to improve accuracy. Interface guidelines from Apple [27] state the size for keys should be 6.7 mm for touchscreen interfaces. Schildbach and Rukzio [26] increased target size to 9.5 mm and showed this improved tapping performance when users were walking. However, these recommended target sizes are less effective if the user is also encumbered. Our results for targeting error suggest a larger target size is required to assist interaction while carrying objects and on the move. Also, increasing target size on screen limited mobile devices can cause other interaction issues such as increasing the amount of scrolling needed to reach all items, as reported by Kane *et al.* [12]. Designers will also need to carefully consider the trade-off between input accuracy and selection time when developing new interaction techniques for encumbrance. The cost of an incorrect selection and subsequent reattempts at selecting a target can result in a frustrating user experience when the user has to multitask while on the move.

CONCLUSIONS

The main contribution of the study presented in this paper is the comparison of two mobile evaluation methods to see if these approaches were appropriate to examine the impact of walking while encumbered. The aim was to measure targeting performance on a touchscreen mobile phone while encumbered and, since users can trade walking speed with input performance, the PWS was controlled. The results and observations from our experiment showed the ground walking method yielded a better representation of the user's PWS than using a treadmill. Despite the variation in walking speed, the differences in terms of targeting performance between the two evaluation methods were small. Both walking techniques are suitable to examine the effects of encumbrance while on the move but each approach has its limitations and care is required when designing encumbered walking experiments.

Our study has also extended the limited literature on the effects of encumbrance. The highest targeting error recorded in our experiment is greater than previous encumbered studies, which shows the extent to which input performance is affected when the user is walking and carrying cumbersome objects at the same time. We hope researchers and user interface designers will be more aware of the usability issues that are caused by the common situation of encumbrance while interacting. At present, there are no input techniques to assist the user to interact in a more effective manner when encumbered yet the popularity of touchscreen mobile devices will continue to grow and present designers with new and unforeseen challenges.

ACKNOWLEDGEMENTS

We thank Dr. Ron Baxendale for his assistance with the treadmill.

REFERENCES

1. Alton, F., Baldey, L., Caplan, S., and Morrissey, M.C. A kinematic comparison of overground and treadmill

walking. *Clinical biomechanics (Bristol, Avon) 13*, 6 (1998), 434–440.

2. Azenkot, S. and Zhai, S. Touch behavior with different postures on soft smartphone keyboards. *In Proc. MobileHCI 2012*, ACM Press (2012), 251–260.
3. Barnard, L., Yi, J.S., Jacko, J.A., and Sears, A. An empirical comparison of use-in-motion evaluation scenarios for mobile computing devices. *International Journal of Human-Computer Studies 62*, 4 (2005), 487–520.
4. Bergstrom-Lehtovirta, J., Oulasvirta, A., and Brewster, S. The effects of walking speed on target acquisition on a touchscreen interface. *In Proc. MobileHCI 2011*, ACM (2011), 143–146.
5. Brewster, S. Overcoming the Lack of Screen Space on Mobile Computers. *Personal and Ubiquitous Computing 6*, 3 (2002), 188–205.
6. Crossan, A., Murray-Smith, R., Brewster, S., Kelly, J., and Musizza, B. Gait phase effects in mobile interaction. *Ext. Abstracts CHI 2005*, ACM Press (2005), 1312–1315.
7. Crossan, A., Williamson, J., Brewster, S., and Murray-Smith, R. Wrist rotation for interaction in mobile contexts. *In Proc. MobileHCI 2008*, ACM Press (2008), 435–438.
8. Goel, M., Findlater, L., and Wobbrock, J. WalkType: using accelerometer data to accomodate situational impairments in mobile touch screen text entry. *In Proc. CHI 2012*, ACM Press (2012), 2687–2696.
9. Hoober, S. How Do Users Really Hold Mobile Devices? http://www.uxmatters.com/mt/archives/2013/02/how-do-users-really-hold-mobile-devices.php.
10. Hyman, I.E., Boss, S.M., Wise, B.M., Mckenzie, K.E., and Caggiano, J.M. Did You See the Unicycling Clown? Inattentional Blindness while Walking and Talking on a Cell Phone. *Applied Cognitive Psychology 24*, 5 (2010), 597–607.
11. Jain, S.S.L. The means of mobility. *Journal of Consumer Culture 2*, 3 (2002), 419–438.
12. Kane, S.K., Wobbrock, J.O., and Smith, I.E. Getting off the treadmill: evaluating walking user interfaces for mobile devices in public spaces. *In Proc. MobileHCI 2008*, ACM Press (2008), 109–118.
13. Kjeldskov, J. and Stage, J. New techniques for usability evaluation of mobile systems. *International Journal of Human-Computer Studies 60*, 5-6 (2004), 599–620.
14. Lim, J.J. and Feria, C. Visual search on a mobile device while walking. *In Proc. CHI 2012*, ACM Press (2012), 295–304.
15. Lin, M., Goldman, R., Price, K.J., Sears, A., and Jacko, J. How do people tap when walking? An empirical investigation of nomadic data entry. *International Journal of Human-Computer Studies 65*, 9 (2007), 759–769.
16. MacKay, B., Dearman, D., Inkpen, K., and Watters, C. Walk 'n scroll: a comparison of software-based navigation techniques for different levels of mobility. *In Proc. MobileHCI 2005*, ACM Press (2005), 183–190.
17. Mainwaring, S.D., Anderson, K., and Chang, M.F. Living for the global city: mobile kits, urban interfaces, and ubicomp. *In Proc. UbiComp 2005*, Springer-Verlag (2005), 269–286.
18. Mizobuchi, S., Chignell, M., and Newton, D. Mobile text entry: relationship between walking speed and text input task difficult. *In Proc. MobileHCI 2005*, ACM Press (2005), 122–128.
19. Murray, M.P., Spurr, G.B., Sepic, S.B., Gardner, G.M., and Mollinger, L. a. Treadmill vs. floor walking: kinematics, electromyogram, and heart rate. *Journal of applied physiology 59*, 1 (1985), 87–91.
20. Ng, A., Brewster, S., and Crossan, A. The effects of encumbrance on mobile gesture interactions. *In Body, Movement, Gestures & Tactility in Interaction with Mobile Devices Workshop, MobileHCI 2011*, (2011).
21. Ng, A., Brewster, S., and Williamson, J. The Impact of Encumbrance on Mobile Interactions. *In Proc. INTERACT 2013*, Springer-Verlag (2013), 92–109.
22. Ng, A., Brewster, S., and Williamson, J. Investigating the Effects of Encumbrance on One- and Two- Handed Interactions with Mobile Devices. *In Proc. CHI 2014*, (2014), 1981–1990.
23. Oulasvirta, A. and Bergstrom-Lehtovirta, J. Ease of juggling: studying the effects of manual multitasking. *In Proc. CHI 2011*, ACM Press (2011), 3103–3112.
24. Oulasvirta, A., Tamminen, S., Roto, V., and Kuorelahti, J. Interaction in 4-second bursts: the fragmented nature of attentional resources in mobile HCI. *In Proc. CHI 2005*, ACM Press (2005), 919–928.
25. Pirhonen, A., Brewster, S., and Holguin, C. Gestural and audio metaphors as a means of control for mobile devices. *In Proc. CHI 2002*, ACM Press (2002), 291–298.
26. Schildbach, B. and Rukzio, E. Investigating selection and reading performance on a mobile phone while walking. *In Proc. MobileHCI 2010*, ACM Press (2010), 93–102.
27. Apple Inc. iPhone Human Interface Guidelines. 2009.

Field Evaluation of a Camera-Based Mobile Health System in Low-Resource Settings

Nicola Dell[1] Ian Francis[2] Haynes Sheppard[2] Raiva Simbi[3] Gaetano Borriello[1]

[1]Computer Science and Engineering
University of Washington
{nixdell;gaetano}@cs.washington.edu

[2]Global Solutions for
Infectious Diseases
ifrancis@gsid.org; haynes.sheppard@gmail.com

[3]Zimbabwe Ministry of
Health and Child Care
raivasimbi@gmail.com

ABSTRACT
The worldwide adoption of mobile devices presents an opportunity to build mobile systems to support health workers in low-resource settings. This paper presents an in-depth field evaluation of a mobile system that uses a smartphone's built-in camera and computer vision to capture and analyze diagnostic tests for infectious diseases. We describe how health workers integrate the system into their daily clinical workflow and detail important differences in system usage between small clinics and large hospitals that could inform the design of future mobile health systems. We also describe a variety of strategies that health workers developed to overcome poor network connectivity and transmit data to a central database. Finally, we show strong agreement between our system's computed diagnoses and trained health workers' visual diagnoses, which suggests that our system could aid disease diagnosis in a variety of scenarios. Our findings will help to guide ministries of health and other stakeholders working to deploy mobile health systems in similar environments.

Author Keywords
Mobile phone; smartphone; mHealth; point-of-care diagnostics; camera; sensors; vision; ICTD; HCI4D.

ACM Classification Keywords
H.5.m. Information interfaces and presentation (e.g., HCI): Miscellaneous.

INTRODUCTION
The rapid increase in mobile device penetration throughout the world is providing an opportunity for mobile systems to play an important role in the delivery of health and information services to people in developing countries. Mobile devices are portable, battery-powered, relatively low-cost and can connect to the Internet via cellular networks. These properties make them more suitable for deployment in low-resource environments than traditional desktop computing platforms. As a result, the emerging research area of mobile health has evolved to study the design and use of mobile systems for healthcare delivery in low-resource settings. Categories of research include informing people about health issues [5], improving adherence to medical protocols [6], providing remote consultation [13] and collecting data in survey format [11].

MobileHCI '14, September 23 - 26 2014, Toronto, ON, Canada
Copyright 2014 ACM 978-1-4503-3004-6/14/09…$15.00
http://dx.doi.org/10.1145/2628363.2628366

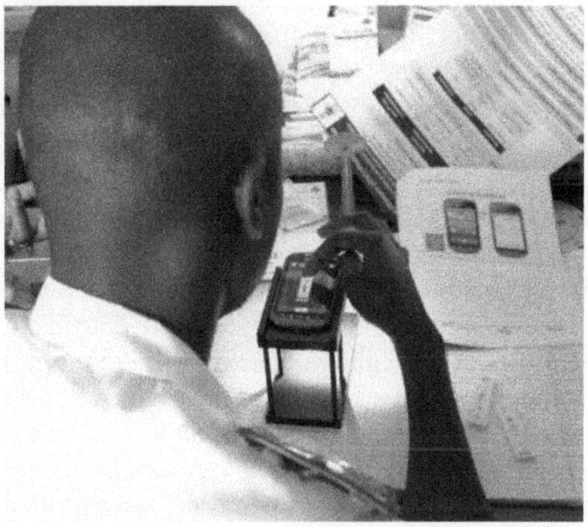

Figure 1: A health worker uses our system in a rural clinic in Zimbabwe to analyze diagnostic tests for malaria.

In addition, a variety of emerging technologies aim to transform a mobile device into a portable medical platform using sensors built-in or attached to the device. SpiroSmart [9] uses the built-in microphone to measure lung function, CellScope [20] uses a lens attachment to turn the camera into a microscope, while NETRA [16] attaches an optical probe to the camera to detect eye anomalies. Although these sensor-based systems may have the potential to transform healthcare in low-resource settings, the majority of them are yet to be evaluated with health workers in the field. As a result, little is known about the challenges and issues that might arise when health workers attempt to integrate mobile sensor-based systems into their patient care routines.

Our work extends the state-of-the-art by exploring the user interaction and deployment challenges that arise when health workers in low-resource settings integrate a mobile camera-based system into their clinical workflow. We designed a system that uses a smartphone's built-in camera and computer vision to capture, analyze and report diagnostic tests for infectious diseases (see Figure 1). Previous research [3] describes an initial implementation of the system's image analysis algorithms. In this paper, we provide an extensive field evaluation of the system with sixty health workers at five hospitals and clinics in Zimbabwe. This is the first time the system has been evaluated with real users in low-resource settings. We explore how health workers are able to integrate the system into their daily patient care routines, both at small, rural clinics and at large, urban hospitals, and we expose a variety of issues that are generally applicable to a range of mobile sensor-based systems (such as data collection issues, user errors, infrastructure challenges, etc.).

Our field evaluation focuses on three important research questions: (i) the impact of the mobile system on health workers' patient care routines, (ii) the impact of poor infrastructure on system usage and data collection, and (iii) the quality of the mobile system's automatically computed diagnoses. Our findings show that health workers were able to integrate the system into their clinical workflow and successfully collect extensive amounts of test data after only sixty minutes of training. Furthermore, health workers used our system to capture and analyze diagnostic tests consistently over an eight-week period. In addition, health workers developed a variety of strategies to overcome poor network connectivity and transmit data to a centralized database. Finally, we show strong agreement between the system's computed diagnoses and the visual diagnoses provided by well-trained health workers, which suggests that the system could assist with disease diagnosis in a variety of scenarios. Taken together, our findings will help ministries of health and other stakeholders to assess the viability and acceptability of deploying mobile sensor-based systems to assist health workers in the field. In addition, our insights will guide future researchers working to deploy mobile health systems in similar environments.

BACKGROUND AND RELATED WORK

Rapid Diagnostic Tests for Low-Resource Settings

Health workers in low-resource settings often lack access to convenient, affordable and usable diagnostic technologies that could help them to quickly diagnose and treat infectious diseases. To address this challenge, low-cost, commercially available rapid diagnostic tests (see Figure 2) have been developed and are now routinely used throughout the world to diagnose a variety of common diseases [12]. For example, the 2013 World Malaria Report [21] showed that a total of 205 million rapid diagnostic tests for malaria were manufactured and sold globally in 2012.

Although the potential benefits of these new diagnostic technologies are immense, little attention has been paid to the challenges faced by the health workers responsible for administering tests and interpreting their results. To run a test, a health worker places a drop of blood on the test, waits a recommended amount of time (usually 10-20 minutes) and then interprets a series of colored control and test lines (see Figure 2) to determine the result. Although interpreting tests may appear to be simple, there are many challenges involved in reading the tests by eye, particularly for health workers in low-resource settings. Human interpretation is subjective and health workers often lack confidence in their ability to read test results correctly [18]. The variety of tests available is also expanding rapidly [12] and the numbers and positions of result lines vary across diseases and test brands, which increases the potential for human error. Researchers are also in the process of developing more complex tests whose results will require quantification [1] or time-sensitive analysis [4] that will be extremely difficult or impossible to analyze by eye. Finally, health workers in low-resource settings may have poor eyesight that could impair their ability to interpret the test.

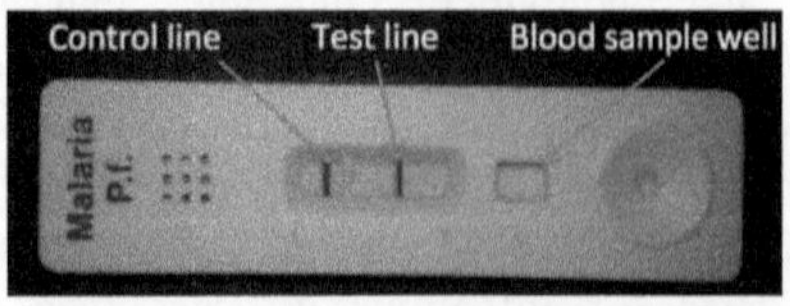

Figure 2: A low-cost rapid diagnostic test for malaria.

In our work, we address these challenges by building a mobile system to objectively interpret the tests. Analysis of tests can become a standardized, auditable and adjustable process that can be changed without retraining users. Commodity smartphones can analyze a variety of tests, negating the need for specialized reader devices, and new tests can be added to the system as they become available. Furthermore, a mobile system can also collect and transmit relevant patient and disease data to a central database. Providing governments and epidemiologists with timely, accurate statistics regarding the diseases detected could aid outbreak detection, supply chain management, evidence-based decision-making, health system evaluation and global disease surveillance and control efforts.

Mobile Health Systems for Low-Resource Settings

A range of prior research highlights the potential for mobile systems to improve healthcare in low-resource settings. Research areas include informing people about health issues [5] and improving adherence to medical protocols [6]. Several mobile data collection systems have also been widely deployed [5, 8, 11]. However, these deployments focus on manually collecting textual data in survey format rather than processing rich data collected from sensors. Telemedicine systems allow users to capture images in the field and transmit them for remote analysis, either by a human expert [13], or by complex image processing algorithms running in a data center [17]. However, many health facilities in low-resource settings lack the reliable network connection required to transmit high-resolution images for off-site analysis. In addition, the expert analyzing the images is likely to be a busy medical professional and it may take days to send a result back to the health worker. These challenges suggest that it may be beneficial to perform any necessary computation locally on the device rather than transmitting it for off-site analysis.

As discussed in the previous section, innovative mobile health systems have also recently been developed that aim to process data collected from sensors built-in or attached to the device [9, 18, 22]. Although these systems have the potential to transform healthcare delivery in low-resource settings, they are yet to be evaluated with real users in the field, and little is known about the issues that might arise when these systems are integrated into the clinical workflow. A notable exception by Chaudri et al. [2] uses an external temperature sensor attached to a smartphone to monitor the pasteurization of human breast milk. The system was evaluated in two South African hospitals with promising preliminary results, although the study did not consider how the system may be used in small, rural clinics.

Mobile Systems for Analyzing Diagnostic Tests

In addition to our work, several recent mobile systems also target the capture and analysis of rapid diagnostic tests. Matthews et al. [14] describe a mobile system that uses image processing to automatically interpret a paper-based test for dengue fever. However, the algorithm has not yet been fully evaluated and only targets a single, special-purpose test for dengue rather than a range of tests for a variety of diseases. Mudanyali et al. [15] developed a smartphone-based diagnostic test reader that controls the environment in which images of tests using lighting. By contrast, our system uses only the device's built-in flash to light the image, which is advantageous since requiring additional battery-powered parts increases the likelihood that one of the parts will run out of charge and render the system non-functional.

The FIO Corporation [7] markets a smartphone-based diagnostic test reader capable of imaging a variety of tests. However, the device is enclosed in a specialized container, which limits it to reading diagnostic tests and prevents it from becoming a general-purpose medical platform. In addition, users must purchase the company's proprietary devices and cloud-based services. By contrast, our system is open-source, allows users to add their own tests to the system, and works with a variety of mobile devices and server solutions. Lastly, to the best of our knowledge, FIO's system is the only smartphone-based diagnostic test reader that has been evaluated in the field [19]. However, the study focused solely on the accuracy of the system's medical diagnoses and did not consider any data collection, usability or infrastructure challenges faced by users in the field.

SYSTEM DESIGN

Our work extends the state-of-the-art by exploring the user interaction and deployment challenges that arise when health workers in low-resource settings integrate a mobile camera-based system into their clinical workflow. Specifically, we designed and built a smartphone system that uses the device's built-in camera to capture and analyze rapid diagnostic tests for infectious diseases. The rest of this section describes our design principles, user interaction and system workflow, and implementation details.

Usage Scenario and Design Principles

We target the following usage scenario: a health worker in a rural clinic has been issued a mobile device to assist with clinical tasks. The health worker enters a patient exam room to assess a patient. After spending time interacting with the patient and using the device to collect patient data, the health worker decides to perform a diagnostic test for malaria. (S)he obtains a blood sample from the patient and administers a rapid diagnostic test for malaria. Then, (s)he uses the device's built-in camera to capture an image of the test. The system processes the image, displays the test result on the screen, and transmits the data to a database if and when there is sufficient connectivity. Finally, based on the test result, the health worker recommends the appropriate treatment or selects another test to run.

In addition to being appropriate for our target problem of interpreting diagnostic tests, many of our design principles are also applicable to a range of other mobile sensor-based systems. For example, similar usage scenarios might apply to capturing images for cell-phone microscopy [16] or sound to analyze lung function [9].

Commercially available devices

Requiring users to import, configure and maintain custom hardware systems may present a significant barrier for many users in low-resource settings. Therefore, our system runs on commercially available Android devices and only uses sensors that come built into these devices. The system does not use any additional hardware or specialized reader device and analyzes rapid diagnostic tests using only images captured from the built-in camera. We have tested the system using a variety of smartphones with 5 mega-pixel cameras and above. The variety of Android devices available in low-resource settings will allow users with varying needs and budgets to choose devices that best fit their requirements. In addition, smartphones are multi-purpose devices that can also provide utility beyond diagnostics (such as voice and text communications, patient management or data reporting).

Local computation

Prior research explores the idea of transmitting images for remote analysis [13, 19]. However, many low-resource settings lack sufficient Internet connectivity to reliably transmit high-resolution images. Thus, our system performs all of the computation and image processing on the device, which allows the system to be fully functional in the absence of a network connection.

Asynchronous transmission

In many low-resource settings, the quality of the network connection might vary with network traffic, time of day and power outages. Thus, our system supports asynchronous data transmission in which collected images and data are stored locally on the device until a network connection or sufficient bandwidth becomes available for transmission.

Data collection

In addition to capturing and processing images, our system allows users to collect and report data (including text, barcodes, GPS data, *etc.*) about the patients seen and diseases detected. Rather than building a new data collection platform, we integrated the image processing components of the system with CommCare [5], a widely used data collection platform based on Open Data Kit [11].

Easily configurable

We wanted to make it easy for test manufacturers and clinical experts to add new rapid diagnostic tests to the system and to control the sensitivity of the image-processing algorithm for their specific test. To add a new test, a clinical expert creates a simple text file, called a *test description file*, which specifies the size and location of the regions that contain the test results. The test description file is uploaded to the device and used to configure the mobile system for use by health workers in the field. The health workers will not adjust the system parameters. Instead, health workers will simply use the smartphone's built-in camera to capture images of tests that have previously been added to the system by clinical experts. A typical test description file consists of about ten lines of text and may be created using any text editor or using a graphical web tool that we developed. Thus far, clinical experts in the laboratory have created and tested description files a variety of rapid diagnostic tests for different diseases and test brands, including tests for malaria, HIV and syphilis [3].

Interaction Design and System Workflow

A prior paper describes the system architecture and image processing algorithms in detail [3]. Here, we provide an overview of the steps required for a health worker to interact with the system to capture and process a diagnostic test. A health worker begins by launching the system and using the mobile application to record any relevant patient data (such as age, gender, *etc.*) They then select the type of diagnostic test from a menu on the screen that contains a list of all the tests that have been added to the system. Selecting a test automatically launches the Android camera application, which allows users to take (and, if necessary, re-take) and image of the relevant diagnostic test. When the user is happy with the image that they captured, they press a button to save and process the image.

The next step in the workflow is to align the captured image, which involves separating the part of the image that contains the diagnostic test cartridge from the background. After aligning the image, the system displays the test on the screen, and provides users with an opportunity to re-take the image should the test appear to be misaligned. If the test has aligned correctly, the user presses a button to compute the diagnosis. The system uses test description file that corresponds to the chosen diagnostic test to locate and process each region on the test that the clinical expert specified as showing a result. For each region, the system uses a thresholding algorithm (described in detail in [3]) to determine if a line is present in that region. Finally, the system uses the combination of detected lines to determine the final test result. After the result has been computed, it is displayed on the screen with an image that shows the user the results of processing so that they can verify the diagnosis. Figure 3 shows the system's user interface for a processed malaria test with a positive result. After checking the result, the user saves and exits the application. The system then stores all of the data associated with the captured test locally on the smartphone, and transmits this data, along with an image of the captured test, to a central database if and when a network connection is available.

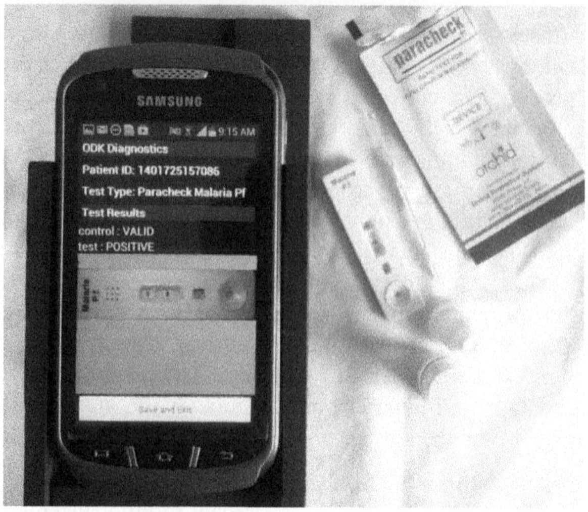

Figure 3: The mobile system's user interface, showing a processed diagnostic test for malaria with a positive result.

FIELD EVALUATION

We conducted an eight-week field study with sixty users at five hospitals and clinics in Zimbabwe to explore the impact that using our mobile camera-based system had on health workers' patient care routines. Although we have extensively tested the system with rapid diagnostic tests for multiple diseases in the laboratory, including tests for HIV, syphilis and flu [3], our field evaluation in Zimbabwe targeted only diagnostic tests for malaria. The practical constraints of integrating a new system into government public health facilities limited our deployment to diagnostic tests that are already routinely purchased and distributed by the Ministry of Health and Child Care. Rapid diagnostic tests for malaria are available at all hospitals and clinics in Zimbabwe and are used to test and treat patients in a variety of clinical departments, including the maternal and child health, outpatient, opportunistic infections and maternity departments. Health workers in Zimbabwe have been trained to administer rapid diagnostic tests for malaria and use them on a daily basis, and the Ministry of Health allowed us to analyze these tests. We acknowledge that only evaluating the mobile system with malaria tests is a limitation of our study. However, since the process of administering rapid diagnostic tests for other diseases is the same as administering tests for malaria, the workflow to analyze tests for other diseases would be identical.

Research Questions

This study was the first time that the system has been evaluated with health workers in low-resource settings. We formalize our study into three research questions:

Q1: To what extent are health workers in low-resource settings willing and able to integrate a mobile camera-based system into their daily patient care routine?

Although many health workers in Zimbabwe own basic mobile phones, the majority have never used a touchscreen device. We wanted to assess how easily health workers learned to interact with these new devices, how easily groups of health workers within a clinic were able to use a single device as a shared resource, and how system usage might vary across health facilities of different sizes. Finally, we wanted to explore the range of user errors that occurred when health workers used the system in the field.

Q2: What infrastructure challenges are faced by health facilities using the system and what strategies might be used to overcome these challenges?

The rapid growth of mobile networks in developing regions has led to the widespread deployment of 2G/3G networks. However, network data speeds are usually erratic and availability can be intermittent. We wanted to examine how network connectivity varied at different sites and see if the sites possessed sufficient bandwidth to transmit collected data and images. In addition, we were interested in what strategies were used to keep the devices safe and charged.

Q3: To what extent do the automatically processed diagnoses computed by the mobile system agree with the visual diagnoses made by trained health workers?

One of our long-term goals is for the system to help health workers who may not have much medical background to correctly diagnose patients. However, since this study is the first field evaluation of the system, we did not want to affect the standard of patient care at this stage. Thus, health workers who participated in our study were trained nurses whose interpretation of tests is currently used to guide patient care. All patient treatment was based on their visual diagnoses collected prior to image processing. This enabled a blinded comparison of the visual diagnoses and the system diagnoses to assess if the system might be used to direct patient care in the future.

Study Sites

Following approval of the study protocols by the IRB, we identified five clinical study sites in the Manicaland province: the Mutare provincial hospital, the Hauna and Nyanga district hospitals, and the Tombo and Zindi rural health centers. We selected sites that typically have a high prevalence of malaria testing and deliberately targeted facilities that ranged in size from large urban hospitals to small rural clinics to explore how system usage varied at different levels of the healthcare hierarchy. Mutare hospital, located in Zimbabwe's third largest city, is the biggest hospital in Manicaland province. Nyanga district hospital is in a town roughly 100km from Mutare. Hauna hospital is located in a substantially more rural and difficult to access valley roughly 100km from Nyanga. Finally, the Tombo and Zindi clinics are in small, rural villages roughly 80km from Nyanga and 60km from Hauna respectively.

Table 1: Summary of study sites, participants and devices.

Study site	No. of Participants	No. of Devices
Mutare hospital	27	4
Nyanga hospital	17	4
Hauna hospital	11	4
Zindi clinic	3	2
Tombo clinic	2	1
All sites	**60**	**15**

Participants

We recruited 60 health workers (47 female) across the five study sites (see Table 1). Participation was limited to trained health workers who conduct malaria diagnostic tests regularly as part of their job. Participants ranged in age from 24 to 64 years (M = 35) and had between 1 and 42 years (M = 6) of experience employed as health workers. Most participants owned basic mobile phones, but 32 had never used a touchscreen device and another 15 had less than six months experience using a touchscreen device.

Apparatus

We configured our mobile application to collect patient data and capture diagnostic tests for malaria. Since our study deals with sensitive personal health information, all the data we collected was anonymized. We recorded the patient's gender, age, location, test type, date, time, the health worker's visual diagnosis and the system's computed diagnosis. The application was also instrumented to record the times at which the test started and ended and the time at which the captured data was transmitted to the server.

We deployed the mobile system on Samsung Galaxy XCover 2 Android devices because they were readily available and moderately priced in Zimbabwe. The XCover 2 has a 1 GHz dual core processor, a 5 mega-pixel built-in camera, a 4-inch capacitive touchscreen and a ruggedized plastic cover to protect the device from dust and moisture. Each device was loaded with a 2GB external SD card and a local SIM card with a 300MB prepaid data bundle. As shown in Table 1, the provincial and district hospitals received four devices each, with one device placed in each of the clinical departments that perform the most malaria diagnostic tests (the maternal and child health department, the outpatient department, the maternity department and the opportunistic infections department). Since rural clinics typically employ fewer health workers than hospitals, each clinic was issued with one or two devices to cover their patient load. In total, we deployed 15 devices across five study sites. Each device was accompanied by a simple plastic stand (see Figure 4) designed to provide stability and a fixed focal length for the device's camera. In addition, we distributed printed user manuals to provide support and guidance for participants in the absence of the researchers.

Figure 4: A simple plastic stand holds the mobile device in a convenient position above the diagnostic test.

Procedure

Preliminary Site Assessment

Before beginning the study, we visited Zimbabwe to assess the selected study sites, understand the health workers' current routines, and gain insight into how a mobile system might be successfully integrated into the clinical workflow. We also tested the network connectivity and data transmission rates at each site.

Adding Diagnostic Tests to the System

During our site assessment, we obtained the details of the three brands of malaria tests currently in use at the sites. Following this, a clinical expert at Global Solutions for Infectious Diseases (San Francisco, USA) [10] created the test description files to add the malaria tests to the system. Encouragingly, creating new test description files was relatively quick, taking roughly 30 minutes per test. Rigorously testing the system parameters for each test took longer, typically several days, since it was necessary to prepare and administer series' of tests with differing dilutions of malaria infected blood under a variety of lighting conditions, before empirically determining the parameters that resulted in the optimal sensitivity and specificity. To make the optimization phase easier, we created a version of the system that could batch process a variety of different test images and parameters at once, which allowed the clinical expert to more quickly narrow in on the optimal algorithm parameters for each test.

Training and Deployment

After adding the malaria tests to the system, we returned to Zimbabwe and conducted participant training sessions at each study site. Each training session lasted approximately 60 minutes and began by demonstrating the system to a group of participants. Participants were then divided into pairs and given time to read user manuals, ask questions and practice capturing and reporting diagnostic test data. The amount of practice that participants required varied depending on their familiarity with technology, although all participants mastered the system within the training session. During each session, we explained that this was the first time the mobile system was being field tested and that all patient care should continue to be based on participants' visual diagnoses. At the end of each session we collected demographic data regarding each participant's age, work experience and familiarity with technology.

After the training sessions, participants were asked to integrate the system into their daily patient care routine and to capture and transmit data every time that they performed a malaria test. At the hospitals, we explained that each of the main clinical departments that conducted malaria tests would receive one device and that participants working in these departments would share the device accordingly. We conducted follow-up visits at each site one week and six weeks after the training sessions to assess how easily participants were able to integrate the technology into their workflow. During these visits, we observed participants using the system and conducted semi-structured interviews to collect data about participants' opinions and experiences.

RESULTS AND DISCUSSION

Q1: Integrating the System into the Clinical Workflow

Our first research question explores the extent to which participants were able to integrate the system into their clinical workflow, including how they used the system and what errors they made when interacting with the system.

Analyzing System Usage and Data Collection

Health workers reacted positively to the introduction of the mobile system into their daily clinical workflow. Most participants were eager to learn the new technology and excited that the system represented progress for Zimbabwe's national health system. Figure 5 shows the number of tests captured by each site. In total, participants captured and transmitted 1828 malaria tests over the two-month study period. The median time that it took to capture and process a test and record patient data was 1.5 minutes (ranging from an average of 2.5 minutes at Mutare to 1.3 minutes at Nyanga).

In addition, a large proportion of participants immediately identified the potential for the system to reduce their paperwork burden by automatically generating aggregated monthly reports. Participants at the small clinics told us that they were currently responsible for manually maintaining a large number of paper-based patient registers, several of which required the same data to be repeated and most of which required a written monthly report. They were eager to show us which registers could be replaced by collecting data using the mobile system, and they requested that the system be extended to enable them to collect a broader range of health information beyond diagnostic test data.

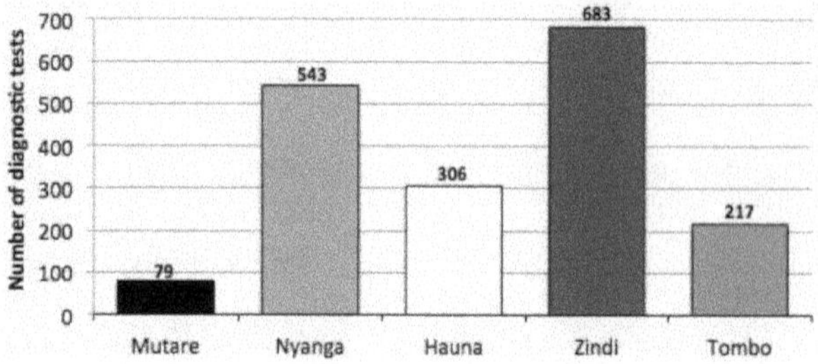

Figure 5: Total number of malaria diagnostic tests captured by each study site.

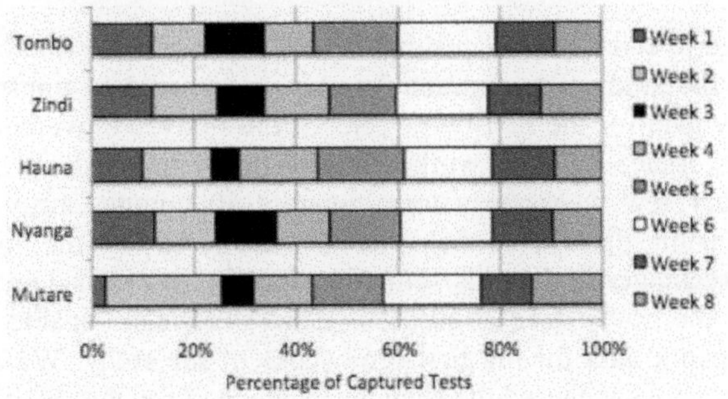

Figure 6: Proportion of each site's total tests that were collected during each week of the study.

Figure 6 shows the proportion of each site's captured tests that were collected during each week of the study. Encouragingly, participants used the system regularly to collect data for the duration of the study, which suggests that they were generally able to integrate the system into their daily clinical routines. In addition, several participants mentioned that patients responded favorably to the new system, believing that it was important for their diagnostic test data to be reported directly to the Ministry of Health.

Somewhat surprisingly Zindi, one of the small rural clinics, captured the largest number of tests (see Figure 5). This could be explained by several factors. First, Zindi is located in the most malaria endemic region of all the study sites and typically performs a large number of diagnostic tests during the malaria season. In addition, small clinics are usually a patient's first point of contact with the health system and represent an ideal place at which to quickly diagnose and treat malaria. Finally, we found that the health workers at Zindi set up a dedicated desk that they used exclusively for performing malaria tests. Placing the mobile device on the same desk made it easy for them to integrate the system into their current workflow and capture tests as necessary.

By contrast, Mutare, the largest hospital in the study, captured the smallest number of tests (see Figure 5). There are several possible explanations for this. First, since visiting the hospital is substantially more expensive than visiting a clinic, many patients only visit the hospital if they are referred there by a clinic. In these cases, patients often already received a diagnostic test at the clinic and there is no need to perform another test at the hospital. In addition, the clinical departments at Mutare hospital are much larger than those at the district hospitals and have many patient exam rooms, and it was challenging for participants to coordinate usage of a single device across multiple rooms. Several participants explained that sometimes when they needed to use the device, it was already being used in another room. Thus, for large hospitals, a better deployment model may be to provide one device per exam room.

We also discovered that the large number of patients at the hospital increased participants' fear that the devices would get stolen if left in a room unattended. As a result, participants frequently locked the device in a cabinet when they left the room. Other participants were then unable to access the device until they found the health worker with the key. During a follow-up visit, we explained to participants that it would be better to use the system and risk theft of the device than keep it locked away. This encouragement may have been responsible for the larger number of tests collected in Mutare in the second week of the study (see Figure 6) although the number of tests decreased again in subsequent weeks. At the end of the study several participants suggested that it would be better for each health worker to have a device and carry it around the hospital. However, this would substantially increase the number of devices and overall cost of deploying the system.

Analyzing User Errors

To analyze the errors that participants made when they interacted with the system, we manually examined all of the captured images and coded any anomalies. User errors fell into five categories: (1) *no image captured* - users collected patient data but failed to capture an image of a test; (2) *captured image is not of a diagnostic test* – in these cases the image was usually of the desk or stand and probably captured accidentally; (3) *incorrect test selected* – the type of test shown in the image is different to the test type selected by the user; (4) *test placed upside-down* – the test in the image was placed the wrong way up; and (5) *unusable image* – the captured image is not usable for analysis because it is out of focus, overexposed or the device was not positioned in the stand correctly.

Figure 7 shows the percentage of each site's captured tests that contained each type of error. Overall, we identified errors in 114 out of 1828 tests (6.2%). The most common error was placing the test upside-down (53/1828 or 2.9%), followed by incorrectly selecting the test type (31/1828 or 1.7%). The other error types were more infrequent, with users failing to capture an image in 11/1828 or 0.6%, capturing an image of something other than a test in 6/1828 or 0.3%, and placing the device incorrectly in 13/1828 or 0.7%. Zindi had the lowest error rate at 2.2%, while Tombo had the highest error rate at 11.5%. One reason for the high error rate at Tombo was due to one participant repeatedly placing the device incorrectly in the stand (see Figure 7).

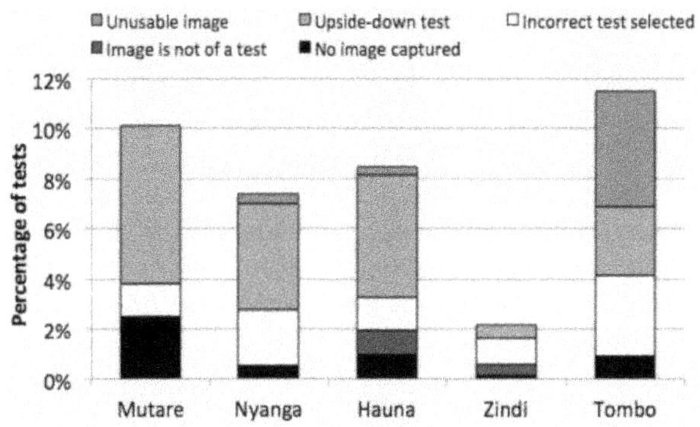

Figure 7: Percentage of each site's total tests that contained each type of user error.

Figure 8: A diagnostic test that contains too much red background to yield a valid diagnosis.

We plan to address several error types through additions to the algorithm. We have already updated the system to make it impossible for users to submit data without capturing an image. In addition, for tests that contain any identifying markings (such as a brand name), it should be relatively straightforward to automatically detect the test type and/or if the test is upside-down. Finally, additional or repeated training sessions would likely also decrease user errors.

Using the System for Quality Control

Our findings also show that the system has the potential to be a valuable quality control tool. Early in the study, our analysis revealed a series of transmitted images in which the tests had been incorrectly administered since the test strip had a dark red background (see Figure 8). This could be the result of health workers either using too much blood on the test or of reading the test result too early. In either case, the dark red background could easily obscure a weak positive result and the test should be discarded. Instead, health workers were incorrectly reporting these tests as valid, usually negative, diagnoses. This problem occurred in a total of 58 tests (3.2%), of which 34 were from Tombo clinic. Based on this data, we alerted the relevant supervisor who reviewed the test manufacturer's guidelines with the health workers. In the future, it will be relatively simple to automatically identify tests that have a dark red background and instruct the user to discard the test and run another test.

Q2: Infrastructure Challenges

Our second research question explores the infrastructure challenges faced by participants using the system. None of the devices were broken, lost or stolen during the study. In addition, participants at each study site were able to keep the devices sufficiently charged despite experiencing frequent electricity outages, which confirms the benefits of deploying portable, battery-charged devices.

We observed substantial variations in network connectivity between the study sites. Mutare and Nyanga had fairly reliable 3G connections, Hauna and Zindi had much slower, unreliable 2G connections, and although Tombo appeared to have a 2G connection, the distance from the clinic to the cell tower made transmitting any data extremely challenging. Thus, although we initially planned to transmit relatively high quality images (roughly 300KB), we decided to instead transmit low-quality, compressed images, which decreased the amount of data to about 70KB per test.

Our findings show several interesting differences in data transmission between the sites. Figure 9 shows the proportion of each site's total tests that were transmitted during each week of the study. Mutare and Nyanga were able to reliably transmit data to the server for the duration of the study. By contrast, Tombo was unable to transmit any data for the first two weeks of the study. To overcome this issue, a health worker from Tombo traveled by bus every few weeks to a town roughly 40 minutes away to transmit data. This behavior is illustrated by the high percentages of data transmitted by Tombo in weeks 3 and 6 of the study (see Figure 9). Zindi was also unable to transmit data for the first few weeks of the study. We are unsure what caused the changes in connectivity that enabled Zindi to transmit large amounts of data in weeks 6-8 of the study, although we hypothesize that the network provider installed a new cell tower or signal-boosting hardware in the area. Finally, health workers at Hauna also struggled initially to transmit data. However, after noticing that connectivity seemed to be more reliable at night, health workers began leaving the devices on to transmit overnight. In total, Hauna transmitted 34% of their tests between 10pm and 4am, compared to 4% by Mutare, 2% by Tombo and 0% by Zindi and Nyanga during the same time frame.

Our findings also show large variations between sites in the delays between capturing tests and transmitting them to the server. Mutare and Nyanga experienced the smallest delays in transmission, with geometric means of 33 seconds (*SD* = 23 hrs) and 45 seconds (*SD* =17 hrs) respectively, compared to mean delays of 2 hrs (*SD* = 129 hrs) at Hauna, 2 hrs (*SD* = 250 hrs) at Zindi and 6 hrs (*SD* = 140 hrs) at Tombo.

These findings can inform the design of other mobile health systems. Many systems that target low-resource settings face challenges relating to network connectivity, and our study highlights the importance of supporting asynchronous data transmission. Depending on the site, it took anywhere from a few seconds to a few weeks for a captured test to be transmitted to the server, which also highlights the need for mobile systems to process data locally rather than transmit it for off-site analysis. Furthermore, several of the strategies that our participants developed for transmitting data could be generalized to other contexts.

Q3: Comparison of System and Human Diagnoses

Our final research question explores the extent to which the system's diagnoses agreed with the health workers' diagnoses. Although the Ministry of Health informed us prior to the study that the sites used three brands of malaria

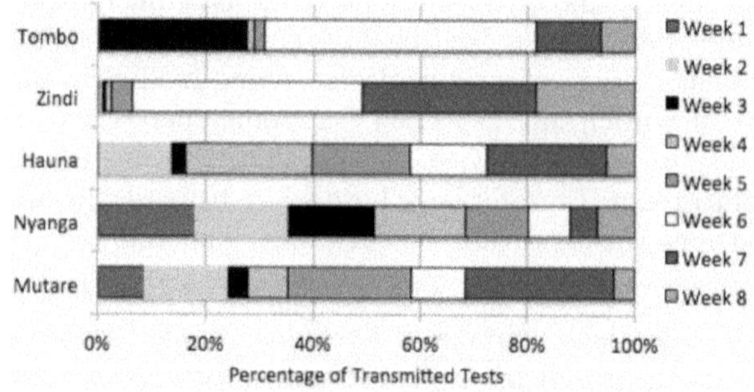

Figure 9: Proportion of each site's total tests that were transmitted during each week of the study.

Table 2: Summary of agreement between (A) the system and visual diagnoses, (B) the review and visual diagnoses and (C) the review and system diagnoses.

A

		System Positive	System Negative	Kappa (95% CI)
Visual	Positive	345	26	
	Negative	70	1273	0.84 (0.81-0.87)

B

		Review Positive	Review Negative	Kappa (95% CI)
Visual	Positive	352	19	
	Negative	22	1321	0.93 (0.91-0.95)

C

		Review Positive	Review Negative	Kappa (95% CI)
System	Positive	367	50	
	Negative	7	1290	0.91 (0.88-0.93)

tests, we found that in practice all the tests they performed were of a single brand (Paracheck Pf®, see Figure 2). Our analysis of agreement did not include tests that contained user errors (shown in Figure 7). Thus, our dataset consisted of 1714 Paracheck tests. As shown in Table 2(A), the system and visual diagnoses agreed in 1618 tests (94.3%). We used Cohen's Kappa [22] to compute a statistical level of agreement between the two diagnoses. The measured Cohen's Kappa for these results was 0.84 (95% CI:[0.81,0.87]), indicating strong agreement.

Further analysis revealed several sources of disagreement. In some cases, the correct diagnosis was clear and either the system or the health worker made an obvious error. Unfortunately, we cannot determine if visual errors were the result of data entry mistakes or if the participants in fact diagnosed a patient incorrectly. In addition, a large portion of tests (430 or 25%) contained at least some amount of red background coloring, which caused a substantial number of the errors made by the system (often these were false positive results). As discussed previously, the red coloring may result from health workers using too much blood on the test or reading the test result too early. In testing the system prior to the study, we always used the correct amount of blood and waited the right amount of time before reading the result. Thus, we did not test the system on images with colored backgrounds. Further adjustments to the algorithm may be required to deal with this issue. Finally, there were tests with equivocal results at the limit of detection. In these cases, either the system or the health worker reported a positive result. However, since our study did not include microscopy-based analysis of blood samples by a clinician (considered the gold standard of malaria diagnostics), we do not know which diagnosis was correct.

To further analyze differences between the system and visual diagnoses, we created a *review* diagnosis for each test. We asked three researchers to examine each test image and provide a diagnosis, and we recorded their majority opinion as the *review* diagnosis. As shown in Table 2(B), the review and visual diagnoses matched in 1673 tests (97.6%). The measured Cohen's Kappa for these results was 0.93 (95% CI: [0.91, 0.95]), indicating a stronger agreement than observed between the system and visual diagnoses (Table 2(A)). Finally, the review and system diagnoses agreed in 1657 tests (96.7%) (see Table 2(C)). The measured Cohen's Kappa for these results was 0.91 (95% CI: [0.88, 0.93]), which is only slightly lower than observed between the review and visual diagnoses (Table 2(B)).

We were interested to see how our results compared to those obtained in the clinical study of the FIO mobile diagnostic system [19]. Their study was conducted at a single site in Tanzania and analyzed SD Bioline malaria tests. Our study took place at five sites in Zimbabwe and analyzed Paracheck malaria tests. The different test brands used somewhat limits the comparisons that can be made between the two systems, since variations could be due to differences in the tests. In addition, their study was able to compare their system's results to a microscopy-based gold standard, finding that the system had an overall accuracy of 95% (95% CI: [93.7, 96.0]). In our deployment, we were not able to obtain additional blood tests for every patient and perform microscopy-based analysis. Indeed, one reason that rapid diagnostic tests are currently used at our study sites is because microscopy-based analysis is infeasible. Finally, their study focuses solely on the medical outcomes of using the system, whereas our study also discusses findings related to health workers' usage of the system and strategies to overcome infrastructural challenges.

The strength of our findings is highly encouraging and will allow us to explore several future deployment scenarios. For example, if health workers are well trained, the system could simply focus quality control efforts on tests in which the human diagnosis differs from the system diagnosis. Alternatively, in situations where health workers are less experienced, the system could provide a second opinion and instruct health workers to run another test if there is disagreement. Finally, in situations where health workers are untrained, the system could perform the diagnosis and inform the health worker of the outcome.

Deployment Costs

The cost of deploying and sustaining a new technology is an important consideration in low-resource settings. The XCover devices that we deployed cost roughly USD $250 each in Zimbabwe. The devices were loaded with 2GB SD cards that cost $5 each and 300MB data bundles that cost $15 each. The plastic stands to hold the devices cost $10 each. Transmitting a single test required roughly 70KB of data, which equates to a transmission cost of 0.35 cents per test. Storing data from all 15 devices in an online database cost less than $10 per month. Health workers were trained during regular work hours and did not receive additional compensation for participating in the study. Thus, the entire deployment cost approximately $4200, or $280 per device. In fact, the travel, transport and lodging costs for four researchers and two accompanying ministry of health staff were 4 to 5 times more than the costs of the deployment.

Future Work and Limitations

Our study has several limitations that provide opportunities for future work. We only analyze tests for malaria and would like to field test the system with tests for a variety of other diseases. In addition, our participants were well trained and we want to explore the potential for the system to aid health workers that have less medical background. Our system also uses a stand to hold the device in position above the test. Systems that require users to capture images using a handheld device may be more convenient to use, but will likely experience additional image capture issues. Finally, we focus on a camera-based mobile system. Although some of our findings apply to sensor-based systems in general (such as data transmission issues), future research will likely expose additional challenges for systems that use external sensors attached to the device.

CONCLUSION

The availability of mobile devices in low-resource settings has led to the creation of mobile health systems that target disadvantaged populations. This paper presents findings from an eight-week field deployment of a mobile system that captures and analyzes rapid diagnostic tests. Health workers in Zimbabwe used the system for the duration of the study to analyze thousands of tests for malaria. In addition, they employed a variety of strategies to overcome poor network connectivity and transmit test data to a server. Finally, the system's computed diagnoses strongly agreed with the visual diagnoses provided by trained health workers. Taken together, our findings show the potential for mobile systems to aid the delivery of healthcare in low-resource settings and provide valuable insights for HCI researchers working in similar environments.

ACKNOWLEDGEMENTS

This work was funded by Econet Wireless Zimbabwe, NSF Grant 1111433 and a Facebook Graduate Fellowship. We thank the Zimbabwe Ministry of Health and Child Care, Global Solutions for Infectious Diseases (GSID), Dimagi Inc. and all of our study participants.

REFERENCES

1. Boyle D., Hawkins K., Steele M., Singhal M., and Cheng X. (2012) Emerging technologies for point-of-care CD4 T-lymphocyte counting. *Trends in Biotechnology*, 30(1):45-54
2. Chaudhri, R., Vlachos, D., Borriello, G., Israel-Ballard, K., Coutsoudis, A., Reimers, P., and Perin, N. (2013) Decentralized human milk banking with ODK sensors. *Proc. DEV '13* New York: ACM Press p. 4.
3. Dell, N., and Borriello, G. Mobile Tools for Point-of-Care Diagnostics in the Developing World. *Proc. DEV '13.*
4. Dell N., Venkatachalam S., Stevens D., Yager P., and Borriello G. (2011) Towards a Point-of-Care Diagnostic System: Automated Analysis of Immunoassay Test Data on a Cell Phone. *Proc. NSDR '11.*
5. DeRenzi B., Borriello G., Jackson J., Kumar V, Parikh T., Virk P., and Lesh N. (2011). Mobile phone tools for field-based health care workers in low-income countries. *The Mount Sinai Journal of Medicine*, 78(3):406-418.
6. DeRenzi, B., Lesh, N., Parikh, T., Sims, C., Maokla, W., Chemba, M., Hamisi, Y., Hellenberg, D., Mitchell, M. and Borriello, G. (2008) e-IMCI: Improving Pediatric Health Care in Low-Income Countries. *Proc. CHI '08*. pp. 753-762.
7. FIO Corporation. http://www.fio.com/.
8. FrontlineSMS. http://www.frontlinesms.com/.
9. Goel, M., Larson, E., Borriello, G., Heltshe, S., Rosenfeld, M., Patel, S. (2012). SpiroSmart: Using a Microphone to Measure Lung Function on a Mobile Phone. *Proc. Ubicomp '12.*
10. Global Solutions for Infectious Diseases. http://gsid.org/
11. Hartung, C., Lerer, A., Anokwa, Y., Tseng, C., Brunette, W. and Borriello, G. (2010) Open Data Kit: Tools to Build Information Services for Developing Regions. *Proc. ICTD '10*. New York: ACM Press. Article 18.
12. List of known commercially-available antigen-detecting malaria RDTs. http://209.61.208.233/LinkFiles/Malaria_in_the_SEAR_manufat_rdt3.pdf.
13. Martinez A., Phillips S., Whitesides G., and Carrilho E. (2010) Diagnostics for the Developing World: Microfluidic Paper-Based Analytical Devices. *Analytical Chemistry*. 82(1):3-10.
14. Matthews J., Kulkarni R., Gerla, M., and Massey T. (2012) Rapid Dengue and Outbreak Detection with Mobile Systems and Social Networks. *Mobile Netw. and Appl.* 17(2):178-191.
15. Mudanyali O., Dimitrov S., Sikora U., Padmanabhan S., Navruz I., and Ozcan A. (2012) Integrated Rapid-Diagnostic-Test Reader Platform on a Cellphone. *Lab on a Chip* 12(15):2678-86.
16. Pamplona V., Mohan A., Oliveira M., and Raskar R. (2010) NETRA: interactive display for estimating refractive errors and focal range. ACM Trans. on Graphics. 29(4), Article 77.
17. Ramanathan, N., Lukac, M., Ahmed, T., Kar, A., Siva, P., Honles, T., Leong, I., Rehman, I, Schauer, J. & Ramanathan, V. (2011) A cellphone based system for large scale monitoring of black carbon. *Atmospheric Environment*. 45:4481-7.
18. Rennie W., Phetsouvanh R., Lupisan S., Vanisaveth V., Hongvanthong B., Phompida S., Alday P., Fulache M., Lumagui R., Jorgensen P., Bell D., and Harvey, S. (2007) Minimizing human error in malaria rapid diagnosis: clarity of written instructions and health worker performance. *The Royal Society of Tropical Medicine and Hygiene* 10(1):9-18.
19. Shekalaghe, S., Cancino, M., Mavere, C., Juma, O., Mohammed, A., Abdulla, S., & Ferro, S. (2013). Clinical performance of an automated reader in interpreting malaria rapid diagnostic tests in Tanzania. *Malaria Journal*, 12(1):141.
20. Tapley A., Switz N., Reber C., Davis J., Miller C., Matovu J., Worodria W., Huang L., Fletcher D., Cattamanchi A. (2013) Mobile digital fluorescence microscopy for diagnosis of tuberculosis. *Clinical Microbiology*. 51(6):1774-8.
21. World Health Organization, 2013 World Malaria Report. http://www.who.int/malaria/publications/world_malaria_report_2013/report/en/index.html.
22. Cohen, J. (1960). "A coefficient of agreement for nominal scales". *Educ. Psychol. Meas.* 20 (1): 37–46.

Was it Worth the Hassle? Ten Years of Mobile HCI Research Discussions on Lab and Field Evaluations

Jesper Kjeldskov and Mikael B. Skov
Centre for Socio-Interactive Design, Department of Computer Science
Aalborg University, Selma Lagerlöfs Vej 300, DK-9220 Aalborg East, Denmark
{jesper, dubois}@cs.aau.dk

ABSTRACT
Evaluation is considered one of the major cornerstones of human-computer interaction (HCI). During the last decade, several studies have discussed pros and cons of lab and field evaluations. Based on these discussions, we conduct a review to explore the past decade of mobile HCI research on field and lab evaluation, investigating responses in the literature to the "is it worth the hassle?" paper from 2004. We find that while our knowledge and experience with both lab and field studies have grown considerably, there is still no definite answer to the lab versus field question. In response we suggest that the real question is not *if* – but *when* and *how* – to go into the field. In response we suggest moving beyond usability evaluations, and to engage with field studies that are truly in-the-wild, and longitudinal.

Author Keywords
Evaluation; study; lab; field; in-the-wild; in-situ

ACM Classification Keywords
H.5.m. Information interfaces and presentation (e.g., HCI): Miscellaneous.

INTRODUCTION
Evaluation of technologies is generally considered one of the major cornerstones in interaction design and human-computer interaction, and it is well known that most HCI design processes include evaluation as a key component. This is also true for mobile HCI. When the field of mobile HCI began to evolve into a distinct area within human-computer interaction about 15 years ago, the issue of evaluation naturally appeared on the agenda almost immediately. In the proceedings of Mobile HCI 1998, Johnson encouraged researchers and practitioners to investigate further into the methods and data collection for evaluating mobile devices, and he suggested that *"the conventional usability laboratory would not be able to adequately simulate such important aspects as the weather and could not easily provide for the wide range of competing activities and demands on users that might arise in a natural setting"* and he continued by saying that *"data collection methods would be needed that were outside the common range of usability studies"* [28].

MobileHCI '14, September 23 - 26 2014, Toronto, ON, Canada
Copyright 2014 ACM 978-1-4503-3004-6/14/09…$15.00.
http://dx.doi.org/10.1145/2628363.2628398

Despite these initial suggestions, Kjeldskov and Graham's survey of mobile HCI research between 2000-02 showed no research focusing on mobile evaluation methodology, and that 71% of all evaluations of mobile devices and services were done in the lab [35]. In direct response to this, we conducted a comparative study on field and lab evaluations of a mobile system with the purpose of investigating the value of evaluating usability in the field [36]. In this study we found – surprisingly – little added value in the field setting, prompting us to ask the somewhat provocative question "is it worth the hassle?" This study raised a heated debate when presented at the 2004 Mobile HCI conference, as observed by Iachello and Terrenghi [25], and sparked a long lasting discussion in the mobile HCI research field of what methods and techniques are appropriate.

Our comparison study [36] influenced a number of follow-up studies contrasting lab-based approaches with field-based ones, and somewhat polarising the research field into two distinct camps of thought, one taking an ethnographic research approach, the other one taking a usability engineering one. As a result of this, as of February 2014 the "is it worth the hassle" paper has 191 citations according to Google Scholar, and it is fair to say that it has had a strong impact on the research field by putting the discussion of empirical methodology in mobile HCI on the agenda – as originally suggested by Johnson [28].

Following up on these discussions, we have reviewed the publications that have responded to the *"is it worth the hassle"* question posed in 2004 [36], and considered whether posing this provocative question a decade ago *was worth the hassle* in terms of subsequent research on the topic. We have done this to investigate and understand how the last ten years of mobile HCI research discussions on lab and field evaluations have unfolded – what we have learned and where we are at today, what challenges we are faced with in the discussion of conducting lab and field studies, and what opportunities for future thinking in this discussion have emerged.

BACKGROUND

The discussion about where and how to do evaluations in mobile HCI is based on the distinction between field and lab studies in research methodology. As space here is limited we are not going to provide a lengthy discussion of research methodology definitions, but only briefly outline what is meant by research in the field and in the lab as this distinction is important for the following discussion.

Field studies are characterized by taking place in "the real world" with researchers spending considerable amounts of time in the real social and cultural context of their study. Data is typically gathered through observations, interviews and surveying techniques. The major advantages are the gathering of large amount of rich and grounded data, and a high level of *ecological validity*. Disadvantages are unknown biases, unknown external validity/generalizability – and typically *low level of control.*

In contrast, lab studies take place in controlled environments created for the purpose of research. Data is typically gathered with precise instruments, such as video recording, logging and questionnaires, and the studied phenomena is placed in an artificial environment where it cannot be disturbed from the outside. Major advantages are the ability to focus on detail, with high replicability, and with large *experimental control.* Disadvantages are the limited relations to the real world, unknown external validity – and typically *low level of ecological validity.*

The "Hassle" paper

In 2004 we published a comparative study of evaluating the usability of a mobile system in a field study and in a lab study [36]. In that paper, which we will refer to as the "Hassle" paper, the purpose of the study was firstly *"to compare the outcome of evaluating the usability of a mobile system in a laboratory setting and in the field in relation to identified usability problems and time spent on conducting the evaluations"* and secondly *to "describe two techniques used for 1) improving the realism of laboratory settings by including mobility and context, and 2) supporting high-quality video data collection when evaluating usability of mobile devices in the field"* [36].

Both evaluations involved six professional nurses with the same amount of work and IT expertise. All nurses used and interacted with the same mobile system (a context-aware handheld patient record), and in both evaluations close-up display video was recorded using a wireless micro-camera mounted on the mobile device. The field evaluation took place in a hospital during ordinary work activities at the ward over a couple of days. The lab evaluation took place in a traditional usability laboratory that was transformed to simulate a hospital ward with a hallway and several rooms (furnished with beds, tables etc.) and with actors acting as patients. The data analysis produced two lists of usability problems – one for each setting. Each problem was classified as cosmetic, serious, or critical, and it was noted how many test subjects it had been experienced by. Time spent by the investigators was calculated from a log for both conditions. These metrics on usability problems and time spent were used for comparing the two conditions.

We found that the lab study revealed more usability problems than the field study, where the lab condition found 36 usability problems while the field found 23 usability problems. Out of the total number of usability problems (N=37), 14 problems were unique to the lab, and only one problem was unique to the field. Looking at the 14 unique lab problems, 9 were classified as serious and one as critical. When considering effort spent, the lab took 34 person-hours while the field took 65 person-hours.

Based on these empirical findings, the Hassle paper discusses the added value of evaluating usability in the field compared to in a lab and state that *"quite surprisingly, our study shows that compared to setting up a realistic laboratory study evaluators achieve little added value when taking a usability evaluation of a context-aware mobile device into the field".* Since the lab evaluations were able to identify the exact same usability problems, except one, and using less effort in man-hours, we pose a confronting question of whether such field evaluations are "*worth the hassle*". We do, however, not provide a direct answer to the question in the 2004 paper. However, we summarize that simulating context in a lab evaluation can facilitate solid identification of usability problems, and that the lack experimental control in the field can undermine the ability to focus an evaluation on specific parts of a system. Ultimately, we suggest that *"expensive time in the field should perhaps not be spent on usability evaluation if its possible to create a realistic laboratory setup including elements of context and requiring mobility"* and that *"field studies may instead be more suitable for obtaining insight needed to design the system right in the first place"* [36].

As argued in the introduction, the Hassle paper triggered a debate about lab and field evaluations in mobile HCI and it has been cited and used significantly for the past decade. We wish to investigate what kinds of discussions we have seen in this period and what we have learned about field and lab studies in mobile HCI.

METHOD

We have conducted a literature review examining the research discussions on lab and field evaluations in mobile HCI following on from the Hassle paper [36] from 2004. According to Google Scholar, the Hassle paper was cited 191 times as of February 2014. Out of these citing publications we were able to obtain 165 electronically. These included conference papers, workshop papers, journal articles, book chapters, and Ph.D. theses. 12 of these publications turned out to be in a language we could not read (e.g. French, Spanish, Chinese, Finish) and were therefore disregarded. The remaining 153 publications were then printed, catalogued and reviewed.

We reviewed each publication by identifying what topic it was addressing, what its contribution was, where the Hassle paper had been cited, and what it had been cited for. We then gave each publication a number of key words that described it briefly (e.g. "lab", "field", "experiment", "longitudinal"). After having reviewed roughly half of the publications, we used the key words to group the papers. We then continued reviewing the rest of the papers using these groups in addition to individual key words. After all publications had been reviewed and grouped, we went through each of them again for a "sanity check" on our first round of reviewing. As the final step we clustered the groups into 3 overall themes. The 3 identified themes covered 142 of the publications (Table 1). Another 7 publications cited the Hassle paper for (sometimes obscure) reasons that were not related to its core focus and content (such as mobile devices having small displays), and in 4 of the publications, the paper was listed in the references, but was not actually referred to in the body text.

Theme	No. of publications
Using lab or field	N=62 (24)
Comparing lab and field	N= 16 (13)
Discussing lab and field	N=64 (22)
Total	N=142 (59)

Table 1. Themes and their number of publications. Numbers in parentheses count the publications referred to in this paper.

The first theme of "Using" covered publications where the Hassle paper is referenced in studies using either field or lab for evaluating a mobile device or service. Within these publications 23 reported findings from the lab and 39 from the field. The lab studies very often involved a simulation of the real use context and cited the Hassle paper for the appropriateness of doing so. The field studies typically reported from an evaluation of a system in real world use, usually voicing the authors' disagreement with the Hassle paper. The second theme of "Comparing" covered publications where an actual empirical study had been carried out that investigated into the relative strengths and weaknesses of lab and field approaches. The third theme of "Discussing" covered publications that took up the topic of where and how to study and evaluate mobile devices and services, typically reviewing the literature and proposing new methods and techniques for the lab or the field.

In the following we will take a closer look at the different research represented by these themes, exemplified by selected representative papers.

FINDINGS

Using Lab or Field Studies

Out of the total 142 publications, we identified 62 papers that present mobile HCI studies conducted in either the lab or in the field, typically using the Hassle paper (and others) to justify the chosen evaluation setting.

Lab studies

The findings presented in the Hassle paper appears to have inspired research on exploring ways of increasing realism in controlled environments, in similar ways to the imitation of a hospital ward in a usability lab in [36]. Of the 23 papers reporting from lab evaluations, 14 involved some kind of context simulation. These simulation studies range from high-fidelity setups such as the use of a ship simulator in [38], to experimental setups where the level of simulation is rather low. As an example of the latter, Holzinger et al. report from a study where the real life environment of an ambulance officer is simulated by the participant sitting on a chair in an office holding the PDA in his hands without laying down the elbows [23].

The group of lab simulation studies shows great variation in what aspects of use context is being simulated, and great creativity in how they are simulated. Firstly, a notable body of lab studies simulates the physical real world environment in great detail. Examples of this include the work of Alsos and Dabelow [2] who carried out a usability evaluation of three PDA based medication systems in a full-scale model of a section of a hospital ward allowing them to effectively collect data from 56 simulated ward rounds with 14 physicians. In a similar manner, Holone et al. [21] evaluate an indoor navigation system for wheelchair users in a "close to real world setting" by turning two floors of a building into a controlled environment that could be observed by the researchers. In the work of Vastenburg et al. [60] evaluations were carried out in a dedicated living room laboratory simulating a home environment.

Some lab studies attempt to reconstruct different ambient aspects of a real world setting like noise, signs of potential danger, or presence and activity of other people. Examples of this include the work of Kondratova et al. [40] who simulate elements of a construction site that would potentially influence a technician's use of a multimodal data entry. Similarly, Lumsden et al. [45] simulate a city street using a surround sound system in the lab to deliver recorded city street noise, and projections on the floor to create virtual obstacles that the user should try to avoid when walking around the lab. Such simulation of mobility is also found in other lab studies, for example in the work by Wilson et al. [62] and Maly et al. [48] where test subjects were asked to walk and navigate a track with a number of obstacles, or in Banard et al. [6] where they are asked to walk on a treadmill. An example of including the presence and activity of other people in a lab study is found in the work of Leitner et al. [44] who simulate a traffic accident to users of an emergency response system.

Most of the rest of the papers referring to a lab evaluation justify this by the need for more control, replicability, easier data capture, and less time required. Only 2 papers justify the lab approach with reference to the Hassle paper by stating simply that the lab is as good as the field, or that field studies have not proven to be better.

Field studies

Most field study papers report from empirical studies where researchers have introduced different forms of experimental control in a natural environment. Using the research method categories of [39] these studies can be characterized as "field experiments", covering the body of *"natural setting research where a number of independent variables are manipulated in the study of a particular phenomenon under controlled but realistic conditions"*. Of the 39 papers reporting from a field study, 17 involved some controlled experimentation such as usability tests, randomized trial, or quasi experiments in real use contexts.

A highly cited field experiment paper is that of Oulasvirta et al. [51] who investigated the fragmented nature of attention when interacting with mobile devices in real world settings, comparing the performance of 28 subjects across two conditions. Data was collected by means of wireless cameras capturing views of the user, the mobile device and the physical surroundings. By comparing their findings to results from earlier lab based studies of the same matter they were able to provide evidence for a difference between lab and field findings, and thereby justification for the importance of field experiments. Another example of a field experiment is the work of Dearman et al. [16] where 48 subjects were assigned to one of three mobile technology conditions in the field, and asked to carry out three different scenarios of rendezvousing with a partner. Data was then collected by means of field notes, audio recordings, data logging, questionnaires and interviews, allowing the researchers to gain insight about the participants' behavior, interactions, performance, and opinions. Finally, Howell et al. [22] report from a controlled field experiment where 56 subjects were divided into two groups in a study with three independent variables of interface metaphors and context of use for a speech-based mobile city guide.

Another notable body of mobile HCI field study research responding to the Hassle paper reports from what can be characterized as "field ethnographies" using *"qualitative and quantitative approaches to natural setting research where the researcher is present in the field from full-scale ethnographic studies of phenomena in their social and cultural context to smaller scale observational studies and contextual inquiry"* [39]. Of the 39 field study papers, 11 reported the use of ethnographic techniques with minimal researcher involvement and no controlled manipulation of variables. Some, but not many, of these studies are in-depth and longitudinal qualitative enquiries of potential areas for mobile technology deployment, such as Wilson et al.'s study of medical shift handover [63], Tolmie et al.'s study of researchers' deployment of UbiComp technologies in private homes [59], and Skattør' study of Norwegian building constructors using a PDA system over four months [56]. The largest group, however, report from shorter studies of prototype systems in use in realistic settings, using various ethnographic-style observational techniques. These include Kalnikaite et al. [32] reporting from the use of a mobile shopping application in a supermarket, Davies et al. [15] reporting from the use of a mobile guide at a historical site, and Wilfinger et al. [61] reporting from the use of an interactive TV system in people's homes.

Another eleven papers are "field surveys" using *"natural setting research where survey techniques such as questionnaires, diaries, log files, interviews etc. are use for data collection rather than the researcher being present in the field"* [39]. These 11 papers report from studies where mobile systems have been deployed in real world settings without researcher presence. A comprehensive example of this is the study by Streefkerk et al. [57] where a notification system for police officers was deployed with 30 users for four months using primarily questionnaires and data logging for data collection. In fact, data logging have played an important role in several field surveys making use of the range of sensors built in to mobile phones today. As an example, Larsen et al. [43] deployed a mobile media player for two weeks collecting data about what media was being played when, where, and in what social contexts. In another example, Jambon and Meillon [27] equipped a group of skiers with a self-performance system, which relayed usage data from a camera, accelerometer and GPS back to the researchers via wireless Internet.

Comparing Lab and Field Studies

As the second theme of research we identified 16 papers that empirically compare lab and field evaluation conditions for mobile systems. Among these some papers conduct studies where they directly compare field and lab conditions, for example [17, 30, 47, 50, 58] while other papers add extra conditions to their comparison and not only consider field and lab, for example eye tracking in lab-based testing [19], or heuristic inspection [18, 37].

In light of the passionate discussions generated by the Hassle paper when presented at Mobile HCI 2004, as observed in [25], it is interesting to observe that no study has aimed at replicating it to confirm or reject its findings. Quite the opposite, all of the comparison papers we have reviewed report from studies where the focus, test subjects, tested system, or the field and lab environments have been very different from the study reported in the Hassle paper. Three studies [17, 30, 50] are similar to the Hassle study in that they address the topic of field versus lab evaluations directly, but they nevertheless differ quite significantly in their experimental setup. For example, in [50] the test subjects were all apprentices at a technical school, and not professional/experienced workers. In [17] the study compared test subjects seated at a table (lab) with test subjects on a train (field). In [30] the study was carried out in an office district, the system was a mobile system for transferring files, and the number of test subjects was considerably higher (20 per condition versus only 6 in the Hassle study). Thus, while replication is fundamental in many other scientific disciplines (i.e. medicine or physics), it seems to play an insignificant role in mobile HCI.

Despite the lack of actual replication, some of the reviewed studies claim to confirm the findings in the Hassle study, while others claim to reject them. Several studies, for example [5, 18, 19, 26, 30, 47], find that properly conducted *lab* usability evaluations can identify many of the usability issues (i.e. usability problems) identified in field evaluations. In a sense, these studies repeat the question posed in the Hassle paper if it is worth doing usability evaluations in the field? As an example, Kaikkonen et al. [30] state that field-testing may not be the optimal way for testing a mobile user interface, as they found no difference in the number of problems between the two test settings. On the hand, Duh et al. [17] found that the field led to the identification of additional usability problems compared to the lab. This was also the case in the study by Nielsen et al. [50] who coarsely state in their title that "it's worth the hassle!" regardless that their field condition was a simulation in a controlled environment (with great resemblance to the *lab* condition in the Hassle paper), thus making it questionable if any claims about real world use can be made from this study. The observation of added value in the field in a comparative study is, however, validly supported by Baillie and Schatz [4] who found that the overall system usability (effectiveness, efficiency, and satisfaction) was rated more highly in the field than in the lab, thus showing a difference between lab and field not addressed in the Hassle paper.

Several comparison papers address the lab and field discussion in quantitative studies focusing comprehensively on statistical differences, for example [5, 29, 58], and as a consequence include a higher number of test subjects than in the Hassle study (which had 6 in each condition). Kaikkonen et al. [30] reports from 20 subjects in each condition, and Barnard [5] from 41 in each. In relation to this, Kaikkonen et al. discuss the number of subjects needed and argue that while six subjects may be adequate for conducting a usability test, the number of subjects needed is different when *comparing* approaches, and that a higher number of subjects *"can increase the power of the test to find differences between two test settings"* [30].

While almost all 16 comparison-papers explicitly apply the terminology lab and field to describe their study conditions, it is quite obvious that there are rather varied understandings on what constitutes a field environment and what constitutes a lab environment. In [58] the lab condition was set up to resemble parts of a sports stadium, while in [50] the lab evaluations was done in a room where subjects were sitting at a table. In [30] the field evaluations were done in the a city center during rush hour, while in [50] the "field" environment was a technical high school warehouse that was *"similar to real working environment"*. Similarly to [50] for the comparison between lab and field environments Khanum et al. [34] *"created two labs at in the school, one for field testing sessions, and one for laboratory testing sessions"*. In our discussion section, we will return to such use and understanding of field and lab.

Several studies conclude that field studies and field evaluations are time-consuming and costly [18, 26, 30]. Kaikkonen et al. report that studies showed that usability field-testing required double the time compared their lab testing [30], while Jambon et al. found that their field tests required almost triple the time compared to lab tests [26].

Discussing Lab and Field Studies

As the third theme, we identified 64 papers that discuss the need, opportunities, implications, or limitations of field and lab evaluations in mobile HCI. Compared to the two other groups of papers (using and comparing) these papers go beyond the more practical use of lab or field studies, but they don't empirically compare the two conditions as the 16 comparison papers. Having said that, these 64 papers are nevertheless rather different in their discussion focus and approach, but they typically integrate a quite strong and detailed discussion on field or lab evaluation approaches in mobile HCI and ubiquitous computing.

From a research methodology perspective, we identified both theoretical and empirical discussion papers. E.g. some papers pursue theoretical perspectives where they outline opportunities or challenges of conducting field or lab-based evaluations. For example several papers are extensive paper reviews [1, 3, 7, 10, 11, 20, 55]. As an illustrative example, Carter et al. describe a comprehensive study on ecological validity in ubiquitous computing stressing that we as designers and researchers should focus on evaluation methods, and prototyping tools, that support realistic use in realistic settings [11]. Other papers are empirically based and typically tend to focus their discussions on either field evaluations or lab evaluations, for example [8, 9, 49, 54]. Brown et al. illustrate how we as researchers need to re-focus our approaches but also views of solid studies when evaluating and understanding experimental systems in the wild [8]. They argue that replication of studies is impossible and infeasible for field trials, and they reject those researchers who advocate more standardized approaches to trials. They argue this by the fact that *"social settings involving humans and technology contain far too much variability to be reproducible in any straightforward way"*.

As noted by Iachello and Terrenghi [25], the lab versus field discussion is associated with passionate and strong opinion and world-views. This is also observable in the group of discussion papers reviewed. In a number of papers the authors argue quite strongly for conducting field studies or evaluations in the field, for example [8, 41, 52, 53, 54]. Explicitly exploring the field approach, TOCHI ran a special issue in 2013 on "The Turn to the Wild" [12] where the editors and contributing authors focused on in-the-wild studies that *"seek to understand and shape new technology interventions within everyday living"* with the purpose of examining the insights, demands and concerns that this has for HCI theory, practice and design. Preceding this special issue, Rogers et al. [54] already in 2007 provided strong and well grounded argumentations on the importance of field (or in-situ) studies in mobile HCI and ubicomp, in the directly responding paper called *"why it's worth the hassle"*. In this paper Rogers et al. stress that traditional evaluation methods and metrics (derived from laboratory settings) fail to capture the complexities and richness of the real world in which systems or technologies are placed and used. As an example it was specifically found that even something as simple as the changing nature of the physical environment, like particular time of year, can have quite significant impact on user experience.

As a consequence of these aspects, several researchers have set out to provide guidelines and techniques for improving studies and evaluations conducted in the field [7, 8, 31, 33, 55]. Roto et al. present and discuss best practices for capturing context when studying technology in the wild. They propose 18 practices, for example that you should identify and select realistic contexts for the tasks during the planning phase, and you should minimize the effects of research setup on participants and the context during the data collection phase [55]. Kaikkonen et al. also identify social context as important and argue that studies should consider the social location of the evaluation, e.g. other people if making phone calls [31]. On the other hand, Burghardt et al. provide a discussion of techniques for collecting data in the field, for example thinking-aloud, video recording, interview [9]. Brown et al. suggest that we should re-focus our paper method sections going away from illustrating replicable results to be more explicit about the natural contingencies and events that happen during trials and that these are vital in understanding the different trials contexts [8]. Finally, some provide inspiration on how to capture user interaction and experiences from a more low-level and practical point of view, for example hardware and equipment configurations for data collection [24, 52].

While the importance of field studies is rather evident (as shown above), several papers bring up field study obstacles or challenges. Two issues seem to play a significant role in these discussions namely lack of control and cost. Kellar et al. stress the lack of control when conducting studies in-situ and identify control challenges in the field, for example weather, social considerations [33]. Secondly, several researchers point to the fact that field studies are nevertheless costly in terms of time and effort spent [53, 54]. Thus, partly as a result of these challenges, some papers work with, and argue in favor of lab evaluations for mobile computing for example [7, 13, 14, 42, 46]. Kray et al. discusses lab studies using immersive video as a technique [42] and Lumsden et al. explore how to conduct meaningful lab-based usability evaluations of mobile systems [46], which is also proposed by Dahl et al. [13, 14] who suggest to simulate the use setting and environment – in their particular case they explore the role of fidelity in recreating hospital settings in laboratories, like in [36]. Finally, Billi et al. propose a methodology for evaluating usability of mobile system including mobile heuristics [7].

DISCUSSION

We have now illustrated ten years of mobile HCI research on field and lab evaluations through three identified themes namely using, comparing, and discussing. We will now turn our attention towards issues that span the three themes and address these issues in the following sections. We will start by looking at how far we have come and where we are today. We will then take up a number of issues that we feel are important to address in order to re-rail the discussion. Lastly we will put forward some points for future thinking in the lab-field study discussion, and some questions that we believe needs to be addressed and considered in our research community in order to move forward.

Status in 2014: Mobile HCI Evaluation Research

Looking back at ten years of research in mobile HCI, we think it is clear that empirical methodologies have been central. A very large body of research has discussed, at length, the pros and cons of different empirical methods for evaluating mobile technology, and several studies have made empirical comparisons between different approaches. Furthermore, as also pointed out in a recent mobile HCI research methods survey [39], there has been a huge increase in the amount of empirical studies in HCI (in the lab as well as in the field) – both absolute and relative to the amount of mobile HCI research as a whole. This research has involved significant effort into evolving our toolbox of empirical methods in mobile HCI. From the lab study side our community has arrived at new ways of simulating context, and from the field study side it has arrived at news ways of experimentation in situ. In that sense it is fair to say that we, as a research community, have responded quite well to Johnson's encouragements at the first Mobile HCI workshop in 1998 in terms of building a body of knowledge and experience with both lab and field studies that are *"outside the common range of usability studies"* [28].

It is, however, also quite clear that the research discussions and comparisons between lab and field approaches has not produced an answer to the question of whether mobile systems should be evaluated in the lab or in the field. There appears to be a general agreement that contextual realism plays an important role when evaluating mobile HCI, but this may be achieved both by simulating contextual factors in the lab or by taking the study "outside" into the field. Further, there appears to be agreement that researcher control plays an important role, but again this may be achieved both by experimentation in the field or by taking the study "inside" into the lab. This discussion basically comes down to the question of balancing *ecological validity* and *control,* and while the lab simulation and field experimentation research are quite distinct, and often done by researchers with very different backgrounds, its important to observe that they actually converge towards the same goal. Hence it appears that both approaches are valid, if paired thoughtfully with ones research aims (and claims), and if carried out well. If this is true, then the important question is not *if* or *why* one should do lab or field studies, but rather *when* we should do what, and *how* we should then do it, so that its done well. These questions remains largely unanswered in a way that does not simply restate existing disciplinary doctrines. They are, however, not for us to attempt to answer here either, as they are much bigger than what one literature review can resolve. They are questions for the broader community of researchers to address through joint efforts. But creating a catalogue of guidelines and best practices in lab and field studies would certainly be a timely and relevant effort.

Different Understandings of the Field

As we illustrated earlier, some researchers argue strongly in favor of conducting field studies as laboratories potentially fail to capture the complexities and richness of the real world [54]. While we agree with this, we interestingly found extensive discrepancies in the way different studies applied (and thus understand) what constitutes a "field setting" in evaluations. The research studies reviewed in this paper involved quite diverse field settings, such as sitting in a train [17], walking around the center of a city [30], being in shops [19], sitting at a sports stadium [58] while others, for example [4] conducted their field study in the immediate area outside their research center building. This obviously raises the questions – *what is the field?* And *when can we say that a setting is in the field?* These essential questions remain partly unanswered.

Perhaps much more importantly, we think it is worth raising the question *does it make sense to engage in field versus lab discussions when we clearly lack common understandings of the things we compare*? It is quite clear that several of the 16 comparison papers are comparing different kinds of field and lab environments, and it makes little (or even no) sense to compare these papers against each other. For example, Nielsen et al. argue that *"it is definitely worth the hassle to conduct field evaluations"* [50] as a response to the Hassle study, but the field and lab conditions are very different in those two studies. Further, while several researchers argue for field studies as they increase realism and uninstructed use of technology [8, 54], other researchers strangely state that if we want to compare field and lab settings *"the field evaluation will have to be less realistic"* [50]. But less realism in field studies is in contrast with both Rogers et al. and Brown et al. who use the term "In the Wild" studies or in-situ studies to illustrate appropriation of technologies in the *real* world under *realistic* conditions. Such fundamental disagreements have highly influenced the discussion over the past decade.

Replication or Novelty

The HCI discipline (including mobile HCI) does not have a strong history of replicating previous studies. Wilson et al. state that replication is a cornerstone of good science where results can be validated to ensure a solid foundation for progress, but HCI research rewards novelty and is typically focused on new results [64]. This clearly seems to hold for mobile HCI research as well. In our opinion, some of the field versus lab discussions from the last decade seem to have failed as they have tried to achieve both replication and novelty at the same time – for example they have attempted to replicate the argumentation of field versus lab (e.g. tried to explore the added value of field studies), but at the same time they have aimed for novelty by evaluating a new type of system, in a different setting etc. But does novelty prevent replication, and does replication prevent novelty? Related to these concerns, we found that several of the comparison studies, for example [17, 30, 36, 50] apply usability problems as their primary metric for their comparison. As a result, the studies report quantitative data (number of problems and severity) that are easy to compare, but perhaps also leave out some of the richness that field studies offer (as illustrated in [54]). Further, usability problem identification and classification has been extensively criticized over the past years especially when applied in research studies for quantitative measures due to the evaluator effect.

Perhaps we need to refocus our discussion on field and lab studies to better reflect the inherent nature of our research discipline namely that we are concerned with discussing *the challenges, potential solutions and innovations towards effective interaction with mobile systems and services* [Mobile HCI conference series website]. As part of this discussion, we definitely need to investigate and understand how technologies are being used and adapted in real world settings – therefore **we need field studies**. But we should focus our field study research to better reflect and embrace the complexity and richness of real world interaction with technology as suggested by Rogers et al. [54]. As argued by Brown [8], we need to address the reality of in-situ studies including innovation in methods that are not replicable.

Beyond Usability and Usability Evaluations

Looking ahead, there are a number of points for future thinking in the lab-field study discussion that we would like to put forward for consideration. The first is to question whether *usability evaluations* are even what we ought to be doing in the first place when studying mobile HCI? In line with the argumentation by Rogers et al. [54] we think that a focus on *usability* simply fails to capture what it is that we really need to learn more about when we study our mobile interaction designs in use. We would argue that after 15 years of mobile HCI research and design, we have become pretty good at designing interfaces that people can operate on a mobile device in a mobile context. That is perhaps not the key research challenge anymore. Where the research challenge 15 years ago was to achieve usability on small displays and with limited means of input, processing power and network speed, for people away from their desk, the research challenge today, and what we need to learn more about, is about designing services, devices and interactions that fit well into people's complex lives, for work and leisure, and that fit well with the abundance of other technologies that we surround ourselves with. This entails a shift from designing for interacting with individual devices, to designing for "orchestration" of *digital ecosystems* made up by a multitude of different systems and devices across ever-changing and overlapping contexts. In this challenge usability is just a basic condition, like bug-free code is. It will not get us there in itself, and therefore neither will usability evaluations – regardless of them being in the lab or in the field. Therefore we should also not use usability problems as a metric when comparing the performance of one method against another.

Beyond Non-Wild, Snap-Shot Field Studies

Moving beyond a focus on usability might be a useful prompt for approaching field studies in a different way. Rather than trying to "fix" the issue of limited control in the field by introducing experimentation, such as usability evaluations, why not consider going in the opposite direction and purposely let go of researcher control? Field experiments are fine as ecologically valid alternatives to lab experiments, but perhaps not as a controlled alternative to field ethnographies. As discussed earlier, the main value of the field is that it is *real* and perhaps *messy,* and not an amputated version of reality. That is perhaps also why the labels "in-situ" and "in-the-wild" have been adapted by some papers (e.g. [8, 12, 24, 27, 54, 55, 63]) as they are really much better at capturing the essence of what field studies should be about. So, just like a lab study without control and replicability would be considered a poor one, a field study that does not really take the researcher into an uncontrolled real world situation is perhaps not a good one either. When going out of the lab, we ought to actually make across the parking lot outside our buildings, and go all the way in to the wild. Studies in the field should embrace the wilderness and not be half-tame.

Moving beyond non-wild field studies of mobile systems should include a second element namely being longitudinal. As another piece of legacy from the tradition of usability evaluation, we have grown accustomed to grounding our knowledge in "snapshots of use" rather than repeated and sustained use over longer periods of time. This is not only true for the lab, but also for several field studies, especially the growing body of field experiments, but also most of the ones using field ethnographies for evaluation. If we are to address issues beyond usability and truly embrace going into the wild, we should also to start embracing longitudinal studies more, perhaps even entertain the thought of sometimes sacrificing some of the direct researcher involvement on order to stretch out the time in use of our systems in the field. Studies like that already exist amongst the group of field surveys described earlier, with [57] being a prime example of a longitudinal study in the wild that does not focus on usability. We definitely believe that more studies like that will give us valuable information on mobile systems use over the coming years.

CONCLUSION

"Was it Worth the Hassle?" We posed that question to investigate and understand what we have learned from the last ten years of mobile HCI research discussions on lab and field evaluations in the slipstream of the 2004 Kjeldskov et al. paper [36] that ignited much of this discussion.

We have shown that lab and field evaluation has been discussed extensively, and been a topic for many authors. We have also shown that over the course of 10 years of empirical evaluations our methodological toolbox have evolved substantially, and that today we have considerable knowledge and experience with both lab and field studies for mobile HCI. Since no answer to the lab versus field question seems to be found, we have argued that the important question is not *if* or *why* one should do lab or field studies, but rather *when* we should do what, and *how* we should then do it. As input to moving the discussion of empirical methodology forward, we have suggested that mobile HCI research should move beyond focus on usability and usability evaluation, that we should embrace field studies that are truly wild and longitudinal in nature in order to fully experience and explore real world use. Currently only a few examples of such studies exist.

To conclude, we believe that the last ten years of empirical work and research discussions of lab and field evaluations have been highly valuable for the mobile HCI research field, and therefore also that engaging with this topic of research has been *worth the hassle*.

REFERENCES

1. Abdulrazak, B. and Malik, Y. Review of Challenges, Requirements, and Approaches of Pervasive Computing System Evaluation. *IETE Technical Review 29,* 6 (2012), 506-522
2. Alsos, O.A. and Dabelow, B. A comparative evaluation study of basic interaction techniques for PDAs in point-of-care situations. *Proc. P-Health'10,* IEEE (2010), 1-8.
3. Axup, J. Building a Path For Future Communities. In *Handbook of Research on Socio-Technical Design,* (2008), 3-20.
4. Baillie, L. and Schatz, R. Exploring Multimodality in the Laboratory and the Field. *Proc. CMI'05,* ACM (2005), 100-107.
5. Barnard, L., Y, J. S., Jacko, J. A. and Sears, A. An empirical comparison of use-in-motion evaluation scenarios for mobile computing devices. *IJHCS 62* (2005), 487-520.
6. Barnard, L., Yi, J.S., Jacko, J. and Sears, A. Capturing the effect of context on human performance in mobile computing. *Pers Ubiquit Comput 11* (2007), 81-96.
7. Billi, M., Burzagli, L., Catarci, T., Santucci, G., Bertini, E., Gabbanini, F. and Palchetti, E. Unified methodology for evaluation of accessibility and usability of mobile applications. *Univ. Access Inf. Soc.,* 9 (2010), 337–356.

8. Brown, B., Reeves, S., and Sherwood, S. Into the Wild: Challenges and Opportunities for Field Trial Methods. *Proc. CHI'11,* ACM (2011), 1657-1666.

9. Burghardt, D. and Wirth, K. Comparison of Evaluation Methods for Field-Based Usability Studies of Mobile Map Applications. *Proc. International Cartographic Conference* (2011).

10. Carter, S. *Techniques and tools for field-based early-stage study and iteration of ubicomp applications: A dissertation proposal.* University of California, 2005.

11. Carter, S., Mankoff, J., Klemmer, S. R. and Matthews, T. Exiting the Cleanroom: On Ecological Validity and Ubiquitous Computing. *Human-Computer Interaction 23,* 1, (2008), 47-99.

12. Crabtree, A., Chamberlain, A., Grinter, R. E., Jones, M., Rodden, T. and Rogers, Y. Introduction to the Special Issue of "The Turn to The Wild". *TOCHI 20,* 3 (2013).

13. Dahl, Y., Alsos, O. A. and Svanæs, D. Evaluating Mobile Usability: The Role of Fidelity in Full-Scale Laboratory Simulations with Mobile ICT for Hospitals, *Proc. HCII'09,* Springer (2009), 232–241.

14. Dahl, Y. Seeking a Theoretical Foundation for Design of In Sitro Usability Assessments. *Proc. NordiCHI'10,* ACM (2010), 623-626.

15. Davies, N., Cheverst, K., Dix, A. and Hesse, A. Understanding the Role of Image Recognition in Mobile Tour Guides. Proc. Mobile HCI'05, ACM (2005), 191-198.

16. Dearman, D., Hawkey, K. and Inkpen, K.M. Rendezvousing with location-aware devices. *IwC 17* (2005), 524-566.

17. Duh, H. B., Tan, G. and Chen, V.H. Usability Evaluation for Mobile Devices: A Comparison of Laboratory and Field Tests. *Proc. Mobile HCI'06,* ACM (2006), 181-186.

18. Fiotakis, G., Raptis, D. and Avouris, N. Considering Cost in Usability Evaluation of Mobile Applications: Who, Where and When. *Proc. Interact'09,* Springer (2009), 231-234.

19. Gelderblom, H., Bruin, J. and Singh, A. Three Methods for Evaluating Mobile Phone Applications Aimed Users in a Developing Environment: AComparative Case Study. *Proc. M4D'12* (2012), 321-334.

20. Hagen, P., Robertson, T., Kan, M. and Sadler, K. Emerging research methods for understanding mobile technology use. Proc. OzCHI'05, CHISIG (2005), 1-10.

21. Holone, H., Mislund, G., Tolsby, H. and Kristoffersen, S. Aspects of personal navigation with collaborative feedback. *Proc. NordiCHI'08,* ACM (2008), 182-191.

22. Howell, M., Love, S. and Turner, M. The impact of interface metaphor and context of use on the usability of a speech-based mobile city guide service. *Behaviour & Information Technology 24,* 1 (2005): 67-78.

23. Holzinger, A., Schlögl, M., Peischl, B. and Debevc, M. Optimization of a handwriting recognition algorithm for a mobile enterprise health information system on the basis of real-life usability research. *Proc. ICETE'10,* Springer (2010), 97-111.

24. Høegh, R. T., Kjeldskov, J., Skov, M. B. and Stage J. Setting Up A Field Laboratory for Evaluating In Situ. In *Handbook of Research on User Interface Design and Evaluation for Mobile Technology,* ISR, 2008.

25. Iachello, G. and Terrenghi, L. Mobile HCI 2004: Experience and Reflection. *Pervasive Computing,* Jan-Mar (2005), 88-91.

26. Jambon, F., Golanski, C. and Pommier, P.J. Meta-evaluation of a context-aware mobile device usability. *Proc. UBICOMM,* IEEE (2007), pp. 21-26.

27. Jambon, F. and Meillon, B. User Experience in the Wild. *Proc. CHI'09 EA,* ACM (2009), 4069-4074.

28. Johnson, P. Usability and Mobility; Interactions on the move. Proc. Mobile HCI'98, GIST Technical Report G98-1 (1998)

29. Jumisko-Pyykkö, S. and Utriainen, T. (2011) A Hybrid Method for Quality Evaluation in the Context of Use for Mobile (3D) Television. Multimedia Tools and Applications, 55(2): 185-225.

30. Kaikkonen, A., Kekäläinen, A., Cankar, M., Kallio, T. and Kankainen, A. Usability Testing of Mobile Applications: A Comparison between Laboratory and Field Testing. *Journal of Usability Studies 1,* 1 (2005), 4-16.

31. Kaikkonen, A., Kekäläinen, A., Cankar, M., Kallio, T., and Kankainen, A. Will laboratory test results be valid in mobile contexts? In *Handbook of Research on User Interface Design and Evaluation for Mobile Technology,* ISR, 2008.

32. Kalnikaite, V., Bird, J. and Rogers, Y. Decision-making in the aisles: informing, overwhelming or nudging supermarket shoppers? *Pers Ubiquit Comput 17* (2013), 1247-1259.

33. Kellar, M., Inkpen, K., Dearman, D., et al. Evaluation of Mobile Collaboration: Learning from our Mistakes. Technical Report 2004-13, Dalhousie University, 2004.

34. Khanum, M. A. and Trivedi, M. C. Comparison of Testing Environments with Children for Usability Problem Identification. *International Journal of Engineering and Technology 5,* 3 (2013), 2048-2053.

35. Kjeldskov J. and Graham C. A Review of Mobile HCI Research *Methods. Proc. Mobile HCI'03,* Springer (2003), 317-335.

36. Kjeldskov, J., Skov, M.B., Als, B.S. and Høegh, R.T. Is it Worth the Hassle? Exploring the Added Value of Evaluating the Usability of Context-Aware Mobile Systems in the Field. *Proc. Mobile HCI'04,* Springer (2004), 61-73.

37. Kjeldskov, J., Graham, C., Pedell, S., Vetere, F., Howard, S., Balbo, S. and Davies, J. Evaluating the usability of a mobile guide: The influence of location, participants and resources. *Behaviour & Information Technology 24,* 1 (2005), 51-65.

38. Kjeldskov, J. and Stage, J. Exploring 'Canned Communication' for coordinating distributed mobile work activities. *IwC 18* (2006) 1310-1335.

39. Kjeldskov, J. and Paay, J. A Longitudinal Review of Mobile HCI Research Methods. *Proc. Mobile HCI'12,* ACM (2012), 69-78.

40. Kondratova, I., Lumsden, J. and Langton, N. Multimodal Field Data Entry: Performance and Usability Issues. *Proc. International Conference on Computing and Decision Making* NRC-CNRC (2006).

41. Korn, M. and Bødker, S. Looking ahead: how field trials can work in iterative and exploratory design of ubicomp systems. *Proc. UbiComp'12,* ACM (2012), 21-30.

42. Kray, C., Olivier, P., Guo, A. W., Singh, P., Ha, H. N. and Blythe, P. Taming Context: A Key Challenge in Evaluating the Usability of Ubiquitous Systems. *Proc. USE'07 Workshop at Ubicomp'07* (2007).

43. Larsen, J.E., Petersen, M.K., Handler, R. and Zandi, N. Observing the Context of Use of a Media Player on Mobile Phones using Embedded and Virtual Sensors. *Proc. NordiCHI'10,* ACM (2010), 33-36.

44. Leitner, G., Ahlström, D. and Hitz, M. Usability of Mobile Computing in Emergency Response Systems – Lessons Learned and Future Directions. *Proc. USAB'07.* Springer (2007), 241-254.

45. Lumsden, J., Kondratova, I. and Durling, S. Investigating microphone efficacy for mobile speech-based data entry. *Proc. HCI'07,* Springer (2007), 89-97.

46. Lumsden, J. and MacLean, R. A Comparison of Pseudo-Paper and Paper Prototyping Methods for Mobile Evaluations. *Proc. MONET'08* (2008), 538-457.

47. Lumsden, J., Langton, N., and Kondratova, I. Bringing the High Seas into the Lab to Evaluate Speech Input Feasibility: A Case Study. *Proc. SiMPE Workshop at Mobile HCI'10* (2010).

48. Maly, I., Mikovec, Z., Vystrcil, J., Franc, J. and Slavik, P. An evaluation tool for research of user behavior in a realistic mobile environment. *Pers Ubiquit Comput 17* (2013), 3-14.

49. Morrison, A., McMillan, D., Reeves, S., Sherwood, S., and Chalmers, M. A Hybrid Mass Participation Approach to Mobile Software Trials. *Proc. CHI'12,* ACM (2012), 1311-1320.

50. Nielsen, C. M., Overgaard, M., Pedersen, M. B., Stage, J. and Stenild, S. It's Worth the Hassle! The Added Value of Evaluating the Usability of Mobile Systems in the Field. *Proc. NordiCHI'06,* ACM (2006), 272-280.

51. Oulasvirta, A., Tamminen, S., Roto, V. and Kuorelahti Interaction in 4-second Bursts: The Fragmented Nature of Attentional Resources in Mobile HCI. *Proc. CHI'05,* ACM (2005), 919-928.

52. Oulasvirta, A. and Nyyssönen, T. Flexible Hardware Configurations for Studying Mobile Usability. *Journal of Usability Studies 4,* 2 (2009), 93-105.

53. Oulasvirta, A. Rethinking Experimental Designs for Field Evaluations. *Pervasive Computing,* Oct-Dec (2012), 60-67.

54. Rogers, Y., Connelly, K., Tedesco, L., Hazlewood, W., Kurtz, A., Hall, R. E., Hursey, J., and Toscos, T. Why It's Worth the Hassle: The Value of In-Situ Studies When Designing Ubicomp. *Proc. UbiComp'07,* Springer (2007), 336–353.

55. Roto, V., Väätäjä, H., Jumisko-Pyykkö, S., and Väänänen-Vainio-Mattila, K. Best Practices for Capturing Context in User Experience Studies in the Wild. *Proc. MindTrek'11* (2011), 91-98.

56. Skattør, B. Training and Deployment as a basis for Usability Engineering of Mobile Systems. *Proc. ACHI,* IEEE (2008), 277-284.

57. Streefkerk, J.W., van Esch-Bussemakers, M.P. and Neerincx, M.A. Field Evaluation of a Mobile Location-Based Notification System for Police Officers. *Proc. Mobile HCI'08,* ACM (2008), 101-108.

58. Sun, X. and May, A. A Comparison of Field-Based and Lab-Based Experiments to Evaluate User Experience of Personalised Mobile Devices. *Adv. in Hum.-Comp. Int.,* Hindawi (2013), Article 2.

59. Tolmie, P., Crabtree, A., Egglestone, S., Humble, J., Greenhalgh, C. and Rodden, T. Digital Plumbing: the mundane work of deploying UbiComp in the home. *Pers Ubiquit Comput 14* (2010), 181-196.

60. Vastenburg, M.H., Keyson, D.V. and de Ridder, H. Measuring User Experiences of Prototypical Autonomous Products in a Simulated Home Environment. *Proc. HCII'07,* Springer (2007), 998-1007.

61. Wilfinger, D., Pirker, M., Bernhaupt, R. and Tscheligi, M. Evaluating and Investigating an iTV Concept in the Field. *Proc. EuroITV'09,* ACM (2009), 175-178.

62. Wilson, M.L, Russel, A., Smith, D.A. and schraefel, m.c. mSpace Mobile: Exploring Support for Mobile Tasks. *Proc. HCI'06,* Springer (2006), 193-202.

63. Wilson, S., Galliers, J. and Fone, J. (2007) Cognitive Artifacts in Support of Medical Shift Handover: An in Use, in Situ Evaluation. *IJHCS 22,* 1&2 (2007), 59-80

64. Wilson, M. L., Mackay, W., Chi, E., Berstein, M., Russell, D. and Thimbleby, H. RepliCHI - CHI should be replicating and validating results more: discuss. *Proc. CHI'11 EA,* ACM (2011), 463-466.

Comparing Pointing Techniques for Grasping Hands on Tablets

Katrin Wolf
University of Stuttgart
katrin.wolf@vis.uni-stuttgart.de

Niels Henze
University of Stuttgart
niels.henze@vis.uni-stuttgart.de

ABSTRACT
With the recent success of tablet devices a new device type became available for mobile interaction. Just as for mobile phones, touch is the dominant way people interact with tablets. In contrast to the much smaller phones a firm grip with both hands is needed to securely hold tablet devices. While a large body of work has investigated touch interaction on smaller devices, is little empirical research has been carried out on touch-based pointing while holding the device with both hands. To understand touch-based interactions using tablet devices, we conducted an experiment to compare four pointing techniques on both the front and back of the devices while it was held in landscape format. We compare direct touch with the following alternatives for selecting targets, indirect pointing on a virtual touchpad, an inverse cursor, and a miniature interaction area. While direct touch is 35% faster than the fastest alternative, only 74% of the touchscreen and 64% of a back-of-device can be reached by each hand. We show that among the indirect pointing techniques, the miniaturized interaction area is significantly faster and received the best subjective ratings. We conclude that a miniaturized interaction area is a viable alternative to direct touch especially on the backside of tablet devices.

Author Keywords
Tablet; pointing; touch; direct; indirect; grasp.

ACM Classification Keywords
H.5.2. User Interfaces: Ergonomics.

INTRODUCTION
Over the last decade, touchscreens have arguably become the most common way to interact with computing devices. A large body of work has investigated how mobile devices with touchscreens are used in daily life and, in particular, developed novel interaction techniques for them. As direct manipulation is the dominant interaction paradigm for touch devices, investigating pointing techniques received major attention. Previous work has focused either on the interaction with mobile phones that can easily be held in one hand (leaving the other hand free to interact) or on interaction with a much larger stationary touch display.

MobileHCI 2014, September 23–26, 2014, Toronto, ON, Canada.

http://dx.doi.org/10.1145/2628363.2628371

With the commercial success of tablet computers a third category of touch screen devices has become widely used. While tablets are small enough to be used "on the go" they are often too large to be held comfortably with one hand.

Indeed one of the most common ways to hold the device is using a two-handed grip (particularly if used in landscape format). Grasp-based pointing on tablets can cause ergonomic problems. Due to the large size of tablets, the thumbs and fingers are sometimes unable to reach the center of the display, while the device is being held [12, 21]. Therefore, direct touch, which is the most common pointing technique for touchscreens, may be not the most appropriated one for tablet devices.

The technology company Apple filed a patent on back-of-device interaction in 2006 [9]; and Wigdor et al. [20] demonstrated in 2007 how back-of-device interaction when using a tablet-sized device solves the *fat-finger* problem [16]. Since the release of the Motorola CHARM in 2010 and the Sony Playstation Vita in 2012, mobile devices with a touch-sensitive back are commercially available. It can be expected that touchpads will soon be embedded in the back of many devices. Users' performance when pointing through back-of-device interaction on tablet has not been study in-depth, and consequently, corresponding design guidelines are not available. Thus, we consider both, pointing on touchscreens as well as on touchpads built in the back of the device.

Pointing performance with grasping hands is constrained by parameters, such as reachability and joint flexion of the pointing digit. To understand touch-based interaction using tablet devices, we conduct an experiment that compares four pointing techniques on the front and on the backside of tablet devices while the device is being held in landscape format. We compare direct touch with selecting targets using a touchpad, an inverse cursor, and a miniature interaction area.

The contribution of this paper is threefold: (1) Describing the area that is easily accessible using direct touch while the tablet is held in landscape format based on empirical data. (2) Comparing four pointing techniques on both sides of tablet devices to show which technique is the best alternative to direct touch. (3) Proposing a combination of direct touch on the front and a miniature representation of the tablet's interaction area on the back that makes the whole screen accessible.

In the following sections we first provide an overview about previous work on pointing techniques. Afterwards, a description of the conducted study and its results is given. Finally, we discuss our findings and conclude the paper with a summary and an outlook on future work.

RELATED WORK

This paper aims to increase our understanding of pointing on tablets. The aim is to overcome the current limitations caused by occlusion and limited target accessibility in the center of the device. Research with respect to pointing on tablet devices is rare. Thus we present here works on pointing with hand-held devices in general, which includes mobile phones. We identified four categories of pointing techniques: direct and relative pointing, remote direct pointing, and inverse direct pointing, which are presented in the following sections.

Direct pointing

Direct pointing is known to be very immediate and intuitive as touching the desired target corresponds directly to the way people interact in the physical world. In contrast to the physical world however, virtual targets are often very small. This can result in a phenomenon known as the *fat-finger-problem* [16], which means that the finger that touches the target is occluding it, thereby decreasing precision. *LucidTouch* [20] is a tablet-sized device that enables back-of-device interaction; and thus the fingers can select targets from the back side without occluding the content that is displayed on the front. *LucidTouch* uses a camera mounted at the rear of the device, which results in a rather bulky prototype. The concept of back-of-device interaction has been improved by Baudisch and Cheng: *NanoTouch* [1] uses a back-mounted touchpad instead of a camera and thus, enables back-of-device interactions even with very small devices.

If a user holds the device while pointing, the hand has to solve multiple tasks, meaning that direct pointing becomes more challenging due to the hands bio-mechanics. Thus, in addition to occlusion, a second problem of direct touch is the accessibility of targets that are further away or very close. The center of the tablet is hard to reach if the device is held in landscape format with both hands [12, 21]. For one-handed pointing on mobile phones it was found that the thumb performance varies with its posture. Poorest pointing performances results from excessive thumb flexion. When tapping on targets closest to the base of the thumb in the bottom right corner of the screen the performance is low. The highest performance is achieved when the thumb is in a rested posture, neither significantly flexed nor fully extended [17]. De Luca et al. [5] showed that back-of-device pointing without visual feedback has a too low accuracy to be considered a valuable input method for authentication. Finally, Buschek et al. developed a model to improve text entry on the back of the device but did not compare direct touch with other pointing techniques [2].

Inverse direct pointing

Roudeau *et al.* [14] introduced *MagStick*, which is a thumb interaction technique for target acquisition on mobile devices with small touch-screens. The technique addresses screen accessibility as well as target selection accuracy and occlusion. The user controls a cursor through an inverse drag motion and thus can select a target without occluding it with the thumb. While *MagStick* enables to access a larger area than the thumb can reach via direct touch, Roudeau *et al.* found that it is slower.

Kim *et al.* [10] proposed an expandable cursor called *Large Touch* that also moves inversely to the user's finger. In contrast to *MagStick*, the cursor moves a larger distance than the thumb that slides across the touchscreen. Thereby, *Large Touch* enables to reach locations that are further away from the thumb. Also in contrast to Roudaut *et al.* [14], Kim *et al.* found no difference in target selection time between the inverse cursor technique (*Large Touch*) and the common direct touch technique in a conducted study [10].

Miniature interaction area

ThumbSpace [8] introduced one-handed thumb interaction for small targets that are spread out wide on mobile phones' screens. The problem addressed is similar to the problem of pointing on targets that are hard to reach due to the size of a tablet. The approach taken is to shrink the screen into a small screen that is defined by drawing it with the thumb. This ensures that the thumb can reach all targets. Thus, *ThumbSpace* improves accuracy for selecting targets that are out of thumb reach, but it is slower than target selections with direct touch. A similar concept was proposed by Kim et al. [10] who presented *Sliding-screen* to address the limited target accessibility on phone touchscreens. A drag from the edge of the screen towards its center dynamically shrinks the interaction area, meaning that a tap can easily reach targets on the smaller display that may have been too far away on the interaction area before it was shrunk. Like *ThumbSpace*, this technique was found to be slower than direct touch for one-handed target selections with mobile phones.

The *ARC-Pad* [11] links the touchscreen of a phone to a large display in a one-to-one mapping. It enables to use the phone's touchscreen to be used as both an absolute and a relative touchpad for large displays. *ARC-Pad* combined absolute and relative cursor positioning. Tapping on the *ARC-Pad* causes the cursor to jump to the corresponding location on the screen, providing rapid movement across large distances. For fine position control, users can use a relative cursor control technique.

Relative pointing

Relative pointing is often used for remote-selections, such as mouse and touchpads that are built in laptops. Forlines *et al.* [6] compared direct touch versus mouse input for unimanual and bimanual tasks on tabletop displays. Analyses of quantitative performance and subjective preference indicate that users may be better off using a mouse for unimanual input and their fingers for bimanual input when working on a large, horizontal display. Cockburn *et al.* [4] compared performance in touch selections on a touchscreen that was horizontally placed on a table in front of the user. They found that direct touch is faster than relative pointing (tap is faster than drag) using the finger. The error rate is high for small targets and further increases using direct pointing methods for target acquisitions over longer distances.

Hasan et al. compared relative pointing with direct touch for back-of-device interaction [7]. They found that relative pointing is faster and more accurate on the back of the device.

A comparison of *ARC-Pad* [11], which was described above, with relative pointing showed that ARC-Pad is faster than relative pointing. Moreover, relative pointing was more accurate. Thus, the *ARC-Pad* was, just like direct touch usually is, namely faster but less accurate than relative pointing.

Summary
Previous work developed and compared pointing techniques for tabletop displays [4, 6], for mobile phones' touchscreens [8, 10, 11, 14], and for the backside of phones [7]. Tablets are, however, a third device type that has almost been entirely neglected. Their size/weight requires a certain grip that not only affects pointing performance but also makes parts of the screen inaccessible using direct touch. In the following sections we reduce this research gap through a controlled experiment. Four target pointing techniques, which represent the four categories discussed above, are compared. We consider front- as well as back-of-tablet interaction using both the dominant and the non-dominant hand. The aim is to provide a fundamental understanding of pointing on tablets with grasping hands.

POINTING TECHNIQUES
Previous work proposed the following four categories of touch-based pointing techniques: direct pointing, inverse direct pointing, relative pointing, and remote direct pointing. In our experiment, we evaluate four pointing techniques (see Figure 1); and each of them represents one of the categories. Direct pointing is represented through *direct touch* (1). The *inverse cursor* (2) stands for the direct inverse pointing techniques. The *touchPad* (3) allows relative pointing; and the *miniature area* (4) enables direct remote pointing using a miniaturized display that represented the entire interaction area of the tablet.

(1) Direct touch
Direct touch is the common pointing technique for touchscreen interactions. The digit is directly touching the

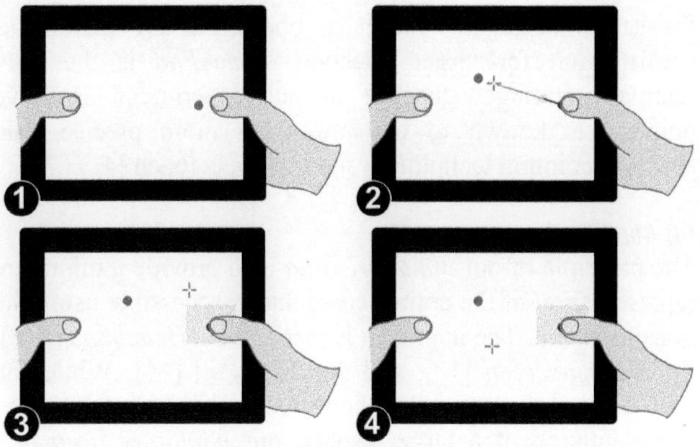

Figure 1. This paper investigates pointing techniques that are performed without losing the tablet grip: (1) direct touch (2) inverse cursor (3) touchPad (4) miniature area.

location where a target is displayed. If the direct touch is performed with the hands that hold a tablet in a symmetric bimanual grip, the thumb can execute direct touch on the front of the device and a finger does it on the back side. Direct touch is known to cause occlusion problems with touchscreens. This problem is addressed through back-of-device pointing proposed by Wigdor *et al.* [20]. Moreover, direct touch can make it difficult to access the center of tablets that are held with both hands [12, 21].

(2) Inverse cursor
The inverse cursor technique refers to *MagStick* [14] and *Large Touch* [10], which were developed for one-handed phone interactions. Similar to both approaches, the *inverse cursor* is controlled by setting an initial anchor point through a touch; and a drag gesture from that initial touch point pulls a cursor in the opposite direction. While the distance the cursor is moved using *MagStick* is similar to the length of the drag gesture; *Large Touch* translates the drag gesture to a larger cursor movement to overcome accessibility problems in one-handed phone interaction. The amount of movement of the *inverse cursor* is adaptive to allow for the entire interaction area to be always accessible when interacting with the hand that grasps the device. The cursor motion depends on the position of the start of the drag gesture. As the cursor movement is defined by an inverse digit movement, dragging the digit to the very outer touchscreen boarder will move the cursor to the touchscreen's very outer opposite edge. This ensures that every screen position is accessible.

(3) TouchPad
The *touchPad* technique is a virtual reference to physical touchpads that are commonly built in laptop computers. Researchers found that there are many ways to hold a tablet device [13, 19]; and Cheng *et al.* [3] proposed placing GUI components (such as virtual keyboards) where people grasp a tablet. Accordingly, our *touchPad* appears after an initial touch. A drag gesture on the *touchPad* moves a cursor relatively. For target acquisition using the *touchPad*, several drag gestures may be required to point on a target. Thus, a release cannot be used to confirm a target acquisition to

finish the selection. We have chosen a tap gesture as confirmation for target selection. *TouchPad* is the only relative pointing technique in our experiment. Relative pointing is known to be slower but more precise than absolute pointing techniques, such as direct touch [4, 7].

(4) Miniature area

The principle of our *miniature area* is to provide a miniature representation of the entire screen that is accessible using the grasping hand. The approach is inspired by *ThumbSpace* [8], the *Sliding-screen* [10], and the *ARC-Pad* [11]. While the *ARC-Pad* uses a mobile phone as a physical one-to-one representation of a large display; our *miniature area* is a virtual miniature one-to-one representation of the tablet's interaction area. Unlike *ThumbSpace* and *Sliding-screen*, which require defining the interaction area size with a drag gesture; *miniature area* does not require an extra interaction step to size the interaction area. The miniature display representation is pre-defined in size and is dynamically placed through a touch gesture. That is similar to the adaptive placement of the *touchPad* and ensures that the *miniature area* is always well accessible aiming for faster interaction. Unlike the *touchPad* that requires a tap gesture to confirm a target selection process, the *miniature area* in more immediate. Target acquisition is realized through touching the *miniature area* at the position that is mapped to the corresponding target position on the tablet's display. The position on the large screen that a touch on the *miniature area* is referring to is visualized through a cursor. Drag gestures allow for moving a cursor. A touch release confirms the target acquisition and ends the selection process.

EXPERIMENT

To provide foundational knowledge about grasp-based pointing on tablets, and to help designers to understand the human factors, we compared four pointing techniques in a controlled experiment. We evaluate the pointing techniques to determine their performance as well as perceived effort and usability. Performance provides insights in target accessibility and selection time. Effort and usability help understanding which pointing technique is preferred for what reason.

Design

Our study had a 4x2x2x3 within subject design with the independent variables *pointing technique* (direct touch, inverse cursor, touchPad, miniature area), *hand* (right, left), *device side* (front-, back-of-device), and *target size* (5, 7, 10mm). The targets were arranged in a 10x7 grid that was equally distributed over the touchscreen, excluding 2 positions of "start" buttons at the vertical center of both most left and right outer x-positions. One target per size appeared per target position in each condition. Thus, 204 targets had to be selected (or rejected if not accessible) per condition, resulting in 3264 targets per participant. The dependent variables were *target selection time, selection effectiveness, perceived effort*, and *usability*. Touch events (for each *pointing technique, hand, device side, target size,* and *target position*) were recorded in logfiles. Perceived effort (for each *pointing technique* and each *device side*) was measured using the SMEQ scale, because it is known to be very sensitive with small sample sizes [15]. The usability of each pointing technique was recorded using the AttrakDiff questionnaire.

Participants

We recruited 14 right-handed participants (6 females) with different academic backgrounds, such as computer science, history of art, and media design. The participants had an average age of 29.6 years (SD=4.3).

Apparatus

A tablet sandwich was used to present the experimental task and to record logfiles. It consisted of two tablet devices glued with their rear sides together and connected via Bluetooth. This allowed for sensing touch events on the back of the apparatus and to update the GUI of the device at the front accordingly. The resolution of the screen was 1280x742 pixels (without bottom menu bar) with a size of 21.7cm x 13.6cm.

Procedure

For each pointing technique, we asked the participants to select targets that appeared after pressing a "start" button as fast and precise as possible. During the tasks, the participants were holding the apparatus in landscape format with two hands in a symmetric grip. Each pointing technique was used on both device sides using one hand after the other. If a target by any reason was perceived to be not easily selectable, the participants were asked to press a "cancel" button. We randomized the order of the 16 conditions. Each participant was asked to perform the tasks using each condition after a short training phase. After completing a condition, the participants filled the SMEQ and the AttrakDiff questionnaires. The experiment was split into two sessions. Each session lasted between 1.5 and 2 hours. When all conditions were completed, a demographic questionnaire was filled.

RESULTS

Our results contain effectiveness (measured as percentage of targets that could successfully be selected), efficiency (measured as task completion time), selection time per target position, number of attempts to select a target, perceived effort, and usability.

Effectiveness

Effectiveness represents the target accessibility for the different pointing techniques. If the participants were not able to select a target, for instance because they could not reach it, they could skip that task with a "cancel" button. The cancelled selection tasks per pointing technique are presented in Table 1.

pointing technique	direct touch	inverse cursor	touchPad	mini. area
		Front of the device		
right hand	50.95%	0.00%	0.00%	0.00%
left hand	51.65%	0.00%	0.00%	0.00%
		Back of the device		
right hand	52.71%	0.00%	0.00%	0.09%
left hand	54.34%	0.17%	0.04%	1.57%

Table 1. Cancelled selections tasks per pointing technique.

While the target accessibility for *inverse cursor, touchPad*, and *miniature area* was 100% on the front side and above 98% on the back of the device. Pointing with direct touch was cancelled in more than half of the cases. As it is expected, targets that are further away from the grasping hand are not reachable via direct touch. The target positions that were accessible in at least 90% of the attempts cover 37% of the front sided interaction area for each hand as well as 34% of the back of the tablet using the left hand and 30% using the right hand, as shown in Figure 2.

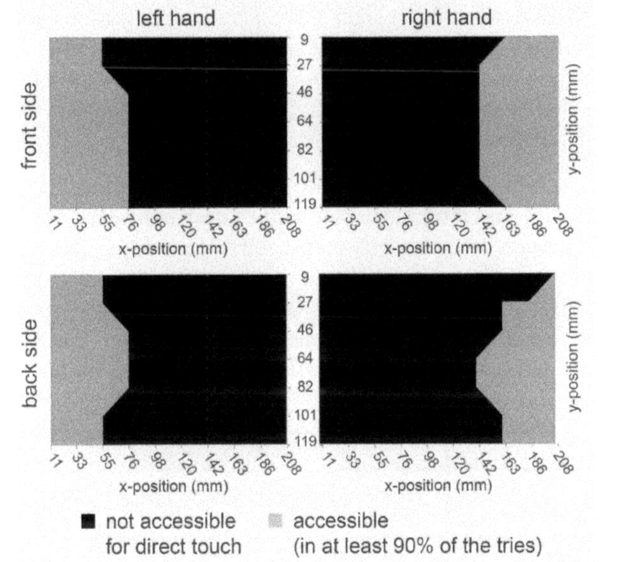

Figure 2. Locations of the targets that are accessible using direct touch.

Efficiency

Efficiency is measured as *target selection time* for the targets that were successfully selected. The selection tasks that were cancelled are not considered in this analysis. We removed 528 of the 45.696 tasks that were more than three standard deviations from the mean and took longer than 8.644s [18]. The average selection times (Mean) and the standard deviations (SD) are presented in Table 2.

A Kolmogorov-Smirnov-Test shows that our data is normally distributed. Mauchly's test indicated that the assumption of sphericity has been violated for the interaction effects *technique* * *hand* (p<.001).

	pointing technique			
	direct touch	inverse cursor	touchPad	mini. area
Mean	1.28s	2.93s	2.53s	1.97s
SD	0.74s	1.29s	0.92s	0.87s
	device side		hand	
	front	back	left	right
Mean	2.06s	2.57s	2.40s	2.22s
SD	1.06s	1.17s	1.15s	1.13s
	target size			
	5mm	7mm	10mm	
Mean	2.51s	2.30s	2.13s	
SD	1.24s	1.13s	1.03s	

Table 2. Mean and SD for target selection time in seconds.

Therefore degrees of freedom were corrected using Greenhouse-Geisser estimates of sphericity for the respective tests. There was a significant main effect of *pointing technique* on the task completion time ($F_{3,36}$=124.24, *p*<.001). Bonferroni corrected pair-wise t-tests revealed significant differences between the four *pointing techniques* (*p*=.007 for *inverse cursor* vs. *touchPad* and *p*<.001 for all other comparisons, see Figure 3). Similarly, *hand* ($F_{1,12}$=20.77, *p*=.001), *device side* ($F_{1,12}$=60.64, *p*<.001, Figure 4), and *target size* ($F_{2,24}$=167.80, *p*<.001) had a significant effect on the task completion time. Bonferroni corrected pair-wise t-tests revealed significant differences between the three *target sizes* (*p*<.001, see Figure 5). We found interaction effects for *technique* * *device side* ($F_{3,36}$=10.33, *p*<.001), *hand* * *device side* ($F_{1,12}$=6.88, *p*=.022, Figure 6), and *technique* * *target size* ($F_{6,72}$=21.22, *p*<.001). In contrast, there were neither significant interaction effects for *technique* * *hand* ($F_{1.27,15.19}$=0.76, *p*=.43), *hand* * *target size* ($F_{2,24}$=0.15, I=.87), nor for *device side* * *target size* ($F_{2,24}$=2.98, *p*=.07).

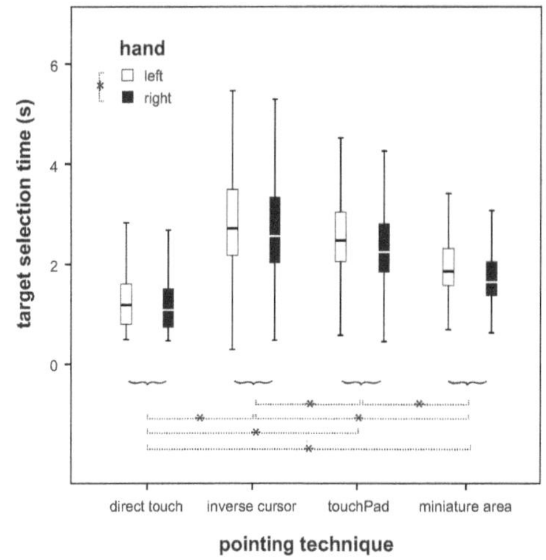

Figure 3. Selection times over pointing technique per hand and sign. differences (*).

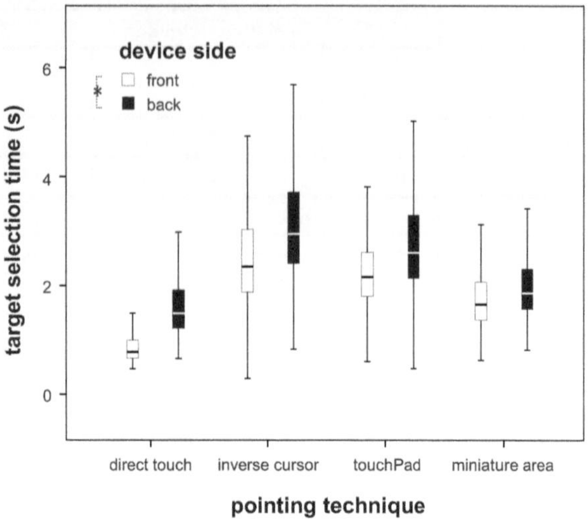

Figure 4. Selection times over pointing techniques per device side.

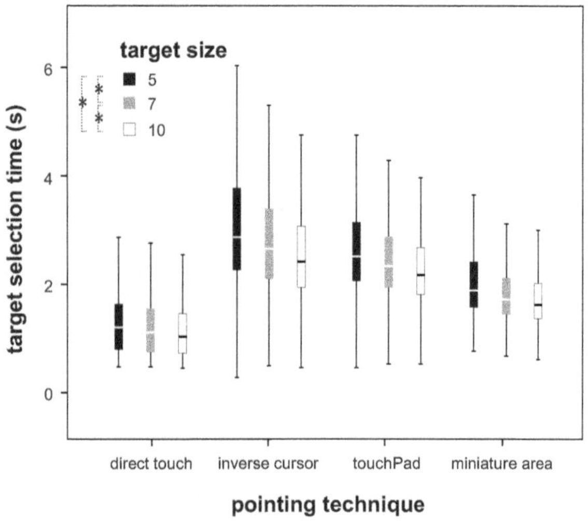

Figure 5. Selection times over pointing techniques per target size.

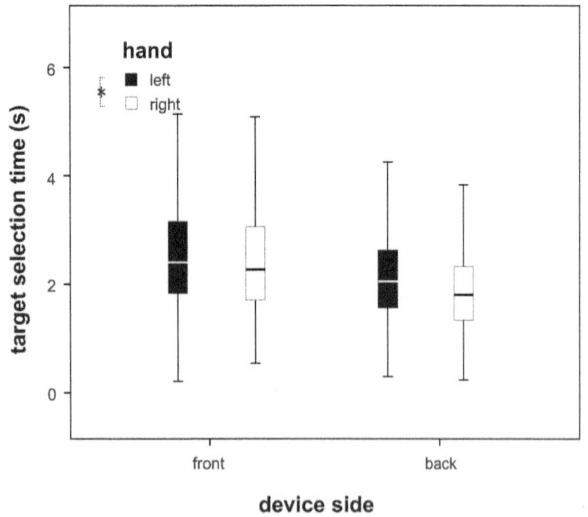

Figure 6. Selection times over device side per hand.

Selection time per target position

Selection time for each *target position* was calculated if the target was at least successfully selected in at least 90% of the attempts. Otherwise the target position was identified to be not accessible. The median time needed to select a target at a certain position is presented in Figure 7. *Direct touch* just allows for accessing targets that are located close to the hand that is selecting it. The other three techniques allow accessing the entire interaction area on both, the front and the back of the device. As shown in Figure 3; the *inverse cursor* has the lowest performance. Selection time increases the further the target is from the selecting hand for the *inverse cursor* and the *touchPad* technique. The *miniature area* results in an almost constant time across the screen and also in the highest selection performance over the entire interaction area on both device sides.

Number of attempts per target selection

We counted how many attempts participants needed to successfully select a target. The numbers of attempts are given by the number of touch downs/releases. Cancelled attempts were ignored for this calculation. We removed all tasks that were more than three standard deviations from the mean and took more than 10.4 attempts [18]. The average number of attempts (Mean) and the standard deviations (SD) for each *pointing technique*, *device side*, *hand*, and *target size* are presented in Table 3.

Again, a Kolmogorov-Smirnov-Test shows that our data is normally distributed, and Mauchly's test indicated that the assumption of sphericity has been violated for the main effect technique ($p<.001$) as well as for the interaction effects *technique * hand* ($p<.001$), and *technique * device side* ($p=.001$).Therefore degrees of freedom were corrected using Greenhouse-Geisser estimates of sphericity for the respective tests.

	Pointing technique			
	direct touch	inverse cursor	touchPad	mini. area
Mean	1.2	1.2	3.1	1.1
SD	0.6	0.6	1.1	0.4
	device side		hand	
	front	back	left	right
Mean	1.7	1.7	1.7	1.7
SD	1.2	1.2	1.2	1.2
	target size			
	5mm	7mm	10mm	
Mean	1.8	1.7	1.7	
SD	1.2	1.2	1.1	

Table 3. Mean and SD for number of attempts to select a target.

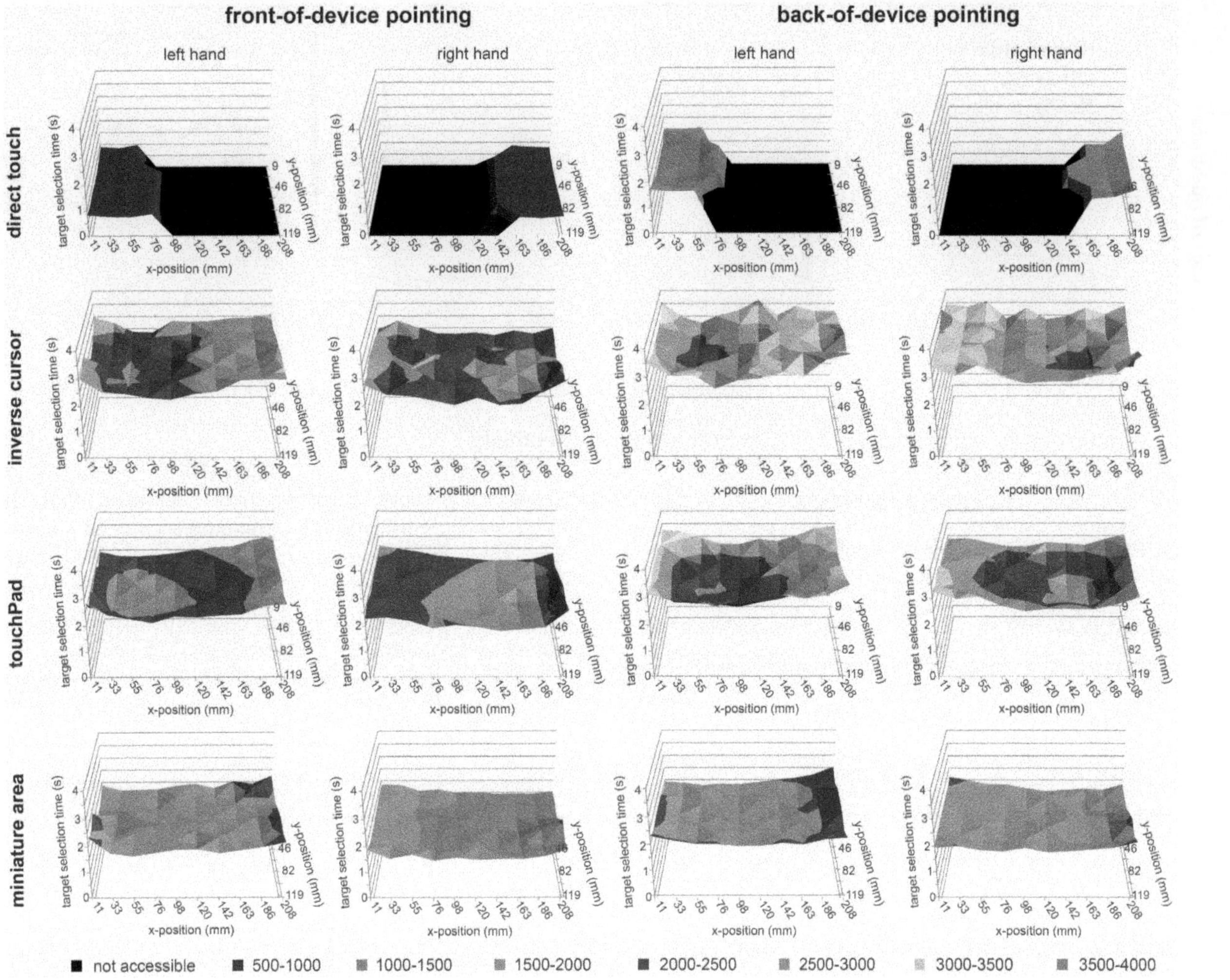

Figure 7. Target selection time (median) for each target position at the front and the back of a tablet (counted in mm from the top left). If the target could not be selected in 90% of the attempts in a certain position, this position is labelled as not accessible.

There was a significant main effect of the *pointing technique* on the number of attempts participants needed to select a target ($F_{1.07,12.87}$=175.89, p<.001. Bonferroni corrected pair-wise t-tests revealed significant differences between *inverse cursor* and *touchPad* (p<.001), *direct touch* and *touchPad* (p<.001), *direct touch* and *miniature area* (p=.002), as well as *touchPad* and *miniature area* (p<.001), see Figure 8. There were no significant main effects for *hand* ($F_{1,12}$=0.001, p=.97) or *device side* ($F_{1,12}$=0.03, p=.87). *Target size* ($F_{2,24}$=33.17, p<.001) had a significant effect on the number of attempts. Bonferroni corrected pair-wise t-tests revealed significant differences between all *target sizes* (p=.047 for 5mm vs. 7mm, p<.001 for 5mm vs. 10mm, and p=.001 for 7mm vs. 10mm). We found significant interaction effects *for technique * target size* ($F_{6,72}$=11.14, p<.001) and *device side * target size* ($F_{2,24}$=8.93, p<.001). There were neither significant interaction effects for *technique * hand* ($F_{1.53,18.35}$=0.52, p=.07), *technique * device side* ($F_{1.91,22.89}$=2.73, p=.09, Figure 9), *hand * device side* ($F_{1,12}$=0.13, p=0.91), nor for *hand * target size* ($F_{2,24}$=0.26, p=.97).

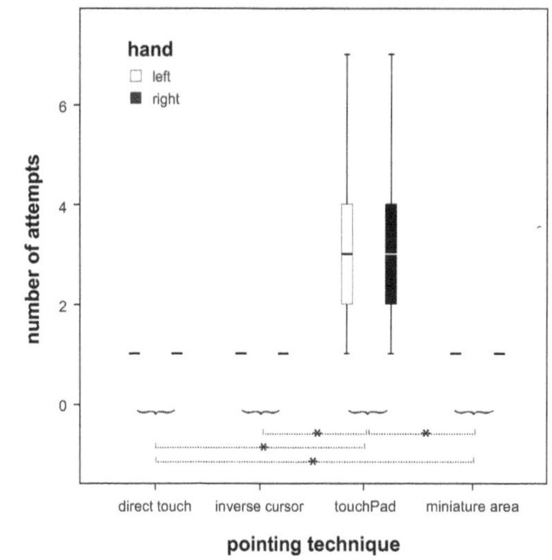

Figure 8. Number of attempts over pointing technique per hand and sign. differences (*).

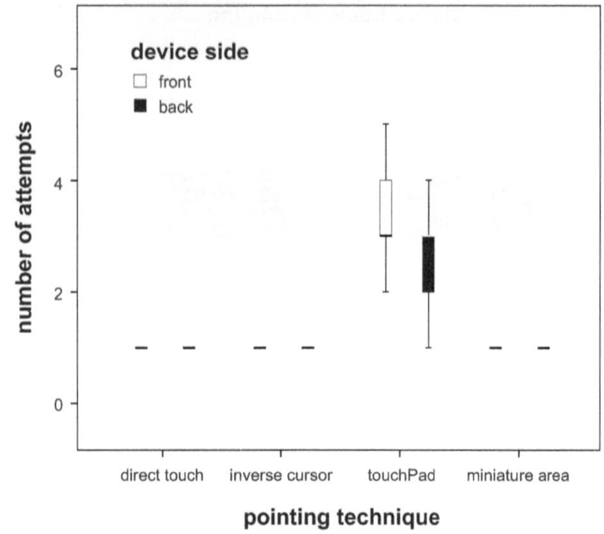

Figure 9. Number of attempts over pointing techniques per device side.

Perceived effort

The perceived effort was measured using the SMEG on a scale from 0 (no effort) to 220 (high effort). The average perceived effort (Mean) and the standard deviations (SD) as well as the according effort description are presented in Table 4.

Pointing techniques	direct touch	inverse cursor	touchPad	miniature area
Mean	81.3	104.8	54.9	49.2
SD	14.0	14.0	14.0	14.0
Description	fairly hard	pretty hard	a bit hard	a bit hard
Device side	**front**		**back**	
Mean	65.3		79.8	
SD	10.8		10.8	
Description	fairly hard		fairly hard	

Table 4. Perceived effort with Mean, SD, and description.

A repeated measure ANOVA yielded a significant different perceived effort for *pointing technique* ($F_{3,80}$=7.2, p<.001). For *device side* it was shown that interacting on the front was perceived significantly easier ($F_{1,92}$=7.9, p=.006). Moreover, we found an interaction effect for *pointing technique* * *device side* ($F_{3,81}$=3.1, p=.030).

While Bonferroni-corrected pairwise comparisons (see Figure 10) showed that the *inverse cursor* technique was perceived to be significantly harder than the *touchPad* (p=.021) as well as than the *miniature area* (p<.001), no significant difference was found between *direct touch* and any other technique (*direct touch* vs. *inverse cursor*: p=1.000, *direct touch* vs. *touchPad*: p=.221, and *direct touch* vs. *miniature area*: p=.336). Furthermore, we found no significant difference between the *touchPad* and the *miniature area* (p=1.000).

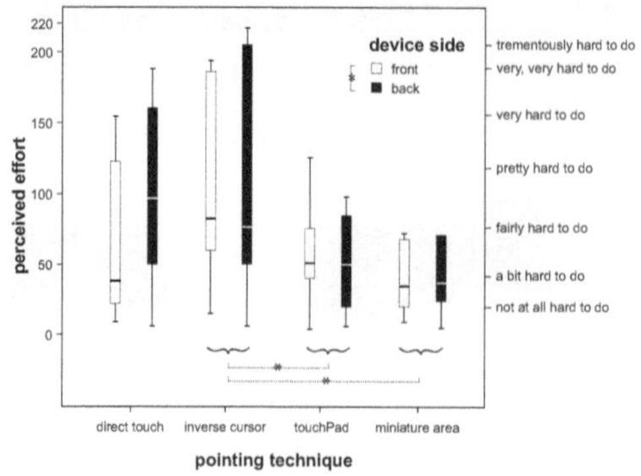

Figure 10. Perceived effort over pointing techn. per device side.

Usability

The four sub-scales of the AttrakDiff questionnaire, which describe usability, are pragmatic qualities, the hedonic quality of identification, the hedonic quality of stimulation, and global attractiveness. All four scales have as minimum 1 and as maximum 7, while high values refer to high qualities. The average usability qualities (Mean) and the standard deviations (SD) are presented in Table 5.

Pointing techniques	direct touch	inverse cursor	touchPad	miniature area
	Pragmatic quality			
Mean	4.8	3.9	5.2	5.2
SD	0.2	0.4	0.2	0.3
	Hedonic quality: Identification			
Mean	4.1	4.2	4.4	4.7
SD	0.2	0.2	0.2	0.2
	Hedonic quality: Stimulation			
Mean	4.4	4.2	4.4	4.4
SD	0.3	0.3	0.3	0.3
	Attractiveness			
Mean	4.6	3.8	4.9	5.2
SD	0.3	0.3	0.2	0.3
Device side	**front**		**back**	
	Pragmatic quality			
Mean	5.0		4.6	
SD	0.2		0.3	
	Hedonic quality: Identification			
Mean	4.3		4.4	
SD	0.2		0.2	
	Hedonic quality: Stimulation			
Mean	4.1		4.5	
SD	0.3		0.2	
	Attractiveness			
Mean	4.9		4.4	
SD	0.2		0.3	

Table 5. Mean values and SD for the AttrakDiff sub-scales.

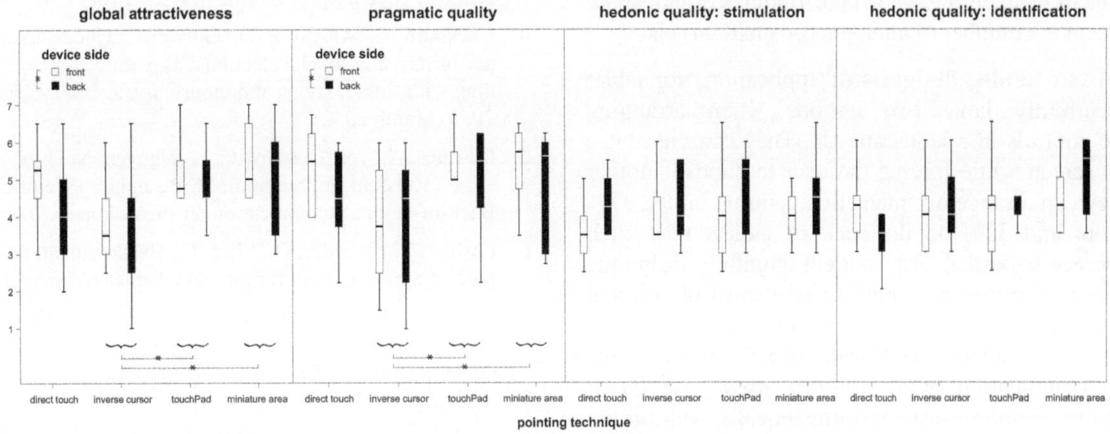

Figure 11: Usability scales: global attractiveness, pragmatic quality, hedonic quality stimulation, hedonic quality identification to rate the four pointing techniques from 1=low rating to 7=high rating.

A MANOVA yielded significantly different ratings per *pointing technique* for the global attractiveness and the pragmatic qualities (global attractiveness: $F_{3,114}$=9.2, p<.001, pragmatic quality: $F_{3,114}$=10.2, p<.001). Both hedonic qualities, identification and stimulation were not rated differently (identification: $F_{3,114}$=2.5, p=.071, stimulation: $F_{3,144}$=1.8, p=.155). Moreover, the attractiveness and the pragmatic qualities were rated significantly different for both, pointing on the front and the back of the device (global attractiveness: $F_{1,10}$=6.7, p=.023, pragmatic quality: $F_{1,10}$=8.9, p=.011). Again, the hedonic qualities were not rated differently for both device sides (identification: $F_{3,114}$=1.4, p=.517, stimulation: $F_{3,144}$=4.5, p=.054). No interaction effect was found between the *pointing techniques* and *device side* (global attractiveness: $F_{3,114}$=1.3, p=.291, pragmatic quality: $F_{3,114}$=1.4, p=.268, stimulation: $F_{3,144}$=2.2, p=.103, identification: $F_{3,114}$=2.0, p=.128).

For attractiveness, Bonferroni-corrected pairwise comparisons (see Figure 11) showed that the *inverse cursor* technique received significantly lower ratings than the *miniature area* (p=.003) and the *touchPad* (p=.006). According pragmatic qualities, Bonferroni corrected post-hoc tests showed again that the *inverse cursor* was rated worse than the *miniature area* (p<.001) as well as than the *touchPad* (p=.002).

Comments

During the experiment, participants gave additional comments about their experience with the different pointing techniques. Four participants appreciated that targets were not occluded when interacting on the back of the device. Targets are always occluded when pointing via *direct touch* on the front side but also through the other three techniques if the targets were located on bottom positions where the thumb is rested while holding the device. One participant mentioned that a tap was sometimes misinterpreted as a drag using the *touchPad.*

DISCUSSION

Analyzing the collected data, we found that only 37% of the front and 32% of the back of tablets is accessible using *direct touch* with one hand. Even with two hands, only 74% of the front and 64% of the back. While *direct touch* is the fastest pointing technique, we found that it is only usable for areas at the screen's border. Among the other pointing technique, the *miniature area* is 28.4% faster than the *touchPad* and 48.7% faster than the *inverse cursor.* In contrast to the other techniques, the target selection time varies little across the screen using the *miniature area.* Looking at the subjective measures of all four techniques, using the *miniature area* resulted in the lowest perceived effort and the highest score on all sub-scales of the AttrakDiff questionnaire even in comparison with *direct touch.*

Our results are in line with Odell et al. [12] as well as with Wolf et al. [21] who found that the center areas of tablet touchscreens and for back-of-device interaction are not accessible with *direct touch.* Moreover, we have shown that *direct touch* on the back of the device results in the same problem. While Kim et al. [10] found that their inverse cursor *Large Touch* is as fast as *direct touch* when pointing on mobile phones, our results are contradictory to these but in line with those of Roudaut *et al.* [14] who found that *direct touch* is faster than the *inverse cursor* technique using mobile phones. The miniature areas *ThumbSpace* [8] and *Sliding-screen* [10] implemented for mobile phones were slower than direct touch, which is in line with our findings using the *miniature area* on the front as well as on the back of tablet devices. Moreover, our *miniature area* is (similar to the *ARC-Pad*) faster than relative pointing, which is represented through the *touchPad* technique in our study. While Hasan *et al.* [7] found that relative pointing performs better than direct touch for one-handed back-of-phone interaction in terms of target selection time as well as accuracy, we found like Cockburn *et al.* [4] that *direct touch* is faster than relative pointing, using our *touchPad* on both the front as well as the back of a tablet. In contrast to the findings of Cockburn *et al.* [4] our findings do not show an increase in the number of attempts for small targets.

In light of our results, designers of applications for tablet devices currently have two options when arranging interactive controls in a landscape UI. They can either use the whole screen while forcing the user to choose another grip or they can arrange all interactive controls on the 37% on the front and 32% on the back of tablets near each vertical screen's border. An indirect pointing technique such as the *miniature area* could offer a third option and make the whole screen easily accessible. As all indirect techniques we considered are slower than *direct touch*, we propose a combination of a *miniature area* with *direct touch*. As the *miniature area* performs equally well on the front as on the back a viable option is to combine direct touch on the front with the *miniature area* on the back. This approach has the advantage that a dedicated pointing technique is used on each device side which helps to avoid confusion of the user. Furthermore, the whole screen becomes easily accessible and thus usable for designers.

CONCLUSION AND FUTURE WORK

In this paper, we investigated pointing on tablet devices. We compared four pointing techniques while participants held the device with both hands in landscape format. For this setup, we showed that only 74% on the front and 64% on the back of tablets can be easily reached using *direct touch*. Among the three alternatives, the *miniature area*, a virtual miniature one-to-one representation of the tablet's interaction area, is the fastest option. As this *miniature area* received the best subjective ratings, even compared to direct touch, we propose to combine direct touch on the front of tablet devices with the *miniature area* on the back. This combination would make the whole screen accessible and avoid mixing interaction techniques.

The conducted study focuses on one of the most common ways to hold tablet devices and as participants were comfortably seated the setup mimics the typical usage context. Future work should nonetheless investigate if the results hold true for other postures and situations. Furthermore, the screen size of the used device was 10.1"; and future work should investigate additional screen sizes. The fraction of the screen that is easily accessible will become even smaller for larger screens. It would be interesting to investigate if our results can be transferred to much larger tabletops where interaction is not restricted by hand size but by arm length.

REFERENCES

1. Baudisch, P., Chu, G. Back-of-device interaction allows creating very small touch devices. *Proc. CHI'09.*
2. Buschek, D., Schoenleben, O., Oulasvirta, A. Improving accuracy in back-of-device multitouch typing: a clustering-based approach to keyboard updating. *Proc. IUI'14.*
3. Cheng, L., Liang, H., Wu, C., Chen, M. iGrasp: grasp-based adaptive keyboard for mobile devices. *Proc. CHI'13.*
4. Cockburn, A., Ahlström, D., Gutwin, C. Understanding performance in touch selections: Tap, drag and radial pointing drag with finger, stylus and mouse. *Int. J. Hum.-Comput. Stud.* 70, 3 (March 2012).
5. De Luca, A., von Zezschwitz, E., Nguyen, N. D. H., Maurer, M.-E., Rubegni, E., Scipioni, M. P., and Langheinrich, M.. Back-of-device authentication on smartphones. *Proc. CHI'13.*
6. Forlines, C., Wigdor, D., Shen, C., Balakrishnan, R. Direct-touch vs. mouse input for tabletop displays. *Proc. CHI'07.*
7. Hasan, K., Yang, X.-D., Liang, H.-N., Irani, P. How to position the cursor?: an exploration of absolute and relative cursor positioning for back-of-device input. *Proc. MobileHCI'12.*
8. Karlson, A.K., Bederson, B.B. ThumbSpace: generalized one-handed input for touchscreen-based mobile devices. In *Proc. INTERACT'07.*
9. Kerr, D. R., Hotelling, S., Huppi, B. Q. 2010. U.S. Patent No. 7,800,592. Washington, DC: U.S. Patent and Trademark Office.
10. Kim, S., Yu, J., and Lee, G. Interaction techniques for unreachable objects on the touchscreen. *Proc. OzCHI'12.*
11. McCallum, D. C. and Irani, P. ARC-Pad: absolute+relative cursor positioning for large displays with a mobile touchscreen. *Proc. UIST'09.*
12. Odell, D., Chandrasekaran, V. Enabling comfortable thumb interaction in tablet computers: a Windows 8 case study. In *Proceedings of the Human Factors and Ergonomics Society Annual Meeting*, 2012.
13. Oulasvirta, A., Reichel, A., Li, W., Zhang, Y., Bachynskyi, M., Vertanen, K., Kristensson, P. O. Improving two-thumb text entry on touchscreen devices. *Proc. CHI'13.*
14. Roudaut, A., Huot, S., Lecolinet, E. TapTap and MagStick: improving one-handed target acquisition on small touch-screens. *Proc. AVI'08.*
15. Sauro, J., Dumas, J. S. Comparison of three one-question, post-task usability questionnaires. *Proc. CHI'09.*
16. Siek, K.A., Rogers, Y., Connelly, K.H. Fat finger worries: how older and younger users physically interact with PDAs. *Proc. INTERACT'05.*
17. Trudeau, M. B., Young, J. G., Jindrich, D. L., Dennerlein, J. T. Thumb motor performance varies with thumb and wrist posture during single-handed mobile phone use. *Journal of biomechanics* (2012).
18. Tukey, J. W. Exploratory data analysis. *Reading, Ma*'77.
19. Wagner, J., Huot, S., Mackay, W.E. BiTouch and BiPad: designing bimanual interaction for hand-held tablets. *Proc. CHI'12.*
20. Wigdor, D., Forlines, C., Baudisch, P., Barnwell, J., Shen, C. Lucid touch: a see-through mobile device. *Proc. UIST'07.*
21. Wolf, K., Schleicher, R., Rohs, M. Touch Accessibility on the Front and the Back of held Tablet Devices. *Proc. EuroHaptics'14.*

BoD Taps: An Improved Back-of-Device Authentication Technique on Smartphones

Luis A. Leiva*
PRHLT Research Center
Universitat Politècnica de València
luileito@prhlt.upv.es

Alejandro Catalá
ISSI-DSIC
Universitat Politècnica de València
acatala@dsic.upv.es

ABSTRACT

Previous work in the literature has shown that back-of-device (BoD) authentication is significantly more secure than standard front-facing approaches. However, the only BoD method available to date (*BoD Shapes*) is difficult to perform, especially with one hand. In this paper we propose *BoD Taps*, a novel approach that simplifies BoD authentication while improving its usage. A controlled evaluation with 12 users revealed that *BoD Taps* and *BoD Shapes* perform equally good at unlocking the device, but *BoD Taps* allows users to enter passwords about twice faster than *BoD Shapes*. Moreover, *BoD Taps* is perceived as being more usable and less frustrating than *BoD Shapes*, either using one or two hands.

Author Keywords

Back of device interaction; Unlocking; Passwords

ACM Classification Keywords

H.5.2 User Interfaces: Input devices and strategies; K.6.5 Security and Protection: Authentication

INTRODUCTION

There is an increasing need to improve protection in mobile devices due to the sensitive data that they give access to, e.g., private chats or online banking. If a smartphone is stolen or accidentally lost, it is important for its owner to gain enough time so that he can use a computer and lock the SIM, deactivate online accounts, or even wipe the device remotely. In this regard, we are particularly interested in exploring the authentication problem, or that of verifying that the user is the one trying to access his device.

A common approach to authenticating a user consists in locking the device so that a *secret* (e.g., a code or password) has to be entered to unlock it. Typical methods to this end are PINs (numerical passwords) or Gridlocks (drawing patterns that connect predefined dots). However, given the frequency of unlocking actions in public or shared spaces, shoulder surfing [12] and smudge attacks [1] could become a threat.

*Authorship determined by coin tossing.

MobileHCI 2014, September 23–26, 2014, Toronto, ON, Canada.

ACM 978-1-4503-3004-6/14/09 ...$15.00.
http://dx.doi.org/10.1145/2628363.2628372

With these two issues in mind, De Luca *et al.* [8] explored the use of Back of Device (BoD) interaction and designed *BoD Shapes*, a pattern-based BoD authentication method that uses relative movements to describe shapes consisting of combinations of horizontal and vertical strokes. It was found that such method provides better security features against shoulder surfing attacks, for which "average" curious people will have it harder to authenticate. Unfortunately, the method presents some weaknesses. For instance, having to slide the finger to describe horizontal and vertical strokes can be difficult to perform due to the anatomy of the human finger, which is especially true for describing corner strokes with the same hand that grabs the device. In fact, as stated by their authors, *BoD Shapes* seemed to be not usable with one hand.

These observations made us wonder if it would be still possible to provide an acceptable alternative to BoD authentication. We believe that a method that supports one-handed BoD authentication would be of particular importance, as the second hand is often occupied with a primary or secondary task [9]. Moreover, as authentication is occurring very often in our daily lives, it is important that the process can be executed fast and effortless.

This paper presents *BoD Taps*, a novel BoD authentication method that is highly usable and theoretically more secure than *BoD Shapes*. We found that users can successfully unlock their smartphones with *BoD Taps*, either with one hand or two hands, as indicated by usability and cognitive effort indicators. We also found that *BoD Taps* allows users to create and enter passwords about twice faster than *BoD Shapes*.

RELATED WORK

Common unlock methods shipped in current mobile devices include Slide, PIN, Password, Face or Voice Unlock, and Pattern (also known as Gridlock). These methods are simple and effective, though they are susceptible to observation attacks. In the research literature we can find a number of alternatives to make devices less susceptible to shoulder surfing. For instance, drawing geometric shapes over a dial pad [13], using tactile cues to obfuscate a PIN entry [7], multi-touch braille-like input [2], or a sequence of user-generated pictures [11]. More esoteric approaches include rotating dials [4] and virtual wheels [3], accelerometer-based gestures [10], or keystroke analysis [6].

Ultimately, preventing shoulder surfing attacks is difficult as long as authentication takes place at the front of the device [8]. A possible alternative would be using biometric-based methods, such as iPhone's Touch ID, however to date the iPhone is the only mobile device that has a fingerprint reader. Moreover, people may have privacy concerns. This is especially true when providing biometric data to service providers or employers [13]. We believe that moving authentication to the back of the device is a compromise solution worth exploring. In fact, some mobile devices already have BoD touch capabilities like the Playstation Vita or the Docomo F-04D smartphone, thus it is likely that this topic will be appealing in the near future.

METHOD DESCRIPTION

A fundamental design consideration is that of unintentional interaction at the beginning of the authentication process. Indeed, De Luca *et al.* [8] detected accidental BoD strokes before users actually meant to start entering a password. We thus considered an activation gesture (a long tap, circa 1 second) to indicate that a password will be entered. This way, spurious touches and movements while grasping the device are easily ignored. Also, an advantage of the long tap gesture is the possibility to include several fingers for activation, so that the number of fingers involved in the process matters.

With the aim of making the BoD authentication process easier to use, we considered tap contacts as main primitives for the design of *BoD Taps*. This decision should address some of the difficulties presented by *BoD Shapes*, such as the need to describe corners, allowing users to unlock their devices more comfortably; see Figure 1.

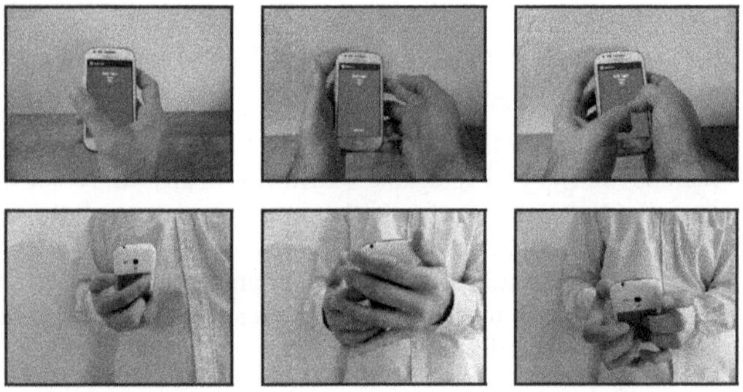

Figure 1: Different ways of interacting with *BoD Taps*, simulating a BoD-capable device. Top row: shoulder surfer view. Bottom row: front view.

The underlying password in *BoD Taps* consists of the number of activation fingers plus a sequence of tokens after activation. Each token is a tap described by relative positions of the fingers according to a 9-directional code. This code considers the typical eight directions (L=Left, U=Up, R=Right, D=Down, LU=Left-Up,...) along with a neutral position (N=Neutral) that represents the same position of the previous token in the sequence. Figure 2 illustrates the kind of codes that are defined in *BoD Taps* and *BoD Shapes*. We should remark that in *BoD Taps* several fingers can be involved in the process, both before and after activation, and so the number of touching fingers are advantageously taken into account. This should in turn help making passwords more resilient against shoulder surfer attacks.

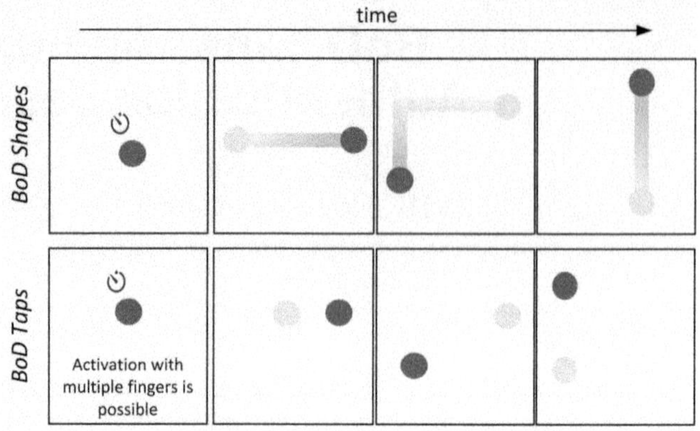

Figure 2: One-finger conceptual comparison. In *BoD Shapes* this password would be encoded as `"1.R.LD.U"` while in *BoD Taps* it would be encoded as `"1.1R.1LD.1U"`.

Theoretical Security Analysis

Information entropy is a common measure of password strength, indicating how robust a technique is to guessing or brute-force attacks [5]. In this metric, the information entropy of a password of n symbols from a symbol set of size m is $\log_2 m^n$, measured in bits. In other words, the information entropy of a password technique is the minimum number of bits needed to encode the set of all possible passwords, assuming all symbols are equally likely [2].

In one *BoD Taps* token there are $3 \times 2 \times 9$ possible combinations: one finger is always touching, but up to 3 fingers can be either touching or not and 9 relative positions are available for each finger. Therefore, a password with 3 tokens has information entropy of $\log_2(54^3) = 17.2$ bits. Moreover, if two hands are used entropy increases more than twice, given all possible combinations regarding the number of fingers involved. By contrast, one *BoD Shapes* token can have up to 3 strokes, where each stroke can be performed in 4 directions and two consecutive strokes cannot have the same direction, making a total of 36 possibilities. Therefore a *BoD Shapes* password with 3 tokens has information entropy of $\log_2(36^3) = 15.5$ bits. Now consider the information entropy of a 4-digit PIN. Each digit has 10 possible inputs, so the PIN has $\log_2(10^4) = 13.2$ bits of information entropy. In sum, the information entropy of *BoD Taps* is higher, indicating that it is theoretically stronger.

USER STUDY

We ran a controlled experiment using BoD unlock tests with both one hand and two hands. The main goal was to evaluate the feasibility of *BoD Taps* as well as comparing it against *BoD Shapes*, its closest peer. Four hypotheses were stated:

1. *BoD Taps* is less error-prone than *BoD Shapes*.
2. *BoD Taps* is faster to perform than *BoD Shapes*.
3. *BoD Taps* is more usable than *BoD Shapes*.
4. *BoD Taps* is less frustrating than *BoD Shapes*.

Apparatus

We used a Google Nexus 4 (4.7" screen, 1280x768 px at 320 ppi) running Android 4.4.2 (KitKat). Using the same smartphone for all participants eliminates the effect of device and the effect of screen size. Moreover, this is a very light device (140 g of weight) so it can simulate a BoD-capable device by placing the touchscreen face down to enable BoD interaction. We put a sticker in the rear side to simulate the front of the phone (Figure 3b). Rubber bands were attached to the edges of the screen to avoid palm interactions (Figure 3a).

(a) (b) (c)

Figure 3: Experimental BoD phone setup (3a, 3b) and screenshot of the acquisition tool (3c).

The Android app we used for gathering data (Figure 3c) featured a practice mode, so that participants could try different methods and hand poses before entering the actual record mode. Since the screen of the smartphone would not be visible to participants, we included haptic response through vibration on touch events and different audio cues—one sound for each type of "key event", e.g., system activated, password entered, successful/unsuccessful unlocks.

Participants

We recruited 12 right-handed participants (4 female) aged 21–35 (*M*=26.3, *SD*=2.1) using our University's mailing lists. Participants were either university staff or students, with no technical background in security or privacy topics. The unlock methods they use were PIN (3 participants), slide (4), grid (4), and none (1). When asked about their unlock choice, the most common agreement was *"because it is fast and easy to perform."* People stated that they use to unlock their devices about 30 times a day (*M*=29.5, *SD*=11.7), either with one hand (5 participants), two hands (3), or both (4).

Design

We considered two independent factors with 2 levels each: *Method* (shapes or taps) and *Pose* (1 or 2 hands). We measured authentication attempts and errors, speed of password creation and execution, and usability plus work load. We used a repeated measures within-subjects design, i.e., participants were assigned to all treatment levels. We used Latin squares to counterbalance the order of the conditions and reduce learning effects. For the statistical analysis, data were accumulated for each participant and were analyzed with the two-way ANOVA test (data met the required test conditions).

Procedure

To begin, we briefly described the purpose of the study. Participants signed in a consent form followed by a demographics questionnaire. Then, both authentication techniques were demoed front-of-device with one and two hands, respectively. After each demo, participants were asked to try themselves on the simulated BoD device (Figure 3). Next, the actual evaluation began. All interactions were performed at the back, as the touchscreen was facing down (Figure 3b).

Each participant was told to define up to 3 self-selected BoD passwords (*record* mode) under the 4 conditions, so that each participant would perform at least 12 BoD unlock tests overall. Once each password was defined, the following distraction task was used. The evaluator grabbed the phone and put the app in *test* mode, then the phone was given back to the participant, with the touchscreen facing down, who had to re-enter the BoD password. As in commercial smartphones or ATMs, participants could retry up to 3 times. When each condition was finished, participants were asked to answer the SUS and NASA-TLX questionnaires on a nearby laptop.

Results

Participants were mostly successful at unlocking the device (Table 1). ANOVA revealed no significant differences regarding *Method* and *Pose* ($p > .05$), and no significant *Method*Pose* interaction was found, suggesting that both authentication methods are comparable under the tested conditions. Therefore, our first hypothesis was rejected.

	1 hand		2 hands	
Method	Attempts	Successful	Attempts	Successful
BoD Shapes	2.25 (0.8)	74.9%	2.83 (0.5)	94.4%
BoD Taps	2.41 (1.0)	80.5%	2.08 (0.9)	69.4%

Table 1: Mean (and SD) number of unlock attempts and overall authentication success rate.

To fairly test our second hypothesis, i.e., password entry speed (Table 2), we considered the *effective* time, i.e., the time required to enter each password after activation. Both methods used the same long tap gesture (1 s) for activation.

Regarding password creation speed, we found that *BoD Taps* allows users to define and enter passwords nearly twice faster than *BoD Shapes*. However, no significant differences were found regarding *Method* and *Pose*, and no significant *Method*Pose* interaction was found. This reveals that participants invested a comparable amount of time defining their own passwords under the tested conditions.

Regarding authentication speed, significant differences were found between *Method* [$F_{1,44} = 10.367, p = .002, \eta_p^2 = 24.12$] but not in terms of *Pose*. No significant *Method*Pose* interaction was found. No pairwise comparisons were performed because each factor has only two levels. Therefore, our second hypothesis was thus partially verified, i.e., users entered BoD passwords with *BoD Taps* faster that *BoD Shapes* just in terms of authentication speed.

On the other hand, participants preferred *BoD Taps* over *BoD Shapes* both in terms of usability and task load (Table 3). ANOVA revealed that differences were significant regarding *Method* [SUS: $F_{1,44} = 13.062, p < .001, \eta_p^2 = 2.25$;

	Creation speed		Authentication speed	
Method	1 hand	2 hands	1 hand	2 hands
BoD Shapes	5.5 (0.5)	5.1 (0.4)	3.4 (0.2)	4.0 (0.3)
BoD Taps	4.4 (0.9)	3.7 (0.2)	2.1 (0.1)	2.6 (0.2)

Table 2: Mean (and SD) password entry speed, in seconds.

TLX: $F_{1,44} = 13.874, p < .001, \eta_p^2 = 1.61$] and *Pose* [SUS: $F_{1,44} = 5.806, p = .020, \eta_p^2 = 1$; TLX: $F_{1,44} = 8.581, p < .01, \eta_p^2 = 1$]. A significant *Method*Pose* interaction effects was found in terms of SUS [$F_{1,44} = 4.483, p = .039, \eta_p^2 = 0.77$] but not in terms of TLX. No pairwise comparisons were performed because each factor has only two levels. Therefore, our third and fourth hypotheses were both verified, i.e., *BoD Taps* was significantly perceived as being more usable and less frustrating than *BoD Shapes*.

	SUS score		TLX score	
Method	1 hand	2 hands	1 hand	2 hands
BoD Shapes	47.7 (29.2)	73.5 (18.7)	5.6 (1.3)	4.2 (1.1)
BoD Taps	80.4 (14.3)	82.1 (12.2)	3.9 (1.1)	3.4 (0.7)

Table 3: Mean (and SD) usability scores (SUS $\in [0, 100]$, higher is better) and work load scores (TLX $\in [0, 100]$, lower is better).

DISCUSSION AND CONCLUSIONS

It is worth pointing out that both BoD authentication methods were new to all participants. Still, evaluation results were quite good. Especially for one-handed authentication, the smartphone's form factor proved to be a burden for the participants using *BoD Shapes*. However, for *BoD Taps* it did not seem to be the case.

We performed an additional analysis on the effect of diagonal *BoD Taps* on authentication errors. In 51% of the one-handed trials and 58% of the two-handed trials the error was due to a difference of at least 1 token between created and entered password; c.f., `"2.1D.2R.1D"` vs. `"2.1D.2R.1DL"`. These results suggest that ignoring diagonal taps should improve accuracy and make *BoD Taps* work better in practice. Further, users commented that they took riskier decisions while defining their own passwords with *BoD Taps*, often when using both hands. This may explain the fact that users performed more successful unlocks using *BoD Taps* with one hand than with two hands.

One user commented that *"I personally was having trouble making corner-like shapes. Hence the shapes I defined were very simple, mostly straight lines."* A deeper analysis of all user-defined passwords, using the mean string distance (MSD) over all password combinations, revealed that there were consistently more variability in those created with *BoD Taps* [MSD_{1hand} = 5.85, *SD*=3.1; MSD_{2hands} = 6.62, *SD*=3.0] than in those created with *BoD Shapes* [MSD_{1hand} = 3.46, *SD*=1.9; MSD_{2hands} = 4.98, *SD*=3.2]. This suggests not only that participants were more creative using *BoD Taps*, but also that users defined simpler *BoD Shapes* passwords apparently to increase their usability and performance.

Participants also commented that unlocking the device with two hands provides more password choices, which in turn allows for defining more complex token combinations. This was mentioned for both authentication methods and is in fact corroborated by the aforementioned MSD computations. Finally, we acknowledge that further analysis should be conducted with a larger sample size, possibly in the wild, in order to draw definitive conclusions. All in all, it is our hope that this work will provide designers and researchers with a new understanding of BoD authentication methods.

ACKNOWLEDGMENTS

We thank Alexander De Luca, Alireza Sahami, Niels Henze, and Albrecht Schmidt for fruitful discussions. We also thank the anonymous MobileHCI reviewers for providing suggestions to strengthen this paper. Work supported by the EU FP7 program (grant 600707), GVA VALi+d program (grant APOSTD/2013/013), and MINECO (grant TIN2010-20488).

REFERENCES

1. Aviv, A. J., Gibson, K., Mossop, E., Blaze, M., and Smith, J. M. Smudge attacks on smartphone touch screens. In *Proc. USENIX WOOT* (2010), 1–7.
2. Azenkot, S., Rector, K., Ladner, R., and Wobbrock, J. Passchords: secure multi-touch authentication for blind people. In *Proc. ASSETS* (2012), 159–166.
3. Bianchi, A., Oakley, I., Kostakos, V., and Kwon, D. S. The phone lock: audio and haptic shoulder-surfing resistant PIN entry methods for mobile devices. In *Proc. TEI* (2011).
4. Bianchi, A., Oakley, I., and Kwon, D. Spinlock: A single-cue haptic and audio PIN input technique for authentication. In *Proc. Haptic and Audio Interaction Design* (2011), 81–90.
5. Burr, W. E., Dodson, D. F., Newton, E. M., Perlner, R. A., Polk, W. T., Gupta, S., and Nabbus, E. A. Electronic authentication guideline. NIST Special Publication 800-63-1, 2011.
6. Clarke, N., and Furnell, S. Authenticating mobile phone users using keystroke analysis. *Intl. J. of Inf. Security 6*, 1 (2007), 1–14.
7. De Luca, A., von Zezschwitz, E., and Hussmann, H. Vibrapass: secure authentication based on shared lies. In *Proc. CHI* (2009), 913–916.
8. De Luca, A., von Zezschwitz, E., Nguyen, N. D. H., Maurer, M.-E., Rubegni, E., Scipioni, M. P., and Langheinrich, M. Back-of-device authentication on smartphones. In *Proc. CHI* (2013), 2389–2398.
9. Hirotaka, N. Reassessing current cell phone designs: using thumb input effectively. In *Proc. CHI EA* (2003), 938–939.
10. Patel, S. N., Pierce, J. S., and Abowd, G. D. A gesture-based authentication scheme for untrusted public terminals. In *Proc. UIST* (2004), 157–160.
11. Takada, T., and Koike, H. Awase-e: Image-based authentication for mobile phones using user's favorite images. In *Proc. MHCI* (2003), 347–351.
12. Tari, F., Ozok, A. A., and Holden, S. H. A comparison of perceived and real shoulder-surfing risks between alphanumeric and graphical passwords. In *Proc. SOUPS* (2006), 56–66.
13. Weiss, R., and De Luca, A. Passshapes - utilizing stroke based authentication to increase password memorability. In *Proc. NordiCHI* (2008), 383–392.

Toffee: Enabling Ad Hoc, Around-Device Interaction with Acoustic Time-of-Arrival Correlation

Robert Xiao[1] Greg Lew[2] James Marsanico[2] Divya Hariharan[2] Scott E. Hudson[1] Chris Harrison[1]
[1]Human-Computer Interaction Institute [2]Electrical and Computer Engineering
Carnegie Mellon University, 5000 Forbes Avenue, Pittsburgh PA 15213
[1]{brx, scott.hudson, chris.harrison}@cs.cmu.edu [2]{glew, jmarsani, dharihar}@andrew.cmu.edu

ABSTRACT
The simple fact that human fingers are large and mobile devices are small has led to the perennial issue of limited surface area for touch-based interactive tasks. In response, we have developed *Toffee*, a sensing approach that extends touch interaction beyond the small confines of a mobile device and onto ad hoc adjacent surfaces, most notably tabletops. This is achieved using a novel application of acoustic time differences of arrival (TDOA) correlation. Previous time-of-arrival based systems have required semi-permanent instrumentation of the surface and were too large for use in mobile devices. Our approach requires only a hard tabletop and gravity – the latter acoustically couples mobile devices to surfaces. We conducted an evaluation, which shows that *Toffee* can accurately resolve the bearings of touch events (mean error of 4.3° with a laptop prototype). This enables radial interactions in an area many times larger than a mobile device; for example, virtual buttons that lie above, below and to the left and right.

ACM Classification: H.5.2 [Information interfaces and presentation]: User Interfaces - Input devices and strategies, Graphical user interfaces.

Keywords: Time of flight correlation; time difference of arrival; TDOA; TOA; TOF; ADI; everyday surfaces; touch interaction; interfaces everywhere; vibro-acoustic sensors; around device interaction.

INTRODUCTION
In order for mobile devices to fit into our pockets and bags, they are generally designed with small screens and physical controls. Simultaneously, human fingers are relatively large (and are unlikely to shrink anytime soon). This has led to the recurring problem of limited surface area for touch-based interactive tasks. Thus, there is a pressing need to develop novel sensing approaches and interaction techniques that aim to mitigate this fundamental constraint.

One option is to transiently appropriate surface area from the environment around us [14]. This allows devices to remain small, but opportunistically provide large areas for accurate and comfortable input (and potentially graphical output if e.g., projectors are used). Tables, in particular, have presented an attractive target for researchers. Foremost, mobile devices often reside on tables, enabling several ad hoc sensing approaches (e.g., vibro-acoustic [13,18] and optical [7,20]). Moreover, unlike e.g., painted walls, tables are accepted areas for work, have durable surfaces, and typically have surface area available for interactive use.

We present *Toffee*, a system that allows devices to appropriate tables and other hard, flat surfaces they are placed on for ad hoc radial tap input. This is achieved using a novel application of acoustic time differences of arrival (TDOA) analysis [4,8,9,16,23,24,25] – bringing the technique, for the first time, to small devices in a way that is compatible with their inherent mobility. At a high level, *Toffee* allows users to define virtual, ad hoc buttons on a table's surface, which can then be used to trigger a variety of interactive functions, including application launching, desktop switching, music player control, and gaming. Leveraging the large surface area of the table, users can potentially trigger simple functionality eyes free.

OPERATION
Our *Toffee*-augmented devices have four vibro-acoustic piezo sensors, located on the underside of each corner (Figure 1). Their exact configuration is discussed in depth in the next section. When a finger or object taps a table, mechanical vibrations (i.e. structural acoustics) propagate outward from the point of contact [11,23]. The speed of propagation depends on the host medium and the frequency

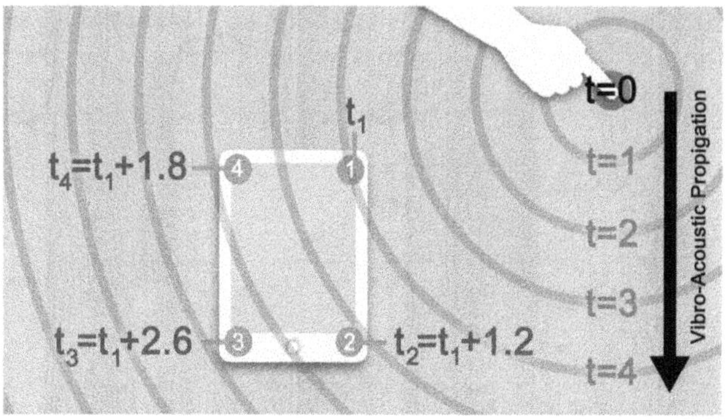

Figure 1. When a finger taps a table, mechanical vibration propagates outward from the point of contact (red concentric circles). Vibro-acoustic sensors (green) can detect when the leading edge of the wave reaches them. From these timing offsets (blue), it is possible to estimate the originating position of the finger tap.

ACM 978-1-4503-3004-6/14/09 $15.00. http://dx.doi.org/10.1145/2628363.2628383

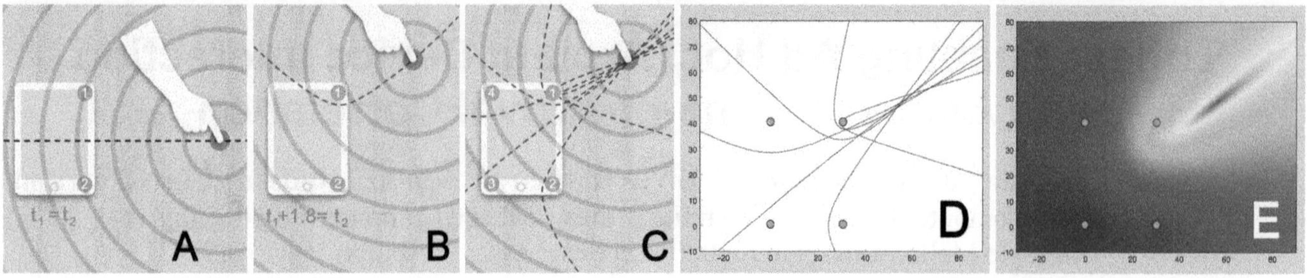

Figure 2. A: When a finger taps equidistant to two sensors, such that arrival time $t_1=t_2$, it is only possible to infer that the finger tapped somewhere along a line (dashed). B: If the finger lies closer to one sensor, this function becomes hyperbolic. C: In a four-sensor setup, six hyperbolas can be computed; intersections are solutions for the originating touch location. D: Real world data of the scenario in C plotted in matplotlib. E: A visualization of total squared error.

of the vibration. In solid materials, such as wood, waves typically propagate at around 600 meters per second [16]. Impulses will tend to disperse into their individual frequency components as they travel through the medium due to differences in propagation velocity between different frequencies. Importantly, because the propagation is not instantaneous, the leading edge of the fastest frequency component in the vibro-acoustic impulse reaches each of the four sensors at different times (Figure 1). Furthermore, this leading edge arrives at each sensor before any reflected wave, so that measurement of the leading edge is expected to be relatively robust to multipath propagation effects. Please see [23,24] for an extended discussion of the related physics.

From the timing data, we can estimate the originating point of contact. First, let us consider an example setup with only a pair of sensors (Figure 2A). If a touch occurs equidistant to the two sensors, the time difference of arrival will be the same. From this, the system can infer that the touch must have occurred somewhere along a straight line equidistant from the two sensors (Figure 2A, dashed line). However, if the touch is closer to one sensor than the other, the touch can be inferred to lie somewhere along a hyperbolic curve – the locus of points having a constant difference between distances to two fixed points (Figure 2B, dashed line).

With three sensors, there are two non-redundant pairings and thus the touch can be inferred to lie at one of the two intersections of two hyperbolic curves. To disambiguate between these two possibilities, we need one more sensor.

With four sensors there are six combinations of sensor pairs, which allow us to compute six hyperbolic functions (Figure 2C). In a perfect system with absolute accuracy, three of these pairings would be redundant, as the curves would all intersect at the location of the touch. In a system with some error (i.e., the real world), these loosely intersect at the probable location of the touch, and the additional "redundant" functions are used to reduce the error. Figures 2D and 2E show real world data for the scenario illustrated in Figure 2C.

HARDWARE IMPLEMENTATION

We constructed three prototype platforms to demonstrate the feasibility of our approach with devices of different size. Specifically, we augmented a Samsung Galaxy S3 smartphone, an Apple iPad 2 tablet, and a 15" Apple Macbook Pro (see Figures 3, 4 and 8). An acrylic frame was attached to the bottom of each device. This provided a flat surface, to which we affixed 20mm piezo discs at each corner. These piezo discs sense acoustic vibrations by bending slightly and compressing the piezoelectric material, generating a voltage differential. For our laptop and tablet prototypes, the acrylic frame is separated into four pieces connected by soft foam tape. This dampens the transmission of mechanical vibrations through the frame (Figure 4, center).

Each piezo disc is connected to a simple analog circuit. This is configured as an operational amplifier with unity gain (i.e., no amplification). Amplification is not necessary because the piezo sensors easily produce voltages in the

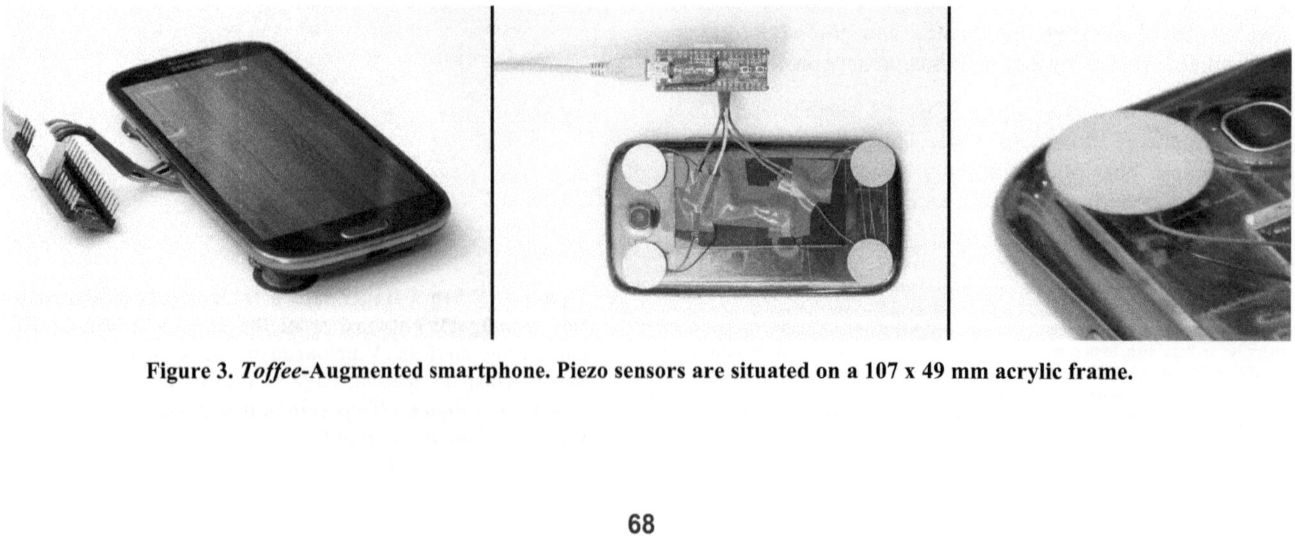

Figure 3. *Toffee*-Augmented smartphone. Piezo sensors are situated on a 107 x 49 mm acrylic frame.

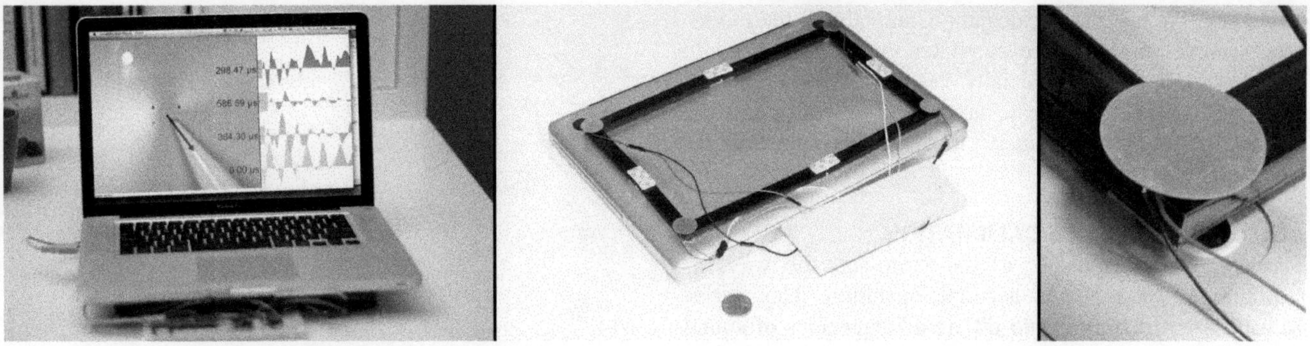

Figure 4. *Toffee*-Augmented laptop. Piezo sensors are situated on a 280 x 167 mm acrylic frame.

range of -10V to +10V. The circuit is used to provide the high input impedance (approximately 1MΩ) required by the piezo sensor, and to add a DC bias to enable our ADC to sample the full range of the signal. Due to limited space, this circuit was omitted for our smartphone prototype and the piezos were directly connected to the microcontroller.

The signal is sampled by the analog-to-digital converter (ADC) of an ARM Cortex M3-based Maple Mini micro-controller running at 72MHz [22]. Our embedded software samples the four piezo sensors at 85kHz (roughly 344,000 data points per second, the fastest possible rate on this hardware). This high sampling rate is required for capturing the tiny differences in the arrival time of the rapidly-propagating vibro-acoustic wave. However, due to the low frequency of the vibro-acoustic waveforms (Figure 5), using even higher sampling speeds will only marginally improve accuracy. When the magnitude of a converted analog value exceeds a predefined threshold, the Maple board delays for a short period to buffer the waveforms. Finally, four waveforms representing 18ms of data (one for each piezo sensor) are sent over USB to a computer for analysis, described in the next section.

SOFTWARE IMPLEMENTATION

Our *Toffee* engine (Figure 5) was developed in Java and performs the calculations necessary to localize a touch. As described above, when a touch occurs, the Maple board sends four waveforms captured by the four piezo sensors (Figure 5D). First, to reduce noise, the signal is smoothed using an exponentially-weighted moving average. The system then computes the discrete derivative of the smoothed signal. The first point (across all four waveforms) at which the derivative exceeds a predefined threshold is assumed to be the impulse resulting from the fastest frequency component of the vibro-acoustic wave. This time index anchors all further calculations (Figure 5D, top waveform).

We initially experimented with using cross-correlation to determine the propagation delay for the other three sensors. However, we discovered that the waveforms from the other sensors were often very different due to attenuation, multi-path interference, acoustic dispersion, and other effects (see e.g., [11,31] for an extended discussion of the relevant structural acoustics). This made cross-correlation a poor estimator of propagation delay – a result also found in [28]. Instead, we use the first impulse in the other waveforms as the time delta, measured in microseconds. We record the relative delay between each pair of sensors and use this information to estimate the position of the tap.

As noted previously, the time difference in the signal's arrival between a pair of sensors defines a hyperbola of possible origination points (Figure 2). Mathematically, if p is the position of the tap, s_i and s_j are the positions of the sensors, Δt_{ij} is the difference in the arrival times of the two sensors, and c is the speed of sound in the surface, then

$$\|p - s_i\| - \|p - s_j\| = c\Delta t_{ij}$$

Figure 2 illustrates an example scenario. In the ideal case (Figure 2C), there would be no error and we would simply solve the set of six equations for each pair *(i,j)* and derive the position of the tap. In the presence of measurement error, we instead aim to minimize the *squared error*

$$\sum_{i \neq j} (\|p - s_i\| - \|p - s_j\| - c\Delta t_{ij})^2$$

over all possible points p. Figures 2E and 5A show this total squared error plotted over all points near the sensors. Note that this equation depends on knowing the speed of sound in the surface, which is obtained through a calibration process described later.

The next step is to solve this optimization problem (see e.g., [10] for additional background). We employ a gradient descent approach with a small step size to avoid ill-conditioned behavior. This gradient descent takes on average about 100 iterations to converge. On our 2011 MacBook Pro (2GHz Intel Core i7), this calculation takes ~700 microseconds. The output of this optimization process is the point that minimizes the total squared error, i.e. that point which best fits the available data (Figures 2E and 5C)

Overall, the processing performed on the laptop is computationally inexpensive, and thus it would be feasible to implement the necessary calculations directly on the microprocessor (eliminating the computer entirely). We could even imagine using a specially designed ASIC that performs both sampling and calculation, and simply returns the x/y position of the touch, much like contemporary touchscreen controllers.

AUTOMATIC SURFACE CALIBRATION

The propagation speed *c* of the vibro-acoustic wave is required for reliable and accurate operation. This varies with different materials and different frequencies of sound [11,31]. Thus, before operating on a surface, it is necessary to perform a quick calibration. A manual calibration is achieved by tapping next to one of the corners of the device, and recording the time offsets to the other sensors. Because the size of the frame is known (Figures 3 and 4), the propagation speed is trivially calculated. Note that this method only examines the leading edge of the impulse, and thus we obtain only the propagation speed of the fastest frequency component in the medium.

However, relying on users for calibration is not ideal. In response, we briefly experimented with two auto-calibration approaches, which we implemented on our laptop prototype (Figure 4). One approach used a solenoid, which programmatically struck the table (much like a finger would) and allowed for the propagation speed calculation. However, this setup was bulky, required extra components, and had a power draw incompatible with mobile devices.

Our second and superior approach repurposed the piezo sensors as piezo actuators. When applying a high voltage with a transformer-based piezo driver circuit (~90V, but very low current and thus low power), the piezo discs flex, imparting a mechanical impulse to the table's surface. As a proof of concept, we modified our laptop prototype, pulsing one piezo and using the other three sensors for timing information (sensing the leading edge of the impulse using the same implementation as *Toffee)*. This approach could be further extended by pulsing all four piezo elements in sequence and averaging the results.

RELATED WORK

There are two significant bodies of work relating to our approach. Conceptually, our approach aligns with other efforts to enable around-device interaction. From a technical standpoint, *Toffee* is a novel application and extension of acoustic TDOA methods, which date back to the 1930's for use in aircraft navigation (see e.g., [5] for a comprehensive history of such systems).

Around Device Interaction

The problem of fat fingers and small devices has long been recognized, and the literature on around-device interaction as a strategy to overcome this has become significant (see [17] for an excellent overview).

Magnetic sensing has been particularly popular, as magnets are unpowered, can be small, and generally avoid issues relating to occlusion and line of sight. Abracadabra [12], MagiTact [19] and similar systems have put forward a range of free-space interactive uses, including radial buttons, in-pocket gestures, and behind device interaction. Electric field [36] and capacitive sensing [32] have similar benefits without the need to wear a magnet, though typically at the cost of reduced spatial resolution.

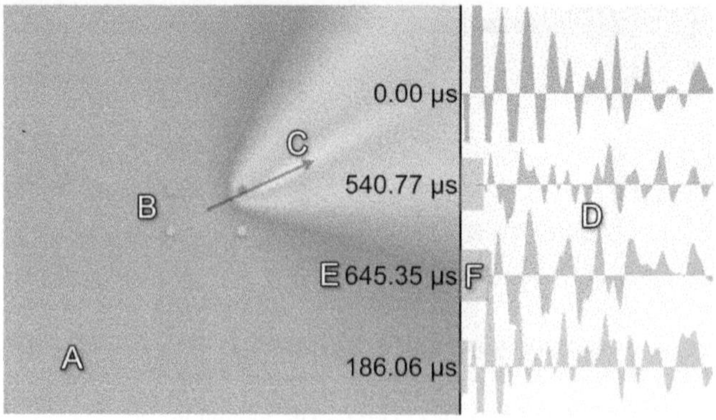

Figure 5. A screenshot of the *Toffee* engine. The multicolored area on the left is a visualization of the total squared error (A). The device with its four sensors (B) is located in the center. Note the error minima visualized as a yellow depression (C) - this is the estimated location of the touch. The waveforms captured by the four sensors are shown on the right (D). In this example, sensor 1 (top most) was triggered first. Note the computed time deltas for the other three sensors (E), also seen as grey periods prefixing the waveforms (F).

There are several optical methods that have proven successful. SideSight [7] and HoverFlow [20] use infrared emitter/receive pairs to sense proximate hands and fingers (which are reflective to infrared light). SideSight in particular is like Toffee in that it utilizes the table as an ad hoc surface for touch input. Cameras can also be used: the Portico system [2] used a pair of stilted cameras that look downward onto an interactive play space. The advent of compact, low-cost depth cameras has recently enabled researchers to consider how they might be used to support around-device interaction in mobile contexts, for example, the PalmSpace system [21].

More similar to *Toffee* are systems relying on passive acoustics. For example, Bonfire [18] used a laptop's accelerometer to detect the vibro-acoustic signal of a touch on a table surface; a separate camera-based system was used to track finger positions. BLUI [26] allows users to blow air at different areas of a laptop screen for interaction, using the built-in microphone to capture the sound of the airflow.

Finally, most similar to our ad hoc approach is Scratch Input [13]. Both systems take advantage of gravity acoustically coupling mobile devices to tables and vibro-acoustics being faithfully preserved inside of solid materials. However, instead of performing multi-sensor TDOA correlation, Scratch Input uses a single microphone and tracks gross variations in amplitude over time to infer a set of basic gestures ([33] uses a similar approach for pen-on-surface classification). Although finger taps were part of Scratch Input's gesture vocabulary, they were not localized, only recognized, offering different interactive capabilities.

Active Acoustic Localization

There are several approaches for localizing interactive events with *active* acoustics. For example, active sonar emits pulses of sound and waits for reflected signals [9]. The Cricket system [30] used a series of ultrasonic beacons fixed in the environment, from which devices could triangulate their location based on relative timing differences. Another example is surface acoustic wave (SAW) touchscreens, which emit pulses of ultrasonic sound. A finger or other object touching the screen dampens the wave locally, which appears as a gap in the signal received by separate acoustic sensors. Using this data, continuous touch tracking is possible.

Passive Acoustic Localization

In addition to the *active* approaches discussed above, there are also several *passive* approaches for localizing signals. The most popular approach, which we utilize, is *time distance of arrival* (TDOA) correlation. This is a well-known technique used in a variety of applications, including the Global Positioning System (GPS) [4] and cell phone tower triangulation [8]. Both of these examples use TDOA analysis on signals in the electromagnetic domain.

More directly related to our approach are systems that employ *acoustic* TDOA analysis [16,23,24,25,34,35]. Most notable among these are the PingPongPlus [16] and Interactive Window [23,24,25] projects. The latter two systems have similar hardware configurations: four contact microphones located at the outermost corners of the desired interactive region. When a Ping-Pong ball or finger touches inside of this region, the signal arrives to the four sensors at different times, enabling a similar all-pairs hyperbolic intersection optimization approach. PingPongPlus uses a linear approximation to the hyperbolic intersection problem to produce an approximated position within the bounds of the microphones. Interactive Window uses a binary search approach to locate the point of minimum error within a predefined range.

Another acoustic approach is time reversal (TR) analysis. When a touch occurs, TR simulates the reverse propagation of the waves received at each sensor. The simulated waves are reflected off the surface boundaries and eventually result in a peak at the original touch point. See [3] for an example system and more in-depth discussion of related work and operational principles. A downside to this approach is that a precise physical model of the surface, including surface boundaries, is required. Due to this significant setup and calibration, ad hoc uses are precluded.

Pham et al. have put forward a series of approaches for performing tap localization on instrumented surfaces. A location template matching approach is employed in [27], which uses a calibrated database of acoustic signatures to identify tap points using a single sensor (see also [6]). Later work by Pham et al. [28] demonstrated a method of decomposing and analyzing TDOA signals using a continuous wavelet transform. In [29], a Kalman filter approach is described that enables continuous tracking of touch inputs when combined with the continuous wavelet transform.

The aforementioned passive acoustic systems differ from *Toffee* in three important respects:

Foremost, the above systems required touch inputs to land *within* the perimeter of the sensors, whereas *Toffee* operates exclusively *outside* of this area (a partial exception to this is the Interactive Window, which offered degraded position sensing when taps occurred just outside the perimeter [23]).

Secondly, the above systems had sensors separated by no less than 20cm, and often on the order of meters. Importantly, the further the sensors are apart, the larger the potential difference in the arrival times, enabling considerably more accurate position sensing. *Toffee* is the first system to demonstrate the ability to scale down to mobile devices, where the technique is potentially most useful.

Third, the above systems permanently instrumented a highly controlled surface (e.g., a glass window, Ping-Pong table). This allowed for tight calibration and excellent (rigid) acoustic coupling of the sensing elements. However, this type of instrumentation and calibration is antithetical to the ad hoc settings we believe makes *Toffee* valuable (e.g., kitchen counter, desk at work, airplane tray table, and café table). *Toffee* is the first system to apply TDOA principles to surfaces in an ad hoc, non-permanent manner for interactive purposes. This means our approach is mobile, whereas previous systems were static. This is made possible in large part due to *Toffee*'s novel, surface auto-calibration method.

Passive Sonar

Functionally, our system most closely resembles passive range-finding sonar systems used in maritime applications [9], though obviously the context, scale and use are significantly different. Passive sonar systems are most frequently employed in military applications, as active sonar is subject to enemy detection. A typical system uses multiple microphones mounted to the vessel exterior in a known configuration (e.g., in a line along the hull – much like the piezos mounted to the underside of our devices). The system calculates time differences by correlating signals (transmitted through an uncontrolled water medium) from each sensor. Using TDOA hyperbolic estimation techniques, sound sources *external* to the submarine can be localized [9,10]. As far as we are aware, *Toffee* is the first system to use these underlying principles for interactive purposes.

Figure 6. Users can navigate between active desktops by tapping to the left and right of the laptop.

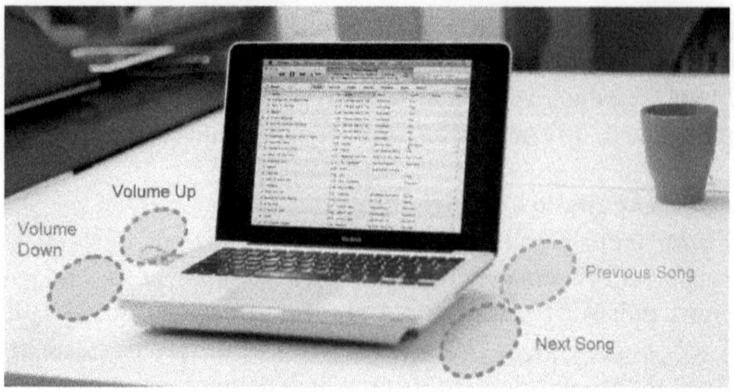

Figure 7. Music player controls can be bound to regions around the laptop, e.g., volume up and down.

EXAMPLE APPLICATIONS

To illustrate some potential uses of *Toffee* – and the surround device interactions it enables – we created proof of concept applications for our three prototype platforms. Please also see the Video Figure.

For our laptop, we created a desktop switching application. Using *Toffee*, areas to the left and right of the keyboard can be tapped to slide left and right, respectively, between active desktops (Figure 6).For a second application, we connected virtual tabletop buttons to the previous/next song and volume up/down controls in iTunes (Figure 7). Users can use these large radial buttons without needing to look at or interact with the screen, enabling inattentive or peripheral use of the interface.

For our tablet prototype, we created a game that spills interaction out onto the surrounding table. At the center of the screen is the player's tank; from all sides, enemies advance towards the player (Figure 8). Tapping on the table orients the tank's turret to the corresponding angle, and fires one projectile. This not only embeds interaction more deeply into the environment, but also opens opportunities for multiplayer experiences.

Finally, on our smartphone, we created an app launcher, where taps above, below, left and right launch the address book, map, calendar and browser respectively (Figure 9).

EVALUATION

We conducted an experimental evaluation to assess the feasibility, accuracy, and ultimately the utility of our approach. We varied a number of experimental parameters to isolate different performance characteristics of our system. In particular, we tested 1) tap angular position, 2) tap distance, 3) tap implement (finger/stylus), and 4) sensor distance (smartphone/laptop).

As an experimental compromise to mitigate a combinatorial explosion of conditions, we selected a single surface for all tests: an unmodified Ikea Galant table (particleboard with wood veneer). This decision was made in part because TDOA has already been shown to work on many surfaces, including glass [23,24,25] and whiteboard [29].

In our first experiment, we sought to understand the angular accuracy of *Toffee*. To do this, we used an overhead digital projector to render a ring around our test device, with rays at 5° intervals (72 angles). A simple interface running on a standalone laptop requested an angle (e.g., 155°), at which time the experimenter tapped the table at the requested angle. The live angular result (e.g., 158°) from *Toffee* was then saved for later analysis. Each angle was requested three times, in randomly interleaved order.

We repeated the above procedure at two different distances (45cm and 65cm), with two different tap types (finger and

Figure 8. The Tank vs. Aliens game we created for our *Toffee*-augmented tablet. When the player taps the table, the tank fires a shell outwards in the direction of the tap.

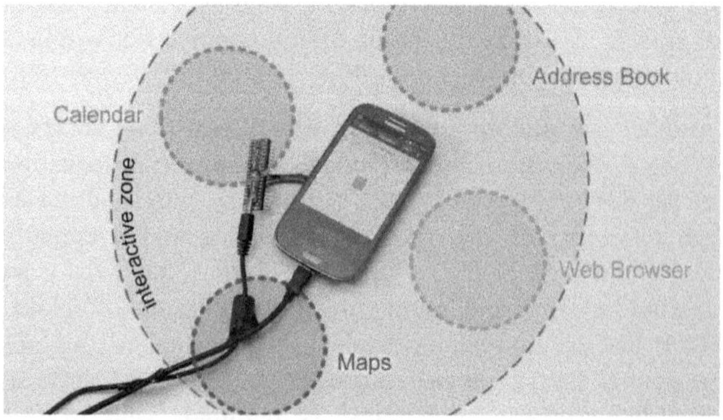

Figure 9. Common applications could be bound to regions immediately surrounding a smartphone (i.e., areas lying within a proximate interactive zone; taps outside this area are attenuated).

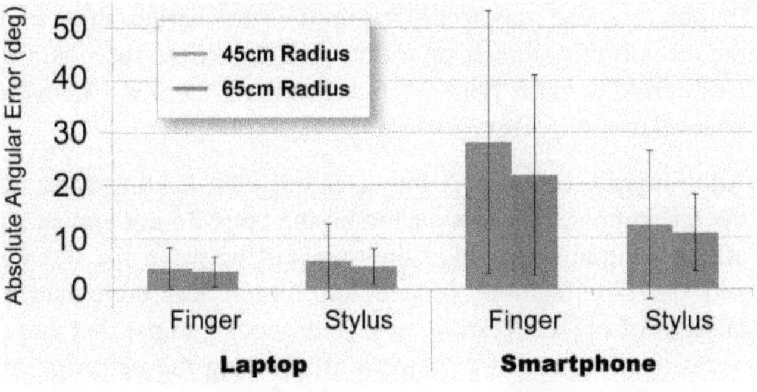

Figure 10. A summary of results in Figure 12. Mean absolute error of estimated angle across eight conditions. Error bars are standard deviation.

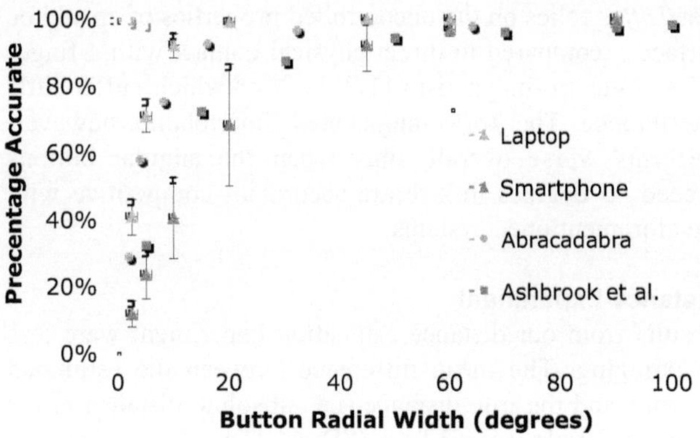

Figure 11. Post hoc simulation of mean input accuracy for different sized angular buttons with our *Toffee*-augmented laptop and smartphone. For comparison, results from two other radial input systems [1,12] are plotted. Error bars illustrate the standard deviation of accuracy across the four sub-conditions for laptop and smartphone trials.

stylus), and with two different device sizes (laptop and smartphone), for a total of eight conditions. This yielded 1728 tap trials (eight conditions x 72 unique angles x repeated three times).

The inclusion of two devices of radically different sizes was purposeful. As the distances between the sensors shrink, the timing deltas also shrink. Because our sampling rate is constant, this means our precision decreases as devices get smaller. We also decided to include both finger and stylus taps. These produce significantly different waveforms (fundamental frequencies of around 380Hz and 1400Hz respectively). As described previously, our sensors trigger in response to an exponentially-averaged derivative exceeding a threshold. A higher frequency signal (larger derivative) is more likely to trigger the system accurately.

Our second experiment was designed to understand *Toffee*'s ability to estimate distance. Seven concentric rings were projected around our laptop prototype, starting with a diameter of 36cm, and increasing in 6cm intervals, up to 72cm. To avoid combinatorial explosion, we tested eight angles (0°, 45°, 90°, ... 315°). As before, each trial (e.g., 155° @ 42cm) was requested three times to reduce noise in the data, yielding 168 data points. This experiment was run twice, once with finger taps and once with stylus taps, for a total of 336 trials.

RESULTS AND DISCUSSION

Overall, *Toffee* performs well at estimating the angle of touch events. However, distance estimation is too poor for practical use at this time. When compared against existing systems, *Toffee* offers competitive performance, despite using an ad hoc surface.

Angular Accuracy

Combining near and far distances, and finger and stylus conditions, the mean angular error (Figures 10 and 12) for our laptop prototype was 4.3° (mean SD = 4.4°). To put this in context, if we were to build a system with eighteen 20° radial buttons (which allows for a ±10° tolerance in the angle estimation) the system would trigger the correct button 91.8% of the time. If we provided eight 45° buttons (e.g., above / below / left / right and the four diagonals), the system would be 99.1% accurate; four 90° buttons would be 99.9% accurate. Figure 11 illustrates this this accuracy curve based on post hoc analysis of the collected data.

The smartphone performed worse, primarily due to loss of precision resulting from its tightly packed sensors. Combining near/far and finger/stylus conditions, the mean angular error for our smartphone prototype was 18.3° (mean SD = 16.5°; see Figures 10 and 12). Stylus taps performed better than finger taps (mean of 11.6° vs. 25.0° respectively), though not significantly so, primarily due to high variance (SDs of 10.9° and 22.1° respectively).

Framing this again in terms of radial interactors: Eight 45° radial buttons would perform at 72.7% accuracy on the smartphone (Figure 11); four 90° buttons would be 91.9% accurate. To approach 100% accuracy, it would be necessary to use just two buttons, perhaps the areas to the left and right of the device. Although this provides less input bandwidth and interactive options than the laptop, this still opens several interesting opportunities.

The results indicate that *Toffee* is viable out to at least 65cm from the device, which enables an interaction area 1m^2 in size centered over the device. This allows for operation across a substantial portion of a typical desk surface, an area most users would consider "near" the device.

Comparison to Prior Work

We designed our radial input experiment so that our results could be plotted against two notable pieces of prior work, which offer a benchmark (Figure 11). The first system is a capacitive-sensing, direct-touch watch bezel developed by Ashbrook et al. [1]. The second system, Abracadabra [12], is a magnetically driven free-space finger-tracking watch.

The laptop condition of *Toffee* exceeds the radial accuracy of both of these systems. This is particularly notable given that *Toffee* relies on the uncontrolled properties of an ad hoc surface – compared to direct physical contact with a finger [1] and electro-magnetism [12], both of which suffer little interference. The *Toffee*-augmented Smartphone, however, performs worse overall; only when the angular buttons exceed 45 degrees in size are accuracies competitive with the aforementioned systems.

Distance Experiment

Results from our distance estimation experiment were less encouraging. The mean difference between the estimated distance and the true distance (i.e., absolute distance error) for finger trials was 51.9cm (SD=44.1cm). Given that our distances ranged from 36cm to 72cm, this should be considered a failure. Stylus taps are more promising: the mean absolute distance error was 10.2cm (SD=8.6cm). From post hoc analysis, it is clear that the higher frequency waveforms generated by the hard tip of the stylus more reliably trigger the sensors. This leads to tighter time delta estimates, which produces a tighter intersection of the hyperbolas, and ultimately yields a superior estimate of location.

Importantly, moving outward along a ray results in very small changes to the arrival time differences, which is inherently less accurate. This stands in contrast to changing the touch angle, which dramatically alters the relative timing differences among the sensors. Further, this problem is exacerbated at larger distances. The only way to overcome this issue is faster and more precise sensing to obtain more accurate timing estimates.

Robustness

Although we tested accuracy, we did not specifically test robustness outside the lab. However, we did note a few properties of the system during piloting, the study, and application development.

Foremost, the system requires a fairly "sharp" finger or knuckle tap in order to work reliably. Soft taps will fail to trigger the system, particularly as our ADC precision was reduced (to 8 bits) to allow for the faster read rate. In practice, the tap force required is no harder than one would normally knock on a door, i.e. excessive force is not required to operate *Toffee*. However, the system works even with relatively soft stylus taps.

Additionally, because *Toffee* uses only the leading edge of the tap impulse, objects placed on the table do not appear to affect accuracy, provided they are not between the device and the tap location. Indeed, our initial test table had a number of objects resting on it (e.g., books, cups) that were occasionally repositioned without affecting the behavior of *Toffee*. Also, as the leading edge of the acoustic impulse arrives before any reflections, *Toffee* appears fairly robust to multipath acoustic interference.

However, we do note that *Toffee* is subject to false positive input, as with any touch interface. Dropping objects on the table near the device, moving the device or table, or striking the device itself can potentially all produce false positives. In the latter two cases, the effect can be mitigated by rejecting input taps that appear to emanate from within the boundaries of the device. In the former case, the device can be equipped with a lock or sleep feature to ignore inputs when not in use (much like a smartphone is usually locked when in a pocket to avoid accidental input). A classification approach may also be used to distinguish the acoustic signature of a knuckle or finger tap from the sound of a larger object being dropped or placed on the surface [15]. Presently, our only implemented approach is to reject acoustic events that result in excessive total squared error (i.e., a preset threshold).

CONCLUSION

We have presented our work on *Toffee*, a system that allows (small) mobile devices to appropriate (large) tabletops for interaction. This was achieved through time-difference-of-arrival correlation of structural vibro-acoustic signals captured by sensors located at the four corners of a device. Our study results suggest that resolving a true, 2D position (angle and distance) is not sufficiently robust to enable accurate interactive use. However, angle estimation is

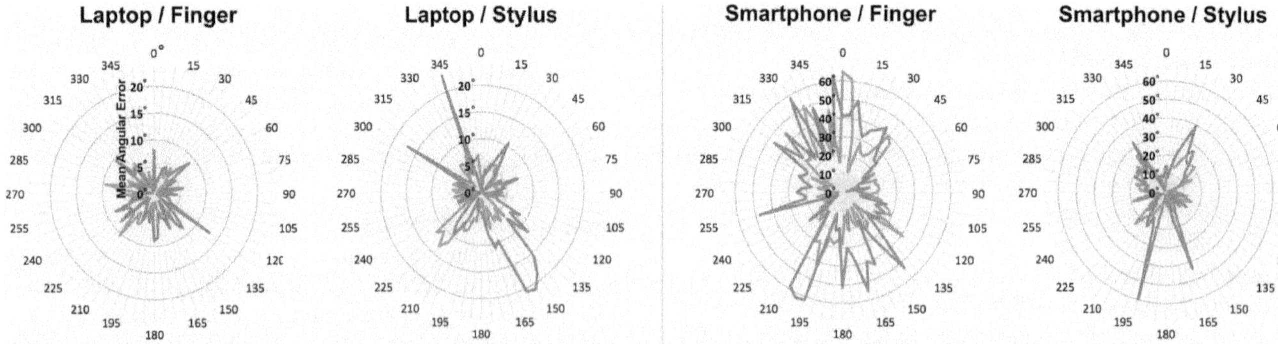

Figure 12. The mean angular error (radial axis) for taps performed in a 360° circumference at two different distances (45 and 65cm). Note the radial axis scale is different for the laptop (20°) and smartphone (60°).

robust, with an average error of 4.3° on a laptop sized setup. Thus, we suggest that interactions should be built around radial interaction, similar to bezel interactions [1] and peripheral free-space gesturing [12]. Our example applications are built using this interaction paradigm, and allow users to make use of the expanded envelope of interactive space surrounding laptops, tablets, and smartphones.

ACKNOWLEDGEMENTS

We would like to thank Bhiksha Raj for encouraging this research as a class project for his Machine Learning for Signal Processing class at Carnegie Mellon University. This work was also supported in part by a Qualcomm Innovation Fellowship, Google Ph.D. Fellowship, Natural Sciences and Engineering Research Council of Canada (NSERC) and NSF grant IIS-1217929.

REFERENCES

1. Ashbrook, D., Lyons, K., and Starner, T. An investigation into round touchscreen wristwatch interaction. In Proc. MobileHCI '08. 311-314.
2. Avrahami, D., Wobbrock, J., and Izadi, S. Portico: tangible interaction on and around a tablet. In *Proc. UIST '11*. 347-356.
3. Bai, M. R. and Tsai Y. K. Impact localization combined with haptic feedback for touch panel applications based on the time-reversal approach. *Journal of the Acoustical Society of America,* vol. 129, no. 3, pp. 1297-1305, March 2011.
4. Bancroft, S. An algebraic solution of the GPS equations. *IEEE Trans. Aerospace and Electronic Systems*, vol. AES-21, pp. 56-59, Jan. 1985.
5. Blanchard, W. F. Hyperbolic Airborne Radio Navigation Aids – A Navigator's View of their History and Development. *The Journal Of Navigation*, vol. 44, no. 3, pp. 285-315, Sept 1991.
6. Bornand, C., Camurri, A., Castellano, G., Catheline, S., Crevoisier, A., Roesch, E. B., Scherer, K. R., and Volpe, G. Usability evaluation and comparison of prototypes of tangible acoustic interfaces. In P*roc. ENACTIVE '05*.
7. Butler, A., Izadi, S., and Hodges, S. SideSight: multi-"touch" interaction around small devices. In *Proc. UIST '08*. 201-204.
8. Caffery, J. and Stuber, G. L. Overview of radiolocation in CDMA cellular systems. *IEEE Commun. Mag.*, 36(4), pp. 38-45, Apr. 1998.
9. Carter, G. C. Time delay estimation for passive sonar signal processing. *IEEE Trans. on Acoustics, Speech and Signal Processing*, vol. ASSP-29, pp. 463-470, June 1981.
10. Chan, Y. T. A Simple and Efficient Estimator for Hyperbolic Location. *IEEE Trans. on Signal Processing*, vol. 42, no. 8, pp. 1905-1915, August 1994.
11. Fahy, F. and Gardonio, P. (2007). Sound and Structural Vibration, 2nd Ed. Academic Press. Oxford, UK.
12. Harrison, C. and Hudson, S. Abracadabra: wireless, high-precision, and unpowered finger input for very small mobile devices. In *Proc. UIST '09*. 121-124.
13. Harrison, C. and Hudson, S. Scratch input: creating large, inexpensive, unpowered and mobile finger input surfaces. In *Proc. UIST '08*. 205-208.
14. Harrison, C. Appropriated Interaction Surfaces. *IEEE Computer Magazine*, June 2010, 43(6). 86-89
15. Harrison, C., Schwarz, J., and Hudson, S.E. TapSense: enhancing finger interaction on touch surfaces. In Proc. UIST '11, 627-636.
16. Ishii, H., Wisneski, C., Orbanes, J., Chun, C., and Paradiso, J. PingPongPlus: design of an athletic-tangible interface for computer-supported cooperative play. In *Proc. CHI '99*. 394-401.
17. Jones, B., Sodhi, R., Forsyth, D., Bailey, B. and Maciocci, G. Around device interaction for multiscale navigation. In *Proc. MobileHCI '12*. 83-92.
18. Kane, S., Avrahami, D., Wobbrock, J., Harrison, B., Rea, A., Philipose, M., and LaMarca, A. Bonfire: a nomadic system for hybrid laptop-tabletop interaction. In *Proc. UIST '09*. 129-138.
19. Ketabdar, H., Roshandel, M. and Yüksel, K. Towards using embedded magnetic field sensor for around mobile device 3D interaction. In *Proc. MobileHCI '10*. 153-156.
20. Kratz, S. and Rohs, M. HoverFlow: expanding the design space of around-device interaction. In *Proc. MobileHCI '09*. Article 4, 8 pages.
21. Kratz, S., Rohs, M., Guse, D., Müller, J., Bailly, G. and Nischt, M. PalmSpace: continuous around-device gestures vs. multitouch for 3D rotation tasks on mobile devices. In *Proc. AVI '12*. 181-188.
22. LeafLabs. Maple Mini. http://leaflabs.com/devices
23. Leo, C. K. Contact and Free-Gesture Tracking for Large Interactive Surfaces. MEng Thesis, MIT Dept. of EECS and MIT Media Lab, May 2002.
24. Paradiso, J. and Leo, C. Tracking and Characterizing Knocks Atop Large Interactive Displays. *Sensor Review*, vol. 25, no. 2, pp. 134-143, 2005.
25. Paradiso, J., Leo, C., Checka, N., and Hsiao, K. Passive acoustic sensing for tracking knocks atop large interactive displays. In *Proc. IEEE Sensors '02*. 521-527.

26. Patel, S. N. and Abowd, G. D. Blui: low-cost localized blowable user interfaces. In *Proc. UIST '07*. 217-220.

27. Pham, D.T., Al-Kutubi, M., Ji, Z., Yang, M., Wang, Z. and Catheline, S. Tangible acoustic interface approaches. In *Proc. IPROMS '05*. 497–502.

28. Pham, D.T., Ji, Z., Peyroutet, O., Yang, M., Wang, Z. and Al-Kutubi, M. Localisation of impacts on solid objects using the wavelet transform and maximum likelihood estimation. In *Proc. IPROMS '06*. 541–547.

29. Pham, D. T., Ji, Z., Yang, M., Wang, Z., and Al-Kutubi, M. A novel human-computer interface based on passive acoustic localisation. In *Proc. HCI '07*. 901-909.

30. Priyantha, N. B. Chakraborty, A., and Balakrishnan, H. The Cricket Location-Support system. In *Proc. MOBICOM '00*. 32-43.

31. Prosser, W. H., Gorman, M. R., and Humes, D. H. Acoustic emission signals in thin plates produced by impact damage. *Journal of Acoustic Emission*, vol. 17, no. 1–2, pp. 29–36, 1999.

32. Sato, M., Poupyrev, I., and Harrison, C. Touché: enhancing touch interaction on humans, screens, liquids, and everyday objects. In *Proc. CHI '12*. 483-492.

33. Seniuk, A. and Blostein, D. Pen Acoustic Emissions for Text and Gesture Recognition. In *Proc. ICDAR '09*. 872-876.

34. Urashima, A. and Toriyama, T. Ubiquitous Character Input Device Using Multiple Acoustic Sensors on a Flat Surface. In *Proc. ICAT '10*. 39-43.

35. Yang, M. Al-Kutubi, M., and Pham, D. T. In-Solid Acoustic Source Localization Using Likelihood Mapping Algorithm. *Open Journal of Acoustics*, vol. 1, no. 2, pp. 34-40, Sept. 2011.

36. Zimmerman, T., Smith, J., Paradiso, J., Allport, D., and Gershenfeld, N. Applying electric field sensing to human-computer interfaces. In *Proc. CHI '95*. 280-287.

BackPat: One-Handed Off-Screen Patting Gestures

Karsten Seipp
Goldsmiths College, University of London
London SE14 6NW
k.seipp@gold.ac.uk

Kate Devlin
Goldsmiths College, University of London
London SE14 6NW
k.devlin@gold.ac.uk

ABSTRACT
We present *BackPat* – a technique for supporting one-handed smartphone operation by using pats of the index finger, middle finger or thumb on the back or side of the device. We devise a novel method using the device's microphone and gyroscope that enables finger-specific gesture detection and explore efficiency and user acceptance of gesture execution for each finger in three user studies with novice *BackPat* users.

Author Keywords
Back-of-device; pat; thumb; movement; sound; off-screen

ACM Classification Keywords
H.5.2 User Interfaces–Interaction styles: .

INTRODUCTION AND PREVIOUS RESEARCH
Using a phone with only one hand is the preferred mode of operation for many users [5]. However, input via the thumb is often limited. Research to overcome this and enrich the one-handed input vocabulary can be divided into three groups:

Motion as input: JerkTilts [8] uses the accelerometer to define a set of eight quick jerk gestures performed with the wrist. However, this technique seems unsuitable for continuous input, as moving the whole device could be tiring and requires the user to refocus on the interface after each jerk. ForceTap [3] uses the accelerometer to determine a tap's force on the screen to enrich input, but does not solve problems such as interface occlusion and reaching distant targets. TapPrints [7] infers tap location on the front of the device by analysing accelerometer and gyroscope data, but does not show if and how this can be achieved on the device's back.
Sound as input: [6] and [2] use the different sounds of the finger nail, tip, pad or knuckle on the device's screen, extracted via a stethoscope. However, these gestures are largely unsuitable for one-handed input.
Back-of-device interaction: Wobbrock et al. [13] recommend complementing thumb input on the front of the device with index finger input on the back of the device. In [1] researchers use an additional touch pad on the back to improve bimanual input, whereas [12] shows how a button on the back of a phone can be used to show contextual information, but does not explore its capabilities for continuous input. The Unifone [4] uses additional, touch-sensitive hardware on the side of a phone to use squeezes of the device for input. Although a prototype, the system seems prone to inadvertent operation, especially if sensors were attached to both sides for ambidextrous users or if the users corrected their grip. TimeTilt[10] shows how the phone's accelerometer can be used to detect a tap on the back for switching a mode, whereas [9] uses a sound created by tapping the back of the phone to control voice services. Finally, [14] shows how taps on a tablet's corners can be detected using internal sensors. However, the researchers only use sound volume and device motion for classification, but not frequency analysis (FA) and do not explore the technique's applicability to one-handed interaction or finger differentiation.
Altogether, previous work uses either additional hardware, is not suitable for continuous input, does not solve the problem of interface occlusion or does not exhaust the sensors' potential. Thus, it remains unclear to what extent sound volume, sound profile and motion can be combined to enrich one-handed input without external hardware. Also, which finger is most suitable for a technique using these properties on the device's back or side, which applications can benefit, and can the technique be used for continuous input while addressing problems of interface occlusion and thumb mobility?

DESCRIPTION
To approach these questions, we present *BackPat* (BP): A technique for supporting one-handed input by using pats of either the index finger, middle finger or thumb on the back or the side of the device – not to *replace* but to *supplement* existing on-screen input via the thumb. This way, users can choose their preferred input method and use the BP gestures for more functionality or facilitation of hard-to-perform tasks. The gestures (Fig. 1) we refer to in this paper are:

- BP-index: Using the index finger to pat the upper part of the device's back.
- BP-middle: Using the middle finger to pat the middle outer part of the device's back.
- BP-thumb: Using the thumb to pat the device's side.

For activation, the user long-taps the screen with their thumb. Subsequent "patting" of the device's back with index or middle finger, or of the device's side with the thumb, will be interpreted as input by the system. To perform a patting gesture, users can either lift their thumb off the screen and then pat the back of the device, or leave it pressed down while patting. This is subject to user preference and app configuration. A

MobileHCI 2014, September 23–26, 2014, Toronto, ON, Canada.

ACM 978-1-4503-3004-6/14/09 ...$15.00.
http://dx.doi.org/10.1145/2628363.2628396

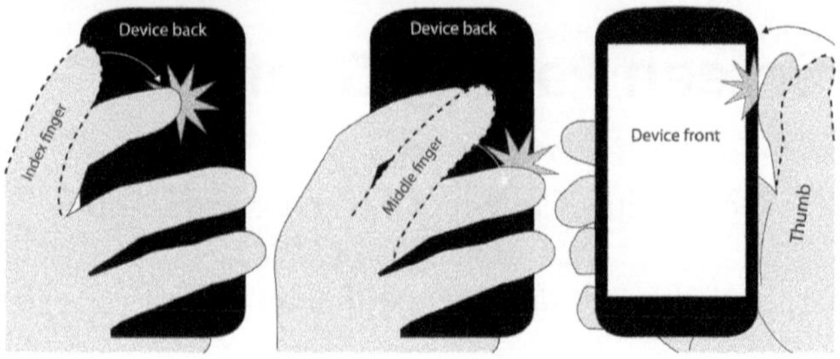

Figure 1. The 3 *BackPat* gestures: BP-index, BP-middle, BP-thumb.

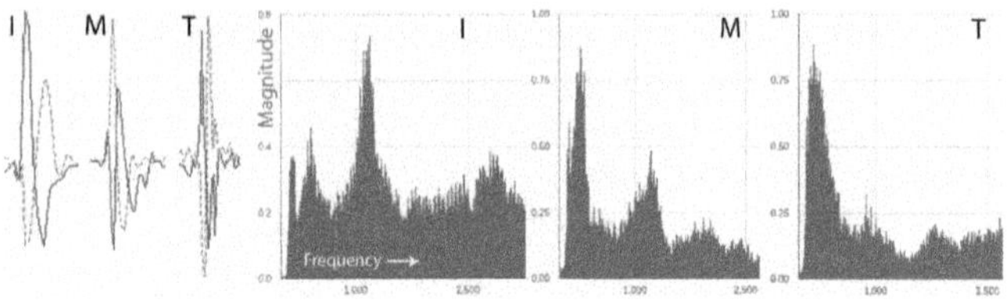

Figure 2. LEFT: The typical gyroscope patterns of BP-index (I), BP-middle (M) and BP-thumb (T) when holding the device with one hand. The full line represents the angular velocity around the x-axis, the dashed line the angular velocity around the y-axis. For BP-index and BP-middle the angular velocity around the z-axis is not noteworthy, but is very high for pats of the thumb on the side of the device, supporting correct pat detection of the otherwise rather similar patterns T and I. RIGHT: Averaged frequency (x-axis) magnitudes (y-axis) of each pat between 0–2500Hz. A pat of the thumb shows a characteristic profile between 0–1200 Hz, the middle finger between 0 and 2300 Hz – partially resembling the thumb – and the index finger between 400 and 2700 Hz.

demo of the technique [11] showed great user interest and learnability, but in this paper, we detail the gesture detection and evaluate each gesture's performance and user preference in three applications.

Finger-specific gesture detection

To configure our gesture detector, we recorded gyroscope and sound properties of pats made with the index and middle finger of each hand from six users (3 F, mean age 32, SD 3.74). The gyroscope data shows characteristic patterns for each pat (Fig. 2), allowing easy detection. However, gestures can be falsely detected by inadvertent movement. Thus we chose the sharp, brief changes in the volume of the microphone to act as gesture delimiters, which are detectable even while talking in close proximity to the phone. If the volume input rises above a certain threshold, we compare the volume values in a short window before and after the peak. If a pat (a high rise and fall in a very short time) is detected we analyse the gyroscope data to determine the finger used. This approach has two advantages. First, by analysing a short window around the volume peak, the pat can be easily distinguished from background noise, providing a relatively reliable delimiter. Second, the windowing delay allows enough time for the characteristic velocity changes to be interpreted. In a following study with the same users we adjusted the detection parameters for index and middle finger pats and added the gyroscope characteristics for pats of the thumb on the side of the device.

To further improve gesture detection, we examined the sound created by each pat. For this we recorded the patting sounds for all gestures from three users (1 F, mean age 30.3, SD 4.1). A Fast Fourier Transform of the data and visualisation of the magnitude of the frequencies gives a distinctive image for each pat (Fig. 2). We used the averaged data as a comparative basis for a detection algorithm which extracts three frequency ranges we defined to be representative of the pats (Fig. 2) from the microphone input and calculates the Pearson Correlation Coefficient (PCC) in relation to the comparative data. The highest value designates the "winner" and registers a pat of the respective finger when found to be above or equal to 0.5. Tab. 1 shows that a differentiation of index, middle finger and thumb patting gestures is possible due to the characteristic audio profiles created by the different angles and locations in which each finger connects with the device when patting. However, talking partly overwrites the frequencies of the pats and can lower the PCC down to 0.32, which is too low for reliable detection, as this is close to the PCC observed when comparing the pats to speech or music (Tab. 1).

Pat sound	Speech	Music	Thumb	Index	Middle
Thumb	0.00 – 0.14	-0.10 – 0.20	0.58	0.37	0.44
Index	0.10 – 0.30	0.00 – 0.31	0.37	0.48	0.35
Middle	0.10 – 0.30	0.10 – 0.30	0.44	0.35	0.56

Table 1. PCC range for the pat sounds compared to a recorded parliamentary speech (Speech) and to a Jungle tune (Music). Measurements were taken twice per pat sound and sound source. PCC range is based on the rounded average of the lowest and highest PCC measured during 60s of playback. Table also shows mean PCC of pats by six users (2 F, mean age: 31.8, SD:3.7) compared to the pat data.

	Pk (L)	Pk (T)	G (L)	G (W)	FA (L)	FA (T)	All (L)
T	87%	87%	85%	75%	77%	35%	91%
I	98%	98%	83%	70%	78%	63%	73%
M	97%	85%	87%	68%	78%	73%	80%

Table 2. Percentage of correctly interpreted pats by six users (1 F, mean age: 33.2, SD:4.5, 10 pats/module) for each module (Gyro (G), Peak (Pk) and Frequency Analysis (FA), separately in % under lab conditions (L = sitting, low noise level), with recorded talking (T) at -0.6 to -0.3 db in the background, while walking (W), and all modules active (All) with equal weighting. Column All shows the importance of a tiered approach over an equally weighted one, as overall accuracy can be lowered.

As Tab. 1 suggests a minimum PCC of 0.38 for reliable detection, we decided to define the following thresholds for our accuracy test to improve detection under non-lab conditions: Thumb: PCC >= 0.45, index and middle finger: PCC >= 0.38. We changed the minimum PCC for the thumb to 0.45 as opposed to 0.38 to reduce false identification as a middle finger pat, which is similar (Fig. 2). Tab. 2 shows the average detection rates per pat and module in various conditions. Peak and gyroscope pattern detection are the most reliable modules, but the reliability of the latter is impacted by walking. Good frequency and peak detection is possible under lab conditions, but is reduced with background noise. While pat detection based on FA might be improved with frequency filtering, per-user calibration, a larger sample size or contact microphones as recommended by [6], we consider it not sufficiently reliable in a real life environment when used as the sole classifier. Therefore, we allocated a minor role to the FA: If a pat has occurred (peak) and a finger could not be reliably determined (gyroscope) the FA is used as a fallback method if the PCC is sufficiently high. This way, the FA can support detection especially when the gyroscope is impacted by walking (Tab. 2). In return, gyroscope analysis allows more reliable detection in a noisy environment than the FA (Tab. 2). If a peak has been incorrectly detected, either the gyroscope or FA pattern has to be characteristic of one of the three pats to reduce false positives. This tiered approach provides a relatively robust gesture detector which can be used with either right or left hand, without extra hardware and per-user calibration. However, the FA is likely to require calibration per device, as different casings may create different sounds. To gain an impression of the technique's performance, we conducted three user studies in a quiet office, using a PCC threshold of 0.5 for the FA module:

User study: Text selection

Text selection can be challenging when operating the phone with only one hand. We wanted to find out if BP could improve selection speed and which BP gesture is the most efficient and preferred by users. In particular, we compared the performance of the BP gestures with "normal mode" (i.e. moving the thumb left or right to drag the selection bracket).

A BP gesture extended or reduced the selection one word per "pat". The study was conducted using a text field 24 lines high, a font size of 27 pixels (px) and line height of 32 px, using the Roboto Regular font in black on a HTC Sensation XE with a resolution of 540 x 960 px at 256 PPI. The text field filled the whole screen, with six words per line (Fig. 3), each in the form of "xxxxx", surrounded by spaces. Tasks started in the horizontal and vertical centre of the field, where users had to select 0.5 lines, 1 line and 1.5 lines of text in either direction using each technique three times, recorded in milliseconds (ms). Selection of the correct words had to be maintained for 500ms to be considered successful. Errors, such as choosing the wrong start point or overshooting by one word, resulted in users restarting the test round. 20 users took part (5 F, mean age: 25.4, SD: 4.57, 18 right-handed, 2 left-handed). The study was counterbalanced by mode (normal/BP), task, and finger. We scanned for outliers using scatter plots and a rule of thumb looking for values significantly smaller or greater than three times the SD. Two participants were removed due to missing data, one was removed due to being unable to hold the phone, leaving 17 cases.

Results and Discussion

A Greenhouse-Geisser corrected ANOVA showed a main effect of amount of text to select $F(1.81, 28.95) = 16.00$, $p < .001$; a main effect of mode, $F(1.83, 29.24) = 6.19$, $p = .007$; and an interaction of mode and amount, $F(4.23, 67.66) = 10.78$, $p < .001$. A Wilcoxon test shows that when selecting 0.5 lines of text beginning in the centre and ending at the edge (Fig. 3), any BP method is faster than normal mode. As shown in Tab. 3, BP-index is the fastest technique – significantly faster than moving the thumb left ($Z = 3.62$, $p < .001$) or to the right ($Z = 2.68$, $p = .007$) in normal mode. BP-index is also significantly faster than BP-thumb, and BP-middle is faster than normal mode. However, selecting 1 line of text that starts in the middle of a line and ends in the middle of the following line (Fig. 3) is fastest when moving the thumb in normal mode. While faster than the normal mode of operation in some cases, for longer selection tasks BP-thumb is less suitable as it requires change in the grip of the phone.

Selecting 1.5 lines of text (Fig. 3), with the start in the screen centre and the end at the screen edge, is fastest using the

M	0.5	*SD*	1	*SD*	1.5	*SD*
BP-T	3535	*818*	5395	*1643*	5702	*2448*
BP-I	2669	*366*	3521	*583*	4642	*642*
BP-M	2971	*649*	3775	*710*	4495	*1400*
N-R	3663	*1384*	3406	*1575*	3273	*1048*
N-L	4059	*2548*	3622	*1479*	3474	*1894*

Table 3. Rounded median task times (left column) and *SD (right column)* of the text selection user study for each mode (M: BP and normal left and right (N-L, N-R)) in ms for 0.5, 1 and 1.5 lines.

Figure 3. LEFT: The text selection tasks marked in red. To allow beginning the selection tasks from the middle of the line, three words were broken down into "xxx" and an "i" was appended to one. MIDDLE: List selection task where the user has to select the grey list elements starting at item 5. RIGHT: The target positions of the Pat-into-place study.

thumb in normal selection mode (Tab. 3). The fastest BP technique is BP-index, which is faster than BP-thumb ($Z = 2.81$, $p = .005$. Bonferroni-Holm correction applied to each test, starting with a divider of 10). For larger amounts of text, normal mode outperforms BP as it allows quick jumping between lines of text which otherwise would have to be "patted" down word by word. Thus, we recommend complementing normal text selection via the thumb with BP: Users can cover large areas of text by moving their thumb over the display and fine-adjust their selection with a few pats. The better performance of BP-index corresponds with the results of the user feedback who judged BP-index to be easier to perform than BP-middle and BP-middle to be easier than BP-thumb.

User study: Multiple selection

Another application of BP is multiple selection of list items. Users create an initial selection using their thumb, and subsequent BP-index or BP-thumb gestures extend the selection upwards. Using a BP-middle gesture will shrink the selection or extend it downwards. This configuration was deemed logical by users. We asked 24 users (6 F, 21 right-handed, 2 left-handed, 1 ambidextrous) to select either three, six or eleven consecutive list items (Fig. 3) three times. Selection started mid-list and mid-screen and had to be performed up and down, with task completion time recorded in ms. This way, we compared the performance of BP-index, BP-middle, BP-thumb and moving the thumb up and down using direct tap (normal mode). The study was counterbalanced by mode (BP/normal) and task. The data had no outliers.

Results and discussion

An ANOVA showed a main effect of amount, $F(1.28, 29.52) = 353.21$, $p < .001$; a main effect of mode, $F(1.96, 45.18) = 8.10$, $p = .001$; and an interaction of amount and mode, $F(4.54, 104.51) = 10.40$, $p < .001$ (G-G correction applied).

Here, BP shows potential for reducing selection time for six items or more. A Wilcoxon test (Bonferroni-Holm correction

M	3	*SD*	6	*SD*	11	*SD*
BP-T	1236	*646*	2436	*1466*	3680	*1975*
BP-I	1073	*548*	1837	*534*	3071	*991*
BP-M	1728	*2071*	2764	*1732*	4352	*3147*
N-U	939	*482*	2544	*1276*	5704	*1139*
N-D	920	*393*	2439	*815*	5660	*1520*

Table 4. Rounded median task times (left column) and *SD (right column)* for each mode (M: BP and normal up and down (N-U, N-D)) in ms for selecting 3, 6 and 11 items in a list.

applied starting with a divider of 10) showed that when selecting 11 items in a list, BP-index is the fastest approach, being faster than BP-thumb ($Z = 3.11$, $p = .002$), BP-middle ($Z = 3.51$, $p < .001$) and normal mode ($Z = 3.97$, $p < .001$). BP-thumb is also faster than normal mode. When selecting six items, BP-index is again the fastest technique (Tab. 4), being significantly faster than using the thumb downwards in normal mode ($Z = 3.34$, $p = .001$); faster than using the thumb upwards in normal mode ($Z = 3.26$, $p = .001$); faster than using BP-middle ($Z = 4.09$, $p < .001$); and faster than using BP-thumb ($Z = 3.26$, $p = .001$). BP-thumb is also faster than moving the thumb up in normal mode ($Z = 3.97$, $p < .001$). When selecting three items (Tab. 4), normal mode outperforms BP mode. The fastest BP method is BP-index, which is significantly faster than BP-middle, $Z = 3.26$, $p = .001$). BP-middle is the slowest, being significantly slower than BP-thumb ($Z = 3.20$, $p = .001$). For selecting only three items, direct selection seems fastest due to the cost of grip adjustment.

We recommend using BP as a complementary method: Small selections should be performed using direct tap, whereas larger selections can benefit greatly from using the BP technique. With BP-middle being the slowest BP technique, we recommend BP-index for extending a selection upwards and BP-thumb for extending a selection downwards. This correlates with the evaluation of the user feedback, who preferred BP-index over BP-thumb and BP-thumb over BP-middle.

User study: Reaching distant targets

In a third study we examined BP's applicability to facilitating interaction with distant targets, which we termed *Pat-into-place* (PIP). Users can perform a BP gesture to move targets into the thumb's reach by touching the screen and subsequently patting the device. This will move targets at the top or bottom of the screen to the level of the thumb, using either BP-index or BP-middle (Fig. 3). While selecting targets directly was faster than using PIP, users felt that PIP made reaching the elements faster and easier than direct access.

CONCLUSION AND FUTURE WORK

This paper has contributed the following over previous work:

- Synthesis of audio profiles, volume changes and gyroscope data can be used to produce three novel off-screen patting gestures to support one-handed input, allowing reaching distant targets as well as continuous input without interface occlusion and extra hardware or per-user calibration for both hands. Using these properties in a tiered approach, gestures can be detected even if one component fails.
- The quantitative performance of thumb, index and middle finger for performing these off-screen patting gestures and user preference for each. This varies by application, but users generally prefer index finger gestures.

This paper shows that *BackPat* can help to improve one-handed interaction, either as a means of direct input or as a "facilitator". However, future work will involve extensive comparison to existing techniques to better judge its impact.

REFERENCES

1. Baudisch, P., and Chu, G. Back-of-device interaction allows creating very small touch devices. In *Proc. CHI'09*, ACM (2009), 1923–1932.
2. Harrison, C., Schwarz, J., and Hudson, S. E. TapSense: enhancing finger interaction on touch surfaces. In *Proc. UIST'11*, ACM (2011), 627–636.
3. Heo, S., and Lee, G. Forcetap: Extending the input vocabulary of mobile touch screens by adding tap gestures. In *Proc. MobileHCI'11*, ACM (2011), 113–122.
4. Holman, D., Hollatz, A., Banerjee, A., and Vertegaal, R. Unifone: designing for auxiliary finger input in one-handed mobile interactions. In *Proc. TEI'13*, ACM (2013), 177–184.
5. Karlson, A. K., and Bederson, B. B. Studies in one-handed mobile design: Habit, desire and agility. Tech. rep., Comp. Sci. Dept., Univ. of Maryland, 2006.
6. Lopes, P., Jota, R., and Jorge, J. A. Augmenting touch interaction through acoustic sensing. In *Proc. ITS'11*, ACM (2011), 53–56.
7. Miluzzo, E., Varshavsky, A., Balakrishnan, S., and Choudhury, R. R. Tapprints: Your finger taps have fingerprints. In *Proc. MobiSys'12*, ACM (2012), 323–336.
8. Oakley, I., and Park, J. A motion-based marking menu system. In *CHI'07 E.A.*, ACM (2007), 2597–2602.
9. Robinson, S., Rajput, N., Jones, M., Jain, A., Sahay, S., and Nanavati, A. TapBack: towards richer mobile interfaces in impoverished contexts. In *Proc. CHI'11*, ACM (2011), 2733–2736.
10. Roudaut, A., Baglioni, M., and Lecolinet, E. TimeTilt: using sensor-based gestures to travel through multiple applications on a mobile device. In *INTERACT 2009*, vol. 5726 of *Lecture Notes in Computer Science*. Springer Berlin Heidelberg.
11. Seipp, K., and Devlin, K. Backpat: Improving one-handed touchscreen operation by patting the back of the device. In *CHI'14 E.A.*, ACM (2014), 555–558.
12. Stienstra, J., Overbeeke, K., and Wensveen, S. There is more in a single touch. In *Proc. CHItaly*, ACM (2011), 27–32.
13. Wobbrock, J. O., Myers, B. A., and Aung, H. H. The performance of hand postures in front- and back-of-device interaction for mobile computing. *Int. J. Hum.-Comput. Stud. 66*, 12 (Dec. 2008), 857–875.
14. Zhang, C., Parnami, A., Southern, C., Thomaz, E., Reyes, G., Arriaga, R., and Abowd, G. D. BackTap: robust four-point tapping on the back of an off-the-shelf smartphone. In *Proc. UIST'13*, ACM (2013), 111–112.

Around-Device Devices: My Coffee Mug is a Volume Dial

Henning Pohl, Michael Rohs
FG Mensch-Computer Interaktion
University of Hannover
Hannover, Germany
{henning.pohl, michael.rohs}@hci.uni-hannover.de

ABSTRACT
For many people their phones have become their main everyday tool. While phones can fulfill many different roles they also require users to (1) make do with affordance not specialized for the specific task, and (2) closely engage with the device itself. We propose utilizing the space and objects around the phone to offer better task affordance and to create an opportunity for casual interactions. Such around-device devices are a class of interactors that do not require users to bring special tangibles, but repurpose items already found in the user's surroundings. In a survey study, we determine which places and objects are available to around-device devices. Furthermore, in an elicitation study, we observe what objects users would use for ten interactions.

Author Keywords
spatial interaction; imaginary interface; tangible user interfaces; affordance

ACM Classification Keywords
H.5.2 [Information Interfaces and Presentation]: User Interfaces—*Input devices and strategies, Interaction styles*

INTRODUCTION
For many of us our mobile devices have become our most important everyday tool. Especially our phones, which we focus on here, are with us most of the day, wherever we go. Like a swiss army knife, we use them for a number of tasks in various roles. For example, phones can play the part of the alarm clock, remote control, cook book, level, game controller, or baby monitor. Their computing capabilities and range of sensors, give current phones enough flexibility to handle those scenarios.

While this allows phones to fulfill those roles, they also box the user into a rather restrictive interaction model. Where specialized devices can offer tailored affordances, the phone is usually a small brick-shaped device that requires the user to touch it for almost all interactions. Not only might this not be the best interaction for a given scenario, but this also requires a close engagement with the device. In contrast, interaction with a specialized device can be more casual in nature.

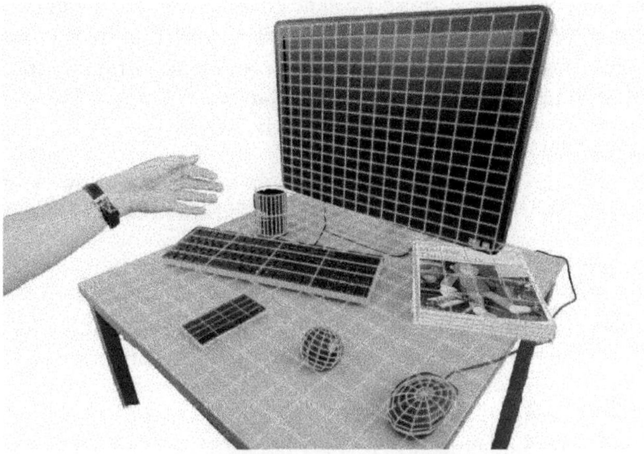

Figure 1. Instead of requiring the user to interact directly with the phone, around-device devices make use of the space and objects in the environment to offer more casual means of interaction. In this conceptual visualization the phone tracks the user's hand and detects objects nearby as geometric primitives, enabling interaction with them.

To take advantage of specialized physical affordances, tangibles can be introduced to the interaction. However, such tangibles are not always readily available. Requiring users to bring along tangibles for each desired affordance could encumber them too much for a mobile experience. Even when restricting themselves to a smaller subset of tangibles, the individual tangible could still be unacceptably bulky or heavy.

Instead, we propose repurposing objects and space around the phone for interactions. We notice that many of the objects that are in proximity to our phones over the course of a day offer good affordances for many common interaction tasks. For example, hacky sacks lying around in a room have a natural affordance for usage as push buttons, e.g., to snooze an alarm. Compared to virtual buttons on a phone screen, such physical *ad hoc buttons* allow pressing with less targeting effort (due to increased size) and allows for interactions with more varying force (we can hit the snooze button hard, if we want to).

Around-device devices are not necessarily bound to a physical object though. Instead, such a device can also be imaginary. While we cannot have real input devices floating in the air next to the user, we can have users pretend to interact with such a non-existing device. Such in-the-air input can also be gestures not directly tied to a specific device.

MobileHCI 2014, September 23–26, Toronto, ON, Canada.

ACM 978-1-4503-3004-6/14/09...$15.00.
http://dx.doi.org/10.1145/2628363.2628401

Around-device devices can provide better affordance, appropriateness, and casualness to phone interactions. On the other hand, such interactions around the device will usually not be as precise as direct touch interaction on the phone. Users do retain the choice to pick up their phone for more fine-grained interaction. They can pick the level of control they desire in the *casual interaction continuum* [33].

In this paper, we investigate scenarios where around-device devices could be used. Using collected ground truth data on what kind of objects people have available near their phones, we determine *which* objects and settings should be more closely considered for around-device devices. Based on those results, we furthermore present an investigation of actual behavior exhibited by users when asked to refrain from close interaction and instead tackle a series of tasks with the kind of around-device devices discussed here.

RELATED WORK

Around-device devices primarily build upon previous work in ad hoc interfaces, and around-device and tangible interaction.

Around-Device Interaction

Much around-device interaction works strives to increase the space available for user input. Kratz and Rohs, e.g., use around-device hand gestures for scrolling and selection [26]. The *BeThere* system projects around-device movements from a local space to a remote one [36]. This allows users to collaborate spatially when not collocated.

Yang et al. added an omnidirectional lens to a phone's camera to enable interaction and tracking all around the phone [43]. They use computer vision to (1) identify nearby objects, (2) detect activity, and (3) track users hands. Similar to our concept, users can trigger actions by pointing at nearby objects. However, we also explore using those objects as tangibles.

Tangible Interaction

Tangibles [22] are a way to increase the affordance of an interface, making possible manipulations more apparent [18]. As in our work, Carvey et al. investigated using everyday objects as tangibles, differentiating objects by weight, so that placing an object on an attached scale triggers actions [4]. Corsten et al. used objects with modifiable weight to allow changing of the objects' haptic properties [9].

Portico and *Bonfire* enable tangible interactions around portable devices. Camera-arms are attached to a tablet for *Portico*, where objects on and around the tablet are detected using classifier methods such as template matching [1]. Users can, e.g., roll a physical ball against the tablet to shoot a virtual ball in a game. In *Bonfire* cameras on a laptop detect objects (via color histograms) in two interaction zones to its sides [23]. While *Portico* is input only, *Bonfire* also includes projection output. In contrast to both systems, we investigate tracking that is built directly into a phone and does not require setup, such as *Portico's* extension of the attachment arms.

Ad Hoc Interfaces

Around-device devices repurpose existing objects for interactions. Similarly, Henderson and Feiner used existing features in the environment to add passive haptics to augmented reality controls like sliders and buttons [17]. Buttons, e.g., are placed on existing protrusions and spinning, bending or sliding objects are used for 3D widgets. Cheng et al. in their *iCon* system added markers to everyday objects found on users' desks and enable toggle and consecutive control by moving or touching [6]. While *iCon* looked at desktop systems with tracking above or under the desk, we investigate mobile device scenarios. However, this includes a desk setting similar to *iCon's*. Steins et al. instructed users to use imaginary input controllers and infer the used controller from a user's hand posture [37]. This enables fast device switching between the simulated controller set. *SketchSpace* is a rapid prototyping tool, that allows designers to attach virtual sensors to objects for fast and easy prototyping [19].

Corsten et al. proposed using objects as ad hoc stand-ins for currently unavailable controllers [10]. While our work is similar to theirs, we specifically investigate repurposing objects and space around a mobile device and thus place special emphasis on determining appropriate settings. Instead of focusing on *tracking* and *object association*, we focus more on aspects of *what* can be used and *how* it would be used.

AROUND-DEVICE DEVICES

Many current mobile devices constrain interaction to touch on the device. Around-device devices, on the other hand, strive to *repurpose* surrounding space and objects for interactions.

The idea of making a space *"active"* through the act of placing a device is similar to *PlayAnywhere*, where Wilson proposed a device to be placed on any table in order to enable interactions on it [41]. One could argue that many of the benefits of around-device devices described in this paper could be achieved by installing tracking systems in those locations we investigate, like the office. However, we believe there are intrinsic advantages to an approach that concentrates on sensors built into a device, observing the space around it.

First of all, instrumented rooms require a much larger amount of equipment. This increases costs and costs scale with the number of places in which a user would like to use around-device devices. Furthermore, there are important privacy concerns: would users, e.g., accept offices that constantly track them and would a date be accepting of a bedroom with cameras in the corners? By having the tracking inside their personal device, users can more conveniently customize their tracking (e.g., by defining different gestures) and ensure their setup always comes with them. This also ensures detection can be tailored better to a specific user, whereas room-based systems have to cater to the requirements of a larger number of potential users. Furthermore, containing the system in their personal devices allows users to retain a sense of control. It is clear *when* the system is tracking (the phone is on the table) and tracking can be easily blocked temporarily by turning the phone around, placing a hand over it or putting it away.

Benefits

Looking at the main benefits of around-device devices, they allow users to (1) choose interactors with more suitable affordances, (2) interact more casually when they do not want to grab their phone, and (3) extend their interaction space, no longer restricting them to interaction on the device itself.

Suitable Affordances
Current phones cannot morph into different shapes, and thus cannot adapt to the affordance most appropriate at the moment. Tangibles, on the other hand, are purposely designed to offer specific affordances (e.g., to invite turning in a knob). Unfortunately, users do not always carry such tangibles with them or have them ready at home or at work. For many tasks, we can instead make use of objects already available nearby.

Casual Interactions
Interaction with mobile phones generally requires users to closely engage with them. For physical, social or mental reasons, however, this is not possible or desirable in every situation. Instead of constraining users to a single engagement level, Pohl and Murray-Smith have proposed allowing them to pick their desired level of engagement on the *casual interaction continuum* [33]. They showed, that when given a choice, users naturally adapt their level of engagement (how closely they interact with a device) according to the task difficulty.

Around-device devices can fill an important role in casual interactions. They essentially offer users a more casual interaction possibility for situations when they need less engaging interaction or are ok with relinquishing some control. For example, in situations where close interaction with a mobile phone is frowned upon (e.g., in a meeting), it might still be acceptable to interact with other objects nearby. This could be something as basic as scrolling through a list of upcoming appointments on a *glance screen*[1] by turning a mug. While users might not universally be able to give detailed commands this way, they could still provide coarser input. Some coarse interactions such as slapping, more forceful touching or hitting are only acceptable with objects more resilient than mobile phones. This user-chosen trade-off between interaction fidelity and engagement defines casual interactions.

Extended Interaction Space
While phones have been getting bigger recently, the interaction space is still comparatively limited. Enabling input in the space around the device and with objects around it substantially increases the available space. The space is tied to the sensing in the phone, making it inherently personal. We are less inclined to place our phones next to strangers, thus are also not extending our interaction space towards them.

Challenges
A general problem with any around-device device (and also tangible and gestural interaction in general) is how users inform, e.g., their phone about an around-device device. Ideally, users would not need to retrain such an association every time they intend to reuse an around-device device. However, more ad hoc situations require a fast way to define associations.

When phones track objects around them, those can be offered to the user for associations. In Figure 2 we present an example, with off-screen visualization to show surrounding objects. Avrahami et al. indicate tracked around-device devices in a similar way [1]. This can be reactive—the phone detects an object nearby was pressed and asks the user whether an association should be made. Such a prompt is transient and disappears if the user does not engage further with the device.

[1] http://conversations.nokia.com/2013/06/25/a-closer-look-at-glance

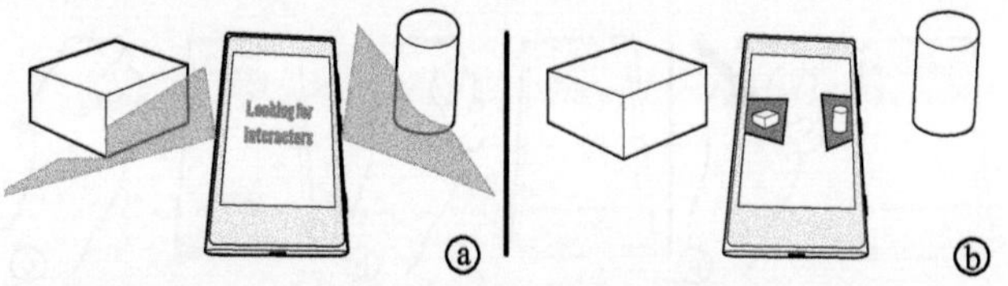

Figure 2. Here we show one way users can define around-device devices. When (a) the phone scans the surrounding space it finds two objects suitable for interaction and (b) uses *Wedge* [13] to inform the user about their type and location. Users can then click on an object to, e.g., associate it with an action in a next step.

In cases a more temporary association is desired, it will often be sufficient to offer the user to grab any object or just use their hands. Figure 3 shows an example of a game that on startup allows the user to either touch the virtual joystick on the screen or place the hands next to the device for an around-device joystick. The association in this case is established in a dedicated specification mode.

Mappings can also be implicit, offering a kind of plausible default mode, based on a state constraint. For example, when music is playing on a phone a user could expect nearby objects to automatically take on a role in the control of the audio. A nearby object with button affordance could, e.g., be assumed to be a play/pause button, a nearby tube to be usable as a volume slider. We can envision similar situations when an alarm is ringing, a call is coming in, or a beep signals an incoming message. For casual interactions it is important that the overall interaction costs are low. Thus, implicit and temporary mappings are more appropriate in that context.

Mobile projection from the phone could be used to indicate the default objects and possible interactors. Thus projection is also possible along the same optical path. Devices would not project on their surrounding space all the time, but would only do so when queried by the user. Projection can also be substituted by off-screen visualizations of the current mappings on the device itself.

Fundamental constraints are imposed through occlusion. If the phone cannot see an object it cannot be tracked for interactions, which may not be clear to a user. While this is a general problem of vision based systems, around-device devices can avoid this limitation to some extent by assuming shape constraints. For example, when the phone sees the front of a bottle it can detect it as a cylindrical shape and *infer* interactions on the back. Thus, occlusion in some situations does not impede interaction. Projection could also demarcate a phone's sensing limits to the user.

AROUND-DEVICE DEVICE TYPES
In this section, we categorize around-device widgets and outline how they can improve interactions.

Around-Device Trigger Controls
Phone applications such as alarm clocks, stopwatches, or call response are centered around simple trigger interactions (e.g., stopping the alarm). With touch control, this requires acquiring targets on the screen and sometimes unlocking the screen to start the interaction. There is no haptic feedback or tactile sensation to pressing those on-screen buttons.

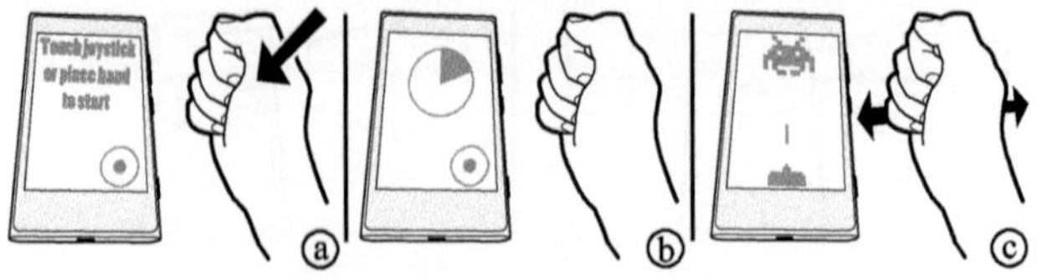

Figure 3. Mobile phones with sideways hand detection can offer players an alternative to on-screen joystick controls. (a) At the start of a game, the player is given the choice on what control to use. (b) When placing her hand next to the phone and holding it still for a short moment, the hand is detected as a joystick replacement. (c) The player can then control her ship's movements by moving the hand next to the phone as if she was holding a physical joystick.

For around-device devices, we propose repurposing objects in the environment as trigger controls. A trigger could be any prominent protrusion [17], but would often ideally be an object inviting pushing. A hacky sack or stress ball, for example, invite slapping and allow users to apply substantially more force to the button than phones would allow (making turning off an alarm that much more satisfying). Apart from tapping or pushing on objects, actions could also be triggered via object arrangements or manipulations (e.g., flipping an object around).

Around-Device Linear Controls

Increasing or decreasing some value is a recurring task in many applications. Most mobile phones, e.g., offer dedicated buttons to control the volume level. Linear control is also required for adjusting the screen brightness, seeking in media, or setting a numeric value with a spinner control. An example of a tangible linear control are *Fillables* by Corsten et al. who, e.g., propose allowing users to scroll through video by moving a glass [9].

Henderson et al. have proposed utilizing edges, pipes, or cords as a base for around-device linear controls, making use of their haptic properties [17]. As we will show later, a number of objects found near mobile phones fit into this category (e.g., pens, candle holders, or cables). Any object that can be moved closer to or further away from the phone could also be used by mapping distance to value.

Around-Device Game Controllers

In contrast to dedicated portable game devices, phones do not offer physical game controls. This constraint has yielded many games specifically designed around touch/gesture control. However, this is not always possible and thus we can find a plethora of on-screen buttons and joysticks. Compared to physical controls, those digital substitutes provide no haptic feedback, making zeroing and not overshooting challenging. Furthermore, large parts of the screen are occluded by the player's hand when using such on-screen controls.

Around-device joysticks or steering wheels could be just tracking the hands themselves (as shown in Figure 3). This has recently been explored by Steins et al. [37]. While this enables fast device switching, those *imaginary devices* do not provide haptic sensations. To get zeroing, plungers could be given to players to grab as around-device joysticks. Any round object (e.g., a plate) would be appropriate to form the base of a steering wheel controller. Thus, children could, e.g., be playing a driving game while waiting for lunch.

Around-Device Input Devices

Researchers have investigated replicating traditional desktop input controllers as imaginary ones. Most prominently, Mistry and Maes built *Mouseless*, where a user's hand is tracked next to a device for an impromptu mouse emulation [30]. Terajima et al. show how fingers could be tracked for in-air typing [39]. Canesta in the past offered a commercial projection keyboard for ad hoc typing capability. In-air typing is also available for the Leap Motion controller through the *DexType*[2] application. Instead of specific shapes for each device, *Visual Panel* tracks a quadrangle and maps user touches to pointing or typing interactions on a desktop [44].

We can envision other input devices being emulated as well. For example, tracking a pen or pen-shaped object around a phone could enable around-device writing or drawing [21]. Simple devices like remote controls can be replaced by gestures [2], but could also map to nearby objects with a more casual interface (i.e., restricting the set of operations, while retaining control of the main task, e.g., changing channels) [33].

Around-Device State Control

Instead of directly interacting with objects, their presence and arrangement itself can encode state. For example, if the phone were to detect several mugs together it could switch to a silent mode as not to disturb a conversation. Arranging common objects on a desk gives a subtle control opportunity, were, e.g., a bottle's proximity to the monitor could affect an application. Users could deliberately reveal or hide arrangements to put their phone in different modes.

Around-Device Storage

While this paper focuses on controls around a device, the objects and space investigated here, could also be used for storing data. For example, Hasan et al. discretized the space in a plane around a device into bins and allowed users to store and browse content there [16]. In addition to such 2D approaches, storing data in 3D space around the user has also been explored [28].

SENSING AROUND-DEVICE INPUT

Current mobile phones do not include the capability for sensing around-device interactions to the extent necessary for around-device devices. However, we think there are no fundamental problems in bringing this kind of sensing to future mobile devices. There has been substantial previous work exploring how this could be done as well as new sensors in mobile form factors from industry. In this section we look at the state of the art for around-device sensing. We believe the approaches described here paint a clear picture that our envisioned around-device devices scenario is grounded in technology that can be expected to be available soon.

Instrumentation

Instrumenting the user, the environment, or objects is one approach to sensing around-device interaction. This could be a worn color glove [40] or markers put on objects. Instead of a glove, *Digits* has users wear a device on the wrist that is able to track hand gestures [25].

[2] http://dextype.com

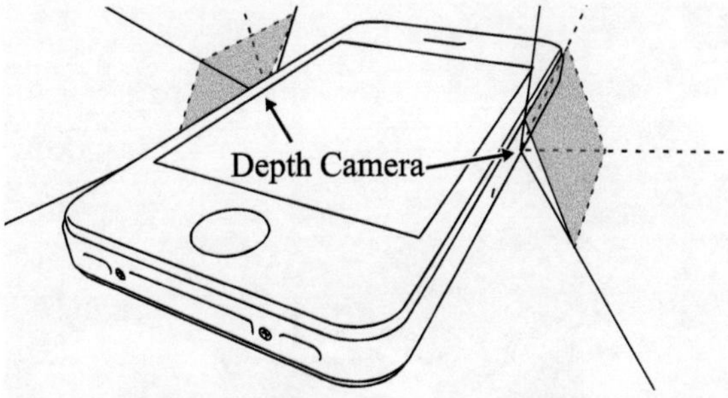

Figure 4. Future mobile devices are likely to include depth cameras with a large field of view in the sides of the device. The field of view shown here is equivalent to the one of a Leap Motion controller. Shading does not indicate sensor range but only highlights the field of view.

Devices incorporating magnetometers, can track fingers wearing magnetic rings [15] or users holding magnets or objects containing magnets [24]. Hwang et al.'s *MagGetz* are physical widgets (e.g., buttons) with embedded magnets that can be placed around mobile devices for customizable around device tangible controls [20]. *EyeRing* is a more sophisticated ring with a built-in camera, that was designed around pointing gesture interaction [32].

Researchers have also looked at using eletromyography to sense muscle activity to, e.g., recognize hand gestures [35]. However, instrumentation restricts interaction to specific rooms or encumbers the user. Thus, we believe a different approach would be more suitable for around-device devices.

Electric Field Sensing

Many touchscreens on mobile devices make use of capacitive sensing. While this technology works well for 2D tracking, it can also be used to track conductive objects (including humans) in 3D. This approach has recently regained interest with researchers looking at tracking users in rooms [8], fine grained hand tracking [11], and tracking for mobile devices [27].

To sense in 3D, electric field sensing requires usage of more than one electrode. Electrode placement has to be such that field lines pass through the desired sensing space. Thus, only having electrodes in a mobile device would most likely not be sufficient for tracking interactions in a larger space. One solution would be to have retractable electrodes that can be pulled out and placed where desired or integrate this technology in earpieces, attached to the phone anyway.

Optical Sensing

Most phones today already include cameras and we believe it would only be a small step from the status quo to integrating depth sensing sensors. In *SideSight* infra-red sensors were embedded along the sides of a mobile device, enabling finger tracking for tasks such as panning on-screen content [3]. Choi et al. arranged the same kind of sensors in a touchpad for *ThickPad*, to enable hover-tracking above the touchpad [7]. Instead of individual infra-red sensors, *Z-Touch* uses infrared laser planes and detects fingers crossing them [38], an approach similar to the one used in *Mouseless* [30].

Depth cameras have also been shrinking and could soon be generally available in mobile form factors. For example, PrimeSense was offering the *Capri* sensor, an embedded design delivering VGA resolution from 0.9 m to 4.0 m before being bought by Apple. Occipital is planning to make the *Structure Sensor*[3], a mobile depth sensor attachment, available in late 2014. Google's *Project Tango*[4] is set to make a prototype phone with a depth sensor embedded in the back available this year.

Other Sensing

More exotic approaches to sense around-device input include *SoundWave*, where the doppler effect is used to detect gestures [12], or using steerable lasers to track fingers in 3D [5].

NOMADIC TANGIBLES FOR MOBILE DEVICES

Around-device devices can be used when the phone is lying around somewhere. While phones are mobile, we posit that most of the time they will, in fact, be placed somewhere. We investigate scenarios where this is the case and what interactions are suitable in those situations. Furthermore, we collected ground truth data on actual device contexts via a crowd sourcing task.

Envisioned Scenarios

We initially brainstormed to collected a set of locations where we think phones would be lying around. In the brainstorming, we identified four such locations:

Office: When brought to the office, people will often place their phone on their desk.

Bedroom: Many people will be using their phones till the end of the day and/or use them as alarms, making placement on the nightstand near the bed a likely option.

Kitchen: During breakfast or dinner, phones might just lay around on the dining table.

Living Room: While relaxing in the evening, phones might be placed on the couch or coffee table.

For each of those locations, we determined what kind of objects we expect to be available for interactions. We do not claim these lists are exhaustive, but they provide a rough bearing of what is characteristic for such places.

Office: staplers, monitors, keyboards, mice, landline phones, mugs, books, pens, office toys (e.g., Newton's cradles).

Bedroom: pillows, books, lamps, glasses cases

Kitchen: cereal boxes, bowls, cups, mugs, glasses, silverware, candle holders

Living Room: remote controls, pillows, books, lamps, bowls, boxes

Depending on the location, different kinds of interactions are appropriate. In an office setting, around-device devices could, e.g., be useful for more casual interactions during a meeting (see earlier scenario) or to support peripheral tasks at the desk. At home, we see the role of around-device devices also primarily as enabler for casual interactions when sitting on a couch or lying in bed. When in the kitchen, users could also benefit from around-device interactions when not willing to interact with their device, e.g., because of dirty hands.

[3]http://structure.io

[4]http://www.google.com/atap/projecttango

Figure 5. Photos depicting settings where phones are lying around. Overall 510 photos were collected via the Scoopshot crowdsourcing service. Copyright of shown photos (numbered clockwise from top-left corner): Ricardo Alves (3), Jens Bloszyk (4), Sarah Jenkins (2, 6, 9, 11, 12), Petra Larsson (8), Sem Lemmers (1), Brad McDougal (10), Rostislav Sedlacek (5), and Chaichan Srisawat (7).

Phone Context Ground Truth

While we established a rough idea of places and objects for around-device devices with the brainstorming, we felt this does not give a full picture of the space. Previous work gave us additional data on those settings. For example, Harrison and Hudson visited ten participants at home and at work to look at placement locations of their phones [14]. Unfortunately, their list focuses on the materials at those locations and does not include details on the space and the objects available. Another six users were visited by Carvey et al., who looked at nearby objects and interviewed them [4]. This investigation, however, does not focus on phone locations. On the other hand, they made interesting observations on people's object mappings, e.g., how in *transient couplings* users were inclined to repurpose any nearby object for simple and immediate tasks. Finally, Cheng et al. in a field study collected photos of 33 desks and the objects on them [6]. This study also focused on desktop scenarios and the paper unfortunately does not provide detailed object information. However, they did learn that most participants placed phones on their desk.

To get some qualitative validation of our own for our envisioned scenarios, we set out to gather real-world data on the places where people lay down their phones. We used the Scoopshot[5] photo crowdsourcing service to collect photos for this purpose (a subset of the photos can be seen in Figure 5). On Scoopshot, users can create tasks to ask other users for photos, matching the task's description. We created several tasks asking users to send in *"photos of places where people usually have their phones lying around"*, where *"the phone and the context (e.g. objects around the phone) should both be visible in the photo"*. Tasks can be assigned to a geographic region, where users get a notification of the new task on their phone. However, users from elsewhere are able to submit photos as well when seeing the task on the Scoopshot website. We ran the task in several regions with high user density: around Amsterdam, Berlin, Copenhagen, Essen, Frankfurt, and Istanbul.

We collected a total of 510 photos[6] from 249 different users. We were able to collect photos from a wide range of locations, not restricted to only those we advertised the task in (note that not all photos included location information). The majority of submissions still comes from Europe (91.9%, including Turkey), so there might be some cultural bias in the dataset. While the majority of users followed the task description, many sent in photos not in line with our requirements (e.g. no phone visible in the photo). Hence, we removed those contributions, leaving us with 286 valid photos. For each photo, we manually annotated the location of the phone and the nearby objects. We only included objects visible in the photo and did not infer other objects (i.e., no mouse is assumed just because a keyboard and a computer are visible). We also only included objects in the range of the phone, if, e.g., an object is only visible in the far distance (beach, outside, ...) it was not counted. Table 1 shows the most common locations, while Table 2 shows the most common nearby objects.

Location	Count	Location	Count
Table	94	Bathroom	7
Desk	50	Shelf	5
Bed	20	Dresser	5
Kitchen	11	Bag	4
Couch	10	Car	4
Restaurant	8	Nightstand	3
Garden	8	Boat	3

Table 1. Most common phone locations in the photo dataset.

Many participants also left comments in a field reserved for the photo description. While mostly just describing their photo, some left more general comments, e.g.:

- *"my mobile phone must lay beside the bed when i'm sleeping"*
- *"Wherever I am, my phone is too! It even comes with when I'm making food and is usually playing music!"*
- *"If I was cooking. My smartpohne is in the kitchen too."*
- *"Das Smartphone liegt zwischen allem anderen auf dem Schreibtisch, immer griffbereit." (The phone is lying on the desk between all that other stuff, always available.)*
- *"It is always near me"*

Discussion

The locations we got from ground truth roughly match up with the set we expected. Additionally, we saw some that were more surprising to us, such as boats, bathrooms, or window ledges.

[5] http://www.scoopshot.com

[6] Photos for each task available at http://www.scoopshot.com/v2/task/{bdwnmsxpvvhdd | cnqlcbltsgxvr | bxvhlnmpwqcgx | bnnqhlrcbrlzg | lrdljhdppddxm | bxcjxxpvlsbzk} respectively.

Object	Count	Object	Count
Cable	38	Tray	12
Phone	37	Container	12
Glass	35	Can	12
Box	33	Flower	11
Paper	32	Notebook	11
Bottle	30	Candle holder	11
Laptop	28	Lamp	11
Bowl	28	Charger	11
Cup	27	Ashtray	10
Keyboard	24	Saucer	10
Mouse	24	Headphones	10
Pillow	23	Figurine	9
Pen	18	Handle	9
Monitor	16	Spoon	8
Book	15	Fruit	8
Sunglasses	13	Pot	8
Tablet	12	Post-its	8
Mug	12	Vase	8
Plate	12	Keychain	8
Bag	12	Remote	7

Table 2. Most common objects near phones in the photo dataset (corresponding geometric primitives given where applicable)

Objects found near phones also largely overlap with our expectations. Bottles, glasses, bowls, and lamps are rather common, while we did not expect the amount of nearby other phones (which supports collaborative usage scenarios such as [29]). Generalizing the found object set, we can sort the found objects into a set of five categories (also illustrated with proxies in Figure 6):

- Spherical objects, such as balls or some fruits
- Dome-like objects, such as plates, bowls, or cups
- Cylindrical objects, such as bottles, cans, mugs, or candles
- Rectangular cuboids, such as boxes, monitors, books, or other phones
- Complex shapes, such as sunglasses, crumbled paper, or figurines

While each object may have additional semantic cues for how people perceive it to be used, their shape already imbues them with certain affordances. For example, spherical objects invite rolling, while cylindrical objects invite turning around the up-axis.

For many of the observed objects, we can make additional assumptions according to Gestalt law. For example, seeing the front of a glass one can assume that the back is similar. By focusing on interaction with objects corresponding to geometric primitives, we can use those assumptions to, e.g., alleviate occlusion problems somewhat. Just because a part of an object is not seen, does not mean it cannot be tracked or that touch on that part could not be inferred.

USER PREFERENCES IN AROUND-DEVICE DEVICES

The collected images have provided us with a good overview of what objects would be *available* for users to incorporate into their interactions. However, most likely not all those

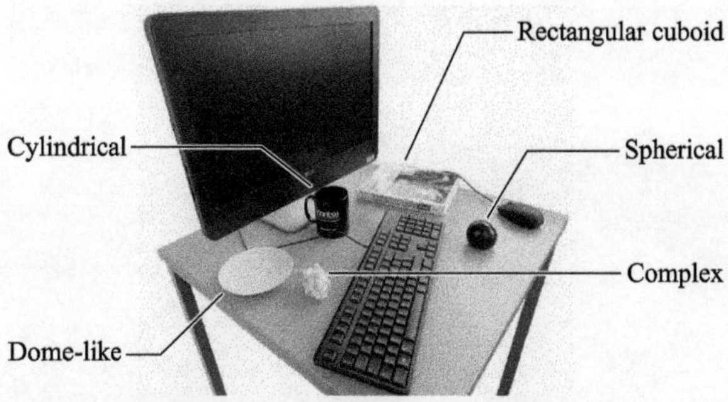

Figure 6. Exemplary object arrangement for a desk scenario, including all shape catagories found in the ground truth study.

objects would be considered equally by actual users. Thus, we designed an elicitation study to collect additional data on which objects would potentially be *used* for interactions if available. This is similar to a previous study by Wobbrock et al., who asked users to come up with tabletop gestures to achieve a shown effect [42].

Participants

We recruited 15 participants (5 female, age 20–46, $\bar{x} = 29.07$, $\sigma = 6.88$) from our institution. The study took approximately 30 minutes and after completion, participants received a small non-monetary gratuity.

Task

We defined a set of ten tasks we felt were an appropriate subset of possible around-device device input scenarios. While covering many phone-specific tasks, we did not include tasks requiring prolonged interaction. Thus, the task list does, e.g., not include a task where participants could be expected to use an object as an ad hoc joystick. However, the used tasks allowed participants to potentially make use of around-device buttons, sliders, or state control.

During the study, participants were asked to find the interaction they deemed most suitable for:

1. Changing the volume of music already playing
2. Rejecting an incoming phone call
3. Dimming the lights
4. Check whether any (email, SMS, IM, ...) new message has arrived
5. Notifying their next appointment they would be a bit late
6. Skipping to the next song
7. Setting an alert/notification for when to leave to catch the next train
8. Querying their sport team's current score (game still running)
9. Querying the status of their ongoing ebay auction
10. Muting their phone

Participants were told that the system has any task-relevant context information available (e.g., calendar with upcoming appointments, information on favorite sport team, or train schedules) and they would not need to relay that information and could limit their interaction to communicating intent.

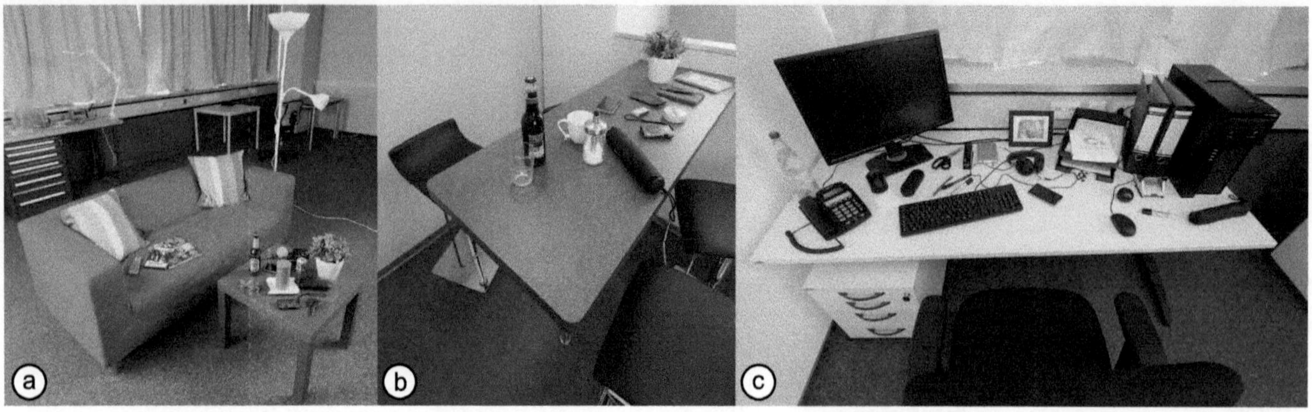

Figure 7. We asked participants how they would perform a series of ten tasks when limited to casual around-device interactions (object movement, object arrangement, gestures, coarse touch, . . .). This was repeated for (a) living room, (b) café, and (c) office scenarios with different objects available.

Procedure

We instructed participants not to consider speech input and close interactions with the phone (such as unlocking and starting an app). As this was an out of the ordinary requirement for many, we used a *priming* technique [31] and pointed out several other approaches they could use with objects instead: (1) moving or rotating, (2) changing arrangement, (3) placing them on top of others, (4) appropriating features or surfaces for touch, (5) performing gestures relative to them, or even (6) performing gestures independent of any object. We did not ask them to restrict themselves to these examples or indicated any preference. As we were only interested in input, we told participants not to worry about output and just assume any feedback would be presented at an appropriate location or provided via audio. Furthermore, we assured participants any answer would be okay including reuse of previously performed interactions. To ensure participants would not concern themselves with recognizability, we told them to assume having previously defined that interaction and that sensing would be capable of picking up any interaction they perform.

In line with the most common settings determined earlier, we choose three different scenes for the study (shown in Figure 7): a living room, a café, and an office. The objects available in each varied, but there was always a mobile phone present in the scene. Other objects present in multiple scenes include: notebooks, bottles, books, umbrellas, pens and markers (see Figure 7 for shots of all present objects). Even though we found multiple phones were often present in the collected dataset, we chose to concentrate on single-user scenarios here were this is not the case. All of the ten tasks were repeated in every scene. We counterbalanced scene order using a reduced latin square design and randomized task order for each scene.

Results

Overall, participants provided a wide range of interaction choices. There was substantial agreement for some tasks, but generally we observed many different approaches.

1. Change Music Volume

Participants almost exclusively followed one of three strategies: (1) turning some object (mostly the phone) on the table, (2) performing a circle gesture on a nearby object (often on the headphones, if available, or on furniture, especially armrests), or (3) using a hand up/down gesture. This behavior was sometimes coupled with an activation step such as clapping three times or pointing at speakers.

2. Reject Phone Call

The most common interaction used by participants was flipping the phone upside down. A close second is performing a "brush aside" gesture over or towards the phone. Some participants also knocked or patted the phone, placed an object on the phone, or performed a "put handset down" gesture.

3. Dim Lights

Here participants used interactions similar to those in task 1. However, they would often point at the lights first before initiating a gesture and use different objects, such as the candle. In the living room scene, several participants used parts of the lamp as base for sliders. Additionally, some participants used hand open/close gestures.

4. Check for New Messages

Most participants here chose to just tap the phone once, stating that any interaction should prompt the phone to display such information. When using gestures, participants would draw question marks on, or circles (like a "refresh" gesture) next to the phone. Many participants associated the notebook with checking for new messages and expected opening the notebook to display the status. Two participant used subtle cues such as glancing at the phone or turning it towards them.

5. Send Delay Message

Generally, participants made three mental connections here: (1) associating the task with leaving and thus, e.g., placing the umbrella or the phone itself ready to go (e.g., at table edge), (2) tapping on their watch or mimicking a clock hand with a pen, stressing the task's association with time, or (3) interacting with the notebook (often described as calendar) because it is associated with the appointment itself.

6. Skip to Next Song

Here participants almost universally waved right, swiped right, or moved objects to the right. They would also tap on the right side of objects (e.g., headphones or chairs) or on the right of two objects (pillows). This was sometimes coupled with claps or pointing to speakers like in the volume changing task.

7. Catch-a-Train Notification
Similarly to task 5, many associations were formed around leaving, the most common one being placing the phone or the umbrella in a "ready to leave"–spot. Many participants also performed a "walking fingers" gesture for the same purpose. Some also placed objects so they would point to the door.

8. Sport Team Status
Most participants here thought of soccer and thus interacted with a ball (or other roundish object if no ball was available) to query the status. One participant arranged three objects in a row to query Formula One rankings. When not referring to a specific sport, participants often just tapped the phone, assuming this would also show game scores (similar to message status in task 4). Some also used notebooks, associating those with a general information lookup action.

9. Auction Status
There was little agreement in this task and participants used a diverse set of interactions. Some made connections to physical auctions, e.g., mimicking use of a gavel. Several times an object (often the camera) was picked and determined to be a stand-in for the auction. Often participants pointed out this task falls under a generic "query status" category and reused tap-on-phone gestures like in task 4.

10. Mute Phone
Almost all participants flipped the phone and placed it screen down for this task. Some also used variations of a shush gesture or placed objects on the phone to cover it.

Discussion
Looking at the interactions picked by participants, we see a strong preference for some (e.g., flipping the phone) and less consensus for others. Overall, we expected participants to make more use of available objects. Instead, participants often used gestures, frequently near or on specific objects, and placed objects in dedicated zones. We speculate this might be due to unfamiliarity with this kind of interaction and *legacy bias* [31]. Correspondingly, phone flipping might have been frequently used because it is already available in some phones for silencing an incoming call. However, we were impressed by the diverse set of associations participants were able to make. Ranging from the very abstract (three paper clips in a row ⇒ Formula One ranking) to the very concrete (writing "ebay" with a finger on the table ⇒ check auction status).

While we told participants to assume context awareness in the system, we still did not expect how much many participants relied on this. For tasks that can be grouped under *check status*, participants very often just looked for trigger interactions and expected the system to show all their desired information. It would be worthwhile to further investigate how we can design systems with more adaptive notification mechanisms that take those expectations into account.

CONCLUSION
In this paper we have looked at around-device devices, a future class of interactors for depth sensing mobiles. We have shown how such devices have beneficial properties with respect to (1) affordance, (2) casual interactions, and (3) interaction space. Furthermore, we conducted a ground truth investigation into what objects would be available for the kind of interaction presented here. We hence gained a quantitative insight into what objects designers could assume to be most likely available. Furthermore, we conducted a study to determine which of those objects users would actually use for a range of tasks and three different settings.

Around-device devices enable users to imbue objects around them with rich interaction capabilities. With many objects sufficiently described by geometric primitives, this also allows for interaction in settings with light occlusion. Mobile phones, our everyday companion device, can be the sensing center for those interactions. This ensures a sense of control and personalization hard to achieve with instrumented rooms.

FUTURE WORK
Small size depth sensing is not yet universally available, however, we expect it to be in the near future. Once available, actual mobile devices with around the device depth sensing can be built. While we investigated which objects are available to these kind of devices, and which ones participants would pick in a lab study, future prototypes with integrated depth sensing will allow in-the field studies of how people actually use such a system under in-the-wild conditions.

We have not investigated the combination of around-device input with around-device output. Especially the combination of mobile depth sensing with mobile projection would enable new interaction possibilities. Around-device devices are also a good fit for experiments in combination with more subtle output possibilities (e.g., ambient indicators in phones [34]).

ACKNOWLEDGEMENTS
Thanks to Roderick Murray-Smith for very helpful feedback.

REFERENCES
1. Avrahami, D., Wobbrock, J. O., and Izadi, S. Portico: Tangible Interaction on and Around a Tablet. *Proc. UIST '11*, 347–356.
2. Baudel, T., and Beaudouin-Lafon, M. Charade: Remote Control of Objects Using Free-Hand Gestures. *Communications of the ACM*, 36(7), July 1993: 28–35.
3. Butler, A., Izadi, S., and Hodges, S. SideSight: Multi-"Touch" Interaction Around Small Devices. *Proc. UIST '08*, 201–204.
4. Carvey, A., Gouldstone, J., Vedurumudi, P., Whiton, A., and Ishii, H. Rubber Shark as User Interface. *Proc. CHI EA '06*, 634–639.
5. Cassinelli, A., Perrin, S., and Ishikawa, M. Smart Laser-Scanner for 3D Human-Machine Interface. *Proc. CHI EA '05*, 1138–1139.
6. Cheng, K.-Y., Liang, R.-H., Chen, B.-Y., Laing, R.-H., and Kuo, S.-Y. iCon: Utilizing Everyday Objects as Additional , Auxiliary and Instant Tabletop Controllers. *Proc. CHI '10*, 1155–1164.
7. Choi, S., Han, J., Kim, S., Heo, S., and Lee, G. ThickPad: A Hover-Tracking Touchpad for a Laptop. *Proc. UIST '11*, 15–16.
8. Cohn, G., Morris, D., Patel, S., and Tan, D. Humantenna: Using the Body as an Antenna for Real-Time Whole-Body Interaction. *Proc. CHI '12*, 1901–1910.

9. Corsten, C., Wacharamanotham, C., and Borchers, J. Fillables: Everyday Vessels As Tangible Controllers with Adjustable Haptics. *Proc. CHI EA '13*, 2129–2138.
10. Corsten, C., Avellino, I., Möllers, M., and Borchers, J. Instant User Interfaces: Repurposing Everyday Objects as Input Devices. *Proc. ITS '13*, 71–80.
11. Grosse-Puppendahl, T., Braun, A., Kamieth, F., and Kuijper, A. Swiss-Cheese Extended: An Object Recognition Method for Ubiquitous Interfaces based on Capacitive Proximity Sensing. *Proc. CHI '13*, 1401–1410.
12. Gupta, S., Morris, D., Patel, S., and Tan, D. SoundWave: Using the Doppler Effect to Sense Gestures. *Proc. CHI '12*, 1911–1914.
13. Gustafson, S., Baudisch, P., Gutwin, C., and Irani, P. Wedge: Clutter-Free Visualization of Off-Screen Locations. *Proc. CHI '08*, 787–796.
14. Harrison, C., and Hudson, S. E. Lightweight Material Detection for Placement-aware Mobile Computing. *Proc. UIST '08*, 279–282.
15. Harrison, C., and Hudson, S. E. Abracadabra: Wireless, High-Precision, and Unpowered Finger Input for Very Small Mobile Devices. *Proc. UIST '09*, 121–124.
16. Hasan, K., Ahlström, D., and Irani, P. AD-Binning: Leveraging Around-Device Space for Storing , Browsing and Retrieving Mobile Device Content. *Proc. CHI '13*, 899–908.
17. Henderson, S. J., and Feiner, S. Opportunistic Controls: Leveraging Natural Affordances as Tangible User Interfaces for Augmented Reality. *Proc. VRST '08*, 211–218.
18. Hinckley, K., Pausch, R., Goble, J. C., and Kassell, N. F. Passive Real-world Interface Props for Neurosurgical Visualization. *Proc. CHI '94*, 452–458.
19. Holman, D., and Benko, H. SketchSpace: Designing Interactive Behaviors with Passive Materials. *Proc. CHI EA '11*, 1987–1992.
20. Hwang, S., Ahn, M., and Wohn, K.-y. MagGetz: Customizable Passive Tangible Controllers on and Around Conventional Mobile Devices. *Proc. UIST '13*, 411–416.
21. Hwang, S., Bianchi, A., Ahn, M., and Wohn, K. MagPen: Magnetically Driven Pen Interaction On and Around Conventional Smartphones. *Proc. MobileHCI '13*, 412–415.
22. Ishii, H., and Ullmer, B. Tangible Bits: Towards Seamless Interfaces between People, Bits and Atoms. *Proc. CHI '97*, 234–241.
23. Kane, S. K., Avrahami, D., Wobbrock, J. O., Harrison, B., Rea, A. D., Philipose, M., and LaMarca, A. Bonfire: A Nomadic System for Hybrid Laptop-Tabletop Interaction. *Proc. UIST '09*, 129–138.
24. Ketabdar, H., Roshandel, M., and Yüksel, K. A. Towards Using Embedded Magnetic Field Sensor for Around Mobile Device 3D Interaction. *Proc. MobileHCI '10*, 153–156.
25. Kim, D., Hilliges, O., Izadi, S., Butler, A. D., Chen, J., Oikonomidis, I., and Olivier, P. Digits: Freehand 3D Interactions Anywhere Using a Wrist-Worn Gloveless Sensor. *Proc. UIST '12*, 167–176.
26. Kratz, S., and Rohs, M. HoverFlow: Expanding the Design Space of Around-Device Interaction. *Proc. MobileHCI '09*, 4:1–4:8.
27. Le Goc, M., Taylor, S., Izadi, S., and Keskin, C. A Low-cost Transparent Electric Field Sensor for 3D Interaction on Mobile Devices. *Proc. CHI '14*, 3167–3170.
28. Li, F. C. Y., Dearman, D., and Truong, K. N. Virtual Shelves: Interactions with Orientation Aware Devices. *Proc. UIST '09*, 125–128.
29. Lucero, A., Holopainen, J., and Jokela, T. Pass-Them-Around: Collaborative Use of Mobile Phones for Photo Sharing. *Proc. CHI '11*, 1787–1796.
30. Mistry, P., and Maes, P. Mouseless: A Computer Mouse as Small as Invisible. *Proc. CHI EA '11*, 1099–1104.
31. Morris, M. R., Danielescu, A., Drucker, S., Fisher, D., Lee, B., Schraefel, C., and Wobbrock, J. O. Reducing Legacy Bias in Gesture Elicitation Studies. *interactions*, 21(3), May 2014: 40–45.
32. Nanayakkara, S., Shilkrot, R., Yeo, K. P., and Maes, P. EyeRing: A Finger-Worn Input Device for Seamless Interactions with our Surroundings. *Proc. AH '13*, 13–20.
33. Pohl, H., and Murray-Smith, R. Focused and Casual Interactions: Allowing Users to Vary Their Level of Engagement. *Proc. CHI '13*, 2223–2232.
34. Qin, Q., Rohs, M., and Kratz, S. Dynamic Ambient Lighting for Mobile Devices. *Proc. UIST '11*, 51–52.
35. Saponas, T. S., Tan, D. S., Morris, D., Balakrishnan, R., Turner, J., and Landay, J. a. Enabling Always-available Input with Muscle-computer Interfaces. *Proc. UIST '09*, 167–176.
36. Sodhi, R. S., Jones, B. R., Forsyth, D., Bailey, B. P., and Maciocci, G. BeThere: 3D Mobile Collaboration with Spatial Input. *Proc. CHI '13*, 179–188.
37. Steins, C., Gustafson, S., Holz, C., and Baudisch, P. Imaginary Devices: Gesture-Based Interaction Mimicking Traditional Input Devices. *Proc. MobileHCI '13*, 123–126.
38. Takeoka, Y., Miyaki, T., and Rekimoto, J. Z-touch: An Infrastructure for 3D Gesture Interaction in the Proximity of Tabletop Surfaces. *Proc. ITS '10*, 91–94.
39. Terajima, K., Komuro, T., and Ishikawa, M. Fast Finger Tracking System for In-Air Typing Interface. *Proc. CHI EA '09*, 3739–3744.
40. Wang, R. Y., and Popović, J. Real-time Hand-tracking with a Color Glove. *ACM Transactions on Graphics*, 28(3), July 2009: 63:1–63:8.
41. Wilson, A. D. PlayAnywhere: A Compact Interactive Tabletop Projection-Vision System. *Proc. UIST '05*, 83–92.
42. Wobbrock, J. O., Morris, M. R., and Wilson, A. D. User-defined Gestures for Surface Computing. *Proc. CHI '09*, 1083–1092.
43. Yang, X.-d., Hasan, K., Bruce, N., and Irani, P. Surround-See: Enabling Peripheral Vision on Smartphones during Active Use. *Proc. UIST '13*, 291–300.
44. Zhang, Z., Wu, Y., Shan, Y., and Shafer, S. Visual Panel: Virtual Mouse, Keyboard and 3D Controller with an Ordinary Piece of Paper. *Proc. PUI '01*, 1–8.

Contextual Experience Sampling of Mobile Application Micro-Usage

Denzil Ferreira, Jorge Goncalves, Vassilis Kostakos
Dep. Computer Science and Engineering
University of Oulu
Oulu, Finland
{denzil.ferreira; jgoncalv; vassilis}@ee.oulu.fi

Louise Barkhuus
Stockholm University
Forum 100
Stockholm, Sweden
barkhuus@dsv.su.se

Anind K. Dey
Human-Computer Interaction Institute
Carnegie Mellon University
Pittsburgh, USA
anind@cs.cmu.edu

ABSTRACT
Research suggests smartphone users face "application overload", but literature lacks an in-depth investigation of how users manage their time on smartphones. In a 3-week study we collected smartphone application usage patterns from 21 participants to study how they manage their time interacting with the device. We identified events we term *application micro-usage*: brief bursts of interaction with applications. While this practice has been reported before, it has not been investigated in terms of the context in which it occurs (*e.g.*, location, time, trigger and social context). In a 2-week follow-up study with 15 participants, we captured participants' context while micro-using, with a mobile experience sampling method (ESM) and weekly interviews. Our results show that about approximately 40% of application launches last less than 15 seconds and happen most frequently when the user is at home and alone. We further discuss the context, taxonomy and implications of application micro-usage in our field. We conclude with a brief reflection on the relevance of short-term interaction observations for other domains beyond mobile phones.

Author Keywords
Context-Awareness; Mobile Automated Logging; Design Implications.

ACM Classification Keywords
H5.m. Information interfaces and presentation (e.g., HCI): Miscellaneous.

INTRODUCTION
Mobile phones have evolved from simple communication devices into multifunctional information and communication devices [4]. Today, application stores allow for the ad-hoc installation of applications, extending and customizing mobile phones' functionality with games, navigation, social networking, news and music among others [13]. With the increase in functionality and diversity of use, applications on mobile phones are accessed frequently: constantly checking for updates on social networks and email has become a part of our daily routine. As continuous updates from several sources can be disruptive, mobile operating systems offer several techniques to keep the user updated without disturbing their mobile usage flow and mitigating information overload [24]. For example, Android and iOS use background notifications to alert the user of application events and messages. Android also provides application status widgets for glanceable information as a secondary interface.

Yan *et al.* [29] reported that a lot of mobile device usage is brief and competes for human attention with the real world. They found that 50% of mobile phone engagement (the time period between the user unlocking and relocking the device) lasts less than 30 seconds. With more granularity, here we explore whether individual mobile applications are also used for short periods of time, from application launch to exit (*i.e.*, application session). We want to uncover the taxonomy of the applications that encourage brief bursts of usage (henceforth *micro-usage*) and the context in which micro-usage is more likely to take place. We approach mobile phone usage as a particular manifestation of HCI in daily life [2].

Our key contributions then, lie not within prescribing design guidelines for the seamless integration of technologies into daily life, but instead by describing daily life with mobile technologies as a fragmented type of interaction. By exploring the situations around this practice and uncovering possible reasons why some applications are used so briefly, we aim to contribute to a broader understanding of mobile phone usage practices that in turn will inform the design of mobile applications and mobile technologies in the future.

RELATED WORK
The existence of brief bursts of application usage on smartphones has been reported in previous literature, but typically as a secondary or inadvertent finding. Falaki *et al.*'s [12] study on diversity in smartphone battery usage reported finding short-term application usage (10-250 seconds) among their participants. Similarly, Böhmer *et al.*'s [4] large-scale study on mobile application usage revealed that mobile phone owners use their device for an average of 59 minutes daily, with the average application session lasting 72 seconds.

MobileHCI '14, September 23 - 26 2014, Toronto, ON, Canada
Copyright 2014 ACM 978-1-4503-3004-6/14/09…$15.00.
http://dx.doi.org/10.1145/2628363.2628367

Considering routine and focusing on mobile phone users' habits, Oulasvirta *et al.* [24] suggest that mobile phones are "habit-forming" devices. Particularly closely related to our work is the "checking habit: brief, repetitive inspection of dynamic content quickly accessible on the device." This habit was found to comprise a large part of mobile phone usage. We believe that the checking habit is one of the behavioral characteristics that leads to mobile application micro-usage, and that it is manifested as short bursts of interaction with applications.

Interestingly, micro-use of applications is not exclusively mobile; multitasking and the management of multiple tasks occur on desktop computers as well [8, 15]. These studies found that desktop users were focused on goals but within these goals they embedded a set of secondary goals that were completed through multitasking. This observation led to the technical advances within multitasking and the options that almost all multipurpose technical devices support: being able to seamlessly switch from one application (and often from one task) to another.

Multitasking is not without consequences for use practices and users' overall wellbeing. For example, Mark *et al.* [21] reported that while workers compensate for interruptions to their work, these interruptions also mean users experience "a higher workload, more stress, higher frustration, more time pressure, and effort." Much of this literature, however, focuses on external interruption, but many interruptions within workflows are in fact "self-inflicted" [16], which multitasking also alludes to.

Here we argue that multitasking is an inherent characteristic of technology use practices and that micro-usage is yet another consequence of our mobile multitasking devices being available throughout the day. But where desktop use often takes place over longer stretches of time (hours, often full work days), mobile phone use is intermittent. So albeit related, we seek to extend the work on interruptions and multitasking to mobile phone use. Here we address micro-usage of mobile phone applications by exploring its characteristics and discussing implications of this practice.

We conducted two field studies to explore micro-usage. Study 1 sought to understand how users spend time interacting with their mobile phones. Subsequently, we wanted to unobtrusively gain enough understanding in order to design and build a mobile Experience Sampling Method (ESM) tool to collect *in situ* real-time qualitative data on application micro-usage while minimizing user burden and annoyance. In Study 2 we deployed the tool on participants' phones to understand the situational factors (*e.g.*, place, with whom) and motivations for mobile application micro-usage. We recruited participants by affixing posters, advertising on a local mailing list and through Facebook. We took extra care in selecting participants with diverse backgrounds as to reduce the risk of selection bias and for a more reliable representation of a wider population.

STUDY 1: MOBILE APPLICATION USAGE

We recruited 21 participants (17 male, 4 female), aged between 22 and 40, with a range of technical skills and professions, and owning an Android mobile phone (Android 2.3+). The study lasted for 3 weeks and participants were compensated with two movie tickets. We conducted a semi-structured interview prior to the study to collect their perception of their application usage behavior.

We designed a logging tool using AWARE [1], deployed on participants' own devices as a background application. Both the Android operating system and AWARE are event-driven so collecting data did not have a noticeable impact on device usability or battery usage. Our logging tool collected:

- *Application session*: when, for how long and which applications were active and visible to the user.
- *Screen usage*: current screen status (on/off) and for how long it was on/off.

The application session listens to events about changes in which applications are active, provided by the Accessibility Services APIs, thus capturing interaction with the applications. The screen usage captures every time the users interact with the mobile phone, by listening to screen on/off events sent by the operating system.

Participants' Perceptions of Mobile Application Usage

In our first interview before deploying the logging tool, we discussed with participants which applications they use the most, and when during the day and week. Not surprising, all participants used their mobile phones for *more* than just calls and messages, mentioning using email, navigation (*e.g.*, Google Maps), browser, games and social applications (*e.g.*, Facebook) *intermittently* throughout the day. More interestingly, some revealed following some *routine*: they would use mobile applications more often *indoors* than outdoors, more *during the day* than evening. However, the use of mobile applications "would depend" on *where* and *with whom* they were at a *given time*.

Elusive Nature of Micro-Usage

Our interviews emphasized the challenge in collecting reliable data on application micro-usage. Particularly, they highlight the need to *capture micro-usage as it happens*, to understand the context in which it occurs. Our first step towards gaining this understanding was to establish an empirical time frame for exploring micro-usage. This is a temporal threshold, below which we choose to flag an application session as micro-usage, based on our data analysis. An *application session* begins when an application is launched, and ends *when the screen is turned off* or the user *exits the application*. Figure 1 shows a probability distribution function of application usage in Study 1. Specifically it shows the duration of sessions for "All apps" across all participants, in relationship with the top-10 most used applications. We used Jenks optimization method [18] to determine the best arrangement of our data values into two clusters. We found a natural break in the data at approximately the 15-second mark indicated with the dashed vertical line, dividing the application sessions' probability into two categories: *micro-used* below the 15 seconds time frame (41.5% cumulative probability) and not micro-used when above (58.5%).

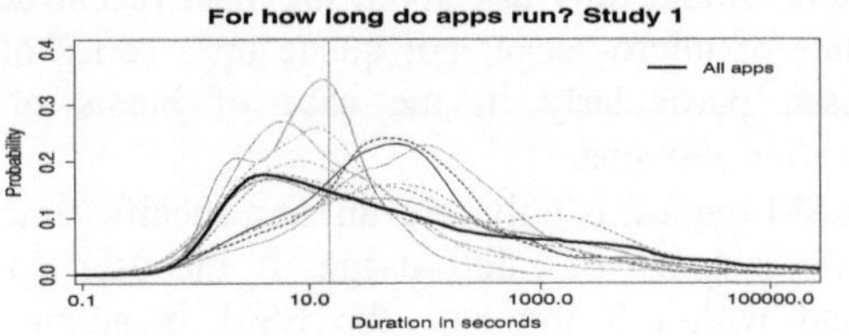

Figure 1: Probability of application session length in Study 1, across all users, regarding the top-10 applications (15-second threshold for micro-usage - dashed vertical line).

Yan *et al.* [29] had a similar number of participants (25) as our Study 1, and their application analysis of these participants reported that 50% of application usage is under 30 seconds and 90% under 4 minutes. Our results were 61% and 78%, respectively. Böhmer *et al.* [4] with a larger sample further shortens the application sessions: 49.9% of all recorded application sessions were *under* 5 seconds, while the average application session lasted about 70 seconds.

To contextualize *micro-usage* behavior in terms of mobile application usage, we conducted a follow-up interview. Participants indicated that checking notifications for email or other notifications took them less than "a minute". They noted that if the notifications were not interesting or if the emails were not urgent, they would quickly dismiss the application. This analysis led us to adopt *15 seconds as an upper threshold to further investigate micro-usage*: it is brief, yet accounts for 41.5% of the application sessions we observed for our participants in Study 1.

Note that 15 seconds is not a definite threshold but an approximate boundary within which we decided to explore micro-usage behavior. Therefore, we are interested in investigating application usage that lasts *up to* 15 seconds, including for example application sessions that last just 1, 5 or 10 seconds.

Usage or Micro-Usage

The most frequently used applications across all users in Study 1 were Facebook, Google Mail and the browser. More interestingly, we note that *micro-usage does not occur equally* with all the applications (*e.g.*, Facebook (22.4%); Google Mail (52.0%) micro-used), in Figure 2.

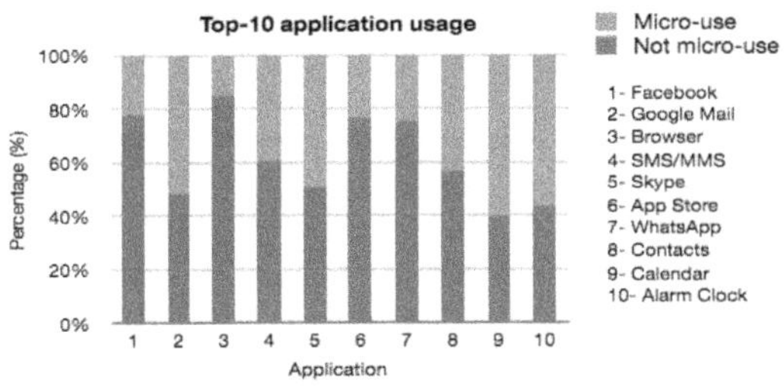

Figure 2: The 10 most frequently used applications in Study 1.

The fact that all applications may at some point be micro-used is not surprising because mobile phones are increasingly used to fill an *undetermined* amount of time. Various applications were used between scheduled activities such as traveling from work to home, "killing time" on games [10] or very briefly while waiting for the elevator or for someone.

Summary of results from Study 1

Our results indicate a cumulative probability of 41.5% of application micro-usage across all participants and applications. However, how much micro-usage occurs *depends on the application*; of the most frequently used applications, some were micro-used as low as 15% (*e.g.*, Browser) while others were as high as 60% (*e.g.*, Calendar) (see Figure 2). As the participants could use *any application* at any given *time* and at any given *location*, our next step was to gain an understanding of the situations in which application micro-usage occurs.

Since we are most interested in instances when our participants interact with their devices for brief periods of time, our critical requirement was to develop a reliable data-collection mechanism that allowed participants to respond quickly. The interview feedback regarding application usage helped inform our data collection strategy for the follow-up study and deciding what questions to ask. From our initial interviews on Study 1, participants revealed that using mobile applications "would depend" on *where* and *with whom* they were at a *given time*. This motivated us to include *location* and *social* context into our micro-usage probe. We discuss this next.

STUDY 2: UNDERSTANDING MICRO-USAGE

We conducted a 2-week follow-up study with a *different* set of 15 participants (gender: 9 male, 6 female; age: 23-50), with varied professions and technical skills, to understand the context of use and the intentions of the user when micro-usage takes place. Previous studies have used diaries [6, 24, 28] and mobile ESM [7, 14] to capture qualitative data on mobile phone usage. Micro-usage is extremely brief and frequent, and thus any reliance on recall methods is likely to be subject to response bias or unreliable recall. Asking participants to reflect on a brief event that happened a few hours or days in the past is likely to result in unreliable data. Therefore, we used mobile ESM to capture *intermittent* micro-usage as it occurs on the device, wherever the user is.

We extended Study 1's software to display a short ESM questionnaire:

- *Micro-Usage ESM dialog*: automatically captured *what* application was micro-used and *when*; asked the user *what* triggered the micro-usage; *where* was the user; and *who* was with the user.

We identified instances of micro-usage by measuring the duration of application sessions in runtime. If an application session lasted *less than* 15 seconds, a micro-usage ESM dialog was scheduled (See Mobile ESM Scheduling section for details).

Mobile ESM Design

The software adopts a 3-step approach in the design of the ESM task for reporting on different context categories for micro-usage. Dey *et al.*'s [10] context categories were used to aggregate the questions we asked (*i.e.*, *Location* (where), *Identity* (who), *Activity* (what), *Time* (when)), and the *Trigger* (why) for the particular micro-usage instance. More importantly, we explicitly chose to minimize the amount of free-text typing required of participants, to minimize their burden (Figure 3). We used the results from our Study 1 interviews to specify the answers to questions, as follows:

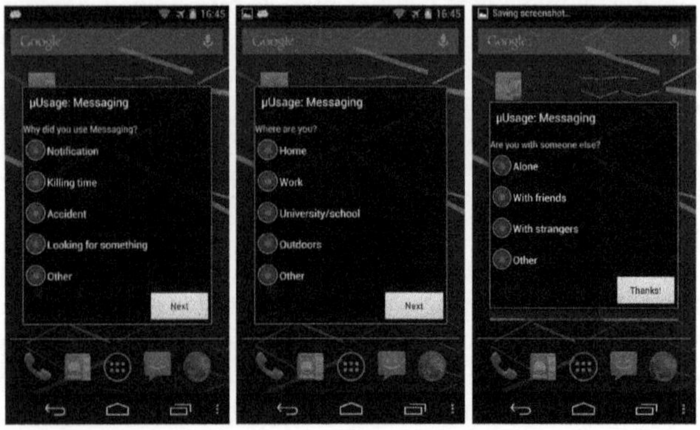

a) b) c)

Figure 3: Mobile ESM shown when micro-usage is detected.

- Step 1 (Figure 3a) *Activity*, *Time* and *Trigger* contexts: A group of radio-buttons displayed: "Notification"; "Killing time"; "Accident"; "Looking for something"; and "Other." These categories reflect Study 1 participants' feedback on perceived mobile phone application usage. "Killing time" refers to instances in which participants used the phone as an entertainment device. "Looking for something" refers to when the participants used the devices to search for information, such as navigation instructions or the Internet, and "Notifications" to instances when the device indicates new information is available (*e.g.*, new email has arrived). Lastly, we included "Accident" for cases where participants launched an application by mistake, and "Other" for other reasons we could not foresee but still wished to capture. The "Other" option would create a modal textbox above the first question, asking the user to be more specific. The current time and application name is automatically captured by the ESMs.
- Step 2 (Figure 3b) *Location* context: A group of radio-buttons displayed: "Home"; "Work"; "University/ School"; "Outdoors"; and "Other." The participants provided the most common locations in which they used mobile phone applications. We clustered the locations into categories that summarize participants' answers.
- Step 3 (Figure 3c) *Identity* context: A group of radio-buttons displayed: "Alone"; "With friends"; "With strangers"; and "Other." Once again, we included "Other" to capture other social contexts.

Further design decisions pertain to the quality of the data:

- The tool should only ask about the *most recent* detected instance of micro-usage, not queue up a series of ESM requests, particularly in the case of bursts of short application sessions.
- The ESM request is only relevant at a specific time, for a specific instance of micro-usage. If the user does not respond within 3 minutes, the ESM is automatically dismissed.
- The user should be able to dismiss an ESM request, by explicitly closing the ESM questionnaire (*e.g.*, pressing the "Back" or the "Home" button on Android devices).
- If the user micro-used an application but immediately turned the screen off, the ESM tool would *vibrate* the mobile phone to prompt the user to answer the ESM.
- The ESM questions did not have default answers to reduce response bias.

Mobile ESM Scheduling

An important issue to consider is the frequency of issuing ESMs. In their work, Consolvo & Walker used randomly triggered ESMs spaced equally during the day [7]. They suggest issuing up to 10 ESMs per day to each participant to keep participant burden manageable. They also advise that proper scheduling requires a flexible and adaptive approach to issuing ESMs, otherwise there is a high risk of missing important events.

We conducted a simulation using Study 1's data and found that if we issued an ESM every time micro-usage took place, participants would have to complete more than 20 ESMs per day, posing a high burden on participants in Study 2. As a compromise, we set a cap of 10 daily ESMs as recommended by [7], and the system considered triggering ESMs only if an application was used for 15 seconds or less. To ensure that the maximum of 10 ESMs per day were distributed throughout the day, as opposed to all being issued successively in the morning and none in the evening, we decided to space out the ESMs by introducing a timeout after each time an ESM was answered. We set this timeout to 15 minutes, such that no two ESMs would be issued within 15 minutes of each other. This value was chosen after analyzing how participants in Study 1 locked and unlocked their phone using a cumulative probability function (CDF) on our screen usage data. Specifically, we looked at how long the screen remains off once it has been turned off (Figure 4).

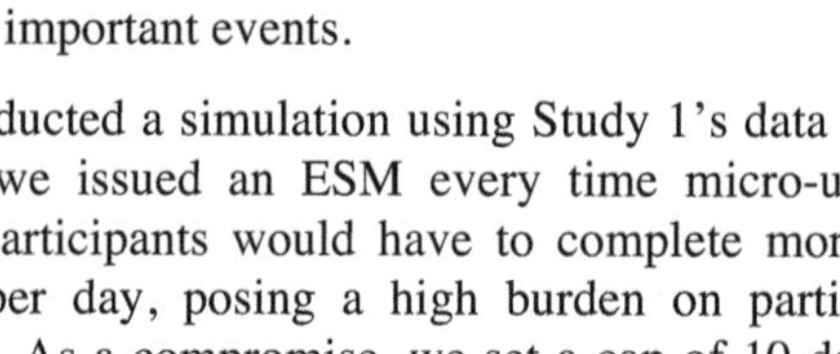

Figure 4: Cumulative probability of screen off duration.

If the screen is on, it is very likely the user is using the mobile phone. Therefore, it makes sense to consider the instances of time when the screen is off to infer periods of inactivity from the user. Using the Jenks optimization [18] we identified a natural break in the data at the 1000-second mark (vertical line), which is approximately 15 minutes, and simulation using Study 1's data confirmed that the cap of 10 ESMs per day was not crossed. This means that participants were relatively more likely to turn their screen on after 15 minutes of inactivity, and therefore this posed as a good threshold for issuing a new ESM if micro-usage occurred.

Recording Micro-usage

Our examination of the results from Study 2 confirmed that the micro-usage followed a similar pattern to Study 1, despite the different set of participants. We analyzed our data to identify any potential links between demographics (*e.g.*, age, gender, profession) and micro-usage: we found no significant effect of age (χ^2=0.78, df=2, p=0.677) or gender (χ^2=0.18, df=1, p=0.672) on micro-usage frequency, for each study independently (Table 1).

Study 1					Study 2				
#	Gender	Age	Profession	Micro-usage (%)	#	Gender	Age	Profession	Micro-usage (%)
1	male	27	Student	20,66	1	male	34	Researcher	60,15
2	male	30	Unemployed	53,29	2	male	28	Student	18,15
3	male	40	Senior Researcher	56,09	3	male	30	Researcher	44,79
4	male	37	Senior Researcher	66,26	4	female	50	Development Manager	12,80
5	male	34	Researcher	25,09	5	male	32	Student / Waiter	44,40
6	male	29	Researcher	24,23	6	male	49	Project manager	55,5
7	female	28	Secretary	49,79	7	male	27	Designer	25,83
8	female	37	Secretary	64,48	8	male	30	Student	66,00
9	male	26	Networks Researcher	31,68	9	male	37	HW & SW Engineer	25,93
10	male	28	Networks Researcher	59,64	10	female	23	Student	52,50
11	male	27	Networks Researcher	40,84	11	female	34	Biologist	48,36
12	male	25	Student	19,66	12	male	27	Student	65,63
13	male	24	Civil Engineer	40,64	13	female	31	Chemist	22,45
14	female	25	Accountant	35,06	14	female	28	Student	40,23
15	male	23	Student	20,61	15	female	42	Researcher	27,1
16	male	29	Student	46,58					
17	female	22	Biology Researcher	42,89					
18	male	32	Robotics Researcher	26,07					
19	male	36	Researcher	65,25					
20	male	30	Researcher	27,36					
21	male	29	Researcher	55,32					

Table 1: Participants' demographic information for both studies. Highlighted in grey are the selected participants for interview in Study 2.

Similarly to Study 1, the cumulative probability of micro-usage for all application instances across all participants is 36% at the 15-second threshold, and we found that certain applications exhibit a higher likelihood of micro-usage than others. Application micro-use also varied between participants, with an average of 41.5% (min=19.7%; max=66.3%; SD=16.1%).

Our mobile ESM was able to capture micro-usage reliably throughout the day (with a maximum limit of 10 ESM per day, per participant)(Figure 5). In total, we detected 14,229 micro-use instances. The logging tool scheduled 762 ESMs questionnaires and recorded 642 complete ESM responses over the 14 days from our 15 participants. We did not consider incomplete, dismissed and expired ESMs in our data analysis. 642 ESM responses correspond to an average of 3 complete ESM answers per participant, per day, and a 76% response rate.

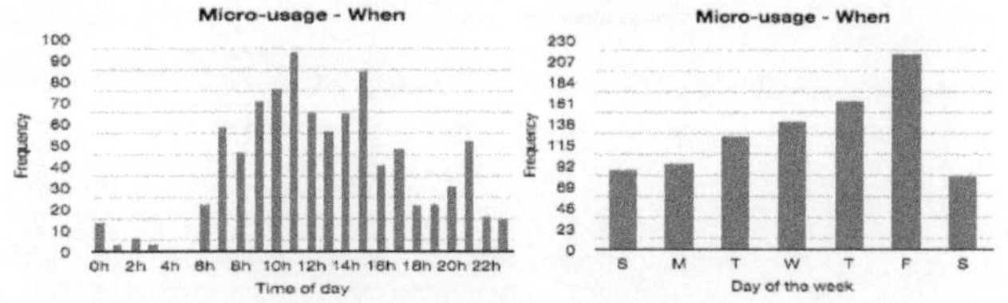

Figure 5: Distribution of time context for micro-usage.

Micro-Usage Context

The most micro-used application categories in Study 2 were Email (40%), instant messaging (*i.e.*, Google Talk, Skype, WhatsApp) (21%) and text messaging (16%)(Figure 6, top left).

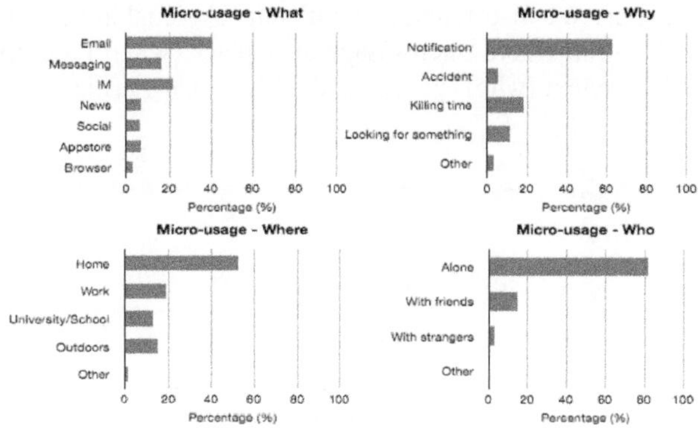

Figure 6: Micro-usage incidence depending on different contexts.

The most frequent triggers for micro-usage were notifications (62%), "Killing time" (18%) and "Looking for something" (11%). Participants micro-used applications by accident 6% of the time. When denoting the "Other" category, 2 participants indicated using their mobile phone for making a translation and writing a message (3%)(Figure 6, top right).

We did not capture location automatically (*e.g.*, using GPS or network triangulation) with our software, to minimize power consumption on the mobile phone. Instead, we asked participants to indicate a coarse-grained category of location. Mobile phones spend more time at home than anywhere else, including time during the night [25], and not surprisingly, our results indicate that micro-usage happens more at home than in other locations (53% *vs.* 47%, respectively)(Figure 6, bottom left). Similar to [11], our participants reported that, when at home, they quickly check their devices for new emails, calls, or messages, regardless of notifications. The results show that micro-usage is most likely to take place when the user is alone (82%). We also found that it happens least often amongst strangers (Figure 6, bottom right).

A chi-squared analysis showed that there was a significant relationship between the trigger of micro-usage (why) and the location where this happened (where) (χ^2=107.8, df=16, p<0.001)(Figure 7).

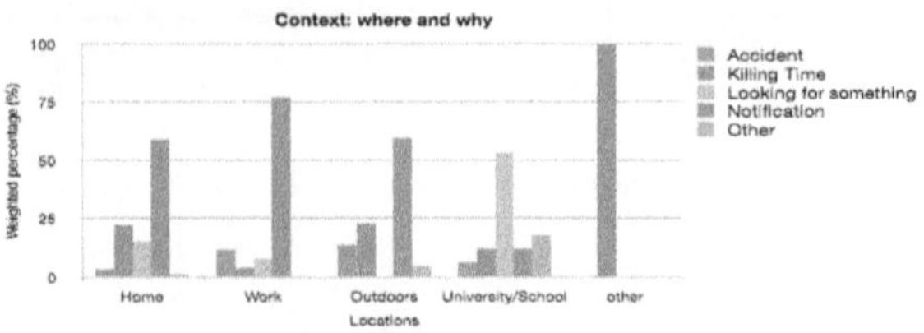

Figure 7: Weighted percentages of micro-usage context by trigger and location context.

Specifically, we found that *system-initiated* micro-usage takes place at home, work or outdoors, mostly due to notifications, whereas *user-initiated* micro-usage happens more frequently at the university, school and other locations. We also found a significant relationship between the location where micro-usage took place (where) and the social context (who) (χ^2=114.2, df=12, p<0.001) (Figure 8).

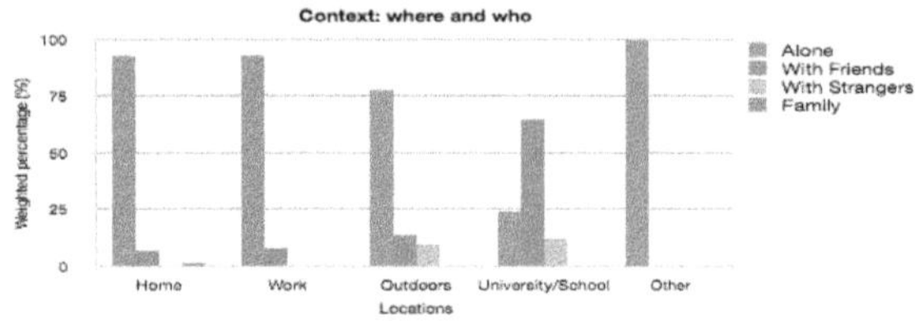

Figure 8: Weighted percentages of micro-usage context by location and social context.

Despite micro-use happening more often at home (Figure 6, bottom left), Figure 8 suggests that application micro-use happens in other locations too, especially when the user is alone. Our participants often reported using their devices to "spend time" or reach out to others, while commuting and at random locations. Less frequently however, micro-use happens too with friends and co-workers. Participants reported showcasing emails, pictures and game high-scores on the phone to each other. We also found a significant relationship between the triggers for micro-usage (why) and the social context (who) (χ^2=30.9, df=12, p=0.002) (Figure 9).

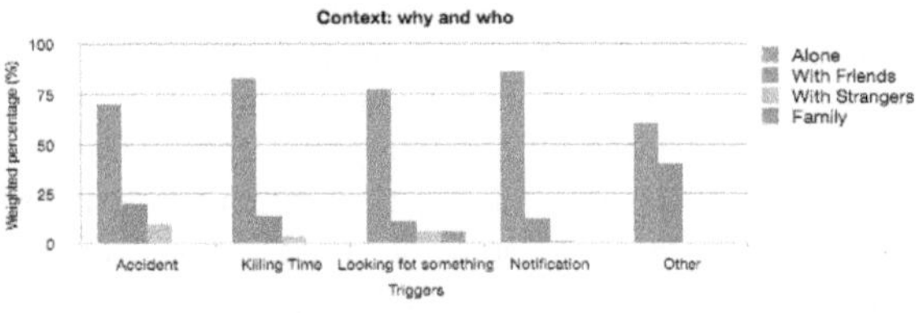

Figure 9: Weighted percentages of micro-usage context by trigger and social context.

Figure 9 further iterates that *user-initiated* micro-use is often to "kill time", while *system-initiated* micro-use is triggered by a notification, especially if the user is alone.

"Other" Context

Please note that the ESM allowed users to input text when an appropriate choice was not provided. We have combined this input text into an "Other" category.) As seen in Figure 6, there were few instances where text input was used. We can only hypothesize about whether our participants purposefully avoided entering time-consuming answers [7], or whether the provided answer-choices were sufficient to capture their micro-usage context. However, as the number of "other" instances is so small, it is *not* statistically significant context, and has not been included in our discussion and conclusions.

Participant Views on Micro-Usage

At the end of Study 2, we interviewed 9 of our Study 2 participants, all those who had exhibited above 40% (min=40.2%; max=66.0%; mean=53.1%; SD=9.4%) of application micro-usage (Table 1 – highlighted in grey). In other words, these participants closed an application within 15 seconds of launching it for at least 4 out of 10 times they used it.

Since we had purposely omitted the true nature of our study to our participants, as an application usage study, we began by introducing micro-usage. Participants were presented with a data analysis on their micro-usage behavior (as in Figure 2). We started the discussion with whether they were aware of such behavior and if they had any thoughts about it. All participants reported that they *never* recognized their micro-usage behavior before. We further inquired about their thoughts on micro-usage happening most often when they are alone, except when with friends at University/School. All participants acknowledged that they often used their mobile phone when alone, as the device is theirs.

"Mostly alone, yes. It is my phone. People check for something, new email, Facebook, then they don't find anything and then they jump to another application." – P5

Also using their device while with others is regarded as normal, especially when the device is used for *information retrieval.*

"The world changed... people before got together and discussed and now they use their phones, on the table or in front of them all the time. Maybe to text or just to show something to others..." – P6

Participants attributed their micro-usage to *system-initiated* triggers (*i.e.,* notifications) or *user-initiated* (*i.e.,* opening an application by mistake, quickly checking email for something new or the calendar, or spending time). In the majority of cases however, participants believed that micro-usage happened simply because *15 seconds was enough* for them to get the information they required.

"I use the phone to control what I need to do and I check it regularly. Also when waiting for my kids, I use my phone to browse the web and play a game or video..." – P8

Interestingly, 4 out of the 9 participants noted that they frequently and swiftly checked specific applications throughout the day, most often those social in nature (*e.g.,* Facebook, Google+, Twitter or email).

"Google+... I don't contribute there much. I go browse what the notification was and close it. I use Facebook more." – P8

We questioned if notifications were the reason why they used an application and what they thought about them.

Participants had split opinions regarding notifications, with 5 out of the 9 participants considering them as an essential or important feature, while others saw notifications as a nuisance.

"I use it [Facebook] on Chrome. I don't like the application because it keeps buzzing" – P5

"I check the notification bar [...] I check the email, calendar, and messages. I don't spend time there." – P8

Participants did not associate notifications with the reason for using a particular application, but regarded it as a part of an application, *i.e.*, participants *expect* notifications from specific applications, such as a notification from a message, or an update in Facebook.

"I send a text there [Google Talk] and they reply when they can. It's not urgent but it's like saying Hi!" – P8

Surprisingly, 2 participants associated not having notifications as distressing or an indicator of connectivity malfunction.

"They [notifications] should be there. If there is nothing there, I would assume something is wrong with my connection." – P8

We concluded the interview with the participants' thoughts on how they felt about their mobile phone usage in the context of micro-usage. Participants repetitively used "to check" their phones as an explanation for their micro-usage behavior, thus confirming our initial belief that the previously reported "checking habit" [24] is often manifested as micro-usage.

"I can't imagine not being able to check... [...], I can't know what is happening, it's not good..." – P6

ANALYSIS & DISCUSSION

The purpose of this paper is to highlight mobile application micro-usage as an important practice, and to investigate the context in which it occurs in order to suggest why it occurs and to identify what consequences it has. Our work also relates to the more general topic of multitasking and interruptions. Previous investigations of mobile application usage [4, 12, 24, 29] reported that the bulk of our interactions are brief, but have not further investigated the reasons *why* this is the case, *how probable it is* and the *context* in which it manifests.

In Study 1, we captured micro-usage behavior as reliably as possible without intervention as to better study this phenomenon. In Study 2, we intervened with ESMs. Our ESMs did not affect *detecting* the *context* of application micro-usage, allowing us to better understand it.

Micro-Usage Timescale

Our findings indicate that micro-usage is indeed a prevalent practice with mobile phones. In line with previous studies [29], we showed that a lot of application launches are either terminated or dismissed *within* 15 seconds (Figure 1) (cumulative probability of 41.5% and 36%, in Study 1 and 2 respectively). The probability of micro-usage is different between our studies due to different application usage patterns and participant samples.

The heavily skewed distribution in our data encouraged us to consider micro-usage as "individual application use that lasts *up to* 15 seconds" for our micro-usage software and our data analysis. Please note *micro-usage should not be treated as having a rigid time frame of 15 seconds*, but for our participants and study, this threshold provided a lens for investigating micro-usage behavior. An application usage session depends on several performance factors that are challenging to consider beforehand:

- *Device*: time to load the application (*e.g.*, CPU, memory, operating system);
- *Network*: time to load network content (*e.g.*, Facebook, browser);
- *User*: time spent on the keyboard, clicking, reading content.

More importantly, our studies and interviews are evidence that *15 seconds is enough for many uses of an application*, such as checking and dismissing a notification, quickly responding to a message or searching for something in the mobile phone browser. As such, our work provides the first study to specifically study *micro-usage in-situ and in real-time.* The exact figure of 15 seconds is defined based on our collected data, and future studies will likely broaden or narrow it. In our own study, this time frame allowed us to identify micro-usage, characterize it and understand it.

Context of Micro-Usage

Our results from Study 2 provide evidence regarding the context in which micro-usage occurs. The most important question is *why* does micro-usage occur, in other words, what triggers micro-usage. Micro-usage triggers are *system-initiated* for application usage sessions initiated by notifications, otherwise as *user-initiated*, *i.e.*, due to users' natural application usage. It is apparent that a substantial amount of micro-usage was not *user-initiated* but *system-initiated*: participants attributed 62% of micro-usage instances to notifications (Figure 6, top right). This raises a further question regarding micro-usage: is it a 'naturally-occurring' behavior or is it mainly system driven? Since most applications, such as Facebook and email, let the user configure notification alerts, it is notable that the users in these cases had not specifically turned notifications off, and on some level found them useful.

Our interviews provide insight into *user-initiated* micro-use. Mobile phone use has changed and we use them as replacements for watches, cameras, game consoles, just to name a few. Mobile phones are 'companions' in moments of potential 'boredom' and fill in the gaps when waiting or on a bus, for example. By far the most popular place where micro-usage occurred was at "home" (Figure 6, bottom left) and "alone" (Figure 6, bottom right). User-initiated micro-use is *unique* to the user and is *diverse*, as expected. However, a distinct characteristic of our data was that the top-10 most frequently used and micro-used applications, for both studies, were for people's *social connections* (See Figure 2 and Figure 6 - top left).

This finding suggests that applications designed to help us remain connected and "keep in touch" are most likely to be used and also micro-used. "Keeping in touch" is a vital social lifeline, essential to human social, psychological and even physical wellbeing [9]. As one participant expressed about her routine: *"It is pleasant, [...] when I go home, certain things always happen. I eat and then I sit on the sofa, I see what is on the telly and at the same time I check [Facebook]. And during weekend it happens many times, I go there and I check."*

Other previous research [3] has highlighted how smart phone users would 'control' their own use of communication by checking email and other communication on their smart phone and wait to reply until they could get to a larger device such as their laptop. This way *they would only spend minimal time checking if anything was in need of immediate attention* but specifically not reply on the device itself. This resonates well with our participants' micro-use of social applications; they were often used for brief checking.

Yet, these social applications rely on new information and updates (providing or consuming) that are being *pushed* to or *pulled* from the device. It is therefore likely that they are popular because they lend themselves well to micro-usage. Just like a telephone ringing in a home 20 years ago prompted immediate answer by the nearest family member, the notifications may trigger our innate need for social interaction [26].

Furthermore, our participants perceived mobile notifications as an integral part of using a mobile application, especially social applications, and as an indicator of contact; therefore their existence has a reassuring effect on users. Similarly, in the context of desktop application usage [21], responding fast and often to notifications, was perceived not as a nuisance but instead alerts were seen as a useful awareness mechanism.

Considering the participants' description of place where *system-initiated* micro-usage took place, interestingly, few instances took place outdoors (16%) but more than half of the notification-prompted micro-usage took place at home (52%). Although there is a slight bias in our data collection method that could influence the answer (perhaps people are more likely to answer the EMS following micro-use at home, than, for example, outdoors), it indicates that people are more open towards interruptions at home, compared to the university and work where only 4% and 28% of the micro-use was prompted by notifications, respectively.

Applications with micro-usage behavior in mind

Applications are very likely to be used very briefly (41.5% under 15 seconds) but also for substantial durations (58.5% above). Mobile phone screen real estate is limited to displaying one application at a time on almost all phones, and these devices do not truly support multi-tasking in comparison to desktop computers. According to our analysis, *15 seconds is often enough to use an application* and switch to another. How should this attention time frame affect application interface design?

We provide evidence that not all applications are micro-used to the same extent (Figure 2). We identified four categories of applications regarding micro-use probability: *focused, social, information seeking* and *leisure* applications:

- *Most likely* to be micro-used are *focused applications*, applications with limited functionalities or that are task-oriented, such as Alarm Clock, Calendar; and *social applications*, applications that rely on frequent notifications to update the user, such as Facebook, email. Of the top four micro-used applications in Study 1, three are communication applications (Facebook can arguably also be used as such with the built-in messaging system), similarly to what Iqbal & Horvitz [16] found with desktop use. They found that the vast majority of diversions took place in the users' email applications.
- *Least likely* to be micro-used are *information seeking applications*, applications that the user uses for information retrieval, such as Google Maps, browsers, news readers; and *leisure applications*, applications meant to entertain the user for longer periods of time, such as sports trackers, games and multimedia.

The applications' purpose of use is a concern that designers address at the *interface* level (*e.g.*, simple or complex interface), developers at the *implementation* level (*e.g.*, widget, notification, full application), and architects at the *system* level (*e.g.*, power consumption, resource management, caching, *etc.*). Similar to multitasking with desktop applications [16], fundamentally mobile application micro-usage emphasizes *fragmented and brief* application usage, that is, switching to, and resuming from another application very quickly. In addition to traditional HCI usability heuristics [23], we further provide micro-usage application interface recommendations, motivated by our studies:

- Allow transitioning between streamlined and full interface; default to the streamlined interface for those applications that are most likely to be micro-used (*e.g.*, focused and social applications), and to the full interface otherwise (*e.g.*, information seeking and leisure applications);
- Support intermittent application usage and transparent resume (*e.g.*, automatically save and resume from changes, provide visual cues for incomplete tasks [20]) to tackle multi-tasking and fast application switching;
- Support brief (*e.g.*, quick reply to new content without launching the application) and long application sessions (*e.g.*, review previous content, exploring new content).

The existence of micro-usage is not a sign of bad design. On the contrary, our studies and interviews indicate that micro-usage is a form of *experiencing* a mobile application and some applications do support it very well (*e.g.*, Gmail – Figure 10), allowing the user to quickly interact with an application (*e.g.*, quickly archive, delete or reply to an email) without launching the application itself.

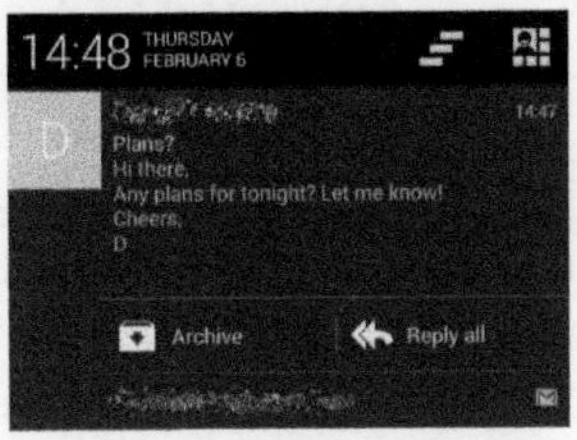

Figure 10: Example of Gmail micro-usage support.

Moreover, we show that notification functions are an important trigger for application usage and micro-usage and application designers should explicitly support these different behaviors. Should the user be presented with all her emails when opening a notification for new emails? What if the interface only displayed what is new for faster readability? The high-level question is, what information should be *emphasized* if the user interface will only remain *visible* for a few seconds?

As the time between phone usage instances is about 15 minutes (Figure 4), and since notifications are the main trigger for micro-usage, phones can optimally pull information from social applications, rather than pushing notifications to the user on every single update. In return, phones can ultimately reduce the nuisance of notifications reported in our interviews yet maintain the perception that applications are working properly. Moreover, when at home, users keep their devices 83% of the time in the same room [11]. As micro-usage is more frequent at home and when the user is alone, applications should take advantage of peripheral notifications, *i.e.*, no sound or vibration, by using device's LEDs or display for feedback and alerts.

From a systems perspective, the FALCON application manager [29] improved the loading times of applications by preemptively loading applications with high probability of use, thereby improving resource management and power efficiency. In considering the impact of micro-use, we could extend the predictions to the allocation and recovery of memory and other resources. We extend the micro-usage application recommendations to include recommendations developers:

- Provide succinct notifications with relevant up-to-date information, at approximately 15 minutes of inactivity, since the users are more likely to use their device again then (see Figure 4);
- If not time-critical, use peripheral notifications, especially if the user is at home (Figure 5 – bottom left);
- Unobtrusive and preemptive loading of newer content, so users do not have to wait for this content, nor search manually for it, for more likely micro-used applications (*e.g.*, social applications);
- For applications that are likely to be micro-used, have the OS make short-term resource optimizations for allocating memory, CPU, *etc*., since the resources will only be needed for a very short time.

We must emphasize that micro-use is *not just* a mobile phone phenomenon. For example, while reporting on their analysis of 1 billion search queries and search sessions, Silverstein *et al.* note: "*[...]most of them are very short. [...] 63.7% of all sessions consist of only one request.*"[27:8]. Users' propensity to disproportionately exhibit short bursts of inquiry are closely reflected by users' website visiting patterns, where about 50% of visits to a website typically involve visiting just a single page [17]. Similarly, for TV channel-watching behavior, 60% of channel holding times are shorter than 10 seconds [5].

As a ubiquitously available media solution, mobile phones naturally compete against other information sources for users' attention. It is not a surprise that, in both of our studies, Facebook and Google Mail are ranked as the most-frequently-used mobile services. Frequent interaction with the mobile phones, such as checking notifications, gave our participants a sense of gratification, and these activities increase in frequency when the cost to perform these activities decreases. We expect increased micro-usage to follow advances in computing devices such as wearable [17], as the effort required for interaction is increasingly minimized. The phenomenon of micro-usage is far from confined to smartphones; rather it is an instance of a broader human mechanism in how we allocate time to activities and how we regulate the rate of our activities.

Contributions

Our work has provided the following contributions: 1) we highlight a temporal dichotomy in application usage: *micro-use* (vs. non-micro use) and describe the distinct characteristics related to the brief spurs of application use that is found to be very common with mobile devices; 2) we identify a close relationship between notification-driven micro-use and how social applications in particular are being used in this way, and finally, 3) we emphasize how micro-use is an important phenomenon across platforms. This manifestation in a variety of domains makes micro-use relevant for the design of future applications and services, and we highlight implications for design and guidelines.

Limitations

Despite our best efforts, we must acknowledge the limitations of studying micro-usage with a sample of 36 participants and that our findings might not be indicative of the behavior of a larger sample. We did not find any potential link between participants' demographics and micro-usage behavior, but we must acknowledge that this might be due to our sample diversity. Despite our effort in designing the ESM to capture as much context as possible, the answer-choices could have limited users' micro-usage context [22]. Nonetheless, through our studies, we were able for the first time to *specifically* investigate micro-usage and the context in which it occurs.

CONCLUSION

The purpose of this paper is to highlight mobile application micro-usage as a distinct phenomenon, and to investigate the context in which it occurs. Our findings suggest that micro-usage is a frequently occurring phenomenon that is most likely to happen when users are alone. Our results provide further evidence that location and purpose are likely to affect the occurrence of micro-usage behavior.

Our results have also raised a number of issues regarding micro-usage that remains to be addressed. Specifically, it is not clear whether micro-usage is in fact wanted at times, or becomes a nuisance due to the existence of system notifications that alert users. Furthermore, our findings suggest a dichotomy in how mobile applications are used, and therefore we argue that designers and developers should consider how this affects their applications' usability and users' experience.

Acknowledgements

Funded by the Academy of Finland project 137736 and TEKES project 2932/31/2009.

REFERENCES

1. AWARE: Android Mobile Context Framework. http://www.awareframework.com
2. Barkhuus, L., and Polichar, V.E. Empowerment through seamfulness: smart phones in everyday life. *Personal and Ubiquitous Computing 15*, 6 (2010), 629-639.
3. Bell, G., and Dourish, P. Yesterday's tomorrows: notes on ubiquitous computing's dominant vision. *Personal and Ubiquitous Computing 11*, 2 (2007), 133-143.
4. Böhmer, M., Hecht, B., Schöning, J., Krüger, A., and Bauer, G. Falling Asleep with Angry Birds, Facebook and Kindle – A Large Scale Study on Mobile Application Usage. *MobileHCI'11*, 47-56.
5. Cha, M., Rodriguez, P., Crowcroft, J., Moon, S., and Amatriain, X. Watching television over an IP network. *SIGCOMM IMC'08*, 71-84.
6. Church, K., and Smyth, B., Understanding the Intent Behind Mobile Information Needs, *IUI'09*, 247-256.
7. Consolvo, S., and Walker, M., Using the experience sampling method to evaluate ubicomp applications. *Pervasive Computing 2*, 2 (2003), 24-31.
8. Dabbish, L., Mark, G., and Gonzalez, V. Why Do I Keep Interrupting Myself?: Environment, Habit and Self-Interruption. *CHI'11*, 3127-3130.
9. Davie, R., Panting, C., and Charlton, T. Mobile phone ownership and usage among pre-adolescents. *Telematics and Informatics 4*, 21 (2004), 359-373.
10. Dey, A.K., and Abowd, G.D. Towards a Better Understanding of Context and Context-Awareness. *Adj. CHI'00, Workshop on the What, Who, Where, When, Why and How of Context-Awareness*.
11. Dey, A., Wac, K., Ferreira, D., Tassini, K., Hong, J-H., and Ramos, J. Getting closer: an empirical investigation of the proximity of user to their smartphone. *UbiComp'11*, 163-172.
12. Falaki, H., Mahajan, R., Kandula, S., Lymberopoulos, D., Govindan, R., and Estrin, D. Diversity in Smartphone Usage. *MobiSys'10*, 179-194.
13. Ferreira, D., Kostakos, V., and Dey, A. K. Lessons Learned from Large-Scale User Studies: Using Android Market as a Source of Data. *IJ. Mobile Human Computer Interaction 3*, 4 (2011), 28-43.
14. Froehlich, J., Chen, M.Y., Consolvo, S., Harrison, B., and Landay J.A. MyExperience: A System for In situ Tracing and Capturing of User Feedback on Mobile Phones. *MobiSys'07*, 57-70.
15. González, V.M., and Mark, G. "Constant, Constant, Multi-tasking Craziness": Managing Multiple Working Spheres. *CHI'04*, 113-120.
16. Iqbal, S., and Horvitz, E. Disruption and recovery of computing tasks: field study, analysis, and directions. *CHI'07*, 677-686.
17. Jansen, B.J., Spink, A., and Saracevic, T. Real life, real users, and real needs: a study and analysis of user queries on the web. *Information Processing & Management 36*, 2 (2000), 207-227.
18. Jenks, George F. The Data Model Concept in Statistical Mapping, *International Yearbook of Cartography 7* (1967), 186-190.
19. Klug, T. and Mühlhäuser, M. Modeling Human Interaction Resources to Support the Design of Wearable Multimodal Systems. *ICMI'07*, 299-306.
20. Leiva, L.A., Böhmer, M., Gehring, S. and Krüger, A. Back to the app: the costs of mobile application interruptions. *MobileHCI'12*, 291-294.
21. Mark, G., Gudith, D., and Klocke, U. The Cost of Interrupted Work: More Speed and Stress. *CHI'08*, 107-110.
22. Möller, A., Kranz, M., Schmid, B., Roalter, L. and Diewald, S. Investigating Self-reporting Behavior in Long-term Studies. *CHI'13*, 2931-2940.
23. Nielsen, J. Enhancing the explanatory power of usability heuristics. *CHI'94*, 152-158.
24. Oulasvirta, A., Rattenbury, T., Ma, L., and Raita, E. Habits make smartphone more pervasive. *Personal and Ubiquitous Computing 16*, 1 (2011), 105-114.
25. Rahmati, A., and Zhong, L. A Longitudinal Study of Non-Voice Mobile Phone Usage by Teens from an Underserved Urban Community. TR0515-09, Rice University, 2009.
26. Sarker, S., and Wells, J., Understanding Mobile Handheld Device Use And Adoption. *ACM Communications 46*, 12 (2003), 35-40.
27. Silverstein, C., Marais, H., Henzinger, M., and Moricz, M. Analysis of a very large web search engine query log. *SIGIR 33*, 1 (1999), 6-12.
28. Sohn, T., Li, K.A., Griswold, W.G., and Hollan, J.D. A Diary Study of Mobile Information Needs. *CHI'08*, 433-442.
29. Yan, T., Chu, D., Ganesan, D., Kansal, A., and Liu, J. Fast App Launching for Mobile Devices Using Predictive User Context. *MobiSys'12*, 113-126.

Mobile Cloud Storage: A Contextual Experience

Karel Vandenbroucke
iMinds-MICT-Ghent University
Ghent, Belgium
karela.vandenbroucke@ugent.be

Denzil Ferreira*, Jorge Goncalves*, Vassilis Kostakos*
University of Oulu
Oulu, Finland
{dteixeir;jgoncalv;vassilis}@ee.oulu.fi

Katrien De Moor
ITEM-NTNU
Trondheim, Norway
katrienr.demoor@ugent.be

ABSTRACT
In an increasingly connected world, users access personal or shared data, stored "in the cloud" (*e.g.*, Dropbox, Skydrive, iCloud) with multiple devices. Despite the popularity of cloud storage services, little work has focused on investigating cloud storage users' Quality of Experience (QoE), in particular on mobile devices. Moreover, it is not clear how users' context might affect QoE. We conducted an online survey with 349 cloud service users to gain insight into their usage and affordances. In a 2-week follow-up study, we monitored mobile cloud service usage on tablets and smartphones, in real-time using a mobile-based Experience Sampling Method (ESM) questionnaire. We collected 156 responses on *in-situ* context of use for Dropbox on mobile devices. We provide insights for future QoE-aware cloud services by highlighting the most important mobile contextual factors (*e.g.,* connectivity, location, social, device), and how they affect users' experiences while using such services on their mobile devices.

Author Keywords
Context-aware; mobile; Quality of Experience (QoE); cloud storage services.

ACM Classification Keywords
H.5.m. Information interfaces and presentation (*e.g.,* HCI): Miscellaneous.

General Terms
Human Factors; Design; Measurement.

INTRODUCTION
Mobile smart devices such as smartphones and tablets are increasingly intertwined with our lives: Forecasts from 2012 predicted that by 2016, the number of mobile-connected devices will amount up to 10.3 billion [5], while for 2013, expected sales of mobile smart devices were close to 1.2 billion units [9]. These devices offer a vast range of new affordances to users and enable connectivity anywhere, at any time and from any device. However, one unyielding disadvantage of these lightweight, mobile devices is their limited storage capacity, which also limits their possible uses. It is also more common to find services and applications that work across different mobile devices and platforms. As a result, the related user behavior and usage patterns have become more complex and a range of problems has emerged. One recurring challenge is to connect multiple devices that have vastly different characteristics and requirements and how to synchronize the stored data across these devices in an effortless way. With recent improvements on network speed, reliability and increased availability, and based on principles of cloud computing, a growing number of consumer market and business-oriented providers of cloud storage have started to address these and other challenges.

MobileHCI '14, September 23 - 26 2014, Toronto, ON, Canada
Copyright 2014 ACM 978-1-4503-3004-6/14/09…$15.00.
http://dx.doi.org/10.1145/2628363.2628386

In spite of the controversy surrounding the notion of 'cloud computing' and whether it is really new or just a new wrapping [22], cloud computing is (re-)shaping the Internet and the services it provides [1]. Infrastructure and scalability management are hidden away onto the "cloud." Services such as Amazon's Elastic Compute Cloud, Microsoft's Azure and Google's AppEngine provide "flexible" hardware and storage availability in a cost-effective approach. Currently, Dropbox is one of the most popular cloud computing services, available on desktop and mobile environments [7]. It offers almost unlimited cloud storage on the go, given the availability of Internet connection (except when accessing cached files). Files can be easily accessed and automatically synchronized across a range of devices: laptops, smartphones, and tablets.

However, from a cloud service provider's perspective, it is challenging to gain insight into the users' expectations and experiences, *i.e.*, users' Quality of Experience (QoE). This is crucial to practitioners and service providers to evaluate service performance and to detect and overcome the technical challenges that come along with these applications. Moreover, as personal cloud storage services and applications may be used in different contexts and from diverse other devices, the key influence factors on the QoE need to be investigated and better understood. We find in literature for example, that users' QoE is influenced by waiting times [17] and the availability of services [4] in a desktop environment. However, nearly no previous work has assessed mobile contextual factors influencing users' QoE when using cloud storage services on mobile devices such as smartphones and tablets. In this paper, we therefore assess users' Quality of Experience (QoE) when using cloud storage services on mobile devices and how it is affected by the users' context.

RELATED WORK

Quality of Experience

Over the last decades, increased attention was given to the world of technology users/society, the actual use and the meaning of technology (*e.g.,* in research, policy and practice). Especially in the context of ICT research and innovation, there has been a growing awareness that users and consumers are demanding, powerful, and self-conscious stakeholders that cannot be simply ignored [15]. In various research fields (*e.g.*, HCI, telecommunications, multimedia and vision research, service management) an effort is being made to measure and understand how users *experience* ICT products, applications and services.

Traditionally, emphasis was put on *technological* excellence and *quality*. Since the 90's however, experiences rendered through the encounters with a product, brand, service or application, have notably been emphasized as a basis for differentiation [19]. The quality of users' experiences have been linked to market success or failure of new and existing products, applications, services [16]. This renewed focus on *experience* is reflected in the literature by relatively young concepts such as User Experience, Quality of Experience and Customer Experience, which stem from distinct disciplines and research traditions, but which nevertheless have some common grounds. We *must* acknowledge that experiences are *subjective*, *individual* and highly *complex* and therefore it is necessary to investigate them from a multi-disciplinary perspective and through involvement of actual users. Other unknown factors may influence users' experiences and should therefore be investigated and better understood.

'Quality of Experience' has its roots in the field of Telecommunications, but over the last decade it has also acquired a more prominent role other fields and disciplines. In 2012, a more holistic and broadly supported perspective on QoE was introduced, defining it in terms of *affective states*, as the: '*degree of delight or annoyance of the user of an application or service. It results from the fulfillment of his or her expectations with respect to the utility and / or enjoyment of the application or service in the light of the user's personality and current state*'[3]. In addition, it is argued that a range of factors situated at the human level, system level and context level may have an impact on a user's Quality of Experience[20].

In the domain of communication services, QoE has been shown to be influenced by service, content, network, device, application, and context of use (divided into several dimensions – Where, What, When, Why, Who and How [6]). Whereas much previous work has already focused on factors at the system level (*e.g.,* network-, device-, media- or content-related) and to some extent at the human level, the influence of contextual factors on QoE is still poorly understood and very challenging to investigate. Here, we explicitly focus on the role of contextual factors of and in relation to QoE.

QoE & Cloud Computing Services

For end-users, cloud computing promises advantages in terms of services, computation and data access. The migration of services to the cloud is associated with new affordances such as sharing and accessing personal data in a flexible way and from different types of devices, easy collaboration amongst multiple users, and others [11]. However, in order to manage the available resources in an efficient way, while at the same time trying to enable a pleasurable and positive Quality of Experience at the user side, it is necessary to better understand which aspects meet users' expectations, enable delight or lead to frustration (and potentially a decision to stop using a service). Moreover, it should be better understood which contextual factors play an influencing role.

Casas *et al.* [4] argues that due to the explosion of cloud-based services in the mobile domain – characterized by dynamic and volatile network conditions – QoE has become problematic, 'a real bottleneck.' In order to establish QoE within applications, Hoßfeld *et al.* [12] monitored network environment and conditions, terminal capabilities, Service Level Agreements (SLAs) and service and application-specific information. However, QoE is not solely influenced by network, technical and Quality of Service (QoS)-related parameters.

It has been shown that contextual and human factors may also play a major role[20]. For example, in the context of Web QoE, memory effects, *i.e.*, the psychological influence of past experiences, bear a strong influence [11]. Furthermore, a recent study on adoption of cloud services suggests that security and privacy issues impose strong barriers to user adoption [23]. As a result, it is important to look beyond the technical aspects in order to gain a better understanding of the experiences and practices related to the use of personal cloud storage services and applications.

METHODOLOGY

We attempt to understand better the mobile context in which users' expectations and experiences change, *immediately* after using a cloud storage service (*e.g.*, Dropbox). Our goal is to study the link between QoE and users' mobile context. To accomplish this, we surveyed 349 cloud storage service users on different aspects of QoE (Study 1). In a follow-up 2-week empirical study, we collected 13 users' perceptions on Dropbox mobile phone usage with a mobile Experience Sampling Method (ESM) (Study 2). The ESMs allowed us to collect *in-situ* qualitative and quantitative contextual data, right after the participants used Dropbox. Our work provides evidence of the effects the user's mobile context (*e.g.,* location, network connectivity (speed, signal strength, network type), time of day, social context) has on users' QoE while using Dropbox on their smartphones and tablets.

Study 1: Mobile cloud storage services survey

Our goal is to better understand the cloud storage services users, as to gain better insight into the users' expectations when using these services. We developed an online survey based on [2, 16] for the use of personal cloud services, with a total of 26 questions divided into 10 groups:

- ***Cloud services:*** what services and applications are used; how frequent are they used;
- ***Context of use:*** in what locations are clouds services used; how frequent are they used in different locations;
- ***Devices:*** what devices are used to access cloud services; what content is consulted on which devices;
- ***Connection:*** what connection is used to access cloud services; how frequent are the connection types used;
- ***Data:*** what amount (GB) and type of data is stored;
- ***Motivation for usage:*** why are cloud services used; importance of service affordances (sharing, back-up) and QoE influencing factors (availability, privacy, cost, security,...);
- ***Financial:*** does the respondent pay for usage; how much does he pay; willingness to pay for greater storage capacity; maximum fee per month;
- ***Sharing:*** with whom is data shared;
- ***User experience:*** how long does the respondent already use cloud services; perceived benefits and drawbacks of using personal cloud services;
- ***Socio-demographic information:*** gender; year of birth; residence; diploma; occupation;

We promoted the survey using mailing lists, advertising at Facebook and online forums, including dedicated online groups with interest on the field of cloud computing. In total, 349 users of personal cloud services and applications completed the survey (66.2% male; 33.8% female). The mean age of the respondents is 33.63 years (SD=12.32; min=18; max=62).

Study 2: Dropbox QoE

In Study 2, our primary goal was to observe the context in which Dropbox mobile application is used, as to understand better users' QoE while using such services in a resource constrained device. More importantly, we wanted to investigate the relationship between context and QoE and how they affect one another, with a real world deployment, *i.e.,* not in a laboratory setting.

We recruited 13 mobile Dropbox users, owning an Android smartphone or tablet (Android 2.3+) as to minimize novelty bias. Additionally, we selected participants whose Dropbox usage varied between several times a day (*i.e.*, frequent user) to 3 or 4 times a week (*i.e.*, occasional user), as to capture diverse cloud service usage (Table 1).

In a 2-week deployment, we used AWARE [8], an open-source Android framework dedicated to infer, log and share mobile context information to acquire data from our participants' phones:

- ***Device***: type (*e.g.*, tablet, phone), hardware specifications (*e.g.*, manufacturer, model) and Android OS version (*e.g.*, 2.3 or higher);
- ***Location***: date, time, and GPS or network triangulation location (as a fallback of a GPS failure);
- ***Network access***: active network connection (*e.g.*, Wi-Fi, network) and network type (*e.g.*, 3G, 2G);
- ***Network traffic***: received and transmitted bytes and packets for active network connection;
- ***Network quality***: signal strength (*i.e.*, RSSI) to connected network point (*e.g.*, Wi-Fi access point, network tower);
- ***Battery life***: battery depletion over time.

Participant	Gender	Age	Occupation	Device	Brand	Model	MOS ESM	MOS Debriefing	# ratings
PP1	M	20	Student	S	Sony	LT22i	4.33	4	3
PP2	M	27	Student	S	HTC	Desire X	4.00	4	3
PP3	M	26	Translator	S	Samsung	GT-I9300	3.62	4	8
PP4	M	23	Student	T	Samsung	GT-P7500	3.30	4	20
PP5	F	26	Student	T	Asus	Prime TF201	3.30	5	10
PP6	F	26	Officer Shipping	S	Samsung	GT-I9300	2.89	3	29
PP7	F	23	Student	T	Samsung	GT-P5110	3.86	4	7
PP8	M	29	Banker	S	HTC	One X	3.75	4	12
PP9	M	24	Developer	T	Samsung	GT-P7320	4.12	4	41
PP10	F	24	Student	S	Sony	LT22i	4.00	4	1
PP11	M	26	Developer	T	Samsung	GT-P7510	5.00	5	3
PP12	M	33	Consultant	S	Sony Ericsson	LT18i	4.07	4	15
PP13	M	28	Student	T	Samsung	GT-P3110	3.50	4	4
M - Male, F - Female, S - Smartphone, T - Tablet							Mean=3.68 SD=1.11	Mean=4.08 SD=0.49	N=156

Table 1. Participants' QoE ratings, socio-demographics and device related information.

In addition to the metrics collected via AWARE, we added the functionality to collect traces on the Dropbox app, such as date, time and amount of time spent using the application. To capture QoE-relevant usage information *in-situ* and independently of the current user's context and to avoid missing data (*e.g.*, daily diaries [14]), we used the Experience Sampling Method (ESM). ESM is a "*research procedure for studying what people do, feel, and think during their everyday lives. It consists of asking individuals to provide systematic self-reports at non-deterministic occasions during the waking hours of their lives*" [10]. Our software (CloudUX) triggered a short on-device step-by-step questionnaire when Dropbox is closed (Figure 1).

This data was collected after the user finished using Dropbox and while responding to this questionnaire, as to not affect routinely device and application usage. We could not determine specific implementation problems within Dropbox. Instead, we asked the participants to report if they had encountered any problems retrospectively to the current session.

- ***Dropbox session expectation*** [16]: the users' rating of their user experience with Dropbox (*e.g.*, -2 much worse; -1 worse; 0 as expected; +1 better; +2 much better);
- ***Purpose of Use***: why is the user using Dropbox? (*e.g.*, uploading, viewing, sharing file, other);
- ***Location context***: where the user is at the moment (*e.g.*, at home, at work/school, indoors, outdoors, on the way somewhere);
- ***Mobility context***: sitting/lying down, standing, walking, in vehicle, other;

- ***Social context***: how many people were around the user, in different scales (*e.g.*, 0, 1-2, 3-4, 5-6, 6+);
- ***Social disturbance***: if social presence disturbed the application use;
- ***Troubleshooting***: if the user encountered problems while using Dropbox;
- ***QoE metrics*** [3]: delight, frustration, surprise, annoyance metric (*e.g.*, not at all, slightly, moderately, fairly, extremely);
- ***Mean Opinion Score (MOS)*** [13]: the users' rating of the Dropbox experience (*e.g.*, between 5 stars (*i.e.*, excellent) and 1 star (*i.e.*, bad).

We collected 156 fully answered (64.5% of a total of 242) ESMs. To complement the ESMs, and as a final step of our study, we collected qualitative feedback from our participants to better understand their opinions of the contextual factors of Dropbox's QoE.

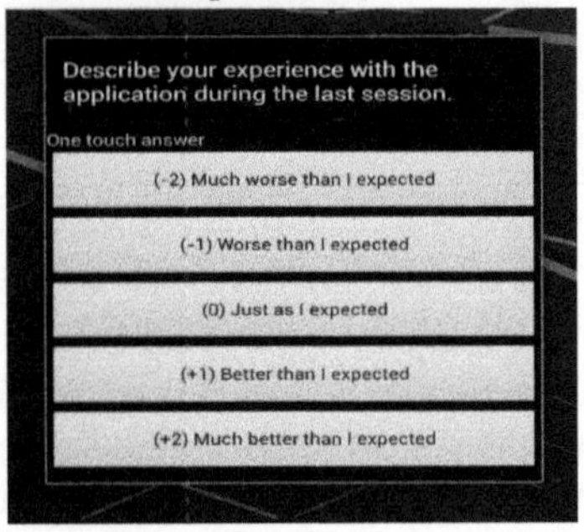

Figure 1. Example of one QoE question.

RESULTS FROM STUDY 1

Service Affordances & Mode of Access

A total of 72% of the respondents have been using personal cloud services for longer than one year, where 56.4% use cloud storage daily, several times in a day. Dropbox (86.5%) and Google Services (*e.g.*, Gmail, Picasa) (55.3%) are used the most, followed by Google Drive (43.6%), Microsoft Hotmail (35.8%), iCloud (29.2%) and Microsoft Skydrive (24.9%).

The most prevalent content stored were text files (95%) (*e.g.,* PDF files, Word documents, spreadsheets,…), followed by pictures (74%), e-mail (50%), calendar (46%) and contacts (42%). 94% of respondents use several portable computer for accessing their personal cloud applications (*e.g.*, smartphone (72%), desktop computer (66%) and tablet (46%)).

This is not surprising since, according to our respondents, the most important affordance of cloud computing applications is their *transversal availability*, *i.e.*, they enable that data and media can be accessed from different devices at any time, with sharing of and backup of data being also considered important affordances (Figure 2).

In contrast, 16% of respondents indicated that they did not share data with others. A total of 50.6% of the respondents uses cloud services at home and 44.2% at school/work on a daily basis, several times a day. While nomadic, *i.e.*, going from one place to another (*e.g.*, in a car, bus, train), only 11.8% of our respondents used cloud services.

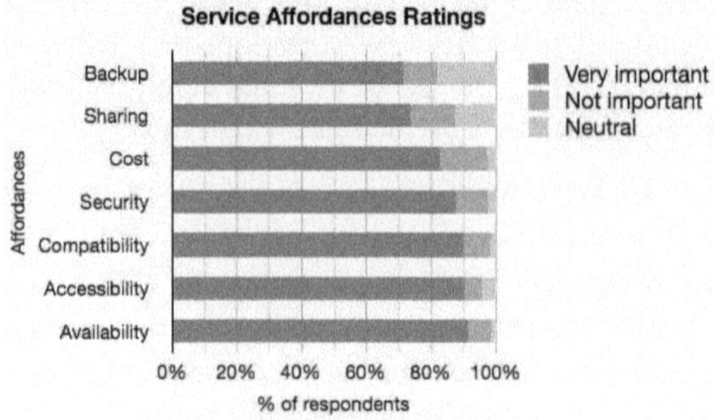

Figure 2. User ratings per service affordances and factors influencing users' QoE

Based on a subjective rating on usage of different access networks, we notice that access to cloud computing services is the lowest when connected to a mobile network (Figure 3).

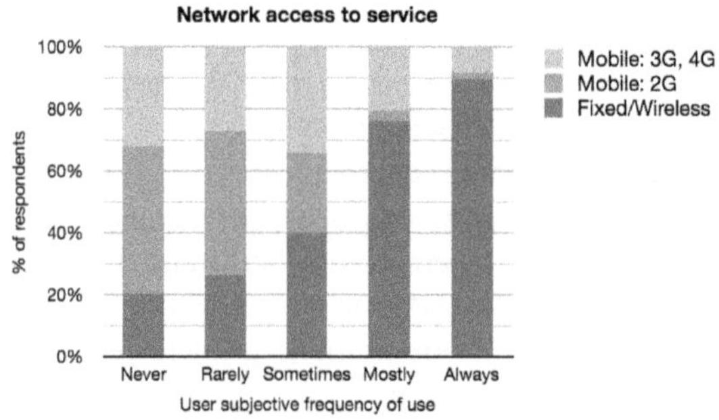

Figure 3. User ratings per network access.

Cloud User Profiles

Using K-Means Cluster Analysis (KMCA) on the respondents' use frequency (on a monthly basis: not at all (1) to several times per day (7)) in different contexts (home, school/work and mobile), we found 3 cloud user profiles: *low*-cloud, *medium*-cloud and *high*-cloud users (Table 2). KMCA is used to cluster respondents into internally homogeneous and externally heterogeneous groups. We found significant differences between the clusters on socio-demographic variables:

- ***Low*-cloud**: a younger population, with balanced gender distribution. The majority are students or employees using 2 devices to connect between 1-3 personal cloud services. With the lowest amount of data stored in their personal clouds, the majority is not paying and have the lowest market potential, *i.e.*, only 10.7% of them are willing to pay for any larger storage capacity. They also use cloud storage the least (75.3% uses cloud services less than weekly). The majority is novice (a user for less than a year) and rarely resorts to a mobile network to access their data. Only 33% of these respondents use cloud storage for professional reasons.
- ***Medium*-cloud**: predominantly a male population (71.6% male), with a higher counts of employees, independent and managerial professionals. The majority uses 3

devices to access their personal cloud data, amongst 4 or more different cloud service providers and are experienced users accessing the services several times in a day. These users are more inclined to pay for the extra storage space and use it for professional purposes.

- ***High*-cloud**: the most mature and predominantly male cluster (83.1% male). Not surprising, this cluster contains the lowest amount of students, with higher number of independent and managerial professionals. These experienced users have 4 or more devices that connect to several cloud storage providers (4 or more), storing the largest amount of data "in the cloud" using any available network anytime and anywhere. Almost half of these users are willing to pay for such services (47.2%), where 73.9% of the users use cloud storage for professional purposes.

		Low	Medium	High
Respondents		118	139	92
Mean age (years)		29,8	32,9	36,3
SD age		11,4	12,2	12,4
		Percentage of respondents		
Gender	Male	46,4	71,6	83,1
	Female	53,6	28,4	16,9
Occupation	Student	48,2	42,2	24,7
	Employee	19,6	22,4	21,3
	Independent	10,7	17,2	23,6
	Management	8,1	13,8	19,1
	Other	13,4	4,4	11,3
Devices	One	20,6	9,5	2,2
	Two	46,4	31,0	20,2
	Three	21,4	41,4	31,5
	Four or more	11,6	18,1	46,1
Cloud Services	One	11,6	11,2	2,2
	Two	22,3	13,8	11,2
	Three	27,8	23,3	13,5
	Four or more	38,3	51,7	73,1
Data stored	< 10 GB	63,6	64,5	45,6
	10-20 GB	7,6	11,6	17,4
	> 20 GB	6,8	15,2	28,3
	Unknown	22,0	8,7	8,7
Never use mobile data plan		65,9	42,9	20,7
Longer than 1 year (%)		51,4	83,6	82,0
Several times a day (%)		16,2	76,7	87,5
Paying		3,9	16,1	25,9
Willing to pay more		10,7	25,9	47,2
Professional cloud user		33,0	73,0	73,9

Table 2. Respondents' demographics and clustered profiles.

In summary, a key affordance of personal cloud applications is *availability* and the possibility to *share* and *backup* data at a *minimal cost*. Other important affordances are *compatibility*, *privacy* and *security*. The use of personal cloud services seems to be constrained by *contextual* factors, such as network availability, device performance (CPU, operating system), location, all of which influence the *availability* and the users' QoE while using cloud storage services on their mobile devices.

RESULTS FROM STUDY 2

We conducted Study 2 to obtain a better understanding of the roles of these contextual factors have in users' QoE and cloud storage services.

Effect of location and mobility context

On average and across all our participants, Dropbox is used the most frequently at home (49.4%), followed by school/work (21.8%), other indoor (12.8%) and outdoor locations (1.3%). However, Dropbox is reported to perform better at School/Work (96.6% sessions without problems) and at home (89.7%), and was less reliably in other indoor (60% sessions without problems) and outdoor locations (43.5%)(Figure 4 - left). There is a significant effect between the location and users' mobility state (*e.g.*, sitting/lying, standing, nomadic) in regard to MOS: users rated Dropbox poorly in outdoor locations and when nomadic ($p<0.01$, Fisher's exact tests) (Figure 4 - right).

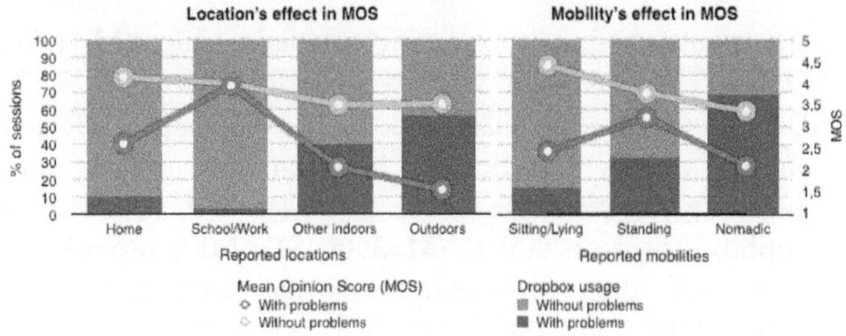

Figure 4. MOS (Mean Opinion Score) per location and mobility states and reported problems.

Effect of network context

Our participants predominantly used Wi-Fi (56.4%), otherwise, they preferably used high-speed mobile network access (HSPA+, HSPA – including HSDPA)(32.4%) or a slower network (EDGE)(8%). In seldom occasions, users had no network connection (3.2%). On average, participants rated using Dropbox on high-speed mobile network higher than when using Wi-Fi ($p<0.01$, Fisher's exact test) (Figure 5). We found no significant effect of network signal strength and QoE, however we know this to not be true [18], surely a consequence of our limited samples of signal strength while on a mobile network (N=49).

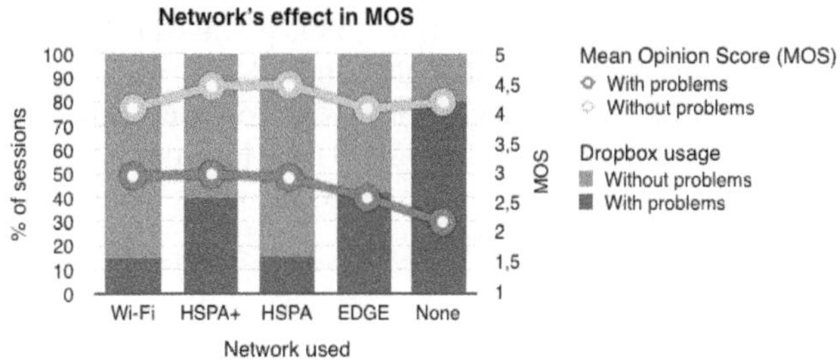

Figure 5. MOS (Mean Opinion Score) per network access.

Effect of device context and affordances

We sampled data from 6 tablet and 7 smartphone users (Table 2). Our participants used Dropbox mostly to visualize images (38.5%), read (24.4%) or access other miscellaneous files (8.3%). On occasion, participants uploaded files (9.6%) or shared data with others (2.6%). Our participants also reported doing "other" things (10.9%), such as sharing files between personal devices and replicating files. Surprisingly, on average our

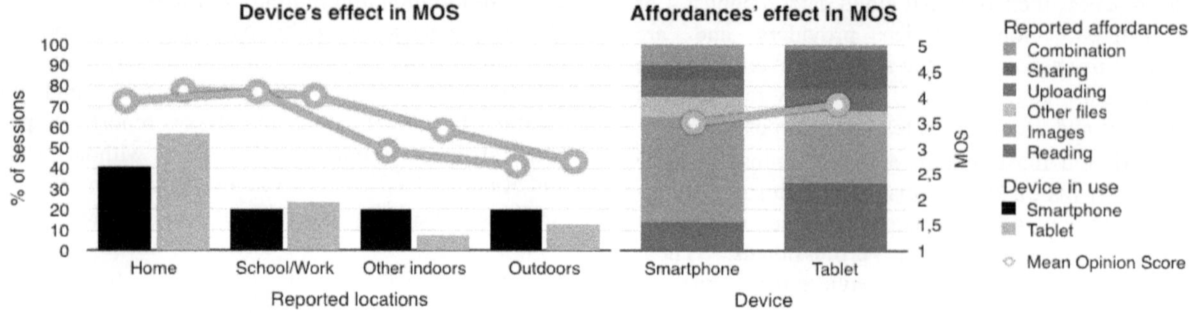

Figure 6. MOS (Mean Opinion Score) per location, and device affordances (*e.g.*, smartphone, tablet).

participants rated their experience uploading files (M=4.47, SD=0.64) higher than when visualizing them (M=3.33, SD=1.17)(Figure 6). The use of Dropbox in different contexts differs significantly between smartphones and tablets (χ^2(1, N=156)=8.116, p=0.04). We found that Dropbox usage on tablets (M=3.85, SD=1.09) provided a better QoE than on smartphones (M=3.49, SD=1.10); t(154)=-2.011, p=0.046, especially when the user is at home (M(tablet, home)=4.10, SD=1.08) or at school/work (M(tablet,school/work)=4.00, SD=0.79).

When outdoors and in other indoor locations, the preferred device is the smartphone (62.2% of instances). Also, we notice that the affordances of Dropbox differ significantly between smartphones and tablets (χ^2(1, N=154)=19.040, p<0.01): smartphones are mostly used for viewing images (50.7%), while tablets are mostly used for reading documents (32.9%). We found no correlation between the device used and the occurrence of problems.

Effect of social context

Most of the time, participants used Dropbox alone (35.9%) or within a small group (1-2 people)(36.5%). A Spearman correlation analysis between MOS and amount of people around the user while using Dropbox shows a significant indirect social effect (r(154) = -.389, p < 0.01). In other words, participants rated higher their MOS when alone (M=4.07, SD=0.98), lower when with someone (M=3.80, SD=0.87) or others (M=2.57, SD=1.39). Five out of the 13 participants considered the presence of others "annoying" (12.2%)(M=2.35, SD=0.99).

Effect of time context

On average, a Dropbox session lasted 44.8 seconds (SD=55). The elevated standard deviation is due to the ESM mechanism: the questionnaire would only be shown to the users when idle (*i.e.*, not interacting with Dropbox), as to not interrupt them. Consequently, a Dropbox session was inadvertently prolonged. However, it did not affect *detecting* the mobile context.

Dropbox is more frequently used on the weekdays (85%), mostly throughout the afternoon (31.8%) and evening (40.3%). We did not find any significant effect of hour of day, weekday or weekend on MOS (Figure 7).

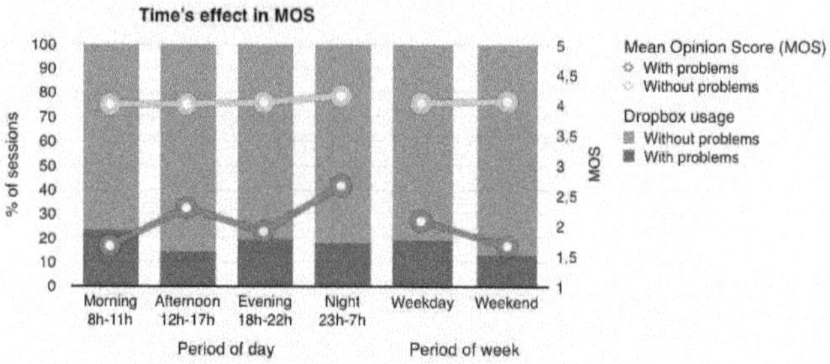

Figure 7. MOS (Mean Opinion Score) per period of day/week.

Effect of emotional context

Our participants rated (*e.g.*, 1 is "Not at all", 5 is "Extremely") 4 emotional states that drive QoE [3]: delight; frustration; annoyance; and surprise. We assessed the effect of these emotions in the users' QoE (Figure 8). We found a strong negative correlation between MOS and frustration (Pearson r(154)=-0.72, p<0.01) and annoyance (Pearson r(154)=-0.71, p<0.01). In other words, users rated poorly Dropbox whether they felt frustrated or annoyed. On the other hand, we found a direct correlation between MOS and users' delight (Pearson r(154)=0.40, p=0.01), but no significant correlation to users' surprise. The emotional states' rating, except for surprise, differs significantly from the scores given when there were no problems (t-test for Equality of Means: p=0.001).

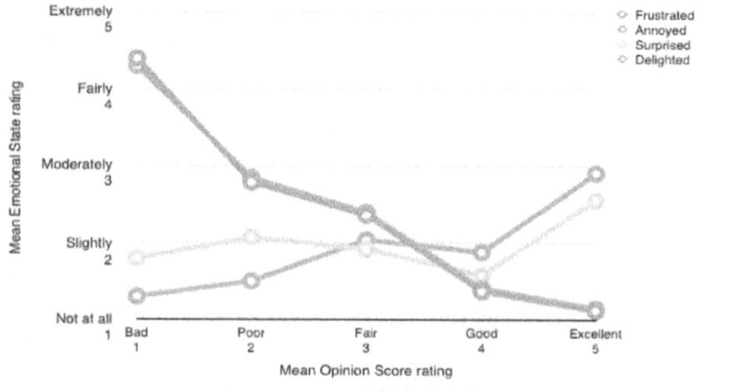

Figure 8. Users' emotions vs MOS (Mean Opinion Score)

Qualitative QoE

At the end of Study 2, we retrieved all participants' data and invited them to fill out an online debriefing survey. We asked 19 questions, 10 of them open-ended. We aimed to investigate further the users' experiences and context by focusing on positive and negative aspects of Dropbox and any perceived external factors influencing users' QoE. We describe the different aspects explored in the debriefing survey in the following paragraphs.

Device satisfaction
On user's satisfaction towards the mobile device itself, 10 participants indicated that were very satisfied, while 3 had concerns. Surprisingly, good software and hardware, proper function, constant Internet access and apps crashing were *rarely* mentioned as positive aspects. On the other hand, participants with a smartphone frequently indicated the insufficient phone memory, limited text editing possibilities and battery discharging too fast as disadvantages of their device.

Mobile Dropbox application
We also inquired participants about the mobile Dropbox application usage and other aspects perceived as positive or negative. Reported positive aspects of Dropbox were: usability (ease of use); easy to upload; download and share data; automatic synchronization; the ability to not only view files but also to (jointly) modify them; stable application (*i.e.,* rare crashes); easy folder navigation and the fact that there is only one non-conflicting application between different machines or users (*i.e.,* platform compatibility). Similarly reported as positive is the ability to secure their files with a pin code, so nobody else has access to them (privacy and security). Accessibility was also mentioned, *i.e.*, the ability to access their data on different (mobile) devices.

Cached files or favorite files can be accessed even when there is no Internet access. However, this can easily be a nuisance of Dropbox: when files are not available and there is a poor Internet connection – or none at all – users are unable to open them, thus frustration arises. Also problematic is the inability to upload a complete folder, Dropbox not supporting all file formats and often slow synchronization between fixed and mobile devices.

Besides the mobile Dropbox application itself, we also found other aspects of mobile devices that affect Dropbox's QoE: a good Internet connection, a device that functions well and short waiting times are good QoE factors. On the other hand, having a device with limited memory, slow, too small screen (smartphone), poor battery life, delays and a poor Internet connection are negative QoE factors.

Social surroundings
We asked our participants if the presence of others in the immediate surroundings possibly influenced the user experience. As PP9 points out: *"I only use Dropbox when I'm alone or when I want to show something to a colleague at work. It's really an advantage that I can show files to others with my tablet and that I don't have to open my laptop to show it. When people in my immediate surroundings are disturbing, I probably won't use Dropbox or any other app until its calm."* In another instance, PP6 used Dropbox in a train with free Wi-Fi during rush hour and there were many other people in the train using this Internet access, causing longer waiting times resulting in lower QoE. Nonetheless, most participants mentioned that other people had no influence because the use of a mobile device is mainly personal and mostly there is no interaction with the immediate surroundings while using Dropbox.

Real-world deployment
We also asked if participants had encountered any problems with Dropbox during Study 2. Several participants mentioned that they could not always open their files due to unreliable mobile Internet connection, someone sending an unrecognizable file or simply having low battery level at the time.

Lastly, the participants were asked to rate their overall experience with Dropbox during the past two weeks based on the Mean Opinion Score. Dropbox was rated as Good by almost all of the respondents *retrospectively* (M=4.08, SD=0.49)(see Table 2 and Figure 5).

This rating is slightly, but not significantly, higher than the MOS on the ESM questionnaires (M=3.68, SD=1.11). Since the ESM mechanism prompted the users for their opinion immediately after using the application, we suspect that any *momentary* frustration could have affected their scores negatively. In other words, the participants' post-usage QoE is better because these problems do not occur often enough and participants continue to use Dropbox regardless.

DISCUSSION

Cloud users' profiles

We found 3 kinds of cloud users from our Study 1 results. The *low*-cloud profile fits the younger population; in our sample they were mostly students. These are novice users to cloud services and only a small percent (10.7%) of them are willing to pay to use cloud services, as they often do not need hefty amounts of cloud space.

In the interest of cloud service providers, the associated *financial cost* (or absence) of the cloud services is affected in two scenarios: first, there are costs of mobile internet usage, not always appreciated by their users especially with high data roaming costs to use cloud storage while travelling; secondly, is their cost for personal cloud services. Only 15.2% of respondents currently pay for cloud computing services and the non-paying users are admittedly satisfied with the offered storage capacity (between 5 to 20 GB, depending on the provider), and only 1:3 respondents indicated that they would actually be willing to pay in exchange for more storage capacity. Most of cloud services providers offer a free plan for 'standard' users. We anticipated a *medium*-cloud user to be a better (*i.e.*, as in paying) customer (25.9% says they would pay if needed). However, we found that these users often juggle between different free cloud services to store their data, thus avoiding further expenses. Their expense is however, on service access. Many of our respondents use mobile data plan interchangeably with Wi-Fi for storage access. On the other hand, *high*-cloud users are often paying customers, as 47.2% are willing to pay. They host large amount of data on the "cloud" (28.3% have more than 20GB) by any means possible (*i.e.,* any network available) and for professional purposes (73.9%). From a market perspective, future research could focus on adoption potential, market potential and domestication of cloud applications, *i.e.*, the shift from usage in a professional context to usage in a domestic context.

Users' expectation versus users' experience

An optimal QoE is a direct match between the *pre-usage* expectations and the actual *post-usage* experience [16]. In our ESMs, we first asked the participants to describe their Dropbox session expectation (*e.g.*, "Much worse than I expected" or "Much better than I expected") and lastly to rate their Dropbox experience using MOS (*e.g.*, 1 is "Poor", 5 is "Excellent"). Within the same context, we investigated the relationship between pre-usage expectations and post-usage experience and found a direct correlation (Pearson $r=0.60$, $N=156$, $p<0.01$) between both measures. In other words, Dropbox QoE is indeed *lower* when the users' experience *does not meet* the users' *expectations*.

Contextual Factors of QoE

Users' QoE is a highly subjective and complex measure[21]. We found evidence that it is partly influenced by the users' mobile context. Taking into account these different contexts can help provide a better understanding when assessing users' QoE. We know that the different contexts are no secluded but interdependent factors effecting each other and users' QoE. However, to provide better understanding, we will discuss the contextual dimensions separately. For each specific context, we discuss how we could meet the users' expectations.

Device context and affordances

Obs. 1: Users demand connectivity from any device

Migration to the cloud is associated with new affordances such as sharing and accessing personal data in a flexible way and from different types of (mobile) devices. However, challenges rise in terms of connecting and synchronizing data between these resources constrained devices. 94% of Study 1 respondents indicated that they use several devices to connect to the cloud, thus, transversal availability is of major importance.

Study 1 shows that prevalent data stored in the cloud are text files (including e-mail) and pictures, whereas Study 2 shows that Dropbox was used most of all for visualizing images or reading text files. Also, smartphones are mostly used for viewing images and tablets for reading documents. Study 2 also showed that uploading data is better experienced than visualizing data. The reason for this is the fact that uploading data is often a background process, not burdening the user unless it actually fails. On the other hand, visualizing data can be influenced by device performance and waiting times. One option for cloud service providers to overcome low QoE when visualizing data is to utilize compressed and memory-efficient file formats (*e.g.,* generate a .pdf automatically from a .doc for mobile consultation; re-encode multimedia files to lower bitrates).

Time Context

Obs. 2: Users demand access to their cloud services at any time.

Our survey shows that 56.4% of respondents use cloud storage daily (one or several times per day). When cloud services are not available, lower QoE are reported. Study 2 shows that 85% of Dropbox sessions took place on weekdays and 72,1% of them occurred during the afternoon and evening (between 12h and 22h). Surprisingly, participants were more tolerant when problems were encountered at night than in the morning (Figure 6). Hence, we recommend service providers to optimize their services during the first half of the day, as to improve QoE during these sessions (*e.g.*, dynamically add redundancy servers to satisfy burst of requests for data).

Location context

Obs. 3: Users demand cloud connectivity anywhere

A core requirement is *mobility*: we need to be able to access data and media at any place. While cloud usage is reported mostly at Home or at School/Work, we found a low percentage of Study 1 and Study 2 participants using cloud services when being outside or nomadic. Associated to this, Dropbox seems to perform better at Home and at School/Work (fewer problems) and poor ratings are given when the user is nomadic and/or in outdoor locations. A recommendation to overcome this low QoE in outdoor locations can be to rescale images to lower quality, download text files page per page (so the document can download while the user is already reading), warn the users when waiting times longer than 5 seconds can occur or display a download progress bar as to inform the users of the waiting times.

Network context

Obs. 4: Users demand high-speed (mobile) networks

Previous research has shown that QoE in mobile services is influenced by network conditions, but due to the explosion of cloud services in the mobile domain, QoE has become problematic [4]. Besides signal strength [17] and availability of services [4], waiting times (*i.e.,* user perceived delays) have a high impact on QoE [16].

When connected to a mobile network, cloud access is lowest (Figure 2), confirmed by Study 2's data, where 56.4% Wi-Fi, 32.4% high-speed mobile network, 8% slow network and 3.2% no network usage was reported. However, Dropbox is rated higher on high-speed mobile networks than on Wi-Fi, even though more problems were reported on mobile network than on Wi-Fi (Figure 5). According to our analysis and survey, this is because the user has *lower expectations towards the network capabilities when connected to a mobile network*. Thus, when files can be accessed flawlessly, good QoE comes as a great outcome. When connected to Wi-Fi, we found the users to be more demanding and less tolerant when problems are encountered. Obviously, when there is no network connection available and if the users want to see a non-cached file, a low QoE is reported.

Although, steps have been taken to improve users' QoE in terms of network connectivity and QoS measures, we suggest future QoE-aware cloud computing applications to transfer changes (synchronize data) when a better signal/network access is available, to warn the user if a network is not good enough as to better meet the user's expectations and take accountability from the user and place it on the current context influencing factors we have less control over.

Social context

Obs. 5: Users demand collaboration amongst multiple users but not directly

One of the key features of cloud computing applications is that they enable to share and (jointly) edit files via the cloud. Only 16% of the survey respondents say they do not share data with others. When looking at social environment, Study 2 showed that Dropbox is mostly used alone (35.9%) or with 1 or 2 people (36.5%). Strikingly, when the user is alone, higher QoE is reported than when with others. Also, a reasonable part of participants considered the presence of others "annoying."

However, in the debriefing survey following Study 2, those same participants said that the presence of others mostly has no influence on their overall experience and that jointly modifying files is considered to be a positive QoE factor. Our study shows that sharing data via the cloud is key, but direct interpersonal contact during the use of Dropbox affects QoE, although users do not realize this *a posteriori*.

Emotional context

Obs. 6: users demand security and privacy in cloud computing

In contrast to QoS as an objective measure, QoE is a highly subjective measure influenced by the user's emotions [20]. In the Qualinet white paper, QoE has been defined in terms of affective states [3]. In Study 2, 8 out of the 13 participants reported experiencing problems while using Dropbox. Our analysis (see Figure 8) confirms that QoE is indeed lower when users are frustrated or annoyed and higher when delighted. Similar to [16], this is a result statistically different from when there were no problems at all. Experiencing the occurrence of problems, that also has a major impact on QoE [20], is also highly subjective to the users' emotions. 80.3% of our Study 1 respondents indicate that it is frustrating when they are not able to access personal cloud applications due to slow mobile Internet access or facing technical problems (*i.e.,* service availability). However, problems are not always related to service availability, but can also be caused by the user's expectations and preferences, emotional state and memory effects [22]. A suggestion to overcome low QoE caused by user-related problems is using persuasive messages (*e.g.*, marketing an application update with: "We are really better now", as to convince users of the improved application).

Other factors that are perceived subjectively are privacy and security [22]. With Study 1 respondents initially indicating that they were not concerned about privacy infringement or to lose the data stored in their personal cloud, they later indicated to not be eager to store files that might contain confidential or private personal information in the cloud. In an open question on the disadvantages of personal cloud services, a third of the respondents mentioned possible violation of privacy and security issues, such as dependency of the provider (*i.e.,* not fully controlling the data); the location of the servers; and who else might have access. The ability to secure files with a pin code is therefore considered as a positive QoE factor. From a cloud provider's point-of-view, it is important to make its users aware of the precautions that have been taken towards file securing, data ownership and privacy protection.

Limitations

We acknowledge the limited sample of Study 2 (N=13). We consciously decided not to recruit many participants because of the possibility of privacy issues, especially since we were tracking their mobile (cloud) application usage. Furthermore, since each participants had to answer an ESM questionnaire *every time* they used Dropbox, we decided to limit the study to 2 weeks, as to not overburden our participants and to not bias our data collection.

Also, we acknowledge that not all *possible* contextual dimensions were taken into account in this study. To provide a broader, more holistic vision on context and subsequently users' QoE, we could for example, have mapped meteorological (weather, temperature, humidity), organizational, psychological and cultural context.

Other contextual factors that we initially wanted to measure but were unable to during Study 2, was battery life and network traffic. We could have assessed cloud-storage efficiency in terms of mobile battery and network traffic (stored versus transferred). This can be used to make a contribution to cloud-storage as a means to overcome mobile devices' storage limitations and possibly highlight quality assurances for a better cloud-service for mobile devices.

However, collecting network traffic data is battery intensive, as we need to constantly request this data from Android OS (*i.e.,* no event is shared regarding network traffic) so we decided against it. Lastly, a hiatus in Study 2 is that we only logged signal strength in a mobile context and not in a fixed (Wi-Fi) environment. Therefore, we were not able to link QoE to Wi-Fi signal strength, although we assume this to be related [18]. This might provide a better understanding of fluctuations in QoE ratings in a Wi-Fi context. Another aspect of Dropbox that was not highlighted in this study is evaluating QoE when sharing data (*i.e.,* How does the user know that his/her shared data on Dropbox is perceived by the other end without problems?) This should be studied on both ends to conclude the QoE evaluation.

CONCLUSION

The purpose of this paper is to gain insights in the use- and QoE-related aspects of cloud storage services and how users' context might affect QoE. Firstly, an online survey with 349 users of cloud computing services was conducted. In an exploratory follow-up study, the use of Dropbox on mobile devices was monitored in real-time using a mobile-based Experience Sampling Method (ESM) questionnaire. In total, we collected 156 responses on *in-situ* context of use for Dropbox on smartphones and tablets. Future QoE-aware cloud services should take into account a number of observations to meet users' expectations: users demand connectivity from any device, at any time and from any place. Also, users expect high-speed (mobile) networks, collaboration amongst multiple users and lastly, they demand security and privacy in their cloud computing services.

Acknowledgements

Authors* were funded by the Academy of Finland project 137736 and TEKES project 2932/31/2009.

REFERENCES

1. Armbrust, M., Stoica, I., Zaharia, M., et al. A view of cloud computing. *Communications of the ACM 53*, 4 (2010), 50.
2. Bevan, N. Quality in use: Meeting user needs for quality. *J. Systems and Software 49*, 1999, 89–96.
3. Callet, P. Le, Möller, S., and Perkis, A. Qualinet white paper on definitions of quality of experience. *European Network on Quality of Experience in Multimedia Systems and Services* (2012).
4. Casas, P., Seufert, M., Egger, S., and Schatz, R. Quality of experience in remote virtual desktop services, *IEEE IM 2013*, (2013), 1352–1357.
5. Cisco. Cisco Visual Networking Index : Forecast and Methodology , 2010 – 2015. *Middle East June*, (2011), 2010–2015.
6. Dey, A.K., Abowd, G.D., and Salber, D. A Conceptual Framework and a Toolkit for Supporting the Rapid Prototyping of Context-Aware Applications. *Human-Computer Interaction 16*, 2 (2001), 97–166.
7. Drago, I., Mellia, M., Munafò, M., and Sperotto, A. Inside Dropbox : Understanding Personal Cloud Storage Services. *Internet Measurement Conference - IMC '12*, (2012), 481–494.
8. Ferreira, D. AWARE: A mobile context instrumentation middleware to collaboratively understand human behavior. *University of Oulu,* (2013).
9. Gartner. Gartner Says 821 Millon Smart Devices Will Be Purchased Worldwide In 2012; Sales to Rise to 1.2 Billion in 2013. *http://gtnr.it/1kw0t87*, 2012.
10. Hektner, J.M., Schmidt, J.A., and Csikszentmihalyi, M. *Experience Sampling Method: Measuring the Quality of Everyday Life*, (2007).
11. Hobfeld, T., Biedermann, S., Schatz, R., Platzer, A., Egger, S., and Fiedler, M. The memory effect and its implications on Web QoE modeling. *Int. Teletraffic Congress (ITC)*, (2011), 103–110.
12. Hobfeld, T., Schatz, R., Varela, M., and Timmerer, C. Challenges of QoE management for cloud applications. *IEEE Communications Magazine 50*, 2012, 28–36.
13. Ickin, S., Wac, K., Fiedler, M., Janowski, L., Hong, J.-H., and Dey, A.K. Factors influencing quality of experience of commonly used mobile applications. *IEEE Communications Magazine 50*, 4 (2012), 48–56.
14. Kahneman, D., Krueger, A.B., Schkade, D.A., Schwarz, N., and Stone, A.A. A survey method for characterizing daily life experience: the day reconstruction method. *Science 306*, (2004), 1776–1780.
15. Kotler, P., Keller, K., Brady, M., Goodman, M., and Hansen, T. Marketing management. *Marketing Management*, (2009), 40–47.
16. Marez, L. De and Moor, K. De. The Challenge Of User- And QoE-Centric Research And Product Development In Today's ICT-Environment. *Observatorio Journal*, (2007), 1–22.
17. Medhi, D. and Trivedi, K. A hierarchical model to evaluate quality of experience of online services hosted by cloud computing. *Integrated Network Management (IM 2011)*, (2011), 105–112.
18. De Moor, K., Joseph, W., Ketykó, I., et al. Linking Users' Subjective QoE Evaluation to Signal Strength in an IEEE 802.11b/g Wireless LAN Environment. *J. Wireless Communications and Networking 2010*, (2010), 541568.
19. Pine, B.J. and Gilmore, J.H. *The experience economy: work is theatre & every business a stage*. (1999).
20. Reiter, U., Brunnström, K., De Moor, K., et al. Factors influencing Quality of Experience. *Advanced Concepts, Applications and Methods*, (2014), In press.
21. Staelens, N., Moens, S., Broeck, W. Van den, et al. Assessing Quality of Experience of IPTV and Video on Demand Services in Real-Life Environments. *IEEE Transactions on Broadcasting 56*, (2010).
22. Voas, J. and Zhang, J. Cloud Computing: New Wine or Just a New Bottle? *IT Professional 11*, (2009).
23. Zhou, M., Zhang, R., Xie, W., Qian, W., and Zhou, A. Security and Privacy in Cloud Computing: A Survey. *Semantics, Knowledge and Grids*, (2010), 105–112.

A Wearable Virtual Guide for Context-Aware Cognitive Indoor Navigation

Qianli Xu, Liyuan Li, Joo Hwee Lim, Cheston Tan, Michal Mukawa, Gang Wang
Institute for Infocomm Research, Agency for Science, Technology and Research
1 Fusionopolis Way, #21-01 Connexis (South Tower), Singapore
{qxu, lyli, joohwee, cheston-tan, stumam, gswang}@i2r.a-star.edu.sg

ABSTRACT
In this paper, we explore a new way to provide context-aware assistance for indoor navigation using a wearable vision system. We investigate how to represent the cognitive knowledge of wayfinding based on first-person-view videos in real-time and how to provide context-aware navigation instructions in a human-like manner. Inspired by the human cognitive process of wayfinding, we propose a novel cognitive model that represents visual concepts as a hierarchical structure. It facilitates efficient and robust localization based on cognitive visual concepts. Next, we design a prototype system that provides intelligent context-aware assistance based on the cognitive indoor navigation knowledge model. We conduct field tests to evaluate the system's efficacy by benchmarking it against traditional 2D maps and human guidance. The results show that context-awareness built on cognitive visual perception enables the system to emulate the efficacy of a human guide, leading to positive user experience.

Author Keywords
Indoor navigation; cognitive spatial model; context-aware; wearable camera; visual perception.

ACM Classification Keywords
H.5.2 Information Interfaces and Presentation: User Interfaces – *interaction styles*; H.1.2 Models and Principles: User/Machine Systems – *human factors*.

INTRODUCTION
Indoor localization and navigation have great potential for personal assistance and context-aware services [23, 31]. Existing technologies are mostly based on sensing specific signals, such as, GPS, infrared, WIFI, and RFID [21]. There are several challenges faced by these sensor-based technologies in indoor environments [16, 31], e.g., the high cost of infrastructure construction, the accuracy of localization, and the reliability of signals in complex indoor environments. Moreover, sensor-based localization methods normally anchor the user's location on a 2D map, which requires the users to interpret the map and associate it with the egocentric perception of the environment [18].

MobileHCI 2014, September 23–26, 2014, Toronto, ON, Canada.
Copyright © ACM 978-1-4503-3004-6/14/09...$15.00.
http://dx.doi.org/10.1145/2628363.2628390

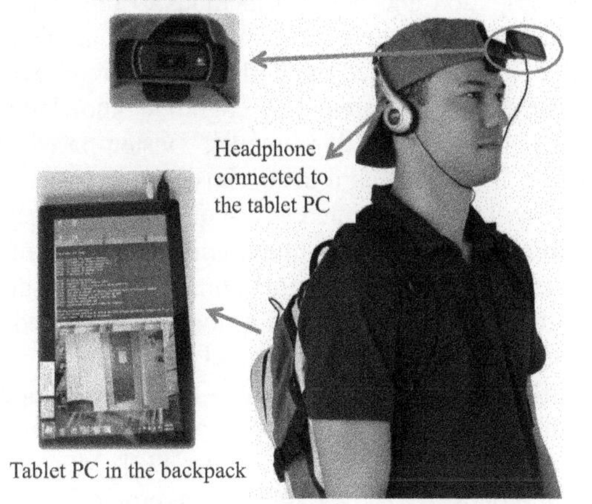

Figure 1. Prototype system for a wearable navigation guide based on cognitive vision for indoor wayfinding

Recently, advancements in wearable cameras (e.g., Google Glass) and mobile computing provide a way to achieve an egocentric perception from the first-person-view (FPV) vision [19, 24]. Unlike sensor-based systems, a vision-based system does not require signal sending devices. Rather, it only requires a camera to receive the visual information. Therefore, it alleviates the need of special building infrastructure for spatial sensing and enables hands-free operations. However, light-weight wearable devices are not sufficient. From a user-centered perspective, there are two major challenges to build such a system: (1) the representation of navigation knowledge that is consistent with the human cognition of wayfinding, and (2) the design of interactions that specify the cognitive communications between the system and the user.

One could resort to human intelligence in assisting wayfinding when designing an intelligent, vision-based navigation guide. If a human usher accompanies a visitor to an indoor destination, she will first (often implicitly) retrieve knowledge of the building and destination, and forms a mental model of the route. Then, along the route she will give instructions typically with reference to some spatial positions (e.g., "*Go through the glass door and turn left*") based on the egocentric visual perception of the current scene, as well as the knowledge of the route [3].

This makes the instructions effective and incurs less mental effort, thus reducing the visitor's stress in a new environment. Existing sensor-based methods could not provide such navigation service because they do not possess the cognitive knowledge of wayfinding built on an egocentric perception of scenes.

The motivation of this research is to provide aided wayfinding using a wearable virtual guide. Inspired by the cognitive process of human-aided wayfinding, we intend to build a cognitive model of knowledge representation for indoor navigation and develop methods to provide context-aware navigation instructions. We propose a hierarchical cognitive model aligned with the concepts of egocentric visual scenes to represent the cognitive knowledge of a building. Based on this model, vision-based indoor navigation is defined as a state transition problem where a complex route is represented as a sequence of trip segments. These trip segments embody the cognitive concepts of indoor scenes. Further, by analyzing the human behaviors in indoor wayfinding, we design navigation instructions based on the egocentric perception of scenes and the changing contexts along a route. Such a capacity makes the system adaptable to the status of the user and the conditions of the environment, which is known as context-awareness [23]. Moreover, this research proposes a novel interaction protocol for indoor navigation that consolidates multiple aspects of contexts, including the physical space, time, and user's cognitive ability. Therefore, the navigation instructions are designed for human cognitive states based on egocentric perception. Hence, we call it cognitive context-aware indoor navigation.

To evaluate the effectiveness of the proposed model, we built a prototype system and conducted user studies involving a few navigation tasks in a complex office building. It is shown that the system was able to provide accurate and robust navigation aid. Moreover, it was perceived as a useful and intelligent tool that enhanced user experience, similar to a human guide in certain aspects.

In this paper, we focus on the contexts related to human cognitive knowledge of wayfinding in indoor environments based on egocentric visual perceptions. In comparison with existing indoor navigation tools, notably those built on mobile devices [6, 7, 9, 28, 31, 32, 38], our system has two main advantages. First, owing to the cognitive concepts of indoor scenes, our method provides more comprehensive navigation knowledge beyond simple decision points. It also alleviates the need of landmarks or fiduciary markers for localization. Second, it is wearable and supports hands-free interaction for context-aware navigation. In this regard, the main contributions of this paper are:

1. A new model for representing egocentric-based cognitive knowledge for indoor navigation;
2. A novel interaction protocol for context-aware navigation that employs egocentric views.

RELATED WORK

Wayfinding and Navigation

Wayfinding and navigation is a persistent requirement of daily life and has received much attention from cognitive scientists and interaction designers [35]. Traditionally, a user uses a map to find the way in a new environment. Recent advances in wayfinding and navigation resorted to spatial models that accommodate an egocentric perspective and human cognition [2, 21, 22, 31]. Irrespective of the medium used for spatial representation, three sources of information are involved in a wayfinding model [17], namely, the environment (physical reality), the topological representation in the form of a map, and the mental representation (cognitive knowledge) possessed by an agent. An agent perceives the egocentric view of the environment and associates the egocentric observations with the allocentric representation for spatial localization and wayfinding. Such a process usually relies on various mental capabilities and efforts [17].

According to the classical cognitive model of wayfinding [40], three levels of cognitive knowledge are required: (1) *survey knowledge* (knowledge about the environment), (2) *route knowledge* (knowledge about the path), and (3) *destination knowledge* (knowledge about the target). The survey knowledge is considered as a mental representation of a familiar area, including information about regions, routes, topography, and landmarks. The route knowledge is the mental representation of a path to a destination that is beyond the immediate field of vision. The destination knowledge is about landmarks along the path to the destination. Many theories have been proposed, focusing on the relationship between the environments and agents [17, 35, 40]. For example, the route knowledge is represented as a sequence of decision points/action pairs, where a landmark is usually associated with a decision point [35].

Existing cognitive models for wayfinding mainly deal with the topological representation of the environment and design of landmark/action pairs for route directions in outdoor environments [35]. Current vision-based navigation methods require a sequence of front views along a route in memory and perform image-matching for navigation [25]. As such they are not computationally effective for indoor navigation because: (1) few salient landmarks are available indoors [37], and (2) there is a misalignment between the allocentric nature of the model and the egocentric perception of the user. Due to these limitations, existing systems usually provide sparse navigation guidance at specific points (e.g., landmarks). It is difficult to provide navigation assistance in real-time to accommodate the user needs. For example, it may require a user to self-locate herself based on the current scenes [3]. It is desirable to develop a computational model for indoor wayfinding based on the egocentric perception and mental concepts of indoor scenes. Such a capacity enables the cognitive-level communication between a system and a user in navigation.

Context-aware Interaction

Context can be defined as characterizing the situation of entities that are relevant to the interaction between a user and an application [14]. A context-aware system can adapt the information content to the users' status [27]. Early work on context-aware interaction focused on mobile computing that was sensitive to the location of users and objects [26, 36]. Recently, more advanced sensors, powerful mobile devices, and enhanced computational intelligence have enriched the implications of context. The scope of context has been expanded to include the physical environment, users' social setting [8], their activities [5, 27], past experience [15], time, weather, the display medium [12], etc. Of particular interest is the user's cognitive ability and familiarity with the environment [6, 9]. In fact, context-awareness was considered as an essential element for building the information models in navigation applications [26]. A few systems with context-awareness include the Aixplore [1], GUIDE [11], HIPS [34], etc. However, in the respective work, the navigation information was mostly tailored to the capability of the system (e.g., its sensibility and accuracy) rather than the user-specific factors.

Some systems have been built to customize interaction modalities and information content to the user's needs [13, 39]. However, these systems usually address only the static and long-term user needs, which are not particularly useful in real-time task-specific navigation. Some researchers proposed activity-based navigation [7, 32], which resorted to recognizing users' activities (e.g., walking or standing still) to inform the format and content of instructions. However, these simple activities may not effectively reflect the user's actual needs. Moreover, for interaction design, users are expected to find navigation instructions on the displays of mobile devices, which require additional cognitive efforts and shifts of attentions. Finally, it requires the user to hold the device upright in most circumstances [31]. Therefore, it is suitable for sporadic usage rather than long-term and frequent use.

METHODOLOGY

Cognitive Knowledge Representation

To achieve egocentric perception of an indoor environment with a wearable vision system, we propose a hierarchical context model for spatial perception based on cognitive conceptualization of FPV indoor scenes (Figure 2).

The model has three layers. At the top layer, a root node is used to represent a specific building. At the next layer, the nodes represent functional areas in the building. In the subsequent case example, it contains three nodes that represent the following cognitive spatial concepts: (1) *Shopping* area, (2) *Transition* area (paths connecting the shopping area and other functional areas), and (3) *Office* area. The bottom level contains sub-classes of locations in each area. For example, the conceptual locations in the *Shopping* area are *Lobby*, *MainEntrance*, *Shop*, *GateToLiftLobby*, etc.; the locations in *Transition* area are *LiftLobby*, *InLift*, *Entrance*, etc.; and the *Office* area has *MeetingRoom*, *Junction*, *Corridor*, *Entrance/Exit* etc. The nodes within each level are connected if there is a direct path between them, as indicated by the dash lines in Figure 2. For example, in layer II, the nodes of *Shopping* and *Transition* are connected, and in layer III, the *MainEntrance* and *Lobby* are connected.

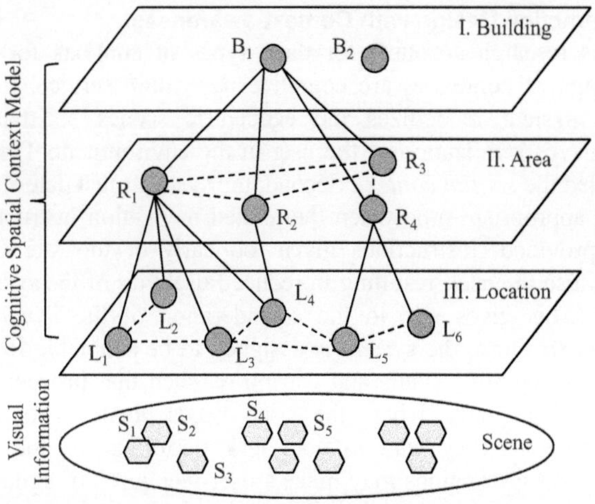

Figure 2. A structure of cognitive spatial context model

The above spatial concepts and their relations collectively constitute the cognitive spatial context model. It represents the survey knowledge for wayfinding. Further, a scene layer is defined as visual information in the form of image sequences (videos) (Bottom of Figure 2), which correspond to the nodes in the cognitive spatial model. In other words, these scenes can be mapped to the location/area/building concepts as defined above. The mapping relationship is established using scene recognition based on image classification algorithms [29].

Next, a cognitive route model can be generated from the hierarchical context model for a specific navigation task in the following process. Given an origin and a destination, two chains of nodes can be generated in the area and location levels, respectively. That is, the route model consists of a chain of area nodes and a chain of location nodes. The area nodes are connected to their child location nodes according to the hierarchical structure. Importantly, we define a trip segment as all information (including the visual scenes) associated with two connected locations. In this way, navigation is reduced to a state transition problem, where a complex indoor route is represented as a sequence of trip segments.

In an actual navigation task with a given origin and destination, scenes (i.e., image sequences) are captured continuously using the wearable camera. The scenes are categorized into area nodes and location nodes, which are compared with the nodes in the cognitive route model. Once a match is found between a recognized node and that in the cognitive route model, specific navigation instructions are retrieved according to predefined rules.

Interaction Design with Context-awareness

This research accounts for three types of contexts for the design of context-aware cognitive navigation service. First, the system recognizes the egocentric scenes so that it achieves localization of the user in the environment. This is called the *spatial context*. Second, the system must determine the appropriate time when the related navigation instruction is provided. Instructions given too early or too late may confuse the user, resulting in reduced usability of the system [4]. This gives rise to the consideration of the *temporal context*. Third, the system is designed to be adaptable to the user's cognitive status and capability, such that instructions are given only when the user needs them. Too few instructions may lead to poor task performance; and too frequent instructions may make a user feel bored or agitated. We consider an individual's status and spatial cognition capability as the *user context*.

Data collection

To align the different types of contexts with the indoor scenes along trip segments, we conducted an experiment to collect visual information related to the typical indoor segments and the actual user behaviors. The experiment involved subjects who were new to the building to go to three destinations in sequence: (1) from the main entrance outside the building (denoted as M_0) to a meeting room M_1 in the *Office* area, (2) from M_1 to meeting room M_2, and (3) from M_2 to meeting room M_3. M_0~M_3 are located at different floors and different parts (towers) of the building. Six subjects were involved in the experiment.

At the beginning of the experiment, a subject's self-reported ability of spatial cognition was collected using the Santa Barbara Sense-of-Direction (SBSOD) scale [20]. The SBSOD score is used to adjust the system's behavior to accommodate the subject's cognitive spatial capability. Before each task, a subject was informed of the next destination and was asked to find it. Along the route, the FPV video was recorded using the vision system, which comprises a webcam connected to a tablet PC running Windows 7 OS. The head-mounted webcam captures color images with a resolution of 640×480 pixels at 8 frames per second. These images are streamed to the tablet PC using a USB cable. In the meantime, a human usher who was familiar with the route accompanied the subject and provided assistance when needed. Such a need is recognized if a subject explicitly said that s/he needed help, or if the usher observed subtle signs of confusion of the subject. Notes were taken of the times and locations of the need for assistance.

Localization using cognitive visual scenes

Videos captured in the navigation tasks were analyzed to build the task-specific route knowledge. Sample scenes in the route from M_0 to M_1 are shown in Figure 3, with 10 scenes/locations belonging to 3 areas (i.e., *Shopping*, *Transition*, and *Office*), respectively. The trip segments,

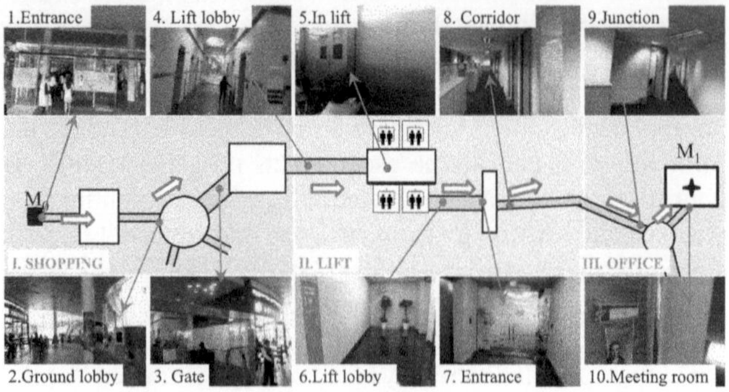

Figure 3. Scenes (images) and locations along a task route (M_0-M_1)

including the scenes, constitute the video-based, task-specific domain knowledge.

Once the route model is built, it can be used to determine the location of a user in an actual navigation task. Specifically, when a user goes along a route, the visual scenes are captured continuously and are used to infer the locations. Two cues are used to determine the location, namely, image categorization and time. The research adopts the extended spectral regression method to infer the location category based on image sequences [29]. This method uses a few learning algorithms to map the raw low-level image features into a manifold subspace with reduced dimensionality. It significantly reduces the load of feature computing, making it possible to recognize scenes using a lightweight computational device. According to [29], the image-driven localization can achieve 84.1% accuracy.

To further improve the robustness of localization, our model includes temporal inference (time). This is intended to tackle the dynamics of a wayfinding task. For example, it takes less time if a user walks faster than others; and the time in a lift may be unusually long when many people are entering/leaving the lift at different floors. The mean travel time of each trip segment is determined roughly on the distance of the segment. First, the time when a location (L_i) is reliably identified (based on image recognition) is denoted as t_i^0. Next, the travel time of a trip segment (T_i) is defined as the average interval between two adjacent locations (L_i, L_{i+1}), i.e., $T_i = avg\left(t_{i+1}^0 - t_i^0\right)$. The information is used in the subsequent probability model for localization (Figure 4).

Next, a probability distribution function is built for each trip segment to specify the probability that a visual scene is associated with that segment. In this study, we adopt a normal distribution $N(t_i, \sigma_i)$, where $t_i = t_i^0 + \sigma_i$ and σ_i is initialized empirically as a value that is slightly larger than the minimum travel time of the segment. It changes dynamically during a specific navigation task.

In a navigation task, after a scene is registered, the probability distribution function for the respective trip segment is retrieved and used to determine the user's location, i.e., the probability that a user is located in trip segment *i* is dictated by the current scenes and how long the scene is in the view since scene registration (t_i^0). With the increase of a user's staying time in the segment, σ_i increases gradually until the next scene is correctly recognized as the subsequent location. For example, at time t_i^0, the scene recognition module identifies the present scenes as location L_i. Accordingly, the distribution function $N(t_i, \sigma_i)$ is retrieved. Note that the distribution function of the previous location $N(t_{i-1}, \sigma_{i-1})$ is still active, i.e., there is typically an overlap between the probability distribution function for adjacent locations. With the probabilities $p_{i-1}(t)$ and $p_i(t)$ computed according to the Gaussian distribution models, the current location is determined based on:

$$L(t) = \arg\left(\max\left(Rand\left(p_{i-1}(t)\right), Rand\left(p_i(t)\right)\right)\right) \quad (1)$$

where *Rand*(*p*) represents a random number in the range of [0, *p*]. At the time t_i^0, the likelihood of recognizing the location as *i* and *i*+1 is identical. As time passes, there is higher probability that the location is recognized as *i*+1. The mechanism is similar to dead reckoning in a typical navigation process. However, unlike activity- or movement-based dead reckoning which suffers drift and loses accuracy over time [33], the time step parameter is calibrated each time a new location is correctly recognized.

Context-aware navigation instructions

The above process allows the system to determine the location of a visitor when s/he traverses the route. The next issue is how to provide effective navigation aids based on the location information. We design an interaction protocol such that navigation instructions are given timely and unambiguously according to the cognitive needs of the user and the egocentric visual perception.

First, we define a decision point along a trip segment as the place where a user needs certain guidance. The decision points are extracted based on the subjects' behaviors in the wayfinding experiment. We found that a need for guidance may or may not be associated with an intersection. For example, when walking along a main corridor, the users did not hesitate in continuing along this direction even if there were sideways leading to an irrelevant place (e.g., a toilet or a pantry). Conversely, users may need certain kind of help even if there were no alternative routes. This happened when the user was unsure if s/he was on the correct route after a prolonged period of unassisted walking. In such a situation, it is useful to affirm the user to continue in that direction. This user-centered approach is consistent with the heuristics of instruction chunking and controlled granularity for lowering the user cognitive load in wayfinding [35]. However, by exploiting the actual user behavioral patterns, our approach alleviates the need to explicitly define the heuristics to optimize the instructions.

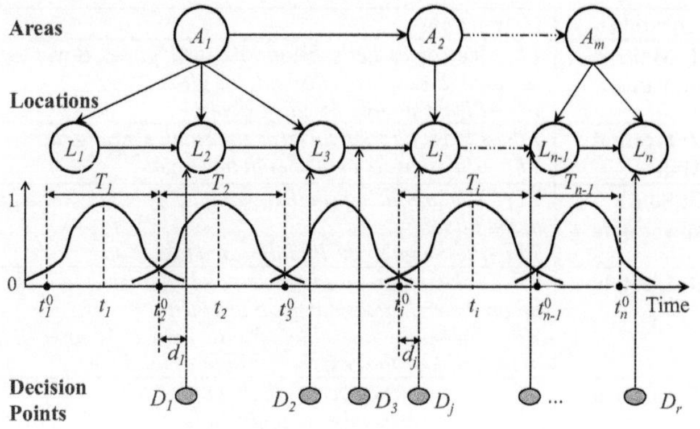

Figure 4. A stochastic model that accommodates multiple aspects of the context

Based on our experiment, if one or a few subjects explicitly requested navigation guidance or showed signs of confusion or hesitation at a position, the respective location was considered as a decision point (D_j). Such decisions reflect the cognitive need of a human subject in wayfinding. A probability value (P_j) is defined on the number of subjects (n) who requested aids at D_j.

$$P_j = \begin{cases} 0.2n, 1 \le n \le 5 \\ 1 \quad n = 6 \end{cases} \quad (2)$$

This model shows that the more subjects required assistance in the vicinity of a decision point, the more likely an assistance instruction is needed. This probability will be used to determine if an instruction is given at an appropriate position. Based on the training data, 10 decision points are identified for task 1, 11 for task 2, and 10 for task 3.

Next, the starting time of the navigation instruction is determined based on the user's cognitive behavior in a trip segment. We design a model that specifies the time attribute of a decision point based on the average interval between the time when a location is identified (t_i^0) and the time of a subject's request for help. The mean value of the time interval between t_i^0 and decision point (D_j) is d_j. Accordingly, the navigation instruction should be provided at time $t_i^0 + d_j$.

To tackle the possibility that a user does not comply with the instructions or there is a significant delay in a user's action due to unforeseen circumstances, the system repeats the instructions (the instructions are rephrased to avoid being considered to be too rigid). We use TT_{j-1} to denote the narration at decision point D_j, and TT_{j-2} to denote the rephrased narration. As an example, when a user reaches the lift lobby, a voice instruction TT_{4-1} is given (Table 1). In case the user stays in the lift lobby for a time longer than expected, another instruction TT_{4-2} is given. Table 1 shows the list of instructions associated with the trip segments along the route $M_0 \rightarrow M_1$ (ref. Figure 3). These navigation instructions are generated and presented as voice instructions using the text-to-speech module.

Location	Instructions
1: Main entrance	$TT_{1.1}$-*Welcome. Let's begin. We will go to Bayes at level ten. Please walk through the glass doors.* $TT_{1.2}$-*Please go into the glass doors.*
2: Ground Hall	$TT_{2.1}$-*Please turn left towards the South Tower gate.* $TT_{2.2}$ -*Please walk to the South tower gate.*
3: South tower gate	$TT_{3.1}$-*You are facing south tower gate. Please go ahead to the lift lobby.* $TT_{3.2}$-*Please go to the lift lobby and take a lift.*
4: Lift lobby	$TT_{4.1}$-*Take a lift on the left side; and go to level ten. The lift on the right does not go to level ten.* $TT_{4.2}$-*Take a lift to level ten. Please look at the top right of the lift door to see if the lift stops at level ten.*
5: Inside lift	$TT_{5.1}$-*Please remember to alight at level ten.* $TT_{5.2}$-*Please remember to alight at level ten.*
6: Lift lobby, Info Board	$TT_{6.1}$-*Please stand in front of the information board and check if you are at level ten.* $TT_{6.2}$-*Proceed to the glass door and get in.*
7: Entrance	$TT_{7.1}$-*Turn right after you enter the glass door.* $TT_{7.2}$-*Please make a right turn after the glass door.*
8: Corridor	$TT_{8.1}$-*Go straight ahead for about 30 meters.* $TT_{8.2}$-*Please go ahead until the junction.*
9: Junction, meeting room	$TT_{9.1}$-*We are close to Bayes. It is the room on the left side of the junction.* $TT_{9.2}$-*Bayes room is around. Please check the name on the door.*
10: Meeting room door	$TT_{10.1}$-*Here we are. You have reached meeting room Bayes. Congratulations!* $TT_{10.2}$-*You have reached meeting room Bayes. Congratulations!*

Table 1. Navigation instructions along route 1: M_0-M_1

In addition, the orientation of a user is critical for correct guidance. In our system, since the scenes are defined on egocentric view, the orientation information is embedded into the scene categories. For example, when a user walks from *LiftLobby* to *Office* along the entrance, the scenes are categorized as *EntranceToOffice*; if the user walks along the same link from *Office* to *LiftLobby*, the scenes are categorized as *ExitToLiftLobby*. We have also considered this issue at decision points where different orientations will lead to different instructions. As an example, in a lift lobby, our system identifies the different information boards on the opposite sides of the lift lobby.

Finally, to account for user's mental capability of spatial cognition, we used the SBSOD score as a parameter to modulate the probability that an instruction is provided at the decision point. Let C_p be a subject's spatial cognition level which is derived from the SBSOD. At any time t_k, a navigation instruction is provided according to three rules:

1. If: $t_k = t_i^0 + d_j$ AND $P_j \geq \min\left(1, \frac{C_p - C_L}{C_H - C_L}\right)$, Then: $TT_{j\text{-}1}$;
2. If: $t_k = t_i^0 + 2\sigma_i$ AND $t_k > t_i^0 + d_j$, Then: $TT_{j\text{-}2}$;
3. If: $t_k \geq t_i + 3\sigma_i$; Then: $TT_{j\text{-}3}$.

Note that in rule 1, C_L (=0.36) and C_H (=0.67) are the smallest and largest scores of the spatial cognitive capability level, respectively, as derived from the six subjects who participated in the data collection experiment. P_j is defined in Eq. 2. This rule determines if an instruction should be given or not depending on the user's cognitive spatial ability. In rules 2 and 3, $\sigma_i = T_i/2$ is used to specify the time property. $TT_{j\text{-}3}$ ("*You seem to be lost. Please talk to the experimenter.*") is used to allow the user to recover from a situation when the location is persistently not identified or if it does not change for an exceptionally long time.

EXPERIMENTAL EVALUATION

We tested the context-ware cognitive navigation guide (denoted as CNG) by comparing it with two other types of navigation aids, namely, a 2D map (denoted as MAP) and a human guide (denoted as HUG). For the MAP condition, the subject was given the floor plans of the routes for which three destinations were marked out. The subjects were supposed to find the destinations without further external aid. In the HUG condition, an experimenter followed the subject and gave instructions when there was a need.

Participants

We recruited 12 participants (6 male, 6 female; mean age 27.7 years with a standard deviation of 8.6 years). The experiment was carried out for individual subjects. Each navigation mechanism (MAP, CNG, and HUG) was used once for each person. The order of the tasks was identical across all test sessions, namely, task1: $M_0 \rightarrow M_1$, task2: $M_1 \rightarrow M_2$, and task3: $M_2 \rightarrow M_3$. On the other hand, the order of navigation mechanisms was different and counter- balanced for the order of usage. This is to cancel out the learning effect, as well as the effect of task difficulty.

Experiment Design

A general procedure of the experiment is as follows. First, the SBSOD questionnaire was used to evaluate the subject's self-reported spatial cognition. The subject's SBSOD score was input into the system as a configuration parameter. Next, the subject was led to the starting point (M_0), where the wearable system was attached. Based on the predetermined order of assistance for that experiment session (Note that the order is different for different subjects), the voice feedback was provided through earphones if the CNG was to be used for the respective task. Otherwise the system ran in a recording mode.

Upon completion of an individual task, a questionnaire was given to the subject to collect the feedback on the respective navigation assistance. After three tasks were completed, a visual memory retention test was carried out whereby the subject was shown a series of 80 photos of the interior of the building. Half of the photos (40) were taken along the task route, and the other half were not. Each image was shown in the tablet screen for a maximum of 5 seconds during which the subject decided if s/he had seen the scene along the route. This was intended to estimate how much visual information the subject could remember.

Finally, the subject was requested to backtrack to the destinations ($M_3 \rightarrow M_2 \rightarrow M_1 \rightarrow M_0$). No navigation assistance of any kind was provided. The experimenter recorded the time that the subject finished each backtracking task. When the participant returned to the origin (M_0), s/he received a $15 shopping voucher as a token of appreciation.

Measures

The efficacy of the system is evaluated using both objective and subjective measures. Objective measures include:

- The time taken to complete an individual task ($O_{\_Time}$),
- Time taken to backtrack in a task ($O_{\_BTime}$),
- Memory retention of scene along the route ($O_{\_Mem}$).

For $O_{\_Time}$ and $O_{\_BTime}$, we normalized the time for each task. The normalization was intended to cancel out the effect of route length and other conditions. From the data collection experiment, we computed the mean (μ_i) and standard deviation (σ_i) of the time for each task (i=1, 2, 3). The normalized time t_i^n for a subject in task i was computed as: $t_i^n = (t_i - \mu_i)/\sigma_i$. The same normalization scheme was applied to the backtracking time.

Subjective evaluation of user experience is conducted on seven measures, each consisting of 3-4 items.

- Usefulness ($S_{\_Use}$) – how useful the guide/tool is for the navigate task.
- Ease-of-use ($S_{\_Eou}$) – how easy it is to use the guide/tool in the task.
- Cognitive load ($S_{\_Cog}$) – how much mental effort the subject has to make to complete the task.
- Enjoyment ($S_{\_Enj}$) – how enjoyable it is to use the guide/tool.
- Stress level ($S_{\_Stress}$) – how stressful the subject feels in the course of the task.
- Intelligence ($S_{\_Int}$) – to what extent the guide/tool can make decisions like a human.
- Trust ($S_{\_Trust}$) – how trustful the advices/information are, as provided by the guide/tool [30].

Hypotheses

We expect that the wearable navigation guide emulates a human guide to achieve equivalent performance with respect to both objective and subjective measures. At the same time, it should outperform the 2D map in most measures, except those related to backtracking time ($O_{\_BTime}$), scene memory ($O_{\_Mem}$), and trust ($S_{\_Trust}$). For $O_{\_BTime}$ and $O_{\_Mem}$, it is expected that the subjects who used MAP would be able to memorize more information of the route because: (1) a map provides an allocentric representation of the entire space (topological knowledge) which may lead to better spatial memory [41], and (2) the users may make more effort to observe the environment in the wayfinding [17]. In comparison, both CNG and HUG provide navigation directions and require less mental effort of the subjects. Therefore, the time taken for backtracking should be shorter in the MAP condition, and more scene images would be correctly recognized. For trust, we expect that the users will trust MAP and HUG more than CNG.

Measurements		Hypotheses	
Task completion time	($O_{\_Time}$)	H1	MAP>CNG=HUG
Backtracking time	($O_{\_BTime}$)	H2	MAP<CNG=HUG
Scene memory	($O_{\_Mem}$)	H3	MAP>CNG=HUG
Usefulness	($S_{\_Use}$)	H4	MAP<CNG=HUG
Ease of use	($S_{\_Eou}$)	H5	MAP<CNG=HUG
Cognitive load	($S_{\_Cog}$)	H6	MAP>CNG=HUG
Enjoyment	($S_{\_Enj}$)	H7	MAP<CNG=HUG
Stress	($S_{\_Stress}$)	H8	MAP>CNG=HUG
Intelligence	($S_{\_Int}$)	H9	MAP<CNG=HUG
Trust	($S_{\_Trust}$)	H10	MAP>CNG<HUG

Table 2. Hypotheses (MAP - 2D map, CNG - Cognitive navigation guide, HUG - Human guide)

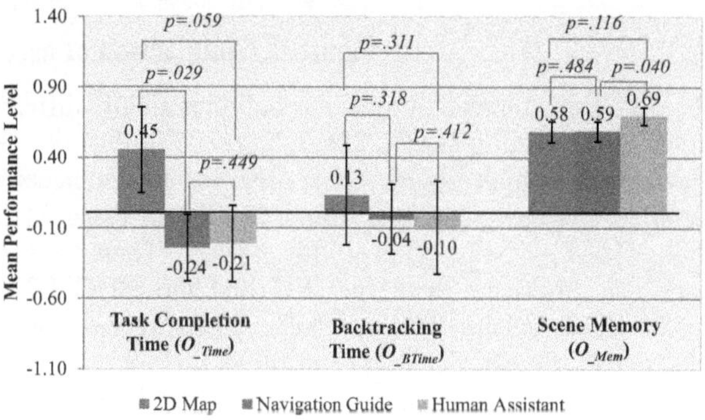

Figure 5. Comparison of task performance using objective measures.

This is because a map gives objective information that is supposed to be credible; a human guide with knowledge of the place is supposed to give trustful information.

The hypotheses in the study are presented in Table 2. The comparison is made with respect to the values of individual measurements. The formula "*X*>*Y*" means the value of the respective measurement is significantly higher in condition *X* than in condition *Y*. "*X*=*Y*" means there is no statistical difference in the measures in two conditions. For example, H1 is concerned with the task completion time ($O_{\_Time}$): MAP>CNG=HUG. It means that: (1) the task completion time is longer when the subjects use MAP than when they use CNG or HUG, and (2) CNG and HUG lead to equivalent task completion time.

RESULTS

Task Performance

We analyzed the effects of different navigation methods using one-way ANOVA with repeated measures for three objective measurements ($O_{\_Time}$, $O_{\_BTime}$ and $O_{\_Mem}$). Post- hoc analysis with paired *t*-test was conducted with a Bonferroni correction (a significance level set at p < 0.017). It is expected that the task performance is higher when subjects use CNG and HUG than when they use MAP. In addition, CNG and HUG would lead to identical performance. Hypothesis 1 (Task completion time) was partially supported, whereas H2 (Backtracking time) and H3 (Scene memory) were not supported. The results are shown in Figure 5.

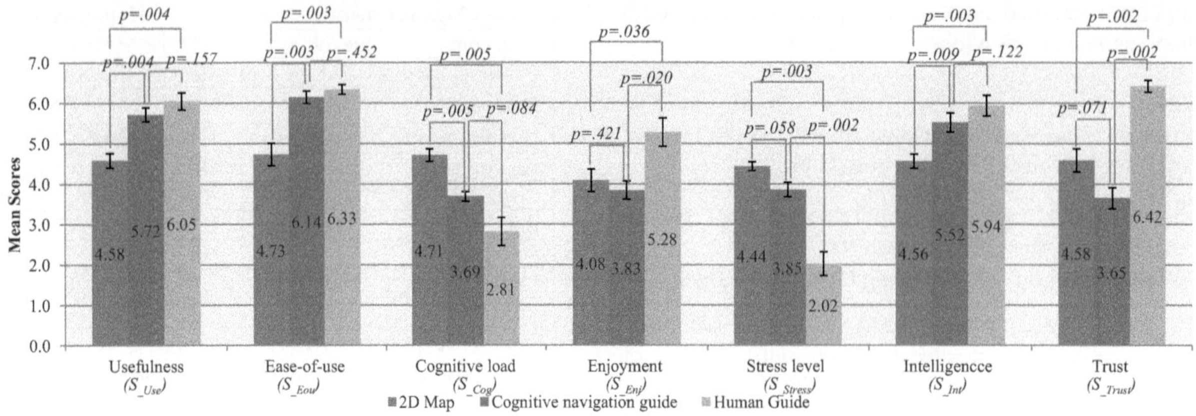

Figure 6. Comparison of user experience using subjective measures.

First, the task completion time was only marginally different among three conditions ($F(2,22)=3.40, p=.051$). Post-hoc test shows that it took slightly less time for the subjects to complete the navigation task using CNG than using MAP: $O_{\_Time}$ (MAP, CNG): $t(11)=2.114$, $p=.029$. There was no statistical difference between CNG and the HUG [$O_{\_Time}$ (CNG, HUG): $t(11)=-0.131$, $p=.449$], nor between MAP and HUG: $O_{\_Time}$ (MAP, HUG): $t(11) = 1.694$, $p=.059$.

Furthermore, no statistical difference was found among three conditions with respect to the backtracking time [$O_{\_BTime}$: ($F(2,22)=0.567$, $p=.575$] and the scene memory [$O_{\_Mem}$: ($F(2,22)=1.907$, $p=.172$]. For the backtracking task, the subjects generally completed the task fairly fast as seen from the near zero mean values of the normalized backtracking time. Similar observation was made for scene memory testing, whereas we found that the memory retention of the visual scenes was slightly worse in the CNG condition than in the HUG condition [$O_{\_Mem}$ (CNG, HUG): $t(11)=-1.978$, $p=.040$]. Overall, the task performance among the three conditions did not show much difference. The reasons will be discussed later.

Subjective Evaluation

We conducted Friedman test with post-hoc analysis using Wilcoxon signed ranks with Bonferroni correction (a significant level set at $p<0.017$) for evaluating the subjective measures. We found significant differences in all seven subjective measures across three conditions. Post-hoc analysis showed a positive effect of the CNG's context-aware capability on the user experience as compared to the MAP, except for the measurements of enjoyment, stress, and trust (Figure 6). In particular, users perceived the cognitive navigation guide to be more useful than the 2D map [$S_{\_Use}$ (CNG, MAP): $z=2.849$, $p=.004$]; it was easier-to-use [$S_{\_Eou}$ (CNG, MAP): $z=2.937$, $p=.003$]; it reduced users' cognitive load [$S_{\_Cog}$ (CNG, MAP): $z=-2.82$, $p=.005$]; and it was considered to be more intelligent [$S_{\_Int}$ (CNG, MAP): $z=2.608$, $p=.009$]. However, the enjoyment level was identical in both conditions [$S_{\_Enj}$(CNG, MAP):$z=-0.804$, $p=.421$]. No statistical difference was found with respect to the stress level [$S_{\_Stress}$ (CNG, MAP): $z=-1.896$, $p=.058$] and trust [$S_{\_Trust}$ (CNG, MAP): $S_{\_Trust}$: $z=-1.806$, $p=.071$.

As compared to the human guide, the CNG achieved equivalent performance in terms of usefulness [$S_{\_Use}$ (CNG, HUG): $z=-1.414$, $p=.157$], ease-of-use [$S_{\_Eou}$ (CNG, HUG): $z=-0.751$, $p=.452$], cognitive load [$S_{\_Cog}$ (CNG, HUG): $z=1.730$, $p=.084$], and intelligence [$S_{\_Int}$ (CNG, HUG): $z=-1.548$, $p=.122$]. It was inferior to a human guide in terms of perceived stress [$S_{\_Stress}$ (CNG, HUG): $z=3.056$, $p=.002$] and trust [$S_{\_Trust}$ (CNG, HUG): $z=-3.070$, $p=.002$]. A marginal difference was observed in favor of the human guide for the enjoyment level [$S_{\_Enj}$ (CNG, HUG): $z=2.317$, $p=0.020$].

DISCUSSION

From the evaluation, it was found that the wearable navigation guide with context-awareness effectively realized cognitive navigation. The measures for which the cognitive navigation guide emulated a human guide were related to the functional aspects of the system. In particular, its performance in usefulness, ease-of-use, intelligence, and cognitive load was equivalent to the human guide. Thus, it is functionally competent in providing navigation guidance for the tasks. This result shows that it is technically feasible to realize real time cognitive indoor navigation based solely on the FPV-based vision system.

The absence of differences in the performance indicators, namely, task completion time, backtracking time, and scene memory was unexpected. The effect of navigation tools seemed to have played little role in the users' memorability of the route and visual scenes. This can be explained in two aspects. First, in a new environment, the subjects' arousal level is typically high, i.e., they paid much attention to observe the scenes when traveling in the building, irrespective of the navigation tools used. Second, the cognitive load for wayfinding and scene memory might be confounded. In fact, the subjects needed to make much effort to reckon the correct route when using a 2D map (which can be seen from the higher level of cognitive load). Thus, the resource allocated to scene memory is reduced.

The lack of difference between MAP and CNG in enjoyment ($S_{\_Enj}$) turned out to be surprising. We had expected that the MAP, as a passive tool, would lead to lower enjoyment level.

However, the absolute value of enjoyment was higher in MAP (M=4.083, SD=0.975) than in CNG (M=3.830, SD=0.797). We suspected that the subjects might have confused the enjoyment of using the device with that of the task. It has been shown that a moderate level of challenge in completing a task may lead to positive enjoyment [10]. Considering that the MAP condition incurred more cognitive load, the subjects might have enjoyed meeting the challenge of the navigation task.

Further, we predicted that users have less trust in the CNG than in the MAP. This hypothesis was not supported with statistical significance. Nevertheless, with a relatively lower level of trust, there was a sign of users' reluctance in trusting the CNG, even though the device did not make any apparent mistakes. Some subjects showed their concerns during the post-experiment survey, i.e., they wondered how the CNG were able to determine the location and give instructions solely using a camera. Thus, they thought the navigation instructions were hardcoded and might be faulty. Such observations gave rise to an important design implication, i.e., unfamiliarity and lack of knowledge of the system may negatively influence users' trust. It is advisable to give users basic knowledge of the system in order to enhance trust and acceptance.

On the other hand, the vision system did not achieve a level of performance that is equivalent to a human guide with respect to enjoyment, stress level, and trust. These measures are largely concerned with the emotional aspects of users' experience. This can be partially attributed to the scope of the study, i.e., to ensure accurate and timely navigation based on the perceptual ability of the system. The design of context-awareness emphasized more on enhancing system performance than on delivering enjoyable experience. This inadequacy can be compensated by adding more features that enhance the users' emotional engagement.

Another observation is related to system reliability. There were no apparent errors during the navigation tasks in all three conditions. However, when using the 2D map, subjects occasionally paused and looked at the map for directions. This might have contributed to the slightly longer task completion time using the map. On the other hand, a few errors happened during the backtracking task when the subjects deviated from the correct route; and the number of errors were similar in three conditions (MAP: 2; CNG: 2, HUG: 3). It might have contributed to the larger variances in backtracking time, thus causing the lack of statistical difference in backtracking time.

Limitations and future work

Benchmarking strategy: In this research, the proposed system is benchmarked against a 2D map and a human guide, rather than with the latest technologies built on smartphones [6, 7, 9, 28, 31, 32, 38]. The reasons for choosing these two benchmarking navigation mechanisms are: (1) they are the prevalent navigation aids that are familiar to the subjects, (2) these two methods require different mental efforts in wayfinding, and (3) smartphone-based navigation systems are still not available in the test building. Moreover, the current work focuses on the technical feasibility of a wearable cognitive usher, i.e., the benefit over traditional maps and its competency compared to human. A comparison with smartphone-based navigation technologies will lead to details of usability evaluation, which is beyond the scope of this research. Notwithstanding, an apparent benefit of using the wearable device is its support to hands-free operation in navigation.

User-specific context: The current research has a simplified mechanism to deal with the cognitive context related to the user. In the proposed model, we trained the model to estimate the decision points where users were likely to request assistance. This strategy could only deal with the "average" needs of users. It falls short as an adaptable mechanism to account for the individual needs of users. In the future, we will collect visual cues that directly reflect a user's needs based on his/her activities [32], e.g., head movement patterns for showing hesitation, eye gaze for indicating intentions, etc. The ability to assess user's cognitive states more accurately and adaptively will endow the system with refined context-awareness for desired personalization. In addition, the current application required additional effort to collect the subject's SBSOD score. However, this is solely for purpose of experimental validation. In future, the respective feature may be designed as a customized function, i.e., users may optionally provide their level of spatial cognition. If so, the system will adapt its feature based on such information. Otherwise, the system provides standard instructions as if the user has "average" cognitive ability.

Scalability and learning: A few parameters of the proposed system are determined by the training data from six videos, and the current test includes a few specific routes. It might not support navigation along unexplored routes. However, the proposed cognitive spatial model is not contingent on the specific routes and can host alternative routes of interest. Data collection at a larger scale can be carried out by observing users' activities along other routes such that the navigational information can be incorporated into all the trip segments. Moreover, the system can be expanded to the entire building provided that wearable cameras, such as, Google Glass, become prevalent. Possibly, during the system development stage, visitors to a host building may voluntarily participate in the program. A glass-type device can be leased out and the navigation process can be recorded. Different routes will be covered in this process. The navigation information can be aggregated, such that route segments may be extracted from users who follow different routes. Therefore, the need for a huge data set for each and every route is exempted.

CONCLUSION

Wearable vision systems provide tremendous opportunities for real-time and context-aware services, e.g., navigation. In this research we investigated if vision-based wearable guides with proper cognitive knowledge and interaction modalities are beneficial to the users. We addressed two critical issues in the implementation of such a system, namely, the representation of cognitive knowledge for wayfinding based on egocentric visual information and the design of cognitive interaction with context-awareness. The hierarchical spatial information structure establishes the foundation for cognitive visual information processing. The interaction model with context awareness serves as a useful basis for developing personalized navigation services. Our research leads to useful implications for the design of wearable vision systems in navigation assistance in indoor environments.

ACKNOWLEDGMENTS

This research is partially supported by the Singapore A*STAR, SERC grant on HFE (#092 1530095).

REFERENCES

1. Aixplorer. http://www.aixplorer.de/.
2. Arikawa, M., Konomi, S.I. and Ohnishi, K. NAVITIME: Supporting pedestrian navigation in the real world. *Pervasive Computing*, *6*, 3, (2007), 21-29.
3. Baras, K., Moreira, A. and Meneses, F., Navigation based on symbolic space models. in *IPIN'10*, (2010), 1-5.
4. Barberis, C., Bottino, A., Malnati, G. and Montuschi, P. Experiencing indoor navigation on mobile devices. *IT Professional*, *14*,1, (2014), 50-57.
5. Bardram, J.E. Activity-based computing for medical work in hospitals. *ACM T. Comput-Hum. Int.*, *16*, 2, (2009), 10:11-36.
6. Baus, J., Krüger, A. and Wahlster, W., A resource-adaptive mobile navigation system. in *IUI'02*, (2002), 15-22.
7. Brush, A.J., Karlson, A.K., Scott, J., Sarin, R., Jacobs, A., Bond, B., Murillo, O., Hunt, G., Sinclair, M., Hammil, K. and Levi, S. User experiences with activity-based navigation on mobile devices *MobileHCI'10*, ACM Press (2010).
8. Bulling, A., Weichel, C. and Gellersen, H., EyeContext: Recognition of high-level contextual cues from human visual behaviour. in *CHI'13*, (2013), 305-308.
9. Butz, A., Baus, J., Krüger, A. and Lohse, M., A hybrid indoor navigation system. in *IUI'01*, (2001), 25-32.
10. Chatting, D.J., Action and reaction for physical map interfaces. in *TEI'08*, (2008), 187-190.
11. Cheverst, K., Davies, N., Mitchell, K. and Friday, A., Experiences of developing and deploying a context-aware tourist guide: The guide project. in *MobiCom'00*, (2000), 20-31.
12. Cheverst, K., Davies, N., Mitchell, K., Friday, A. and Efstratiou, C., Developing a context-aware electronic tourist guide: Some issues and experiences. in *CHI'00*, (2000), 17-24.
13. Davies, N., Cheverst, K., Mitchell, K. and Efrat, A. Using and determining location in a context-sensitive tour guide. *Computer*, *34*, 8, (2001), 35-41.
14. Dey, A.K., Abowd, G.D. and Salber, D. A conceptual framework and a toolkit for supporting the rapid prototyping of context-aware applications. *Human-Computer Interaction*, *16*, 2, (2001), 97-166.
15. Etzion, O., Skarbovsky, I., Magid, Y., Zolotorevsky, N. and Rabinovich, E., Context aware computing and its utilization in event-based systems. in *DEBS'10*, (2010), 270-281.
16. Fallah, N., Apostolopoulos, I., Bekris, K. and Folmer, E. Indoor human navigation systems - A survey. *Interacting with Computers*, *25*, 1, (2013), 21-33.
17. Freksa, C., Klippel, A. and Winter, S. A cognitive perspective on spatial context. in Cohn, A.G., Freksa, C. and Nebel, B. eds. *Spatial Cognition: Specialization and Integration*, Dagstuhl, 2007.
18. Giudice, N.A., Bakdash, J.Z., Legge, G.E. and Roy, R. Spatial learning and navigation using a virtual verbal display. *ACM Trans. Applied Perception*, *7*, 1, (2010), No. 10.
19. Hanheide, M. *A Cognitive Ego-Vision System for Interactive Assistance*, Ph.D Thesis, University of Bielefeld, Bielefeld, 2006.
20. Hegartya, M., Richardsona, A.E., Montellob, D.R., Lovelacea, K. and Subbiah, I. Development of a self-report measure of environmental spatial ability. *Intelligence*, *30*, (2002), 425-447.
21. Heiniz, P., Krempels, K.H., Terwelp, C. and Wüller, S., Landmark-based navigation in complex buildings. in *IPIN'12*, (2012), 1-9.
22. Hile, H., Grzeszczuk, R., Liu, A., Vedantham, R., Košecka, J. and Borriello, G. Landmark-based pedestrian navigation with enhanced spatial reasoning. *Lecture Notes in Computer Science - Pervasive Computing*, *5538*, (2009), 59-76.
23. Hong, J., Suh, E.-H. and Kim, S.-J. Context-aware systems: A literature review and classification. *Expert Systems with Applications*, *36*, 4, (2009), 8509-8522.
24. Kanade, T. and Hebert, M. First-person vision. *Proceedings of the IEEE*, *100*, 8, (2012) 2442-2453.
25. Kaneko, Y. and Miura, J. View sequence generation for view-based outdoor navigation. in *ACPR'11*, (2011), 139-143.
26. Kenteris, M., Gavalas, D. and Economou, D. Electronic mobile guides: A survey. *Pers. & Ubiquit. Comput.*, *15*, 1, (2011), 97-111.
27. Kjeldskov, J. and Paay, J. Indexicality: Understanding mobile human-computer interaction in context. *ACM Trans. Computer-Human Interaction*, *17*, 4, (2010), 14:11-28.
28. Kray, C., Elting, C., Laakso, K. and Coors, V., Presenting route instructions on mobile devices. in *IUI'03*, (2003), 117-124.
29. Li, L., Goh, W., Lim, J.H. and Pan, S.J. Extended spectral regression for efficient scene recognition. *Pattern Recognition*, *47*, 9, (2014), 2940-2951.
30. McKnight, D.H., Carter, M., Thatcher, J.B. and Clay, P. Trust in a specific technology: An investigation of its components and measures. *ACM T. Inform . Syst.*, *2*, 2, (2011), 1-15.
31. Möller, A., Kranz, M., Huitl, R., Diewald, S. and Roalter, L. A mobile indoor navigation system interface adapted to vision-based localization, in *MUM'12*, (2012), No.4.
32. Mulloni, A., Seichter, H. and Schmalstieg, D., Handheld augmented reality indoor navigation with activity-based instructions. in *MobileHCI'11*, (2011), 211-220.
33. Mulloni, A., Seichter, H. and Schmalstieg, D., Indoor navigation with mixed reality world-in-miniature views and sparse localization on mobile devices. in *AVI'12*, (2012), 212-215.
34. Opperman, R. and Specht, M., A context-sensitive nomadic exhibition guide, in *HUC'00*, (2000), 127-149.
35. Richter, K.-F. and Klippel, A. A model for context-specific route directions. in Freksa, C. et al.(eds). *Spatial Cognition IV. Reasoning, Action, and Interaction*, (2004), 58-78.
36. Schilit, B. and Theimer, M. Disseminating active map information to mobile hosts. *IEEE Network*, *88*, 5, (1994), 22-32.
37. Snowdon, C. and Kray, C., Exploring the use of landmarks for mobile navigation support in natural environments. in *MobileHCI '09*, (2009), No. 13.
38. Taher, F. and Cheverst, K., Exploring user preferences for indoor navigation support through a combination of mobile and fixed displays. in *MobileHCI'11*, (2011), 201-210.
39. Wang, S.-L. and Wub, C.-Y. Application of context-aware and personalized recommendation to implement an adaptive ubiquitous learning system. *Expert Syst. Appl.*, *38*, 9, (2011), 10831-38.
40. Wiener, J.M., Buchner, S.J. and Holscher, C. Towards a taxonomy of wayfinding tasks: A knowledge-based approach. *Spatial Cognition and Computation*, *9*, 2, (2009), 152-165.
41 Willis, K.S., Hölscher, C., Wilbertz, G. and Li, C. Comparison of spatial knowledge acquisition with maps and mobile maps. *Computers, Environment and Urban Systems*, *33*, 2, (2009), 100-110

Learning to Recognise Disruptive Smartphone Notifications

Jeremiah Smith, Anna Lavygina, Jiefei Ma, Alessandra Russo, Naranker Dulay
Department of Computing, Imperial College London
180 Queen's Gate, SW7 1AZ, London, UK
{jeremiah, a.lavygina, jiefei.ma, a.russo, n.dulay}@imperial.ac.uk

ABSTRACT
Short term studies in controlled environments have shown that user behaviour is consistent enough to predict disruptive smartphone notifications. However, in practice, user behaviour changes over time (concept drift) and individual user preferences need to be considered. There is a lack of research on which methods are best suited for predicting disruptive smartphone notifications longer-term, taking into account varying error costs. In this paper we report on a 16 week field study comparing how well different learners perform at mitigating disruptive incoming phone calls.

Author Keywords
Interruptions; Machine Learning; Smartphone; Experience sampling;

ACM Classification Keywords
H.5.m. Information Interfaces and Presentation (e.g. HCI)

INTRODUCTION
Various studies have shown that smartphone notifications can be disruptive[2, 11, 7]. A disruptive notification is one that interrupts the recipient such that the disturbance of receiving the notification outweighs the perceived benefit. Notification disruptiveness is also context and content dependent. Approaches to address disruptive notifications can be classified into: *receiver scheduling* [2, 4], where notifications are delayed by the receiving smartphone until a more opportune moment, *sender scheduling* where the receiving smartphone's context is used help a potential sender estimate appropriate moments to send a notification to the user, and *mitigation* [3, 8, 13, 16], where the delivery of a notification is purposely modified to lessen its disruptiveness, for instance decreasing ringtone volume or flashing an LED light.

In this paper, we restrict ourselves to detecting disruptive incoming phone calls, which represent a major source of irritation to some users [11]. We benchmark 6 different machine-learners and analyse how well they work on a 16-week dataset collected using a custom Android application. The learners used are SVM, NB, kNN, RUSBoost, Genetic Programming (GP) and Association Rule learning (AR).

In contrast to previous research we take into account dataset imbalances, varying costs for the different types of classification errors, changes in user behaviours, online windowed learning vs offline learning. We also compare learners qualitatively, in terms of interpretability of predictions taking HCI aspects into account.

MobileHCI 2014, September 23–26, 2014, Toronto, ON, Canada.

http://dx.doi.org/10.1145/2628363.2628404

BACKGROUND
Smartphone interruptions have mostly been researched using short term (5 day to 4 week) studies and experience sampling experiments. Research in [2, 5, 6, 7] focuses on predicting opportune moments to deliver notifications such as after a phone call or at physical activity breakpoints and are suited for textual and task notifications. Most of these approaches use external body-worn accelerometers to gather context, which we think is impractical.

We are interested in incoming calls for which delivery cannot be delayed [3, 16, 14]. The approach in [3] combines *implicit* experience sampling (monitoring phone ringer status changes) with an *explicit* experience sampling heuristic that prompts the user to label contexts that have high ground truth uncertainty. This minimises interruptions due to the sampling process while maintaining high accuracy. While the authors focus on predicting the smartphone ringer setting, i.e. silent or ring, we focus on *individual call signalling preferences* which is more flexible as consecutive calls from different contacts can have different ringer preferences. The approach in [16] uses a sampling heuristic that queries users only when a label covers a wide range of contexts, to lessen the number of samples required as time goes by. The work recognises the need for intelligible learner predictions while also uncovering concept drift in their 4-week dataset.

We follow the approach taken in [14] which uses *implicit* experience sampling i.e. silently gathering labels for contexts based on user actions. This has the disadvantage that there is no control over the amount of data collected, but provides a practical, unobtrusive and long-term data gathering technique which is crucial from an HCI point of view. Virtually all existing works recognise that user notification preferences are user dependent, none address the related problem of varying prediction error costs – a call incorrectly predicted as non-disruptive could potentially affect the user more than the converse. We also address dataset imbalance, which can lead to classifier inaccuracies and is likely to happen in practice.

DATA AND EXPERIMENT

Measuring Learner Performance

One of the main challenges in addressing smartphone interruptions is that users are dissimilar in the way they rate their interruptibility [3, 6, 7, 8, 16].

We set the positive class to be non-disruptive calls and propose to use the following weighted accuracy measure:

$$wp = \frac{w * sensitivity * |c^+| + specificity * |c^-|}{w * |c^+| + |c^-|} \quad (1)$$

where $w = \frac{\text{true positive weight}}{\text{true negative weight}} \in [0, \infty)$ is the user preference ratio of true positive importance (non-disruptive calls predicted as such), over true negative importance (disruptive calls predicted as such). Choosing this class assignment, a false positive could be receiving an audible incoming call during a job interview and a false negative could be silencing an incoming call for a sought after job interview. We also constrain the true positive weight to be in $[0, \infty)$ and the true negative weight to be in $(0, \infty)$. c^+ and c^- are the set of positive and negative class instances respectively. Note that wp takes into account users that prefer a high sensitivity/recall rate (the percentage of correctly recognised non-disruptive calls), preferring to be interrupted by some unimportant calls to avoid potentially missing important ones, i.e. $w > 1$. While $w < 1$ indicates that a user prefers to miss some important calls instead of being interrupted, commanding high specificity (the percentage of correctly recognised disruptive calls) and $w = 1$ is the typically reported accuracy.

Collected Data

We are interested in naturally occurring smartphone interruptions over long periods of time [11] and the associated practical challenges. Intrinsically, explicit experience sampling methods cannot be used to collect such data.

To avoid *experiment fatigue* and the need to observe experiment subjects continuously we developed an Android application that would intercept an incoming call, and let the user answer or decline the call in the usual way with the addition of a new Silent Answer 4th button (plus Answer, Decline and Ignore) that would label the call as disruptive while letting the user answer it anyway, for cases such as receiving an important call at an inappropriate moment. The App shown in Figure 1 had a single screen when opened in the Android App launcher which explained the purpose and how to use the app, while a broadcast receiver would launch the above mentioned custom incoming call screen with a small customisable delay to overlay on the Android default incoming screen. A more detailed explanation of the App can be found in [17].

The collected features were: *day of week*, *month*, *incoming call time*, *incoming phone number (-1 if unavailable)*, *cell tower id*, and *WiFi SSID*. GPS data was also collected but we found that users often turned it off to preserve their battery so we discarded the readings due to many missing values. Polling of other onboard sensors data would require a lot of attention to energy management techniques and was not done to avoid user dissatisfaction with the application.

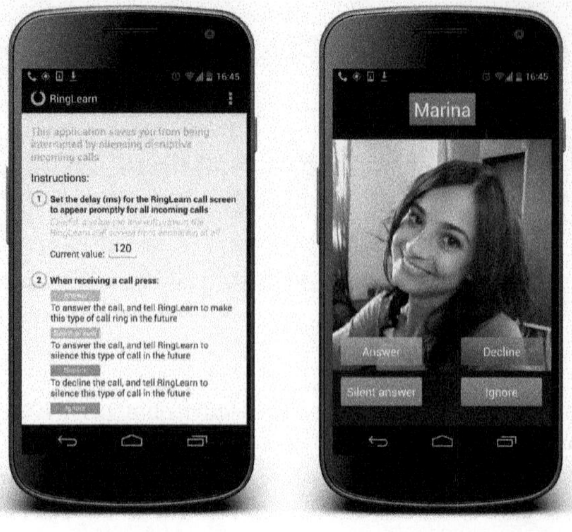

Figure 1. The Android app used to collect the experimental data

To test our learners we collected data from 11 subjects over 16 weeks. Small datasets and corrupted datasets (due to manufacturer incompatibilities with our App) were dropped from the analysis leaving the 3 larger ones belonging to PhD students. For each set, we used the first 60% of data points to train learners and made 10 different test sets, corresponding to 10 different scenarios, by randomly undersampling 90% of the 40% remaining (most recent) datapoints without replacement.

Set name	A	B	C
span (days)	111	118	113
training set size	141	176	115
training $\|c^-\|$	19(13%)	59(33%)	30(26%)
test set size	81	107	71
typical test $\|c^-\|$	12(14%)	19(17%)	15(21%)

Table 1. Summary of our three collected datasets, c^- denotes the set of calls labelled as disruptive

Machine Learning Techniques for Interruption Prediction

The following learners were evaluated:

1. A Support Vector Machine (SVM).
2. A Naive Bayes classifier (NB).
3. A k-Nearest Neighbors classifier (kNN) – a lazy learner.
4. Random Under Sampling ensemble with decision trees (RUS). Uses boosting tailored for imbalanced sets.
5. Genetic programming (GP). A heuristic approach that operates with a large set of feasible solutions represented in the form of trees that are mutated, crossed-over and evaluated over several generations to produce new solutions that are then ranked by a specific utility (fitness) function and can be translated into human readable rules [9].
6. Association Rule learning (AR) that uses data mining to find *class association rules* between the features and the classes, and uses them for predictive classification [12].

Results were benchmarked against the current 'naive' choices users have, putting the phone into a silent mode (Ringer off) or an audible incoming call alert mode (Ringer on).

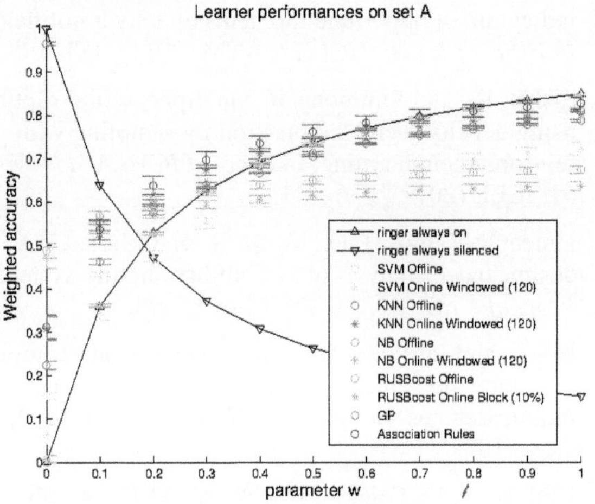

Figure 2. Benchmarked algorithms on set A

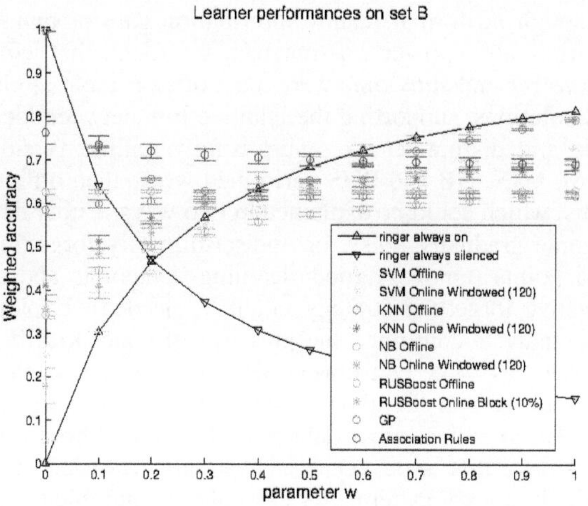

Figure 3. Benchmarked algorithms on set B

Most learners were benchmarked offline and in a sliding-window/block, online learning setting to test for changes in user behaviour, which would be uncovered if incrementally 'forgetting' older datapoints had a positive effect on performance [10]. SVM, NB, kNN were tried with different window sizes from 100% to 30% of the total data by incrementally retraining using with the data label received after each prediction, while RUS used 10 instances at a time due to high training costs.

Cost sensitivity for SVMs was considered by oversampling of the minority class based on the w parameter but did not bring any significant performance gain and is thus not reported. Cost sensitivity for NB classifiers was considered by weighing the predicted probabilities of class membership by w which increased the performance for small values of w but also markedly increased the standard error for larger values of w and is also not reported. The kNN classifier is by default cost insensitive. We did not try any cost sensitive variations of it. RUS, GP and AR are by nature cost sensitive.

Because of the limited size of the number of features collected, we were able to test all combinations (63) of features and found that using any subset of them, either reduced performance or did not yield any significant gain.

RESULTS

Our results show that for each subject there is a range for the w parameter (approximately 0.15 to 0.4) for which machine-learners perform better than a naive solution. This corresponds to a disruptive call weighing between approximately 2 and 7 times that of a non-disruptive call. If users are very concerned about disruptive calls (very low values of w) only GP was able to learn the silent mode behaviour (Figures 2–4). When w approaches 1 i.e. disruptive and non-disruptive calls are weighted the same, users are better off leaving their ringer on due to class imbalance: if the cost of misclassifying a disruptive call is low enough the number of incoming disruptive calls is also low enough so that the aggregate error does not outweigh the benefit of not silencing non-disruptive calls by mistake.

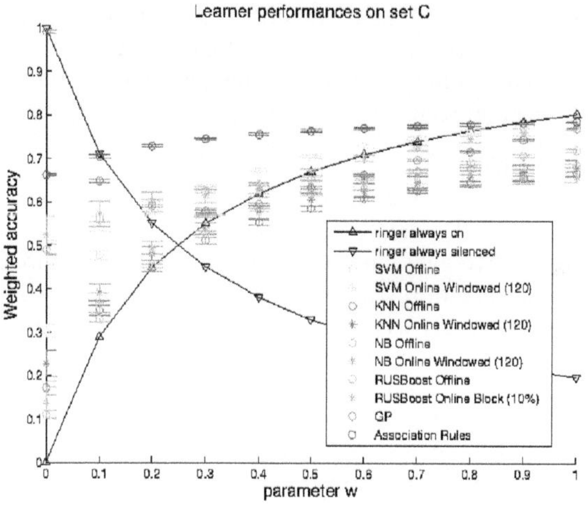

Figure 4. Benchmarked algorithms on set C

The best performing machine-learner was AR, outperformed all others on the w parameter's range of interest. GP came second and was more responsive to different values of w. Both AR and GP potentially have the ability to inform the user the reason for their prediction, which is an important consideration from an HCI perspective. For instance, one of the solutions obtained by GP for dataset C can be represented by the following rule:

```
IF (ssid != 1 OR celltower != 56) AND
   ((contact != 29 AND ssid != -1) AND
    (celltower = 27 OR celltower !=42 AND
     starttime <= 22.54)) THEN disruptive
```

The example of the solution provided by AR for the set C is the following set of rules which are matched with test points from top to bottom or until the default condition is hit:

```
1) IF day = Monday THEN not disruptive
2) IF ssid=-1 AND starttime=14 THEN not disruptive
...
21) IF celltower=56 AND ssid=1 THEN disruptive
...
33) IF day=Saturday AND ssid=2 THEN not disruptive
34) OTHERWISE disruptive
```

Although no formal feature information gain or ranking of discriminative power was pursued, we found that *wifi_ssid*, *cell_tower* and *start_time* were most often present in GP and AR solutions, supporting the intuitive link between location, time and disruptiveness. Surprisingly, online versions of SVM, kNN, NB and RUS performed worse than offline versions, which could be explained in two ways. Either datasets become gradually noisy, or, indiscriminately forgetting old data points removes 'good' learning datapoints and an alternative forgetting strategy might be needed. Exploratory data analysis confirmed the presence of concept drift in all datasets, as some cell towers ids only appeared in the testing sets, so that the above result is even more surprising – we plan to collect more data from the same users to further investigate this issue. Data analysis also revealed that it is difficult to learn patterns, for example, on multiple occasions users would decline incoming calls before picking up creating contradicting labels for very similar datapoints.

Although we accounted for different users preferences by means of a class preference weight parameter w, the way in which to determine a suitable parameter for a user remains an open question which we plan to explore in the future.

DISCUSSION

Our results show that based on the relative importance a user associates with detecting disruptive incoming calls versus non-disruptive calls, machine-learners can be used to lessen the occurrence of disruptive calls (for example, by silencing the phone's ringer when such a call is detected) without fully removing incoming call notifications, as putting the phone in a silent mode would. The best learner, an association rule classifier, outperformed all other benchmarked techniques but also outputs human readable rules which could be used to inform a user why a (non-)disruptive call prediction was made, an important HCI consideration. Moreover it is lightweight and could easily be deployed on a phone.

In a post-experiment survey of the 11 participants, 9 found the App easy to use and the incoming call screen did not confuse of bother them. 7 said they would continue to use the App beyond the experimental setting. 4 participants said they would only do so there was a way to relabel incoming calls, again highlighting the link between disruptiveness and the content of notifications – it is impossible to entirely predict the disruptiveness of a notification without knowing its content.

Other studies [1, 15] have demonstrated that device usage activity such as the amount of time since the user was active on the device are significant features for recognising the disruptiveness of notifications. Incorporating user activity into our features should improve the classifier's predictive power.

Acknowledgements

This work was supported by EU FP7 projects iCareNet (grant 264738) and Allow Ensembles (grant 600792).

REFERENCES

1. Avrahami, D., and Hudson, S. E. Responsiveness in instant messaging: Predictive models supporting inter-personal communication. In *CHI* (2006).
2. Fischer, J. E., Greenhalgh, C., and Benford, S. Investigating episodes of mobile phone activity as indicators of opportune moments to deliver notifications. In *Proc. of MobileHCI '11*, ACM (2011), 181–190.
3. Fisher, R., and Simmons, R. Smartphone interruptibility using density-weighted uncertainty sampling with reinforcement learning. In *Proc. of ICMLA '11 - Volume 01*, IEEE (2011), 436–441.
4. Hincapié-Ramos, J. D., Voida, S., and Mark, G. A design space analysis of availability-sharing systems. In *Proc. of UIST '11*, ACM (2011), 85–96.
5. Ho, J., and Intille, S. S. Using context-aware computing to reduce the perceived burden of interruptions from mobile devices. In *Proc. of CHI '05*, ACM (2005), 909–918.
6. Hudson, S. E., Fogarty, J., Atkeson, C. G., Avrahami, D., Forlizzi, J., Kiesler, S. B., Lee, J. C., and Yang, J. Predicting human interruptibility with sensors: a wizard of oz feasibility study. In *CHI*, ACM (2003), 257–264.
7. Kern, N., and Schiele, B. Towards personalized mobile interruptibility estimation. In *Proc. of LoCA'06*, Springer (2006), 134–150.
8. Khalil, A., and Connelly, K. Improving cell phone awareness by using calendar information. In *Proc. of INTERACT'05*, Springer-Verlag (2005), 588–600.
9. Koza, J. R., Bennett III, F. H., and Stiffelman, O. *Genetic programming as a Darwinian invention machine*. Springer, 1999.
10. Lazarescu, M., Venkatesh, S., and Bui, H. H. Using multiple windows to track concept drift. *Intell. Data Anal. 8*, 1 (2004), 29–59.
11. Leiva, L. A., Böhmer, M., Gehring, S., and Krüger, A. Back to the app: the costs of mobile application interruptions. In *Mobile HCI* (2012), 291–294.
12. Liu, B., Hsu, W., and Ma, Y. Integrating classification and association rule mining. In *KDD* (1998), 80–86.
13. Markitanis, A. Learning mobile user behaviours. Master's thesis, Imperial College London, 2011.
14. Markitanis, A., Corapi, D., Russo, A., and Lupu, E. C. Learning user behaviours in real mobile domains. In *Proc. of ILP'11* (2011).
15. Pielot, M., de Oliveira, R., Kwak, H., and Oliver, N. Didn't you see my message?: Predicting attentiveness to mobile instant messages. In *CHI* (2014).
16. Rosenthal, S., Dey, A. K., and Veloso, M. Using decision-theoretic experience sampling to build personalized mobile phone interruption models. In *Proc. of Pervasive'11*, Springer-Verlag (2011), 170–187.
17. Smith, J., and Dulay, N. Ringlearn: Long-term mitigation of disruptive smartphone interruptions. In *ACOMORE*, PerCom '14 (2014).
18. ter Hofte, G. H. H. Xensible interruptions from your mobile phone. In *Proc. of MobileHCI '07*, ACM (2007), 178–181.

Exploring Smartphone-Based Interaction with Overview+Detail Interfaces on 3D Public Displays

Louis-Pierre Bergé, Marcos Serrano, Gary Perelman, Emmanuel Dubois
IRIT – University of Toulouse
118 Route de Narbonne, 31062 Toulouse, France
{Louis-Pierre.Berge, Marcos.Serrano, Gary.Perelman, Emmanuel.Dubois}@irit.fr

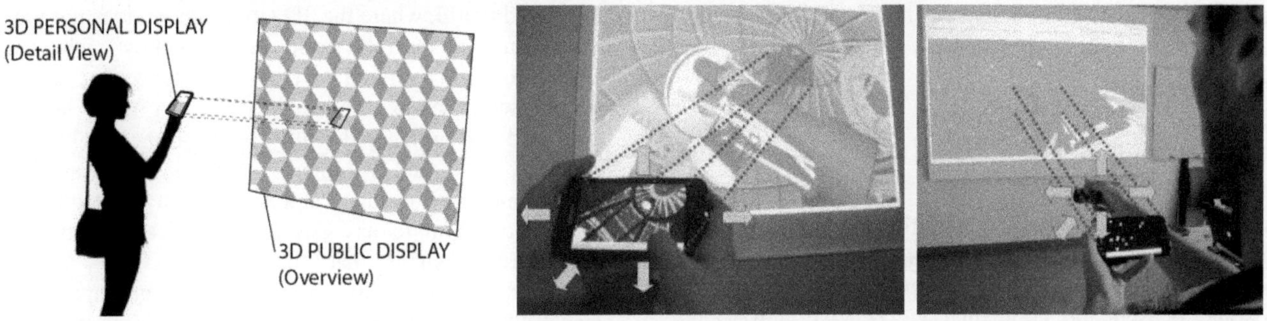

Figure 1: a) General setting of smartphone-based Overview+Detail interface on a 3D Public Display. We used two mid-air navigation techniques in a public installation to explore a 3D telescope visualization: b) Mid-Air Phone and c) Mid-Air Hand.

ABSTRACT
As public displays integrate 3D content, Overview+Detail (O+D) interfaces on mobile devices will allow for a personal 3D exploration of the public display. In this paper we study the properties of mobile-based interaction with O+D interfaces on 3D public displays. We evaluate three types of existing interaction techniques for the 3D translation of the Detail view: touchscreen input, mid-air movement of the mobile device (Mid-Air Phone) and mid-air movement of the hand around the device (Mid-Air Hand). In a first experiment, we compare the performance and user preference of these three types of techniques with previous training. In a second experiment, we study how well the two mid-air techniques perform with no training or human help to imitate usual conditions in public context. Results reveal that Mid-Air Phone and Hand perform best with training. However, without training or human help Mid-Air Phone is more intuitive and performs better on the first trial. Interestingly, on both experiments users preferred Mid-Air Hand. We conclude with a discussion on the use of mobile devices to interact with public O+D interfaces.

Author Keywords
Overview + detail; 3D interfaces; public display; mid-air interaction; personal displays

ACM Classification Keywords
H.5.2. Information interfaces and presentation: Interaction.

MobileHCI 2014, September 23–26, 2014, Toronto, ON, Canada.

http://dx.doi.org/10.1145/2628363.2628374

INTRODUCTION
Public displays allow pedestrians to interact with 2D content such as city maps or tourism information [29]. In this context, existing systems have used smartphones as personal views (Detail) of the public display (Overview), leveraging multi-user access to one display [12]. Visualisation of 3D content on public displays is emerging to visualize scientific 3D data [37]; to explore culture heritage 3D scanned objects [1]; to teach history through virtual tours of 3D reconstructed historical sites [1]; to play public 3D games [42] or to navigate a city 3D map [44].

Most of these examples already include the use of a personal device to interact with the 3D content (to orient and position a slice plane [37] or to navigate in the 3D environment [44]) but few consider how to apply the Overview and Detail (O+D) paradigm using the smartphone. Using the O+D on mobile devices will provide the user with the ability to privately visualize details of the 3D environment while still taking advantage of the mobile device input to interact with the 3D content. However, the public context imposes certain constraints in terms of user's profiles (mainly beginners) and appropriate interaction techniques (which need to be easy to understand and perform).

In this paper we focus on the translation task, i.e. how to move the Detail view (displayed on the smartphone) on a 3D environment, the Overview (displayed on the public display). We report on the evaluation of three interaction techniques for controlling the translation of the Detail view: mid-air hand gestures around the mobile device like [27], mid-air movements of the mobile device itself and classical touchscreen pad. We performed two experiments. The first one is a controlled experiment with training: its goal is to evaluate the three techniques in terms of performance, usability and user preference. The second experiment aims at studying the difficulty of performing the two mid-air gesture-based techniques in a situation imitating a public space, i.e. without the experimenter help or training.

Our contributions include: 1) An elicitation of the design space for mobile 3D O+D, 2) a controlled evaluation of three techniques for the 3D translation of the Detail view and 3) an evaluation of the difficulty to perform the mid-air techniques with no human help or training. We also report about an exhibition in public context for several days.

RELATED WORK

Our research is inspired by previous works on using mobile devices to visualize large datasets, to navigate 3D scenes and to interact with public displays.

Large information space visualization on mobile phone

To explore large information spaces such as web pages or maps, research on visualization proposes three solutions to separate focused and contextual views: Overview+Detail (spatial separation), Zooming (temporal separation) and Focus+Context (seamless focus in context) [12]. On desktop environments, previous research established that Overview+Detail (O+D) is worse than Zooming or Focus+Context (F+C) in terms of task completion time [4, 12]. However, users usually prefer O+D because it helps them build a mental model of the explored information [31]. In addition, display size has less impact on O+D than Zooming or F+C [34].

Recent implementations of these types of interfaces involved mobile devices [10] to support information search on a webpage [35], a map [9] or a scatterplot [40]. Results are mixed: O+D is faster with off-screen objects and maps but slower with scatterplots. And yet, participants prefer O+D for navigation on webpages [35]. They also are better in spatial recall of targets when using O+D [9]. Still, none of these previous works explored the use of focused or contextual views for 3D content.

Our goal is to explore interaction with a large screen providing the 3D contextual view and a mobile phone displaying the 3D focused view. F+C and Zooming interface are not in line with our setting because we have two separate views. Moreover, using F+C interface involve intentional distortion view such as fisheye or lens [12]. Using Zooming interface raises the risk of perturbing user's position and losing the user in the 3D volume. O+D interface seems to be good alternative for our context.

3D navigation with a mobile phone

We focus our analysis on navigation techniques for 3D content [8] on smartphones and where the user controlled the navigation, i.e. active navigation. Existing solutions can be divided into three main types: using the touchscreen, moving the smartphone and interacting around the smartphone (around-device interaction).

Touchscreen is the standard input on mobile 3D games, usually through a rate-based pad [39]. Research works explored touchscreen input with one [5, 13, 18] or two fingers [10, 39]. To reduce finger occlusion, Hachet et al. extended the mobile phone with a 3-DOF elastic controller attached to the device [17].

Using built-in sensors or adding new ones, researchers proposed different techniques based on moving the smartphone. Hurst et al. explored two different metaphors [22]: fixed world, where the 3D environment does not move in relation with the real world, and "shoebox", where the 3D environment is fixed to the smartphone. The idea of pointing with the smartphone as if it was a magic lens has been used for augmented reality applications [1, 32] or to interact with virtual volumetric data [38]. A less direct solution based on tilting gestures has been compared with touchscreen input to navigate a virtual reality panoramic [21]. Results show that the gesture-based technique performed twice as well as the touchscreen input in an orientation task and was preferred by 80% of the users. More recent works investigated around-device interaction as a novel approach to interact with 3D content [36, 26, 27]. PalmSpace is a mid-air gesture technique to rotate 3D objects on the mobile display [27]. Around-device gestures have also been used to navigate 2D multi-scale maps [26].

In our research we compare these three different types of interactions in the context of 3D O+D public displays.

Public Display and mobile phone

To interact with public displays, researchers explored using multi-touch input [14] or mid-air gestures [43]. Another strategy inspired by the prevalence of mobile devices is the use of smartphones as remote controllers [28, 30]. For instance, touchscreen input is used to control a distant cursor [28], to select an item [7] or to pan and zoom [30]. Mid-air gesture with the phone has also been used for some of these tasks [6, 32].

Few works explored interaction with 3D content on public displays. Smartphones have been used to reveal hidden 3D content on augmented posters [16]. In the context of large displays (not necessarily in public context), Song et al. investigated the use of multi-touch interaction and mid-air gestures to explore and annotate 3D data [37].

An important aspect to consider on public displays is how to reveal the interaction technique to the user. This aspect has been barely addressed in the state of the art. Walter et al. [43] investigated different strategies to reveal mid-air gestures to interact with a public display. Their study indicates that users intuitively discover gestures by imitating or extending other user's gestures.

Our work is inspired by solutions using the mobile phone as the means to interact with public displays. For the task of interacting with a 3D O+D interface, existing interaction approaches need to be compared and evaluated. In particular, the public context imposes constraints on how to reveal and learn these interaction techniques. The goal of our work is to deepen existing research on using mobile phones to interact with 3D interfaces on public displays.

INTERACTION TECHNIQUE DESIGN: APPROACH

Among the considerations addressed in the literature, we focus on the main properties for mobile-based interaction with 3D Overview+Detail (O+D) interfaces.

3D Tasks

In our work we focus on the 3D navigation task and more precisely the *travel* subcategory defined by Bowman [8]. Generally the user controls 3 degrees of freedom (DOF) to translate the point of view and 3-DOF to rotate the point of view. Many metaphors have been explored to reduce these DOFs, such as the flying vehicle control metaphor or avatar metaphor [8]. In our work, we limit user control of the Detail view to a 3-DOF translation. This task is sufficient to explore public 3D content such as museum objects and it simplifies the task in a public setting, where interaction needs to be intuitive and straightforward.

Types of interaction techniques

Works presented in the literature report about different approaches to interact with 3D content. Among them using a touchscreen [18], moving the device [5] or around the device [27] have been implemented on mobile phone. We explore these three different approaches to control the position of the Detail view:

- **Mid-Air Hand** (Figure 2–a): the position of smartphone serves as a spatial reference. The position of the hand in this referential is mapped to the virtual position of the Detail view. We constrain the movement of the hand to the area behind the mobile phone. A virtual button on the mobile screen (de)activates this navigation mode.
- **Mid-Air Phone** (Figure 2–b): similar to [22], translations applied to the mobile phone translate the virtual position of the Detail view. As for Mid-Air Hand, a virtual button on the mobile display (de)activates this navigation mode.
- **Touchscreen** (Figure 2–c): inspired by commercial mobile 3D games, we use two rate-based joysticks to control the virtual position of the Detail view. The left circular joystick controls the 2D translation along the X and Y axis. The right cylinder joystick controls the 1D translation along the Z axis. Both pads can be used at the same time to control the 3-DOF navigation.

Mapping

Two ways of mapping a gesture with a 3D translation are illustrated in the literature: direct or indirect [26, 38]. In the direct mapping, the absolute position or gesture offset (in mid-air) is directly mapped to a 3D position on the virtual environment. Both the Mid-air Phone and the Mid-air Hand techniques are based on direct mapping. In the indirect mapping, the gesture controls the velocity and direction of the camera movement in the virtual environment. The Touchscreen technique is based on indirect mapping.

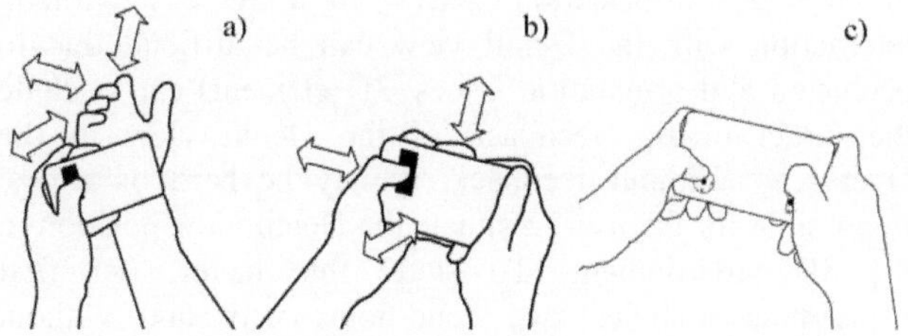

Figure 2: Three types of techniques: a) Mid-Air Hand, b) Mid-Air Phone and c) Touchscreen.

Mid-air gestures reference

Another factor concerning mid-air gestures is whether these gestures relate to a reference position in the real world. We can divide gestures into absolute or relative. Absolute gestures are not linked to a particular position in the real world. For instance, the Mid-Air Phone is absolute: when the user presses the button the virtual camera moves according to the absolute displacement of the phone in the real world. Relative mid-air gestures are linked to a real-world reference object. The Mid-Air Hand technique is relative as it uses the phone as a reference: the movements of the hand are linked to the position of the phone and limited in space around this reference. Previous work suggests that using a reference is useful for mid-air input without visual feedback [15] and for 3D interaction [20].

O+D visualization

To design the representational aspect of O+D interfaces, a set of parameters can be adjusted [10]: 1) the overlap of O+D views (usually not overlapping), 2) the relative size of both views (Overview is usually smaller than Detail view, as in PowerPoint or Google Maps), 3) the volume of space displayed by the Detail view, 4) the number of Detail views and 5) the feedback of the Detail view's position in the Overview (typically a polygonal outline or a shaded area).

In our work, we fixed these visual parameters in order to focus on input interaction. Thereby, the two views are non-overlapping and are displayed on two different displays: the Overview on the Public Display and the Detail view on the smartphone. As opposed to usual O+D, the Detail view is smaller than the Overview. In public context, this setting allows a personal view and multi-user access to the public display. The Detail view displays the 3D environment with no depth limitation. In terms of feedback, a coloured 3D pyramid on the Overview indicates the position of the Detail view: one color is assigned to each user.

Revealing message

Another important factor on public displays is how to inform the user of the interaction to perform. This has already been explored for full-body interaction with a large public display [43]. Different types of feedback (text, icon, video…) were explored. In our work we designed textual and image-based revealing messages to assess the suitability of studied interactions to public context.

3D environment: occlusion and orientation

Previous work on the use of O+D interfaces mainly refers to large 2D information spaces. In a 3D environment, interaction with the Detail view can be difficult due to occlusion and orientation issues. 3D elements can occlude the target or the feedback of the Detail view in the Overview. Without feedback, it may be hard or almost impossible for the user to situate the Detail view position in the 3D environment. To study this factor, our first experiment includes two conditions: with and without occlusion objects.

In next sections we report on two experiments to explore these properties. The first study evaluates the three types of gestures with previous training and with different occlusions. The second study evaluates the two mid-air techniques without training or indications from the experimenter.

SYSTEM DEVELOPMENT

In this section we describe the implementation of the 3D O+D environment and the three interaction techniques illustrated in Figure 2.

3D environment

Our implementation runs synced 3D content both on a mobile device and on a large display. We used a Samsung Galaxy S2 smartphone (6.6x12.5x0.8cm, 116 gr., 4.3" screen) running Android 4.1.2. The large display was a 24" monitor with a resolution of 1920x1080px. To implement all 3D content, we used a C++ open source engine based on OpenGL, Irrlicht [23]. The same C++ 3D code executed on the smartphone and on the large display: to run it on Android we compiled it with a JNI-based tool. The 3D scene on the smartphone ran at 20fps and the scene on the large display ran at 300fps. This difference of frequency was barely perceivable and no user commented on this.

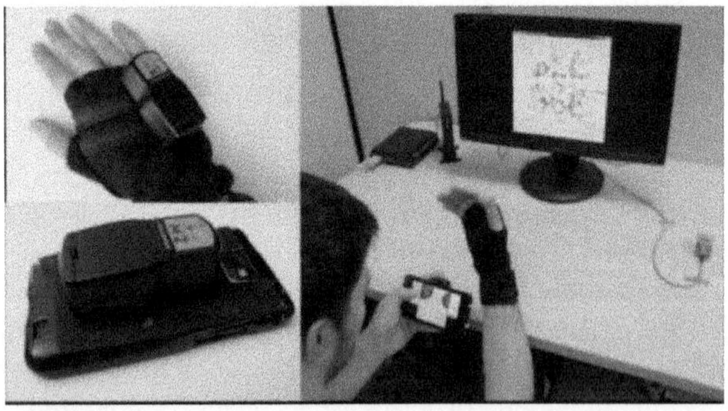

Figure 3. Tracker on hand and on smartphone (left) and user performing the Mid-Air Hand technique (right).

Mid-air gestures tracking

To prototype the mid-air gestures we used two Polhemus Patriot Wireless trackers (7x3x2.5cm, 79.4gr.) [33]. One tracker was attached to the back of the smartphone using Velcro touch fastener. For the Mid-Air Hand technique, the tracker was attached to the hand using a glove and Velcro (Figure 3). We consider in the discussion section envisioned solutions to implement the mid-air tracking.

The trackers communicate wirelessly with a magnetic receptor, USB-connected to the computer running the 3D scene on the large display. The computer and the mobile phone communicated wireless through sockets using the IVY-bus library [24]. We filtered data using the 1€ filter [11]. The tracking system runs at a maximum frequency of 50Hz. Overall, the latency was negligible and no user commented on this.

EXPERIMENT 1: TRANSLATION OF THE DETAIL VIEW

The goal of this experiment is to evaluate the comparative performance of the three techniques presented in the previous section for the 3D translation of the Detail view.

Task and mapping

We asked users to reach a target on a 3D scene using the Detail view. A sphere represented the target. Virtual walls limited the 3D scene to a cubic area. We divided the cube into a matrix of 2x9 equal smaller cubes. We placed the target in the center of one of the 18 small cubes (Figure 4-left). The Detail view, displayed on the mobile screen, is initially situated on the front-center position (red cube in Figure 4-left). The Detail view does not show the entire 3D scene and so the user needs to look at the large display to find the target.

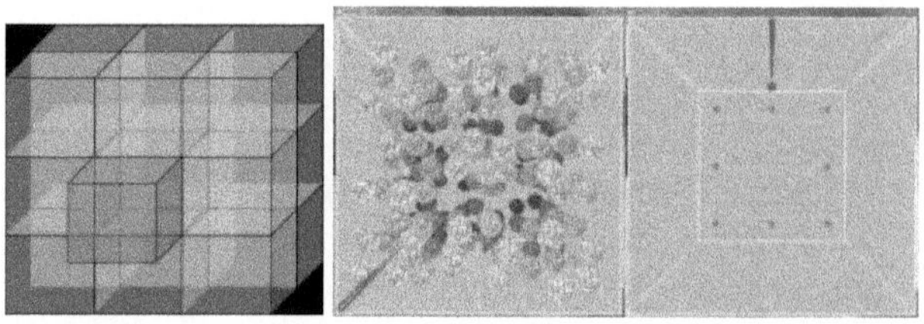

Figure 4: The 3D environment was divided into 18 areas (left), and displayed with or without occlusion objects (center/right).

The participant moves the Detail view until it is close enough to the target: on the Detail view, the target color changes to indicate the user reached it. We studied two occlusion conditions: with occlusion objects (10 spheres randomly distributed inside each of the 18 smaller areas) and without occlusion objects (Figure 4-center, right). We added a feedback on the target position: a ray attached to the target, parallel to the depth axis of the square area.

Apparatus

We used the apparatus described in the previous section.

Participants

We recruited 12 participants (3 female) aged 28.6 years on average (SD=5.2). Two of them had previously played 3D games on mobile phones and 10 of them had used mid-air interaction (Wiimote or Kinect).

Design and procedure

The experiment followed a 3x2 within-participant design, with *Technique* (Mid-Air Hand, Mid-Air Phone or Touchscreen pad) and *Occlusion* (True or False) as factors. Three blocks were run for each technique, the Techniques factor being counterbalanced by means of a 3X3 Latin Square. Trials in a block were grouped by the Occlusion factor, which was always ordered by increasing difficulty (first without Occlusion, then with Occlusion). Each block of trials required 18 selections per Occlusion factor. The 18 targets were randomly ordered. Each subject performed 3 techniques x 3 blocks x 2 occlusions x 18 targets = 324 trials. On average, the experiment lasted 97 minutes, with 1 min. 21 sec. of training for each *Technique*. The training period was performed before each technique and consisted of a minimum of 5 successful trials.

Collected data

We logged all tracking data as well as touch events from the touchscreen. We measured trial completion time from stimulus onset to target reached. Beside time, we collected user preference through a set of techniques: usability via the System Usability Scale questionnaire (SUS) [3] and attractiveness via the AttrakDiff questionnaire [19]. AttrakDiff [19] informs on the attractiveness of a technique according to three distinct dimensions: the pragmatic quality (PQ) indicates whether the user can achieve his goals; the hedonic quality (HQ) indicates to what extent the technique enhances the possibilities of the user; finally the attractiveness (ATT) gives an idea on how the user values each technique based on its quality and engagement.

EXPERIMENT 1: RESULTS

We collected 324 trials/user x 12 users = 3888 trials in total.

Quantitative results

Task completion times

A Shapiro-Wilk test shows that task completion time data does not follow a normal distribution ($p < 2.2 \times 10^{-16}$). We did not find any data transformation that would allow us to use parametric tests. Our statistical analysis is thus based on non-parametric tests. Figure 5 (left) summarizes the task completion times for each technique with and without occlusion. Three different Wilcoxon tests reveal that the occlusion factor has a significant effect on task completion time for each interaction technique: +32.8% (+1.1s, p<0.01) for Mid-Air Hand, +33.6% (+1.21s, p<0.01) for Mid-Air Phone and +38.9% (+1.66s, p<0.01). As expected, the completion time is longer with occlusion.

For the condition without occlusion, a Friedman test reveals a significant effect of the interaction technique on task completion times ($\chi^2(2)$=7.17, p=0.028). A post-hoc test using Wilcoxon with Bonferroni correction shows a significant difference between Mid-Air Hand and Touchscreen Pad (p=0.032). Without occlusion, only one direct mapping technique is significantly faster than the indirect mapping technique. For the condition with occlusion, a Friedman test reveals a significant effect of the interaction technique ($\chi^2(2)$=15.17, p<0.01). A post-hoc test using Wilcoxon with Bonferroni correction shows a significant difference between Mid-Air Hand and Touchscreen Pad (p<0.01) and between Mid-Air Phone and Touchscreen Pad (p=0.016).

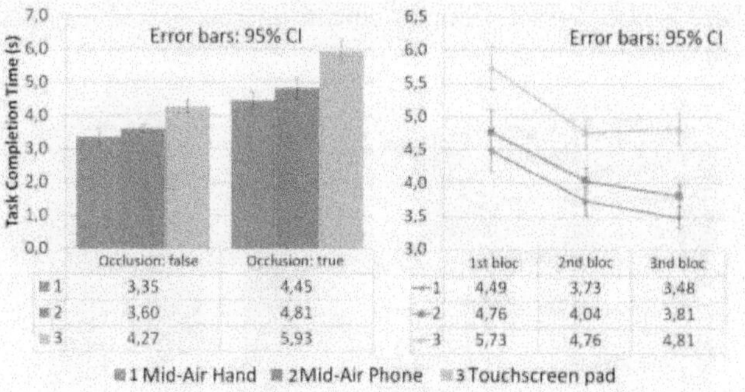

Figure 5: Task completion times (in s) for each technique according to the Occlusion factor (left) and learning effect for each technique (right).

Learning effect

Friedman tests reveal a significant effect of the block order on task completion time for each different interaction technique (Mid-Air Hand: $\chi^2(2)$=10.67, p<0.01; Mid-Air Phone: $\chi^2(2)$=8.17, p=0.017; Touchscreen: $\chi^2(2)$=18, p<0.01). A post-hoc test using Wilcoxon with Bonferroni correction showed a significant difference between the first and the last block for all techniques (Figure 5-right). This confirms a learning effect. Completion time improves 22.5% for Mid-Air Hand (p=0.003), 20.0% for Mid-Air Phone (p=0.05) and 16.0% for Touchscreen (p<0.0001). Further studies are required to establish if a longer use of these techniques would increase the observed improvement as suggested in Figure 5 (right), especially for the Mid-Air Hand and Mid-Air Phone techniques.

Qualitative results

Three aspects have been considered in the qualitative evaluation: usability, attractiveness and user preference.

Usability evaluation

A SUS score was computed for each technique [3]: 81.04 (SD=12.94) for the Mid-Air Hand, 77.50 (SD=18.59) for the Mid-Air Phone and 72.5 (SD=22.69) for the Touchscreen. A Friedman test did not reveal any significant effect of the interaction techniques on the SUS score ($\chi^2(2)$=0.13, p=0.94). According to [3] the usability of the three techniques can be rate as "good".

Attractiveness

To measure the attractiveness of the three techniques we relied on the Attrakdiff method [19]. We summarize in Figure 6-a, the results of the Pragmatic Quality (PQ) and Hedonic Quality (HQ) dimensions. According to the Attrakdiff report, Mid-Air Hand is rated as "desired". More precisely, with regards to PQ, the technique is very pragmatic and assists the user optimally. With regards to HQ the report establishes the technique is very hedonic: the user identifies with the technique, which motivates and stimulates him. On the other hand, Mid-Air Phone is rated as "task-oriented". With regards to PQ and HQ dimensions, the Attrakdiff report concludes there is room for improvement in terms of usability and user's stimulation. Finally the Touchscreen technique is rated as "neutral":

there is also room for improvement in terms of usability and stimulation.

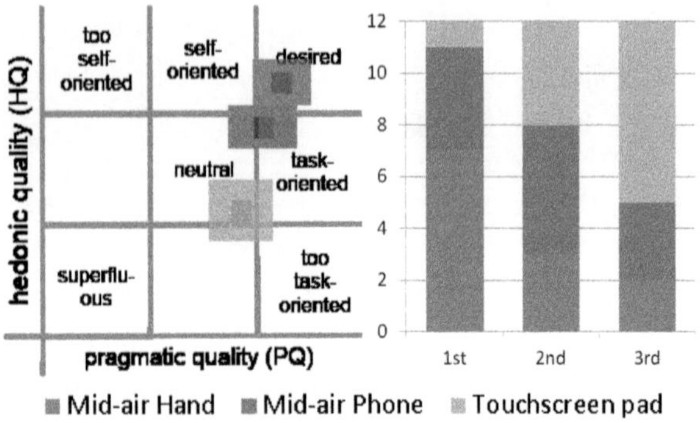

Figure 6: a) Portfolio generated using the AttrakDiff method, and b) user ranking of the three techniques.

In addition the overall user's impression of Mid-Air Hand and Mid-Air Phone is that they are very attractive (Attractiveness ATT> 1). For Touchscreen the overall impression is moderately attractive (ATT = 0.5).

User preference

We asked participants to rank the three techniques in order of preference. 7 participants rated Mid-Air Hand as the preferred technique, 4 the Mid-Air Phone and 1 the Touchscreen pad. 7 participants ranked Touchscreen pad in last position. For the statistical analysis, we marked the most preferred technique with one and the least preferred technique with three. A Friedman test did not reveal any significant effect on the mark representing the user preference on interaction technique ($\chi^2(2)=5.17$, $p=0.075$).

Finally the most frequently mentioned positive comments refer to an accurate, funny and intuitive technique for Mid-Air Hand (P1, P3); an intuitive and easy to use technique for Mid-Air Phone (P3, P5); and a familiar technique for Touchscreen (P6, P12). The most frequently mentioned negative comments relate to the weight of the smartphone and the fatigue for Mid-Air Hand and Phone (P1); the lack of accuracy with distant targets and the loss of reference with quick movement for Mid-Air Phone (P3, P10); and the lack of accuracy, the two-handed aspect and the difficulty to combine movements in 3-DOF for Touchscreen (P6, P5).

Summary

Our study reveals that techniques based on direct mapping (Mid-Air Hand and Phone) are better than those based on indirect mapping (Touchscreen) for controlling the 3D translation of a Detail view. The study also reveals Mid-Air Hand scores better in terms of attractiveness and user preference, although there is no significant difference concerning SUS score. An interesting result of our study is that Touchscreen, i.e. the most common technique, is the worst in terms of performance, of perceived attractiveness and of user preference. These results are very encouraging and lead us to further explore the two mid-air techniques in a second experiment: the goal is to better investigate their use in the context of interaction with a public display.

EXPERIMENT 2: UNCOVERING THE GESTURES

The goal of this second experiment is to evaluate the difficulty of performing the two mid-air techniques in usual public context, i.e. without training and without human explanation. We thus study the impact of revealing strategies.

Task and apparatus

The task is the same as in the previous experiment: reach a target in a 3D space. We decided to display the 3D space without occlusion objects.

The apparatus is the same than in previous experiment: one sensor was attached to the smartphone while the other was attached to the hand.

Revealing strategies

Inspired by [43], we explore different revealing strategies. In the context of smartphone-based interaction with a public display, we focus on personal feedback on the smartphone. We study two different strategies to reveal the mid-air gestures: image (Figure 2) or a text explaining the gesture to perform. The text to explain the Mid-Air Hand was: "To move the view in the 3D scene, move your right hand in mid-air behind the smartphone while pressing the on-screen button". The text to explain the Mid-Air Phone was: "To move the view in the 3D scene, move the smartphone in mid-air while pressing the on-screen button".

Participants

We recruited 24 participants (4 females) from the local university, aged 27.54 years on average (SD=5.44). 8 of them had experience with 3D on mobile devices and 22 with mid-air gestures (Wiimote or Kinect). None of them participated in the previous experiment and we ensured they had not heard of it.

Design

To evaluate the different revealing strategies, our experiment followed a 2x2 between-participants design with Technique (Mid-Air Hand or Mid-Air Phone) and Revealing strategy (Text or Image) as factors. Every participant performed the two Techniques using one of the two Revealing strategies only. We counterbalanced the order of the Technique factor across participants: half of the participants started with one technique and half with the other. For every technique, each participant performed 8 selections on randomly selected targets (all at the same distance from the initial position).

Procedure

We decided to conduct a controlled experiment in order to exclude the imitation effect of public context [43], i.e. to reveal the gestures to future participants. Moreover the apparatus implied that participants could not perform the tasks with their own mobile device, excluding a large field study in a public space.

The study was performed in the presence of the interviewer. Participants were equipped with the sensors and explained the task (reach a target) without describing the interaction techniques. We informed them of the contextual revealing message (text or image) that would describe the technique. Participants watched the revealing message and then performed the task eight times for each technique. In case the participant took more than 2 minutes to understand the technique (i.e. perform the first trial), we ended the technique's block and marked it as a failure. This time (120 s) has been identified as the maximum time a user will try to perform an interaction in public spaces [43].

To diminish the influence of the sensor on the hand (that could partially reveal the nature of the Mid-Air Hand gesture), both sensors were attached during all the experiment. We did not inform users of what these sensors were used for.

Collected data

We logged all tracking data and measured time to complete the task from stimulus onset (including the time to read the help message). We measured user preference and perceived difficulty using a 5-points Likert scale.

EXPERIMENT 2 : RESULTS

Some participants failed to use some techniques since they were unable to understand the gesture. We first report on success rate and on data collected before analyzing quantitative and qualitative results.

Success rate and data collected

Among the 24 participants, 2 of them (8.3%) did not understand the Mid-Air Hand gesture and 1 (4.15%) the Mid-Air Phone gesture. These 3 participants were unable to understand in less than 2 minutes the technique, which was the first one to be used in the experiment. The Revealing strategy of these three failed conditions was 1 Text and 1 Image for the two Mid-Air Hand failures, and 1 Image for the Mid-Air Phone failure. Once these participants failed to perform the technique (always the first one), we asked them to perform the second technique while still providing the same revealing message: they all succeeded.

Consequently we collected a different number of trials for these three participants than for the others. For the 3 participants that failed to perform one technique we collected 8 trials (1 technique x 1 revealing strategy x 8 repetitions) x 3 users = 24 trials. For the 21 other participants, we collected 16 trials (2 techniques x 1 revealing strategy x 8 repetitions) x 21 users = 336 trials. In total we collected 360 trials.

Quantitative results

Task completion time

A Shapiro-Wilk test shows that the task completion time data do not follow a normal distribution ($p < 2.2 \times 10^{-16}$). None of the data transformations we tried allowed us to use parametric tests. The statistical analysis is thus based on non-parametric tests. We first compare for each technique the task completion time between trials when the technique was performed first or second. A Mann-Whitney test indicates that the order of techniques does not have a significant effect on task completion time (Z=6.62, p=0.2755 for Mid-Air Hand used first and Z=6.0, p=0.7956 for Mid-Air Phone used first). Thus we use all collected trials (including the 3 participants that failed one technique) for our analysis.

A Mann-Whitney test reveals the overall difference between the two techniques is not statistically significant (Z=9.0, p=0.38). The average task completion time for Mid-Air Hand is $24.54s$ (SD = 34.85) and for Mid-Air Phone $21.50s$ (SD = 26.57). We refine this analysis to distinguish the results obtained for each of the 8 trials performed by participants (Figure 7). For the first trial a Mann-Whitney test reveals a significant difference between the two techniques (Z=4.73, p=0.04), Mid-Air Hand being slower ($95.55s$ SD = 53.71) than Mid-Air Phone ($63.39s$ SD = 43.99). But for the other seven trials the difference is not significant (Figure 7). We note that the results obtained for these seven trials match the measures observed during the training session of experiment 1 (on average 81 second for five successfully repeated trials).

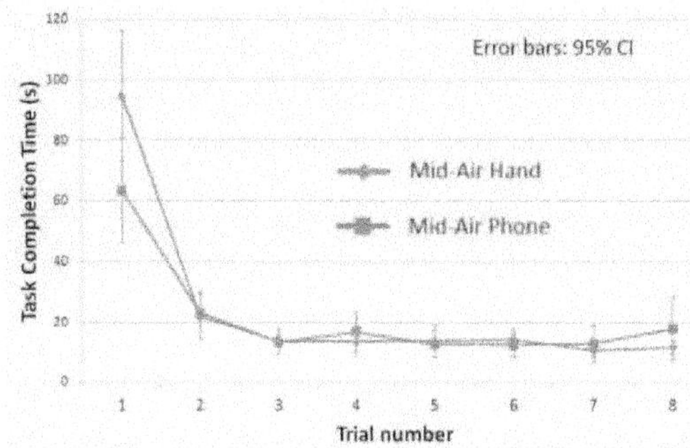

Figure 7: Task Completion Time (in s) for the 8 trials

Effect of the revealing strategies

A Mann-Whitney test reveals there is no significant effect of the revealing strategy factor (Z=4.71, p=0.35 for Mid-Air Hand and Z=5.08, p=0.50 for Mid-Air Phone).

Qualitative results

Both techniques get similar results in terms of perceived difficulty: 58% of participants find the Mid-Air Hand easy to use ("agree" or "strongly agree") vs. 63% for Mid-Air Phone. A Mann-Witney's test shows that there is no significant effect of the technique on the perceived difficulty expressed on the 5-Likert scale question (Z=-0.13, p=0.90). Interestingly, user preference produces different results for both techniques: 71% of participants like the Mid-Air Hand ("agree" or "strongly agree") whereas only 46% like the Mid-Air Phone technique (Figure 8). A Mann-Witney's test shows a significant effect of the technique on the overall user's rating expressed on the 5-Likert scale question (Z=2.23, p=0.026). This last result permits to reinforce the trend highlighted in the experiment 1 with regards to the hypothesis H3: user prefers interacting with Mid-Air Hand than with Mid-Air Phone.

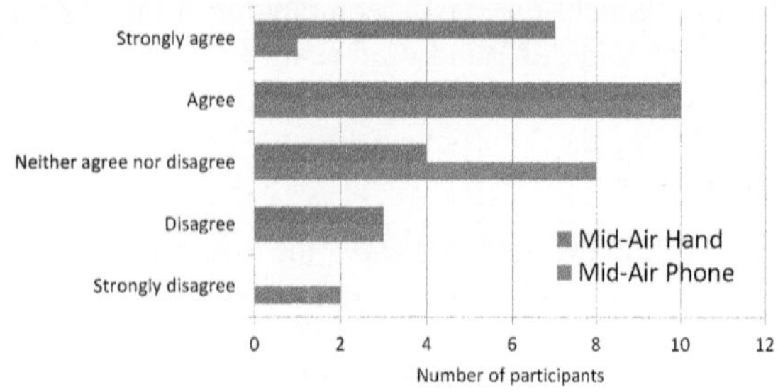

Figure 8: Likert scale results on the user preference for the two interaction techniques

Summary

Overall, results confirm that mid-air gestures can effectively be used to interact with O+D interface on 3D public display: 91.7% of participants have successfully used the Mid-Air Hand technique and 95.8% the Mid-Air Phone without any training or human explanation. These percentages would probably rise in a public context since users would be able to imitate other participants as observed in [43], thus enhancing the overall understanding of the gesture to perform.

A surprising outcome of our study is that the Mid-Air Hand gesture is more difficult to understand and to perform at first than the Mid-Air Phone. Not only the success rate is higher for the Mid-Air Phone, but it also allows a faster interaction during the first trial. However, our results also reveal that after the first trial, both techniques are comparable in terms of task completion time. Interestingly our study shows that despite the initial difficulty, participants preferred the Mid-Air Hand technique.

DISCUSSION

Based on the results of our two experiments we draw a set of design guidelines for smartphone-based interaction with Overview+Detail (O+D) interfaces on 3D public displays.

Gesture type and spatial mapping

One of the main findings of our experiments is that mid-air gestures are more efficient and preferred than touchscreen input for 3D interaction. Previous works on mid-air interaction with 2D content showed mixed results: some found mid-air interaction to perform as well as touchscreen [26], while others found touchscreen input to perform better [30]. Our results indicate that mid-air interaction is the best solution for interacting with 3D content. This result can be explained by the straightforward mapping between the gestures and the 3D translation.

Mid-air gestures reference

Our study establishes that with some training relative gestures (Mid-Air Hand) are as efficient and more preferred than absolute gestures (Mid-Air Phone). This result is in line with previous work on the use of spatial references for gestures [15,20]. One drawback is that the length of user's arms limits the Mid-Air Hand interaction. To overcome this limitation, the physical space behind the smartphone could be split into two areas: hand movements in the closest area would drive a position control interaction while movements in the furthest area would drive a rate-based control interaction, as explored in [41].

Gestures according to expertise

Our study also highlights that Mid-Air Hand performance depends on the user's expertise. To understand the gesture and perform it correctly, a novice user with only a text or an image as instructions is facing more difficulties than with the Mid-Air Phone (Figure 7). However, after the first trial users' performances are similar. The novelty of the Mid-Air Hand interaction, which is still far from being established, can explain this result.

Gesture information

A direct implication of the previous finding is that designers of 3D public applications should pay attention to the message used to reveal the interaction. Based on the experiments reported in [43] on 2D public displays and gestures, our second experiment compared the use of text and image revealing messages. As opposed to [43], we did not observe any significant differences. Given the unusual interaction, a more concrete instruction (e.g. video based or a combination of image and text) might be more appropriate. These results motivate us to keep investigating in the future the use of other revealing messages to explain how to physically operate a 3D mid-air input interaction.

Differences between our study and public context

Our second experiment was a controlled study representing a worst-case scenario. This experiment consisted in asking a user to perform a gesture never seen before. In a public place like a museum, the visitor is not alone and chances are s/he will observe others interacting with the system. The user will then benefit from an imitation effect [43] and the Mid-Air Hand performance will probably enhance.

To validate the interest of mid-air gestures for interacting with 3D O+D interfaces, we have employed the two mid-air techniques (Mid-Air Hand and Mid-Air Phone) in a concrete case study (Figure 1-b, c). The 3D scene, projected on a public display in the local university hall, represents a large telescope. The goal is to explore the different parts of the telescope and understand how it works. During two days, a large and varied audience (approx. 100 visitors composed of students, teachers and external public) virtually explored the dome of the telescope. This in-situ evaluation enriched the feedback from our experiments and permitted us to identify some limitations about the techniques.

Limitations

The addition of a sensor on the mobile phone and the hand makes them slightly heavier. As a result, several participants pointed out some muscle fatigue when using the Mid-Air Phone and Hand techniques. The size and weight of the mobile device should be limited to take fully advantage of these techniques. In the future, we will consider a better use of the embedded sensors to address this problem and the use of vision tracking to detect the hand position on the Mid-Air Hand technique.

To perform the Mid-Air Hand technique, we used the back area of the device as in [27]. This area was established after a preliminary study aimed at selecting the optimal width, height and depth of the mid-air interaction area. During the experiments, some participants wished to perform larger gestures. It should be possible for a user to calibrate his hand movement or to adjust the interaction area. In the future, we plan to consider other areas such as the side of the device as in [26].

Finally, the in-situ installation revealed a limitation when selecting an object in the 3D scene with the Mid-Air Hand technique. Newcomers were facing problems when trying to validate the selection with the hand handling the mobile phone instead of the hand behind the phone. This sometimes resulted in very difficult thumbs motions, especially when the target was close to the border of the screen. Using the hand behind the device is neither optimal, as it induces mid-air clutching. Designing different selection procedures, such as finger gestures (pinching for instance) or device actions (such as pressing a physical button), should be considered and offered as an alternative to touchscreen input.

CONCLUSION AND FUTURE WORK

In this paper, we explored the design space of mobile-based interaction with Overview+Detail (O+D) interfaces on 3D public displays. We evaluated three mobile-based techniques from the literature to navigate in a 3D scene: mid-air gesture around the mobile device (Mid-Air Hand), mid-air gesture with the mobile device (Mid-Air Phone) and touchscreen input. Our two controlled experiments show that Mid-Air Hand and Mid-Air Phone perform better than touchscreen input. However, the Mid-Air Phone gesture is easier to understand than the Mid-Air Hand gesture in usual public conditions, i.e. without training and with only a text message or an image as revealing information.

In the future we plan to increase the degrees of freedom of the navigation task by integrating the 3D rotation. For instance the Mid-Air Hand technique could be extended using gestures similar to [27]. To better implement mid-air solutions, we plan to remove the additional tracker: we will explore the combination of integrated sensors (gyroscope, accelerometer) and camera-based detection. Finally, we will extend our research to consider the selection and manipulation of the 3D objects in the 3D scene.

ACKNOWLEDGMENTS

We would like to thank the OMP-TBL members and all the participants who generously shared their time for the study. We are also grateful to the anonymous reviewers for their valuable comments and suggestions to improve the quality of the paper.

REFERENCES

1. 3D Ancient Wonders, archeological reconstruction online virtual museum. 2014. *http://www.3dancient wonders.com/*. Accessed: 2014-05.
2. Alessio, P., & Topol, A. 2011. A Public 3D Visualization Tool for the Musée des Arts et Métiers de Paris. Entertainment Computing – *ICEC 2011*, 6972, 136–142.
3. Bangor, A., Kortum, P.T., and Miller, J.T. 2008. An Empirical Evaluation of the System Usability Scale. In Proc. of *IJHCI, 24*, 6, 574–594.
4. Baudisch, P., Good, N., Bellotti, V. and Schraedley, P. 2002. Keeping things in context: a comparative evaluation of focus plus context screens, overviews, and zooming. In Proc. of *CHI '02*, ACM, 259-266.
5. Benzina, A., Dey, A., Toennis, M. and Klinker, G. 2012. Empirical evaluation of mapping functions for navigation in virtual reality using phones with integrated sensors. In Proc. of *APCHI '12*, ACM, 149–158.
6. Boring, S. et al. 2009. Scroll, tilt or move it: using mobile phones to continuously control pointers on large public displays. In Proc. of *OZCHI '09*, ACM, 161–168.
7. Boring, S, Baur, D., Butz, A., Gustafson, S. and Baudisch, P. 2010. Touch projector: mobile interaction through video. In Proc. of *CHI '10*, ACM, 2287-2296.
8. Bowman, D., Kruijff, E., LaViola, J. and Poupyrev, I. 2004. 3D User Interfaces: Theory and Practice. Addison Wesley Longman, Redwood City, CA, USA.
9. Burigat, S., Chittaro, L., and Vianello, A. 2012. Dynamic visualization of large numbers of off-screen objects on mobile devices. In Proc. of *MobileHCI '12*, ACM, 93-102.
10. Burigat, S. and Chittaro, L. 2011. On the effectiveness of Overview+Detail visualization on mobile devices. *Personal and Ubiquitous Computing*. 17, 371–385.
11. Casiez, G., Roussel, N., and Vogel, D. 2012. 1 € filter: a simple speed-based low-pass filter for noisy input in interactive systems. In Proc. of *CHI'12*, ACM, 2527-2530.
12. Cockburn, A., Karlson, A., and Bederson, B. 2008. A review of overview+detail, zooming, and focus+context interfaces. *ACM Computing Surveys 41*, 1, 1–31.
13. Decle, F. and Hachet, M. 2009. A Study of Direct Versus Planned 3D Camera Manipulation on Touch-Based Mobile Phones. In Proc. of *MobileHCI '09*, ACM, 32–35.
14. Fu, C, Goh, W. and Allen, J. 2010. Multi-touch techniques for exploring large-scale 3D astrophysical simulations. In Proc. of *CHI '10*, ACM, 2213–2222.
15. Gustafson, S., Bierwirth, D., and Baudisch, P. 2010. Imaginary interfaces: spatial interaction with empty hands and without visual feedback. In Proc. of *UIST '10*, ACM, 3-12.

16. Grubert, J. Grasset, R. and Reitmayr, G. 2012. Exploring the design of hybrid interfaces for augmented posters in public spaces. In Proc. of *NordiCHI '12*, ACM, 238-246.

17. Hachet, M. et al. 2008. 3D Elastic Control for Mobile Devices. *IEEE Computer Graphics and Applications*. 28, 4, 58–62.

18. Hachet, M. et al. 2009. Navidget for 3D interaction: Camera positioning and further uses. *International Journal of Human-Computer Studies*. 67, 3, 225–236.

19. Hassenzahl, M., Burmester, M., and Koller, F. AttrakDiff. 2014, http://attrakdiff.de/index–en.html.

20. Hinckley, K., Pausch, R., Goble, J., and Kassell, N. 1994. A survey of design issues in spatial input. In Proc. of *UIST '94*, ACM, 213-222.

21. Hürst, W. and Bilyalov, T. 2010. Dynamic versus static peephole navigation of VR panoramas on handheld devices. In Proc. of *MUM '10*, ACM, Article 25.

22. Hürst, W. and Helder, M. 2011. Mobile 3D graphics and virtual reality interaction. In Proc. of *ACE '11*, ACM, Article 28.

23. Irrlicht Engine - A free open source 3D engine. 2014. *http://irrlicht.sourceforge.net/*. Accessed: 2014-02.

24. Ivy software bus: *http://www.eei.cena.fr/products/ivy/*. Accessed: 2014-02.

25. Jacob, R. J. K., & Sibert, L. E. 1992. The perceptual structure of multidimensional input device selection. In Proc. of *CHI '92*, ACM. 211–218.

26. Jones, B., Sodhi, R., Forsyth, D., Bailey, B., and Maciocci, G. 2012. Around device interaction for multiscale navigation. In Proc. of *MobileHCI '12*, ACM, 83-92.

27. Kratz, S. et al. 2012. PalmSpace: continuous around-device gestures vs. multitouch for 3D rotation tasks on mobile devices. In Proc. of *AVI '12*, ACM, 181-188.

28. McCallum, D.C. and Irani, P. 2009. ARC-Pad: absolute+relative cursor positioning for large displays with a mobile touchscreen. In Proc. of *UIST '09,* ACM, 153-156.

29. Müller, J., Jentsch, M., Kray, C., and Krüger, A. 2008. Exploring factors that influence the combined use of mobile devices and public displays for pedestrian navigation. In Proc. of *NordiCHI '08*, ACM, 308-317.

30. Nancel, M., Wagner, J., Pietriga, E., Chapuis, O., & Mackay, W. 2011. Mid-air pan-and-zoom on wall-sized displays. In Proc. of *CHI '11*, ACM, 177-186.

31. Nekrasovski, D. et al. 2006. An evaluation of pan & zoom and rubber sheet navigation with and without an overview. In Proc. of *CHI '06*, ACM, 11-20.

32. Ouilhet, H. 2010. Google Sky Map: using your phone as an interface. In Proc. of *MobileHCI '10*, ACM, 419-422.

33. Polhemus Patriot Wireless - Polhemus. 2014. *http://www.polhemus.com/motion-tracking/all-trackers/patriot-wireless/*. Accessed: 2014-01.

34. Rønne Jakobsen, M. and Hornbæk, K. 2011. Sizing up visualizations. In Proc. of *CHI '11*, ACM, 1451-1460.

35. Roto, V. et al. 2006. Minimap: a web page visualization method for mobile phones. In Proc. of *CHI '06*, ACM, 35–44.

36. Serrano, M., Hildebrandt, D. and Irani, P. 2014. Identifying Suitable Projection Parameters and Display Configurations for Mobile True-3D Displays. In Proc. of *MobileHCI '14*, ACM, 9 pages.

37. Song, P., Goh, W.B., Fu, C.-W., Meng, Q., and Heng, P.-A. 2011. WYSIWYF: exploring and annotating volume data with a tangible handheld device. In Proc. of *CHI '11*, ACM, 1333–1342.

38. Tangible Media Group. *http://tangible.media.mit.edu /project/tether*. Accessed: 2014-01.

39. Telkenaroglu, C. and Capin, T. 2012. Dual-Finger 3D Interaction Techniques for mobile devices. *Personal and Ubiquitous Computing*. 17, 7, 1551–1572.

40. Thorsten B, et al. 2006. Usability of overview-supported zooming on small screens with regard to individual differences in spatial ability. In Proc. of *AVI'06*, ACM, 233-240.

41. Tsandilas, T., Dubois, E., and Raynal, M. 2013. Modeless Pointing with Low-Precision Wrist Movements. In Proc. of *Interact '13*, Springer, 494–511.

42. Vajk, T., Coulton, P., Bamford, W., & Edwards, R. 2008. Using a Mobile Phone as a "Wii-like" Controller for Playing Games on a Large Public Display. *International Journal of Computer Games Technology*, 2008, 1–6.

43. Walter, R., Bailly, G., and Müller, J. 2013. StrikeAPose: revealing mid-air gestures on public displays. In Proc. of *CHI '13*, ACM, 841-850.

44. Zhai, Y., Zhao, G., Alatalo, T., Heikkilä, J., Ojala, T., & Huang, X. 2013. Gesture interaction for wall-sized touchscreen display. In Proc. *UbiComp '13*, ACM, 175-178.

Identifying Suitable Projection Parameters and Display Configurations for Mobile True-3D Displays

Marcos Serrano[1,2], Dale Hildebrandt[1], Sriram Subramanian[3], Pourang Irani[1]

[1]University of Manitoba
Winnipeg, MB, R3T 2N2, Canada
{umhilde6,irani}@cs.umanitoba.ca

[2]IRIT - University of Toulouse
Toulouse, 31062, France
marcos.serrano@irit.fr

[3]University of Bristol
Woodland Road, BS81UB UK
sriram@cs.bris.ac.uk

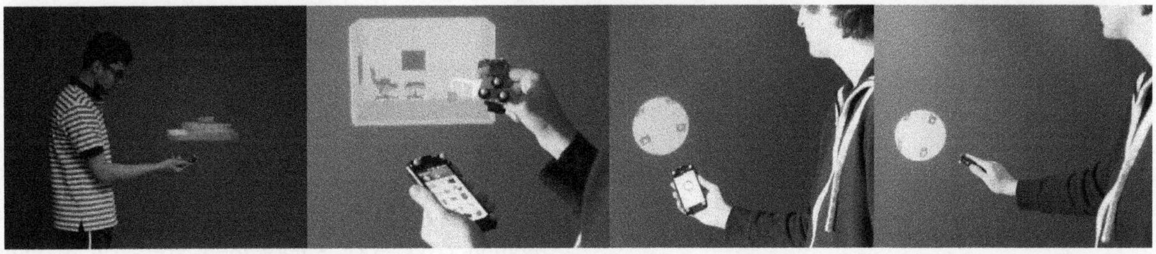

Figure 1. a) Illustration of a true-3D visualization on a mobile device. b) We implemented a 3D interior design application in our true-3D mobile prototype. c-d) Subject doing visual search during the first experiment.

ABSTRACT
We present a two-part exploration on mobile true-3D displays, i.e. displaying volumetric 3D content in mid-air. We first identify and study the parameters of a mobile true-3D projection, in terms of the projection's distance to the phone, angle to the phone, display volume and position within the display. We identify suitable parameters and constraints, which we propose as requirements for developing mobile true-3D systems. We build on the first outcomes to explore methods for coordinating the display configurations of the mobile true-3D setup. We explore the resulting design space through two applications: 3D map navigation and 3D interior design. We discuss the implications of our results for the future design of mobile true-3D displays.

Author Keywords
Mobile True-3D, intangible displays, mid-air pointing, displays.

ACM Classification Keywords
H.5.2. Information interfaces and presentation: Interaction.

INTRODUCTION
Benefiting from 3D on mobile devices is pertinent, beyond video games, for mobile scenarios such as 3D interior design or 3D map exploration. Mobile devices (smartphones and gaming consoles) incorporate at present

MobileHCI '14, September 23 - 26 2014, Toronto, ON, Canada
Copyright 2014 ACM 978-1-4503-3004-6/14/09 $15.00.
http://dx.doi.org/10.1145/2628363.2628375

auto-stereoscopic displays as a first step toward achieving true-3D content [21]. True-3D, i.e. displaying volumetric 3D content in mid-air, can be accomplished through different means: stereoscopic displays with head-tracking, optical illusions, moving parts or augmented reality glasses [14,15,17,20,27]. Integrating true-3D on mobile devices, apart from facing hardware challenges, presents a number of unresolved human factors questions concerning its use.

We possess limited knowledge on both the numerous constraints imposed on viewing and interacting with mobile true-3D interfaces and the usage scenarios suitable for such displays. These include knowing about the ideal angular position, size and distance of the volumetric projection, relative to the mobile device, the projection limits on visual search and direct interaction and how to coordinate the mobile and true-3D views. Answers to such questions will equip manufacturers and designers with tools to begin exploring a range of technologies that can be tailored for true-3D input on mobile devices.

We study the various factors that can potentially influence the effective deployment of true-3D on mobile devices in an emulated environment (Figure 1). We focus on mobile-mounted 3D projection, which means that the true-3D projection moves with the mobile device as if both were attached. We systematically address the above listed fundamental questions for this form of Mobile Multi-Display Environment (MMDE).

Our contributions include: 1) an identification of suitable display parameters and constraints for true-3D mobile display; 2) an exploration of the coordinated display configurations for the 2D mobile and true-3D displays; and 3) the application of these configurations to the design of two proof-of-concept applications, a 3D map and a 3D interior design application (Figure 1).

STATE OF THE ART

True-3D

True-3D refers to any 3D digital display capable of producing mid-air, full-depth-cue (or volumetric), multi-angle and/or multi-user images without the need for user instrumentation [15,17].

Recent work studying the value of 'true' 3D displays has relied on emulation for recreating this type of display [1,15,20]. To produce intangible and mid-air images, most systems use optical illusions. Vermeer is an interactive 360° viewable 3D display based on the optical illusion of using two parabolic mirrors [2]. HoloDesk is a system that exploits a see through display with kinetic motion for creating a 'true' 3D effect [15]. Virtual Reality (VR) has mostly emulated the 'true' 3D experience using stereoscopic projections, an approach we adopt to evaluate the display projection parameters for true-3D mobile displays. Head-mounted augmented reality systems have largely evolved and can facilitate 3D stereo viewing capabilities, with lighter glasses and see-through displays, such as the Vuzix Star 1200 [28]. Depth cues can be produced using auto-stereoscopic displays, which have appeared on mobile and handheld gaming devices. Such screens can be viewed by only one user and have a narrow viewing angle. Coupling such displays with head-tracking allows various angles of view, as in Fuwa-Vision [20], an auto-stereoscopic display presenting images in mid-air.

Aside from good 'emulations', the last few years witnessed 'true' 3D displays developing at an accelerated pace. The HelioDisplay generates a mid-air display using floating particles as a projection surface [14], but is limited to projection on a two-dimensional plane. Researchers more recently have demonstrated the use of laser plasma technology to produce 3D-objects with light dot arrays in space [17]. This method does not allow for direct interaction with the true-3D display.

While such advances bring us closer to experiencing true-3D, we possess limited knowledge on how to design for such displays to co-exist with other forms of displays, such as mobile devices. To our knowledge, this work is the first exploration of the human factors considerations for a true-3D mobile multi-display environment.

Mobile Multi-Display Environments

Previous works have classified Mobile Multi-Display Environments (MMDE) on a continuum from being partially mobile (one mobile phone used with fixed displays [1]) to fully mobile systems [5]. Fully mobile can be further divided into multi-device-single-display and single-device-multi-display [5] MMDEs. We focus our explorations on the category of fully mobile, single-device and multi-display systems.

Foldable mobile devices such as the Nintendo 3DS [21] integrate a second screen to extend its display capabilities. Using an additional screen has the disadvantage of increasing the overall size and weight of the device. Pico-projectors alleviate the above problem by allowing use of a secondary display as needed [25]. Their main limitations are the need for a flat projection surface and the large distance between the projected display and the main display. While the latter drawback can be resolved by finding a closer projection surface [5] or by using steerable projectors [6], the former still limits where such systems can be used. The use of a true-3D display could overcome this limitation.

Interaction with mobile 3D and true-3D interfaces

Recent work demonstrates methods for interacting with 3D content using different smartphone interaction capabilities such as the touchscreen, the accelerometer or the camera [29,18]. Song et al. presented a set of techniques for visual exploration of volumetric data [29]. PalmSpace proposes the use of continuous around-device gestures for 3D rotation tasks [18]. Sitcky tools are a set of multi-touch techniques for 6DOF manipulation on flat tabletops [13]. However it is unobvious whether such solutions transfer well to handheld mobile true-3D, where the 3D content moves with the device.

In the case of true-3D displays, we can borrow knowledge from the literature on 3D user interfaces [11,19]. However, with actual systems very few results exist. Chan et al. investigated direct-touch interaction for 2D intangible displays [7]. The apparatus was based on the use of a Fresnel lens to create the optical illusion of true-3D. Results showed users performed poorly in distinguishing the z-coordinate of the targets. The use of visual pseudo-shadow feedback improved user performance. Vermeer [1] and HoloDesk [15] present interactions with holographic images, such as direct-touch, scooping and grasping. The growing body of literature on 3D user interfaces [12, 13] inspires the design of the basic direct input methods we developed in our prototype applications.

DISPLAY PROPERTIES

The following factors, which we derive in part from the MMDE literature, can influence the display properties of a true-3D mobile multi-display environment.

Projection area

While pico-projectors need a projection surface, true-3D projectors may display an image in mid-air around the mobile device. Prior work has generally kept the mobile projection pointing downward [5], straight [30] or steerable (using a motor to direct the projector) [6]. These solutions provide significant flexibility in finding a suitable projection surface. A true-3D mobile display needs not be constrained by the position of the projection throw. Therefore after considering the potential projection areas around the smartphone, we decided to focus on the top area of the phone (Figure 2-left). This area always remains visible when the user rotates the phone to inspect the 360° true-3D image.

Projection distance to the 3D object

The distance between the mid-air 3D projection area and the smartphone (Figure 2-center) may have an impact on users' visual perception and direct input. If the projection is far from the device, it may affect the continuity of the visual search [5] but even further limit direct-touch interaction with the true-3D and require indirect forms of interaction. Previous research has investigated the effect of visual separation (angle and distance between displays) on MMDE [5]. Results show there was no effect on task performance but a higher number of eye context switches occurred if both displays were not in the same field of view (approximately 30% higher). We further investigate this factor in our first experiment.

Projection angle

We define the projection angle as the angle between the phone's y-axis and the 3D object. Traditional depictions of mobile true-3D envision the 3D content at a 90° angle relative to the phone's plane (Figure 2-right) or displayed directly over the touchscreen (see Samsung's concept vision in [26]). These depictions assume the best projection 'extends' the mobile display into a 3D volume. However, this projection style presents several drawbacks. First, it is unclear how both displays would properly overlay as there could be issues with color mixing and light intensity since the touchscreen would likely be brighter than the true-3D. Second, this vision is limited as it considers the true-3D simply as an extension of the touchscreen instead of viewing it as a secondary display that can extend the mobile phone's capabilities. Our first experiment examines this factor, studying angles from 90°, perpendicular to the phone's plane, to 0°, collinear to the phone's plane (Figure 2-right).

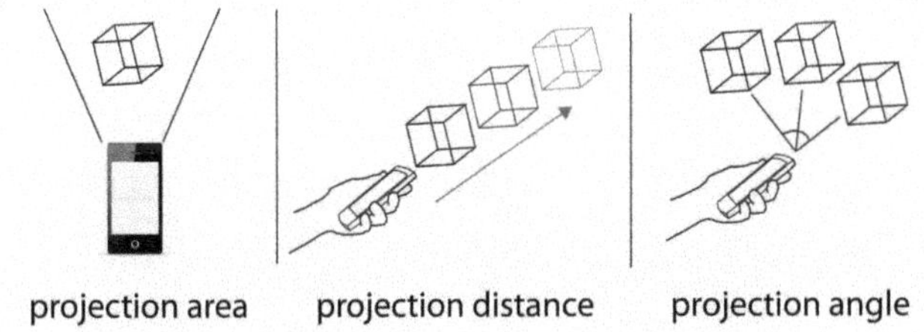

Figure 2. Projection area, distance and angle properties.

Projection volume

On traditional MMDE, display sizes are heterogeneous (i.e. pico-projection and mobile touchscreen will vary in size) and further can change while being used if the device is hand held. Some studies with fixed displays show better performance for identical size compared to different size displays [5,24]. In the case of mobile true-3D, its volume may affect visual search as well as direct-touch interaction, a factor we investigate in our experiment.

Point-of-view

The visual exploration of a mobile true-3D display can rely on wrist rotation dexterity to avoid complex interactions for rotating it. There are three main rotation axes around the wrist: flexion/extension, pronation/supination and ulnar/radial deviation. Previous work on wrist dexterity has identified that the maximum angles are 60°-45° for flexion/ extension, 65°-60° for pronation/supination, and 15°-30° for ulnar/radial deviation [23]. We thus expect limited accessibility to occluded areas on the true-3D projection, which we explore across the entire 360° true-3D display using wrist dexterity alone.

MOBILE MULTI-DISPLAY TRUE-3D PROTOTYPE

To gain an understanding of the various properties that could influence the human factors aspects with mobile multi-display true-3D we implemented a running emulation.

Prototype

Our implementation was based on a stereoscopic display coupled with head tracking, on the VisCube [27] platform, an immersive environment composed of a projection wall and floor (Figure 3). In this system the user has to wear polarized glasses with IR markers to allow visual head-tracking. 3D content was developed using GLUT. We used an LG-P925 smartphone (4.3'' screen, weight 6oz, dimensions 5"(H)×2.7"(W)×0.4"(D)) running Android 2.3. The position of the mobile device in the environment was tracked using a Vicon IR motion tracking system and IR markers.

Figure 3. We built our prototype in a VisCube 3D [27] immersive system, tracking the mobile device using optical tracking.

Emulating True-3D

Emulating true-3D in a CAVE environment has been achieved by others. The Personal Cockpit project investigated the use of virtual windows around the user through emulation in a VisCube immersive system [9].

EXPERIMENT 1: DISPLAY PROPERTIES

The goal of this experiment was to identify the best spatial configuration for the projection of a mobile true-3D display to ensure effective visual search. We explore the case of natural user interaction, i.e. wrist rotation for search without interface support, but do not explore any type of user input. We focus on the properties described in the previous section (Figure 2): projection's **angle** to the phone plane, **distance** to the phone, **volume** and **pattern position** on the true-3D (point-of-view).

Apparatus, task and instructions

We used the VisCube prototype described previously. Participants were required to identify the location of a graphical pattern on a 3D opaque sphere on the true-3D display. The sphere was separated into eight parts, each one containing a unique pattern. All eight patterns had the same volume and were symmetrically positioned on the sphere (Figure 4).

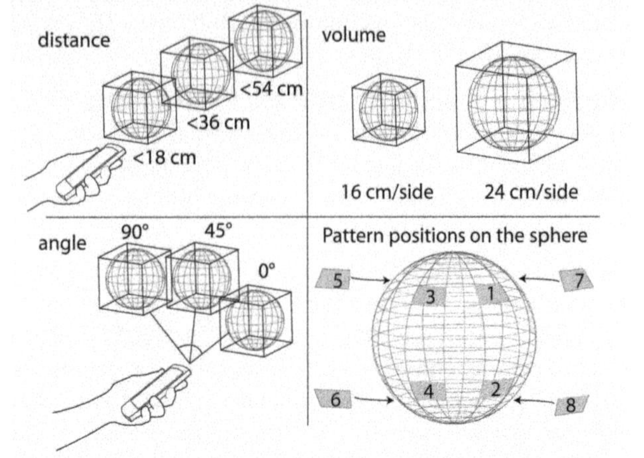

Figure 4. Properties evaluated in the first experiment: true-3D display's distance to the phone, volume size, angle to the phone and item position on the sphere (4 positions on the front and 4 symmetrical positions on the back).

We used a basic geometrical shape as the stimulus pattern: circle, triangle, square or star. The stimulus was displayed on the mobile screen to ensure that all users would start the task with a focus at the same location. Once the stimulus was displayed, in black and white, users had to find its coloured version on the sphere (three possible colors) and click a button of the same color on a wand (held with the other hand) to select the answer (Figure 1). Color allowed differentiating correct and false answers with minimum cognitive load. We used the wand merely as an experimental input to collect answers from users. Buttons on the wand are disposed overall at the same distance of the thumb. In case of an error, we recorded the number of attempts it took the user to find the correct answer. We asked participants to minimize selection time (primary demand) without neglecting the error rate (secondary demand).

The position of the sphere was determined by the angle and distance factors (Figure 4). The angle represents the position of the sphere in relation to the mobile device plane: 0°, 45° and 90°. We defined three approximate distances to the center of the sphere: *close* when the sphere center is 18cm away from the top of the device, *middle* when it is 36cm away and *far* when it is 54cm away. The volume factor represents the volume of the sphere's bounding cube (Figure 4): the small cube was approximately 16cm/side and the big cube 24cm/side.

Participants

11 men and 1 woman, aged 25.25 years on average, volunteered for the experiment. All of them were right handed; 9 held the mobile device in the right hand while 3 preferred to hold it with the left hand. We mirrored the results from those 3 participants for the position factor (others factors not being dependent on the hand used).

Procedure

We used a 3×3×2×8 within-subject design with Angle (0°, 45° and 90°), Distance (close<18cm, medium<36cm and far<54cm), Volume (small=16cm/side and big=24cm/side) and Item Position (8 areas of the sphere) as factors. We ran three blocks of trials for each condition. Angle was counter-balanced using a 3×3 Latin square while other factors were presented randomly. We ran one training block before the experiment. The experiment consisted of 144 conditions×3 blocks×12 users = 5184 trials.

Data Collection

We recorded the smartphone's position and angle with the Vicon. Besides success rate, we measured trial completion time, from stimulus onset to button pressed. Participants filled a 5-point Likert scale with nine questions to indicate preference for the four factors. The ninth question asked whether users liked the concept of mobile true-3D.

Results and Discussion

We used the univariate ANOVA with post-hoc comparisons using the Bonferroni adjustment for all our analyses. Results reveal a main effect of angle ($F_{2,22}$=97.6, p<.001), distance ($F_{2,22}$=91.6, p<.001) and position ($F_{7,77}$=139.7, p<.001) on completion time. There was no consistent effect of volume ($F_{1,11}$=.116 p=.734). We found an interaction between angle and distance ($F_{4,44}$=12.6, p<.001) and volume and distance ($F_{2,22}$=5.5, p=.004). We also found interaction effects for position and angle ($F_{14,154}$=11.7, p<.001) and position and distance ($F_{14,154}$=11.6, p<.001). We did not find any main effects for accuracy rate, with an average success rate of 97.8% (std. dev. 0.2%).

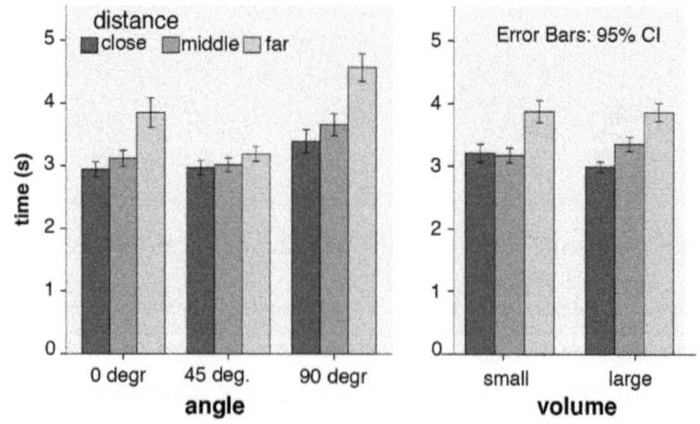

Figure 5. Completion time (s) for Distance at each Angle (left) and Distance at each Volume (right).

Angle and distance interaction: Overall, completion time increased with distance and angle (Figure 5). Post-hoc analysis revealed a significant difference between all three angle positions, 45° (3.0s on average) being slightly faster than 0° (3.3s) and considerably faster than 90° (3.8s). Surprisingly, the worst projection angle for a visual search task on a mobile true-3D display is 90°, which contradicts popular conceptions of such displays. Subject 4 reported "when the sphere is farther horizontally it is easier to search than if it is vertically distant". Concerning distance, we also found a significant effect between all three distances. Performance with the close (3.0s) being slightly better than with middle (3.2s) and considerably better than far (3.8s). The results do not reveal a linear degradation of distance on visual search (while distances values are linear) and can thus expect a stronger negative impact with further positions. Concerning the interaction between both factors, we notice in the case of 45° that the difference between all three distances is less important than for the other two angles, which are particularly bad when the 3D image is far.

Position on the sphere: As expected, the front hemisphere is significantly faster than the back (2.7s vs. 4s). Our experiment required searching for objects in the back part of the projection to capture conditions such as 3D object occlusion. We find a significant difference between the back right (3.7s) and left elements (4.4s) (Figure 6). Several users reported severe difficulty reaching the back left elements and particularly the top left object (4.6s) due to a physiological limitation in wrist rotation. This result is consistent with previous works on wrist rotation [23].

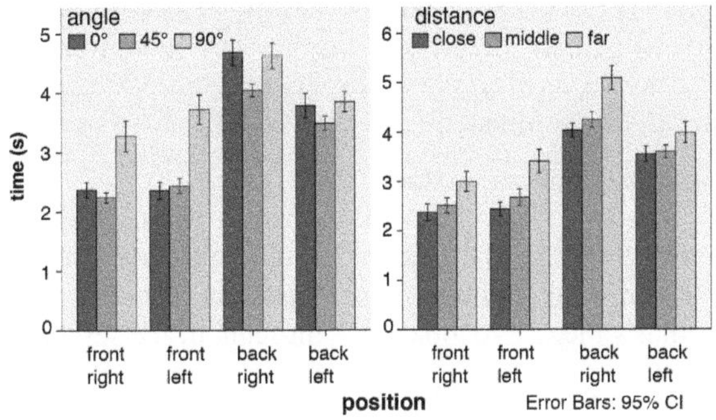

Figure 6. Completion time (s) for Position at each Angle (left) and Position at each Distance (right).

User Preference

From the 5-point Likert scale most participants found it difficult to search for content on the large sphere (Q1), did not show a specific preference for projection at 0° or 45° (Q7), and generally preferred the closer distance (Q6). All participants liked the concept of having mobile true-3D.

Summary of Experiment 1 Results

This first study demonstrates that a 3D object positioned at an angle of 0° or 45° and at a distance of less than 36 cm (middle or closer) performs best for visual search. We also found that the region in the back and opposite to the hand holding the device is the weakest for object search. This is primarily due to the wrist dexterity as observed during the experiment and from participant feedback. Wrist dexterity also affects objects located further away, i.e. these become hard to inspect under all angles. Thus, our results recommend shorter distances if the device is to solely rely on wrist rotation for viewing the display. We consider these constraints in experiment 2.

EXPERIMENT 2: DIRECT-TOUCH INTERACTION

The goal of this experiment is to investigate the effect of volume size on visual search and direct input.

Task and instructions

Participants were required to identify the location of a graphical pattern on the true-3D display and to select it with direct mid-air touch. To complete the task, they used their finger, equipped with IR markers, to touch the pattern on the sphere. We added one larger volume size than in experiment 1 to further investigate this factor (note we did not see effects of the volume sizes selected in the previous study). The small volume was approximately 16cm/side, the medium 24cm/side and the large 36cm/side (the volume is constant and does not scale to the distance to the user).

Participants

Ten men and two women, of an average age of 26.3 years volunteered for the experiment. Five participated in the first experiment. Eleven were right handed and one left-handed. They all held the mobile device with their left hand and used their right index finger for interaction.

Procedure and data collection

This experiment followed a 3×2×8 within-subject design with Volume (small, medium and large), Angle (0° and 45°) and Item Position (8 areas of the sphere) as factors. We set the Distance factor to *middle (<36cm) to allow enough space for the large Volume to be displayed.* Three blocks of trials were run for each condition, the angle factor being counter-balanced while others were selected randomly. We also ran one training block before the experiment to reduce the learning effect between new participants and those who participated in the first study. The experiment consisted of 48 conditions×3 blocks×12 users = 1728 trials. We collected the same data as in the previous experiment.

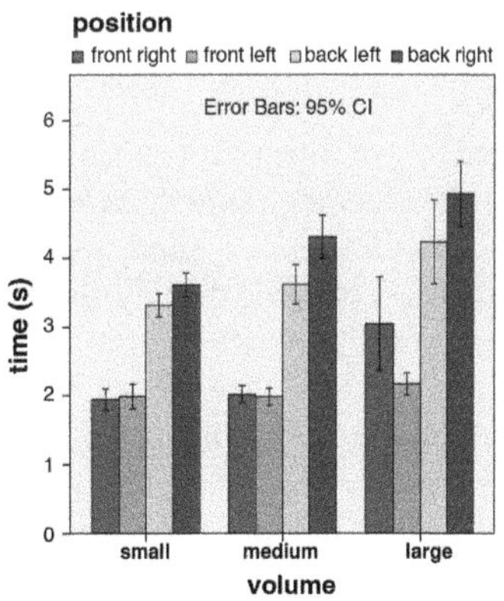

Figure 7. Completion time (s) for Volume at each Position.

Results and Discussion

We used the univariate ANOVA with post-hoc comparisons using the Bonferroni adjustment for all our analyses. Results revealed a main effect of volume ($F_{2,22}$=8.4, p<.001) and of position ($F_{7,77}$=38.8, p<.001) on completion time. We found an interaction between volume and position ($F_{14,154}$=2.5, p=.002). There was no consistent effect of angle. Concerning error rate, there was a significant effect of volume ($F_{2,22}$=9.6, p<.001) but no significant effect of other factors (position and angle).

Volume: Overall, completion time increased with the volume of the display (Figure 7). A post-hoc analysis revealed there is no significant difference between the mean time for the small (2715 ms) and the medium volumes (2980 ms). There was however a significant difference between those two times and the mean time for the large volume (3594 ms). Results showed that success rate increased with volume: 91.3% for the small volume, 95.8% for the medium volume and 97.2% for the larger volume. Most of the errors were due to the intangible nature of the display. In some cases users had a bad perception of 3D depth and touched a back or adjacent item while pointing: this happened more often on the small volume, since items were closer, thus explaining the difference in success rate. In other cases users inadvertently touched another item on the way to the target.

Position: Overall, as in the previous experiment, post-hoc analysis revealed a significant difference between the front (2.6s) and the back items (4s). On the back, the right side (4.3s) was significantly slower than the left side (3.7ms). This can be explained as users held the phone with the left hand and most of the selection time corresponds to the visual search (back right items are more difficult to see).

Summary of Exp. 2

This second experiment allowed us to explore suitable values for the projection volume for direct interaction. Projections smaller than 24cm/side improved efficiency. The slight cost in accuracy at smaller volumes suggests that target sizes need to be considered carefully for such displays, and may be limited by the 3D input tracking capabilities. Other forms of feedback for mid-air input, as proposed in [7], could also help improve targeting accuracy. We leave this exploration for future work.

IMPLICATIONS OF EXPERIMENTS 1 AND 2

From this first exploration of mobile-mounted true-3D displays we identified suitable display parameters along with some display constraints.

Suitable display parameters

Our two experiments enabled us to identify the suitable values for the explored display factors (angle, distance, volume and position of true-3D content). To improve user search and direct input interaction, a true-3D display should be positioned at an angle between 0 and 45 degrees. The center of the projection should be less than 36cm away from the mobile device. The volume of the display should be smaller than a cube of 24cm/side. The back area of the display opposite to that of the hand holding the device is difficult to access. This suggests target reaching techniques could be developed for such displays as with large displays or tabletops [30]. We apply these parameters in the design of our applications, as described later.

Implications

Display Volume: Based on our experiments, mobile true-3D displays may consider a limited volume if users are to rely on direct input and wrist rotation as their primary means of interacting with the display. This limitation suggests that if 3D content is larger than this volume (for example if displaying a very large map) or if the user wishes to translate 3D objects, the content should be clipped to the boundaries of the volume space. Our applications are restricted to displaying content within such limits. However, alternative methods for space allocation and effective space management need to be considered.

Occlusion: Both viewing and touching the back of the mobile true-3D are particularly difficult. We deduce two main implications from this constraint. First, when creating 3D content for this display, designers should avoid including important content (such as controls or interactive objects) on the back region. The second implication is that to allow easier access to the back region, applications should include rotation techniques for rotating the content of the true-3D and not solely rely on wrist control. The user could then access the back region by rotating the content instead of rotating his wrist.

We use our derived parameters and constraints in the rest of our work: first to frame and define usage scenarios, and second as requirements for our applications.

ILLUSTRATIVE EXAMPLES

Our implementation of the two representative examples was informed by two participatory design sessions. These sessions helped us define the display configurations for mobile true-3D displays: how the 2D and the 3D displays content can be coordinated.

Participatory design sessions

In both sessions participants filled Post-it notes with their ideas on how users should interact with mobile true-3D. All Post-it notes were read and participants could comment on one another's ideas. We took notes throughout the sessions.

Design session 1: The goal of this first session was to collect general mobile true-3D design ideas. We first asked participants to describe how they envision using mobile true-3D and then to think specifically about the map application and give ideas on display content and interaction. Eight HCI graduate students took part in this session. Participants' ideas for mobile true-3D included: maps, instruction delivery (Chinese calligraphy, sign language), online shopping and 3D sculpting. Concerning the 3D map participants suggested displaying "volumetric buildings" and "3D signposts and landmarks". Several general ideas emerged on the relation between mobile and true-3D displays, such as "2D cross-sections" of the 3D image, "screen replication" to avoid the fat finger problem and "real pop-ups" in 3D. Concerning the input, some participants would like to touch the true-3D image ("nice to touch 3D") while others imagined ways of indirect interaction ("3D cursor at a distance from the finger").

Design session 2: The goal of the second design session was to collect ideas on how to interact in our 3D environment. Ten students with HCI background participated. On the mobile phone, participants cited "moving/rotating the phone for rotating the true-3D content" and "using the device angle to initiate scale". On the true-3D space, some participants indicated the use of 3D gestures such as "pinching" for selecting or translating and using the "distance from the hand in mid-air to the phone" for zooming. A participant also cited using "eye tracking" for rotation, and another one using "face tracking" for translation.

Coordinated display configurations

From these design sessions and the results from the first exploration, we identified a set of display coordination configurations for mobile true-3D. Our configurations are compliant with the **volume constraint** identified in the first exploration: we only consider configurations with a limited true-3D volume. We define four dimensions to characterize the coordinated display configurations (CDC) of 3D and 2D displays:

CDC1: Independent (Figure 8-a): both displays show separate content. For example, a GUI on the mobile display used to control the 3D content on the true-3D display.

CDC2: Extruded replication (Figure 8-b): the true-3D display extrudes the content of the mobile display in 3D. For example, the 3D view of a map or spatial workspace.

CDC3: Cross-section (Figure 8-c): the mobile display shows a cross-section view of the true-3D display. An example is views in 3D Computer Aided-Design (CAD) or in architecture visualization.

CDC4: Extruded detail (Figure 8-d): the true-3D display extrudes a detailed 3D view of a section of the content presented on the mobile display. This corresponds to the idea of a "3D pop-up" in design session 1.

In terms of input, we used three interaction modes: on the mobile, on the true-3D area and mixed true-3D + mobile. Interaction can be single handed (on the mobile) or bi-manual (one hand on the mobile, one on the true-3D).

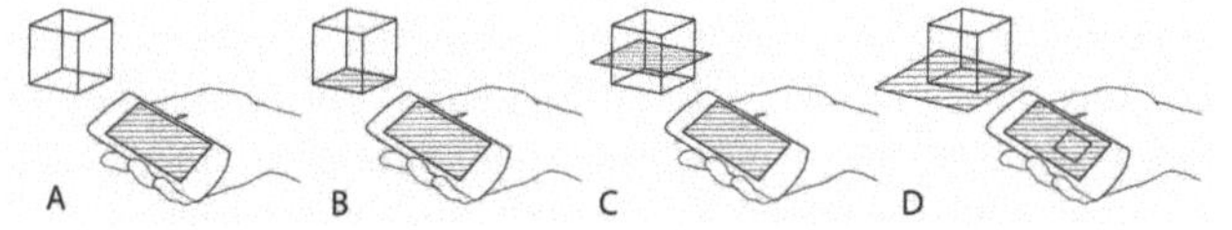

Figure 8. Coordinated Display Configurations of 2D mobile and true-3D displays.

We apply our coordinated display configurations in two applications: the 3D map and the interior design application. Our applications were designed based on the projection parameters we obtained from the first two experiments.

Illustrative application 1: 3D map

3D maps can provide information on terrain height. This is useful for military personnel and hikers, who often traverse areas with many rapid changes in elevation. 3D maps provide advantages over conventional 2D maps as landmarks on the former closely resemble their physical counterparts. They also decrease mental load in comparison to 2D maps [22]. True-3D display maps enable users to align their viewpoint with objects in the real-world. Such 3D maps are being constructed in projects such as the Urban Photonic Sandtable Display [8].

Our application consists of a top-down view of a 2D map on the mobile device's display, while a 3D version of the map is shown on the true-3D display (**CDC2**, Figure 9-b). The 3D map is clipped to the volume of the true-3D display (**volume constraint** from our first exploration). Interactions can be performed through either the touchscreen or by using pinch gestures in the true-3D display volume. Various overlay information, such as paths and points/regions of interest can be placed by interacting with the 3D map. These are represented by visual markers on the 3D map, which are replicated on the 2D map as well. This display relationship allows for modification of markers on one display, with all changes appearing on both displays. This design helps overcome the difficulty of interacting with the back region of the display (**occlusion constraint** from our first exploration); the 2D view can be used to verify the position of an out-of-sight marker as it is being placed in 3D. Map content can be filtered based on a number of different properties. In our application, we focus on height filtering. A user can move their hand up or down to control a horizontal selection plane, which intersects the 3D map (**CDC3**, Figure 9-c). The 2D view displays a horizontal slice of the 3D map at the intersection height. This takes advantage of the 3D and multi-display setup by allowing a visualization of the selected height on the original 3D map, while the 2D version displays the height-filtered map.

Illustrative application 2: Interior design

Interior design is a field with a long history in computer-aided design (CAD). Recently, with the advent of mobile devices, interior design applications such as AutoCAD provide mobile support with great success (more than 5 million downloads on the Android Market). They facilitate the design process in the field and as a result can integrate features into this process, such as taking pictures of the real

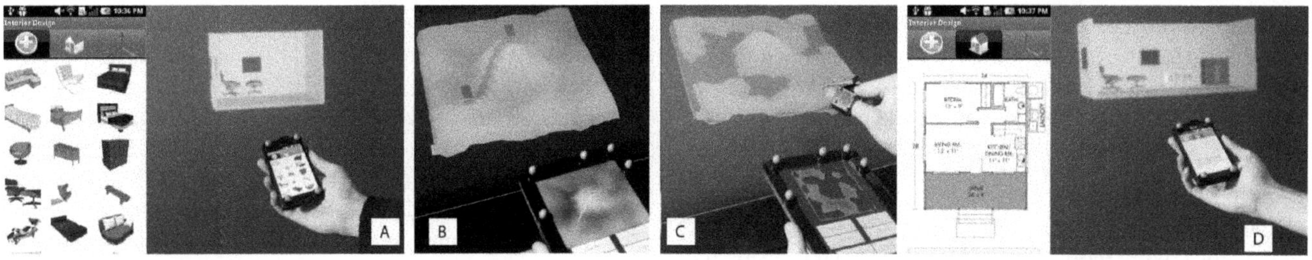

Figure 9. Illustration of the display configurations: A. Independent; B. Extruded replication; C.Cross-section; D. Extruded detail

space being designed. An obvious limitation of such applications is the difficulty of manipulating 3D content on a mobile device. Mobile true-3D displays could be used to perform and brainstorm 3D interior design in the field.

Our interior design application consists of a 3D representation of the room to design and a mobile interface with three views. The room occupies the true-3D volume and cannot be translated outside of it (a solution to accommodate the **volume constraint**). The front wall is transparent to allow the user to easily inspect and position the 3D furniture (a solution to the **occlusion constraint).** The three views of the mobile phone illustrate different aspects of our display configurations: the first view displays a set of images of furniture (**CDC1**, Figure 9-a). When the user selects furniture, it is added to the 3D room (it appears in mid-air so that the user can select it and position it). The second view represents the floor plan of the house. On the floor plan, the room currently selected is displayed in a different color (**CDC4,** Figure 9-d). The user can select another room to change the 3D room on the true-3D display. The third view allows users to rotate and scale the selected furniture by using a slider or by setting the direct-touch mode to "rotate" or "scale" so that the user can rotate or scale the 3D furniture using his/her fingers by pinching. The user can rotate and position the object at the same time by performing a bi-manual interaction: with the right hand he/she directly rotates the object on the 3D environment, while translating the phone can be delegated to the left hand, thus moving the room.

DISCUSSION

Lessons learned

Mobile true-3D - opening new usages. Most previous works on MMDE were motivated by the need for expanding mobile displays. One lesson learned from our explorations is that mobile true-3D displays will represent a shift in how users interact with mobile platforms. Accordingly designers will need guidelines to create content for this novel interaction environment.

Design guidelines: Our Coordinated Display Configurations (CDC) can help designers explore design alternatives for usage applications. For example, an application to view 3D photos can be implemented using the Extruded detail configuration (CDC4). A 3D image is shown on the true-3D projection while the mobile phone displays the collection of images. Another view can be based on the Independent configuration (CDC1), for example to provide an interface to also allow editing the image. In reality, various CDCs will co-exist in a single application, as we demonstrated in our two proof-of-concept applications. By integrating several CDCs in their applications designers will enrich mobile true-3D interfaces and user interaction capabilities.

Display properties: In the context of natural user interactions with mobile true-3D, we can take away the resulting properties that emerged from our first two experiments. These were designed specifically to allow full content viewing through wrist rotation, and interaction using direct input. The use of other interaction techniques with mobile true-3D may allow overcoming some of these constraints: for example, a technique for content rotation can replace natural wrist-based rotation and allow access to occluded elements on the true-3D.

Limitations and future work

Our work is built upon some assumptions on the capabilities and limitations of future mobile true-3D displays. We assumed mobile true-3D projectors will be able to display a volumetric image of any volume, at any distance and any angle of the phone. We made this assumption to evaluate the user limitations independently from technology capabilities.

The results of our experiments are influenced by the technology we used to emulate the true-3D displays. The obvious differences between this technology and the final true-3D display, in terms of color, brightness or 3D perception, may alter the results from our experiments. However, most of those results are strongly influenced by human physiological limitations on wrist-based rotation and arm reach. Thus we believe these technical differences do not have a fundamental impact on our findings. Moreover, researchers have used such platforms for developing and testing novel technologies.

There is still much to learn on how mobile true-3D displays will be used in a real mobile situation. A next step in our work will be to use existing mobile augmented reality glasses [28] to evaluate the display properties in mobile situation. A second perspective to our work is to explore the input space of mobile true-3D. In our work we have identified some input configurations and implemented several interaction techniques, including finger gestures such as pinching. We will explore the input configurations space to propose a full suite of interaction techniques. Finally, a third perspective derives from user collaboration on the true-3D display. This will allow us to elaborate on our coordinated display and input configurations.

CONCLUSION

In this paper we present a two-part exploration of the concept of mobile true-3D. In the first exploration we do the first ever study on mobile true-3D display properties. Results reveal the best distance to phone, angle to phone, display volume and positions on the display for good visual search and direct touch input interaction on mobile true-3D displays. We use these results to guide the design of our applications. Finally, in the last exploration we identify coordinated display configurations between the 2D mobile display and the true-3D display. We define four display configurations named Independent, Extruded replication, Extruded detail and Cross-section. We illustrate those configurations using our two proof-of-concept applications.

In HCI we find numerous examples of novel technologies whose adoption, from discovery to commercial use, take decades [4]. Buxton refers to this process as the Long Nose of Innovation [3]. Our paper is motivated by our will to reduce the long nose for mobile true-3D. While extensive research is taking place to engineer mobile true-3D [8,10,16,20] we provide a contribution in this vein to identify application guidelines, limitations and scenarios to help future adoption of this technology.

REFERENCES

1. Bergé, L.-P., Serrano, M., Perelman, G., and Dubois, E. 2014. Exploring Smartphone-Based Interaction with Overview+Detail Interfaces on 3D Public Displays. In *Proc. of MobileHCI '14*, ACM, 10 pages.
2. Butler, A. et al. 2011. Vermeer: direct interaction with a 360° viewable 3D display. In *Proc. of UIST '11*, ACM, 569-576.
3. Buxton, B. The Long Nose of Innovation. CHI 2011 Keynote.
4. Buxton, B. Buxton Collection (last accessed February 2014). *http://*research.microsoft.com/buxtoncollection
5. Cauchard, J., et al. 2011. Visual separation in mobile multi-display environments. In *Proc. of UIST'11,* ACM, 451-460.
6. Cauchard, J., et al. 2012. Steerable projection: exploring alignment in interactive mobile displays. *Personal Ubiquitous Comput.* 16, 1 (January 2012), 27-37.
7. Chan, L. et al. 2010.Touching the void:direct-touch interaction for intangible displays. In *Proc. of CHI'10*, ACM, 2625-2634.
8. DARPA (last accessed February 2014), http://www.darpa.mil/newsevents/releases/2011/11/23.aspx
9. Ens, B., Finnegan, R. and Irani, P. 2014. The Personal Cockpit: A Spatial Interface for Effective Task Switching on Head-Worn Displays. In Proc. of CHI '14. ACM, 10 pages (to appear).
10. Fattal, D. et al. 2013. A Multi-Directional Backlight for a Wide-Angle Glasses-Free Three-Dimensional Display. In Nature 495, 348-351 (21 March 2013).
11. Froehlich, B. et al. 2006. The GlobeFish and the GlobeMouse: two new six degree of freedom input devices for graphics applications. In *Proc. of CHI '06*, ACM, 191-199.
12. Hancock, M. et al. 2007. Shallow-depth 3d interaction: design and evaluation of one-, two- and three-touch techniques. In *Proc. of CHI'07*, ACM, 1147-1156.
13. Hancock, M., Ten Cate, T., and Carpendale, S. 2009. Sticky tools: full 6DOF force-based interaction for multi-touch tables. In *Proc. of ITS '09*, ACM, 133-140.
14. HelioDisplay, http://www.io2technology.com
15. Hilliges, O., Kim, D., Izadi, S., Weiss, M. and Wilson, A. 2012. HoloDesk: direct 3d interactions with a situated see-through display. In *Proc. of* CHI '12, ACM, 2421-2430.
16. Karlsson, N et al. 2012. iAR: an exploratory augmented reality system for mobile devices. In *Proc. of VRST '12*, ACM, 33-40.
17. Kimura, H., et al. 2011. True 3D display. In *ACM SIGGRAPH 2011 Emerging Technologies*. ACM, Article 20, 1 pages.
18. Kratz, S. et al. 2012. PalmSpace: continuous around-device gestures vs. multitouch for 3D rotation tasks on mobile devices. In *Proc. of AVI'12*, ACM, 181-188.
19. Martinet, A., Casiez, G. and Grisoni, L. 2010. The effect of DOF separation in 3D manipulation tasks with multi-touch displays. In *Proc of* VRST '10. ACM, 111-118.
20. Nii, H. et al. 2012. Fuwa-Vision: an auto-stereoscopic floating-image display. In *SIGGRAPH Asia 2012 Emerging Technologies*. ACM, Article 13, 4 pages.
21. Nintendo 3ds, http://www.nintendo.com/3ds
22. Nurminen, A. and Oulasvirta, A. 2008. Designing interactions for navigation in 3D mobile maps. In Lecture Notes in Geoinformation and Cartography, Springer, pp. 198-224
23. Rahman, M., Gustafson, S., Irani, P. and Subramanian, S. 2009. Tilt techniques: investigating the dexterity of wrist-based input. In *Proc. of CHI'09*, ACM, 1943-52.
24. Rashid, U. Nacenta, M. and Quigley, A. 2012. The cost of display switching: a comparison of mobile, large display and hybrid UI configurations. In *Proc. of* AVI '12, ACM, 99-106.
25. Rukzio, E., Holleis, P. and Gellersen, H. 2012. Personal Projectors for Pervasive Computing. *IEEE Pervasive Computing* 11, 2 (April 2012), 30-37.
26. Samsung Flexible Amoled vision (last accessed Feb. 2014), http://youtube.com/watch?v=f4AhTiQkWwk
27. Visbox, http://www.visbox.com/
28. Vuzix, http://www.vuzix.com/home/
29. Song, P. et al. 2011. WYSIWYF: exploring and annotating volume data with a tangible handheld device. In *Proc. of CHI'11*, ACM, 1333-1342.
30. Winkler, C., Pfeuffer, K. and Rukzio, E. 2012. Investigating mid-air pointing interaction for projector phones. In *Proc. of ITS '12*, ACM, 85-94.

Portallax: Bringing 3D Displays Capabilities to Handhelds

Diego Martinez Plasencia[1], Abhijit Karnik[1,2], Jonatan Martinez Muñoz[1], Sriram Subramanian[1]
[1]Department of Computer Science, University of Bristol, UK
[2]School of Computing and Communications, Lancaster University, UK
{diego.martinez-plasencia, sriram.subramanian}@bristol.ac.uk, a.karnik@lancs.ac.uk,
jonatan.m@gmail.com

ABSTRACT

We present Portallax, a clip-on technology to retrofit mobile devices with 3D display capabilities. Available technologies (e.g. Nintendo 3DS or LG Optimus) and clip-on solutions (e.g. 3DeeSlide and Grilli3D) force users to have a fixed head and device positions. This is contradictory to the nature of a mobile scenario, and limits the usage of interaction techniques such as tilting the device to control a game. Portallax uses an actuated parallax barrier and face tracking to realign the barrier's position to the user's position. This allows us to provide stereo, motion parallax and perspective correction cues in 60 degrees in front of the device. Our optimized design of the barrier minimizes colour distortion, maximizes resolution and produces bigger *view-zones*, which support ~81% of adults' interpupillary distances and allow eye tracking implemented with the front camera. We present a reference implementation, evaluate its key features and provide example applications illustrating the potential of Portallax.

Author Keywords

Mobile 3D; Clip-on; Autostereoscopic; parallax barrier; handheld device; face-tracking.

ACM Classification Keywords

H.5.2 [Information interfaces and presentation]: User Interfaces - Graphical user interfaces;

INTRODUCTION

3D stereoscopic systems and content have attracted the interest of users throughout the years. After Avatar (2009), twenty eight 3D titles were released in 2010, thirty six in 2011 and over forty in 2012 and 2013 [4]. Multiuser 3D TVs technologies have also been proposed [15], and glasses-free TVs, like Toshiba 55ZL2, reached the market in 2012.

The market of mobile devices joined this 3D trend a few years ago. Sharp mova SH251iS, the first stereo 3D enabled mobile phone, was released in 2002 and since 2010 we have witnessed a new generation of 3D enabled handheld devices, with the HTC Evo 3D, Sharp Lynx 3D, Samsung SCH-B710 or LG Optimus as just some of the latest examples. Clip-on solutions, like 3DeeSlide [1] or Grilli3D [3] allow retrofitting other non-3D devices with similar 3D capabilities.

MobileHCI '14, September 23 - 26 2014, Toronto, ON, Canada
Copyright 2014 ACM 978-1-4503-3004-6/14/09…$15.00.
http://dx.doi.org/10.1145/2628363.2628392

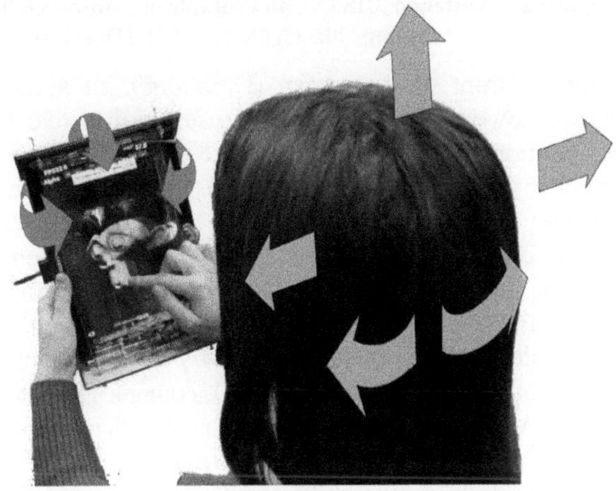

Figure 1. Portallax is the first clip-on technology that provides 3D visualization even when users move their head or their device. It uses an actuated parallax barrier, providing stereoscopy, motion parallax and perspective correction through face tracking

With the arrival of these mobile 3D display technologies, the stage seemed to be ready to allow mobile devices fully supporting 3D experiences. The graphical capabilities of mobile devices allow compelling scenes, as demonstrated by the ever growing mobile gaming industry. Interesting usage scenarios have been identified (e.g. stereo games [30], mobile 3D TV [20] and user interfaces [16]). The capability of these devices to process 3D video contents has also been demonstrated[37]. Finally, 3D gestural input can be used to interact with the 3D contents shown on these devices, either using magnets attached to the users' hands and fingers [17, 22, 23] or even with the bare hands[6, 35]. However, the acceptance of these stereo 3D mobile devices has been low. According to *M&M* only 16 million of the 1.1 billion smart phones sold in 2013 were 3D enabled [2].

The exact reason behind the slow uptake is not fully clear, but we believe that the limitations of current mobile 3D display technologies are an important factor. Existing technologies rely on static parallax barriers or lenticular arrays, which show a correct 3D effect only at a fixed

Figure 2. : Nintendo 3DS (A), an example of commercially available mobile 3D device, features a static parallax barrier. Clip-on solutions like Grilli3D (B) or 3DeeSlide (C) use static parallax barriers or static lenticular arrays.

position in front of the screen (*view-zone)*. In a mobile scenario, however, it is likely that users will move their head, or more importantly their devices. Such a situation frequently occurs while playing games, either because the interaction involves tilting the device to control an avatar, or simply because users are too absorbed in their action and move the device to try to influence an action. In this context, if the user moves out of the 'sweet spot', the stereoscopic effect breaks. Also, *motion parallax* which is a strong depth cue for perceiving 3D content [19] is not available. Many techniques relevant for 3D navigation (e.g. gaze steering [5]) or 3D manipulation using touch screens [14, 28] also rely on the ability of the users to move their heads, and thus cannot be supported by current mobile 3D technologies.

Finding an alternative mobile 3D display technology that allows users to move and is also well suited for handheld use is difficult. Such technology should avoid instrumenting the user (e.g. no glasses) and adapt to a wide range of users (e.g. variable interpupillary distance –IPD). It should rely on self-contained computing and fit within a thin form factor. It cannot interfere with the typical use of conventional 2D applications, and should be cheap to produce, to qualify as a successful clip-on solution.

We explore the existing range of mobile 3D display technologies, looking for an alternative that complies with the stated requirements. We then present Portallax (Figure 1), a *clip-on* solution that uses a mechanically actuated parallax barrier and face tracking to support a working volume of 60°. The 3D position of the observer's eyes is used to realign the barrier in real time, and provide perspective correction. Given that the user can move in front of the display, motion parallax as well as 3D interaction techniques can be supported. We provide a proof of concept implementation which achieves all this with just clip-on hardware made from off-the-shelf components and without compromising the interactive capabilities of the device. Portallax implements an improved version of parallax barrier which increases the size of the *view-zones*, eliminates *hue shift* and has better effective resolution than classical parallax barriers.

We present the design of the device as well as example applications that illustrate its key capabilities. We then show the results of a quantitative evaluation of its most relevant features: working volume, tracking response and resilience to *ghosting*. Finally, we provide a discussion on the capabilities and limitations of our approach, as well as of improvement and the potential of this type of devices.

PORTALLAX: GOALS AND DESIGN

The current paper focuses on the possibility to retrofit existing devices with 3D display capabilities. Thus we consider three factors to guide our design. The first one was to overcome the limitations in existing approaches. Secondly, the context of use of these devices was also considered, based on the observations reported by Jumisko-Pyykkö [20]. Finally, technical aspects, like the computing capabilities of current mobile devices or costs have been considered. The following set of goals was established to guide the design of Portallax:

- *Support for a big working volume*: As opposed to existing mobile 3D solutions, the working volume of the clip-on should be as big as possible. This feature facilitates its usage, as users do not need to align and stay at fixed positions to see the effect. Freedom of movement within a bigger volume adapts better to the contexts of use (e.g. public transport, walking through cities) described in [20]. Interaction techniques relying on accelerometers [30] or user head movements [5, 14, 28] can be used together with the 3D effect.
- *Support for additional depth perception cues*: The clip-on should provide binocular disparity (*stereopsis*) and also support *motion parallax* with *perspective correction.* These cues are known to greatly enhance the perception of 3D content [19]. Eye tracking within the working volume might be required to provide perspective correction when a limited number of views are generated.
- *Support seamless integration:* Jumisko-Pyykkö [20] suggests that 3D contents should be available for short periods. Thus the attachment should allow seamless transitions between stereo 3D and 2D applications. It should not limit the existing capabilities of the device (e.g. access to the touch screen) or the way it is used.
- *Self-contained operation:* A wide variety of contexts of use are envisioned (indoor, outdoor, cafes, parks, etc). In order to support the contexts of use envisioned, the clip-

on attachment should not require extra hardware on the user (e.g. glasses) or require connections to non portable external devices (e.g. computers, fixed tracking systems).

- *Form factor and quality considerations:* To be really useful, the design should add minimally to the form factor of mobile devices. Being a clip-on solution, the overall cost of the elements used and the simplicity to mount it become critical factors.

ANALYSIS OF MOBILE 3D DISPLAY TECHNOLOGIES

One of the most critical factors for the design of Portallax is the choice of the appropriate 3D display technology. Most mobile 3D displays technologies are *autostereoscopic* (the user does not need any eyewear) and also are *multiview* displays (deliver several views to different *view-zones*). The most common approaches used to achieve these capabilities are parallax barriers [10], lenticular arrays [27] and directional backlighting [38].

Each of these three approaches has been applied to the mobile context. Consoles like Nintendo 3DS (Figure 2 A); mobile devices like HTC Evo 3D, Sharp Lynx 3D, Samsung SCH-B710 or LG Optimus; and even cameras, like Fuji FinePix, use a fixed two view parallax barrier. A dedicated LC panel displays or hides the barrier allowing the device to switch between 2D and 3D modes. Flack et al. [13] proposed a mobile device that allows this same feature for a lenticular array. 3M manufactures *lightguide plus retardation* film, which transforms mobile devices' backlighting making the pixels of the TFT only visible from certain positions. Clip-on solutions have also been proposed using both parallax barriers (Grilli3D [3] in Figure 2 B) and lenticular arrays (3DeeSlide [1] in Figure 2 C). They can be attached to the mobile device while still being able to use its multitouch screen.

In all the previous approaches, the barrier is static. They generate two fixed *view-zones* and, thus, the stereo effect only works at a fixed position in front of the display.

Other multiview displays use information about the position of the user to support a bigger working volume. Woodgate et al. [38] and Dodgson [7] propose displays with three or four *view-zones*, each smaller than a fraction of the user's interpupillary distance (IPD). The positions of the user's eyes are detected and the contents (left eye or right eye views) are swapped to the appropriate *view-zones* for the user to perceive correct 3D imagery. The NEC HxDP display [34] uses this technique, adapting it for a mobile device and lenticular arrays.

However, this technique also imposes some limitations. For an average IPD distance of 63 mm [8], the four *view-zones* would measure 63/4 ~ 16 mm. The tracking system would need to support an accuracy of 8 mm, which is not achievable with the front facing camera found in most devices. Creating these *view-zones* might require additional spacing between the display and the parallax barrier (e.g. up to 5 mm, for a Galaxy Tab like the one we use in our prototype), which adds to the form factor and would prevent the usage of the touch screen. Finally, using four views the resolution for each eye would be, at best, 25% of the original screen resolution.

Instead of swapping, other approaches physically move the *view-zones* according to the user position. This can be done by mechanically rearranging parts of the display [9, 11, 18, 38], but other approaches have also been proposed.

The Varrier [33] and Dynallax [32] use passive barriers, but they rearrange the image at a subpixel level, aligning it to the user's eyes. This requires a rendering overhead of, at least, three rendering passes per eye (excessive in a mobile context) and only provide an effective resolution of 25% for each eye. Their working volume is also small if the user is located close to the display, as would be the case with a handheld device.

Perlin et al.'s autostereoscopic display [31] and MUSTARD [21] use an LC arrangement that allows them to rearrange the position of the parallax barrier and random hole mask respectively, to the current position of the observer. However, current mobile devices do not support synchronized dual graphical outputs (similar to NVIDIA Quadro GSync cards), which are required to operate these displays. The additional LC panel would also require an external power source, occlude the touch screen and drive up the cost of the implementation, which should be ideally low for a clip-on solution.

Following a different approach, non-tracked multiview displays create a large number of views of the 3D imagery. This allows observers to see correct 3D independently of their position, does not require tracking and allows for multiuser operation. However the real-time generation of all the views might be problematic and the resolution of each view is reduced (i.e. display resolution divided by number of views). Recently Fattal et al. [12] reported a backlighting technology capable of creating up to 64 views in a compact form factor. Lanman et al. introduced a new approach that uses stacked LC panels to create an approximation of the constrained 4D lightfield of a 3D scene [24, 25]. This allows multiple full resolution views around the display and the authors propose it as a valid solution for mobile devices. These solutions open interesting opportunities for future mobile devices, but current devices do not have the resolution or the computing power required to operate these displays or create 3D imagery in real time.

Instead, Portallax uses a two view parallax barrier which is mechanically actuated using a microcontroller and two servo motors, all powered through the USB connection. *View-zones* are aligned to the position of the observer using eye tracking and the device's onboard camera. This reduces the costs and power requirements of the solution.

Portallax relies on a novel approach for barrier design that provides wider *view-zones*, to cope with the relatively low

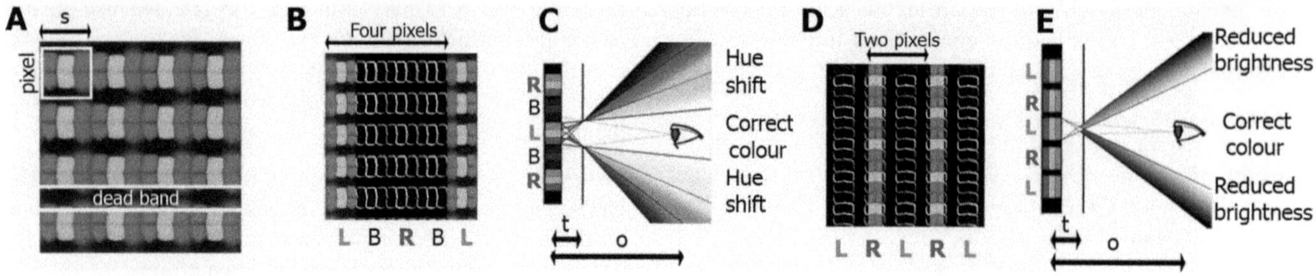

Figure 3. Parallax Barrier Configuration: (A) Microscope photo of panel (B) Classical barrier setup resulting in (C) *hue shift*, small focal regions and four pixel patterns (reduced resolution). (D,E) The Portallax approach uses a two-pixel pattern and has increased resolution and visibility.

precision of our tracking system. It also reduces *hue shift* and provides 50% effective resolution for each eye, maximizing image quality.

Portallax's Parallax Barrier

In a standard LCD panel, the pixel is made up of red, green and blue subpixels arranged in a horizontal row (Figure 3 A). The rows are separated by gaps (~25% of pixel pitch '*s*') where the ITO circuitry resides (*dead bands*). Most parallax barriers (Figure 3 B) use vertical slits (running perpendicular to the pixel rows) or slanted slits (~30% from the vertical [33]). These arrangements have beneficial features, such as support for subpixel algorithms or alleviating Moiré effects. However, as the user moves to the sides, red and blue subpixels get partially occluded (see Figure 3 C), varying their relative contribution and distorting the colour perceived (*hue shift*).

To compensate for this, slit width can be made equal to or greater than the width of a pixel. Due to this, the neighbouring pixels become unintentionally visible, leading to *ghosting*. *Ghosting* can be minimized by blanking out the neighbouring pixels (usually called *pixel guardbands*). The resulting arrangement is the classical barrier design with repeating blocks four pixels wide [32, 33]: one pixel each for left (L) and right (R) eyes interleaved with one pixel wide *pixel guardbands* (B). Note the L-B-R-B pattern in Figures 3 B and 3 C. The effective resolution is 25% of the horizontal display resolution for each eye. Another important parameter is the barrier's *duty cycle*, that is, the percentage of the barrier pattern that the slit occupies (*slit/(slit+barrier)*). The typical *duty cycle* is 25% and can go up to 50% to get brighter images (but smaller *view-zones*).

Portallax manages to avoid *hue shift* and allows a higher resolution per eye by using a novel barrier design based on three heuristic features: *rotated barrier*, *narrower slit* size and *hardware guardbands*. These are described next.

Rotated barrier to avoid hue shift

Portallax uses a barrier rotated by 90° to the pixel rows (see Figure 3 D). The rotated barrier reduces the *hue shift* as all three subpixels are equivalently and simultaneously occluded by the barrier. The proportion to the *view-zones* free of *hue shift* is bigger than before and this effect is mostly replaced by a linear loss of brightness at the boundaries of the *view-zones* (see Figure 3 E).

Narrower slits to increase resolution

Unlike classic barriers, our slits are narrower than one pixel ($slit<s\cdot(o-t)/o$). Neighbouring pixels are not visible through these slits. Thus Portallax eliminates *pixel guardbands* and uses a pattern of two pixels (one for each eye) instead of the four pixel pattern in classical barriers. Note the L-R pattern in Figure 3 D and 3 E. Portallax thus delivers 50% of the display's resolution to each eye, instead of the usual 25%.

Hardware guardbands to reduce ghosting

Portallax also makes use of the *dead band* (shown in Figure 3 A) to further reduce *ghosting*. The *dead band* acts as an implicit *hardware guardband* that prevents *ghosting* when the user reaches the limits of the *view-zone*. At the same time, these are not *pixel guardbands*, so the full resolution of the LC panel remains usable. The *hardware guardbands* can also be used to help optimize the width of the *view-zones* as explained in the next section.

Slit size computations

A large *view-zone* is vital for the success of Portallax. In an ideal classical barrier (Figure 4 A), the size of the *view-zones* '$\omega(o)$' at the optimal viewing distance 'o' is, at best, as wide as the conflict region '$c(o)$' (region where both R and L views are visible). This ratio is even smaller as the observer moves forward or backwards.

Our barriers minimize the width of the conflict zone. The relation between the size of the *view-zone* and conflict zone in Portallax can be described by:

$$\omega(o) = (o - f) \cdot tan\alpha; \; c(o) = (o - t) \cdot tan\beta - \omega(o) \qquad Eq. 1.$$

For e.g., at o = 350 mm, a comparable classical barrier will have $\omega(o) = c(o) = 36.79$ mm. Our barrier, using a typical duty cycle of 25%, results in $\omega(o) = 55.44$ mm and $c(o) = 18.32$ mm (Figure 4 B). The third arrangement (see Figure 4 C) shows a barrier where the slit is as big as the *hardware guardband*, resulting in optimal regions of $\omega(o) = 73.7$ mm and constant-size conflict regions of $c(o) = 0.04$ mm.

Using an LC panel with *hardware guardbands* as big as pixels (Figure 4 D) would produce the best brightness (33% *duty cycle*) and constant size conflict regions (similar to

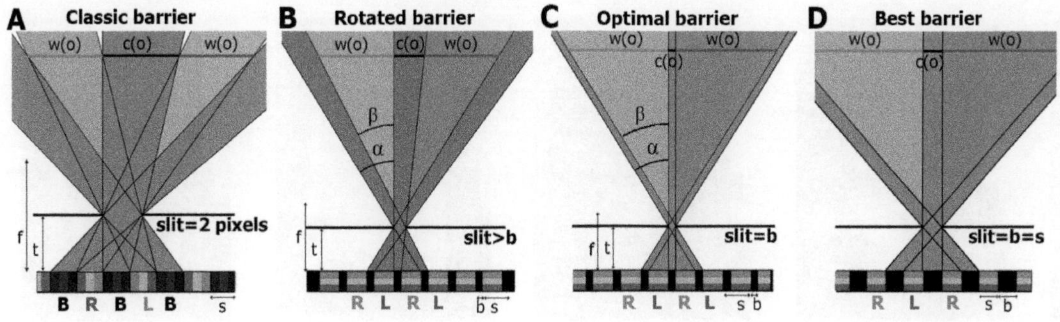

Figure 4. Comparison focal region sizes: (A) Classical parallax barrier. Example Portallax barriers with varying slit sizes (B) slit > guardband (C) slit = guardband and (D) a specially manufactured panel with *hardware guardbands* of the size of a pixel.

Figure 3 C). This arrangement is beyond the scope of this paper as it requires changes at LC fabrication level.

Brightness v/s accuracy trade-off

The previous section describes how the slit size can be used to minimize the conflict zone. However, at the same time, the slit size affects the brightness too. A wider slit (as in Figure 4 B) will produce brighter images, but the size of the *view-zone*s reduces proportionally. A narrower slit (equalling width of the *dead bands*, as in Figure 4 C) produces wider *view-zone*s, but we also see reduction in brightness.

The choice of the appropriate size is actually driven by a third factor: the quality of the tracking technology available. The barrier needs to be repositioned to align the *view-zone*s to the current position of the user's eyes. Errors in registration of the position of the user's eyes will result in misalignments of the barrier, which can break the stereo effect. Thus, the error of the tracking system must be smaller than that allowed by the size of the *view-zones*.

While it can be hard to eliminate the sources of error (tracking, actuation, etc.) it is possible to evaluate these, and select a slit size, which is as bright as possible, but at the same time produces *view-zone*s wide enough to deal with tracking errors. Our implementation of Portallax's barrier takes this into account as described below.

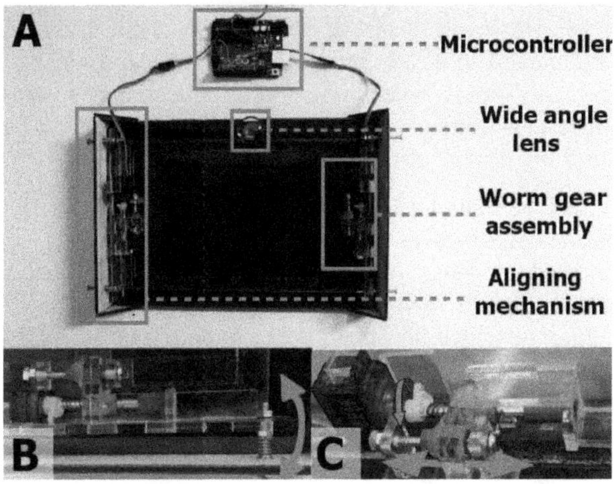

Figure 5. (A) Elements in Portallax. Details of the aligning mechanism (B) and worm gear assembly (C).

IMPLEMENTATION OF PORTALLAX

We provide a reference implementation of Portallax for a Samsung Galaxy Tab 10.1 as shown in Figure 5 A. Additional hardware consisted of the actuation assembly driving the parallax barrier. The parallax barrier was printed on a transparency, to allow *multitouch gestures* to work through it. A mounting frame allows us to fix and align the barrier to the screen (See Figure 5 B). Once installed, no Moiré effects are observed. During operation, the screen is displaced sideways using two servos and a worm gear coupler (Figure 5 C).

An Arduino UNO microcontroller is used to communicate with the device and operate the servos. This additional hardware derives its power from the USB port on the tablet allowing the device to be fully self-contained. One 25 mm off-the-shelf plano-concave lens is included to increase the field of view of the front camera. The current prototype supports a working volume of ~60°, with an optimal observer distance $o=350 \pm 100$ *mm* and an IPD range $e=63 \pm 5$ *mm*, which fits approximately the *~81%* of the adult population [8].

Barrier specifications

The barrier is designed to conform to the working volume we desired to achieve. ($o=350 \pm 100$ *mm, 60°*). Based on the thickness of the display ($t=0.8$ *mm*), its pixel pitch ($s=0.169$ *mm*) and size of the *hardware guardband* ($b=0.042$ *mm*). The pattern pitch '*p*' (size of one slit and one barrier band) is $2 \cdot s \cdot (o - t) / o = 0.337$ *mm* and its *duty cycle* is *18.75%*. This duty cycle complies with the error produced by our tracking system (*26.4 mm*, as described later) and maximizes brightness. The resulting barrier creates *view-zone*s of up to *64.51 mm*, with conflict zones of 9.25 mm. The resulting tolerance to tracking errors is $\mathcal{E} = (63 - 9.25)/2 = 26.8$ *mm*.

This barrier is the best approximation that our printer (1200 dpi) can provide to the optimum slit size. Error tolerance of *26.4 mm* would require a duty cycle of *19.38%*.

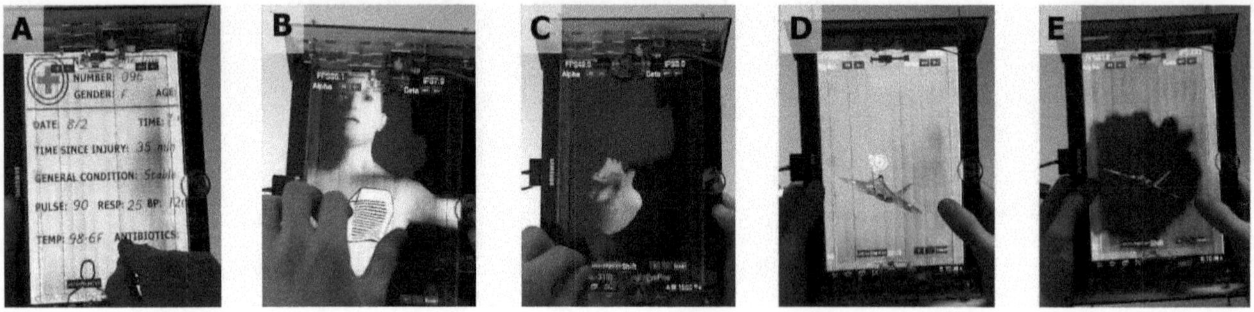

Figure 6. Two examples illustrate key features: (A-C) Users can interact with 2D and 3D contents in a medical application. (D and E) The jet application uses the position of the user relative to the screen to control the direction and speed of the fighter.

Actuation and alignment of the barrier
According to the thickness of the display (t = 0.8 mm) and the angle covered by our working volume (*FOV*), the barrier must be displaced up to $2 \cdot t \cdot tan(FOV/2) = 0.924\ mm$.

We use a paired worm gear assembly [29] powered by two servos to perform this actuation (Figure 5 C). This speed reduction coupling ensures high precision control over the displacements of the barrier. The coupling maps the 256 steps of the servo to the *0.924 mm* we need to displace the screen, achieving a resolution of $0.004 \pm 0.002\ mm$. The misalignment due to this error for an ideal observer (located at *350 mm*) is *1.75 mm*, which is considerably smaller than the error introduced by the tracking system.

The coupling increments the power of the servo proportionally (i.e. our servos' torque of *1.5 Kg/cm*, corresponds to *1.5 Kg/0.924 mm ~1600Kg*). It is also a non reversible coupling, assuring that users' displacements of the screen (e.g. when using finger gestures) will not affect/destroy the servo.

The servo features a rotation speed of 500 degrees per second. This would correspond to a user moving from one end of the working volume to the opposite (*350mm*) in *340 ms* (i.e. *1.03 m/s* observer speed). Maximum observer speed is mostly constrained by the frame rate of the front camera (up to 15 fps in our device and most current devices), rather than to the capabilities of our clip-on solution.

Tracking Algorithm
Portallax uses the front camera to perform an approximate 3D tracking of the user's eyes. This information is used to realign the position of the barrier (to support *stereopsis*) and to correct the perspective according to the relative position of the observer to the screen (to support *motion parallax*). The camera resolution used is 640×480 and covers a volume of up to 60° horizontally in front of the screen (once the wide angle lens is added). It provides up to 15 fps, but its frame rate can decrease in poor lighting conditions.

The tracking algorithm is an OpenCV implementation of the face tracking algorithm by Viola and Jones [36]. Template matching is used to detect the pupils. The 3D position is then estimated using an assumed eye separation of 63 mm and that the user is looking head-on at the display. An α-β filter is used to smooth the measures returned by the algorithm and forward predict the current location of the observer.

Rendering algorithm
Portallax uses a modified version of Rajawali (https://github.com/MasDennis/Rajawali) to generate 3D graphics. We use the stencil buffer to interleave odd and even columns in the display for the left and right eyes, in a similar way to how interlaced stereo was generated in old HMDs. Each frame is rendered twice, once from the point of view of each eye. Off-axis projection of the frustum, according to the relative position of the eye to the screen is performed to correct the perspective.

This implementation incurs the minimum overhead possible for a stereo rendering. The stencil buffer does not need to be recomputed, as pixel columns are always assigned to the same eye, so only the left and right images need to be recomputed.

EXAMPLE APPLICATIONS
Portallax opens an exciting spectrum of new interaction possibilities. Its support for additional stereo cues, allows the replication/adaptation of techniques proposed in the context of 3D user interfaces and tabletop 3D interaction [5, 14, 28]. However, its mobile nature allows these techniques to be applied in novel contexts, like augmented reality. Its ability to interweave these 3D applications with the applications users use in their day to day life creates a very interesting design space.

We feel we cannot do justice to exploring the complexity of this design space in the current paper. The applications presented are thus only intended to illustrate what we consider to be two key aspects: The possibility to seamlessly switch between 2D and stereo 3D tasks and the support for interaction techniques that allow the user to move in front of the device.

The first example replicates a medical application to visualize annotated 2D and 3D information, easily switching among both types of contexts (Figure 6 A-C). The users can browse 2D reports of their patients using

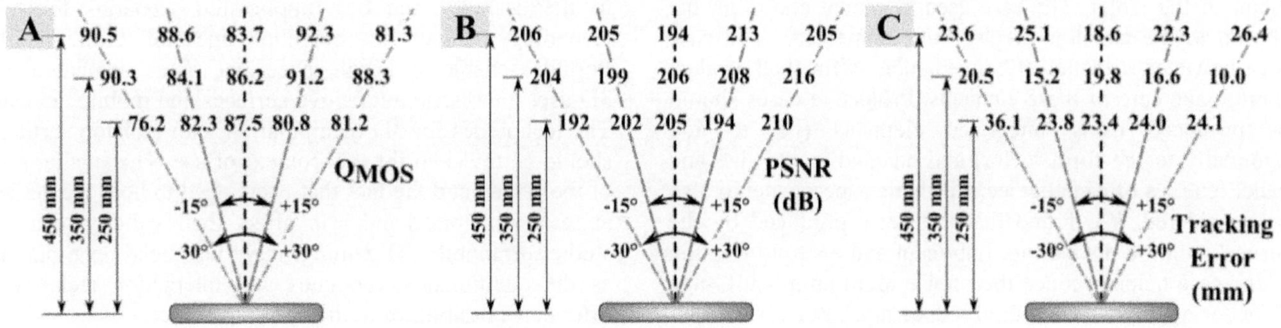

Figure 7. Results table: (A) QMOS and (B) PSNR were used to evaluate the presence of ghosting in the system. (C) The tracking error was also evaluated, confirming that it stays within the margins allowed by our barrier.

conventional gestures (e.g. swipe to scroll, two finger gestures to zoom in and out). 3D models of the anatomy of their patient are embedded in these reports, which the user can visualize by clicking them. Finger touches translate the 3D model and two finger gestures can be used to scale and rotate it. This 3D model contains annotated information, that can be clicked to reveal other relevant pieces of information i.e. other 2D content like reports or 3D models.

The second application is a flight simulation game (Figure 6 D, E). The control of the jet relies mostly on the way the user moves relative to the tablet. The observer distance (Z coordinate) is used to control acceleration. If the user moves further than 40 cm, the velocity is increased, if he approaches closer than 30 cm, the speed of the jet is reduced. This way, kinaesthetic cues are used alongside 3D cues to improve the player's sense of immersion. The roll and pitch of the aircraft is determined by the X and Y position of the user's head. This allows the user to control the direction of the jet in two different ways, by tilting the display or by moving himself. In this last case the tablet serves as a window, revealing the parts of the 3D world the aircraft flies in.

In both examples stereo images, corrected perspective and motion parallax are provided all the time. Objects are placed behind the screen for visual comfort.

EVALUATION OF THE DISPLAY

We performed a quantitative evaluation of the view quality of the prototype to determine how well Portallax fulfils its design requirements. Specifically we measured *ghosting* to measure the quality of the stereo effect within the working volume and the accuracy of the eye tracking algorithm.

Ghosting

We placed a camera behind the right eye of a dummy human face. The face was positioned such that the right eye would be at distances of 250, 350 and 450 mm from the screen (minimum, optimum and maximum distances of our working volume). At each of these, the position was further offset horizontally to emulate 30°, 15°, 0°, -15° and -30° positions. The resulting positions mimicked a user tilting the display and moving in front of it. At each position, six photographs were captured. The first was used as a reference image with right eye seeing a solid blue rectangle and the left eye view turned off. The other five test images were taken with the same right eye view and a solid green rectangle as the left eye view. We also recorded the eye position as detected by the eye tracker every time.

The view quality was analysed using HDR-VDP2 [26] using their reference implementation to compute a Q_{MOS} score ([0→100], 100 is best). This metric measures perceivable differences for an average human observer. PSNR value was also computed, to measure objective interference due to ghosting. The results are shown in Figure 7 A, B. Q_{MOS} scores had a mean value of 85.64 (σ=4.68), indicating that the *ghosting* is minimal and not easily visible to the human eye. PSNR, with an average value of 203.97 dB (σ=6.79), also aligns with these results. Both results confirm our informal observations that no noticeable *ghosting* is present.

Tracking accuracy

As discussed previously, the precision of the tracking system affects the design of the barrier. More accurate tracking allows wider slits, which result in smaller *view-zone*s but also a brighter image. We evaluated the accuracy of our tracking algorithm twice, once to design our barrier and a second time to validate our design. We only report the results from the second study, as they are similar to the ones from the first study.

The values returned by our tracking algorithm were recorded while taking the pictures for the *ghosting* evaluation. As shown in Figure 7 C, the tracking error (distance to actual position) is always within the error range of our barrier. The only exception is the set of measures at the left extreme angle, at 250mm. The fact the Q_{MOS} and PSNR also reveal lower scores at this position pushes us to believe that there could be an alignment error on the wide angle lens of our device. This could cause errors in our tracking system, which in turn would cause the barrier to be incorrectly aligned, producing more *ghosting*

DISCUSSION

Limitations

The demonstrated prototype is not without limitations. The usage of off-the-shelf elements adds too much to the form factor of the tablet. The case used to mount and align the clip-on to the tablet is precise but rudimentary. The case was, however, a matter of convenience. A finished product should take care of these elements. Protective cases should be produced using integrated elements (i.e. to add minimally to the form factor) and adapted to the size and panel features of each device. Aesthetic aspects should also be considered. We found that the noise produced by the servos could be distracting. Lubricant and a strong fixation to the case helped reduce their noise to a minimum. Usage of better quality servos would reduce noise eve further, but increase the cost of the solution.

The possible interference of the attachment with other applications also requires consideration. During our development, we realized that the minimum font size had to be 3mm (8.5 pt) to be readable. The wide FOV lens could also affect the experience of the user with videoconference applications such as Skype. The overall brightness of the device is diminished, as a result of the barrier. The orientation of the barrier limits the stereoscopic operation to the portrait mode of the device. This may be useful for applications like 3D video conferencing but not for others. Also the frame rate of the camera decreases in poor lighting conditions. This affects the tracking speed thus slowing down the responsiveness of the barrier.

The impact that these limitations have on the user experience is beyond the scope of this paper and could be dealt with in future work.

Going beyond Portallax

We firmly believe the design of Portallax provides a clip-on solution that could benefit a huge number of mobile devices. However during our implementations, we did note that certain small design changes in the manufacturing of the devices could prepare them to work nicely with this kind of *clip-on* solutions. For example, if it was possible to pre-select the pixel pitch (s), the thickness of the display (t), the *hardware guardband* size (b), the device would have a pre-optimized *view-zone*s. Ideally, *view-zone*s of 75 mm can adapt to the vast majority of adults [8]. Products designed for children could equally be adjusted. Likewise, a *hardware guardband* of the same size as the pixels would allow for barriers that maximize brightness and size of *view-zone*s, as illustrated in Figure 4 D.

Increasing the frame rate of the front cameras, would improve the tracking quality (i.e. no blurring due to high speed head movements). This could lead to less restrictive barriers (wider slits) and brighter images. In addition to this, removing the IR filter from the front camera would enable the use of IR illumination to enhance the visibility of the user's pupils (i.e. better accuracy) and maintaining a high frame rate even in dark environments.

CONCLUSIONS AND FUTURE WORK

The current paper focuses on the engineering aspects related to Portallax. As already mentioned, aspects related to the usability and best application scenarios for this technology remain as potential lines of future work. Portallax enables a design space that mixes elements from 3D user interfaces, interactive surfaces and mobile devices. The techniques for 3D manipulation with tabletop surfaces should be revisited for this context of use. The smaller size of the screen and the fact that users need to hold the device at least with one hand, can affect their validity. Current studies on mobile 3D gaming might also need revalidation, as the additional stereo cues and interaction techniques offer new possibilities to the user experience.

This paper has presented Portallax, an improved version of an actuated parallax barrier that converts an existing handheld device into a stereoscopic 3D enabled device without limiting the device's interactive capabilities. Portallax provides and optimized design of parallax barriers, alleviating traditional issues. *Ghosting* and *hue shift* are reduced by reorienting the barrier and making use of the implicit *hardware guardbands*. The usage of *narrow slits* supports an increased resolution of 50% per eye. Finally, careful selection of *slits* and *duty cycle* allow us to cope with the error introduced by the eye tracking while maximizing the brightness. Portallax also supports a wider working volume, when compared to existing commercial devices. Finally we tested the device for its performance and are able to see that it meets the high requirements we set for retrofitting a handheld device.

ACKNOWLEDGEMENTS

This work is supported by European Research Council (Starting Grant Agreement 278576) under the Seventh Framework Programme.

REFERENCES

1. *3DeeSlide*. 2013; Available from: http://www.spatialview.com/product/3deeslide/.
2. *Global mobile statistics 2013 Part A: Mobile subscribers; handset market share; mobile operators*. 2013; Available from: http://mobithinking.com/mobile-marketing-tools/latest-mobile-stats/a#mobiletablet.
3. *Grilli3D*. 2013; Available from: http://www.grilli3d.com/.
4. *List of 3D films*. 2013; Available from: http://en.wikipedia.org/wiki/List_of_3D_films.
5. Bowman, D.A., Kruijff, E., LaViola Jr, J.J., and Poupyrev, I., *3D user interfaces: theory and practice*. 2004: Addison-Wesley Professional.
6. Caballero, M.L., Chang, T.-R., Menendez, M., and Occhialini, V. *Behand: augmented virtuality gestural interaction for mobile phones*. In Proc. of *ACM MobileHCI*. 2010. Lisbon, Portugal: ACM Press.
7. Dodgson, N.A. *On the number of viewing zones required for head-tracked autostereoscopic display. In Proc. of Stereoscopic Displays and Virtual Reality Systems XIII*. 2006. SPIE.

8. Dodgson, N.A. *Variation and extrema of human interpupillary distance*. In Proc. of *SPIE 5291*. 2004.

9. Eichenlaub, J.B. *Autostereoscopic display with high brightness and power efficiency*. In Proc. of *Stereoscopic Displays and Virtual Reality Systems I*. 1994. SPIE.

10. Eichenlaub, J.B. *Developments in autosterioscopic technology at Dimension Technologies Inc*. In Proc. of *Stereoscopic Displays and Applications IV*. 1993. SPIE.

11. Ezra, D., Woodgate, G.J., Omar, B.A., Holliman, N.S., Harrold, J., and Shapiro, L.S. *New autostereoscopic display system*. In Proc. of *Stereoscopic Displays and Virtual Reality Systems II*. 1995. SPIE.

12. Fattal, D., Peng, Z., Tran, T., Vo, S., Fiorentino, M., Brug, J., and Beausoleil, R.G., *A multi-directional backlight for a wide-angle, glasses-free 3D display*. Nature, 2013. **495**(7441): p. 348-351.

13. Flack, J., Harrold, J., and Woodgate, G.J. *A prototype 3D mobile phone equipped with a next-generation autostereoscopic display*. In Proc. of *Stereoscopic Displays and Virtual Reality Systems XIV*. 2007. SPIE.

14. Hachet, M., Bossavit, B., Cohé, A., and de la Rivière, J.-B. *Toucheo: multitouch and stereo combined in a seamless workspace*. In Proc. of *ACM UIST*. 2011. Santa Barbara, California, USA: ACM Press.

15. Harrold, J. and Woodgate, G.J. *Autostereoscopic display technology for mobile 3DTV applications*. In Proc. of *Stereoscopic Displays and Virtual Reality Systems XIV*. 2007. SPIE.

16. Huhtala, J., Karukka, M., Salmimaa, M., and Häkkilä, J. *Evaluating depth illusion as method of adding emphasis in autostereoscopic mobile displays*. In Proc. of *MobileHCI*. 2011. Stockholm, Sweden: ACM Press.

17. Hwang, S., Ahn, M., and Wohn, K.-y. *MagGetz: customizable passive tangible controllers on and around conventional mobile devices. In Proc. of ACM UIST*. 2013. S*t. Andrews, S*cotland: ACM Press.

18. Jewell, M., Chamberlin, G., Sheat, *D., Cochrane, P., and McCartney, D. 3-D imaging systems for video communication applications. In Proc. of Stereoscopic Displays and Virtual Reality Systems II*. 1995. SPIE.

19. Johnston, E.B., Cumming, B.G., and Landy, M.S., *Integration of stereopsis and motion shape cues*. Vision Research, 1994. **34**(17): p. 2259-2275.

20. Jumisko-Pyykkö, S., Weitzel, M., and Strohmeier, D. *Designing for user experience: what to expect from mobile 3D TV and video?* In Proc. of *ACM UXTV*. 2008. ACM Press.

21. Karnik, A., Mayol-Cuevas, W., and Subramanian, S. *MUSTARD: A Multi User See Through AR Display*. In Proc. of *ACM SIGCHI*. 2012. Austin, Texas, USA: ACM Press.

22. Ketabdar, H., Moghadam, P., Naderi, B., and Roshandel, M. *Magnetic signatures in air for mobile devices*. In Proc. of *ACM MobileHCI*. 2012. San Francisco, California, USA: ACM Press.

23. Ketabdar, H., Roshandel, M. and Yuksel, K. A. *Towards using embedded magnetic field sensor for around mobile device 3D interaction*. In Proc. of *ACM MobileHCI*. 2010. Lisbon, Portugal: ACM Press.

24. Lanman, D., Hirsch, M., Kim, Y., and Raskar, R., *Content-adaptive parallax barriers: optimizing dual-layer 3D displays using low-rank light field factorization*. *ACM* Trans. Graphics, 2010. **29**(6): p. 1-10.

25. Lanman, D., Wetzstein, G., Hirsch, M., Heidrich, W., and Raskar, R. *Polarization fields: dynamic light field display using multi-layer LCDs*. In Proc. of *ACM SIGGRAPH Asia* 2011. Hong Kong, China: ACM Press.

26. Mantiuk, R., Kim, K.J., Rempel, A.G., and Heidrich, W. *HDR-VDP-2: a calibrated visual metric for visibility and quality predictions in all luminance conditions*. In Proc. of *ACM SIGGRAPH*. 2011. ACM Press.

27. McAllister, D.F., *Stereo computer graphics: and other true 3D technologies*. 1993: Princeton University Press.

28. Möllers, M., Zimmer, P., and Borchers, J. *Direct manipulation and the third dimension: co-planar dragging on 3d displays*. In Proc. of *ACM ITS*. 2012. Cambridge, Massachusetts, USA: ACM Press.

29. Oberg, E., *Spiral and Worm Gearing: A Treatise on the Principles, Dimensions, Calculation and Design of Spiral and Worm Gearing . 2008:* Kessinger Publishing.

30. Ogniewski, J. and Ragnemalm, I., *Autostereoscopy and Motion Parallax for Mobile Computer Games Using Commercially Available Hardware*. IJCISIM, 2011. **3**: p. 480-488.

31. Perlin, K., Paxia, S., and Kollin, J.S. *An auto-stereoscopic display*. In proc of *ACM SIGGRAPH* 2000.

32. Peterka, T., Kooima, R.L., Girado, J.I., Ge, J., Sandin, D.J., Johnson, A., Leigh, J., Schulze, J., and DeFanti, T.A. *Dynallax: Solid state dynamic parallax barrier autostereoscopic vr display*. In Proc. of *IEEE VR*. 2007. IEEE Computer Society.

33. Sandin, D.J., Margolis, T., Ge, J., Girado, J., Peterka, T., and DeFanti, T.A., *The Varrier autostereoscopic virtual reality display*. ACM Transactions on Graphics, 2005. **24**(3): p. 894-903.

34. Shigemura, K., Niioka, S., Masumura, K., and Asada, H., *P-5: A High Resolution Multi-View 2D/3D Display with HxDP Arrangement and its Optical Characterization.* SID Symposium Digest of Technical Papers, 2011. **42**(1): p. 1109-1112.

35. Sodhi, R.S., Jones, B.R., Forsyth, D., Bailey, B.P., and Maciocci, G. *BeThere: 3D mobile collaboration with spatial input*. In Proc. of *ACM SIGCHI*. 2013. Paris, France: ACM Press.

36. Viola, P. and Jones, M. *Rapid object detection using a boosted cascade of simple features.* In proc *CVPR2001.*

37. Willner, K., *Ugur, K.*, Salmimaa, M., Hallapuro, A., and Lainema, J. *Mobile 3D Video Using MVC and N800 Internet Tablet*. In Proc. of *3DTV Conference*. 2008.

38. Woodgate, G.J., Ezra, D., Harrold, J., Holliman, N.S., Jones, G.R., and Moseley, R.R. *Observer-tracking autostereoscopic 3D display systems.* In Proc. of *Stereoscopic Displays and VR Systems IV*. 1997. SPIE.

Spaces of Innovation in Complex UX Design

Mark Vanderbeeken
Experientia
Turin, Italy
mark@experientia.com

Author Keywords
User Interaction

ACM Classification: H.5.m

Abstract
Leading practice in mobile user experience design presents complex opportunities and challenges not always fully revealed in academic exploration and research. Addressing users with cultural and behavioural differences; understanding economic imbalances and wide demographic ranges amongst individuals and networks; including ethical considerations such as right to privacy and confidentiality, authorship, and transparency; perception and cognition; larger sustainability concerns; and understanding often ignored biases within the client group - these many factors define the contemporary user experience design landscape. How can we create a space for innovation that takes these constraints and people's context and aspirations into account? Mark Vanderbeeken will illustrate these challenges with examples from Experientia's practice, particularly through a project they recently conducted with Intel.

MobileHCI 2014, September 23–26, 2014, Toronto, ON, Canada.
ACM 978-1-4503-3004-6/14/09.
http://dx.doi.org/10.1145/2628363.2634236

Related Work
Experientia works with clients around the world to envision design strategies, develop policies, and establish strategic communications platforms. They work with ethnographic research and information architecture to develop scenarios and user profiles, experience prototyping, physical computing and software prototyping. A strong focus of their work involves heuristic evaluations, international usability, research and testing, and website usability.

Speaker's Bio

Mark Vanderbeeken is a founding partner of Experientia, where he is involved with management, project supervision, editorial contributions, design policy and strategic communications.

Prior to starting Experientia, he was communications manager of Interaction Design Institute Ivrea (Ivrea, Italy), European communications coordinator for the World Wide Fund for Nature (or WWF, Copenhagen, Denmark), marketing director of Gwathmey Siegel & Associates Architects (New York, USA) and chief press officer of Antwerp 93, Cultural Capital of Europe (Antwerp, Belgium).

He is the author of Experientia's successful experience design blog Putting People First, has set up a professional blog on e-democracy, and writes for Core77, the well-known USA-based online design magazine.

He studied visual and cognitive psychology at the University of Leuven, Belgium and obtained a master's degree in cognitive psychology at Columbia University, New York. He speaks English, French, German, Italian and Dutch.

Interaction for Reading Comprehension on Mobile Devices

Rafael Veras*, Erik Paluka*, Meng-Wei Chang*, Vivian Tsang†, Fraser Shein†, Christopher Collins*

*University of Ontario Institute of Technology
Oshawa, Canada
{rafael.verasguimaraes, erik.paluka, meng-wei.chang, christopher.collins}@uoit.ca

†Quillsoft Ltd.
Toronto, Canada
{vtsang, fshein}@quillsoft.ca

ABSTRACT
This paper introduces a touch-based reading interface for tablets designed to support vocabulary acquisition, text comprehension, and reduction of reading anxiety. Touch interaction is leveraged to allow direct replacement of words with synonyms, easy access to word definitions and seamless dialogue with a personalized model of the reader's vocabulary. We discuss how fluid interaction and direct manipulation coupled with natural language processing can help address the reading needs of audiences such as school-age children and English as Second Language learners.

Author Keywords
e-reading; mobile; touch interaction

ACM Classification Keywords
H.5.2. Information Interfaces and Presentation (e.g. HCI): User Interfaces

INTRODUCTION
Reading in the mobile HCI landscape is largely dominated by applications designed for proficient readers, featuring a variety of supports for active reading tasks, in particular, annotation. The needs of a large audience, composed of children, English as Second Language (ESL) learners, and struggling readers have not been well-addressed. Such needs consist mainly of support for vocabulary acquisition and text comprehension.

School-age children are faced each year with a massive number of new English words. Printed school English for grades three through nine contains about 88,500 word families, with over 100,000 distinct meanings, and the average number of words learnt yearly by children until the end of high school, when they know on average 40,000 words, is around 3,000 [13].

Research has shown that much of the vocabulary learning occurs incidentally while reading, with strategies that include using contextual cues, morphological information, cognate knowledge, and dictionaries [3]. The consensus is that the best way to improve vocabulary is by reading difficult texts, but texts with a high density of unknown words can quickly become unintelligible and frustrating [4, 10]. Moreover, there is evidence in the literature showing that ESL learners experience reading anxiety, the anxiety levels correlate with the reader's perception of the difficulty of the text, and the reading performance of learners decreases in conjunction with increased reading anxiety [16, 17].

In this paper, we present a novel reading interface for tablet devices aimed at improving the experience of struggling readers. Our design focuses on fluid interaction with the goal of empowering readers and relieving the anxiety that comes with reading unfamiliar texts. We take touch interaction beyond marking and highlighting to direct manipulation of the text's content. The main features of our prototype are a visual representation of text difficulty, interactive replacement of words with synonyms, a word definition lens, and a personalized model of the reader's vocabulary.

RELATED WORK
Several publications present multitouch tools for active reading, with some interaction design similarities to this work. LiquidText is a desktop application that leverages multitouch interaction to create a fluid reading experience where the main design goal is flexibility [18]. It supports annotation, highlighting and novel ways to manipulate the representation of content. Similarly, there are tools that explore pen and touch interaction for active reading on tabletops [12] and tablets [9]. Although these tools aim to develop more fluid ways to interact with text, they focus on active reading tasks, mainly annotation; therefore, they lack support for text comprehension and vocabulary acquisition.

Other publications propose user interfaces or methods to make texts easier to understand. For example, Zeng-Treitler et al. replace difficult words in electronic health records (EHR) with easier synonyms to improve comprehensibility for customers [21]. Unlike our prototype, their system is non-interactive and its scope is limited to improving sentences for EHR systems. Yu and Miller propose a method for transformation of content on web pages centred on sentence separation and spacing to enhance readability and comprehension for non-native readers [20]. Eom et al. offer sense-specific word definitions for texts on the web through a rudimentary HTML interface; their experiments demonstrated that the system can help ESL learners enhance vocabulary and understanding of texts [7].

MobileHCI 2014, September 23–26, 2014, Toronto, ON, Canada.

ACM 978-1-4503-3004-6/14/09 ...$15.00.
http://dx.doi.org/10.1145/2628363.2628387

Microsoft Word 2013 has functionalities that can be used to improve comprehension of texts, although this feature is targeted at writing, instead of reading. Readers can access dictionary definitions and synonyms of any selected word. Through the "touch mode" in hybrid laptops, these functions can be accessed by tapping on the screen, creating an experience somewhat similar to the one presented in this paper. The fundamental difference is that Word is still a desktop application based on the WIMP paradigm. The dictionary and thesaurus are add-ons that perform in isolation from the overall context of the word of interest. For example, the dictionary presents multiple definitions, some of them not corresponding to the word's part-of-speech (POS) in the text.

In the commercial mobile landscape, a large number of educational applications are meant to improve reading comprehension and vocabulary. However, the great majority is composed of games for kindergarten-aged children aimed at teaching words in isolation (reproducing the flashcard experience) [11], distinguishing facts from opinions [5], identifying the five W's of reading [6], or reading out loud curated stories [15]. Our application creates a mobile reading experience for older children, aimed at vocabulary acquisition and easing reading anxiety. It can be used with any text chosen by the learner or suggested by a teacher.

In summary, there is a gap left unaddressed between out-of-context, kindergarten word learning and independent reading. In other words, there is yet a system that provides the appropriate scaffolding leading to sustained, independent and critical reading, for which some of the cited systems provided support. Our proposed system provides one such scaffold. To the best of our knowledge, no publication or commercial system has brought together solutions for vocabulary acquisition and text comprehension in a highly interactive, general purpose, mobile reading system.

PROTOTYPE

We developed a multitouch web reading interface tailored to tablets. The prototype allows the creation of a personal profile and accepts as input plain text documents. In this section we introduce the main features of the prototype.

Breaking Down the Wall of Grey

When faced with a page of dense text, colloquially called a "wall of grey," readers can become intimidated and discouraged before even beginning to read. One of the authors of this work relates an anecdote in which his child was intimidated by a reading challenge and refused to begin to read a new book. The parent discovered that by pointing out how many words his child already knew on the page, the reading anxiety was reduced. This observation inspired our first design feature, the Personal Vocabulary View (PVV) which "breaks down" the wall of grey text by showing the reader how much of the text they already know how to read, based on a record of their personal vocabulary. The technique also isolates the proportion and location of unknown words, which leads the reader to use the other tools, described later, to expand their vocabulary. An interaction mechanism allows readers to inform the application of additional words they know. With a

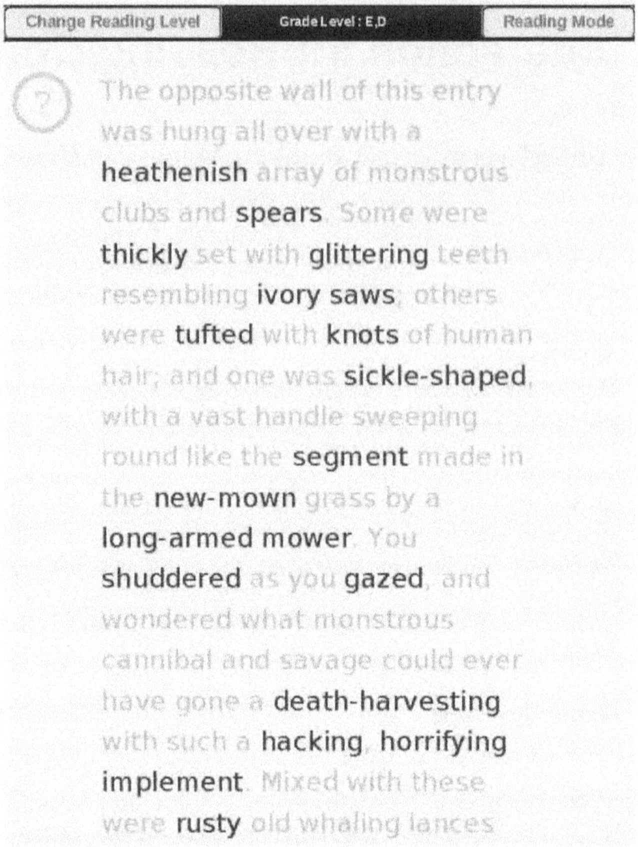

Figure 1: The Personal Vocabulary View highlighting unknown words according to a personalized model of the reader's vocabulary. Excerpt of Moby Dick by Herman Melville.

personalized, incremental model of the reader's vocabulary knowledge, our Personal Vocabulary View conveys a personalized visual representation of the text difficulty.

The PVV (Figure 1) fades out the words that are known by the reader, while the unknown words are highlighted in black. Every word in the text can be toggled with a single tap gesture. Tapping an unknown word informs the tool's internal model that the word (with the current part-of-speech) is known by the reader, preventing it from appearing as unknown in the future. If the word appears in other context playing a different syntactical role, it will be considered unknown. Document scrolling is constrained to dragging in the margins of the text to prevent gesture ambiguity.

One of the challenges related to this approach is inferring the initial vocabulary of the reader. Biemiller, using partly empirical methods, roughly estimated the vocabulary of pre-elementary and elementary students in a list of 11,000 root word meanings categorized as: useful to teach during the primary grades (K–2), easy by second grade, useful to teach during the upper elementary grades, and difficult for elementary children at grade 6 or earlier [1]. We use that list, along with a list of stop words, to populate the tool's vocabulary model of the reader at profile creation time, based on the reader's

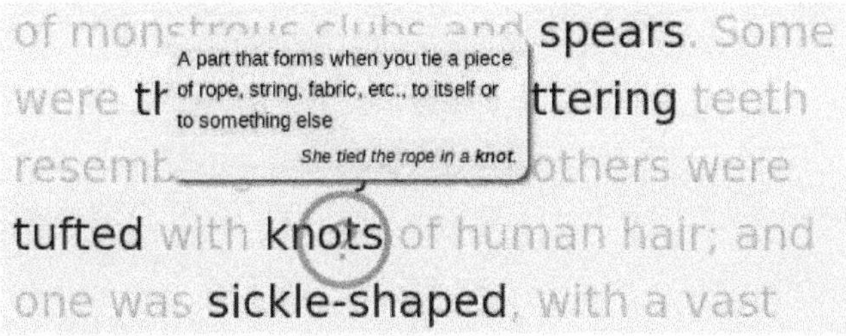

Figure 2: The word definition lens being used on the word *knots*.

selection of school level: a) lower than grade 2, b) lower than grade 6 or c) higher or at grade 6. Note that this level system is most appropriate for native readers, as it refers to school grades. We consider alternative methods for inititalizing the personal vocabulary list in the future work section.

Interactive Replacement of Words with Synonyms

The data-driven learning paradigm advocates that systems should provide evidence (as opposed to answers) and rely on users' intelligence to reach the correct conclusions. For example, researchers have shown that corpus-based usage examples, based on concordances, can be just as effective as dictionary definitions in conveying the meaning of words for L2 learners [8]. In favour of a minimal switch in the focus of attention, we take the inverse approach: instead of showing different contexts where the target word appears, we allow readers to browse synonyms suitable to the context. Evidence for the efficacy of synonyms for text comprehension can be found in Wittrock et al., where the authors demonstrate that stories whose rare words were replaced by more frequent synonyms were significantly better comprehended by children in sixth grade [19]. We hypothesize the replacement of words with (more familiar) synonyms can make the understanding of rare words easier and faster than dictionary definitions. Moreover, through exploring an array of nearly equivalent words in a real usage context, readers have more opportunities to improve their vocabulary.

In our prototype, readers can manipulate the words of a document directly using their fingers. Building upon a roller metaphor, as in a combination lock, the application allows readers to "roll" over several choices of synonyms for any word in the document, as illustrated in Figure 3. The rolling gesture is registered by touching and holding a word for at least 600ms, causing the word to subtly shake, as if it were "detached" from the document. Then readers can drag their fingers up and down to roll over synonyms. Lifting the finger terminates the gesture and replaces the original word with the synonym chosen. To relieve the constraint of having fingers down during the whole gesture (there may be many synonyms), we delay the termination by 2 seconds after the finger is lifted; any touch on the word within the delay is interpreted as a continuation of rolling, allowing one to perform multiple swipes, as opposed to a continuous dragging motion. The substitute words remain underlined to facilitate their identification. Compared with dictionary definitions, which usually appear in pop-ups and carry longer text with their own unfamiliar words [14], we believe this design is more fluid and less distracting.

Note that we intentionally did not include a visual affordance indicating which words have synonyms available. As the view is both an exploratory interface as well as a reading application, we felt this would be distracting. Also, through engaging with the text in an exploratory way, we hypothesize that learners will develop a deeper connection to the vocabulary.

Ranking Synonyms

The order in which the list of synonyms is made available to the reader is important to minimize the time spent browsing, and it can implicitly inform the user of the most appropriate synonyms, since the semantic equivalence of words varies across contexts. Also, the knowledge about the reader's vocabulary captured by the PVV can be leveraged to prioritize more familiar words, as the utmost purpose of the tool is to make the text more comprehensible.

Thus, the ranking of synonyms is based on two attributes, in order of importance: familiarity and fitness to context. Upon registration of the rolling gesture, a list S of synonyms of the target word with matching part-of-speech is retrieved from the Merriam-Webster's Dictionary Public API and sorted in two stages according to the ranking criteria. The sorting determines the order the words appear while the reader is performing the rolling gesture.

The *familiarity score* of each $s \in S$, where s is a tuple of the form $\{word, POS\}$, is determined straightforwardly based on its membership in the set of the reader's known words (0 or 1). The *fitness score* is computed according to the frequency of s in a large N-gram corpus, within the context of the next word w_1. Therefore, the fitness score $F(s, w_1)$ is defined as $C(s, w_1)/C(*, w_1)$, where the numerator corresponds to the frequency that s occurs before w_1, and the denominator corresponds to the frequency that w_1 occurs after any word. As a source for the frequencies, we employ the bigram collection of the Contemporary Corpus of American English, containing over 48 million rows with POS information.

After sorting, S is further trimmed by removing the words for which $F = 0$. This ensures that synonyms that never occur in a certain context are cut off, preventing sentences such as "a strong cup of tea" being erroneously turned into "a powerful cup of tea". Finally, we change the inflection of the synonym, if necessary, to match the same conjugation of the original word, in case of a verb, or the same number, in case of a noun.

Word Definition Lens

The replacement of words with synonyms does not always lead to comprehension, as sometimes the replacement is just as unfamiliar as the original word; in addition, the algorithm described in the previous section might return an empty list, in case no appropriate replacement is found. In order to cover these cases, we designed a minimalistic, gesture-based word definition lens. Many of the available tools that offer word definitions, such as the built-in iPad dictionary, present the user with an overwhelming amount of information, usually containing definitions for several senses of the word, along with phonetic symbols and usage examples. The goal behind our word definition lens was to make it simpler and more interactive.

The lens is represented by a question mark icon placed in the upper left corner of the screen (Figure 1). The lens can be dragged around freely; holding it over any word triggers the appearance of a box showing the first, main definition of the word along with a usage example from Webster's Learner's Dictionary (Figure 2). The word definitions presented correspond to the POS of the target word (distinguishing, for example "sit in a chair" from "chair a meeting"). Swiping the definition box brings up additional definitions of the word, if they exist. Any touch out of the definition box cancels it. The lens returns to its home position when released, allowing reading to resume quickly. The word definition lens allows readers to investigate the meanings of many words quickly by just dragging the lens over them.

Implementation Details

Our prototype is implemented in a client-server architecture. The client-side is based on HTML5, CSS3, and JavaScript, powered by the D3 library. The server-side is based on Python, and uses NLTK and nodebox for the natural language processing. Communication is done via JSON documents.

When the reader inputs the text in the client, the text is sent to the server for processing and returns with POS tags. Every interaction in the client requires the target word to be sent along with surrounding words and POS tags to the server. The personal vocabulary of each reader is held on the server side. Latency depends on requests to the third-party API (Webster's) where it gathers synonyms and definitions from. The server maintains the N-gram corpus in a fully indexed database, so that lookup is done without compromise to interaction. POS tagging is done following the Brill algorithm [2]. All interactions with the text (tapping words, activating synonym replacement, and requests for definitions) are tracked in order to build a data resource about reading behavior and vocabulary development on an individual and community basis. Leveraging this data for educational analytics, and investigating the privacy issues related to its collection are left for future work.

FUTURE WORK

Future work includes a study to evaluate our tool using instruments for measuring reading performance and anxiety. There are also many opportunities to expand the capabilities of our prototype. The current estimation of the reader's initial vocabulary does not support groups other than English first language children; estimates of ESL learners' vocabulary, for example, are necessary. Ideas to initialize the model include creating a self-adjusting model of learner vocabulary based on community statistics. At first deployment of our software, the vocabulary initialization would be based upon rough estimates and models taken from the grade-level vocabulary dataset. Then, leveraging the collective knowledge about vocabulary encoded in the usage statistics from the system, and

Figure 3: Direct replacement of words with synonyms. The word "heathenish" is replaced with the more familiar word "wild" through a rolling gesture, captured here in three snapshots. The grey circle represents the touch point.

meta-data about the learner, we could create an increasingly accurate estimate of initial learner vocabulary for new users. Another potential avenue for vocabulary estimation could be through analyzing some writing or reading samples provided by the learner. When considering how this prototype could fit into a larger learning ecology, the data collected by the interactions of readers with the software, if properly protected and anonymized, could be useful for educators to mine in curriculum planning.

The suggestions of synonyms and dictionary definitions are currently based on part-of-speech and bigram frequency of use statistics. Future work will investigate how grammar (parsing) and word sense disambiguation (semantics) can improve the quality of the suggestions. For example, rather than looking only at bigrams of the candidate word and next word to filter synonym candidates, we could examine counts of the candidate word and syntactically related verbs or nouns using the parse tree.

Currently, a single tap on a word in the PVV is taken as a permanent indication that a word is known by the reader. This design decision needs to be tested with an empirical study. It may take multiple exposures to a new term before a reader is comfortable with it. We are investigating ways to adapt the number of exposures required before the word is marked as known. One idea is to require multiple exposures (and taps) on words that are ranked as significantly above the reading level of the learner, as determined by community statistics. In addition, it may be useful to employ a time function, requiring multiple exposures of a term in a specified time period before it is permanently marked as learned, or a morphology function, requiring exposure to multiple variants of a word in a variety of contexts.

The PVV currently only shows the difficulty of the words that are within the viewport. A more abstract representation that can portray the difficulty of the words across the entire text could make this view more powerful and should be considered.

CONCLUSION

With the design proposed in the current paper, we hope to have empowered struggling readers with tools to effectively overcome reading anxiety and comprehension difficulty using mobile technology. Recognizing that the main obstacle for reading is vocabulary difficulty, we designed a view where readers can easily visualize the unknown words in a text, an interaction mechanism by which readers can substitute difficult words with familiar synonyms and a minimalistic word definition lens. Furthermore, we believe the direct manipulation and the fluidity of our interaction play a significant role in connecting the reader to the text, which might also be a factor in reducing anxiety.

REFERENCES

1. Biemiller, A. *Words Worth Teaching: Closing the Vocabulary Gap*. McGraw-Hill SRA, 2009.
2. Brill, E. A simple rule-based part of speech tagger. In *Proc. of the Workshop on Speech and Natural Language*, HLT '91, Association for Computational Linguistics (1992), 112–116.
3. Carlo, M. S., August, D., McLaughlin, B., Snow, C. E., Dressler, C., Lippman, D. N., Lively, T. J., and White, C. E. Closing the gap: Addressing the vocabulary needs of english-language learners in bilingual and mainstream classrooms. *Reading Research Quarterly 39*, 2 (2004), 188–215.
4. Carver, R. P. Percentage of unknown vocabulary words in text as a function of the relative difficulty of the text: Implications for instruction. *Journal of Literacy Research 26*, 4 (1994), 413–437.
5. E. Skills Learning, LLC. MiniMod Fact or Opinion Lite. `https://itunes.apple.com/ca/app/minimod-fact-or-opinion-lite/id492491726`, 2013.
6. E. Skills Learning, LLC. MiniMod Reading for Details Lite. `https://itunes.apple.com/ca/app/minimod-reading-for-details/id409669762`, 2013.
7. Eom, S., Dickinson, M., and Sachs, R. Sense-specific lexical information for reading assistance. In *Proc. of the Seventh Workshop on Building Educational Applications Using NLP*, Association for Computational Linguistics (2012), 316–325.
8. Frankenberg-Garcia, A. The use of corpus examples for language comprehension and production. *ReCALL 26*, 02 (2014), 128–146.
9. Hinckley, K., Bi, X., Pahud, M., and Buxton, B. Informal information gathering techniques for active reading. In *Proc. of the SIGCHI Conference on Human Factors in Computing Systems*, CHI '12, ACM (2012), 1893–1896.
10. Hsueh-Chao, M. H., and Nation, P. Unknown vocabulary density and reading comprehension. *Reading in a Foreign Language 13*, 1 (2000), 403–30.
11. Innovative Mobile Apps. Sight Words List. `https://itunes.apple.com/ca/app/sight-words-list-learn-to/id445708245`, 2013.
12. Matulic, F., and Norrie, M. C. Supporting active reading on pen and touch-operated tabletops. In *Proc. of the International Working Conference on Advanced Visual Interfaces*, AVI '12, ACM (2012), 612–619.
13. Nagy, W., and Herman, P. Limitations of vocabulary instruction (tech. rep. no. 326). *Center for the Study of Reading. Urbana: University of Illinois* (1984).
14. Nesi, H., and Haill, R. A study of dictionary use by international students at a british university. *International Journal of Lexicography 15*, 4 (2002), 277–305.
15. Rock 'N Learn, Inc. Rock 'n Learn Phonics Easy Reader. `http://rocknlearn.com/html/EasyReadersiPad.htm`, 2011.
16. Saito, Y., Garza, T. J., and Horwitz, E. K. Foreign language reading anxiety. *The Modern Language Journal 83*, 2 (1999), 202–218.
17. Sellers, V. D. Anxiety and reading comprehension in spanish as a foreign language. *Foreign Language Annals 33*, 5 (2000), 512–520.
18. Tashman, C. S., and Edwards, W. K. Liquidtext: A flexible, multitouch environment to support active reading. In *Proc. of the SIGCHI Conference on Human Factors in Computing Systems*, CHI '11 (2011), 3285–3294.
19. Wittrock, M. C., Marks, C., and Doctorow, M. Reading as a generative process. *Journal of Educational Psychology 67*, 4 (1975), 484.
20. Yu, C.-H., and Miller, R. C. Enhancing web page readability for non-native readers. In *Proc. of the SIGCHI Conference on Human Factors in Computing Systems*, CHI '10, ACM (2010), 2523–2532.
21. Zeng-Treitler, Q., Goryachev, S., Kim, H., Keselman, A., and Rosendale, D. Making texts in electronic health records comprehensible to consumers: A prototype translator. In *Proc. of the AMIA Annual Symposium*, vol. 2007, American Medical Informatics Association (2007), 846.

A Long-Term Field Study on the Adoption of Smartphones by Children in Panama

Elba del Carmen Valderrama Bahamndez
FISC, Technological University of Panama
P.O. Box 0819-07289, El Dorado, Panama City, Panama
elba.valderrama@utp.ac.pa

Bastian Pfleging, Niels Henze, Albrecht Schmidt
VIS, University of Stuttgart
Pfaffenwaldring 5a, 70569 Stuttgart, Germany
{firstname.lastname}@vis.uni-stuttgart.de

ABSTRACT
Computing technology is currently adopted in emerging countries. Especially mobile phones and smart phones become widely used – with a much higher penetration than traditional computers. In our work we investigate how computing technologies and particularly mobile devices can support education. While previous work focused on controlled experiments, in this paper we present the results of a 20 weeks long study of mobile phone usage in an emerging region. Our aim was not only to investigate how the phones are used for education but also to learn how they are adopted by children in daily life. By logging screenshots, we used an unsupervised approach that allowed to unobtrusively observe usage patterns without the presence of researchers. Instead of offering tailored teaching applications, we used general-purpose applications to support teaching and found that the phone itself was an empowering technology similar to pen and paper. Based on a detailed analysis of actual use in a natural setting, we derived a set of typical use cases for mobile phones in education and describe how they change learning. From in-depth interviews with a teacher, selected guardians and pupils we show that introducing mobiles phones has great potential for supporting education in emerging regions.

Author Keywords
Adopting mobile phones; children; education; emerging countries; learning; mobile phones.

ACM Classification Keywords
H.5.2. Information Interfaces and Presentation (e.g., HCI): User Interfaces

General Terms
Human Factors

INTRODUCTION
Over the last decade, mobile phones have become the most ubiquitous devices in developed countries. In emerging regions, however, the adoption of mobile phones is even more disruptive. They are often the first computing platform that people get access to. In our previous work we investigated how mobile phones and smart phones can be used to support education in developing regions. Offering high quality education in rural areas of emerging countries is difficult.

MobileHCI 2014, September 23–26, 2014, Toronto, ON, Canada.

ACM 978-1-4503-3004-6/14/09 ...$15.00.
http://dx.doi.org/10.1145/2628363.2628403.

Figure 1. Children in class working with their phones.

The use of computers to support education has been proposed over the last decade. Experiments with computer labs have been conducted and the idea of one laptop per child (OLPC[1]) has been explored. The use of conventional computers has been less successful than many expected. The usage model (e.g., a computer lab), as well as the administration and maintenance of computers in schools has made widespread and sustained use difficult. New devices are costly; hence, economic constraints often prohibited their uptake.

Recent projects have observed that mobile phones and in particular smart phones are a viable alternative to conventional computers. Over the last years mobile phones have become ubiquitous around the world and the dominant computing platform in many emerging regions. Research has shown that phones can provide myriad opportunities to support teaching and learning activities. However, previous work mainly focused on rather short and supervised deployments. Studies were highly supported by the researchers, who provided exciting new teaching material.

In this paper we report from a long-term study that we conducted to not only understand how mobile phones are used as teaching and learning tools but also to learn how they are adopted in daily life. We conducted a 20 weeks long study

[1]OLPC. Last access: 2014-02-21, `http://one.laptop.org/`

with school children in a small town in rural Panama. We aimed at learning about the opportunities and challenges that arise when phones become available as personal tools.

In our study a class of 23 pupils aged 10 to 12 were equipped with simple touchscreen cell phones (see Figure 1). The children were required to bring their phones to school every day, but they could also use them in their spare time and take them home. During the study, almost no on-site support by the researchers was given and the teacher was completely free in the way he used the phones in his teaching. In order to understand how children used the phones and how they were integrated with the teaching we automatically recorded time-stamped screenshots every 20 seconds on each phone (while being in use). By using parts of the about 1,663,000 screenshots we analyzed how the children used their phones for learning and recreational activities.

Additionally, we conducted extensive interviews with teachers, children, and selected parents to understand how phones impacted them in teaching, learning, and their lives. Our results suggest that phones are a very useful and versatile tool for a variety of different subjects and tasks in schools. For the pupils, the phones provided new and efficient ways for information gathering and also became an alternative to copying machines, which are not available in the school. For the teacher it became apparent, that once accustomed to the availability of the phone as a tool, there was little to no extra effort in utilizing the phones across many school subjects.

The main contributions of this paper are:

- A report of the results of a 20 weeklong unsupervised study of mobile phone usage in a school in an emerging region.
- A set of typical use cases for mobile phone usage in education based on a detailed analysis of actual use in a natural setting.
- In-depth analysis of responses from children, parents, and a teacher on the impact of mobile phone usage in school.

RELATED WORK

A large body of work investigates (mobile) learning for children. For stationary devices, various projects such as the "hole in the wall" project [2] investigated how implementation of technology impacts learning. In the following, we focus on work that explored the use of mobile phones for learning in emerging regions. Most authors have analyzed different features of mobile phones for learning like audio [3, 4, 13], image and videos for creating content [11], and learning games [6, 8, 9, 10]. In all cases above the approach was to create a learning application or game as a use case. Educational applications that support the curriculum where children can review lessons, play quizzes, and monitor their progress have for instance been explored for teaching in Africa [5, 12].

Kam et al. [8] explored learning games for English language in after-school settings in India; they developed learning games based on traditional games known by children in India [9]. In contrast, Jain et al. [6] explored the use of pico projectors in collaborative learning games. Mathur et al. [11] developed an annotation tool that allows teachers to create content to share with pupils using pico projectors.

Audio recording and playback was also explored for learning. While Frohlich [4] and Reitmaier et al. [13] developed a minimal textual application to support storytelling with adults in rural India and Africa respectively; Ford and Leionen [3] implemented an audio wiki to create and access audio content. The use case was evaluated with high school students in South Africa.

The usage and adoption of mobile phones by children was also explored [1, 7, 10, 14]. While Bell et al. [1] and Jarievich et al. [7] explored the adoption of mobile phones in the developed world, Kumar et al. [10] explored the usage of mobile phones in an emerging country. Similarly, we explored mobile phone usage in an emerging country in a previous project where we conducted an exploratory short-term study to explore the adoption of mobile phones by children and teachers in classroom settings in rural Panama [14] . In contrast to the work in this paper, our previous study focused on the adoption of using mobile phones exclusively for learning activities. In addition, the children used the phones only for a very short time in the previous study. In contrast, our current study analyzes the long-term effect on the behavior and adoption of mobile phones in two settings – at school and after-school/at home – as well as both for learning and recreational use. Kumar et al. [10] explored the usage of mobile learning outside of classroom settings. They observed the use of a preinstalled customized application for learning outside of classroom settings with a text logger, while we were interested in the adoption of the mobile phones and not a specific application in both settings inside and outside of the school. In addition, our study was also supported by the analysis of the screenshots. As previous work was mainly conducted in very different cultural, social, and economic settings (e.g., India, [10]), we show how different cultures impact the acceptance and use of technologies for education and beyond.

LONG-TERM FIELD STUDY

Method and Design

In order to gain knowledge about how touchscreen phones can become a personal tool at school and at home in an emerging country, we conducted a long-term field study over a period of 20 weeks. The study was conducted with pupils of an elementary school in the Panamanian countryside. Besides studying the opportunities and challenges when touchscreen phones are introduced as personal tools, we also wanted to study longer-term motivational effects.

In contrast to other projects, we did not install specific learning applications but provided and explained some general-purpose applications. To allow an unobtrusive observation and to prevent influences by observing researchers, we impemented an application to generate automatic screenshots of the phones screen to create application usage logs and installed it onto each phone.We did a manual post-hoc analysis of the usage of applications after the study by collecting and looking at the corresponding log files, screenshots, and videos stored on each phone. We especially investigated the usage pattern once the children were more experienced by analyzing in detail 10 selected days towards the end of the study. We also conducted open interviews with pupils, the teacher involved as well as with the pupils parents. In addition, we distributed questionnaires to all pupils to evaluate the use of mobile phones.

Participants and Location

We conducted the study at the public primary school Angelina M. de Tirones in Rio Hato. This school was randomly selected based on voluntary applications during a meeting with 200 teachers from different public schools in Panama. From the applicants, the school Angelina M. de Tirones was selected as a typical public primary school in the countryside of Panama regarding to infrastructure, class size (2-shift school for smaller classes), and discipline (e.g., school uniform). Rio Hato is an average village in the Panamanian countryside. The inhabitants are mainly working as fishermen or service staff (e.g., in hotels) and have a low income. Although located in a rather rural area, the primary school Angelina M. de Tirones is still classified as an urban school. It has about 1200 pupils from grade one to six as well as kindergarten classes. In order to comfortably accommodate all pupils, classes are offered in two school shifts: The morning shift last from 7:00 am to noon (12:00 pm) while the afternoon shift lasts from 12:30 pm to 5:30 pm. With respect to technology, the school owns a TV set, a DVD player, and a computer lab with 12 desktop computers and one video projector. The school has access to the Internet through a portable Internet connection via satellite that is shared via WiFi. However, the signal quality of the satellite link only allows for Internet connectivity when set up near to the computer lab, in the front schoolyard, or at the director's office.

The study was conducted with a 6th grade class ("6C") of the morning shift. In total 23 children (11 male, 12 female) participated in our field study. With the exception of one student (14 years), participants were between 11 and 13 years old ($M = 11.7$ years). Eight children had access to a computer at home that is connected to the Internet; three pupils had access to a computer without Internet connectivity. In contrast to computer ownership, almost all families possessed a mobile phone: 22 pupils reported that their family owns at least one (basic) mobile phone, including four families with a touchscreen phone. Only in one household, a student reported that they do not have electricity at home. Five children had never used a mobile phone before. In contrast, about one half of all pupils (10 pupils) reported to own a mobile phone.

Besides the pupils also their form teacher participated in this field study. He reported that he had never used a touchscreen phone before the start of the study. As primary school teacher in Panama have a rather low monthly gross income (450–700 USD), he owned a very low-end phone that only allowed him to make calls and send SMS.

Apparatus

In order to investigate our research goals, we provided 24 touchscreen phones (Nokia 5530 Xpress Music[2]) to all students of the selected class as well as to the teacher. This type of mobile touchscreen phones comprises amongst other (general) phone features an integrated video camera, music player functions, and a voice recorder. We did not install any customized learning application on the devices. Instead, we added two general purpose applications to complement to the default features and software set of the selected phone model: The PaintPad[3] application was installed as a drawing tool and StickyNotes Touch[4] as another application allowed to write notes analog to post-it notes.

We installed a logging and screenshot application on each handset in order to have a better insight in how the children use their mobile phone. This application includes a screenshot application, which automatically takes a screen shot of the active screen every 20 seconds while the phone is in use. The screenshots are then stored on a SD card. During the study, these cards (and the phones) were collected four times in order to retrieve and centrally store all screenshots and to empty the SD cards afterwards. Similar to the screenshots, the logging application also creates log files containing time stamps and the currently active applications in order to continuously log the use of the phone. Each time a new application is started, a new log file entry is generated. Besides allowing a detailed analysis of the phone usage of every pupil, a second goal of the application was to prevent inappropriate use, which could have been revealed by looking at the screenshots.

Participants Consent

During the initiation phase of our study, we contacted the schoolmaster of the school via e-mail in order to get the permission to conduct the study at his school. Once we had received the permission, the schoolmaster introduced our experimenter to the corresponding class teacher and class. Being in class, the phones were presented to the students. First, the phones were only handed out for in-school use, but only during times when the teacher requested to use the phones. The pupils were allowed to explore every feature of their phone. They were warned to properly use the phone: The experimenter explained to the children that the logging application will post-hoc allow the researcher to see any activity on the phone, and that inadequate behavior and use will thereby be revealed to teachers and parents. Within the first days of the study, a meeting was held with the schoolmaster and all parents. During this meeting, the purpose and procedure (including the logging application and process) of the project were presented to the parents. An explanatory letter about the project was handed out to the parents, which also contained a consent form that – once signed – allowed the pupils to participate in the project. Once the consent form had been signed, the children were allowed and encouraged to also carrying and using their phones outside of the school during their spare time. During their spare time, the children were allowed to use their phones for any purpose.

Procedure

Besides the general introduction of the phones, certain features of the phones were explained throughout the course of

[2] `http://www.nokia.com/in-en/support/product-archive/?action=productArchive&tid=1845426`

[3] `http://mobile.zensis.com/showproduct.php?pid=117`

[4] `http://store.ovi.com/content/14200`

the study: On the first day, when the phones were initially handed out to the students, the video and photo recording and playback functionalities were shown and discussed. After two weeks, the PaintPad application was introduced. The experimenter in class demonstrated another week later how the pupils could use Bluetooth to connect phones and share objects. Using the Internet was neither explicitly explained nor did the phones come with a SIM card. Throughout the study, technical issues were solved either via e-mails between experimenter and teacher or by the experimenter visiting the school and fixing problems in situ.

The study started in May 2012 and ended 7 months later in November 2012. Initially, the study was only planned from May to June but was extended due to the positive experiences teachers and pupils had during the first two months. As the size of the SD cards limited the storage of screenshots, the SD cards and phones had to be collected four times throughout the study. It took about one week each time to empty the SD cards. Also, the Panamanian vacation schedule contains quite a few holidays that resulted in phones being only used at home or on vacation during these times. Holidays were from June 4, 2012 to June 10, 2013 and from September 10, 2012 to September 16, 2012. Additionally, November is traditionally a month with many holidays, extra activities and celebrations outside of the ordinary school life. All together, the phones were used for 20 weeks, including 16 weeks with school days. In November, the experimenter collected all phones. Besides four SD cards (damaged or lost), all phones were returned without a single phone being lost.

Ethical Considerations

Using the screenshot logger application to collect usage information actually means that sensible private data is recorded. We explained to all the persons involved in our study (teacher, principal, and in particular parents and students) how the screenshot logger application works and which data is collected. We followed the required steps for conducting research with school children in Panama and we followed the policies and regulations of the involved institutions.

ANALYZING PHONE USAGE

Based on the large sets of screenshots that were recorded we are able to analyze how children used the phones over the course of the study. Overall, about 1,663,000 screenshots have been taken that documented the phone usage. Figure 2 shows typical screenshots that have been observed. As screenshots were taken every 20 seconds, longer interaction periods with the same application resulted in several images of the same application that allow seeing which progress in a task or game was made. For applications that were used shorter than 20 seconds it may be the case that no screenshot was recorded. In this case, only an entry in the log file existed. We especially analyzed (manually) about 200,000 screenshots and logs of 10 selected days toward the end of the study period. In our analysis we were interested in:

- Identification of main use cases of the phone at school
- Identification of main use cases at home (educational and recreational)

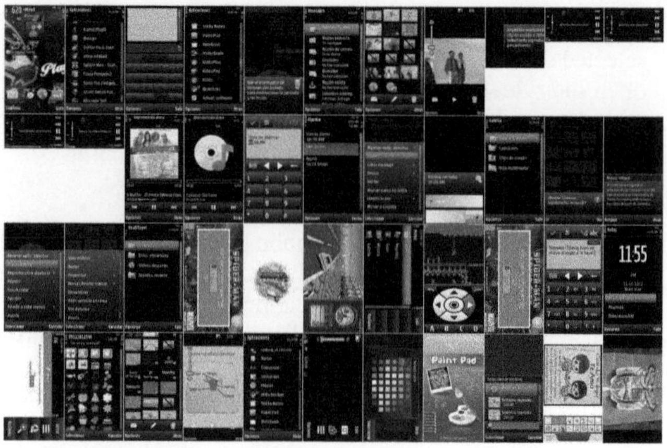

Figure 2. Sample screenshots that were automatically taken on one of the pupils mobile phones for a post-hoc analysis. The picture shows the usage of different applications.

- Long term changes in the use of the phones
- Comparison between users over the time of the study

The analysis was conducted manually by inspection and interpretation of the screenshots.

During the field study the teacher did not receive instructions on how to use the phone or in what context the phone should be used. From the very beginning of the study we could observe that the teacher incorporated the phone as a tool in his teaching approach. In our initial briefing with the teacher and the students we did not provide information on how to access the Internet through the phones. Getting online and accessing the Internet using the school infrastructure was discovered by children from sixth grade, who explained it to their teacher. The teacher took this up and immediately started to use the phones for information gathering in class. In our conversations during the study he stated that he found access to Internet in the classroom the most useful function of the mobile phone, which impacted the way he could teach. He designed more and more learning activities in which the children should use the phone to gather information from the Internet.

Within the classroom there was only limited connectivity and, hence, most of the time the teacher allowed the pupils to access the Internet from the schoolyard where the connection quality was better. Even though the bandwidth of the data connection at the school was very limited, it provided a tolerable speed and experience when using the Internet on a phone.

We provided the phones without SIM cards. As the pupils were allowed to take the phones home, some of their parents bought prepaid SIM cards to use the phone as well as to have mobile Internet access (about 1US$ for 500 MB). At the end of the study, about 16 % of the participating children used mobile Internet with a prepaid card.

In our analysis we identified the following major actives that occurred throughout the study: *information gathering* using online sources, *image capture* as replacement for a copying machine, *imanipulation of captured images*, *iusage of the phone as a tool*, *listening to music*, and *playing games*. In the

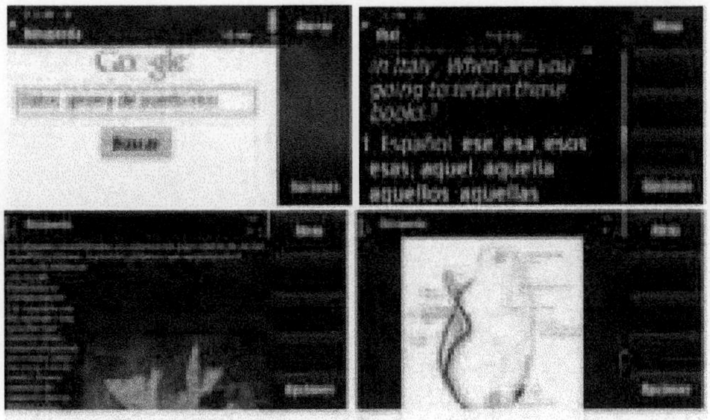

Figure 3. Examples of typical tasks done during a lecture (top left: information gathering task; top right: dictionary use; bottom: information gathering on the web

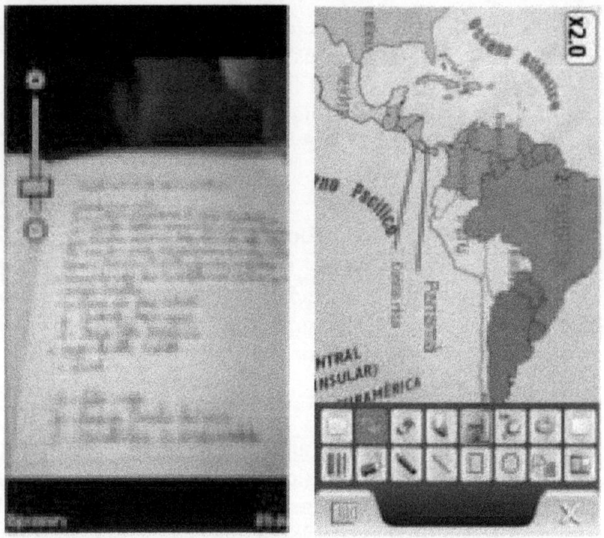

Figure 4. Images captured with the phones camera. Left: copying written notes; right: annotating a captured map

remainder of this section we discuss these activities in detail. We also observed that watching and recording videos with the phone was a major feature used for teaching and learning. We will discuss this in the following section.

Information Gathering

Once all children understood how to access the Internet on their phone, this feature was widely used across different subjects. From the screenshots we could observe that information gathering tasks were done in the following subjects: In *Spanish* the tasks were to get information about prepositions, conjugations and accents. In *Natural Sciences* pupils received an open task to learn about invertebrates. In the context of *Religion* the tasks included finding a list with the 10 commandments. A further example task was to find details on the history Panama Canal as well as images. The information sources used by the pupils were very diverse and contributed according to the teacher to the discussion in the classroom. In Figure 3 screenshots from different information seeking tasks are displayed. During the Olympic Games 2012 students used the phones to get news about the events. The teacher took this as an opportunity to discuss the event with his pupils.

Overall, the phone provides an easy means for individual Internet access for pupils. Looking for information on the phone is cumbersome, but sufficient in many situations. Over the course of the study the use of the phone for searching information increased and pupils made use of this function to suit their personal information needs both in the context of education as well as for recreation.

Image Capture

As reported in one of our previous papers [14] multimedia-enabled phones allow pupils to use the camera to capture worksheets and fill them out virtually by using a paint application. In this study, we were able to observe this usage pattern again. The convenience of this approach seems to be a main driver. The teacher does not need to prepare work sheets but can directly use material from books and the children can capture this content on their devices. This approach is especially important for differentiation. For instance, if a child has already finished a given task this method allows the teachers to provide additional material with more challenges to such students.

From the screenshots we collected during the field study, we found that eight pupils used the camera phones to take pictures of books, blackboards, and classmates annotations and notes. When asking the children about the images there were different reasons for capturing content. Photos of the blackboards were taken by children who expected that this information would help them with their homework. When one child was away from class, photos of the black-board and of certain written notes (e.g., a text written by the classmate, see Figure 4) were taken to allow the child to rework what happened at school.

We also saw that children used the camera of the phone to take photos when they forgot books at home that they were required to work with in class.

Before the use of the camera, children typically had to copy the written information by hand. In general, all these cases show that the phone replaces the function of a copying machine, which is not available at this particular school.

Manipulation of Captured Images

The most common step after capturing a photo of a worksheet or a form was to use the installed image manipulation software Paint. Using this app, the pupils were able to digitally fill in missing numbers or words into worksheets and cloze tests. Obviously, well-equipped schools either use (physical) workbooks or the pupils receive actual copies to fill in the missing elemenst. If this option is not available, as in the case of the school in Panama we worked with, having the opportunity to capture images and fill out forms digitally is a welcome alternative. This is especially helpful for math as this increases the number of tasks a student can solve compared to the situation where they have to copy the tasks first. Figure 4 shows an example of a captured and annotated map.

We observed that children preferred to use the virtual keyboard to fill out cloze tests or forms (manipulating photos taken of book exercises), rather than filling them by handwriting. In our interviews, the pupils stated that they would like handwriting as input modality if the writing would be digitized and converted into text.

Usage of the Phone as a Tool

From the screenshots we see that the children often used the calculator application, especially to support them to when calculating with negative numbers. Further tools employed were dictionary and translator applications (Figure 3).

Listening to music

During the ten days that we analyzed in detail, the maximum time a child listened to music on one day was 167 minutes (min.: 0 minutes). The average daily listening time differed between 18 seconds/day and 128 minutes/day among the pupils. In that time the children listened to 808 songs (771 in Spanish, 36 in English, one in Portuguese). Although the number of songs downloaded was quite high, only 20 songs were commonly listened to and downloaded by almost all children. The children mainly listened to Latin American music. Furthermore, all children had at least one religious song on their phone, one child only had religious songs.

The pupils shared the music they downloaded from the Internet with their peers using Bluetooth. The transfer of files was usually done at school, either early in the morning before class or during the morning breaks.

Playing Games

Based on our detailed analysis (10 days), the children spent on average between one and two hours per day on playing games. In most cases they played at least three different games. Most of these games were downloaded from the Internet. With this regard, we found interesting gender differences: Most girls downloaded the same games. Therefore they were able to interchange information about games they had downloaded. In contrast, most of the boys downloaded different games. Furthermore, girls played different games than boys. While boys preferred to play action games, girls preferred to play adventure games. The most popular game played by girls was WonderZoo[5] where the player has to uncage locked up animals. To our surprise, during the days we analyzed girls spent more time on playing games than boys. Only four of children actually played some kind educational game (e.g., arithmetic trainer / English trainer) during the analyzed period.

Non-Educational Pictures and Images

Taking photos was one of the main activities done by the children. We analyzed the pictures taken by all children that were not part of some learning assignments. The children took a variety of pictures that we classified by using the following categories:

- People: photos of family members or friends, teachers or classmates, and pictures of the children themselves.

[5] `http://www.gameloft.com/mobile-games/wonder-zoo/`

Figure 5. Example use of mobile phones at school: A student records an explanation of his class teacher.

- Nature: photos of animals in their environment like dogs, chicken, horses, but also picture of the landscape
- Sport: pictures related to their favorite football team.
- Other: objects photographed like cars, bikes, etc. This also includes pictures of hand-made drawings and paintings.
- Religion: images related to Christianity.
- School related: pictures of books, blackboards, events, and contests at school

The main topics photographed by boys and girls were family/friends, either at home or during special events. Self-portrait photos were more common for girls than for boys.

With respect to images downloaded, the most frequently category found were friends and love messages (e.g., a teddy bear with hearts), followed by showbiz (e.g., singers) and religious images. Photos of singers were especially shared using Bluetooth.

Video Recording and Playback

When categorizing videos filmed at school, we distinguish between different recording settings: Individual shooting in this case refers to one child filming his/her own video. In contrast, a class shooting refers to the situation when all children simultaneously film the same object. Accordingly, in a collaborative shooting children work together, e.g., when they were acting. For videos filmed at school the children preferred individual and group shootings compared to collaborative shootings. The reason is that filming in teams collaboratively and simultaneously was not suitable inside the classroom. There are children who speak loud and those who speak more quiet. For instance, dialogs to be recorded by one team group can accidentally be captured by a different group and overlapped the own voice of the latter group. As the school selected for our study does not have a big garden, such student teams could not go outside and create videos without interrupting other grades. A very common approach among the students was therefore to simply film the teachers explanations (Figure 5) in order to play them back later at home. Also, the teacher requested the children to record films at home.

Video Playback

As children already had the experience of watching educational videos in the computer lab, we asked them to compare watching videos on a computer to wathing them on a mobile phone. Most children stated that they prefer watching videos on the phone because it is more accessible. P#1: "The videos are easier to find." P#3: "On the PC I forget where to find the videos." P#4: "I can find the videos faster." The children also reported that it gives them freedom: "I can see the video as long as I want."(P#2) "I can replay a video until I really understand the subject."(P#1) "I can watch the video again the other day."(P#6) "I can watch the video without time pressure."(P#10)

Mobility was another reason why the children preferred to watch videos on the mobile phone rather than on a desktop computer: "I can see a video at any place I am in contrast to PCs [that] are difficult to carry," "It easier to carry with me." Concentration was also mentioned as a factor for preferring mobile phones to watch videos. "[It] helps me to memorize." "I can concentrate more." "I can learn more." The reduced screen size and resolution of a phone displays was the main complaint of the children with regard to watching videos on mobile phones: "I can see the video bigger and clearer [on the computer screen]". A few pupils did not prefer one solution over the other.

INTERVIEW WITH A TEACHER

Three months after starting the study as well as at the end of the study we conducted open interviews (30 minutes each) with the form teacher. In these interviews, we addressed the following topics: impact on teaching and learning, discipline and motivation, effect on interaction between children, opportunities that arise with phones in the classroom, and finally risks and how to deal with them. In the following we report some of the insights that were most interesting to us. We have to point out that the teacher knows his pupils quite well as he had been teaching them for three years.

Motivation to Learn

Just before the field study, three pupils of the selected class (it had 25 pupils before) showed a peculiar behavior. They did not show up regularly at school and showed a bad behavior at school. The teacher reported: "I have students with really serious problems at home, like parents in jail because of drugs, [. . .] who show a bad behavior and a bad performance in class." In fact, two of them finally left school permanently. The third student instead changed his behavior with the begin of the study. According to the teacher, this person showed a radical change in his behavior, attended the classes regularly, and became much more active in class. "[The student] has made a 180 degree change, at the beginning of the school year he was undisciplined, did not attended classes, did not do assignments, etc. Now he started to be more engaged at school, improved his grades, and finally passed the exam to continue to grade seven. And I think that the use of a mobile phone has positively influenced this change."

The teacher also noted a change in the conduct of his pupils: "There was a positive change. Students who were not used to participate in class or work on assignment,[. . .] one [could] see them working and being engaged in the learning tasks. . . Students who were timid and did not ask questions [. . .] started to put their hands up."

The Phone as a Tool for Learning and Teaching

When asked about what features the mobile phone needs to have to be the perfect tool for learning, the teacher answered that "it would be the possibility to have a good Internet connection available, a good antenna, that allows downloadind information and educational videos faster without the need to buy mobile Internet or to move to the front yard. This would be perfect. We used the Internet several times but the Internet was very slow and inconsistent [unreliable]. Mainly those kids who paid [mobile Internet] get better access to it. . . With all these phone companies in Panama, could not one of them install a good Internet antenna at school? "

Internet for mobile phones was considered as a very useful tool for learning: "Children can gather Information about the topic we are introducing and discussing [. . .] or they can look for videos and then download them to their phones and watch them later, it is simply fantastic."

As a final note, the teacher underlined the increase mobility of the phones: "[. . .] if I could give a mobile phone to each child instead to a computer... it would be easier to transport... The student has direct access to the information in his/her pocket, s/he do not have to move [to the lab] and does not to have to install all these tools and it would be more pragmatic. You look for something, store it, and you can review it whenever you want to."

Multigrade Schools

In very remote regions of Panama with less population, one can also find multigrade schools, i.e., schools where one teacher is teaching a class consisting of pupils from different grades at the same time. We also wanted to know if it would be possible to use touch screen phones in such schools and classes as well. When asked about such multigrade schools, the teacher first explained his previous experiences about teaching at such a school:

"I was a multigrade teacher for about 10 years, I worked with a tribe in the mountains[. . .]. This is a community that lives in extreme poverty [. . .] under inhuman conditions. I had 20 to 25 students from three [different] grades together . . . I had to be like MacGyver. . . This tool would be incredible for multigrade since we could assign a task to each child to develop while the teacher attends the other group. [Mobile] phones can support the teacher to better manage and distribute learning task according to age similar to the approach followed in multigrade schools."

When we asked further about the access to technology and electricity in such schools, he answered: "To get there you need to drive two hours by car with a four-wheel drive and during winter, instead of the car carrying people, people have to carry [push] the car. . . People there have simple cell phones and there is signal [i.e., network coverage]. . . And nowadays I hear it has electricity."

Social Impact

The use of mobile phone caused other positive social effects to the pupils behavior. Usually, only the child with the best grades gets awarded or is considered to take part in special or new academic projects. As we distributed a phone to every child, pupils felt that they were equally important and included by the school regardless their academic profile. The teachers underlined this positive effect and commented:

"The pupils feel more motivated and with a higher commitment to work with mobile phones as they feel themselves important. This arouses their responsibility to take care of the phone... No phone got damaged or lost." Also, the use of mobile phones seems to be also influenced in the engagement in non-academic activities done at school. As the school has a large number of students, it is often selected to participate in contests or other extracurricular activities. In those cases, not all children participated in former times. Reasons to not doing so were related shyness or because the kids simply did not want to.

"X. is a girl who never participated [in such activities], I mean, she is good academically, but she does not want to participate in external activities... She [only] cares to get good marks ... I have told her mom, education is more: Behavior, performance, and attitude. It is not [the] only [goal] to have the best marks. [...] N.N. is the best student [academically] of the whole school, but she is a very timid girl, and she does not participate in extra activities. But the main problem with her is that she is too quiet, and shy... I organized an activity where students had to give a speech about moral values in groups of four to children of lower grades who attended also classes in the morning. [...] I always did these extra activities at school, but now I wanted them to do it. Using the phone to record a video, watching the video, one can see the qualities everyone has [...] We have [students with] outstanding voices... I wanted them to go to the other class and see that it is not easy to get other children to pay attention to whom is talking in front ... I accomplished for the very first time that X. participated and N. overcame her shyness."

Recording videos was a way that the teacher considered as helpful for children to lose their shyness about talking in public. "Some pupils look nervous when they film and then watch the video showing themselves... [They realize] it is normal that everyone needs to get rid of the fear to talk in front of an audience. [...] But the engagement has been high..." In addition he could observe that "[s]tudents also have improved a lot [with regard to] their self-confidence".

However, the teacher will not recommend using phone every day for teaching: "I would use the mobile phone [only] two days a week [...] Part of maintaining the childrens motivation for learning is to vary between activities. Therefore I assume that using [it] daily will considerably decrease the motivation and engagement of the children."

Discipline

Filming has helped the teacher to witness and control the behavior of problematic students as he explained: "Although I have no discipline problem with most of my pupils, there are two pupils who are tremendous... When I complain to their parents or guardians on how they sometimes behave at school, their parents do not believe me. They think their kids are godsend [...] The other day I used the [mobile phone] camera and filmed one of them while he was fighting against a child of another group before I proceeded to separate them. When I showed the video to his grandmother she was deeply shocked. [...] That was the last fight."

The students learning discipline also improved by using mobile phones as the teacher explained: "Definitively the discipline is the first that thing improved, when the student works with the cell phone s/he is completely concentrated [...] doing the assignment, or watching a video."

He also talked about the importance for teachers to know the latest technology: "Teachers should adapt to the [new] time [...] Sometime we [docents] say I do not like that, but we have to keep up-to-date ourselves [...] The Pupils already known all these technologies and if not they are fast in adopting them. We teachers have to keep up with the children in the use of technology."

Supervision at Home

With regard to letting the pupils use their phones at home, the teacher would recommend usage with caution and clear rules: "While I found the use of mobile phones for learning an excellent tool, I think their use at home needs to be controlled. At school, teachers can easily control who is working and who not. However, there are bad addresses [inappropriate web sites] that children should not have access to. Parents should carefully supervise the proper use of the phone as with any other technology. But the main problem is rather than some parents do not supervise what their children do at all."

When asked if we provide with mechanisms that parents set what children access he answered to us: "I do not think that any technical mechanism can help parents to manage what children access on the web because simply parents do not know about technologies [...] In fact, also the parents have a low level of education."

INTERVIEWS WITH CHILDREN

In order to understand the pupils' opinion on using mobile phones at school and at home, we conducted a group interview with all students. We wanted to know their impressions of using a phone during the study in general and the use of applications in specific. Due to time constraints it was not possible to do individual interviews. In order to minimize any bias due to group influence, we distributed an open questionnaire to each participant that had to be completed and returned the same day and before the interview.

The children stated that there was no problem with learning how to use the phone. This is consistent to what we observed in the screenshots analysis: "Although it was the first time I used a cell phone [...] it was easy to work with the phone. [...] No function was difficult to use for me [...]."

The children admitted that they mainly used their phones for recreation at home: "At home I used the phone to get [download] and listen to music I like." "Racing cars was my favorite game, I played almost every day." "After having done my homework I watched photos [on the web] and [listened to] songs of Prince Royce [teenager singer]. The best photo I put on the screen [as a wallpaper]."

Also, the children used the phones as status symbol: "Now I can show my friends that I also have a music player." In fact, only 3 participants owned a real MP3 player. Another pupil added: "When I was bored at home I looked for new games to play on OVI [. . .] Then I showed them to my friend the other day."

The experience of painting was mainly received well by the pupils: "Painting with a phone [i.e., Paintpad application], is similar to painting with pencils only that here I can erase something without holing the paper." Further the students liked that they "can change colors while painting". However, other children preferred traditional painting due to being more creative or having more freedom.

The children found it useful to video record own presentations; some comments received were: "[Giving a live presentation in the classroom] makes me nervous and [I] make mistakes", "in front of others I get nervous and forget everything what I have to say", "[by filming my presentation] with the mobile phone I do not get nervous", "it is important to use new technologies" and "if I forget something I can record the presentation again".

INTERVIEWS WITH PARENTS / GUARDIANS

At the end of the study, we discussed the concept of using mobile devices with 13 of the children guardians (all female relatives; either mothers, grandmothers, or aunts). Although we tried to have a lively conversation, they were rather timid. Only six of them engaged a little more with us. We think that the shyness is due to their low schooling, and that they are, in case of older women, technology illiterate. However, only one woman did not own a mobile phone. Their main concern was the loss of a device: "My main concern was that the mobile phone gets lost and that I have to pay for it." 't is an expensive phone [. . .] so I warned my daughter to really take care of it. [. . .] I was always watching that she took care [of it] properly."

They were also worried about a proper use of the mobile phone: "In the news they always show the risk of young children when using such technology improperly. I was worry about a bad use of this device, is there a way to control [access to the] Internet?" Another guardian stated: "I find it positive and like that N.N. did assignments with more enthusiasm than before. But I dislike how addicted he became to the device. I have to forbid usage while we eat."

One guardian also commented on the social impact of the use of the phone: "I observed a new attitude and behavior of my grandson at home and at school. He was motivated to attend classes, an engagement that was not there before the [study]." Later we figured that she was actually talking about the child who almost had left school forever.

Also, one participant commented how surprised she was about how fast their children adopted the technology and how they learned from them: "I tried to help my child to film a video at home, my child explained everything in detail although he has never had such a modern phone before. This really impressed me [. . .] how fast kids learn new technologies.'. As a response, one mother added: "My daughter taught me how to use Bluetooth on my phone."

The fact that all children were considered for the study was also pointed out by one mother: "Finally all children and not only the best pupils were considered to take part in the project. They usually only award children with good marks[. . .] I think that all children should receive the same treatment."

Using a projector, we showed some examples of the content created by the class while using the phone. "I am still surprised that all this can be created with modern phones. It is amazing!"

LIMITATIONS

As the study was conducted in a natural environment with no researcher present for most of the time we based our findings on the automatically recorded screenshots as well as on interviews conduced in the middle and at the end of the study. While most of the phones worked well, we observed that some phones ran out of memory and did not record all screens. The screen capture software did for technical reasons not capture the content of video recordings. Hence, information about video recording was based on the recordings the pupils kept on their phones.

The screen capture software ran in the background and slightly affected the stability of the system software. From time to time, this resulted in some of the phones freezing (every few days). In this case children rebooted the phones, but their task was interrupted.

As phones may be passed between people, we have no information whether or not others used the phone. During school time this was to our knowledge very rare, as all children had their phone available. For use at home we are less certain as parents, siblings, or friends may have used the phones, too.

Concerns about abuse and misuse of the technology were prevalent among the parents. The software for taking screenshots, initially designed as research tool, served a second purpose: supervision. As children knew their actions were monitored, we did not observe inappropriate use. However we did not explore this issue in detail and it remains to further research to investigate how effective and acceptable monitoring can be realized, without violating the need for private spaces in the use of mobile technologies.

CONCLUSION

In this paper we investigated the adoption of mobile phones by children in rural Panama. Our goal was to understand the impact of using mobile phones both as educational tools on teaching and learning and for recreational use beyond the novelty effect. We provided 23 pupils with touchscreen phones over the course of 20 weeks.

During the study there was almost no interference by the researchers and the data was collected automatically by capturing screenshots every 20 s. Over the course of the study more than 1.5 million screenshots were taken and analyzed in parts. Using this logging approach, we were able to investigate user habits and their use of technology. In contrast to other methods (e.g., direct observation), this approach allowed an unobtrusive observation with a comparably low effort and without observers being present. Having no observer present during the experiment and running a long-term study, we think that this approach allows a higher validity of the results and will be interesting for other research projects that want to explore new fields with a similar methodology in educational contexts. Since the pupils were also allowed to take the phones home with them, our observation also reveals insights into how children in Panama adopt mobile phone usage.

Our research is an example of how to study emerging technology use over a longer term. During the experiment, we did neither enforce certain usage patterns (e.g., by providing tailored educational applications or content) nor did we prescribe how the phones should be used. It was deliberately set up so that the teacher and pupils could use the phone in ways they considered useful for teaching/learning and beneficial. Our analysis showed that pupils used the phones for different subjects and tasks during their lessons at school. It was exciting to see the how well the participants could appropriate the devices for the use even if they had only little/no prior knowledge.

Another finding of our research is that mobile phones even without specific learning applications empower teachers to create learning activities in the way they are used to teach. We see this approach similar to providing students with pen and paper where the versatility of the tool (pen/paper/phone) actually supports the teaching and learning process.

Most prominent use cases were accessing the Internet using the phone as a camera, as a playback devices, or as a replacement for copying machines. Having the phones available at all times allowed the teacher to spontaneously make use of information available on the Internet and enabled him to give different task to students and hence to differentiate based on the pupils ability. Through interviews with the teacher, children, and guardians we learned about a strong motivational effect of using phones as educational tool. This effect lasted over the duration of the entire study. Overall our results suggest that mobile phones are a versatile and powerful tool that can be used across a wide range of subjects.

ACKNOWLEDGEMENTS

This project was partly funded from the German Research Foundation within the Cluster of Excellence in Simulation Technology (EXC 310/1) at the University of Stuttgart.

REFERENCES

1. Bell, M., Chalmers, M., Barkhuus, L., Hall, M., Sherwood, S., Tennent, P., Brown, B., Rowland, D., Benford, S., Capra, M., and Hampshire, A. Interweaving mobile games with everyday life. In *Proc. CHI '06*, ACM (New York, NY, USA, 2006), 417–426.
2. Dangwal, R., and Kapur, P. Children's learning processes using unsupervised "hole in the wall" computers in shared public spaces. *Australasian Journal of Educational Technology 24*, 3 (2008), 339–354.
3. Ford, M.; Leionen, T. A mobile tool and service framework for formal and informal learning. In *mLearn 2006*, AU Press (2006), 195–214.
4. Frohlich, D. M., Rachovides, D., Riga, K., Bhat, R., Frank, M., Edirisinghe, E., Wickramanayaka, D., Jones, M., and Harwood, W. Storybank: Mobile digital storytelling in a development context. In *Proc. CHI '09*, ACM (New York, NY, USA, 2009), 1761–1770.
5. Hollow, D., and Masperi, P. An evaluation of the use of ict within primary education in malawi. In *Proc. ICTD '09* (April 2009), 27–34.
6. Jain, M., Birnholtz, J., Cutrell, E., and Balakrishnan, R. Exploring display techniques for mobile collaborative learning in developing regions. In *Proc. MobileHCI '11*, MobileHCI '11, ACM (New York, NY, USA, 2011), 81–90.
7. Jarkiewicz, P., Frankhammar, M., and Fernaeus, Y. In the hands of children: Exploring the use of mobile phone functionality in casual play settings. In *Proc. MobileHCI '08*, ACM (New York, NY, USA, 2008), 375–378.
8. Kam, M., Kumar, A., Jain, S., Mathur, A., and Canny, J. Improving literacy in rural india: cellphone games in an after-school program. In *Proc. ICTD '09* (April 2009), 139–149.
9. Kam, M., Mathur, A., Kumar, A., and Canny, J. Designing digital games for rural children: A study of traditional village games in india. In *Proc. CHI '09*, CHI '09, ACM (New York, NY, USA, 2009), 31–40.
10. Kumar, A., Tewari, A., Shroff, G., Chittamuru, D., Kam, M., and Canny, J. An exploratory study of unsupervised mobile learning in rural india. In *Proc. CHI '10*, CHI '10, ACM (New York, NY, USA, 2010), 743–752.
11. Mathur, A., Ramachandran, D., Cutrell, E., and Balakrishnan, R. An exploratory study on the use of camera phones and pico projectors in rural india. In *Proc. MobileHCI '11*, ACM (New York, NY, USA, 2011), 347–356.
12. Nokia. Momath nokia mobile mathematics. `https://projects.developer.nokia.com/Momaths/`, 09 2013.
13. Reitmaier, T., Bidwell, N. J., and Marsden, G. Field testing mobile digital storytelling software in rural kenya. In *Proc. MobileHCI '10*, MobileHCI '10, ACM (New York, NY, USA, 2010), 283–286.
14. Valderrama Bahamondez, E. d. C., Winkler, C., and Schmidt, A. Utilizing multimedia capabilities of mobile phones to support teaching in schools in rural panama. In *Proc. CHI '11*, ACM (New York, NY, USA, 2011), 935–944.

Understanding Shortcut Gestures on Mobile Touch Devices

Benjamin Poppinga[1], Alireza Sahami Shirazi[2], Niels Henze[2], Wilko Heuten[3], Susanne Boll[1]

[1]University of Oldenburg
Oldenburg, Germany
firstname.lastname@uni-oldenburg.de

[2]VIS, University of Stuttgart
Stuttgart, Germany
firstname.lastname@vis.uni-stuttgart.de

[3]OFFIS - Institute for Information Technology
Oldenburg, Germany
heuten@offis.de

ABSTRACT

Touch gestures become steadily more important with the ongoing success of touch screen devices. Compared to traditional user interfaces, gestures have the potential to lower cognitive load and the need for visual attention. However, nowadays gestures are defined by designers and developers and it is questionable if these meet all user requirements. In this paper, we present two exploratory studies that investigate how users would use unistroke touch gestures for shortcut access to a mobile phone's key functionalities. We study the functions that users want to access, the preferred activators for gesture execution, and the shapes of the user-invented gestures. We found that most gestures trigger applications, letter-shaped gestures are preferred, and the gestures should be accessible from the lock screen, the wallpaper, and the notification bar. We conclude with a coherent, unambiguous set of gestures for the 20 most frequently accessed functions, which can inform the design of future gesture-controlled applications.

Author Keywords

Touch gestures; shortcut; mobile phone; gesture recognition; instant access; quick launch.

ACM Classification Keywords

H.5.2 Information Interfaces and Presentation: User Interfaces—*Input devices and strategies*

INTRODUCTION

Over the past years, mobile devices, such as smart phones, tablets or wearable devices, started to replace traditional desktop computers as the most successful computing devices. Many of these mobile devices use touch-sensitive displays or surfaces as primary means of interaction, often mimicking traditional user interfaces like keyboards. However, with smaller form factors and display sizes, touch-based interaction runs into limitations as buttons and other interactive elements become too small to be operated accurately. Thus, alternative interaction techniques have been invented and studied. Most observable, we saw a breakthrough of gesture-based interaction on many recent mobile devices.

On nowadays devices a small set of simple touch gestures is used for zooming, rotating, and scrolling. Further, touch gestures are also used to provide users with a *shortcut* to certain functionalities, e.g., a swipe gesture to unlock the phone or to show the device's camera. Typically, these gestures were defined by the designers and developers of a system [13], although previous work showed that gesture sets that are mainly informed by the designers' intuition might not satisfy the users' requirements [23]. Beyond a basic set of well-established gestures, touch gestures for mobile phones are still not completely understood. For designers and developers it is unclear which action a gesture should cause, how the gesture should be shaped, and where the gestures should be executed.

In this paper, we study unistroke touch gestures for instant access to a mobile phones' core functions in the wild and from a user's perspective. To do this we design our apparatus, Gestify, which allows users to train and recognize custom gestures on Android phones. We deploy this application on the Google Play store and observe how users create and use gestures in their real life. Further, we conduct a supplemental lab study with 18 participants to substantiate these observations and to collect additional qualitative insights. We study which actions users prefer to cause with their gestures, which shapes their gestures have, and how users trigger gestures in their everyday life.

The contributions of this paper are as follows:

- We show that gestures are a valuable means for instant access and they should be executable on phones' lock screens, notification bars, and wallpapers.
- We highlight the 20 most important functions that should be accessible through shortcut gestures.
- We identify that *letter*-shaped gestures, which represent the first character of a related action, are used most commonly.
- We provide a consistent gesture set for the 20 most important functions.

MobileHCI 2014, September 23–26, 2014, Toronto, ON, Canada.

ACM 978-1-4503-3004-6/14/09...$15.00.
http://dx.doi.org/10.1145/2628363.2628378

In the next section, we provide an overview of previous work on touch and shortcut gestures on mobile devices. Afterwards, we describe the apparatus that we used to conduct two users studies. We describe an 'in the wild' field study to observe users' real life behavior, and a controlled lab study to substantiate the findings. We discuss the results of the studies and derive a consistent gesture set for the 20 most important functions. Finally, we conclude and provide potential directions for future work.

RELATED WORK

Gestures have a long history in human-computer interaction (HCI). They are one facet of interaction techniques that are sometimes dubbed natural user interfaces [22], and their exists a large body of work which investigated a broad range of different gestural interfaces (see [4] for an overview).

Previous work mainly investigated three different types of gestural interfaces: free-hand gestures in mid-air, gestures as alternatives for traditional user interface elements, and touch gestures. Work on free-hand gestures that are executed in mid-air most closely resemble gestures that humans use for communicating with each other [5]. With the release of the Wii and the Kinect, free-hand gestures became widely used for gaming and different applications in HCI research [19]. In desktop computing, gestures were mostly investigated as alternatives or complements for direct manipulation interfaces. Moyle and Cockburn, for example, analyzed mouse and pen flick gestures [14]. With the recent success of touch screen devices, touch gestures became the most widely used type of gestural interface and a focus in HCI research.

Touch gestures are meaningful strokes which are executed on a touch-sensitive surface, like a mobile phone, a tablet or a larger tabletop computer (see [26] for a review). It has been shown that touch gestures have a similar performance as keyboard shortcuts, but come with significant cognitive advantages, i.e., they are easier to learn and recall [3]. In addition, stroke gestures can be used eyes-free and are particularly beneficial for selecting frequently executed commands [17]. The variety of different application domains, settings, and techniques is huge, e.g., [8, 6, 12, 20]. The most of these domains and applications are investigated on a by-case basis. Consequently, a practical, coherent understanding of touch gestures is hardly existing and no comprehensive guidelines for gestural control are available [25].

Previous work not only investigated the design of touch gestures but also explored design processes for gestural interfaces. In general, it has been found that user-defined gestures are easier to memorize than pre-designed gestures [15]. Actual designs for user-defined gestures are typically identified in participatory design studies [23, 10, 9, 20]. Most prominently, Wobbrock et al. [23] presented an approach to design tabletop gestures with the help of potential users. They showed the actual effect a gesture would cause and then ask the user to define an appropriate action, i.e., gesture. In a lab study with 20 participants they recorded gestures, performed with one or two hands. They found that users prefer to execute gestures with one hand and mostly do not care about how many fingers are used. Wobbrock et al. conclude with a user-defined standard gesture set for common surface computer tasks and a taxonomy of surface gestures. Seyed et al. applied a similar approach for multi-display environments [20].

Ouyang and Li explored user-defined gesture shortcuts on mobile phones to realize a crowdsourced gesture recognition system [16]. They explored user-defined gesture shortcuts of 26 Android users and found that about 72 % of all gestures were of alphanumeric nature, i.e., a character or letter. They observed that users often define similar gestures for different actions, resulting in ambiguity and a decrease of recognition rate to about 70 %. Further, they reported that only a few gesture actions were shared by all users. Thus, in most cases the users defined gestures for very individual actions.

Another interest for the community lies in the application and everyday use of gestures [11, 21]. Gesture Search by Li [11] allows users to search their mobile phone for apps, contacts, and media files with the help of letter-shaped stroke gestures. Thereby, a variety of actions can be controlled, e.g., application launches, phone book access, or music playback. The research focuses on how the gesture recognition can be combined with traditional user interface elements. They concluded that Gesture Search enables a quick and easy way to access mobile data and users appreciate the usefulness and usability.

In summary, most of existing work provides valuable insights into a single research question, e.g., what do users want to control via gestures, how should a gesture look like, and how can gestures be applied in various settings or scenarios. Few papers study gestures in context or in the wild, and come with other limitations. For example, Gesture Search [11] was limited to letter-shaped gestures and their quick start application wasn't accessible from anywhere in the operating system. In contrast, we follow an exploratory approach and investigate the overall nature of touch gestures for shortcut access on mobile phones. With this approach we derive a coherent gesture set, which combines our findings on the gesture actions and ideal gesture shapes, that should be accessible through a phone's lock screen, notification bar, and wallpaper.

APPARATUS: GESTIFY

To investigate how touch gestures as shortcut to the phone's functionalities are used, we developed the Gestify application, that enables users to define gestures and use them to access various functions of their phone. In the following, we describe the design of the application, the used gesture recognition algorithm and the data that is recorded.

Creating and Managing Gestures

Gestify is an Android application, running on Android 3.0 or newer, that consists of two sub applications: *Gesture Manager* and *Gesture Recognizer*. With installation of the application both sub applications are installed and added to the home screen. The Gesture Manager allows users to manage existing gestures and define new ones, the Gesture Recognizer does the actual gesture recognition.

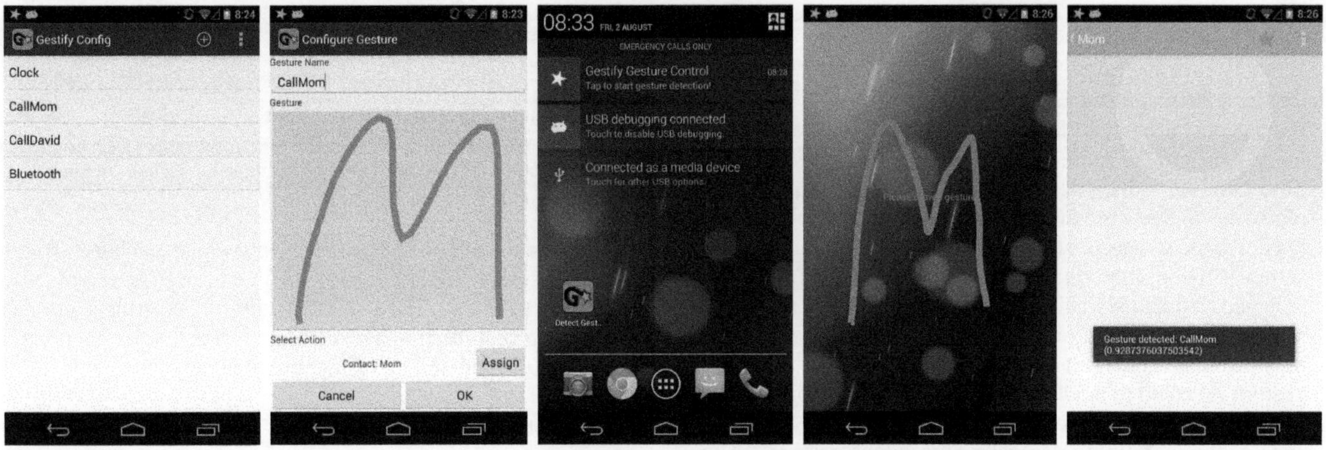

(a) List of existing gestures. (b) Add a new gesture. (c) Trigger detection through one of the provided activators, e.g., notification bar. (d) Draw gesture in recognition activity. (e) A pop-up indicates that the gesture is detected.

Figure 1. Gestify is an Android application that allows users to define and execute their own shortcut gestures. If gestures were trained to the system they can be recognized via different activators, i.e., through the lock screen, the notification bar, the wallpaper, and through a separate activity. If a gesture is detected, a toast is shown and the linked action is executed.

When the Gesture Manager is launched, an initially empty list shows the names of all existing gestures (see Figure 1a). A new gesture can be created by pressing the add button in the top right menu. The subsequently appearing dialogue is shown in Figure 1b and first asks the user to name the new gesture. The name can consist of alphanumerical characters and is recorded solely to allow users to maintain an overview over existing gestures (as shown in Figure 1a).

Gestify only supports unistroke gestures as defined in [26]. Thus, the touch movement for defining a gesture has to be a single, continuous movement that can have a theoretically unlimited complexity and length. Consequently, a single tap or two successive strokes are no valid gestures. Although there are multistroke gesture recognition engines available, e.g., [2], we decided for a unistroke recognition to emphasize the shortcut characteristic of the gestures.

In the last step of the creation process an action needs to be defined, which is triggered once the gesture is recognized. The user can select to start any application that is installed on his or her phone (*application gestures*), show a contact from the phone book (*contact gestures*) or change a system setting (*setting gesture*). While any application or contact can be selected, only core system settings, i.e., Bluetooth, Wi-Fi, Ringer, Vibration, can be changed for technical reasons. The user can decide to enable, disable or toggle one of these system settings. A tap on the *OK* button initiates the actual gesture training, closes the dialogue, and guides the user back to the gesture overview.

To simplify the analysis of recorded gestures, once created, a gesture cannot be updated. After a gesture has been designed and associated with an action, neither the name, the shape nor the action can be modified. If the user wants to change a gesture, it must be deleted and a new one has to be created.

Using Shortcut Gestures

The second sub application, Gesture Recognizer, is the interface for the actual gesture recognition. The app includes a single, full screen view in which the user can draw a gesture. A drawn gesture is taken as input for the gesture recognition engine and, based on the gesture recognition result, the corresponding action assigned to the gesture is executed. The view can be reached through four different ways, namely, (1) the lock screen, (2) the phone's notification bar, (3) directly launching the Gesture Recognizer app, and (4) a live wallpaper. In the following, we refer to these different ways to trigger the gesture recognition view as *activators*.

By installing Gestify and respectively the Gesture Recognizer app, the gesture recognition view automatically replaces the device's current lock screen. Further, this view can be reached through a short cut in the Android notification bar (see Figure 1c). The lock screen and notification bar activators are enabled by default, although they can be individually disabled through the application settings. In addition, the gesture recognition view can serve as a live wallpaper, which allows to recognize gestures straight from the phone's home screen. Due to technical restrictions users need to manually enable the wallpaper activator. To avoid confusion with other wallpaper-related interactions, e.g., changing the home screen with a sideways swipe, the gesture recognition needs to be initiated through a double tap onto an empty area. A pop-up briefs the user about this procedure.

Visual feedback is provided while drawing a gesture (see Figure 1d) to increase the drawing accuracy [1]. The actual recognition is triggered once the finger is lifted from the screen. The result for each recognition trial is displayed as a pop-up, which either shows the gesture label and recognition probability or that no gesture could be detected (see

Figure 1e). If a gesture is recognized, the according action is immediately executed.

Gesture Recognition Engine

Because the user should not be asked to provide several training gestures of the same type, we decided for a gesture recognition engine, which achieves high accuracies for few sample sizes. Gestify uses the $1 recognizer by Wobbrock et al. [24], which is based on geometric template matching, and achieves recognition rates of over 97 % with a single training instance. Although we did some empirical testing on the individual parameters of the engine, we eventually went with the best-performing default configuration [24]. That means every gesture is scaled to a 500x500 pixel square and consists of 64 points. The gesture recognition engine has some limitations, such as the inability to deal with ambiguous gestures. These limitations were not communicated to the users to avoid limiting them in their creativity.

Data Logging

The Gestify application is accompanied by a custom logging framework. Once the application is installed, various device information are recorded, e.g., the manufacturer, the model and the locale. Further, the logging framework records each created gesture, including their label and action, and when a gesture is deleted. All recognition attempts are stored with their origin, i.e., wallpaper, lock screen, notification bar, or the activity itself, and their recognition result. For ethical reasons no personal information, e.g., the contact name for gestures which trigger a phone call, is logged. The log data is transferred to a central server every two minutes.

'IN THE WILD' FIELD STUDY

In our first study, we investigate how people use the Gestify app 'in the wild', i.e., in their everyday life. We determine the actions that are triggered, the gesture shapes that are drawn, and the activators which are used to do the gesture recognition.

Recruitment

We published Gestify in the Google Play store in April 2013. Until January 2014 the application was downloaded and used by 388 users. The majority, 259 users (66.75 %) had an English locale, e.g., en_US, en_GB followed by German locales (de_DE) with 24 users (6.19 %). In total, 124 users (31.96 %) had an European/African time zone, i.e., GMT/0 to GMT/2 and 70 (18.04 %) an American timezone, i.e., GMT/-4 to GMT/-8. This shows that our application was mostly used by English- or German-speaking EU citizens and US Americans, which has to be considered when interpreting the results [7]. All users were using phones with Android 4.0 or newer.

Dataset

Gestify recorded information about the device, trained gestures and gesture recognition attempts. This data was transferred over the Internet and stored on a server. It was analyzed using the R software environment for statistical computing.

Our analysis shows that the 388 users trained 1134 gestures, whereby the number of trained gestures per user ranges from 1 to a maximum of 25 gestures. On average, each user trained 2.92 gestures (SD 3.61, median 1) and used the application for 5.15 days (SD 22.10, median 0.002). Given these numbers it is clear that the majority of users just tested the application for a short time and then stopped using it.

Abstract Geometric Icon Letter Word

Figure 2. We empirically identified five different shapes each gesture can be assigned to. This figure shows an example for each of the shapes.

Application Categorization

In total, 303 unique applications were launched using Gestify. To investigate for which application category the gesture action was used, we retrieved application categories from the Google Play marketplace. However, as also reported by Sahami et al. [18], we realized that the categories are too generic to differentiate between application functionalities. Further, also the class/package names are inconsistent, rarely self-explaining and, thus, don't allow for a classification. Consequently, we manually investigated the underlying functionality of each application and assigned it to a unique and illustrative category. Thereby, we followed the approach by Sahami et al., but successively added more categories, when we realized this was necessary. This resulted in 17 categories. Categories had between 4 and 155 unique applications (mean 17.82, SD 35.80, median 7).

Gesture Shape Categorization

Gestify allows a user to use any type of gesture shape. For a better characterization and discussion of the various shapes, we manually analyzed and classified all gestures in a two-step process. In the first step, we went through all gestures and identified a set of five shape classes: *abstract*, *geometric*, *icon*, *letter* and *word* shapes (see Figure 2). *Abstract* gestures consists of not inherently meaningful, not closed movements, e.g., a straight swipe or a wave-like movement. *Geometric* gestures look like well-known, closed geometric shapes, e.g., a circle, a square, or a heart. *Icon* gestures recap parts of an app-icon or other well-known icons, e.g., an envelope (for a messenger application) or a pentagram. *Letter* gestures look like an alphabetic character or digit, and *word* gestures contain more than one letter or whole words. In the second step, we went through all gestures again and assigned each of them to a single category. In the majority of all cases the classification was obvious. In borderline cases we assigned a gesture to the more generic class, e.g., an f-shaped gesture for the Facebook application was assigned to the *letter* category and not to the *icon* category.

'Power Users' Subsample

To obtain a better understanding about how gestures are used, we extracted a sub-sample of users who used the application for a longer period. This allows us to study if the gesture actions, shapes, or activators differ between short-term and long-term users. We call these users *power users* and include

n	All Users		Power Users		n
471	Other	41.53 %	Other	44.66 %	113
111	Messenger	11.50 %	Messenger	13.76 %	30
82	Phone	8.50 %	Phone	10.55 %	23
75	Browser	7.78 %	Social Netw.	6.42 %	14
71	Camera	7.36 %	Music Player	5.96 %	13
58	Music Player	6.01 %	Camera	5.96 %	13
54	Gallery	5.60 %	Mail	5.50 %	12
52	Social Netw.	5.39 %	Gallery	4.59 %	10
41	Mail	4.25 %	Browser	3.21 %	7
27	Settings	2.80 %	Settings	2.29 %	5

Table 1. The top ten categories of application gestures. Most gestures were defined for messaging apps, such as WhatsApp or SMS.

only users who actively used the application for at least a full week, i.e., 7 days, and trained and used at least 1 gesture. This resulted in a set of 36 users, which closely resemble the original sample characteristics, i.e., locale and time zone. These power users trained a total number of 253 gestures. Each power users trained on average 7.03 gestures (SD 5.13, median 5.5) and used the application for 52.72 days (SD 53.18, median 29.79).

Results

In the following, we present the user-defined *actions* and visual *shapes* of gestures. Further, we study which *activator* users preferred to use and draw their gestures on. We do this analysis for both, all users and the identified 'power users' subsample.

Gesture Actions

Gestify differentiates between three types of possible gestures: start an application, show contact details, or modify a system setting. Of the 1134 recorded gestures, 965 gestures (85.10 %) were *application gestures.* 87 gestures (7.67 %) were *contact gestures*, and 82 gestures (7.23 %) were *setting gestures.* Power users contributed 253 gestures, of which 218 (86.16) are *application*, 19 (7.51 %) *settings*, and 16 (6.32 %) *contact gestures.*

An analysis of the application categories shows that messaging applications, such as WhatsApp or SMS/MMS messengers, were the most frequently launched applications (111 gestures, 11.50 %). Phone-related apps, such as the phone book or the dialer activity were the second most frequent applications (82 gestures, 8.50 %) followed by browser applications (the Android default browser, Chrome or Firefox) with 75 gestures (7.78 %) of the total 965 application gestures. For power users a similar trend was observed, except that the third-most often triggered functionality were social networks instead of browsers (14 of 218 gestures, 6.42 %). About one third of all application gestures (302 of 965, 31.30 % and 78 of 218, 35.78 % for power users) were not of a particular popular functionality, and therefore assigned to the 'other' category. For example, these gestures were used to trigger specific games or niche applications, which are of importance for the individual user, but not of general relevance. An overview of the top ten actions for both user groups can be found in Table 1.

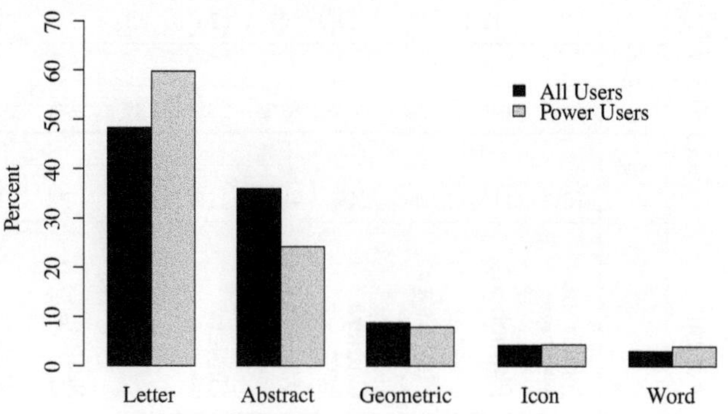

Figure 3. Gesture shapes for all users and power users. Letter-shaped gestures are the most prominent among both user groups, observed in about half of all cases.

From 82 *setting gestures* observed 9 were identified as erroneous and therefore were excluded from analysis. Of the remaining 73 gestures, 17 (23.29 %) were configured to toggle Wi-Fi, 14 (19.18 %) toggled Bluetooth, and 8 (10.96 %) enabled vibration. On average, each user uses a single gesture to toggle a system settings, i.e., turn on or off a setting depending on its current state. About 89.04 % of all gestures were configured to control Wi-Fi, Bluetooth, or vibration (about 30 % each). Only 10.96 % were used to change ringer settings.

We made slightly different observations for power users. They contribute 19 *setting gestures* in total, of which none was invalid. Of these, 6 gestures (31.58 %) were configured to enable vibration. 5 gestures (26.32 %) toggled Wi-Fi and 3 gestures (15.79 %) disabled vibration. 2 gestures each (10.53 %) were used to toggle Bluetooth or vibration. A single gesture (5.26 %) was set up to toggle the ringer. Similar to the set of all users, the majority of gestures (94.74 %) operates Wi-Fi, Bluetooth, or the vibration actuator.

Further, we observed 87 *contact gestures* for all users and 16 *contact gestures* for power users. However, for ethical reasons we did not record the meaning of any contact gestures, as this would allow us to track intimate contact details.

Gesture Shapes

Of the 1134 recorded gestures, *letter*-shaped gestures were the most frequent ones with 546 gestures (48.15 %) (see Figure 3). 407 gestures (35.89 %) matched the *abstract* shape, consisting of mostly simple swipes. The *geometric* shape included 99 gestures (8.73 %), the *icon* shape 48 gestures (4.23 %) and the *word* shape 34 gestures (3.00 %). We observed a similar distribution for power users, although the power users tend to have less *abstract* and more *letter*-shaped gestures.

For a more in-depth analysis of the gesture shapes, we extracted a set of gestures for the most commonly actions used. The set consists of the top 3 applications from the largest category, i.e., other applications (Play Store, YouTube, Google Maps), the top 2 applications from the second largest category, i.e., messenger applications (WhatsApp, SMS Composer), and the first application of every other category with

Study		Facebook (Social Network)	Phonebook (Phone)	Play Store (Others)	Camera (Camera)	WhatsApp (Messaging)	Gallery (Gallery)	Browser (Browser)	Settings (Settings)	SMS (Messaging)	Youtube (Other)	Mail (Mail)	Clock (Clock)	Calculator (Calculator)	Google Maps (Other)	Music (Music Player)	Calendar (Organiser)	Launcher (Launcher)	Flashlight (Flashlight)	Fav. Contact	Toggle Wifi
Field Study	n	39	37	32	29	27	26	25	24	16	15	13	13	13	13	13	11	5	2	87	17
Field Study	1st	f	/	P	C	W	g	B	S	M	Y	e	O	C	M	M	C	✓	L	M	W
		31%	14%	28%	34%	81%	23%	28%	29%	38%	60%	38%	31%	23%	31%	31%	36%	20%	50%	9%	71%
Field Study	2nd	F	P	e	O	B	G	e	O	✉	▷	M	✓	P	↑	☆	Gl	O	|	S	\
		18%	11%	9%	21%	4%	12%	12%	13%	19%	13%	31%	15%	15%	15%	23%	18%	20%	50%	8%	12%
Lab Study	1st	f	C	P	O	W	G	\	✿	✉	Y	✉	◷	+	M	♪	C	⌂	💡	♡	W
		59%	15%	39%	24%	61%	33%	21%	29%	28%	71%	28%	28%	47%	44%	41%	28%	28%	28%	30%	22%
Lab Study	2nd	r	웃	▷	▣	P	□	B	S	S	▷	M	O	1	◫	▷	□	/	✓	☆	O
		18%	15%	22%	18%	6%	28%	16%	24%	22%	12%	17%	22%	18%	17%	18%	22%	17%	17%	24%	11%
Lab Study	n	17	18	18	17	18	18	18	17	18	17	18	18	17	18	17	18	18	18	17	18

Table 2. A visualization of the top two gestures for the twenty most popular gesture actions. For some actions the gestures are very consistent among users and studies, e.g., with about 71 % in the field study and 61 % in the lab study most people agree that WhatsApp should be triggered with a *W* gesture.

more than 10 trained gestures. Further, we included the most prominent *settings gesture* (i.e., Toggle Wi-Fi), and all *contact gestures*. The resulting set consists of 20 representative actions for the most commonly controlled functionalities and is shown in Table 2.

Regarding the shape of *application gestures*, we found that 459 of the 965 gestures (47.56 %) were classified to have a *letter* shape. Further, we identified 344 (35.65 %) *abstract*, 85 (8.81 %) *geometric*, 47 (4.87 %) *icon*, and 30 (3.11 %) *word* gestures. The in-depth analysis shows that there is often a strong consensus among users on which gesture shape should be used for which application (see Table 2). In fact, users often select the first letter of the application name, e.g., *W* to start WhatsApp or *f* to start *f*acebook. For power users we observed the same order with a similar distribution, i.e., 56.77 % were *letter* gestures, 24.77 % *abstract*, 8.72 % *geometric*, 5.05 % *icon*, and 4.59 % *word* gestures.

Again, the 9 erroneous *setting gestures* were excluded from the analysis. Of the remaining 73 *setting gestures*, 35 (47.95 %) were of *letter*, 25 (34.25 %) of *abstract*, 9 (12.33 %) of *geometric*, and 4 (5.48 %) of *word* shape. None of the gestures had an *icon* shape. *Setting gestures* of power users were 78.95 % *letter*-shaped, 15.79 % *abstract*-shaped, and 5.26 % of *geometric* shape. The two most common actions for all users, i.e., toggle Wi-Fi and toggle Bluetooth, were most frequently triggered with a *w*/*W*-shaped (12 of 17, 70.59 %) respectively *B*-shaped (7 of 14, 50.00 %) *letter* gesture (see Table 2).

We observed that 50 of 87 (57.47 %) *contact gestures* were *letter* shaped. 32 gestures (36.78 %) had an *abstract*, 4 (4.60 %) a *geometric*, and 1 (1.15 %) an *icon* shape. No *word*-shaped gestures were observed. Power users created 12 (75.00 %) *letter*-shaped *contact gestures*, and 4 (25.00 %) *abstract* gestures.

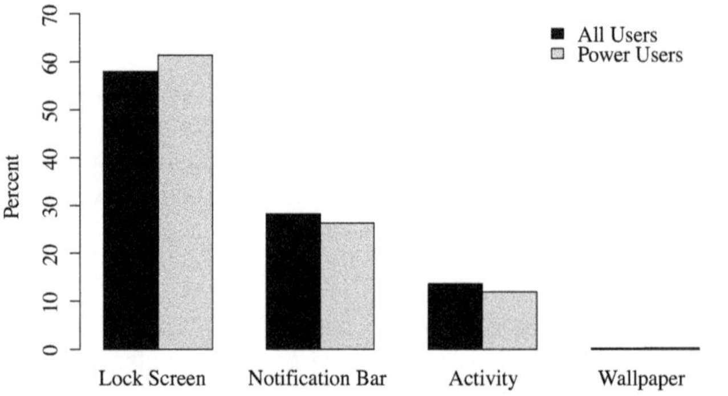

Figure 4. Users most frequently used the lock screen as activator for the gestures recognition. The wallpaper activator was hardly used at all, although study participants rated it best in the lab study.

Gesture Activators

Gestify offers four activators to start the gesture recognition. A user could use the lock screen, the wallpaper, a separate activity or the notification bar. Overall, 12531 gesture recognition attempts by 321 different users were recorded. Of these, 7263 (57.96 %) were performed on the lock screen, 3537 (28.23 %) via the notification bar, 1708 (13.63 %) via the activity, and 23 (0.18 %) on the wallpaper (see Figure 4). A similar distribution was observed for power users. Overall, the lock screen seems to be the preferred activator to launch applications, change settings or open a contact.

We further studied which activator is most frequently used per user. 135 users (42.06 %) most frequently used the lock screen to execute a gesture. 130 users (40.50 %) used the notification bar, and 56 users (17.45 %) used the activity most frequently. None of the users used the wallpaper as their most frequent activator. On average, 85.56 % (SD 15.16 %) of a users gesture recognition attempts were done using the same activator. This indicates that most users prefer to permanently use a single activator instead of various activators in parallel.

6164 of 12531 gesture recognition attempts, i.e., 49.19 % (48.22 % for power users), led to a successful recognition of a gesture. Thereby, the recognition rate varies between the individual activators, i.e., 34.78 % for the wallpaper and 67.01 % for the notification bar. We argue that the limited recognition performance can mostly be credited to users, who studied the limitations of the recognition, and accidental gesture recognition attempts, e.g., caused by unintentional lock screen or wallpaper use.

LAB STUDY

The study through the marketplace was conducted in an uncontrolled setting and its findings have high external validity. In the following, we complement these findings through a lab study, which will provide us with insights of internal validity. We study if lab users of Gestify create similar shaped gestures and what their preferred activators are.

Method

We recruited 18 participants (7 female) with an average age of 26.4 years (SD 5.20). The participants were recruited through the university's mailing lists. Twelve participants were students in different subjects such as Informatics, Electrical Engineering, etc. All participants owned an Android phone and 67 % used it for more than a year. None of the participants had used the Gestify application or another application with similar functionality prior to the study.

We installed Gestify on a Nexus 5 mobile phone and used it during the study to collect data. After welcoming and signing the consent form, participants were asked to fill in a demographic questionnaire. Then, we introduced Gestify through a short demo and explained its functionality. The participants were then asked to specify and train gestures for the 20 most popular actions, which we identified in the field study. The actions' order was randomized to reduce sequence effects. Finally, we asked the participants to answer a questionnaire, which assesses the participants' current and desired future use of activators for gesture shortcuts. Further, the questionnaire provided room to leave qualitative feedback about the participants' impressions of using Gestify. The study lasted approximately 30 minutes. Each participant was compensated with 5€.

Results

In total, 360 gestures were performed by the participants. However, because of a technical failure 7 gestures could not be recorded. Consequently, our analysis is done with 353 gestures. To have an overview on the gesture shapes we reviewed all gestures collected for each action and assigned them to one of the five shape categories, which we identified in the field study (see Figure 2). Based on these results, *letter*-shaped gestures were the most frequent gestures (35.41 %), followed by *icon*-shaped (26.91 %), *abstract*-shaped (26.62 %), *geometric*-shaped (9.06 %), and *word*-shaped (1.42 %) gestures. The two most frequent gestures for each action are shown in Table 2.

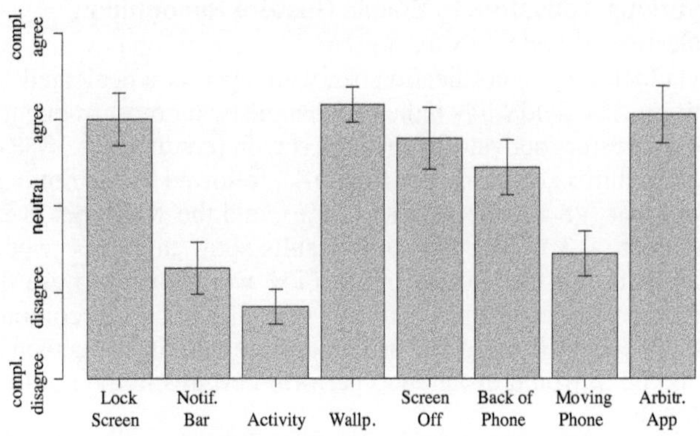

Figure 5. Lab study participants were asked to provide their level of agreement to a set of possible gesture activators. The results show that on average, participants mostly agree with performing gestures on the wallpaper. The error bars show the standard error.

In the questionnaire we asked the participants to rate a statement on each of the four different activators, e.g., *I would like to perform the gesture on the wallpaper*, using a 5-point Likert scale from (1) 'completely disagree' to (5) 'completely agree'. The analysis shows that 83.00 % of participants (mean 4.16, SD 0.85, median 4) would agree to use the wallpaper for gesture recognition. 77 % would agree to use the lock screen (mean 4, SD 1.28, median 4.5). 83 % of the participants disagreed with the statement on performing gestures in a separate application (mean 1.83, SD 0.85, median 2) as it—according to received qualitative feedback—would require more interaction steps and, thus, is cumbersome. Furthermore, 66 % disagreed with a gesture performance in the notification bar (mean 2.27, SD 1.27, median 2).

We further asked the participants to provide feedback on four other possible activators, i.e., the back of the phone, moving the phone itself, drawing gestures on the phone's screen when it is off, and draw a gesture while using arbitrary applications. The results reveal that 78 % of all users would agree to perform a gesture while using any arbitrary application (mean 4.05, SD 1.39, median 5). Further, 72 % agreed to perform gestures while the phone screen is off (mean 3.77, SD 1.51, median 4) and 56 % agreed with the back of the phone as an activator (mean 3.44, SD 1.33, median 4). 56 % disagree with moving the phone for performing a gesture (mean 2.44, SD 1.09, median 2). A visualization of these results is provided in Figure 5.

The qualitative feedback shows that the participants consider simpler gestures for frequently used actions, since these are easier to memorize. Furthermore, it was mentioned that existing symbols and icons, e.g., characters taken from the alphabet, can be a good starting point for the definition of gesture sets.

DISCUSSION AND RECOMMENDATIONS

In the following, we discuss our results and provide recommendations for designers and developers of future gesture recognition systems on mobile touchscreen devices, such as mobile phones.

Various Activators to Enable Gesture Recognition

Gestify offered four ways to start the recognition process, i.e., via lock screen, notification bar, wallpaper, or a dedicated activity. The field study indicated that the by far most frequently used gesture activator is the lock screen (credited for 58 % of all gesture executions, see Figure 4), followed by the notification bar (28 %), the activity (14 %), and the wallpaper (very close to 0 %). The lab study results show that 83 % would agree to use the wallpaper and 77 % would agree to use the lock screen as gesture activator (see Figure 5). In contrast, 83 % would disagree to use a separate activity as activator, and 66 % would disagree to perform gestures in the notification bar.

The lab study results indicate that users prefer the wallpaper activator, although the field study findings indicate that it was hardly used in practice. A potential reason for this gap could be that the field study users were not fully aware of the wallpaper activator, although it was equally well advertised as other activators. Another potential reason could be that the technique to enable the activator, i.e., a double tap on empty space on the wallpaper, was too complex to create a real advantage over using the regular launcher. Further, it could have been confusing or misleading that also the regular home screen keeps reacting to touch input during gesture execution, which can lead to minor icon movement.

Future gesture recognition systems should definitively respect the desire for diversity and offer various ways to recognize a gesture. For mobile phones, gesture recognition should be available through the lock screen, the notification bar, and through the wallpaper. However, because of our observations we recommend that the gesture interaction with the wallpaper needs further research. For example, it should be clarified how users exactly want an ideal gesture wallpaper to behave. Because we did not observe an intense use of the application activator and because people don't have a desire to use gesture recognition in a separate activity, this option could be omitted in future systems.

We further identified that the preferred activator is user specific. In about 85 % of all gesture recognitions, users use their most frequently used activator. For example, if a user's most frequently used activator is the lock screen, about 85 % of all gesture executions are done here. Thus, if for any reasons a user has to decide for a certain approach, most users will probably be able to make such a decision comfortably. Future research could investigate if gesture actions for individual activators differ, e.g., if messaging gestures are more often triggered from the lock screen or the notification bar.

Applications Are Most Popular Gesture Action

Gestify allowed users to use three types of gesture actions: *application gestures* to start applications, *contact gestures* to quickly reach for contacts, and *settings gestures* to modify system settings. In fact, *any* application and *any* contact could be assigned to a gesture. Further, Gestify provides a functionality, which—similar to existing quick settings applications—allows to instantly change system settings. Consequently, we argue that Gestify can be used to control these functionalities without any limitations.

Our results show that 85.10 % of all trained gestures in the field study were *application gestures*. Consequently, only a minority of *setting gestures* and *contact gestures* were created. This contradicts with earlier findings reported by Li [11], who observed that *contact gestures* (66 %) are preferred over *application gestures* (28 %). Even applications from the communication category and *contact gestures* together only sum up to 32.72 % of communication-related gestures, which is still half of the percentage that Li reported [11].

We argue that the reason for this difference lies in the slightly different interaction concepts. The app *Gesture Search* by Li consists of a single activity, which needs to be started and which then recognizes predefined character gestures. These are concatenated to words that serve as filter for a list of all available phone actions, such as 'start application' and 'show contact'. In contrast, Gestify can be accessed directly via various activators, allowing to trigger an action with a single user-defined gesture.

Thus, the omnipresence of gesture activators and the self-contained, 'single stroke' character of a gesture seem to be two key criteria for appreciated shortcut gesture recognizers. This is supported by our lab study, where users preferred to execute gestures, e.g., on the wallpaper, in every application or on the lock screen. All these activators are very present and often just a button press away. Further, we hardly observed *word*-shaped gestures in our studies. Instead, most users created letter, icon or abstract gestures.

Designers and developers should consider these findings in their future touch gesture recognition systems for shortcut access. Future research could investigate which of the proposed gesture activators perform best in everyday use. Further, also the execution speed of various gesture types could be studied and how this affects the overall user experience.

Pre-defined Gesture Set

We observed that many gestures were created for a small set of actions. In fact, we analyzed 1134 gestures from 388 users to identify a set of 20 popular actions. This set is shown in Table 2 and consists of 18 *application gestures*, one *settings gesture* and one *contact gesture*. We argue that this set is a good representation of the average user's preferred actions and, therefore, makes a good starting point for the definition of future shortcut tools for mobile devices.

Similar to Ouyang and Li [16], we observed that half of all 1134 gestures, i.e., 47.12 %, were *letter*-shaped. 35.89 % were of *abstract* shape, 8.73 % of *geometric* shape, 4.23 % of *icon* shape, and 3.00 % of *word* shape. This dominance is also present within our top 20 set of actions (see Table 2). Qualitative statements from the lab study indicate that some users used the alphabet and the action name as a reference for their gestures.

Overall, our findings show a clear preference for *letter*-shaped gestures. We argue that this is the case because they are powerful enough to represent and differentiate between advanced information, such as various apps. At the same time letters are simple enough to be memorized and remembered. In contrast, *abstract* and *geometric* gestures have a limited

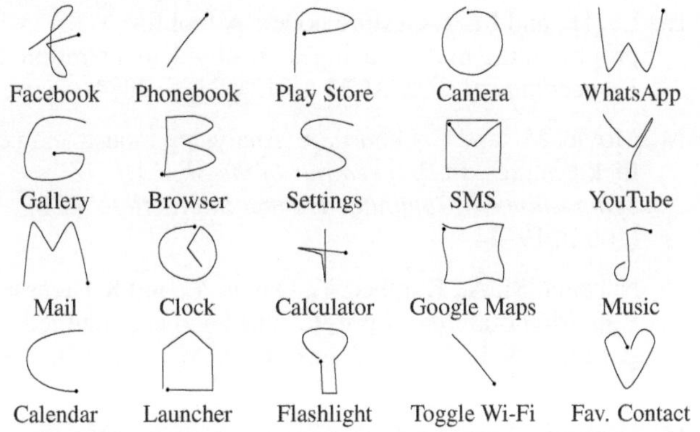

Figure 6. By analysing and combining gestures from both studies, we derived a comprehensive gesture set for the top 20 actions. This gesture set can serve as the default configuration for future mobile touch interfaces.

expressiveness, *icon* gestures can be too hard to remember, and *word* gestures can be too complex to draw.

Both, the identification of common actions and the subsequent analysis of gesture shapes, allow us to design a coherent and unambiguous gesture set. To derive this set we analyzed all gestures that we observed in both studies. We used the absolute number of gestures, which were observed in the field study, as a global indicator for importance. Starting from the most important gesture (left hand side in Table 2), we calculated an overall percentage for each identified shape by combining data from both studies. If the gesture shape with the highest percentage is not already used for a more important action, it was assigned to this gesture. Otherwise the next-most prominent shape is considered until an yet unused shape was found. This procedure allows us to consider both, i.e., how often a gesture was used, and which gesture shape was used most frequently.

The resulting set is shown in Figure 6 and could be used as a default working configuration, likely suiting the needs of most users. A deployment of this set could allow users to trigger actions without the need to train gestures in advance. This can positively affect the user experience and potentially reduce the time to learn and understand the gesture recognition application. Nevertheless, it must be clear that this set might also contradict the user's desires. Therefore, it should still be customizable to ensure greatest flexibility and to address users' individual needs.

Future research should study how gesture actions, shapes, and activators are designed for other user groups, e.g., users with a non-Latin alphabet, and if and how the availability of a default gesture set affects the user experience. Further, it would be interesting to know if the importance of individual actions change over time, and if and in which cases users re-define a gesture.

CONCLUSIONS

Touch gestures are becoming a more and more popular interaction technique on nowadays smart phones, tablets, and wearables. Existing touch gestures, e.g., a sideways slide to unlock a device, are typically defined by designers and developers, although it is unclear if these gestures meet the end-user requirements.

In this paper, we studied the users' needs and desires regarding gestures from the ground up. We designed and developed a flexible gesture recognition application, Gestify, which aims to fulfill most of the potential user needs. Users could define their own gesture actions, gesture shapes, and use different activators to initiate the gesture recognition. Using the Gestify application we conducted two exploratory user studies in two different settings: a field study in the Google Play marketplace and a supplemental lab study with 18 participants.

Our results show that the majority, i.e., 85 %, of all analyzed gestures are set up to control the user's applications. About 7 % each modify system settings or show contact information. Half of all gestures, i.e., 48 %, have a *letter* shape, typically mimicking the first letter of the controlled application name, e.g., *W* for *W*hatsApp. 36 % have an *abstract* shape, representing, e.g., a single swipe. Our field study results show that the lock screen (58 %) and the notification bar (28 %) are the most frequently used activators to trigger the gesture recognizer. However, the lab study reveals that the live wallpaper and back of the phone are also in the user's preference for triggering gestures.

We conclude that touch gestures are a valuable means for instant access to a variety of actions, e.g., to start applications, to show contact details, or to toggle system settings. We found that users prefer gesture activators, which are omnipresent and ideally less than a button press away. In fact, our results indicate that gesture execution should be possible on the lock screen, on the wallpaper, and in the notification bar. We observed that users rarely switch between various activators. Instead, they decide for a single activator and continue to use it. We argue that future gesture recognition systems should consider the need for diversity, but may ask users to decide for a single activator if necessary.

We further highlight the 20 most important actions which should be accessible through shortcut gestures. Of these 20 actions the majority are *application gestures*, such as Facebook, WhatsApp, or the Camera application. One action each is dedicated to access contact information or toggle system settings. We identify that about half of all gestures are *letter*-shaped, and the second most prominent gestures are of *abstract* shape. Overall, only a few gestures are of *icon*, *word*, or *geometric* shape. *Letter* shapes typically represent the first character of a related action, whereby *icon* gestures typically mimic the application icon. Through our two complementing studies we provide a comprehensive, unambiguous gesture set for the 20 most important actions (see Figure 6), which can serve as a customizable default gesture set for future touch devices and thereby avoids time-consuming gesture training efforts.

In our future work, we want to apply this proposed gesture set in the wild and study if users are satisfied or if they apply any modifications. Further, we are interested to investigate how gestures are used in everyday life. We plan to research which gestures are used most frequently over the day, and if certain activators are preferred to execute certain gestures. Further, it remains questionable to what extend our proposed gesture set can be transferred to future mobile devices, like wearable glasses or smart watches.

ACKNOWLEDGEMENTS

This work is partially supported by the German Research Foundation within the SimTech Cluster of Excellence (EXC 310/1).

REFERENCES

1. Anthony, L., Brown, Q., Nias, J., and Tate, B. Examining the need for visual feedback during gesture interaction on mobile touchscreen devices for kids. In *Proceedings of the 12th International Conference on Interaction Design and Children*, IDC '13, ACM (2013), 157–164.
2. Anthony, L., and Wobbrock, J. O. $n-protractor: A fast and accurate multistroke recognizer. In *Proceedings of Graphics Interface* (2012), 117–120.
3. Appert, C., and Zhai, S. Using strokes as command shortcuts: Cognitive benefits and toolkit support. In *Proceedings of CHI*, ACM (2009), 2289–2298.
4. Billinghurst, M. Gesture based interaction. In *Haptic input*, B. Buxton, Ed. Cambridge University Press, 2009.
5. Bolt, R. A. “put-that-there”: Voice and gesture at the graphics interface. In *Proceedings of SIGGRAPH*, ACM (1980), 262–270.
6. Döring, T., Kern, D., Marshall, P., Pfeiffer, M., Schöning, J., Gruhn, V., and Schmidt, A. Gestural interaction on the steering wheel: Reducing the visual demand. In *Proceedings of CHI*, ACM (2011), 483–492.
7. Henze, N., Pielot, M., Poppinga, B., Schinke, T., and Boll, S. My app is an experiment: Experience from user studies in mobile app stores. *Int. J. Mob. Hum. Comput. Interact. 3*, 4 (Oct. 2011), 71–91.
8. Hinrichs, U., and Carpendale, S. Gestures in the wild: Studying multi-touch gesture sequences on interactive tabletop exhibits. In *Proceedings of CHI*, ACM (2011), 3023–3032.
9. Lahey, B., Girouard, A., Burleson, W., and Vertegaal, R. Paperphone: Understanding the use of bend gestures in mobile devices with flexible electronic paper displays. In *Proceedings of CHI*, ACM (2011), 1303–1312.
10. Lee, J. C., Hudson, S. E., and Tse, E. Foldable interactive displays. In *Proceedings of UIST*, ACM (2008), 287–290.
11. Li, Y. Gesture search: A tool for fast mobile data access. In *Proceedings of UIST*, ACM (2010), 87–96.
12. Lü, H., and Li, Y. Gesture avatar: A technique for operating mobile user interfaces using gestures. In *Proceedings of CHI*, ACM (2011), 207–216.
13. Lü, H., and Li, Y. Gesture coder: A tool for programming multi-touch gestures by demonstration. In *Proceedings of CHI*, ACM (2012), 2875–2884.
14. Moyle, M., and Cockburn, A. Analysing mouse and pen flick gestures. In *Proceedings of the SIGCHI-NZ Symposium On Computer-Human Interaction*, ACM (2002), 19–24.
15. Nacenta, M. A., Kamber, Y., Qiang, Y., and Kristensson, P. O. Memorability of pre-designed and user-defined gesture sets. In *Proceedings of CHI*, ACM (2013), 1099–1108.
16. Ouyang, T., and Li, Y. Bootstrapping personal gesture shortcuts with the wisdom of the crowd and handwriting recognition. In *Proceedings of CHI*, ACM (2012), 2895–2904.
17. Roudaut, A., Bailly, G., Lecolinet, E., and Nigay, L. Leaf menus: Linear menus with stroke shortcuts for small handheld devices. In *Human-Computer Interaction – INTERACT 2009*, vol. 5726 of *Lecture Notes in Computer Science*. Springer Berlin Heidelberg, 2009, 616–619.
18. Sahami Shirazi, A., Henze, N., Dingler, T., Pielot, M., Weber, D., and Schmidt, A. Large-scale assessment of mobile notifications. In *Proceedings of CHI*, ACM (2014), 3055–3064.
19. Schlömer, T., Poppinga, B., Henze, N., and Boll, S. Gesture recognition with a wii controller. In *Proceedings of TEI*, ACM (2008), 11–14.
20. Seyed, T., Burns, C., Costa Sousa, M., Maurer, F., and Tang, A. Eliciting usable gestures for multi-display environments. In *Proceedings of ITS*, ACM (2012), 41–50.
21. Tran, J. J., Trewin, S., Swart, C., John, B. E., and Thomas, J. C. Exploring pinch and spread gestures on mobile devices. In *Proceedings of MobileHCI*, ACM (2013), 151–160.
22. Wigdor, D., and Wixon, D. *Brave NUI world: designing natural user interfaces for touch and gesture*. Elsevier, 2011.
23. Wobbrock, J. O., Morris, M. R., and Wilson, A. D. User-defined gestures for surface computing. In *Proceedings of CHI*, ACM (2009), 1083–1092.
24. Wobbrock, J. O., Wilson, A. D., and Li, Y. Gestures without libraries, toolkits or training: A $1 recognizer for user interface prototypes. In *Proceedings of UIST*, ACM (2007), 159–168.
25. Wolf, K., McGee-Lennon, M., and Brewster, S. A study of on-device gestures. In *Proceedings of MobileHCI*, ACM (2012), 11–16.
26. Zhai, S., Kristensson, P. O., and Appert, C. *Foundational Issues in Touch-Surface Stroke Gesture Design*. Now Publishers Inc., Hanover, MA, USA, 2012.

JuxtaPinch: Exploring Multi-Device Interaction in Collocated Photo Sharing

Heidi Selmer Nielsen, Marius Pallisgaard Olsen, Mikael B. Skov, Jesper Kjeldskov
Centre for Socio-Interactive Design, Aalborg University
Selma Lagerlöfs Vej 300, DK-9220 Aalborg East, Denmark
{hsn.mobil, marius.pallisgaard}@gmail.com, {dubois, jesper}@cs.aau.dk

ABSTRACT
Mobile HCI research has started to investigate multi-device interaction as we often have more devices at our immediate disposal. We present an application called JuxtaPinch that allows users to share photos while being collocated using several different devices, i.e. mobile phones and tablets, at the same time. JuxtaPinch use pinching to connect devices and it enables flexible physical positioning of devices and supports partial viewing of photos. Our evaluation showed that JuxtaPinch enabled participants to experience their own familiar photos in new ways known as defamiliarization. It further enabled participants to engage jointly in playful interaction with the photos and with each other. However, we also found that multiple device collocated photo sharing challenges aspects of synchronization and coordination.

Author Keywords
Collocated photo sharing; pinching; multi device

ACM Classification Keywords
H.5.2 Information interfaces and presentation (e.g., HCI): Miscellaneous.

INTRODUCTION
With the continuously growing number of smart phones and tablets, we are currently using and adapting these devices and technologies in more and more contexts and for many purposes. With more than 1.75 billion smart phones sold in 2012, these mobile devices have become deeply embedded into our everyday life, supporting work, social interaction, leisure, and collaboration. With such diffusion of smart phones and tablets in people's everyday lives, we see that people often have not only one, but several, of such devices at one's immediate disposal. HCI and mobile HCI research has consequently begun to explore and study opportunities and challenges of user interaction across several platforms. Often referred to as multi-device interaction or cross-device interaction, using several devices at the same time provides new opportunities for interaction and open avenues for new application areas. But currently we have only witnessed few studies on multi-device interaction, for example interaction techniques [4, 12, 14] or collaboration [3].

http://dx.doi.org/10.1145/2628363.2628369

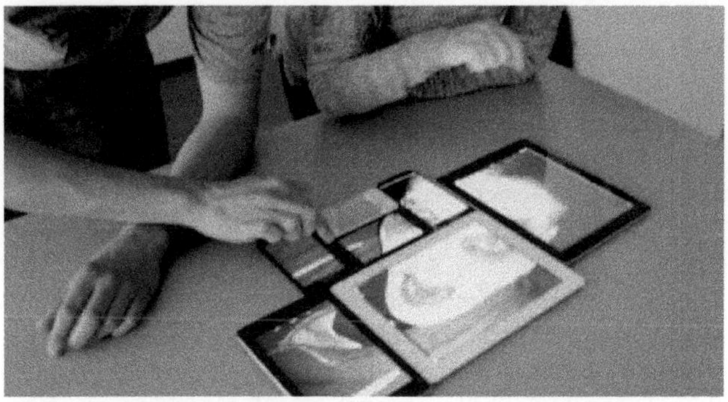

Figure 1. Collocated photo sharing where two users share a photo using JuxtaPinch and they employ seven devices namely three tablets and four smartphones.

Ohta and Tanaka [14] illustrate a pinching technique called Pinch that enables multiple devices to be connected as one device and they call for studies on cross-device interaction application designs. One such application design is photo sharing as we increasingly use smart phones and their built-in photo features [8] and especially collocated photo sharing where more people gather to share and view photos while being collocated. Often referred to as collocated photo sharing [10], this plays an important role socially and individually as it develops people's self-image, as well as creating and strengthening relationships within social groups [20]. Current collocated photo sharing HCI research attempt to investigate how to overcome some of the inherent problems when sharing photos with others on small screens [19], but also how can we utilize multiple devices for such photo sharing as people would bring not only phones but sometimes also tablets when gathered in social groups.

We present a multi-device application called JuxtaPinch that supports collocated photo sharing on multiple devices (shown in figure 1). JuxtaPinch allows flexible side-by-side positioning of devices and stitching their display areas together through a pinching gesture and allows partial photo viewing by scaling photos. Our contribution is two-folded. Firstly, we contribute to multi-device interaction research through a qualitative study on opportunities and challenges related to using several devices at the same time. Secondly, we contribute the collocated photo sharing research through illustration of emerging patterns of use and exploration of familiar photos.

RELATED WORK

We investigate multi-device interaction through the design of JuxtaPinch and three areas of related research work have influenced JuxtaPinch: multi-device interaction, collocated photo sharing, and multi-device photo sharing applications.

Multi-Device Interaction

With the rapidly increasing proliferation of smartphones and tablets in people's everyday lives, it is now not uncommon to have several of such devices at one's immediate disposal. This creates new use situations and new opportunities for exploring interaction designs that span across multiple devices rather than being limited to just one. Researchers have responded to these opportunities by exploring a new class of "multi-device applications" that allow users to link individual mobile devices and use them as one joint interface. Examples of this include *Pass-Them-Around* by Lucero et al. [11], *Junkyard Jumbotron* by Borovoy & Knep [15], and *Pinch* by Ohta and Tanaka [14], These all create and make use of larger screen real estate by physically placing a number of mobile devices next to each other and treating their combined display surface as joint. Pass-Them-Around [11] does this with up to four devices, placed side-by-side, using a pinching gesture across two devices at a time. As a very different approach, Junkyard Jumbotron [15] combines several displays, in arbitrary arrangements, through a calibration process with an external camera and QR codes displayed on each device. Finally, Pinch [14] allows the display surfaces of iOS devices, placed next to each other, to be joint using pinch gestures. The multi-display layout can then be changed dynamically, allowing for great interactivity, and content automatically adapts to the size of the combined display. This, the creators speculate, may be useful in many different types of multi-device applications, for example for viewing videos and playing games.

While specific application areas for multi-device interaction are still underexplored, some call for further explorations [14], and one of the areas where this approach may have immediate value is for collocated viewing and sharing of photos as people gather and bring their own devices. We will return to this choice in our discussion and relate our findings to other areas of potential application.

Collocated Photo Sharing

Even in today's technologically mediated, distributed, and digital world, collocated photo sharing is an important social activity. In [20] van House present and discuss three themes that describe why this is. The first theme is related to *memory, storytelling, and identity*. Memories and narratives related to a photo are dynamic and change over time. How we remember a story related to a photo may not be the same today, as it will be in five years [20]. The stories that are told about photos help constructing the self-image of the individual as well as the group. When we tell our stories to other people, we then make sense of our lives for ourselves.

The second theme is related to the role of photo sharing in *relationships*. Sharing photos, and their stories, with someone face-to-face enacts the relationships between the people involved. This typically happens either through *storytelling,* linking it to the previous theme, or through *reminiscing* [1, 6, 19, 20]. Storytelling here describe the situation where a person presents a photo where the viewers were not present, and often happens around photos of events where the owner feels that the viewers should have been there too. Reminiscing, on the other hand, happens around photos with several of the viewers present, giving them an opportunity to relive parts of a shared past, and through this reinforce their relationship in the present [19].

The third theme is related to the *orality* of collocated photo sharing. When co-located, people are able to tell stories, and reminisce orally rather than through writing, as in for example online sharing services like Flickr, this gives the storyteller dynamic control over the story as told in that specific moment. This allows him or her to adjust the story in an ad-hoc manner in response to the specific audience, their interests, and their reactions along the way [20].

In today's digital and connected world, many people have access to large portions of their personal photo collection at all times through smart phones, tablets and cloud services [11, 20]. Combined with the role of collocated photo sharing this has created a growing interest in photo sharing applications for mobile devices that allows people to share, view and explore photos together. One of the most commonly used ways of digital collocated photo sharing is to pass devices (usually mobile phones or tablets) around and letting people see the photo one person at a time [19]. However, research studies have identified several limitations. Firstly, smartphone screens are rather small for viewing photos [5, 19], making it hard to identify what is happening on the photo, and easy to lose details. Secondly, it is difficult to use the photo as anchor point in a shared social interaction as one can't "point-and-tell" and because only a few people can see the photo at the same time [19]. When only people in close proximity can see what is on the screen and what is pointed at, it becomes difficult for the whole group to follow any story and take part in the social interaction, leaving part of the group as outsiders and thus impairing the photo sharing experience.

Collocated Photo Sharing on Multi-Device Applications

Several studies have addressed the identified limitations of collocated photo sharing on single devices. Schmidt et al. [16] and Greaves and Rukzio [7] explore transferring photos to larger display areas such as an interactive surface or a projector. However, such infrastructure is far from as commonly available as mobile devices. Another solution, proposed by Kun and Marsden [1], suggests transferring photos to everyone in a group, and then looking at it on one's own device. This allows simultaneous viewing, but complicates point-and-tell and also takes attention away from a common focus and the shared social interaction. Also, the limitation of small screens, i.e. viewing details, remains unsolved. As an alternative, Stelmaszewska et al. [19] propose combining multiple mobile device displays to compose one larger one screen or display. This allows simultaneous viewing, point-and-tell, a common focus, and adds screen real estate.

Most of the systems exploring this approach make use of some sort of multi-device interaction as we have discussed earlier. Systems such as *Phone as a Pixel* [17] and *Junkyard Jumbotron* [15] use camera infrastructure to assess the geometry of individual devices being used, and then use this information to split a shared into smaller sections that are then transferred to and displayed on the appropriate device. However, as the approaches suggested by Schmidt et al. [16] and Greaves and Rukzio [7], this approach is somewhat cumbersome due to the need for extra hardware infrastructure besides people's individual mobile devices.

Taking a different approach, as mentioned earlier, *Pass-Them-Around* [11] is a collocated photo sharing application that allows viewing on composite display surfaces without the need for additional hardware. In this system, up to four devices can be made into one larger display by placing them side-by-side and connecting them using a pinching gesture across two devices. The use of this system has been studied extensively, in a controlled environment, involving different tasks of storytelling and reminiscing, and with very promising results. Similarly, the Pinch system [14] also allows collocated photo sharing on a composite display surface made up by several devices, in this case in arbitrary geometrical configurations, and also using the pinching gesture to configure the layout.

Opportunities for Design and Research

Based on related research we see a number of opportunities for exploring multi-device applications for collocated photo sharing. Firstly, we need additional studies on multi-device interaction in different application domains to explore and understand opportunities and limitations of interacting with several devices at the same time. As part of this exploration, we would like to facilitate flexible physical side-by-side device positioning, as seen in Junkyard Jumbotron [15], but using more simple interaction mechanisms for aligning and connecting devices without external hardware. Secondly, for collocated photo sharing on multiple devices, we would like to explore what happens when allowing partial viewing of photos. Rather than including as much of a photo as possible on a sometimes odd-shaped shared display canvas by zooming out and adding white space (as seen in Pass-Them-Around [14]), we would like to see what happens when photos always fill the canvas, and thereby removing parts of the photo.

JUXTAPINCH

JuxtaPinch is an application that supports collocated photo sharing and exploration on multiple handheld and mobile devices. JuxtaPinch combines ***juxtapositioning***, which is the act of positioning objects (i.e. devices) side-by-side, and ***pinching***, which is the act of stitching devices together. The basic idea of JuxtaPinch is that photos from one device can shown across multiple devices as illustrated in figure 1, by connecting them through the act of pinching (and removing through lifting and moving of devices).

We employ cross-device pinching as a simple and intuitive interaction technique as Otha and Tanaka argue that cross-device pinching resembles the action of stitching something together [14]. Lucero et al [11] also found that the pinch technique to be natural for connecting devices. JuxtaPinch combines the screens of several devices to appear as one. This means that a photo shown on the system will extend over a multitude of devices. We would like to stress that it is not our purpose to investigate issues of effectiveness or efficiency of the pinching interaction technique nor is it the purpose to understand basic usability of the JuxtaPinch application. Instead, we wish to investigate opportunities and challenges of multi-device interaction in the domain of sharing photos with others, and we want to explore how people experience their own photos when shown across several devices.

Functionality

JuxtaPinch basically offers three different functionalities for exploring photos over several mobile and handheld devices namely selecting a new photo, connecting devices, and disconnecting devices.

JuxtaPinch allows the users to select photos among the photos stored in the library on the device. Users can access the gallery of their device and choose any photo from it. When a new photo has been chosen, all connected devices will disconnect such that the system provides a clean screen to build the new photo.

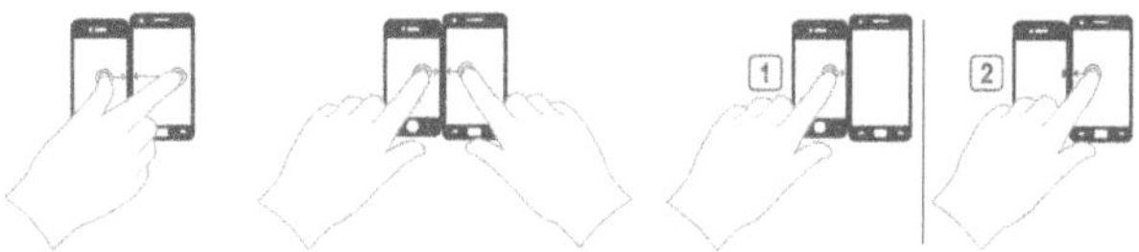

Figure 2. The three pinching techniques in JuxtaPinch for connecting devices: one-hand pinching (left), two-hand pinching (middle), and two-step pinching (right)

JuxtaPinch allows three cross-device pinching techniques to connect devices: One-hand pinching, two-hand pinching, and two-step pinching. Inspired by Otha and Tanaka [14], we implemented one-hand pinching where users typically use their thumb and index finger on the two devices. The user then slides the fingers towards each other to connect

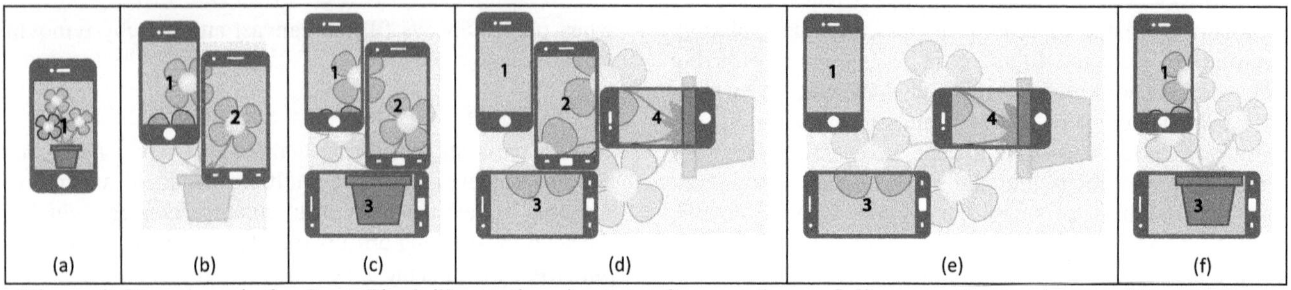

Figure 3. Use scenario for JuxtaPinch illustrating six steps of connecting and disconnecting devices – with up to four different devices and rotation and scaling of the photo

the devices at the adjoining edges (as illustrated in figure 2, left). Two-hand pinching inspired by Lucero et al [11] uses two hands. Here the users typically uses index fingers on both devices and slides them towards each other (see figure 2, middle). Finally, we developed a two-step pinching technique during the testing phase of JuxtaPinch. Here the user slides his index finger to the edge of one device and then afterwards to the edge of the other device (as shown in figure 2, right).

JuxtaPinch allows the user to use all the above pinching techniques for the sake of flexibility in the interaction. We also chose to allow all three pinching techniques because we were not interested in assessing or comparing these individual techniques (for such studies please refer to [11, 14]). Finally, JuxtaPinch permits users to remove and reposition devices when exploring photos. In order to reposition (or remove) a device, the user simply moves or lifts the device. Inspired by the repositioning in Otha and Tanaka [14], we utilize the accelerometer and gyroscope to detect movement as it is recognized as both tilting the device from side-to-side or top-to-bottom as well as acceleration on all axes.

Implementation

We implemented JuxtaPinch as a web application enabling cross platform interaction through the use of browsers. The client was implemented in HTML5 and we developed Android and iOS wrappers to let the users experience the system as a full application. However it is also possible to use the system directly from a web browser. JuxtaPinch was implemented using the socket.io library for a Node.js websocket server. The accelerometer and gyroscope was used to detect when devices were being moved around in order to disconnect the moved device from the photo, i.e. a detected acceleration above zero or tilting the device more than 10 degrees would disconnect the device. The Hammer.js library was used for detecting swipe, drag, and hold gestures.

We implemented pinching as swiping or dragging on two devices in opposite directions. When swipes (or drags) are detected on two devices, we then collect device data on screen size, resolution, pinch location, and pinch direction using JavaScript. We use the four-step algorithm from Ohta and Tanaka [14] to calculate the relative positions of the devices according to the following: 1) we position screens from the two devices (A and B) as overlapping completely, 2) afterwards we move screen B by the distance between swipe A's location and center position of screen A, 3) then we rotate screen B by the difference of the two devices' directions, and 4) finally we move screen B further by the distance between the location of the swipe on screen B and the center position of screen B (please refer to [14] for further explanation of this algorithm). Finally, from the calculated positions and sizes, we calculate the joined size of all connected devices that make up the viewing display. The relation between the size of the viewing display and the size of the photo is then used to determine the photo scaling and rotation.

Use Scenario

We exemplify how JuxtaPinch operates in the following use scenario and also visualized in figure 3. The scenario shows a photo of flowers in a pot where up to four devices (mobile phones) are used in different configurations.

Alice wants to share a photo of a flower to her friend Bob while being collocated. At first, the photo is on her device only (#1) (figure 3a). Bob then connects his device through pinch and the photo is now shown on two devices (#1 and #2) but only partially as parts of the photo is now hidden (b). They then connect a third device (#3), which shows the lower part of the photo (c). Alice wants to show Bob a detail in the photo and connects a fourth device to make the photo bigger (#4 is pinched together with #2). As a result of adding device #4 the joint canvas is now longer horizontally than vertically and therefore the photo is rotated 90 degrees (d). Bob wants to tease Alice, so he removes device #2 from the configuration, which creates a hole between the devices, as they are no longer positioned side-by-side (e). Finally Alice removes devices #4 making the photo smaller rotating it 90 degrees (f).

EVALUATION

We evaluated JuxtaPinch in a lab evaluation. Our aim was to explore how people would interact with JuxtaPinch as a multi-device application and it supported collocated photo sharing. In particular we were interested in investigating the three opportunities raised earlier in the paper on flexible physical positioning of devices, partial viewing of digital photos, and multi-device collocated photo sharing that works across different mobile operating systems.

Participants

22 people (6 females) participated in the lab condition in six different groups. The participants were between 21 and 49 years old (M=27.6) and they had different backgrounds including 12 university students, two high school students, and eight work professionals. We recruited participants through Facebook, our extended network, and snowball sampling. Participants were required to use their own devices (mobile phones or tablets) during the evaluation with either iOS version 6.0 or later or Android version 4.0 or later.

Our participants participated as groups (six groups in total) and we included four groups with four participants and two groups with three participants. As suggested by Miller and Edwards [13] and Stelmaszewska et al. [19] who report that people primarily share photos within their social network, we required that participants knew each other in advance, for example work colleagues, family, roommates, and friends. We furthermore required that they were able to bring at least one photo from a joint event, for example a holiday or attending a party together.

Procedure

The lab evaluation was conducted in the usability lab at Aalborg University in Denmark. The lab allowed us to video record the tests for later analysis. The evaluation consisted of six sessions – one session with each of the six groups of participants. The three or four group participants arrived at the lab facilities together. All participants were required to bring at least one personal device – typically their mobile phone, but some brought tablets as well. The evaluation was conducted around a high table without chairs allowing the participants to freely move around while interacting with JuxtaPinch and the mobile devices.

Participants were asked to bring at least one personal photo that would enable them to tell a story about the photo, i.e. story telling according to Van House [20], and one photo that could support a conversation between the group members, i.e. reminiscing Van House [20]. This could be a photo from a shared group event where all participants were present. The photos had to be stored on their own device, which allowed JuxtaPinch to access the photos during the test. Since they brought their own devices, the sessions featured different combinations of devices ranging from a session where all participants brought their own smartphone to a session where all three participants brought both a smartphone and a tablet.

Each session consisted of four parts and the session would last approximately one hour. First, we gave an introduction to JuxtaPinch (approx. 10 minutes) where we introduced the overall idea behind the application and gave a quick tour of the functionality with a particular focus on the implemented pinching techniques and how to connect and disconnect the devices. Participants were then allowed to try out JuxtaPinch to get comfortable with using the application and the pinching techniques. Secondly, the actual evaluation started where participants were asked to share their own photos with each other (approx. 20 minutes). They were asked to talk about and discuss their photos (both the story telling and reminiscing photos). They could freely choose the order among the members of the group. Thirdly, we gave them five devices (two Samsung Galaxy SII, one iPad 3, one Nexus 7 and one Acer Iconia Tab A200) to enable further exploration of the photos. Participants were then told to play and interact with the system and freely choose any photos from their devices (approx. 10 minutes). Fourthly, we had a debriefing session where we had them to fill out an AttrakDiff questionnaire and we conducted a semi-structured interview (approx. 20 minutes). The interview consisted of a set of open-ended questions. The goal of the interview was to understand personal experiences the participants had during the session. Also, we wanted to ask into their relationships to each other, to their photos and to their own versus other's versus public devices.

Figure 4. JuxtaPinch in use from two of our lab evaluations where participants are connecting and disconnecting mobile phones and tablets.

Data Collection and Analysis

We automatically logged the number of viewed photos (from the different devices), the number and type of pinches (connects), and the number of movements (disconnects) during our evaluation. The recorded video sessions from the evaluation were divided into smaller segments containing interaction with one single photo. We then analyzed these video segments from a quantitative point view where we identified pinch techniques (which one of the three pinching techniques), movement of devices and whether participants moved their own device, another persons device, or a public (shared) device.

Interviews were transcribed and afterwards analyzed by grouping answers for each of the 23 questions from the interview guideline. Homogeneous answers were color-coded to emphasize repeated answers. We used inductive analysis to analyze the qualitative data. Through repeated assessment of the interviews and viewing of the videos, we identified a number of topics and themes.

FINDINGS

In the following, we present findings from the evaluation of JuxtaPinch. We have identified themes evolving around the use and application of JuxtaPinch as a multi-device system that supports collocated photo sharing. Participants have been renamed for anonymity.

Organizing Multi-Device Interaction in Groups

The inherent collaborative nature of using multiple devices in groups was tackled in several ways. Here we observed different collaboration behavior between the six groups during the first part of the lab sessions (where they viewed and explored photos using only own devices). As an example, participants in one of the groups took turn when interacting with JuxtaPinch and the devices. Here the photo owner would control and organize the session. Other groups employed a more chaotic process where participants would all attempt to connect and disconnect at the same time resulting in application errors. As third example of how collocated photo sharing took place, we saw one group where all participants brought their own mobile phones and they shared one tablet. In this evaluation session, the tablet primarily served as a stationary or fixed-place device left in the same spot during the whole session and the participants would only connect and disconnect their mobile phones, i.e. they would only move these devices.

Considering the interactions made, we found 871 pinches and 583 device movements were made. We counted and classified all pinches made in the six lab sessions and the single most used pinch technique was one-hand pinch with 55.6%, followed by the two-step pinch 34.9%, and two-hand pinches with 9.5%. We observed that some groups would employ the same pinching technique again and again throughout an entire evaluation session, as an illustrative example we saw one group that used the two-step pinch 96.4% of the time during their session, while another group used the one-hand pinch 93.6% of the time, and finally a third group used the two-step pinch 88.9% of the time. Furthermore, we also observed that participants would move mobile phones more often than tablets (64% of the movements).

Our participant argued that they found it unproblematic to interact with other participants' devices, but perhaps more surprisingly they also found it unproblematic that the other participants interacted with their personal device. Lucero et al. [11] made a similar observation, but their participants used handed-out mobile phones and not their own phones. All participants expressed that they did not think of this during the session and some of them further articulated that they experienced the situation and environment as safe involving people they knew and trusted and this made the sharing of devices uncomplicated. While these statements point in one direction, our analysis of the interaction with the devices shows that 66.3% of the pinches (connects) was made on own devices and 53.8% of the movements (disconnects) were made with own devices.

Using Devices to Create Irregular Viewing Shapes

As argued above, we deliberately designed JuxtaPinch to support flexible viewing configurations where users can create various shapes using the devices – as opposed to, for example, the application *Pass-Them-Around* [11] that solely enables rectangular viewing canvas. This feature of JuxtaPinch led to different kinds of photo explorations and encouraged playfulness.

We observed that several groups started their sessions by creating rectangular viewing area in attempt to simulate a larger screen where they were able view the whole photo. Most groups would actually try to imitate a rectangular screen as much as possible for the first couple of photos. Some groups would keep constructing rectangular shapes throughout their entire session and one of the groups even repositioned the devices beforehand to display as much of the photo as possible, as this example illustrates. Before selecting his photo the owner, Hans, said: "*Now we want to try something else, because this is a tall photo*" and he restructured all the devices. *"Now you are making it wide?"* Walter asked and he responded: *"Yes, it is on purpose. The photo is long and tall"* as he pinched all devices together. However, he had to disconnect and re-connect one device to ensure that the whole photo could be seen correctly on all the included devices.

Opposed to the above, some participants started creating more irregular shapes of their photos. Here they utilized the opportunity for flexible positioning in JuxtaPinch to shape irregularly viewing displays as the example in figure 7, right or photo in figure 5, left where participants created a partial view to show a beer bong. We found that JuxtaPinch sometimes encouraged playfulness when exploring photos. This was visible in more ways namely to show specific parts, to hide specific parts, and to create funny views.

Figure 5. Using JuxtaPinch to create partial views of photos (left) and to create playful situation where people are "removed" from the photo

Playfulness

Our participants would occasionally use the multitude of device to create playful situations where they intentionally played with the photos to create funny layouts. Five of the six lab groups used the flexibility of positioning devices in JuxtaPinch to create funny views, i.e. devices were positioned to make a face span across two devices, which created funny optical illusions due to the gap between the actual screens. As an example of the creation of a funny view, Zoe, a female participant, mentioned that by positioning the devices in different ways, she was able to split the photo in ways, which made it humorous to look at. *"In an old photo I have a 1000Kr. bill in my mouth I could [by repositioning] get the bill to be on one device and my face to be on another, which was quite funny to look at".*

Several participants discovered (some of them by chance) that if they carefully moved the devices around, they would not detach from the photo (disconnect) as they would not activate the disconnect functionality (e.g. tilting over 10 degrees or acceleration). Thus, participants were then able to carefully rearrange devices, for example to switch bodies or heads of two people. Also, "incorrectly" pinching with a device not positioned to the edge of it, meant that the photo would be showed more like a swap-tile puzzle.

Other groups used the flexible positioning of JuxtaPinch to reconfigure the viewing display repeatedly. One of our lab groups would constantly change positions of the devices to either display other parts of the photo or hide parts that were currently visible. This was a family (mother, daughter, and son in law) who were looking at a photo from a family vacation and the photo included several family members. As they played with the photo, a new family member appeared on the display several times, which is illustrated in the following example: *"well, that was lovely! [ironic] Now Trudy is in the photo again. That was not the plan" the son in law argued and he quickly repositioned the device "There we go! Much better! Now I am in focus!"* For several photos, this group of participants kept repositioning devices to hide certain parts and to highlight other parts. A similar situation of playfulness occurred in another lab groups where they removed the father from the other devices while exploring and discussing the photo (as illustrated in figure 5).

Defamiliarization through Multi-Devices

Our evaluation showed that several participants experienced their own familiar photos in new ways – sometimes referred to as defamiliarization. Shklovsky [18] originally proposed the concept of defamiliarization in 1917 as a technique for presenting something familiar in an unfamiliar or "strange" way. Our evaluation showed that some participants would uncover new details of an otherwise familiar photo while using JuxtaPinch. Originally, Shklovsky used the term to illustrate how art could defamiliarize [18], but recently we have seen how defamiliarization can been applied within HCI [2, 9].

We identified defamiliarization in several situations as it occurred during our lab evaluations. Actually, all six groups experienced aspects of defamiliarization where familiar photos were experienced in new and sometimes surprising ways. Defamiliarization typically occurred unintentionally when participants were connecting and disconnecting their devices. Usually our participants would discover details that they had never seen or noticed before. For example, some discovered a lamppost on a photo of a bike trail and made comments on that and explored the photo even further, while another group learned that a specific football club was 50 years old as they noticed details on a birthday cake. In both situations the participants had never noticed these details before.

We observed characteristics of defamiliarization in three different but somewhat related ways – we refer to these as defamiliarization through segregation, through scaling, and through hiding. These will be explained and illustrated in the following.

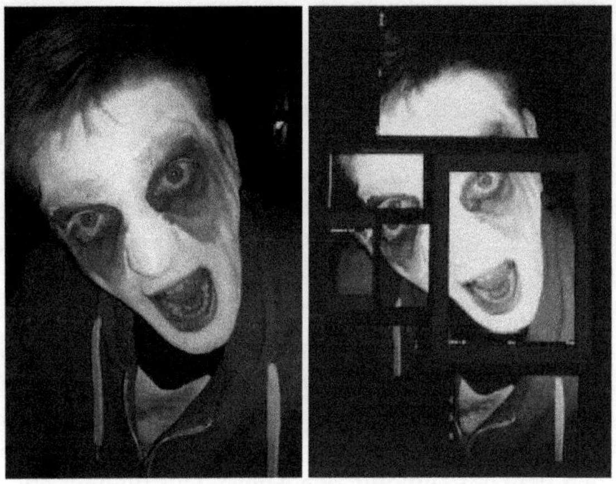

Figure 6. Situation where defamiliarization through segregation was experienced with a photo of a person wearing a t-shirt with a Nicki Minaj print.

Defamiliarization through segregation happened when parts of a photo was segregated (or isolated) on one single device such that particular details would stand more out and thus be emphasized by the isolation and framing of the device. One group (with student participants) viewed and explored a photo from their group room at the university; suddenly one of them discovered that one group member was looking at his Facebook-page in the photo, as this part of the photo was isolated on one device. Another group was viewing and exploring the photo illustrated in figure 6 (left) on multiple devices. They were discussing and talking about the photo (which is a little spooky and unusual) when suddenly one of the group participants, Carl, asked, *"What is that"*, pointing to a specific part of the shirt of the person in the photo (figure 6, lower right). Parts of the t-shirt had been isolated or segregated on one device and the image on this device looked strange by itself (as illustrated in figure 6, lower right). The other participants from the group looked closer at the photo on the device and after a short period of time, Oscar, the photo owner said *"Aaah, it's a t-shirt with a Nicki Minaj print on it. Because it is black outside the print [points at the black spot and the print], it looks as if he has cleavage" The rest of group started laughing and one of them said "It looks very weird".*

This particular element of the photo, and the interpretation of it, had never been experienced by the owner of the photo before. The participants elaborated this during the interview, for example Carl stating, *"it [JuxtaPinch] was brilliant for experiencing new details in a photo you already know, because they suddenly appear on a single screen"*. The photo owner, Oscar, further elaborated this, stating, *"for instance, Dave's t-shirt – I never noticed before that it really looked weird"*. This particular situation illustrated how defamiliarization through segregation occurred when using JuxtaPinch. One could argue that the t-shirt was not the main objective of the photo and the isolation of parts of the photo on individual device screens empathized other qualities of the photo.

Defamiliarization through scaling happened as participants used multiple devices to view a photo and the scaling of the photo would occasionally magnify and thus highlight new details in the photo. As an example, one participant, Victor, was showing a photo of an ambulance bus. Suddenly, they noticed a new detail on the bus indicating defamiliarization through scaling (but also through segregation). Victor explained the experience as *"Suddenly, someone noticed that you could read the full technical specification on the right front wheel of the bus ... these small details would normally disappear in the entirety but they are suddenly visible"*. The group noticed the technical specification of the bus, which they had never seen before. However, as it was now isolated on one screen and scaled compared to viewing the photo on only one device. Our findings suggest that randomness can be used to incite defamiliarization, which is in agreement with Leong et al. [9] who used randomness to provoke defamiliarization in photos.

Figure 7. Defamiliarization through hiding (on the left) where participants noticed details in the photo when the kayak was not visible on any device, and on the right a situation where participants created irregular photo shapes through flexible positioning of devices

Finally, defamiliarization through hiding happened when participants on purpose or accidently hid the primary element of a photo, and thereby caused other elements to become more notable or emphasized. As an example, we observed a group looking at a photo of a kayak at sea (figure 7, left). Since the kayak was so dominant (due to its placement and color), other parts of the photo were not noticed at first. However, when this part of the photo was left out, the group experienced it in a new way, and suddenly noticed new details on the shore behind it.

AttrakDiff Questionnaire

The result of the AttrakDiff questionnaire showed that JuxtaPinch scored above average in both Hedonic Quality - Stimulation (HQ-S) and Attractiveness (ATT). Above-average on HQ-S means that JuxtaPinch stimulates the users, awakens curiosity and motivates the users. Words such as inventive, creative and captivating are rated high by the users to describe JuxtaPinch in terms of HQ-S. Above-average on ATT means that the overall impression of the product is very attractive.

DISCUSSION

We investigated multi-device interaction through the design of JuxtaPinch an application that allows sharing of photos across multiple devices. JuxtaPinch allow partial viewing of photos, which seemed to stimulate our study participants to create irregular viewing canvases with their devices and this led to defamiliarization where participants experienced new details in familiar photos or experienced details in new and different ways. Extending previous research on collocated photo sharing, our findings illustrate that the combination of multiple devices do not equal the same experience as a bigger screen. It creates new experiences and interactions. We found that the opportunity for flexible configurations of devices encouraged playful sharing of photos where our participants would intentionally attempt to create funny situations in the photos. While the insights on multi-device interaction constitute one key contribution of the paper, the unique features of JuxtaPinch also formed basis for some additional themes that constitute a second contribution of the paper. These are discussed in the following.

Creative Device Configurations

As illustrated above, the partial viewing of photos enabled by JuxtaPinch led to creative exploration where our users configured their devices in many ways. During this, they arranged the devices in rather irregular configurations.

Lucero et al. [11] designed their application differently as they deliberately chose configurations where devices were strictly aligned either as 2x1, 3x1, 2x1x1, or 2x2. While this removes some of the complexity of calculating photo presentation, as basic assumptions can be made about devices aligned side-by-side, it also prevents users from applying devices of different sizes. We observed that users particularly welcomed this type of challenge of putting their devices together in unconventional ways in order to obtain a particular result, for example showing specific parts of a photo, or leaving a particular part out. Because the system scale and rotate the photo continuously when devices are added, moved, or removed, this was a highly social and interactive activity, which appeared to challenge the users akin to solving a puzzle together. Thus, they engaged more actively with each other and with the shared photo.

Using Different Kinds of Devices

JuxtaPinch supports an extensive range of mobile devices, i.e. smartphones and tablets (and more operating systems), to enable more realistic use. As illustrated in our findings, the effects of using different devices contributed positively to aspects of defamiliarization and participants experienced photos in new and sometimes more interesting ways.

Lucero et al. [11] stress that the flexibility of devices may introduce challenges when trying to combine devices with very different properties and physical form factors. This was confirmed in our study. We observed three factors of device difference that influenced people's interactions and use: different display qualities, different size frames/bezels, and varying screen sizes and aspect ratios. Variance in display quality included properties such as brightness, contrast, and colors, making individual parts of photos appear different when distributed over several devices. This would, for example, sometimes made it difficult for people to see if two displays were pinched together correctly. Variance in frame/bezel size happened very often when devices of different make were pinched together. This sometimes caused the composite photo to appear distorted, for example, making a head look taller if spanning two devices. In response to this effect, some participants suggested omitting the part of the photo that would sit "behind" the area with no display, but others expressed concerns that this would make parts of the photos impossible to see. Finally, variance in screen sizes and aspect ratios caused participants to interact with devices differently. Here, we observed a tendency towards placing larger devices (tablets) stationary in the middle of the table, while moving smaller devices (Smartphones) around more frequently, like satellites.

Sharing Your Own Device

Another unique feature of JuxtaPinch was the possibility for our test participants to use their own mobile devices. We did this so that the social interaction would not be impeded by different preferences for operating systems, and also to investigate further the questions raised by Lucero et al. [11] and Stelmaszewska et al. [19] about people's comfort with using someone else's personal mobile devices, and letting others use theirs.

Our findings somewhat confirm those in Lucero et al. [11] that people are generally willing to share their own device with others, but with the added detail that this is more likely accepted with *familiar people* and not so much with strangers. This observation confirm those in [19] where it was reported that digital photo sharing rarely involves strangers, as people generally do not trust unfamiliar people with their own mobile devices or digital content. Adding to this, we often observed that people who had stated that sharing their own device, and using someone else's, was not a problem, in reality in fact kept mostly to their own.

Multi-Device Interaction: Other Use Applications

While we have explored collocated photo sharing as one potential area for multi-device interaction, our work points potentially a number of other applications of multi-platform interaction that may be useful and explored further. We saw that our participants used JuxtaPinch to hide parts of the photo when they were trying to focus on selected elements in a photo. Such hiding could potentially inform other kinds of applications, for example, when planning a route on a map or inspecting building blue prints. Secondly, an increasing number of digital games are utilizing several devices to support the game play, for example, card games and racing games where some devices are used as controllers while others (usually a tablet) is used a the shared gaming space.

CONCLUSION

We have implemented and evaluated JuxtaPinch, which is an application for flexible multi device collocated photo sharing. JuxtaPinch supports a wide range of devices through the use of web technologies. The application allows users to combine several mobile device displays to form a larger display area for joint sharing and viewing of photos. JuxtaPinch will scale and rotate the photos to show as much of a photo as possible.

Our evaluation suggested that our participants experienced their own familiar photos in new ways also known as defamiliarization where we identified three causes namely segregation, scaling, and hiding. We also found that JuxtaPinch would encourage participants to play with their photos where they created new views and re-composed photos by moving the different devices around. Participants expressed no direct concerns about sharing their personal mobile device with other participants (in this case friends, family members or work colleagues), but we also found that our participants would predominantly interact with and move their own devices.

Our work with JuxtaPinch proposes a number of avenues for future work. First, we need to further investigate how to control the interaction and synchronization for a multiple device collocated photo-sharing application. We identified situations where JuxtaPinch had to be restarted, as our users simultaneously attempted to connect or disconnect devices. Part of this can be explained by the prototypical nature of our implementation of JuxtaPinch, but some problems were also a result of the simultaneous and collaborative nature of use. Secondly, using pinching (or other techniques) for multiple device interaction could be further investigated for other applications within collaboration or social interaction. It could, for example, be interesting to explore how different pinching techniques can be used for collaborative technologies using large interactive displays or boards in connection with small handheld devices such as mobile phones or tablets.

ACKNOWLEDGMENTS
We would like to thank several anonymous reviewers for comments on previous versions of the paper and also the participants in our evaluations.

REFERENCES
1. Ah Kun, L. M., and Marsden, G. Co-present photo sharing on mobile devices. In *Proceedings of the 9th international conference on Human computer interaction with mobile devices and services*, MobileHCI '07, ACM (New York, NY, USA, 2007), 277–284.
2. Bell, G., Blythe, M., and Sengers, P. Making by making strange: Defamiliarization and the design of domestic technologies. *ACM Trans. Comput.-Hum. Interact. 12*, 2 (June 2005), 149–173.
3. Boring, S., Jurmu, M., and Butz, A. Scroll, tilt or move it: using mobile phones to continuously control pointers on large public displays. In *Proceedings of the 21st Annual Conference of the Australian Computer-Human Interaction Special Interest Group: Design: Open 24/7, OZCHI '09*, ACM (New York, USA, 2009), 161–168
4. Chen, X. A., Grossman, T., Wigdor, D. J., and Firzmaurice, G. Duet: exploring joint interactions on a smart phone and a smart watch. In *Proceedings of the Human Factors in Computing Systems (CHI'14), ACM,* (Toronto, Canada, 2014) *159-168*
5. Fails, J. A., Druin, A., and Guha, M. L. Content splitting & space sharing: collaboratively reading & sharing children's stories on mobile devices. In *Proceedings of the 13th International Conference on Human Computer Interaction with Mobile Devices and Services*, MobileHCI '11, ACM (New York, NY, USA, 2011), 361–370.
6. Frohlich, D., Kuchinsky, A., Pering, C., Don, A., and Ariss, S. Requirements for photoware. In *Proceedings of the 2002 ACM conference on Computer supported cooperative work*, CSCW '02, ACM (New York, NY, USA, 2002), 166–175.
7. Greaves, A., and Rukzio, E. View & share: supporting co-present viewing and sharing of media using personal projection. In *Proceedings of the 11th International Conference on Human-Computer Interaction with Mobile Devices and Services*, MobileHCI '09, ACM (New York, NY, USA, 2009), 44:1–44:4.
8. Kindberg, T., Spasojevic, M., Fleck, R., and Sellen, A. The ubiquitous camera: An in-depth study of camera phone use. *IEEE Pervasive Computing 4*, 2 (Apr. 2005), 42–50.
9. Leong, T. W., Harper, R., and Regan, T. Nudging towards serendipity: a case with personal digital photos. In *Proceedings of the 25th BCS Conference on Human-Computer Interaction*, BCS-HCI '11, British Computer Society (Swinton, UK, UK, 2011), 385–394.
10. Lindley, S., and Monk, A. Designing appropriate affordances for electronic photo sharing media. In *CHI '06 Extended Abstracts on Human Factors in Computing Systems*, CHI EA '06, ACM (New York, NY, USA, 2006), 1031–1036.
11. Lucero, A., Holopainen, J., and Jokela, T. Pass-them-around: collaborative use of mobile phones for photo sharing. In *Proceedings of the SIGCHI Conference on Human Factors in Computing Systems*, CHI '11, ACM (New York, NY, USA, 2011), 1787–1796.
12. Miller, A. D., and Edwards, W. K. Give and take: a study of consumer photo-sharing culture and practice. In *Proceedings of the SIGCHI Conference on Human Factors in Computing Systems*, CHI '07, ACM (New York, NY, USA, 2007), 347–356.
13. Marquardt, N., Hinckley, K., and Greenberg, S. Cross-device interaction via micro-mobility and f-formations. In Proceedings of the 25th annual ACM 10 symposium on User interface software and technology, UIST '12, ACM (New York, NY, USA, 2012), 13–22.
14. Ohta, T., and Tanaka, J. Pinch: An interface that relates applications on multiple touch-screen by pinching gesture. In *Advances in Computer Entertainment*, A. Nijholt, T. Romo, and D. Reidsma, Eds., vol. 7624 of *Lecture Notes in Computer Science*. Springer Berlin Heidelberg, 2012, 320–335.
15. Rick, B., and Brian, K. Junkyard jumbotron. http://jumbotron.media.mit.edu/, June 2011.
16. Schmidt, D., Chehimi, F., Rukzio, E., and Gellersen, H. Phonetouch: a technique for direct phone interaction on surfaces. In *Proceedings of the 23nd annual ACM symposium on User interface software and technology*, UIST '10, ACM (New York, NY, USA, 2010), 13–16.
17. Schwarz, J., Klionsky, D., Harrison, C., Dietz, P., and Wilson, A. Phone as a pixel: enabling ad-hoc, large-scale displays using mobile devices. In *Proceedings of the 2012 ACM annual conference on Human Factors in Computing Systems*, CHI '12, ACM (New York, NY, USA, 2012), 2235–2238.
18. Shklovsky, V. Art as technique. In *Contemporary Literary Criticism: Modernism through Poststructuralism*, R. C. Davis, Ed., Longman (1917).
19. Stelmaszewska, H., Fields, B., and Blandford, A. The roles of time, place, value and relationships in collocated photo sharing with camera phones. In *Proceedings of the 22nd British HCI Group Annual Conference,* Volume 1, BCS-HCI '08, British Computer Society (Swinton, UK, UK, 2008), 141–150.
20. Van House, N. A. Collocated photo sharing, story-telling, and the performance of self. *Int. J. Hum.-Comput. Stud. 67*, 12 (Dec. 2009), 1073–1086.

Are You Comfortable Doing That?: Acceptance Studies of Around-Device Gestures in and for Public Settings

David Ahlström[1], Khalad Hasan[2], Pourang Irani[2]

[1]Alpen-Adria-Universität Klagenfurt
Klagenfurt, Austria
david.ahlstroem@aau.at

[2]University of Manitoba
Winnipeg, Manitoba, Canada
{khalad, irani}@cs.umanitoba.ca

ABSTRACT

Several research groups have demonstrated advantages of extending a mobile device's input vocabulary with in-air gestures. Such gestures show promise but are not yet being integrated onto commercial devices. One reason for this might be the uncertainty about users' perceptions regarding the social acceptance of such around-device gestures. In three studies, performed in public settings, we explore users' and spectators' attitudes about using around-device gestures in public. The results show that people are concerned about others' reactions. They are also sensitive and selective regarding where and in front of whom they would feel comfortable using around-device gestures. However, acceptance and comfort are strongly linked to gesture characteristics, such as, gesture size, duration and in-air position. Based on our findings we present recommendations for around-device input designers and suggest new approaches for evaluating the social acceptability of novel input methods.

Author Keywords

Around-Device Input; User Acceptance; Gesture Design.

ACM Classification Keywords

H.5.2. Information interfaces and presentation (e.g., HCI): User Interfaces.

INTRODUCTION

Hardware and software advances in motion sensing technology have compelled researchers to demonstrate the rich potential of interactions that can take place in the air around a mobile device. Such 'Around Device' (AD) interactions has been shown to facilitate input on very small devices such as wristwatches [5], can be used to extend the input vocabulary of mobile phones [8, 10], minimize the likelihood of occluding the screen with the input hand [1] and were shown to be more efficient for search and retrieval tasks in analytic settings [6]. Commercial devices (e.g., Samsung Galaxy S4), inspired by such work, are enabling AD-interactions such as scrolling by swiping the hand above the screen. However, commercial advances are still limited.

While several user studies [1, 6, 7, 10, 19] performed in laboratory settings have shown the potential and benefits of AD-input in a number of tasks, little is known about users' attitudes and comfort levels using these innovative interactions. Particularly when performed in a public setting hand movements and finger gestures around the device may attract by-passers' undesired attention or intrude into areas 'owned' by others (e.g., when sitting on a bus), and thus may evoke feelings such as embarrassment or discomfort. Accordingly, the acceptance and willingness to perform AD-gestures may be limited to certain settings. This speculation is supported by previous studies [13, 14, 17, 18] on device-based gestures (e.g., swinging or tilting the device) and body-based gestures (e.g., a wrist rotation, nods, or foot taps) for mobile phone interaction. These studies have demonstrated that users are indeed very concerned about others' reactions and that users are sensitive and selective regarding where and in front of whom they would use such gestures.

These prior studies, however, classify gestures as either being acceptable or not. In contrast, we hypothesize that gestures and AD-interactions – the focus of this paper – belong to an acceptability-continuum and that various gesture properties influence acceptance differently. Research has not teased out or studied what gesture properties, and specifically AD-features, could lead to higher acceptance and thus lead to quicker adoption of this emerging interaction style. In this paper, we take a first step in this direction. We explore how socially comfortable (we term this as *comfortable* throughout the remainder of the paper) users feel when performing AD-gestures in a public place. We also survey users for which locations and in front of whom they would feel comfortable using AD-interactions. In our first two studies we examine the influence of four fundamental AD-gesture features – the distance from the device, the position relative to the device, gesture size and gesture duration – on users' level of comfort. We further examine whether such perceptions are related to a user's introversion/extroversion personality trait. Finally, in a third study, we elicit opinions from people observing others using AD-gestures in public.

In this work we: i) identify how specific AD-gesture features influence user comfort and acceptance; ii) reveal

MobileHCI 2014, September 23–26, 2014, Toronto, ON, Canada.
Copyright © 2014 ACM 978-1-4503-3004-6/14/09…$15.00.
http://dx.doi.org/10.1145/2628363.2628381

that AD-gestures are perceived as equally acceptable by users with introversion or extroversion traits; and, iii) propose a set of recommendations to assist AD-interaction designers. A minor contribution also consists in proposing methodology improvements for future acceptability studies.

RELATED WORK AND MOTIVATION

Our research is motivated and inspired by the many applications for mobile devices made possible using sensing technology (e.g., magnetic and infrared sensors or cameras-based solutions) to detect in-air finger and hand movements. We first provide a brief overview of this work and then discuss previous studies that have investigated user acceptance of novel mobile interactions.

Previous work has demonstrated that AD-input can be used to facilitate many elementary interactions, such as button selection [5], menu navigation [1], pan and zoom [1, 7], and digit entry [8, 20]. Researchers have also shown how to capitalize on AD-space in more complex tasks or situations, including rotation of on-screen objects [1, 10], the operation of media players [9], for item search and retrieval in analytic settings [6], for cursor control on projector phones [19], and in mobile collaboration scenarios [16]. Most of these projects were focused on hardware solutions. Only a few projects have attended to the human factors involved when designing AD-interactions. Ens et al. [2] modeled user performance in off-screen target acquisition tasks and Jones et al. [7] examined user performance and preferences for multi-scale navigation in AD-space. Hasan et al. [6] proposed a framework consisting of numerous design parameters relevant to AD-interactions, such as the range for user input, suitable in-air target sizes, selection methods and techniques for placing and retrieving content in AD-space.

All of the above projects have studied AD-interactions in a lab setting and have focused on hardware solutions or user performance. The acceptance and users' comfort levels when performing these interactions have received very little attention. To our knowledge, only Jones et al. [7] and Kratz et al. [10] have, although only very briefly, considered how users would feel about using AD-interactions in a public setting. Jones et al. who compared various AD-methods for panning and zooming also asked their study participants how comfortable they would feel using the AD-methods in public places. Jones et al. report that although the enlarged interaction space provided by the AD-methods was valued, participants said they were less likely to use these in public settings. Similarly, Kratz et al. who studied AD-techniques for rotating on-screen objects found that participants were split regarding using these in public. These findings, together with recent studies [13, 14, 15, 17, 18] regarding users' concerns and feelings about performing body or device-based gestures in public settings – e.g., tapping the shoulder or shaking the phone to mute a call – warrant caution and further investigations. Probing user perceptions of novel AD-interactions could allow designers to rule out unwanted styles of input before they get implemented. What is needed is an understanding of how such interactions work in ecologically valid settings.

Ronkainen et al. [15] introduced the idea of studying social acceptance of gesture input on mobile devices. In an online survey they used short video clips of people performing different device-based gestures (e.g., swinging and slapping the device) for various tasks and in different settings (café, library, while walking). Participants were asked to decide and comment on whether they would use the featured gestures themselves. As participants were not explicitly instructed to consider the social setting in their responses Ronkainen et al. were surprised to find that roughly half of the participants mentioned context-related and social issues in their rationales when rejecting a gesture.

Rico and Brewster [14] expanded on this finding and studied how the social setting influences the acceptance of device-based and body-based gestures (e.g., tapping the nose, squeezing the forearm). Again, participants watched short video clips showing a person using the examined gestures while being alone in a room. From this, participants were asked to state where and in front of whom they would use the gestures themselves. Rico and Brewster found that participants were very sensitive and selective regarding the usage context: both locations (e.g., at home, on a sidewalk, in a café) and audience (e.g., colleagues, family, strangers) affected participants' willingness to use the gestures. In a follow-up, user reactions were elicited from eleven persons having performed some of the gestures both, in a private room and on a busy sidewalk. Most participants commented on how different they felt when performing the gestures in public, feeling uncomfortable and worrying about what others might think. Several participants also reported having felt somewhat less uncomfortable in later stages of the exercise. These findings demonstrate the potential limits of only letting participants imagine usage without having had a firsthand experience with strangers watching or being cognizant of their own behaviour.

Williamson et al. [17, 18] collected user experiences and insights from real-world usage situations. They asked participants to use a mobile phone application operated though body gestures (nods, rotating and shaking the wrist) as often as possible during a couple of days. The majority of registered usage situations took place in private while at home or in semi-private settings at work or when walking. Only a few participants decided to use the application during public transport. Many worried about what others would think and worked out strategies to appropriate or disguise the gestures in order to avoid attention from potential spectators. Williamson et al. also report that several participants noted a large, and unanticipated, difference between how they felt about 'transitory' and 'sustained' spectatorship (e.g., a person catching a glimpse of the interaction while walking by resp. a fellow passenger on a train that watches the interaction for a longer time).

Montero et al. [13] also used video clip demonstrations of device-based gestures. They asked participants to indicate on a scale from 'embarrassed' to 'comfortable' how they would feel performing the example gestures in a public place. Their results demonstrate that factors, such as gesture category, 'suspenseful' or 'magical', have an impact on the acceptability of device-based gestures. Interestingly, their results also show that early and late technology adopters perceive suspenseful gestures, those with a clear action that is easily seen by bystanders but without a noticeable outcome, as being less acceptable. These results could suggest that AD-gestures, which can be considered to be suspenseful, may not be accepted for public use.

In summary, previous work clearly demonstrates that people are very concerned about what others think and how they will react when observing them perform unusual interactions. Previous studies also show that people are sensitive and selective regarding which gestures they would feel comfortable with in various social settings. However, AD-gestures – as well as many body-based and device-based gestures – possess several attributes, such as area of input and duration that can affect comfort and acceptance. No prior study has explored whether and how user attitudes and acceptance vary depending on such features, a task necessary to refine and propose novel AD-interactions. We are also unaware of any prior work that examines the role of personality traits when investigating acceptance and user perceptions about gesture interfaces. In the next section we present three studies designed to provide initial insights regarding these open questions.

THREE ACCEPTABILITY STUDIES

With our first two studies we aim at clarifying how four elementary gesture-design factors influence users' acceptability of AD-gestures. In Study 1 we explore how users' comfort levels vary when they perform gestures in different regions around the device and at different distances from the device. We also explore whether users' perceptions about AD-gestures are related to extroversion personality traits. In Study 2 we focus on the size and duration of gestures and investigate how these parameters affect users' comfort. In Study 3 we switch to a spectator's point of view and examine peoples' reactions when having observed someone else using AD-gestures.

Compatible with our focus on general gesture-design factors, the involved gestures are simple and consist of 'drawing' one-digit numbers in the air around the device. Such abstract drawing-gestures are easy to perform, are context free and reduce the likelihood that participants' responses are influenced by any uncontrolled factors such as previous experiences, cultural background, and associations to interface tasks or functionality.

In our three studies we elicit participant impressions through questionnaires and use Rico and Brewster's [14] 'audience-and-location' axes to determine levels of "social acceptability". We ask participants to state in front of whom and in what locations they think they would feel comfortable using AD-gestures. To determine the influence of gesture parameters we ask participants to indicate how comfortable ('very comfortable', 'comfortable', 'neutral', 'uncomfortable', 'very uncomfortable') they felt when performing the gestures. We acknowledge that the central usage of the word 'comfort' in our questions may leave room for diverse and individual interpretations. However, we carefully instructed participants of the intended and desired interpretation and we explicitly asked participants to relate 'comfort' to social and mental aspects rather than physical ones. Furthermore, our terminology finds support in previous studies on social acceptance of gestures for mobile use [13, 14, 15, 17, 18] where both, authors and participants have used similar wordings. We also recognize that user acceptance is multifaceted and by far not limited to the perceived or expected levels of confidence and comfort [3].

In contrast to all prior studies on AD-input and the majority of earlier studies on user acceptance of gestures for mobile devices, our studies were conducted in public places. We believe this is important since it provides participants with firsthand usage experiences before making their judgements, unlike in video-based surveys where participants are asked to imagine future use and possible feelings.

Study 1 – Region and Distance

The first study was conducted in a shopping mall. Without being informed about the exact purpose of the study, the participant was asked to perform a set of AD-gestures in a busy entrance zone of the mall. The participant was standing and held the smartphone in the non-dominant hand at a natural viewing distance. A set of 45 images guided the participant through the study task. The images were viewed in full-screen size using the device's default image browser. Each image showed a position in the air around the device and a one-digit number to 'draw' at the indicated in-air position. Figure 1 (a and b) shows two example images.

As illustrated in Figure 1c, five different drawing regions were used: *Above* and *Below* the device, to the *Left* and to the *Right* of the device, and in *Front* of the device. Each region was divided in three distance ranges, measured from the device: *Close*, *Mid*, and *Far*. *Close* corresponds to the area 0 to 15cm away from the device, *Mid* to 15 to 30cm from the device, and *Far* to more than 30cm away from the

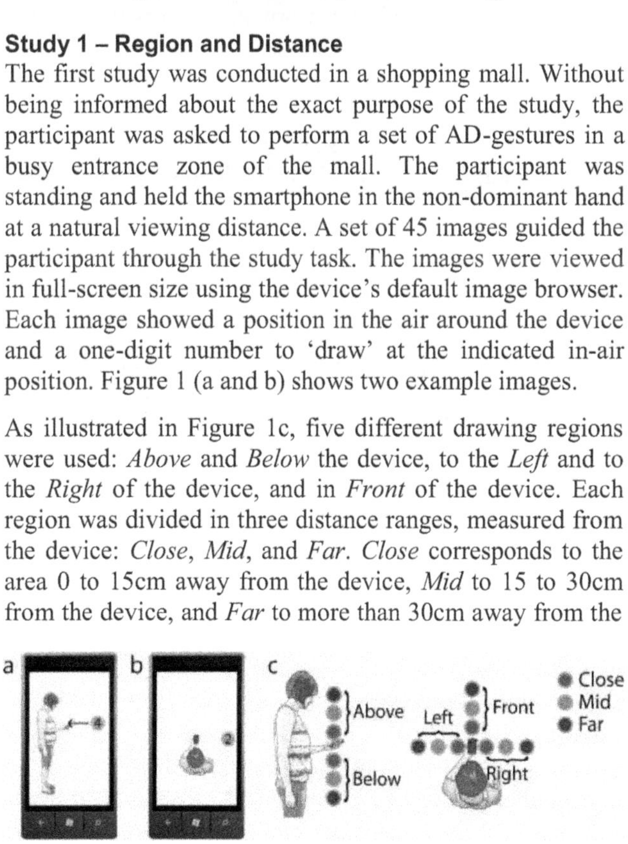

Figure 1. Example task prompts for (a) a gesture in the *Above* region at the *Close* distance and for (b) a gesture in the *Right* region at the *Far* distance. (c) Gesture distances and regions.

device. The furthest distance roughly corresponds to the maximum comfortable reaching range around a handheld device [6], which is also the border area between the 'intimate' and 'personal' space as defined in studies on proxemics [4]. Five regions and three distances yield 15 around-device positions prompted to the participant. In practice trials we explained how to interpret the 15 different gesture positions shown in the task images and to "anchor" the positions in relation to body parts (such as face, chest, shoulder, and beyond shoulder).

The experiment was self-paced and the participant was instructed to work through the images and to draw the prompted numbers at a moderate speed. The next image in the set was loaded with a flick gesture on the touchscreen.

The image set was divided into three sub-sets of 15 images, with one image for each of the 15 gesture positions. The order of gesture positions and the prompted number to draw in the air was randomized within the three sub-sets. All participants used the same image set (and image sequence) in two rounds, for a total of 90 gestures.

After completing the two rounds of gestures the participant was debriefed and asked to answer four questions regarding (Q1) the overall impression/emotion during the task, (Q2) in front of whom and (Q3) in what locations he/she would feel comfortable using AD-gestures, and (Q4) how comfortable he/she felt when performing the gestures in the various in-air positions. Figure 2 shows the used questionnaire. We instructed the participant to answer these questions and to interpret the central word 'comfort' from a social perspective and to ignore issues related to physical comfort and practicability. The participant also completed a Big Five Personality Test [12], which is a standard psychology test that assesses a person's personality on five broad dimensions: conscientiousness, openness, extraversion, agreeableness, and neuroticism. We used the test

Q1) On a scale from 1 to 6, what was your overall impression/emotion during the task?

1☐ 2☐ 3☐ 4☐ 5☐ 6☐

I hated it, it felt terribly awkward — I enjoyed it, it felt comfortable

Q2) Imagine your mobile phone could be operated through similar gestures as those you recently performed. Now, **in front of whom** do you think you would **feel comfortable** using such gestures? Select **one or more** items from the list below.

☐ I would **not** feel comfortable using them even when alone

or

☐ when alone ☐ in front of my partner ☐ in front of friends

☐ in front of family ☐ in front of colleagues ☐ in front of strangers

Q3) Now, **in which locations** do you think you would **feel comfortable** using such gestures? Select **one or more** items from the list below.

☐ I would **not** feel comfortable using them no matter where I am

or

☐ at home ☐ on the sidewalk ☐ in a pub, café, or restaurant

☐ in a shop ☐ in a museum ☐ as a passenger on a bus or train

☐ at my workplace

Q4) In the figures to the right, write a number from 1 to 5 in **each of the circles** to indicate how **comfortable** you felt performing a gesture at that particular position.

1=very comfortable 4=uncomfortable
2=comfortable 5=very uncomfortable
3=neutral

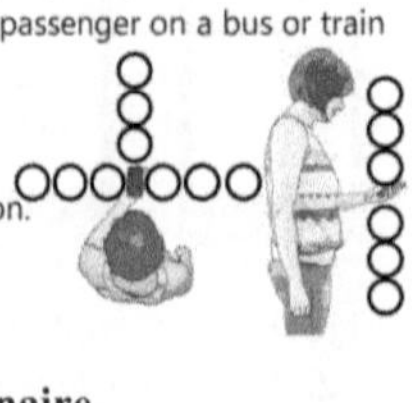

Figure 2. Study 1 questionnaire.

available at http://www.outofservice.com. We were primarily interested in identifying whether scores on extraversion correlated with perceptions of AD-gestures.

Eighteen right-handed smartphone owners (6 female) aged between 24 and 51 years (mean 31.1 years, s.d. 6.6) participated. Participation lasted roughly 30 minutes.[1]

Results

Question 1: Only four participants indicated that their impressions/emotions during the task were more negative than positive by selecting a rating of 3. The other fourteen participants indicated having had more of a positive impression/emotion during the task: ten gave a rating of 4, three gave a rating of 5, and one participant indicated enjoyment/comfort (rating 6).

Question 2 and 3: No participant completely rejected the idea of using AD-gestures by stating that he/she would not feel comfortable using gestures even when alone. Only one stated that he would only feel comfortable using the gestures if alone and at home. Sixteen participants indicated they would be comfortable doing the gestures in at least one of the non-private settings (i.e., when not at home and when not alone). One participant thought he would feel comfortable using AD-gestures in all locations and in front of all audiences listed in the questions.

To analyze the answers to Question 2 and 3, we established an acceptance rate for each given audience and location by calculating the percentage of participants who selected each audience/location in their answers. As visible in Figure 3, the more familiar audiences, family, partner, and friends, were accepted by most participants. Only 6 of 18 participants indicated they would comfortably use AD-gestures in front of colleagues and strangers. A Cochran's Q test showed a significant difference between the audiences ($\chi^2_{(5,N=18)} = 46.9$, $p < 0.001$). Post-hoc McNemar tests (Bonferroni: α-levels from 0.05 to 0.003) showed that the acceptance rates for the least familiar audiences, colleagues and strangers, were significantly lower than the rates for the other audiences.

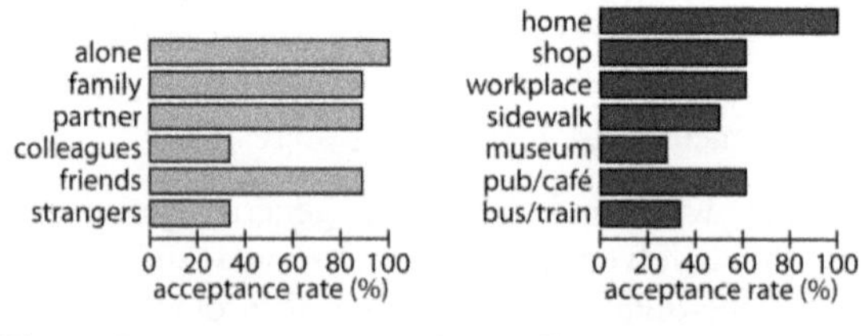

Figure 3. Acceptance rates for audiences and locations.

Also the location influenced the willingness to use AD-gestures (Cochran's Q test: $\chi^2_{(6,N=18)} = 27.2$, $p < 0.001$). However, the results are slightly more controversial with

[1] The anonymous data from our studies can be retrieved at http://ias.aau.at/experiments/.

acceptance rates around 50% for four locations (shop, workplace, sidewalk, and pub/café). All participants indicated they would feel comfortable using AD-gestures at home. Post-hoc pairwise tests McNemar tests (Bonferroni: α-levels from 0.05 to 0.002) showed that the rate for home was significantly higher than for the two most rejected locations, museum and bus/train (with rates of 28% resp. 33%). No other pairwise comparisons were significant.

We also examined whether there was a connection between acceptance rates and participants' extraversion personality trait. On the Big-5 test, nine of the 18 participants had an extraversion percentile score below 50, and nine a score above 50. That is, 50% of our participants were less extraverted than 50% of all persons (over 10,000 persons) that have completed the online Big-5 test service we used. As visible in Figure 4, introverts and extroverts provided similar ratings for most audiences and locations. We did not find any significant differences in the ratings.

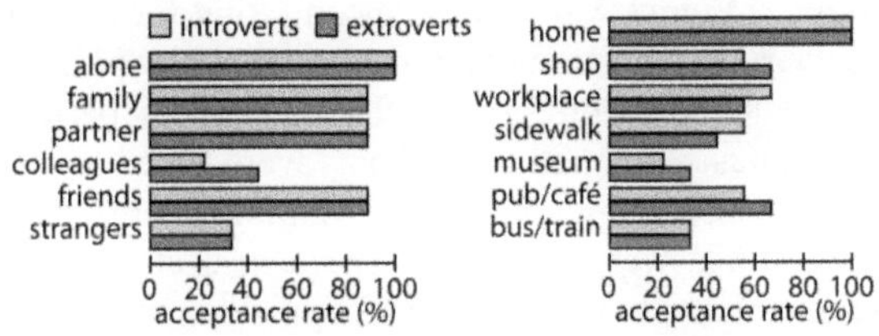

Figure 4. Acceptance rates for audiences and locations split by introverted and extroverted users.

We can conclude that the majority of our participants, not only extroverted persons but also persons with a more introverted personality, were quite open to the idea of AD-gestures. Only one participant indicated a strong hesitance to perform AD-gestures in the public or in front of someone else. All other participants responded that they would feel comfortable using AD-gestures outside the privacy of their home: in four of the six non-private locations 50% or more of our participants would feel comfortable using AD-gestures. Overall, our results confirm Rico and Brewster's [14] results, which also showed that both audience and location are important factors that influence the willingness to use gestures.

Given the low acceptance rate for strangers in the audience category, the fairly high acceptance rates for shop, sidewalk, and pub/café – where one would expect to be seen by strangers – are somewhat surprising. However, we assume that participants indeed focused on the various locations and the circumstances that are typical for these. For example, in a pub an AD-gesture could be more easily disguised, e.g., under a table, than in a bus with a passenger sitting close by. We also suspect that acceptance depends on the frequency with which the gestures are used, their size and duration. Particularly for locations such as in a crowded bus or on a busy sidewalk where large or lengthy gestures are likely to be perceived as more inappropriate than small or quick ones. We evaluate these factors in Study 2.

Question 4: Figure 5 shows the mean rating for each of the 15 gesture positions that were rated by participants according to how comfortable they felt when doing gestures in these positions. In all five regions, the position furthest away from the device had the worst rating. Most participants stated they felt either uncomfortable or very uncomfortable doing AD-gestures far away from the device. The majority of participants indicated they felt comfortable or very comfortable when gesturing at a close distance from the device, no matter what region they used.

A Friedman test showed that, across the five regions, the ratings for the far, mid, and close distances (with mean rating of 4.3, 2.8, and 1.5, respectively) differed ($\chi^2_{(2,N=18)}$ = 36.0, $p < 0.001$). Post-hoc Wilcoxon tests (Bonferroni: α-levels from 0.05 to 0.016) showed differences for all three pairwise comparisons.

We also found significant differences in the ratings for the five regions ($\chi^2_{(4,N=18)}$ = 36.0, $p < 0.0001$). The mean rating for each region was: 2.8 (above), 3.6 (below), 3.1 (left), 2.6 (front), and 2.3 (right). Post-hoc Wilcoxon tests (Bonferroni: α-levels from 0.05 to 0.005) showed significant differences between the left and right region, and between the below region and each of the above, right and front regions. No other comparisons were significant.

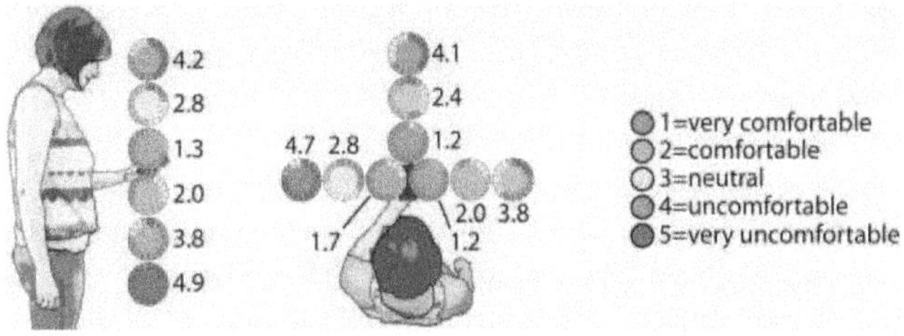

Figure 5. Comfort-ratings of the 15 gesture positions (segments around each middle circle show individual ratings, best viewed in color).

Again, as with acceptance rates for audiences and locations, we did not find any differences in the distance ratings or region ratings between introverted and extroverted persons.

We can conclude that the distance between the device and the region in which AD-gestures are made strongly influence how comfortable users feel performing AD-gestures in a public setting. The level of comfort depends on the position of the gestures: gestures below the device evoke feelings of discomfort (more so the further away they are from the device) and gestures to the right of the device are preferable (we note that all our participants were right-handed, we assume the results regarding the left and right regions should be mirrored for left-handed users).

Summary

Our results suggest that we could expect the majority of future around-device gesture users to have a neutral feeling when they use AD-gestures in the public (Q1), but that how comfortable they feel using the gestures will depend on where and in front of whom the gestures are used (Q2 and Q3). The results also suggest that most users think that AD-gestures are compatible with many public settings, but that the acceptance for some settings is quite divergent. The results do not show that acceptance is related to the extraversion personality trait. Furthermore, our results (Q4) show that, generally, users feel more comfortable when gesturing within 30cm from the device (i.e., distances corresponding to the Close and Mid distances in the study).

Study 2 – Size and Duration

With the knowledge that most of the participants in our first study showed a neutral attitude towards using AD-gestures in public and that none completely rejected the idea of doing so, we conducted our second study to investigate how the size and duration of AD-gestures affect users' attitudes. Since Study 1 showed that there was no relationship between users' extraversion personality trait and how they perceived using AD-gestures in public, we decided not to use the Big-5 test.

For Study 2 we used the busy main entrance hall of the local university. The task and materials were similar to those used in Study 1. A set of images guided the participant through the task. As in Study 1, the images prompted one-digit numbers to be 'drawn' in the air at a specific in-air position around the device. A Silverlight Windows Phone application displayed the task images and randomized the image sequences for each new participant. One task image is shown in Figure 6. A task counter was shown in the top right corner, and a label in the top left corner indicated to the participant for how long he/she was required to draw the prompted number. When the 'start' button was pressed, the timer in the bottom right corner of the screen started. The participant was asked to re-draw the digit in the indicated location as long as the current task screen was shown. The next task screen was loaded when the timer reached the prompted duration.

We used small and large gestures. Small gestures were required to cover an area of about 15×15cm, large gestures 30×30cm. These sizes roughly correspond to half respectively the full distance of the preferred gesture distances defined by Study 1 results (Close and Mid). Two small gestures were prompted in each of the *Left*, *Front*, and *Right* regions (corresponding to distance *Close* and *Mid* in Study 1) and one large gesture was prompted in each of the three regions. We used three gesture durations: 3, 6, and 9 seconds (typical AD-gesture durations reported in the literature [6, 7, 9]). In total 27 task images were used. The used combinations of gesture size, duration and location are shown in Figure 6. Each combination was repeated twice, for a total of 54 images. After completing the 54 gestures the participant was debriefed and asked to complete the questionnaire shown in Figure 6. As in Study 1, we instructed the participant to answer these questions and to interpret the central word 'comfort' from a social perspective and to ignore issues related to physical comfort and practicability. Participation lasted around 25 min. Eighteen right-handed smartphone owners (3 female), aged 21 to 32 years (mean 26.1, s.d. 3.6) participated. Five had participated in Study 1.

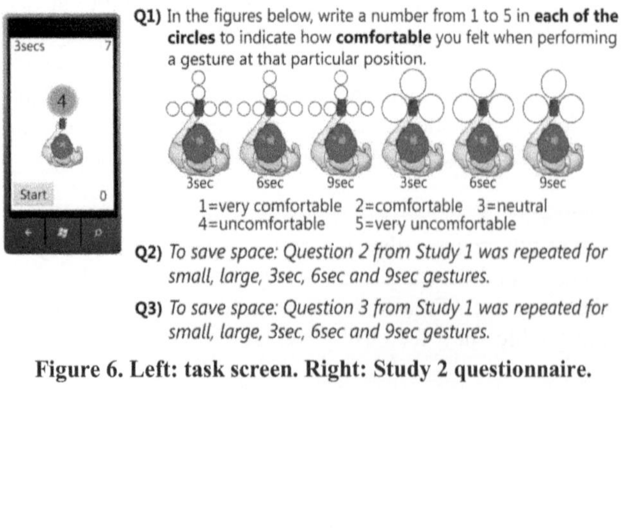

Figure 6. Left: task screen. Right: Study 2 questionnaire.

Results

Question 1: Figure 7 shows the mean rating for each of the 27 size/duration/location combinations rated by participants according to how comfortable they felt when performing these gestures. Although participants were asked to provide twice as many ratings for small than for large gestures (small gestures were performed twice in each region), we chose to make a comparison for guidance. The mean comfort-rating was 3.0 for small gestures and 3.5 for large gestures. A Wilcoxon test showed a significant difference ($Z = -2.9$, $p < 0.01$). Understandably, smaller gestures felt more comfortable as these are likely to attract less attention.

The average comfort-rating was 2.4 for 3sec gestures and 3.1 and 3.8 for 6sec and 9sec gestures, respectively. A Friedman test showed differences between the three gesture durations ($\chi^2_{(2,N=18)} = 34.5$, $p < 0.0001$) and post-hoc Wilcoxon tests (Bonferroni: α-levels from 0.05 to 0.016) showed differences for all pairwise comparisons. We also found significant differences among the three regions (Friedman: $\chi^2_{(2,N=18)} = 24.4$, $p < 0.0001$) with post-hoc Wilcoxon tests (Bonferroni: α-levels from 0.05 to 0.016) showing that the right region, with a mean rating of 2.6, was significantly different from both the front (mean 3.1)

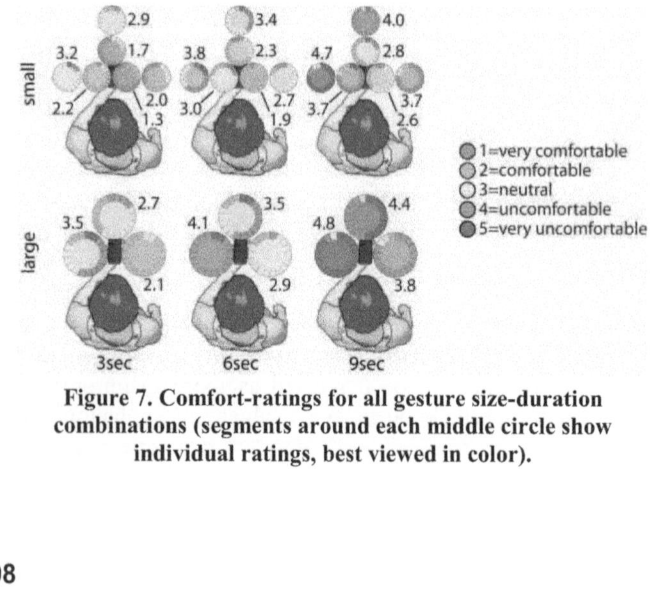

Figure 7. Comfort-ratings for all gesture size-duration combinations (segments around each middle circle show individual ratings, best viewed in color).

and the left (mean 3.7). Also left and front differed. Again we note that all participants were right-handed and assume the results would be mirrored for left-handed users.

In Figure 7 we also see an interesting interplay between position, size and duration indicating that the drawbacks of large gestures can be compensated if they are done in a favourable location and if they are quick (e.g., to the right/3sec). Likewise, a small 3sec gesture in a less favourable region (e.g., far away in the left or front region) is rated similarly to a large 6sec gesture in the preferred right region. We also note how small 3sec gestures are consistently rated about 0.5 points higher than in Study 1 at the corresponding gesture positions (close and mid distance, compare middle part of Figure 5). Since small 3sec gestures take longer than the gestures in Study 1, where participants only had to draw one quick digit, the higher ratings in Study 2 are reasonable and confirm the robustness of our rating-based approach. We can conclude that both gesture size and duration have a significant influence on how comfortable users feel when performing AD-gestures in public. Most users indicated that they felt comfortable or neutral using small gestures and were less comfortable with large ones.

Questions 2 and 3: We analyzed acceptance rates for audiences and locations aggregated across gesture sizes and durations. The results are shown in the left part of Figure 8. A Friedman test showed a significant difference between audiences ($\chi^2_{(5,N=18)}$ = 59.8, $p < 0.001$) and post-hoc Wilcoxon tests (Bonferroni: α-level 0.05 to 0.003) showed that the least desired audiences – colleagues and strangers – differed from all other audiences, as in Study 1. The rates for the audiences were similar to those in Study 1 (±10%).

A Friedman test showed differences among locations ($\chi^2_{(5,N=18)}$ = 40.1, $p < 0.001$) and post-hoc Wilcoxon tests (Bonferroni: α-level 0.05 to 0.002) showed that home differed from all other locations. In Study 1, home only differed from museum and bus/train.

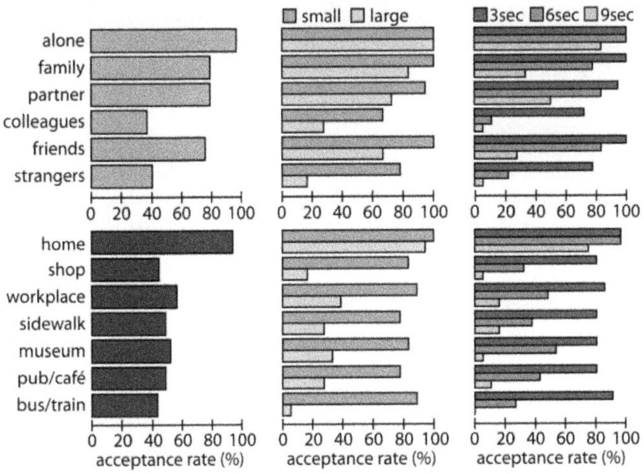

Figure 8. Acceptance rates for audiences (top) and locations (bottom). Rates aggregated across size and duration (left), split by size (middle), and split by duration (right).

The ratings for gesture sizes and gesture durations are shown in the middle and right parts of Figure 8. Clearly, for private settings (alone and home) size and duration had little or no effect. For familiar audiences (family, partner and friends) size and duration were more important. For the least familiar audiences, colleagues and strangers, we see pronounced differences with the rates for large, 6sec and 9sec gestures around 25% or below. We also see such pronounced differences for all non-private locations. In particular we note the great difference between 3sec and 9sec gestures in the location ratings: 3sec gestures have an acceptance rate close to, or above, 80% for all locations whereas 9sec gestures have rates below 10% (ignoring the private home setting). We conclude that, indeed, both gesture size and gesture duration have a great influence on how comfortable users feel about performing AD-gestures in public places (and to some extent even at home).

Summary

To our knowledge, considering unique gesture features has not been explored in prior acceptability studies. The results of Study 2 further confirm the need to examine the acceptability of gesture features separately. Gesture size and duration, both impact the acceptability of AD-interactions. We notice that acceptance drops rapidly after the 6-second mark. Furthermore, for all locations and audiences (except home and alone), larger gestures are seen as being less acceptable.

Study 3 – Spectators

After Study 2 and 3 where we investigated users' attitudes about the acceptability of AD-gestures we were also interested in the reactions of persons who have watched someone else using this type of input modality. We call these persons "spectators". We are unaware of any previous work on mobile gestures that investigates spectators' reactions by probing people in public. Another important aim with the study was to compare the effect of having participants perform interactions themselves – as in Study 1 and 2 – to the effect of only letting participants watch another person and then ask them to imagine their own future usage without having had the opportunity to try out the interaction themselves (as in previous video-based acceptance assessments of mobile gestures [13, 14, 15]).

One of the authors acted as an AD-gesture user in five different locations: in a commuter train, in a café, in a library, in a restaurant, and at a birthday party. The author worked through the same image set as was used in Study 1 until noticing having caught someone's attention. This spectator was then asked to answer the questions shown in Figure 9. Answers were collected from 24 spectators aged between 17 and 43 years (mean 26.7, s.d. 9.6). Eleven were female and all but one owned a smartphone.

Results

Question 1: In Question 1 spectators were asked to select one or more statements to describe his/her thoughts when

Q1) What were you thinking watching me gesturing around my phone, the way I just did? Select **one or more** items from the list below.

- ☐ I was wondering what you were doing
- ☐ I thought "what a weird behaviour"
- ☐ I did not think much about it
- ☐ I thought it looked stupid / strange
- ☐ I thought it was annoying / disturbing
- ☐ I thought the movements were inappropriate
- ☐ I thought it looked fancy / interesting
- ☐ I thought / my impression was:______________________

Q2) Imagine you could operate your mobile phone using gestures in the air (similar to what I was doing). Now, **in front of whom** do you think you would **feel comfortable** using such gestures? Select **one or more** items from the list below.

- ☐ I would **not** feel comfortable using them even when alone

or

- ☐ when alone
- ☐ in front of my partner
- ☐ in front of friends
- ☐ in front of family
- ☐ in front of colleagues
- ☐ in front of strangers

Q3) Now, **in which locations** do you think you would **feel comfortable** using such gestures? Select **one or more** items from the list below.

- ☐ I would **not** feel comfortable using them no matter where I am

or

- ☐ at home
- ☐ on the sidewalk
- ☐ in a pub, café, or restaurant
- ☐ in a shop
- ☐ in a museum
- ☐ as a passenger on a bus or train
- ☐ at my workplace

Figure 9. Study 3 questionnaire.

watching the AD-gestures. Twelve spectators (50%) indicated that they became curious, wondering what the user was doing. Twelve indicated that they did not think much about what they had seen and two commented that it looked "cool". One thought that it looked "fancy". Only five spectators thought it was a weird behaviour and one thought it looked stupid or strange. No one thought it was annoying or disturbing. These initial reactions were given by the spectators before they were informed about the idea of AD-gestures and before they knew what the user actually did. This suggests that most spectators perceived the gestures in a neutral or curious way. Very few perceived the gestures as something negative or disturbing.

Question 2 and 3: Spectators' acceptance rates, generated from answers to Question 2 and 3 (in front of whom and in what locations they thought they would feel comfortable using AD-gestures), are shown in Figure 10. As the users in Study 1, all spectators answered that they would comfortably use AD-gestures when alone and 92% said they would feel comfortable using the gestures in front of their partner and friends. The acceptance rate for family, colleagues, and strangers amount to 83%, 79%, and 67%, respectively. We found a significant difference between the audiences (Cochran's Q test: $\chi^2_{(5,N=24)} = 15.4$, $p < 0.01$). But post-hoc pairwise McNemar tests with the conservative Bonferroni correction (α-level 0.05 to 0.003) showed no significant differences among pairs of audiences.

When compared to the acceptance rates in Study 1 (Figure 3) where Question 2 was answered after a firsthand

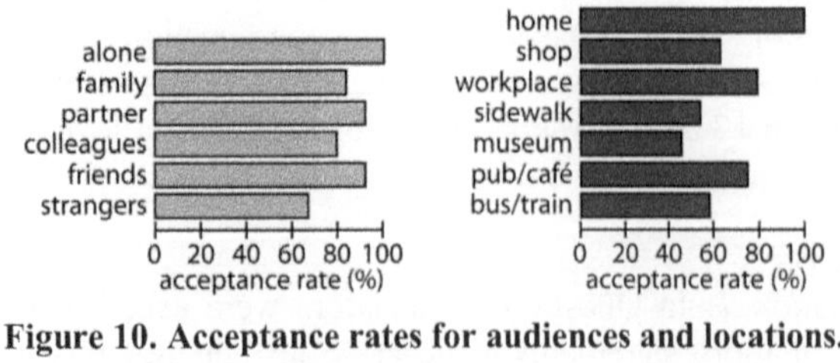

Figure 10. Acceptance rates for audiences and locations.

experience of performing AD-gestures in a public setting, we see markedly higher rates in Study 3 for the least familiar and most critical audiences, colleagues (79% vs. 33%) and strangers (67% vs. 33%). The results for the more familiar audiences are similar in the two studies. We also find higher acceptance rates in Study 3 for most locations. Rates for home and shop were the same in both studies, for the other locations we find higher rates in Study 3. The differences vary between four percent points (sidewalk) and 25 percent points (bus/train). A Cochran's Q test showed a significant overall difference among locations ($\chi^2_{(6,N=24)} = 28.3$, $p < 0.0001$). Post-hoc McNemar tests (Bonferroni: α-level 0.05 to 0.002) showed that the acceptance rate for home was significantly higher than for shop, sidewalk, museum, and bus/train (no other pairwise comparison was significant).

In conclusion, the results from our spectator study indicate that AD-gestures are not likely to be perceived as obtrusive (Q1). None of the spectators we asked thought the gestures were inappropriate or annoying. Indeed, many did not think much about the gesturing they had watched, 50% got interested and curious. Furthermore, as most users in Study 1 and 2, most spectators were quite open to the idea of AD-gestures and thought they would feel comfortable using them in public locations and in front of strangers. However, acceptance rates were generally much higher in Study 3 than in Study 1, indicating an over-estimation. A likely reason for this is the absence of an actual usage experience to relate to when providing the answers.

DISCUSSION

In this section, we discuss the lessons we learned and insights we gained from our studies. We also demonstrate how our findings can be applied to existing around-device interactions, reflect on limitations in our approach, and point at directions for future work.

AD-Input Design Considerations & Recommendations

Intuition may provide initial guidance regarding AD-input design, suggesting general directions such that a small or quick gesture is more likely to be acceptable than a large or lengthy one. However, without experience or empirical data it is difficult to estimate what size is small enough; when does a gesture start to feel too lengthy; and to correctly predict the consequences of changes regarding such gesture parameters. With our results we can provide opening design considerations and recommendations.

It is evident from our results that AD-gestures belong to an acceptability-continuum where a combination of several gesture properties influences user perceptions and how comfortable users feel about performing the gestures in a social setting. Our results demonstrate that users are sensitive to the parameterization of the examined properties – distance from the device, input region, gesture size and gesture duration – and that rather small differences in parameter settings may result in large shifts on the acceptability-continuum.

The following considerations and design recommendations emerge from our exploration of AD-gesture acceptability:

• *Distance*: AD-gestures that are closer to the device are more acceptable. Our results suggest a critical point approximately 30cm away from the device. Input beyond this distance is likely to be considered as "socially awkward" and thus should be avoided if possible (the region from the device extending to this point is slightly smaller than the intimate space defined in studies on proxemics [4]). The critical distance is applicable for all tested regions: to the left and right, in front, above, and below the device.

• *Input region*: Our results reveal a strong preference for gestures to the right of the device for AD-gestures, then the front region (for right-handed users, and the reverse otherwise). This suggests that AD-input designers need to consider user handedness (which should be reflected in the operation of the system) and that they should design for input to the right and in the front of the device. However, also the regions above, below and to the left of the device are acceptable given that the critical distance is attended to.

• *Size*: When in public, users indicated a strong preference for small gestures. Our results indicate that caution is warranted when the gesture size approaches 15×15cm, larger gestures should be avoided.

• *Duration*: Gesture duration strongly affects users' comfort levels, even after a few seconds of AD-input users are likely to start feeling uncomfortable. Acceptance drops rapidly after the 6-second mark.

• *Gesture property interplays*: The strong interplays we found between gesture properties suggest that AD-interaction designers can achieve socially acceptable designs even when their interactions require less favourable property characteristics. For example, the negative effects of an over-sized gesture can be reduced if input is allowed very close to the device or in a favourable region. Thus, designers are good advised to carefully consider such interplays and to examine possibilities to encounter critical features by making changes to other gesture properties.

Adaptations to AD-Interactions

Our findings can be directly applied to several existing AD-input techniques. For example, Hoverflow [9] uses a small space (5-7cm) above the device for simple interactions such as to sweep or to rotate an image. Similarly, SideSight [1] uses proximity sensors that are capable of detecting limited space (8cm) along each side of the device. In contrast, our results suggest that socially acceptable AD-input space could be larger (30cm) and could be used for complex 3D gestures such as Cyclo [11] for continuous zooming. Such gestures could extend up to 6 seconds in length without impairing users' perception of comfort.

Few AD-techniques utilize the valuable – and acceptable – space below the device. For example, the AD-Binning technique [6] relies on a large 2D space, extending up to 40cm away from the device, to allow users to store, browse and retrieve contents through gestures issued within storage bins that are positioned in AD-space. Our results revealed that people feel uncomfortable using far distances for AD-input. This finding diminishes the potential value of AD-Binning. However, our results can suggest alternatives and still allow users to benefit from AD-Binning. Using the space above and below the device, we could reorganize bins in a layered structure into a small 3D space. This avoids large reaching distances and thus likely improves the acceptance of the technique.

Improved Methods for Acceptance Studies

Our studies included two new approaches to collecting user opinions related to social acceptance. The first consisted of teasing apart specific gesture features. Whereas in prior work results would indicate whether a gesture is viewed as either acceptable or not, our approach is to examine unique elements of gestures. This may not be possible with all types of gestural input. However, when the interaction modality affords this, such as with AD-input, we recommend that studies tease these apart. In our case we found that rather small changes on the studied variables had a large influence on user perception. Furthermore, teasing apart gesture features may reveal new opportunities to improve the acceptability though intelligent combinations or adjustments to the individual parameters.

The second adjustment we included was to ask participants to rate their view of a gesture after having experienced using this in a public setting. Prior work has relied on visual demonstrations of the studied gestures and on participants' imagination of a future usage situation. In our case, we found that having a person rate gestures without having had a firsthand usage experience resulted in much higher acceptance rates. Overly positive responses in early design phases may allude to sub-optimal designs that future users may avoid in public settings. However, more targeted methodological research endeavours are needed to systematically disentangle the effects of firsthand usage experiences in acceptability related matters.

We also introduced a new dimension to social acceptability studies by exploring possible linkages between personality traits and user perception. Our results did not reveal any relations between the extroversion trait and user perceptions. One explanation might be that people are starting to get familiar with mid-air sensing mechanisms, through systems such as gaming consoles. Our surprising finding may also be related to the small number of participants used in Study 1. We acknowledge the limitations of the Big-Five personality test. It provides one aspect of a person's traits. Additional work is needed to identify how social acceptability tests can be linked to personality types.

Limitations

We acknowledge the limited methodological support for our central use of perceived 'mental comfort' as a predictor of social acceptance. However, as numerous previous study designers [13, 14, 15, 17, 18] and many of their participants have used a similar terminology, our choice was not a farfetched one. We also recognize that user acceptance and social acceptance are multifaceted concepts, by fare not limited to the perceived or expected levels of mental comfort [3, 13]. In our studies we focused on social settings and ignored important cultural factors, such as participants' cultural background. Our studies were conducted in Canada and Austria with persons living there. Little is known about how cultural aspects influences user perceptions about, and the social acceptance of novel interaction techniques [17]. Accordingly, and with all our participants living in a western culture, we are wary of generalizing our results to non-western users and cultures. We suspect that examining culture-dependent differences of technology adoption and social acceptance would be a challenging but very fruitful path for future work. Finally, we are also wary of assuming our results apply to other age groups. Most of our 60 participants were 25 to 35 years old (mean 27.8, s.d. 7.6).

CONCLUSION

In this paper, we have presented three studies that explored the acceptability of hand gesture input in 3D space around a smartphone. The studies were performed in various public locations. We surveyed users that performed such Around-Device gestures and people who passed by about their impressions. Most users and spectators answered they would use such interactions if available on their smartphone, but also indicated they would be concerned about others' reactions. Our results show that people are selective regarding in what public settings they would use gestures. Moreover, gesture properties, such as duration and distance from the device, have a great influence on how comfortable users feel when using Around-Device gestures in public. Acceptance and perceived mental comfort markedly sink if gestures are done further than 30cm away from the device or last longer than 6 seconds. Gesture size and region (e.g., on the side, above or below the device) also matter. According to our findings and study experiences, we presented recommendations for around-device input designers and suggestions about how to improve methods used in studies related to the social acceptance of novel interaction techniques.

REFERENCES

1. Butler, A., Izadi, S., and Hodges, S. SideSight: Multi-"touch" interaction around small devices. In *Proc. UIST 2008*, 201-204.
2. Ens, B., Ahlström, D., Cockburn, A., and Irani, P. Characterizing user performance with assisted direct off-screen pointing. In *Proc. MobileHCI 2011*, 485-494.
3. Davis, F.D., Bagozzi, R.P., and Warshaw, P.R. User acceptance of computer technology: a comparison of two theoretical models. *Management Science 35,* 8 (1989), 982-1103.
4. Hall, E.T. *The Hidden Dimension.* Garden City, Doubleday, NY, USA, 1966.
5. Harrison, C. and Hudson, S.E. Abracadabra: wireless, high-precision, and unpowered finger input for very small mobile devices. In *Proc. UIST 2009*, 121-124.
6. Hasan, K., Ahlström, D., and Irani, P. AD-Binning: leveraging around-device space for storing, browsing and retrieving mobile device content. In *Proc. CHI 2013*, 899-908.
7. Jones, B., Sodhi, R., Forsyth, D., Bailey, B. and Maciocci, G. Around device interaction for multiscale navigation. In *Proc. MobileHCI 2012*, 83-92.
8. Ketabdar, H., Roshandel, M., and Yüksel, K. A. MagiWrite: towards touchless digit entry using 3D space around mobile devices. In *Proc. MobileHCI 2010*, 443-446.
9. Kratz, S. and Rohs, M. Hoverflow: exploring around-device interaction with IR distance sensors. In *Proc. MobileHCI 2009*, 1-4.
10. Kratz, S., Rohs, M., Guse, D., Müller, J., Bailly, G., and Nischt, M. PalmSpace: continuous around-device gestures vs. multitouch for 3D rotation tasks on mobile devices. In *Proc. AVI 2012*, 181-188.
11. Malacria, S., Lecolinet, E., and Guiard, Y. Clutch-free panning and integrated pan-zoom control on touch-sensitive surfaces: the cyclostar approach. In *Proc. CHI 2010*, 2615–2624.
12. McCrae, R.R. and John, O.P. An introduction to the Five-Factor model and its applications. *Journal of Personality 60*, 2 (1992), 175-215.
13. Montero, C.S., Alexander, J., Marshall, M.T., and Subramanian, S. Would you do that?: understanding social acceptance of gestural interfaces. In *Proc. MobileHCI 2010*, 275-278.
14. Rico, J. and Brewster, S. Usable gestures for mobile interfaces: evaluating social acceptability. In *Proc. CHI 2010*, 887-896.
15. Ronkainen, S., Häkkilä, J., Kaleva, S., Colley, A., and Linjama, J. Tap input as an embedded interaction method for mobile devices. In *Proc. TEI 2007*, 263-270.
16. Sodhi, R.S., Jones, B.R., Forsyth, D., Bailey, B.P., and Maciocci, G. BeThere: 3D mobile collaboration with spatial input. In *Proc. CHI 2013*, 179-188.
17. Williamson, J.R., Brewster, S., and Vennelakanti, R. Mo!games: evaluating mobile gestures in the wild. In *Proc. ICMI 2013*, 173-180.
18. Williamson, J.R., Crossan, A., and Brewster, S. Multimodal mobile interactions: usability studies in real world settings. In *Proc. ICMI 2011*, 361-368.
19. Winkler, C., Pfeuffer, K., and Rukzio, E. Investigating mid-air pointing interaction for projector phones. In *Proc. ITS 2012*, 85-94.
20. Yang, X.D., Hasan, K., Bruce, N., and Irani, P. Surround-See: enabling peripheral vision on smartphones during active use. In *Proc. UIST 2013*, 291-300.

Monox: Extensible Gesture Notation for Mobile Devices

Roman Ganhör
Vienna University of Technology
Favoritenstrasse 9-11/187
1040 Vienna, Austria
roman.ganhoer@tuwien.ac.at

Wolfgang Spreicer
Vienna University of Technology
Argentinierstrasse 8/187
1040 Vienna, Austria
wolfgang.spreicer@tuwien.ac.at

ABSTRACT
The rise of modern smartphones brought gesture-based interaction to our daily lives. As the number of different operating systems and graphical user interfaces increases, designers and researchers can benefit from a common notation for mobile interaction design. In this paper, we present a concept of an extensible sketching notation for mobile gestures. The proposed notation, *Monox*, provides a common basis for collaborative design and analysis of mobile interactions. *Monox* is platform independent and enables general discussions and negotiations on topics of mobile gestures. An extensive evaluation showed the practicability and ability of *Monox* to serve as a common denominator for discussion and communication within interdisciplinary groups of researchers, designers and developers.

Author Keywords
Design; Interaction Design; Interface Design; Mobile Interaction; Gesture; Expression; Interaction Pattern; Fitts' Law; GOMS;Software Engineering; KLM.

ACM Classification Keywords
H.5.m. Information interfaces and presentation (e.g., HCI): Miscellaneous.

INTRODUCTION
Sketching is a useful tool when discussing novel interaction mechanisms and application designs [2]. Regardless of whether researchers scrutinizing new approaches for mobile interactions or a team of developers exploring different variations of an interface design, they all utilize sketches to communicate their ideas. However, since there is no commonly accepted general notation for mobile gestures researchers and designers use their very own notation or use one of the notations provided by one of various mobile operating systems.

The mobile operating systems with the biggest market shares are Google Android, Apple iOS and Microsoft Windows Phone [11]. In addition to these widely known operating systems, there exist some less popular ones such as Asha and MeeGo (Nokia), Blackberry or Bada (Samsung). According to recent announcements new mobile operating systems such as Ubuntu Phone (Canonical), Firefox OS (Mozilla) and Tizen (Samsung, Intel) have already entered the market or will enter the market soon [5].

Despite the variations in the underlying platforms and the targeted markets, all of these operating systems utilize touch-based gestures as their main interaction concept. Basic interaction gestures such as *tap* or *swipe* are part of all mobile operating systems. However, there are differences and thus, every implementation is unique in its own sense. For example, the number of fixed hardware and software buttons ranges from zero (Meego on Nokia N9) to four (Android on HTC Sensation).

The number of hardware buttons is a basic design decision that influences the overall interaction concept. Devices with dedicated buttons can rely on them and thus, can provide a consistent user experience for every application (home or search). On the other hand, devices with no buttons have to provide different strategies to compensate for the lack of dedicated buttons. As a result, every platform promotes its own style guide to ensure a consistent user experience for all their applications. Consequently, there exist various notations and expressions for the same gesture. This is not only potentially confusing when discussing sketches, it also complicates the comparability and interchangeability of sketches and design ideas. Moreover, evaluating user experience is unnecessarily cumbersome due to the lack of a standardized set of gesture expressions.

In this paper, we propose an extensible notation for gestures (*Monox*, MObile NOtation - eXtensible) on touch-based devices. *Monox* can support comparability over different platforms and provides extensibility for the pre-defined basic set of gesture expressions. *Monox* comprises of a superset of gestures for mobile devices and serves as a common ground for researchers, designers, programmers and executives. Through its handwriting-like notation it is suitable for collaborative sketching in early phases of design sessions. Furthermore, due to its platform-independency, *Monox* can be a first step in building a cross-platform analysis tool. We envision a standardized set of gesture expressions that supports discussions in

MobileHCI 2014, September 23–26, 2014, Toronto, ON, Canada.

ACM 978-1-4503-3004-6/14/09...$15.00.
http://dx.doi.org/10.1145/2628363.2628394

interdisciplinary groups consisting of individuals with various professional backgrounds.

BACKGROUND & RELATED WORK

Every company or organization on the market distributing mobile operating systems provides guidelines on how applications should be written and how specific interactions should be referred to [1,3,7]. Besides, various independent designers made exhaustive compilations of existing gestures [17,24]. However, simpler and more dynamic collaborative evaluation tools could assist in making decisions and in finding a common ground for discussions. Existing tools focus on software supporting design [12] or distributed collaboration tools [16]. In the following, we provide a short overview of existing approaches for describing and evaluating touch based mobile interaction.

Mobile Extensions to GOMS/KLM

Various methods for measuring and analyzing usability and design issues on desktop interfaces have been introduced, such as Fitts' Law, GOMS and KLM [4]. However, exploring novel methods for quantifying user experience is still an active research area [14], especially for mobile interfaces. Using regular expressions is such an approach to describe user interaction mechanisms [12]. Other approaches are KLM-qt [22] or the framework suggested by Heo et al [8].

Holleis et.al. [9] added "gestures" to the standard KLM making the method more applicable for modern mobile devices. Moreover, the authors specified existing parameters in more detail, e.g. splitting "attention shift" in two categories: a minor attention shift happens within the mobile device, whereas a major attention shift happens between the mobile device and the "real" world. The evaluation of the proposed mobile extension brought up promising results. However, the extensions in their publication focus on feature phones and not on smartphones. Thus, all possible gestures for touch interaction are subsumed into a single category "gesture", which is not appropriate for modern smartphones.

Jung et.al. [10] extended KLM for smartphone interaction by introducing more detailed gesture elements. For their experiment, the authors compared a novel *flick and press* gesture that outperformed the standard gestures for selecting a web-link on mobile devices. To underline the superiority of their design the authors used an adapted GOMS model for mobile phones.

To better apply GOMS for the mobile domain an extension was presented by Lee and Paik [15]. The authors introduced the term of *mental preparation time*, which depends on the experience of the user and the difficulty of the task. For example, it is much more challenging for an inexperienced user to deal with applications that regularly swap the whole content of the screen than it is for an experienced user who is familiar with the workflow of a given application. The experience of users influence their mental load and thus, *mental preparations time* can vary significantly among users. However, complex interactions are hardly covered by the proposed extensions.

Gesture Notations

While GOMS and KLM are useful for measuring interactions these methods are of limited use during the design phase where basic ideas are discussed. Sketches are widely used in early stages of design [2]. Thus, designing and discussing applications for touch-based devices involves both, sketching the elements of the interface and sketching the user interaction (gestures).

Notations for gestures are provided by most mobile platforms (e.g. Android, Ubuntu). At least written guidelines are supplied (e.g. Apple). Figure 1 depicts the notation styles of Windows Phone and Ubuntu Phone.

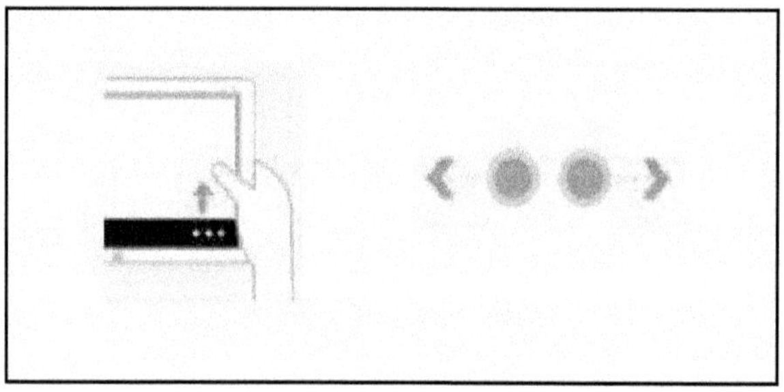

Figure 1: Gesture notation of Windows Phone (left) and Ubuntu Phone (right)

Comparing these guidelines and notation styles reveals various issues on interoperability, accuracy and extensibility.

Interoperability: since the guidelines differ in look and appearance designers have to agree on one notation and its implicit meaning. This implicates a limited interoperability between groups due to limited definitions of existing notations.

Accuracy: existing guidelines illustrate just the gesture and leave out additional information. For example, in certain scenarios it can be important to define the start area and the stop area of a *"swipe"* or *"fling"*. Communicating this extra information with a gesture expression can be crucial for the understanding of its usefulness.

Extensibility: none of the guidelines offer explicit rules to extend the given notation. Especially when exploring novel gestures it can be tedious to discuss the meaning and boundaries of newly generated expressions.

To overcome the limitation of interoperability designers already published vendor-independent gesture collections [24,6]. However, the artwork of these collections is thoroughly advanced and not primarily designed for quick sketches. Furthermore, these compilations do not provide particular accuracy (exact start of and end of a gesture) nor do they provide extensibility.

Models and Diagrams

In the domain of software engineering applications are often described with diagrams such as UML. Diagrams provide graphical representation of tasks and subtasks and express their relationship amongst each other [18]. Thus, diagrams can help to set a common ground for communicating and discussing ideas. Ambiguity and other problematic cases can be identified in early process stages.

Programming software for gesture recognition raises the need for appropriate gesture sketches. During the design phase sufficient precise sketches help to identify and pinpoint the gestures and afterwards the same sketches can be used in a manual to describe the operating principles of the software [13,19,21,23]. Figure 2 depicts various styles used to sketch and notate gestures. The drawings range from formal (left) to descriptive (center) and artistic (right).

Figure 2: Various notations styles for gestures

A useful gesture notation would both serve as a base for measuring user experience (GOMS, KLM and other) and provide a set of extensible gesture expressions for designers (sketches for discussion). In the next section we propose *Monox*, out approach to such a gesture notation.

MONOX - GESTURE GRAPHICS

Monox addresses the need for distinct and extensible expressions for mobile gestures. One aim is to provide graphical representations for the gestures offered by various mobile platforms. In the following, the expressions are described in detail. Since the notation should be easy to draw by hand - especially by non-artists - all sketches throughout this paper are kept simple in their appearance.

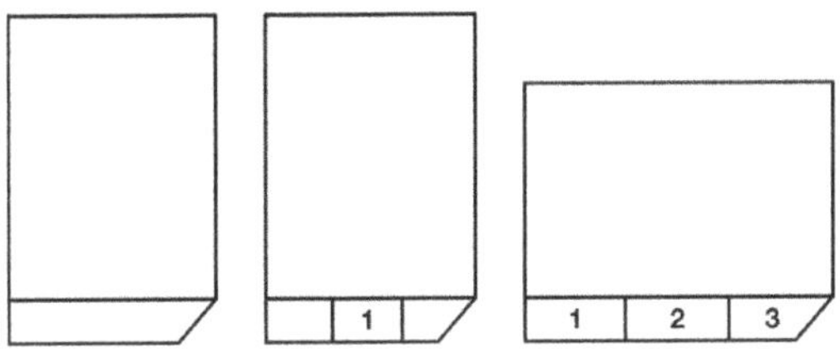

Figure 3: Phone outline with platform-dependent buttons

The primary layout of a *Monox* sketch is a simple rectangle representing the front side of the mobile device. The skewed corner indicates the lower right corner of the device when holding it in its intended position, portrait for mobile phones, landscape for tablets. Whenever the device rotates the skewed corner rotates in the same direction. The lower part of the phone is separated from the screen and contains the platform-dependent buttons (software buttons or hardware buttons). The buttons are numbered from left to right in an increasing order. If a phone does not provide any buttons, this area stays empty. Figure 3 depicts three devices: a smartphone with no buttons (left), a smartphone with one button (middle), and a tablet with three buttons (right). The skewed corner indicates the device's orientation.

Tapping Gesture

A common gesture on touch-based devices is pointing and clicking a specific icon (tapping). This gesture is covered by most guidelines and gesture collections. However, optional definition of a launch area is missing. The launch area defines the boundaries within the tap must be performed. The bigger the launch area is, the easier it is to hit it (Fitts 'Law [4]). In *Monox*, the launch area is defined by a rectangle around the pointing icon. If a user misses the launch area, the system can ignore the pointing gesture or accept it as a (unintentional) pointing to a different item. The earlier is without consequences for the user the latter leads to an unintended input.

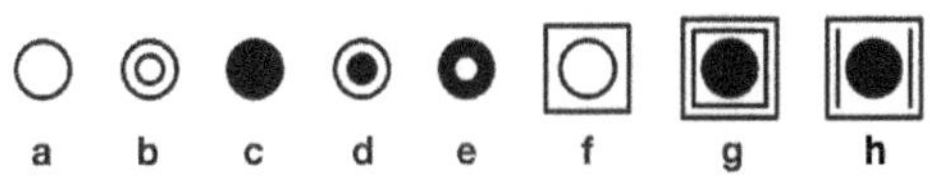

Figure 4: Pointing gesture with launching area

Figure 4 depicts: (a) a normal tap; (b) a double tap; (c) a long tap. Combining a short and a long tap is shown in (d) and (e): (d) starts with a short tap and ends with a long tap; (e) starts with a long tap and ends with a short tap. (f) and (g) add additional information to the basic tap gesture. A single outline (f) indicates the area wherein the tap can be carried out. This single outline can be narrow like in (f) or as big as the whole screen. For the sake of clarity every tap should be encircled. A single outline as shown in (f) indicates, that a tap outside the outline has no further consequences. In contrast, the double outline of (g) indicates that a tap outside the outline has consequences like closing the application or entering unintended input. (h) hints to consequences left and right of the outline and no consequences above and below the outline.

Extending the presented basic pointing gestures can be achieved by using the basic rules presented above. A thin round outline represents a short tap, a thick round outline represents a long tap. Sketching short and long taps around each other combines them to tap sequences (like (b), (d) or (e)). To perform a tap sequence the user starts with the outermost circle and end with the innermost circle. If an interaction is intended for two fingers two tap sketches are drawn next to each other. The same applies for three or four fingers.

Moving Gesture

While tapping gestures have just one coordinate, *swipes* and *moves* have two: the start coordinate and the end coordinate of the gesture. The time needed to carry out a gesture is another important variable. While a *swipe* is a more swinging movement of a person's hand (little time is needed) a *move* can be slower and thus, more time consuming. However, both gestures start within a starting area and end within a landing area. Another similarity is the presence of a directional movement.

In *Monox,* a (slow) moving gesture is indicated with an arrowhead (Figure 5a), whereas a (fast) swiping gesture is drafted with a double arrowhead (Figure 5b). Moving or swiping in either way is depicted with arrowheads on both ends (Figure 5c). Whenever a *move* or *swipe* should carried out with more than one finger, the number of fingers is hinted by the number of dashes crossing the arrow (Figure 5d).

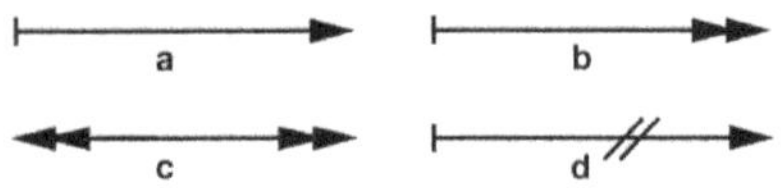

Figure 5: Move, swipe, drag and drop

The meaning of *move* and *swipe* gestures can depend on their starting and landing areas. These areas are notated as follows: a starting area is drawn as a rectangle with sharp corners, whereas the landing area has rounded corners (Figure 6a). If both areas overlap, just the sharp corners are drawn (Figure 6b). An arrow starts and ends within the boundaries of a starting or landing area, usually touching the boarder.

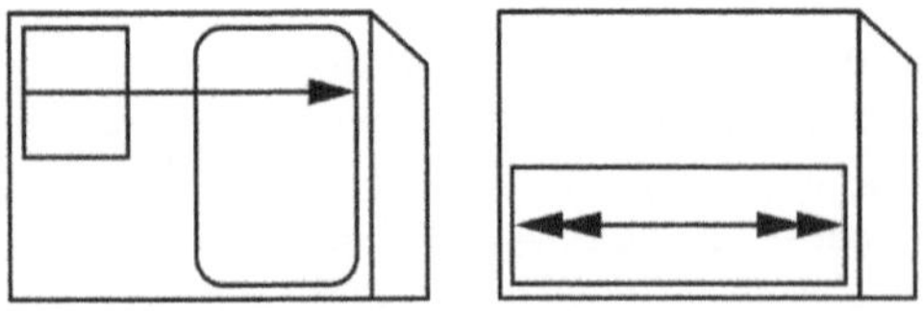

Figure 6: Move, swipe

The *move* and *swipe* gesture can be extended with the tapping gesture to create known or new interaction mechanisms. Figure 7 shows such a combination to form a drag and drop gesture.

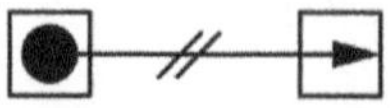

Figure 7: Drag and drop, move with 2 fingers

Multi-Touch Gestures

Multi-touch gestures are carried out with two or more fingers and include gesture like spreading (Figure 8a), pinching (Figure 8b) and rotating (Figure 8c and 8d).

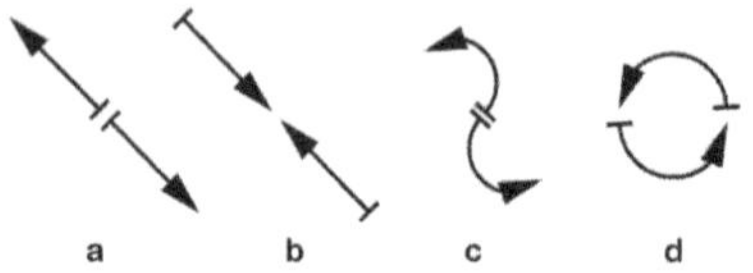

Figure 8: Multi touch gestures

Again, multi-touch gestures can be combined with existing gestures such as the tapping or starting and landing areas.

Screen Change

Due to the small screen sizes of mobile devices the entire screen is usually utilized by a single application. Typically, every interaction leads to a new screen and thus, to a (minimal) cognitive load for the user who has to remember the content of the previous screen. This cognitive load depends on the familiarity with the application and on the importance of the (now not visible) information. However, depending on the application and its implementation not every interaction changes the whole content of a screen. Often only a partial area is changed. Since the way the screen is updated can influence the 'flow' of the interaction, it seems practical to distinguish between *full* and *partial* screen update.

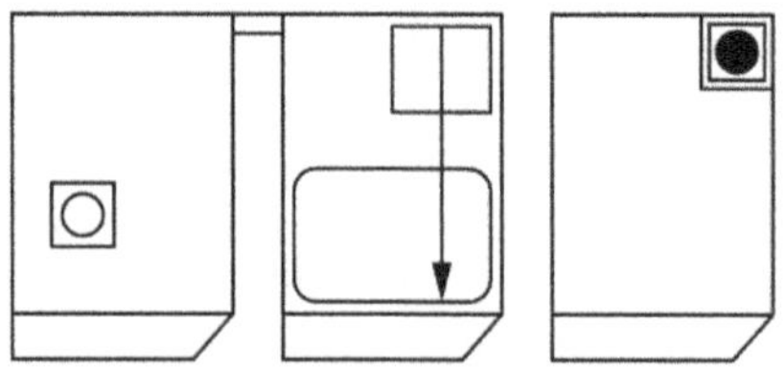

Figure 9: New screen and updated screen

The connection on the upper edge between Figure 9a and Figure 9b indicates a partial screen update when carrying out a short tap (Figure 9a). After the *move* in Figure 9b the screen performs a complete screen update since there is no connection between (b) and (c) on the upper edge between Figure 9b and Figure 9c.

Rare Gestures

Rare gestures are uncommon or novel gestures. Such gestures can be illustrated by combining the appropriate expressions presented above. An example for an uncommon gesture is a Bezel Swipe [20] or Edge Swipe used by MeeGo and Ubuntu Phone (Figure 10).

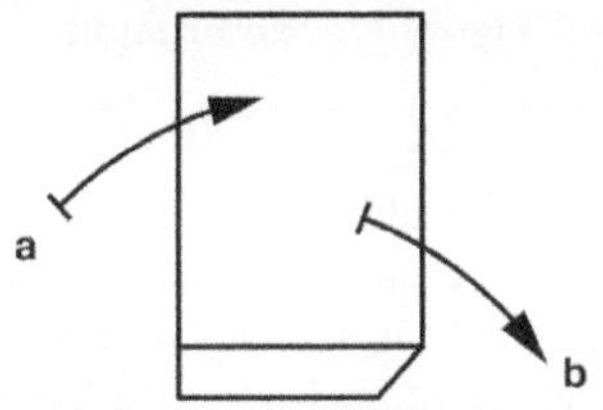

Figure 10: Bezel Swipe as an uncommon or novel gesture

Especially the field of mobile gaming creates novel an unique gestures. In *Monox*, new gestures can be introduced by combining the given set of expressions.

EVALUATION

We conducted an iterative evaluation process to evaluate our approach and identify missing expressions. In the first iteration (initial study) we discussed *Monox* with HCI experts to set the general direction for the notation. In the second iteration (usability study) we conducted an evaluation with a large number of students to proof the basic concept of *Monox*. The findings of these two iterations completed the set of gesture expressions of *Monox*. This extended notation formed the basis for the third iteration (field study), which evaluated *Monox* in real world settings.

First Iteration (Initial Study)

A first iteration was carried out with four HCI experts in a workshop setting to test the basic idea of the proposed gesture notation. The participants were asked to carry out four different tasks. Each participant used a different platform on a daily basis: Apple iOS, Google Android, Microsoft Windows Phone and Nokia MeeGo. The tasks involved two low-level tasks (turning on wireless network and switching between two applications) and two high-level tasks (writing an e-mail and bookmarking a website). In conducting the workshop we were able to do both evaluate the applicability of *Monox* and compare existing interaction designs over various platforms.

The gestures made to fulfill the given tasks were observed by the authors and notated using *Monox* expressions. Afterwards, the tasks were discussed with the participants. During the discussion, we got a detailed picture of the different approaches made by each smartphone manufacturer. Some participants were able to derive basic guidelines for an operating system (unknown to them) just by observing the collected gesture expressions. Furthermore, potentially weak or error-prone interaction techniques were spotted during discussing the collected gesture expressions.

However, this initial evaluation showed the possible potential of the proposed notation. Through *Monox*, HCI experts were able to compare different interactions on various applications spanning over different platforms. Furthermore, the participants were able to discuss improvements for platforms they were not aware of through a unified gesture set.

Second Iteration (Usability Study)

Although the insights of the workshop with HCI experts helped to resolve minor issues with the expressions, we wanted to evaluate our approach with a large user base. Furthermore, we intended to find missing expressions and issues with existing expressions. Thus, we instructed 120 bachelor students in a HCI course (M=23,7yr, SD=3,5) to sketch one of the following tasks: 1) take a photo and change its brightness 2) plan a route to a given destination 3) follow a given user on Twitter or 4) describe a mobile game you recently played. The prerequisites were carrying out the task on a mobile touch-based device and using *Monox* notation. The students were asked to give hints about missing expressions and their overall experience when using *Monox*.

Categorization

The feedback from the students was analyzed and grouped in categories. Based on these categories we identified missing expressions and extended the existing expressions. In the following we present the most often mentioned categories: text input, sensor input, hardware buttons and gesture macros.

Text Input: this category addresses the possibility to type alphanumeric characters by means of a software-emulated keyboard. Participants criticized the exaggerated effort to illustrate arbitrary textual input in *Monox*. An often-proposed approach by the students was a single expression that covers general alphanumeric input, such as a stylized keyboard.

Sensor Input: modern mobile devices are equipped with numerous sensors (accelerator, gyroscope, GPS, NFC, etc.). This category summarizes the possibilities to express sensor input using *Monox*. Participants suggested expressions for shaking, rotating, contactless cross-device communications and audio-based input.

Hardware Buttons: besides touch-based input, mobile devices possess a number of hardware-based buttons to interact with the user, such as volume and power buttons. As these buttons can be an integral part of an interaction sequence visualizing user interaction with hardware buttons should be considered.

Gesture Macros: various interaction sequences contain recurring steps. Often mentioned repetitious tasks were power on and unlock the phone as well as repeating touch interactions in complex applications such as mobile games. To condense such recurring interaction steps in a single *Monox* expression we gathered suggestions for gesture macros made by the participants.

These four categories form the basis for a revision of *Monox*. In the next section we present and discuss the additions we made to complete the proposed notation.

Results

The overall purpose of *Monox* is to foster a systematic approach towards a useable illustration of mobile user interaction. Therefore a basic set of expressions was reduced to a necessary minimum in order to support learnability as well as usability. The idea and notation were well received by the participants, however, the findings of the iterative evaluation with HCI experts and 120 students showed some missing basic, and hence important expressions. These missing expressions belong to four categories we defined above: text input, sensor input, hardware buttons, gesture macros.

Text Input: To achieve a simple and useful illustration for text input the context of the user interaction should be considered. Text input can be letters only, numbers only, mixed, lower case, upper case or special characters. Therefore, we propose following solutions for *Monox* (Figure 11).

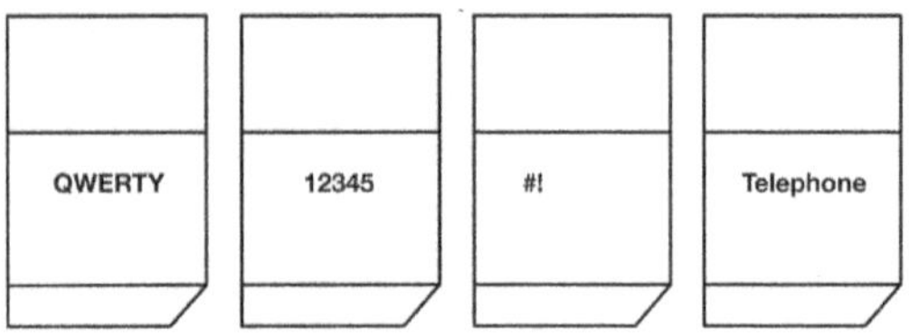

Figure 11: Text input

A software-emulated keyboard usually allocates approximately the lower half of a mobile screen. *Monox* reflects this with a simple schematic depiction of such a keyboard. Additionally, the preset of the keyboard layout is written in the stylized keyboard: "QWERTY" for alphanumerical input, "12345" for numerical input, "#!" for special characters and "Telephone" for a phone like keyboard. Considering the keyboard layout during the sketching phase in a design process can support the awareness of the proper keyboard layout and thus, can lead to more consistent interfaces.

Sensor Input: Sensor data is part of a growing number of mobile applications and should be reflected in *Monox*. Sensor input can be generated actively by moving or shaking the device (accelerometer, gyroscope, NFC) or can be collected passively without direct user involvement (GPS, iBeacon). Figure 12 depicts the notation in *Monox*.

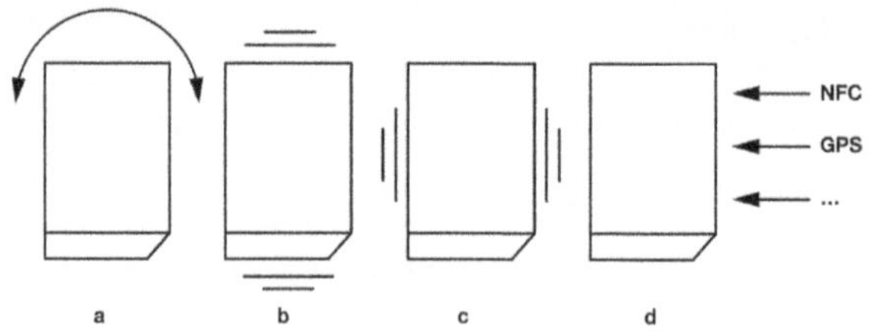

Figure 12: Sensor input

Hardware Button: In addition to input via touch screen mobile devices often use hardware buttons to perform certain functions, such as setting volume or adjusting the camera zoom. Such interaction is notated using the tap expressions (long tap, short tap, etc.) and located outside the device (Figure 13). The expression of hardware buttons in *Monox* follows the principle of simplicity and the idea of re-using given expressions. In this way, the hardware buttons follow the interaction logic already described and do not introduce an additional type of expression.

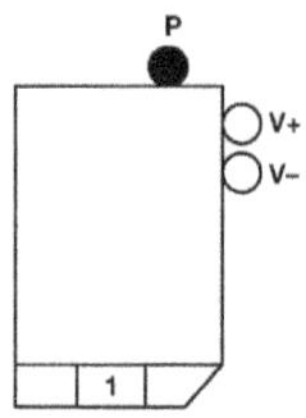

Figure 13: Hardware buttons; long tap on power (P) and short taps on volume up/down (V+/V-)

Gesture Macros: Macros represent a sequence of interactions as a single expression, making the notation task less tedious and error-prone. Using gesture macros follows a two-step process. First, defining a macro by putting the desired interaction sequence in brackets and labeling the sequence with a unique name. Second, using the macro by adding an empty device outline with the desired label on top of it (Figure 14).

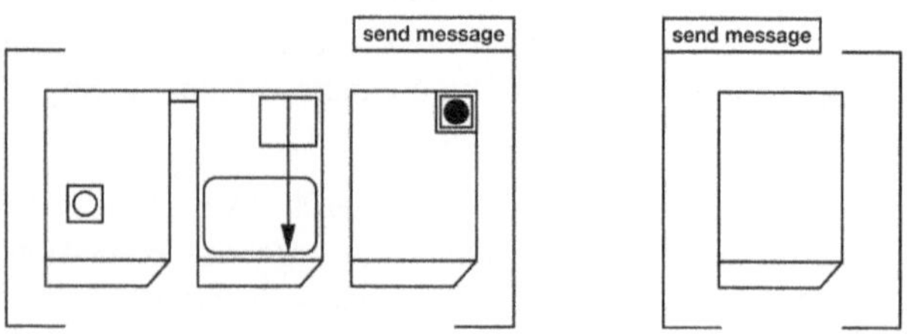

Figure 14: Gesture macros

Together with our initial suggestions for a mobile gesture notation, these additional expressions form an extended version of *Monox*. An evaluation of this new version was realized by means of a field study in real world setting.

Third Iteration (Field Study)

For the field study we visited three different project teams. Every team was in a different stage of the development cycle (setting up the project, defining the requirements, redesigning an existing implementation). To evaluate *Monox* in real world settings, we asked each team to use *Monox* in one of their design sessions.

mApp - discussing ideas for a mobile application

mApp is a small company that focuses on mobile applications. We conducted a design session and an interview with one employee who acts as a technical project manager. The design session and the interview were set up in the office of the company. In the design session the participant (employee) was asked to draw a few sketches (using his own expressions) and explain the idea of the upcoming project. This was done to reveal any similarities in his expressions with *Monox*. It turned out that the company followed a completely different strategy to communicate and discuss interaction design ideas.

Figure 15: Sketches made by the project manager

Figure 15 on the left depicts a typical sketch used in this company. The sketch is numbered all the way through and on an additional sheet of paper the meaning of the numbers is explained in detail with additional sketches. The participant agreed on the argument of a messy sketch and the potential usefulness of a standardized notation. *"However, I doubt this (standardized expressions) will help us much. It is not about the notation itself. It is just the people are ignorant about anything new"*, he explained. Furthermore, the participant revealed an use-case which is not covered by *Monox* now (Figure 15, middle). *"Mobile apps are more and more going to be a single page. You can jump here and there within this page. I guess, in a few years time page flipping will be dead anyhow"*.

After the design session an interview about *Monox* was conducted. Asking the participant where he thinks *Monox* could fit best in their existing workflow he answered "*... wireframe tools like balsamiq.com or similar*". He drew the shaking-sketch from *Monox*, which he found particularly useful (depicted in Figure 15, right), and explained his thought: "*... every tool comes up with its own notation. This is weird and makes group work impossible. If you add a small hint to the sketches this would help a lot. In a context like wireframing tools this make complete sense for me*".

Prool - designing a mobile prototyping tool

Prool is intended to be a mobile application to ease process how mobile prototypes are built and evaluated. In a first design session the process of initializing the application was found too complicated. The goal of this design session was to simplify the initialization process. Two participants with interface- and interaction design background took part in the design session. During the previous development of Prool both participants used a self-made notation that was continuously adapted to the current situations and problems. Thus, depending on situation and problem an expression could have diverse meanings. The participants did not considered this as a major problem although it sometimes led to lengthy and unnecessary discussions.

However, the participants agreed on the presumption that their approach could be problematic on larger projects with more people involved. They further agreed on the idea that a standardized notation could be useful in general. To gather information about the strengths and weaknesses of *Monox* in the described setting we chose the following setup: one participant (Person M=*Monox*) was introduced to the notation of *Monox* and explained its expected advantages like unambiguousness and reproducibility. Person M was also encouraged to use *Monox* throughout and explain the expressions while drawing them. The second participant (Person Z) was just informed about *Monox*, but not instructed. The idea was to see how these two notations (*Monox* vs. non-standardized ad-hoc) "compete" against each other and what kind of discussion starts between the participants about the new notation. Therefore both participants were asked to think out loud.

The design session was set up at the participants' workplace, where the sketches were drawn on whiteboards. Person M (aware of the *Monox* notation) used *Monox* consequently from the beginning whereas Person Z used the informal notation he was used to. Both participants explained the meaning of their sketches during drawing. After a short period of time Person Z began to adopt touch-expressions from *Monox*. Person Z commented this with: "*... these touch expressions are somehow well defined and easy to remember. So I don't have to explain every small change in the interaction design*". In contrast, Person M fell back to the old behavior every now and then and had to redraw sketches. This could be observed especially with small/little interactions. In this case Person M wanted to avoid drawing a complete new sketch and added the interaction to the previous sketch (Figure 16 right).

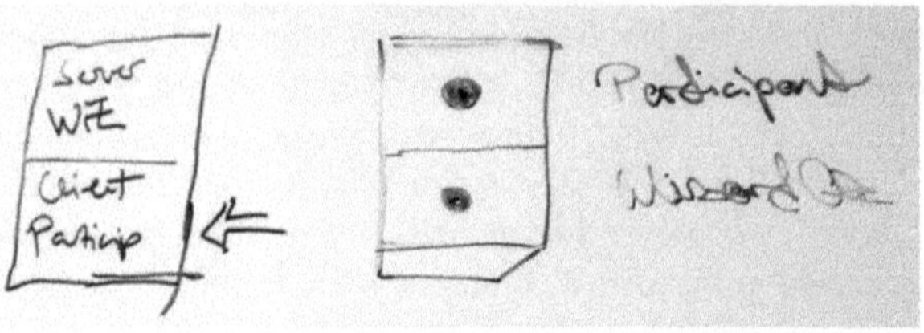

Figure 16: Participants's informal notation (left), Monox (right)

Figure 16 depicts a sketch in both notations used during this session. On the left hand side the informal notation, whereas the right hand side shows the same interaction with *Monox* (with all interaction possibilities on the screen at one time). This contrasting juxtaposition shows the different approaches of these two notations quite well. The informal notation concentrates on the content on the screen and not the interaction. The interaction is explained verbally while sketching and is marked with arbitrary markers (in this case an arrow). *Monox* in contrast prioritizes the interaction. This difference was made the subject of a discussion during the session and the following statements are pointing in this direction:

"*I agree on the idea of Monox, but wouldn't it be nice to have both world (interface design and interaction design) in one sketch?* " (Person Z)

"*Sometimes it is hard to draw a full sketch from scratch just to add a minor interaction. It sometimes feels more natural to add a second interaction to an existing sketch*" (Person M).

After the design session both participants were familiar with the idea of *Monox* and a short interview was conducted. Hereafter a few statements made during the interview.

"*I see the advantage when working over distance. Monox is much clearer and above all, specified. This leaves out a lot of confusion and misunderstandings. Definitely can make things easier.* " (Person Z)

"*You have to learn it, but I guess, when you know it, you just use it like you use hand writing*" (Person M)

"*Does extensible mean, everybody can extend it their way they want?* " (Person Z)

The interview revealed the need for standardization and the participants back ambitions for standardization. At the same time the participants emphasized the (assumed) advantages of case-dependent notations. However, extensible notations like Monox could be both, standardized and open for case-dependent ad-hoc notations as well.

Private Banking - redesigning a Tablet Application

We were able to take part in a usability workshop for a tablet application in the private banking sector. The application in question runs on Windows 8 and is implemented with C# .NET. The workshop participants consisted of a software engineer, who was part of the development team, a graphic designer, an executive of the IT company running this project and one of the authors for moderation and assisting the participants in the usage of *Monox*. The workshop was organized to evaluate the user experience of the application. The participants agreed on redesigning "*investment consultancy*" as the primary use case for this session.

After an introduction to *Monox* by the moderator, the workshop participants started a heuristic evaluation of the consultancy workflow. Whenever a flaw was detected the team utilized *Monox* to discus the problem and potential solutions. In the following we provide an example of an interaction design issue that was discussed by the workshop participants.

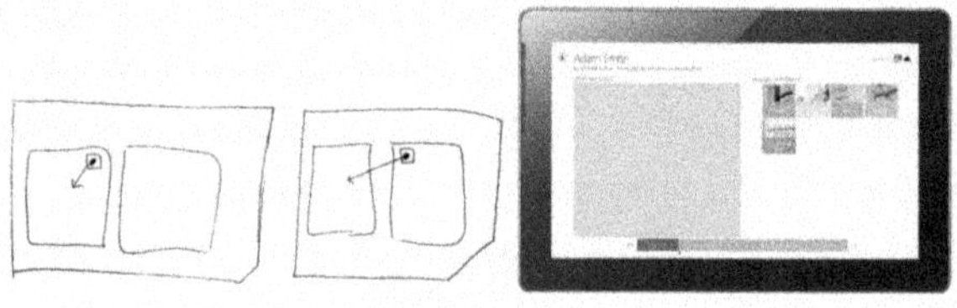

Figure 17: Drag and drop interface elements (courtesy of CPB Software Austria GmbH)

The example shows a problem with an inconsistency following a drag and drop interaction. The interaction is meant to add interface elements to the grey area on the left side of the screen (Figure 17c, right). Therefore the user has to choose one of the interface elements provided on the right side of the screen and move it to the grey area via drag and drop. The *Monox* sketch for this interaction is shown in Figure 17b (center). After this interaction a pop-up window appears providing additional parameters for the element. Figure 17a (left) shows the interaction design problem found by the programmer: whenever the user applies a drag and drop option to one of the elements already added to the grey area on the left the application also instantiates a new element and calls the corresponding pop-up, which should not be the case. The programmer made a sketch of the problem using *Monox*. He said in the direction of the moderator: "*Because of you, I have to renounce my own notation*". Although it would have been easier for the programmer to use his own notation, the graphic designer and the executive were not aware of this notation. This shows, that a common notation like *Monox* supports cooperative discussions about interaction design, especially when working in interdisciplinary teams. By sketching the problem on paper the programmer could do both, explaining the problem to the other participants and taking the paper sketch with him as a reminder and guide how to fix the problem.

DISCUSSION AND CONCLUSION

In this paper we presented a flexible, combinable and extensible notation (*Monox* - MObile NOtations eXtensible) for touch-based gestures on mobile devices. The proposed expressions are intended to be simple to sketch and easy to extend. *Monox* allows the illustration of interaction tasks and the comparison of interaction patterns regardless of the platform. Thus, *Monox* can help to discuss and pinpoint strenghts and weaknesses in an interaction design for mobile applications. Our findings show that the proposed notation can provide a common ground for discussing and exchanging ideas during all phases in a project (design, implementation, evaluation).

Monox was developed in an iterative process and reflects multiple aspects of touch-based interaction on modern mobile devices. The first two iterations included an initial workshop with HCI-experts and a usability evaluation with 120 participants. Based on the results of the evaluation we designed a revised version of *Monox* with additional expressions. The third iteration was a field study utilizing *Monox* in three different real world settings. The field study included various stakeholders like researcher, project manager, programmer and designer.

During the first field study *Monox* was proposed as a tool for detached groups supporting collaborative working. The participant explained the different settings the groups had to work in. These groups include persons who are not willing to learn something new, like *Monox*. However, the participant also suggested that a unified and well-defined notation could form the basis for XML- or JSON-based gesture descriptions. And these technical descriptions could be used as an interchange format for wireframing tools.

The second field study was conducted with two participants who were designing a mobile application for rapid prototyping. During the observed design session various interaction sequences were discussed by the participants utilizing both, *Monox* and their own non-standardized expression set. Depending on the particular interaction sequence they decided in-situ which notation would fit best. Both participants agreed on the idea of a unified and expandable notation for mobile applications. The participants saw the main advantage of *Monox* in its unambiguity that eases discussions about complex interaction sequences. However, especially one participant urged for joining the content and interaction expression in one sketch.

In the third field study we applied *Monox* in a redesign workshop for a tablet application in the private banking sector. The results showed, that the usage of *Monox* provides a common ground for discussing usability issues in an interdisciplinary team. This allowed the team members to focus on redesigning user interaction rather than struggling with different self-defined notations. However, we noted that the participants of the workshop focused on a basic set of expressions ignoring the more advanced expressions. The participants mentioned that they would enjoy a tool for tablets or mobile phones, which provides the possibility to add *Monox* sketches as an overlay to the current screen.

In each iteration of our design process we gathered useful feedback from the participants. Thus, we propose future work should further explore how to merge content with expressions, avoiding ambiguity of screen elements and interaction expressions at the same time. Furthermore, the integration of *Monox* into existing tools and applications could beneficial for rapid prototyping. Both could increase the usefulness and acceptance of the notation.

Extensive work has been done to qualify and quantify touch-based gestures, mostly utilizing proprietary vendor-specific notations.

An open alternative could help to compare designs across platforms and to gain more valuable insights. Therefore we see *Monox* as a first step in establishing a common, unified notation easing the burden of finding best practices in interaction design across various platforms and applications. Serving as a tool for researchers, designers and programmers, *Monox* can also lower the gap between distinct professions whenever discussing or evaluating novel ideas and designs. We hope, that the ideas presented in this paper will motivate others to contribute to the process of establishing a comprehensive notation for touch-based gestures.

ACKNOWLEDGMENTS

We thank all the participants involved in the studies and everyone who helped to shape this paper.

REFERENCES

1. Apple Inc. 2013. iOS Human Interface Guidelines. http://developer.apple.com/library/ios/#documentation/userexperience/conceptual/mobilehig/Characteristics/Characteristi cs.html
2. Buxton, B. 2010. Sketching User Experiences: Getting the Design Right and the Right Design: Getting the Design Right and the Right Design. Morgan Kaufmann, 2010.
3. Canonical Ltd. 2013. Ubuntu Gestures http://design.ubuntu.com/apps/get-started/gestures
4. Fitts, P.M. 1954. The information capacity of the human motor system in controlling the amplitude of movement. Journal of Experimental Psychology. 47(6): p. 381-391.
5. Gandhe, S. 2014. Press render of Samsung's Tizen-based ZEQ 9000 leaks online. Neowin LLC. http://www.neowin.net/news/press-render-of-samsungs-tizen-based-zeq-9000-leaks-online
6. Gesture Works. 2013. http://gestureworks.com/pages/core-features-gestures

7. Google, Inc. 2013. Android Patterns and Gestures http://developer.android.com/design/patterns/gestures.html

8. Heo, J., Ham, D-H., Park, S., Song, C. and Yoon. W.C. 2009. A framework for evaluating the usability of mobile phones based on multi-level, hierarchical model of usability factors. Interaction Computing 21, 4 (August 2009), 263-275.

9. Holleis, P., Otto, F., Hussmann, H. and Schmidt, A. 2007. Keystroke-level model for advanced mobile phone interaction. In *Proceedings of the SIGCHI Conference on Human Factors in Computing Systems* (CHI '07). ACM, New York, NY, USA, 1505-1514.

10. Jung, K. and Jang, J. 2013. A Two-Step Click Interaction for Mobile Internet on Smartphone. In *Communications in Computer and Information Science - Posters' Extended Abstracts*. Springer Berlin Heidelberg 2013.

11. Kantar Worldpanel Comtech Report 2013 http://www.kantarworldpanel.com/dwl.php?sn=news_downl oads&id=151 03.08.2013

12. Kin, K., Hartmann, B., DeRose, T. and Agrawala, M. 2012. Proton: multitouch gestures as regular expressions. In *Proceedings of the 2012 ACM annual conference on Human Factors in Computing Systems* (CHI '12). ACM, New York, NY, USA, 2885-2894.

13. Kin, K., Hartmann, B., DeRose, T. and Agrawala, M. 2012. Proton++: a customizable declarative multitouch framework. In *Proceedings of the 25th annual ACM symposium on User interface software and technology* (UIST '12). ACM, New York, NY, USA, 477-486. DOI=10.1145/2380116.2380176 http://doi.acm.org/10.1145/2380116.2380176

14. Law, E.L-C. 2011. The measurability and predictability of user experience. In *Proceedings of the 3rd ACM SIGCHI symposium on Engineering interactive computing systems* (EICS '11). ACM, New York, NY, USA, 1-10.

15. Lee, J. and Paik, D. 2007. Human-Computer Interaction. Interaction Platforms and Techniques. In *Human-Computer Interaction, Part II, HCII 2007*, Springer-Verlag Berling Heidelberg. LNCS 4551, p. 401-407.

16. Li, G., Cao, X., Paolantonio, S. and Tian, F. 2012. SketchComm: a tool to support rich and flexible asynchronous communication of early design ideas. In *Proceedings of the ACM 2012 conference on Computer Supported Cooperative Work* (CSCW '12). ACM, New York, NY , USA, 359-368.

17. McMahon, K. 2013. App Dev Wiki. http://appdevwiki.com/wiki/show/HomePage

18. Paternò, F., Mancini, C. and Meniconi, S. 1997. ConcurTaskTrees: A Diagrammatic Notation for Specifying Task Models. In *Proceedings of the IFIP TC13 International Conference on Human-Computer Interaction* (INTERACT '97), Steve Howard, Judy Hammond, and Gitte Lindgaard (Eds.). Chapman & Hall, Ltd., London, UK, UK, 362-369.

19. Ramanahally, P., Gilbert, S., Niedzielski, T., Velázquez, D. and Anagnost C. 2009. Sparsh UI: A Multi-Touch Framework for Collaboration and Modular Gesture Recognition. In *Proceedings of World Conference on Innovative Virtual Reality*. ASME-AFM.

20. Roth. V. and Turner, T. 2009. Bezel swipe: conflict-free scrolling and multiple selection on mobile touch screen devices. In *Proceedings of the SIGCHI Conference on Human Factors in Computing Systems* (CHI '09). ACM, New York, NY , USA, 1523-1526.

21. Schmidt, M. and Weber, G. 2013. Template based classification of multi-touch gestures. Journal of Pattern Recognition. Elsevier. DOI=http://dx.doi.org/10.1016/j.patcog.2013.02.001

22. Schulz, T. 2008. Using the Keystroke-Level Model to Evaluate Mobile Phones. Trolltech ASA. University of Oslo. http://hdl.handle.net/10852/9883

23. Wobbrock, J.O., Ringel Morris, M. and Wilson, A.D. 2009. User-defined gestures for surface computing. In *Proceedings of the SIGCHI Conference on Human Factors in Computing Systems* (CHI '09). ACM, New York, NY, USA, 1083-1092. DOI=10.1145/1518701.1518866 http://doi.acm.org/10.1145/1518701.1518866

24. Wroblewski, L. 2013. Touch Gesture Reference Guide http://www.lukew.com/ff/entry.asp

Automating UI Tests for Mobile Applications with Formal Gesture Descriptions

Marc Hesenius
marc.hesenius@paluno.uni-due.de

Tobias Griebe
tobias.griebe@paluno.uni-due.de

Stefan Gries
stefan.gries@paluno.uni-due.de

Volker Gruhn
volker.gruhn@paluno.uni-due.de

paluno - The Ruhr Institute for Software Technology
University of Duisburg-Essen
Gerlingstr. 16, 45127 Essen, Germany

ABSTRACT
Touch- and gesture-based interfaces are common in applications for mobile devices. By evolving into mass market products, smartphones and tablets created an increased need for specialized software engineering methods. To ensure high quality applications, constant and efficient testing is crucial in software development. However, testing mobile applications is still cumbersome, time-consuming and error-prone. One reason is the devices' focus on touch-based interaction – gestures cannot be easily incorporated into automated application tests. We present an extension to the popular Calabash testing framework solving this problem by allowing to describe gestures with a formal language in tests scripts.

Author Keywords
Software Engineering; Testing; Test Automation; Mobile Applications; Gestures; Gesture Formalization;

ACM Classification Keywords
H.5.2. User Interfaces: Evaluation/methodology; D.2.5. Testing and Debugging: Testing Tools

INTRODUCTION
In recent years mobile devices have emerged in a variety of types ranging from portable music players to highly specialized custom-built devices (e.g. ticket validation in public transport). Especially general purpose smartphones aiming at mass audiences evolved into an everyday tool and have become an important platform for digital service distribution. While there is a large number of device manufacturers and several different operating systems – usually deeply embedded into provider-specific operating environments – smartphones typically offer a set of similar features, such as a multitude of sensors and, predominantly, a touch screen interface.

Smartphones introduced touch screens as a common tool into daily life, accompanied by an interaction paradigm shift. They enable users to touch and manipulate virtual elements directly on the display of a mobile handset without the need for mediating technology (e.g. mouse, keyboard or similar), leading to a more natural and intuitive way of interaction. Besides, touch screen interfaces also allow for touch gestures.

MobileHCI'14, September 23 - 26 2014, Toronto, ON, Canada
Copyright 2014 ACM 978-1-4503-3004-6/14/09$15.00.
http://dx.doi.org/10.1145/2628363.2628391

While users benefit from the interaction improvements and the multitude of available devices, the overall situation poses major challenges to software developers. Gesture-based interaction is harder to process than classic point'n'click interaction and is even more difficult to test. Additionally, tests have to be performed on a large number of devices to cover as many different configurations (i.e. display size, display orientation, operating system) as possible. Automating User Interface (UI) tests is generally hard and troublesome but is presently almost impossible for mobile applications. Current automation technology typically only allows to record and replay gestures or to flood the Application Under Test (AUT) with random input events. Both are insufficient strategies for effective testing: replaying the same gesture suffers from uniformity (gestures by human users will slightly differ on every execution) and flooding applications with random input events is not useful in structured testing scenarios.

We present an extension to the test framework Calabash[1] allowing developers to formally describe touch gestures within a specification for UI tests. Running the test mimics human users by translating the specified gesture into corresponding touch events injected into the AUT upon test case execution. Developers and testers can write test scenarios in Calabash's Gherkin language and directly include touch gesture expressions without the need for manual recording. In order to create realistic testing scenarios, the described gestures are simulated with noise and drift to reflect human users' inaccuracy.

The remainder of this paper is structured as follows: First, we introduce common techniques and problems in mobile application testing with a focus on gesture-intensive applications. Then we briefly discuss an overview of formal gesture definition languages. In the following sections, we will present our approach to automating mobile application testing and discuss an evaluation of our approach. Our contribution concludes with a review of related work and a discussion of future research on the topic.

[1] `http://calaba.sh`

TESTING GESTURE-INTENSIVE MOBILE APPLICATIONS

Testing is a crucial activity for software developers that claims a major portion of up to 90% [19] of the total development effort. Effective application testing is vital for the economic success of a development project, especially in highly competitive environments such as the mobile application market. Short release cycles are common and an alternative app can be installed with just a few clicks via app stores.

The economical challenges and changing dynamics of the software market expose developers and testers to additional pressure in terms of quality management and time to market. In response, highly agile, iterative development processes such as Scrum have gained popularity. While powerful tools for mobile app development were made available to the general public, manufacturers have failed to introduce sufficient testing facilities into their respective Software Development Kit (SDK) and – even more important – their devices.

Mobile Application Testing

Testing software for mobile devices differs from testing software for desktop computers or server/host environments in several aspects. Traditional testing tasks, e.g. selecting an appropriate and representative and yet economically reasonable set of test cases, determining adequate test oracles and specifying test input data, still persist in mobile testing. Additionally, test activities are predominantly driven by mobile- and device-specific factors significantly increasing an application's vulnerability to potential defects. Mobile-specific factors include context-specific properties of the device, the execution environment and the user (e.g. type, availability and quality of network connection, sensor data, location information). Device-specific factors include properties that are inherently bound to different handsets, such as operating system, form factor (tablet computer vs. smartphone), display size and orientation. These factors multiply the testing effort, as the typical testing process (unit-tests, integration tests, smoke tests, system tests, acceptance tests and regression tests) is extended by *device tests* and *testing in the wild* [9], where the AUT is deployed on a set of handsets and executed under the appropriate conditions. This may include visiting off-site locations, provoking roaming scenarios and traveling long distances.

When executing test cases for mobile applications, the AUT needs to be exposed to an adequate selection of mobile-specific factors paired with device-specific factors, immediately creating a test case explosion problem even for simple test cases: a representative selection of devices and – depending on the application's purpose – different locations to cover potential dependency on GPS, sensor data or roaming scenarios that might affect the AUT are necessary.

Dealing with the large number of test cases required to assure adequate coverage of mobile-specific as well as device-specific factors easily exceeds a single developer's or tester's – or even a mid-sized company's – capabilities in terms of effort invested in testing time as well as in budget. Using appropriate test automation technology can help to remedy the mismatch between the required effort and the available budget. Unfortunately, test automation technology barely meets the immediate requirements in terms of adequately handling mobile- and device-specific factors as well as device heterogeneity and interaction concepts in test case execution.

While close-to-code tests probing an application's core logic can be created using similar technology as used for testing desktop and web applications (e.g. unit tests using designated testing frameworks), for UI testing the AUT needs to be executed, stimulated with user interaction events and carefully observed. Since the AUT is executed on a different machine than the one used for development, there is only limited access to the AUT at runtime. To decouple the observation of the AUT and the subsequent classification of defective application behavior from manual interaction, interfaces to the AUT are needed that allow for the inspection of application properties at runtime. On most contemporary platforms this is achieved by instrumentation technology, where some aspects of the AUT can be observed at runtime and artificial user interface events can be generated to remote-control and manipulate the AUT.

Gesture-intensive Application Testing

In addition to the economic impact of testing activities, interaction specification causes an increased communication need. Natural language is highly ambiguous and error-prone. Hence, misunderstandings between stakeholders are common. Requirements engineers and UI designers have to translate customer demands into written specifications and UI mock-ups, typically incorporating some sort of interaction concept in form of graphical and textual annotations. These documents provide the basic foundation for development and testing. Therefore, developers and testers must gain a common understanding with requirements engineers and UI designers regarding the interaction. To overcome this communication gap, techniques such as Behavior-Driven Development (BDD) [22] have been created.

The problems arising from the communication gap hold especially true for applications based on touch gestures. Since modern smartphones and tablets commonly feature touch-sensitive displays as the primary interaction channel, developers actively incorporate touch gesture recognition into their applications. Common examples range from very simple gestures like swipes to complex multi-touch gestures involving various fingers and movements.

From the developer's perspective, the recognition of touch gestures introduces new complexity to an application's source code. Contemporary mobile platforms support a rudimentary set of basic gestures (i.e. touch/double touch, long press, swipe/drag, pinch open/close) accessible via the respective platform SDK. However, the recognition of custom gestures is cumbersome. As long as there are no convenience frameworks such as the *Android Gesture Libraries* [2], the developer has no option but to analyze the set of individual points returned by low-level UI events for gestures. While this approach promises the most flexible gesture recognition algorithms, it is also the most error-prone. Very likely an inadequately large portion of the overall code will be focused on gesture recognition rather than functional logic.

From the testing perspective, gesture-intensive applications create two major challenges: gestures need to be exactly specified and reliably reproduced. Both – specifically the absence thereof – represent key challenges in mobile application testing and can be overcome by formal gesture specification in conjunction with instrumentation technology.

The lack of formal gesture specifications prevents the use of test automation technology, even in cases where existing technology could automate the testing process in other aspects. Current test automation tools can at best replay pre-recorded gestures, making the process highly dependent on specific handset configuration (i.e. platform, display orientation, display size). To our knowledge, formal gesture description is currently not supported in existing test automation tools.

At the same time, the absence of formal gesture specification also requires testers to have in-depth understanding of the requirements documentation. There is a risk that inaccurate interpretation of natural language test case descriptions yields unreliable test results. Hence, the set of efficient testers is reduced to stakeholders directly involved in development, effectively excluding budget-friendly testing methods (e.g. crowd-testing, cloud testing services, offshoring) and especially test automation tools from the available options.

Automation, on the other hand, is a key technology to reliable test execution reproduction, which in environments of extreme device heterogeneity is a constraining prerequisite since the AUT needs to be tested on a large selection of mobile devices. Also, in mobile environments the testing effort is driven by additional triggers [9], since mobile platforms evolve rather quickly and major updates are to be expected frequently. The need for (regression) testing arises in response to mobile platform evolution. We therefore introduce an approach to test automation for gesture-intensive mobile applications that uses a formal gesture specification language to describe touch gestures within the Cucumber/Gherkin-based test automation technology Calabash.

FORMALIZING MULTI-TOUCH GESTURES

SDKs to develop mobile apps typically ship with predefined gesture-based UI-components (e.g. scrolling with a finger in Android's ListView UI element). Additionally, components are included that allow developers to easily identify a set of basic gestures like swipes and pinches (e.g. the latter can be detected using Android's *ScaleGestureDetector*). However, implementing custom gestures leaves developers without further support. For a gesture with the complexity of Figure 1, analyzing the incoming stream of UI events to identify the gesture's different elements in correlation is necessary – an error-prone and mathematically sophisticated task.

Declarative descriptions can be used to simplify the implementation of gesture recognition. Formal languages to define gestures and accompanying tool sets provide an abstraction layer from the underlying touch events, effectively freeing developers from the necessity of manually processing touch coordinates to derive gestures. Several approaches have been developed in recent years using different techniques and formal foundations.

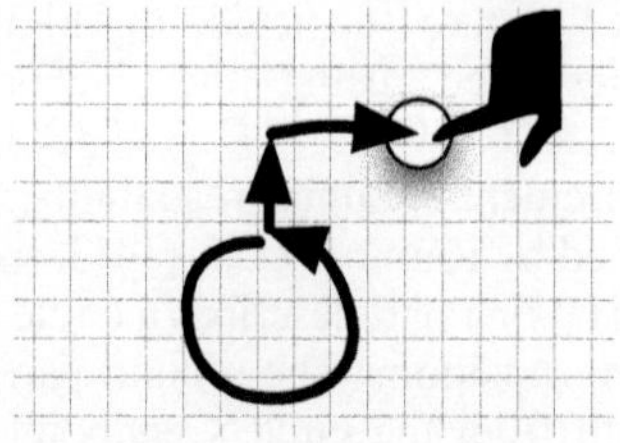

Figure 1. Complex touch gesture where one finger performs a counter-clockwise circle, followed by a line in northern direction and a line in eastern direction.

Proton [16, 17] describes gestures using Regular Expressions (RegEx). It strictly corresponds to the fingers' movements on the surface – a description starts with a D (down), followed by a series of M (move) and different operators, and ends with an U (up). Different fingers can be identified with indices. Additionally, attributes can be used to describe different customized parameters (e.g. movement direction). Complex gestures result in complex and hard to read RegEx.

GISpL [7] describes gestures using a JSON representation. It has the advantage that it can be used to describe alternative gesture-based interaction modalities and is not bound to multi-touch applications. Gestures are defined as a set of *features* to be executed in customizable *regions*. Features include attributes such as the number of fingers used or the direction of movement. The JSON representation is basically human-readable, but the use of vectors and other specialized notations makes a sound technical background necessary.

GeForMT [13, 14] uses a simple grammar-based approach to gesture definition. Complex gestures can be composed from a basic set of atomic gestures, such as $LINE$, $SEMICIRCLE$, $MOVE$ or $HOLD$. Atomic gestures can be attributed by adding movement directions using a compass notation. $MOVE\_N$ describes a movement upward, $MOVE\_NE$ describes a movement towards the right upper corner. $SEMICIRCLE\_S\_CW$ describes a semicircle rotating clockwise and ending south of the starting point. While GeForMT's reduced syntax allows for the fast and easy creation of gestures and is human-readable without a technical background, it lacks the possibility to add custom attributes such as length or speed.

These languages and frameworks have been developed with simplifying gesture specification and subsequent *detection* in mind. As we target gesture *simulation* within our testing framework, we have different requirements for gesture specification languages. We aim for a natural-language-oriented approach to test case specification as discussed in the next section. Hence, we require the gesture specification to be easily readable – for humans as well as for machines – and to be concise enough to be included in test case specifications. Due to this constraint, Proton and GISpL (and similar languages) have been ruled out as their RegEx- and JSON-based approaches do not fit the constraint of human readability. We settled on using GeForMT in our approach due to its grammar-based approach resulting in a concise, clear and easily readable syntax.

The complex gesture depicted in Figure 1, for example, is described using the GeForMT expression $1F(CIRCLE\_N\_CCW, LINE\_N, LINE\_E)$, which satisfies our requirement of human readability. According to the grammar defined by Kammer et al. [14] it specifies three partial gestures: The first part describes a circle starting and ending in the north position. The second part describes a line extending north from the circle's endpoint. The third part specifies a line extending east from the previous line's endpoint.

AUTOMATING MOBILE APPLICATION TESTING

Recently, a number of test automation frameworks (e.g. JUnit[2], CUnit[3], Calabash, Robotium[4], Calculon[5]) have appeared that build on top of application instrumentation technology. Some of these are code-based (i.e. test cases are written in platform-native code, e.g. Java for Android or Objective-C for iOS), while others employ a Domain Specific Language (DSL) to express test cases. The latter are useful when test cases are written by non-developers. This is especially beneficial in environments where communication barriers exist between developers, who focus exclusively on the technical implementation, and the business department, who focus exclusively on the business logic. However, existing test execution automation tools are only marginally suitable for testing gesture-intensive mobile applications.

Test Execution Automation

To overcome this limitation, we have extended an existing test execution automation tool to support the inclusion of complex gesture-based interaction in the test case specification. At the current stage of our research, we have selected Calabash-Android[6] as the target automation technology. Calabash is a functional test automation technology available for the platforms Android and iOS, where test cases are expressed as Cucumber[7] features. Cucumber is an acceptance test automation technology that allows for the specification of test cases using the DSL Gherkin[8]. We have decided on Calabash because of its ability to accept near-natural language test specifications as input and because of its extensibility.

Calabash consists of a complex technology stack running test cases partially on a host system, where the test specification is interpreted, and partially on the AUT, where the actual test – including simulated user interaction – is executed. A HTTP-based communication via link (a) in Figure 2 is used to send commands extracted from the test case specification to the Robotium-based test server on the target system. The test server is deployed together with the AUT on the device. This enables the use of the Android-specific native instrumentation technology to interact with the AUT (i.e. injecting user interface events and inspecting/reporting the state of UI elements).

[2] `http://junit.org`
[3] `http://cunit.sourceforge.net`
[4] `https://code.google.com/p/robotium/`
[5] `https://github.com/mttkay/calculon`
[6] `https://github.com/calabash/calabash-android`
[7] `http://cukes.info`
[8] `https://github.com/cucumber/cucumber/wiki/Gherkin`

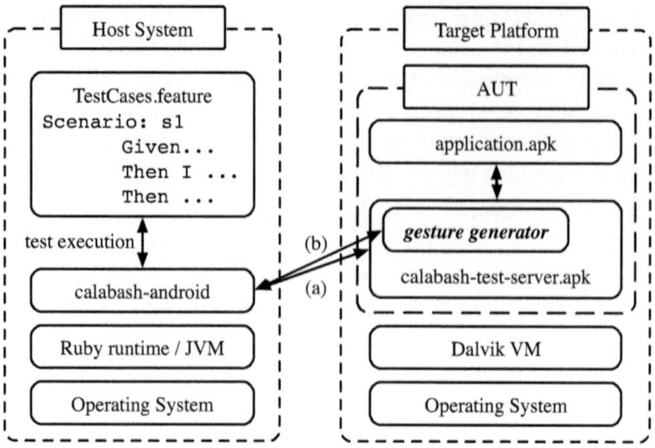

Figure 2. The Calabash test execution automation technology stack extended with our gesture generator module.

Gesture-intensive Test Execution Automation

While basic gestures such as swipe and drag are already included in Calabash, complex and custom gestures are not supported. Hence we created the *gesture generator* module based on the technology discussed in the next section, which can be directly addressed by Calabash using communication link (b) in Figure 2.

For this purpose we created a custom implementation of the Calabash framework. The gesture generator module accepts GeForMT expressions and transforms them into a series of touch events. We designed the gesture generator to accept various parameters to respond to device- and use-case-specific requirements (e.g. display size, resolution and orientation). Using this approach, the gesture simulation can be limited to certain areas of the screen (e.g. the upper half) or the area of a specific UI element.

Along with the custom Calabash implementation, we prepared a number of Gherkin templates that accept GeForMT expressions and a set of parameters specifying the absolute/relative location, duration and pseudo-random variance of the gesture. When test cases containing GeForMT expressions are executed, the command is transferred into the client-side compartment of the Calabash stack (see Figure 2) and sent to the gesture generator. A corresponding stream of touch events is injected into the AUT, which is expected to recognize the gesture, eventually forming the actual test case.

Gesture recognition within the AUT at this point is left to the developer, who may opt for a recognition technology of his personal preference (e.g. [4, 20, 21]). A test case is treated as a success if the stream of touch events is correctly interpreted by the AUT.

Using our approach to formally express touch gestures in test case specifications provides a solid base for reliable, automated gesture-intensive application testing. Test specifications can be created in near-natural language including complex gesture-based interactions with an application's user interface. An example of a Cucumber feature accepted by Calabash expressed in Gherkin and featuring a formal gesture description in GeForMT is depicted in Listing 1.

```
1 Scenario: Activation of push services
2 Given my app is running
3 Then the "GameMain" activity should be open
4 Then the view with id "push-ind" should
      have property "visibility" = "FALSE"
5 Then I perform gesture "1F(CIRCLE_N_CW,
      LINE_N,LINE_E)"
6 Then the view with id "push-ind" should
      have property "visibility" = "TRUE"
```

Listing 1. Example of a Calabash test case expressed in Gherkin featuring a GeForMT expression in line 5 to specify a touch gesture.

In the example presented in Listing 1, a test case is specified where the automation technology – and specifically the gesture generator – is instructed to perform a $1F(CIRCLE\_N\_CW, LINE\_N, LINE\_E)$ gesture. After performing the gesture, the UI of the AUT is queried for the desired outcome. In the specific case in Listing 1, an applications' push service can be enabled performing a clockwise circle followed by a line in north direction followed by another line in east direction. A mismatch between the expected and the actual outcome is counted as an application defect, since the application did not respond correctly to the touch gesture.

Gesture Simulation

To enable Calabash to accept GeForMT expressions in test cases and subsequently execute them as simulated touch gestures, we extended Calabash with an additional module. The *gesture generator* (see Figure 2) receives GeForMT expressions and converts them into a series of touch events injected into the AUT. Gesture simulation is done in two phases: in phase one the GeForMT expression is analyzed; in phase two the result of the analysis is used to extrapolate touch coordinates from atomic gestures and inject corresponding touch events into the AUT.

Mimicking human users as closely as possible is desirable in order to execute realistic test cases, but – to our best knowledge – little is currently known about gesture variance and execution patterns. We performed an experiment to find out how gestures differ between human users and used the acquired data to improve the gesture simulation algorithm with suitable signal noise. We expect our approach to be in an early but useful development stage. With related research (e.g. [3, 8]) recently starting to elicit more important details, we are interested in a deeper elaboration and optimization of our current simulation approach in future work.

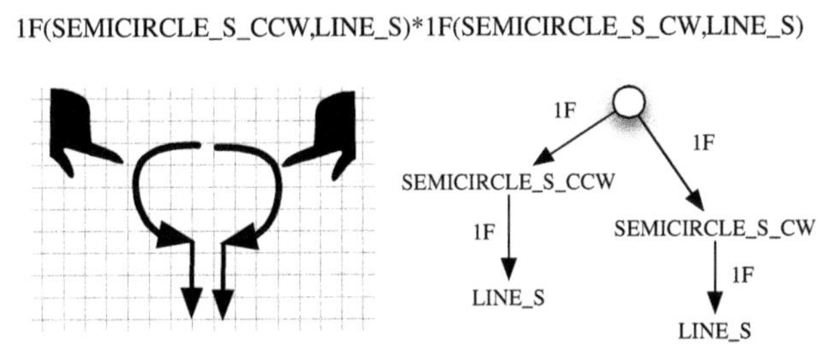

Figure 3. Syntax tree of a complex GeForMT expression where two fingers each perform a semicircle follows by a line in south direction.

GeForMT Expression Analysis

Our gesture generator starts by decomposing GeForMT expressions into executable parts. A syntax tree is used to identify atomic gestures executed either concurrently or sequentially. Each node with more than one child branch describes a multi-touch gesture and introduces additional parallelization. The example in Figure 3 represents the GeForMT expression $1F(SEMICIRCLE\_S\_CCW, LINE\_S) * 1F(SEMICIRCLE\_S\_CW, LINE\_S)$: two fingers perform mirrored semicircles ending in the south direction followed by a line. This expression is decomposed into four atomic gestures representing the syntax tree's nodes. The $*$-operator denotes parallel gesture execution.

On touch-based devices, the area where the gesture input is detected may cover the display completely or may be limited to certain display regions. With the large number of different devices using various display sizes available, touch gestures vary significantly in dimension and location relative to the device's display. GeForMT, however, has neither a notion of a gesture's dimension nor its location. To overcome this issue, we assign a virtual dimension to each atomic gesture identified in the syntax analysis within the range $[-1, 1]$ on both axes of a cartesian coordinate plane, where the start point of the atomic gesture is at the coordinate system's origin. For example, the gesture expression $LINE\_N$, a vertical line extending from south to north, extents from $0, 0$ to $0, 1$, while $LINE\_SW$ extends from $0, 0$ to $-1, -1$. The atomic gesture expression $SEMICIRCLE\_N\_CW$, a circle drawn clockwise ending in the north position, is 0.5 units in width and 1 unit in height.

Overall gesture dimension is calculated by successively building the maximum required dimension from atomic gestures and subsequently adding the maximum atomic gesture's dimensions to the endpoint of the previous atomic gesture. Figure 4 shows an example of the gesture $1F(LINE\_N, SEMICIRCLE\_N\_CCW)$ having the overall dimension of 2 units in height and 0.5 units in width. For each atomic gesture, a pair of coordinates for the start and end point is stored and used during the next phase to extrapolate touch coordinates.

The first gesture generation phase results in a set of atomic gestures stored in a tree structure representing their structural relation and their bounding boxes. This data structure is used in the second phase, which extrapolates coordinates on a device's display used for touch event injection.

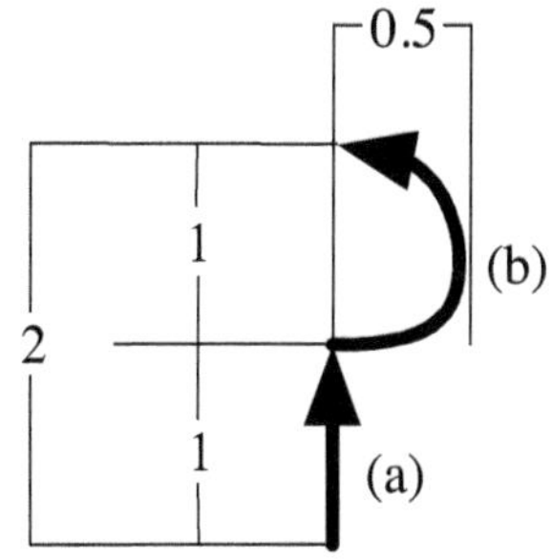

Figure 4. A gesture having the overall dimension of 2 units in height and 0.5 units in width.

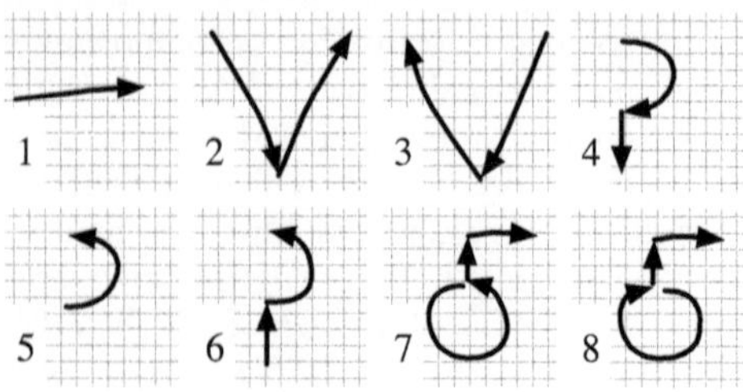

Figure 5. The selection of gestures used to evaluate our gesture generator within the test case execution automation technology.

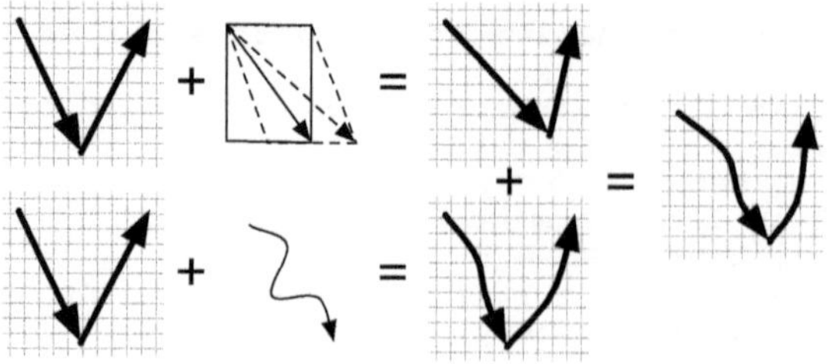

Figure 7. The GeForMT gesture $1F(LINE\_SE, LINE\_NE)$ drawn accurately (left side) and with drift and jittering (right side).

Gesture Simulation Algorithm

In the second phase, our gesture generator uses the data structure created in the GeForMT expression analysis to determine a set of coordinates and injects corresponding touch events into the AUT. In a first step, the individual bounding boxes of atomic gestures are aggregated to an overall bounding box, which subsequently is scaled down to fit a unity bounding box while preserving the aspect ratio. Then the total bounding box is mapped to a handset's display or a region on the touch sensitive display specified in the Gherkin statement (total display area is used if region specification is omitted).

Since GeForMT expressions are built from a finite set of atomic gestures, we defined a coordinate extrapolation algorithms accepting atomic gesture expressions and a bounding box as input (e.g. $LINE\_SE$ in a rectangle from 100, 100 to 400, 400 in display coordinates). Due to the limited set of atomic gestures, simple line and circle equations were sufficient to extrapolate individual touch coordinates. The time based extrapolation equations create a set of coordinates mapped to the atomic gesture's bounding box parameterized with an atomic gesture's duration.

The equations used to extrapolate touch coordinates originally created perfect gestures. For example, the atomic gesture expression $LINE\_W$ resulted in a set of touch coordinates evenly distributed on a perfectly straight line. Obviously, no human user is able to perform touch gestures with this geometric accuracy. Dealing with signal noise is a major challenge in gesture recognition and the quality of recognition algorithms significantly depends on the ability to handle noisy/fuzzy gestures with good confidence. For effectively testing touch-based input, gestures must be simulated with a realistic amount of signal noise, hence we enhanced our gesture generator with capabilities to mimic close-to-human user touch input blur.

We conducted an experiment to obtain a data set of coordinates from touch gestures performed by human users to determine adequate artificial signal noise parameters. We created

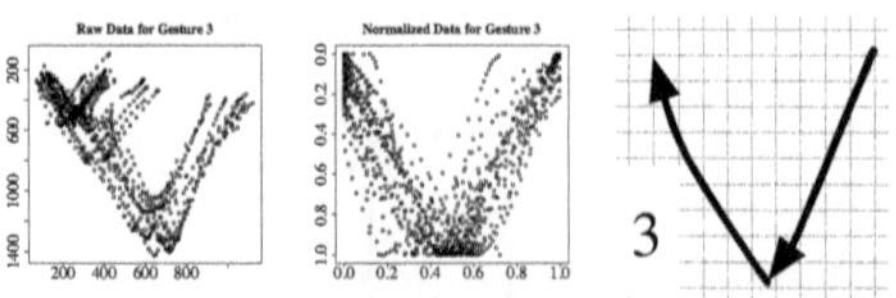

Figure 6. Touch coordinate data collected in our experiment versus gesture ideal (gesture 3, Figure 5) as described by a GeForMT expression.

an Android application showing a series of graphical touch gesture representations (see Figure 5). Test subjects had a couple of seconds to memorize the displayed gesture until it faded out and were subsequently asked to perform it. The touch coordinates were recorded and sent to a web service for aggregation and analysis. We obtained touch coordinate data along with metadata from a total of 479 gestures performed on ten different device models[9]. The gestures had to be performed in landscape and portrait device orientation, resulting in an average of 30 samples per gesture.

The first insight into human user gesture execution we gained was that the average duration of gesture execution varied with gesture complexity ranging from 330 milliseconds (gesture 1) to 1200 milliseconds (gesture 3). The correlation between gesture duration and complexity appears to be non-trivial and needs further investigation. For our current implementation, we concluded to simulate gestures with a standard duration of 350 milliseconds per atomic gesture.

We individually analyzed the data obtained in our experiment to identify classes of noise. Figure 6 depicts 31 raw data samples for gesture 3 in portrait orientation and the normalized samples to compensate for varying gesture size and location.

We settled to implement two generalized classes of signal noise we derived from our experimentation data: gesture drift and jittering. The drift causes gestures to lose geometric accuracy and jittering causes touch coordinates to deviate from the perfect path. Figure 7 depicts these effects. The magnitude of the parameters can be specified in Gherkin scenarios; omission will trigger the use of standard values derived from our experimentation data. For standard drift values, we averaged the coordinate deviations of pivot points (i.e. points where atomic gestures connect) in normalized experimentation data from corresponding pivot points in our prototype gestures (see Figure 5). For standard jitter value we apply a harmonic oscillation whose parameters are derived from overall gesture dimension and type (i.e. less jitter for circular-type motion, more jitter in line-type motion, amplitude by average deviation in data obtained in the experiment).

To inject touch events into the AUT, we modified the original target platform compartment of Calabash. Upon test case execution, the gesture generator creates a set of threads corresponding to the scheduling of the atomic gestures in the syntax tree created in phase one of the gesture simulation. Each

[9]Galaxy Nexus, GT-I9100, HTC Desire S, LG-P920, LT30p, Nexus 4, Nexus 5, Nexus 7, XT1030, XT890

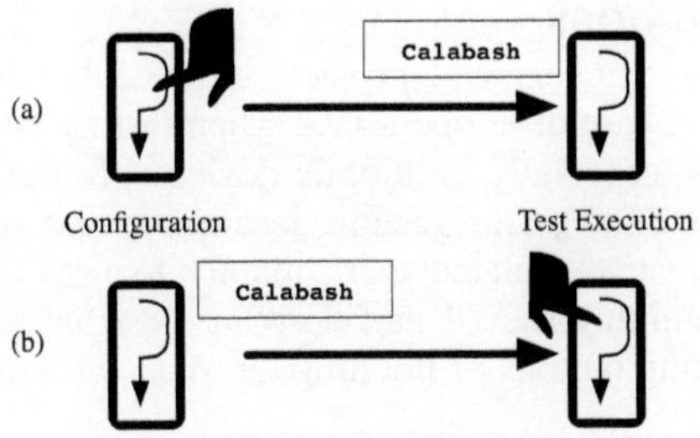

Figure 8. Testing scheme for laboratory evaluation.

thread (for multi-touch gestures) calculates the touch coordinates according to atomic gesture template and drift/noise. We then create touch events and send them into the AUT using the Application Programming Interface (API) functions provided by Android native instrumentation technology.

EVALUATION

To evaluate our approach and verify its suitability for test automation for gesture-intensive applications, we aimed to show that from the perspective of the AUT it cannot be determined whether the origin of a touch interaction is a human user or our gesture generator. If a AUT cannot distinguish a touch gestures' origin, both are accepted to be equivalent.

To verify this equivalence, we followed a testing scheme (see Figure 8) where test applications were stimulated with manual and generated gesture input. We determine our gesture generator to be adequate for test automation if manual and automated gesture execution yield identical results.

To cross-validate our findings, we set up two test environments. The first consists of a specifically designed application that accepts pre-defined gesture input and runs a recognition algorithm based on training data to determine which gesture has been performed. This approach allows for the intensive testing of our technology by confining potential errors to malfunctioning gesture detection and excluding other possible causes of failures. The second setup involves two applications from the Google Play Store, which – besides proving our approach's black-box testing ability – provides us with real world examples of gesture-based user interaction in publicly available applications.

We expect our gesture generator to create touch events equivalent to human user input. Hence, we expect both test setups to yield identical results when executed by a human user and by our automation technology.

We defined a set of eight gestures depicted in Figure 5 to test for the equivalence of gestures performed by a human user and the gesture generator. These gestures have been specifically selected to include common gestures (e.g. swipe, semicircle) as well as a number of complex gestures.

In our first test scenario, denoted in part (a) of Figure 8, a specifically designed application was expected to correctly recognize gestures using the *Android Gesture Libraries*. We manually recorded our gesture test set using the *Gesture Builder* application (provided by the Android SDK). We implemented an application to listen for this set of gestures and display the identifier of the particular gesture recognized with the highest confidence accessible for Calabash. Next, we executed a set of Calabash test cases with GeForMT expressions corresponding to the gestures in Figure 5.

In the second step of test scenario one, part (b) in Figure 8, we prepared a set of Calabash test cases targeting the *Gesture Builder* application. This time, we used GeForMT expressions in Calabash test cases to record the gestures. The recorded gestures obtained in this process where then imported into the AUT we created for the first step. We then conducted a series of manual test cases by performing the gestures.

We repeated the first and the second step of the validation process on a variety of different Android devices[10]. Since the gesture generator operates with random values within a specified margin to create noise, we ran ten test series on each device. We found that the manually recorded gestures were correctly recognized by stimulating the AUT with the corresponding GeForMT expression in part (a) of the testing scheme. Using part (b) of our scheme, the AUT accepted all the gestures performed manually using the GeForMT-based machine-recorded gesture descriptions.

All configurations of gesture records created either manually or using our gesture generator were accepted by the AUTs, no matter whether test cases were executed manually or using our custom Calabash implementation. Hence, from the perspective of the AUT, the origin of gesture input cannot be determined. This leads to the conclusion that our gesture generator can mimic human users close enough and therefore can be used for test automation.

To evaluate the influence of noise, we ran test series with progressive values for drift and jitter. We found that generated gestures could not be successfully recognized when drift and jitter exceeded gesture-specific threshold values. Of course, recognition of fuzzy gestures is a quality of the recognizer algorithm. In our work, however, we focus on gesture simulation rather than recognition. We discovered the threshold values for drift and jitter to be gesture-specific. For most of the gestures in Figure 5 we where able to get positive test results for extreme drift and noise values. However, for complex gestures (7 and 8 in Figure 5) we observed failures for drift and jitter values mediocrely larger than average deviations at gesture pivot points. We plan to investigate this issue in our future work.

The results of the above experiments demonstrated that our gesture generator performed up to our expectations under laboratory conditions for the first test setup. To verify its usability under realistic conditions, we applied our solution to applications available at the Google Play Store (the second setup). We used the two Android applications *Gesture Way*[11] and *Google Gesture Search*[12].

[10] HTC Desire S, Nexus 4, Nexus 5, Nexus 7, Galaxy Tab 10.1

[11] `https://play.google.com/store/apps/details?id=sk.cep.gesturesway`

[12] `https://play.google.com/store/apps/details?id=com.google.android.apps.gesturesearch`

Gesture Way is a customizable launcher that maps custom user-defined gestures to commands, e.g. launching an application and accessing system settings. We successfully created a test script that uses the gestures denoted in Figure 5 to launch different applications on the devices used in the first test and different virtual device configurations on the Android emulator. In all test cases, the manually defined gesture to launch an application could successfully be produced by our gesture generator as well as machine-generated gestures cross-checked manually.

Google Gesture Search indexes information on the device and allows the user to perform searches on this information by *writing* characters via touch gestures on the screen. In order to search for the Google Play Store app, a user could perform the three gestures denoted in Figure 9, which will result in a list of all information items (e.g. apps, contacts) containing the sequence of letters "STO". The angular shape will be treated as the letter "T" by Google Gesture Search.

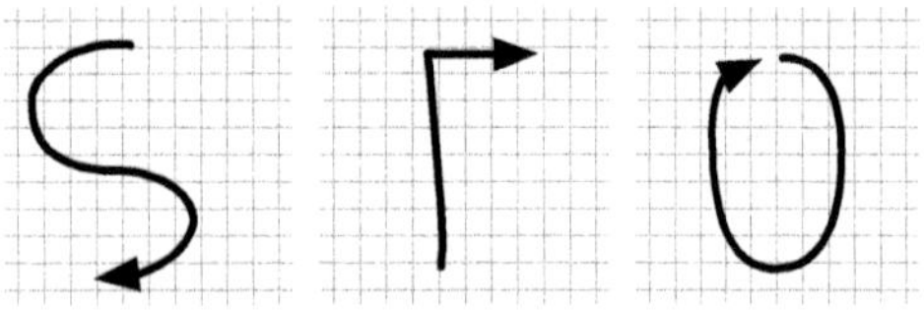

Figure 9. The graphical representation of the gesture-based search term "STO".

The GeForMT expressions corresponding to the graphical representation of the gestures we used to denote the search term "STO" in Figure 9 are $1F(SEMICIRCLE\_S\_CCW, SEMICIRCLE\_S\_CW)$, $1F(LINE\_N, LINE\_E)$ and $1F(CIRCLE\_N\_CW)$. These have been restricted to a rectangular region of the screen.

Our implementation of the Calabash framework could successfully run the code in Listing 2. On the Android handsets we used in our evaluation the test case succeeded and the Google Gesture Search app identified – among other results – the Google Play Store app.

The experiments under laboratory and real application conditions prove our approach to automated gesture-intensive application testing to be feasible. The automation technology allows for the frequent execution of gesture-based test cases consuming only a minimum of human workforce and can easily be integrated in automated build environments or continuous integration systems.

```
Feature: Google Gesture Search Test
Scenario: Gesture Test 01
Given my app is running
Then I perform gesture "1F(SEMICIRCLE_S_CCW
     ,SEMICIRCLE_S_CW)" in relative region
     from 25:25 to 80:80
Then I perform gesture "1F(LINE_N,LINE_E)"
     in relative region from 25:25 to 80:80
Then I perform gesture "1F(CIRCLE_N_CW)" in
     relative region from 25:25 to 80:80
Then I wait for a second
Then I see the text "Play Store"
```

Listing 2. A Calabash test case searching for the Play Store application in Google Gesture Search.

RELATED WORK

Several researchers and projects have dealt with the challenges software developers face when testing interactive applications, especially on mobile devices. To our best knowledge, none integrates gesture description and simulation as we do. Instead, related work mainly focuses on automatically examining the UI and deriving possible test states by e.g. clicking buttons or flooding the AUT with random input events.

Haller analyzes the special requirements of mobile application testing [9]. The author identifies two new test types: *device tests* and *tests in the wild*. These new types address the problems of device heterogeneity in mobile environments and the situational context-specific properties of an AUT. While these factors are also addressed in our work, the main challenge Haller identifies is the need for sufficient automation technology to efficiently handle the testing demands imposed by quickly evolving platforms introducing new test triggers. With our approach, we also address these issues by automating the testing process for gesture-intensive applications.

Choi et al. present a testing algorithm called *SwiftHand* based on a model learning the AUT's UI and generating new input sequences that take the app to untested states [6]. They increase the tests' efficiency by reducing the amount of necessary restarts and constantly improving the model during test execution. The improvements lead to a UI model closer to the real application interface, hence allowing for a faster exploration of untested states. The created input sequences are inferred from the AUT's UI component tree – UI elements with an event handler are triggered with corresponding touch events. They do not take gestures specifically into account and there is no possibility to configure them.

Testdroid, an online platform for conducting UI tests on different physical devices, is presented by Kaasila et al. [12]. Developers can upload a test script generated from a manually recorded session with the AUT, which is translated into an automated test using the Robotium platform. The recorded test is then uploaded to the authors' system that runs the test cases on a set of physical Android devices and reports back to the developer about the outcome. Although their system solves a common problem especially for Android developers (device heterogeneity), they specifically state that Testdroid is limited when the AUT depends on speech, movement or gesture input.

AndroidRipper is presented by Amalfitano et al. and demonstrates how Android UIs can be automatically explored and tested [1]. The hierarchical structure created by UI elements and widgets is analyzed in order to determine sequences of possible input events, which are seen as possible test cases and subsequently fired. The authors demonstrate that their approach is more efficient than Android's built-in testing mechanisms – specifically the aforementioned UI monkey – and finds more bugs. AndroidRipper's main purpose is to detect application crashes and not to examine its interaction behavior in detail. As test cases are created from detected UI elements and widgets, gestural input is not tested.

Hu & Neamtiu conducted a bug study and revealed that UI bugs are a common source of errors in mobile applications [11]. They present a framework for automatically generating and performing test cases resulting in a collection of log files that are analyzed afterwards. With these techniques, they were able to rediscover known bugs as well as reveal new ones in the examined applications. However, they do not use a structured approach to write test cases – instead, they rely on the pseudo-random user events create by Android's UI/Application Exerciser Monkey. Hence, they have no control about the tested user interaction.

Khandkar et al. present TouchToolkit [15], an automated testing tool for .NET-based applications allowing testers to run unit tests with recorded gestures. A drawback of this approach is that the test is repeated with exactly the same gesture over and over again – an unlikely scenario. To repeat tests under realistic conditions multiple times, gestures must be slightly different on each run.

Hou et al. demonstrate how to automatically create a testing model and test cases from a mobile application and a corresponding specification [10]. Their approach analyzes the AUT and derives a finite state machine model used for further test creation. Although they claim to reduce the necessary amount of manual testing and record/replay scenarios, they do not take gesture-based interfaces into account.

Hermes is a tool for mobile application testing demonstrated by She et al. [18]. With Hermes, developers can write XML-based test cases consisting of an action and different assertions for the AUT's response. Test cases can be of different types, e.g UI, functional, or environmental tests. In their testing environments, *test agents* are used as virtual users, providing necessary input to the AUT. As with most automation approaches, UI elements can be automatically processed, but gestures are not specifically included.

Bo et al. demonstrate MobileTest [5], an early attempt to incorporate automated testing mechanisms in mobile software development. The system provides agents running on mobile devices that receive commands generated from test scripts. The authors emphasize the use of *sensitive events* such as *incoming call*, *inbox full* or *memory low*. An interesting feature MobileTest provides is the ability to have tests running simultaneously on different interacting devices. The system can trigger an SMS on one device and capture the reception on another, making cross-device tests possible. User interaction is tested by recording and replaying scenarios consisting of button clicks. The authors do not explicitly state whether or not gesture-based interaction can be tested.

Related research also deals with the generation of gestures. Galbally et al. demonstrate how to use hand-written human signatures as templates to automatically generate derivatives [8]. As with gestures, no human can make exactly the same signature again. While their approach resembles what we called the record-and-replay approach to testing (recording a gesture and replaying it during automated test execution), their research provides interesting insights into how to calculate deviations in human gesture execution.

CONCLUSION & FUTURE WORK

We presented an extension to the Calabash testing framework allowing for test automation for gesture-based mobile applications. Gestures can be formally specified as GeForMT expressions in Gherkin scenarios. An artificial stream of touch events is derived from the gesture description and injected into the AUT, effectively simulating human user interaction. To mimic human behavior, our gesture generator distorts gestures by adding pseudo-random signal noise. We also prepared a set of Gherkin templates for the specification of complex gestures with a set of additional parameters, namely execution duration and area on a device's display.

We evaluated our approach by applying a set of gestures to a specifically designed Android application implementing a gesture recognizer. We furthermore cross-validated the test setup by teaching the gesture recognizer algorithm manually performed gestures and gestures performed by our gesture generator. In both setups, the gestures were successfully recognized using test automation and manual testing. We also evaluated our approach using two apps available from the Google Play Store. Here we found the outcome of the gestures performed by our gesture generator to be equivalent to gestures performed manually.

We expect that our approach to test execution automation simplifies and improves mobile application testing by removing the need to manually test gesture-based apps or use static record and replay techniques. The modified Calabash implementation and all related sources will be made publicly available in the near future.

In order to optimize the simulation algorithm and create more realistic test cases, our future work targets a deeper investigation of how inaccurately users perform certain gestures to determine a better understanding for the necessary noise parameters used in our current implementation, especially regarding gesture execution dynamics (i.e. speed, time variation between individual touch events).

The use of GeForMT for gesture description has some drawbacks due to GeForMT's limited expressiveness (e.g. duration, dimension, dynamics). Especially for complex gestures, atomic gesture duration may be a significant characteristic. In our future work, we plan to investigate how to incorporate additional expressiveness into GeForMT.

Apart from the current dominance of touch gestures, interaction with mobile devices is evolving. As mobile devices get more powerful and incorporate more sensors, additional interaction modalities become available. Each new modality brings different challenges to developers and testers alike, e.g. speech recognition or device motion gestures need to be tested thoroughly. In our future research, we aim for the inclusion of motion gestures into our gesture generator module.

Finally, as more and more alternative modalities appear in the classic world of personal computing on desktop machines (e.g. *Microsoft Kinect* or the *Leap Motion Controller*), a completely new field of interactive applications emerges. Hence, integration into other Gherkin-based frameworks in non-mobile environments is also of interest.

REFERENCES

1. Amalfitano, D., Fasolino, A. R., Tramontana, P., De Carmine, S., and Memon, A. M. Using GUI Ripping for Automated Testing of Android Applications. In *Proceedings of the 27th IEEE/ACM International Conference on Automated Software Engineering*, ASE 2012, ACM (New York, NY, USA, 2012), 258–261.
2. Android Developer Network. Android GestureLibraries. `http://developer.android.com/reference/android/gesture/GestureLibraries.html` [accessed 2014-02-15].
3. Anthony, L., Vatavu, R.-D., and Wobbrock, J. O. Understanding the Consistency of Users' Pen and Finger Stroke Gesture Articulation. In *Proceedings of Graphics Interface 2013*, GI '13, Canadian Information Processing Society (Toronto, Ont., Canada, Canada, 2013), 87–94.
4. Anthony, L., and Wobbrock, J. O. A Lightweight Multistroke Recognizer for User Interface Prototypes. In *Proceedings of Graphics Interface 2010*, GI '10, Canadian Information Processing Society (Toronto, Ont., Canada, Canada, 2010), 245–252.
5. Bo, J., Xiang, L., and Xiaopeng, G. MobileTest: A Tool Supporting Automatic Black Box Test for Software on Smart Mobile Devices. In *AST '07: Proceedings of the Second International Workshop on Automation of Software Test*, IEEE Computer Society (Washington, DC, USA, 2007), 8.
6. Choi, W., Necula, G., and Sen, K. Guided GUI Testing of Android Apps with Minimal Restart and Approximate Learning. In *Proceedings of the 2013 ACM SIGPLAN International Conference on Object Oriented Programming Systems Languages & Applications*, OOPSLA '13, ACM (New York, NY, USA, 2013), 623–640.
7. Echtler, F., and Butz, A. GISpL: Gestures Made Easy. In *Proceedings of the Sixth International Conference on Tangible, Embedded and Embodied Interaction*, TEI '12, 233–240.
8. Galbally, J., Plamondon, R., Fierrez, J., and Ortega-Garcia, J. Synthetic On-Line Signature Generation. Part I: Methodology and Algorithms. *Pattern Recognition 45*, 7 (2012), 2610 – 2621.
9. Haller, K. Mobile Testing. *SIGSOFT Softw. Eng. Notes 38*, 6 (Nov. 2013), 1–8.
10. Hou, Y., Chen, R., and Du, Z. Automated GUI Testing for J2ME Software Based on FSM. In *SCALCOM-EMBEDDEDCOM '09: Proceedings of the 2009 International Conference on Scalable Computing and Communications; Eighth International Conference on Embedded Computing*, IEEE Computer Society (Washington, DC, USA, 2009), 341–346.
11. Hu, C., and Neamtiu, I. Automating GUI Testing for Android Applications. In *Proceedings of the 6th International Workshop on Automation of Software Test*, AST '11, ACM (New York, NY, USA, 2011), 77–83.
12. Kaasila, J., Ferreira, D., Kostakos, V., and Ojala, T. Testdroid: Automated Remote UI Testing on Android. In *Proceedings of the 11th International Conference on Mobile and Ubiquitous Multimedia*, MUM '12, ACM (New York, NY, USA, 2012), 28:1–28:4.
13. Kammer, D., Henkens, D., Henzen, C., and Groh, R. Gesture Formalization for Multitouch. *Software: Practice and Experience* (2013).
14. Kammer, D., Wojdziak, J., Keck, M., Groh, R., and Taranko, S. Towards a Formalization of Multi-Touch Gestures. In *Proceedings of ITS'10*, 49.
15. Khandkar, S. H., Sohan, S. M., Sillito, J., and Maurer, F. Tool Support for Testing Complex Multi-Touch Gestures. In *ACM International Conference on Interactive Tabletops and Surfaces*, ITS '10, ACM (New York, NY, USA, 2010), 59–68.
16. Kin, K., Hartmann, B., DeRose, T., and Agrawala, M. Proton++: A Customizable Declarative Multitouch Framework. In *Proceedings of the 25th Annual ACM Symposium on User Interface Software and Technology*, UIST '12, 477–486.
17. Kin, K., Hartmann, B., DeRose, T., and Agrawala, M. Proton: Multitouch Gestures As Regular Expressions. In *Proceedings of the SIGCHI Conference on Human Factors in Computing Systems*, CHI '12, 2885–2894.
18. She, S., Sivapalan, S., and Warren, I. Hermes: A Tool for Testing Mobile Device Applications. In *ASWEC '09: Proceedings of the 2009 Australian Software Engineering Conference*, IEEE Computer Society (Washington, DC, USA, 2009), 121–130.
19. Tassey, G. The Economic Impacts of Inadequate Infrastructure for Software Testing. Tech. rep., National Institute of Standards and Technology, 2002.
20. Vatavu, R.-D., Anthony, L., and Wobbrock, J. O. Gestures As Point Clouds: A $P Recognizer for User Interface Prototypes. In *Proceedings of the 14th ACM International Conference on Multimodal Interaction*, ICMI '12, ACM (New York, NY, USA, 2012), 273–280.
21. Wobbrock, J. O., Wilson, A. D., and Li, Y. Gestures Without Libraries, Toolkits or Training: A $1 Recognizer for User Interface Prototypes. In *Proceedings of the 20th Annual ACM Symposium on User Interface Software and Technology*, UIST '07, ACM (New York, NY, USA, 2007), 159–168.
22. Wynne, M., and Hellesoy, A. *The Cucumber Book: Behaviour-Driven Development for Testers and Developers*. Pragmatic Bookshelf, 2012.

100 Days of iPhone Use: Understanding the Details of Mobile Device Use

Barry Brown, Moira McGregor, Donald McMillan
Mobile Life @ Stockholm University
SE-164, Kista, Sweden
{Barry, Moira, Don}@mobilelifecentre.org

ABSTRACT

Internet connected mobile devices are an increasingly ubiquitous part of our everyday lives and we present here the results from unobtrusive audio-video recordings of iPhone use – over 100 days of device use collected from 15 users. The data reveals for analysis the everyday, moment-by-moment use of contemporary mobile phones. Through video analysis of usage we observed how messages, social media and internet use are integrated and threaded into daily life, interaction with others, and everyday events such as transport, delays, establishment choice and entertainment. We document various aspects of end-user mobile device usage, starting with understanding how it is occasioned by context. We then characterise the temporal and sequential nature of use. Lastly, we discuss the social nature of mobile phone usage. Beyond this analysis, we reflect on how to draw these points into ideas for design.

Author Keywords

iPhone; Screen Recording; Device Use; Video Analysis

ACM Classification Keywords

H.5.1. Evaluation/methodology

INTRODUCTION

The growth of the mobile device as the paramount platform for computing is increasingly difficult to dismiss, with growing sales and usage, as well continuous innovation in hardware and applications. Indeed, the range of applications and services available through the Android and iOS app stores already compete with the range available for desktop computers, and with the web as a general online interface for services and goods. New technical opportunities such as near field communication, barcode scanning and Bluetooth LE (low energy) also offer increasing opportunities for integrating mobile devices into the environment.

Yet integration of devices goes beyond the tangible and technical: devices play an ever increasing part in our everyday activity and conversation, interrupting but also augmenting our lives in new ways. Some have gone as far as to claim that our human sociality is being damaged by the spread of internet connected devices [22, 21] (drawing us into shallow online interactions at the cost of more valuable face to face ones) yet there is little empirical data here. Indeed, more broadly, there is only a schematic understanding of user behaviour on modern internet connected mobile phones – one of the most important contemporary sites of technology innovation.

MobileHCI 2014, September 23–26, 2014, Toronto, ON, Canada.

ACM 978-1-4503-3004-6/14/09...$15.00.
http://dx.doi.org/10.1145/2628363.2628377

We present here results from a study of iPhone use, using video recording to gain a more empirically informed understanding of mobile phone use in everyday life. We developed a software application (app) that ran on our participants' own iPhone to record all screen interactions. The app also recorded ambient and device audio, GPS location and app launches. We used this to collect naturalistic data from 15 iPhone users in Sweden, the UK and the USA. The corpus collected consists of 1,695 video clips of use – over 70 video hours of iPhone use. The videos present a distinctive view, allowing us to study device use in situations as diverse as workplaces, bars, transport, outdoors, shopping malls, dinner parties, even toilets.

Our analysis is framed by the concept of the 'occasioned' nature of device use – how context influences the initiation of device at particular point in place and time. We explore the temporality and sequentiality of device use through what we call episodic organisation. Thirdly, our data revealed interaction with others while using a mobile phone to be surprisingly common. To conclude, we discuss the potential opportunities in using video to study mobile device usage.

LITERATURE

Some of the first attempts to understand mobile device usage involved logging software. One of the most notable long-term deployments of such a mobile logging application is Cenceme [15], an application that used context sensing to automatically update social networking sites with each user's current activity. Initially developed for the Nokia N95 and trialled among 30 locally based participants, the software was then ported to the iPhone when the App Store was first launched. Other apps include AppAware [9], which allows users to share, via existing social networks location-tagged information on which applications they are installing. In doing so, users are able to explore applications being used in their current location and the popularity and lifecycle of mobile applications are trackable for research.

An alternative approach was adopted in [2] where interview data documented some of the ways in which mobile phones are used as part of communication and work tasks. While Church et al. [7] use a diary study augmented by interviews to document the situations in which mobile Internet was accessed. They reported that more than 70% of search on the mobile devices was *not* carried out in a mobile context (out of the house), and that only 17% of recorded searches were directly related to the location of the search. Church et al. [6] also examined reasons for engaging in mobile search.

One related approach has been to use video to study mobile device use. Video recordings has been one longstanding method used in HCI for a range of different analytic purposes, but particularly to document interaction with and around technical artifacts [10]. Video has proven valuable in illuminating aspects of activities neglected by previous methods, particularly drawing on conversation analysis to understand mobile device use [5,14]. Video can focus attention on the moment-by-moment production of technologically mediated action. These papers make use of interactional analysis to study the details of interaction that takes place either through or around a technology with an ethnomethodological orientation deployed to understand the details of particular usage situations.

METHODS

In this earlier work a predominant method of studying phone use has been through analysis of log data from large numbers of participants, [11]. While these methods are powerful in identifying failings in form factors relating to specific physical attributes of the phone (such as errors in touch or keyboard input), for this study we wanted to design an approach to provide us access to the details of activities undertaken concurrent to any interaction with the phone, as well as the immediate contextual environment.

We adopted video methods to study screen recordings of phone use and also audio recordings of surrounding talk in interaction [10]. The data collection system consisted of a local recording application installed on participants' iPhones, and a website that allowed participants to review and annotate their data recordings (figure 1). The recording application itself was designed to run in the background on the phone and capture the screen of the device, it's location, the apps used during each session, and the surrounding audio from the microphone. Recording would stop during phone calls or when the device was put into sleep mode. The video data and associated meta-data were uploaded opportunistically when the device was locked and simultaneously connected to both a power supply and wifi.

During the use of applications (except full screen apps such as games), a red bar was shown at the top of the screen reminding users that recording was taking place. Participants had multiple options to hide data both before and after it was recorded; one option being to simply turn the recording application off. After the data had been uploaded, the participants were asked to review the videos and annotate them with diary entries providing the reason for each device use. Here they also had the opportunity to hide confidential recordings from the researchers. Exit interviews with all participants were conducted at end of each week either face to face or over Skype, to discuss interesting behaviour or ambiguities captured in their video data, and extracts included in this report were all discussed

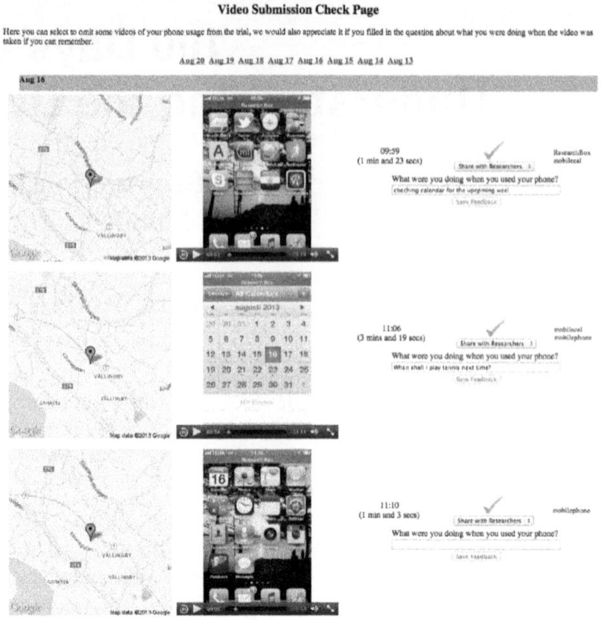

Figure 1: Participants' video review and diary entry

in exit interviews. Alongside the diary entries, these interviews clarified areas of uncertainty in the recorded data. Lastly, audio analysis techniques were used to establish the number of speakers on each recorded video.

Our analytic approach is built upon the lengthy and detailed examination of video recordings of actual use in focused analytic sessions. The purpose here is to remain anti-reductionist and avoid coding for patterns, as this leads to an analysis of the general not the specific, and loses the nature of the phenomena being investigated. This is the approach we have taken in previous work, such as [5], where video data of phone use was collected using wearable cameras during a 'day trip' in a city. While that paper presented rich video of device use, the usage was to an extent influenced by frequency of map use, navigation, and searching for establishments to visit – as would be expected on a 'day out' in a city. In contrast, here our method allow the capture of a broader range of usage data.

In total, 15 mobile phone users participated in the study; 10 of whom were recruited through adverts on social media and student websites, and the remaining participants were recruited using Mechanical Turk. All participation was rewarded with either gift tokens or Mechanical Turk payment. Of the 15 participants, six were female and nine male – all participants fell within age range 22-50 years and lived in Sweden, the UK and USA. They were recruited with the request that they be regular iPhone users and they use their phones naturally throughout the period of the sessions. Eight of the participants were first language English speakers, and all interaction with and surrounding the phone was conducted in English – while seven participants used a mixture of Swedish and English throughout their sessions. In terms of occupation, our participants represented a diverse range including: opera producer, lecturer, actuary, creative director, massage therapist, nanny, HR consultant and student.

DATA AND ANALYSIS

The corpus we collected consists of 1,695 video clips of use, with additional 62 videos hidden by our participants. There was a total of over 70 video hours of iPhone use. The median clip was 38 seconds long, although 10% of our clips were over 277 seconds (4 minutes 37 seconds) long. Participants each contributed from 22 to 440 video clips of use, with a median of 123 clips submitted per user. 40% of our clips have user entered diary entries.

A large corpus like this presents challenges for analysis. Some of the clips only have the video of the device available – there is no talk, ambient noise, or user's diary entry that might help identify surrounding activity. For other clips, while there is no talk there are aspects of the audio which, when combined with the location data, can identify the use as being on public transport, driving or walking. For the clips with diary entries, however, it is possible to reconstruct more of the situation of use. Moroever, often analysis is supported by talk around the clips in that the reaction of others provides a rich source for understanding the context of use.

All the video clips were logged and watched soon after being uploaded. The corpus was categorised broadly by the activity, apps used, and by the number of people co-present. We did not count numbers of clips in each category but rather moved analytically between the rough categories, comparing and refining the categories as we investigated further video clips. Through this grounded process 55 interesting clips were identified for further investigation. Over two days all three authors watched these clips and selected twenty for transcription and in-depth analysis which, combined with understanding of the broader corpus, forms the basis for results given here.

Communication Apps	**43,30%**	**Productivity and Admin**	**8,97%**
Messages	23,40%	Preferences	2,58%
Mobile Mail	11,50%	Calendar	1,30%
Phone	5,20%	App Store	1,11%
Skype	0,80%	Clock	0,96%
Google Hangouts	0,70%		
Whats App	0,60%		
Internet, News, Search	**18,90%**	**Music and Sound**	**4,94%**
Mobile Safari	12,10%	Spotify	2,16%
BBC News App	1,30%	Podcasts	1,46%
Chrome	1,10%	Music	0,71%
Feedly	0,60%	Pandora	0,28%
Youtube	0,50%		
Social Media	**16,30%**	**Games**	**1,14%**
Facebook	7,60%	Temple Run 2	0,23%
Instagram	5,80%	Talking Tom	0,11%
Pintrest	1,30%	Candy Crush	0,11%
Twitter	1,10%	Cave Man Feast	0,10%
AlienBlue	0,30%		
LinkedIn	0,10%		
Grindr	0,10%	**Photo and Camera**	**1,39%**
		Photos	0,74%
Maps and Geoinfo	**5,00%**	Camera	0,65%
Google Maps	2,8%		
Stockholm Subway Info	1,1%	**Other (98 apps)**	**2,21%**
Apple Maps	0,5%		
Yelp	0,3%	**Total**	**100%**

Figure 2: App usage as % of total phone use time, Categorised by type of application. Only the top applications from each category are listed

A number of video clips are included in this paper, represented by screenshots and written transcripts of the audio. The transcripts make use of simplified notation to indicate [overlaps], ↑raising and ↓falling tone and pauses (length in brackets). Asterisks [*] show when screenshots displayed alongside the transcription were taken.

RESULTS

It is clear that modern mobile phone use – iPhone use in our study – is incredibly varied. There is a variety of different situations of use, and ways in which context is hooked into and connected with use. The first rather broad question we asked of the data was simply what are mobiles used for? To answer this question in we categorised the apps used by function, analysing time spent by users in each application and category and figure 2 provides the high level statistical results.

Further, and digging deeper, we attempt to address the *Temporality of mobile device use*. We examine why a device is used at a particular time and how the use integrates with concurrent activity. We explore with the data how task and situation create temporal 'slots' of sorts for a user to interact with their device, and how the resulting usage emerges to an extent from the nature of its slot. We ask what in the environment 'occasions' any given phone usage.

Nearly all our sessions of use are relatively short and although there are longer, more complex examples there are clearly certain time constraints that can influence device use. Within those time constraints, usage is further shaped by the episodic nature of the completion of different tasks.

This led us to characterise different 'styles' of phone use that were common in the data: *Micro-breaks* are user-initiated instances where the phone was checked for messages or social media – relatively short and frequent, often during the working day or another task. We see *Filling time* as similar, yet temporally motivated behaviour, which is more acutely determined by the amount of time available. We describe the type of mobile reading in relation to the temporal 'slot' available for it.

Finally, we address *Sociality of use* – one of our most surprising findings is the prevalence of multi-party interaction during device use. *Digital knitting* describes a mode of use we observed, where the phone was used for a longer period of time while the user was also involved in another activity such as conversation with those around; we describe situations in which the device is central to the current co-present conversation, and others where the phone is used for complex, multi-party communication and collaboration.

Application Use

The first question is simply what was done on the mobile devices during the video recordings we captured. Figure 2 shows the percentage of seconds of use for each application, based on its duration in the foreground during recorded usage. Since we tracked a relatively small sample (15 users), these numbers perhaps give only a rough picture of broader application usage. There are also gaps in recording time when users turned off the application or did not share usage videos with us. Also, applications which are used mainly in the background – such as the music and sound applications – will be under-represented. This said, these results are broadly in line with other reported application usage, such as [3].

Communication, internet and search, and social media comprise 78.5% of the time that our participants were on their mobile phones – clearly demonstrating that mobile phones are heavily used for these activities. A surprisingly small percentage of time was accounted for by games, given that games are top sellers in the application stores on both the Android and iOS store. This, however, may be explained by the age demographics of our participants who were all over the age of 20.

Perhaps most striking is the relatively small amount of phone calls on what are, after all, still "mobile phones". Indeed, there was more Instagram use that phone calls taken or received in the study. A related statistic is the average number of application launches per day – Messages is launched on average 11.6 times a day, Mail 7, Phone 3 and Facebook 3.5. While this shows frequent use of Facebook, even when combined with the other social networking applications it does not entirely fit with the notion of out of control, compulsive social media consumption.

Temporality of Use

One way of looking at the application use is by clock time. This shows the lowest usage at 4am, and phone usage peaking between 3-4pm. Around 7am usage jumps with a spike both in messaging and social media use, corresponding with typical waking up time. Looking at the length of use, participants used their phones for an median of 37 minutes per day, with a max of 14 hours and a minimum of 3 seconds.

However, since we have a relatively small number of participants, perhaps a better approach is to dig deeper and look at what actually was involved in usage at particular times. In particular, we started with the question: what actually made a participant use a phone at a particular time?

Occasioning use

Perhaps the most straightforward example of use being initiated is when a notification (such as a message) arrives (figure 3). This is an example of the device 'occasioning' use – the arriving message creates a slot where a user can

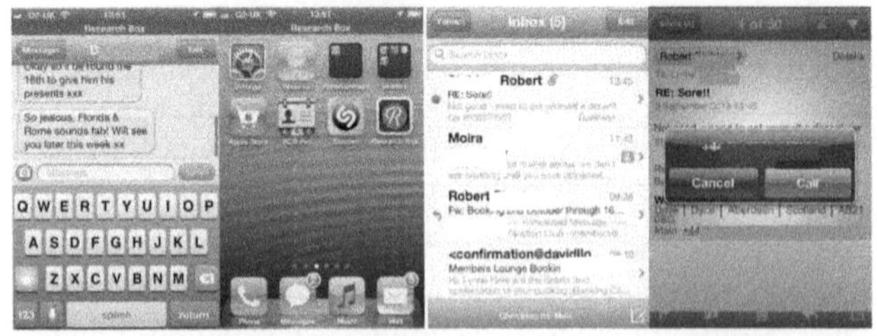

Participant receives a notification of a message and unlocks their iPhone, seeing a message from a relative. The participant then exits the SMS app and opens their email, the participant reads the email, then clicks on a link in the signature of the message to call the sender directly on their mobile telephone number.

Figure 3: A simple form of occasioned use – a message arrives, leads to reading email then a call

then naturally attend to their device, perhaps by replying to the message. Of course, this is not to say that the device *compels* a user to initiate use – many messages go ignored. It is that an occasion has been created where device use is natural and likely. This does not mean usage is determined or produced, but rather that one of the most basic resources needed for mobile phone use – something to do with the phone – is made available by the incoming message.

More broadly, context can occasion many different forms of use. One straightforward example of this is when there is a need for some sort of information that can be found using the phone. A common example of this was searching for directions using the map. We noted many of these sorts of location and information searches at the transitions of events – such as when leaving home or work, or about to arrive at a public transport. Searches seen at this point could be for another establishment to visit, public transport times, or navigation information to the next destination.

Circumstances outside a participant's control can also occasion the use of the device. In figure 4 a delayed train leads to a search for information. The participant's train has stood still at a station for longer than she expected. Not understanding the announcement made in Swedish, she searches on the Internet, eventually turning to a popular

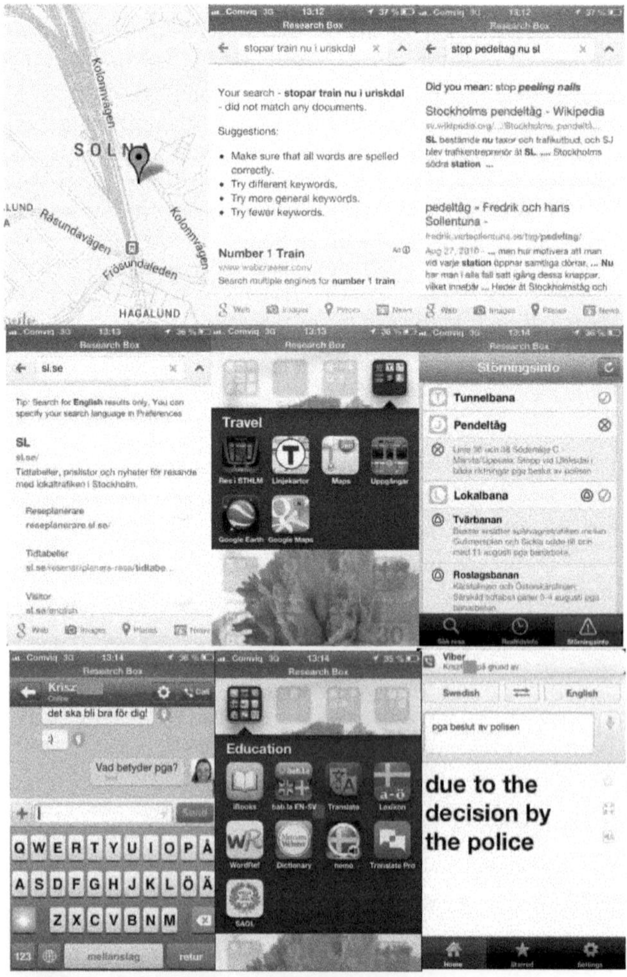

Figure 4: Diary entry reads: "in the train going home - try to figure it out why the train was stopped at the station." The train is a reason to search – it occasions use.

Stockholm transport information app (RES i STHLM). The information page explains that the pendletåg (commuter train) is delayed, but uses the abbreviation "pga". The participant messages a friend to ask what "pga" means, and also uses google translate – with a reply to her message and the translation arriving at the same time. In this clip there was no conversation, so we include screenshots from the recording of the mobile phone use.

There are also cases in which the the use of a device makes it possible to exploit a feature of the situation itself. For example, in one clip a son plays a video game while talking with their mother in the car. The mother is driving and the two converse about how television shows change as they become popular. As the mother's secondary involvement is driving, the son themselves also takes up a secondary involvement by playing a video game. In another extract, a participant at a dinner party finds the conversation drifting onto family issues that do not concern them directly, so they pull out their phone and start browsing YouTube videos, while still monitoring the conversation and engaging with it sporadically.

These are situations where the user has some 'free' attention, even if they are engaged in one activity, and thus can interact with their device and another activity simultaneously. This was seen during television watching – commonly know as 'second screen' activity.

Filling Time

A related – and commonly familiar – variant on this situation is using the mobile while waiting in some capacity, such as for a friend or an event (such as a train to arrive). These sorts of 'filling time' events are common in the data – echoing early data on the use of phones by mobile workers [17], the phone enables otherwise 'dead time' be put to some use. Rather than simply killing time though, it is more the case that these short intervals can be put to something useful, be it enjoying a quick video game or browsing social media.

One interesting feature of this sort of 'waiting' device use is that it is often time constrained, and as such users thus tend to take up activities which can be completed very quickly or abandoned easily, such as browsing social media. So, in one extract a participant browses potential partners on Grindr dating app while waiting to meet a friend – an activity which takes him only a minute or so, before the device is put away. As Licoppe puts it [14], the 'temporal projection' of cellphone activities is such that the decision of what to do with the device relies to an extent on how long the 'gap' that the user has to fill can be reasonably expected to be.

Micro-breaks

Another common, yet related, situation of use was that of 'Micro-breaks' – where, in contrast to the user employing free attention or free time to engage with the mobile device, the user actively carves time for their mobile device use from their ongoing tasks. Examples of this use are often quite short and distributed throughout the day in short bursts. Looking more closely, we find that much of this short use was checking the mobile for updates, at times triggered by a notification or incoming message, but at other times this is simply a check of social media, or that check is combined with reading incoming emails or messages. This echoes Oulasvirta et al's [18] discussion of 'checking behaviours', which still seem prevalent despite the advance in technology to support push notification rather than pull modes for media.

One example of this was a participant who worked at a newspaper designing websites. Even though she was at her computer for much of the day, we noticed a pattern of intermittent small 'snacks' where she would check her phone, navigating between Facebook, messaging, her work and personal email. These clips would often be less than a minute, and although similar to figure 3, they would be self-initiated rather than in response to a notification. The applications that would be accessed during these micro-breaks also seemed to be fairly habitual – a favourite website, a news application, social media or messaging. Since micro-breaks were frequent this could lead to these applications being checked many times.

Interestingly, the ergonomic literature has long advocated taking 'micro breaks' to prevent posture issues. While the management literature [1, 13] is more mixed on the productivity value of micro-breaks, their adoption as a method for dealing with work appeared common in our data. Related literature concerns 'self interruptions' [12] – daydreams, thoughts about bodily state (e.g. hunger) or simply one's mind wandering from the current task or activity. These micro-breaks on the mobile device can be viewed as a form of self-interruption, possibly helping concentration in the long term by the short change in task and attention.

Episodic task completion and sequences of use

Pulling back from individual types of use, our videos also give us a view of the overall structure of device interaction. In particular, individual user actions can be seen to fit together into 'episodes' of use – multiple actions with the phone that complete a single task. To a competent user there is a natural sequence to interaction – a 'next' action which follows what has been done previously. In searching for a route home, for example, there is a sequence that proceeds through entering the destination and then reading off the route. If one is searching for information, not finding the correct item leads to a repeat search. These sequences of actions bind together in what we characterise as an 'episode' of use. These discrete episodes encourage their completion, with the end of an episode of use acting as a natural point to end device use. This leads to a certain "I've started so I'll finish" nature of device use – a compulsion to complete an activity before putting the device down.

A 'compulsive' aspect of use can be seen in the nature of communication on mobile devices; messages often demand a reply. Within conversation analysis this is referred to as 'adjacency pairs'; questions demand answers, and so conversationalists make use of questions to manage participation. This does not determine or control behaviour but again acts as a structure that can be used by those interacting with a device – messages can be replied to (although again, frequently, they might not be).

The episodic and sequential nature of use might explain some other compulsive aspects of mobile device use; that there is a desire to complete particular actions and to answer messages received. Sometimes this is in conflict with other requirements such as politeness to those who are co-present. In figure 5, for example, a participant is in conversation with someone they have met in a local pub. While the conversationalist is telling a story, the participant has started to enter their contact details into the phone. They get to the 'email field' and ask for the storyteller's email four times, interrupting the story being told. This clip gives a sense of the 'compulsion' that the sequentiality of the task of creating a new contact can produce. This clip is also one of the clearest examples we have of "disruption" to the conversation caused by the device. Despite being engrossed in their phone (and asking so many times for the email address) the participant does properly engage in the story telling, offering their own evaluation "I'm not surprised..." at a suitable point in the conversation.

'Episodes' of task-oriented use like this can be contrasted with others which are more open-ended. Some activities, such as reading social media, can continue almost indefinitely – for as long as there is new content available. These are activities which can be dropped quickly and without consequence. Yet even here there is a sort of 'mini-episodic' nature in that there are natural breaks to reading at the end of a sentence, paragraph or status update.

Mobile reading

While video and music are fairly common media types; the dominant media consumption activity on mobile phones is *reading* in some form or another. Our video of use are full of text of different sorts: news, messages, emails, websites, games, reviews, maps, notes and so on. The majority of smartphone use, then, is textual in some form, even though it may be supplemented with rich graphics.

The forms of reading we identify entail different commitments by the reader. These differences lie in the length of time required and the concentration involved. One of the most demanding reading commitments is book reading – only one participant read books, using both the Kindle application and iBook on their iPhone, reading for twenty minutes or so during their commute to work. This sort of intensive reading requires a commitment that can be considered long when compared to the average device session of only 38 seconds. Social media, however, can be enjoyed with a much smaller time commitment – the same participant later spends 4 minutes on social media reading (Twitter and Facebook) during a lunch break. Reading Twitter she then switches to a third form of reading – a webpage review of a new film. Lastly, when at home that evening she checks the BBC news application, (figure 6).

Media consumption on mobile devices has been the subject of some attention previously. Yet we are not simply saying that mobile phones are used sporadically, or as Dimmick et al. [8] put it, during 'niches'; "the utilization of media in the interstices of people's schedules, those odd crevices of time/space that routinely occur in our daily lives where no common assumptions or norms exist with regard to how to spend time". The model proposed by Dimmick is a passive model of media consumption in that mobile phone use is something that fits into the interstices in our life. We argue that dedicated slots – micro-breaks – are proactively created in which media can be usefully consumed, but with the media use selected to fit the constraints of the particular micro-break.

Moreover, drawing again on Licoppe [14], we would argue for the importance of the temporal organisation of activity in choosing the reading activity to be undertaken. The reading should fit with the expected time interval that the user has free. So a micro-break at the work desk, for example might only be 5 minutes and so the type of reading chosen will fit with that time slot. A lunch hour might support a different, longer, reading session – or time spent relaxing in the evening different again. The media type, then, will be chosen not just because of its intrinsic interest, but also because of the demands it makes on the user. To this we might add the nature of the attention demanded, and the opportunity to thread this into other activities such as conversation with others. The granularity of social media, with its small snippets, fits well with other tasks since it can be stopped and started, and each snippet can possibly

```
B: I'll tell you what was absolutely clas-
   sic. At the time I was talking, eh,
   first started talking to an [*]---------
   agency about Daewoo I was also talking
   to another agency about Nissan - they've
   got a place out at Guildford. And they
   wanted to do the same
A: What's your email address [*]----------
B: And the last I heard from them (.) was
   that (.) that um that they wanted a
   crowd of engineers to go in there and
   blitz the place basically and then-
A: What's-what's your email address
B: And the last I heard from them was the
   agency rang me said just to sort of
   keep me up to date, they've come back
   and said none of the people you put for-
   ward have, they said that none of the
   people that we put forward would be
   suitable but also it turns out that they
   didn't realise that SEC were in charge
   of it, and apparently have been sacked
   from the job as well now
A: I'm not surprised, they're shit
C: heh heh heh
B: I know, I know-
A: what's your email address?
B: I mean I was (.) ...I was working for
   SEC at eh network rail and that's why I
   had to leave
A: yeh
B: because they're a bunch of fuckin idiots they really are
A: They're almost, they're worse than the computer centre
   and that's sayin, that's saying something
B: I know, I know-
A: what's your email address?
B: (.) keith underscore hotmail dot com
```

Figure 5: Entering new contact details vs. the conversation

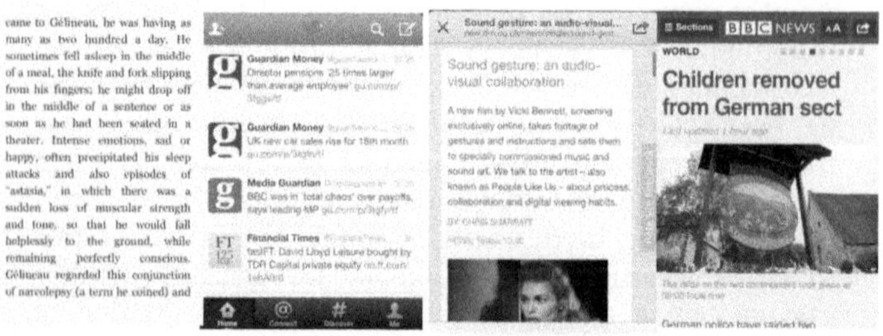

Figure 6: Four forms of mobile reading

contribute to conversation, while books (although they have other advantages of depth and immersion) require a greater level of temporal commitment.

Using the phone with others

One of the clearest aspects of the data is how social use of mobile devices was. We describe this in three ways, first how much co-present conversation went on around the phone, second how the phone itself allowed users to maintain complex multi-party collaborations, and lastly a form of use we have named "digital knitting".

Talk around the phone

The frequency of multiple parties talking around the phone in our data was a considerable surprise. In particular, the ways in which devices came to be used and brought into conversational settings. While it is impossible to obtain exact results due to the ambiguity of the audio data, we identified that 25% of our videos had more than one voice speaking while the device was being used, indicating some sort of interaction taking place around the phone. While in many cases this was just a device being used alongside an interaction, in our analysis it was surprisingly common for the mobile phone to be brought into the interaction in some way – such as occasioning a use of some sort. In figure 7, for example, social media consumption leads to a short conversation between the participant and their partner, with a short question, and explanation, then followed by discussion of a message received from a relation.

We are reminded here of Sacks' [20, vol ii, p92] comments on the ways in which 'local resources' (he meant physical objects in the environment) provide topical resources for conversation. What we find here is talk sparked off by something that (once it is found) is common to the conversationalists. Indeed, we were struck by how much co-present social media consumption there was in the data – with social media offering an array of topic resources to be introduced and discussed. The device then acts as something that can rather naturally be brought into conversation or discarded – it supports a form of multi activity, conversation and device use.

A related common multi-party interaction in which the mobile is brought into the interaction is search – social search having been remarked upon and researched in other publications [6]. That is, a conversation topic which generates some sort of object which can be found on the internet (such as a video or an answer to a question). This all said, the majority of our clips are actually of individuals using their devices on their own. Of course the iPhone is, by design, a device intended for single party use with a small screen and a form factor making it difficult to maintain multi-party interactions over a long period of time. Nevertheless it is also, by design, a device made for communication. The top application usage on the device is communication and socialising with others – as can be seen in figure 2. The iPhone then is still a device predominantly for sociability and communication, even if it is no longer predominantly used for voice calls.

```
[A opens Facebook app on phone and scrolls through New
updates]

A: We? [*]-------------------
B: °What's that↑°
   ((Participant B responds from
   the other side of the room,
   where they can be heard typ-
   ing on a keyboard))
A: we:e:e↑ ((A repeats the ques-
   tion about B's status up-
   date))
B: we wha:at?
A: You said WE
B: oh (.) Whee↑eee
A: oh my gawd
   ((muffled groans as partici-
   pant A gets the joke))
   ((A opens a FaceBook message
   from his aunt)) (12s) [*]----
A: Aunt Jo-leen wants us to move
   to Bakersfield
   ((While telling B about the
   message, A closes Facebook,
   opens Mail and begins to
   review and delete, without
   opening, a number of emails
   in the inbox))
A: you're too far away ((Adopts
   an 'Aunt' accent while continuing to explain the
   Facebook message)) (.) to which I would have to
   say, something to the effect of, we:e:ell you
   haven't seen me in fortee (.) no, thurty eight
   years
```

Figure 7: Conversation around a Facebook entry

Multi-party collaboration

Although we commented above on the relatively small number of phone calls made we would not want to downplay the importance of communication in our videos. As one would expect much mobile communication took place (in particular using Facebook and iMessage – the iPhone's messaging system). In figure 8, for example, a participant is booking cinema tickets for a group, and manages the details of the time of the showing, and how many tickets are to be booked simultaneously. The extract starts with the participant asking on Facebook if anyone wants to go to see the film, Pacific Rim. After a Facebook discussion he gets ready to book three tickets with the cinema app. He stops and checks if a third friend would like to go. He asks him, waits, does not receive a definite reply but eventually reserves four tickets. This communication takes place through Facebook direct messages, Facebook group messages as well as comments on a Facebook status message. Moreover, the asynchronous nature of the message allows the participant to move between the cinema booking application, the message itself as well as playing a game on the phone while waiting for replies.

Digital Knitting

While micro-breaks are relatively short episodes of use, we also observed longer episodes where content was consumed or games played while the user was also involved in some other activity. Above we mentioned cases where use exploits some 'spare attention' made available by the situation. In this category we see instances where the use of the device is combined with another activity, with attention moving between the mobile and the other activity dynamically, and where the device itself is at times connected to that activity.

Figure 8: Cinema ticket booking (Translations from Swedish have been superimposed)

So, for example, in figure 9 a massage therapist finds herself with a spare time slot as her customer has not turned up for their appointment, allowing her time to start a Solitaire game with a fellow therapist. However, the game is also combined with a conversation – centering on a story about two colleagues. We draw an analogy with conversations in knitting circles, where conversation can continue alongside and around the knitting. In this clip concentration moves from the Solitaire game to sporadic conversation around television, and a story about their boss, finally ending when both players admit to being stuck.

> *Participants at knitting groups are participating in handwork – their hands are busy but their minds can easily stray to other matters. In this way knitting is conducive to chatting, and chatting is justified because participants are still being productive. For this reason, knitting groups are increasingly termed "Stitch & Bitch' since participants can use the gathering to share not only skills but everyday life information.* [19]

In this case the two therapists are playing a shared game on their phones, while other examples include editing photographs with Instagram, or browsing and reading webpages while jointly watching television at home. What is interesting here is that as well as supporting enjoyable or creative activities, the mobile phone also allows for that activity to occur simultaneously with a secondary activity. The device also provides topics which can be brought up in conversation – such as the game itself.

DISCUSSION

The results here gives us a start on understanding how mobile phone use has developed beyond phone calls and SMS. A key focus has been on how context occasions use, and how use is managed to fit circumstances. We have tried to document the 'why' of use, how it is that usage itself is structured, and the differences between different styles of use. In discussion we relate three lessons we can draw from this work. First we address the issues of distraction around mobile phone use, and popular discussion that mobile phones are distracting or interfering with ordinary life. Drawing on the results here we can see how mobile phones usage has been shaped to fit with, and become part of our everyday interactions and life and we have some scepticism towards the notion of disruption. Second, we discuss the

```
A: Playing solitaire? [*]
B: Su:re
A: I'm gonna be really surprised if this girls comes back
   in like em not kidding
B: Really
A: yeah like cos she has been on the shit
   list and I'm trying to remember I've got
   a feeling she's no-showed on you before,
   lemme look, i swear she has (8)
A: it doesnt say-euw
B: she's never actually successfully been in
A: nope
B: she was physically here this morning, so
   that gives me hope that maybe she'll be
   here, [maybe]
A:        [wouldn't count on it]
B: you wouldn't count on it↑
A: not gonna count on it
B: dang
  ((fanfare music to start the joint game
   of Solitaire))
A: oh my gawsh that was like in stereo i
   heard it from over there and here
  ((A and B play a 5-min game of 'Multi-
   player Solitaire'. Each of them play on
   their own phone, and are able to see
   the other's score at the bottom of the
   screen, while the time counts down at
   top)) [*]
B: shoot player down, okay (16s)
A: beep
A: beeep (8s)
A: figure i'll watch emperors new groove
   tonight
B: aw maaan
A: I'm like in that mood heh heh heh
A: and what is that music, s'not even music
   (3s)
B: it's very slow kind of thing
A: slow and annoying
B: h-h-h heh slow and depressing
A: yes (20s)
A: Alex was like so funny he was like cos
   when Melinda was like up here the other
   day like she was like now quiet we can't have fun
   while she's around (.) and he like comes in from lunch
   and walks through here and we're like Melinda's here
   and he like scurries off to his room. And then like
   whenever she's went to the back he came up and he was
   like I knew Melinda was gawn and I'm like how and hes
   like cos you two started having fun again
B: hah hah awww
A: he wis like really quiet
B: can't believe I'm stuck
A: I think I'm stuck too, quite frankly [*]
A: shit
A: where did I go wrong, it was going so well
```

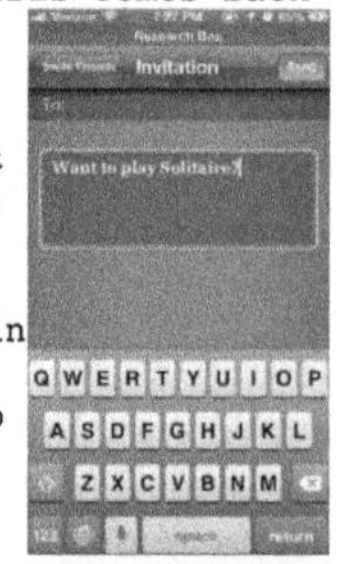

Figure 9: Diary entry reads: *"Almost 1 hour of solitaire with one of my favorite therapists Sue ^_^"* In this extract, attention moves fluidly between the game and conversation between the two therapists

importance of availability in the temporal structuring of mobile phone use. Finally, we touch briefly on the role of research design in this study – we argue that this paper supports the power of video as a technique for studying and understanding distributed mobile device use.

Distraction and mobile phone use

As with any new technology, the advent and adoption of the 'smartphone' has generated concerns over its effects on sociality and interaction. The New York Times, for example, commented on politicians in the recent mayoral race as suffering from 'distracted campaigning' in reaction to them checking their mobile phones at electoral hustings; "The phenomenon is in part a fact of contemporary life – people everywhere check their cellphones constantly" [16]. Slade goes further and writes of the mobile phone effects: "Human relationships are still in decline. We no longer have the time to take time even with those closest to us. [...] our focus on the tiny devices that fill the void left by social connection has surprising consequences." [21]. Even Turkle writes: "Our face-to-face conversations are routinely interrupted by incoming calls and text messages [...] When someone holds a phone, it can be hard to know if you have that person's attention. A parent, partner, or child glances down and is lost to another place" [22, p161].

Few seem to compliment the mobile phone's impact on our lives. Yet to these worries we can bring two aspects of our data. The first is the shared nature of much of the device use we recorded – as we mentioned above, 25% of our videos involved a conversation that took place around the activities on the smartphone. As can be seen in the examples above mobiles can also enhance sociality, with the device brought into the conversation and interaction. Device use becomes managed as any other aspect of the interaction. One might take the opinion that device use distracts from conversation, and that using a phone simultaneously is likely to be detrimental to that communication. Yet human interaction is something that is nearly always connected with the surroundings (with the exception of phone calls). Objects offer a set of rich resources that support not only conversation but also joint activity. So it is with mobile devices, in that they themselves are just objects in the environment that may be shared or ignored.

Secondly, it is worth remarking the majority of the use of mobiles is in a sense social – either communication or social media consumption. While there are those who would argue about the status of such sociability *vis a vis* face to face contact, it is worth remembering that while we might see people looking down at their phone screen there is an engagement with others through the device itself.

Portability and ubiquity

One of the key questions raised in our analysis above was the question of 'why now' – why would a mobile phone be brought out and used at a certain point in time. We described this in terms of the 'temporality' of device use. Yet one rather simple answer is that devices are brought out because they can be – they are actually carried on the person, or are available locally, so that for much of the time the effort involved in getting them out is low. This might seem a trivial point – that mobile phones are mobile – yet it sets a context of 'low threshold' use that other technologies might not have – iPads and laptops still need to be brought out of containers and carrying bags, or found in the environment. While the mobile makes some demands, it is remarkable to the extent that it is available in the settings where people find themselves, rather than having to have a place carved out for itself where it can be used.

When we are waiting to meet someone, we pull our phones out. The device is available and can be brought into situations determined not by the device, but by the requirements of the context. The importance of the mobility of the mobile device then is that it can be threaded into such a wide range of settings and activities because of its physical portability, stash-ability and pocket-ability. This a form of local computation that can be easily brought into whatever situation an individual might find themselves in. A related temporality that we have only touched on briefly is in turn how the routines of daily life figure in the use of the device. It is not that these devices change our daily routines as such. We, after all, have to go to work and care for our loved ones under the same temporal regimes as before. Rather, the mobile exploits these existing regimes, such as in post-waking and pre-sleeping use, or micro-breaks during the working day.

Designing from understanding use

This paper has focused on analysing use rather than specific design implications. A positive development in recent years has been the growing acceptance in developing the HCI field through both empirical and theoretical work, before the need to jump to specific design takeaways. This said, there are a few aspects of our analysis above which are worth mentioning. The first concerns the question of the temporality of usage. Predicting when and where a device will come to be used could have implications for battery life and the frequency of network updates. This can be done to an extent through time statistics, a system could also potentially attempt to work out the 'situation of use' – to predict situations in which a particular form of usage might dominate. So, for example, predicting waiting situations, or matching modes of transport with usage patterns.

Alternatively, phones could detect situations from talk around the device – potentially activate aspects of the system to fit better with the device being 'presented' to others. If modes of use (such as waiting or using an app while only partially involved in another interaction) could be identified, app usage clusters of those used in certain contexts of use might be identified, and a phone OS could update the content in these apps in the background. Broader inputs to this process again might include transport mode, time of day, if there is conversation and so on to produce an approximation of the likely 'situation of use' – watching for clusters such as morning social media updates, second screen television watching or reading messages at work.

More broadly however, this paper points to the role of video as a data collection method for understanding and improving the design of mobile applications. While the goal here has been on understanding usage more holistically, it seems to us that the trend for automated testing could be usefully augmented by video data that could explain particular mobile use outcomes, as well as developing understandings of how the context of use has such a major role on mobile device use. Video could potentially help us move on from understanding that a particular design is more popular to understanding why it is more popular.

CONCLUSION

We have presented analysis of an exciting new corpus of data on naturalistic mobile device use. Through recording software deployed on end users' iPhones, we collected a library of over one hundred days of ordinary iPhone use. Analysing this data allowed us to answer key questions about actual usage: What is done on mobiles? When are mobile used? Why are mobiles used? Who is present when mobiles are used? In discussion we focused on the temporal and sequential aspects of use, the opportunities of the sociality of mobile phones, before briefly commenting on how to draw these points into broad ideas for design.

The paper contributes to the growing interest in understanding end-user mobile behaviour. That the context of use is a major characteristic of mobile device use is clear, and existing research techniques where usage is represented artificially in some way miss out on much of this.

ACKNOWLEDGEMENTS

We acknowledge financial support from Yahoo Inc. FREP program, and Vinnova's funding of the Mobile Life Vinnova Excellence Centre.

REFERENCES

1. Ariga, A., Lleras, A., 2011. Brief and rare mental "breaks" keep you focused: Deactivation and reactivation of task goals preempt vigilance decrements. Cognition 118, 439–443.
2. Barkhuus, L., Polichar, V.E., 2011. Empowerment through seamfulness: smart phones in everyday life. Pers Ubiquit Comput 15, 629–639.
3. Böhmer, M., Hecht, B., Schöning, J., Krüger, A., Bauer, G., 2011. Falling Asleep with Angry Birds, Facebook and Kindle: A Large Scale Study on Mobile Application Usage, in: Proceedings of MobileHCI '11. ACM, New York, NY, USA, pp. 47–56.
4. Brown, B., Laurier, E., 2012. The Normal Natural Troubles of Driving with GPS, in: Proceedings of the CHI '12. ACM, New York, NY, USA, pp. 1621–1630.
5. Brown, B., McGregor, M., Laurier, E., 2013. iPhone in Vivo: Video Analysis of Mobile Device Use, in: Proceedings of CHI '13. ACM, New York, NY, USA, pp. 1031–1040.
6. Church, K., Cousin, A., Oliver, N., 2012. I Wanted to Settle a Bet!: Understanding Why and How People Use Mobile Search in Social Settings, in: Proceedings of MobileHCI '12. ACM, New York, NY, USA, pp. 393–402.
7. Church, K., Oliver, N., 2011. Understanding Mobile Web and Mobile Search Use in Today's Dynamic Mobile Landscape, in: Proceedings of MobileHCI '11. ACM, New York, NY, USA, pp. 67–76.
8. Dimmick, J., Feaster, J.C., Hoplamazian, G.J., 2010. News in the Interstices: The niches of mobile media in space and time. New Media Society. doi:10.1177/1461444810363452
9. Girardello, A., Michahelles, F., 2010. AppAware: Which Mobile Applications Are Hot?, in: Proceedings of MobileHCI '10. ACM, New York, USA, pp. 431.
10. Heath, C., Luff, P., 2000. Technology in Action. Cambridge University Press.
11. Henze, N., Rukzio, E., Boll, S., 2011. 100,000,000 Taps: Analysis and Improvement of Touch Performance in the Large, in: Proceedings of the 13th International Conference on Human Computer Interaction with Mobile Devices and Services, MobileHCI '11. ACM, New York, NY, USA, pp. 133–142.
12. Jin, J., Dabbish, L.A., 2009. Self-interruption on the Computer: A Typology of Discretionary Task Interleaving, in: Proceedings of CHI '09. ACM, New York, NY, USA, pp. 1799–1808.
13. John P. Trougakos, I.H., 2009. Momentary work recovery: The role of within-day work breaks. Research in Occupational Stress and Well-being 7, 37–84.
14. Licoppe, C., Figeac, J., 2013. Patterns of Gaze Switching in the "Naturally-Occurring" Uses of Smartphones in Urban Mobile Settings.
15. Miluzzo, E., Lane, N.D., Lu, H., Campbell, A.T., n.d. Research in the App Store Era: Experiences from the CenceMe App Deployment on the iPhone.
16. Nir, S.M., 2013. Mayoral Candidates Wedded to Smartphones While Campaigning. The New York Times.
17. O'Hara, K., Perry, M., Sellen, A., Brown, B., 2002. Exploring the relationship between mobile phone and document activity during business travel, in: Wireless World. Springer London, pp. 180–194.
18. Oulasvirta, A., Rattenbury, T., Ma, L., Raita, E., 2012. Habits Make Smartphone Use More Pervasive. Personal Ubiquitous Comput. 16, 105–114.
19. Prigoda, E., McKenzie, P.J., 2007. Purls of wisdom: A collectivist study of human information behaviour in a public library knitting group. Journal of Documentation 63, 90–114.
20. Sacks, H., 1995. Lectures on Conversation. Blackwell.
21. Slade, G., 2012. The Big Disconnect: The Story of Technology and Loneliness. Prometheus Books, Amherst, N.Y.
22. Turkle, S., 2012. Alone Together: Why We Expect More from Technology and Less from Each Other, First Trade Paper Edition edition. ed. Basic Books, New York.

An In-Situ Study of Mobile Phone Notifications

Martin Pielot
Telefonica Research
Barcelona, Spain
martin.pielot@telefonica.com

Karen Church *
Telefonica Research
Barcelona, Spain
kchurch@yahoo-inc.com

Rodrigo de Oliveira †
Telefonica Research
Barcelona, Spain
oliveirar@google.com

ABSTRACT

Notifications on mobile phones alert users about new messages, emails, social network updates, and other events. However, little is understood about the nature and effect of such notifications on the daily lives of mobile users. We report from a one-week, in-situ study involving 15 mobile phones users, where we collected real-world notifications through a smartphone logging application alongside subjective perceptions of those notifications through an online diary. We found that our participants had to deal with 63.5 notifications on average per day, mostly from messengers and email. Whether the phone is in silent mode or not, notifications were typically viewed within minutes. Social pressure in personal communication was amongst the main reasons given. While an increasing number of notifications was associated with an increase in negative emotions, receiving more messages and social network updates also made our participants feel more connected with others. Our findings imply that avoiding interruptions from notifications may be viable for professional communication, while in personal communication, approaches should focus on managing expectations.

Author Keywords

Notifications; Asynchronous Communication; Interruptions; Mobile Phones; Empirical Study

ACM Classification Keywords

H.5.2 Information interfaces and presentation: Miscellaneous; H.4.3 Communications Applications: Other.

INTRODUCTION

Smartphones have evolved to become a constant, pervasive companion to almost 1 billion people across the globe. Applications like messaging, email, and online social networks, allow smartphone users to connect to their family, friends and even co-workers wherever they go. Most of these communication apps are asynchronous, i.e. the receiving person is not expected or required to respond to a message/email/social network update right-away. However, the majority of these apps use proactive, push-based notifications, *i.e.*, visual, auditory, and/or haptic alerts, to inform mobile users about new, unattended messages or events, even when the user is not actively using the application in question. On arrival, these notifications alert users via sounds, vibrations, icons, and badges on the app's icon.

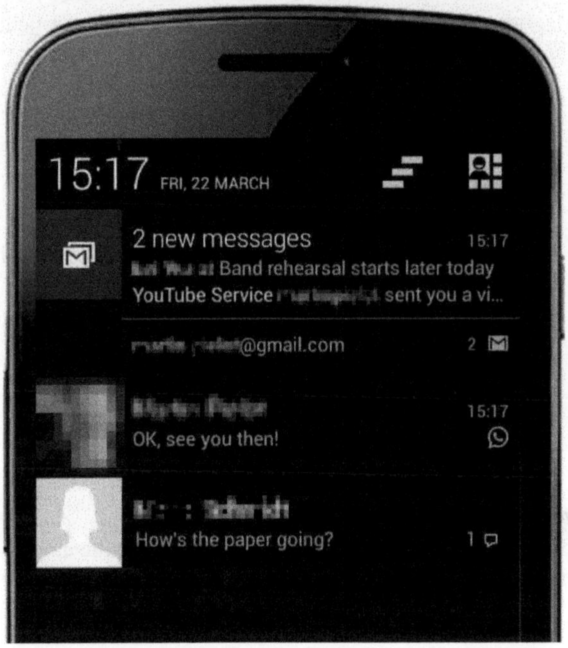

Figure 1. Notification drawer on Android OS, which can be opened by pulling down the notification area. Here, users can see pending notifications and preview sender and content.

This forms a stark contrast to the *quiet and invisible servants* that Weiser foresaw in his vision of ubiquitous, calm technology [31]. Push notifications have the ability to turn our mobile and ubiquitous communication devices into loud, disruptive machines. And the increased volume of communication exchanges among smartphone users highlights just how disruptive smartphones have become. For example, WhatsApp, a free messaging service that uses the internet to relay SMS-like exchanges, currently handles over 50 billion messages per day[1]. Finally, at the end of 2012, more users connected to Facebook every day via their mobile phones than via the desktop[2]. Given that notifications are at the core of many of

*The author is currently affiliated with Yahoo Inc., USA.

†The author is currently affiliated with Google Inc., USA.

[1]On Dec 31st [2013] [WhatsApp] users sent 18B msgs and received 36B = 54 Billion total messages in a day, See `https://twitter.com/WhatsApp/status/420373902980689920`

[2]Facebook Now TRULY a Mobile Company, Beats Expectations, see `http://www.cnbc.com/id/100420893`

MobileHCI '14, September 23 - 26 2014, Toronto, ON, Canada

http://dx.doi.org/10.1145/2628363.2628364

these applications, it's likely that mobile users have to deal with dozens and even hundreds of notifications per day.

While the effect of notifications in desktop environments, particularly in work settings, has been studied thoroughly [8, 9, 16, 18, 20, 22, 32], little is understood about the nature and effect of *mobile notifications* on *everyday life*. Since we carry our phone with us throughout the day, mobile notifications continually cross the boundaries of work and private life and as such have the potential to interrupt us in a wider range of situations and contexts. To shed light on what notifications phone users have to cope with and how these affect them, we conducted a one-week, in-situ study involving 15 mobile phone users, where we collected objective and subjective data about mobile notifications. The contribution of this work is:

- A quantitative analysis of the notifications that our participants receive and how they dealt with them,
- the fusion of this data with daily subjective ratings and stories describing events around notifications, and
- a discussion of previously explored approaches to improve notifications and asynchronous communication.

RELATED WORK

Notifications and their Interruptive Nature

Iqbal and Bailey [19] define a *notification* as a visual cue, auditory signal, or haptic alert generated by an application or service that relays information to a user outside her current focus of attention. On mobile phones, notifications are typically delivered instantly, *e.g.,* when the user receives a call or a message. In general, they only arrive when a corresponding application is closed, *e.g.,* when the user has an email application open, no notification will be generated by the OS if a new email arrives.

To date, the majority of research on notifications has focused on information workers in desktop environments. This previous work has repeatedly highlighted the negative effects of notifications on work efficiency. On the basis of the results of a study with 11 information workers, Czerwinski *et al.* [10] conclude that people find it difficult to return to a previous task after having been interrupted by *e.g.,* instant messages, calls, or an engagement with a colleague. Cutrell et al. [8] found that the effect is more pronounced when the task is cognitively demanding. Leiva *et al.* [21] found that phone calls interrupting the use of an app, though occurring rarely, significantly increase the time a user spends completing the initial task. De Vries *et al.* [11] showed that, depending on the mental workload, the level of politeness of a notification affects how annoyed and disrupted users feel. In their study, the participants preferred polite notifications during low-workload tasks and neutral notifications during high-workload tasks.

Mark *et al.* [22] conducted a deprivation study where they completely cut off email access to 13 information workers for 5 work days. Their results show that without email, the workers multitasked less, spent more consecutive time on tasks, and had decreased levels of stress. Similarly, Iqbal *et al.* [20] found that disabling email notifications leads to less frequent opportunistic email checking. However, while participants were aware of the disruptive effects, they appreciated the awareness provided by the notifications [20].

In mobile phones, notifications play an even more central role to "notify" users of new messages, events or actions. Previous work has shown that the perception towards mobile notifications varies strongly. If apps which are not perceived as useful keep sending notifications, users become annoyed and consider deleting those apps [12]. According to a field study with 11 co-workers by Fischer et al. [14], the user's receptiveness is determined by message content, i.e. how interesting, entertaining, relevant, and actionable a message is. The time of delivery, in contrast, did not affect receptivity. Sahami *et al.* [28] conducted a large-scale study with more than 40,000 Android phone users, and found via experience sampling that notifications from communication applications the most important.

Computer-Mediated Communication and Social Pressure

Communication via such channels has become essential for young people in particular [3, 29]. Skierkowski and Wood [29] report that when they restricted messaging as part of a user study, the participants not only showed increased anxiety, but many also did not comply. Communication applications, such as messengers, email, or social networks, rely on notifications to draw its users' attention to new messages or content. Holtgraves *et al.* [17] describes the unspoken rule of immediacy and pressure felt by people to carry their personal mobile devices at all times. Notifications are an essential part to supporting immediacy, as otherwise people would have to check their phone frequently. And despite the availability of notifications, Oulasvirta *et al.* [24] found that mobile phones force user's to adopt the habit of frequently checking for new messages and notifications, which is perceived as annoying rather than useful. Birnholtz *et al.* [5] found that one way to counter this social pressure is through "butler lies", *i.e.,* pretending that a message wasn't seen on time.

Mediating Interruptions and Expectations

To counter the disruptive effects on notifications, previous work has investigated to delay their delivery until a suitable point. In a study with 16 graduate students, Adamczyk *et al.* [1] found that their participants felt higher workloads when notifications were delivered while they were in the middle of a work task, such as correcting or writing text, or conducting a web search. Horvitz *et al.* [18] proposed deferring email notifications by 1 to 5 minutes to minimize their disruptive nature. Iqbal and Bailey [19] showed that delivering emails at so-called *breakpoints*, *i.e.* events when a person has just mentally finished a task, reduces frustration and makes users react to them faster.

Another approach in the case of communication is to shape expectations by estimating and/or communicating the availability of the recipient. Nardi *et al.* [23] explored the use of desktop instant messengers in work settings and highlight that when starting a conversation, time and topic are convenient for the initiator, but not necessarily for the recipient.

Fogarty *et al.* [15] conducted a series of studies that show that in an office environment, simple, low-costs sensor, such as a microphone, can infer the interruptibility of an information worker with the same accuracy as humans. Avrahami and Hudson [2] showed that it is possible to predict how fast a receiver of a message is going to respond by utilizing the *status* of the user and general activity events, such as key presses or mouse clicks. While Teevan and Hehmeyer [30] found that for desktop instant messaging, "busy" workers are more likely to accept a call, because they believe that the call is important.

Research in this regard has also been conducted in the mobile space. For example, Ho and Intille [16] explored delivering notifications at the transition between physical activities. Their results suggest that notifications might be considered more positively when being delivered between two physical activities, such as sitting and walking. Fischer *et al.* [13] conducted an experience-sampling study, where they created notifications that asked users to provide feedback about their context, such as taking a picture of the current activity. The participants reacted faster to notifications, when they are delivered right after finishing a phone call or reading a text message. However, Fischer *et al.* could not show whether the subjective experience improves, presumably because the artificial notifications created extra work. Rosenthal et al. [27] contributed to a method to learn, in a personalized way, when to mute a phone on a call or a notification to avoid embarrassing interruptions.

In summary, most of prior work has focused on desktop environments and office settings. While some past work has studied notifications in the context of mobile devices, none of those studies investigated *real-world* notifications in natural, un-biased settings. Given that mobile phone notifications are often related to communication, and thus highly personal, what is missing from the literature are insights on the basis of unobtrusive, in-situ data collection, which explore how mobile phone users deal with the fact that notifications now reach them everywhere and all the time.

METHOD

In order to study the nature and effect of notifications on the lives of mobile phone users, we conducted a one-week, in-situ field study. Given the goal of this work was to investigate mobile notifications in natural settings, we needed to employ a study methodology that would (1) avoid generating extra notifications that would potentially bias the nature of the phenomenon being studied — as would have been the case with experience sampling, and (2) would enable us to gather *actual* notification data in real-world contexts and in an unobtrusive manner. Thus, we used a mixed-method approach, where we collected both objective and subjective data.

For the objective data, we collected and analyzed real-world logs of all notifications that our participants received during the study period and how fast the participants viewed them after they arrived to their phone. For the subjective data, we conducted an online-diary study, where our participants reflected on the notifications they received each day, and they provided insights into their perceptions regarding those notifications.

Participants

For security reasons, the ability to monitor notifications is restricted on most popular mobile platforms. At the time the study was conducted, the only way was to use Android OS and intercept notifications through its accessibility API. Hence, we recruited Android participants via announcements on social networks and community forums. In total, 15 English-speaking participants (6 female, 9 male) aged 24-43 (Mdn = 28, M = 30.46, SD = 6.04) successfully completed all aspects of the study[3]. All of the participants lived in either North America or Europe, and their professions included engineering, teaching, graduate and undergraduate students.In terms of incentives, participants were rewarded with a 40 EUR Amazon Gift Card for taking part. In addition, we raffled three 100 EUR gift cards amongst them.

All participants indicated that on average they use email and *WhatsApp* several times per day, *Google Talk* once per day, *SMS* several times per week, and *Facebook Messenger* about once per week. Other messengers like *Line*, *TuMe*, or *KakaoTalk* were only reported by few participants, or were used infrequently. When asked to gauge how fast they typically respond to messages, half of the participants indicated that they generally respond to notifications within a few minutes, while the other half indicated that they tend to respond within an hour. Participants also estimated that others expect them to respond within similar time frames, i.e. half within a few minutes, half within an hour.

Procedure

The study was conducted in February and March 2013. Prior to the beginning of the study, the participants installed our logging app, the *Notification Monitor*, distributed as .apk, on their mobile phone. This Android app collected data regarding the notifications received along with details of when and how participants attended to those notifications. The Notification Monitor app ran as a background service on the user's phone. Once installed, the participants were asked to send us their participation ID, which was automatically generated by the app on their behalf. From the point of installation, the notification logging began and continued until the end of the study. The main phase of study commenced once the application was running on all participants' phones.

This main phase ran for one week, beginning on a Monday and ending on a Sunday. On each day during this period, participants were asked to provide subjective feedback regarding their perceptions and experiences with notifications through the daily diary which was delivered in form of a survey. Every morning, we sent an email to participants with a link to the survey asking them to reflect upon the notifications received on the previous day.

Given past work has shown that many mobile app interactions, in particular with social networking apps [6] and text

[3]In total, 27 participants started the project, but due to our strict compliance requirements, we discarded the data of 12 of them.

messaging [3], occur most often in the late evening / at night-time (between 7pm - 1am), we chose to prompt users to fill out the diary every morning of the following day, so that participants could reflect on the whole past day. This conscious design choice turned out to be an important as it allowed us capture periods of communication that take place late at night. To not bias the participants, no statistics of the data collected on previous day was presented. Participants were informed that in order to be eligible for the study incentives, they were required to fill out all 7 diary entries.

The diary included a mix of open-ended and closed questions, of which there were 9 in total, focusing on the 3 key areas:

- *Subjective perceptions* of the volume of received notifications and the time to react to them by category.
- *Attitudes and emotions* felt towards all notifications.
- *Personal stories*, collected via open-text fields, highlighting actual cases encountered by the participant where notifications kept them from doing something they had to, caused feelings of pressure to respond and/or induced feelings of wanting to respond to a notification faster than was possible.

Finally, at the end of the study, participants were debriefed and provided with their compensation. In the following sections, we describe the notification logging and diary portion of the study in more detail.

Quantitative Measures

To understand the quantitative measures, it's important to understand how notifications are implemented in Android OS[4]. When a notification arrives, the phone, depending on its mode, creates a buzz and an audible notification sound. At the same time, a little icon appears in the top left part of the phone screen, the so-called *notification area*. To see more details about the notification, the user can pull down this area and extend it into the *notification drawer*, which is shown in Figure 1 on page 1. In this notification drawer, users are provided with more details about the notifications. For short messages, the whole message can be read there. For longer messages, such as email, the user can read the subject line.

We tracked two events: the reception of a notification, i.e. *Notification Received* and the time between receiving and viewing of a notification, i.e. *Notification Viewed*.

Notification Received

On Android OS, notifications are generated by a number of applications which cannot be considered *true notifications* in the sense of the definition by Iqbal and Bailey [20]. For example, a weather widget that shows the current temperature in the notification area will constantly generate notification events, however, there will be no alert to the user whenever the temperature is updated. To overcome this issue, we created a white-list of applications that deliver true push notifications in the sense of Iqbal and Bailey. We then grouped these notifications into four categories: *Messengers*, (e.g. WhatsApp, SMS, Line), *Emails* (any email client), *Social network* updates (e.g. Twitter, Facebook, Google+), and *Other* notifications (e.g. system messages, calendar reminders, application updates). For each of these notifications, we store the local time of the notification arrival and the package name of the corresponding application (*e.g.*, com.whatsapp), which serves as a unique identifier for apps on the Google Play Store.

Notification Viewed

There are two ways of viewing notifications. When opening the notification drawer, we consider all pending notifications shown in the drawer as viewed. When the user opens an application, we consider all pending notifications associated with this application as viewed. For the scope of this study, *viewing* is the key event, as in this moment users have clearly become aware of the notification. For each of these *view events*, we store the name of the notification (*e.g.*, com.whatsapp) and the local time at which the message was viewed. How users actually react to notifications, *i.e.*, whether they respond, dismiss it, or ignore it, is out of the scope of this work.

RESULTS

Quantitative Results from Logs

In total, our Notification Monitor application logged 15 person weeks (105 days) of real mobile notification events which equates to 75 weekdays and 30 weekend days. Due to the non-normal distribution of some measurements, we report median rather than mean values (unless otherwise noted) and use non-parametric methods for inferential statistics. Therefore, null-hypothesis testing was performed using the Friedman test and the Wilcoxon rank sum test for matched pairs. Correlations were computed using the Spearman's Rho coefficient and pairwise deletion.

Basic Descriptive Statistics

In the first step, we cleaned the data set by removing instances of misused notifications. Examples are, the Android keyboard that creates a notification event whenever opened, the app market that uses a notification icon to present the percentage of downloaded data – generating 100 events in the process of each update, or a custom battery indicator which used a notification icon to display the battery level. We removed notification events from 64 applications in the process.

The remaining 33 applications were clustered into messengers, email, social networks, and other, as described above. By applying these filters, we ended up with 6854 notifications as defined by Iqbal and Bailey [19]. Thus, each participants received a mean number of 65.3 notifications per day. Table 1 shows the number of notifications received per category.

Cat.	#	Top apps
Msger	**3340**	WhatsApp, Google Talk, SMS
Email	**2210**	GMail, K-9 Mail, Android Email
Social	**269**	TweakDeck, Facebook, Google Plus
Other	**1035**	Updates, Calendar, Pea Pod

Table 1. Notifications by category.

[4]See `http://developer.android.com/guide/topics/ui/notifiers/notifications.html` for the official description

Since we wanted to study the effect of the notifications that people *actually* receive, we did not require the participants to turn on notifications they typically have disabled. All of the participants received notifications from messengers and other apps. All but two received emails notifications, and 8 received notifications from social networking apps.

5374 (78.4%) of the notifications arrived during a weekday and 1480 (21.6 %) during the weekend, which means that the number of notifications dropped during the weekend. Thus, we split our analysis by weekday and day in weekend to determine if more interesting differences emerge.

Figure 2 shows the average number of notifications received per day for each category, split by weekday versus weekend day. The number of notifications received per day differed significantly by category of notification ($\chi^2(3) = 44.64, p < .001$). Pairwise comparisons using Bonferroni-corrected Mann-Whitney tests showed that our participants received significantly more messages and emails than social network updates and other notifications (all differences significant at $p < .001$).

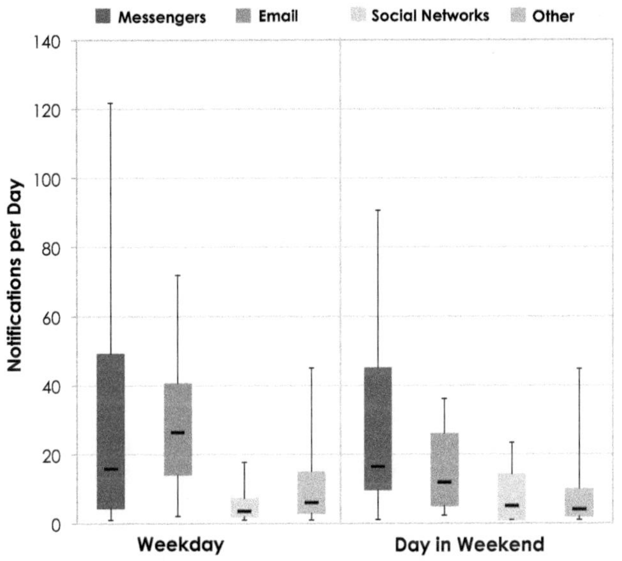

Figure 2. Median number of notifications received per participant by day, split by weekday versus weekend day

Temporal Patterns

Figure 3 shows at what (local) time notifications arrived. In general, the number of notifications dropped during the night. Most emails arrived during working hours, which two peaks before and after lunch. Messages, in contrast, filled the gaps and arrived primarily during lunchtime and after working hours.

Mostly Viewed Through Notification Drawer

4837 (70.6%) of notifications were first viewed through the notification drawer, the remaining 1966 (28.7%) by directly opening the app. When viewing the notification in the drawer, the participants continued to the app in 1988 (41.1%) of cases, and they did not in 2849 (58.9%) of cases. When any notification was viewed, either through the notification drawer or through the app, on average there were other un-viewed notifications ($Mdn = 1$, $M = 3.8$, $SD = 6.0$). This means that our participants typically did not let notifications accumulate.

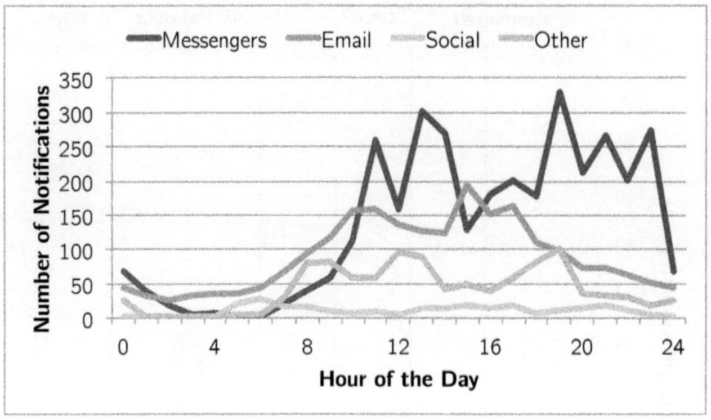

Figure 3. Notifications by hour of the day

Notification Viewed Times

Figure 4 shows the average time between the arrival of a notification until it was viewed, for each of the categories of notifications, split by day of the week and day of the weekend. The median time ranges from 3.5 min for messengers on weekends to 27.7 min for email on weekends. The fastest attended notifications were those generated from messengers (6.6 and 3.5 min) and social network applications (3.8 and 7.0 min / weekday and weekend day, respectively).

The box plots indicates that half of the notifications were viewed within a few minutes, and that the majority were attended to within hour (email on weekends being the exception), which confirms the subjective perception of the participants from the recruitment survey. When notifications arrived, the screen had been off in 69.2% of the cases. Given how fast people attended to notifications, this indicates that notifications often triggered interaction with the phone.

The speed at which notifications were viewed on average during the day differed significantly by type ($\chi^2(3) = 9.13, p < .05$). Pairwise comparisons using Bonferroni-corrected Mann-Whitney tests showed that our participants viewed messages significantly faster than emails ($p = .025$).

The Effect of Ringer Mode

One element of mobile phone technology that may or may not effect the interaction with and perceptions of mobile notifications relates to the ringer mode of the mobile phone. Android phones have three different ringer modes: normal mode (sound and vibration), vibration-only, and silent mode (neither sound nor vibration). It might be assumed that users turn the phone to silent mode if they want to avoid interruptions. Of the recorded notifications, 46.2% were received in normal mode, 41.5% in vibration-only mode, and 12.2% in silent mode. This indicates that people frequently disable sound, but rarely disable all alerts. Plotting the distribution, we could not identify any time-related patterns, such as that non-sound modes are prevalent during working hours or night time.

We compared the median time until viewing notifications between the ringer modes and found a significant effect

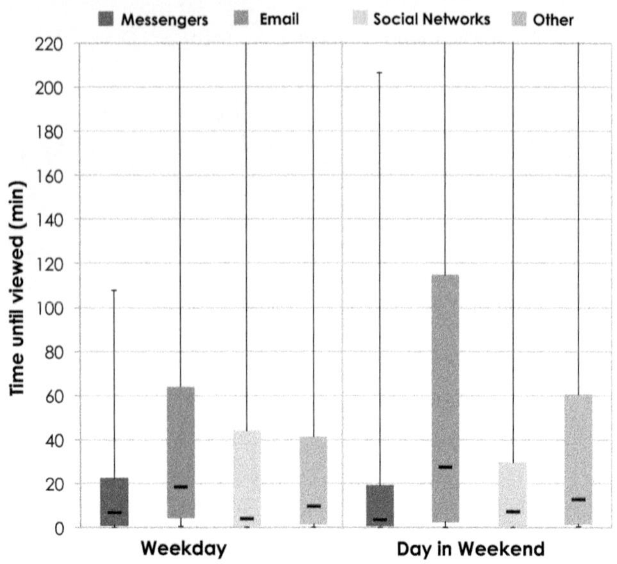

Figure 4. Median delay between receiving and viewing notifications, split by weekday versus weekend day.

($F(2) = 7.6609, p < .001$). Notifications were viewed significantly faster when the phone was in vibration mode compared to silent mode ($p < .001$) and normal mode ($p < .001$). Notably, the data does not contain any evidence that putting the phone into silent mode – the absence of audio-tactile alerts – leads to slower response times. Thus, it appears that having the phone in silent mode does not appear to help escape the effects of notifications.

Qualitative Results from Diary

In total we collected 97 diary entries over the 1-week period with an average of 6.5 diary entries per participant (Min=4, Max=7, SD=1.1). All diary responses were manually analyzed by two of the authors in an iterative manner to extract emergent themes. This manual analysis took a number of rounds to identify and cluster reoccurring themes.

In order to get further insights into how notifications affected the emotional states of our participants, where possible, we correlated the objective log data from each day with the subjective diary responses for the same day. In our notation, ρ_{obj} indicates correlations with the actual number of notifications received and ρ_{sub} the subjective notification volume, as shown in Figure 5.

Number of Notifications

While in the majority of cases, participants felt as though they received their "usual" amount of notifications per day, we did find differences in their perceptions depending on the type of notification (Figure 5). For example, for messengers and social networks, a significant proportion of participants felt that they received fewer or way fewer notifications than usual over the course of our study (30.5% and 23.7% respectively). Thus, although the number of notifications logged in our study was high (6854 notifications in total, 65.3 notifications per user per day on average), our participants didn't feel as though they received *more* or *way more* notifications than usual. This implies that participants general perception of their "usual" number of daily notifications is generally very high.

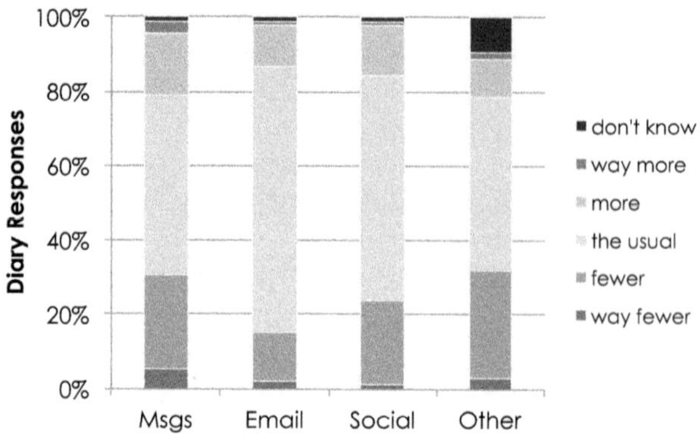

Figure 5. Subjective perceptions of the number of notifications received compared with the "usual".

Perceptions of Interruptions

One of the questions explicitly asked in the diary related was how much the majority of their daily notifications interrupted the participants. Based on the responses to that question, we find that mobile messenger applications and emails are the two primary sources of perceptions of interruptions. Participants reported that these apps interrupted them (occasional, frequently, or very frequently) in almost 50% of cases (Figure 6). Taking a closer look at the personal stories surrounding the apps or notifications that cause the most distractions we find that email was *explicitly mentioned* more often than messaging apps (50% vs. 28%).

The amount of emails received during a day was correlated with increased self-reports of negative emotions. Both, subjective and objective email count, lead to higher feelings of being stressed ($\rho_{obj} = 0.356$ and $\rho_{sub} = 0.238$), interrupted ($\rho_{obj} = 0.499$ and $\rho_{sub} = 0.315$), and annoyed (0.412 and $\rho_{sub} = 0.213$). The subjective amount of emails correlated with the feeling of having to deal with a lot of notifications ($\rho_{sub} = 0.374$) and with being overwhelmed ($\rho_{sub} = 0.290$). Additionally, we found a significant correlation between the actual volume of received emails and the number of reported instances where participants felt as though they were kept from doing something ($\rho_{obj} = 0.340$) and pressure to respond ($\rho_{obj} = 0.398$). According to the diary responses, email was mostly associated with work and their impact was generally considered to be interrupting due to their volume, their nature and their unclear urgency, e.g.:

> *Nastja: Email notifications are usually from exchange server, so they are work related. It means if I am not near my computer, I should get to my computer and reply.*
>
> *Cynthia: Email notifications seem to be the most distracting consistently. There are more of them and they are longer.*
>
> *Nico: Email notification is most disturbing because the urgency often varies widely.*

Having objectively and subjectively received more notifications from messenger apps during a day correlated with a

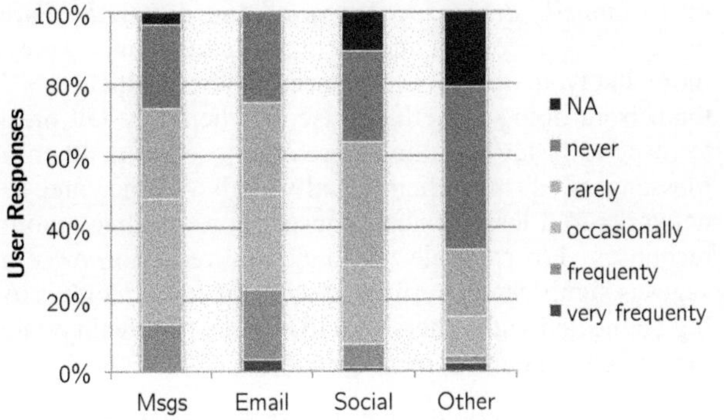

Figure 6. Subjective perceptions as to how much the majority of these notifications interrupted from daily tasks

stronger feeling of having to deal with a lot of messages ($\rho_{obj} = 0.264$ and $\rho_{sub} = 0.464$) and being overwhelmed ($\rho_{obj} = 0.241$ and $\rho_{sub} = 0.241$). In the diary responses, participants often mentioned messenger apps in this context when being focused on work tasks or when they were busy engaging in other social / leisure activities. In most cases there was an underlying feeling of social pressure, in particular for applications like WhatsApp:

Christina: Yesterday, I was working from home and had my phone next to me all day, so I saw all notifications as they came in. Therefore, I was frequently distracted... specially with WhatsApp notifications.

Adrian: Also WhatsApp was distracting a bit in the evening when I was out at the opera and then for birthday drinks with friends. It was not important to answer, but still a matter of politeness I had to answer in a reasonable time span.

Social network updates also had an impact on emotional states. An increasing subjective volume of social network updates correlated with increased feelings of having to deal with a lot of notifications ($\rho_{sub} = 0.387$), feeling stressed ($\rho_{sub} = 0.224$), interrupted ($\rho_{sub} = 0.221$), and annoyed ($\rho_{sub} = 0.218$). One of the key themes related to social network notifications that emerged from our study is the fact that while social networks are designed to connect people to one another, the many of the notifications generated by social networks are neither directed at the receiver nor are they relevant to the receiver:

John: Facebook distract me most, because it notifies all the comments that people made in some trending, so a lot of this messages are not for me.

While receiving too many emails and social network updates were related to stress or annoyance, we did not find any of such evidence for messengers. In contrast we found that receiving more messages is significantly correlated with increased feelings of being connected with others ($\rho_{obj} = 0.291$). The same positive correlation was found for the amount of social network updates and feeling connected to others ($\rho_{obj} = 0.205$). Overall this implies that while these services are at times interrupting and overwhelming, the fact that they help users to keep in touch with friends, family and others appears to also have positive effects.

Perceptions of Response Time

Our log data revealed that most notifications are viewed within a few minutes of reception, and both messenger and social app notifications in particular were viewed very quickly (3.5min - 7min depending on day of week and app type). When we asked our participants about how long it took them to *actually respond to the majority of these notifications*, we found a different pattern. While our participants perceived that they responded to around 30% of messenger notifications within a few minutes and almost 62% of messenger notifications within 1 hour, the perception of responding to email and social app notifications was notably lower (around 30% within an hour), see Figure 7.

Looking to the diary responses we find that social pressure plays a role in how fast users respond to notifications from messenger apps. Specifically we found 3 predominant sources for this pressure, all of which are in line with [7]. First, related to the expectations of others:

Yoshio: WhatsApp, as users don't have option to stop other side of users knowing if you have already read or not [...] people tend to expect immediate answers.

Second, relates to exchanging important, time-critical information, in particular for coordination activities:

Christina: I was pending to meet with someone, and was cautious to receiving any WhatsApp from him and be able to reply fast.

Nico: I was trying to find out if I should pick up a friend on my way to a meeting.

And finally, the relationship with the receiver seemed to play a role. Given instant messages were mainly used to communicate with loved ones, family, and friends, they seem to generate an increased expectation for faster responses:

Michael: In this case, [it] was my girlfriend who asked for some immediate stuff and I should better answer fast if I want to keep her stress less :D

Bob: I was talking to my sister. She was sad [and] I wanted to respond immediately to comfort her.

For email and social network updates, in contrast, our data shows that participants deferred attending to these notifications when they started feeling overwhelmed. The more often participants reported that notifications kept them from doing something, the slower they attended to notifications from email ($\rho = 0.255$) and social network updates ($\rho = 0.376$). Participants reported deferring viewing notifications because of other priorities or because of the increased the effort it takes to view and respond to these notifications compared to other communications apps. For example,

Nastja: Sometimes I take time to respond, because I see it is not urgent and there are other priorities at the moment, so it is my free choice.

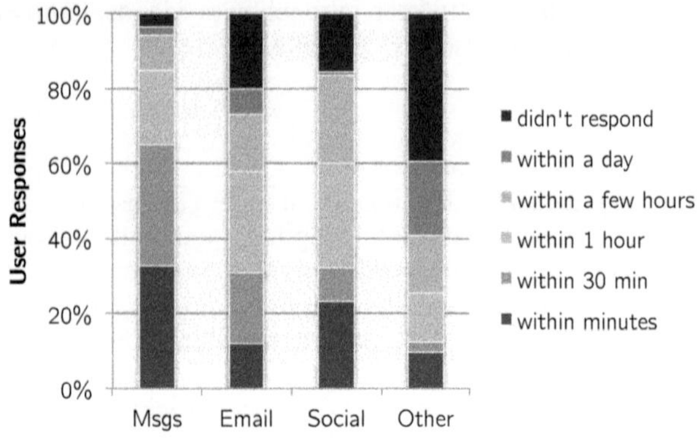

Figure 7. Subjective perceptions of the time it took to respond to the "majority" of their notification.

> *Cynthia: I receive more emails than any other type of notification; and these take more effort to check because you cannot read the message without fully opening the email client. They take longer to read and also require more effort to sort or delete when compared to other messages.*

DISCUSSION

Our participants had to deal with a daily mean number of 65 notifications, mostly from communication apps. The majority of the notifications were generated by messengers, such as SMS or WhatsApp, as well as email applications. This implies that mobile notifications are inherently social. When asked about their perceptions of the volume of notifications in the diary, we found that on average our participants largely indicated to have received the "usual" amount of notifications. This implies that our study captured a representative time period of mobile usage and that our participants perception of their "usual" number of daily notifications is generally very high. We found that email notifications were mostly associated with work and were intuitively received more often during work hours, while messenger notifications were mostly associated with personal life and as a result were received during downtimes (lunch breaks) and after work hours.

Notifications were viewed within a few minutes of their reception, with messengers and social network notifications being the fastest attended (3.5-6.6 min and 3.8 -7.0 min respectively), which is inline with the 6 minutes reported by Battestini *et al.* [3] regarding SMS. Notifications were largely prescreening in the notification drawer. In the diary, the participants indicated that, apart from notifications from the "other" category, they attend to the majority of notifications within an hour. Thus, objectively, participants reacted even faster than subjectively perceived. Overall the fast view times can be attributed to factors like expectations of a response from others, time-critical communication, and the relationship between the sender/receiver (with close-knit relationships appearing to lead to the more feelings of social pressure).

Our analysis revealed a significant relationship between the number of notifications and emotional effects. We found that emails and social networks were correlated with negative emotional responses, in particular to feelings of being *overwhelmed, stressed, interrupted* and *annoyed*. Furthermore, when receiving more emails, participants were also more likely to report experiences where notifications kept them from doing something else or when they felt pressure to respond faster than they were able to. On the other hand, messengers, despite their equally high volume, and social networks to a lesser extent, caused more positive emotional responses. For example we found that receiving more messages is significantly correlated with increased feelings of being connected with others. It's likely that this again relates to the personal nature of messaging apps.

Our participants could have turned the ringer mode of their phone off, i.e. set their phone to silent mode to escape notifications. However we found that just 12.2% of the recorded notifications were received when the phone was in silent mode. Interestingly, setting the phone to silent mode did not have an effect on how fast our participants viewed the notification. That is, we did not find any evidence that people viewed notifications slower when the phone was in silent mode while they arrived. This could be an indicator that our participants, despite enabling silent mode, still frequently check their phone [24], adhering to the "rule" of immediacy [17]. Thus putting the phone to silent mode does not help to escape the effects of notifications.

In the diary, we found several reports where our participants indicated that they postponed attending to their notifications. Increased feelings of having to deal with a lot of messages correlated with longer delays until emails and social network updates were viewed. Thus, rather than these longer view times being associated with the phone being in silent mode, it appears that at times people make an explicit decision to delay *dealing with notifications*.

During 2013, the number of messages that WhatsApp handled rose from 10B to 56B. Furthermore, younger populations than the sample we studied, particularly teens, have been found to send and receive even more messages per day. Our work represents a snapshot of the situation in March 2013. Given that the volume of communications done via mobile phones is on the rise, as well as the fact that new mobile apps are continually released which rely on notifications, the effects we found in our study might be more pronounced in the future and amongst other user groups.

The presented study has two limitations. First, the data reported in this paper reflects 15 Android users across 7 days. While this is inline with related landmark in-situ studies, which studied between 11 to 20 [10, 13] subjects for 5 to 14 days [22, 20], our findings may not be generalizable to other populations, such as teens or older adults. Initially, we had aimed for more participants, but many volunteers dropped out because they did not comply to filling out the diary every day. As such there are clear opportunities for more research in this domain, focusing on other mobile platforms and other populations over longer time periods.

Second, the notifications we monitored by not only be viewed via the notification centre or the phone apps. For example, on receiving an email notification, our participants might have checked their emails on their desktop computer rather than on their phone. Or, the user might have glanced at the notification summary that briefly appears in the notification area when the notification arrives. In this case, the delay between reception and viewing of the notification in our data set would be longer than it actually was. Thus, we have to assume that the actual time between receiving and viewing notifications reported in our current work represent a lower bound (i.e. they are likely to be faster than the 3.2 to 22.0 minutes per category), in particular for emails and social network updates.

IMPLICATIONS

Reducing Interruptions

Reducing the number of interruptions by notifications may seem like an intuitive approach, given the large volume of notifications phone users have to deal with every day. For example, Rosenthal *et al.* [27] have shown that phones can be trained to automatically mute according to contextual information. Previous work has shown the benefits of not being exposed to email notifications: information workers checked their emails less opportunistically [20], spent more time on tasks and felt less stressed [22]. They still appreciated the awareness that notifications provide, and all but one participant reverted to the use of notifications [20].

Our work confirms the negative emotions associated with receiving too many emails found in [22]. However, we also found a generally positive attitude towards notifications and even an increased feeling of being connected with others in the case of messaging and social network updates. Given that our participants typically viewed messages and social networks updates within minutes, and given that muting notifications had no effect on those viewing times, we would expect that even if these notifications are reduced, it's likely that mobile users will check their phones more frequently to make sure that no "important" or "urgent" message has been missed. This should be considered when designing systems to reduce the number of interruptions from notifications.

Delivering Notifications at the Right Time

Some prior work has focused on *when* to delivery notifications. Examples include deferring the delivery of emails by a few minutes when the user is busy [18], delivering emails during the transition between two work tasks [20], and delivering phone notifications between physical activities [16] or after finishing a phone call or text message [13].

Our data shows that some participants delayed attending to emails and social network updates when they were busy. On the other hand, notifications from messengers and social networks were typically viewed within minutes, even if they interrupted the receivers. Thus, systems that delay notifications need to consider this level of immediacy, in particular in personal communication. For example, a system that delays the delivery of a message until the end of a meeting may at times violate user expectations.

Communicating Availability

A rich body of past literature has focused on understanding a persons *availability* to allow people to judge whether it is a good time to engage in a conversation. Proposals for automatically inferring a persons availability in office spaces [15] and desktop instant messengers [2], phone calls [25] and mobile instant messengers [26] have been explored. Other researchers have investigated the use of rich-presence information including motion, location and music to enable users to determine when and how to contact an individual in mobile environments [4].

In our study, we found that participants at times decided to defer viewing or attending to notifications because they were busy with other tasks or priorities. In such cases, we believe that providing information about a person's *availability* is the most promising approach to a better user experience. One of the key challenges in detecting availability to be solved in future work, however, is that in daily life, a person is not strictly available or unavailable. Rather, a person is available for different people or in different situations at different times [4]. Thus, understanding availability is a complex, pervasive problem and one that has not been fully solved by past work, especially for always-connected mobile phone users.

CONCLUSIONS

We found that mobile phone users have to deal with a large volume of notifications, mostly from messengers and email, each day (63.5 on average per day), which was perceived as the usual. Notifications were largely checked within a few minutes of arrival, regardless of whether the phone was in silent mode or not. In particular in the case of personal communication, explanations for these fast reaction times related to high social expectations and the exchange of time-critical information. Increasing numbers of notifications, in particular from email and social networks, correlated with negative emotions, such as stress and feeling overwhelmed. Personal communication, on the other hand, also related to increased feelings of being connected with others.

These findings highlight that strategies are needed to lower negative emotions. Reviewing previously explored approaches, our findings imply that reducing interruptions and deferring notifications may work in a professional context. For a personal context, strategies around communicating (un)availability and managing expectations appear more suited.

While our work sheds first light on the relationship between received notifications and subjective emotional responses, more work is needed to extend our knowledge to other populations. Our findings encourage future work, in particular given that asynchronous communication via mobile phones is still on the rise and becoming a more and more essential form of communication for large groups in our societies.

ACKNOWLEDGEMENTS

We thank the participants for their contributions.

REFERENCES

1. Adamczyk, P. D., and Bailey, B. P. If not now, when?: the effects of interruption at different moments within task execution. In *Proc. CHI '04*, ACM (2004).

2. Avrahami, D., and Hudson, S. E. Responsiveness in instant messaging: predictive models supporting inter-personal communication. In *Proc. CHI '06*, ACM (2006).
3. Battestini, A., Setlur, V., and Sohn, T. A large scale study of text-messaging use. In *Proc. MobileHCI '10*, ACM (2010), 229–238.
4. Bentley, F., and Metcalf, C. J. The use of mobile social presence. *IEEE Pervasive Computing 8*, 4 (Oct. 2009), 35–41.
5. Birnholtz, J., Reynolds, L., Smith, M. E., and Hancock, J. "everyone has to do it: " a joint action approach to managing social inattention. *Comput. Hum. Behav. 29*, 6 (Nov. 2013), 2230–2238.
6. Böhmer, M., Hecht, B., Schöning, J., Krüger, A., and Bauer, G. Falling asleep with angry birds, facebook and kindle: a large scale study on mobile application usage. In *Proc. of MobileHCI '11*, ACM (2011), 47–56.
7. Church, K., and de Oliveira, R. What's up with whatsapp? comparing mobile instant messaging behaviors with traditional sms. In *Proc. MobileHCI '13*, ACM (2013).
8. Cutrell, E., Czerwinski, M., and Horvitz, E. Notification, disruption, and memory: Effects of messaging interruptions on memory and performance. In *Proc. INTERACT '11* (2001).
9. Czerwinski, M., Cutrell, E., and Horvitz, E. Instant messaging and interruption: Influence of task type on performance. In *Proc. OZCHI '00* (2000).
10. Czerwinski, M., Horvitz, E., and Wilhite, S. A diary study of task switching and interruptions. In *Proc. CHI '04*, ACM (2004).
11. de Vries, R. A. J., Lohse, M., Winterboer, A., Groen, F. C., and Evers, V. Combining social strategies and workload: a new design to reduce the negative effects of task interruptions. In *Proc. CHI '13 EA*, ACM (2013).
12. Felt, A. P., Egelman, S., and Wagner, D. I've got 99 problems, but vibration ain't one: a survey of smartphone users' concerns. In *Proc SPSM '12*, ACM (2012).
13. Fischer, J. E., Greenhalgh, C., and Benford, S. Investigating episodes of mobile phone activity as indicators of opportune moments to deliver notifications. In *Proc. MobileHCI '11*, ACM (2011).
14. Fischer, J. E., Yee, N., Bellotti, V., Good, N., Benford, S., and Greenhalgh, C. Effects of content and time of delivery on receptivity to mobile interruptions. In *Proc. MobileHCI '10*, ACM (2010).
15. Fogarty, J., Hudson, S. E., Atkeson, C. G., Avrahami, D., Forlizzi, J., Kiesler, S., Lee, J. C., and Yang, J. Predicting human interruptibility with sensors. *ACM Trans. Comput.-Hum. Interact. 12*, 1 (Mar 2005), 119–146.
16. Ho, J., and Intille, S. S. Using context-aware computing to reduce the perceived burden of interruptions from mobile devices. In *Proc. CHI '05*, ACM (2005).
17. Holtgraves, T., and Paul, K. Texting versus talking: An exploration in telecommunication language. *Telemat. Inf. 30*, 4 (Nov. 2013), 289–295.
18. Horvitz, E., Apacible, J., and Subramani, M. Balancing awareness and interruption: investigation of notification deferral policies. In *Proc. UM '05*, Springer-Verlag (2005).
19. Iqbal, S. T., and Bailey, B. P. Effects of intelligent notification management on users and their tasks. In *Proc. CHI '08*, ACM (2008).
20. Iqbal, S. T., and Horvitz, E. Notifications and awareness: a field study of alert usage and preferences. In *Proc. CSCW '10*, ACM (2010).
21. Leiva, L., Böhmer, M., Gehring, S., and Krüger, A. Back to the app: the costs of mobile application interruptions. In *Proc. MobileHCI '12*, ACM (2012).
22. Mark, G., Voida, S., and Cardello, A. "a pace not dictated by electrons": an empirical study of work without email. In *Proc. CHI '12*, ACM (2012).
23. Nardi, B. A., Whittaker, S., and Bradner, E. Interaction and outeraction: instant messaging in action. In *CSCW '00*, ACM (2000).
24. Oulasvirta, A., Rattenbury, T., Ma, L., and Raita, E. Habits make smartphone use more pervasive. *Personal Ubiquitous Comput. 16*, 1 (Jan 2012), 105–114.
25. Pielot, M. Large-scale evaluation of call availability prediction. In *Proc. UbiComp '14* (2014).
26. Pielot, M., de Oliveira, R., Kwak, H., and Oliver, N. Didn't you see my message? predicting attentiveness in mobile instant messaging. In *Proc CHI '14*, ACM (2014).
27. Rosenthal, S., Dey, A. K., and Veloso, M. Using decision-theoretic experience sampling to build personalized mobile phone interruption models. In *Proc. Pervasive '11*, Springer-Verlag (2011).
28. Sahami Shirazi, A., Henze, N., Pielot, M., Weber, D., and Schmidt, A. Large-scale assessment of mobile notifications. In *Proc. CHI '14*, ACM (2014).
29. Skierkowski, D., and Wood, R. M. To text or not to text? the importance of text messaging among college-aged youth. *Comput. Hum. Behav. 28*, 2 (Mar. 2012), 744–756.
30. Teevan, J., and Hehmeyer, A. Understanding how the projection of availability state impacts the reception incoming communication. In *Proc. CSCW '13*, ACM (2013).
31. Weiser, M. The computer for the 21st century. *Scientific American 265*, 3 (1991), 66–75.
32. Whittaker, S., and Sidner, C. Email overload: exploring personal information management of email. In *Proc. CHI '96*, ACM (1996).

ProactiveTasks: the Short of Mobile Device Use Sessions

Nikola Banovic, Christina Brant, Jennifer Mankoff, Anind K. Dey
Human-Computer Interaction Institute
Carnegie Mellon University
5000 Forbes Ave., Pittsburgh, PA 15213, USA
{nbanovic, jmankoff, anind}@cs.cmu.edu, cbrant@andrew.cmu.edu

ABSTRACT
Mobile devices have become powerful ultra-portable personal computers supporting not only communication but also running a variety of complex, interactive applications. Because of the unique characteristics of mobile interaction, a better understanding of the time duration and context of mobile device uses could help to improve and streamline the user experience. In this paper, we first explore the anatomy of mobile device use and propose a classification of use based on duration and interaction type: *glance*, *review*, and *engage*. We then focus our investigation on short *review* interactions and identify opportunities for streamlining these mobile device uses through proactively suggesting short tasks to the user that go beyond simple application notifications. We evaluate the concept through a user evaluation of an interactive lock screen prototype, called ProactiveTasks. We use the findings from our study to create and explore the design space for proactively presenting tasks to the users. Our findings underline the need for a more nuanced set of interactions that support short mobile device uses, in particular *review* sessions.

Author Keywords
Interaction types; mobile devices; duration; proactive tasks.

ACM Classification Keywords
H.5.2. User interfaces: User-centered design.

INTRODUCTION
Mobile devices have made the transition from simple communication tools to fully functioning general-purpose computing devices. One of the main reasons for the success of mobile devices is the wide range of functionalities they support and the users' ability to pick those functions that best suit their needs [4]. Despite advances in the past few years, appropriate interaction models for these computers are still evolving, as application interfaces are often not designed to provide information at an appropriate time and quickly enough for the interaction to be worthwhile [20]. Therefore, a better understanding of the different ways that mobile devices are used is needed to help improve and streamline the mobile device interactions.

Time duration of mobile device interactions is one aspect of mobile device use that has been underexplored. Although time duration seems to be a critical component of a user's experience with a mobile phone [10, 17, 23], most current mobile applications provide a monolithic interface that does not change regardless of whether the user intends to spend a lot of time with the interface, or just glance at it. Notifications and wallpaper widgets on smartphone platforms are a step in the right direction because they enable the user to quickly check for new information of interest. However, questions remain regarding the extent to which the existing mobile device user interfaces support interactions based on the amount of time the user can or is willing to dedicate to the task at hand.

In this paper, we first briefly explore the anatomy of mobile device use based on data collected from 10 participants over a period of 18 to 36 days. We distinguish three types of interactions based on their duration and interaction type (Figure 1): 1) *glance* sessions, where the user only looks at the information on the locked screen or home screen of the phone, 2) *review* sessions, where the user briefly interacts with one or more applications on the device, and 3) *engage* sessions, where the user engages in longer interaction with applications. We then investigate how existing mobile user interfaces support these use types. Our results indicate that existing interface elements, such as notifications and wallpaper widgets, although very good at streamlining both *glance* and *engage* sessions, leave room for improvement in supporting short *review* uses.

Insights from our first study suggest that proactively providing short tasks to users on their mobile device could streamline *review* sessions, making the overall interaction with mobile devices more efficient. We present the concept of proactive tasks through a prototype of ProactiveTasks interactive lock screen that goes beyond simple application notifications and widgets. We evaluated the prototype with 27 users over a period of four weeks in a real-world setting. Findings from the study informed the design space for proactively suggesting tasks to users, and identified different useful ProactiveTasks. We present two alternative ProactiveTasks designs to further explore the design space. Our exploration results in design recommendations on how to improve short *review* interactions with mobile devices.

MobileHCI 2014, September 23–26, 2014, Toronto, ON, Canada.

http://dx.doi.org/10.1145/2628363.2628380

CHARACTERIZING OVERALL MOBILE DEVICE USE

Past research has shown that users perform a variety of tasks, from entertainment to productivity, to satisfy a wide range of needs using mobile devices in different contexts [4, 20], and even identified different kinds of cognitive [16] and psychological factors that guide mobile device use [5, 12, 19]. In this section we review past research on different aspects of mobile device use and the context, or environmental information relevant to the current interaction between the user and the device [8], in which the user interacts with mobile devices.

Researchers have explored different high-level aspects of mobile device use, such as overall amount and duration of mobile device use sessions [10, 17, 23]. In that work, sessions are defined by the user's active interactions when the device screen is on or when the user is on a phone call. Mean session duration varies significantly between users, from 10 to 250 seconds [10]. The distribution of session durations follows a long-tail distribution where the majority of sessions have short durations, with duration independent of the length of previous sessions [10]. Furthermore, 35% of sessions are very short interactions where the user turns the screen on, then turns it off again quickly [17]. Duration of device use, from when the user unlocks the screen until the user turns the screen off, are shorter than 30 seconds in 50% of cases, with 90% being less than 4 minutes [25].

Breaking these high level trends down further, use may differ based on context such as a user's location [23], time of day [23], and social context [9]. For example, time of day and location impact which applications the user is more likely to interact with [6]. The location, time of day, and duration between application uses are predictive of the user's next application [25]. Also, a large portion of application use is triggered through notification events such as incoming phone calls or SMS [25]. However, we know very little about how such context impacts overall device use irrespective of applications users interact with.

Given the prevalence of short sessions, it is not surprising that today's mobile platforms increasingly provide user interface components that allow the user to briefly view a summary of application data (often through application widgets) and that support faster application invocation (as is the case with application shortcuts). Application designers have begun to appropriate the device lock screen and launcher (or home screen) in order to present valuable information to the user as often as possible. However, most existing widgets support no or limited interactions, and therefore still require the user to invoke the corresponding application to interact with data from the widget. Recent interactive widgets have shown that frequent mobile device use could power crowd-sourced data collection [21, 22], but such solutions do not focus on reducing the time to interact with the mobile device or streamlining mobile device use.

Past research has identified invocation of applications as one of the bottlenecks to efficient device use [18]: notifications provide a partial solution, but only help the user streamline interaction with those applications that have immediate notifications pending. Strategies for reducing invocation times include using contextual data to predict different applications [14, 18, 24, 25, 26] or Web content [11] that the user will interact with next, and even automating mobile tasks [15]. However, that body of work focuses on a very specific aspect of mobile device use, and not on understanding and streamlining overall device use, and therefore, overall mobile user experience.

STUDY OF GLANCE, REVIEW AND ENGAGE SESSIONS

We conducted a formative study of mobile device use in a real-world setting to explore the different types of mobile device use associated with different session lengths. We analyzed the data collected in the study to understand the anatomy of mobile device use and identify areas in which interaction with mobile devices can be further improved.

Study Method

We collected data from 10 participants (7 male and 3 female) who were recruited through online postings and social media. Participants were between 20 and 50 (median=25) years old. Data collection lasted between 18 and 36 days (median=31). Participants were not compensated for taking part in the study.

Task and Procedure

Participants downloaded and installed our tracking application from the Android Play Store onto their primary (personal) phone. We focus on the Android OS because it is the dominant mobile phone operating system that offers all major user interface elements (*e.g.*, lock screen, home screen, application notifications, *etc.*) present on other mobile platforms. We collected data using the AWARE Framework (www.awareframework.com), which ran unobtrusively on participants' devices as a background service without any user interface. We did not use an experience sampling method (ESM) on the mobile device because it could have impacted the duration of mobile device use.

Data Collection and Preparation

Our application collected the following data: screen events (on, unlock, and off); application use events (launches and exits); phone calls, SMS, and other device and application notifications; Global Positioning System (GPS) location data, and activity data (still, walking, cycling, in vehicle).

Characterizing Mobile Device Use Sessions

Device use sessions start when the screen is turned on and end when the screen is turned off. When two sessions are 5 seconds or less apart, we merge them into one session to account for accidental timeouts and unintentional breaks in interaction. For example, the user might be reading a Web page on the device when the device screen times-out and turns itself off, and the user has to unlock the device and continue the task. All the events that occur during the time from screen on to screen off, such as application launches or notifications, are considered to be part of the session.

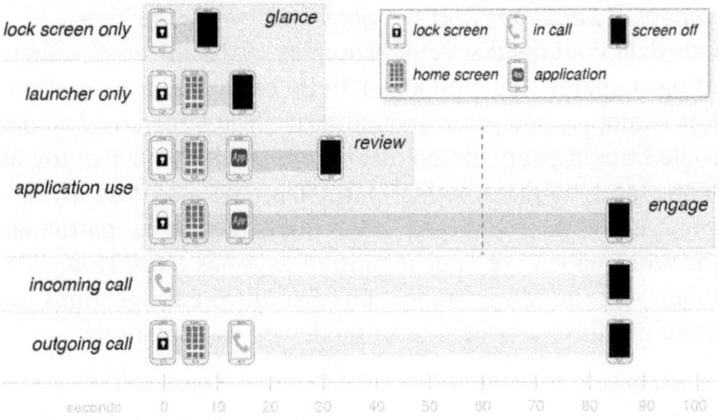

Figure 1. Examples of common mobile device uses: 1) lock screen only (median=30.2% of uses in our study), 2) launcher only (median=8.0% uses), 3) application use (median=49.1% uses), and 4) phone call (median=10.7% uses).

During a session, users interact with their mobile devices in one of four well-established ways that are quite consistent across different mobile phone platforms, such as glancing at a lock screen, visiting a home or launcher screen (screen containing a set of application icons), launching an application, or making or receiving a phone call. Figure 1 shows examples of steps the users often make during those interactions. In the lock screen only interaction, the users check information on the locked screen (*e.g.*, time, or non-interactive application widgets) with no other interaction. In the launcher only interactions, the users often only read information from widgets within the home or launcher screens. While in the launcher screen, users can invoke and use an application. Alternatively, the users might receive or make a phone call. However, note that our focus in this work is on interactions that do not involve phone calls.

The categorization of mobile device activity based these interaction types does not account for interaction duration. However, duration could be very important, especially in mobile situations where the user has limited time to interact with the device. As shown in Figure 2, most device use sessions are short, although there is a long tail. The median duration across all sessions in our study was 30.5 seconds. Note that because so much of our analysis is characterized by a long tail distribution, we typically use a median statistic rather than mean in describing our results.

One way to characterize these short device uses is to empirically determine temporal boundaries characteristic of different interaction types. We use a statistical technique that performs well on skewed data: head/tail breaks classification [13]. The natural break that we found at around 60 seconds (dashed line in Figures 1 and 2) also coincides with the screen timeout for most of our participants. Thus, for all sessions shorter than 60 seconds, participants indicated that they completed their tasks by

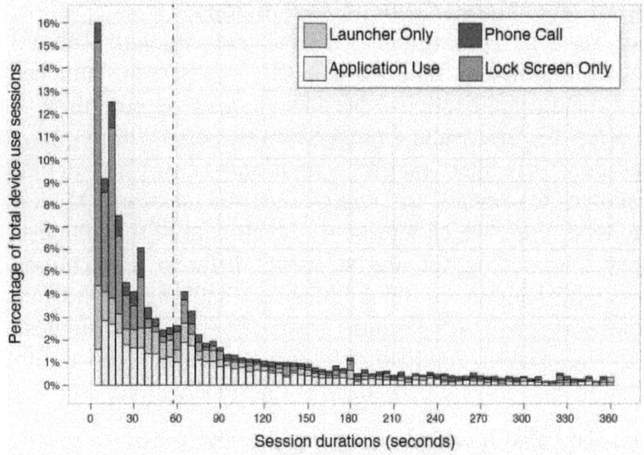

Figure 2. Histogram of interaction types durations across participants for durations less than 360 seconds (95% of all device use sessions). Dashed line represents a natural break.

turning off their screen before the timeout. Note that, although lock screen and some launcher only interactions dominate these short sessions, application use is also a significant component of sessions of 10 seconds and longer. Combining interaction types with the duration of the interaction and removing phone call usage, we see three major groups of device uses, illustrated in Figure 1:

Glance sessions are brief interactions, where the user turns the screen on, checks the information on the lock screen, and then turns the screen off or the screen timeout is reached, with no other interaction (median=46.6% of device uses in our study). Alternatively, the user might unlock the phone and glance at the application widgets displayed on the home screen. These typically involved no input and had a median duration of 13.5 seconds. Two examples of *glance* sessions found in our data are checking the time or checking a recently received notification.

Review sessions are interactions that last 60 seconds or less, involving one or two applications (median=24.6% of device uses). The median duration of *review* sessions is 22.5 seconds. Review sessions involve users both consuming content from the phone and providing quick input to the phone. Most often *review* sessions involve only a single application (median=65.4%). An example found in our data is opening an email application and briefly scrolling through existing email messages.

Engage sessions involve longer application use interactions that last more than 60 seconds (median=22.1% of device uses). These interactions could last several minutes in our data, with the median length being 130.25 seconds. They often, but not always, involve multiple applications. Examples from our data include playing a game or using the web browser to search and view Internet content.

Duration of Mobile Device Use Sessions

For session types (*glance, review* and *engage),* Table 1 shows the median time spent in the lock screen, launcher, and using applications. Median locked screen time is shorter for *review* and *engage* sessions compared to *glance* sessions. It is likely that the user in most cases had already decided to *review* or *engage* in the session. Median launcher time, which represents the amount of time the user spends searching for and selecting different applications, was surprisingly low for both *review* and *engage* sessions (median=1 and 4.5 seconds, respectively). This suggests that the existing application invocation mechanisms do not present such a great bottleneck as previously thought [18].

Our data also revealed very frequent device use (over 50% percent of all sessions are within 5 minutes of another session). Table 2 shows the median transition time between different device use session types. The short transition times from long *engage* sessions to all other types of use suggests that users seem likely to *glance, review,* or *engage* again about 5 minutes after a long session ends. This could indicate chunking of longer or related tasks into multiple sessions. However, few existing interaction techniques support or take advantage of such frequent device use bursts. Further investigation is required to validate whether consecutive device use sessions are in fact related.

The Context of Mobile Device Use Sessions

Mobile devices support interactions in a wide range of contexts that could impact the frequency and duration of device use. For example, a user might be more likely to engage in browsing a social website at leisure, but glance at the phone repeatedly when expecting an important email. In this section, we explore specific aspects of context that could impact session type in order to identify opportunities to streamline mobile device use.

Table 1. Median times of different components of mobile device interactions for different device use session types.

	Glance	*Review*	*Engage*
Lock screen time	5 sec	2 sec	2 sec
Total launcher time	0 sec	1* (3**) sec	4.5* (8.5**) sec
Total application time	N/A	15 sec	118 sec

* no launcher sessions included, ** launcher sessions only

Table 2. Median transition times between different device use session types.

To: / From:	*Glance*	*Review*	*Engage*
Glance	412 sec	481 sec	391 sec
Review	326 sec	263 sec	316 sec
Engage	301 sec	388 sec	225 sec

Impact of Locations and Activities on Device Use Types

Our data contained several examples of the different effects of participants' location and activity on device use duration. For example, one participant almost always *reviewed* a bike route tracking application just before leaving and arriving at home and work. Another participant was almost always *engaged* with email and SMS messages at a particular location, which we later identified as a bus stop. However, there was no clear indication that different locations or activities have a large impact on device use durations.

Applications Associated with Device Use Session Types

The set of applications users interacted with was very diverse, with a median of 35 different applications per user across the entire study. We treat each application separately instead of categorizing applications based on semantics because they varied too much due to the large and dynamic nature of the mobile device application market.

Figure 4 shows the distribution of session types per application, sorted by frequency of use. Participants invoked 36.6% (median) of applications 95% or more times in *engage* sessions. However, participants both *reviewed* and *engaged* many different frequently used applications (median=48.3%). Only 14.5% (median) of all applications were used more in *review* than *engage* sessions. We found that applications with more *review* sessions are those that support short tasks (*e.g.*, read or respond to an SMS).

This could indicate that for many of the tasks that the users perform on their mobile devices with their applications, there are portions of these tasks that can be accomplished very quickly. For example, although it might take a long time for the user to compose an important email, quickly scanning the inbox and archiving a few unimportant emails could be a quick task. This highlights an opportunity for making these already short tasks even more efficient.

Our findings also indicate that some tasks are inherently interaction heavy or require longer time to process (*e.g.*, reading news articles or watching video clips). Participants might also prefer to *engage* with applications when passing time or bored. However, the median duration of *engage* sessions is less than 2 minutes, and it is likely that a large portion of *engages* could be streamlined further and either reduced to *reviews* or simply be made easier to access.

Effect of Notifications on Device Use Sessions

Notifications alert the user to events on the mobile device and enable quick access to important application data. Most notifications on Android platform are persistently presented at the top of the user's screen until the user notices and dismisses them or acts upon them. Some notifications, such as phone calls, are more obtrusive, and demand the user's immediate attention. Contrary to findings from [25], our data shows that 75.4% (median) of all device use sessions are not preceded by any notifications, suggesting that the users are mostly proactively using their devices, rather than reacting to notifications.

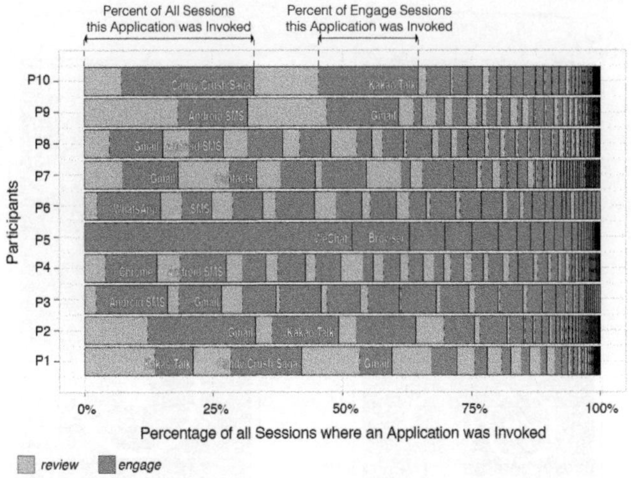

Figure 4. Distribution of session types per application and user. Each rectangle is an application. Color represents session type. Width represents application frequency.

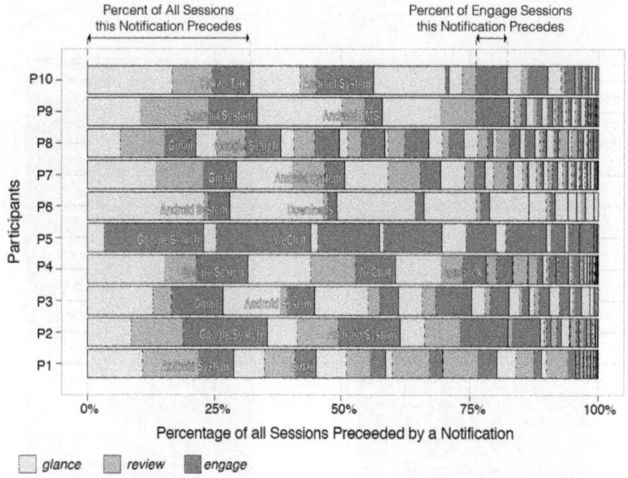

Figure 3. Distribution of session types per notification and user. Each rectangle is a notification. Color represents session type this notification preceded. Width represents frequency.

We thus explore the effects of notifications on different device use types. Figure 3 shows stacked bar charts for each user indicating the percentage of time each notification type preceded different use types. Frequent notifications mostly precede *glance* sessions. Of sessions preceded by at least one notification, 43.6% (median) were *glance* sessions, 29.9% were *review* sessions, and 32.7% were *engage* sessions. Examples from our data show that notifications that require no input from the user, such as application update notifications, precede fewer *review* or *engage* sessions compared to notifications that might require immediate response, such as email or SMS notifications.

Discussion

Our classification of mobile device use sessions based on session duration and the interaction type sheds new light on how users interact with their devices. Our results show that current user interface components, such as notifications and static widgets allow the users to quickly invoke applications when there is new incoming data. Almost half of all device uses were *glance* sessions. A glance at an application widget allows the user to review an application's data without having to start the application. A glance at a notification enables the user to determine if the incoming data is important enough to warrant a *review* or an *engage.*

However, our results showed that most device use sessions do not follow a notification, which means that users often interrupt themselves throughout the day (at times every 5 minutes) to check their mobile device for new data. Lacking notifications, application prediction [14, 18, 25, 26] could be used to suggest the next likely application to the user based on the context. This would not address the bottleneck for short device uses because the user still needs to navigate the application interface to access the data.

Predicting device use type ahead of time would allow applications to dynamically present the user with the best user interfaces given likely use duration. However, whether or not prediction succeeds, interactions that complement notifications and widgets could further streamline mobile device use for short *review* sessions.

Such an interface could proactively suggest short tasks that the users can accomplish on their mobile devices without having to invoke the corresponding applications. This could enable faster and more efficient interactions by allowing the users to glance at data and immediately act on it whenever they initiate device use. For example, the system could show unread emails from the users' inbox on the lock or home screen and allow the users to mark important emails or purge emails that they have no intention of reading. This could allow users to focus on important messages once they choose to *engage* by loading the full application.

SUPPORTING PROACTIVE DEVICE USE

The goal of proactively presenting tasks is to enable users to *glance* at and *review* task data without impeding them from engaging in longer interactions with the device. We present an initial prototype of ProactiveTasks, a concrete example of an interaction that enables quicker access to application data through proactively suggesting tasks. We deploy this prototype in a user study to further explore how users interact with ProactiveTasks in a real-world setting.

Initial ProactiveTasks Prototype

Considering that our goal is to make available tasks as prominent to the user as possible, we implemented an initial prototype of ProactiveTasks as an interactive application widget that can be deployed to the user's lock screen (Figure 5.A). ProactiveTasks displays the description of the tasks and available actions the user can perform on those tasks (Figure 5.A1). The user performs the actions by swiping over the task action buttons, reminiscent of the CrossY system [1]. In order to apply the actions, the user must end the swipe in the commit or unlock regions (Figure 5.A2). This guards against unintended actions (*e.g.*, accidently applying actions when the phone is in a pocket).

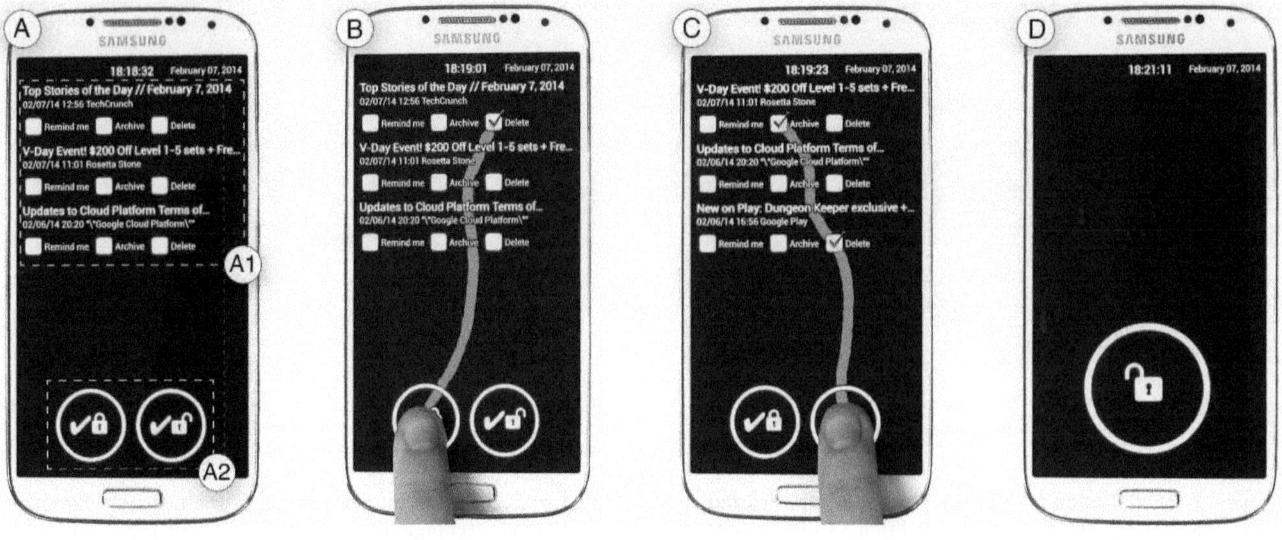

Figure 5. The initial prototype of ProactiveTasks: A) ProactiveTasks interactive lock screen widget with email tasks (A1) and the commit and unlock regions (A2); B) the user swipes over an action and into the commit region to delete a message without unlocking the screen; C) the user applies actions to two different messages and unlocks the screen by finishing a swipe in the unlock region; D) the ProactiveTasks lock screen without any tasks.

Swiping into the commit region applies the actions and displays more tasks instead of unlocking the screen (Figure 5.B). Swiping into the unlock region applies the actions, if any were selected, and unlocks the screen (Figure 5.C).

Good task candidates for ProactiveTasks are easy to glance at and understand the task purpose and available actions. Users should be able to quickly accomplish tasks in *review* sessions, even if their intended primary goal when turning on the screen was to *engage* in use with other applications. Such tasks should allow the users to do this without having to invoke the application and navigate the application user interface. Thus, ProactiveTasks allow only limited feedback and further interactions after the user applies the actions.

In our prototype, we chose email tasks because users frequently *reviewed* and *engaged* email applications in our formative study. The lock screen widget presents up to three recent unread email messages from the user's inbox, or no tasks if there are no such messages. We presented the subject line, email sender, and time the message was received for each message. This enables the user to quickly glance if there are any messages that need reviewing. The lock screen enables the user to perform three actions from the lock screen on the unread emails (Figure 5.A.1): 1) request a reminder, which removes the message from the inbox for a certain duration (4 hours in our example), after which it sends the message back into the inbox, 2) archive the message, which removes the message from the inbox and places it in a special archive folder, or 3) delete the message, which removes the email from the inbox and places it into the trash for final deletion. We did not include an action to start the email application that could derail the users from their original intended tasks. Alternatively, the user could unlock the phone without performing any action.

User Study of ProactiveTasks

Our formative study suggests opportunities to streamline mobile device use by proactively presenting tasks to the user. However, questions remain about how users would interact with ProactiveTasks. We thus conducted a user study to evaluate our prototype in a real-world setting.

Participants

A total of 30 participants (16 male and 14 female) took part in our study. Participants were recruited through online postings and social media. Participants were between 18 and 50 (median=23) years old. Study lasted four weeks. Participants received $40 for taking part in the study.

Study Method

Participants came to our lab to install the ProactiveTasks prototype and the AWARE tracking application onto their primary, personal phone. The study software ran on touch-screen smartphones running Android 4.0 and newer. We excluded Motorola and HTC phones because they were not compatible with our study software. We noted participants' lock screen, and configured the prototype with participants' primary Gmail account to display and manage emails. We explained how the prototype works without instructing participants to perform the tasks during the study.

During the first seven days, participants did not have any ProactiveTasks displayed on their screen even if they had unread emails. This allowed us to compare their normal device use with ProactiveTasks use. After seven days, the lock screen started showing the emails and the participants could choose to perform the email actions. After four weeks from the date they started the study, participants took part in a short interview that asked neutrally stated, open-ended questions about their experience using the lock screen. We asked them to identify other proactive tasks and scenarios that they felt would streamline their mobile device use.

Data Collection and Preparation

We again collected data using the AWARE Framework, which ran unobtrusively on participants' devices as a background service without a user interface. We collected screen events (on, unlock, and off), emails displayed on participants' lock screen, and actions they performed on the emails. We measured how many times participants saw the lock screen (with and without emails), and how many times they applied actions by either only committing the actions or unlocking the screen. We removed any use sessions that did not contain a lock screen (*e.g.*, when the lock screen is overridden by the incoming call screen).

User Study Results

In this section we discuss the results of our data collection and the post-study interviews. We analyzed the data of 27 participants that completed our study. One participant quit the study after two days because she worked for a financial institution and required a more secure lock screen. We also removed data from two other participants who re-enabled their more secure lock screens during the study.

Frequency of Use

Figure 6 shows the task use across all participants during the 4 weeks. Although our formative study only had 10 participants, our user study with 30 participants revealed a similar distribution of lock screen only *glances* and other device use sessions. We define ProactiveTasks use only when the user applied actions to emails because we cannot determine when the participants only glanced at the emails. Overall, participants used ProactiveTasks in 9.5% (median) of all of their device use sessions in which they had email tasks present on the screen. This might appear low, but it is also expected because interaction with ProactiveTasks was not supposed to be participants' primary goal. Instead, ProactiveTasks provide a mechanism to manage emails when participants had time or found it convenient.

We identified four different types of ProactiveTasks users: 1) non-users, 2) normal users, 3) power users, and 4) cleaners. Figure 6 shows examples of each user type.

Non-users (10 participants) were participants that never applied any actions or applied actions only to a few emails in the first few days of week 2. Most stated that they simply do not manage their email on their phones or, as in case of three participants, that they simply leave old unread emails in their inbox. However, four of these participants mentioned that seeing new available emails was helpful.

Normal users (9 participants) applied actions to their emails occasionally over the period of three weeks. Most of these participants interacted with ProactiveTasks when they had time or as *P20* pointed out: *"when bored or nothing better to do."* Participants stated that ProactiveTasks allowed them to unobtrusively access their phone when they did not want to perform the tasks.

Power users (5 participants) on the other hand applied actions to emails for more than a third of their mobile device uses when the tasks were present. These participants had a large number of incoming emails, and ProactiveTasks allowed them to manage their inbox better by clearing out unwanted messages or setting reminders for important ones.

Cleaners (3 participants), a special group of power users, tried to maintain their inbox free of any unread messages, but unlike power users they had fewer emails in their inbox at any given time. As *P4* put it: *"[ProactiveTasks] helped me clear the inbox, so it's faster to use Gmail later."* Therefore, ProactiveTasks enabled these participants to clear out any distraction notifications or messages quickly and without having to start the email application.

Subjective Feedback about ProactiveTasks

Confirming the findings from our device use study, all participants said that they used their lock screens primarily

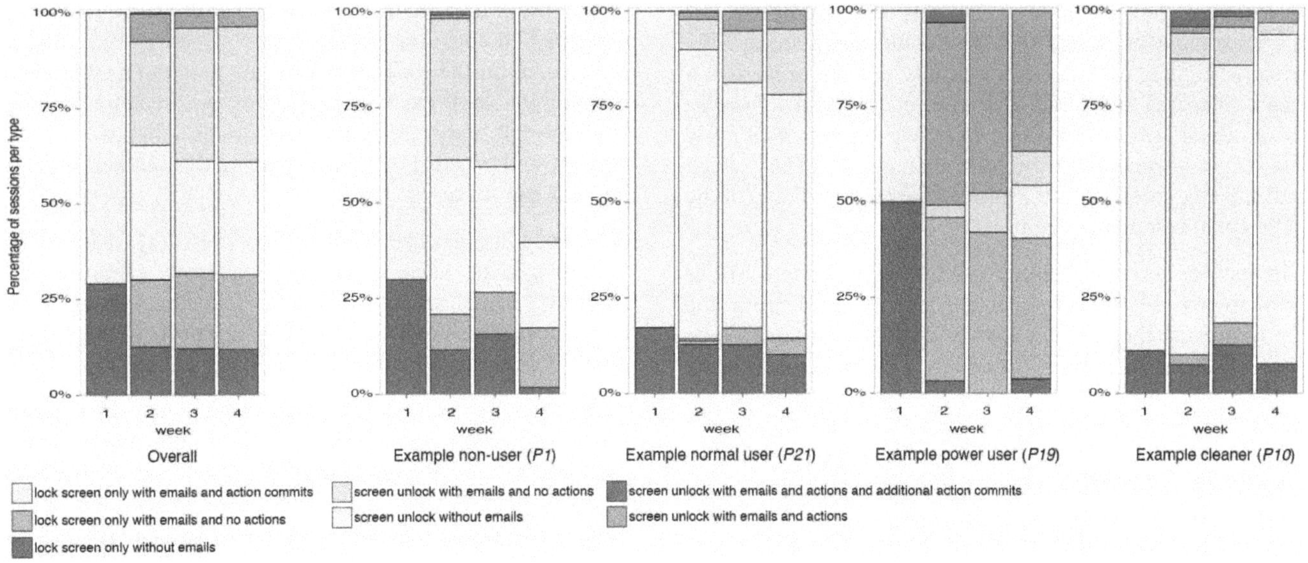

Figure 6. Median percentage of total number of mobile device use sessions per ProactiveTasks use type.

to check the time or notifications. Participants only used the system-defined lock screen widgets that appeared when notifications arrive (*e.g.*, on a calendar event, alarm, *etc.*). One participant used the Google Now widget on his lock screen. Thus, few existing widgets are truly interactive and interaction with existing lock screens mostly happens in response to application notifications.

Most participants stated that ProactiveTasks allowed them to manage emails faster than existing applications. Those that used the tasks said that it helped them filter unwanted or easily addressed information. As *P4* said: *"Once, I found an email that was important and I never noticed it before."* Managing their inbox enabled them to focus on important data once they *engage* with the application.

Participants also changed the way they use their email. For example, *P5* said: *"I like to keep my inbox clear. But usually I would be too lazy to do it. I would do it less often without ProactiveTasks." P19* also stated: *"It actually changed how I use and organize my Gmail. I will start taking care of more of my email for work."* This is likely because raising exposure and awareness of these advanced features [3] made participants realize the benefits of customizing and managing their inbox.

Only three participants used the commit feature without unlocking the phone. We expected to see power users take advantage of their *glances* to complete tasks and then turn the screen off. However, as *P7* stated: *"When I decide to perform tasks, then I just unlock my phone and check other things."* However, the distribution of lock screen glances does not appear to change between the first week and the last three weeks. Thus, it is not likely that ProactiveTasks reduce *glances*. Instead, the participants likely interacted with ProactiveTasks when they already decided to *review* or *engage* with their phone beforehand.

The cognitive load of having to deal with ProactiveTasks every time the screen turns on was not a problem for participants. Most stated that they could just disregard the tasks when they did not want to deal with them or were in a hurry to access the phone. *P19* even commented: *"I prefer to see three email tasks rather than one because then I feel like I can accomplish more with one swipe."* Thus, when participants decide to use ProactiveTasks, they prefer to be efficient at completing the tasks.

The lack of security features was the main concern of our participants. Three participants were removed from the study because they did not want to disable their secure lock screens. Prior to starting the study, 14 participants used secure lock screens (*e.g.*, gesture- or pin-based security), and all of them stated that they would not feel comfortable using their phone without a security feature. A few of these participants also had privacy concerns about displaying sensitive information on the lock screen.

All participants were positive about the concept of ProactiveTasks. All except two participants (including the non-users) suggested ProactiveTasks for other applications that they use on their phones. For example, 21 participants said that they would like to use ProactiveTasks with other messages (*e.g.*, SMS, WhatsApp, *etc.*). Few asked for an ability to respond to an SMS message with a predefined set of answers (*e.g.*, "yes" or "no") from their lock screen. Similarly, one participant suggested using ProactiveTasks in collaborative tools for approving changes.

Other proposed tasks included: tracking productivity by managing calendars and to-do lists (8 participants); social networking (*e.g.*, up-voting and sharing/retweeting posts, accepting friends) (7 participants); managing RSS feeds (3 participants); managing music playlists (*e.g.*, rating recently played songs) (3 participants); and downloading recently accessed files from cloud storage to the mobile device (1 participant). Participants also proposed ProactiveTasks with interactive feedback. For example, a map application could proactively ask the user to select her next destination just before she leaves a location and provide bus times for nearby stops (3 participants).

THE DESIGN SPACE OF PROACTIVETASKS

In this section we explore the tradeoffs inherent in proactive presentation of tasks through a design space based on the findings from our studies. To help us illustrate dimensions of the design space, we present two new ProactiveTasks designs, which focus on the impact of privacy and security on the user experience.

The first alternative (Figure 7.A) combines an existing gesture-based lock screen and ability to perform tasks. When the user performs the secure gesture successfully, ProactiveTasks presents one task to the user. The user can then choose to continue swiping and perform the task, or lift her finger to dismiss the task and go to the home screen. This design emphasizes security at the expense of the number of tasks that the user can perform at the same time.

In the second alternative (Figure 7.B), ProactiveTasks are presented to the user on the home screen as an overlay rather than on the lock screen as in our initial design. The user can invoke ProactiveTasks from any screen by swiping from the left and right bezel. This design emphasizes both security and privacy, while maximizing the number of tasks the user can see at one time.

Our study highlighted tradeoffs between key features of ProactiveTasks, such as security and task visibility and cognitive demand and efficiency. The three designs we have discussed illustrate some of the tradeoffs in our design space (Figure 8). We discuss each dimension below.

Visibility refers to the level of engagement needed to reach ProactiveTasks. Lock screen is highly visible, and provides an immediate advantage when participants self-interrupted to check their phones (a frequent occurrence in our data). Since self-interruption is usually internal and difficult to control [7], it makes sense to leverage it for ProactiveTasks.

Intrusiveness expresses how much ProactiveTasks impact the time it takes for the user to get to her intended task. Intrusive designs can help increase visibility. However, ProactiveTasks should enable the user to only *glance* at any available tasks (new and old), similarly to how notifications currently notify the users of new data. Unlike notifications, ProactiveTasks should not derail users from their original intended tasks by requiring them to invoke the application.

Efficiency defines how quickly and how many different tasks the user can accomplish at any given time. However, our user study showed that the users chose to perform their tasks mostly when they already had time, and thus, the time to complete the tasks might not be an important factor. The two designs in Figure 7 illustrate low and high efficiency.

Cognitive and physical demand represent the difficulty of ProactiveTasks interaction. In order to reduce cognitive and physical demand, ProactiveTasks should present fewer tasks at a time. However, our designs illustrate a trade off between showing fewer tasks to reduce task difficulty and added efficiency of performing multiple tasks at a time.

Multiplicity refers to how many different applications and task categories are presented at any given time. Our user study identified many tasks that could be implemented as ProactiveTasks, some of which fall in the same category and have similar actions (*e.g.*, email, instant messages, and SMS). These could be combined and presented together in a single task list (Figure 7.B). Although this might increase efficiency, it will likely also increase cognitive demand.

Security and privacy should be considered when designing ProactiveTasks. A naïve way to secure ProactiveTasks is to display the tasks on the home screen, as is the case with our home screen ProactiveTasks design. This increases security and privacy, but hiding ProactiveTasks behind a lock screen decreases visibility and efficiency. Adding ProactiveTasks

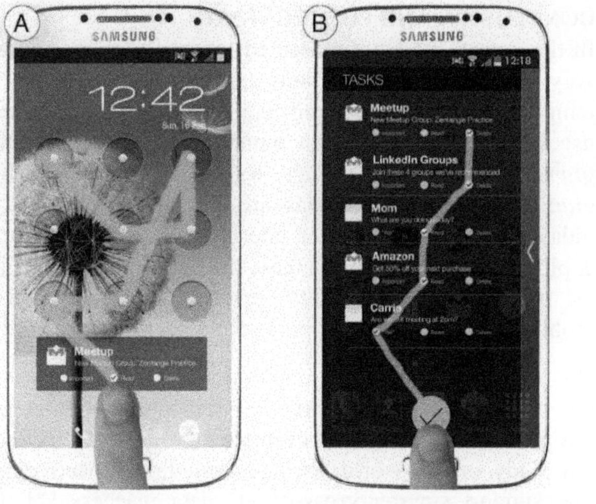

Figure 7. Two new ProactiveTasks designs: a) lock screen ProactiveTasks with built-in security features, and b) home screen ProactiveTasks.

to existing secure lock screens (Figure 7.A) might not increase efficiency, but increases the visibility of tasks.

Presentation strategy refers to how and when to present a proactive task to the user. Our designs present tasks when there is available data. Increasing tasks multiplicity for this strategy could quickly lead to high cognitive demand if there are many available tasks from different applications. Proactively presenting the tasks from the user's next likely applications could limit the number of presented tasks and lead to a higher task completion rate. However, care should be taken not to prevent users from serendipitously learning about tasks from their infrequently used applications.

Although our designs only explored a portion of the design space, making the design space explicit makes it easier to design future ProactiveTasks to meet a chosen set of goals.

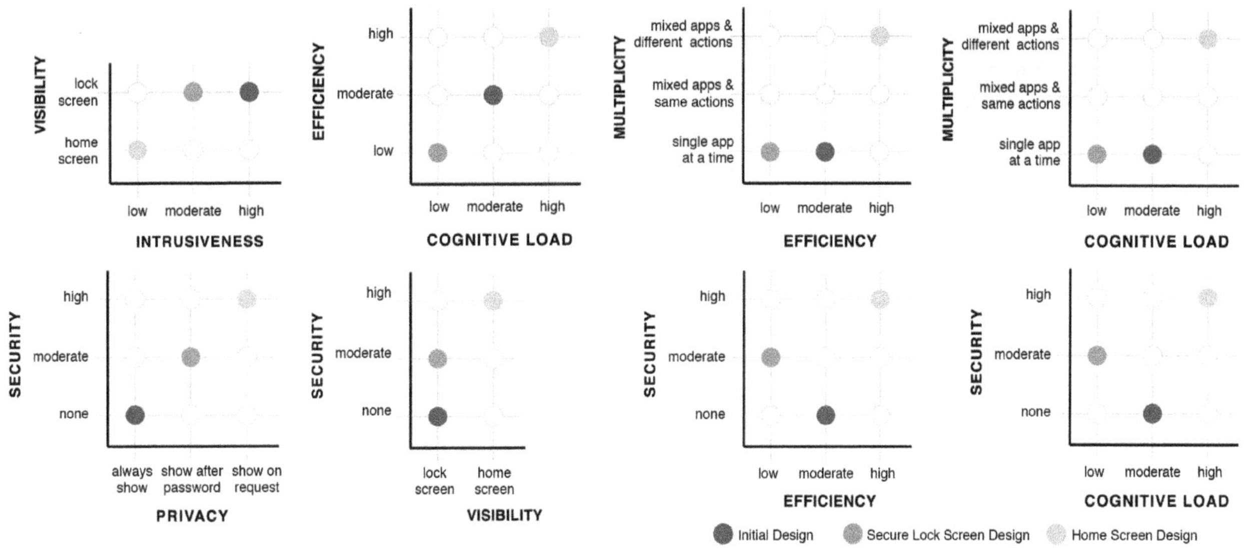

Figure 8. The three different ProactiveTasks designs mapped to the dimensions of the design space.

CONCLUSION AND FUTURE WORK

In this paper, we have presented evidence for existence of very short mobile interactions and empirically determined temporal boundaries of three distinct types of mobile device use sessions based on their duration and interaction type: *glance*, *review*, and *engage* sessions. Surprisingly brief *glance* and *review* sessions are the most common, yet today's mobile device user interfaces are only starting to explore ways to streamline these diverse device uses. Thus, we propose different design opportunities to improve the mobile user experience by proactively suggesting tasks.

Our work opens up many opportunities for future work. In our initial prototype we explored only one particular task, but future research should evaluate other tasks identified in our study in real-world settings, including ProactiveTasks that support smarter cross-device data reaccess [2]. Our prototype presented tasks when they were available, but future research should explore both adaptable and adaptive tasks based on the user's context. ProactiveTasks provide motivation for design of new interfaces based on interaction duration. Our design space informs the design of a new generation of interfaces that allow easy transition from glancing to reviewing to engaging mobile devices.

ACKNOWLEDGEMENTS

This work was funded by NSERC, NSF (CAREER Grant 0746428, IIS 1217929), LG Electronics, and Microsoft. We thank Dan Tasse and Samuel Drucker for their help with the early iterations of this work.

REFERENCES

1. Apitz, G. and Guimbretière, F. (2004) CrossY: a crossing-based drawing application. *UIST '04*, 3-12.
2. Bales, E., Sohn, T., and Setlur, V. (2011) Planning, apps, and the high-end smartphone: exploring the landscape of modern cross-device reaccess. *Pervasive'11*, 1-18.
3. Banovic, N., Chevalier, F., Grossman, T., and Fitzmaurice, G. (2012) Triggering triggers and burying barriers to customizing software. *CHI '12*, 2717-2726.
4. Barkhuus, L., and Polichar, V. E. (2011) Empowerment through seamfulness: smart phones in everyday life. *Person. Ubiquit Comput.*, *15*(6), 629-639.
5. Bianchi, A. and Phillips, J. G. (2005) Psychological predictors of problem mobile phone use. *CyberPsychology & Behavior*, *8*(1), 39-51.
6. Böhmer, M., Hecht, B., Schöning, J., Krüger, A., and Bauer, G. (2011) Falling asleep with angry birds, facebook and kindle – a large scale study on mobile application usage. *MobileHCI '11*, 47-56.
7. Dabbish, L., Mark, G., and Gonzalez, V. (2011) Why do I keep interrupting myself?: environment, habit and self-interruption. *CHI '11*, 3127-3130.
8. Dey, A. K. 2001. Understanding and using context. *Person. Ubiquit. Comput.*, *5*(1), 4-7.
9. Do, T. M. T., Blom, J., and Gatica-Perez, D. (2011) Smartphone usage in the wild: A large-scale analysis of applications and context. *ICMI '11*, 353-360.
10. Falaki, H., Mahajan, R., Kandula, S., Lymberopoulos, D., Govindan, R., and Estrin, D. (2010) Diversity in Smartphone Usage. *MobiSys '10*, ACM, 179-194.
11. Google. (2014) *Google Now*. Retrieved February 17, 2014, from http://www.google.com/landing/now/.
12. Ha, J. H., Chin, B., Park, D. H., Ryu, S. H., and Yu, J. (2008) Characteristics of excessive cellular phone use in Korean adolescents. *CyberPsychol. Behav.*, *11*(6).
13. Jiang, B. (2012) Head/Tail Breaks: A New Classification Scheme for Data with a Heavy-Tailed Distribution. *The Professional Geographer*.
14. Kamisaka, D., Muramatsu, S., Yokoyama, H., and Iwamoto, T. (2009) Operation prediction for context-aware user interfaces of mobile phones. *SAINT'09*, 16-22.
15. Maués, R. A. and Barbosa, S. D. J. (2013) Keep doing what I just did: automating smartphones by demonstration. *MobileHCI '13*, 295-303.
16. Oulasvirta, A., Tamminen, S., Roto, V., and Kuorelahti, J. (2005) Interaction in 4-second bursts: the fragmented nature of attentional resources in mobile HCI. *CHI '05*, 919-928.
17. Oulasvirta, A., Rattenbury, T., Ma, L., and Raita, E. (2012) Habits make smartphone use more pervasive. *Person. Ubiquit. Comput.*, *16*(1), 105-114.
18. Shin, C., Hong, J. H., and Dey, A. K. (2012) Understanding and prediction of mobile application usage for smart phones. *UbiComp '12*, 173-182.
19. Shin, C. and Dey, A. K. 2013. Automatically detecting problematic use of smartphones. *UbiComp '13*, 335-344.
20. Sohn, T., Li, K. A., Griswold, W. G., and Hollan, J. D. (2008) A diary study of mobile information needs. *CHI '08*, 433-442.
21. Truong K. N., Shihipar, T., and Wigdor, D. (2014) Slide to X: unlocking the potential of smartphone unlocking. *CHI '14*.
22. Vaish, R., Wyngarden, K., Chen, J., Cheung, B., and Bernstein, M. S. (2014) Twitch crowdsourcing: crowd contributions in short bursts of time. *CHI '14*.
23. Verkasalo. H. (2009) Contextual patterns in mobile service usage. *Person. Ubiquit. Comput.* 13, 5, 331-342.
24. Vetek, A., Flanagan, J., Colley, A., and Keränen, T. (2009) Smartactions: Context-aware mobile phone shortcuts. *INTERACT 2009*, 796-799.
25. Yan, T., Chu, D., Ganesan, D., Kansal, A., and Liu, J. (2012) Fast app launching for mobile devices using predictive user context. *MobiSys '12*, 113-126.
26. Zhang, C., Ding, X., Chen, G., Huang, K., Ma, X., and Yan, B. (2013) Nihao: A Predictive Smartphone Application Launcher. *Mobile Computing, Applications, and Services*, 294-313.

User Challenges and Successes with Mobile Payment Services in North America

Serena Hillman, Carman Neustaedter, Erick Oduor and Carolyn Pang
School of Interactive Arts and Technology, Simon Fraser University
250-13450 102nd Avenue, Surrey, British Columbia, Canada
shillman@sfu.ca, carman_neustaedter@sfu.ca, eoduor@sfu.ca, and carolyn_pang@sfu.ca

ABSTRACT
Mobile payment services have recently emerged in North America where users pay for items using their smartphones. Yet we have little understanding of how people are making use of them and what successes and challenges they have experienced. As a result, we conducted a diary and interview study of user behaviors, motivations, and first impressions of mobile payment services in North America in order to understand how to best design for mobile payment experiences. Participants used a variety of services, including Google Wallet, Amazon Payments, LevelUp, Square and company apps geared towards payments (e.g., Starbucks). Our findings show that users experience challenges related to mental model development, pre-purchase anxiety and trust issues, despite enjoying the gamification, ease-of-use, and support for routine purchases with mobile payments. This suggests designing a better mobile payment experience through the incorporation of users' routines and behaviors, gamification and trust mechanism development.

Author Keywords
mobile payment services; Google Wallet; LevelUp; Square; PayPal; ubiquitous commerce; eCommerce; mCommerce; gamification

ACM Classification Keywords
H.5.2 [User Interfaces]: User-Centered Design

INTRODUCTION
It is now possible to pay for items in North America (United States and Canada) using smartphones via a variety of mobile payment services. This includes carrier billing (e.g., Text2Pay), near-field communications (e.g., Google Wallet), closed loop mobile payments (e.g., Starbucks app), and card readers (e.g., Square). With the recent addition of large online players (Google and Amazon), as well as more traditional payment entities (MasterCard and PayPal), and some well-developed startups (e.g., LevelUp and Square), expectations for a societal shift towards ubiquitous commerce—eCommerce activities occurring from virtually any location—is both high and deemed of "critical importance" [16] for the future of mobile and electronic commerce.

While a number of studies have looked at mobile payment services in developing countries [7], and even developed countries in Europe [16,17] and Asia [11], this past body of work has not focused on the North American market and smartphones. These past studies were also focused on SMS-centric mobile payments, rather than smartphone-based payment. Mobile payment services have just started to become available on smartphones in North America; therefore, collecting empirical data on their usage prior to the last couple of years was not possible.

Our research fills this gap with a study of existing and new mobile payment users in North America. We wanted to understand the experience from the perspective of those who had already adopted and integrated mobile payments into their purchasing routines, as well as those who were using it for the first time. The former allows us to understand those who have had relative success with mobile payments, while the latter allows us to understand first impressions and the people who may choose to not adopt the technology for longer term usage. We focused on uncovering the challenges and successes they faced. We also specifically explored trust concerns as they have been cited as a major barrier to the adoption of eCommerce [16].

Our findings showed that designing mobile payment services around routines and habits aids in a positive user experience. Users also appreciate gamification aspects associated with mobile payments and find that transactions create a socially cohesive experience, despite pre-purchase anxiety. Our results also revealed that mobile payments are not without their problems. Some users currently lack the mental model needed to see a clear benefit for mobile payments. Moreover, from a trust perspective, we saw that trust levels between vendor and user are notably worse for mobile payments than that reported for mCommerce activities and that trust mechanisms in this area need to be developed further. Together, this suggests design directions to increase the adoption of mobile payments by users while lessening usability and trust concerns.

RELATED WORK
There exists a variety of research on mCommerce, mobile payment services, and trust in eCommerce. We discuss research in these key areas to inform and situate our study.

MobileHCI '14, September 23 – 26, 2014, Toronto, ON, Canada.

http://dx.doi.org/10.1145/2628363.2628389

mCommerce and Mobile Payment

eCommerce has traditionally been viewed as a stationary act, performed at desktop computers in offices, homes, or other locations. Within this space lies mobile commerce (mCommerce): commerce activities occurring on a mobile device. Mobile payment services have been classified as a subset of mCommerce and a form of eCommerce [17]. The definition of mobile payment services has varied to include payment over any mobile communication device [21] to a more focused definition around just payments on mobile phones [6]. In our study, we adopt the later definition, similar to that of Schierz et al. [17]: "all payments for goods, services and bills authorized, initiated or realized" [17] using a mobile phone. Thus, mobile payments include paying for items in a store using a mobile device, as well as paying bills or transferring money using smartphone apps. The former takes place in a physical store like traditional commerce and the latter could take place in any location. While seemingly valuable, there have been noted shortcomings when comparing mobile payment growth in North America to its expectations [20]. Lack of adoption has been blamed on poor usability [20], social and cultural ideologies [12], and mobile technology limitations [10].

There have also been some studies that look specifically at mobile payments, yet none have focused on North American usage or smartphones. Instead, studies have focused on earlier versions of mobile payments (using SMS) in industrialized countries in Europe. First, Schierz et al. [17] analyzed mobile payment usage in Germany based on the Technology Adoption Model. This model explains that the adoption of technologies is based on the perceived usefulness and ease-of-use of the technology [1,3]. Findings show that perceived ease of use, compatibility, security, and usefulness, along with individual mobility positively affected users' attitudes towards mobile payments.

Second, and the closest study to our own in terms of its findings, Mallat [16] explored mobile payments in Finland in 2002 when they were based solely on SMS (direct billing). Results showed that users found mobile payments faster and more convenient than cash; mobile payments were most compatible with small value payments; and complexities around the use of the systems along with a lack of large merchant acceptance were barriers to adoption [16]. Users also described issues with trust where they had feelings of "vagueness" and "perceived lack of control." Users were also concerned about trust in network reliability and having their phone accessed if it was hacked, lost, or stolen [16]. While valuable, we caution that this study focused on feature-phones, not smartphones. Technology and culture have also dramatically changed since 2002.

Mobile payment services have also been studied in non-industrialized countries. In Kenya M-Pesa has seen tremendous success reporting 19 million subscribed users, which accounts for two-thirds of the entire adult population [19]. China has also found some success with Alipay [18] and GCash has had well documented success in the Philippines [1]. Use for these systems is often fueled by users' lack of trust in their local country's banking systems along with a range of other social and cultural motivators [7,16,17]. Hinman and Matovu [7] investigated opportunities and challenges around mobile-based finances in rural Uganda. Their study found that users had a strong affinity to fixed assets, lacked access to capital, did not understand how mobile payments worked, and, overall, were confused by the mental model used to interact with the service [7]. Unlike developed nations, Ugandans lacked the reference point of transferring funds from person-to-person [7].

Together, the related research on mobile payment services shows a mixture of challenges and successes for the technology. Yet this past research does not explore mobile payments in North America using smartphone technology to understand how present day technology affects shopping behaviors and how to best design for such experiences. This is the focus of our study.

eCommerce Trust

In order to build trust in eCommerce environments, one usually relies on trust mechanisms such as third-party certifications and user-to-user relationships [5,10]. Even still, trust has historically been a major obstacle for the success of eCommerce [15,16]. The notion that users are vulnerable and likely to expose themselves during an online purchase is often a main concern [5]. Thus, past research has shown that the level of trust established in the user-vendor relationship dictates if a transaction will occur and to what scope [15]. Past work has shown that not only does trust play a key role in the adoption of new technologies and the initial trust with a new vendor; it also results in repeat purchases and continued relationships [5].

Moving from traditional eCommerce on computers to mCommerce on mobile devices, we see that trust is less of a concern for users. Hillman et al. [8] studied shopping and purchasing on mobile phones (not mobile payment services) and found that mCommerce users had few trust concerns while making transactions on their mobile devices over the Internet. They found this was because trust was built through: direct brand awareness; the 'app' approval process; and, purchase recommendations by friends and family. Within this, brand played the most significant role in trust for mobile commerce activity.

Turning to mobile payments in North America, we do not see any study of the trust issues that users face or the ways in which such concerns might be mitigated. While part of mCommerce, mobile payments present a mixed-context. On one hand, they are different than mobile shopping activities because they can be performed in a retail store, the same as traditional shopping. Yet they can also be performed outside of a store from nearly any location as a form of bill payment or money transfer online. This mixed-context brings into question the legitimacy of eCommerce trust models for understanding mobile payment services as well as mCommerce trust models. Our study addresses this topic by exploring the trust issues that users face with mobile payments.

STUDY METHODOLOGY

The goal of our study was to understand how people use mobile payments in North America and what successes and challenges they faced. We explored this from the perspective of new and existing mobile payment users.

Participants

We recruited 21 participants (11 female) through postings on online forums and word of mouth. Ages ranged from 21 to 49, with a median age of 27. All participants lived in major metropolitan cities in North America (Canada and the United States). Occupations of participants varied heavily, e.g., engineer, graphic designer, social worker, student, web developer. Participants had average to expert technical abilities and all owned a smartphone. About half of the participants used an iPhone, while the other half used an Android device.

We purposely chose to investigate two groups of participants: existing users and new users. This allowed us to understand the experience from the perspective of those who have had relative success with mobile payments, leading to their repeated usage or long term adoption, as well as the first impressions of new users who may or may not choose to adopt the technology for longer term usage. Based on their own descriptions, we classified eleven users as *existing users* and ten participants as *new users* who had never tried a mobile payment service prior to the study. The amount of experience that existing users had in using mobile payments varied between two weeks and four years with a median of ~6 months. Existing users used mobile payments on average twice a week.

Method

Our study method varied depending on whether a participant was an existing or new user of mobile payment services.

Method 1: Existing Users

Existing users participated in a semi-structured interview that focused on their past and current experiences with mobile payment systems. Interview questions were based on understanding the participant's specific instances of use and why they used the services the way they did. Sample questions included: What mobile payment services have you used? When was the first time you used a mobile payment service and why? When was the last item you purchased using a mobile payment and why did you choose this payment method over another? What time of day was the purchase made and why? Interviews usually lasted between thirty and sixty minutes.

Method 2: New Users

After the data collection of Method 1 was complete, ten new users, who had not used mobile payments before were asked to complete an e-diary over a two-week period while trying out any mobile payment service(s) of their choosing. The diary method was chosen specifically to capture the user's experience in-the-moment over the first two weeks of use. This method has been used in similar studies [8,9]. During the two weeks, participants were asked to complete a minimum of four diary entries though we anticipated that some people may not complete this requirement if they simply found mobile payments too difficult to use or it did not meet their routines. A diary entry was required for every instance of purchasing that they attempted. The four diary entry minimum was chosen as four was the average number of completed transactions by existing users in Method 1 over a two week period.

The diary entry was a web form which had fields asking the participants for the following information: title of the activity, date, time and location of the purchase, if they had any trust concerns when completing this activity, why they used a mobile payment and not cash/credit/debit, a summary of the purchase, and their satisfaction level of the experience. Participants were told to complete the diaries as soon as possible after the purchase. This could be done on their phones in the moment, or later in the evening when at home. Participants opted to do a range of behaviors for recording entries.

After participants completed the diary entry phase, they participated in a semi-structured interview. During the interview, which also took between thirty and sixty minutes, participants were asked to review each of their diary entries and expand and/or clarify their entries. After, they were asked questions about the overall experience.

Existing users did not complete diary entries as we were interested in their summative experiences across their entire experience of using mobile payments, rather than a small portion of time, which would have been captured by diaries.

Participants used a variety of mobile payment options. These fell into one of four categories based on the types of mobile payment methods available in North America:

1. ***Closed Loop Mobile Payments*** (e.g., Starbucks App): the consumer uses an app on their smartphone to pay, typically by scanning a barcode at the register (7 new users, 7 existing users).

2. ***Carrier Billing*** (e.g., Text2Pay): the consumer pays by text message and the charge is added to their phone bill (1 new user, 2 existing users).

3. ***Card Readers*** (e.g., Square): these solutions allow merchants to take payment via a card reader attached to a smartphone or tablet (2 new users, 2 existing users).

4. ***Near-Field Communications*** (e.g., Google Wallet): the consumer can pay at the point of sale by waving their phone in front of a terminal (0 new users, 3 existing users).

As can be seen, most users focused on closed loop payments given that they are currently more widely available in North America. The skew of new users to closed loop payments (e.g., Starbucks app) speaks to what participants were comfortable using mobile payments for and the monetary value and potential risk during the start of their usage. Because our participants used a variety of mobile payment services, our study reveals behaviors across a range of mobile payment options rather than findings specifically on any one payment solution. Despite this diversity, our results are fairly homogenous around all of the mobile payment services that participants used. We also feel this allowed us to explore the mobile payment research space as a whole, rather than a targeted study of just one type of payment option.

Data Collection and Analysis

We collected audio recordings of all interviews, notes from the interviews, and users' diary text. Interview recordings were later transcribed. All data was analyzed using open, axial, and selective coding. Each user group was first analyzed separately. We then reviewed the data from both groups together to compare and contrast experiences. Our coding revealed several main themes that relate to the success and challenges that our participants faced when using mobile payment services. We also found several ways in which existing and new users differed. We outline these differences along with our main themes in our results.

PURCHASING ACTIVITIES

Existing users reported purchasing a wide range of products and services using mobile payments. This included: coffee, clothes, sporting goods, electronics, furniture, extra-curricular activities, and even school tuition. These products ranged in price from a $2 cup of coffee to around $3,000 for school tuition; however, the majority of items were between $2 and $50. Some participants also told us that they paid bills and made bank transfers to individuals using a mobile app. While this was not about purchasing items, it does fall in to the definition of mobile payment services [17].

During the two weeks, new users purchased coffee, and made bill payments and bank transfers to individuals. New users' product prices ranged from $2 to ~$150. Although we asked participants to complete four diary entries over the two weeks, participants completed an average of 2.3 entries. Three new users did not complete any transactions even though they tried or thought about paying but did not understand; we followed up on these instances in our interviews. Without these three outliers, the average number of diary entries / purchases was 3.2. This illustrates that purchasing with mobile payments was an activity that typically occurred a couple of times a week for the new users. Thus, it was not a habitual or routine activity, which is to be expected for new usage when a person is still establishing a routine.

Within these purchase activities and experiences, our findings revealed clear successes that participants had in terms of mobile payments creating positive purchasing experiences. In addition, we also saw clear challenges that mobile payments posed for participants. Our results focus on these two main sections.

USER SUCCESSES WITH MOBILE PAYMENT

Participants had a variety of successes using mobile payments. These focused on routines, ease-of-use and usefulness, gamification, regulatory avoidance, and social perception. We describe each in turn.

Habitual Routines

First, we found that mobile payments were best for habitual purchases—purchases that were frequent and re-occurring. Participants who used mobile payments as a part of habitual purchasing activities felt they worked well and they liked them because they could easily fit in to their 'routine.' Half of the existing users very clearly had a daily habitual-type routine when using their payment service. Some understood this explicitly while others were only tacitly aware of the routine nature of their purchases. For example, when asked how often P6 (existing user) used mobile payments, she told us "everyday". She then described the time of day and variations based on her weekend and weekday schedule.

I rarely go to any other coffee shops [now]... I've just got accustomed to Starbucks... - P6, existing user

Other existing users had similar comments on how they liked mobile payments because they fit well into their routine:

I have my cell phone already in my hand because I listen to a podcast every morning, all it is pause the podcast, get coffee... Always the same time of day... 7:45 in the morning... on my way to work. - P4, existing user

Participants told us that using a mobile payment service made them more loyal to a particular store. For example, P4 told us that the mobile payment process was so "easy" that she frequented the store more often instead of going to a variety of stores. We caution that this did not mean that they increased the frequency in which they made purchases. Instead, it meant they opted for the same store each day as opposed to competitor stores. For example, if they purchased coffee once a day before using a mobile payment, they would continue to purchase coffee once a day. However, now they would avoid stores that did not offer the mobile payment solution.

Three new users also reported that they had a habitual routine for using mobile payments. For example, P12 also found it easy to integrate mobile payments into her daily routine and commented on how surprised she was that it was so easy to integrate:

I think how quickly I became accustomed to doing it. I just don't even think about it anymore, [it's] just how I pay for things now. - P12, new user

Five existing users and three new users had more of a semi-habitual routine. While their purchases were not daily and at a particular time of day, these users reported that they made purchases at the same place in certain time intervals for re-occurring purchases. For example, this included utility bill payments, purchases of coffee a couple of times a week, or tuition payments for school that were paid once each term.

Moreover, participants suggested that the best services for mobile payments were heavily related to transactions that were frequent and routine, such as gas purchases, bill payments, and groceries. For example, P6, an existing user, told us that she wished she could use mobile payments for gasoline purchases, because she filled up her car every few days or so. P4, also an existing user, and P12, a new user, had similar thoughts around grocery store purchases as well:

I wish gas stations and grocery stores accepted mobile payment. - P4, existing user

If my grocery store had it, that would be great. I would be reluctant to use an app like that in a place that I am not a regular patron. - P12, new user

Participants also expressed disappointment when they tried to find ways to use mobile payments to pay their recurring monthly bills. For example, P18, a new user, was unhappy that her power company did not have a mobile payment app:

Another thing that was really surprising for me was that there was no app for paying your hydro bill because... [this is] important for me. - P18, new user

Ease-of-Use and Usefulness

When asked about the benefits of using mobile payments, all participants mentioned ease-of-use, with no bias toward any particular type of mobile payment service. When asked to elaborate, responses mostly included two key elements: The process was *easy* and *faster* than other payment methods. For example, P17, a new user, described how the mobility and shortcut to make a bill payment allowed him to multi-task while in a university class:

It was nice to actually be able to take care of [paying my bills]... when it popped into my head I wasn't doing anything and I was able to [pay some bills], so I just pulled out my phone and did it. Which was kind of a new thing for me and I actually really liked that. It felt very productive too, to get something like that done; I felt like I accomplished something in class today. - P17, new user

Second, and somewhat surprisingly, mobile payments made it so payment methods were more often ready-at-hand and available when needed at a store. For example, a number of existing users mentioned that they often forgot their wallets but never their phones. In fact, these participants described paying by phone as a more natural process than using their wallet.

You always have your cell phone; I mean you forget your wallet nowadays way more than you do your cell phone. It is just easier to use. A lot of people have it in their pocket and it's just right there as opposed to ... trying to get your wallet and everything and so it just makes everything easier, one little device. - P4, existing user

It was just easier to have my phone out than take my wallet out and find a card. - P2, existing user

Gamification and Entertainment

Many mobile payment services that are designed as smartphone apps provide gamification elements where a user can score points, level-up, and receive rewards for purchases. The majority of users mentioned that they enjoyed the gamification of the mobile payment service they used. In fact, they would often describe the experience of purchasing as "more entertaining" and "funner" because of the gamification.

For example, P12, a new user, described how much she enjoyed seeing the stars from the Starbucks app "dropping in the cup," indicating she was getting closer to a free drink. This "elevated" the transactional experience compared to paying by credit card or cash. In this case, Starbucks has taken a desired action, buying Starbucks coffee, which is not normally game related and attached a game mechanism around collecting stars for rewards with every purchase. LevelUp also uses similar game mechanics, and while they are light and simple, it clearly had an added benefit for users. Some users also mentioned gamification as a loyalty draw for them. In the example below, P11, a new user, discusses his first gamification experience through mobile payment:

I think it is cool to be able to use my phone to [participate in gamification]... I am probably more inclined to go to the deli that accepts LevelUp than other delis in my neighborhood... more for the gamification... - P11, new user

Two existing users also mentioned that gamification had a significant role in their positive user experience of mobile payment service. This was even after a year of usage. Specifically, P4 and P10 said that collecting and using loyalty programs made the shopping experience more interesting than using cash or a credit card for payment.

Social Perception

Participants generally felt positive about the social perception of using mobile payments. First, they talked about the positive aspects of being watched by other people when they were using a mobile payment service in a store. Participants often described how they felt "cool" using mobile payments because it was a new technology and not everybody was using it.

Second, they felt that mobile payments allowed them to make payments faster (than debit or credit) which helped the lineup move faster. They felt that this, in turn, eased any social tensions created by impatient employees or customers. This is despite whether others were actually impatient or not.

[Other store patrons] like it because the line moves faster you can see they are impatient if you are looking for cash or a lot of extra steps for [the employee] to key in a credit card purchase. - P21, existing user

Third, participants described that they were sometimes even engaged in a positive discussion around mobile payments with friends or customers during or after purchases. Existing users also described how many of their friends used mobile payment services and they felt they were becoming popular because it was a "topic of discussion" within their work or school environments. In order for them to appear like they were part of their community, they felt they should be able to comment on the new technology.

There was this discussion in the community I am in. It definitely prompted [my mobile payment usage] in that sense... I know a lot of techies... the community would be, I guess, the geek or techie community. - P3, existing user

Regulatory Avoidance

A number of participants also mentioned that they used a form of mobile payment service to get around regulatory restrictions from banks. Some examples included credit limitations, much like pre-paid visas (e.g., PayPal); ordering gaming licenses from countries that did not accept the user's local credit card information; making payments from consumer to consumer or small businesses; and, charities collecting payments without a POS terminal from a bank (e.g., Square). For example, P1, an existing user, told us he used Square for his business so he did not have to set up a merchant account at a bank. Being able to accept credit cards as a small business altered the way he sells merchandise. He described how mobile payment services have allowed him to accept credit cards and thus expand his business.

It is well known that the poor trust relations and fear between banks and patrons have helped drive the success of mobile payment services in developing countries [7]. While North American bank systems do not have the same level of mistrust, our participants still used mobile payment services to avoid bank charges and regulations; however, the reported types of charges and regulations were specific to North America.

USER CHALLENGES WITH MOBILE PAYMENTS

Naturally, like any new technology, users also experienced challenges with mobile payment services. In this section, we present the challenges that users faced, which focused on a lack of payment options around their routines, usability issues, pre-purchase anxiety, and trust issues.

New Users' Routines and a Lack of Benefits

For new users, the value of routines for using mobile payments was still high. Yet not all had a purchasing routine that mapped well to using a mobile payment service. For this reason, four new users did not enjoy the service, while an additional three new users did not make purchases. For example, P19 explains how mobile payments did not fit his purchasing routines:

The Starbucks one is nice, it sounds quite cool but I don't use-- I don't buy Starbucks often enough to use it. - P19, new user

This quote speaks to the fact that mobile payments are currently only available in a small number of instances and stores within North America. As an example, it also illustrates that people who use Starbucks can easily use mobile payments because Starbucks has a payment app. Yet people who drink coffee at another location that does not support mobile payments will not have the same opportunities to use the payment method. This suggests that, over time, if more stores adopt mobile payment services as a payment option, the practices of new users might be different. Until this point, new users may not see the point of using a store "once in a while" simply so they can use a mobile payment option; indeed, this is what our participants told us.

Many new users also told us that they did not see the benefits in using mobile payments instead of a credit card, despite understanding how to use mobile payment options. That is, the mobile payment service seemed to offer the same benefits as a credit card to them, e.g., payment without cash. Yet they were already able to do this with a debit or credit card. Some participants told us in their final interview that they felt they would not use mobile payment services in the near future unless their routines changed.

I think [I would maybe use mobile payments in the future] because it could become more popular and we are moving towards that, maybe when my friends and family start using it and when it becomes a norm. – P19, new user

This illustrates that people are often fairly engrained within their current payment methods. It suggests that unless there is a larger societal shift in payment options and usage that some people simply will not change their practices.

Mental Model Development & Usability Issues

Mental models often help shape behavior and explain a person's thought process on how something works [4]. Some participants within the new user group, described how they just could not understand how paying with their phone worked or how to start the process. For example, P16, a new user, explained during the interview that she had a complete lack of knowledge around what direction to proceed to even start the study. She said she did not know what apps to look for or download. As a technically engaged individual this was shocking for her. She told us:

I didn't know, like when I agreed to do it, I didn't know what apps to download, I didn't even know what to look for. - P16, new user

Other users made specific comments around not having the "mental model" to see their smart phone as a payment source. P20, a new user, was surprised that payment over a phone was even possible. While P17, a new user told us "it never even occurred" to him to use his cell phone to make a purchase. For him the thought of doing something serious like making a payment on the same device he uses to make "stupid text messages" from seemed unheard of. In his mind, the mental model for what a cell phone does did not include paying for items.

Participants also complained about a lack of adequate feedback with mobile payment services. Many participants indicated they did not know how much they were being charged before or during the transaction. This was true for a number of payment methods (e.g., Starbucks app and Square). For example, P11, a new user, talks about the delay in being notified how much he spent at a local deli:

A few minutes later you get a message on your phone saying you just used LevelUp and the amount was X so it's just for the split second when they punch in the number they put in and then they charge your phone [you don't know how much you are being charged]. - P11, new user

A common theme across mobile payment services was a lack of visual or audio indicators for feedback around transactional information. Users felt it was unclear when a transaction went through as there was little indication, leaving them unsure if the transaction was complete. In addition to lack of social cues from the employees, this lead to participants being concerned that they might have been charged twice.

Pre-purchasing Anxiety

A common trend for both user groups was pre-purchase anxiety, despite the previously reported positive social perceptions associated with mobile payments. Before participants made a purchase, they often tried to get their phones ready and were nervous that the phone would not be ready to be scanned when it was their turn in line. They harbored anxiety that the phone would turn to screen saver mode, and then require a password to be entered, or the barcode would not be ready to be scanned. Participants told us that this could cause a longer wait for people in lines, confusing discussions with store clerks, feelings of inadequacy in not being able to know how to use the technology, or the need to switch to another payment form. For example, P12's diary had numerous entries on pre-purchase anxiety:

I like making sure I have the screen ready -- that my screen does not go to sleep. It has more to do with my performance anxieties than the app or the interaction. - P12, new user

Overall, the amount of tension around using mobile payments was far greater than participants thought they would feel. Surprisingly, while these feelings did diminish over time, they were still mentioned by existing users.

Trust Concerns

We found several trust concerns in relation to using mobile payments. These included concerns about around access to information and fragmented payment solutions.

Access to Information

First, four existing users reported having serious issues with information access across a variety of mobile payment systems. They were worried that other people may be able to access their payment information or other data on their smartphones.

For example, P10, an existing user, explained how one mobile payment service he used was tied to his email account. His email account was hacked, which he assumed compromised his financial data. As a result, P10 no longer used that particular service, but still uses other mobile payment services.

P6, also an existing user, described a situation she had when using a pay-by-phone parking service for metered parking. She explained how the system was tied to her phone number when you call in to pay and that she had just recently had her phone number changed. The system did not allow her to change her profile, which resulted in her having access to someone else's account. This, in turn, left her with the assumption that someone had access to her account too. She told us the situation was "worrisome."

Another existing user reported having trust concerns over the security of paying through a barcode displayed on his phone. Because of this, he and his sister did a test where he sent his sister a screenshot of the barcode and she displayed the picture of the barcode at the store to make a purchase. To both their surprise, the barcode scanned successfully at the store and his sister was able to purchase.

Both user groups had trust concerns around security of personal information that they entered over Wi-Fi or other networks. For example, P20 had extreme concerns around the contract he had to sign to use the Starbucks app, as well as little understanding towards how the process would work. He even was concerned that he might be giving the company access to all of the data on his phone.

Issues around access to information also occurred for the viewing of information in person. Some users had concerns about data on their screen being visible to outsiders. For example, P8, an existing user, told us, *"It has to do with money, it's kind of private, so then I try not to show anyone."* P16, a new user, told us that she was nervous entering her credit card information on a bus.

I found [a payment app] which I could add [money] to with a credit card... so I added $20 and paid with my card. I did it on the bus and I think that made me a little nervous, like, can anybody see me taking my card out? - P16, new user

Fragmented Payment Solutions

Second, some participants told us that they did not like to leave money or personal information untouched and not regularly used. As a result, they really disliked the idea of creating multiple mobile payment service accounts for each vendor that they might use. Instead, they wanted just a single global account so they would not accidentally mishandle their money by, perhaps, forgetting about it in an account. They were also concerned that they may not be able to keep track of account charges across multiple account in cases of potential fraud. Participants specifically told us they needed to "touch" their money often (e.g., by spending small amounts with each mobile payment service) to ease trust concerns and overall fear of money loss.

For example, P17, a new user, mentioned how he had information saved in a PayPal account from years ago. He expressed concern about not regularly using the account and felt uneasy about having his information just "languishing" there for years. This ultimately gave him a negative feeling towards PayPal. He mistrusted PayPal as a brand and the information that was stored with them.

Similarly, P19, a new user, also said he would not use a system for payment unless it was accepted at nearly all of the stores he frequented. He, too, disliked the idea of having money in numerous places and was concerned this would lead to a loss of money as it "just sits in an account somewhere."

DISCUSSION

Our findings showed a range of user practices with mobile payment services along with clear successes and challenges in using mobile payments. We discuss the implications of these findings and further reflect back on our related work section, as well as introduce new literature as a lens to interpret key components of our findings.

Mental Model Development and Designing for Routines

First, our results illustrated clear trends around why existing users continue to use mobile payment services long term. In our study, all existing users perceived their mobile payment use as easier and faster than other payment methods. They also described how their smartphone was often a more convenient solution to make payments than money or credit/debit cards. Yet in contrast, our study also revealed why some users may not adopt mobile payment services, or why they may chose to not use them even initially. Here we found that some new users were almost puzzled by why people might find mobile payment services to be easier and faster than the current payment methods they used. Our results also found that some users lacked the mental model of how mobile payments would work. This was a key factor that affected the usefulness of mobile payments.

As mentioned, Hinman and Matovu [7] found similar mental model and conceptual gaps between their users and mobile payment use. While our participants understood the exchange of funds for services, some did not seem to conceptually understand payment through their smartphones and the benefits associated with it. Considering that Hinman and Matovu's study was conducted in 2002—over ten years ago—this result is especially surprising. One would expect that the idea of paying for items using a phone would be more commonly understood than what we saw. Certainly as mobile payment services become more readily available in North America, it is likely that the issues around mental model will slowly disappear as users get used to the idea that smartphones can support payments.

Yet we also feel there are design directions that could help support the uptake of mobile payment services to help increase adoption and the usefulness of the technology. Participants in our study very clearly found mobile payments most valuable when they focused on routine and habitual activities. In fact, both new and existing users expressed this sentiment. We had expected that would be the case for existing users but not new users. This suggests clear benefits for mobile payment services that target habitual or routine activities as a starting point for designs. For example, these may include mobile payment options for gas, groceries, and other routine purchases. Over time, as users develop practices around habitual purchases, they would develop a mental model of how mobile payments work, which could then extend to understanding how mobile payment services could be more broadly used for other non-routine purchases. This extends past work by Mallat [16] who suggested mobile payments are most compatible with small value payments. We now see additional compatibility with routine purchases.

Gamification and Entertainment

Our study also revealed that one of the key benefits for new users of mobile payments over other payment methods was the gamification and reward features. These attributes created a more emotional and exciting experience. Given this, we believe that gamification elements coupled with a mobile payment service that is perceived to be useful will entice new users to adopt mobile payment services. Thus, gamification can act as a complementary component for mobile payment designs.

Yet the question is whether or not such features would continue to attract users longer term. Lindqvist et al. [13] investigated Foursquare users and found that the gamification element of collecting badges was a decreasing motivator for usage over time; users had a slow decline of participation after 200-300 days. In our case, we only had two veteran users comment that gamification in mobile payment services still had long term appeal after a year. This suggests further study of the long-term effects of gamification on mobile payments.

Social Cohesion

Part of the positive experiences we found for mobile payment related to social cohesion. Ling [14] describes social cohesion as a strong 'current' in society and strong bonds linking individuals, which affects how we interact with one another and what we know about each other. This is the opposite of individualism [14]. Related to social cohesion is the idea that people have negative attitudes towards people using mobile phones in public situations and locations [12,14]. That is, using one's mobile phone in public areas has been deemed socially rude and is often met with negative connotation [12,14]. However, in our findings, participants described the opposite. They felt that the use of mobile payments created a positive experience for people around them. They explained that this was because they were using their mobile phone in socially positive ways, which in this case was speeding up a store line and eliminating wait times for others. Participants felt their mobile payment activity allowed them to "help out" fellow patrons resulting in social cohesion [14]. Of course, there is the chance that while the purchaser *thought* the experience was positive for others, it may have in fact been unpleasant or annoying. We did not ask others present during mobile payment purchases about what they thought of the activity to know for sure. This suggests future work that investigates public reactions to mobile payment usage.

Of course, negative experiences around social cohesion can also obviously arise. As discussed in the findings, users 'fiddle' with their phones before use because of pre-purchase anxiety, and this could negatively impact social cohesion if patrons are in groups (face-to-face) when purchasing. This also suggests design opportunities to make mobile payments less distracting for the payee. For example, in recent versions of Apple's iOS software, the phone's camera functionality is available from a locked screen with a single finger swipe. Payment options could similarly be integrated in such a manner if people feel safe with such easy access to payment options.

Mobile payments were also associated with a "coolness" factor when one was using them. Yet once mass adoption occurs, this coolness could easily diminish and it is not clear what feelings people may have toward the appearance of using the technology once this occurs.

Trust Concerns

Our findings also reported significant trust concerns amongst both types of users—new and existing. This differs heavily from work done in past mCommerce studies that have focused on purchasing products over the web [8]. Past work found that mechanisms to mitigate trust issues with mCommerce were prevalent and came in three distinct forms: family and friend recommendations, brand awareness, and leveraging trusted marketplaces such as iTunes and Google Play [8]. As a result, people did not have trust issues with their mCommerce shopping activities. In contrast, participants in our study did not find ways to mitigate their trust concerns. Instead, they simply had to "put up" with the issues, not purchase at all, or use another payment option. This is interesting because a large portion of transactions were done using apps from the same marketplaces reported by Hillman et al. [8]. Thus, brand awareness and trusted marketplaces were not enough to mitigate many users' trust concerns unlike other mCommerce shopping activities. Similarly, trust created by actually being physically present in a store was also not always present.

What is somewhat surprising is that the same trust issues observed by Mallat [16] over ten years ago were also described by participants in our study. Users were still concerned about network security, vagueness of transaction, and lack of control. Not only were users concerned that their mobile phone would get lost, stolen or hacked, we were presented with stories of this *actually occurring*. With these findings, addressing security and trust concerns seems essential to mobile payment success in the future.

Of course, trust concerns could simply go away over time, much like the mental model issues that some people have for mobile payments. Here continued and widening usage of mobile payments could see the easing of trust concerns. Yet there are also possible design avenues that could help speed up the easing of such concerns. First, many people had trust issues that revolved around data transmission. This suggests solutions that further enhance secure data transmission, or mobile payment designs that let users know that data transmission is in fact secure, if it is.

Second, we also recognize that currently mobile payment systems do not offer the same institutional backing as one might find with a credit card company. For example, if fraudulent charges occur on a credit card, most credit card companies are quick to reverse such charges. In the case of mobile payment systems, such services may not exist or users do not know about them. This suggests new models for companies to provide institutional backing against fraud, or designs that highlight such backing, if it exists.

Third, participants also reported issues around strangers seeing one's smartphone screen and private data while transactions were being made. This suggests designs that obscure such information so it is viewable only by the user.

Lastly, participants were concerned about the fragmented nature of mobile payment solutions where one's money may reside in several places (e.g., PayPal, the Starbucks's App). This meant users could easily forget about their balance. This suggests mobile payment designs focused around a centralized hub that manages all transactions and balances. Of course, this type of solution would require partnerships between companies, which may not be possible. Alternative solutions could look at providing better feedback to users of balances (especially if they are untouched for a long time), or the ability to easily move money out of a mobile payment service if it is no longer being used.

Limitations and Generalizability

Our study comes with several limitations that suggest future research in this space. First, we note that our analysis focused on all types of mobile payment services instead of just one particular type. Studying a single service could have revealed more detailed findings about that particular service. Yet, despite this diversity in our study, we did not see variations in responses based on any of the mobile payment types that participants used. That said, because our study was a qualitative study and not a quantitative controlled study, we did not control for such variables nor did we look for cause and effect. Therefore, we suggest additional studies focused on specific types of mobile payments independently.

Second, we studied North Americans as a group and only from major metropolitan cities. We did not see a difference in results from Canadians versus Americans; however, further investigation could be conducted to compare the two with a larger sample, especially if the countries end up developing unique e-wallet solutions.

Third, we caution that our study did not investigate the long-term adoption of mobile payments as might be found in a study that lasts several months to years. Instead, we focused on the first reactions of new users to mobile payment services along with the experiences of existing users who have already adopted the technology. This suggests an additional longitudinal study to complement our research.

CONCLUSION

To summarize, mobile payment services are in their infancy in North America. The potential to enhance users experience with faster and more useful transactions is possible. There is also potential for mobile payments to aid in social cohesion [14], which has previously been missing in mobile use. However, user challenges with mobile payments still exist. These include a perceived lack of need for the technology, and issues around mental model development and trust concerns. In order to move past these obstacles, this paper has outlined key areas for improved user experience: designing around users' routines and behaviors, trust mechanism development, and supporting gamification and social cohesion.

REFERENCES

1. Chemonics. Mobile Phone Banking Expands into Rural Philippines, retrieved from: http://www.chemonics.com/OurStory/OurNews/Pages/Mobile-phone-Banking-Expands-into-Rural-Philippines.aspx
2. Cho, D., Kwon, H., and Lee, H., Analysis of Trust in Internet and Mobile Commerce Adoption, *40th Annual Hawaii International Conference on System Sciences*, pp. 1-10. (2007).
3. Davis, F. D., Perceived Usefulness, Perceived Ease of Use, and User Acceptance in Information Technology, *MIS Quarterly*, 13 (3), pp. 319-340. (1989).
4. Forrester, J., Counterintuitive Behavior of Social Systems, *Theory and Decision*, Volume 2, Issue 2, Springer, pp. 109 - 140. (1970).
5. Head, M. and Hassanein, "Trust in e-Commerce: Evaluating the Impact of Third-Party Seals", *Quarterly Journal of Electronic Commerce*, 3(3), (2002), pp. 307-325.
6. Henkel, J., Handygestützte bezahlverfahren [Mobile payment]. In G. Silberer, J. Wohlfahrt, & T. Wilhelm (Eds.), Mobile commerce (pp. 327–351). Wiesbaden, Germany: Gabler. (2002).
7. Hinman, R., and Matovu, J., Opportunities and Challenges for Mobile-based Financial Services in Rural Uganda, Extended Proceedings of Computer-Human Interaction. pp. 3925-3930. (2010)
8. Hillman, S., Neustaedter, C., Bowes, J., and Antle, A., Soft Trust and mCommerce Shopping Behaviors, MobileHCI 2012. pp. 113 - 122.
9. Hillman, S., Neustaedter, C., Pang, C., and Oduor, E., "Shared Joy is Double Joy": The Social Practices of User Networks within Group Shopping Sites, CHI2013. pp. 2417-2426.
10. Kalakota, R. and Robinson M., M-Business: The Race to Mobility. Mcgraw-Hill Trade, pp.1-84. (2001).
11. Kim, C., Mirusmonov, M., and Lee, I., An Empirical Examination of Factors influencing the intention to use Mobile Payment, Computer in Human Behavior Journal, pp. 310-322, (2010).
12. Kindberg, T., Sellen, Abigail, S., and Erik Geelhoed, Security and Trust in Mobile Interactions: A Study of Users' Perceptions and Reasoning. UbiComp 2004: Ubiquitous Computing. pp. 1-16. (2004).
13. Lindqvist J, Cranshaw J, Wiese J, Hong J, Zimmerman J., I'm the Mayor of my house: examining why people use foursquare—a social-driven location sharing application. In: Proceedings of CHI. ACM Press, New York, pp. 2409–2418. (2011).
14. Ling, R., New Tech, New Ties: How Mobile Communication is Reshaping Social Cohesion, Massachusetts Institute of Technology, (2008).
15. Luo, X., Trust Production and Privacy Concerns on the Internet - A Framework Based on Relationship Marketing & Social Exchange Theory, *IMM,* 31,(2002).
16. Mallat, N., Exploring Consumer Adoption of Mobile Payment – A Qualitative Study, Journal of Strategic Information Systems 16, pp. 413-432, (2007).
17. Ondrus, J., and Pigneur, Y., Towards a Holistic Analysis of Mobile Payments: a Multiple Perspective Approach, Electronic Commerce Research and Applications 5 (3), pp. 246-257, (2006).
18. Ong, J., Alipay Dominates as Online Payment in China Top $150 Billion in Q3: Report, Retrieved from: http://thenextweb.com/asia/2012/12/03/alipay-leads-online-payments-in-china-after-nearly-rmb-1-trillion-in-transactions-in-q3-2012/
19. Twomey, M., Cashless Africa: Kenya's Smash Success with Mobile Money, Retrieved from http://www.cnbc.com/id/101180469, (2013).
20. Ventakesh, V. Ramesh, V., and Massey, A. P. Understanding usability in mobile commerce. Communications of the ACM, Vol. 46(12), pp. 53-56. (2003). Model, Information and Management 42 (5), pp. 719-729, (2005).
21. Zmijewska, A., and Lawrence, E., Implementation Models in Mobile Payment, In Proceedings of the IASTED International Conference, Puerto Vallarta, (2006), pp.19-25.

TalkZones: Section-based Time Support for Presentations

Bahador Saket[1,2], Sijie Yang[1,3], Hong Tan[1], Koji Yatani[1], Darren Edge[1]
[1] Microsoft Research, Beijing, China
[2] University of Arizona, Arizona, USA
[3] Indiana University, Bloomington, Indiana, USA
saket@email.arizona.edu, y1s2j3@gmail.com, {hongtan, koji, darren.edge}@microsoft.com

ABSTRACT
Managing time while presenting is challenging, but mobile devices offer both convenience and flexibility in their ability to support the end-to-end process of setting, refining, and following presentation time targets. From an initial HCI-Q study of 20 presenters, we identified the need to set such targets per "zone" of consecutive slides (rather than per slide or for the whole talk), as well as the need for feedback that accommodates two distinct attitudes towards presentation timing. These findings led to the design of TalkZones, a mobile application for timing support. When giving a 20-slide, 6m40s rehearsed but interrupted talk, 12 participants who used TalkZones registered a mean overrun of only 8s, compared with 1m49s for 12 participants who used a regular timer. We observed a similar 2% overrun in our final study of 8 speakers giving rehearsed 30-minute talks in 20 minutes. Overall, we show that TalkZones can encourage presenters to advance slides before it is too late to recover, even under the adverse timing conditions of short and shortened talks.

Author Keywords
Presentations; Timing; Pacing; HCI-Q Methodology

ACM Classification Keywords
H.5.2. Information interfaces and presentation: User Interfaces

INTRODUCTION
Oral presentations often have predefined time limits that speakers should not exceed out of respect for the audience's time and the following schedule of events. However, the cognitive challenges of dividing attention with the secondary pacing task [11, 31] and the social pressure of maintaining a level of engagement with the audience [1, 3, 7, 8] mean that presenters may not be able to fully attend to their timing while they are speaking. Previous approaches to presentation timing support [17, 26] have also failed to control talk pacing and time overruns adequately. We believe that mobile devices offer a particularly flexible, practical, and contextually-appropriate channel through which to configure and follow talk timing support. Our goal with this research is thus to explore how a mobile application could support all stages of the presentation time management process, from planning and refinement to rehearsals and delivery.

MobileHCI'14, September 23 - 26 2014, Toronto, ON, Canada
Copyright 2014 ACM 978-1-4503-3004-6/14/09…$15.00.
http://dx.doi.org/10.1145/2628363.2628399

We begin by reviewing the related work from the cognitive science literature on pacing, planning, and split attention; the presentation literature on best practices; and presentation systems in the HCI literature and the marketplace. Through this review, we derive a set of concerns that should be considered when designing for timing support.

Next, we describe how we used HCI-Q methodology [20] to elicit presenter feedback on these potential concerns. We translated these concerns into concrete statements of potential stakeholder perspectives, before using these statements as the basis of the card sort (N=20). This helped to characterize contrasting attitudes towards timing based on the level of flexibility of the presenter-timing relationship:

- **Less-flexible attitude:** the presenter wants to stay in control in a well-rehearsed talk, using a glanceable countdown against coarse, well-tested time targets.
- **More-flexible attitude:** the presenter wants to finish on time in a more-improvised talk, following adaptive guidance based on fine-grained, aspirational time targets.

This re-examination of presenter attitudes towards timing support helped us understand why existing approaches might not be optimal. For example, setting a single time target for the whole talk cannot provide adequate pacing information early in the talk (when there is still time to get back on track). Conversely, setting time targets for each individual slide can result in feedback that overemphasizes the importance of following a timing plan precisely (at the expense of other metrics like fluency of slide transitions). Our high-level conclusion and contribution is that planning and following time targets for *zones of slides*, rather than for individual slides or for the whole talk, allows presenters to prepare the timing plan for each talk at the level of detail it requires.

In the design section, we describe our resulting TalkZones prototype: a mobile application that supports flexible target setting for zones of consecutive presentation slides. This mobile application acts as a companion to presentation slideware, supporting time management throughout presentation planning, rehearsal, and delivery. Motivated by the results of our analysis, TalkZones supports customization of the timing feedback visualization along two axes:

- **Target type:** whether time targets are shown as they were *planned* (less-flexible) or targets that are *adaptive* to current progress and time remaining (more-flexible).
- **Detail level:** whether visual feedback is shown for the talk *overall* (less-flexible) or just for the current *zone* emphasizing the immediate situation (more-flexible).

Our evaluation of TalkZones spans two related studies. The first is a between-subjects study (*N*=24) of TalkZones against a regular timer, with participants in the TalkZones condition following a structured elicitation of configuration preferences under various scenarios. In most situations, the majority of TalkZones users would choose our *adaptive-overview* visualization of timing feedback. This visualization combines elements designed for both less-flexible and more-flexible attitudes towards presentation timing, suggesting that it is a satisfactory solution in general. The next task was to deliver a rehearsed 6m40s talk using a deck of 20 slides, each prompting the speaker to describe an aspect of their life. In addition to giving a short talk with many slides, the time pressure was increased further through four interruptions (emulating questions from the audience) in both conditions. All 12 participants in the TalkZones condition used the *adaptive-overview* visualization with 2-5 zones (mode of 4). The mean and maximum overruns were 8s (2% over time) and 35s (9%), compared with 1m49s (27%) and 3m40s (55%) in the control condition using a regular timer. TalkZones thus provides effective timing support for short presentations, even when they are shortened by interruptions.

In our second study (*N*=8), presenters pre-rehearsed 30-minute talks with their own slides before starting the session. At the beginning of the session, we instructed them that the time limit had been shortened from 30 to 20 minutes, and that they could use TalkZones with the *adaptive-overview* visualization to manage their timing. Results were almost identical to the first study: all participants created 3-5 zones (mode of 4) leading to well-controlled mean and maximum overruns of 23s (2% over time) and 2m3s (10%). TalkZones thus provides effective timing support for medium-length presentations, even when the talk is shortened in an unanticipated manner. Overall, we also learned that 4 zones represent a manageable number of opportunities to receive and act upon late signals for a range of talk durations.

RELATED WORK

In this section, we move from general results in cognitive science, via recommendations of best presentation practices, towards concrete systems for presentation timing support. Significant concerns are emphasized with italics.

Cognitive Science Literature

Punctuality in oral presentations is always desired, yet often difficult to achieve. Psychological studies have observed *distortion of time perception* during cognitively-demanding tasks, with people overestimating the passage of time [11]. The attentional-gate model attempts to explain this phenomenon through the *division of attentional resources* between the main task and the secondary task of time tracking [31]. Since the cognitive workload of the main task of delivering presentations is very high, there is often starvation of attention for the secondary task of time tracking. This is especially pronounced for inexperienced presenters, as well as for those anticipating failure or unpleasantness because of *communication apprehension* [2].

Another possible explanation for unsuccessful time tracking during presentations, even for seasoned presenters, is the planning fallacy [14]. The tendency to adhere to an original timing assessment and ignore the potential impact of unanticipated factors on the actual completion time (as shown in [6]) can result in a *distortion of time estimation*. Frequent comparison of actual-to-planned progress, especially in rehearsal, could help to ameliorate this bias.

Timing notifications should not be disruptive to the main task since excessive interruptions can lead to degradation of task completion efficiency [15] and emotional state [4]. The complexity of the interrupting task and its similarity to the main task both impact a person's ability to switch back again [13]. This suggests that *unimodal interference* between audio notifications and the presenter's speech process should be avoided, and that *multimodal notifications* [29], for instance using the haptic channel [26], should be preferred.

Presentation Advice

Presentation expert Nancy Duarte provides several strategies for keeping to time [8]. The first two steps are to "Plan content for 60% of your time slot" and "Trim your slide deck" by moving non-essential slides to an appendix, which we can summarize as *authoring to time limits*. The next step is to "Practice with the clock counting up", first cutting slides to meet the time limit and then iterating until rehearsals consistently fall within the time limit. This is followed by "Practice with the clock counting down" – dividing presentation content into quarters and assigning cumulative time markers to the slides as targets. Such *rehearsing to time targets* could help presenters refine their timing plan into a more fine-grained and accurate guide for the final delivery. Duarte also recommends *preparing to shorten* to guard against talk overruns: plan a shorter version of the talk with the same material or have two natural ending points [8].

One structured approach to *preparing to shorten* is to use the Beyond Bullet Points [3] presentation template, organized hierarchically with Key Point slides, Explanation slides, and Detail slides. While presenting all slides might take 45 minutes, hiding all the Detail slides might shorten the talk to 15 minutes, and presenting only the introduction and Key Point slides might take just 5 minutes. A related strategy for more freeform presentations is *timing by the section* such that if the talk needs to be shortened, the presenter can more easily determine which sections to cut to finish on time [1].

In a timed presentation, *monitoring time while speaking* is important because it is all too easy to lose track of time without any external reference [7]. A large clock on the lectern, a wall clock, or a signaling audience member all enable discrete time checks in ways that are preferable to reading the time from a watch, which "sends the unspoken message that you are either bored or anxious to bolt" [7]. Monitoring time also enables *communicating time plans and progress*, letting the audience know that you are sensitive to time constraints and the value of their time in ways that help to build rapport and maintain audience attention [7].

Presentation Systems

Mamykina et al. [17] were the first researchers to address presentation timing. They describe several problems with using conventional timing tools, such as watches and timers, for pacing tasks: the numeric display is not designed for glanceability (or *preattentive processing* – the unconscious detection of basic visual information [27]); mental resources are consumed by *proactive time checking* and the *calculation of relative progress*; and any *disruption to the prior plan* must be mentally tracked and accommodated in real-time. They then draw on several theories from the behavioral sciences to propose five design goals for pacing interfaces:

1. Minimize cognitive load for regulating a dynamic task.
2. Provide information on the progress of the task.
3. Indicate discrepancies between planned and actual pace.
4. Lead to an optimal recovery strategy.
5. Require less effort than the task being augmented.

Translating these goals into pacing features, they suggest pacing interfaces should include a *task overview*, a *progress report*, *pacing cues*, and *control over the task*. Their resulting Time Aura system [17] uses an *ambient display* [22, 30] to achieve these goals, minimizing the cognitive cost of *detecting and correcting plan deviations*. It comprises a modified slide list at the side of the presenter's private view to communicate progress (Figure 1). Slides are represented at heights proportional to their *slide time target* such that the whole talk fills the height of the screen. An *elapsed time marker* continuously descends along a vertical time-line and a *current slide highlight* moves discretely with advancing slides, with the spatial distance between the two communicating the difference between planned and actual progress. A redundant representation of the pace difference is provided by color interpolation of a transparent slide list overlay (blue=ahead, white=on-time, red=behind).

In an informal, between-subject study of 9 participants presenting ready-made slides according to a predetermined timing plan and 7-minute time limit, presentations with Time Aura resulted in a significantly higher subjective evaluation of pacing as rated by the audience (although no times were reported). Mamykina et al. also observed that the system divided visual attention between the audience, speaking notes, and timing cues, suggesting use of *multimodal cues*. Their conclusion was that future systems should provide *flexible and customizable interfaces* that support a range of *compensatory strategies* (e.g., slide skipping, revisitation), as well as *forgiving feedback* that does not cause presenter alarm when deviations from the timing plan are correctable.

In the second main work on presentation timing support, Tam et al.'s HaNS [26] is a wrist-worn haptic notification system that uses three 10-second *symbolic vibration patterns* to communicate *increasingly urgent notifications* that the talk time is almost up (e.g., 3 minutes, 1 minute, and 0 minutes). It also incorporates a private channel for *session chair communication*, with chair-initiated overtime signals that can be covertly acknowledged by the presenter.

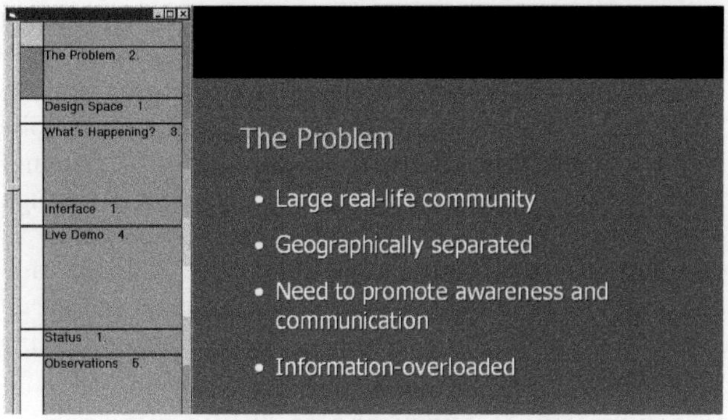

Figure 1. Time Aura pacing interface [17]

Results of field observations at three mid-sized speaking events (where presenters were still free to use their own tools and strategies for time control) indicate that such a haptic notification system can deliver salient cues through *unobtrusive and private notifications* while *minimizing social implications* of chair-speaker timing exchanges. However, speakers using HaNS still went overtime: at one event, 43% (10/23) of speakers opting to use HaNS overran by a mean 51s. At the same event, 45% (9/20) of non-HaNS speakers overran by a mean 32s. Nevertheless, speakers were observed responding to haptic cues by adjusting their pace accordingly. This suggests that *customizable cue timings* and *early indications of lateness* could enhance presenters' time control. The wearable form factor allowed presenters to *leave the lectern* and roam freely, unlike Time Aura [17].

In our prior study on understanding presentation practices [10], we identified *influencing audience with timing* as a major concern for presenters. Informants reported problems associated with interruptions, slide skipping, underrunning, overrunning, and being cut off, all in ways that were perceived to betray nervousness, nonchalance, or inadequate preparation. Our HyperSlides system [10] supports dynamic prototyping of semantically hyperlinked slides through the hierarchical specification of talk structure. The associated approach to time management is to reduce the number of points that are expanded by choosing not to drill down the slide hierarchy. The audience thus remains unaware that the presenter needed to skip some prepared materials, *maintaining speaker credibility*. Another system that uses *non-linear slide paths* as a compensatory strategy is NextSlidePlease [25]. The user first assigns time costs to slides organized in a directed graph, then during delivery the optimum path to timely completion is continuously updated.

We have also previously explored the connection between the activities of rehearsal and time planning. Our PitchPerfect [28] system supports *authoring to time limits* and *rehearsing to time targets* as recommended in the literature. Voice-activated recording and timing also aims to reduce the feelings of anxiety and time pressure resulting from continuous recording of all pauses and mistakes. This conforms to the common strategy of *reducing notes, times, and errors until ready*, and emphasizes the importance of tracking timing progress throughout the rehearsal process.

The marketplaces for mobile applications also contain many examples of *remote controllers* for desktop slideware, which typically use simple indicators tied to slide progress and the elapsed or remaining time (e.g., the Office Remote mobile app for controlling Microsoft PowerPoint [19]). Timing-oriented tools typically offer richer feedback through visualizations and audio and haptic feedback, as well as customizable notification schedules, but without any coupling to slide progress. The *physical comfort* and *social perception* of using a handheld mobile device while presenting also depends on the nature of the talk event.

UNDERSTANDING ATTITUDES TO TIMING SUPPORT

We wanted to understand the importance that potential users of presentation timing support would assign to the various concerns we derived from our literature review, as well as the existence of conflicting attitudes that might arise from differences in presenter personality or talk situation.

We decided to adopt HCI-Q methodology [20] for this purpose since it aligned closely with our study requirements. Firstly, HCI-Q tailors the well-established Q-methodology to solicit stakeholder feedback prior to designing or building any particular system, allowing critical reflection on basic assumptions and avoiding premature prototyping and fixation on preconceived solutions. Secondly, HCI-Q can lend statistical validity (and potential replication) to the qualitative interpretation of subjective data taken from small samples, generating groupings of stakeholder attitudes that provide a strong basis for the crafting of design requirements.

The methodology is based on a Q-Set – a balanced collection of positive and negative statements crafted by designers to represent possible stakeholder attitudes. Explicitly considering the negative implications of a design allows for critical reflection on the impact it could make on people's lives [9]. The complementary Q-Sort involves stakeholders sorting those statements into a forced distribution. Factor analysis then reveals the statistically quantifiable set of underlying perspectives that can be used to ground design.

Participants

We recruited 20 stakeholders from our organization (11 male and 9 female, ages 21–50), with backgrounds in computer science, engineering, design, and marketing and communication. All had experience giving timed talks at formal academic conferences or business events.

Procedure

Our HCI-Q analysis used a Q-Set of 30 concrete statements pertaining to presentation timing support, directly mapped from the more abstract set of concerns we derived from our literature review. The Q-Sort itself was performed with FlashQ [12] and comprised two stages. In the first stage, informants read each statement, asked the experimenter for further explanations if necessary, then provisionally assigned the statement to one of three groups: agree, neutral, and disagree. This familiarized the informant with all statements and began the process of differentiation.

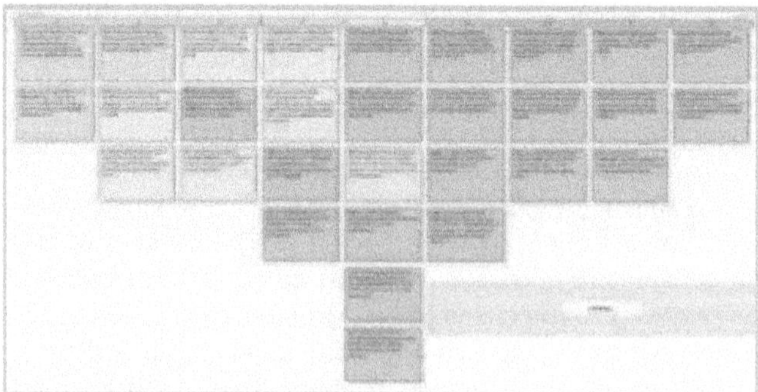

Figure 2. Example Q-Sort of statements into a forced distribution from most disagree (left) to most agree (right). Colors indicate initial assignments of statements to agree (green), disagree (red), and neutral (grey) groups.

In the second stage, informants arranged all statements in a forced distribution table according to the personal significance of the statements in their own experiences. Our table consisted of columns representing 9 ordinal levels of agreement from most disagree to most agree, with 2-3-3-4-6-4-3-3-2 rows of statements respectively. This relatively flat distribution is appropriate when informants are knowledgeable about the subject matter and thus likely to have stronger feelings [5], as was the case with our presenters. Figure 2 shows an example Q-Sort result from one study informant. After completing the Q-Sort, each informant explained their ratings to the experimenter.

Following our HCI-Q sessions with stakeholders, we used the PQMethod tool [23] to analyze the data. Principal Component Analysis extracted 8 factors from which we chose the two factors that explained the greatest variance in the data (21% and 17% compared with 9% and below). Rotation revealed the two factors A and B to be defined by 9 and 11 stakeholders respectively, with no confounds.

Results

The final result is a model Q-Sort for each of Factor A and B that defines the attitudes of a prototypical stakeholder in a way that can inform design. Each factor contains a similar distribution of experience levels for its defining stakeholders. The characterization of both Factor A and Factor B across the 30 statements in our Q-Set is shown in Tables 1 and 2.

Consensus & Conflict between Factors

Table 1 shows that stakeholders in both factors strongly agree that sound-based feedback is likely to be distracting, and in interviews informants reported several bad experiences with audio alerts built into some applications and conference facilities. More surprisingly, both factors strongly disagreed that presentation software should help presenters cover all of the prepared materials without skipping slides or rushing. Interview responses clarified that presenters should always retain the freedom to adjust their pacing as they feel is appropriate (including slide skipping if required), using timing feedback as a guide rather than a rule.

Factor	Agreement	Statement	Z-score
A	Strongly Agree	*Sound-based timing feedback would be distracting for the presenter or the audience or both.*	1.8
		*It should not feel like an emergency or like I have failed if I don't quite hit my time targets.	1.6
		*When there is a time limit for the presentation, it is more important to know the time remaining than the time spent so far.	1.3
		*It is often not socially appropriate to hold a mobile phone while giving a presentation.	1.2
		*I would not use presentation timing support in a live presentation without using it in rehearsals beforehand.	1.1
		*Visual timing feedback should be quickly glanceable even from a distance and focus on essential information only.	1.1
		***I would not use physical timing feedback (e.g., a vibrating phone or wristband) if it had the potential to surprise me.**	1.1
		*It is often physically uncomfortable to hold a mobile phone while giving a presentation	0.9
	Strongly Disagree	*Timing feedback should become harder to ignore if the presenter is in danger of running behind and time is running out.	-1.8
		*I would use physical timing feedback (e.g., a vibrating phone or wristband) because I would not have to remember to check the time.	-1.8
		***When presentations have a time limit, presentation software should help presenters to finish within the allowed time.**	-1.2
		*I would like to receive timing feedback on a handheld mobile device I also use to control my slides.	-1.1
		*Presentation timing support should help me anticipate when I should move to the next slide so I can move on accordingly.	-1.1
		***Timing support should help the presenter adapt to any unexpected changes to the time limit before or during the talk.**	-1.0
		Presentation software should help presenters to cover all of the prepared material without skipping slides or rushing.	-1.0
B	Strongly Agree	***When presentations have a time limit, presentation software should help presenters to finish within the allowed time.**	2.0
		*During a presentation, timing support should adjust time targets based on actual progress rather than targets planned in advance.	1.6
		Sound-based timing feedback would be distracting for the presenter or the audience or both.	1.4
		***Timing support should help the presenter adapt to any unexpected changes to the time limit before or during the talk.**	1.3
		Getting better at meeting time targets during rehearsal would improve my timekeeping and confidence for the live presentation.	1.3
	Strongly Disagree	*I am concerned that feedback from a tool may be more noticeable to the audience than signals from a session chair.	-2.1
		***I would not use physical timing feedback (e.g., a vibrating phone or wristband) if it had the potential to surprise me.**	-1.8
		*I would not be willing to use timing feedback if I had to think about how long I wanted to spend on each slide.	-1.8
		Presentation software should help presenters to cover all of the prepared material without skipping slides or rushing.	*-0.9*
		*I am concerned that continuous timing feedback could make me nervous and result in a poorer performance than without it.	-0.8

Table 1. Results of HCI-Q analysis characterizing two factors at a strong dis/agreement level ($|Z|>0.8$). Positive consensus is shown in green/italic, negative consensus in red/italic and conflict in blue/bold. Starred statements distinguish factors at significance $p<.01$.

Remaining 10 statements that do not distinguish Factor A and Factor B at significance level $p < .01$	Z-score A	Z-score B	Z-score A-B
I would prefer to check my timing when it is convenient rather than risk being distracted by automatic notifications.	0.04	-0.73	0.8
I would be concerned that the mental load of interpreting timing feedback would be greater than mentally tracking my own progress.	0.02	-0.71	0.7
Use of presentation timing support should not be apparent to the audience since it could erode the credibility of the speaker.	0.61	0.39	0.2
I would not want to do any kind of mental calculation to work out whether I should move on or keep talking about the same slide.	0.05	-0.05	0.1
I would typically want my timing feedback to include a numeric representation of the total time spent so far or time remaining.	0.17	0.18	0.0
Rehearsing a presentation should have the beneficial side effect of helping me to set time targets for the final delivery.	0.44	0.56	-0.1
It is more realistic to plan to finish a talk within a certain time window (e.g., 15-18 minutes) than after a precise time.	-0.27	0.21	-0.5
Presenters should always try to finish on time even if they are frequently interrupted or sidetracked by comments and questions.	-0.22	0.28	-0.5
Presenters may not be able to act effectively on timing feedback if they are already too far behind or too late in the talk.	-0.39	0.47	-0.9
Presentation timing support should help me to realize when I am in danger of exceeding up upper time limit at any point in the talk.	-0.80	0.75	-1.5

Table 2. Statements that do not strongly distinguish between factors. Lower/higher Z-scores indicate greater dis/agreement with the corresponding statement within the factor, and greater differences indicate greater conflict for the statement between factors.

Three statements in particular differentiated the two factors. Factor A stakeholders did not believe that presentation software should adapt to any changes in the available time or help presenters finish within the time limit. They would also not use any kind of physical timing feedback (e.g., a vibrating phone or wristband) if it had the potential to surprise them. In contrast, Factor B stakeholders wanted presentation software to adapt to changing talk durations and help them finish within the time limit, using physical timing feedback to attract their attention when necessary. These differences arise from complex interaction between the presenter's personality and the presentation situation, and characterize two contrasting *attitudes* to timing support:

- **Less-flexible attitude (Factor A):** the presenter wants to stay in control in a well-rehearsed talk, using a glanceable countdown against coarse, well-tested time targets.
- **More-flexible attitude (Factor B):** the presenter wants to finish on time in a more-improvised talk, following adaptive guidance based on fine, aspirational time targets.

These prototypical attitudes arising from the HCI-Q study can be seen as the extremes of a continuous scale of flexibility in the presenter-timing relationship. Considering these extremes in the design process should encourage the design of timing support mechanisms that satisfy the needs of presenters who lie anywhere in between these extremes.

Implications for mobile application support

The potential for using mobile devices to support both attitudes is high. Both would want to set time targets in advance, with less-flexible presenters testing them more thoroughly in rehearsal. In delivery, less-flexible presenters would prefer to passively glance at a mobile device propped upright on the lectern or positioned as a remote display within sight of the stage. Presenters with a more-flexible attitude may additionally want to use their mobile device in hand, controlling their slides while continuously receiving multimodal visual and haptic feedback designed to actively guide them to a timely talk completion.

Implications for time target setting

The potential for designing a target setting mechanism appropriate for both attitudes is also high. Setting time targets per slide like Time Aura [17] might satisfy presenters with a more-flexible attitude since they would be willing to think about how long they wanted to spend on each slide – the targets are aspirational rather than refined through practice. More-flexible presenters also value continuous feedback (in contrast to that of HaNS [26]). For presenters with a less-flexible attitude, the converse is true. Given their prior refinement and reinforcement of time targets through rehearsals, they would disagree that timing support should help them anticipate when to move to the next slide, which could translate into the feeling of it being an emergency whenever these targets are missed.

To satisfy the broadest range of presenters, a more customizable approach to target setting is required. Several stakeholders suggested the ability to set time targets for variable-length sequences of slides, starting with a time limit for the whole talk and refining into section targets and then slide targets only when necessary. Such division of a talk into different timing zones would provide multiple further advantages for both types of presenters. Greater spacing between targets would make each more salient, providing stronger active guidance to presenters with a more-flexible attitude and reducing chances to make less-flexible presenters feel uncomfortable if they have diverged from their prior timing plan. Fewer targets from a small number of zones may also be more glanceable at a distance in ways that suit less-flexible presenters while giving more-flexible presenters large enough zones to notice and act upon any adaptive adjustments to their time targets.

Goals for the design of presentation timing support

In summary, we present four high-level goals for the design of mobile presentation timing support:

1. Timing should be considered from authoring to delivery.
2. Target setting should be by variable-length slide zones.
3. Visual feedback should be glanceable and forgiving.
4. Physical notifications should be subtle and optional.

DESIGN

We wanted to design a presentation timing companion that would provide an acceptable solution for presenters with different levels of flexibility in their attitude to timing support. In the following sections, we describe how we translated our four design goals into concrete features of a mobile application called TalkZones. This Windows Phone application communicates with a Microsoft PowerPoint Add-In over Bluetooth, synchronizing time data in the XML of the .pptx file format allowing the same presentation to be paired with any mobile device. TalkZones also provides the high-level capabilities of time planning, time feedback, and remote control of the PowerPoint slideshow.

Timing should be considered from authoring to delivery

We set out to explore the potential of mobile devices for presentation timing support, and we concluded that mobile phones are sufficiently flexible to satisfy the needs of both presenter types in a single form factor (e.g., as a handheld remote control and/or a remote timing display, giving passive visual feedback and/or active haptic notifications). Additional screen real-estate on the mobile phone can also help all presenters to set time targets while authoring slides, as well as attempt to follow them in rehearsals that closely anticipate the conditions of the final presentation delivery.

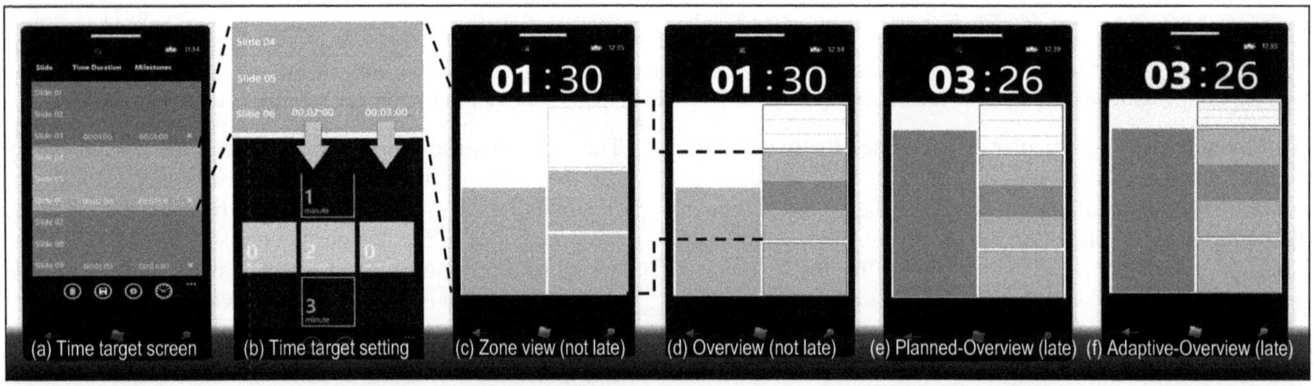

Figure 3. TalkZones presentation timing support. First set time targets by zone (a–b) then select a timing visualization (c, d, e, or f).

(a) Time target screen showing an ordered list of all presentation slides. Tapping on a slide brings up buttons to set the duration or cumulative time milestone for a talk zone ending on that slide. Tapping on a cross removes the corresponding talk zone.

(b) Setting a time target by duration or milestone. Tapping either button opens a time picker that returns to the time target screen.

(c) Zone visualization (not late). 1:30 of the presentation has elapsed and the presenter is on slide 2 of 3 in the current zone. Just over half of the time allocated to the zone has passed. The color follows the color of the zone on the time target screen.

(d) Overview visualization (not late). Showing same timing situation as (c) but in the context of all zones. The darker box indicates the current slide (slide 2 of 3) in the current zone (also zone 2 of 3).

(e) Planned-Overview visualization (late). The time bar becomes darker in color when its height exceeds that of the current zone box, providing redundant visual indications of lateness as measured against the initial timing plan.

(f) Adaptive-Overview visualization (late). Same as (e) with an additional indication of lateness: the ascending time bar, on reaching the top of the current zone box, stretches the current zone box and compresses future zone boxes. Time targets adapt to the delivery.

Target setting should be by variable-length slide zones

We designed a lightweight and flexible approach to time target setting. The user creates time zones as an implicit side effect of assigning a duration or milestone to a slide (Figure 3a-b). Each slide is initially represented as a row in a table that contains columns for the slide index and buttons with which to set the duration or cumulative time milestone of a zone ending on that slide. Tapping either of these takes the user to a time picker control with which they can specify the time period. A zone can be further subdivided by selecting a slide within it or deleted by tapping the cross icon. Usage patterns are free to vary from setting the durations of each slide (like Time Aura [17]) to setting milestones that indicate impending and actual "time up" (like HaNS [26]), as well as supporting the progressive refinement of targets. For example, the user might first set milestones for high-level zones (e.g., 3 sections to finish after 5, 10, and 15 minutes), and then refine these into lower-level slide zones by specifying the durations (e.g., refining the 10-15 minute zone into two zones of 2 and 3 minutes, respectively).

In our target-setting screen, zones are automatically assigned colors in a reverse spectrum from violet to red (Figure 3a). This progression is familiar, uses the widest range of discernable colors, and conveniently represents progress towards the "hot" end of the talk. Using *zone coloring* during delivery (Figure 3c-f), color can provide a glanceable indication of the current zone and the approximate progress through the talk. Iterative rehearsal of a talk and the delivery of multiple talks over time should serve to reinforce this color mapping and accelerate processing of progress made. We also offer *late coloring* – a binary color scheme in which red and blue signify lateness and timeliness according to a blue=cool=on-time and red=hot=late metaphorical mapping. We chose this in preference to a traffic light metaphor since green=speed-up and red=slow-down is contradictory in the context of speaking to presentation slides, and confused users in pilot tests. Red and blue caused no such problems. While *zone coloring* gives feedback about where in the talk the presenter is, *late coloring* provides a simpler indication of how the presenter is doing with respect to time targets.

Visual feedback should be glanceable and forgiving

Our design of a mobile timing companion with flexible target setting supports both less-flexible (Factor A) and more-flexible (Factor B) attitudes through anticipated differences in the number of targets. However, more fundamental differences in visualization preferences could arise from two tensions identified in the HCI-Q study:

- Mental comparison of planned and actual timings (A) vs. Forgiving guidance from adaptive time targets (B)
- Glancing at rough progress against the overall plan (A) vs. Being notified when running late in a zone (B)

We refer to these tensions as *planned vs. adaptive targets* and *overview vs. zone feedback*, creating a 2×2 design space. We filled this design space with a family of timing support visualizations based on the metaphor of a race in which a timing bar on the left, continuously growing upwards, is juxtaposed with boxes stacked on the right representing discrete units of progress. If the presenter moves through their slides at a pace such that the continuous time bar and discrete boxes reach the top of the visualization area together, she will always finish her talk on time.

In our *planned-overview* visualization (Figure 3e), the timing bar represents the passage of time for the whole presentation and the stacked boxes represent presentation zones subdivided into slides (with the current slide highlighted). These zone boxes are shown at a fixed size proportional to their time target planned in advance. In our *adaptive-overview* visualization (Figure 3f), boxes do not remain at an initial fixed size but scale dynamically whenever the presenter is overrunning the zone. These visualizations differ in the quality of forgiveness. *Planned-overview* uses spatial differences between bars to highlight deviations from the prior plan in a way that could be perceived as judgmental or pressurizing. *Adaptive-overview* is more forgiving, stretching the boxes of zones that are being overrun to focus attention on the time remaining (not past lateness).

Our *zone* visualizations (Figure 3c) are full-screen views of the current zone taken from the respective *overview* visualization. The discrete units in this view are the slides of the zone. When moving to a new zone with *adaptive-zone*, the time bar immediately begins filling the screen at a rate determined by the updated target time for that zone. In *planned-zone*, the time bar moves at a pace predetermined by the initial plan and can thus lag behind or already fill part or all of the screen when changing to a new zone. Compared with overviews, zone views have lower resolution, faster visual motion, and larger, full-screen indications of lateness designed to be maximally glanceable.

Physical notifications should be subtle and optional

Presenters with less-flexible and more-flexible attitudes were divided over the use of haptics and its potential to attract/distract the presenter's attention. We therefore focus on visualizations of timing with haptic feedback an optional and redundant representation of lateness. In our system, presenters can choose to receive a one-time vibration of 200ms when they begin overrunning in a zone, as well as each time they physically advances slides within a late-running zone (when speech is momentarily paused and attention to the haptic sensory channel elevated). The initial notification of lateness, while potentially surprising and thus disrupting less-flexible presenters, might be necessary to attract the attention of more-flexible presenters who are overrunning without noticing. Conversely, the notification of lateness on presenter-initiated slide transitions can be anticipated in advance in ways that reduce the potential for surprise, while increasing the continuousness of timing feedback in ways desired by more-flexible presenters.

EVALUATION

Our evaluation of TalkZones spans two related studies. The goals of the first study were to understand how participants choose to configure and use TalkZones under various scenarios, and to compare the performance of TalkZones to that of a regular timer for controlling the pace of a short talk. The second study built on the first by testing how well TalkZones could pace longer talks with speakers' own slides.

Study 1: Presenting Short but Interrupted Talks

We employed a between-subject design because familiarization with materials and timing strategies in one condition could impact performance in the other condition. Half of the participants were asked to use TalkZones after an initial session of training and preference elicitation, while the remaining half of the participants used a minimal TalkZones application configured as a regular countdown timer (showing overruns as negative time in red type).

Participants

We recruited 24 participants (20 male, 4 female) aged 21–32 years (mean 24) from our organization, with backgrounds in science, engineering, and design. All had experience giving timed presentations at international conferences. We divided them into two groups of 12 balanced by self-identified timing attitude from our descriptions (7 less-flexible, 4 more-flexible, 1 neutral in each group). Only the 12 participants in the TalkZones condition participated in the structured elicitation of configuration preferences described below.

Procedure: Collection of TalkZones Preferences

For collecting user preferences, we created a deck of 20 slides each of which contained a prompt the participant could speak to without prior rehearsal. Examples include "My home town" and "My university life". To learn how different numbers of zones might affect visualization preferences, we created three versions of this deck with different targets:

1. Slide targets (20 zones × 1 slide each)
2. Quarter targets (4 zones × 5 slides each)
3. Midpoint target (2 zones × 10 slides each)

To let participants experience the feeling of each combination of these 3 target types and our 4 visualizations, we set the interface to use *zone coloring,* positioned the mobile phone next to the presentation laptop, and gave the participant a handheld clicker to advance slides. We then provided the following instructions for each of the 12 trials combining a target type with a visualization:

1. Speak continuously and maintain good eye contact (as recommended in the presentation literature).
2. Miss early targets by longer times, but gradually catch up (to experience the feeling of recovering from being late).
3. Gradually move back to the longest glanceable distance (to discover the potential of mobile timing display).

For all trials, we preconfigured a talk time limit of 6 minutes 40 seconds. This corresponds to the total time available in the Pecha Kucha [21] talk format of presenting 20 slides, each of which automatically advances after 20 seconds. This

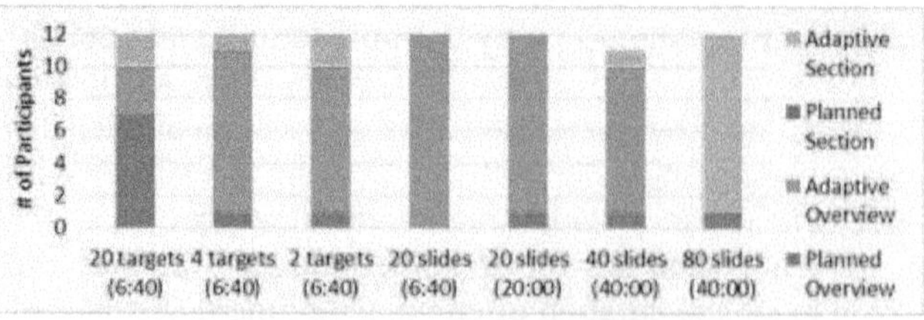

Figure 4. Visualization preferences for different numbers of time targets and talk durations after initial use experiences

format was invented to tackle the problem of presenters overrunning in talks whose allocated time was already longer than needed to communicate the core message. The use of auto-forward is "all important" because "There's no 'next slide' or 'go back one, please' at PechaKucha Nights" [21]. Presenting so many slides in such a short time *without* the use of auto-forward creates a high level of time pressure from the outset, making it an ideal format to test our visualizations.

Following these sensitizing experiences, we invited participants to experiment with the option of *late coloring* (red for late, blue for not late, regardless of the section) as well as the use of handheld control and haptic feedback. We then collected subjective configuration preferences across a range of typical presentation formats: 20 slide, 6m40s Pecha Kucha style talks and 20-40 minute talks with 20-80 slides.

Procedure: Comparison of TalkZones against Timer

For the final task, participants in both TalkZones and Timer conditions spent 15 minutes rehearsing a premade slide deck of personal talking points to be presented on camera in Pecha Kucha style (with manual slide control). TalkZones users were free to configure the application as they preferred. Control group participants had the same rehearsal time, following an introduction to the task, training in the use of the clicker and timer, and familiarization with the presentation deck. To test the ability of the timing support tool to provide an acceptable recovery strategy, we interrupted each presentation with the same four questions.

Study 1 Results

The first three columns of Figure 4 show how preferences shifted from *planned-overview* to *adaptive-overview* as the numbers of zone targets decreased for a 20 slide, 6m40s talk. With one slide per zone, target adaptation happens on each slide transition in ways participants reported to be disruptive. Participants all preferred *overview* to *zone* because of the feelings of confidence and control that come from easy, glanceable access to complete talk information (the different resolutions of *overview* and *zone* did not affect legibility in the 1-3m viewing range). The shift in choice from *planned* to *adaptive* with decreasing zone targets stemmed from the reduced mental load by not needing to compare actual versus planned-progress (only content versus time remaining), the increased salience of late signals when they occur at a few strategic points in the talk, and the clearer signaling of lateness through dynamic changes to zone size *and* color. *Adaptive* targets should thus be used in non-singleton zones.

The preferred number of zones (with participant frequencies) were 2 (1), 3 (2), 4 (8), and 5 (1), with the majority of participants (9/12) preferring *zone coloring* to *late coloring* because a few memorable zone colors reminded them of the similarly colored timing plan. With too many zones, however, they become less identifiable and hence less useful as a glanceable indication of progress. While preferences for *adaptive* continued with increasing time and slides, 11 participants would prefer to use *zone* feedback for decks of 80+ slides at which point *overview* was found to be illegible. Automatically switching from a default *overview* to a *zone* view once a slide threshold is reached would be reasonable.

In situations where it is appropriate to use a mobile phone to control slides, nine participants would choose to use some combination of the two haptic signals they tested (but none did so during their final talk on account of its formality). Several users suggested adding such feedback to a clicker.

Completion times in the TalkZones condition ranged from a 25s underrun to a 35s overrun, with a mean overrun of 8s (*SD*: 18s), or 2% over the target completion time. In contrast, participants using a regular timer in the control condition all ran over by 25-220s, with a mean of 1m49s (*SD*: 1m11s), or 27% over the time limit. A Welch's t-test revealed a significant difference ($t_{(12.7)}$=4.87, p<.0001, Cohen's d=1.97), translating to a 14× improvement with TalkZones.

Overall, participants reported that "it is easy to divide each section [zone]" and that the "smaller goals" of zone targets helped them to "quickly notice the remaining time" when considering slide transitions. When overrunning in a zone, the adaptively "shrinking space" of future zones helped participants to "pre-manage" their timing before it was too late, resulting in a "sense of security" and feeling of control.

Study 2: Presenting Longer but Shortened Talks

Our second study aimed to evaluate whether the effectiveness of TalkZones for pace control of short, intense talks would transfer to longer talks also under time pressure.

Participants & Procedure

We recruited 8 participants (5 male, 3 female) aged 23-38 (mean 27) with backgrounds in science and engineering, with no overlap with participants from earlier studies. Prior to the study, we instructed participants to prepare through prior rehearsal for a 30-minute presentation, using one of their existing presentation decks. Their decks of choice ranged from 37-58 slides, with a mean of 48 slides. On starting the study, we then asked participants to give the actual presentation in just 20 minutes, with the rationale that such enforced, last-minute talk shortening is an unfortunate but common practice in many real-world situations.

Participants used TalkZones preconfigured with the *adaptive-overview* visualization (unanimously preferred by participants in the first study) but could select *zone coloring* or *late coloring*. They were also free to create zones and time allocations as they liked. Talks were video recorded.

Study 2 Results

All participants chose 3-5 zones (mode 4) and the majority (6/8) chose *zone coloring*, consistent with the results of the first study. In their timed talks, the mean and maximum overruns corresponded to 2% (23s) and 10% (2m3s) of the 20 minute time limit, again highly consistent with the 2% and 9% mean and maximum overruns from the first user study.

From these results, we can conclude that TalkZones is an effective means of timing support for short-to-medium length presentations, and that *zone coloring* of fixed but flexible-length talk "quarters" represent a manageable and predictable way to receive and act upon late signals (confirming the expert recommendation in [8]). Taken together, our results suggest that mobile phones are a suitable platform for presentation timing support, and that our TalkZones application gently encourages presenters to advance slides before it is too late to recover, even under the adverse timing conditions of short and shortened talks.

CONCLUSION

We have presented TalkZones – a mobile application and presentation timing companion that supports the setting and following of time targets using variable-length slide zones. Across two user studies, TalkZones consistently controlled presentation pacing in ways that minimized talk overruns, demonstrating its effectiveness even under the adverse timing conditions of short and shortened presentations.

This work makes progress in a problem space well investigated in the literature but not previously addressed by systems validated in empirical studies. In an attempt to understand how to improve upon prior systems, our HCI-Q study revealed two contrasting attitudes towards presentation timing, as well as the potential advantages of mobile application support and the need for a more flexible, zonal approach to working with time targets. Our design process aimed to support both timing attitudes through a family of related visualizations. However, we found that one visualization in particular, which adapts timing targets within the context of an overview of all talk zones, was preferred by all participants for almost all presentation scenarios. For more formal talks like the ones forming the basis of our studies, all participants also preferred to use TalkZones as a remote timing display. In the case of less formal, more improvisational talks, TalkZones can also offer handheld slide control augmented with haptic timing feedback. Overall, we can recommend a single paradigm for timing support in a mobile phone application that embodies convenience, effectiveness, and flexibility in use.

Future work should investigate the design of handheld clickers or wearable devices for multimodal presentation pacing that is not primarily visual. Another area to explore is how to support the timing of non-linear presentations. For example, zoomable presentation systems like Prezi [24] and Fly [16] have a preset path but also support seamless and impromptu navigation away from this path. For such systems, our concept of talk zones could be mapped to spatial areas of the canvas rather than to sequences of slides. Our existing adaptive time guidance could be modified to support such non-linear navigation by treating revisitation as the norm rather than the exception. Exiting a zone early would allow the zone to retain its unused time allocation, while remaining in a zone beyond its time allocation would consume remaining time from all zones with a time surplus (not just unvisited ones). Similarly, for hierarchical presentations such as with HyperSlides [10], time targets could be specified for each of the high-level "scene" slides, with the time allocation cascading down to subordinate "detail" slides. In each case, future work should explore how non-linear visualizations can communicate the spatial or hierarchical distribution of time targets.

Assessing the suitability of the TalkZones visualizations for other display surfaces and activities, such as use on meeting room walls for ambient time management [18], would generalize and extend the current contribution. Finally, within the activity of presenting, larger-scale studies in naturalistic contexts such as academic and business conferences would go even further towards demonstrating the value of TalkZones for presenters and audience alike.

REFERENCES

1. Abela, A. (2008). Advanced Presentations by Design: Creating Communication that Drives Action. Pfeiffer.
2. Ayres, J. (1996). Speech preparation processes and speech apprehension. Communication Education, 45, 228-235.
3. Atkinson, C. (2005). Beyond bullet points: Using Microsoft PowerPoint to create presentations that inform, motivate, and inspire. Microsoft Press.
4. Bailey, B.P., Konstan, J.A., & Carlis, J.V. (2001). The effects of interruptions on task performance, annoyance, and anxiety in the user interface. INTERACT'01, 593-601.
5. Brown, S.R. (1980). Political subjectivity: Applications of Q Methodology in political science. Yale University Press.
6. Buehler, R., Griffin, D., & Ross, M. (1994). Exploring the "planning fallacy": Why people underestimate their task completion times. Journal of personality and social psychology, 67(3), 366-381.
7. Dempsey, D.J. (2010). Present Your Way to the Top. McGraw Hill.
8. Duarte, N. (2012). Harvard Business Review Guide to Persuasive Presentations. Harvard Business Review Press.
9. Dunne, A. & Raby, F. (2001). Design noir: The secret life of electronic objects. August Media.
10. Edge, D. Savage, J. & Yatani, K. (2013). HyperSlides: dynamic presentation prototyping. CHI'13, 671-680.
11. Eisler, H. (1976). Experiments on subjective duration 1868-1975: A collection of power function exponents. Psychological Bulletin, 83(6), 1154-1171.
12. FlashQ. http://www.hackert.biz/flashq/home/
13. Gillie, T., & Broadbent, D. (1989). What makes interruptions disruptive? A study of length, similarity, and complexity. Psychological Research, 50(4), 243-250.
14. Kahneman, D., & Tversky, A. (1977). Intuitive prediction: Biases and corrective procedures. TIMS Studies in Management Science, 12, 313-327.
15. Kreifeldt, J.G., & McCarthy, M.E. (1981). Interruption as a test of the user-computer interface. Annual Meeting of the Human Factors and Ergonomics Society, 87-91.
16. Lichtschlag, L., Hess, T., Karrer, T. & Borchers, J. (2012). Fly: studying recall, macrostructure understanding, and user experience of canvas presentations. CHI'12, 1307-1310.
17. Mamykina, L., Mynatt, E. & Terry, M.A. (2001). Time Aura: Interfaces for Pacing. CHI'01, 144–151.
18. Occhialini, V., van Essen, H. & Eggen, B. (2011). Design and Evaluation of an Ambient Display to Support Time Management during Meetings. INTERACT'11, 263-280.
19. Office Remote. http://research.microsoft.com/en-us/projects/officeremote/
20. O'Leary, K., Wobbrock, J.O. & Riskin, E.A. (2013). Q-Methodology as a Research and Design Tool for HCI. CHI'13, 1941–1950.
21. Pecha Kucha 20x20. http://www.pechakucha.org/faq
22. Pousman, Z. & Stasko, J. (2006). A taxonomy of ambient information systems: 4 patterns of design. AVI'06, 67-74.
23. PQMethod. http://www.lrz.de/~schmolck/qmethod/
24. Prezi. http://prezi.com
25. Spicer, R., Lin, Y. R., Kelliher, A., Sundaram, H. (2012). NextSlidePlease: Authoring and delivering agile multimedia presentations. TOMCCAP, 8(4).
26. Tam, D., MacLean, K.E., McGrenere, J. & Kuchenbecker, K.J. (2013). The Design and Field Observation of a Haptic Notification System for Timing Awareness during Oral Presentations. CHI'13, 1689-1698.
27. Treisman, L. (1985). Preattentive processing in vision. Comp. Vision, Graphics, and Image Proc., 31(2), 156-177.
28. Trinh, H., Yatani, K. & Edge, D. (2014). PitchPerfect: Integrated Rehearsal Environment for Structured Presentation Preparation. CHI'14.
29. Warnock, D., McGee-Lennon, M.R., & Brewster, S. (2011). The impact of unwanted multimodal notifications. ICMI'11, 177-184.
30. Wisneski, C., Ishii, H., Dahley, A., Gorbet, N., Brave, S., Ullmer, B. & Yarin, P. (1998). Ambient Displays: Turning architectural space into an interface between people and digital information. CoBuild, Springer LNCS, 1370.
31. Zakay, D., & Block, R. A. (1997). Temporal cognition. Current Directions in Psychological Science. 6, 12-16.

Direct Manipulation Video Navigation on Touch Screens

Cuong Nguyen[1] **Yuzhen Niu**[2,1] **Feng Liu**[1]
[1]Portland State University [2]Fuzhou University
Portland, OR 97207-0751 USA Fuzhou, Fujian 350108, China
{cuong3,yuzhen,fliu}@cs.pdx.edu

(a) DMVN using a mouse (b) DMVN using a finger

Figure 1. Direct Manipulation Video Navigation (DMVN) using a mouse vs. a finger. With DMVN, a user can directly drag the car along its trajectory to the target location using a mouse as shown in (a). While a touch screen can fit DMVN naturally and enhance the directness, the fat finger problem with touch screens can make dragging the car difficult.

ABSTRACT
Direct Manipulation Video Navigation (DMVN) systems allow a user to directly drag an object of interest along its motion trajectory and have been shown effective for space-centric video browsing tasks. This paper designs touch-based interface techniques to support DMVN on touchscreen devices. While touch screens can suit DMVN systems naturally and enhance the directness during video navigation, the fat finger problems, such as precise selection and occlusion handling, must be properly addressed. In this paper, we discuss the effect of the fat finger problems on DMVN and develop three *touch-based object dragging techniques* for DMVN on touch screens, namely *Offset Drag*, *Window Drag*, and *Drag Anywhere*. We conduct user studies to evaluate our techniques as well as two baseline solutions on a smartphone and a desktop touch screen. Our studies show that two of our techniques can support DMVN on touch screen devices well and perform better than the baseline solutions.

Author Keywords
Video navigation; direct manipulation; mobile devices; touch screens.

ACM Classification Keywords
H.5.2 Information Interfaces and Presentation: User Interfaces

MobileHCI '14, September 23 - 26 2014, Toronto, ON, Canada
Copyright 2014 ACM 978-1-4503-3004-6/14/09...$15.00.
http://dx.doi.org/10.1145/2628363.2628365

INTRODUCTION
Capturing, sharing, and watching videos have now become common daily activities. To better support video navigation and browsing tasks, a variety of novel video browsing technologies have been developed [19, 21, 4, 15]. Among them, Direct Manipulation Video Navigation (DMVN) systems allow a user to navigate a video by directly dragging an object of interest along its motion trajectory, as shown in Figure 1 (a), and have been shown well suited for space-centric video navigation tasks [5, 7, 11, 12, 13, 14, 17].

Meanwhile, many of video-capable devices are now equipped with a touch screen, such as smart phones and tablets. DMVN systems can suit these touch-screen devices naturally. As is well known, touch-based interfaces allow a user to interact with an object directly on the screen without any extra input devices and thus reduce the gap between the user input and the system output [22]. For a DMVN system, allowing a user to directly interact with the object of interest can remove the need to use an extra input device like a mouse and further enhance the directness of the video navigation experience.

However, proper touch-based interfaces must be designed for DMVN. The fat finger problem [25] can severely compromise the performance of DMVN on touch screens, as shown in Figure 1 (b). When a user's finger occludes the content behind the finger, it becomes difficult for a user to precisely select an object of interest. A particularly unique challenge with a DMVN system is that the occlusion problem will prevent the user from receiving the feedback from the DMVN system such as the object location and contextual trajectory information, making it difficult to *drag the object* along its trajectory and to the desired location. To our best knowledge,

[1] `http://graphics.cs.pdx.edu/project/TouchDMVN/`

while various DMVN systems have been developed and some were experimented on touchscreen devices or provided an implementation for touchscreen devices, no touch-based interfaces, which are intended for DMVN systems and handle the fat finger problem, have been reported.

In this paper, we report our designs of touch-based interfaces for DMVN systems. We build upon previous research on precise selection techniques for touchscreen, such as Shift [29] and Offset Cursor [20, 23], and extend them to handle object manipulation in a DMVN system on touchscreen devices. Specifically, we design three *object dragging techniques* for touch-based DMVN interaction, including *Offset Drag*, *Window Drag*, and *Drag Anywhere*, which allow a user to drag an object of interest along its motion trajectory without suffering from the fat finger problem. We evaluate these techniques together with two baseline solutions in user studies on both a large desktop touch screen and a small touch screen on an Android smartphone. Our studies show that two of the three touch-based interfaces that we developed enable significantly better direct manipulation-based video navigation than the baseline solutions.

DMVN on Touch Screen

In our work, we implemented a standard DMVN system similar to what was discussed in [11]. To support direct object manipulation, we first used computer vision techniques, including optical flow [28] and feature tracking [24], to estimate the motion trajectories of the objects in an input video. After a user selects an object to manipulate, the object's trajectory is rendered on the screen to help a user drag the object spatially. When a user drags her finger on the screen, the system calculates and navigates to the video frame where the object is spatio-temporally closest to the user's pointer location. Thus the object of interest always follows the user's pointer, creating a feeling of direct manipulation during video navigation. More detail about the DMVN system can be found in [11].

DMVN consists of two steps: object selection and object dragging. On touchscreen devices, both steps can be difficult due to the fat finger problem, which happens when the finger is bigger than the object [25]. This leads to the precision and occlusion problem, compromising the user experience in manipulating a video on a touch screen. Existing methods for precise object selection on touch screens can be used to solve the problem of object selection [20, 23, 1, 3, 18, 29]. They, however, cannot handle object dragging. Below we discuss the effect of the precision and occlusion problem on DMVN, focusing on object dragging.

Precision

A large corpus of touch-based interface techniques have been developed to facilitate the target acquisition task on touch screens [1, 3, 18, 29]. Different from regular target selection tasks, interacting with a DMVN system requires a user to interact with the motion trajectory. In a DMVN system, the original finger contact point on the screen is mapped to the closest point on the trajectory, progressing the video to the corresponding frame in time. This mapping technique is similar to the Bubble Cursor method [8] where the nearest target around the cursor area is acquired.

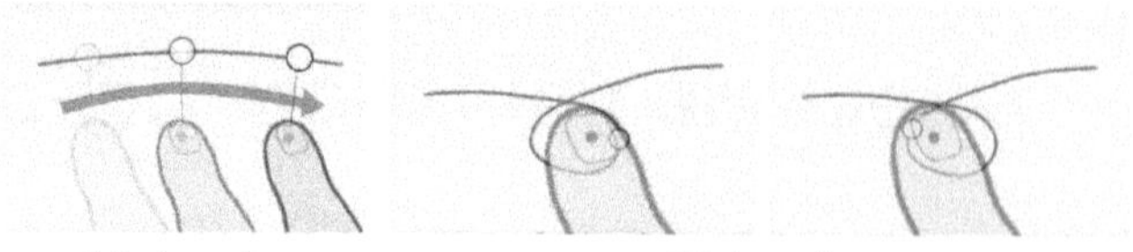

(a) dragging (b) jumping

Figure 2. The effect of the fat finger problem on DMVN. DMVN maps the finger touch point to its spatio-temporally nearest point. This works well for a simple trajectory as shown in (a). For a complex trajectory, the inaccuracy in dragging objects caused by the fat finger problem can make DMVN map the finger touch points to different segments of the trajectory and results in jumping.

Within this context, even if the finger contact point can be ambiguous, a user can easily drag the object along its motion trajectory without worrying about inaccurate selection. Figure 2 (a) illustrates this idea, even though it is difficult to select a specific frame with his finger, the object can still be dragged correctly until it reaches the desired frame. If the trajectory is simple enough, a user can also move her finger away from the object during dragging and still maintain a continuous video navigation while being able to observe the occluded target. This behavior is similar to MobileZoomSlider [10] which allows a user to move the cursor away to adjust the dragging speed. When the trajectory is complicated, such as when it forms a loop or an intersection, the inexact selection point of the finger may make the system accidentally map the touch point to a wrong trajectory segment, as shown in Figure 2 (b). While this problem can be alleviated with the temporal continuity constraint discussed in [11, 5], the same problem will still occur for some complicated trajectories.

Occlusion

Compared to the precision selection issue, occlusion from the fat finger problem downgrades the performance of DMVN on touchscreen devices even more. For space-centric video browsing tasks, a user needs to navigate to a frame with some specific visual properties. This requires a user to pay attention to not only the object that she is dragging, but also the motion trajectory and the video content as well. Due to occlusion, it is difficult for a user to make micro-adjustment for frame-accurate video navigation. When the local trajectory segment is occluded by the finger, in combination of its complex shape, and the ambiguity in selection points as mentioned above, the user is more likely to make an unexpected jump between nearby trajectory segments. Finally, the occluded video content prevents a user from observing and appreciating the video while navigating, compromising the user experience of DMVN.

RELATED WORK

Our work is directly related to research on direct manipulation video navigation and research to address the fat finger problem on touch screens.

Direct Manipulation Video Navigation

Direct manipulation video navigation systems allows for effective space-centric video browsing [5, 7, 11, 12, 13, 14, 17]. These systems estimate motion information using computer vision algorithms, such as optical flow [28], visualize the motion trajectory in the video display window, and allow a user to drag an object of interest along its motion trajectory. Among existing DMVN systems, PocketDragon from Karrer *et al.* was developed to run on Apple iPhone with multi-touch capability [12]. PocketDragon allows a user to navigate an object of interest by directly dragging the object using a finger directly on the screen. To address the occlusion problem when selecting the object of interest to drag, PocketDragon allows a user to pick the most dominant motion trajectory around the finger contact point. While this system provides a good attempt at developing a DMVN system for touchscreen mobile devices, it did not address the fat finger problem with touch screen. Recently, Karrer *et al.* conducted a user study to evaluate their DMVN system in handling spatial-temporal ambiguity problem using a touch screen [13]. Their system does not address the fat finger problem either. Instead, a stylus was provided for a user to manipulate an object of interest.

Precise Selection on Touch Screens

Previous work have been done to improve the selection precision on touch screen devices. Zooming techniques magnify the selection area when an object is very small [1, 3, 18] and can effectively improve the selection precision. These techniques, however, may not suit DMVN well. If we zoom back after selection, the fat finger problem affects dragging. If we do not zoom back and drag while scrolling/panning the screen, video content will move outside the screen. If we use fisheye view warping, the trajectory will be distorted and mislead dragging.

The control-display ratio can also be manipulated to improve the selection precision [1, 3]. These techniques allow a user to modify the control-display ratio - a mapping between the input movement and the system pointer movement. When the control-display ratio is smaller than 1, the pointer will move slower than the input finger. This has two advantages. First, because the pointer moves slower than the finger, the user finger does not occlude the pointer anymore. Second, the slow movement of the pointer allows a user to select a small object more accurately. Although these techniques have been shown effective for small target selection [1, 3], they were not designed for video object dragging in a DMVN system. These techniques either require additional widget manipulation, or need a user to focus on controlling the system pointer to acquire a fix target, which can be inconvenient for object dragging. Our *Drag Anywhere* technique is inspired by the advantages of the CD-ratio manipulation techniques. We map the finger dragging direction and acceleration to the arc-length distance of the motion trajectory. In this way, a user can control the object from anywhere on the screen by dragging her finger according to the motion trajectory.

Occlusion Handling on Touchscreen Devices

Offset cursor by [20, 23] addresses the occlusion problem by allowing a user to select an object without having to position the finger on top of it. When a user touches the interaction screen, this technique displays a cursor on top of the user finger. The orientation and distance between the cursor and the finger contact point are fixed. By maintaining contact with the touch screen, a user can navigate the cursor to the desired location and select the target using the take-off technique: selection is made after lifting the finger from the screen. Offset cursor cannot be directly applied to the task of dragging an object along its motion trajectory as the orientation and the offset distance cannot be dynamically adjusted. This is problematic for DMVN as a fixed orientation can make the finger occlude the motion trajectory when the cursor orientation is similar to the local motion trajectory. We extended the Offset Cursor technique and develop an *Offset Drag* technique for touch-based DMVN. *Offset Drag* allows a user to adjust the orientation and length of the offset cursor dynamically.

Shift addresses the occlusion problem by displaying the content occluded by the finger in a callout window in a non-occluded area [29]. A dash-line connecting the user finger to the center of the window indicates the current pointer location. A user can observe the occluded content in this window and adjust the selection. Shift also uses the take-off technique to trigger selection. It also determines whether it is necessary to escalate the window, allowing a user to use the direct touch technique for a large object. While Shift works well for object selection, it sometimes cannot support object dragging well. During dragging, a user needs to constantly receive feedback from the video content and the motion trajectory to decide where to go next. When the callout window size is fixed, it may not cover enough feedback information for a user to maintain a fluent dragging experience; otherwise a user might have to shift her/his attention from the callout window and the real motion trajectory, causing unnecessary re-orientation effort. Simply increasing the size of the window does not help but distracts the user even more. We design a *Window Drag* technique that changes the callout window size adaptively according to the current trajectory segment.

Specialized Hardware

Hardware-specific techniques have also been designed to address the finger occlusion problem. Back-of-device interaction techniques allow a user to interact with the content on the back of the device, avoiding occlusion completely [27, 31, 32, 2, 9]. A variety of devices have been explored. Wigdor *et al.* designed an interactive touch table that can receive touch inputs from both top and bottom surface [31]. LucidTouch and NanoTouch [30, 2] allow back-of-device interaction for tablet-size and very small-size devices. Back-of-device interaction has also been seen in commercial product such as *Sony PSP Vita* which features a rear touch pad. The recent developed NailDisplay [26] can show the visual content underneath the finger on a small display mounted on the finger. Although these techniques can handle the fat finger problem, they all require specific hardware support. This work addresses the fat finger problem in object dragging during video navigation on general-purpose touch screens.

DESIGN

DMVN consists of two steps: object selection and object dragging. We can use any of the above mentioned state-of-the-art precise selection techniques for the object selection step in DMVN. Thus, we assume that an object of interest has already been selected for manipulation. In this paper, we focus on object dragging and design *Offset Drag*, *Window Drag*,

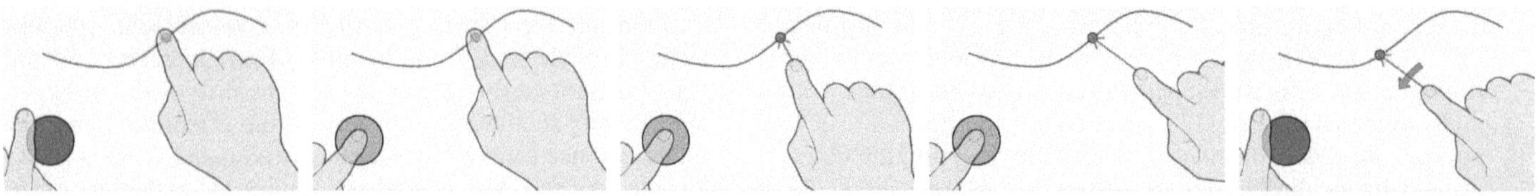

Figure 3. Offset Drag for DMVN. By default, Offset Drag works like direct dragging (a). To set up a cursor or change the cursor orientation/length, a user keeps the primary finger touching the object, and uses the secondary finger to press a button to trigger the cursor (b). By holding the secondary finger on the button on the screen, the user can move the primary finger away from the object to define the offset distance (c) and orientation (d). Once the cursor is defined, the user lifts the second finger and uses the primary finger to drag the object using the cursor (e).

and *Drag Anywhere* for non-occluding direct object manipulation/dragging for DMVN.

Design 1: Offset Drag

We first implemented the basic Offset Cursor technique [20, 23] to support our touch-based DMVN system. When a user touches the screen, we provide a cursor at a fixed distance above the finger's contact point. When triggered, the system takes the offset cursor location as input to find the next frame in the video. In this way, we allow dragging while a user maintains contact with the screen and moves the offset cursor along the motion trajectory. Take-off selection technique was not implemented since we did not need to perform object selection during dragging.

Offset Cursor is good at handling the occlusion problem because the user's finger does not need to be positioned on top of the object. However, this technique still has several limitations when it is applied to touch-based DMVN. First, as discussed in [29], a problem with the Offset Cursor technique is that the user is unable to aim for the actual target when they first interact with the device. When the offset cursor is triggered, it will point to the location above the user's finger, instead of the actual object location. This is problematic for DMVN when the motion trajectory is cluttered. If the cursor is triggered on a different trajectory segment nearby, the object may jump to that part, causing an unexpected scene jump. Second, for DMVN, precise dragging is not always required. Then the effort to trigger the offset cursor can delay navigation. Third, Offset Cursor does not allow a user to access some parts of the screen like the edges as discussed in in [29]. This is because the orientation and length of the offset cursor is fixed. As a result, edge and corner areas become difficult to reach. Moreover, when the cursor orientation is similar to the neighboring motion trajectory segment, only a very short segment ahead of the current position is shown and the rest is occluded by the finger, as shown in Figure 4 (b). This makes it difficult for a user to drag quickly.

To address these issues, we designed an extension of Offset Cursor that satisfies the following requirements,

1. A user should be able to offset the finger selection point to avoid occluding the object of interest.

2. A user should be able to adjust the orientation and length of the offset pointer dynamically.

3. A user needs to trigger the offset cursor only when needed.

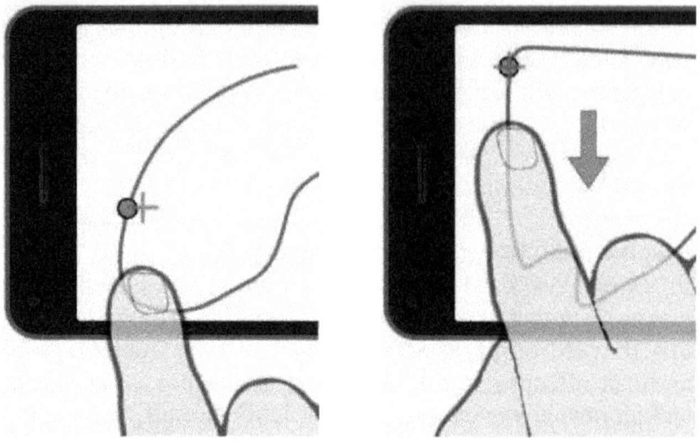

(a) Edge problem (b) Occlusion

Figure 4. Problem with Offset Cursor in a DMVN system.

We followed the design guidelines of Benko *et al.* [3] to design a bi-manual interaction technique for dragging object in DMVN using an offset cursor. We call it *Offset Drag*. Offset Drag allows a user to trigger the offset cursor only when needed. A user can also interactively adjust the offset cursor's orientation and length during video navigation to allow access to all screen regions and avoid occlusion with the neighboring trajectory segment.

Compared with Offset Cursor, Offset Drag has an extra trigger button, located at the bottom left corner of the screen, for a user to trigger and adjust the cursor. With Offset Drag, a user's primary finger is used as the main finger for dragging. By default, Offset Drag works like direct dragging. While the primary finger is on contact with the object, placing the secondary finger onto the trigger button will trigger a cursor. By holding the secondary finger on the screen, moving the primary finger away from the object will not move the object. Instead, by moving it away from the object, a user will be able to define the offset distance and orientation as illustrated in Figure 3. The cursor is always located at the current object location, and the system renders an arrow to depict the current offset distance. Offset Cursor rendered the cursor as a crosshair. We used an arrow instead to better depict the orientation of the cursor. To continue dragging, a user lifts her secondary finger from the screen. The dragging movement now will be offset with the newly defined offset cursor. Then Offset Drag works in the same way as Offset Cursor. Similarly, a user can dynamically adjust the cursor during navigation.

Design 2: Window Drag

Our next technique, *Window Drag*, is inspired by the Shift technique [29], which places a callout window near the finger

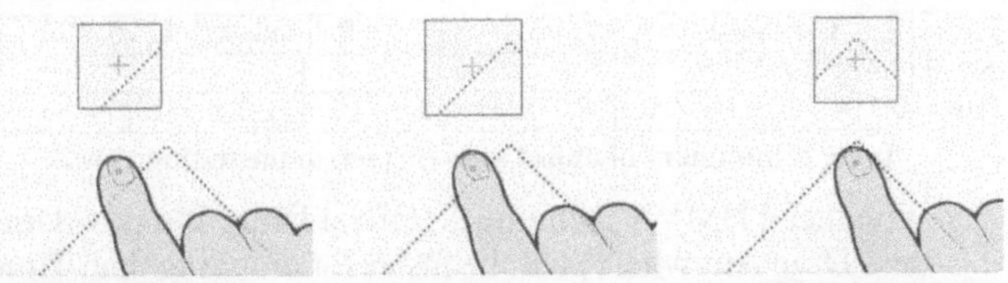

(a) Default size (b) New size (c) Default size

Figure 5. Adaptive window size for *Window Drag*. Two windows with the same size can cover different trajectory lengths. The trajectory segment in (a) is shorter than (c). We adaptively change the window size to maintain a consistent amount of information in the window. For example, we increase the window size from (a) to (b) so more information about the trajectory can be included.

to show a copy of the occluded area underneath the finger. The position of the callout window is calculated to prevent clipping by the screen edges. When a user places a finger on the touch screen, a callout window appears on top of the finger, showing the occluded area under the finger. A crosshair in the center of the window represents the current selection point. The window is displayed as long as a user finger is in contact with the screen. It follows the user's finger to provide additional support for the occluded content. With this window, a user is able to avoid the occlusion problem by observing the content underneath and adjust the current selection during navigation. When a user releases the finger from the touch screen, the window disappears. Note that we made the content inside the callout window fully opaque so that it does not blend into the background and distract the user.

By default, we picked the window size to be slightly larger than the average fingertip size so that it can cover a part of the object and the motion trajectory segment around the object at the current position. For example, the default window size for Google Nexus 4 is $20mm \times 20mm$. The user only needs to observe a part of the motion trajectory around the object to decide where to move next.

Our pilot study showed that this technique allows a user to navigate along the motion trajectory very accurately. However, Shift was originally designed to address the occlusion problem for target acquisition, where the fixed target is usually the main concern of a user. In a DMVN system, in order to drag an object along its motion trajectory, a user needs to pay attention to the shape of the trajectory to follow it. While Shift can display a part of the trajectory in its callout window, due to the fixed window size, there is no guarantee that it can display a consistent amount of motion trajectory segment for a user to navigate the video. Figure 5 shows an example where two trajectory segments with different length are displayed in the same-size windows. Increasing the window size can increase the amount of motion trajectory inside the window and thus reduce the reorientation cost. But a large window is distracting as it occludes too much video content.

We developed a Window Drag technique to address this problem by adaptively changing the window size based on the local motion trajectory information. Window Drag finds such a callout window that contains a trajectory segment that covers at least 20 frames. If the default window does not cover such a trajectory segment, we expand the window to cover it.

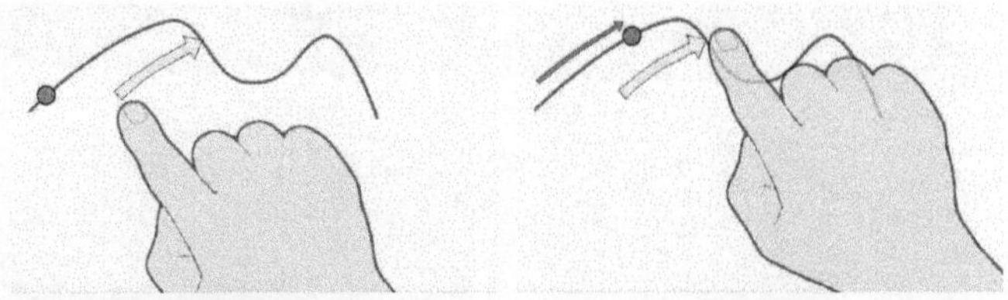

(a) Start (b) End

Figure 6. Drag Anywhere for DMVN. Drag Anywhere allows a user to drag on any location and maps the user drag to the object trajectory.

Design 3: Drag Anywhere

When interacting with a touchscreen device, there are two different mapping modes: direct and indirect [16]. Direct mapping requires the pointer to be positioned directly under the finger, which leads to the fat finger problem. The indirect mapping, in contrast, does not require the pointer to be under the finger. Although not as intuitive as direct mapping, indirect touch clearly does not suffer from the occlusion problem. Previous research on touchscreen interaction [1, 3, 6] has already explored indirect mapping interaction techniques that adjust the control-display ratio to increase or decrease the pointer speed. This has been shown to improve precision in target acquisition tasks.

Inspired by Moscovich and Hughes [16], we designed an indirect mapping navigation technique for our touch-based DMVN system. Moscovich and Hughes argued that designing indirect mapping techniques needs to ensure the perceptuomotor compatibility of the interaction task, which is the degree to which the user's physical actions are similar to the system's visual feedback. Interestingly, this is also the case for designing the DMVN interface. As Dragicevic *et al.* mentioned, the directness of a DMVN interface also depends on the perceptuomotor compatibility [5].

Thus, when a user drags on the touch screen, we map the finger dragging motion to the object trajectory, as shown in Figure 6. Specifically, we compare the finger dragging direction to the tangent of the motion trajectory at the object's position to determine whether the object should be moving forward or backward in time. Then we map the dragging distance to the arc-length of the trajectory to determine how far the object should move along the trajectory. By using the orientation and distance as the mapping parameters, we ensure that the dragging movement closely matches the object movement, thus resulting in a smooth dragging experience without having to put the finger on top of the object.

One drawback of this technique is that a user is unable to quickly skim through the video, a common task in video browsing. This is because the object moves exactly the same distance as the user pointer. We overcome this problem by adaptively adjusting the CD ratio between the finger and the object of interest. This is similar to the classic "mouse acceleration" interface seen in Apple Mac Operating System. When a user moves the finger more quickly, the dragging distance is made larger so that the object can travel quicker along the motion trajectory. Our system keeps track of the finger dragging speed and uses this speed to compute a magnification coefficient to modulate the dragging distance. Our

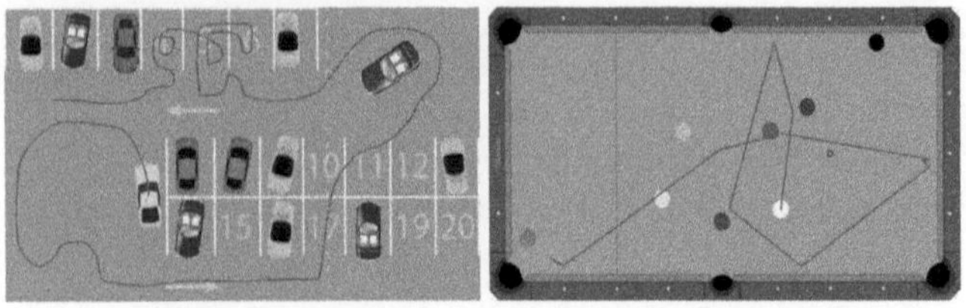

Figure 7. Sample frames of testing videos with trajectories.

system uses the following function to compute the magnification coefficient

$$m = \sqrt{s * a + 1}, \quad (1)$$

where m is the magnification coefficient for the dragging distance, s is the dragging speed, and a is a parameter that be adjusted by a user to control the scaling factor. Our pilot study shows that for the smartphone (Google Nexus 4) and the desktop touch-screen, good values for a are 0.25 and 6.67 respectively.

EXPERIMENTAL EVALUATION

We conducted a user study to evaluate our touch-based DMVN techniques: *Offset Drag*, *Window Drag*, and *Drag Anywhere* on both a large and small touch screen. Our study asked participants to perform spatial video navigation tasks: locate a frame with some specific visual event in a video.

For the baseline techniques, we used the basic DMVN system and the standard timeline slider. For simplicity, we use DMVN and Timeline to denote these two techniques, respectively. DMVN interprets the finger contact point as the pointer location and thus provides no additional support to handle the fat finger problem. Timeline is similar to the timeline interface used in YouTube Video Player on iPhone. It allows a user to offset the cursor on the timeline to address the occlusion problem. We want to understand the performance of DMVN-based techniques against Timeline for space-centric video navigation tasks on touchscreen devices. Early studies have shown that DMVN performs better than the standard timeline slider for space-centric tasks using a mouse or stylus as input; however, no study between them has been reported that directly uses a finger as input on touchscreen devices.

Note, the first step of direct manipulation video navigation is to select an object of interest to manipulate. As precise object selection has been well studied in previous research, we focus on dynamic object dragging during video navigation. Accordingly, an object of interest has already been selected for a user to manipulate beforehand. In the study, we only show the trajectory of the selected object and map the pointer movement to the nearest position on the trajectory.

We hypothesized that:

1. Techniques that can handle the occlusion problem (Timeline, Offset Drag, Window Drag, and Drag Anywhere) would outperform the basic DMVN for small-size objects.
2. The basic DMVN system would perform similarly to the DMVN systems supported by fat finger problem-handling techniques (Offset Drag, Window Drag, and Drag Anywhere) for big objects.

Screen	Car videos (V1, V2, V3)			Ball videos(V4, V5, V6)		
Small	1.4×3.2	5.8×12.8	9.7×21.3	1.5×1.5	9.6×9.6	15.5×15.5
Large	3.1×7.3	9.4×20.8	18.7×41.6	2.5×2.5	11.3×11.3	50.2×50.2

Table 1. Summary of object sizes (in *mm*) in the testing videos.

3. Enhanced DMVN techniques (Offset Drag, Window Drag, and Drag Anywhere) will be faster for dragging than Timeline for space-centric tasks on touch screen devices.

Apparatus

We used a large touchscreen display and a smartphone equipped with a touch screen. For the large display, we used a 23-inch Acer T232HL bmidz capacitive touch screen monitor. The monitor has a 1920×1080 resolution (95.8 pixels per inch). The size of each pixel is about 0.26 *mm*. We take a regular finger size to be 15 *mm* wide [3], which is about 58 pixels on this monitor. For the small display, we used a Google Nexus 4 smartphone running Android 4.3.3. This smartphone comes with a capacitive touch screen. Its active display area resolution is 1280×768 (320 pixels per inch). The size of a pixel is roughly 0.08 *mm*. The width of a regular finger on this small display is about 188 pixels.

Task and Stimuli

For each touch screen, we ask a participant to perform six tasks, each involving a different video. We then have six videos for each display. These six videos cover three object sizes (small, medium, large) and two types of scene content (parking lot and pool ball). The object motion for the parking lot videos is complex and that for the ball videos is simple, as shown in Figure 7. Since the two touch screens have different resolutions, the six videos used for the big screen are different from those for the small screen. We report the object sizes of these videos for each screen in Table 1. The videos range from 305 to 900 frames (10.2 to 30.0 seconds) and were shown at a display window of 1280×768 pixels on both screens. In each task, a participant was asked to use each of the five techniques to navigate a given video and locate a target frame with specific visual content as fast and as accurate as possible. Like the previous research [5], the starting frame in each task is the first frame.

Experimental Setup

There were 15 participants in our study, including 6 female and 9 male current or former students in our university. These participants come from a range of academic departments, including Computer Science, Business, Arts, Architecture, etc. The ages of these participants range from 20 to 30 years. All of them were familiar with touchscreen devices and were right handed. One participant was left handed but preferred to use his right hand for everyday work. We conducted a within-subject study with these users. We tested 5 techniques (Timeline, DMVN, Offset Drag, Window Drag, Drag Anywhere), 2 devices (large and small display), and 6 tasks. This resulted in a total of 60 data points per user.

Our study consisted of two stages. Each participant first performed all the tasks on one screen and then performed the tasks on the other screen. To reduce the carry over effect, after a participant finished studies on one screen, we let the participant rest for around 10 minutes. We used a 2×2 latin square to counterbalance the study order of the large screen and small screen. At each stage, a participant performed the same task using the above mentioned five techniques. In order to reduce the learning effect, we counterbalanced the order of the techniques using a 5 × 5 latin square.

For each task, a participant watched the video twice and was shown the target frame together with the textual instruction to understand the task beforehand. The participant was given a maximal navigation time to finish the task. This maximal navigation time was set to be 2 times of the video length. The task session terminated if the participant successfully achieved the goal or ran out of time. We added a button in our testing interface to allow the participant to submit the navigation result. If the right frame was not reached, the participant was alerted to refine the navigation result by the system. The timer started counting when the participant first touched the screen and stopped counting when the submit button got hit and the right frame was reached. If a participant could not finish the task within the given time, we took the given maximal navigation time as the actual navigation time. We recorded not only the overall navigation time, but also the time a user took to reach the pre-defined neighborhood of the target frame, and the micro-navigation time a user spent inside the neighborhood around the target frame. The target neighborhood was defined to be slightly larger than a typical finger size. Specifically, the neighborhood radii for the small screen and big screen were 8 *mm* and 13 *mm*, respectively.

Results

In our studies, all the participants successfully finished the navigation tasks on the large screen. On the small screen, 4 participants failed to reach the target frame within the given time on Video 1 using DMVN, 1 participant failed on Video 2 using DMVN, 1 participant failed on Video 3 using Timeline, and 2 participants failed on Video 4 using DMVN. We analyzed the temporal measurements with repeated measures ANOVA analysis and pairwise comparisons using t-tests with Bonferroni correction for post-hoc analysis.

Overall Navigation Time

We conducted one-way ANOVA analysis to test whether different methods result in different overall navigation times on both the large and small screen and found a significant effect of method on overall navigation time on both the large screen ($F(4, 56) = 94.13$, $p < 0.001$) and small screen ($F(4, 56) = 16.74$, $p < 0.001$). Figure 8 provides a summary of the performance analysis with respect to the overall navigation time for each of the five techniques. According to the navigation time, the relative performance between (basic) DMVN and Timeline method depends on the object size. On the small screen, DMVN actually took participants longer than Timeline on the small touch screen when the object was significantly smaller than the finger. According to the feedback from the participants, occlusion from the fat finger problem made it difficult for them to navigate to the exact location. When the object was big, DMVN then performed better than Timeline on the small screen. For all the videos on the large screen, they were longer than those on the small screen. At the same time, their objects are larger, as reported

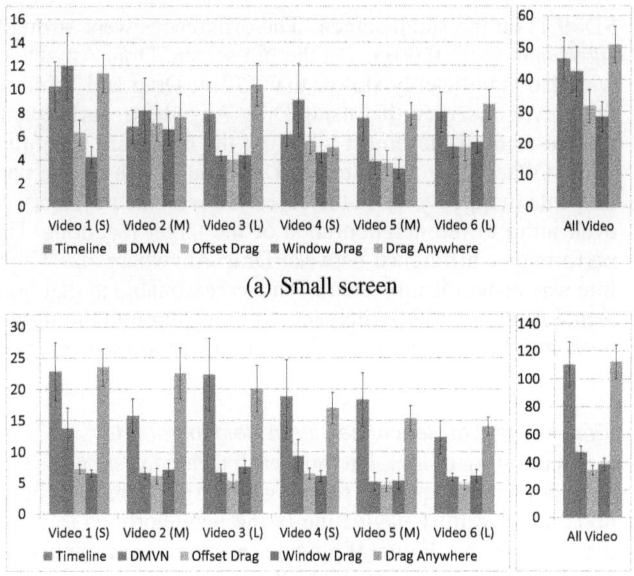

(a) Small screen

(b) Large screen

Figure 8. Navigation time summary (seconds). Left: the average navigation time and 95% confidence interval on each video. Right: the sum of the navigation time on all the six videos for each technique.

in Table 1. As we will discuss in detail in the next subsection, the performance of DMVN, particularly considering the time to reach the neighborhood of the target location, depends less on the video length than Timeline. Then for all the videos on the large screen, DMVN was consistently faster. Looking at the sum of the navigation time on the large screen, the mean times for DMVN and Timeline were 47.1 seconds (SD=9.0) and 110.1 seconds (SD=32.5), respectively. The difference between DMVN and Timeline was strongly significant ($p < 0.001$).

The relative performance between two of our extended DMVN methods (Offset Drag and Window Drag) and DMVN also depended on the object size. When the object was small, Offset Drag and Window Drag could improve DMVN. For example, the average navigation times for DMVN, Offset Drag, and Window Drag for the small object size video (Video 1 on the small screen) were 12.0 seconds (SD=5.5), 6.3 seconds (SD=2.1), and 4.2 seconds (SD=1.8). The difference between DMVN and Offset Drag were strongly significant ($p < 0.001$), so was the difference between DMVN and Window Drag. When the object sizes were comparable to or bigger than the finger size, such as those in Video 3 and 6 on both screens, these three methods performed similarly and their differences were not significant.

On both the small and large screen, Offset Drag was slower than Window Drag when the object was small. We observe that when the object was small, participants tended to use the cursor, which took some time to first set up the cursor. In contrast, Window Drag did not have this cost. When the object became large, Offset Drag was faster. The differences between these two techniques were insignificant in both cases.

According to the sum of the navigation time, Drag Anywhere (M= 50.9, SD=11.3) performed consistently worse than both Offset Drag (M=31.7, SD=10.2) and Window Drag (M=28.3,

SD=9.1) on the small screen. The differences were strongly significant ($p < 0.001$). On the big screen, Drag Anywhere was also significantly slower than Offset Drag and Window Drag. We observed that using Drag Anywhere, participants needed to drag the object all along the trajectory carefully, while Offset Drag and Window Drag could both enable participants to quickly move the object through the trajectory or even jump to the neighborhood of the target location. The performance difference between Drag Anywhere and Timeline was insignificantly small. This is reasonable in that both techniques required participants to move through the trajectory until the neighborhood of the target location was reached.

Time Needed to Reach the Target Neighborhood

It is interesting to look into how each technique supports two navigation tasks: quickly reaching the target frame neighborhood and carefully navigating in the neighborhood to reach the target frame. Figure 9 provides a summary of the performance analysis with respect to the time needed to reach the neighborhood of the target frame for all the five techniques. The neighborhood size is 100 pixels (8 *mm*) and 50 pixels (13 *mm*) for the tasks on the small screen and the large screen, respectively. The ANOVA analysis found a significant effect of method on the time needed to reach the target neighborhood on both the large screen ($F(4, 56) = 111.2$, $p < 0.001$) and small screen ($F(4, 56) = 45.58$, $p < 0.001$).

The three variations of the DMVN techniques, including DMVN, Offset Drag, and Window Drag, enabled a participant to quickly navigate to the neighborhood of the target location. For all the videos on both the small and large screen, these three techniques consistently took a participant around one second to reach the target neighborhood. This clearly showed the advantage of DMVN that allows for quickly dragging an object of interest to the target neighborhood.

The performance of Timeline depended on the temporal location of the target. If the target was temporally close to the starting point, such as those in Video 2 and 4 on the small screen, it took comparable time to the three DMVN methods, as shown in Figure 9. Otherwise, it took much longer to reach the neighborhood. For example, the time differences between Timeline and any DMVN methods were strongly significant on Video 1, 5, 6 on the small screen and Video 5 and 6 on the large screen ($p < 0.001$).

Drag Anywhere required a participant to literally go through the trajectory from the starting point until the target neighborhood was reached. When the spatial arc distance along the trajectory between the target location and the starting point was large, it took Drag Anywhere a long time to reach the target neighborhood. The time differences between each of the three other DMVN techniques (DMVN, Offset Drag, and Window Drag) and Drag Anywhere were all strongly significant with $p < 0.001$ according to the sum of the time needed to reach the target neighborhood, as shown in Figure 9. During the study, we also observed that when the trajectory was straight, participants could quickly move along the trajectory using Drag Anywhere by either flicking on the touch screen very frequently or using a quick long-range dragging action.

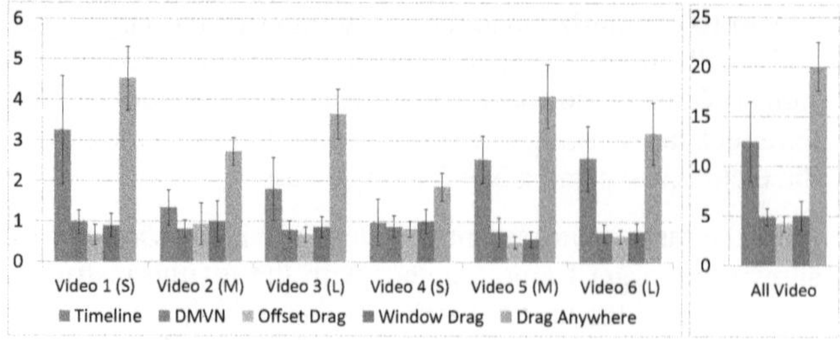

(a) Small screen

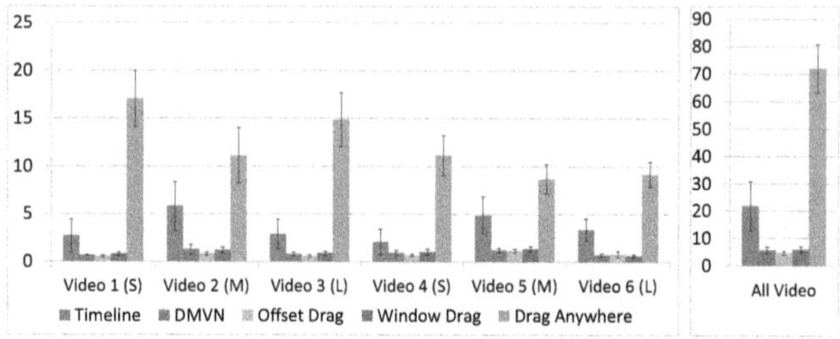

(b) Large screen

Figure 9. Time needed to reach the target neighborhood (seconds). Left: the average time and 95% confidence interval on each video. Right: the sum of the time on all the six videos for each technique.

But around the sharp corners, the participants often got stuck and sometimes even navigated in the opposite direction.

Micro-navigation Time in the Target Neighborhood

We are also interested in how each technique supports a user to perform micro-navigation in the neighborhood of the target frame. Figure 10 provides a summary of the performance analysis with respect to the time needed for micro-navigation in the target neighborhood. The ANOVA analysis found a significant effect of method on the micro-navigation time in the target neighborhood on both the large screen ($F(4, 56) = 50.6$, $p < 0.001$) and small screen ($F(4, 56) = 7.367$, $p < 0.001$).

When the object was small, it took participants longer to navigate to the final target location using DMVN than Timeline. For example, the object in Video 1 on the small screen was very small ($1.4 \times 3.2mm^2$), DMVN (M=11.0, SD=5.7) was significantly slower than Timeline (M=7.0, SD=3.2). The difference was significant ($p = 0.02$). Participants complained that it was difficult to use DMVN for micro-navigation due to the finger occlusion. For videos with big objects, such as V3, V5 and V6 on the small screen, DMVN performed better than Timeline. According to the sum of the micro-navigation time in the target neighborhood, DMVN (M=41.5, SD=8.2) was faster than Timeline (M=88.4, SD=29.7) with $p < 0.001$ on the large screen. While the objects in V1 and V4 on the large screen were smaller than the finger and the occlusion still compromised the user performance using DMVN, Timeline on the big screen caused participants to switch their attention frequently between the timeline and the object they were dragging according to their feedback after the study. This re-orientation cost compromised the user performance with Timeline. Besides, participants also reported that when they were dragging the timeline slowly and carefully, the friction between their fingers and the (big) touch screen often prevented them from smoothly and continuously navigating the video at small steps. On the small touch screen on the smartphone, the friction was less an issue.

As shown in Figure 10, Offset Drag and Window Drag could both improve DMVN on videos with small objects, such as V1 and V4 on the small screen and V1 on the large screen. The time differences between these two techniques and DMVN on these videos were significant ($p < 0.05$). For videos with big objects that are comparable or larger than the finger, such as V3 and V6 on both screens, these three techniques performed similarly.

According to the sum of the micro-navigation time as shown in Figure 10, Drag Anywhere took less time than DMVN and Timeline, and took more time than Offset Drag and Window Drag on both screens. The time differences between Drag Anywhere and the others were not significant except that between Drag Anywhere and Timeline on the big screen. Looking at the data on each video, the performance of Drag Anywhere for micro-navigation varied and was highly dependent on individual video property. If the trajectory in the target neighborhood was smooth, users actually reported Drag Anywhere was very helpful as it did not have the occlusion problem, required no extra widget, and allowed users to drag on any location that they felt comfortable. In practice, a user can drag in an area which is close to the object, having the feeling of directness without any occlusion, distraction from extra widgets, or the re-orientation cost. However, when the trajectory has a sharp angle or a high curvature, Drag Anywhere often confused participants by accidently moving to the wrong direction. In many of the testing videos, the object trajectories were very complex, which contributed to the relative poor performance of Drag Anywhere compared to Offset Drag and Window Drag.

Summary

DMVN and two of our enhanced DMVN techniques (Offset Drag and Window Drag) can quickly navigate to the neighborhood of the target location without regarding to the object size. When the object is small, the occlusion problem compromises the performance of the basic DMVN for micro-navigation tasks. Offset Drag and Window Drag can effectively handle the occlusion problem. Overall, Offset Drag and Window Drag can better support space-centric video navigation tasks than Timeline for both small and big objects. In contrast, the basic DMVN method is helpful to the space-centric tasks only for videos with big objects. A common concern with Window Drag from participants is that the call-out window is sometimes distracting.

The performance of Drag Anywhere depends on the trajectory shape and the distance between the target location and the starting point. Around the trajectory segment that has a high curvature or sharp angle, Drag Anywhere is not convenient for users to drag an object. Accordingly, when the target is faraway from the starting point, Drag Anywhere cannot well support quick navigation to the target neighborhood as a user needs to literally move the object through the trajectory until reaching the target location. For a simple trajectory, Drag Anywhere can support quick navigation well. Participants also reported that Drag Anywhere has advantages, such as handling occlusion without any extra widget and allowing for dragging at any location on the screen.

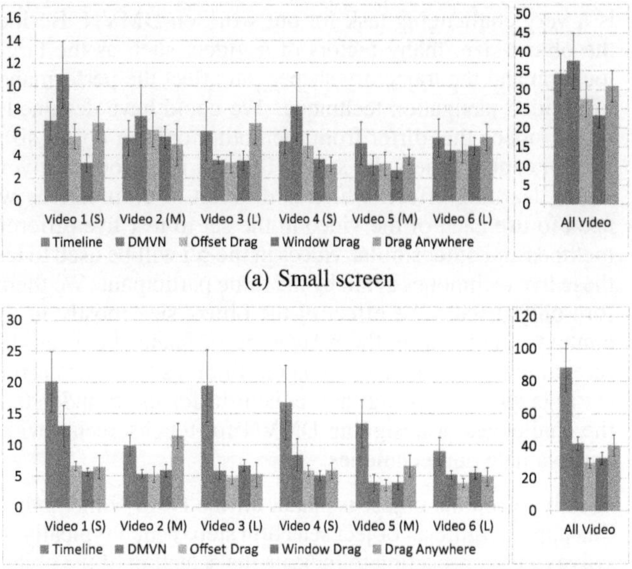

(a) Small screen

(b) Large screen

Figure 10. Micro-navigation time in the target neighborhood (seconds). Left: the average time and 95% confidence interval on each video. Right: the sum of the time on all the six videos for each technique.

Discussion

We would like to note that this paper only studied the performance of each method for object dragging, although DMVN consists of two steps, object selection and dragging. As object selection on touch screens has been well studied, our study omitted this step. Although it will be certainly helpful to involve the object selection step in our studies, we feel that skipping this selection step will not severely jeopardize our study as all the DMVN methods covered in this paper require this step, which can be achieved using any of the state of the art precise selection methods. Thus our conclusion from this study can be applied to the complete DMVN procedures. Meanwhile, we need to clarify that the comparisons between DMVN and Timeline are affected by this omission, as Timeline does not require an object to be selected at all for navigation. We considered this affect during our design of this study and chosen our current design for the following reasons. First, object dragging is a unique problem of DMVN. Therefore, we wanted to focus on this step and make this already complex study controllable. We can borrow from the previous research for object selection performance analysis if needed. Second, this omission will not affect the comparison between different DMVN methods at all. Third, object dragging typically contributes to the majority of time cost of a DMVN task. So in general, our conclusion is still valid between the comparison between DMVN and Timeline although for some particular videos, the results for object dragging may have to be revised to apply to the whole DMVN procedure.

It could also have been nice that we could provide a performance curve that shows the effect of the object size on each individual technique in our study, like those in previous work on precise selection techniques. However, we found that this is a very challenging task for our work on DMVN. Besides the object size, many factors of a video, such as the target location and the trajectory shape, can affect the performance of a video navigation technique. We could have designed a set of videos that differ from each other only in object sizes while keeping others the same. But it will introduce a very strong learning effect, which is difficult to eliminate as we need to use each of the video in the set to test five different methods and other similar videos in the set will be used to test these five techniques again by the same participant. We therefore only discuss the effect of the object size mostly in the context of comparing the relative performance between different methods and we feel that our findings from the current study is still interesting, and is helpful for us to understand the challenges of designing DMVN for touchscreen devices and evaluate our techniques.

Finally, when the object is small, all the DMVN methods in this paper require an object selection step, which typically involves a take-off action to indicate the selection of the object. This breaks DMVN into two separate steps and comprises the directness of DMVN. In future, we plan to eliminate this take-off action and combine object selection and dragging into a single continuous procedure to make DMVN smoother.

CONCLUSION

This paper discussed the effects of the fat finger problem on DMVN systems for touchscreen devices and developed three touch-based interface techniques to support DMVN, including Offset Drag, Window Drag, and Drag Anywhere. Our study showed that Offset Drag and Window Drag could effectively support DMVN on touchscreen devices and enable DMVN to outperform the traditional timeline based video navigation method for space-centric video browsing tasks. While Drag Anywhere did not perform as well as the other two techniques, it offered a few encouraging features.

Acknowledgments. The video and images in this paper are used from YouTube user MSPDawgs, Flickr user John Baer, Wikimedia Commons under Creative Commons licenses and from public domain (http://openclipart.org). This work was supported in part by NSF grants IIS-1344163 and CNS-1205746. Yuzhen Niu was supported by NSFC 61300102.

REFERENCES

1. Albinsson, P.-A., and Zhai, S. High precision touch screen interaction. In *ACM CHI* (2003), 105–112.
2. Baudisch, P., and Chu, G. Back-of-device interaction allows creating very small touch devices. In *ACM CHI* (2009), 1923–1932.
3. Benko, H., Wilson, A. D., and Baudisch, P. Precise selection techniques for multi-touch screens. In *ACM CHI* (2006), 1263–1272.
4. Cheng, K.-Y., Luo, S.-J., Chen, B.-Y., and Chu, H.-H. Smartplayer: user-centric video fast-forwarding. In *ACM CHI* (2009), 789–798.
5. Dragicevic, P., Ramos, G., Bibliowitcz, J., Nowrouzezahrai, D., Balakrishnan, R., and Singh, K. Video browsing by direct manipulation. In *ACM CHI* (2008), 237–246.
6. Forlines, C., Vogel, D., and Balakrishnan, R. Hybridpointing: fluid switching between absolute and relative pointing with a direct input device. In *ACM UIST* (2006), 211–220.
7. Goldman, D. B., Gonterman, C., Curless, B., Salesin, D., and Seitz, S. M. Video object annotation, navigation, and composition. In *ACM UIST* (2008), 3–12.
8. Grossman, T., and Balakrishnan, R. The bubble cursor: enhancing target acquisition by dynamic resizing of the cursor's activation area. In *ACM CHI* (2005), 281–290.
9. Hasan, K., Yang, X.-D., Liang, H.-N., and Irani, P. How to position the cursor?: an exploration of absolute and relative cursor positioning for back-of-device input. In *ACM MobileHCI* (2012), 103–112.
10. Hürst, W., Götz, G., and Welte, M. Interactive video browsing on mobile devices. In *ACM Multimedia* (2007), 247–256.
11. Karrer, T., Weiss, M., Lee, E., and Borchers, J. Dragon: a direct manipulation interface for frame-accurate in-scene video navigation. In *ACM CHI* (2008), 247–250.
12. Karrer, T., Wittenhagen, M., and Borchers, J. Pocketdragon: a direct manipulation video navigation interface for mobile devices. In *MobileHCI* (2009), 47:1–47:3.
13. Karrer, T., Wittenhagen, M., and Borchers, J. Draglocks: handling temporal ambiguities in direct manipulation video navigation. In *ACM CHI* (2012), 623–626.
14. Kimber, D., Dunnigan, T., Girgensohn, A., III, F. M. S., Turner, T., and Yang, T. Trailblazing: Video playback control by direct object manipulation. In *IEEE ICME* (2007), 1015–1018.
15. Matejka, J., Grossman, T., and Fitzmaurice, G. Swifter: improved online video scrubbing. In *ACM CHI* (2013).
16. Moscovich, T., and Hughes, J. F. Indirect mappings of multi-touch input using one and two hands. In *ACM CHI* (2008), 1275–1284.
17. Nguyen, C., Niu, Y., and Liu, F. Direct manipulation video navigation in 3d. In *ACM CHI* (2013), 1169–1172.
18. Olwal, A., and Feiner, S. Rubbing the fisheye: Precise touch-screen interaction with gestures and fisheye views. In *ACM UIST* (2003), 83–84.
19. Pongnumkul, S., Wang, J., and Cohen, M. Creating map-based storyboards for browsing tour videos. In *ACM UIST* (2008), 13–22.
20. Potter, R. L., Weldon, L. J., and Shneiderman, B. Improving the accuracy of touch screens: an experimental evaluation of three strategies. In *ACM CHI* (1988), 27–32.
21. Ramos, G., and Balakrishnan, R. Fluid interaction techniques for the control and annotation of digital video. In *ACM UIST* (2003), 105–114.
22. Sears, A., Plaisant, C., and Shneiderman, B. Advances in human-computer interaction (vol. 3). 1992, ch. A new era for high precision touchscreens, 1–33.
23. Sears, A., and Shneiderman, B. High precision touchscreens: design strategies and comparisons with a mouse. *Int. J. Man-Mach. Stud.* (1991), 593–613.
24. Shi, J., and Tomasi, C. Good features to track. In *IEEE CVPR* (1994), 593–600.
25. Siek, K. A., Rogers, Y., and Connelly, K. H. Fat finger worries: how older and younger users physically interact with pdas. In *Proceedings of the 2005 IFIP TC13 international conference on Human-Computer Interaction*, INTERACT'05 (2005), 267–280.
26. Su, C.-H., Chan, L., Weng, C.-T., Liang, R.-H., Cheng, K.-Y., and Chen, B.-Y. Naildisplay: bringing an always available visual display to fingertips. In *ACM CHI* (2013), 1461–1464.
27. Sugimoto, M., and Hiroki, K. Hybridtouch: an intuitive manipulation technique for pdas using their front and rear surfaces. In *ACM MobileHCI* (2006), 137–140.
28. Sun, D., Roth, S., and Black, M. Secrets of optical flow estimation and their principles. In *IEEE CVPR* (2010).
29. Vogel, D., and Baudisch, P. Shift: a technique for operating pen-based interfaces using touch. In *ACM CHI* (2007), 657–666.
30. Wigdor, D., Forlines, C., Baudisch, P., Barnwell, J., and Shen, C. Lucid touch: a see-through mobile device. In *ACM UIST* (2007), 269–278.
31. Wigdor, D., Leigh, D., Forlines, C., Shipman, S., Barnwell, J., Balakrishnan, R., and Shen, C. Under the table interaction. In *ACM UIST* (2006), 259–268.
32. Wobbrock, J. O., Myers, B. A., and Aung, H. H. The performance of hand postures in front- and back-of-device interaction for mobile computing. *Int. J. Hum.-Comput. Stud.* (2008), 857–875.

Enhancing KLM (Keystroke-Level Model) to Fit Touch Screen Mobile Devices

Karim El Batran
Computer and Information Sciences,
University of Strathclyde
Richmond St, Glasgow, G1 1XH, Scotland, UK.
karim.el-batran@strath.ac.uk

Mark D. Dunlop
Computer and Information Sciences,
University of Strathclyde
Richmond St, Glasgow, G1 1XH, Scotland, UK.
Mark.Dunlop@strath.ac.uk

ABSTRACT
This short paper introduces an enhancement to the Keystroke-Level Model (KLM) by extending it with three new operators to describe interactions on mobile touchscreen devices. Based on Fitts's Law we modelled a performance measure estimate equation for each common touch screen interaction. Three prototypes were developed to serve as a test environment in which to validate Fitts's equations and estimate the parameters for these interactions. A total of 3090 observations were made with a total of 51 users. While the studies confirmed each interaction fitted well to Fitts's Law for most interactions, it was noticed that Fitts's Law does not fit well for interactions with an Index of Difficulty exceeding 4 bits, highlighting a possible maximum comfortable stretch. Based on results, the following approximate movement times for KLM are suggested: 70ms for a short untargeted swipe, 200ms for a half-screen sized zoom, and 80ms for an icon pointing from a home position. These results could be used by developers of mobile phone and tablet applications to describe tasks as a sequence of the operators used and to predict user interaction times prior to creating prototypes.

Author Keywords
Quantitative prediction model; KLM (Keystroke-Level Model); GOMS; Fitts's Law; touch screen interaction.

ACM Classification Keywords
H.5.2 User Interfaces: Input devices and strategies.

General Terms
Design; Measurement.

INTRODUCTION
Quantitative prediction models, such as GOMS (Goals, Operators, Methods, and Selection rules) and KLM (Keystroke-Level Model) have been shown to be useful tools in modeling interaction and in deciding between, and filtering out designs (e.g. [1]). KLM is used to estimate the time taken to complete simple data input tasks by combining small timing constants. On physical-key devices it has been widely used to predict task times (e.g. text entry for Korean Language [10], Text Entry Speed on 12-button Phone Keypads [7] etc.).

MobileHCI '14, September 23 – 26, 2014, Toronto, ON, Canada
Copyright 2014 ACM 978-1-4503-3004-6/14/09...$15.00.
http://dx.doi.org/10.1145/2628363.2628385

Many enhancements to KLM have been proposed in the literature to be able to evaluate different techniques. However, there has been little research that improves user behavior modeling techniques to estimate the time taken to achieve common interactions performed on mobile touchscreen devices. In this paper we report our work on enhancing KLM by extending it with three new operators. In this short paper we report our investigation into modeling three interactions performed on mobile devices and tablets using KLM. Our model is based on suggested times derived from Fitts's Law modelling and analysis of how well these interactions fit Fitts's Law. We believe this gives an enhancement for developers of smart-phone and tablet applications to predict user interaction times without even needing to create prototypes.

KLM-GOMS MODEL
KLM was introduced as part of the wider GOMS-related work of Card, Moran, and Newell on modelling and quantitatively predicting the skilled and error free performance of users interacting with a text editor [1]. KLM is usually applied in situations that require minimal focussed, scripted interaction with a computer interface or software design.

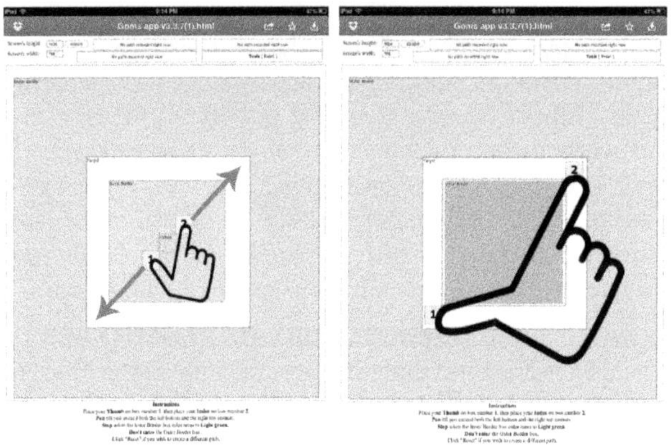

Figure 1 Zoom usability test scenario

Assuming error-free expert user interaction, KLM proved to yield precise estimated results, which is a drawback of similar models [10]. Moreover, when the estimated experimental studies results were considerably different from observed values, the estimated difference between two examined designs still proved to be a strong basis for making design choices.

KLM FOR PHONE USERS

Dunlop and Crossan [2] used KLM operator sequences to compare three different text entry methods for traditional physical-key phones (multitap, predictive, and word completion). How and Kan [5] defined 13 operators that directly map onto the phone keyboard interface according to the different input methods. They used videotaped sessions with a small set of subjects and a message typing task in order to gather new times for these operators. Mori et al. [9] studied how the time values of the original KLM operators apply to mobile phone menu navigation and concluded that the operator values fit well and suggested only minor modifications.

KLM FOR MOBILE DEVICE INTERACTIONS

Until recently the main use of mobile phones was making phone calls, sending text messages, and sometimes basic calendar tasks. Phones used very small displays and small physical buttons as the primary interface. With modern smartphones these buttons have been replaced with larger touch screens. Moreover, other uses are becoming more popular such as taking pictures, surfing the web, social networking, and playing music, videos and games. This adds several new interaction styles that have not yet been fully described by interaction models.

There has been surprisingly little published research that includes new interaction techniques such as swipe, zoom, or tabbing, for mobiles and tablets. Luo and John followed by Teo and John showed that the method could be soundly applied to handheld devices using stylus-based interfaces [6, 11]. They also presented a tool to automatically generate KLM models from storyboard descriptions and stated that they aimed to apply such research to novel interfaces those using speech and gestures. Holleis et al. adopted and defined a set of operators to give study-based estimates of performance measures. They assumed that developers of mobile applications could then describe tasks as a sequence of the operators they added and predict user interaction times without needing to create prototypes [4]. Closest to our work, as part of their research on user performance of multi-touch gestures on mobile devices, Tran et al. conducted an exploratory study of pinch and spread gestures on smartphones and tablets [12]. Their spread gesture on tablet is equivalent to our Zoom interaction.

CONCEPT AND METHODOLOGY OF PROTOTYPES

The development of three prototypes came in the process of enhancing KLM. These prototypes reflected three common interactions used widely on tablets and mobile devices:

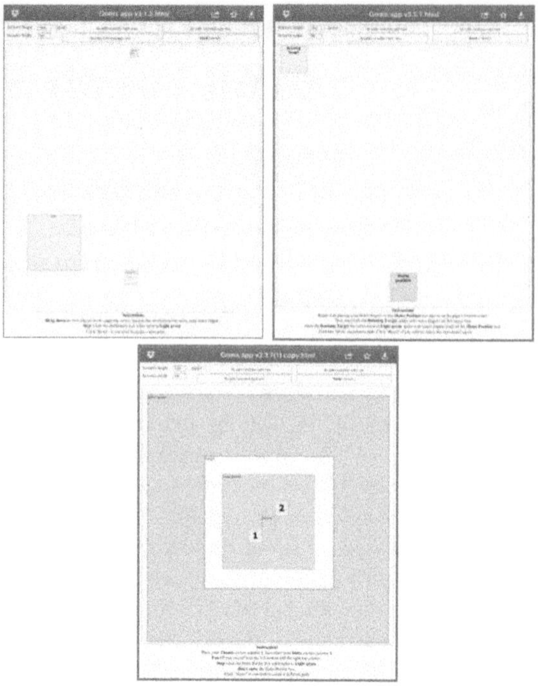

Figure 2. Swipe (left), Tap (right), & Zoom prototypes.

1. Swipe interaction, which enables the user to do different swipe gestures (short or long) to achieve certain tasks (e.g. scrolling through a document etc.).
2. Tap interaction, which estimates the user's tapping response time in comparison to his/her finger travel distance from a home position (e.g. to estimate typing speed or pointing to a target etc.).
3. Zoom interaction, which is used to cause text or other graphics in a window or frame to appear larger on the screen (e.g. zooming, panning a map/photo etc.).

The three prototypes were built to estimate the time taken to conduct these interactions. Fitts's Law [3] as a model is used to analyze the general case of time taken estimation for these interactions. It is primarily used in human–computer interaction and ergonomics to predict the time required to rapidly move to a target area, it is a function of the distance to the target and the size of the target. One of a variety of available formulations, the Shannon formulation is widely used [9] and is defined as:

$$T = a + b * ID, \text{ where } ID = log_2\left(\frac{D}{W} + 1\right).$$

Where

- T is the average time taken to complete the movement. It may also be referred to as MT (mean movement time),
- a represents the incorporating reaction time and/or the time required to execute the operator,
- b represents for the inherent speed of the device,
- D is the distance from start to the center of the target and
- W is the width of the target.

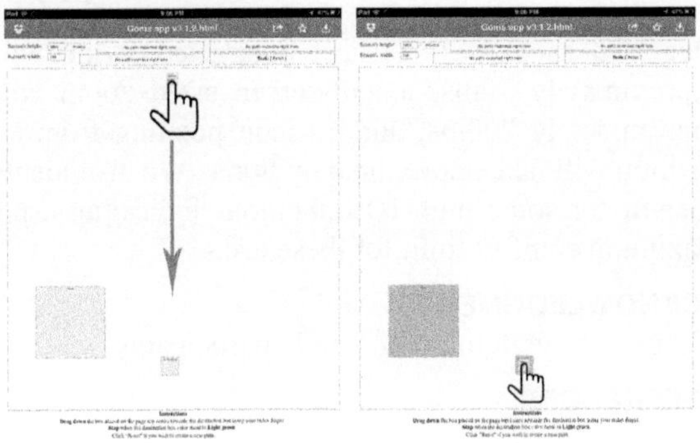

Figure 3 Swipe usability test scenario

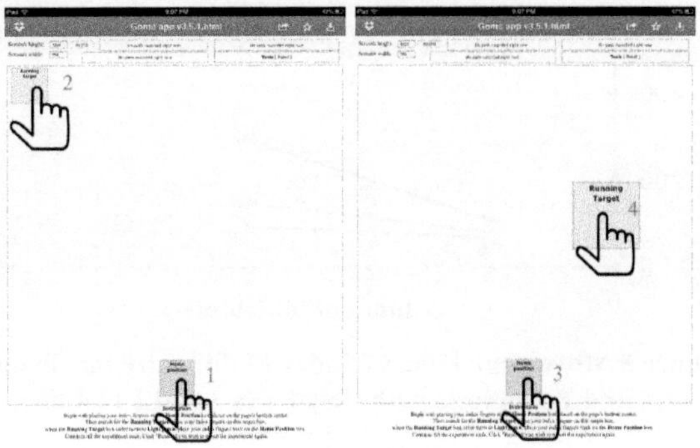

Figure 4 Tap usability test scenario

The constant "1" in the formula made a difference from Fitts's original form, especially for low values of the ratio D/W, given the advantage that the ID is always non-negative. Here we are investigating the ability of modelling the finger touch input for different target sizes and movement distances.

DEVELOPING AND TESTING THE PROTOTYPES

The prototypes were developed in HTML5 / JavaScript and displayed on an iPad Mini (a 7" multi-touch tablet), as shown in figure 2. Three usability studies were conducted to extract completion times (in seconds). For each interaction we tested a range of target size and distances from the starting point to the center of the target (in pixels).

Participants

30 volunteers took part in the Swipe and Zoom usability tests. The participants were aged 22-39, 35% female / 65% male, bachelor graduates, and 70% were familiar with touch screens and 85% were PC users. 21 users conducted the Tap tests, with a similar demographic profile.

Tasks

For the Swipe task, forty eight successive attempts were made. As shown in figure 3, users dragged down a box placed on the top center towards the destination box placed on the bottom center of a web page using the participant's index finger. The participant stopped and removed his/her index finger from the screen when the destination box color turned to light green. This was recorded as a successful attempt.

The Tap task, ten successive attempts were made. As shown in figure 4, users were asked to place their index finger on the "Home Position" box near the bottom of the page. The participant searched for the "Running Target" box and placed his/her index finger on this target box. He/she removed his/her index finger from the "Running Target" box when its color turned to light green. Afterwards, the participant placed his/her index finger back on the "Home Position" box. This was recorded as a successful attempt.

For the Zoom task, twenty six successive attempts were made. As shown in figure 1, each by placing the thumb finger of the participant on the box number 1 and his/her index finger on the box number 2. The participant zoomed till he/she exceeded both the left bottom and the right top corners of the border box, within the target box. He/she stopped and removed his/her thumb and index fingers from the screen when the border box color turned to light green. This was recorded as a successful attempt.

Results

For the Swipe task, as shown in figure 5, target width and target amplitude varied across four levels resulting in IDs of 1 to 4 bits. The target width varied from 50 to 400 pixels, while target amplitude varied from 100 to 800 pixels. Mean movement time ranged from 20ms to 1610ms with each score derived from over 1440 observations. While the Tap task, the target width varied from 50 to 250 pixels, while target amplitude varied from 125 to 900 pixels. Mean movement time ranged from 50ms to 470ms with each score derived from over 210 observations. For the Zoom task, the target width varied from 50 to 150 pixels, while target amplitude varied from 100 to 550 pixels (fixed step of 50 pixels). Mean movement time ranged from 60ms to 1230ms with each score derived from over 1440 observations. Regressing MT on ID yields the following prediction equation for movement time (ms):

- Swipe interaction: $MT = 9.46 + 55.83\ ID$.
- Tap interaction: $MT = 52.12 + 14.62\ ID$.
- Zoom interaction: $MT = 114.86\ ID - 20.45$.

By comparing the results with the previous work of Tran et al. [12], both outcomes are largely in line with slightly different prediction equation and higher correlating MT with ID (R^2 Zoom > 0.884).

POOR FIT FOR ID=4

It was noticed in the Swipe and Zoom usability tests that the 4th ID level does not fit in the straight line, which passes by the other 3 levels of ID. Moreover, the constant "a", representing the incorporating reaction time and/or the time required executing the operator, in the prediction equation for movement time of the Zoom usability test is negative. By excluding ID=4, as shown in figure 5, regressing MT on ID yields the following predictions (ms):

- Swipe interaction: $MT = 44.78 + 34.64\ ID$.

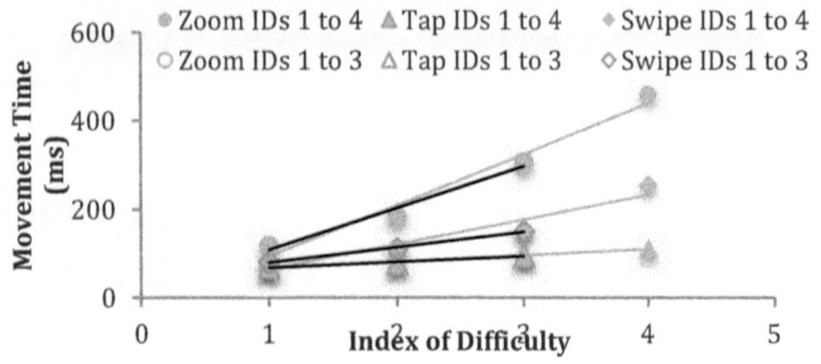

Figure 5 Movement Time vs. Index of difficulty for Swipe, Tap, and Zoom tests with IDs of 1 to 3 and 1 to 4 bits.

Interaction	Time
Short untargeted swipe, ½ width of 5" screen	70ms
½ screen zoom, 100*100 to 350*350px image	200ms
Icon pointing of size 200*200px at a distance of 700px from home position	80ms

Table 1. Suggested approximate movement time for KLM

Interaction	R^2
Swipe usability test with IDs of 1 to 3	0.995 ($p<0.05$)
Swipe usability test with IDs of 1 to 4	0.911 ($p<0.1$)
Tap usability test with IDs of 1 to 3	0.972 ($p<0.05$)
Tap usability test with IDs of 1 to 4	0.985 ($p<0.05$)
Zoom usability test with IDs of 1 to 3	0.972 ($p<0.05$)
Zoom usability test with IDs of 1 to 4	0.971 ($p<0.05$)

Table 2. R^2 values for interaction execution times.

- Tap interaction: $MT = 54.38 + 13.27\ ID.$
- Zoom interaction: $MT = 13.75 + 94.33\ ID.$

The correlating MT with ID for the Swipe test yields $R^2 = 0.995$ ($p<0.01$) instead of $R^2 = 0.911$ ($p<0.1$) (see table 2), which gives a better-fit and more precise prediction.

We believe that the poor fit of ID=4 is indicative the increase in the spread distance required for a Zoom task of this size is too large for comfort, where the target amplitude (D) is between 500px and 550px (about 98 mm) while the target width (W) is 50px. This result parallels what Hoggan et al. found for pinch, where a large pinch distance of over 90mm took significantly longer time to complete tasks and produced an increase in ergonomic failure rate [13].

CONCLUSION

The objective of this paper is to enhance KLM as a quantitative prediction model, by extending it with new operators necessary to describe interactions used on mobile devices and tablets. It was determined, after conducting three usability tests that estimating the movement time for certain interactions is done using Fitts's Law. Furthermore, three equations were formed to estimate the movement time for three interactions; Swipe, Tap, and Zoom. The ID is the variable used to be submitted in any of the three equations in order to calculate the movement time. Based on results, the following approximate movement times for KLM are suggested as shown; a short untargeted swipe will take approximately 70ms, a half-screen sized zoom will take approximately 200ms, and an icon pointing from a home position will take approximately 80ms. We also identified a poor-fit for some high ID operations indicating a possible maximum comfort limit for these tasks.

ACKNOWLEDGMENTS

We are very grateful to our study participants.

REFERENCES

1. Card, S. K., Moran, T. P. and Newell, A. (1983): *The Psychology of Human–Computer Interaction*. Erlbaum.
2. Dunlop, M.D. and Crossan, A. (2000). Predictive Text Entry Methods for Mobile Phones. *Personal Technologies*. 41. 134-143.
3. Fitts's, P. M. (1954). The information capacity of the human motor system in controlling the amplitude of movement. *J. Experimental Psychology*. 47(6). 381-391.
4. Holleis, P., Otto, F., Hussmann, H., and Schmidt, A. (2007). Keystroke-level model for advanced mobile phone interaction. *Proc. CHI 2007*. 1505-1514.
5. How, Y. and Kan, M. Y. (2005). Optimizing Predictive Text Entry for Short Message Service on Mobile Phones. *Proc. HCI International 2005*.
6. Luo, L. and John, B. E. (2005). Predicting Task Execution Time on Handheld Devices Using the Keystroke-Level Model. *Proc CHI 2005*. 1605-1608.
7. Pavlovych, A., Stuerzlinger, W. (2004). Model for Non-expert Text Entry Speed on 12-button Phone Keypads. *Proc. CHI 2004*. 351-358.
8. MacKenzie, I. S. (1992). Fitts's' law as a research and design tool in human–computer interaction. *Human–Computer Interaction*. 7. 91–139.
9. Mori, R., Matsunobe, T., and Yamaoka, T. (2003). A Task Operation Prediction Time Computation Based on GOMS-KLM Improved for the Cellular Phone and the Verification of that Validity. *Proc. ADC 2003*.
10. Myung, R. (2004). Keystroke-level analysis of Korean text entry methods on mobile phones. *Int. J. Human-Computer Studies*. 60(5), 545-563.
11. Teo, L. and John, B. E. (2006). Comparisons of Keystroke-Level Model Predictions to Observed Data. *Extended Abstracts of CHI 2006*. 1421-1426.
12. Tran, J. J., Trewin, S., Swart, C., John, B. E. and Thomas, J. C. (2013). Exploring pinch and spread gestures on mobile devices. *MobileHCI 2013*. 151-16.
13. Hoggan, E., Nacenta, M., Kristensson, P. O., Williamson, J., Oulasvirta, A., and Lehtiö, A. (2013). Multi-touch pinch gestures: performance and ergonomics. *Proc. ACM 2013*. 219- 222.

Around-Body Interaction: Sensing & Interaction Techniques for Proprioception-Enhanced Input with Mobile Devices

Xiang 'Anthony' Chen, Julia Schwarz, Chris Harrison, Jennifer Mankoff, Scott E. Hudson
Human-Computer Interaction Institute, Carnegie Mellon University
{xiangche, julia.schwarz, chris.harrison, jmankoff, scott.hudson}@cs.cmu.edu

ABSTRACT
The space around the body provides a large interaction volume that can allow for big interactions on small mobile devices. However, interaction techniques making use of this opportunity are underexplored, primarily focusing on distributing information in the space around the body. We demonstrate three types of around-body interaction including *canvas*, *modal* and *context-aware* interactions in six demonstration applications. We also present a sensing solution using standard smartphone hardware: a phone's front camera, accelerometer and inertia measurement units. Our solution allows a person to interact with a mobile device by holding and positioning it between a normal field of view and its vicinity around the body. By leveraging a user's proprioceptive sense, around-body Interaction opens a new input channel that enhances conventional interaction on a mobile device without requiring additional hardware.

ACM Classification: H.5.2 [User Interfaces]: Input devices and strategies, Interaction styles.

Keywords: Proprioception; around-body; mobile devices.

INTRODUCTION AND RELATED WORK
Modern mobile devices rely on touch as the primary input modality. However, as devices become smaller, touch interaction gets more difficult, because our fingers do not shrink with our devices. Meanwhile, mobile usage often occurs when a user's attention is divided among multiple tasks, making touch-based interaction increasingly difficult.

By expanding the input space beyond the device's screen, we can situate interaction in the space within arm's reach around the body. This increases the space for interaction, thus mitigating the small screen problem while allowing for expressive input with more degrees of freedom. Further, arm movements naturally leverage *proprioception* [9] – our awareness of the relative position of neighboring body parts – to further reduce the attention required for interacting with a mobile device.

However, the lack of an established, low-cost solution for around-body sensing prevents developers from fully leveraging the space around a user's body to ease the use of miniaturized devices, or to enhance the expressiveness of interactions. Although some prior research has explored the use of proprioception to enable interaction around a user's body [5,8,9,13], the space of such interaction is underexplored, primarily focusing on distributing information in a user's around-body space.

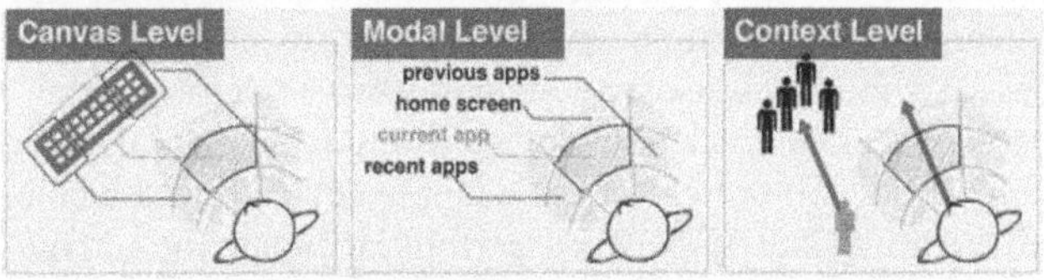

Fig 1. Around-body interaction expands the interaction space (left), mediates the switching between applications/modes (center), and increases context-awareness of the device (right).

The goal of this paper is to provide technical and design solutions that can increase the variety of interactions available between a mobile device and the space around a person's body. To achieve this, we developed a set of around-body, proprioception-enhanced techniques that allow a person to interact with a mobile device in the space around her body for a variety of application scenarios.

To explore these techniques, we built a sensing mechanism to track a smartphone's 3D location relative to a person using its front camera, accelerometer and inertia measurement units. This sensing capability allowed us to rapidly prototype a diverse set of around-body interactions.

In particular, we contribute three categories of interactions demonstrated in six exemplar applications. At the *canvas* level, the around-body space expands the interaction area beyond the screen's boundaries. This allows for placing a UI element, or operating an interactive component in a space that is much larger than the screen (Fig. 1, left). At the *modal* level, around-body movement supports switching between different applications, or different modes within a given application (Fig. 1, center). At the *context* level, the device's spatial relationship to the user may indicate level of privacy. For instance, the farther the device is from the body, the more visible it may be to other people nearby (Fig. 1, right). All these interactions are achieved by leveraging a user's proprioception to hold and position a mobile device around her body, while the device's sensors inform its spatial relationship to the user.

MobileHCI 2014, September 23–26, 2014, Toronto, ON, Canada.
Copyright © 2014 ACM 978-1-4503-3004-6/14/09…$15.00.
http://dx.doi.org/10.1145/2628363.2628402

Although we believe it to be underutilized, the use of proprioception is not entirely new to mobile devices. For example, *Body Mnemonics* associates digital information with different body parts [1]. *Virtual Shelves* makes mobile phones more accessible to visually impaired people by associating programmable shortcuts with locations around the user [8,9]. Proprioception-enabled interactions are also used in virtual reality systems, for example zooming by bimanually setting a rectangular frame [10].

Related to our use of devices' *motion and spatial* awareness for creating interactions, past work also explored using a device's motion sensors to support device-centric motion-based interaction, such as device tilting and gestural input (*e.g.*, [2,11,12]) or to infer and adapt to device-oriented context, e.g., switching between portrait/landscape, or activating the phone when picked up [7]. Others focus on the spatial aspect of devices, such as a device that displays information according to the part of the environment it is situated in [6]. Cao and Balakrishnan turned a handheld projector into a spatially aware device which can be used to project on and interact with multiple information spaces embedded in physical environments [4].

Our sensing and interaction techniques explore and open a space of proprioception-enhanced mobile interaction not covered by previous work. Next we describe sensing solutions that allow devices to be spatially aware around a user's body entirely based on commodity hardware. Following that we present six example applications that demonstrate the variety of interactions supported by our sensing solutions, and that illustrate three categories of around-body interaction.

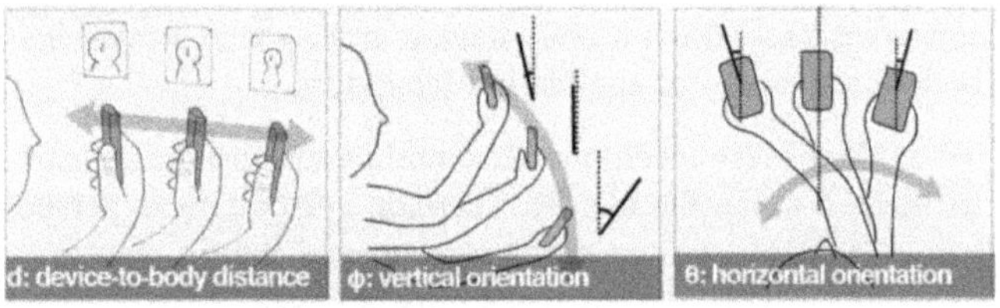

Fig 2. Sensing a device's 3D location: device-to-body distance d; vertical orientation φ; and horizontal orientation θ.

SENSING A DEVICE'S AROUND-BODY LOCATION

We built a sensing mechanism to estimate a smartphone's 3D location (d, θ and φ, as shown in Fig. 2) relative to the person holding and using it. Our system uses four of the phone's built-in sensors: accelerometer, gyroscope, magnetometer and the front camera.

Using front camera to track device-to-body distance ***d***. Using face detection, we estimate the head size (H) of the user from the front camera image. The range of the device-to-body distance corresponds to a minimum (H_{min}) and maximum (H_{max}) head size. For a given head size H, we estimate $d = (H_{max} - H) / (H_{max} - H_{min})$. This normalized value indicates how far away the device is held relative to the face. To calibrate to each particular user's head size and arm length, our system starts with an initial H_{min} and H_{max} (*e.g.*, $H_{min} = \frac{1}{4} W$, $H_{max} = \frac{3}{4} W$, where W is width of the front camera image). Over time, we update H_{min} and H_{max} to match the actual range of the device. This allows our system to adapt to any user and to respond to changes in range of movement for different types of interactions.

Using compass to track horizontal orientation $\boldsymbol{\theta}$. As the device moves horizontally around the body, the compass's value ($\theta_{device\text{-}world}$) changes (Fig. 2 left). When a person brings the device close (normalized $d < 0.25$, face visible), we record the compass' reading as the body's orientation relative to the world ($\theta_{body\text{-}world}$), and subsequently use it to calculate device's orientation relative to the body as $\theta_{device\text{-}body} = \theta_{device\text{-}world} - \theta_{body\text{-}world}$. The value $\theta_{body\text{-}world}$ is only updated when the device is relatively stationary, which can be detected by comparing the sum of the gyroscope reading against a small threshold ε.

Using accelerometer to track vertical orientation $\boldsymbol{\varphi}$. As the device moves vertically around the body, the user naturally tilts the device to make it visible (Fig. 2 center). This behavior allows us to infer the device's vertical orientation (φ) using the accelerometer. The vertical orientation, φ, can be calculated from the degree the device is tilted relative to the accelerometer's x axis. We dynamically update the range of the vertical orientation, similar to how we calculate d.

PROPRIOCEPTIVE, AROUND-BODY INTERACTION

Our sensing techniques leverage a person's proprioceptive sense to provide a large interaction canvas for a mobile phone. Yet it is still unclear how this capability can enhance the expressiveness of interaction beyond simply distributing the interactions equally around the body.

Past work has suggested *dimensions* such as proximal spaces to situate mobile interactions on/around a person's body [5]. In VR, spatial *metrics* were developed to mediate interpersonal communication [3]. In contrast, our goal is to create sensing and interaction techniques that explore categories of interactions to fully make use of the around-body space. Below we demonstrate these three categories: canvas, modes, and context.

Expanding the Canvas for Interaction

At the *canvas* level, the around-body space expands the interaction canvas beyond the screen's boundaries.

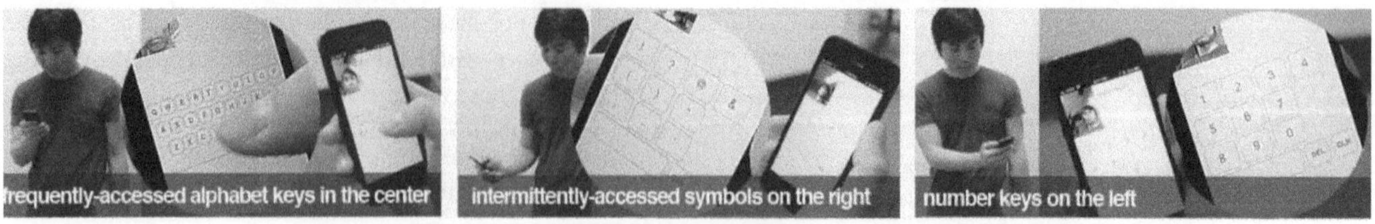

Fig 3. Around-body interaction maps a physical keyboard around the body

Fig 4. Around-body interaction toggles apps and home screen.

Typing around the body. Our spatial and kinesthetic memory allows us to fluently and quickly access keys on a physical keyboard. Likewise, Around-Body Interaction can leverage a user's proprioceptive sense to access a virtual keyboard mapped out beyond the small phone screen. As shown in Fig. 3, our keyboard design centers alphabet keys – the primary keys used in day-to-day typing – in the user's field of view (Fig. 3, center). Intermittently accessed keys – such as symbols and numbers – are placed on the left and right sides of the body (Fig. 3, left & right). Using proprioceptive arm movement to switch between key sets maintains a constant grip for single-handed typing.

Around-body treasure hunt. As another example (shown in our video figure), Around-Body Interaction provides a large gaming area and a range of interaction beyond 'finger poking' the screen. In our 'treasure hunt' game Player 1 places the treasure somewhere near his body and Player 2 moves the device to search for that relative location. The space around the body can be mapped to a variety of game scenes thus adding to the gaming experience for the player.

Mediating Application and Mode Switching

At the *modal* level, the device's around-body movement can mediate the switching between different applications, or different modes within a given application.

Switching between applications. Displaying multiple applications is infeasible on a small screen. Around-body interaction enables toggling between an application and the home screen by holding the phone closer in the field of view vs. farther away (Fig. 4). A person can retrieve previous apps by shifting the device to the right (Fig. 5abc), and return to more recent apps by shifting it to the left (Fig. 5cde). In addition, holding the device to the right or left starts a quasi-mode where one can swipe the screen to go forward/backward in application history.

Switching between modes within an application. With only one thumb available, typical map navigation such as pinch-to-zoom becomes cumbersome. By associating different functions with different around-body locations, we can improve this situation. In the normal field of view, a person can use a thumb to scroll-and-pan the map (Fig 6, left); holding the device further out switches to scroll-and-zoom (Fig. 6, center); shifting to the right shows menus for changing map views (Fig. 6, right). Thus the device's around-body location augments the limited expressivity of the thumb and enables more variety of interactions in a one-handed scenario.

Increasing the System's Context-Awareness

At the context level, the device's spatial relationship to the user can increase the system's *context-awareness*.

Mediating public vs. private phone behavior. During social interactions (*e.g.*, a face-to-face meeting), around-body interaction infers context from the phone's proximity to the body, and mediates its behavior accordingly. Notifications are pushed to the user when the phone is held close, where typically only the user can see the display (Fig 7, right). Holding the phone in a 'public zone' – where it is also visible to the others – will hide notifications. This enables socially appropriate phone behavior without requiring the user to explicitly switch modes.

Inferring states of application usage. When using an application, the device's around-body location can imply different states and provide a way to proactively select UI views that match such states. Our video figure shows a person raising the device up and holding it horizontally as he prepares to take a photo. This is sensed using the device's around-body location (up above the field of view), causing the camera to open. After taking the photos, as the device is lowered relative to the eye level, the change in around-body location switches the view to an image browser.

PERFORMANCE TEST, LIMITATIONS AND TRADEOFFS

We conducted a preliminary performance test of the sensors we used. Our goal is not to run a task-based usability evaluation of the interaction, but to collect sensor data and use machine learning analysis to test the saliency of the this data in estimating the device's around-body locations.

Fig 5. Around-body interaction enables multitasking between previous and more recent apps.

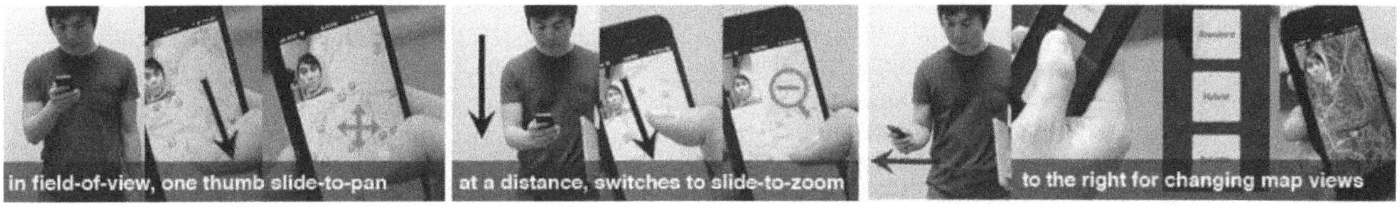

Fig 6. Around-body interaction mediates mode switching in a map app.

Fig 7. Around-body interaction increases context-awareness.

One experimenter held and placed a smart phone at a number of locations pre-calibrated and evenly distributed around a fixed central point (representing the user's body position). We used these locations as ground truth and logged sensor and camera data at each location. We tested all the three axes (d, θ and φ) and varied the sensing resolution (the number of distinct locations) on each axis (3, 5, and 7 for θ and φ; 2, 3, and 4 for d). We repeated the measurement 25 times at each location (975 data points total) by moving the device between that location and the central point.

For each sensing resolution on each axis, we used ten-fold cross validation with a 1R classifier to estimate the accuracy of the best sensor for that dimension (camera-d, accelerometer-θ and magnetometer-φ, respectively). As shown in Table 1, the sensors achieved 100% accuracy in identifying 3×3×3=27 around-body locations (3 on each axis). However, performance dropped on θ and φ axes as sensing resolution increased.

d	# of locations	2	3	4
	Accuracy	100.00%	100.00%	99.04%
	Kappa	1.00	1.00	0.99
θ	# of locations	3	5	7
	Accuracy	100.00%	84.80%	74.73%
	Kappa	1.00	0.81	0.71
φ	# of locations	3	5	7
	Accuracy	100.00%	95.20%	85.71%
	Kappa	1.00	0.94	0.83

Table 1. Performance test of around-body sensing.

Although the accuracy decreases as the number of locations increases, this result still promises a good match for users' needs. Li et al. [8] found people are best at discerning seven or fewer directions around their body. This suggests a simple yet useful division of the around-body space into a normal field of view and six peripheral interactive zones.

Several possible explanations for these errors exist. We assume a user will tilt the device to be visible while holding and positioning it around the body. However in reality such tilting does not always perfectly align with the device's *true* around-body location, thus causing errors.

Beyond this performance test, there are other limitations to address. For example, to reliably track the device's horizontal orientation, our current solution demands a frequent update of the body's orientation, which requires frequently bringing the device into focus while interacting with it. Further, our calculation of device-to-body distance relies on face detection, whose accuracy subjects to the physical environment. To address all these sensor related uncertainties, the interface can provide active feedback as well as allowing for manual overriding false sensing results.

User error is another important consideration. For example, gesturing with a device in hand during conversations could cause false positives. To solve this we can develop ways to detect suspicious device movement. We can also employ explicit activation mechanisms to start an interaction.

CONCLUSION

We presented a series of around-body, proprioception-enhanced interaction techniques that open a new input channel on a commercial smartphone. Our sensing mechanism requires no custom hardware, and performs at high accuracy for the normal field of view and a few periphery zones. We demonstrate three categories of interactions: 1) increasing the interaction space for interactors or an entire interface, 2) mediating application and mode switching, and 3) increasing the device's context-awareness. Collectively, they offer new ways of leveraging the around-body space to enhance mobile interaction. Our future work includes further testing and improving the sensing techniques, and developing around-body interaction at the toolkit level.

REFERENCES

1. Angesleva, J., Oakley, I., Hughes, S. & O'Modhrain, S., Body Mnemonics. *UIST '03*, 2-5.
2. Bartlett, J.F. Rock 'n' Scroll is here to stay [user interface]. *IEEE CG&A* 20, 3 (2000), 40–45.
3. Benford, S. and Fahlén, L. A spatial model of interaction in large virtual environments. *ECSCW'93*, 109–124.
4. Cao, X. and Balakrishnan, R. Interacting with dynamically defined information spaces using a handheld projector and a pen. *UIST '06*, 225-234.
5. Chen, X. A, Marquardt, N., Tang, A., Boring, S., and Greenberg, S. Extending a mobile device's interaction space through body-centric interaction. *MobileHCI '12*, 151-160.
6. Fitzmaurice, G.W. Situated information spaces and spatially aware palmtop computers. *CACM 36*, 7 (1993), 39–49.
7. Hinckley, K., Pierce, J., Sinclair, M., and Horvitz, E. Sensing techniques for mobile interaction. *CHI '00*, 91–100.
8. Li, F.C.Y., Dearman, D., and Truong, K.N. Virtual shelves. *UIST '09*, 125-134.
9. Li, F.C.Y., Dearman, D., and Truong, K.N. Leveraging proprioception to make mobile phones more accessible to users with visual impairments. *ASSETS '10*, 187-194.
10. Mine, M.R., Brooks, F.P., and Sequin, C.H. Moving objects in space. *SIGGRAPH '97*, 19–26.
11. Rekimoto, J. Tilting operations for small screen interfaces. *UIST '96*, 167–168.
12. Small, D. and Ishii, H. Design of spatially aware graspable displays. *CHI '97*, 367-368.
13. Yee, K.-P. Peephole displays. *CHI '03*, 1-8.

Investigating the Effectiveness of Peephole Interaction for Smartwatches in a Map Navigation Task

Frederic Kerber
German Research Center for Artificial Intelligence (DFKI)
Saarbrücken, Germany
frederic.kerber@dfki.de

Antonio Krüger
German Research Center for Artificial Intelligence (DFKI)
Saarbrücken, Germany
krueger@dfki.de

Markus Löchtefeld
German Research Center for Artificial Intelligence (DFKI)
Saarbrücken, Germany
markus.loechtefeld@dfki.de

ABSTRACT
With the increasing availability of smartwatches the question of suited input modalities arises. While direct touch input comes at the cost of the fat-finger problem, we propose to use a dynamic peephole to explore larger content such as websites or maps. In this paper, we present the results of a user study comparing the performance of static and dynamic peephole interactions for a map navigation task on a smartwatch display. As a first method, we investigated the static peephole methaphor where the displayed map is moved on the device via direct touch interaction. In contrast, for the second method – the dynamic peephole – the device is moved and the map is static with respect to an external frame of reference. We compared both methods in terms of task performance and perceived user experience. The results show that the dynamic peephole interaction performs significantly more slowly in terms of task completion time.

Author Keywords
map navigation; smartwatch; mobile devices; dynamic peephole interaction; touch interaction

ACM Classification Keywords
H.5.2. Information Interfaces and Presentation: User Interfaces – input devices and strategies, interaction styles

INTRODUCTION
Smartwatches – small computing devices allowing for in- and output at the users wrist – have already been around since the 1980s with devices such as the Seiko D409 and the Seiko Epson RC-20. The technical limitations back then prevented them from making any impact in the mass market. With current devices such as the Samsung Galaxy Gear or the Sony SmartWatch 2, not only has the computing performance increased drastically, the available interaction techniques have also become much more versatile. In contrast to their predecessors from the 1980s, the devices are equipped with touch input and various sensors (e.g. GPS, accelerometer or camera), and they are extensible through the already well-known mobile app concept. Thus, the devices can be used in varied ways and can supersede specialized versions, e.g. sport watches. Nonetheless, most of the devices are only usable in combination with a smartphone. Besides the lack of meaningful dedicated applications for such devices, the input in particular is still cumbersome. While most of the current devices are equipped with a touch screen, the rather small display size, usually only about 1.5" to 2.5", makes it hard to use due to the fat-finger problem [1].

MobileHCI '14, September 23 – 26 2014, Toronto, ON, Canada
Copyright 2014 ACM 978-1-4503-3004-6/14/09...$15.00.
http://dx.doi.org/10.1145/2628363.2628393

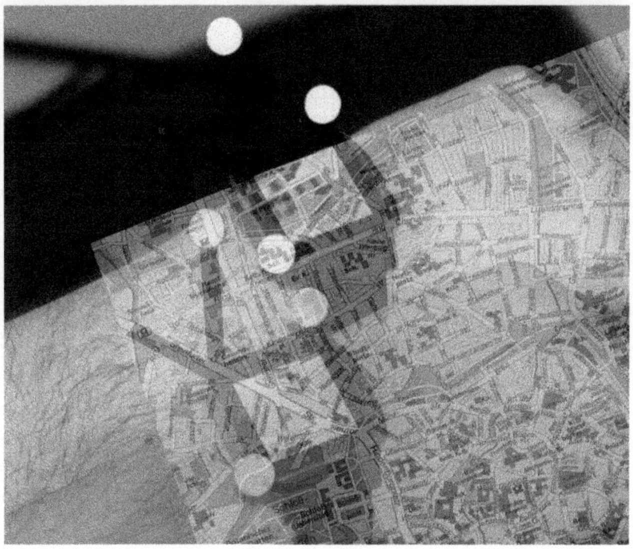

Figure 1. A dynamic peephole map application - The user moves his arm to browse the map (created by blending two photos and the original map)

However, some of the typical use cases of smartphones can be of relevance for smartwatches as well. The exploration of large-scale content such as websites or maps is one of the most common tasks on today's smartphones, for which reason this paper investigates map navigation. This task would come in handy when a user is in a foreign area, with his hands occupied by e.g. luggage. Sophisticated interaction techniques for these tasks might let smartwatches overcome the perception of being only a notification auxiliary.

On current smartphones, this task is typically handled using a static peephole [2]. This means that the map that is presented on the display is only a zoomed-in section of a complete map. Thus, the display provides access to a larger virtual workspace behind through a limited viewport. To be able to explore the complete workspace, it can be moved, e.g. by scrolling or panning, whereas the viewport stays fixed. An

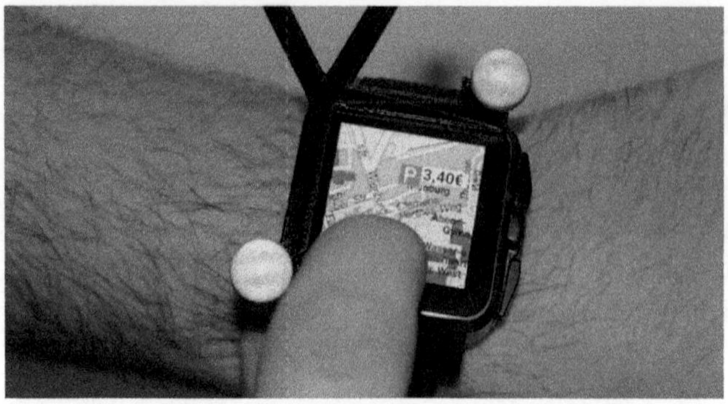

Figure 2. A user exploring a map using the direct touch static peephole interaction technique.

analysis of this interaction method by Guiard et al. [3] shows that the navigation time increases when the view size is reduced. Since smartwatches have a limited form-factor to keep them wearable on the user's wrist, this will decrease task performance on such devices.

To ease this problem, Fitzmaurice et al. [2] introduced the concept of the so-called dynamic peephole. In this technique, the viewport is physically moved above the virtual workspace that is static with respect to an external frame of reference (see Figure 1). With the help of a spatially-aware display, it is detected which part of the virtual workspace should be shown. The sensors embedded in current devices, such as gyroscopes and accelerometers, would allow such devices to track their relative position and thereby allow them to become spatially-aware.

In this paper, we investigate two methods for map navigation for a wrist-worn smartwatch. The first one is the standard static peephole interaction based on direct touch (see Figure 2). The second one is a dynamic peephole interaction technique where the user controls the position of the peephole with his arm movements. We present the results of a user study comparing the performance of these two interaction techniques. Both methods are compared with respect to task performance and perceived user experience. The results show that dynamic peephole interaction performs significantly worse in a map navigation task. Nonetheless, in terms of user preference, the participants favored the dynamic peephole interaction over the static one.

RELATED WORK

Initial work on dynamic peephole interaction has been conducted by Fitzmaurice et al. [2]. They presented the Chameleon prototype, a virtual cubic spreadsheet accessible by a spatially aware handheld device. An extension of this approach is provided by Yee [12] who investigated menu selection, note taking and map navigation on four prototypes of peephole display hardware. A comparison of the static and dynamic peephole metaphor by Mehra et al. [9] shows the superiority of the dynamic approach for a line length discrimination task: Both discrimination thresholds and required time for discrimination are lower, if line length exceeds the peephole area. Additionally, it has been shown that the majority of participants preferred the dynamic approach. Similar results could be gained by Hürst and Bilyalov in their comparison study of dynamic and static peephole navigation of virtual reality panoramas on handheld devices [5]. In recent years, investigations of map navigation with mobile phones have also been conducted. Rohs and Essl examined in [10] sensing methods for an abstract map navigation task. In [11], Rohs et al. present a study comparing the dynamic peephole method, joystick navigation and the magic lens paradigm. Among those, joystick navigation was found to be inferior in terms of search time and degree of search space exploration.

In [8], Kaufmann and Ahlström investigated collaborative map usage by comparing classical touchscreen interaction and dynamic peephole interaction with a mobile projector. Although their results showed equal map navigation performance, they could show that spatial memory performance was better using the peephole interaction with the projector phone. In contrast to the aforementioned work, we investigate a device with a distinctly smaller display. Furthermore, the typical movement patterns are expected to be different when using a smartwatch, as it is directly attached to the user's arm.

Another suitable interaction technique for smartwatches would be touch input on the back of the device, as was proposed by Baudisch and Chu [1]. Unfortunately, their investigation focused only on small displays that allowed for touch input directly on the back. This is not possible on smartwatches since they are wrist-worn. The forearm between the watch and a possible touch area might lead to interferences between the perceived touches by the user and the sensed touches, and would therefore need further investigation.

EXPERIMENT

To evaluate the effectiveness of dynamic peephole interaction with a smartwatch, we conducted a user study to compare a dynamic peephole against a static one using the touch screen of a smartwatch. Similar to [10], we provided a virtual city map on which parking lot symbols are displayed, providing information on the hourly parking rates. The task for the participants was to find and select the cheapest parking option. For solving the task, an exhaustive map search was required while at the same time, location and cost of the currently-cheapest parking space had to be remembered. Finally, navigation back to the memorized target place was necessary. Thus, the experiment combines a navigation task on a small display with spatial memory components.

Apparatus

We used a smartwatch by simvalley (AW-414.Go) with a screen diagonal of 1.5" and a screen resolution of 240 pixels $\times$ 240 pixels running Android 4.2.2. The 1 GHz dual-core processor enables an implementation without any observable delay. The implementation of the dynamic peephole interface was done using an optical tracking system from NaturalPoint (OptiTrack V120:Trio) attached to an additional computer handling the position computation. To be able to track the watch, we equipped it with a thin 3D-printed frame carrying IR-reflective material (see Figure 1). For the static peephole navigation task the same device was used, but without being tracked by the OptiTrack system. In all settings, the target spot had to be selected by double-tapping on the display.

Participants and Experimental Design

We recruited 12 participants (6 female), aged 21-32 (M=27.2, SD=3.1). All participants are daily smartphone users, but had no prior experience with smartwatches. We split the experiment into two conditions: 6 participants (3 female) started in the static peephole condition, whereas the rest first completed the dynamic peephole condition. In both conditions, the participant first pushes a virtual start button on the smartwatch and then explores the presented map, beginning in its center, to find the cheapest parking spot. The underlying map was presented in a size of 1725 pixels × 1725 pixels. For the dynamic condition, this area was mapped to a physical movement space of 20.1 cm × 20.1 cm. This mapping represents an exact mapping of device to pixel movement. If the device is moved by 2mm the pixels on the screen are moved accordingly. The covered movement space of 20.1 cm × 20.1 cm was determined in a pre-study in which we tested comfortable arm movements for three participants with different arm lenghts. The covered area was easily accessible for all of them. In both conditions, zooming was not possible.

After finishing the first condition, participants were required to take a 5 minute break before they started with the second condition. After completing each condition, all participants were requested to fill out a short post-session questionnaire consisting of a NASA TLX[4], an ISO 9241-9 [6] questionnaire as well as personal preference questions. Overall, the whole procedure took around 45 minutes.

Tasks

The scenario for both map navigation methods was the same. Users had to find the cheapest among a varying number of parking lots on a map. Three different numbers of parking lot symbols were shown on the map: 4, 8 and 16. The presented city map was unknown to all participants. Each parking lot was marked with a white P symbol on blue background. The rates were randomly assigned to the P symbols and displayed next to each of them (compare Figure 2). We made sure that no more than one target was ever displayed at the same time. A single trial consisted of exploring the map using the given method and finally selecting the target. Selecting was done by double-tapping the P symbol. After each selection, the subject was informed about success or failure of the trial and the next trial could be started. However, it was assured that no parking spots were presented in the initial view directly after pressing the start button. Five trials were conducted for each condition and P symbol count. Overall, this sums up to 360 trials (12 users × 2 conditions × 3 P symbol counts × 5 trials). We counterbalanced the two conditions as well as the P symbol counts to eliminate possible learning effects.

Measures

- *Task completion time*: Time between starting the task and selecting a target (including trials with wrongly selected targets).

- *Error rate*: Percentage of selected parking spots that were note cheapest over all performed trials.

- *Map coverage*: The amount of the map that was explored (pixels displayed at least once) using the different techniques (including trials with wrongly selected targets).

- *Personal preference*: NASA TLX and ISO 9241-9 questionnaire assessing subjective information on a 7-point scale.

Hypotheses

Based on our review of prior work, we expected the dynamic peephole interaction to be significantly faster compared to using a static peephole with direct touch (*H1*). We did not expect any difference in error rate (*H2*) or covered map area (*H3*) between the two interaction techniques.

Results

We used a two-way ANOVA test with the different interaction technique and number of targets as factors for task completion time, map coverage and number of errors. We used the univariate ANOVA test for the NASA TLX and ISO 9241-9 results analysis with the subject as a random factor.

Task completion time: There was no significant effect of target number, but we found a significant difference for interaction techniques ($F_{1,358} = 7.28, p < 0.01$). The dynamic peephole interaction was significantly slower (M=65.56 sec, SD=28.63 sec) compared to the static one using direct touch (M=58.46 sec, SD=22.45 sec).

Error rate: Target number as well as interaction technique had no significant effect on error rate (M_{Touch}=8.9%, M_{Peephole}=8.3%).

Map coverage: There was no significant effect of target number on the covered map area. Nonetheless, interaction technique again had a significant effect ($F_{1,358} = 11.69, p < 0.01$). With the dynamic peephole technique, the participants explored a significantly larger area of the map (M=87.7%, SD=11.7%) compared to the static peephole implementation using direct touch interaction (M=82.2%, SD=18.4%).

Personal preference: We found no significant differences for the NASA TLX questions. However, for the following parts of the ISO 9241-9 (see Figure 3) questionnaire, we found significant differences ($p < 0.05$): Users rated the dynamic peephole technique as causing less strain for their fingers (M=1.08, SD=0.28) compared to the static peephole (M=2.92, SD=1.71). On the other hand, the operation using the dynamic peephole was rated as being less accurate and not as smooth as the static one. Nevertheless, when asked whether they would rather use the dynamic peephole or the static one with direct touch interaction, eight of the twelve participants chose the dynamic peephole.

DISCUSSION

In contrast to the related work, the dynamic peephole interaction performed significantly worse in terms of task completion time. With an on-average 12% slower task completion time, we have to reject *H1*. The main reason for this might be the limited degrees of freedom of possible arm movements, compared to a hand-held device that was used in the related

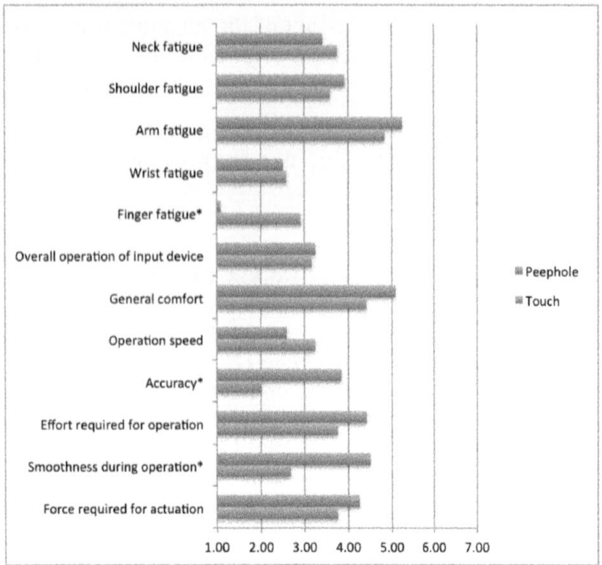

Figure 3. Results of the ISO 9241-9 questionnaire (lower values represent a better rating). For values marked with a *, a significant difference was found ($p < 0.05$).

works. Another reason could be that the users on average explored a significantly larger part of the map (rejects *H3* as well). But the increase in coverage map area could be explained with the overshooting behavior that is generally observed when using dynamic peephole interaction [7].

As we could not find any significant differences or a correlation in error rate between the two techniques, *H2* can neither be confirmed nor rejected. Even though the dynamic peephole performed objectively worse compared to the static one using direct touch, it was the favorite technique in subjective preference selected by eight out of twelve participants.

Overall, it is questionable whether the dynamic peephole technique is a reasonable interaction technique for wrist-worn smartwatches. The 12% higher task completion time compared to direct touch interaction would argue against using it. Nonetheless, the advantage of exploring large-scale content with one hand might compensate for the slower speed. This is also reflected in the user preferences.

CONCLUSION AND FUTURE WORK

In this paper, we presented the results of our user study investigating the usefulness of a dynamic peephole interaction for wrist-worn smartwatches that can be controlled by arm movements. Our results show that compared to the static peephole using direct touch interaction, the dynamic peephole performs significantly worse in terms of task completion time. In terms of user preference, the dynamic peephole was favored by eight out of twelve participants. Keeping in mind the advantage of one-handed interaction, we would argue for further investigation of this interaction technique.

As future work, we want to analyze whether the slower task completion time is an effect of the restricted arm movements or the result of overshooting. One possibility would be to investigate different mappings for the dynamic peephole, i.e. non-linear mappings of arm and pixel movement. Another approach could be to map the radial movements of the arm to the y-direction of the dynamic peephole.

Furthermore, we want to develop a system that is based only on the internal sensors, i.e. accelerometer, magnetometer and gyroscope, instead of relying on an external tracking system.

REFERENCES

1. Baudisch, P., and Chu, G. Back-of-device Interaction Allows Creating Very Small Touch Devices. In *Proc. CHI '09*, ACM (New York, NY, USA, 2009), 1923–1932.
2. Fitzmaurice, G. W., Zhai, S., and Chignell, M. H. Virtual Reality for Palmtop Computers. *ACM Trans. Inf. Syst. 11*, 3 (July 1993), 197–218.
3. Guiard, Y., Beaudouin-Lafon, M., Bastin, J., Pasveer, D., and Zhai, S. View Size and Pointing Difficulty in Multi-scale Navigation. In *Proc. AVI '04*, ACM (New York, NY, USA, 2004), 117–124.
4. Hart, S. G., and Stavenland, L. E. Development of NASA-TLX (Task Load Index): Results of empirical and theoretical research. In *Human Mental Workload*, P. A. Hancock and N. Meshkati, Eds. Elsevier, 1988, ch. 7, 139–183.
5. Hürst, W., and Bilyalov, T. Dynamic Versus Static Peephole Navigation of VR Panoramas on Handheld Devices. In *Proc. MUM '10*, ACM (New York, NY, USA, 2010), 25:1–25:8.
6. ISO. *ISO 9241-9 Ergonomic requirements for office work with visual display terminals (VDTs) - Part 9: Requirements for non-keyboard input devices.* ISO copyright office, 2000.
7. Kaufmann, B., and Ahlström, D. Revisiting Peephole Pointing: A Study of Target Acquisition with a Handheld Projector. In *Proc. MobileHCI '12*, ACM (New York, NY, USA, 2012), 211–220.
8. Kaufmann, B., and Ahlström, D. Studying Spatial Memory and Map Navigation Performance on Projector Phones with Peephole Interaction. In *Proc. CHI '13*, ACM (New York, NY, USA, 2013), 3173–3176.
9. Mehra, S., Werkhoven, P., and Worring, M. Navigating on Handheld Displays: Dynamic Versus Static Peephole Navigation. *ACM Trans. Comput.-Hum. Interact. 13*, 4 (Dec. 2006), 448–457.
10. Rohs, M., and Essl, G. Sensing-based Interaction for Information Navigation on Handheld Displays. In *Proc. MobileHCI '07*, ACM (New York, NY, USA, 2007), 387–394.
11. Rohs, M., Schöning, J., Raubal, M., Essl, G., and Krüger, A. Map Navigation with Mobile Devices: Virtual Versus Physical Movement with and Without Visual Context. In *Proc. ICMI '07*, ACM (New York, NY, USA, 2007), 146–153.
12. Yee, K.-P. Peephole Displays: Pen Interaction on Spatially Aware Handheld Computers. In *Proc. CHI '03*, ACM (New York, NY, USA, 2003), 1–8.

ambiPad - Enriching Mobile Digital Media With Ambient Feedback

Markus Löchtefeld, Nadine Lautemann, Sven Gehring and Antonio Krüger
German Research Center for Artificial Intelligence (DFKI)
Stuhlsatzenhausweg 3, Saarbrücken, Germany
firstname.lastname@dfki.de

ABSTRACT
With the recent increase in sales figures of tablet computers, a corresponding boost of mobile media consumption on such devices can be observed. Even though tablets provide a comparably larger screen in contrast to smartphones — which are taking the main share of mobile media consumption — the experience of consuming media content on tablets is still limited. For movie theaters the notion of 4 dimensional (4D) films exist, describing a 3D movie that is enhanced with ambient feedback such as environmental light, air streams or moist. In this paper we present *ambiPad* , a tablet prototype that enriches mobile digital media with ambient feedback around the tablet's display. Besides a light emitting frame, *ambiPad* allows for thermal stimuli as well. We report on the results of a qualitative user study, in which the feedback channels of *ambiPad* were rated as highly attractive and desirable by the participants.

Author Keywords
Tablet; Thermal Feedback; Ambient Light

ACM Classification Keywords
H.5.m. Information Interfaces and Presentation (e.g. HCI): Miscellaneous

INTRODUCTION
Today's mobile devices allow for a variety of different activities including accessing everyday information, playing games as well as the increasing consumption of digital media such as images, videos or even complete movies. One important factor contributing to the current growth in mobile media consumption is the expanding distribution of tablets [3]. Their increasing number brought a new, larger display form factor allowing for convenient media consumption while being (semi-) mobile.

Nevertheless, the viewing experiences of theatrical motion pictures on such devices is still limited. Besides frequently appearing bad audio quality, which might be resolved by using adequate headphones, the screen of a tablet simply does not provide the immersion featured by a cinema with its enormous screen size. The development of sensor-based enhancements for cinematic experiences exist since the early 1960's, with developments such as the Sensorama [6]. This device allowed the viewer to immerse into a 3D movie through vibrotactile, aromatic and wind feedback. Nowadays, the term 4D movie is regularly used for such kind of cinematic experiences. This term describes systems that enhance 3D movies with synchronized physical effects. A different variety of such effects exists, such as dedicated-lighting, smoke, rain, air bubbles or special smells. While the augmentation of a movie with such physical effects requires a large amount of additional work, this approach is common in theme parks. One of the earliest examples of such attractions is Disneyland's Captain EO[1] from 1986 which incorporated lasers and smoke as additional effects. Similar approaches for enhancing the user experience while consuming digital media have been transferred to our living rooms as well. The Philips Ambilight system [2] for example creates immersive light effects around the television that are in synchronization with the displayed video content.

In this paper we present *ambiPad*, a mobile tablet computer

MobileHCI '14, September 23 – 26 2014, Toronto, ON, Canada
Copyright 2014 ACM 978-1-4503-3004-6/14/09...$15.00.
http://dx.doi.org/10.1145/2628363.2628395

Figure 1. ***ambiPad*** **is an Android tablet modified with (1) an ambient light frame that enhances the perception of the screen as well as (2) Peltier elements on the back allowing for thermal stimuli.**

[1] https://disneyland.disney.go.com/attractions/disneyland/captain-eo/

[2] http://www.philips.co.uk/c/televisions/33092/cat/#/hue

augmented with thermal feedback mechanisms as well as an ambient lighting frame around the display. We developed a media player application that allows for synchronizing the ambient light and thermal stimuli with the video. While for classic media settings augmentations exists since the 1960s, such enhancements have only been sporadically implemented and studied for mobile settings. We evaluated *ambiPad* in a qualitative user study focusing on the user experience. The study outlined the desirability of the proposed features. Especially the proposed thermal stimuli enhanced the subjective emotional responses of the users.

DESIGN CONSIDERATIONS

The design goal of *ambiPad* is to enhance the experience of digital visual media through ambient feedback on a mobile device. Since *ambiPad* is meant to be a fully mobile device this limits the possible feedback channels. Therefore, we decided to focus on thermal stimuli and ambient light, which have been proven to be implementable and efficient on mobile devices [9, 12].

Ambient light has been shown to reduce visual fatigue [4] but can also be used to express additional information and enhance the immersion [7, 10]. Therefore, we adapt the Philips Ambilight concept by adding a light emitting frame to the tablet. The Philips Ambilight emits light from the back of the device. In our early evaluations on a tablet, this turned out to only work well when the tablet is lying on a table. When holding it, the effect was perceived stronger with the light emitting frame mounted on the front of the tablet. The study of Müller et al. showed that most of the time, tablets are used in home environments [8]. Additionally, users also tend to use their tablets rather at night-times [3]. In such a setting, the ambient lighting around the tablet can easily be perceived and without disturbing people in the vicinity of the user. Lately, thermal stimuli have been studied as an additional output channel [11]. The results of Halvey et al. show great potential to enhance emotional perception of media [5]. As thermal feedback can be easily perceived through the hands while holding it [8], the thermal feedback elements can be incorporated into the tablet.

We expect these elements to enrich the emotional response towards visual media. For example reflecting emotions such as anger through different colors and heat. Additionally also contextual artifacts of videos such as explosions might be enhanced by adding heat and appropriate coloring.

PROTOTYPE

Our prototype is based on a Samsung Nexus 10 tablet running an Android system. For the ambient lighting frame around the tablet we laser-cutted a plexiglas frame fitting the non-touch enabled edges of the tablet. For emitting colored light, we attached 2 RGB LEDs to each of the corners. Furthermore, we sanded the plexiglass frame in order to ensure an even dispersion of the colored light around the edges of the tablet.

For the thermal stimuli we attached two Peltier elements on the back of the device. Due to limited space in our casing, we implemented a polarity reversal for the Peltier elements. Therefore, they are only enabled to either heat up or cool

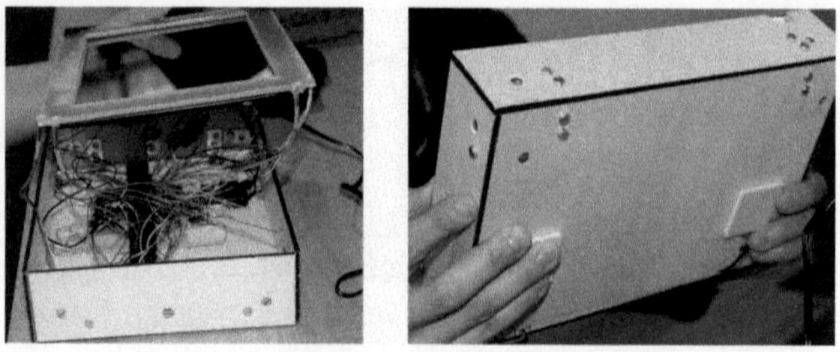

Figure 3. Our *ambiPad* prototype consisting of a custom manufactured casing containing an Arduino Mega ADK (left), two Peltier elements on the back (right) and the plexi-glass frame with integrated RGB LEDs (left).

down, but with an additional circuit both feedback mechanisms would be possible. The 8 RGB LEDs and the two Peltier elements are controlled using an Arduino Mega ADK, that is connected to the Tablet. As the LEDs and the Peltier elements need more power then the Arduino ADK can provide, an additional power supply was used. All components — except for the power supply — are contained in a custom manufactured wooden casing which has a height of 45mm and can still be hold comfortably while providing sufficient mobility.

To control the light frame and the Peltier elements we developed a custom media player. When a video is loaded, we approximate the ambient light by averaging the color of 10% of the video frames in each corner with an update rate of 27 frames per second. We did not implement a mechanism that allows the automatic creation of thermal feedback elements, as it would require extensive analysis of the video. Instead, we do this manually by creating an external file for each video that contains the time stamps at which the thermal feedback should peak and how long it should last. The media player loads the file and controls the Peltier elements accordingly by activating them 100ms before the peak to ensure that they reach the peak temperature of 38 °C.

USER EXPERIENCE EVALUATION

Since *ambiPad* aims at enhancing hedonistic factors of media consumption on tablet computers, our evaluation focuses on such factors. We do not expect the device to increase performance in productive settings, even though scenarios exist where the unique features of the *ambiPad* might be beneficial. E.g., the ambient light frame could be used for off-screen visualization similar to [9].

Method

To assess the participant's experience and perception of *ambiPad* we utilized an adapted version of the Microsoft Production Reaction Cards [2]. Even though this method was originally designed to evaluate the emotional response and desirability of a software design, it has also been applied to product design [1]. Instead of presenting separate cards, we presented a sheet of paper with 26 antonym word pairs to each participant. The participants where asked to select five out of these 52 words that they found to describe their experience most accurately.

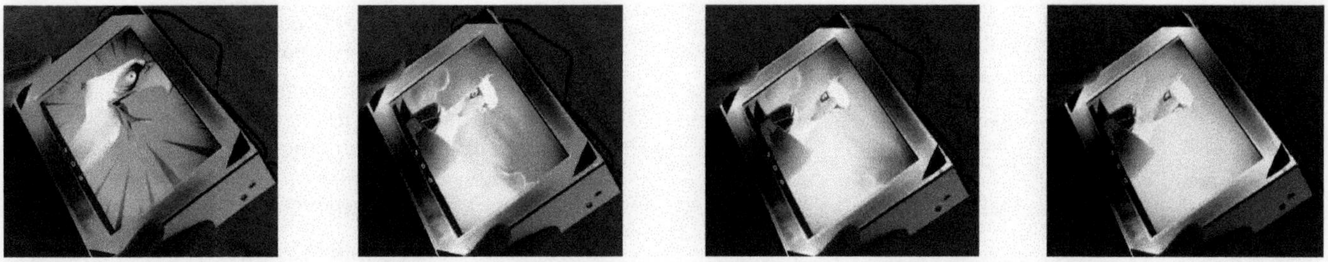

Figure 2. ***ambiPad*** **allows to enhance the emotions in videos using its Ambilight style framing. From left to right it is visible how the fading rage of the main character is also reflected in the color of the light frame.**

Study Set-up

For our study we recruited 21 participants (8 female) from our university (staff members as well as students). The participants age varied between 22 and 35 years with an average age of 28 years. All participants owned a smartphone with a touch-screen. All except one participant (female, 29 years) had used a standard tablet before and 10 of them owned one which they stated to use on a daily basis.

We also asked the users to rate their experience in terms of entertainment, excitement, whether they found it innovative, hard to use or annoying on a 5-point likert scale.

As our focus was on investigating the effect of the different introduced feedback channels, we presented three conditions to the participants. First, *ambiPad* without additional feedback channels. Second, only light is added and third, the *ambiPad* with light and thermal feedback. The users where presented three different videos containing still images with feedback. The still images containing a rather warm ambience were enhanced with thermal feedback. The videos were 90 seconds long, contained 9 images (10 seconds per image). For each video, we added three images with thermal feedback. For the study, we used the aforementioned *ambiPad* prototype.

We counterbalanced the videos as well as the conditions to ensure that the different videos had no effects on the users perception. Additionally, we only explained the current condition shortly before the videos were shown. After each condition, the participants were asked to fill out a questionnaire. Besides this, the participants where asked to think out loud through the whole study. Finally the participants where shown a 3D animated short movie[3], enriched with light and thermal feedback. The average duration of the study per user was 20 minutes.

Results

In total, for the standard condition 25/52 terms have been selected, for the light only condition 31/52 terms and for the light and thermal feedback condition 30/52. For the standard tablet condition 16/25 terms where negative, 6 neutral and 3 positive. In the light only condition 5/31 terms were negative, 10/31 were neutral and 16/31 were positive. For the light and thermal condition 4/30 terms were negative, 8/30 were neutral and 18/30 were positive. The six most selected terms for each condition can be found in Table 1.

[3]http://www.youtube.com/watch?v=3mEGDWkKhBI

Overall, the results of the Microsoft Reaction Cards show a clear difference in selected adjectives between the standard tablet and the two conditions with added feedback channels. The terms selected for the proposed feedback channels where generally more positive, which was also represented in the comments of the users during the study. One issue that the participants found annoying was the brightness of the light feedback. Since the study was conducted in a rather dark environment, the emitted light seemed really strong.

Standard	Light	Light & Thermal
Ordinary (12/21)	Creative (12/21)	Creative (13/21)
Familiar (9/21)	Attractive (9/21)	Exciting (12/21)
Simplistic (9/21)	Clear (9/21)	Entertaining (8/21)
Calm (8/21)	Entertaining (9/21)	Fun (8/21)
Old (8/21)	Comfortable (8/21)	Innovative (8/21)
Boring (7/21)	Calm (6/21)	Attractive (7/21)

Table 1. The six most common terms selected by the paricipants to describe the standard tablet -, light enhanced tablet - and the light & heat enhanced tablet user interfaces (n = 21)

We used a pairwise univariate ANOVA test for the experience ranking questionnaire results analysis with subject as a random factor. For the user experience ranking, the conditions light and light&thermal where significantly better ($p < 0.05$) ranked as the standard condition, with no difference between the two in terms of Entertainment. The same result was found for Excitement. With regards to how innovative the experience was perceived, the participants not only rated the two novel conditions of *ambiPad* significantly better ($p < 0.01$) but there was also a difference between the light and light&thermal condition, with light&thermal being rated significantly better ($p < 0.05$). For the other two questions no difference where found. An overview of the results can be found in Figure 4.

Discussion

The results of our study outline that the added features of *ambiPad* drastically enhance the experience of mobile media consumption. Most users stated that the light emitting frame was more invasive compared to the thermal stimuli. Still, they rated it to be eminently valuable for the overall experience. Especially interesting was that 6 users explicitly expressed that they felt more immersed with the added components. One participant (Female, 22) stated: "wow. the heat really makes me feel the sun of this lovely spring day" when

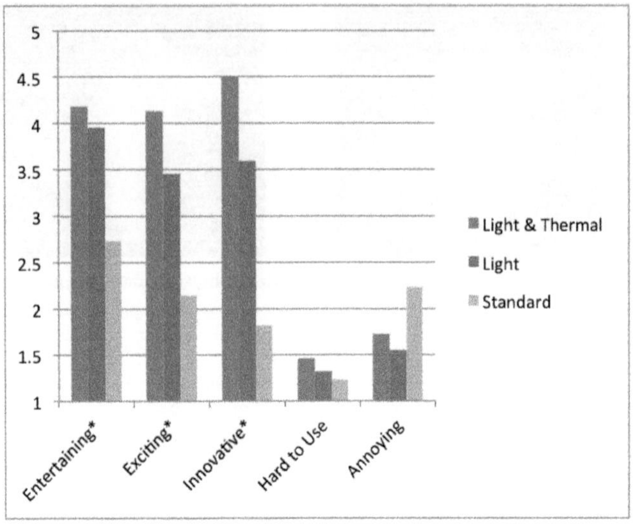

Figure 4. Averages of the answers on the question: I find the investigated user interface... (1 - Completely disagree, 5 - completely agree). For items marked with a "*" we found a significant difference.

showed the picture that can be seen in Figure 1. This is in accordance with the findings of [5].

Even though 4 users stated the brightness of ambient light was to high, this might even out in settings with more environmental light. Furthermore this problem could be easily solved by dimming the light using the ambient light sensor of the tablet. A very similar problem occurred for the heat, as two users felt that the stimuli were to hot. Since individual difference can occur for thermal stimuli [11] we suggest to introduce a simple calibration phase to adapt the stimuli to the users preferences.

CONCLUSION AND FUTURE WORK

In this paper we presented *ambiPad* , a tablet prototype for enriching the consumption of mobile media with ambient feedback. In addition to a light emitting frame around the tablet device, we also added thermal stimuli to enhance the emotional response as well the user experience. The results of our study show that *ambiPad* succeeds in enriching the user experience for mobile media consumption.

For future work, we will to transform the process of adding the thermal stimuli to the videos in an automatic or at least semi-automatic process. This could be achieved by an algorithm that infers emotions from the video features.

REFERENCES

1. Barnum, C. M., and Palmer, L. A. More than a feeling: Understanding the desirability factor in user experience. In *CHI '10 Extended Abstracts on Human Factors in Computing Systems*, CHI EA '10, ACM (New York, NY, USA, 2010), 4703–4716.
2. Benedek, J., and Miner, T. Microsoft product reaction cards. In *http://www.microsoft.com/usability/uepostings/productreactioncards.doc* (2002). (Online; last accessed 15th of February 2014).
3. Blog, G. A. Tablets are changing the way consumers engage with content. In *http://googlemobileads.blogspot.de/2011/04/tablets-are-changing-way-consumers.html* (2011). (Online; last accessed 15th of February 2014).
4. Bullough, J. D., Akashi, Y., Fay, C. R., and Figueiro, M. G. Impact of surrounding illumination on visual fatigue and eyestrain while viewing television. In *Journal of Applied Sciences 6,8* (2006), 1664–1670.
5. Halvey, M., Henderson, M., Brewster, S. A., Wilson, G., and Hughes, S. A. Augmenting media with thermal stimulation. In *Proceedings of the 7th International Conference on Haptic and Audio Interaction Design*, HAID'12, Springer-Verlag (Berlin, Heidelberg, 2012), 91–100.
6. Heilig, M. L. Sensorama simulator. U.S. Patent Number 3050870 (1962).
7. Jones, B. R., Benko, H., Ofek, E., and Wilson, A. D. Illumiroom: Peripheral projected illusions for interactive experiences. In *Proceedings of the SIGCHI Conference on Human Factors in Computing Systems*, CHI '13, ACM (New York, NY, USA, 2013), 869–878.
8. Müller, H., Gove, J., and Webb, J. Understanding tablet use: A multi-method exploration. In *Proceedings of the 14th International Conference on Human-computer Interaction with Mobile Devices and Services*, MobileHCI '12, ACM (New York, NY, USA, 2012), 1–10.
9. Qin, Q., Rohs, M., and Kratz, S. Dynamic ambient lighting for mobile devices. In *Proceedings of the 24th Annual ACM Symposium Adjunct on User Interface Software and Technology*, UIST '11 Adjunct, ACM (New York, NY, USA, 2011), 51–52.
10. Vatavu, R.-D. There's a world outside your tv: Exploring interactions beyond the physical tv screen. In *Proceedings of the 11th European Conference on Interactive TV and Video*, EuroITV '13, ACM (New York, NY, USA, 2013), 143–152.
11. Wilson, G., Brewster, S., Halvey, M., and Hughes, S. Thermal icons: Evaluating structured thermal feedback for mobile interaction. In *Proceedings of the 14th International Conference on Human-computer Interaction with Mobile Devices and Services*, MobileHCI '12, ACM (New York, NY, USA, 2012), 309–312.
12. Wilson, G., Halvey, M., Brewster, S. A., and Hughes, S. A. Some like it hot: Thermal feedback for mobile devices. In *Proceedings of the SIGCHI Conference on Human Factors in Computing Systems*, CHI '11, ACM (New York, NY, USA, 2011), 2555–2564.

Cuenesics: Using Mid-Air Gestures to Select Items on Interactive Public Displays

Robert Walter[1] robert.walter@tu-berlin.de
Gilles Bailly[2] gbailly@mpi-inf.mpg.de
Nina Valkanova[1,3] nina.valkanova@upf.edu
Jörg Müller[1,4] joerg.mueller@acm.org

[1]Quality and Usability Lab, Telekom Innovation Laboratories, TU Berlin, Germany
[2]Graphics, Max-Planck-Institut für Informatik, Saarbrücken, Saarland, Germany
[3]Music Technology Group, Universitat Pompeu Fabra, Barcelona, Catalonia, Spain
[4]Alexander von Humboldt Institute for Internet and Society, Berlin, Germany

Figure 1. People performing mid-air gestures to select items on interactive public displays. The system was installed at three locations: (L1) on a large wall-projection in a coworking space, (L2) on a rear-projection screen in a students' cafeteria, (L3) on an LCD at a venue's opening event

ABSTRACT
Most of today's public displays only show predefined contents that passers-by are not able to change. We argue that interactive public displays would benefit from immediately usable mid-air techniques for choosing options, expressing opinions or more generally selecting one among several items. We propose a design space for hand-gesture based mid-air selection techniques on interactive public displays, along with four specific techniques that we evaluated at three different locations in the the field. Our findings include: 1) if no hint is provided, people successfully use *Point+Dwell* for selecting items, 2) the user representation could be switched from *Mirror* to *Cursor* after registration without causing confusion, 3) people tend to explore items before confirming one, 4) in a public context, people frequently interact inadvertently (without looking at the screen). We conclude by providing recommendations for designers of interactive public displays to support immediate usability for mid-air selection.

Author Keywords
Interactive Public Displays; Selection Techniques; Mid-air gestures; Immediate Usability

ACM Classification Keywords
H.5.m. Information Interfaces and Presentation (e.g. HCI): Miscellaneous

MobileHCI'14, September 23 - 26 2014, Toronto, Canada.

ACM 978-1-4503-3004-6/14/09 $15.00.
http://dx.doi.org/10.1145/2628363.2628368

INTRODUCTION
The focus of public displays is transitioning from static broadcast displays to interactive displays. In particular, this enables displays to become multi-purpose [12] by enabling users to choose between different content and applications, thereby increasing their usefulness. However, multi-purpose public displays also raise new challenges for interaction [12]: How to enable users to switch between applications and games, browse content or express their opinion (e.g. voting [27])?

Interactive public displays raise challenges for both the choice of the *input modality* and the design of the *interaction technique*. Traditional input devices like keyboards and mice are typically not available in public spaces. Touch screens can also be inappropriate due to hygienic reasons or because the display is installed at locations that are not within the physical reach of passers-by [29]. Finally, remotely using an input device for input (e.g. a smartphone) does not allow users to interact instantly, as they have to fetch their phone and install/launch the corresponding app before.

Selection techniques for public displays have to fulfill certain requirements that are very different from those on personal computers or mobile phones. On personal devices, users usually perform thousands of selections, causing selection time and error rate to be the most important factors. In contrast, most users of public displays are expected to be first time users [29], only performing relatively few consecutive selections. Thus, immediate usability becomes much more important than performance. Furthermore, users may give up if they do not immediately succeed with the interaction [17].

In this paper we investigate how to support users to select items on public displays using mid-air gestures. Mid-air gestures have several advantages for interactive public displays

[29]. They allow users to interact from a distance, may foster discoverability and collaboration and are fun to perform [19, 26, 29]. However, it is not clear how to design immediately usable mid-air selection techniques for public displays.

To guide this process, we present a design space with five dimensions: *Selection Gesture*, *Confirmation Gesture*, *Input Space*, *Layout*, and *User Representation*. The design space aims at highlighting important design choices and helps designers to categorized existing techniques. We illustrate the applicability of our design space by comparing mid-air selection techniques used in the context of distant displays.

As an application for mid-air selection on public displays we implemented an interactive polling tool, that allows users to make a vote on a given topic. We conducted a field study to evaluate four selection techniques and investigate the impact of user representation and input space on immediate usability. We deployed the system at three different locations for a total period of three weeks. We report on our findings of three studies, which include:

- After a guided registration, no further instruction is required to allow people to successfully select and confirm items using *Point+Dwell*. Some people tend to perform other confirmation gestures than dwelling (push, grasp, wave, etc).
- The user representation can be switched from *Mirror* to *Cursor* after registration without confusing users.
- People explore the options before confirming one item. In our studies, they selected 2.5 (out of 6) items in average before confirmation.
- In a public setting, people may interact inadvertently with the display, without even looking at it.

We believe that these findings, our design space, and the proposed selection techniques are useful for researchers and practitioners of public displays and digital signage. For researchers, our techniques provide a baseline for developing novel selection techniques. The availability of immediately usable mid-air selection techniques may support the investigation of more complex interactions with public displays. Both users and practitioners can benefit from multi-purpose public display applications.

RELATED WORK

We first discuss the challenges of interactive public displays, highlighting different phases of interaction and then discuss related work on techniques for choosing options with a focus on mid-air techniques.

Interaction with Public Displays

Before users can interact with the system, they need to (1) notice the display, (2) understand that the system is interactive, (3) understand how to interact, and finally (4) be motivated to interact. The challenging aspect is that the system only has a couple of seconds or minutes for communicating how it works [29], otherwise users may just leave. Additionally, a public display generally has only "one shot": Users may give up if they do not immediately succeed with the interaction [17].

Noticing Displays

Sometimes people do not even notice public displays. Huang [9] has shown that most public displays receive very few glances. Müller [20] finds that people often expect nothing useful on public displays and speculates that therefore, they may intentionally ignore them. These works, as well as [10, 11, 18] investigate some factors that attract attention for public displays, like installation height, motion, context, etc.

Communicating Interactivity

Once passers-by have noticed the display, they need to understand that it is interactive. For communicating interactivity, techniques like *call-to-action* [14] have been proposed. The *Honeypot* effect [5] is effective in demonstrating interactivity when other users already interact with the system.

Understanding Initiation of Interaction

When users have understood that a display is interactive, they need to understand how to initiate interaction, or more specifically how to *register* [30] a gesture. While this appears apparent for touch-screens [22] (touching the screen), it is less obvious for mid-air gestures. In previous work [29] we have investigated how to provide hints for mid-air gesture registration. We found that a descriptive textual hint, combined with an icon representation of the gestures presented at the bottom of the screen (space division) is most effective.

Understanding Interaction Techniques

After these steps, users need to understand *how* to interact with the display, e.g., how to select an item. This question has not yet been addressed for mid-air gestures in the context of public displays. Therefore, we take inspiration from other device classes, such as desktop computers and large displays.

Selecting Items

Items are often selected through menu bars, context menus, toolbars, palettes, etc. In particular, menus received a lot of attention in literature including empirical studies (e.g. [21]), predictive models or various interaction techniques (e.g. [15]). However, most of these works focus on dedicated input devices (e.g. keyboard or mice) rather than mid-air gestures.

Several menus have been designed to exploit various input or output modalities such as multi-touch [1, 16], pen interaction [25], mobile devices [31, 7], remote control [2] or virtual reality [4]. In [8] a set of five pre-defined mid-air selection gestures for large displays is evaluated in a laboratory study regarding their *intuitiveness* and *effectiveness*, showing that *Dwelling* is the most *intuitive* gesture for selection. In our work we build on that finding and evaluate different designs of selection techniques in a field study, focusing on one specific selection gesture (*Point+Dwell*).

Mid-air Gestures and Large Displays

While we are not aware of existing work on selecting items using mid-air gestures on public displays, a few systems focusing on large displays have been proposed [8, 13, 24, 28,

3]. For instance, Bailly et al. [3] proposed a mid-air menu technique for large displays. Users are able to select a command in a linear menus by extending a certain number of fingers towards the displays. However, these different menus are not well suited for public displays because they are not compatible with immediate usability since they require explicit teaching.

DESIGN SPACE

We propose a design space of hand-gesture based mid-air selection techniques for public displays. It aims at helping designers and practitioners to design selection techniques by describing and comparing their main features. This design space has been derived from the analysis of differences and similarities of existing mid-air selection techniques in NUI frameworks, commercial products and related work.

We distinguish three phases for selecting items on a public display using mid-air gestures (see Figure 9):

1. *Registration:* Users express their intention to make a selection by performing a specific action to display a list of available items. This phase has been particularly investigated in *StrikeAPose* [29]. In this paper we distinguish three different modalities of registration.
    - *Modeless:* Selection is possible at any time. As soon as a users steps in front of the screen, they are instantly able to select an item. This registration technique is useful when the selection itself is an essential element of the system, as in [27].
    - *Quasimode:* For the *quasimode*, or *user-maintained* registration, a dedicated action (e.g. a posture) has to be actively maintained by the user to allow for selection (similar to modifier keys on keyboards). This technique has been proposed in [29].
    - *Modal:* After registration, the application switches to a special mode, that is only dedicated to the act of selection. The list of options is displayed once a dedicated registration gesture has been performed until the selection has been confirmed or explicitly canceled.
2. *Selection:* The display shows all the different selectable items, and users can select and explore them.
3. *Confirmation:* Once users have decided on an item, they confirm that selection in this phase. Only after this phase a command is triggered to the system.

While several design spaces of selection techniques and menus have been proposed in the literature (e.g. [23]), they mainly focus on mouse or keyboard-based interaction. As mentioned in the related work section, *public displays* is a specific context requiring to revisit existing techniques to accommodate immediate usability [19, 29]. In this design space we focus on mid-air hand gestures. We do not intend to cover other body-based selection techniques (e.g. finger-based [2] or position-based techniques [27]). Furthermore we only focus on selection and confirmation (phase 2. and 3. above). In the following, we discuss the different dimension of our design space.

D1: *Selection Gesture* (Figure 2). During selection, users may explore different options before confirming one. While several hand gestures have been proposed, we focus our analysis on easily guessable gestures in favor of immediate usability.

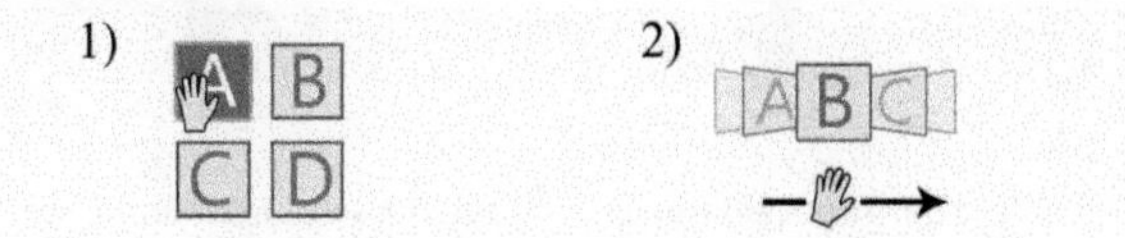

Figure 2. Selection Gesture: 1) Point, 2) Swipe

1) *Point*: Cursor-based pointing: users move the representation of their hands over the desired item in order to change the selection (similar to hovering with a mouse cursor on items before clicking). Among the systems we analyzed (Table 1), pointing is the most commonly applied selection technique.
2) *Swipe*: Users swipe with their hand in mid-air over a certain region on the screen in order to change the current selection. This can be compared to a *scrolling* mechanism.

D2: *Confirmation Gesture* (Figure 3). After users selected the item, they confirm their selection, which marks their final decision. The following hand gestures may be used to confirm selections.

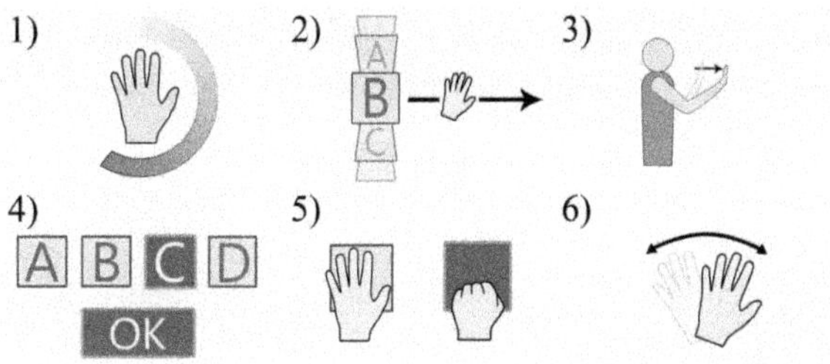

Figure 3. Confirmation Gesture: 1) Dwell, 2) Swipe, 3) Push, 4) Pointing, 5) Grip, 6) Wave

1) *Dwell*: Users rest their hand over an item. This is one of the most commonly used confirmation gestures. To define an appropriate dwell time is challenging as it may be perceived too short by novices and too long by expert users [6].
2) *Swipe*: Users swipe their hand in mid-air over an item in order to confirm their selection. This technique may be combined with both *Swiping* (different direction) and *Pointing* for selection (D1).
3) *Push*: Similar to *Swipe*, a quick movement along a dedicated axis is performed to confirm a selection. An additional DoF (depth) is used for that confirmation gesture, which enables the technique to be combined with both *One-Dimensional* and *Two-Dimensional* layouts (see D4).
4) *Point*: Users point in a second stage to a dedicated item (similar to touching *OK* button on touch screens). This approach reduces the necessity for dwell times but could hamper immediate usability, as a second pointing stage is required.
5) *Grip*: Users perform a grip or grasp motion hovering over the selected item in mid-air.
6) *Wave*: Users wave with their hand over the selected item.

D3: *Input Space* - As we focus on hand gestures, there are mainly two ways to extend the arm in order to invoke a selection (Figure 4).

Figure 4. Input Space: 1) In Front of User, 2) Around User

1) *In Front of User*: Users reach out their arm to the front in order to select items, as they would typically do for pointing gestures (D1).
2) *Around User*: Users may also reach out to their sides (left, right and top) to reach for items that are available for selection. If a *Silhouette* or *Avatar* user representation (D5) is applied, using this input space reduces occlusion with the users' representation and the selectable items.

D4: *Layout* - Different ways to layout items in the selection are possible that mainly differ in dimensionality (Figure 5).

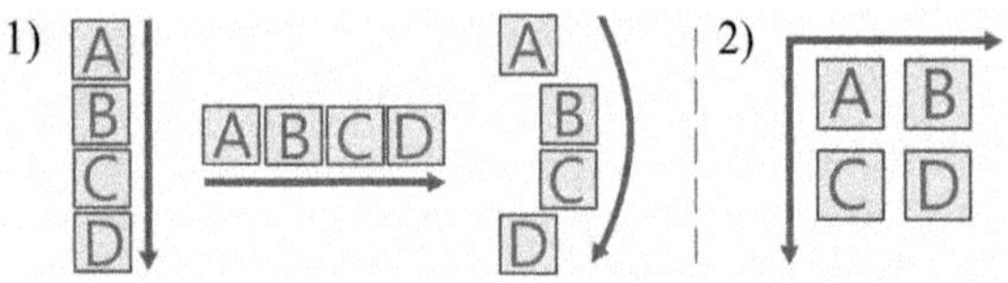

Figure 5. Layout: 1) One-dimensional, 2) Two-dimensional

1) *One-dimensional*: Selections can only be changed in one direction. Users move their hand along a straight or curved axis to select items. While one-dimensional layouts typically require less constrained hand movements than two-dimensional ones, the number of selectable items at a time is smaller.
2) *Two-dimensional*: Users exploit two degrees of freedom in hand movement to change selections, typically x and y-direction. Such a layout is used in the *Kinect Hub* menu system on the *Microsoft Xbox 360*.

D5: *User Representation*. Mid-air interaction techniques mostly require some sort of visual feedback representing the user (Figure 6). This dimension has already been investigated for communicating the interactivity of a public display [19].

Figure 6. User Representation: 1) Cursor, 2) Avatar, 3) Mirror Image

1) *Cursor*: The user is reduced to a small pointer or cursor on the screen that moves according to the users' hands. This kind of representation only requires a small amount of screen space. It may not be immediately obvious to which of the both hands the cursor is attached. Users have to trial-and-error for both hands and observe the feedback in order to determine the correct hand. Moreover, in a multi-user scenario,

	D1		D2						D3		D4		D5		
System	Point	Swipe	Dwell	Swipe	Push	Point	Grip	Wave	Front	Around	1D	2D	Cursor	Avatar	Mirror
Kinect Hub [1]	✓		✓						✓			✓	✓		
Kinect Adventures [1]	✓		✓						✓		✓		✓	(✓)	
Dance Central [1]	✓			✓						✓	✓		✓		(✓)
Sonic Free Riders [1]		✓		✓					✓		✓		✓		
Your Shape [1]	✓		(✓)			✓				✓	✓				✓
Video-place [13]	✓		✓							✓	✓				✓
Samsung Smart TV	✓						✓		✓			✓	✓		
K4W SDK [2]	✓				✓		(✓)		✓			✓	✓		(✓)
OpenNI NiTE	✓	(✓)	✓	(✓)	(✓)			(✓)	✓			✓	✓		

Table 1. Categorization of techniques according to the design space (✓: technique is applied; ✓: technique is applied secondarily)

which is common for public displays [19], it may be challenging for users to identify the cursor that belongs to themselves.
2) *Avatar*: The user is represented by a virtual avatar that mimics their motions. Not only the hand movements are mapped to the representation of the user, but also the movements of other joints. As a downside, significantly more screen space is required for that representation. While this technique does not help to notice interactivity [19] of the display, it may work well after the registration phase, when the user is already aware that the display is interactive.
3) *Mirror Image*: The user is represented by a mirror image, or sometimes only by a simplified version of it: a silhouette on the screen. Unlike an *Avatar*, not just the movements but also the shape or outline and the colors of the representation correspond to the user. This representation provides the highest fidelity. It also works best for communicating the interactivity of a public display [19].

Table 1 categorizes a set of mainly commercial products and systems according to the dimensions of this design space. The (primarily) applied features of a system are checked (✓) in the table. Potential secondary techniques are marked with light-gray check mark (✓). For example *Kinect Adventures* primarily uses a *Cursor* user representation, but also shows an *Avatar* representation in the background (secondary).

[1] Available for Microsoft XBox 360
[2] Microsoft Kinect for Windows

As shown in Table 1, there is already a large variety of techniques among this exemplary set. A commonly used standard or gestural language for mid-air selecting has not yet been established. Also it is not yet clear, which of the techniques support immediate usability best. For this reason we investigated the dimensions of this design space in a series of three studies. In an initial pilot study, we focus on gestural input, represented by the first two dimensions (*Selection* and *Confirmation* gesture).

PILOT STUDY

To better understand the mental model of users, we conducted a preliminary study with 23 participants. The goal of this study was to identify immediately usable actions for *Selection Gesture* (D1) and *Confirmation Gesture* (D2), based on a *Mirror Image* representation (D5) and *Around User* as input space (D3). We presented participants a large real-time silhouette representation of themselves, along with a minimalistic body-centric menu-like overview of selectable items (Figure 7). We conducted the study as a Wizard of Oz experiment: after observing the registration gesture, the wizard manually activated the menu showing the items.

Participants were asked to select the highlighted item and confirm their selection, using what they think would be the most "intuitive" actions while no further hint was provided. They were free to try multiple actions consecutively. The experimenter highlighted that there are no wrong or right actions, and asked the participants to *think aloud* and freely express their thoughts and considerations during the task. After participants stated to have finished the task, the experimenter proceeded with a semi-structured interview asking to describe the actions they performed in detail.

To see if selecting items at different positions in the selection would afford different gestures for selection and confirmation, we randomly changed the highlighted item after each participant. We counted the frequencies of all observed gestures. We analyzed both *first* gestures and alternatives of actions that people investigate *after* performing the first gesture.

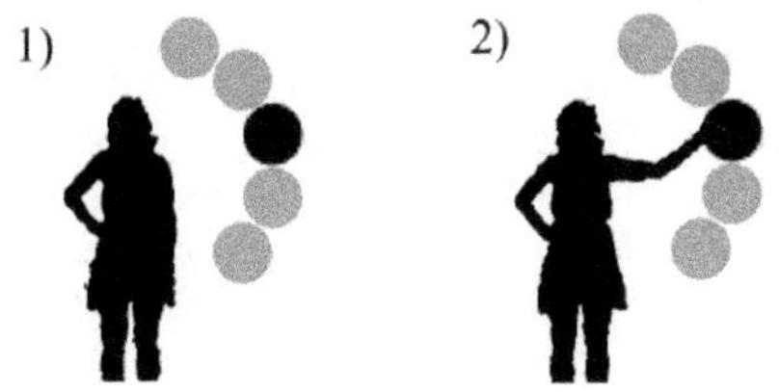

Figure 7. *Mirror Image* user representation with five items attached. Participants were asked to demonstrate how they would select and confirm the highlighted item.

Results

The following gestures and actions were used by the participants in order to select items and confirm their selections.

Selection Gesture: For a large majority of participants (22 of 23) we observed *Point* to be the most frequently performed gesture for selection: Users moved their hand over the highlighted item to signal their choice (Figure 7.2). Even after trying different actions consecutively, people sticked to pointing as a general behavior, only altering in hand postures. Considerable variations include pointing with 1) open hand, palm facing towards screen (18 of 23), 2) palm turned away from the screen (4 of 23). 3) only index finger extended (3 of 23), Six unique hand postures while pointing were observed. No effect of the item position on the performed selection gesture was identified.

Confirmation Gesture: Confirming [8], we observed *Dwell* to be the most frequently performed first action (15 of 23 participants) for confirming a selection. Still, there was a large variety of observed gestures including *Grip* (4 of 23) in different variations: grip once and dwell, grip repetitively, *Plucking* (grip and pull towards themselves). Plucking was also among the most popular alternative actions that people performed after their first action (3 of 23). Furthermore, we observed people repetitively tilting their palm towards and away from the screen (3 of 23). In total we noted 15 unique gestures for confirmation. We observed no effect of the item position on the performed confirmation gesture.

We have learned, that most people would point and dwell to select items if no hint is provided. For our design (Figure 7), different item positions did not afford different gestures. Yet, it is not clear if other designs would trigger different user behavior. We decided to implement *Point+Dwell* as selection and confirmation gesture and investigate further dimensions of the design space in a iterative design study.

ITERATIVE DESIGN STUDY

The goal of this user study was to investigate two dimensions of the design space: input space (D3) and user representation (D5). We are particularly interested in *Mirror Image* and *Cursor* user representations in the selection phase. We iteratively improved two techniques that use two different user representations (D5) to improve immediate usability of both. For the registration phase we use a technique proposed in *StrikeA-Pose* [29]: Users are represented by a virtual *Mirror Image* on the screen, and an animated *Text+Icon* label describing the registration gesture is shown (compare Figure 9 left). As proposed [29] we use the *Teapot* gesture for registration: User may use their left (right respectively) hand to touch their left (right) hip. In the initial state of the study, the registration was implemented as *quasimode*: As users release their hip, the selectable items would disappear again.

Selection Techniques

We used two selection techniques that were inspired by commercial systems as a starting point, and iteratively adjusted them during the study to improve immediate usability.

Cursor-Front: This technique uses a *Cursor* user representation and an *In Front of User* input space. It was inspired by the *Kinect Hub* menu system for *Xbox 360* (Figure 8 left). While the *Kinect Hub* version uses a *Two-Dimensional* layout, we decided to use a *One-Dimensional* one to remain consistent with the other technique. Additionally to the cursor, there is a real-time PiP (picture-in-picture) *Mirror Image* representation of the user shown in the bottom right corner, with the hands highlighted. For the registration phase, a *Mirror Image* user representation is used, that is switched to *Cursor* for the selection phase.

Mirror-Around: This technique uses a *Mirror Image* representation and an *Around User* input space. It was inspired by the *Your Shape* menu system for *Xbox 360* (Figure 8 right). Since we also use a *Mirror Image* user representation in the registration phase, the visualization does not change after registration.

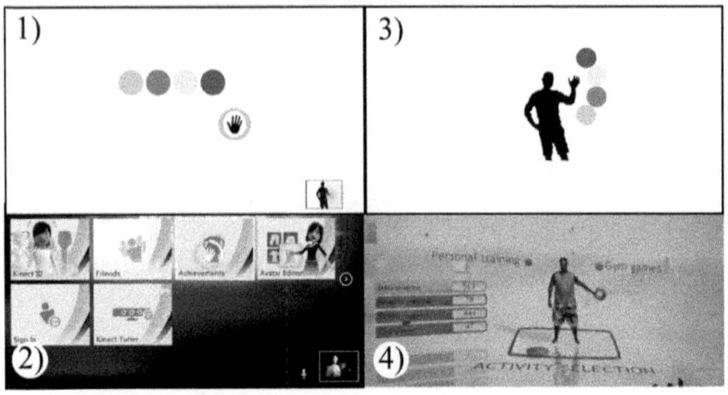

Figure 8. The two iterative design study conditions in their initial states: 1) Cursor-Front, 3) Mirror-Around, and in-game screenshots of the two corresponding systems that they were inspired by: 2) Kinect Hub, 4) Your Shape.

Apparatus and Participants

The system was installed for four days in a passage in close proximity to the main entrance of an university building. We randomly invited passers-by in the entrance to participate in a five-minute experiment. In total 51 passers-by participated in the test. For the entire time of the interaction the system logged the raw depth video, a screen capture, a camera recording and various user events to a text file. We noted user comments during the test and conducted a semi-structured interview at the end of each test. The questions included 1) how they selected the item, 2) what problems they encountered, 3) what improvements they suggested, and 4) which technique they preferred and why. Based on observations and user feedback, we adjusted the initial techniques on a daily basis.

Instructions and Task

We informed each participant, that the study is about interactive public displays and selecting items. As we focus on immediate usability, no further specific information was provided to resemble a field-situation. Each participant was asked to initially select an arbitrary item (color) using one of the two techniques (switched after each participant). After this first trial, we introduced the participants to the other technique and asked them to select ten consecutive items with each of the two techniques.

General Learnings

Modal Registration is less confusing: We observed problems with the *quasimode* registration, because it requires both hands. Especially in the first trial participants unintentionally released their hand from their hip while trying to select an item with the other hand. Some users even tried to use the same hand that they used for registration (e.g. touched their hip with the right hand and tried to make the selection with the right hand as well, consequently releasing their hip and causing the menu to disappear). It appears to be too complex for novice users to use both hands for two different sub-tasks (one for registration and one for selection). For this reason we introduced *modal* registration: after performing the registration gesture, the system switched to selection mode. The registration posture may be released for selecting. Using modal registration also allows to use one hand only for both registration and selection. Switching from quasimode to modal registration appeared to introduce less confusion to participants, especially in the first trial. As a downside, this step introduces another dwell time for entering the selection mode.

Registration Gesture should be meaningful: During the interviews some participants mentioned that while they understood and performed the registration gesture (touching the hip with one hand), they kept asking themselves for the reason: "I was confused. Do I have to touch my hip for calibration?", "I didn't know why it wanted me to touch my hip.", "Why touching the hip?", "Why do I have to touch my hip before the colors appear?". It seems that people do not wonder about the registration itself, but about the unusual gesture which is generally not used for human communication. For this reason we decided to change the gesture to a more meaningful one: raising the hand [27]. Though this gesture is less subtle, it's more clear for users of the system and onlookers that they raise their hand in order to communicate with the system. This gesture is socially used to gain attention, so people may wonder less why they have to do it to initialize the selection.

Cursor-Front - Learnings

Dual-Cursor makes selection easier: Participants reported that they were confused about which hand they should use for selection: "You have to try which hand you can use!". We observed both behaviors: using the same hand that was used for registration and using the opposite one. For this reason we implemented two cursors to allow users to decide which hand to use. They could either use their left hand to control the left cursor (displaying a left hand), or their right hand to control the right cursor (displaying a right hand). This change appeared to reduce the confusion about what hand ought to be used for selection.

Representation switch does not cause confusion: As mentioned earlier, for this technique the representation of the user switches from *Mirror Image* to *Cursor* after the registration (compare Figure 9.1 to 9.2). During the switch, the mapping between hand position in space and pixel coordinates on the screen was preserved: the cursor appeared at the exact same position on the screen as the hand of the users' mirror representation. Initial concerns that this could confuse users were not confirmed. However, it is not yet clear if this could become a problem in a multi-user scenario.

PiP hint is ignored: After the first ten participants, we observed that seven of them did not notice the Picture-in-Picture (PiP) hint showing a *Mirror-Image* representation of the user at all (see Figure 8 left). Two participants noticed but ignored it, and only one actually looked at it. One even reported that he was distracted by it. We did not observe a change in user behavior after removing the picture.

Mirror-Around - Learnings
Dual-Selection causes confusion: We observed the same confusion about what hand to be used as in the *Cursor-Front* technique. Initially, the items appeared on the opposite side than the one that was used for registration (Figure 8.3), suggesting to use the opposite hand. Still we observed that participants used the same hand that they used for registration also for the selection (for example trying to use the right hand to reach for items that are displayed at the left side of their body). For this reason, as an analogy to the dual-cursor, we decided to put two identical, mirrored sets of items to both sides of the user. However this lead to even more confusion, as people were not sure if it makes a difference if they select items from the left or right side. To avoid constraining the free choice of the user what hand to be used to select items, we moved the items from the side to the top of the users' representation (compare Figure 8.3 to 10.4). At this position the selection can be reached with both hands equally well, allowing users to freely choose which hand they use for selection.

We have iteratively developed two selection techniques using different user representations (D5) and input spaces (D3) that support immediate usability on public displays. We have learned that 1) quasimode registration causes confusion, 2) the registration gesture should be meaningful to users in the given context, 3) users should be able to freely choose which hand to use, 4) a switch of the user representation after registration does not necessarily cause confusion, 5) PiP hints may be ignore by users. To investigate if these findings also apply in an ecologically valid in-the-wild setting and to explore additional combinations of user representation (D5) and input space (D3), we decided to conduct a field study.

FIELD STUDY

We conducted a field study to evaluate the techniques and analyze user behavior in an ecologically valid setting. We deployed the system at three different locations (Figure 1):

Coworking Space (L1): We installed the system for two weeks in the cafeteria of Betahaus Berlin, a well visited coworking space. Visitors mainly include entrepreneurs, freelance software developers, as well as artists and designers.

Student's Cafeteria (L2): The system was also installed for four consecutive days in a large student's cafeteria. The deployment location was mainly visited around noon by students or staff of the Technical University of Berlin and Berlin University of the Arts, as well as locals living nearby.

Venue Opening (L3): On the occasion of the Summer Fair for Factory Berlin, a large campus for start-ups and technology-driven companies in the city of Berlin, we deployed the system for one evening in a passage close to the entrance.

System: As an application for our selection techniques, we implemented an interactive public survey tool, that allows users to place a vote for one out of six different options to a given topic. We adapted these topics to the particular location in order to increase the participation rate. For example at the coworking space, we invited passers-by to "Tell us your passion!" (written in large letters in the upper area of the display, see Figure 1). The selectable options in the coworking

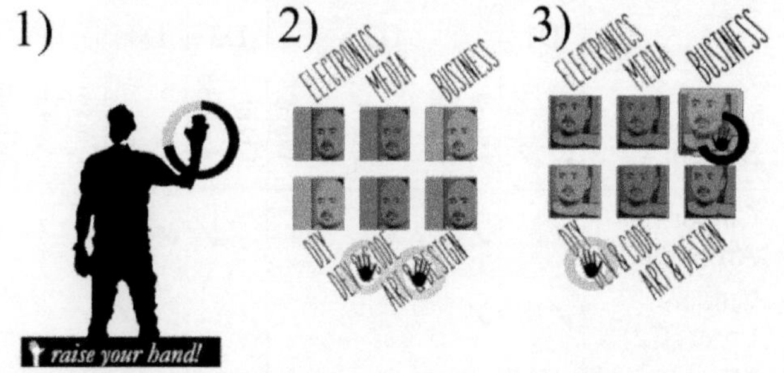

Figure 9. The three phases of interaction - 1) registration: a user represented by a *Mirror Image*, a registration-gesture hint is shown at the bottom. 2) selection: user moves their hand over an item. 3) confirmation: user dwells over desired item; displayed Technique is *Cursor-Front*

space were 1) *Dev & Code*, 2) *DIY*, 3) *Media*, 4) *Electronics*, 5) *Art & Design*, and 6) *Business*. While for the registration phase a *Text+Icon* hint was provided, no further instructions for selection and confirmation were presented (Figure 9). The order of the items was randomly altered on a daily basis for all locations. As users choose one of the options, the system takes a photo of the their face and adds it to a tile-based poll visualization [27], that shows the distribution of users across the different options (Figure 1).

Implementation: The system is using the *Kinect* camera to capture passers-by. For visualization, the *Processing*[1] library is used. The software implementation is based on the prototypes of the first two experiments. It uses the *OpenNI*[2] framework and the skeletal tracking features of the *NiTE* middleware.

Techniques: We tested four techniques (Figure 10) in total. *Cursor-Front* and *Mirror-Around* are the results of the iterative design study. The aim was to evaluate two dimensions of the design space (User Representation and Input Space). As User Representation (D5) we use *Cursor* and *Mirror Image*. As Input Space (D3) we use *In Front of User* and *Around User*. This dimension also affects the item layout (D4): if the input space is *In Front of User*, items can be arranged in a *Two-dimensional* layout, while for the other case the items are arranged in a *One-Dimensional* layout. The condition was changed randomly every ten selections.

Data Analysis: We recorded a screen capture, the raw depth video from the sensor, as well as various user events in a log file for the entire time of the deployment in all the locations. The most important automatically captured events in the log file include when users 1) step in front of the display, 2) perform the registration gesture, 3) make a selection, and 4) leave the display. During that time two researchers gathered data from on-site observations and semi-structured interviews with users. In particular we were interested in 1) if users are able to select the item they want, 2) what they think how to select items, and 3) how they knew how to select items. The recorded videos and material were later reviewed. Each instance of a user performing a selection was annotated by a researcher. Finally data for each selection include 1) which

[1] http://processing.org/
[2] http://www.openni.org/

System	D1		D2						D3		D4		D5		
	Point	Swipe	Dwell	Swipe	Push	Point	Grip	Wave	Front	Around	1D	2D	Cursor	Avatar	Mirror
Cursor-Around (C1)	✓		✓							✓	✓		✓		
Cursor-Front (C2)	✓		✓						✓			✓	✓		
Mirror-Around (C3)	✓		✓							✓	✓				✓
Mirror-Front (C4)	✓		✓						✓			✓			✓

Table 2. Techniques that were investigated in the field study mapped to the design space

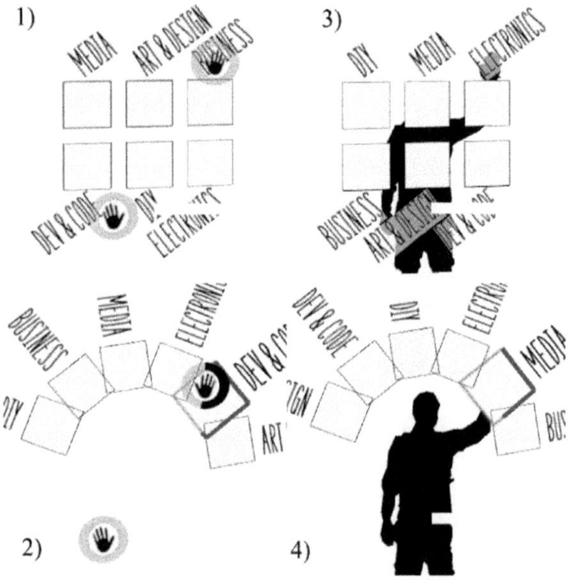

Figure 10. The four fieldstudy conditions: 1) *Cursor-Front*, 2) *Cursor-Around*, 3) *Mirror-Front*, 4) *Mirror-Around*

item / option was selected, 2) which condition was active, 3) which hand was used for registration / selection, 4) how long it took for users to register / select / confirm, 5) which hand postures / confirmation gestures they use.

We report on 405 unique observed selections, excluding 1) repetitive selections of one user, 2) cases of wrongly recognized registration gestures, 3) researchers of the team and other people that are familiar with the system, and 4) unintended user interaction from the data.

Results

People explore the system before selecting: The average time from stepping in front of the screen until registering for selection was 13 seconds, using similar hints as in [29]. After registration, most users confirmed a selection within 10 seconds. This time includes 1) understanding how to select items, 2) exploration of the options and 3) temporal demand to execute selection gestures, as well as 4) dwell time (2 seconds). In average people selected 2.5 items before they finally confirmed one. They spent about 5 to 7 seconds for that exploration process. We did not observe an effect of the condition on the selection time, or on the amount of exploration.

No hint for selection required: One question in the interview was "Did you successfully select the item you wanted?" 47 (of 49) participants reported that they did, which indicates that throughout all techniques, most people were able to use the system and select the items they want. In the data we could not identify one significantly least, or most frequently selected position in the selection. Randomly altering the order of the options did not affect the survey results. Both indicates that selections were not random. We also asked people how they knew how to select an item. The majority of interviewed people (33 of 49) reported that they were able to make the selection based on their "intuition" or "gut feeling" and by just trying. Five participants reported that someone else explained them how to use the system, four participants reported to have experience with the *Kinect* and one stated he has learned from observing other people how to interact with the system. However, the majority (39 of 49) of people report that did not observe other people before trying to interact with the system.

Representation switch does not cause confusion: As in the lab study, for the cursor conditions (*Cursor-Front, Cursor-Around*) the user representation was switched from *Mirror* to *Cursor* after registration. We did not observe a difference in selection time (required time from registration to confirmation) and conversion (percentage of people that actually select an item after registration) between the techniques. Both indicates that this switch of the user representation does not cause confusion also in a field scenario. This confirms findings from the laboratory study and shows that they also apply in a field scenario.

People perform different confirmation gestures: We asked interviewees to recap the interaction and explain us what steps they went through until they finally confirmed a selection. While the last step (confirmation) was not explicitly mentioned by a majority of participants, most of the others (17) reported to have "rested" their hand over the corresponding item. 12 of them explicitly refer to the dwell-time visualization (Figure 9, 10) and mentioned that they have dwelled until "the circle was fully charged". However, as observed in the pilot study, some people tend to perform other confirmation gestures than dwelling. Two participants reported to have performed a *Push*, and one mentioned he performed a *Grip* gesture to select the item. In the annotated videos we observed that 90% of users *Point+Dwell* to select items, as suggested by the visualization. 4% perform a *Push* gesture, 3.5% decide to *Grip* and another 1% *Wave* over the item.

People stick to one hand: From those users that could potentially use both of their hands (none occupied), 80% decide to use the same hand for registration as for selection. Even if they could use the left hand to better reach an item at the left side of their body, they would still use the right hand, if they already have registered with that one. Surprisingly, we did not observe an effect of the position of the item on the used hand. It appears that mainly the choice of the registration hand determines what hand would be used for selection.

Reasons of errors: We observed 25% of all registrations to be unintended: people inadvertently performed the registration gestures without even looking at the screen. In most of these cases they were raising their hand while pointing to the menu of the cafeteria in order to place an order next to our screen. About 28% of all users were carrying objects (mugs, bottles, phones, tablet computers, bags etc.) in one hand. This constraint leads to false selections where people were pointing with one hand at an item, but unintentionally selected another item with the other hand (lifted as well). This scenario was observed 11 times, while in five of these cases, one hand of the user was occupied. We only observed this kind of false selections when the *In Front of User* input space was active. Unlike to *Around User*, people use this space as a resting position for their hands (e.g. arms crossed in front of body).

RECOMMENDATIONS

From the insights and findings we collected during our three studies we provide the following recommendations for designers of interactive public displays, that want to allow users to select options using mid-air gestures.

No hint for point+dwell required: In all of the three studies we observed that people would point and dwell at items that they want to select, if no further hint or instruction is provided. This confirms the finding of [8] and shows that this also applies in the field. Given one of the four presented selection techniques, designers are free omit or delay hints as "move your hand to the item" for the selection and confirmation phase.

Design for one-handed interaction: Many people in public spaces carry objects in their hands. To allow people with one hand occupied to interact with the display, we recommend to only require one hand for a successful interaction. From the the field study we learned that users tend to use one hand only, so this behavior should be supported. However, we also observed that some people do switch hands, so the application should also not *require* to stick to one hand. The best solution could be to use one hand only, that can be switched at any time, i.e. all items are within reach of both hands.

Handle unintentional interactions: Especially in public space, we can not expect that users who gesture in front of the display are actually addressing it. Many people may unintentionally trigger actions (especially registration gestures) on the screen. We are not aware of an appropriate registration gesture that would avoid this problem. The application should either be designed to cope with unintentional interactions, or use techniques to detect if peoples are addressing the screen with their gestures (e.g. face detection or gaze tracking).

Support exploration: Most users of interactive public displays are first-time users, who are not familiar with the interface and the options to choose from. In the field study we observed that users in average explore 2.5 (out of 6) items before they select one. This behavior should be supported for example by using higher dwell times in the beginning.

User representation may be switched: From the laboratory study and the field study, we have learned that it is not necessary to stick to one user representation for the entire interaction. In our studies we did not observe that a switch from *Mirror Image* to *Cursor* after registration would introduce any confusion to users. If the mapping between hand position and screen coordinates is preserved during the switch, the user representation may be changed after registration. This way, designers could take advantage of both representations: high fidelity and strong communication of interactivity of the *Mirror Image* representation, as well as reduced screen space consumption of the *Cursor* representation.

CONCLUSION

In this paper we presented a design space for hand-gesture-based mid-air selection techniques on interactive public displays. From two laboratory studies, we derived four different selection techniques supporting immediate usability. These technique vary in dimensions of *Input Space* (D3) and *User Representation* (D5). In a field study we showed that the four techniques perform equally well in an in-the-wild scenario, so designers may choose freely among them.

Our findings allow designers of interactive public displays to create applications that go beyond playful interaction. Allowing users to easily make selections or change contents, allows public display applications to evolve towards multi-purpose applications. We believe that this will make the platform of interactive public display more attractive to users, practitioners and advertisers.

Yet, the design space of hand gesture-based mid-air selection techniques for interactive public displays is not yet fully explored experimentally. As the main scope of the field studies in this paper is on the dimensions of *Input Space* and *User Representation*, further investigations on the other dimensions is yet to be done. Besides, future work is necessary to show if the techniques also apply in a wider demographical and cultural context, as the public installations of this work were addressed to a defined audience.

ACKNOWLEDGMENTS

This research was funded by the European Institute of Innovation and Technology, the German Federal Ministry of Education and Research (grant number 01IS12056), the Max Planck Center for Visual Computing and Communication and the Cluster of Excellence Multimodal Computing and Interaction of Saarland University. Special thanks go to Betahaus Berlin, Factory Berlin and TU Berlin Mensa for facilitating our field study locations and to Ines Ben Said, Céline Coutrix, Tiare Feuchtner, David Lindlbauer and Moritz Behrens for their valuable support.

REFERENCES

1. Bailly, G., Lecolinet, E., and Guiard, Y. Finger-count & radial-stroke shortcuts: 2 techniques for augmenting linear menus on multi-touch surfaces. In *CHI'10*, ACM (2010), 591–594.
2. Bailly, G., Vo, D.-B., Lecolinet, E., and Guiard, Y. Gesture-aware remote controls: guidelines and

interaction technique. In *ICMI'11*, ACM (2011), 263–270.

3. Bailly, G., Walter, R., Müller, J., Ning, T., and Lecolinet, E. Comparing free hand menu techniques for distant displays using linear, marking and finger-count menus. In *INTERACT'11*, Springer (2011), 248–262.
4. Bowman, D. A., and Wingrave, C. A. Design and evaluation of menu systems for immersive virtual environments. In *VR'01*, IEEE (2001), 149–.
5. Brignull, H., and Rogers, Y. Enticing people to interact with large public displays in public spaces. In *INTERACT'03* (2003), 17–24.
6. Cockburn, A., and Gin, A. Faster cascading menu selections with enlarged activation areas. In *GI'06*, Canadian Information Processing Society (2006), 65–71.
7. Francone, J., Bailly, G., Lecolinet, E., Mandran, N., and Nigay, L. Wavelet menus on handheld devices: stacking metaphor for novice mode and eyes-free selection for expert mode. In *AVI'10*, ACM (2010), 173–180.
8. Hespanhol, L., Tomitsch, M., Grace, K., Collins, A., and Kay, J. Investigating intuitiveness and effectiveness of gestures for free spatial interaction with large displays. In *PerDis'12*, ACM (2012), 6:1–6:6.
9. Huang, E. M., Koster, A., and Borchers, J. Overcoming assumptions and uncovering practices: When does the public really look at public displays? In *Pervasive '08*, Springer-Verlag (Berlin, Heidelberg, 2008), 228–243.
10. Jacucci, G., Morrison, A., Richard, G. T., Kleimola, J., Peltonen, P., Parisi, L., and Laitinen, T. Worlds of information: designing for engagement at a public multi-touch display. In *CHI'10*, ACM (2010), 2267–2276.
11. Ju, W., and Sirkin, D. Animate objects: how physical motion encourages public interaction. In *PERSUASIVE'10*, Springer (2010), 40–51.
12. Kostakos, V., Kukka, H., Goncalves, J., Tselios, N., and Ojala, T. Multipurpose public displays: How shortcut menus affect usage. *Computer Graphics and Applications, IEEE 33*, 2 (2013), 56–63.
13. Krueger, M. *Artificial reality II*. Addison-Wesley, 1991.
14. Kules, B., Kang, H., Plaisant, C., Rose, A., and Shneiderman, B. Immediate usability: a case study of public access design for a community photo library. *Interacting with Computers 16*, 6 (2004), 1171–1193.
15. Kurtenbach, G., and Buxton, W. User learning and performance with marking menus. In *CHI'94*, ACM (1994), 258–264.
16. Lepinski, G. J., Grossman, T., and Fitzmaurice, G. The design and evaluation of multitouch marking menus. In *CHI'10*, ACM (2010), 2233–2242.
17. Marshall, P., Morris, R., Rogers, Y., Kreitmayer, S., and Davies, M. Rethinking 'multi-user': an in-the-wild study of how groups approach a walk-up-and-use tabletop interface. In *CHI'11*, ACM (New York, NY, USA, 2011), 3033–3042.
18. Müller, J., Alt, F., Michelis, D., and Schmidt, A. Requirements and design space for interactive public displays. In *MM'10*, ACM (2010), 1285–1294.
19. Müller, J., Walter, R., Bailly, G., Nischt, M., and Alt, F. Looking glass: a field study on noticing interactivity of a shop window. In *CHI'12*, ACM (2012), 297–306.
20. Müller, J., Wilmsmann, D., Exeler, J., Buzeck, M., Schmidt, A., Jay, T., and Krüger, A. Display blindness: The effect of expectations on attention towards digital signage. In *Pervasive'09*, Springer (2009), 1–8.
21. Nilsen, E. L. *Perceptual-motor control in human-computer interaction*. PhD thesis, Ann Arbor, MI, USA, 1991. UMI Order No. GAX91-35659.
22. Peltonen, P., Kurvinen, E., Salovaara, A., Jacucci, G., Ilmonen, T., Evans, J., Oulasvirta, A., and Saarikko, P. It's mine, don't touch!: interactions at a large multi-touch display in a city centre. In *CHI'08*, ACM (2008), 1285–1294.
23. Samp, K. Designing graphical menus for novices and experts: connecting design characteristics with design goals. In *CHI'13*, ACM (2013), 3159–3168.
24. Shoemaker, G., Tsukitani, T., Kitamura, Y., and Booth, K. S. Body-centric interaction techniques for very large wall displays. In *NordiCHI'10*, ACM (2010), 463–472.
25. Song, H., Grossman, T., Fitzmaurice, G., Guimbretiere, F., Khan, A., Attar, R., and Kurtenbach, G. Penlight: combining a mobile projector and a digital pen for dynamic visual overlay. In *CHI'09*, ACM (2009), 143–152.
26. Ten Koppel, M., Bailly, G., Müller, J., and Walter, R. Chained displays: configurations of public displays can be used to influence actor-, audience-, and passer-by behavior. In *CHI'12*, ACM (2012), 317–326.
27. Valkanova, N., Walter, R., Vande Moere, A., and Müller, J. Myposition: Sparking civic discourse by a public interactive poll visualization. In *CSCW '14*, ACM (New York, NY, USA, 2014), 1323–1332.
28. Vogel, D., and Balakrishnan, R. Interactive public ambient displays: transitioning from implicit to explicit, public to personal, interaction with multiple users. In *UIST'04*, ACM (2004), 137–146.
29. Walter, R., Bailly, G., and Müller, J. Strikeapose: revealing mid-air gestures on public displays. In *CHI'13*, ACM (2013), 841–850.
30. Wu, M., Shen, C., Ryall, K., Forlines, C., and Balakrishnan, R. Gesture registration, relaxation, and reuse for multi-point direct-touch surfaces. In *TABLETOP'06*, IEEE (2006), 185–192.
31. Zhao, S., Dragicevic, P., Chignell, M., Balakrishnan, R., and Baudisch, P. Earpod: eyes-free menu selection using touch input and reactive audio feedback. In *CHI'07*, ACM (2007), 1395–1404.

AirAuth: Evaluating In-Air Hand Gestures for Authentication

Md Tanvir Islam Aumi
UbiComp Lab, DUB Group
University of Washington
Seattle, WA, 98195, USA
tanvir@cs.washington.edu

Sven Kratz
FX Palo Alto Laboratory
3174 Porter Drive
Palo Alto, CA, 94304, USA
kratz@fxpal.com

ABSTRACT

Secure authentication with devices or services that store sensitive and personal information is highly important. However, traditional password and pin-based authentication methods compromise between the level of security and user experience. *AirAuth* is a biometric authentication technique that uses in-air gesture input to authenticate users. We evaluated our technique on a predefined (*simple*) gesture set and our classifier achieved an average accuracy of 96.6% in an equal error rate (EER-)based study. We obtained an accuracy of 100% when exclusively using personal (*complex*) user gestures. In a further user study, we found that AirAuth is highly resilient to video-based shoulder surfing attacks, with a measured false acceptance rate of just 2.2%. Furthermore, a longitudinal study demonstrates AirAuth's repeatability and accuracy over time. AirAuth is relatively simple, robust and requires only a low amount of computational power and is hence deployable on embedded or mobile hardware. Unlike traditional authentication methods, our system's security is positively aligned with user-rated pleasure and excitement levels. In addition, AirAuth attained acceptability ratings in personal, office, and public spaces that are comparable to an existing stroke-based on-screen authentication technique. Based on the results presented in this paper, we believe that AirAuth shows great promise as a novel, secure, ubiquitous, and highly usable authentication method.

Author Keywords

In-air gestures; authentication; shoulder surfing; user experience; acceptability.

ACM Classification Keywords

H.5.m. Information Interfaces and Presentation (e.g. HCI): Miscellaneous

INTRODUCTION

A growing number of users store and manipulate important and sensitive information online, on their personal computers and mobile devices. As such, finding methods of secure and easy-to-use authentication is of increasing importance, since tradeoffs exist between the users' desire for security and the compromises in user experience they are willing to take [10].

MobileHCI '14, September 23 - 26 2014, Toronto, ON, Canada

ACM 978-1-4503-3004-6/14/09. . .$15.00.
http://dx.doi.org/10.1145/2628363.2628388

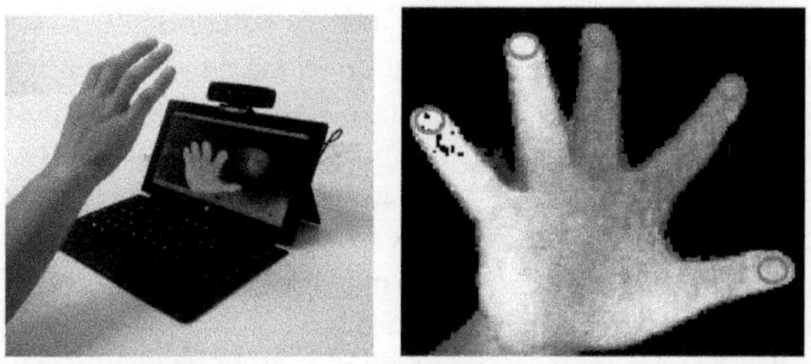

(a) (b)

Figure 1. (a) A user is performing an authentication gesture in front of a short range depth camera. (b) Hand features (3D locations of finger tips and hand center) captured and used by AirAuth.

At present, passwords and PIN numbers are the most widely-used authentication methods for gaining access to PCs, mobile devices and online accounts, and they are well-understood by the users. However, such knowledge-based systems can have disadvantages, such as requiring the user to learn complex passwords (for increased security vs. "trivial" passwords). Also, as the number of accounts or devices the user needs to access grows, the mental burden increases for the user to remember multiple passwords or variants thereof. That is one reason why a number of users resort to using only a few passwords (perhaps with simple variants) used for all of their authentication activity [27], which puts the users at significant risk if one of these passwords is compromised.

Traditional password entry can be prone to *shoulder-surfing attacks* [25]. The growing amount of video surveillance in public spaces and the potential of misusing it compounds this danger. In addition to shoulder-surfing attacks, mobile devices equipped with touch screens are prone to *smudge attacks* [2]. In the case of smudge attacks, the attacker attempts to reconstruct the device pin or login stroke from finger smudges left on the device's screen after authentication.

A possible solution to problems of traditional password entry is to use biometric features during the authentication process. Instead of relying solely on the user's knowledge of a secret, biometric authentication systems can enhance security twofold: (1) the systems can directly use distinct physical features of the legitimate user; (2) the system can make use of behavioral traits of the legitimate user during the authentication process as a further authentication layer.

Regarding the user experience, this means that users are permitted to retain less complex secrets, since the biometric adds extra layers of security. Furthermore, the authentication process itself can be made more engaging. We argue that instead of using a keyboard or pinpad for password entry, gestures can be used for authentication, where the system checks for the knowledge of a secret as well as physical and behavioral properties of the user. In daily life, some gestures, such as writing one's signature, are performed very often and can thus be easier and more engaging to use than traditional password or PIN-based authentication.

In this paper, we present a novel authentication system, *AirAuth*, that uses hand gestures made in the vicinity of a computing device (Figure 1(a)). Using a short-range depth camera, our system tracks hand gestures input by the user. In contrast to longer-range systems such as Kinect, the short-range depth camera allows us to track individual finger tips and the center of the user's hand in 3D space (Figure 1(b)). This data provides us with an abundance of features allowing the decoding the user's authentication secret, classifying biometric properties of the user's hand, and classifying the movement style of the user.

Our system achieves a higher authentication accuracy than previous work [12, 22] that does not track multiple points in space. Furthermore, we do not require a large multitouch screen [22] for gestural authentication to work. Also, the mobile device itself does not need to be moved [12], which might prove impractical in some situations.

We present the results of three user evaluations we conducted of our system. In the first study, we analyze the EER-based authentication accuracy of our system and achieved an accuracy of 96.6% including predefined gestures and 100% for personalized gestures only. In a second study, we analyze the susceptibility of our system to shoulder-surfing attacks, by asking a second and distinct set of users attack user models trained in the first study. The results of this study confirm those of previous work [23], demonstrating the resistance of gesture-based approaches to shoulder surfing attacks. A third longitudinal study was conducted to analyze the robustness of AirAuth over time and the effect of a template update strategy on the authentication accuracy. We also evaluated our system in terms of user experience and location acceptability. The results indicate that gestures that are enjoyable to the users are also more secure and difficult to forge, an important characteristic which is not present in traditional password based authentication systems. In addition, our technique was also highly rated by users for use in personal, office, and public spaces when compared to the presently available stroke-based on-screen authentication technique used in Android phones. Finally, our technique is simple, robust, and easy to implement. We used the Dynamic Time Warping (DTW) algorithm [24] which is fast and easily deployable on embedded hardware. This characteristic makes ubiquitous deployment of our system easy: can be used anywhere where secured authentication is crucial, e.g., on door panels, fixed PCs, laptops or mobile devices.

RELATED WORK

We have structured our discussion of related work as follows: first, we discuss *usable security* in general and look at previous works on password-based authentication schemes, to highlight how our proposed method could solve some of the problems of those schemes. Next, we discuss some of the most common *threat models* that are presented in the literature. Following that, we look at *biometric methods* used in previous works. Finally, we discuss previous work done on *gesture-based authentication*.

Usable Security and Password-Based Authentication

Kainda et al. [10] highlighted the tradeoff between usability and security. Security engineers always strive to make systems more secure, but it has been shown that usability suffers as a consequence. New authentication schemes should thus strive to make authentication more usable and engaging, while keeping the authentication process secure.

The vast majority of today's online services, computers and mobile devices use a password or PIN-based scheme for adhoc (immediate) user authentication. Although this type of authentication is well-known by both the user base and also developers of secure systems, it does have some drawbacks. Password-based authentication systems become more secure as the length of the password grows. However, longer passwords are more difficult to remember, and, instead of using a distinct password for different services that require authentication, users commonly use variations of a basic password. Also, users tend to change their password infrequently, once it has been set [20]. Von Zezschwitz et al. report that users use simpler password variations for low-sensitivity authentications. If these low-sensitivity accounts are compromised by attackers, highly sensitive authentications that share the same basic password root are put at risk [27].

Threat Models

As already mentioned in the introduction, *shoulder-surfing* and *smudge attacks* are two very important threats to password-based authentication on mobile devices.

There have been numerous approaches proposed to counter the shoulder-surfing threat, for instance, using fake cursors to confuse attackers [5], making use of relative locations of known password icons and distractor icons [29], using set-intersection techniques to extract a correct pin using binary choices made by the user [21], entering the password out of sight from potential attackers [4] or using haptically-cued false entries [3]. We verified empirically that our proposed method is resilient against shoulder-surfing attacks through a user study with video-based attacks.

A further threat model, especially for touch-based mobile device and perhaps to a somewhat lesser degree on keyboards or keypads is the *smudge attack*, which lets attackers reconstruct password, PIN or stroke entry by imaging or otherwise analyzing the oily residue left by the user's fingers on a precleaned surface after a legitimate user has performed an authentication [2]. On touchscreen devices, smudge attacks can be mitigated by randomizing the locations where user needs to touch the screen for authentication [28]. AirAuth is fully resistant to smudge attacks, since no touch-based interaction whatsoever is required for authentication.

Biometric Techniques

A wide range of input devices and sensors have been used to gather biometric data for authentication. Jorgensen et al. explore mouse dynamics as a biometric for behavioral authentication [9]. Similarly, keystroke dynamics have also been explored [16]. Alpcan et al. propose signature-like strokes on a touchpad as a biometric [1]. This concept has been extended to multi-touch surfaces with good results [22]. Kumar et al. propose gaze-based password entry [11] as method of avoiding shoulder-surfing attacks. Similarly, [14] propose using specific gaze points on still images for authentication. Further biometrics that have been used include fingerprint scanning, retinal scanning, face recognition, voice recognition, and palm vein scanning [13, 30]. However, these techniques are complex and require specialized hardware. In contrast, AirAuth is relatively simple and requires only a depth camera, hardware which may soon be integrated into smartphones [7]. In contrast to pure biometrics, AirAuth also has the additional advantage of requiring the knowledge of a gesture for successful authentication.

Gesture-based Authentication

Motion gestures on mobile phones have been proposed as an authentication biometric. During a gesture input, the user moves the entire phone through the air. The movement is recorded by the mobile phone's motion sensors (typically an accelerometer and a gyroscope). The results presented so far in the literature appear promising [8, 12, 17]. A relatively closely related touch-less biometric has been proposed by Sahami et al. [23], which uses a mobile device's magnetometer to track free-space input via a magnetic widget. The main drawback of their method is that only a single point is tracked in space and the requirement for the magnetic widget. AirAuth tracks multiple points in free space without the requirement for additional user instrumentation. Sae et al. explored multi-touch gestures on on touch screens with positive results [22]. However, that technique may not be suitable for phone-sized devices due to the space required for 5 finger gestures and it also may be susceptible to smudge attacks. Finally, *BroAuth* [15] used full-body gestures tracked by a Kinect for authentication. We believe that using hand gestures as in AirAuth is more practical, because it requires much less interaction space and it also supports small devices such as handsets and tablets.

THE AIRAUTH SYSTEM

In the following, we describe the hardware and software implementation of AirAuth prototype, which we also used during our user studies.

Hardware

Our hardware prototype (Figure 2) consists of a Creative Senz3D[1] short range depth sensor placed on a computing device, in our case a Microsoft Surface Pro Tablet (Figure 1(a)), in such a way that the sensor can image the user's hand while she makes authentication gestures in the vicinity of the device. When the user's hand passes a previously set threshold distance from the device, gesture recording starts. The recording stops when the user's hand moves beyond the threshold distance.

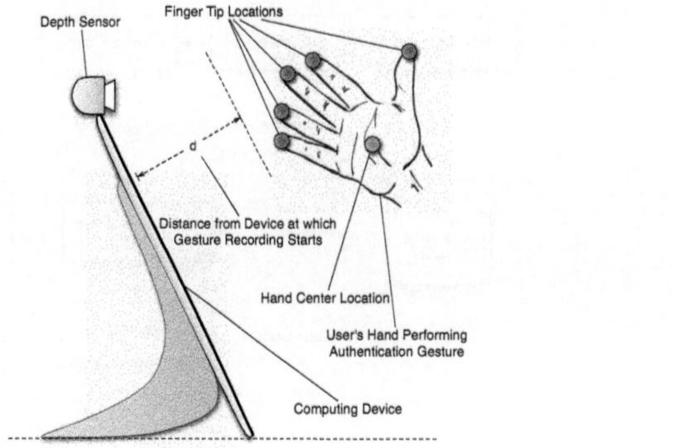

Figure 2. Hardware prototype of our system. A depth sensor is arranged on a computing device so that it can observe the user's hand while it makes in-air gestures for authentication. The depth sensor measures the 3D locations of the user's fingertips and of the hand center.

Software

From the depth image, persistent features can be extracted, i.e., the 3D locations of the users fingertips. The extracted features (tip and hand center locations) are a biometric that our system uses for user authentication. However, our system is not limited to these specific features. Other types of persistent features can also be used given a means to extract them reliably. Since a gesture entry typically takes around 1–2 s to perform, our biometric consists of a time-based stream of the aforementioned features. For our prototype, we used the Intel Perceptual Computing SDK[2] to extract the feature points from the depth image.

In a biometric authentication system, there are usually two operational stages: the *enrollment stage* and the *authentication stage*. In the enrollment stage, the users authentication data is registered with the system by acquiring and storing a biometric template corresponding to a particular user. In the authentication stage, instances of authentication inputs are compared with the registered one(s) in order to authenticate a user.

Figure 3 shows an overview of our software implementation. A new user needs to undergo an enrollment phase (a), where the user performs three authentication gestures. If the gestures are not sufficiently similar to each other, the user has to repeat the task. Once the user passes the enrollment phase, those three gestures are processed and their average is stored by the system as the template. The maximum pairwise distance between the three initial gestures is calculated and stored as a threshold ε. For distance calculation, we used the Dynamic Time Warping (DTW) algorithm [24].

[1] The maximum IR depth resolution of this sensor is 320x240 and its diagonal field of view is 73°. The sensor captures images at a rate of 30 Hz.

[2] `http://software.intel.com/en-us/vcsource/tools/perceptual-computing-sdk`

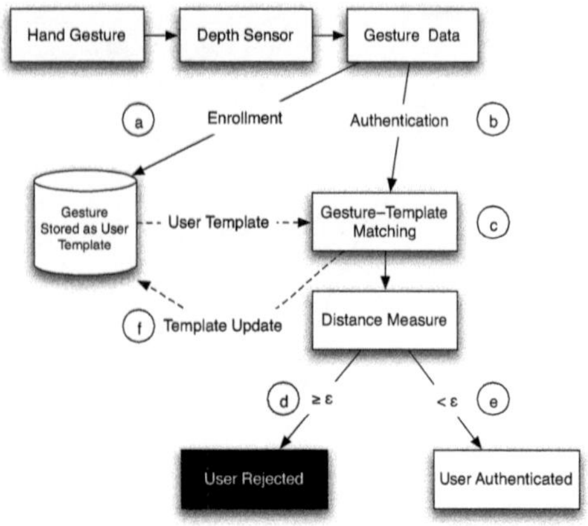

Figure 3. A conceptual overview of the AirAuth software implementation. Note the two main stages of the authentication system—enrollment (a) and authentication (b).

For the authentication phase (b), our system compares the gesture data input by the user with the template and calculates the distance score (c). If the distance score is greater than the threshold ε, the user is rejected (d), since this indicates a fraudulent authentication attempt. If the distance score is below ε, the user is authenticated (e) by our system. To compensate for temporal changes in the biometric, the user template is periodically updated (f) with data from authentication gestures with a low distance to the existing template.

Data Processing

From the depth sensor, we obtain raw 3D coordinates (x, y, and z) of all (visible) fingers of the user and also the user's hand center. However, the location of user's hand with respect to the depth sensor can be anywhere and in any orientation in the air and differ one instance to another. To transform location and orientation of the hand to *relative* coordinates, input data needs to be normalized before applying any matching algorithm. Therefore, at first we normalize the data to a $[0, 1]$ interval by scaling the raw 3D points using the following three equations [26].

$$x_1{}^{i^s} = \frac{x_1{}^i - \min_i(x_1{}^i)}{\max_i(x_1{}^i) - \min_i(x_1{}^i)} \quad (1)$$

$$y_1{}^{i^s} = \frac{y_1{}^i - \min_i(y_1{}^i)}{\max_i(y_1{}^i) - \min_i(y_1{}^i)} \quad (2)$$

$$z_1{}^{i^s} = \frac{z_1{}^i - \min_i(z_1{}^i)}{\max_i(z_1{}^i) - \min_i(z_1{}^i)} \quad (3)$$

Here $x_1{}^i$, $y_1{}^i$, and $z_1{}^i$ are raw coordinates of any single finger or the hand center and $x_1{}^{i^s}$, $y_1{}^{i^s}$, and $z_1{}^{i^s}$ are coordinates after performing scaling operation. After scaling, we translate all the points with respect to the origin by subtracting the mean of the point set from all points:

$$(x_1{}^{i^s})_t = x_1{}^{i^s} - \frac{\sum_{i=1}^{n} x_1{}^{i^s}}{n} \quad (4)$$

$$(y_1{}^{i^s})_t = y_1{}^{i^s} - \frac{\sum_{i=1}^{n} y_1{}^{i^s}}{n} \quad (5)$$

$$(z_1{}^{i^s})_t = z_1{}^{i^s} - \frac{\sum_{i=1}^{n} z_1{}^{i^s}}{n} \quad (6)$$

Here $(x_1{}^{i^s})_t$, $(y_1{}^{i^s})_t$, and $(z_1{}^{i^s})_t$ are scaled coordinates after being translated to the origin.

Matching Gesture Data

While capturing the gesture, the depth sensor collects 3D coordinates of all five fingers and the hand center in each frame. Therefore, data for each input gesture is actually a time-series data of hand locations. So, at first an input gesture is formatted as a time series data of hand locations

$$\text{Input}(t) = [\text{Location}_1, \text{Location}_2, \ldots, \text{Location}_n] \quad (7)$$

where n is the number of frames captured during the entire gesture. Location_i is the ith sequence vector composed of the x,y and z coordinates of the positions of the user's five fingers and his hand center, thus:

$$\text{Location}_i = [x_1^i, y_1^i, z_1^i, x_2^i, y_2^i, z_2^i, \ldots, x_6^i, y_6^i, z_6^i]^\mathsf{T} \quad (8)$$

After processing these raw data points using the scaling and translation equations, DTW is used to calculate the distance between two gesture instances. We used the Euclidian distance as the distance measure for DTW.

USER STUDIES

We conducted four user studies to evaluate AirAuth. First, to find a set of simple gestures users would be willing to use, we conducted a pilot study to obtain a set of gesture suggestions from several test subjects. Second, we conducted a user study that comprised enrollment and authentication phases, with the goal of determining AirAuth's accuracy. Third, we conducted a user study to evaluate the resilience of AirAuth towards shoulder surfing attacks. Finally, we performed a longitudinal study to assess authentication similarity and repeatability over time.

User Study 1: Finding a Set of Simple Gestures

One of the goals of our research was to test the accuracy as well as the vulnerability of predefined, *simple*, in-air gestures. Hence, we tried to identify a set of gestures that are simple and easy to reproduce from a user point of view.

Therefore, as a pilot study, we conducted a short interview session with 10 participants from an industrial research lab. At first we explained to them the purpose of the study and asked them to perform up to three different air gestures that they thought were simple and easy to reproduce. Participants could choose any gesture they wanted. We asked them to find gestures that can be performed with both single and multiple fingers. The whole interview session took only 2–3 minutes per participant. As a result of this study, we found a set of 15 gestures. Figure 4 shows the 2D sketches of the gesture suggestions we obtained from the study.

It should be noted that this gesture set is intended to be simple and reproducible from a user's perspective and also performable with one or multiple fingers. If we examine the gestures closely, we can see that some participants chose their first name initial (gesture IDs 6, 12, 14, and 16), favorite number (gesture IDs 1, 5, and 11), shape, symbol, etc. Participants

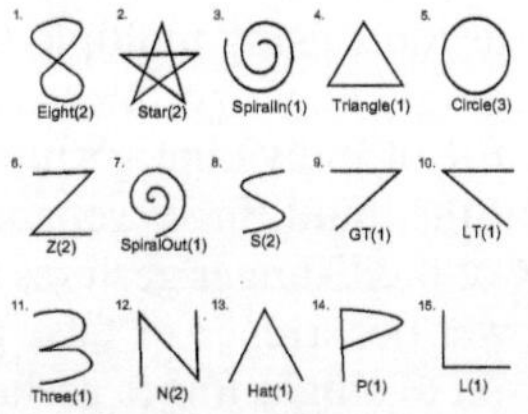

Figure 4. 2D sketches of the user defined *simple* gesture set, consisting of 15 gestures we sourced from 10 participants. The gesture id is denoted on the top left of each gesture symbol. The gesture name and the choice frequency by the study participants are indicated below the gesture symbol.

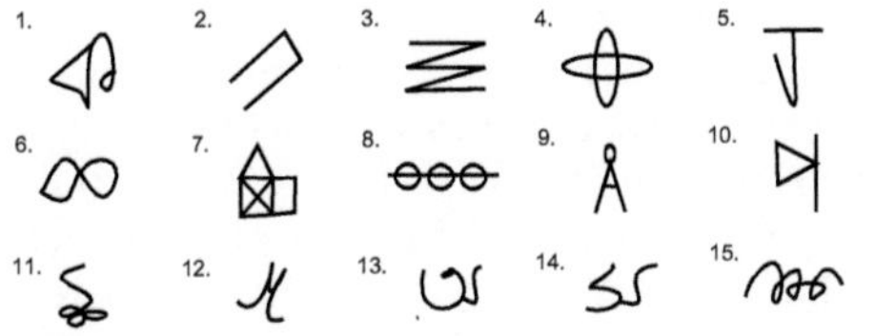

Figure 5. 2D representations of the *complex* gestures the participants of study the 2nd user study chose to enter.

chose certain gestures because, according to them, they were easy for them to perform and also to remember later without any effort. It should also be noted that some of the gestures were chosen more than once by different participants (the choice frequency is indicated after each gesture name in parentheses in Figure 4). This shows that there was at least some consensus regarding the choice of gesture amongst the participants. Some people also chose the existing 2D gesture they use to unlock their touch-based mobile phone since they were already comfortable with the 2D version of the gesture.

User Study 2: Determining AirAuth's Accuracy

In this study, we investigated the accuracy of our system across multiple users. One particular goal when using the fixed gesture set was to measure the accuracy of our system of distinguishing between gesture entries of different users for the same gesture type. For this study, we recruited 15 participants. 11 were male and 14 of them were right handed. All but one of them was fairly experienced with smartphones and computers. 4 of them were familiar with in-air gestures (mostly using Kinect). The participants' age ranged from 18 to 46 (average: 28.3, SD: 6.5).

Before each user study session, we explained our system briefly to the participants. After that, they were asked to fill out a short questionnaire with demographic information and then proceeded to the gesture trials. To test our system with more complex and personalized gestures, we decided to add the participant's signature (performed as a hand movement in the air) and one custom complex gesture for each participant. So, each participant was asked to enter a total of 17 gestures: the 15 fixed gestures from Figure 4, one signature, and one self-defined complex gesture. Figure 5 portrays 2D sketches of the self-defined *complex* gestures each participant came up with. It should be noted that each of these gestures are complex from the participant's point of view. The participants were asked to come up with gestures that they thought would be more secure and less vulnerable to attackers.

Before entering each gesture, the participants were asked to practice the gesture a few times. Once comfortable, we asked them to perform the gesture 20 times: 10 times with single finger and 10 times with multiple fingers. In case of multiple fingers, participants were free to choose any number of fingers they wanted. They were also free to perform the gestures however they wanted, we just instructed them to be consistent among multiple trials of same gesture. To get rid of the carry-over effect, we counterbalanced the order of gestures to enter between participants. Additionally, we took video footage (see Figure 9) of the participants while performing the gestures and used that footage later for our third user study.

We also wanted to measure the participants' feelings and experience about the gestures qualitatively. Therefore, after performing each gesture, the participants rated that gesture in terms of pleasure, excitement, and easiness of use. To obtain excitement and pleasantness ratings for each gesture in an impartial way, we applied the *EmoCard* technique [6]. In addition, we were curious about the location acceptability of our technique. As mentioned in [19], both location and audience play a significant role in determining which gestures are acceptable. Therefore, after completing all the gestures, participants rated both our technique and the stroke-based on-screen authentication technique from Android phones in different hypothetical locations such as private, office, and public environments. Before leaving at the end of the study, participants were given the opportunity to express written opinions about the usability, applicability, and usefulness of the technique. The whole study took approximately 1 hour per participant.

In the following, we detail our findings on *accuracy*, *qualitative feedback*, and *location acceptability*.

Accuracy Analysis

To determine the accuracy of our system across multiple users, we calculated the Equal Error Rate (EER), a point where (at a certain threshold setting) the False Acceptance Rate (FAR) and False Rejection Rate (FRR) are equal. FAR and FRR are inversely related. Thus, decreasing one measure will result in an increase in another. Calculating the EER is a standard method in the literature of measuring the accuracy of authentication systems [1]. We measured FAR and FRR using the following formulae:

$$\text{FAR} = \text{number of accepted forgeries / total number of forgery cases} \quad (9)$$

$$\text{FRR} = \text{number of rejected genuine authentications / total number of genuine authentications} \quad (10)$$

We measured the EER of single and multiple finger gestures separately. For each gesture, we had 10 single and 10 multiple finger samples from each user. As we mentioned previously, in our prototype application, the users had to provide 3 samples of their password gesture during the enrollment stage and the average of those were used as our reference template. Therefore, we decided to do the same for EER calculation and used the average of the first 3 samples for each gesture as a reference template for that gesture. Generating the template gesture in this way reflects the state of a hypothetical

Gesture	EER (Single Finger)	EER (Multiple fingers)
01 (Eight)	0.04	0.03
02 (Star)	0.02	0.02
03 (SpiralIn)	0.04	0.04
04 (Triangle)	0.05	0.04
05 (Circle)	0.04	0.03
06 (Z)	0.05	0.04
07 (SpiralOut)	0.04	0.04
08 (S)	0.05	0.05
09 (GT)	0.04	0.01
10 (LT)	0.04	0.02
11 (Three)	0.06	0.03
12 (N)	0.06	0.04
13 (Hat)	0.04	0.04
14 (P)	0.05	0.02
15 (L)	0.04	0.04
16 (Sign)	**0.0**	**0.0**
17 (Complex)	**0.0**	**0.0**
Average (all gestures)	0.038	0.029

Table 1. Equal Error Rate for each gesture, for single finger input and multiple finger input. Note that the *sign* and *complex* gestures have an EER of 0.

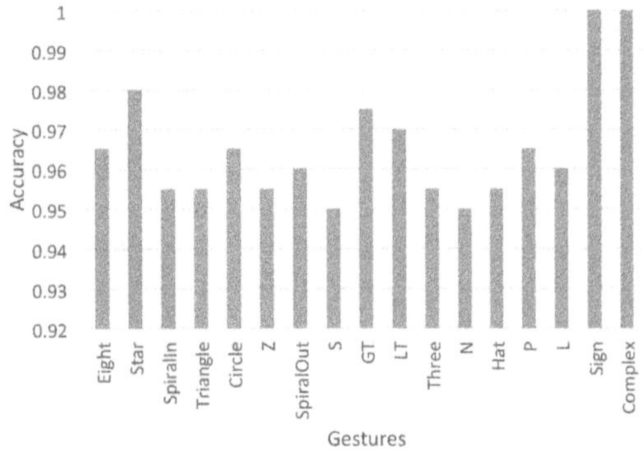

Figure 6. Achieved accuracy of the gestures used in the study. Note that the user-defined gestures (*sign* and *complex*) achieved 100% accuracy.

deployed AirAuth system that has just been enrolled. The last 7 samples were used as a test case. Trials with the same gesture from other participants were used as forgery cases. So, for each gesture performed with single or multiple fingers, we had $7 \times 15 = 105$ gestures to calculate FRR and $10 \times 14 \times 15 = 2100$ gestures to calculate FAR.

To calculate the EER of a particular gesture, it is necessary to determine the threshold ε at which FAR = FRR. As we described previously in our prototype application, we calculated the maximum distance among the first 3 reference samples and set it as our starting threshold, $\varepsilon_{\text{start}}$. Now if the distance between the reference template and the test case is smaller than $\varepsilon_{\text{start}}$, the gesture is verified. Otherwise it is a reject (see also Figure 3 (d, e)). So for each ε, we calculated the FAR and FRR using the previously defined formulas. By varying ε, we obtained different pairs of FAR and FRR for each ε. We plotted all these and obtained a receiver operating characteristic (ROC) curve for each gesture. The particular point of the curve where FAR = FRR is the value of the EER. Table 1 shows the value of EER for our different gestures. Figure 6 also shows a graphical version of the result where we averaged the single and multiple fingers accuracy of each gesture.

From Table 1, we can see that average EER for single and multi finger gestures are 0.038 and 0.029, respectively. So, we observe that gestures using multiple fingers appear to be more secure than single finger gestures. This trend is also observable in the EER of individual gestures, which is always lesser or equal for the multi finger version of a gesture. Due to the lower EER of multi-finger gestures we can assume that there will be a lower occurrence of false positive authentications in comparison to single-finger gestures. A possible explanation for the lower EER we observed for multi-finger gestures is that a larger amount of information usable for authentication can be extracted from the participants during multiple finger gestures.

Qualitative Feedback

As we discussed previously, after each gesture, users rated that gesture in terms of *easiness*, *pleasantness* and *excitement* using the EmoCard approach. Figure 7 (a)–(c) illustrates the user rating for each gesture in terms of excitement, pleasantness, and easiness. We aimed to analyze if there is a relation between these ratings and the authentication accuracy, so we formulated the following hypothesis:

"Gestures that are highly rated by participants achieve a higher accuracy rate for biometric authentication."

To verify this hypothesis, we aggregated the pleasantness, excitement, and easiness rating for each gesture for all the participants and computed an accuracy matrix. We then performed a 3 (pleasantness) × 3 (excitement) × 5 (easiness) within subjects ANOVA. The results of this indicate that both pleasantness ($F_{1,13} = 11.09$, $p < 0.01$) and excitement ($F_{1,13} = 7.33$, $p < 0.01$) had a significant effect on accuracy. However, easiness did not exhibit any significant effect on accuracy ($F_{1,13} = 0.23$, $p > 0.05$). Also, no interactions were significant.

To further analyze the effect of these factors on accuracy, we correlated each of the qualitative measures with accuracy (see Figure 7 (d)–(e)). As we can see, both pleasantness and excitement are positively correlated with accuracy, which means that gestures that are more pleasant and exciting are also more secure from a biometric point of view. However, easiness does not have any relation with accuracy. Furthermore, the above ANOVA result also agrees with these correlation tests.

We investigated these results further and analyzed the effect of easiness on accuracy. The fixed set of 15 gestures (Figure 4) that we used in our evaluation is a set of easy gestures, as defined by the test subjects of the pilot study. That is why during the gesture trials, participants also felt comfortable and rated those gestures as easy. The complex and sign gestures were harder to perform compared to the easy gesture set, as the participants rated them as less easy than most other gestures (see Figure 7 (a)). However, the complex gestures were more accurate than the easy gestures. For all the other gestures in the fixed, simple gesture set, accuracy and easiness does not follow any fixed trend. Both ANOVA and correlation tests also agree with this finding. We can therefore conclude that easiness does not significantly influence the accuracy, in contrast to pleasantness and excitement.

Sae et al. performed a similar analysis [22] and, in contrast to

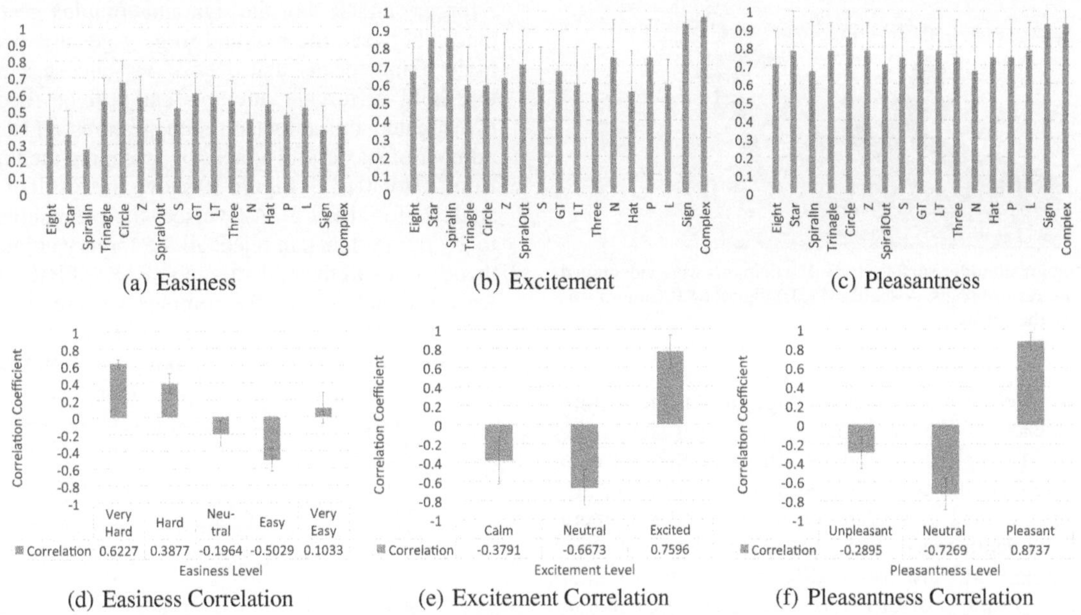

Figure 7. Results of qualitative feedback from the user study. (a)–(c) show the *easiness*, *excitement*, and *pleasantness* rating for different gestures. (d)–(e) show the correlation coefficients for Easiness, Excitement, and Pleasantness associated with gesture accuracy. The error bars show the standard deviation of the mean.

the present study found a positive correlation of accuracy with all three ratings. A possible reason for this might be because the gestures in their study were all exclusively predefined, and required the use of all five fingers. Thus, the participants of that study may have found those gestures harder to perform than their own personalized gestures. In our case, the fixed gestures were explicitly selected for their ease of entry and participants were asked explicitly to design the *complex* gestures to be more difficult than the simple gesture set. This may be an explanation why easiness did not have an effect on accuracy in our study.

Location Acceptability

To assess the location acceptability of our technique, we asked participants to imagine AirAuth being used to unlock their phone. Then we gave them three hypothetical usage situations: private (e.g., home), office, and public (e.g., pub, street). After that, we told them to rate both our technique and on-screen gestural password entry as found on Android devices on a Likert scale from 1 to 5 (1 being the least preferred). We only considered feedback from 14 participants because one of the participants was not familiar with the on-screen gesture technique. Figure 8 shows the normalized results we obtained from the participants. As we can see, participants preferred our technique in all three situations. In the private setting, 10 out of 14 participants chose our technique. 4 participants thought that they would be at less risk in a private setting and hence they chose the on screen gesture. In office and public settings, 12 out of 14 participants chose our technique. 2 participants remarked that it would be slightly socially awkward to perform gestures in front of other people. Also, they felt more comfortable using a standard password or on-screen authentication method in public settings.

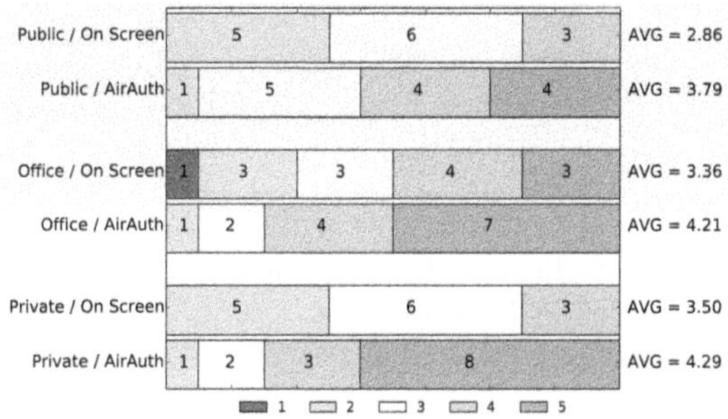

Figure 8. Location acceptability comparison between AirAuth and on screen gestures. The colors represent the given ratings, i.e., 1 (red) = *least preferred* to 5 (green) = *most preferred*. The number within the colored bars show how often the participants rated the technique that way.

We also collected verbal user comments about why they would prefer our technique which included: *"simple and faster"*, *"more secure than traditional approaches"*, *"simply cool"*. One participant commented: *"It's great because I do not have to touch my phone when I am cooking. I would like to use similar techniques to do more stuff like receiving calls and reading text messages"*.

User Study 3: Shoulder Surfing Attack

To evaluate the vulnerability of our system against shoulder surfing attacks, we conducted a further user study. In this study, we recruited 15 participants. 12 were male and 14 of them were right handed ranging in age from 21 to 36 (average: 27.8, SD: 4.6). All participants were fairly proficient with computers and smartphones and one participant was familiar with in-air gestures.

As we mentioned earlier, while participants were doing the

Figure 9. Setup for shoulder surfing study. Participants were videotaped while doing the gesture trials. A standard (2D) digital SLR camera was used to capture the videos.

gesture trials, we recorded video footage of certain gesture entries from each of the participants. Figure 9 shows the setup we used to capture the videos. In particular, we also videotaped the sign and complex gestures from all users. To record video, we used a standard (2D) digital SLR camera instead of a 3D depth sensor (e.g., Kinect), as standard cameras are portable. They are also readily available to potential attackers [23]. In the previous study, we selected a random gesture from each participant and made a set of 15 videos of fixed (simple) set gesture trials from Figure 4. So, in total we had 45 video clips: 15 videos of fixed gestures, 15 of sign gestures, and 15 of complex gestures. Since we observed (see Table 1) that multiple finger gestures were more secure, we decided to only use those gestures for this study. Therefore, all the videos we selected were videos of multiple finger trials. For each of the 45 gestures, we took first 3 trials in terms of DTW distance: T_1, T_2, and T_3. We then calculated the average of the three trials and used that as our template: $T_{\text{reference}}$. The threshold ε was again chosen as the maximum distance between T_1, T_2, and T_3.

Experiment

After explaining the study to all 15 participants, we asked them to complete a short demographic survey. We then explained the shoulder surfing attack procedure to them. Afterwards, we conducted the experiment. At first they were shown the video clips of the gestures. They could watch the clip as many times as they wanted before they proceeded to forge the gesture. They could also slow down the video. The order of the videos was counterbalanced.

We decided to assign each of the participants 15 fixed gesture videos, 3 sign videos, and 3 complex gesture videos. For gestures from the fixed set, participants had 3 attempts to forge the gestures. For sign and complex gestures, they had 5 authentication attempts. So, each participant had $(3 \times 15) + (5 \times 3) + (5 \times 3) = 75$ attempts to forge the video gestures, which resulted in total 1125 attacks. The whole study took approximately 90 minutes per participant. Just like our previous study, for each of the forge trials T_{forge}, we calculate the DTW distance (d) between $T_{\text{reference}}$ and T_{forge}. Now if d is less than ε, the trial T_{forge} is authenticated. Otherwise it is rejected.

Results and Analysis

Out of the total 1125 attacks, only 24 were successful. That means that in 97.8% of times, our system was able to resist a forgery attack. For the sign and complex gestures, the distances between the real and forgery gestures were relatively high. That means that even if we choose a high value of threshold ε, forgery attempts can still be recognized. We investigated this effect on sign gestures and calculated the number of successful attacks by sweeping the threshold value from 20 to 50 [23]. Figure 10 shows the result of the threshold analysis for study 3. As we see, for a threshold value of 20 to 24, our system can reject all the forgery attempts while authenticating all the real attempts (FAR = FRR = 0). Therefore we can conclude that for complex gestures such as a user's signature, user can select a higher threshold value which permits low false acceptance and false rejection rates.

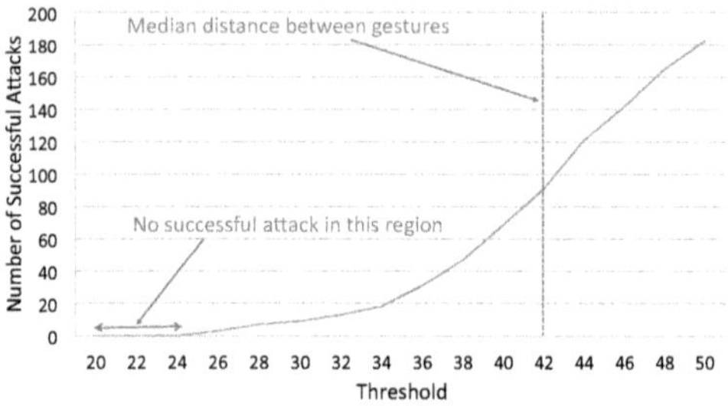

Figure 10. The number of successful attacks is dependent on the threshold setting. For a wide region of the threshold (up to a setting of 24), no successful attacks are possible. The vertical dashed line shows the median distance between gestures, which shows that our system has good overall robustness, since the useful threshold settings are relatively far away from this mark.

User Study 4: Similarity and Repeatability Analysis

To evaluate the similarity and also the repeatability of authentication over time, we performed a longitudal study. We recruited 5 participants ranging in age from 22 to 29 (AVG: 24.8, SD: 2.5). All participants were right handed male. For each participant, gestures were collected in 3 different sessions (S_1, S_2 and S_3) within a period of 10 days. The difference between two consecutive sessions was at least 4 days per participant. In each session, participants performed each of our 17 gestures 10 times. Again, we chose multiple finger gestures as they have a higher accuracy.

As in study 2, we used the average of first three S_1 gestures for each participant as enrollment gesture. Then for each gesture of S_2 and S_3, we calculated the average distance of the gesture to the enrollment gesture. To assess the accuracy under a simulated attack, we also calculated the average *attack distance* of each gesture to video-based attacks performed in Study 3. Figure 11 shows the result of this study. As we see, the average distance from S_1 grows from S_2 to S_3. The average attack distance of each gesture remains considerably larger than the difference between sessions. This indicates that AirAuth is robust enough to accomodate variation of gesture inputs at least for the time span we analyzed. However, the growth of the matching distance between time-separated sessions suggests that periodically updating templates as described previously is important.

To explore the accuracy of our system with template updates, we performed another EER analysis (as in Study 2). Again,

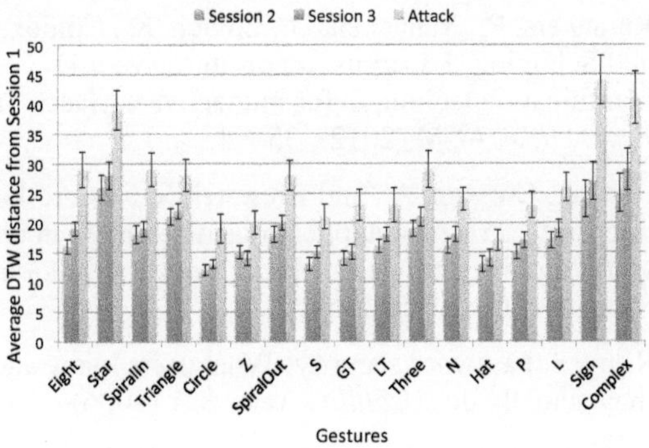

Figure 11. Average distance for each gesture of session 2 (blue) and 3 (red) from session 1. Average distance from study 3 (green) is also shown. The error bars show the standard deviation of the mean.

we considered the average of first three S_1 gestures for each participant as enrollment gestures. As we described earlier, we propose updating the template upon the first valid authentication attempt if the template is older than 24 h. So, when using template updates for this study, the template gesture is updated after the first successful authentication in S_2. Consequently S_3 gestures will be compared to the updated template. Conversely, without template updates, S_3 gestures are compared to the original reference gesture from S_1. We considered both of these cases during EER analysis. For accuracy measurement purposes, all S_3 gestures were considered genuine authentication attempts and all gestures from study 3 were treated as video-based forgery attempts. Figure 12 shows the result.

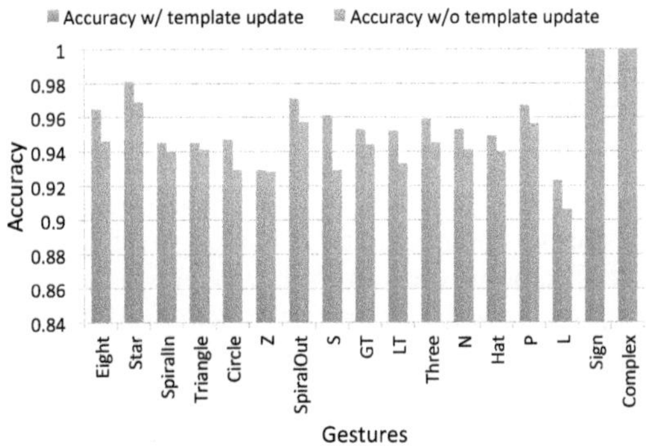

Figure 12. Achieved average accuracy for S_3 gestures with and without template update. User-defined gestures (*sign* and *complex*) achieved an accuracy of 100% in both cases.

We calculated the average across all the gestures and achieved an accuracy of 95.9% and 94.7% with and without template update, respectively. Therefore we can conclude that AirAuth system with template update is more robust against day to day variation of gestures.

CONCLUSION AND FUTURE WORK

In this paper we have presented a novel approach to gesture-based authentication, which makes use of biometric features extracted from in-air gestures tracked by short range depth camera. AirAuth is simple, robust and easy to implement. The DTW algorithm we used does not require large amounts of CPU time, so AirAuth is easily deployable on mobile devices; as well as on desktop systems. We conducted a short survey and found out a set gestures that are simple and easy to perform from user's point of view. Not only did AirAuth show a high EER-bases accuracy of 96.6% for simple and 100 % for complex gestures, in a realistically-designed video-based forgery scenario, AirAuth was able to resist attack for 97.8% of all attack attempts. Our longitudinal repeatability study shows that with a template update mechanism, AirAuth maintains consistent accuracy levels over time.

We obtained qualitative feedback from our participants regarding their experience about each gesture. Based on their rating, we found a positive correlation between the security of the authentication gestures and user experience (expressed as excitement and pleasantness), a characteristic not present in traditional password based systems [27]. Our users also gave our system a higher usage acceptability rating in three different usage situations compared to on screen gesture authentication technique found on Android devices.

Our system allows users to register and use their personalized gestures for authentication. Moreover, the results we obtain indicate that personalized gestures (e.g., signature, complex) are also more secure and rated higher by users in terms of user experience. Therefore, we envision our system to be used in application level security. Whereas in the present work we have studied the immediate validity of AirAuth's authentication technique, in the future, we intend to also put it in more direct comparison with traditional, password-based authentication mechanisms. To accomplish this, we plan to deploy AirAuth to several employees of our laboratory, replacing the standard password-based login for their workstations. We hope that this longitudinal study with a larger user based and vastly more entered gestures will give us further insights on the long-term robustness of the biometric we use, and also how AirAuth will be received in a real-life scenario. Furthermore, we hope to obtain a meaningful comparison to existing authentication methods. On an application level, we also envision using the gesture recognition component of AirAuth to enable controlling device functions, which is useful in situations where the users are unable or reluctant to touch their devices' touch screens, e.g., when cooking. Since many depth cameras are equipped with a combined RGB camera, our biometric could be further strengthened by, for instance, adding face recognition or further 2D visual features of the user's hands (e.g., as in [18]).

REFERENCES

1. Alpcan, T., Kesici, S., Bicher, D., Mihçak, M. K., Bauckhage, C., and Çamtepe, S. A. A lightweight biometric signature scheme for user authentication over networks. In *Proc. 4th international conference on Security and privacy in communication netowrks*, ACM (2008), 33.

2. Aviv, A. J., Gibson, K., Mossop, E., Blaze, M., and Smith, J. M. Smudge attacks on smartphone touch screens. In *Proc. 4th USENIX conference on Offensive technologies*, USENIX Association (2010), 1–7.

3. De Luca, A., Von Zezschwitz, E., and Hußmann, H. Vibrapass: secure authentication based on shared lies. In *Proc. CHI*, ACM (2009), 913–916.
4. De Luca, A., von Zezschwitz, E., Nguyen, N. D. H., Maurer, M.-E., Rubegni, E., Scipioni, M. P., and Langheinrich, M. Back-of-device authentication on smartphones. In *Proc. CHI*, ACM (2013), 2389–2398.
5. De Luca, A., von Zezschwitz, E., Pichler, L., and Hussmann, H. Using fake cursors to secure on-screen password entry. In *Proc. CHI*, ACM (2013), 2399–2402.
6. Desmet, P., Overbeeke, K., and Tax, S. Designing products with added emotional value: Development and appllcation of an approach for research through design. *The design journal 4*, 1 (2001), 32–47.
7. Ehrenberg, R. The digital camera revolution: Instead of imitating film counterparts, new technologies work with light in creative ways. *Science News 181*, 2 (2012), 22–25.
8. Farella, E., OModhrain, S., Benini, L., and Riccó, B. Gesture signature for ambient intelligence applications: a feasibility study. In *Pervasive Computing*. Springer, 2006, 288–304.
9. Jorgensen, Z., and Yu, T. On mouse dynamics as a behavioral biometric for authentication. In *Proc. 6th ACM Symposium on Information, Computer and Communications Security*, ACM (2011), 476–482.
10. Kainda, R., Flechais, I., and Roscoe, W. A. Security and usability: Analysis and evaluation. In *Availability, Reliability, and Security, 2010. ARES'10 International Conference on*, IEEE (2010), 275–282.
11. Kumar, M., Garfinkel, T., Boneh, D., and Winograd, T. Reducing shoulder-surfing by using gaze-based password entry. In *Proc. 3rd symposium on Usable privacy and security*, ACM (2007), 13–19.
12. Liu, J., Zhong, L., Wickramasuriya, J., and Vasudevan, V. uwave: Accelerometer-based personalized gesture recognition and its applications. *Pervasive and Mobile Computing 5*, 6 (2009), 657–675.
13. Liu, S., and Silverman, M. A practical guide to biometric security technology. *IT Professional 3*, 1 (2001), 27–32.
14. Maeder, A., Fookes, C., and Sridharan, S. Gaze based user authentication for personal computer applications. In *Proc. 2004 International Symposium on Intelligent Multimedia, Video and Speech Processing*, IEEE (2004), 727–730.
15. Maurer, M.-E., Waxenberger, R., and Hausen, D. Broauth: evaluating different levels of visual feedback for 3d gesture-based authentication. In *Proc. AVI*, ACM (2012), 737–740.
16. Monrose, F., and Rubin, A. D. Keystroke dynamics as a biometric for authentication. *Future Generation Computer Systems 16*, 4 (2000), 351–359.
17. Patel, S. N., Pierce, J. S., and Abowd, G. D. A gesture-based authentication scheme for untrusted public terminals. In *Proc. UIST*, ACM (2004), 157–160.
18. Ramakers, R., Vanacken, D., Luyten, K., Coninx, K., and Schöning, J. Carpus: a non-intrusive user identification technique for interactive surfaces. In *Proc. UIST*, ACM (2012), 35–44.
19. Rico, J., Crossan, A., and Brewster, S. Gesture-based interfaces: Practical applications of gestures in real world mobile settings. In *Whole Body Interaction*. Springer, 2011, 173–186.
20. Riley, S. Password security: What users know and what they actually do. *Usability News 8*, 1 (2006).
21. Roth, V., Richter, K., and Freidinger, R. A pin-entry method resilient against shoulder surfing. In *Proc. 11th ACM conference on Computer and communications security*, ACM (2004), 236–245.
22. Sae-Bae, N., Ahmed, K., Isbister, K., and Memon, N. Biometric-rich gestures: a novel approach to authentication on multi-touch devices. In *Proc. CHI*, ACM (2012), 977–986.
23. Sahami Shirazi, A., Moghadam, P., Ketabdar, H., and Schmidt, A. Assessing the vulnerability of magnetic gestural authentication to video-based shoulder surfing attacks. In *Proc. CHI*, ACM (New York, NY, USA, 2012), 2045–2048.
24. Sakoe, H., and Chiba, S. Dynamic programming algorithm optimization for spoken word recognition. *IEEE Transactions on Acoustics, Speech and Signal Processing 26*, 1 (1978), 43–49.
25. Tari, F., Ozok, A., and Holden, S. H. A comparison of perceived and real shoulder-surfing risks between alphanumeric and graphical passwords. In *Proc. 2nd symposium on Usable privacy and security*, ACM (2006), 56–66.
26. Vatavu, R.-D., Anthony, L., and Wobbrock, J. O. Gestures as point clouds: a $p recognizer for user interface prototypes. In *Proc. 14th ACM international conference on Multimodal interaction*, ACM (2012), 273–280.
27. von Zezschwitz, E., De Luca, A., and Hussmann, H. Survival of the shortest: A retrospective analysis of influencing factors on password composition. In *Proc. INTERACT 2013*. Springer, 2013, 460–467.
28. von Zezschwitz, E., Koslow, A., De Luca, A., and Hussmann, H. Making graphic-based authentication secure against smudge attacks. In *Proc. IUI*, ACM (New York, NY, USA, 2013), 277–286.
29. Wiedenbeck, S., Waters, J., Sobrado, L., and Birget, J.-C. Design and evaluation of a shoulder-surfing resistant graphical password scheme. In *Proc. AVI*, ACM (2006), 177–184.
30. Zhang, Y.-B., Li, Q., You, J., and Bhattacharya, P. Palm vein extraction and matching for personal authentication. In *Advances in Visual Information Systems*. Springer, 2007, 154–164.

MirrorTouch: Combining Touch and Mid-air Gestures for Public Displays

Jörg Müller[1,2] Gilles Bailly[2,3] Thor Bossuyt[2] Niklas Hillgren[2]
[1]Alexander von Humboldt Institute for Internet and Society, Berlin, Germany
[2]Quality and Usability Lab, Telekom Innovation Laboratories, TU Berlin, Germany
[3]CNRS LTCI, TELECOM ParisTech, Paris, France

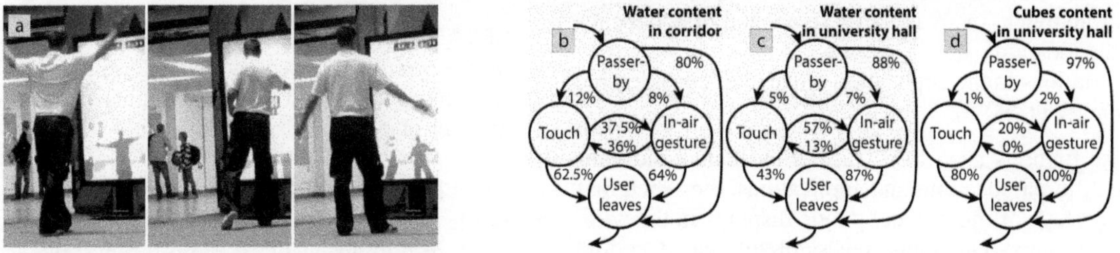

Figure 1. a) A user performs a transition from mid-air gestures to touch and back to mid-air gestures again. b), c) and d) Conversion Diagrams for transitions in two locations (corridor vs. hall) and for two contents (water vs. cubes), each one based on around 350 passers-by.

ABSTRACT

In this paper we present a series of three field studies on the integration of multiple modalities (touch and mid-air gestures) in a public display. We analyze our field studies using Conversion Diagrams, an approach to model and evaluate usage of multimodal public displays. Conversion diagrams highlight the transitions inherent in a multimodal system and provide a systematic approach to investigate which factors affect them and how. We present a semi-automatic annotation technique to obtain Conversion Diagrams. We use Conversion Diagrams to evaluate interaction in the three field studies. We found that 1) clear affordances for touch were necessary when mid-air gestures were present. A call-to-action caused significantly more users to touch than a button (+200%), 2) the order of modality usage was different from what we designed for, and the location impacted which modality was used first, and 3) small variations in the application did lead to considerable user increase (+290%).

Author Keywords

Public Displays; Field Studies; Touch; Mid-air Gestures

ACM Classification Keywords

H.5.m. Information Interfaces and Presentation (e.g. HCI): Miscellaneous

MobileHCI 2014, September 23–26, 2014, Toronto, ON, Canada.

ACM 978-1-4503-3004-6/14/09$15.00.
http://dx.doi.org/10.1145/2628363.2628379

INTRODUCTION

The majority of interactive public displays support either touch or mid-air gestures. Recently, Jurmu et al. [13] presented a study on a public display that combined touch and mid-air gestures. They found that people who already interact in one modality are reluctant to switch to the other modality. Because in their study, interaction was supervised, they propose that future studies should investigate unsupervised interaction with multimodal public displays. They argue that the current lack of models and metrics, as well as variety of objectives hamper research in multimodal public displays. In particular, the order of modality usage, the conditions of modality switching and the impact of the environment and application are unsolved questions. In this paper we address these issues through a series of in-the-wild studies of multimodal public displays. In a prestudy, we observe the same effect as [13] that people are reluctant to switch modalities once they started to interact in one modality.

To address the lack of models and metrics for multimodal public displays, we use Conversion Diagrams. In Conversion Diagrams, the percentage of users converting from usage of one modality to other modalities is explicitly given. They can be used 1) as a conscise description of actual usage of a multimodal public display, 2) as a design guideline to make implicit assumptions about how a display will be used explicit and compare these assumptions to how it is actually used in the wild, and 3) to derive hypotheses regarding the influence of independent variables on transitions.

While data for Conversion Diagrams can be obtained by simple manual counting, we present a semi-automatic coding technique. We capture a depth video of user interactions, as well as interaction logs (e.g., touches). In a first analysis round, video parts with at least one user in front of the screen are extracted. These parts are then manually annotated.

We designed MirrorTouch, a multimodal public display to investigate usage of multimodal public displays through three field experiments. MirrorTouch integrates touch interaction and mid-air gestures.

From the three field studies, we learned that

- Clear affordances for touch were necessary when mid-air gestures were present, with a call-to-action being more effective than a button (+200%).
- Although the displays were designed for using mid-air gestures before touch, many users used touched first, depending on the location.
- Small variations in the application did lead to considerable user increase (+290%).

While these findings need to be further evaluated and validate using different locations and applications, they shed first light on the usage of multimodal public displays in the wild. Further, Conversion Diagrams, the semi-automated coding technique and our field studies are intended as tools for researchers investigating usage of multimodal public displays in field studies.

MOTIVATION

Touch is known to afford highly accurate interaction, which is beneficial for fine-grained interaction like text entry, selection and manipulation of interface objects, selection from complex menus etc. In addition, touch provides a natural delimiter (i.e. when touching the surface). It also provides tactile feedback for the delimiter and structural support for the users' hands, thereby reducing strain. A major drawback of touch is that users may not know whether a surface is a touchscreen or not.

When a mirror image of passers-by is shown on a displays, passers-by may interact inadvertently with the display, thereby capturing their attention [19]. Mid-air gestures can also be a lot of fun, and users do not have to make a detour to approach the display. They also work when the display is out of reach, and have less hygienic issues. On the downside, delimiters for mid-air gestures are difficult to design and communicate [27].

As we see, the benefits of mid-air gestures and touch are largely complementary. In order to highlight the mutual benefits that can arise by combining these two modalities, we provide three scenarios.

S1. *Alice is a tourist in an unknown city. Strolling through a street, she notices her mirror image on a display that she would otherwise not have noticed. She sees that she had inadvertently kicked a few virtual objects, and plays with them a bit. She notices that the display provides a map of the city center with information what is currently going on there. She approaches and touches the display and browses through the events, until finding an art event to attend.*

S2. *Bob goes window shopping on a sunday. He passes by a shop window and sees in it his mirror image augmented with some cool clothes. This attracts his attention, and he approaches the window to touch it and browse through a catalogue. He finds some nice new clothes and orders them to be delivered to his home.*

S3. *Lisa is waiting at a bus stop and sees her contour mirrored on a large display where she can play with a virtual ball. See sees some other people from a different city on the same screen and plays a bit with them. After some time, she approaches the screen where she can use a soft keyboard to chat with them. Finally, she makes some new friends and exchanges email addresses with them.*

RELATED WORK ON MULTIMODAL PUBLIC DISPLAYS

In this section we review related work on public displays combining touch and mid-air gestures and supporting different user phases.

Combining Touch & Mid-air Gestures

While traditionally most interactive devices support either touch or mid-air gestures, more recently the combination of touch and mid-air gestures is receiving increasing attention. Schick [24] proposes a technique to use the pointing direction as an extension to direct touch for very large displays. Hilliges [6] extended a multitouch tabletop through gestural interaction above and enabled to lift virtual objects to put them into containers.

Lightspace [29] uses projectors and depth cameras to enable touch interaction on arbitrary surfaces in a room as well as in mid-air. For example, virtual objects can be picked up from surfaces and carried through the room to other surfaces. Marquardt [16] propose a design concept of a continuous interaction space above interactive surfaces. Bailly proposes finger-count [1], a gesture set and menu technique that can be used in touch as well as mid-air gestures.

For public displays, the combination of touch and mid-air gestures has been proposed by the Interactive Public Ambient Display [26] and the Proxemic Peddler [28]. A first field study of a public display combining touch and mid-air gestures has recently been presented by Jurmu [13]. They deployed a display at a science fair and asked passers-by to interact. One observation was that once users started to interact using one modality, they were reluctant to switch to the other modality. Our paper investigates this issue in more detail in an unsupervised in-the-wild setting.

Kukka et al. [15] present an extensive in-the-wild study investigating which factors entice passers-by to interact with a touchscreen. They found that text is more effective than icons, color more than greyscale, and static more than animated. In comparison, our study focusses on the switching between the touch and mid-air gesture modalities. Our first field study can be interpreted as and extension of the findings of [15]. We compare a call-to-action (icon and text, static and color) to a conventional button (icon and text, static and color). We find that the call-to-action outperforms the button by +200%.

System Design Models for Different User Phases

A number of public display systems have been developed which support different *phases* of user interaction. They mostly provide interaction with different modalities in these phases. The Hello.Wall [21] proposes to recognize whether the user is in an ambient zone, notification zone, or cell interaction zone, and adapt its behavior accordingly. Similarly, the Interactive Public Ambient Display [26] can be in ambient mode, implicit interaction, subtle interaction, or personal interaction mode based on the users' distance and head direction. More recently, the Proxemic Peddler [28] initially scrolls the product list at fast speed, slowing down when the user orients towards the display, and shows more product details when the user walks closer. In contrast to previous models, the Peddler actively tries to move a user from one phase to the next, e.g., to recapture attention once the user turns away.

It is important to distinguish these models for system design from models like Conversion Diagrams that describe actual user behavior based on observations. These models describe how a system should or does react when the user shows a certain behavior, and are not used to evaluate a public display, or to describe observations from a field study.

However, such system models could clearly benefit from descriptive models like Conversion Diagrams. For example, while the Proxemic Peddler actively tries to move the user to a specific phase, it is unclear which techniques (e.g., moving content) can achieve this. Conversion Diagrams allow to systematically investigate the impact of various techniques on conversion probabilities. A system could then use this to predict what a user would do next with which probability when the system applies a certain technique (like moving content). It could then decide to use the technique that maximizes the probability that the user does a certain action (e.g., touch the screen).

EVALUATION METHODS FOR PUBLIC DISPLAYS

In this section we analyze which kinds of field studies have been used for evaluating public displays. We classify the different methods that have been used (see Table 1) and illustrate them with examples of findings. Finally, we extract the metrics that have been used in quantitative field experiments (see Table 2). We show how Conversion Diagrams complement these existing methods. For practitioners, this section provides an overview of evaluation methods for public displays. For researchers, the benefit is to outline the state of the art in public display evaluation and provide them a simple framework (study types and metrics) to select the right study for their problem.

For the evaluation of public displays, almost exclusively field studies have been used. Because the actual situation in-the-wild is hard to predict, it is difficult to design laboratory studies where the results actually transfer to real settings. For example, Marshall et al. [17] have shown that actual multi-user behavior in the wild differs widely from what is usually simulated in laboratory studies for multitouch tables.

Descriptive Field Studies

The majority of field studies of public displays are descriptive. Most often, a single prototype is deployed in the wild, and usage is being described, without variations of the prototype.

Descriptive Qualitative	[23][3][2][10][5]
Descriptive Quantitative	[4][20][11][17][18]
Descriptive Existing Systems	[8][9]
Comparative Qualitative	[25]
Comparative Quantitative	[14][12][19]

Table 1. Categories of Field Studies for Public Displays

Qualitative Descriptive Studies

Blueboard [23] is an early example of large touchscreens in semi-public settings. It was deployed in a longitudinal setting, usage was captured on video and analyzed. Among others, it was found that social learning plays a large role, e.g., people observe others to learn how to use the system. The Vision Kiosk [3] was a touchscreen kiosk with an on-screen avatar that followed passers-by with the eyes. Among others, it was found that the perception of the quality of the system depended strongly on the quality of the content.

Opinionizer [2] was a large screen that enabled users to leave their opinion via a keyboard at a party. Usage was videotaped and analyzed. One of the major findings was that once someone already interacted with the display, also others would start to interact (the Honeypot effect). Dynamo [10] was a multi-user display that enabled users to collaborate and share data that was installed in a school. Usage was also videotaped and analyzed. One finding was that the display was used extensively for performances in front of audiences. Finally, Fischer [5] conducted observations and interviews of usage of the SMS Slingshot. From these observations, he constructed a model of the space around the displays.

Quantitative Descriptive Studies

All studies which collected quantitative data also performed a qualitative analysis of user behavior. Arguably, one of the first quantitative studies of public display usage is the Plasma Poster Network [4]. For a network of large touch-enabled screens, the number of clicks and posted content was logged. For example, it was found that posting behavior was skewed in the population and 8 users were responsible for 75.2% of the posted materials on the screen.

The CityWall [20] was a large multitouch screen installed in downtown Helsinki. Usage was captured with cameras and manually annotated. In particular, the duration of interaction sessions, number of simultaneous active users, and number of bystanders were annotated. One result was that very few passers-by interacted when alone - 72% of all users were in pairs.

Worlds of information [11] extended this system to a 3D interface that was investigated during a trade fair. Usage was logged on video and manually annotated, and in addition questionnaires were collected. In particular, the number of simultaneous users, the duration of interactions, and the number of "interaction spots" was annotated. Among the findings was that almost all interactions started with using only one finger. Because most of the interaction relied on multi-finger gestures, users had difficulties in discovering them.

Marshall et al. [17] observed interaction with a multitouch table in a tourist information office. They conducted observations and captured the durations of interaction sessions as well as the number of users per session. A major finding was that groups of tourists did not approach the table simultaneously. In contrast, one member started interaction, maybe a second joined some time later, the first member left etc. Michelis [18] conducted observations of gesture enabled public displays. They propose the Audience Funnel model, where the number of passers-by showing a certain behavior (e.g., stopping and interacting with the screen) is observed.

Descriptive Field Studies of Existing Systems

A number of studies investigate systems that were already available and were not a research prototype. All of these studies obtained some quantitative data, but, probably because it is difficult to change conditions on a commercial deployment, all of them were of descriptive nature.

Hornecker [8] observed usage of a multitouch table in a museum. Besides a large number of qualitative observations, she counted about 200 passers-by. 40 of them did not look at the table, while 60 looked but did not touch. 40 touched, but only played with the interface, and 70 touched and read some content. Of these, 35 read more than one content item. Huang [9] observed whether passers-by of large screens looked at them. She found that most displays only receive very few glances.

Comparative Field Studies

Only a handful of comparative field studies of public displays have been conducted.

Qualitative Comparative Studies

Very few comparative studies use only qualitative data. Chained Displays [25] was a deployment of a space-invaders game set up on a concave, flat, and convex large display. Usage was observed by nearby researchers. Among others, it was found that for group interactions, the flat arrangement was best. In order to maintain group coherence, it was much more important that the group could see the same thing on the screen (shared focus) than that they could see each other (as with the convex setting).

Quantitative Comparative Studies

Comparative field studys where at least two conditions of an independent variable are compared, a quantitative dependent variable is measured, and subjects are assigned to the conditions randomly, will also be called *field experiments* throughout the paper.

In the Ubidisplays deployment [14], a shortlist menu for applications (the wizard) was compared to a general menu regarding the number of application launches. A single display was used to compare application launches within three non-consecutive phases of 60 days each. It was found that applications were started significantly more often when available in the wizard compared to when available from the menu.

Rogers [22] investigated whether ambient displays (LEDs in the floor) can make more people take the stairs compared to the elevator. They determined the ratio of people using the stairs compared to the elevator in a 6 month period before deployment compared to 8 weeks after deployment, as measured by pressure mats. They could show that the ambient displays could indeed increase the percentage of people taking the stairs significantly.

Absolute Number of Users	[8][9][19]
Percentage of Users	[18][12][22][7]
Number of Interactions	[14]
Duration of Interactions	[20][11][17]
Number of Simultaneous Users	[20][11][17]

Table 2. Metrics for Field Studies for Public Displays

Ju [12] conducted a comparative field study to determine whether an animatronic hand can attract more users to touch a kiosk compared to a projected hand. She also compared the animatronic hand to an animatronic arrow. Conditions were switched every 30 minutes. She manually counted the number of passers-by and how many looked at and touched the kiosk. She found that the physical motion attracted significantly more views and touches, but the hand did not attract more compared to the arrow.

Looking Glass [19] was a field experiment of the effectiveness of different interactivity cues on whether passers-by start to interact. Conditions were switched every 30 minutes, and anonymous depth video of interactions was recorded and manually annotated for number of interaction sessions (with a new session starting when nobody was in front of the screen for at least 2 seconds). It was found that inadvertent interaction through a colored mirror image of the user attracts significant more interactions than other visualizations or a classical call-to-action.

Metrics

The metrics used for quantitative evaluations of public displays can broadly be categorized into five categories (see Table 2).

The *absolute number of users* was used in descriptive studies, for example to determine the number of interactions [8] or views towards displays [9]. These metrics are heavily influenced by variations in numbers of passers-by over time. When used for experiments, conditions need to be switched often to reduce the impact of varying numbers of passers-by on the dependent variable.

The *percentage of users* showing a certain behavior is used in descriptive as well as experimental studies. This percentage can be based on the total number of passers-by [18], sometimes restricted to people walking into a certain direction [12]. In other cases, the percentage is based on the number of users showing a certain behavior. For example, those going upstairs [22] or those using a certain gesture variation to execute a specific command [7].

The absolute *number of interactions* can often be determined easily from automated system logs. For example, [14] used this metric to determine how often an application was started.

Finally, the *duration of interactions* and *number of simultaneous users* or bystanders were used in a descriptive way by [20, 11, 17]. They are usually used to round up the description of usage.

While a number of metrics have been proposed for describing interaction with a public display, none of them are especially suited for *multimodal* public displays. For this reason, in this paper we use Conversion Diagrams provide a concise model of the entire interaction process with a multimodal public display, from passing-by to leaving.

USING CONVERSION DIAGRAMS

Conversion Diagrams (see Figure 2) contain states that can describe the current behavior of the user. For example, a user may be passing by, interact via touch or mid-air gestures, or leave. The frequency with which users transition from one state to another is annotated on the edges and can serve as an estimation of the probability of one particular user transitioning to the other state. Conversion Diagrams reveal how users transition between the modalities or states, which modality they use first, and which modality they use last before leaving. We present different use cases that benefit from the use of Conversion Diagrams.

Conversion Diagrams as a Descriptive Tool

Conversion Diagrams enable the quantitative comparison of usage of different applications, times and locations. In particular, unlike the number of interactions, they are very robust against variations in footfall (number of passers-by) caused by variations in time or location. Importantly, all transitions of all users observed are annotated on the edges. Thus, a conversion diagram is a maximum likelihood estimator of user transitions.

As one consequence, one user transitioning very often can heavily skew the transition probabilities between modalities (but not those entering and exiting the diagram). However, they are a very compact representation of usage. Conversion diagrams also omit important information, like how long each modality is being used, multiuser effects (e.g., whether users are influenced by other simultaneous users), or what users exactly do while they use a certain modality. For these reasons, they should always be augmented with other metrics (see section on enriching Conversion Diagrams).

Conversion Diagrams as Design Guideline

For both researchers and practitioners, Conversion Diagrams are also intended as a design guideline. During the early design phases of a multimodal public display, we recommend creating Conversion Diagrams with the intended transition probabilities annotated (Figure 2 a). This can serve as a tool to more explicitly think about and communicate how the display is intended to be used.

During the design process (field observations, early prototypes, prestudies in the field, and field studies of final prototypes), the Conversion Diagram should then gradually be refined to reflect actual usage of the system. When discrepancies between actual and intended usage are discovered (Figure 2 b), systematic experiments can be conducted regarding

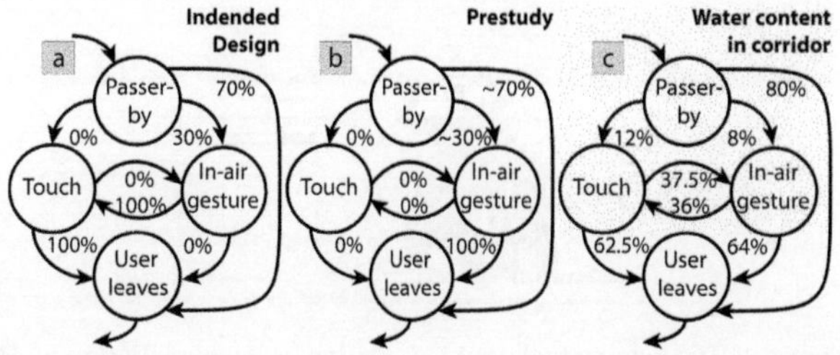

Figure 2. Conversion Diagrams are useful in making implicit assumptions explicit during the design process, and systematically comparing them to reality. For example, we implicitly assumed that people would use mid-air gestures before touching (a). During a first prestudy, we noticed, however, that not a single user touched the screen at all (b). After adding an effective touch affordance, in one location more users touched first than gesturing first (c).

the effectiveness of design changes on particular transition probabilities (Figure 2 c).

Conversion Diagrams for Deriving Experiments

Conversion Diagrams can support the generation of hypotheses and experiments, in particular regarding the impact of various variables on conversions. Regarding the formulation of hypotheses, two equivalent perspectives can be taken. In the state perspective, all users entering or exiting a certain state or set of states can be investigated. In the transition perspective, all users making a certain transition or set of transitions can be investigated.

Conversion Diagrams depict the absolute number of *transitions*, thereby enabling to predict the next action of a user. For experiments, one would generally be more interested in how many *users* make a transition (and only consider each user once). Still, conversion diagrams can help in generating these hypotheses. We will demonstrate which kinds of hypotheses can be derived from Conversion Diagrams during the field studies.

Figure 3. Examples from log files: a) two users perform a high five after reaching the highscore b) two users mime a camel in the university hall c) two children roughhouse the screen in the university corridor.

Obtaining Conversion Diagrams

Conversion Diagrams are useful in particular if it is efficient to generate them. A simple method to obtain Conversion Diagrams would be to manually observe the deployment and keep a list of transitions. Because interactions may be rare, and when they happen, multiple interactions may happen simultaneously, this may be very tedious. Instead, we present a semi-automatic annotation technique.

The presence of a user can be determined using background subtraction. Our prototype (see next section) uses the mirror image of the user to support gesture-based interaction with

Figure 4. The logging tool used for creating conversion diagrams. When a touch is detected, the contour of the closest user turns red. Playback speed is adjustable, and only situations with at least one user in front of the display or a touch detected are shown. Transitions are annotated manually into a spreadsheet program.

virtual objects. We log the anonymous contours of users (see Figure 3). A custom annotation software (Figure 4) is used to play back situations where at least one user was in front of the screen. The annotating researcher could fast-forward, rewind and pause on sequences of interest. When a pause was made, the current timeframe was automatically copied to the clipboard. This way, it could be pasted into an excel sheet for later reference. When observing an entire day in detail, the timestamps of users entering/leaving the scene were noted this way, as well as the sequence of interactions made by that person. This way it was easy to go back from the excel sheet to the corresponding point in the video. The system also logs touch events, and during a touch, the user closest to the screen is highlighted. Finally, the annotations are compiled into Conversion Diagrams.

Enriching Conversion Diagrams

Conversion Diagrams can easily be extended with other metrics and qualitative observations to provide a broader perspective. For example, it always makes sense to annotate the absolute number of users observed. It would also be useful to annotate the average duration of interactions and number of simultaneous users at the phases.

On a qualitative side, they can be extended through data from observations (either manual or automatic) and interviews. Although we keep a complete anonymous interaction video log for later analysis, the narrow field of view of the camera means that usually not the entire situation is captured. Therefore, we use researchers present at the experiment site at all times to perform manual observations. Exemplary cases of how Conversion Diagrams can be extended through observations are provided in the three field studies in the following sections.

MIRRORTOUCH

Conversion Diagrams can be used for any kind of multimodal public displays. We think that the integration of touch and mid-air gestures is a very interesting case, since 1) both modalities are well established, 2) they have complementary benefits, as mid-air gestures are good for attracting users and touch is good for enabling highly accurate extended interactions, and 3) to our knowledge, no field studies investigating public displays that combine touch and mid-air gestures have been done yet. For these reasons, we designed, implemented and deployed MirrorTouch to illustrate the use of Conversion Diagrams for the specific case of a public display that integrates touch and mid-air gestures.

MirrorTouch (Figure 5) is a public display that combines mid-air gestures and touch interaction. People see their own mirror image as a contour and can play with virtual objects. The central idea behind the design was to attract users through mid-air gestures and then enable detailed and accurate interaction (e.g., looking up information) through touch. Gestural interaction was designed so that passers-by would discover the fact that the display was interactive inadvertently while passing-by (as in [19]). Because we were not especially interested in the details of touch interaction, and only in the fact whether people touch at all, the touch interaction was rather simple (looking up information or spawning ducks).

Water and Cubes Designs

We developed two variations of MirrorTouch. In the *water* variant (see Figure 5 b), people can play with water particles that are spawned from a virtual faucet. When they touch the screen, a duck appears that floats on the water. In the *cubes* variant (see Figure 5 a), people can play with virtual cubes, and throw them into a cloud, where they disappear. When they touch the display, an informational screen is shown and the game is interrupted.

Implementation

MirrorTouch uses a Samsung 650TS 65" touchscreen in portrait format. Users are tracked through an Asus Xtion Pro camera. The user contour is extracted using OpenNI. The water variant is 2D and uses Box2D as physics engine and Processing for rendering. The cubes variant is 3D, where the interaction is constrained to a 2D plane. It uses Bullet as physics engine and Java OpenGL for rendering.

Prestudy

As a prestudy we deployed the water prototype for one evening during a university fair. We let passers-by discover interaction by themselves but stood in the vicinity to observe and answer questions. Our system was designed to attract people through mid-air gestures and then enable detailed interaction through touch. Surprisingly, this approach did not

Figure 5. Two types of content used for MirrorTouch: a) cubes, b) water.

Figure 6. During the prestudy, not a single user touched the screen.

work at all. We did not observe a single user (among several hundreds who used mid-air gestures) who touched the screen (see Figure 6). Apparently, once users started to interact through mid-air gestures, they were caught in that interaction modality and did not consider that other modalities were also available. While our implicit design assumption was that users would transition from mid-air gestures to touch, this simple study already showed that the actual Conversion Diagram was very different. The same behavior was also observed by Jurmu et al. [13]. Consequently, we started our field studies with finding efficient affordances for touch.

FIELD EXPERIMENT 1: AFFORDANCES FOR TOUCH

We conducted a field experiment to compare two affordances for touch, a (more classical) button design and a call-to-action "touch here" in combination with a hand icon (see Figures 8 a and 8 b). This study can be interpreted as an extension of the touch affordances study by Kukka et al. [15], who found that static colored text works best. Both our affordances use static colored text, but we compare a button design to a call-to-action.

Method

As apparatus for this field experiment the water prototype was used (see Figure 5 b). We deployed the screen for one day in a corridor leading to a university cafeteria (see Figure 7 a). Participants were mostly students, faculty, and visitors to the university. Most users would come from the elevators, walk past the display towards the cafeteria, or come from the cafeteria and walk towards the elevators. We sat nearby in a student working room to inconspicously observe interaction with the display. The two conditions were switched every 5 minutes. We captured the contours of passers-by as well as touch events. Later all events with at least one user in front of the camera were automatically extracted. These events were then manually annotated regarding the number of users who passed-by and the number who touched the display. The entire data was annotated by two independent coders. Inter-rater reliability was very good (Cohens Kappa=0.82).

Location	University corridor (a)	University hall (b)
Space	narrow	spacious
Audience	students	students
Content	water	water & cubes

Figure 7. Deployment locations: a) the university corridor b) the university hall

Figure 8. Two types of touch affordances: a) standard button, b) call-to-action.

Results

We counted 697 passers-by of whom 66 touched the screen. A Chi-square test revealed that the percentage of passers-by utilizing the touch screen significantly differed with the affordance used ($\chi^2_{1,N=697} = 20.9, p < .05$). The call-to-action affordance had a 15% touch conversion rate, while the button had 5%. To our surprise, however, people did not use the modalities in the order we intended. Instead of gesturing first before touching, some users touched the screens directly without gesturing first.

We also observed some interesting details about user behavior. The display was installed in a distance of about 10m from the elevators. Quite often we observed people leaving the cafeteria, passing by the display without interacting and walking toward the elevators. When they saw that the elevators had not arrived yet, they walked back to the display and interacted. When the elevator arrived, it played a ringing tone, and people hurried towards the elevator, although some missed it. This demonstrates that waiting zones are important even when the display itself is not installed immediately within the waiting zone. It may thus be benefitial to install displays in well-frequented areas (e.g., hallways) but close to this kind of waiting zone. These qualitative observations illustrate that some external factors (like elevators) can have large effects on the transitions, and should be reported. In particular, the duration of interactions in this case may be determined less by the display itself, but rather by the arrival time of the elevator.

Discussion

This study demonstrates that different design of affordances can have large differences in effectiveness (in our case +200%). We learned that the order of modalities was different from what we designed for. Many users touched without gesturing first. The study also demonstrates how to systematically investigate the impact of design decisions on the Conversion Diagram. Although the call-to-action achieved a much higher transition probability than the button, in order to derive a general recommendation, this result should be

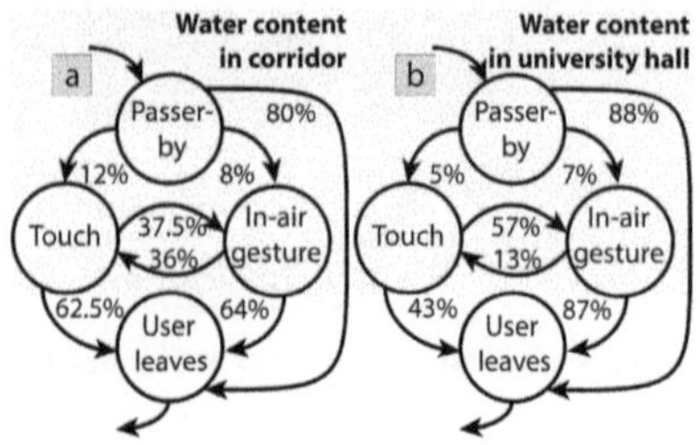

Figure 9. Conversion Diagrams for Field Experiment 2. The water content was deployed in the university corridor (a) and the university hall (b).

validated in different user populations, locations, and applications. For the following study, we decided to investigate in more detail which modality is used first. We proceeded with using the call-to-action as affordance.

FIELD EXPERIMENT 2: IMPACT OF THE LOCATION

After having identified an effective touch affordance (call-to-action) we conducted a second field study to determine whether there would be differences in the Conversion Diagrams between the two locations.

Method

As apparatus, the water content (see Figure 5 b) was used in the university hall (see Figure 7 b) and the university corridor (see Figure 7 a). Both locations had similar participants, being mostly students, but also faculty and visitors to the university. We tested each location for one day. Otherwise, the methodology used was the same as in Field Experiment 1.

Results

During the two days of deployment we observed a total of 117 users and 718 passers-by. A Chi-square test revealed that the first used modality significantly differed with location ($\chi^2_{1,N=117} = 3.9, p < .05$). Passers-by mainly used mid-air gestures as a first modality in the hall (7% vs. 5%) while they mainly used touch first in the corridor (12% vs. 8%). The two Conversion Diagrams are illustrated in Figure 9.

We also observed what seems to be a very interesting interaction effect between playful mid-air gestures and touch interaction. Some people were roughhousing the screen during touch interaction after engaging in intense mid-air gesture interaction. In particular, on one occasion some children were playing with the screen in the university corridor (see Figure 10).

They started with rather modest motion playing with the water. Over time, the motion became increasingly expressive and even agressive. When they then started touching the screen, they started to push it harder and harder (see Figure 3 c). The screen started shaking considerably, and we had to intervene (entering from our concealed position) to prevent damage or accident.

We observed a very similar behavior in the university hall. One employee of the cafeteria also became more and more engaged over time playing with the water through mid-air gestures. When she started touching the screen, she began to shake it violently so we had to intervene. These qualitative observations illustrate that the details of usage of one modality may differ by which other modality was used before. Such unexpected effects can only be discovered by qualitative observations.

Discussion

From this study we learned that not only many users used the modalities in a different order than intended, but the order in which they used the modalities also depended on the location. We do not know the reason why they touched first more often in the corridor, but the corridor was more narrow than the hall. It is possible that the fact that people were closer to the screen when passing by influenced in which order they used the modalities. It would be, however, necessary to validate this hypothesis in different locations and with different applications. The experiment serves to illustrate how to evaluate the ratio between two transitions in a field experiment. It also indicates that mid-air gestures can lead to more violent touches and roughhousing. When validated in further experiments focussing on this aspect, it could mean that touchscreens that also support (playful and engaging) mid-air gestures would need to be very physically robust.

FIELD EXPERIMENT 3: IMPACT OF THE CONTENT

Our third field study aimed at comparing two different contents and keeping the location (university hall) constant. We hypothesized that there would be no differences between the Conversion Diagrams between the cubes and water content (Figure 5).

Method

As apparatus, we compared the two applications described in the MirrorTouch section (Figure 5). Both applications were installed in a university hall close to a major cafeteria (see Figure 7 b). Paricipants were mostly students, faculty, and visitors to the university. People would pass by the display either on their way to the cafeteria or the way back. We used the same data analysis technique as for Field Experiment 1.

Results

The prototypes were deployed during one day each, for a total of 53 users and 700 passers-by. A chi-square test revealed that

Figure 10. Children after roughhousing the screen.

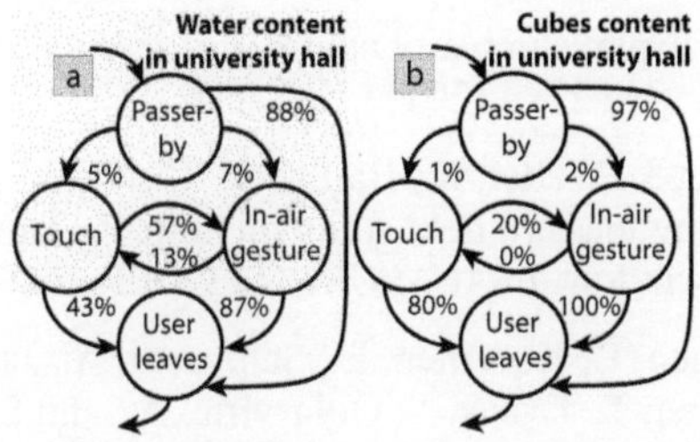

Figure 11. Conversion Diagrams for Field Experiment 3. The water content (a) and the cubes content (b) were deployed in the university hall.

the percentage of passers-by utilizing the public display significantly differed with content ($\chi^2_{1,N=700} = 20.5, p < .05$). The water content increased the number of users by +290%, compared to the cubes content. Furthermore, the content did not have a significant effect on which modality people chose to use first, nor did it affect which one they used last. The Conversion Diagrams are shown in Figure 11.

Mid-air gestures seemed to cause more playful behavior and cause a stronger Honeypot effect (see Figure 12) than touch. We also observed that some users who used touch first never noticed their mirror image (the feedback for mid-air gestures). Because they were very close to the screen, they failed to see their mirror image displayed in the lower area of the display. These observations illustrate that one modality (mid-air gestures) may not even be discovered if another modality (touch) is used before, augmenting the information represented in Conversion Diagrams.

Discussion

We learned two things from this study. First, a variation of content did lead to a huge difference in the number of transitions. We found this surprising as the two applications were quite similar: both were 1) a game with 2) physics simulation, 3) they also had the same affordances and 4) the same modalities (touch and mid-air gestures). Although it is unclear what exactly caused these large differences, it would be interesting to investigate this phenomenon further in different contents and with different locations and user populations.

Second, it may be difficult to combine feedback for touch and mid-air gestures in such a way that users still perceive the feedback when they are touching the screen. As they see only a very small part of the screen, and feedback for mid-air gestures usually requires considerable space, it is a challenge to show the feedback for mid-air gestures in such a way that touching users still perceive it.

CONCLUSION

In this paper we presented a series of three field studies on the integration of multiple modalities (touch and mid-air gestures) in a public display. We used Conversion Diagrams as an approach to evaluate multimodal public displays. We also presented MirrorTouch, a public display combining touch and mid-air gestures. We learned that the actual usage of such displays in the wild can be very different from what was intended. Small variations in affordance, location and application had considerable influence on actual usage. For example, in our case the call-to-action was three times more effective than a traditional button. Contrary to what we designed for, many people touched before mid-air gesturing, and the order of modalities depended on the location. Finally, small variations in the content increased the number of users by 290%. Conversion Diagrams provide a systematic way to address these issues. In particular, they enable us to narrow the (often huge) gap between what we believe how our devices are or should be used and how they are actually used in the wild.

Figure 12. Mid-air gestures seemed to cause stronger Honeypot effect than touch.

ACKNOWLEDGEMENTS

We want to thank Robert Walter for help during the implementation and field studies. This work was supported by the European Institute of Innovation and Technology.

REFERENCES

1. Bailly, G., Müller, J., and Lecolinet, E. Design and evaluation of finger-count interaction: Combining multitouch gestures and menus. *International Journal of Human-Computer Studies* (2012).
2. Brignull, H., and Rogers, Y. Enticing people to interact with large public displays in public spaces. In *INTERACT*, M. Rauterberg, M. Menozzi, and J. Wesson, Eds., IOS Press (2003).
3. Christian, A. D., and Avery, B. L. Speak out and annoy someone: experience with intelligent kiosks. In *ACM CHI'00* (2000), 313–320.
4. Churchill, E. F., Nelson, L., Denoue, L., and Girgensohn, A. The plasma poster network: Posting multimedia content in public places. In *INTERACT'03*, vol. 3 (2003), 599–606.
5. Fischer, P. T., and Hornecker, E. Urban hci: spatial aspects in the design of shared encounters for media facades. In *ACM CHI'12* (2012), 307–316.
6. Hilliges, O., Izadi, S., Wilson, A. D., Hodges, S., Garcia-Mendoza, A., and Butz, A. Interactions in the air: adding further depth to interactive tabletops. In *ACM UIST '09* (2009), 139–148.
7. Hinrichs, U., and Carpendale, S. Gestures in the wild: studying multi-touch gesture sequences on interactive tabletop exhibits. In *ACM CHI '11* (2011), 3023–3032.

8. Hornecker, E. I dont understand it either, but it is cool - visitor interactions with a multi-touch table in a museum. In *IEEE TABLETOP'08* (2008), 113–120.

9. Huang, E., Koster, A., and Borchers, J. Overcoming assumptions and uncovering practices: When does the public really look at public displays? In *Pervasive Computing*, vol. 5013 of *Lecture Notes in Computer Science*. Springer Berlin Heidelberg, (2008), 228–243.

10. Izadi, S., Brignull, H., Rodden, T., Rogers, Y., and Underwood, M. Dynamo: a public interactive surface supporting the cooperative sharing and exchange of media. In *ACM UIST'03* (2003), 159–168.

11. Jacucci, G., Morrison, A., Richard, G. T., Kleimola, J., Peltonen, P., Parisi, L., and Laitinen, T. Worlds of information: designing for engagement at a public multi-touch display. In *ACM CHI'10* (2010), 2267–2276.

12. Ju, W., and Sirkin, D. Animate objects: How physical motion encourages public interaction. In *Persuasive Technology*. Springer Berlin Heidelberg, 2010, 40–51.

13. Jurmu, M., Ogawa, M., Boring, S., Riekki, J., and Tokuda, H. Waving to a touch interface: Descriptive field study of a multipurpose multimodal public display. In *ACM PerDis '13* (2013), 7–12.

14. Kostakos, V., Kukka, H., Goncalves, J., Tselios, N., and Ojala, T. Multipurpose public displays: How shortcut menus affect usage. *Computer Graphics and Applications, IEEE 33*, 2 (March-April), 56–63.

15. Kukka, H., Oja, H., Kostakos, V., Gonçalves, J., and Ojala, T. What makes you click: Exploring visual signals to entice interaction on public displays. In *ACM CHI'13* (2013), 1699–1708.

16. Marquardt, N., Jota, R., Greenberg, S., and Jorge, J. A. The continuous interaction space: interaction techniques unifying touch and gesture on and above a digital surface. INTERACT'11, Springer-Verlag (2011), 461–476.

17. Marshall, P., Morris, R., Rogers, Y., Kreitmayer, S., and Davies, M. Rethinking 'multi-user': an in-the-wild study of how groups approach a walk-up-and-use tabletop interface. In *ACM CHI'11*, ACM (2011), 3033–3042.

18. Michelis, D., and Müller, J. The audience funnel: Observations of gesture based interaction with multiple large displays in a city center. *Int. J. Hum. Comput. Interaction 27*, 6 (2011), 562–579.

19. Müller, J., Walter, R., Bailly, G., Nischt, M., and Alt, F. Looking glass: a field study on noticing interactivity of a shop window. In *ACM CHI '12* (2012), 297–306.

20. Peltonen, P., Kurvinen, E., Salovaara, A., Jacucci, G., Ilmonen, T., Evans, J., Oulasvirta, A., and Saarikko, P. It's mine, don't touch!: interactions at a large multi-touch display in a city centre. In *ACM CHI '08* (2008), 1285–1294.

21. Prante, T., Röcker, C., Streitz, N., Stenzel, R., Magerkurth, C., Van Alphen, D., and Plewe, D. Hello. wall–beyond ambient displays. In *Adjunct Proceedings of Ubicomp* (2003), 277–278.

22. Rogers, Y., Hazlewood, W. R., Marshall, P., Dalton, N., and Hertrich, S. Ambient influence: can twinkly lights lure and abstract representations trigger behavioral change? In *ACM Ubicomp'10* (2010), 261–270.

23. Russell, D., Drews, C., and Sue, A. Social aspects of using large public interactive displays for collaboration. *ACM UbiComp'02* (2002), 663–670.

24. Schick, A., van de Camp, F., Ijsselmuiden, J., and Stiefelhagen, R. Extending touch: towards interaction with large-scale surfaces. In *ACM ITS'09* (2009), 117–124.

25. Ten Koppel, M., Bailly, G., Müller, J., and Walter, R. Chained displays: configurations of public displays can be used to influence actor-, audience-, and passer-by behavior. In *ACM CHI '12* (2012), 317–326.

26. Vogel, D., and Balakrishnan, R. Interactive public ambient displays: transitioning from implicit to explicit, public to personal, interaction with multiple users. In *ACM UIST'04* (2004), 137–146.

27. Walter, R., Bailly, G., and Müller, J. Strikeapose: Revealing mid-air gestures on public displays. In *ACM CHI '13* (2013), 841–850.

28. Wang, M., Boring, S., and Greenberg, S. Proxemic peddler: a public advertising display that captures and preserves the attention of a passerby. In *ACM ISPD'12* (2012), 3.

29. Wilson, A. D., and Benko, H. Combining multiple depth cameras and projectors for interactions on, above and between surfaces. In *ACM UIST '10* (2010), 273–282.

Probabilistic Touchscreen Keyboard Incorporating Gaze Point Information

Toshiyuki Hagiya
KDDI R&D Laboratories, Inc.
to-hagiya@kddilabs.jp

Tsuneo Kato
KDDI R&D Laboratories, Inc.
tkato@kddilabs.jp

ABSTRACT

We propose a novel probabilistic keyboard that takes into account the distance between a gaze point and a touch position in order to improve typing efficiency. The proposed keyboard dynamically changes the size of the search space for predicting candidate words based on a model that estimates the magnitude of touch position errors according to the distance between the gaze point and the touch position. This makes it possible for users to type intended words even when they glance at different areas on the screen. Performance was evaluated in terms of input accuracy in total error rate (TER) and of typing speed in words per minute (WPM). The results showed that the proposed keyboard successfully reduced the TER by 18.2% and increased WPM by 12.7% compared to the conventional keyboard.

Author Keywords

Touchscreen text input; mobile devices; eye tracking; gaze-supported interaction; multi-modal interface

ACM Classification Keywords

H.5.2 **[Information Interfaces and Presentation]**: User Interfaces

INTRODUCTION

In concert with the recent popularity of smartphones and tablets, the touch screen keyboard has also become popular. While a touch screen display provides the benefits of a flexible software keyboard that is able to switch its layout, users tend to make typing errors mainly due to the lack of tactility and the small keys [7]. Users often type text while glancing at different areas of the keyboard to check the typed text or other information, even though typing errors increase under these circumstances. We measured the touch position error from a target associated with the gaze point quantitatively, and found the variance of the touch position error increases in accordance with the distance between the gaze point and the touch target. One solution is to adjust the target areas according to the actual touch distributions as described in the next section. Another solution is to show a number of candidate words guided by sequences of characters associated with the typed characters. This approach is effective for users who select candidate words frequently. On the other hand, this approach has a drawback in that a long list of irrelevant words is confusing when typing carefully, and a lot of time is wasted in searching for target words from the list. As the touch precision is influenced by the gaze point, the operational load on users can be reduced by proper candidate word selection while taking changes in touch precision into consideration.

In this paper, we propose a novel probabilistic keyboard incorporating a model which estimates the magnitude of the touch position error according to the distance between the gaze point and the touch position (hereinafter referred to as the "gaze-touch model"). The size of the search space for candidate words changes dynamically in association with the estimated touch position error by the gaze-touch model. More specifically, the size of the search space for an input is set small when a user types carefully with a steady gaze, while it is set large when a user types carelessly while glancing at different areas.

MobileHCI'14, September 23–26, 2014, Toronto, ON, Canada
Copyright 2014 ACM 978-1-4503-3004-6/14/09···$15.00.
http://dx.doi.org/10.1145/2628363.2628370

RELATED WORK

In order to reduce typing errors, some studies proposed transforming the detection areas based on both the language model and touch model approaches [5, 4, 17]. Joshua *et al.* [5] used character n-grams for the language model and the Gaussian mixture model (GMM) for the touch model. The probability of a character being typed was given by the product of the two probabilities. Arif *et al.* [1] proposed a keyboard taking account of fingertip pressure predicted by the touch-point movement and the time. For practical issues in the real environment, Goel *et al.* [4] analyzed the differences in touch distributions between sitting and walking, and proposed adaptation techniques. Yin *et al.* [17] defined the hierarchical submodels depending on users and hand postures in order to adapt each model according to the amount of data for adaptation.

Some proposals for improving usability of the input combined operation with gaze. Zhai *et al.* [18] proposed the MAGIC pointing approach, which combines mouse and gaze input for item selection. Bieg *et al.* [3] analyzed the relationship between the positions of the mouse and of the eyes in a selection task and found that users automatically minimize the travel distance to targets. To support touch operation, Stellmach *et al.* [14] proposed a method in which the nearest object from the gaze point was selected when a user touched some overlapping objects. However, the relationship between the gaze point and the touch distribution has not been researched.

PROBABILISTIC KEYBOARD WITH GAZE-TOUCH MODEL

The keyboard that we propose here has two features. One is that the gaze-touch model, which models the relationship between the variance of touch position error and the distance between the gaze point and touch position, is incorporated into the probabilistic keyboard. The other is that the number of character sequences for searching candidate words changes dynamically according to the occurrence probability of a character that is controlled by the gaze-touch model.

Formulation of probabilistic keyboard

First, we explain a conventional probabilistic keyboard. The occurrence probability of a character is given by the product of the probability of the touch model and that of the language model using Bayes' theorem as in

$$P(c_j|(x_t, y_t)) = \frac{p((x_t, y_t)|c_j) \cdot p(c_j)}{p(x_t, y_t)} \quad (1)$$

$$\propto p((x_t, y_t)|c_j) \cdot p(c_j) \quad (2)$$

$$= p_T \cdot p_L \quad (3)$$

where p_T is the probability of the touch model and p_L is that of the language model. The probability of touch model p_T can be represented by a single Gaussian distribution in the simplest case. In practice, the performance was improved by a Gaussian Mixture Model (GMM) because the touch distribution is different depending on hand postures, such as the typing hand. The generative model outputs the probability p_T by the following equation

$$p_T = \sum_{k=1}^{K} \omega_k N((x_t, y_t)|\mu_{jk}, \Sigma_{jk}) \quad (4)$$

$$\Sigma_{jk} = diag(\sigma_x^2, \sigma_y^2) \quad (5)$$

where N denotes a Gaussian distribution with a mean vector μ_{jk} and a diagonal covariance matrix Σ_{jk} and K is the number of mixtures. On the other hand, the language model, which defines the probabilities of the subsequent characters, is implemented by a character 3-gram because the probability of c_j greatly depends on the history of character sequences. The probability p_L is shown as follows

$$p_L = p(c_j|h) \quad (6)$$

where h is the history of the character sequences. The probability of a sequence is given by the product of those of all the characters in the sequence.

User adaptation

The touch model is adapted to an individual user based on the maximum likelihood linear regression (MLLR) algorithm that has been reported to be effective for key input [6]. In MLLR, the means of the normal distributions are transformed and re-estimated as

$$\mu_k' = \mathbf{A}\mu_k + b \quad (7)$$

where μ_k is the mean vector of Equation (4), and μ_k' is the adapted mean vector. (**A**, b) are obtained by maximum-likelihood estimation.

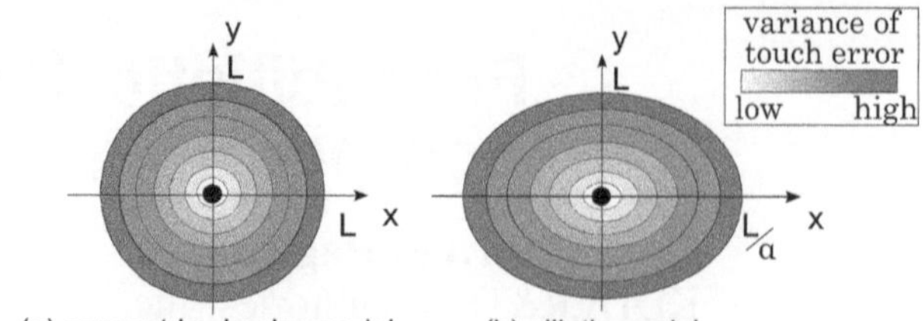

(a) concentric circular model (model A)　(b) elliptic model (model B)

Figure 1. Gaze-touch model

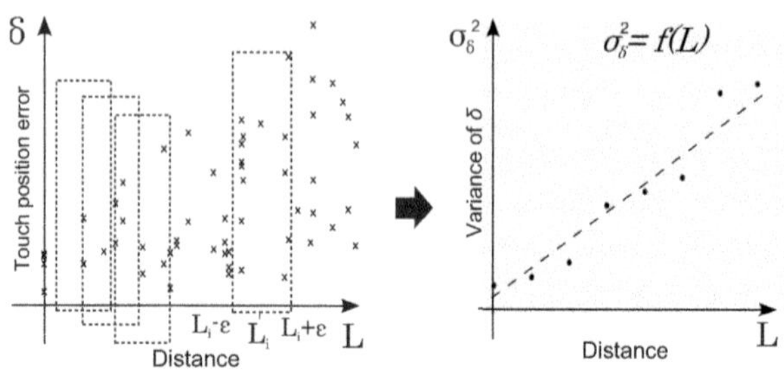

Figure 2. Convert the touch position error to the variance

Formulation of gaze-touch model

In the human visual system, the fovea, the part responsible for visual acuity, spans 1–2 degrees of the visual field [16], and the spatial resolution decreases as the distance from the fovea increases. Touch position error (δ), which is the distance between the touch position and a target, can be expected to increase when users look at a point farther from the target. Consequently, we define the gaze-touch model so that it gives the variance of the touch position error (σ_δ^2) based on the distance (L) between two coordinates (x_g, y_g) and (x_t, y_t). Since it is known that the central visual field is a concentric circle with an angle of 20–30 degrees or an ellipse with a horizontal angle of 30 degrees and a vertical angle of 20 degrees [16], we propose the two gaze-touch models as shown in Figure 1. One is the "concentric circular model" (model A) and the other is the "elliptic model" (model B). Let us formulate the gaze-touch models as shown in the following equations:

$$\sigma_\delta^2 = f(L) \quad (8)$$

$$L = \sqrt{\alpha^2(x_g - x_t)^2 + (y_g - y_t)^2} \quad (9)$$

$$\alpha = \begin{cases} 1 & (model A) \\ \frac{\tan 20^\circ}{\tan 30^\circ} & (model B) \end{cases} \quad (10)$$

where f is a monotonically increasing function, and α is the scaling factor for axis lengths. Figure 2 shows the operation for calculating σ_δ^2 as the variance of δ in a moving window. The function $f(L)$ in (8) is determined by a regression.

Incorporating the gaze-touch model into a keyboard

Figure 3 shows a block diagram of the approach. The coordinates (x_g^i, y_g^i) and (x_t^i, y_t^i) are the gaze point and the touch position on the screen, respectively. The superscript i corresponds to the number in a character sequence. The gaze-touch model outputs an estimated variance of the touch position based on the inputs (x_g^i, y_g^i) and (x_t^i, y_t^i). The touch model is formulated by a GMM for each key. In our method, the variances of the gaze-touch model are used to take into

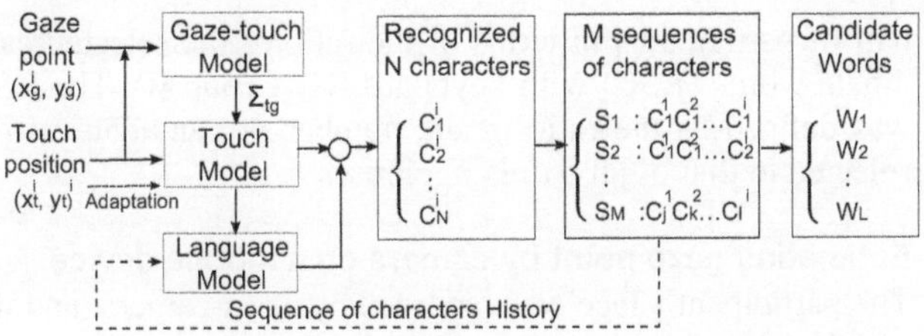

Figure 3. Block diagram of the proposed method

account the influence of the gaze point. The effect of L can be taken into account if we simply replace the variance of the conventional model Σ_{jk} by Σ_{tg}. Specifically, the touch model incorporating the gaze-touch model is shown by the following equation

$$p_T = p((x_t, y_t)|c_j, L) = \sum_{k=1}^{K} \omega_k N((x_t, y_t)|\mu_{jk}, \Sigma_{tg}) \quad (11)$$

$$\Sigma_{tg} = diag(\sigma_\delta^2, \sigma_\delta^2) \quad (12)$$

where σ_δ^2 is given by Equation (8). The occurrence probability of every character is given by the product of those of the touch model and of the language model, in this case character n-grams were used to create the model.

The characters of variable N-best are output according to their probability. The number N changes depending on how many characters have a probability within a range from the highest probability among all the characters as in

$$\mathrm{N} = | \{c_j \,|P(c_j) > P_{max} \times r_{th}\} \,| \quad (13)$$

where r_{th} is a threshold between 0 and 1. The larger the variances from the gaze-touch model are, the smaller the differences between the probabilities of the most probable character and the probabilities of the others are. The number of output characters, N, increases as a result. The probability of a sequence of characters is given by the product of those of the character. M sequences of characters with high probabilities are obtained from the possible combinations of characters. Candidate words are selected from a lexicon by left-hand match to the M sequences. The actual figures are decided from the preliminary experimental results.

DETERMINATION OF GAZE-TOUCH MODEL

In this section, we determine the function of the gaze-touch model, i.e. $f(L)$ in (8), and evaluate the goodness of modeling in terms of the determination coefficients (R^2).

Data collection

We recruited sixteen participants (ten males and six females) between the ages of 25 and 59 (average 35.1). Thirteen of them (eight males and five females) were right-handed. All of them were familiar with typing with a smartphone, although they did not have experience with gaze-based interfaces. The device was the AQUOS PAD SHT21 running Android 4.0 with a 7.0 inch screen having a resolution of 1280 × 800 pixels (216 ppi). The participants were instructed to touch a target (touch-target) while looking at another point

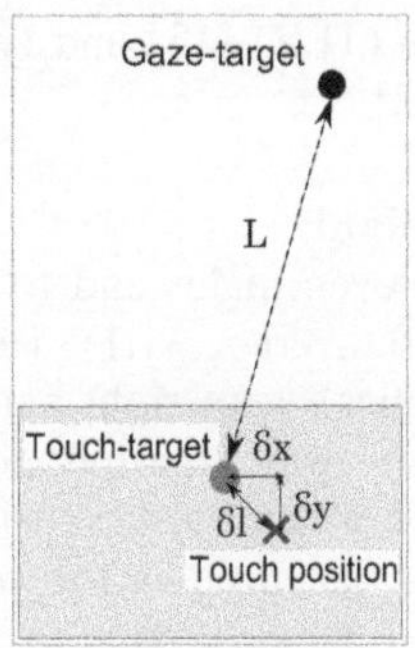

Figure 4. Screenshot of the application for the determination of the gaze-touch model

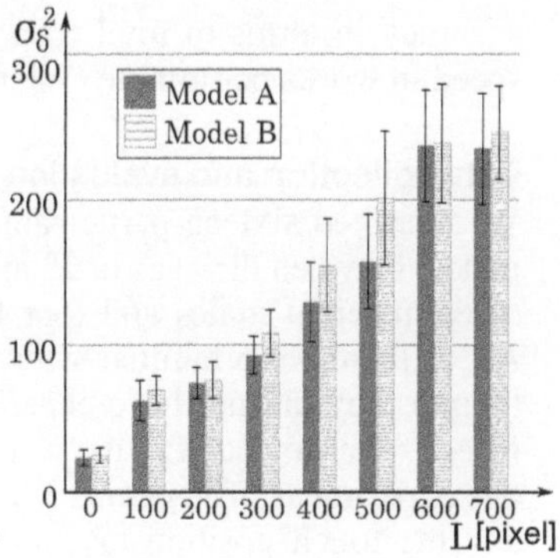

Figure 5. Average of the variances; vertical bars show standard errors

Table 1. Average determination coefficients (R^2) of regression analysis

	Linear	Exponential	Logistic
Model A	0.79	0.77	0.81
Model B	0.81	0.74	0.81

(gaze-target). The touch-target and gaze-target were drawn with a red dot and a black dot with a radius of 15 pixels as shown in Figure 4. Participants touched eight times per set and repeated ten sets of different gaze-targets while holding the device with both hands. The touch-target changed its position in the area corresponding to the keyboard after every touch, while the gaze-target was fixed during a set. The device recorded the coordinates of the touch position (x_t, y_t) in addition to those of the both targets. In the experiment, gaze points were tracked using Tobii Glasses [15]. On the basis of the gaze points, the data when participants did not look at the gaze-target were eliminated by humans off-line.

Determination of the functions of the gaze-touch model

We compared the functions of the "concentric circular model" (Model A) to those of the "elliptic model" (Model B). The variances were computed with a moving window. The window size and the window shift were 200 pixels and 100 pixels, respectively. Figure 5 shows the relation between L and the variance of each model. In general, as we had anticipated, the larger L was, the larger the variance was. For modeling the relation between L and the variance of two models, three regressions, i.e. linear regression, exponential regression with a natural basis, and logistic regression, were examined. Table 1 shows determination coefficients, R^2, for each variance and regression. The R^2s of the regression functions for each model show very little difference. ANOVA did not show a significant difference ($F(6, 90) = 2.31, p \leq 0.05$). Accordingly, we adopted the linear regression of Model A, the simplest model. Hereinafter, the regression is defined as $\sigma_\delta^2 = aL + b(a{=}0.32, b{=}14.7)$.

EVALUATION OF THE PROBABILISTIC KEYBOARD INCORPORATING THE GAZE-TOUCH MODEL

In this section, we evaluate the performance of the proposed keyboard in comparison with two baseline keyboards: the conventional keyboard (B1) and the probabilistic keyboard without the gaze-touch model (B2). We compared the typing accuracy in terms of total error rate (TER) [13] and typing speed in words per minute (WPM) [2]

Data collection and evaluation method

We recruited sixteen participants (eleven males and five females) between the ages of 23 and 40 (average 31.1). Twelve of them (eight males and four females) were right-handed. All of them were familiar with typing with smartphone, although they did not have experience with gaze-based interfaces. The device was the same as that used in the previous experiment. The device recorded the gaze point (x_g, y_g) and the touch position (x_t, y_t). The gaze point was measured in real-time with an eye tracking technique using an in-camera as described in the next subsection instead of the Tobii Glasses, which are limited in terms of their offline data recording capability. The keyboard had a QWERTY layout, which had a fixed key display area. In a sitting position, the participants typed six sets of 20 phrases chosen from MacKenzie's phrase set [10] with each keyboard with a typing application as shown in Figure 6. The calibrations of the gaze point were carried out before each set of input trials. The participants were permitted to correct their inputs and to select candidate words to input the exact-match phrases. The presentation order of the keyboards and the set of phrases were given at random.

For the two probabilistic keyboards, the character 3-gram of the language model was trained by maximum likelihood estimation (MLE) on the Brown corpus [8]. The touch model was also trained by MLE with touch data for 840 phrases typed by participants (five males and two females) between the ages of 23 and 36 (average 29.2). They did not participate in the evaluation experiment. The number of mixtures of the GMM was set to 2. Data for MLLR adaptation were the correctly typed data of the first phrase of each set. We evaluated the remaining 19 phrases except for the first phrase of each set. From the preliminary experimental results, the threshold r_{th} for deciding N of Equation (13) was set to 0.5, and the maximum number of sequences of characters for searching candidate words, M, was set to 6. The candidate words were searched by left-hand match using OpenWnn [11].

The proposed keyboard is considered effective for users who select candidate words frequently. The TER and WPM were tallied in two groups; all participants (Group I) and the upper half of participants in terms of the ratio of the selected candidate words (RSC) with keyboard B1 (Group II). The RSC was defined as the ratio of the number of candidate words selected to that of all words in phrases.

Estimating gaze point by camera on a mobile device

The participant's face was recorded by an in-camera, and the facial and eye data were captured by Snapdragon SDK [12]. The obtained data were as follows: coordinates of eyes and mouth, face leaning (pitch, roll and yaw), horizontal and vertical gaze angle value, and gaze point relative to the position of the camera. The gaze point on the screen is calculated with these pieces of information. The correspondence between the gaze point on the screen and these data was modeled by multiple linear regression before each set of the typing experiment because the coefficients differ from the experimental environment. Figure 7 shows a screenshot of the calibration procedure. Participants looked at the stationary gaze-target that moves after each trial. Participants repeated the trial 60 times. When all of the trials were completed, the coefficients of multiple linear regression were calculated. The coefficients were used in a set of the experiment. A preliminary experiment showed that the participants can focus on the circles having radii of 50 pixels, 100 pixels, and 150 pixels with probabilities of 74.5%, 83.8%, and 97.4%, respectively.

Evaluation of the proposed keyboard

Figure 8 (a) and (b) show the average TER and WPM for the three keyboards. Looking at the results for Group I, the TER and WPM were 6.47% and 10.5 for the conventional keyboard (B1), 5.67% and 10.9 for the probabilistic keyboard (B2), and 5.29% and 11.8 for the proposed keyboard. In other words, the proposed keyboard reduced the TER by 18.2% and 6.7%, and increased WPM by 12.7% and 8.0% compared to the other two keyboards. The major factor influencing the improvement was that the typing counts and editorial operations were reduced owing to more hits in candidate words. Actually, the RSC of the proposed keyboard increased 26% compared to the others; The RSCs were 28.3% for B1, 27.6% for B2, and 38.2% for the proposed keyboard. ANOVA revealed statistically significant differences among the three keyboards in TER ($F(2, 45) = 3.31$, $p \leq 0.05$) and WPM ($F(2, 45) = 3.55$, $p \leq 0.05$). However, a post-hoc Tukey's test did not show any significant difference between B2 and the proposed keyboard.

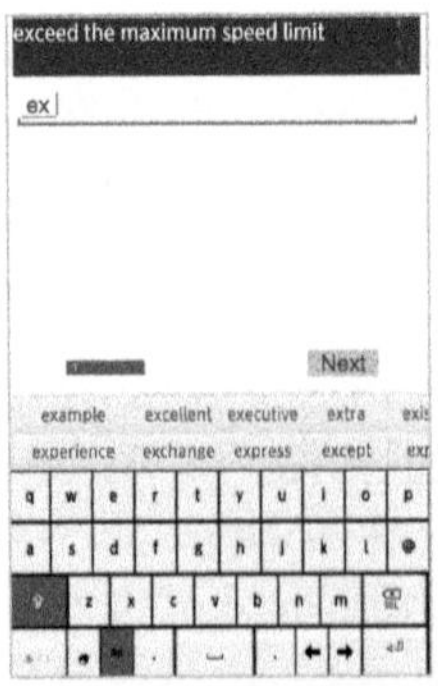

Figure 6. Screenshot of the application for the evaluation experiment

Figure 7. Screenshot of the application for the gaze point calibration

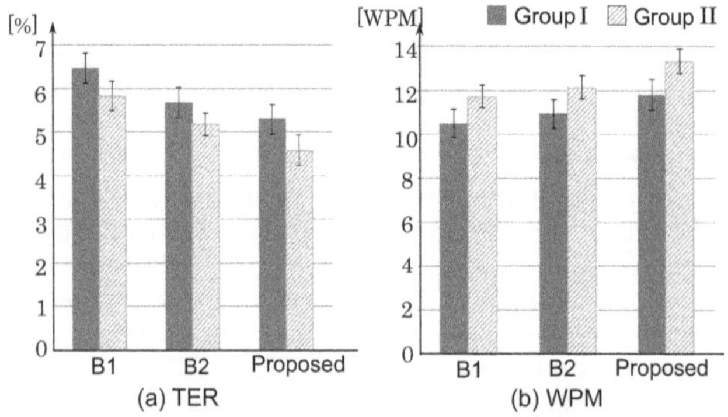

Figure 8. Comparison of total error rate (TER) and words per minute (WPM); vertical bars show standard errors

On the other hand, focusing on Group II in Figure 8 (a) and (b), the proposed keyboard reduced the TER by 21.5% and 11.5%, and increased WPM by 13.5% and 9.7% compared to the others. ANOVA showed statistically significant differences among the three keyboards in TER ($F(2, 21) = 3.89$, $p \leq 0.05$) and WPM ($F(2, 21) = 4.03$, $p \leq 0.05$). A post-hoc Tukey's test also showed significant differences between the proposed keyboard and the other two. These results suggest that the proposed keyboard benefited those who used the list of candidate words frequently.

DISCUSSION AND FUTURE WORK

A significant difference was observed in TER and WPM between the proposed keyboard and keyboard B2 for participants of high RSC. It is possible to automatically categorize those users into a group based on RSC. The proposed keyboard is apparently of benefit to users in this category, which implies that the keyboard should be useful in practice. The effectiveness of the proposed keyboard is particularly significant for long words as it reduced TER by 12.9%, and increased WPM by 14.1% compared to the probabilistic keyboard for words with 5 or more letters. This is probably due to the fact that the longer words are, the more time is needed for correction if the intended words are not displayed.

On the other hand, in actual practice, users adopt a variety of hand postures when using mobile devices. However, switching hand postures was not considered in our experiment although the touch model was adapted to users. A possible solution to this issue is proposed in [17]. They proposed detecting hand postures by touch distributions and changing models accordingly. By incorporating their methods and setting a number of the touch models for the hand postures, the proposed keyboard could be further improved.

In addition, the gaze-touch model could be improved if the performance of the eye tracking could be improved. In this experiment, the eye tracking technique was very simple and needed calibration whenever the user's posture changed. Thereby, the experiments were conducted only in the sitting position even though the distributions of touch and gaze point become large when the user is moving. In addition, it is known that users tend to look at targets before clicking the mouse [9]. It is considered that taking into account the gaze point immediately before the touch operation would make the model more accurate because a similar phenomenon might also happen in the touch operation.

CONCLUSION

In this paper, we proposed a probabilistic keyboard that took gaze point into consideration. The gaze-touch model, which models the relationship between the variance in the touch position error and the distance between the gaze point and the touch position, was incorporated into the Gaussian mixture distributions of the touch model of the probabilistic keyboard. Experimental results showed that the proposed keyboard reduced the total error rate by 18.2% and increased typing speed by 12.7% compared to the conventional keyboard.

REFERENCES

1. Arif, A. S., and Stuerzlinger. Pseudo-pressure detection and its use in predictive text entry on touchscreens. In *Proc. OzCHI 2013*, ACM (2013), 383–392.
2. Arif, A, S., and Stuerzlinger, W. Analysis of Text Entry Performance Metrics. In *Proc. TIC-STH 2009*, IEEE (2009), 100–105.
3. Bieg, H, J., Reiterer, H., and Bulthoff, H, H. Eye and pointer coordination in search and selection tasks. In *Proc. ETRA 2010*, ACM (2010), 89–92.
4. Goel, M., Findlater, L., and Wobbrock, J, O. WalkType: using accelerometer data to accomodate situational impairments in mobile touch screen text entry. In *Proc. CHI 2012*, ACM (2012), 2687–2696.
5. Goodman, J., Venolia, G., Steury, K., and Parker, C. Language Modeling for Soft Keyboards. In *Proc. IUI 2002*, ACM (2002), 194–195.
6. Hagiya, T., and Kato, T. Probabilistic Keyboard Adaptable to User and Operating Style Based on Syllable HMMs. In *Proc. ICPR 2012*, IEEE (2012), 65–68.
7. Hoggan, E., Brewster, S. A., and Johnston, J. Investigating the effectiveness of tactile feedback for mobile touchscreens. In *Proc. CHI 2008*, ACM (2008), 1573–1582.
8. Kucera, H., and Francis, W, N. *Pattern Recognition And Machine Learning*. Brown University Press, 1967.
9. Kumar, M., Paepcke, A., and Winograd, T. EyePoint: Practical Pointing and Selection Using Gaze and Keyboard . In *Proc. CHI 2007*, ACM (2007), 421–430.
10. MacKenzie, I, S., and Soukoreff, R, W. Phrase sets for evaluating text entry techniques. In *Proc. CHI 2003*, ACM (2003), 754–755.
11. OMRON SOFTWARE Co., Ltd. `http://www.omronsoft.com/`.
12. Qualcomm. `https://developer.qualcomm.com/`.
13. Soukoreff, R. W., and MacKenzie, I, S. Recent Developments in Text-Entry Error Rate Measurement. In *Proc. CHI 2004*, ACM (2004), 1425–1428.
14. Stellmach, S., and Dachselt, R. Still Looking: Investigating Seamless Gaze-supported Selection, Positioning, and Manipulation of Distant Targets. In *Proc. CHI 2013*, ACM (2013), 285–294.
15. Tobii Technology. `http://www.tobii.com/`.
16. Walker, H, K., Hall, W, D., and Hurst, J, W. *Clinical Methods: The History, Physical, and Laboratory Examinations*. Boston, Butterworths, 1990.
17. Yin, Y., Ouyang, T, Y., Partridge, K., and Zhai, S. Making Touchscreen Keyboards Adaptive to Keys, Hand Postures, and Individuals - A Hierarchical Spatial Backoff Model Approach. In *Proc. CHI 2013*, ACM (2013), 2775–2784.
18. Zhai, S., Morimoto, C., and Ihde, S. Manual and gaze input cascaded (MAGIC) pointing. In *Proc. CHI 1999*, ACM (1999), 246–253.

The Inviscid Text Entry Rate and its Application as a Grand Goal for Mobile Text Entry

Per Ola Kristensson
University of St Andrews, UK
pok@st-andrews.ac.uk

Keith Vertanen
Montana Tech, USA
kvertanen@mtech.edu

ABSTRACT
We introduce the concept of the inviscid text entry rate: the point when the user's creativity is the bottleneck rather than the text entry method. We then apply the inviscid text entry rate to define a grand goal for mobile text entry. Via a proxy measure we estimate the population mean of the sufficiently inviscid entry rate to be 67 wpm. We then compare existing mobile text entry methods against this estimate and find that the vast majority of text entry methods in the literature are substantially slower. This analysis suggests the mobile text entry field needs to focus on methods that can viably approach the inviscid entry rate.

Author Keywords
Inviscid entry rate; mobile text entry; crowdsourcing

ACM Classification Keywords
H.5.2 Information interfaces and presentation: User Interfaces: Input devices and strategies

INTRODUCTION
It is obvious text entry methods should be fast. However, what is not obvious is how we know when we have created a text entry method that is fast enough. The maximum upper bound for text entry is the speed of light, which is the fundamental limit for how fast physical information can travel. We also note that users can speak very fast, up to 200 wpm [16]. However, can users *compose* non-trivial text at such a high entry rate? The processes of speaking and writing, while related, are significantly different (see Chafe and Tannen [2] for an extensive overview). To put this further into perspective, an A4 sheet of paper contains about 500 words. To be able to write an email at 200 wpm means being able to write a short essay filling an entire A4 sheet in just 2.5 minutes.

We introduce the concept of the *inviscid entry rate*. We argue the search for faster text entry methods is bounded: there is a limit when it is not useful to search for faster text entry methods. This point occurs when the text entry method is not the bottleneck of the process of transferring thoughts into writing. In other words, the point when the user's creativity is the bottleneck rather than the text entry method. We call this point the *inviscid entry rate*. The term *inviscid* is borrowed from fluid dynamics: an inviscid fluid has no viscosity. Similarly, an inviscid text entry method does not hinder the free flow of information from a user's mind to the computer.

MobileHCI 2014, September 23–26, 2014, Toronto, ON, Canada.

http://dx.doi.org/10.1145/2628363.2628405

The inviscid entry rate can be estimated by measuring how fast users can compose novel messages using an inviscid text entry method. An entry rate depends on the amount of text generated and the time it takes to write it. Let us define $T_{compose}$ as the time it takes to a compose a given amount of text and $T_{transcribe}$ as the time to transcribe the same amount of text. $T_{compose}$ can be broken down into two components—the time it takes to conceive the text ($T_{conceive}$), and the time it takes to articulate the text ($T_{articulate}$)[1]:

$$T_{compose} = T_{conceive} + T_{articulate}. \quad (1)$$

In contrast, the time it takes to transcribe memorable[2] text depends solely on the time it takes to articulate the text:

$$T_{transcribe} = T_{articulate}. \quad (2)$$

For a given fixed amount of generated text, an inviscid text entry method will result in $T_{compose}$ being markedly higher than $T_{transcribe}$. This is because when the text entry method is inviscid, it is rate-limited by $T_{conceive}$. At this point, even if $T_{articulate}$ is further reduced, it will only result in a negligible performance improvement.

We currently do not know if a true inviscid text entry method has been discovered. However, we can still identify a *sufficiently* inviscid text entry method. A sufficiently inviscid text entry method is a text entry method in which $T_{compose}$ is markedly higher than $T_{transcribe}$.

We demonstrate how to apply the concept of the inviscid entry rate to form a meaningful grand goal for mobile text entry. If we have a population estimate of users writing with a sufficiently inviscid text entry method, then we have an explicit goal to aspire to in the field of mobile text entry. The creative process of inventing a new mobile text entry method is then not about creating faster text entry methods in comparison to what is out there. Instead, it is about creating mobile text entry methods performing at, or slightly above, the sufficiently inviscid entry rate. After that point, it could be more useful to address other design aspects of text entry (such as for instance user engagement or learnability).

[1] Articulation time includes not only motor actions but also fixed overhead time spent processing visual feedback.

[2] The established experimental paradigm for testing text entry methods is to instruct participants to transcribe memorable sentences.

We hypothesize that we can estimate a sufficiently inviscid entry rate for mobile text entry by measuring how fast users compose small messages on their regular full-sized QWERTY keyboards. The assumption is that the regular full-sized QWERTY keyboard is a sufficiently inviscid text entry method. This is plausible for two reasons. First, the fact that the ubiquitous full-sized QWERTY keyboard has prevailed means that it is likely that most users are satisfied with its speed [4]. Second, as we will show, users compose text significantly slower than they transcribe text when they use their regular full-sized QWERTY keyboards.

This means we can measure the text entry rate from a wide sample of users composing novel messages using their own full-sized keyboards and infer a sufficiently inviscid entry rate. Assuming a normal distribution, by obtaining a population estimate of the mean composition entry rate and adding one standard deviation we acquire a sufficiently inviscid entry rate that represents a text entry rate about 84% of users in the population cannot surpass if they compose original text using a full-sized desktop or laptop keyboard.

As a control, we also measure participants' transcription entry rate. If the mean composition entry rate is markedly lower than the mean transcription entry rate then the bottleneck for composition was not the text entry method per se but the creativity required to invent novel messages.

ESTIMATING A SUFFICIENTLY INVISCID ENTRY RATE

We used data originally collected as part of Experiment 1 in Vertanen and Kristensson [20]. In this paper, we re-analyzed the data using only workers resident in the US. This was done to focus on fluent speakers who are likely faster typists. It also eliminated some non-US workers who appeared to be copying text rather than creating novel compositions. Removing non-US workers reduced the number of participants from 181 to 115. We additionally removed one composition task that was not representative of mobile text entry (the AID condition in [20]). For completeness, we explain the methodology of the original data collection.

We recruited 115 participants from the US using Amazon's Mechanical Turk microtask market. They were compensated $1 for taking part in a single Human Intelligence Task (HIT). The average time to complete the HIT was 27 minutes. Before the first task, we asked participants to provide information such as sex, country, age, English ability, typing ability, and computer type.

Participants were asked to complete four tasks using their full-sized keyboards. In each task they did ten different transcriptions or compositions. The order of the tasks was randomized. In all the composition tasks participants were instructed not to disclose any private information (such as phone numbers, email addresses or names). Participants were prevented from pasting text. For the exact instructions given for each task, see Figure 1 in [20]. The four task types were:

Transcription Task – Participants were presented with a sentence and asked to type it as quickly and as accurately as possible. The sentences were taken from a corpus of email messages written by Enron employees on their BlackBerry mobile devices [19]. This was the COPY condition in [20].

Composition Task 1 – Participants were presented with a short message (e.g. "Wanna go to the park?") and asked to imagine they received this message on a mobile device. They were asked to type a fictitious response. The set of messages used in this task were created by other workers who had been asked to invent things they might send from a mobile device. This was the REPLY condition in [20].

Composition Task 2 – Participants were presented with short fictitious situations (e.g. "Your co-worker Carl will be 29 years old today. Send him a greeting."). They were then asked to imagine they were using a mobile device to compose a response to this situation. This was the SITUATION condition in [20].

Composition Task 3 – Participants were asked to imagine they were using a mobile device and to compose a fictitious message. They were also advised that if they were struggling for ideas to think about things they write on their own mobile device. This was the COMPOSE condition in [20].

Results

The average age of participants (self-reported) was 29 (sd = 10). 64% reported being female. Participants rated their English skill as native (96%) or advanced (4%). Participants reported using a laptop (62%) or a desktop computer (38%). Participants reported their typing ability as fast (37%), moderate (59%) or slow (3%).

For the transcription task, error rate was measured as the minimum edit distance between the stimulus sentence and the participant's response, divided by the number of characters in the stimulus sentence. This provides us with a character-level error rate. We found that the mean error rate was 2.2% and the median error rate was 0%. This is comparable with other text entry experiments (e.g. [14]).

Participants' entry rate was measured in words-per-minute (wpm) and a word was defined as five consecutive characters including spaces. The time required to write a response was defined as the interval between when they first typed a character in response to a new stimulus until their last key press before proceeding to the next stimulus. This meant that if participants paused between stimuli, such pauses did not affect the entry rate measurements. The mean entry rate for the transcription task was 68 wpm. Participants transcribed a little over 11K words.

For the composition tasks, we verified participants' responses were intelligible and sensible, removing from our analysis any participants who did not provide adequate responses. Overall participants created plausible and imaginative compositions (for examples see [20]). Entry rate was measured in the same way as for the transcription task. In total, participants composed a little over 29K words.

Figure 1 shows the entry rate for each task. Participants wrote at 57 wpm (sd = 20) in composition task 1, 43 wpm (sd = 13) in composition task 2, and 55 wpm (sd = 18) in composition

Text entry method	Highest reported entry rate (wpm)
Estimate of the inviscid entry rate	*67*
Physical thumb keyboards	60 [3]
Gesture keyboards	45 [9]
Optimized on-screen keyboards	45 [12]
QWERTY on-screen keyboards	40 [12]
KALQ thumb keyboard	37 [14]
Half-QWERTY	35 [13]
Twiddler	35 [11]
WalkType	31 [5]
ContextType	28 [6]
Disambiguating keypads	26 [7]
Unconstrained handwriting recognition	25 [8]
Dasher	20 [21]
Mobile speech	18 [18]
Quikwriting	16 [15]
Unistrokes	16 [1]
TiltText	14 [22]
Multi-tap	12 [23]
Graffiti	11[1]
EdgeWrite	7 [24]

Table 1. The highest reported entry rate in words-per-minute (wpm) of a variety of mobile text entry interfaces.

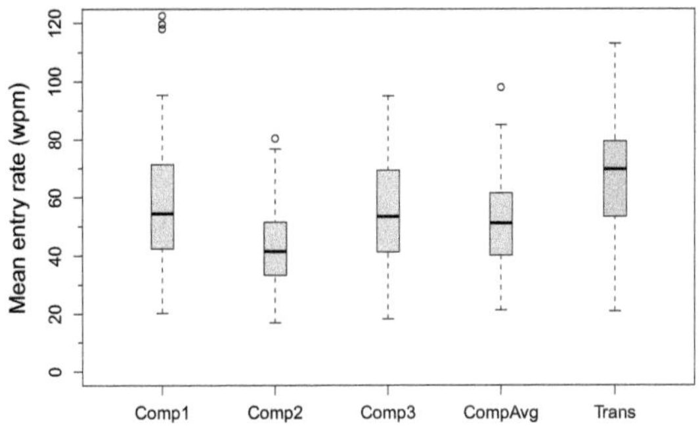

Figure 1. Entry rates for the composition and transcription tasks.

task 3. The grand mean composition entry rate was 52 wpm (sd = 15). For comparison, the transcription entry rate was 68 wpm (sd = 18). According to our previous definition of the inviscid entry rate being equal to a population estimate of the mean composition entry rate plus one standard deviation, the inviscid entry rate in the population is 67 wpm.

Figure 2 shows the entry rate distribution for the transcription task and the three composition tasks. As shown in Figure 2, all composition tasks follow a roughly similar positively skewed distribution with a mode relatively close to each other. Thus, to estimate the inviscid entry rate we averaged the mean composition rates in Figure 1.

The transcription entry rate (68 wpm) was markedly higher than the mean composition entry rate (52 wpm). Thus, it is likely the cognitive process of composing text ($T_{conceive}$) was the bottleneck rather than the operation of a full-sized keyboard ($T_{articulate}$). RM-ANOVA revealed that the difference between mean composition entry rate (averaged over all three composition tasks) and the transcription rate was significant ($F_{1,114}$ = 125.969, η_p^2 = 0.525, $p < 0.001$).

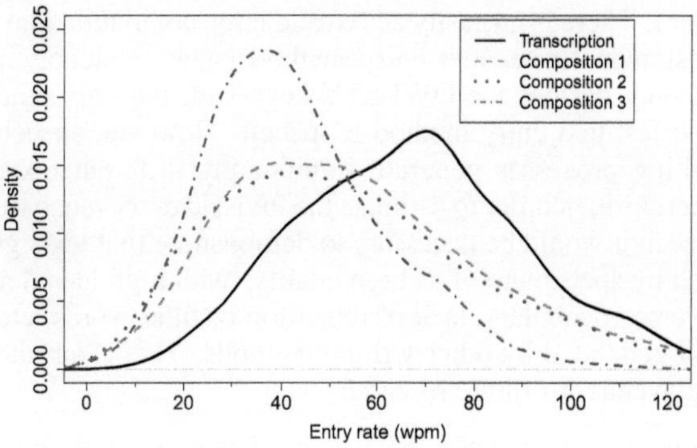

Figure 2. Probability densities for the transcription task and the three different composition tasks.

DISCUSSION

In theory, the inviscid entry rate estimate enables us to assess to what extent a mobile text entry methods hinders users' free-flowing writing. Such an analysis can tell us how far we are from the goal of achieving mobile text entry methods that support the fluid transmission of thoughts into writing. This analysis can in principle be carried out for various text entry methods by, for example, measuring participants' entry rates when they compose novel small messages.

Unfortunately, composition tasks are rarely used in text entry experiments. Instead the dominating method for testing a text entry method is to measure its performance using a transcription task. However, we can make an upper-bound estimate of a mobile text entry method's performance by basing a comparison on its highest reported transcription entry rate. If such an upper-bound estimate does not surpass our 67 wpm estimation of the sufficiently inviscid entry rate then the probability that the text entry method will ever support users' free-flowing writing is low.

We surveyed the literature to find the highest reported entry rates for an array of mobile text entry methods. The results are in Table 1. Note that these entry rates were obtained on transcription tasks rather than composition tasks and thus overestimate the entry rates of the methods in the table. Even so, Table 1 shows that very few text entry methods have reported entry rates near our estimate of the inviscid entry rate. This means there is still room for active research on faster mobile text entry methods.

LIMITATIONS AND FUTURE WORK

We defined the sufficiently inviscid entry rate for mobile text entry to be a population estimate of the mean composition entry rate plus one standard deviation. This definition is to some extent arbitrary. However, our definition has two advantages. First, it has a clear statistical interpretation. Second, even though it could be set higher, no existing mobile text entry method is close to the sufficiently inviscid entry rate.

It is likely there are alternative text entry methods that are already invented or yet to be discovered that could provide a better estimate of the *true* inviscid entry rate. We chose to measure the sufficiently inviscid entry rate based on the QWERTY keyboard for two reasons. First, a large proportion of the population are highly proficient with the QWERTY keyboard. There is no easily accessible large population that have mastered a faster text entry method (such as stenography). Second, besides the QWERTY keyboard, the only other viable fast text entry method is speech. However, speech and writing processes generate significantly different texts [2]. Therefore, in order to estimate the inviscid entry rate based on speech it would be necessary to demonstrate that texts generated by speech are of as high quality (with high idea density, diverse vocabulary, lack of repetition or filler words, etc.) as text generated by other writing methods. This is an interesting avenue for future research.

Previously we defined the time it takes to a compose text as the sum of two variables: the time it takes to conceive the text and the time it takes to articulate the text. However, these two variables may not be independent. For speech, the cognitive resources required to conceive the text will in part be consumed by the additional cognitive resources required to articulate it [17]. Further work is necessary to tease out the relationship between these two variables.

CONCLUSIONS

It is obvious higher entry rates are better, but it is not as obvious when to stop searching for ever higher entry rates and start improving alternative design dimensions [10]. We suggest using the inviscid entry rate as an explicit goal that bounds the otherwise endless search for ever higher text entry rates. We have estimated the sufficiently inviscid text entry rate for mobile text entry to around 67 wpm. We compared existing mobile text entry methods against this estimate and found that the vast majority are substantially slower. Our analysis suggests the mobile text entry field needs to focus on methods that can viably approach the inviscid entry rate.

REFERENCES

1. Castellucci, S. J., and MacKenzie, I. S. Graffiti vs. Unistrokes: an empirical comparison. In *Proc. CHI* (2008), 305–308.
2. Chafe, W., and Tannen, D. The relation between written and spoken language. *Annual Review of Anthropology 16* (1987), 383–407.
3. Clarkson, E., Clawson, J., Lyons, K., and Starner, T. An empirical study of typing rates on mini-QWERTY keyboards. In *Ext. Abstracts CHI 2005* (2005), 1288–1291.
4. David, P. A. Clio and the economics of QWERTY. *American Economic Review 75*, 2 (1985), 332–337.
5. Goel, M., Findlater, L., and Wobbrock, J. WalkType: using accelerometer data to accomodate situational impairments in mobile touch screen text entry. In *Proc. CHI* (2012), 2687–2696.
6. Goel, M., Jansen, A., Mandel, T., Patel, S. N., and Wobbrock, J. O. ContextType: Using hand posture information to improve mobile touch screen text entry. In *Proc. CHI 2013* (2013), 2795–2798.
7. James, C., and Reischel, K. Text input for mobile devices: comparing model prediction to actual performance. In *Proc. CHI 2001* (2001), 365–371.
8. Kristensson, P., and Denby, L. C. Text entry performance of state of the art unconstrained handwriting recognition: a longitudinal user study. In *Proc. CHI 2009* (2009), 567–570.
9. Kristensson, P. O. *Discrete and Continuous Shape Writing for Text Entry and Control*. Doctoral dissertation, Linköping University, 2007.
10. Kristensson, P. O. Five challenges for intelligent text entry methods. *AI Magazine 30*, 4 (2009), 85–94.
11. Lyons, K., Starner, T., and Gane, B. Experimental evaluations of the twiddler one-handed chording mobile keyboard. *Human-Computer Interaction 21*, 4 (2006), 343–392.
12. MacKenzie, I. S., and Zhang, S. X. The design and evaluation of a high-performance soft keyboard. In *Proc. CHI 1999* (1999), 25–31.
13. Matias, E., MacKenzie, I., and Buxton, W. One-handed touch-typing on a qwerty keyboard. *Human-Computer Interaction 11*, 1 (1996), 1–27.
14. Oulasvirta, A., Reichel, A., Li, W., Zhang, Y., Bachynskyi, M., Vertanen, K., and Kristensson, P. O. Improving two-thumb text entry on touchscreen devices. In *Proc. CHI* (2013), 2765–2774.
15. Perlin, K. Quikwriting: continuous stylus-based text entry. In *Proc. UIST* (1998), 215–216.
16. Rosenbaum, D. *Human Motor Control*. Academic Press, 1991.
17. Shneiderman, B. The limits of speech recognition. *Communications of the ACM 43*, 9 (2000), 63–65.
18. Vertanen, K., and Kristensson, P. O. Parakeet: A continuous speech recognition system for mobile touch-screen devices. In *Proc. IUI* (2009), 237–246.
19. Vertanen, K., and Kristensson, P. O. A versatile dataset for text entry evaluations based on genuine mobile emails. In *Proc. MobileHCI* (2011), 295–298.
20. Vertanen, K., and Kristensson, P. O. Complementing text entry evaluations with a composition task. *ACM Transactions on Computer-Human Interaction 21*, 2 (2014), Article No. 8.
21. Ward, D. J., Blackwell, A. F., and MacKay, D. J. C. Dasher: a gesture-driven data entry interface for mobile computing. *Human-Computer Interaction 17*, 2–3 (2002), 199–228.
22. Wigdor, D., and Balakrishnan, R. TiltText: using tilt for text input to mobile phones. In *Proc. UIST* (2003), 81–90.
23. Wigdor, D., and Balakrishnan, R. A comparison of consecutive and concurrent input text entry techniques for mobile phones. In *Proc. CHI* (2004), 81–88.
24. Wobbrock, J. O., Myers, B. A., and Kembel, J. A. EdgeWrite: a stylus-based text entry method designed for high accuracy and stability of motion. In *Proc. UIST* (2003), 61–70.

Texting While Walking: An Evaluation of Mini-QWERTY Text Input while On-the-Go

James Clawson, Thad Starner, Daniel Kohlsdorf, David Quigley, Scott Gilliland
Georgia Institute of Technology
School of Interactive Computing
{jamer,thad,dkohlsdorf,quigs,scott.gilliland}@gatech.edu

ABSTRACT

Interacting with mobile technology while in-motion has become a daily activity for many of us. Common sense leads one to believe that texting with a mini-qwerty keyboard while mobile can be dangerous since users are distracted and not paying attention to the environment. Previous studies have found that mobility negatively impacts text entry performance for novice participants typing on virtual keyboards on touch screen mobile phones. We investigate the impact of mobility on expert users' ability to quickly and accurately input text on mobile phones equipped with fixed-key mini-qwerty keyboards. In total, 36 participants completed 600 minutes of typing on mini-qwerty keyboards (300 minutes training up to expertise) in three mobility conditions (seated, standing, and walking) generating almost 4,000,000 characters across all conditions. Surprisingly, we found that walking has a significant impact on expert typing speeds but does not significantly impact expert accuracy rates.

Author Keywords

expert performance; text entry; mini-qwerty keyboards use-in-motion;

ACM Classification Keywords

H.5.2. Information interfaces and presentation: User Interfaces: Evaluation/methodology; Input devices and strategies

INTRODUCTION

Many individuals carry mobile phones all the time and use these devices in a wide variety of contexts including at work, at home, in the car, while riding public transportation, et cetera [19]. Often, mobile device usage occurs while the user is on-the-go, and interacting with a mobile phone while walking has become common practice. Using a mobile device in this manner can result in distraction since the user is forced to split their attentional resources between their mobile device and the environment [25].

http://dx.doi.org/10.1145/2628363.2628408

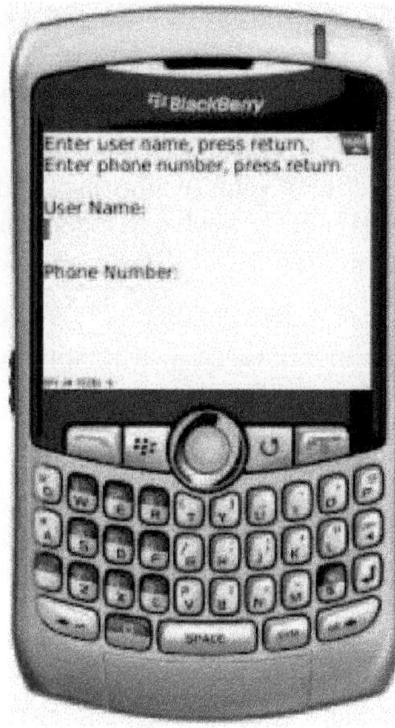

Figure 1. The mini–QWERTY keyboard enabled mobile phone used in the mobile study: the RIM Blackberry Curve 8320.

Kane *et al.* observed that most mobile interfaces are designed to be used by a person who is standing still and attending solely to the task of interacting with the mobile device [14]. However, the portable nature of these devices results in usage that occurs while the user is often on-the-go. When mobile, users must constantly adapt their usage of a device to the demands of their environment [16]. When walking, a user's head and hands both move making it difficult for the user to read the screen or interact with the mobile phone. For example, when attempting to input text on a mobile phone while walking, a user must maintain awareness of her surroundings while at the same time navigating her environment, and interacting with a device that is itself in motion. In these situations, the user's ability to accurately interact with the device is often impaired. Sears *et al.* used the term *situational impairments* to describe the situation that occurs when contextual factors reduce a users ability to successfully interact with a mobile device in a way that is similar to the way in which users with physical or sensory impairments interact with technology [30].

Despite the increasing importance of mobile devices in everyday life, little research has been published that quantifies the impact of mobility on the use of mobile devices. Situational impairments may be triggered by a range of contextual factors, and may exert a range of effects on performance. However, the degree to which those distractions impact performance is unknown. In this paper, we describe an investigation that explores the impacts of mobility on interaction with a mobile device. Specifically, we examine the effects of sitting, standing, and walking on users' ability to quickly and accurately input text into a mobile phone equipped with a physical mini-qwerty keyboard (see Figure 1). We compare words-per-minute and accuracy rates in each condition as well as perform a detailed comparison of errors made in each condition. We conducted these studies using a walking track constructed in our laboratory in order to fully observe the effects of typing on a mini-qwerty keyboard while walking. Our work makes the following contributions to HCI and text entry research communities:

1. We determine the average typing rates and accuracies for expert mini–QWERTY keyboard typists inputing text on physical mini–QWERTY keyboards while sitting, standing, and walking.
2. We present the first detailed investigation of mobile typing errors.
3. We make methodological contributions to the emerging field of controlled use–in–motion studies through the use of a sensor enabled walking track.

RELATED WORK

This section discusses previous work focused on the evaluation of mobile interaction, interfaces, and devices while users are in-motion, with a special emphasis placed on investigations of on-the-go text entry.

Controlled Use–In–Motion Studies

Recently there has been increased interest in evaluating the use of mobile devices (such as mobile phones or on-body interfaces) while the user is in motion. Designing for mobility has been highlighted as an important area in need of additional research for years [3, 5, 9, 13, 23, 26]. Mobile devices create opportunities for users to complete certain tasks (e.g., taking notes or scheduling appointments) on the move, but they also introduce new challenges by creating competition for a user's attentional resources. This competition forces the user to split her attentional resources between interacting with the device and navigating the environment [25]. Interacting with mobile devices under stationary settings is similar to the use of a desktop computer in terms of attention allocation. However, when the user is mobile, attentional demands increase.

Our research is focused on understanding the impact that motion has on interactions with mobile computing devices, specifically inputting text using mini–QWERTY keyboards. Such interactions rely on two fundamental activities: retrieving the information shown on the screen (output) and entering information (e.g., commands or text) into the device (input). To date, researchers have studied the impact of walking on both input– and output–oriented activities. For example, Barnard et al. [2] report that walking affects performance for information retrieval tasks including both reading comprehension tasks and word search tasks. Similarly, Price et al. [28] confirmed that walking can significantly affect the accuracy of speech–based input. Vadas et al. furthered Barnards' work by decoupling input from output and comparing visual and audio output while in motion [32].

Hall et al. compared target selection accuracy on finger–operated touch screens under seated and standing conditions [12]. They found that in order to achieve greater than 99% accuracy, the target area for the standing condition (30 mm^2) had to be larger than that of seated condition (26 mm^2). Although standing is not a mobile condition, it shares one key characteristic with mobile situations: the lack of a stable surface on which to place the mobile device. Schildbach et al. further explored finger–operated touch screen input in a study that examined target acquisition and reading tasks with users both standing and walking [29]. They found negative effects for both reading and selecting targets when walking although the negative effects associated with target selection were mitigated when they increased the size of the targets. Interestingly, the reading task did not see the same compensatory effect with larger text size since increasing the size of the text increased the need for scrolling. This result was not surprising, given that MacKay et al. had earlier compared using scrollbars to two other navigation techniques (tap-and-drag and touch-and-go) in three different mobility conditions (sitting, standing, and walking) and found scrollbars to be the poorest performing navigation technique for mobile users [19].

Brewster [3] explored use–in–motion in an early multimodal study. He investigated the use of a stylus-based calculator application under two conditions: seated in a lab and walking outside. The results showed that walking significantly reduced the amount of data entered and increased the perceived workload, indicating some difficulties associated with stylus–based tapping while walking. The walking route used in this study was a natural setting, but as the researcher himself pointed out:

> "[It] was still quite controlled: users walked along a reasonably quite straight path [3]."

A similar, simple, and safe walking condition was also used in a follow–up study [4]. The decline in performance from seated to walking may have been underestimated by these results due to the simplicity of the walking task. In addition, this study did not collect any error data, which makes it difficult to interpret task completion time and workload results.

In contrast, Chamberlain and Kalawsky [6] did not find a significant difference in error rates between stationary and walking conditions when participants completed stylus–based target selections. They did, however, find an increase in selection times when participants were walking. In their study, a wearable computer was attached to a vest which provided additional support. This added support made the computer more stable than in real-world on-the-go usage, and may help explain why their results differed from those reported elsewhere. Lin et al. also investigated mobile pointing using a stylus while walking [17, 18]. In their first study Lin et al. had participants complete a Fitts' Law pointing task using a stylus while walking. They found impaired performance while walking when targeting small targets [18]. A follow-up study by Lin et al. found that single target selection completion time did not increase while walking, but that overall task completion times did increase as did subjective ratings of cognitive load [17].

Kane et al. examined use–in–motion in an outdoor evaluation and coined the term "walking user interfaces" [14]. They evaluated an adaptive interface that scaled button sizes based on user motion. They found significant interactions between size and movement and demonstrated that dynamic user interfaces performed as well as the equivalent static interfaces without any additional penalty due to adaptation.

Typing on-the-go

Although there has been much work examining both input and output while users are walking, text entry while in motion is an underexplored research area. Mizobuchi and Yatani both investigated touch screen text input using a stylus [21, 34]. Mizobuchi et al. studied the relationship between walking speed and text entry difficulty [21]. They examined four different key sizes ranging from 2.0 X 2.5 to 5.0 X 6.3 mm. Participants entered text using a soft keyboard while either standing or walking. The results showed that text input speed did not differ between the standing and walking conditions. This lack of difference between mobility conditions might be due to the simple–and–safe walking setting used, which was comparable to those in Brewster [3] and Brewster et al. [4]. However, error rates were significantly different between the two conditions, but only because of the high error rate for the smallest target size in the walking situation.

In contrast, Yatani et al. explored the design of a two-handed virtual keyboard for a PDA which utilized the thumb of the hand holding the device to create a chorded input system [34]. They compared their chorded keyboard to other stylus-based text entry methods while participants were seated and walking around a path in the lab. Of note, Yatani et al. reported a difference in performance (WPM, accuracy, and cognitive load) between stationary and mobile conditions when participants typed on a virtual mini-QWERTY keyboard with a stylus. Most recently Goel et al. designed and evaluated an adaptive system for two-thumb text entry on touch screens that leveraged the phone's built-in accelerometer to compensate for the vibrations that result from walking. Their system was shown to both reduce errors and increase typing rates on touch screen mobile phones [10].

WALKING IN A USABILITY EVALUATION

Having surveyed the relevant mobile interaction research exploring input and output while on-the-go, here we discuss the mechanics of how to incorporate walking into a usability evaluation. There are many tradeoffs to be considered when designing an evaluation that explores human mobility. For example, should the study designers dictate walking speed or should participants walk at their own pace? Should participants be able to chose their own route or should the route be dictated by the study designers? Should the participants be exposed to distractions and if so, should these distractions be designed by the researchers so that each participant has the same experience or should the research team allow distractions to occur randomly? These questions get at the heart of the tension between designing an internally valid or ecologically valid task.

In this section, we present a taxonomy of walking conditions (see Table 1). We categorize existing work along two dimensions: mechanisms for controlling participant walking speed and walking route. Both of these dimensions run along a continuum from perfectly controlled, internally valid laboratory study to uncontrolled, ecologically valid, in the wild exploration of user behavior. To the best of our knowledge, no work exists in which a research team has designed and deployed participant distractions in a laboratory style study. Designing ecologically valid, yet controlled distractor tasks is challenging and we consider this to still be an open research question. As such, we have excluded distraction as a variable in our taxonomy.

Many of the early use-in-motion evaluations employed a treadmill in their evaluation to control the walking pace of their participants [22]. The advantage of using a treadmill is that researchers can regulate the pace and direction for every participant or, if they choose to allow the participant to set their own pace, the researcher can reliably measure the pace of a participant over the course of the evaluation. With no distractions or obstacles to avoid, having participants walk in-place using a treadmill affords the researcher the most control over the speed and direction walked by the participant. The disadvantage of using a treadmill is that it artificially fixes participants' pace in a way that is rarely seen in the wild. As an alternative to using a treadmill, several researchers have chosen to use a member of the research team to walk in front of the participant to act as a pace setter for the experiment [10, 14]. The advantage of employing a human pace setter is that the participant experiences a constant but flexible walking pace for the duration of the task. While using a human pacer does help ensure consistency across participants, it has the potential to force participants to commit unnatural errors in their task because the participant may need to slow down to perform particularly difficult tasks but is forced to keep up with the pace setter. Though not to the same degree, using a human pacer introduces some of the same external validity challenges as using a treadmill to evaluate use-in-motion. The participants pace is forced and their ability to make navigational decisions is reduced. Without allowing participants the flexibility to set their own pace and walk their own path researchers are unable to accurately measure the full potential impact of mobility on an individual's ability to interact with mobile technology while on-the-go. At the opposite end of the validity spectrum is allowing participants to set their own pace. This decision has the advantage of improved ecological validity (typically participants slow down when attempting challenging tasks and speed up when completing those tasks or attempting simpler tasks). Affording participants the ability to control their pace however makes it difficult to assess the true impact of mobility. If participants choose not to move while completing a task, this strategy can back fire altogether. It also make comparing performance across participants within the same study challenging as participants walking at different speeds may have radically different results.

In addition to varying the pace of participants in an evaluation, researchers can choose to vary the complexity of the path the participants will be asked to walk. Some researchers choose to let study participants walk on a treadmill opting for control over forcing participants to make directional decisions. Others decide to have participants walk a particular route. The simplest routes found in the literature ask participants to walk unassisted the length of a hallway [22]. The advantage to using a hallway is that participants can choose to walk at their own pace and can do so relatively comfortably as there are typically no obstacles or other distractions to be found in the hallway setting. The limitation of using a hallway to conduct walking studies becomes quickly apparent. If participants are asked to to complete a task that requires them to walk more than several meters, researchers must find long corridors in which to conduct their studies. Also, using a hallway is only a slight improvement in ecological validity over using a treadmill since walking in a straight line in a distraction free hall is still a relatively constrained task.

Several researchers have chosen to conduct mobile evaluations in which they designate a specified walking path for their participants. Depending on the design of the path, studies can be conducted with participants in a head-down condition (typically when the path is laid out by placing tape or string on the floor) [32], or in a head-up condition by placing visual markers at participants' eye-level [15]. One research team even decided to have their participants walk up and down a set of stairs [34].

USING A WALKING TRACK

In this paper, we choose to quantify natural human performance. As such, when in the walking condition, participants were instructed to walk at a normal pace around a track constructed in our laboratory (see Figure 2). The track was approximately 25.2 meters long and was denoted with pairs of flags hanging from the ceiling with their tips 0.75 meters apart. Each flag was hung so the tip was approximately 1.6 meters above the floor. We chose to use flags hanging from the ceiling to ensure that participants were engaged in a head-up task. Had the participants been following a path laid out on the ground, a head-down condition would have ensued which we considered to be inappropriate given the nature of the study (as walking around, head down, is not typical behavior). As the study is conducted with participants walking continuously around the track, they were told they could slow down or stop as needed to complete a trial, but were asked to keep walking at a comfortable pace if possible.

Our decision to allow participants to control their own pace (ecologically valid) while walking on a head-up path (controlled and internally valid) places our work in the top-right cell of Table 1. Though we attempted to find a sweet spot on the continuum between internal and externally valid tasks, our study design decisions are not without their limitations. For example, walking on a short indoor path without distractions affords participants the ability to accommodate to the task over time and does not introduce the same attentional demands typically found in the wild (e.g. traffic or obstacles).

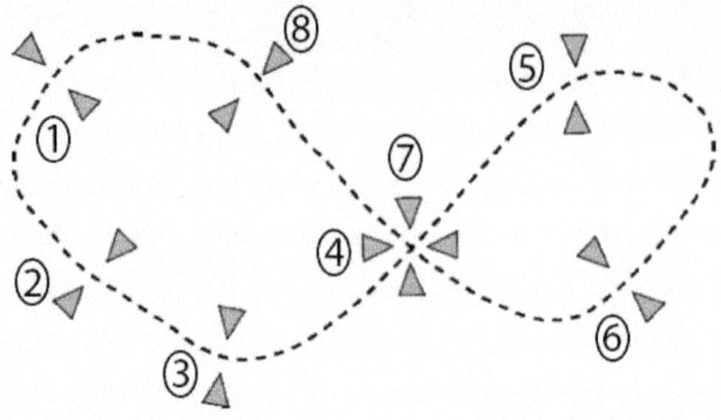

Figure 2. The path participants walked, starting at flag 1 and proceeding either clockwise or counterclockwise.

In an effort to accurately calculate the speed and distance traveled by the participants, we built a set of motion sensors that we mounted in the ceiling of our lab between each pair of flags (see Figure 3). The sensors were connected to a computer in the laboratory via bluetooth. Every time a participant walked between a pair of flags, the sensor would record the time and send that information to the computer. In this way, we could calculate the instantaneous and average speed of the participant as they walked from flag to flag along the track as well as the total distance traveled (see Figure 4). Upon completion of the twenty-minute session, the mobile phone displayed the following message in a large font on the screen "Session over. Please hand the Blackberry to the researcher." Participants were requested to stop where they stood in order to allow the researcher to measure how far they had walked past the last pair of flags. In this way we were able to accurately record the total distance traveled to the nearest half-meter.

Figure 3. The flag and sensor configuration that comprised the walking track.

EVALUATION

Though much research has explored the use of mobile devices while in-motion, current studies have not investigated such topics as typing on physical keyboards, mobile errors,

Walking speed regulation	Walking Route			
	No Path	Hallway	Head-down Path	Head-up Path
Participant controlled	[19, 25]	[21, 27]	[2, 13, 17, 29, 32, 34]	[3, 4, 15]
Paced Walking		[22]		[1, 10, 14]
Treadmill	[1, 17, 18, 22, 28]	N/A	N/A	N/A

Table 1. A taxonomy of different methods used to experimentally explore mobile interaction while walking.

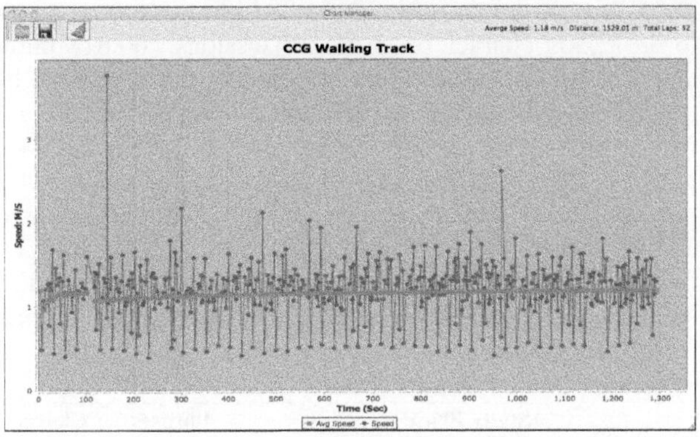

Figure 4. A screenshot of the software we used to capture participant movement data. The y-axis is speed in $\frac{m}{s}$ and the x-axis shows time in seconds. Each blue dot on the chart represents an instance where the participant walked through a pair of flags (under a sensor). The blue dots show instantaneous pace while the red dots show the participant's average speed. Average speed, distance traveled and total number of laps around the track can be seen in the upper right corner.

or the impact of user expertise on on-the-go mobile input. The goal of our evaluation is to investigate the impact of mobility on expert fixed-key mini-QWERTY keyboard text entry performance.

Participants

We recruited 36 participants from our local university (15 female, 21 male) ranging in age from 18 to 25 (M=19.75, SD=1.63) who had not used a mini–QWERTY keyboard more than once. Each participant had at least six years of full–QWERTY keyboard experience (M=11.36, SD=2.86) and at least one year of mobile phone experience (M=5.11, SD=2.19). All participants were native American English speakers who were taught to read and write in an American English education system (it is important from a spelling/errors perspective that participants were American English natives). On average, participants reported sending 27 text messages a day (SD=43). Twenty-nine of the thirty six participants reported that they have sent a text message while walking, sending on average 13 text messages a week while walking (SD=16).

Equipment and Software

Figure 1 shows the mini–QWERTY keyboard enabled mobile phone used in the experiment, a RIM Blackberry Curve 8320. For this study, we ported text entry evaluation software we had used in previous work to the Blackberry platform resulting in the new application. Though it was run on a RIM Blackberry Curve 8320, it can run on any current Blackberry model mobile phone. We are releasing the software package to the public, and it can be found here: `http://www.cc.gatech.edu/ccg/projects/twidor/blacktwidor/`.

As with our previous studies, the software was configured to use the MacKenzie and Soukoreff phrase set [20], a set of 500 phrases representative of the English language. The phrases range from 16 to 43 characters with an average length of 28 characters. The phrase set was modified to use only American English spellings and display only lower case letters and spaces (no punctuation or capitalization). The test software presented a phrase to the participants at the top of the screen. Underneath the presented phrase, participants transcribed the phrase and pressed the return key upon completing the task. The test software provided statistical feedback in the form of typing rate and accuracy data for the most recent sentence typed and the current session average (see Figure 5).

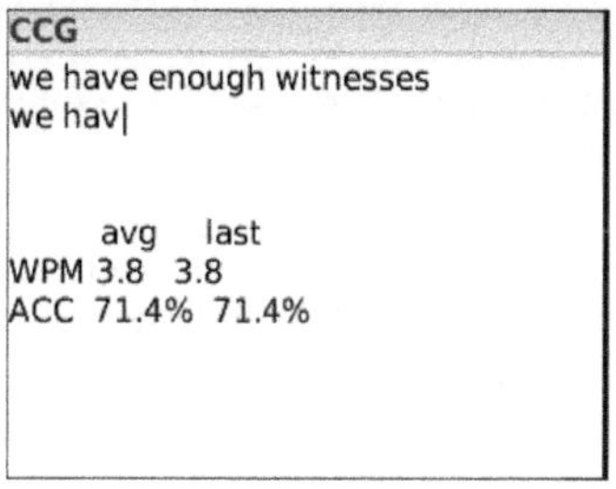

Figure 5. The interface in the study displayed both the presented string and the transcribed string (in progress directly below the presented). It also showed the words per minute (WPM) and accuracy rates (ACC) for the session so far (avg) and the phrase just completed by the participant (last).

Each session was preceded by a warm–up phase, in which the participants were asked to type the phrase "abcd efgh ijkl mnop qrst uvwx yz" twice. Participants were required to type this phrase without mistakes. User performance in the warm–up phase was not counted in the session statistics. Upon completion of the warmup, the twenty-minute session was started. A session was comprised of a number of trial blocks each containing ten randomly selected phrases from the MacKenzie and Soukoreff phrase set [20]. The participants completed as many blocks as possible in a twenty–minute session. At the end of a twenty-minute session the mobile phone displayed a message instructing the participant to find the researcher so that the researcher could collect the data, record the participants performance, and compensate the participant appropriately. Participants were compensated proportional to their typing rate and accuracy over the entire session: $0.125 × WPM × accuracy, with a $4 minimum for each twenty minute session.

Procedure

Prior to beginning the first session of the study, the participants filled in a questionnaire detailing their demographic information and their mobile phone usage history. Upon completion of the questionnaire, participants were given an introduction to the task and were provided a mobile phone to familiarize themselves with the application. Participants were instructed to type using only their two thumbs and to type as quickly and accurately as possible. Participants were allowed to interact with the mobile device and were prompted to ask any clarifying questions prior to beginning the task. When the researchers were confident that the participant was comfortable performing the task, they ushered the participants into the lab wherein they proceeded to input text for the entirety of a twenty-minute session. Two sessions were completed in a 1-hour visit. Participants were asked to take a 5–minute break after the first 20–minute session. Each 1-hour visit was separated by at least two hours and by no more than two days. To complete the study, participants scheduled fifteen session pairs over the course of two to three weeks.

Study Design

To begin, participants were trained to expertise before being introduced to the mobile conditions. In our previous work we have shown that participants' learning curves flatten after 300 minutes of typing on a mini-QWERTY keyboard indicating that participants have become expert typists [7]. In this study, participants were asked to complete 15 twenty-minute sessions seated in our laboratory prior to entering the experimental phase of the evaluation. Having completed 300 minutes inputting text on a mini–QWERTY keyboard enabled mobile phone, our now–expert participants transition into the mobility portion of the study.

The study is designed to investigate expert text entry performance in three different mobility conditions: sitting (the control condition), standing (participants stand in an empty room for the duration of the twenty-minute session) and walking (participants continuously walk the track in our laboratory for the duration of a twenty-minute session). Each participant was assigned an initial mobility condition and rotated through all three conditions over the course of the study. Participants input text for five 20-minute sessions (100 minutes) for each mobility condition. The order of mobility conditions was counterbalanced, and participants were randomly assigned to orders. All 36 expert participants successfully input text for 100 minutes in all three mobility conditions. By the completion of this study, participants had typed for a total of 600 minutes – 300 minutes seated and 300 minutes in the mobile conditions (100 minutes sitting, 100 minutes standing, and 100 minutes walking).

We structured the study as a 3 x 5 within-subjects design. The factors and levels were:

- **Mobility** *Sitting, Standing, Walking*
- **Sessions** *One, Two, Three, Four, Five*

Because our participants were expert typists by the time they began this phase of the evaluation, there was no need to counterbalance conditions at the session level to avoid learning affects. Participants input text for five sessions in each mobility condition before switching to a different condition. Analyzing the subset of participants who went directly from the final training session into the sitting mobility condition (thus typing for 400 minutes while seated) confirmed that our participants' learning curves had flattened. Additionally, running an ANOVA over sessions 16-20 showed no significant effect on either WPM or ACC.

RESULTS

Thirty-six participants input 131,884 phrases, corresponding to 3,872,505 characters across all sessions. 60,818 phrases and 1,793,564 characters were typed in the first three hundred minutes of typing as participants were trained to expertise. In the experimental portion of the study, a total of 24,116 phrases (705,156 characters) were typed while seated, 24,078 phrases (705,014 characters) were typed while standing, and 22,872 phrases (668,771 characters) were typed while walking (see Table 2). Averaged over the five 20-minute walking sessions, participants traveled 912m (SD=300m) or approximately 2.75km/hour.

Study Phase	Phrases	Characters
Training to Expertise (300 minutes)	60,818	1,793,564
Seated (100 minutes)	24,116	705,156
Standing (100 minutes)	24,078	705,014
Walking (100 minutes)	22,872	668,771
Total (600 minutes)	131,884	3,872,505

Table 2. Dataset collected from 36 participants typing for 600 minutes: 300 minutes seated training from novice to expert, 100 minutes seated, 100 minutes standing, and 100 minutes walking.

The main measures collected were speed, calculated as words per minute (WPM); accuracy calculated as 1-total error rate using equations detailed by Soukoreff and MacKenzie [31], and, when participants were mobile, distance traveled and average speed. In the mobility conditions, the mean entry rate for the seated condition was 56.79 WPM (SD=11.51), while the standing condition was 56.61 WPM (SD=10.97), and the walking condition was 52.51 WPM (SD=11.56). The mean accuracy for the seated condition was 95.36% (SD=6.15%), the standing condition was 95.25% (SD=6.54%), and the walking condition was 94.91% (SD=6.59%) (see Table 3 for complete results). On average, participants traveled 911 meters (SD=300m) per 20-minute session. The minimum total distance traveled over the course of 100 minutes was 1,298 meters, while the maximum total distance traveled over the course of 100 minutes was 7,247 meters.

Study Phase	Mean WPM (SD)	Mean ACC (SD)
Training to Expertise (300 mintues)	48.21 (13.11)	96.05% (6.87%)
Seated (100 minutes)	56.79 (11.51)	95.36% (6.15%)
Standing (100 minutes)	56.61 (10.97)	95.25% (6.54%)
Walking (100 minutes)	52.51 (11.56)	94.91% (6.59%)
Total (600 minutes)	52.06 (12.78)	95.58% (6.65%)

Table 3. The average words per minute and accuracies for 36 participants in the training phase of the study and the three mobility conditions (seated, standing, and walking).

Training to expertise

An analysis of variance (ANOVA) of text entry speed shows a main effect for session ($F_{14,490} = 75.158$, $p < 0.0001$). The main effect of session was expected as it is assumed that the participants would learn to type faster over the course of the 15 twenty-minute sessions. We performed the same test for accuracy which also shows a main effect for session ($F_{14,490}$ = 3.205, $p < 0.0001$). Again this effect was expected since accuracy rates typically decrease when typing rates increase due to the speed/accuracy tradeoff.

Mobility Conditions

We tested for effects of condition order on the main measure of typing speed using a 3-way ANOVA with mobility condition order as a between-subjects factor and Session and Mobility as within-subjects factors. No main effect of mobility condition order was found, indicating that overall counterbalancing on the condition level was effective.

The 36 participants typed a total of 71,066 phrases (2,078,941 characters) across all sessions and all mobility conditions. We analyzed the data using a mixed model analysis of variance with fixed effects for Mobility and Session. We found a main effect of Mobility on speed ($F_{2,56} = 13.0076$, p<.0001) as well as a main effect of Session on speed ($F_{4,112}$=15.905, p<.0001). To analyze these effects further, we conducted post-hoc pairwise comparisons using Bonferroni correction. The post-hoc test for Mobility shows a significant effect on speed between the sitting condition and the walking condition (t_{35} = 5.244, p<.0001) and a significant effect on speed between the standing condition and the walking condition (t_{35} = 4.762, p<.001) but no significant effect on Speed between the sitting and standing conditions. The post-hoc test for Session shows a significant effect on speed between Sessions 1 and 3 (t_{35} = -5.251, p<.0001), Sessions 1 and 4 (t_{35} = -4.557, p<.0001), Sessions 1 and 5 (t_{35} = -8.585, p<.0001), Sessions 2 and 3 (t_{35} = -5.201, p<.0001), Sessions 2 and 4 (t_{35} = -3.264, p<.002), and Sessions 2 and 5 (t_{35} = -5.518, p<.0001). No other statistically significant effects on speed were found for Session. We found no main effect of either Mobility on accuracy ($F_{2,56}$=1.316, p=.276) or Session on accuracy ($F_{4,112}$=1.469, p=.216).

Analysis of errors

Errors have long been considered an important source of insight into understanding a users performance of a task. Grudin performed an analysis of error patterns for full-QWERTY desktop typing in an attempt to understand how complex motor task skills are organized and developed [11]. Grudin's analysis segmented errors into groups: substitutions, insertions, deletions and transpositions.

Substitution errors occur when a character is replaced by a different character within a text string. Insertion errors occur when a character is added, and deletion errors occur when a character is omitted. Transposition errors occur when a participant attempts to type a letter combination or word and exchanges two of the letters (for example, typing *teh* but intending *the*). With full–QWERTY keyboard typing Grudin found substitution errors account for the majority of the errors (62.92%). Previous work by Clawson et al. found that errors on mini-QWERTY keyboards are more evenly distributed with substitutions still occurring most frequently (40.2%) followed by insertions (33.2%) and deletions (21.4%). In comparison, there are relatively few transpositions (5.2%) [8].

One significant limitation of the work conducted by Clawson et al., is that they conducted their analysis on data collected from a study run using mini-qwerty keyboards designed as attachments for personal digital assistants. A great deal of research and design has gone into the development of robust mobile keyboards since that time. As such, in an effort to replicate their findings and see if their results still hold, we conducted a similar analysis.

In conducting our analysis however, we opted to use the error classifications described by Wobbrock et al. [33] instead of following exactly the analysis performed by Clawson et al., which took a more rudimentary approach to classifying errors. In their work Wobbrock et al. clarified the error classes used by Grudin by naming the previous error types Uncorrected Substitutions, Uncorrected Insertions, and Uncorrected Omissions. Wobbrock ignored transpositions but added an error-free category termed Uncorrected No–Errors which take place when a user enters a correct character and does not edit it. Wobbrock et al. then introduced *corrected* character–level error types: Corrected No–Errors, Corrected Substitutions, Corrected Insertions, and Corrected Omissions. Corrected No–Errors are characters that are input correctly by the user but later erased. Corrected Substitutions are erroneous characters input by the user in an attempt to correct an existing error. Corrected Insertions are erroneous characters inserted into the input stream that are then noticed and corrected by the user. Corrected insertions exist in the input stream but not in the final transcribed text. Corrected Omissions occur in the input stream when the user initially skips a character but then later replaces the omitted character correcting the omission.

Investigating the training phase of the evaluation in which 36 participants sat and input text in our laboratory for fifteen 20-minute sessions, we found that of the 1,793,564 characters input, 90,710 were errors. Of note, there were far more uncorrected errors than corrected errors in the set (69,721 vs. 20,989 respectively). This finding is unsurprising as participants will often optimize for speed over accuracy in an effort to maximize their earnings from the study. The most common type of error in the dataset was Uncorrected Substitutions which accounted for 34% of the total errors. The second most prevalent error type was Uncorrected Omissions which accounted for almost 26% of the errors. This finding is particularly interesting given that when participants took the time to correct their mistakes, there were significantly fewer Corrected Omissions than either Corrected Substitutions or Corrected Insertions (see Table 4 for a full breakdown of errors that were collected from the first 300 minutes of typing).

Substitution Errors

Though Wobbrock et al.'s error classes have become the standard approach to analyzing text entry errors, Grudin's foundational analysis provides an interesting departure point for further analysis of substitution errors. Grudin identified several different types of substitution errors that occur in full-QWERTY keyboard typing including row errors, column er-

Error Type	Error Count	% of Total Errors	% of Total Chars
Cor No Errors	17,584	n/a	0.98%
Cor Omissions	4,728	5.21%	0.26%
Cor Insertions	5,774	6.37%	0.32%
Cor Substitutions	10,487	11.56%	0.58%
Uncor Omissions	23,339	25.73%	1.30%
Uncor Insertions	15,532	17.12%	0.87%
Uncor Substitutions	30,850	34.01%	1.72%
Uncor No Errors	1,685,270	n/a	93.96%
Total	1,793,564	100.00%	100.00%

Table 4. A breakdown of the errors committed by 36 participants in the training phase of the mobile evaluation. Participants typed for 300 minutes generating a total of 1,793,564 characters and 90,710 errors.

rors, and homologous errors [11]. Row errors occur when the intended character is replaced by a character immediately to the left or the right of the intended character. For example, the user intends to press *"e"* on a QWERTY keyboard but instead types *"w"* or *"r"*. Column errors occur when the correct character is replaced by a character immediately above or below of the intended character (the user intends to press *"d"* but instead types *"e"* or *"x"*). Homologous errors occur when the correct character is replaced by the mirror-image character typed by the same finger in the same position on the other hand (the user intends to press *"d"* but instead types *"k"*). Similar to Grudin's work, Clawson et al. found that the majority of mini-QWERTY keyboard substitution errors were row errors accounting for 55.3% of the substitution errors and 22.2% of the total errors. In the current analysis row substitution errors again account for the majority of the errors. Surprisingly, the prevalence of these errors has not decreased dramatically as keyboard hardware has improved over time. From our data, there were 20,460 row substitution errors. These errors account for 49.50% of the substitution errors and 22.56% of the total errors in our dataset.

Insertion Errors

The prevalence of insertion errors (Corrected and Uncorrected Insertions total 21,306) merits in-depth analysis. Inspired by the number of row errors discovered in the substitution case, we analyzed insertions in a similar manner. We examined insertions that are off by one key to the left or right of the intended key. Row insertions account for 30.69% of the insertions and 7.21% of the total errors. Of note, in their earlier analysis of errors, Clawson et al. found that a combination of row and key repeat insertions accounted for 68.7% of the insertions and 22.8% of the total errors. Adding key repeats to our analysis does not have a large impact as key repeat errors occurred extremely rarely (only 431 key repeats). Including key repeats to our analysis of insertions in an effort to better compare to the results of Clawson et al. shows only a marginal increase in the percentage of row insertions to 32.71% of the insertions and 7.68% of the total errors.

Off–By–One Errors

Of note, recent investigations of errors in two handed touch screen typing [10, 24] have confirmed the earlier findings by Clawson et al. that the off-by-one errors are the most common errors that occur when typing with two thumbs on a mobile phone [8]. We found similar results with 30.24% of our errors falling into the off-by-one category described by Clawson et al. [8].

Differences in keyboard ergonomics can be observed when comparing off-by-one errors from our evaluation to the errors reported in the evaluation by Clawson et al. Table 5 illustrates how the reduction of key repeat insertions impacts the overall off-by-one error rate.

Error Type	% of Error Class	% of Total Errors
Clawson et al. row substitutions	55.3%	22.2%
Mobile row substitutions	49.50%	22.56%
Clawson et al. row insertions	68.7%	22.8%
Mobile row insertions	32.71%	7.68%
Clawson et al. off-by-one errors	N/A	45.0%
Mobile off-by-one errors	N/A	30.24%

Table 5. A comparison of the off-by-one errors committed in the evaluation conducted by Clawson et al. and the off-by-one errors committed in the training phase of the mobile evaluation. The second column shows the number of row errors divided by the total number of errors for each error class per dataset. The third column shows the number of row errors divided by the total number of errors per dataset.

Mobile Errors: Sitting vs. Standing vs. Walking

To investigate mobile errors we decided to perform an analysis similar to the one we performed when analyzing the data from the first 300 minutes of the evaluation. This analysis resulted in the following breakdown of errors across mobility conditions (see Table 6). To investigate the impact of mobility on error type we performed an ANOVA with fixed effects for Mobility and Error Type. As participants typed more slowly when walking they generated less text in a twenty minute period than they did when sitting or standing. As such, we normalized the error data (errors/character) to account for this discrepancy. We did not include either Corrected NoError or Uncorrected NoError classes in our analysis. As we were uninterested in correction behavior at this point, we combined corrected and uncorrected error classes. As such, our ANOVA utilized Mobility with three levels (Sitting, Standing, and Walking) and Error Type with three levels (Omissions, Insertions, and Substitutions). We found no main effect of Mobility on the number of errors committed ($F_{2,70}$=.390, p=.679). We also did not find an interaction effect of Mobility $*$ Error Type on the number of errors committed ($F_{4,140}$=.123, p=.974). However, we did find a main effect of Error Type on the numbers of errors committed ($F_{2,70}$=30.825, p<.0001). To analyze these effects further, we conducted post-hoc pairwise comparisons and employed Bonferroni correction. Unsurprisingly, the post-hoc test for Error Type showed a significant effect on number of errors committed between Omissions and Substitutions (t_{35} =-7.289, p<.0001) and between Insertions and Substitutions (t_{35} = -6.348, p<.0001) but no significant effect on number of errors committed when comparing Omissions and Insertions (t_{35} =1.711, p=.096). Participants generated far more Substitution errors than either Omission or Insertion errors.

Next we investigated correction behavior in an effort to understand if correction behavior changed in the different mobility conditions. To investigate correction behavior in the mobility conditions, we again conducted a repeated measures ANOVA with fixed effects for Mobility (Sitting, Standing, Walking),

	Error Count			% of Total Errors			% of Total Chars		
Error Type	Sitting	Standing	Walking	Sitting	Standing	Walking	Sitting	Standing	Walking
Cor No Errors	3,645	3,663	2,461	n/a			0.52%	0.52%	0.37%
Cor Omissions	1,304	1,277	969	3.52%	3.38%	2.58%	0.18%	0.18%	0.14%
Cor Insertions	1,284	1,243	1,036	3.47%	3.29%	2.76%	0.18%	0.18%	0.15%
Cor Substitutions	2,186	2,073	1,827	5.90%	5.49%	4.87%	0.31%	0.29%	0.27%
Uncor Omissions	9,185	9,521	9,988	24.80%	25.22%	26.62%	1.30%	1.35%	1.49%
Uncor Insertions	6,757	7,012	7,074	18.24%	18.57%	18.86%	0.96%	0.99%	1.06%
Uncor Substitutions	16,320	16,631	16,621	44.07%	44.05%	44.30%	2.31%	2.36%	2.49%
Uncor No Errors	664,475	663,594	628,795	n/a			94.23%	94.12%	94.02%

Table 6. A breakdown of the errors committed by 36 participants in the three mobility conditions: sitting, standing, and walking. Participants typed for 100 minutes in each condition generating 705,156 characters and 37,036 errors while sitting, 705,014 characters and 37,757 errors while standing, and 668,771 characters and 37,515 errors while walking for a total of 1,791,169 characters and 145,971 errors.

Error Type (Omissions, Insertions, Substitutions), and Correction (Uncorrected, Corrected). Again, we saw no main effect for Mobility or interaction effects for Mobility and Error Type, Mobility and Correction ($F_{2,70}$=.604, p=.549), or Mobility, Error Type, and Correction ($F_{4,140}$=.221, p=.926). We did however see main effects for Error Type and Correction ($F_{1,35}$=44.440, p<.0001) as well as an interaction effect of Error Type and Correction ($F_{2,70}$=18.508, p<.0001). To investigate these effects further, we again conducted a series of post-hoc pairwise comparisons employing Bonferroni correction. Comparing all corrected to all uncorrected errors yielded a statistically significant result (t_{35} =-6.666, p<.001). Exploring the interaction effect between Error Type and Correction yielded a significant effect for number of errors for almost every combination of Error Type and Correction. Of note, no significant effect was found when comparing Corrected Omissions to Corrected Insertions (t_{35} =-.166, p=.869) or Uncorrected Omissions to Uncorrected Insertions (t_{35} =1.813, p=.078) implying that participants' took the same approach to correcting (or not correcting as was more typically the case) Insertion and Omission errors. All other comparisons were statistically significant.

DISCUSSION

Our goal with this study was to quantify the impact of mobility on text entry performance. In an effort to definitively demonstrate the impact of mobility on text entry performance, we designed a "best case scenario" study utilizing expert participants typing in a controlled environment on devices that afforded tactile feedback (fixed-key mini-qwerty keyboards). Even in these idealized conditions we still saw a significant impact of mobility on participants text entry rates with mobility inducing a significant negative impact on typing performance.

Most surprisingly we did not see a corresponding impact of mobility on participant accuracy rates. Intrigued by this result, we conducted an in-depth analysis of errors. In comparing errors from the training phase of the evaluation to previous work, we uncovered that changes made to keyboard technology have dramatically reduced the number accidental key repeats made by participants. In the experimental phase of the evaluation we investigated the impacts of sitting, standing and walking on the types of errors committed by participants. We found that participants created statistically significantly more Substitution errors than Insertion or Omissions errors. Comparing corrections in the training phase of the study to corrections in the experimental phase of the study indicates that as participants increase in experience, they correct far fewer mistakes than they do as novices.

FUTURE WORK AND CONCLUSION

Goel et al. demonstrated the potential of correlating instantaneous walking speed with text entry performance [10]. Inspired by this work we are interested in performing an analysis of errors that ties changes in instantaneous walking speed to participant error and correction behaviors.

Though interacting with mobile technology while in-motion has become a daily activity, typing on a phone while on-the-go leads to situational impairments that negatively impact typing rates. We evaluated expert two-thumb typing on fixed-key mini-qwerty keyboard enabled mobile phone. In our longitudinal evaluation, 36 participants who had minimal mini-qwerty experience trained for 300 minutes to become expert mini-qwerty typists and then moved into the mobility phase of the study to type for 100 minutes in each of three conditions: sitting, standing, and walking. Surprisingly, walking has a significant impact on expert word-per-minute rates but not on accuracy rates. We performed an in-depth investigation of errors in both the training and experimental phase of the evaluation. These results illuminate that even under ideal conditions (expert typists receiving tactile feedback from their interactions), mobility impairs users' ability to interact with a mobile phone while on-the-go.

ACKNOWLEDGEMENTS

Thanks to Google for partially funding this work. Thanks also to Bret Brammer, Maggie Markey, Raymond Jabaley, and Alyssa Kuncaitis for all of your help being the core of the mini-qwerty study admins. You were fantastic!

REFERENCES

1. Barnard, L., Yi, J. S., Jacko, J. A., and Sears, A. An empirical comparison of use-in-motion evaluation scenarios for mobile computing devices. *IJHCS 62*, 4 (2005), 487–520.

2. Barnard, L., Yi, J. S., Jacko, J. A., and Sears, A. Capturing the effects of context on human performance in mobile computing systems. *PUC 11*, 2 (2007), 81–96.

3. Brewster, S. Overcoming the lack of screen space on mobile computers. *PUC 6*, 3 (2002), 188–205.
4. Brewster, S., Lumsden, J., Bell, M., Hall, M., and Tasker, S. Multimodal 'eyes-free' interaction techniques for wearable devices. In *CHI '03* (2003), 473–480.
5. Bristow, H. W., Baber, C., Cross, J., Knight, J. F., and Woolley, S. I. Defining and evaluating context for wearable computing. *IJHCS 60*, 5-6 (2004), 798–819.
6. Chamberlain, A., and Kalawsky, R. A comparative investigation into two pointing systems for use with wearable computers while mobile. In *ISWC '04* (2004), 110–117.
7. Clarkson, E., Clawson, J., Lyons, K., and Starner, T. An empirical study of typing rates on mini-qwerty keyboards. In *CHI '05* (2005), 1288–1291.
8. Clawson, J., Lyons, K., Rudnick, A., Robert A. Iannucci, J., and Starner, T. Automatic whiteout++: correcting mini-qwerty typing errors using keypress timing. In *CHI '08*, ACM (2008), 573–582.
9. Dunlop, M., and Brewster, S. The challenge of mobile devices for human computer interaction. *Personal Ubiquitous Computing 6*, 4 (2002), 235–236.
10. Goel, M., Findlater, L., and Wobbrock, J. Walktype: using accelerometer data to accomodate situational impairments in mobile touch screen text entry. In *CHI '12* (2012), 2687–2696.
11. Grudin, J. *Cognitive aspects of skilled typewriting*. Springer–Verlag, New York, 1983, ch. Error Patterns in novice and skilled transcription typing, 121–143.
12. Hall, A. D., Cunningham, J. B., Roache, R. P., and Cox, J. W. Factors affecting performance using touch-entry systems: tactual recognition fields and system accuracy. *Journal of Applied Psychology 73*, 4 (1988), 711–720.
13. Johnson, P. Usability and mobility; interactions on the move. In *MobileHCI '98* (1998).
14. Kane, S. K., Wobbrock, J. O., and Smith, I. E. Getting off the treadmill: evaluating walking user interfaces for mobile devices in public spaces. In *MobileHCI '08*, ACM (2008), 109–118.
15. Komor, N., Gilliland, S., Clawson, J., Bhardwaj, M., Garg, M., Zeagler, C., and Starner, T. Is it gropable? - assessing the impact of mobility on textile interfaces. ISWC '09 (2009), 71–74.
16. Kristoffersen, S., and Ljungberg, F. "making place" to make it work: empirical explorations of hci for mobile cscw. In *GROUP '99* (1999), 276–285.
17. Lin, M., Goldman, R., Price, K. J., Sears, A., and Jacko, J. How do people tap when walking? an empirical investigation of nomadic data entry. *IJHCS 65*, 9 (2007), 759–769.
18. Lin, M., Price, K. J., Goldman, R., Sears, A., and Jacko, J. A. Tapping on the move - fitts' law under mobile conditions. In *IRMA-International* (2005), 132–135.
19. MacKay, B., Dearman, D., Inkpen, K., and Watters, C. Walk 'n scroll: a comparison of software-based navigation techniques for different levels of mobility. MobileHCI '05, ACM (2005), 183–190.
20. MacKenzie, I. S., and Soukoreff, R. W. Phrase sets for evaluating text entry techniques. In *CHI '03 extended abstracts*, ACM Press (2003), 754–755.
21. Mizobuchi, S., Chignell, M., and Newton, D. Mobile text entry: relationship between walking speed and text input task difficulty. In *MobileHCI '05* (2005), 122–128.
22. Mustonen, T., Olkkonen, M., and Hakkinen, J. Examining mobile phone text legibility while walking. In *CHI '04* (2004), 1243–1246.
23. Newell, A. F., and Gregor, P. "user sensitive inclusive design" in search of a new paradigm. CUU '00 (2000), 39–44.
24. Nicolau, H., and Jorge, J. Touch typing using thumbs: understanding the effect of mobility and hand posture. CHI '12, ACM (2012), 2683–2686.
25. Oulasvirta, A., Tamminen, S., Roto, V., and Kuorelahti, J. Interaction in 4-second bursts: the fragmented nature of attentional resources in mobile hci. In *CHI '05* (2005), 919–928.
26. Pascoe, J., Ryan, N., and Morse, D. Using while moving: Hci issues in fieldwork environments. *ACM ToCHI 7*, 3 (2000), 417–437.
27. Pirhonen, A., Brewster, S., and Holguin, C. Gestural and audio metaphors as a means of control for mobile devices. CHI '02 (2002), 291–298.
28. Price, K. J., Lin, M., Feng, J., Goldman, R., Sears, A., and Jacko, J. A. Motion does matter: an examination of speech-based text entry on the move. *Universal Access in the Information Society 4*, 3 (2006), 246–257.
29. Schildbach, B., and Rukzio, E. Investigating selection and reading performance on a mobile phone while walking. MobileHCI '10 (2010), 93–102.
30. Sears, A., Lin, M., Jacko, J., and Xiao, Y. When computers fade pervasive computing and situationally-induced impairments and disabilities. In *HCII*, vol. 2 (2003), 1298–1302.
31. Soukoreff, R. W., and MacKenzie, I. S. Metrics for text entry research: an evaluation of msd and kspc, and a new unified error metric. 113–120.
32. Vadas, K., Patel, N., Lyons, K., Starner, T., and Jacko, J. Reading on-the-go: a comparison of audio and hand-held displays. In *MobileHCI '06* (2006), 219–226.
33. Wobbrock, J. O., and Myers, B. A. Analyzing the input stream for character-level errors in unconstrained text entry evaluations. *ACM ToCHI 13*, 4 (2006), 458–489.
34. Yatani, K., and Truong, K. N. An evaluation of stylus-based text entry methods on handheld devices in stationary and mobile settings. MobileHCI '07, ACM (2007), 487–494.

ReviewCollage: A Mobile Interface for Direct Comparison Using Online Reviews

Haojian Jin[1,2], Tetsuya Sakai[1,3], and Koji Yatani[1]
[1]Microsoft Research Asia Beijing, China
[2]Yahoo! Labs Sunnyvale, CA, USA
[3]Waseda University Tokyo, Japan
haojian.jin@yahoo-inc.com, tetsuyasakai@acm.org, koji@microsoft.com

ABSTRACT
Review comments posted in online websites can help the user decide a product to purchase or place to visit. They can also be useful to closely compare a couple of candidate entities. However, the user may have to read different webpages back and forth for comparison, and this is not desirable particularly when she is using a mobile device. We present ReviewCollage, a mobile interface that aggregates information about two reviewed entities in a one-page view. ReviewCollage uses attribute-value pairs, known to be effective for review text summarization, and highlights the similarities and differences between the entities. Our user study confirms that ReviewCollage can support the user to compare two entities and make a decision within a couple of minutes, at least as quickly as existing summarization interfaces. It also reveals that ReviewCollage could be most useful when two entities are very similar.

Author Keywords
Comparison; summarization; user-generated review; mobile interface; natural language processing.

ACM Classification Keywords
H5.2. Information interfaces and presentation (e.g., HCI): User Interfaces.

General Terms
Human Factors

INTRODUCTION
Marketing research shows that people often perform two-stage decision making to determine their choice of purchase or activities [2, 21]: screening and comparing. Screening means that the user attempts to narrow down to several candidates (in most cases, two or three [13]) from available choices. The user would do this based on her major requirements (e.g., the location and opening hours). This is well supported in many existing websites, such as filtering by several pre-defined parameters.

MobileHCI 2014, September 23–26, 2014, Toronto, ON, Canada.
Copyright © ACM 978-1-4503-3004-6/14/09...$15.00.
http://dx.doi.org/10.1145/2628363.2628373

However, comparing is often not well supported in such websites. In this process, the user would check details of the candidates from different perspectives and make the final decision. The user has to manually compare multiple entities by looking for information about particular aspects or reading review comments. Our pilot study with eight users (explained later) found that this is not desirable particularly when the user is using a mobile device as the screen size is limited. Nevertheless, comparison in a small screen is becoming a common activity; nowadays the user often reads webpages to find a place to visit (e.g., seeking a restaurant in an unfamiliar city) through mobile services.

Summarization systems can help the user read review comments as they allow her to view information quickly. Review Spotlight [27] and RevMiner [12] are found effective for quick impression formation. Their work also shows that tag-cloud interfaces help to overview review text. However, summarization performed independently for each entity may not help the comparing process because it does not fully consider relative relationships between multiple entities. This motivates us to develop a mobile interface providing a one-page view that allows the user to closely compare two entities using review comments.

Our system, ReviewCollage, highlights key descriptions about two entities using a tag-cloud interface. It uses attribute-value word pairs extracted from the original review

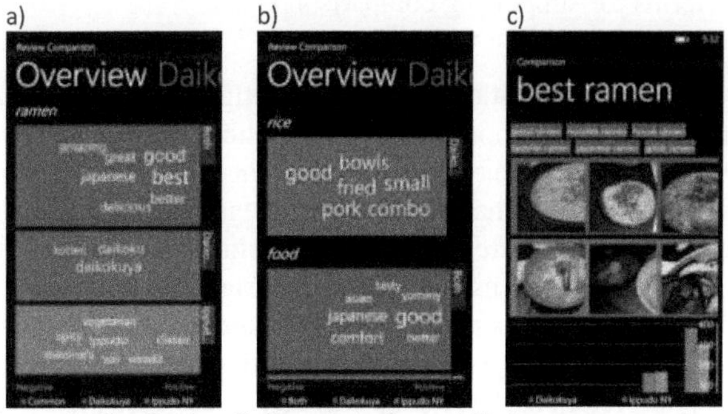

Figure 1. The ReviewCollage interface. a) It shows an overview of two entities (restaurants) by attribute ("ramen" in this view). The three panels show descriptions used for both restaurants (purple) or primarily for one (red and blue). This offers a quick view of how similarly and differently two entities are reviewed; b) The system also shows attributes primarily used for one restaurant; c) The interface also shows details for a clicked word with pictures, rating distributions, and comments.

text, similar to RevMiner [12], to offer an overview of two reviewed entities. Figure 1 shows the ReviewCollage interface with two Japanese restaurants. The three panels show descriptions (values) associated with the attribute "ramen (a soup noodle)". The purple panel contains descriptions representing some features common in the two restaurants. As in Figure 1a, both restaurants are positively described with the terms "best" and "good". The red and blue panels show descriptions used primarily for only one of the restaurants. For example, Daikokuya (in the red panel) is described with "kotteri (thick soup)" whereas the ramen in Ippudo (in the blue panel) is "spicy". In this manner, the user can view how similarly or differently two reviewed entities are described within a one-page view. ReviewCollage also offers the detailed information about a specific word pair (Figure 1c). This view includes pictures, rating distributions, and comments containing the selected word pair, and helps the user deepen their understanding of the entities.

Our comparative user study with existing summarization interfaces using word pairs (Review Spotlight [27] and RevMiner [12]) shows that participants were able to view information about two entities and make a choice at 105 seconds on average. This was significantly faster than RevMiner and comparably fast to Review Spotlight. It also reveals that ReviewCollage could be most useful when two reviewed entities are very similar and summarization for one entity does not highlight differences well.

The contributions of this work are summarized as follows:

- The design of the mobile interface to support a comparison process using review comments;
- The development of Shared-Distinct value, an algorithm to identify attribute-value word pairs used commonly in two entities (shared terms) or primarily for one entity (distinct terms); and
- Our evaluation to confirm the utility of ReviewCollage and highlight different benefits of shared and distinct terms for supporting comparison tasks.

RELATED WORK

Review summarization has been investigated extensively in the field of computational linguistics [11], and user interfaces also have been examined. Liu et al. built a system to visualize how many positive or negative reviews were posted about features of an entity using bar graphs [18]. Carenini et al. [3] used a Treemap visualization to show a summary of reviews although their user study found that participants often preferred text-based summaries because the interpretation of Treemap was often not intuitive.

One common technique used in review summarization is keyword/tag extraction. These keywords and tags allow the user to view information about an entity at a glance. They are often associated with sentiment, in particular, positivity and negativity. Dave et al. [6] built a system to extract tags from product reviews with a sentiment score. Lee et al. [16] developed a system in which the user can manually add tags and their sentiment to an entity, and the rated valence of the tag is shown by the font. The system by Ganesan et al. [9] uses a tag cloud interface with emoticons to visualize eBay seller feedback (e.g., automatically adding a smiley face to a positive tag). Yatani et al. developed Review Spotlight [27] using adjective-noun word pairs in a tag cloud interface. It offers more detailed information at a glance than single-word tag clouds. Their study revealed that Review Spotlight could help the user quickly develop an impression about a reviewed entity (a restaurant in their prototype).

As the screen size is limited on mobile devices, review summarization would become even more beneficial. The study by von Reischach et al. [26] confirms that people prefer ratings and text summaries because they can glance at review comments on a mobile device. Have2eat [8] is a mobile application that offers information about nearby restaurants. It shows its summary about a restaurant by automatically selecting salient sentences in the review text. RevMiner [12] summarizes review text using attribute-value pairs in a manner similar to Review Spotlight [27] to offer a concise overview of how a restaurant is described. But these systems only provide information about one entity, and are not designed to directly support the comparison process.

Prior work has also developed interactive systems that aim to support the comparison process. For example, systems developed by Carenini et al. [4] and Zhang et al. [27] show the distribution of positive and negative reviews or differences about multiple entities along different aspects. ManyLists [19] provides a table view of food nutritional ingredients or product features. It utilizes the spatial layout and animation to indicate similarities between entities as well as their unique features.

These systems categorize information based on pre-determined aspects, and may not highlight the similarities and differences between multiple entities in a flexible and lower-level manner. ReviewCollage addresses this issue by parsing review text and finding descriptions used commonly in two entities and primarily for one of them. Our interface is also designed towards mobile devices, thereby differentiating our work from the projects above.

PILOT STUDY

We conducted a pilot study with eight participants (four male and four female) to inform the interface design for review comment comparison. We chose four sets of two or three restaurant review webpages in the same category. The participants were asked to find out how much they would like to visit each of the restaurants assuming that basic conditions are equal (e.g., distance to the restaurant or budget limit). This design allowed us to focus on examining user behavior on comparison rather than searching or screening. They read the two sets of webpages on a laptop and the other two on a mobile touch-screen device. This experimental design was included to uncover interaction difficulty related to the form-factor of a mobile device.

This pilot study revealed the following behavior which our participants showed often.

Frequent page switching: Participants found that switching multiple webpages needed effort, particularly on a mobile device. Also, this often made it hard for the participants to keep track of which restaurant is good for what, as one participant commented:

"It's quite often that I need to swich back to the former page to check the details since I don't want to remember all the things."

This suggests that the interface should offer a one-page overview of multiple entities.

Looking for similarities and differences: We also found that participants sought how similarly or differently people described the restaurants. For example, one participant provided the reason for her choice by articulating the similarities and differences in the two restaurants:

"Both two restaurants seem good and also provide similar foods, but some people mentioned the service is intolerable in the first restaurant, and I didn't find similar comments on the other. That's why I chose the second one."

This implies that the interface should highlight descriptions which apply to multiple entities or to only one of them.

Comparing visually using pictures: We observed that participants often viewed and compared pictures posted by the reviewers in addition to reading comments. These pictures offered a better understanding of the comments or enhanced their impression about a particular restaurant. Thus, pictures should be incorporated into the interface along with relevant information (e.g., keywords or descriptions which can be associated with them).

These findings motivated us to consider a summarization interface that covers the similarities and differences between two reviewed entities, to facilitate low-level comparison in an efficient manner. Summarization using word pairs and tag-cloud interfaces [12, 27] is found to be effective for quick impression formation. This can also be appropriate for mobile interfaces as it does not require a large visual space. We thus decided to investigate how a tag-cloud interface with word pairs can be extended to support comparison tasks. This requires two improvements over existing systems:

- Determining whether a word pair is frequently used in both entities or primarily in one of them,
- Displaying word pairs to highlight similarities and differences between two entities.

In the following sections, we explain our implementation of ReviewCollage by describing each of the major system components: word pair extraction, word pair ranking, and mobile interface.

WORD PAIR EXTRACTION

We carefully re-implemented the RevMiner extraction method [12]. We first generated attribute-value pairs as initial seeds. We parsed sentences in review text for 20 randomly-chosen restaurants with the Stanford parser [5], and extracted sets of nouns and their modifying adjective. We chose the 50 most frequently used nouns, and the three most frequently used adjectives for each noun, resulting in 150 pairs (the nouns as attributes and the adjectives as values) as the initial seeds. We then performed the bootstrapping algorithm (the details are available in [12]) to collect new attribute-value pairs. The cutoff threshold for our dataset was experimentally set to 11. This needs to be calibrated for other datasets as discussed in [12].

During development, we also came across the same issue of word pair over-generation as RevMiner, such as "happy guys" from the sentence "the guys were happy with the food". These spurious extractions were caused by short templates like "[attribute] were [value]" because it could aggressively match to sentences. To further restrict these short templates, our system also includes templates that consider the words preceding or following the pairs.

We crawled reviews for 48 restaurants in Yelp.com. This resulted in 780k sentences. After performing word-pair extraction, we had 556 templates, 1478 attributes, and 2172 values in our current prototype.

WORD PAIR RANKING

After the extraction, the system attempts to identify which word pairs are used commonly in both restaurants (referred to as "shared terms") or mostly for one restaurant (referred to as "distinct terms"). Monroe et al. [20] examined word classification methods with political content to uncover what word was used primarily by Democrats or Republicans in the United States of America. They tested various approaches, including model-based ones. These approaches could be applicable, but require explicit assumptions for models. These models may need re-training or modifications when they apply for another corpus. We thus sought model-free methods that satisfy the following requirements:

- Req1. Our algorithm must differentiate shared and distinct terms only using the occurrence probabilities in two review text sets.
- Req2. Our algorithm must weigh shared and distinct terms based on the occurrence probabilities in two review text sets. Suppose that one word pair has a 50% occurrence probability in both review sets, and another has 10%. The former should have a larger weight than the latter.

TF-IDF [24] is commonly used to extract words that occur frequently in particular documents but rarely in the rest of the entire document set. We can apply TF-IDF to our case by using its maximum value in the two review text for example:

$$TF\text{-}IDF(tf_A, tf_B) = Max(tf_A, tf_B) \times log\frac{2}{dc(tf_A, tf_B)},$$

where

$$dc(tf_A, tf_B) = \begin{cases} 2 \ (tf_A \neq 0 \text{ and } tf_B \neq 0) \\ 1 \ (\text{otherwise}) \end{cases},$$

and tf_A, tf_B are term frequencies (occurrence probabilities of a term) in the review text for entity A and B, respectively. A term frequency is defined as the number of occurrences of a term over the number of occurrences of all terms of interest. We do not consider the case of $tf_A = tf_B = 0$ as it means that the term does not appear in either of the review text. This TF-IDF is not generally useful for ReviewCollage. For example, TF-IDF can be zero even in a case where the term is used very frequently in one entity, and very rarely, but not at all, in the other. We want to classify such a term as distinct.

To this end, we explored different existing algorithms commonly used for representing similarities or differences, and also developed our own. We present them with mathematical definitions in this section.

Binary Entropy

Binary entropy [25] represents the average uncertainty in a random variable which can take only two values. In our context, this can be regarded as how likely a word pair would be seen in one entity over the other. If a term is distinct, it is more likely to be observed in one entity; thus, an event of word pair occurrences is certain (or a prediction of which entity has this word pair is certain). For shared terms, the event becomes more uncertain. Thus, Binary entropy becomes small for distinct terms and large for shared terms. Therefore, it can be used to represent similarities on phenomena described by two probability values. The binary entropy is defined as follows:

$$BE(A,B) = -\frac{tf_A}{tf_{A+B}}\log_2\left(\frac{tf_A}{tf_{A+B}}\right) - \frac{tf_B}{tf_{A+B}}\log_2\left(\frac{tf_B}{tf_{A+B}}\right),$$

where tf_{A+B} is the sum of the two term frequencies. To make the polarity consistent with the other algorithms we explain below (large values for distinct terms and small for shared terms), we use the inverse binary entropy (IBE):

$$IBE(tf_A, tf_B) = 1 - BE(tf_A, tf_B).$$

IBE takes a value between 0 and 1 by definition; thus, it is already normalized.

Kullback-Leibler Divergence

Kullback-Leibler Divergence (KL-divergence) [14] is used to quantify the difference between two discrete probability distributions. It represents the information lost which happens when one probability distribution is used to approximate the other. It is defined as the difference between cross entropy and self-entropy:

$$D_{KL}(tf_A||tf_B) = -tf_A\,(\log_2(tf_B) - \log_2(tf_A)).$$

Note that KL-divergence is not symmetric; generally, $D_{KL}(tf_A||tf_B) \neq D_{KL}(tf_B||tf_A)$. This is not ideal because our ranking method would otherwise require to calculate and calibrate two directionalities. We thus did not consider KL-divergence for further analysis.

Jensen-Shannon Divergence

Jensen-Shannon Divergence (JS-divergence; JSd) [17] solves the non-symmetric behavior of KL-divergence. It represents the similarity of two probability distributions as the total divergence to the average distribution:

$$D_{JS}(tf_A, tf_B) = \frac{1}{2}D_{KL}(tf_A||tf_M) + \frac{1}{2}D_{KL}(tf_B||tf_B),$$

where tf_M is the mean of the two term frequencies ($tf_M = (tf_A + tf_B)/2$). As D_{JS} takes a value between 0 and 0.5 given that tf_A and tf_B are between 0 and 1, it can be normalized: $D_{JS\_n}(tf_A, tf_B) = 2D_{JS}(tf_A, tf_B)$.

Limitations of the algorithms above

The three algorithms above all satisfy Req1. For example, KL-divergence and JS-divergence are zero when $tf_A = tf_B$, and the values become large when $tf_A \ll tf_B$ or $tf_A \gg tf_B$. But these three algorithms do not satisfy Req2 well, in particular for shared terms (e.g., $D_{JS\_n}(0.5, 0.5) = D_{JS\_n}(0.1, 0.1) = 0$). This problem is also observed in other existing methods we surveyed, such as WordScores [15], frequently used in political science. We chose inverse binary entropy and JS-divergence as examples of existing algorithms mainly because they are commonly used in information theory and still clarify the limitation.

Nevertheless, we found that JS-divergence is close to ideal in a case of distinct terms for the two following reasons. First, JS-divergence is symmetric. Second, JS-divergence gives weights for distinct terms as we desire even when either tf_A or tf_B is equal or close to zero. For example, $D_{JS\_n}(0.5, 0) = 0.5 > D_{JS\_n}(0.1, 0) = 0.1$, but $IBE(0.5, 0) = IBE(0.1, 0) = 1$.

Shared-Distinct value

We developed Shared-Distinct value (SD-value; SDv) to determine whether an adjective is used frequently for both entities or only for one of them. The definition is as follows:

$$SDv(tf_A, tf_B) = Max(tf_A, tf_B) \times \left(\frac{\pi}{8} - \tan^{-1}\frac{Min(tf_A, tf_B)}{Max(tf_A, tf_B)}\right).$$

The first term of the product (the maximum of the occurrence ratios in the review text of two entities) reflects Req2. The second term maps shared and distinct terms into positive and negative values, respectively; thus, it satisfies Req1. It also contributes a weight based on the skewness of the ratios. For example, if the ratios are equal, this part becomes the minimum negative value of $-\pi/8$. But if the ratios are skewed in one way, it gives a large positive value towards $\pi/8$ because the arctangent part is close to zero. In this manner, the SD-value can offer both the shared/distinct polarity and magnitude in a single measure. The deduction from $\pi/8$ also ensures that Req2 is met.

Given that A and B are between 0 and 1, the SD-value can take a value between $-\pi/8$ and $\pi/8$. To maintain the sign, we can normalize SD-value into [-1, 1], defined as:

$$SDv_n(tf_A, tf_B) = \frac{SDv(tf_A, tf_B)}{\pi/8}.$$

Our SD-value is only based on word occurrence frequencies and can be used in different corpora without modifications.

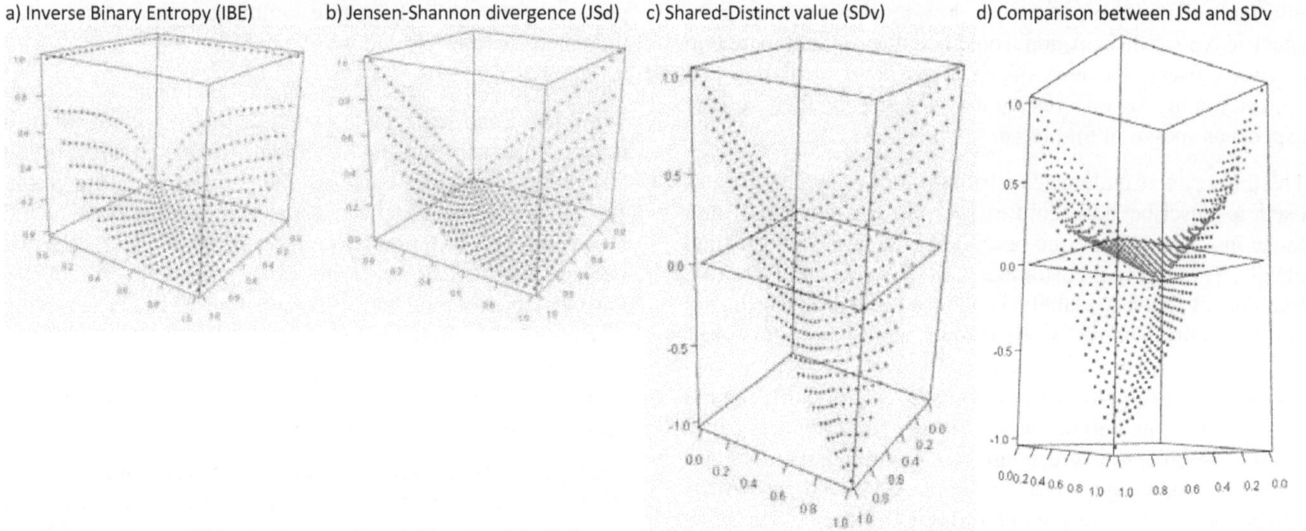

Figure 2. Value distributions of the inverse binary entropy (green), normalized Jensen-Shannon divergence (red), and normalized Shared-Distinct value (blue). In all plots, the horizontal axes represent the occurrence probabilities of a term within each review text of two entities (*A* and *B*). Please refer to the accompanying video to see these plots from different perspectives.

Systematic Examination on Shared-Distinct Value

As we discussed in the previous section, our algorithm must satisfy two major requirements (Req1 and Req2). In addition, it ideally should have a similar characteristic to JS-divergence for distinct terms as it is a commonly-used similarity measurement for two probability distributions.

We conducted simulations to systematically evaluate our SD-value. Figure 2 shows the value distributions of the normalized IBE, JS-divergence, and SD-value by ranging values of tf_A and tf_B from 0 to 1 with an interval of 0.05 (excluding the case of $tf_A = tf_B = 0$). The smoothing factor of 1E-100 was included to avoid the log of zero and division by zero when necessary. The plots of IBE and JS-divergence again illustrate limitations discussed in the previous section. The plot of SD-value shows that shared terms would have negative values, forming the main difference from the other two algorithms. Figure 2d shows plots of JS-divergence and SD-value integrated in one space. As we desired, the distribution of the SD-value closely overlaps with that of JS-divergence for distinct terms. A Pearson's correlation was found highly strong (r^2=.88, p<.001). This also supports that SD-value behaves similarly to JS-divergence for distinct terms and differentiates shared terms based on their occurrence probabilities.

Table 1 shows an example comparison between SD-value and the other algorithms. SD-value can determine whether each word pair is shared or distinct by its sign and absolute value. In the other algorithms, some shared terms are not weighed properly (e.g., TF-IDF and IBE), or distinct terms are likely to be mis-classified as shared (e.g., "awesome food" with JS-divergence).

Based on the evidence gained through our quantitative examination, we decided to use SD-value in ReviewCollage. After the word pair extraction, ReviewCollage first ranks all

Word pair	Term frequency		Algorithms (normalized)			
	A	B	TF-IDF	IBE	JSd	SDv
Good food	0.1013	0.0767	0	0.0138	0.0025	-0.0659
Great food	0.0452	0.0625	0	0.0187	0.0020	-0.0372
Tasty food	0.0095	0.0130	0	0.0175	0.0004	-0.0079
Bad food	0.0047	0.0047	0	0.0000	0.0000	-0.0047
Indian food	0.5948	0	1	1	0.5948	0.5948
Flavorful food	0.0060	0	0.0100	1	0.0060	0.0060
Spicy food	0.0202	0.0035	0	0.3960	0.0094	0.0114
Chinese food	0.0023	0.6033	0	0.9640	0.5838	0.5974
Awesome food	0.0024	0.0106	0	0.3099	0.0040	0.0046

Table 1. An algorithm comparison with word pairs of "food" extracted from two actual restaurant reviews. The values are normalized within each algorithm. Our SD-value can separate shared and distinct terms by its sign and absolute value.

the attributes with the absolute SD-value. It then distinguishes all associated values for each attribute into shared and distinct word pairs using the signed SD-value, and ranks each of them. This ranking result is used to prioritize word pairs to be shown in the interface, as explained in the next section.

REVIEWCOLLAGE INTERFACE DESIGN

After identifying shared and distinct word pairs, ReviewCollage displays them in an interface using tag cloud visualization. ReviewCollage has two views to support the user's comparison: Summary View and Detail View. A complete demonstration of the ReviewCollage interface is available in the accompanying video.

Summary View

When the user chooses two entities, ReviewCollage shows panels of tag clouds in a one-page view (Figure 1a). We use a tag cloud interface because it can visually emphasize representative words [12, 22, 27]. The three panels contain descriptions (values of the extracted word pairs) associated with a particular attribute ("ramen" in Figure 1a). The system does not use high-level or generic concepts; thus, the interface offers comparison on low-level aspects (e.g., a specific type of dishes), and would help the user compare two entities closely. ReviewCollage also shows attributes that appear mainly in one restaurant to highlight their unique aspects as shown in Figure 1b.

The three panels under each attribute show associated values used to describe both entities (purple: Shared panel) and those mostly used for one restaurant (red and blue: Distinct panel). The user can customize the color scheme if desired. Each panel also has a label: "Both" for the shared word pairs and the entity's name for the distinct word pairs. This view thus highlights similarities and differences between the two entities. For example, the interface shows that ramen (soup noodle) in both entities are positively described because "best", "good", and "great" are in the purple panel. But the ramen in Daikokuya (red) can be characterized as "kotteri (thick soup)" whereas the one in Ippudo (blue) is described as "spicy" or "vegetarian".

ReviewCollage uses the absolute SD-value to order the attributes extracted from the review text, starting with the largest to the smallest except for the ones under the threshold. The font size of values for each attribute is set to be proportional to their absolute SD-value to highlight salient words. The system also performs sentiment analysis using SENTIWORDNET [7]. It uses the average sentiment value across all the senses (meanings) for each value. This is used to determine the layout of the adjectives in the panel. Our layout algorithm attempts to loosely place positive and negative adjectives towards right and left sides, respectively. In this manner, the user can glance how positively or negatively entities are mentioned from the word layout.

Detail View

When the user taps a word in a panel, the system provides the details about the selected word pair (Figure 1c). Precise pointing with a finger is difficult, and ReviewCollage employs object-based target selection. When the user makes a tap within a panel, the system calculates the distance from the centroid of each word, and determines the one closest to the contact point under the threshold (4 mm) as the target word. Detail View first shows pictures posted in the original review webpage and associated with the chosen word pair. We found that the interface shows only few pictures for some word pairs because descriptions associated with most of the pictures do not match with them. Thus, we extract pictures associated with the attribute-value word pair as well as with the attribute only, and prioritize the ones associated with the word pair in the view. Our informal study confirmed that participants would prefer to see many pictures even if some do not exactly match to the selected word pair.

The view shows the rating distributions of the reviews associated with the selected word pair. They are based on the overall ratings in the original webpage. Thus, this graph does not offer the exact sentiment distribution about the word pair; however, the graph still provides a quick view of how positively or negatively people comment on the entities when they mention the selected word pair.

The system shows several sentences containing the selected word pair. Each sentence is again associated with the overall rating, and the system attempts to match the rating distribution of the sentences to the one shown in the graph. We also prioritize sentences whose length is between 10 and 30 words. This criterion was chosen based on heuristics that very short sentences would not offer much detail while very long sentences would take too much time to read. The system then orders the candidate sentences by the "usefulness" score (the number of votes given by users who found the review useful in the original webpages), and shows most highly ranked sentences for each rating.

Examples Using Review Text in Other Domains

We have so far explained the interface design and features of ReviewCollage with reviews on restaurants (extracted from Yelp.com), but it can be extended to other types of review text. Figure 3 shows Summary View examples using Amazon and TripAdvisor reviews. Similar to the example shown in Figure 1, the user can see similarities and differences between two entities. For example, in Figure 3b, service in two hotels of interest receive both positive and negative descriptions. But in the panels for distinct terms, one of them shows strongly positive words, such as "amazing" and "outstanding". This indicates that service in that hotel may be substantially better than the other in general.

This demonstration suggests that ReviewCollage generally satisfies our main requirement: highlighting similarities and differences between two reviewed entities from different domains (restaurants, hotels and products). An extensive evaluation on how different domains could influence the word pair extraction and interface is beyond the scope of this work. Instead, we evaluated ReviewCollage through a user study to compare it with other summarization interfaces.

USER STUDY

To validate our design of ReviewCollage, we conducted a comparative study against existing summarization user interfaces using word pairs: Review Spotlight [27] and RevMiner [12]. We opted out original webpages because the experiment otherwise would bias towards ReviewCollage. We decided to include RevMiner as it is the latest mobile summarization interface. Although Review Spotlight was not designed for mobile devices, we decided to include it because ReviewCollage takes a similar approach to summarization. The study on RevMiner [12] also shows some advantages of a mobile interface like Review Spotlight. We re-implemented Review Spotlight and RevMiner as faithfully as we could for our study, as shown in Figure 4.

Experimental Design

We crawled review comments on 16 restaurants (8 restaurant pairs) from Yelp.com. Two of these restaurant pairs were in the same category (American, Barbeque, Chinese, and Japanese). We chose these categories because they

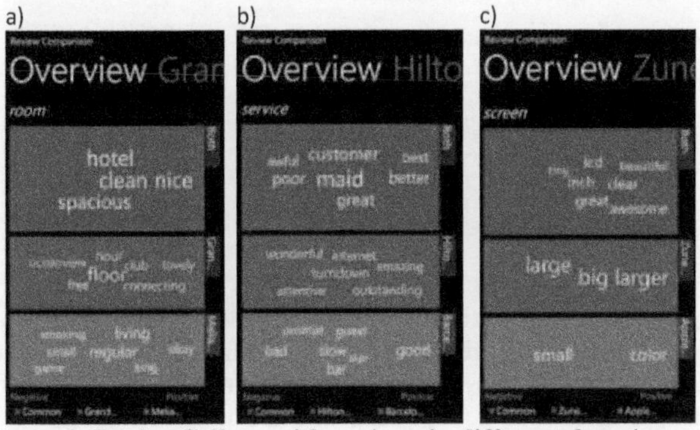

Figure 3. ReviewCollage with reviews in different domains: a, b) hotel reviews ("room" and "service attributes) from TripAdvisor; and c) product reviews (mp3 players) from Amazon.

represented different types of food and places. These restaurants also had a sufficient number of reviews at the time of this experiment. One of the two pairs in the same category was used for comparing ReviewCollage with either Review Spotlight or RevMiner (referred as a *comparison pair*), and the other pair was used as a distractor with the remaining interface (referred as a *distractor pair*). This distractor was introduced to prevent participants from directly using their previous decisions by simply judging the restaurant category. Table 2 shows the two groups randomly assigned to six participant each.

As the Review Spotlight and RevMiner interfaces only show a summary about one restaurant, we prepared two views for each comparison task. Participants could switch between the views by swiping horizontally on the screen. We considered side-by-side views of these reference systems in a landscape mode. But it would require frequent up/down scrolls, and impose another difference (e.g., portrait vs. landscape views) to this experiment. Our re-implementation does require a horizontal swipe, but this is a very quick, transient gesture. The view also offers larger space to show information for each entity. We thus determined that the implementation was acceptable for our purpose. Detail View was available for any value word in ReviewCollage and RevMiner or word pair in Review Spotlight. The names of the restaurants were anonymized in all interfaces.

The presentation order of the twelve tasks (3 interfaces × 4 categories) for each participant was randomized, but the presentation of each comparison pair was separated by at least two tasks. We counter-balanced the presentation order of the interfaces for each comparison pair across participants. As our comparison focuses on the interfaces, we did not analyze the performance across restaurant categories.

Procedure

At the beginning of the experiment, participants were given instructions of the study and system, and time to practice with the interfaces until they felt comfortable with using them. After participants chose one restaurant in each task, the experimenter asked them to describe their reasons. They were instructed to tell a couple of points which made them

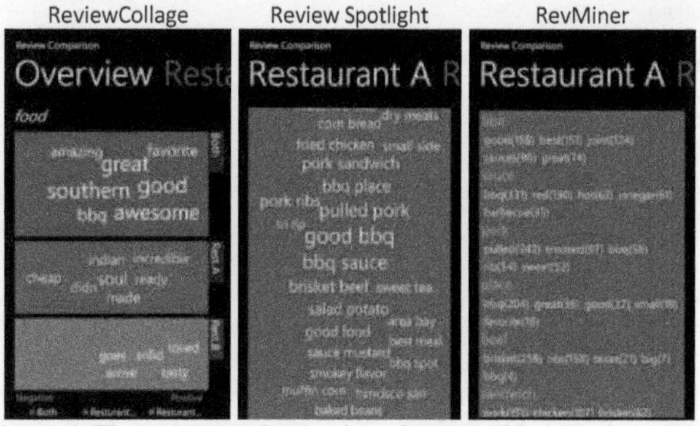

Figure 4. Three summarization interfaces used in our user study. For Review Spotlight and RevMiner, two views were prepared and each showed one restaurant.

Restaurant Category	Group A			Group B		
	RC	RS	RM	RC	RS	RM
American	C	C	d	C	d	C
Barbeque	C	d	C	C	C	d
Chinese	C	C	d	C	d	C
Japanese	C	d	C	C	C	d

RC: Review Collage, RS: Review Spotlight, RM: RevMiner
C: Comparison pair / d: Distractor pair

Table 2. Experimental conditions. Participants were divided into Group A or B randomly. The distractor restaurant pair was introduced to prevent participants from directly using their previous decision.

choose that particular restaurant. For task completion time, we measured the time between when an interface was shown to the participants and when they stopped using it and described their decision to the experimenter.

After the participants completed the twelve tasks, they were invited to a short interview to express their opinions on the three interfaces. We did not directly ask preferences to avoid potential good-subject effect. Rather, we asked them to express what benefits and shortcomings each interface have and how they would use it in a realistic setting. The entire study took approximately one hour. A gift card worth $15 USD was offered as the compensation.

Participant

Twelve participants (P01–P12; seven male and five female; average age 23.3 years old) from our research institute were recruited for this study. They were undergraduate or graduate students with various backgrounds in different universities. Some of the participants were non-native English speakers though all of them were able to understand the instructions and express their opinions in English. All had experience of using mobile touch-screen devices, and were aware of or had used mobile apps showing restaurant information and reviews. None of them participated in our pilot study.

RESULTS

Task Completion Time

Figure 5 shows the average task completion time with the three interfaces. Mauchly's test did not show a violation of sphericity (an assumption of a repeated-measure ANOVA test). This permits direct interpretation of one-way repeated-

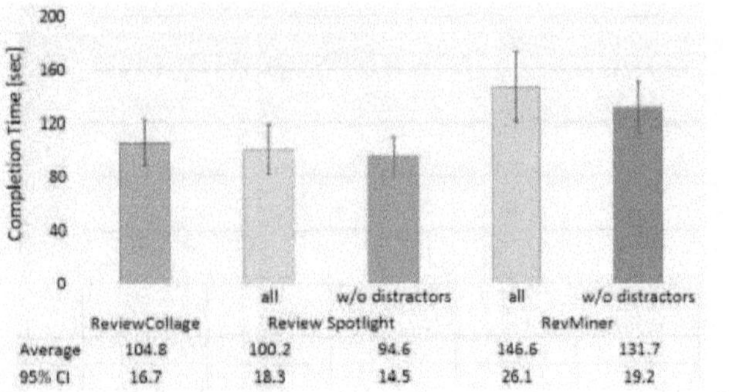

Figure 5. Task completion time. The error bar represents the 95% confidence interval.

measure ANOVA F-test results. An ANOVA test on the completion time against the interface with all tasks showed a significant difference on the completion time ($F_{(2, 22)}$=5.52, p<.05, η_p^2=.33). The post-hoc pairwise comparison with paired t-tests using the Bonferroni correction reveals a significant difference, showing that Review Spotlight were faster than RevMiner (p<.01).

An ANOVA test with all the tasks excluding the distractors also found a significant effect of the interfaces on the completion time ($F_{(2, 22)}$=6.13, p<.05, η_p^2=.36). The post-hoc test reveals significant differences with ReviewCollage and Review Spotlight outperforming RevMiner (p<.05 for both). Figure 6 shows the distribution of completion time differences between ReviewCollage and the other interfaces. This plot confirms that ReviewCollage was comparably fast to Review Spotlight and generally faster than RevMiner.

Effect of Interfaces on Decision-making

The participants made the same restaurant choice for 34 out of the 48 tasks with the comparison pairs (70.8%). We found that the same participants often gave different reasons for their choices even when they chose the same restaurant. For example, one participant was able to express a specific reason on her choice with ReviewCollage:

"I gonna choose Restaurant A. Because I didn't like spicy, salty, hot things. And Restaurant A has Cantonese food, and I haven't tried any Taiwanese food before. I don't want to try something new this time." [P02, ReviewCollage, 135 sec (completion time)]

On the other hand, this participant was struggling to make a decision on the same comparison pair with RevMiner. As a result, she had to spend more time, but was not able to express specific reasons.

"I would say, Restaurant A. It's really hard to choose. Both restaurants' price is reasonable. But Restaurant A has long waiting, and Restaurant B is also the same, long wait. I don't see any obvious thing here." [P02, RevMiner, 201sec]

Some participants often made their decisions with RevMiner based on frequency numbers shown next to words by assuming that higher numbers indicate that more people had visited the place.

Participants used a few word pairs as part of reasons for their choices with RevewCollage. This was also true when they

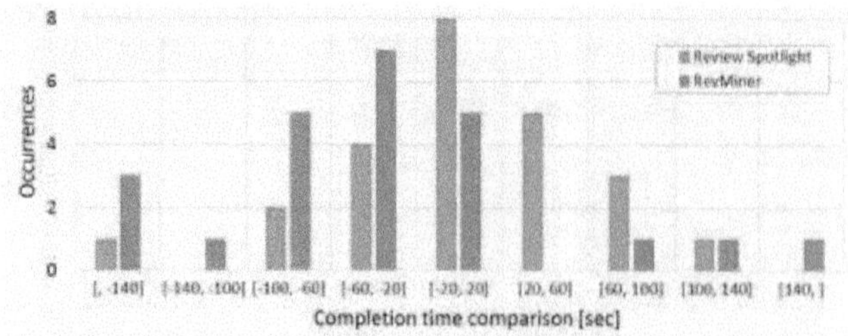

Figure 6. The distribution of the task completion time differences between ReviewCollage and the other interfaces. A negative value represents a case in which participants finished the task more quickly with ReviewCollage than with the other interface.

used Review Spotlight, but they tended to mention the differences rather than the similarities with ReviewCollage:

"I choose Restaurant B because there is a comment like dishes in Restaurant A are dirty or something. And it is about Taiwanese food, and I want to have a try." [P05, ReviewCollage, 102 sec]

"I choose Restaurant B because comments mention more different dishes. And there are a lot of things in common, but comments in Restaurant B have 'cup chicken', which may be a famous Chinese dish. I am more interested in it." [P05, Review Spotlight, 156 sec]

We observed a similar reasoning pattern when participants made different choices. ReviewCollage often helped participants quickly find aspects which they were interested in but was not visible in the other interfaces, and this led to changes in their choices. For instance, P09 described the reasons for his choices with ReviewCollage and Review Spotlight as follows:

"I would choose Restaurant B. Because I am so much into spicy food, and I saw keywords with 'spicy' in Restaurant B, but not in A." [P09, ReviewCollage, 26 sec]

"I choose Restaurant A. I see both of them have Chinese food. I checked the details of them, and thought A is better because I saw more positive comments." [P09, Review Spotlight, 89 sec]

DISCUSSIONS

Our results show that ReviewCollage was able to support comparisons and informed decisions at least as fast as existing interfaces using word pairs. We further examine differences between ReviewCollage and the other interfaces through comments collected in post-experiment interviews.

Uncovering Different Use Scenarios

Our quantitative results show that ReviewCollage and Review Spotlight performed comparably in terms of completion time. One reason is that both interfaces are based on tag clouds, and they were easy to glance. This is in line with findings from prior work [12, 22, 27]. More specifically, participants expressed that Review Spotlight could offer an overview that was quicker to read whereas ReviewCollage could show the details better.

"[ReviewCollage] separates common keywords for both restaurants, so I can focus on something special for each restaurant. But if I want to make a choice quickly, I would use [Review Spotlight] because it is easier to see biggest keywords. But if I want to see more details about two restaurants, I would use [ReviewCollage]." [P03]

Another difference between ReviewCollage and Review Spotlight was that word pairs are grouped by attribute in ReviewCollage, and participants were able to quickly focus on specific aspects of restaurants they were interested in:

"It ha s so me go od thing s. I espe cially like noodles. I want to eat noodles in these restaurants. So I would like to compare feedback on each restaurant about noo dles. And [ReviewCollage] has specific categories, an d that is u seful bec ause it can se parate no odles from sauce and soup, for example." [P02]

These differences indicate that ReviewCollage and Review Spotlight have different benefits despite the similarity in the interface design. In particular, participants considered ReviewCollage to be more useful when the two entities to be compared were very similar as one participant commented:

"To compare two re staurants, I thought this i nterface (ReviewCollage) would be much better especially when they are the same types of restaurants. For example, if I choose the same type of restaurants and I want to c ompare, I want to see what are common things and different thing s. If the re is a diffe rence, for example, a Chinese re staurant and Ja panese rest aurant, I guess, a nother o ne (Review Spotlight) would be better. You would just see keywords for each restaurant, and that would be enough." [P12]

When two entities are relatively dissimilar, Review Spotlight can show many different word pairs between them, and thus can highlight unique aspects of each entity. However, when they are very much alike (e.g., restaurants in the same food category), Review Spotlight would mostly display similar word pairs. This requires the user to visually search different word pairs in two views. ReviewCollage can emphasize the differences between two entities even for such a case.

Advantages of Tag Clouds

Our user study found that ReviewCollage was significantly faster than RevMiner. One reason was that RevMiner does not visually highlight frequently-used word pairs well as compared to ReviewCollage, and participants tended to spend more time finding word pairs they thought were important or representative of restaurants.

"I couldn't clearly see which words were more important because the size of words was the same." [P08]

Participants also found that they often needed to spend much time to identify the differences between two entities in RevMiner, as they did with Review Spotlight, because shared attributes and values were not grouped well.

"I was a little confu sed with la bels. I thoug ht the re were the same labels (attributes) in bot h sc reens, so I was tryi ng to find the same label for comparison. But it was not always the case. So it was often hard to compare." [P09]

Participants liked the number next to each word showing its occurrence frequency. Some participants extrapolated that higher numbers indicate that more people had visited the place, and used it as part of reasons. But, they generally felt that RevMiner is not organized for comparison, and this was also reflected in the performance time.

Different Benefits of Shared and Distinct Terms

ReviewCollage shows word pairs that represent both restaurants (shared word pairs) and ones that apply to only each of the restaurants (distinct word pairs). Our interview revealed that many of our participants used Distinct panels more often than Shared panels.

"I fou nd Both (shared w ord pai rs) i s not helpf ul for me to judg e because I only needed to see the difference between Restaurant A and B. Maybe it is helpful for me to ju dge whether I w ant to go to the se two restaurants." [P10]

However, some participants also found shared panels useful. As we expected, they used Shared panels to ensure that some aspects important to them are equally positive or negative. In addition, they used Detail View for words in Shared panels to perform comparison as P08 commented:

"[ReviewCollage] is useful for comparison, especially when I tapped into a wo rd (in Shared panel s) and it gave me picture s and a cha rt about both restaurants." [P08]

These findings show that ReviewCollage can support different ways to perform comparisons, and validate its interface design of showing the similarities and differences between two reviewed entities in a one-page view.

LIMITATIONS

Our present study has several limitations. First, the user study design did not investigate how satisfied participants would be about decisions they made in light of experience at an actual restaurant. We selected restaurants located in a different city to ensure that the participants would not be able to use prior experience with them. A deployment study would help to examine user satisfaction on decision making through ReviewCollage in a realistic setting.

The sample size is relative small (twelve participants). This could be one reason why we did not see clear quantitative differences among the conditions. However, our qualitative results indicate important differences, and encourage future work to examine them deeply in a larger scale.

Our summarization is not always perfect like other systems. Some heuristics may help, but a generalizable approach would be challenging. This is an active research topic in computational linguistics, and future improvements could be integrated into the ReviewCollage system. We do not claim that SD-value is the optimal solution, and future work should examine various ranking algorithms systematically. This work offers a foundation for such future studies.

CONCLUSION AND FUTURE WORK

Comparison between multiple reviewed entities on a mobile device is becoming a common activity. But current interactive systems do not support this process well because existing summarization methods only take one entity into account. We present ReviewCollage, a mobile interface to support direct comparison between two entities using review comments. ReviewCollage extracts attribute-value word pairs from reviews, and highlights descriptions that apply to both entities and to only one of them. Our user study confirms that ReviewCollage can help comparison and decision-making within a couple of minutes. This was at least as fast as existing summarization interfaces using word pairs. It also reveals that ReviewCollage can be most useful when two entities are very similar.

Future work should test different visualization methods. Word Spectrum [10] could be one approach to showing shared/distinct word pairs in one panel although it requires large landscape view space. Adaptively changing the visualization by the device orientation would be one solution.

We plan to investigate how ReviewCollage can be extended to support the comparison among more than two entities. While our SD-value can be readily extended to more than two entities (e.g., by using an Euler angle for three entities), the interface showing differences among more entities can become very complex, and is a challenge for future work.

ACKNOWLEDGEMENTS
We are grateful to Jeff Huang for providing the details of the implementation of the RevMiner attribute-value extraction method. We also thank all our user study participants.

REFERENCES
1. Baccianella, A., Esuli, A., Sebastiani, F. SentiWordNet 3.0: an enhanced lexical resource for sentiment analysis and opinion mining. In *Proc. LREC 2010*, ELRA, 2200-2204.
2. Beach, L. R. Broadening the definition of decision making: The role of prechoice screening of options. *Psychological Science 4*, 1993, 215-220.
3. Carenini, G., Ng, R. T., Pauls, A. Interactive multimedia summaries of evaluative text. In *Proc. of IUI 2006*, ACM, 124-131.
4. Carenini, G., Rizoli, L. A multimedia interface for facilitating comparisons of opinions. In *Proc. of IUI 2009*, ACM, 325-334.
5. Cer, D., Galley, M., Jurafsky, D., Manning, C. D. Phrasal: a toolkit for statistical machine translation with facilities for extraction and incorporation of arbitrary model features. In *Proc. of HLT-DEMO 2010*, ACL, 9-12.
6. Dave, K., Lawrence, S., Pennock, D. M. Mining the peanut gallery: opinion extraction and semantic classification of product reviews. In *Proc. of WWW 2003*, ACM, 519-528.
7. Esuli A., Sebastiani F. SENTIWORDNET: a publicly available lexical resource for opinion mining. In *Proc. of LREC 2006*, ELRA, 417-422.
8. Fabbrizio, G. D., Gupta, N., Besana, S., Mani, P. Have2eat: a restaurant finder with review summarization for mobile phones. In *Demo Volume of COLING 2010*, ACL, 17-20.
9. Ganesan, K. A., Sundaresan, N., Deo, H. Mining tag clouds and emoticons behind community feedback. In *Proc. of WWW 2008*, ACM, 1181-1182.
10. Harrison, C. Word Spectrum: Visualizing Google's Bi-Gram Data. http://www.chrisharrison.net/index.php/Visualizations/WordSpectrum
11. Hu, M., Liu, B. Mining and summarizing customer reviews. In *Proc. KDD 2004*, ACM, 168-177.
12. Huang, J., Etzioni, O., Zettlemoyer, L., Clark, K., Lee, C. RevMiner: an extractive interface for navigating reviews on a smartphone. In *Proc. of UIST 2012*, ACM, 3-12.
13. Hubl, G., Trifts. V. Consumer decision making in online shopping environments: the effects of interactive decision aids. *Marketing Science 19* (1), 2000, 4-21.
14. Kullback, S, Leibler, R. A. On information and sufficiency. *The Annals of Mathematical Statistics 22.1*, 1951, 79-86.
15. Laver, M., Benoit, K., Garry, J. Extracting policy positions from political texts using words as data. *American Political Science Review 97*, 02 (2003), 311-331.
16. Lee, S. E., Son, D. K., Han, S. S. Qtag: tagging as a means of rating, opinion-expressing, sharing and visualizing. In *Proc. of SIGDOC 2007*, ACM, 189-195.
17. Lin, J. Divergence measures based on the Shannon entropy. *IEEE Transactions on Information Theory 37.1*, 1991, 145-151.
18. Liu, B., Hu, M., Cheng, J. Opinion observer: analyzing and comparing opinions on the Web. In *Proc. of WWW 2005*, ACM, 342-351.
19. Liu, R., Chao, T., Plaisant, C., Shneiderman, B. ManyLists: product comparison tool using spatial layouts with animated transitions. *University of Maryland Technical Report*, 2012.
20. Monroe, B. L., Colaresi, M. P., Quinn, K. M. Fightin'words: Lexical feature selection and evaluation for identifying the content of political conflict. *Political Analysis 16*, 4 (2008), 372-403.
21. Payne, J.W., Bettman, J.R., Johnson, E.J. *The adaptive decision maker*. Cambridge University Press, 1993.
22. Rivadeneira, A. W., Gruen, D. M., Muller, M. J., Millen, D. R. Getting our head in the clouds: toward evaluation studies of tagclouds. In *Proc. of CHI 2007*, ACM, 995-998.
23. Rrnyi, A. On measures of entropy and information. In *Proc. Berkeley Symposium on Mathematical Statistics and Probability*, University of California Press, 1961, 547-561.
24. Salton, G., McGill, M. J. *Introduction to Modern Information Retrieval.* McGraw-Hill Inc., New York, NY, USA, 1986.
25. Shannon, C.E. A Mathematical Theory of Communication, *Bell System Technical Journal 27*, 1948, 379-423, 623-656.
26. von Reischach, F., Dubach, E., Michahelles, F., Schmidt, A. An evaluation of product review modalities for mobile phones. In *Proc. MobileHCI 2010*, ACM, 199-208.
27. Yatani, K., Novati, M., Trusty, A., Truong, K. N. Review spotlight: a user interface for summarizing user-generated reviews using adjective-noun word pairs. In *Proc. CHI 2011*, ACM, 1541-1550.
28. Zhang, J., Jones, N., Pu. P. A visual interface for critiquing-based recommender systems. In *Proc. EC 2008*, ACM, 230-239.

Mobile Interaction Analysis: Towards a Novel Concept for Interaction Sequence Mining

Florian Lettner, Christian Grossauer, Clemens Holzmann
University of Applied Sciences Upper Austria
Department of Mobile Computing
Softwarepark 11, 4232 Hagenberg, Austria
firstname.lastname@fh-hagenberg.at

ABSTRACT

Identifying intentions of users when they launch an application on their smartphone, and understanding which tasks they actually execute, is a key problem in mobile usability analysis. First, knowing which tasks users actually execute is required for calculating common usability metrics such as task efficiency, error rates and effectiveness. Second, understanding how users perform these tasks is important for developers in order to validate designed interaction sequences for tasks (e.g. sequential steps required to successfully perform and complete a task). In this paper, we describe a novel approach for automatically extracting and grouping interaction sequences from users, assigning them to predefined tasks (e.g. writing an email) and visualising them in an intuitive way. Thus, we are able to find out if the designer's intention of how users should perform designed tasks, and how they actually execute them in the field, matches, and where it differs. This allows us to figure out if users find alternate ways of performing certain tasks, which contributes to the application design process. Moreover, if the users' perception of tasks differs from the designer's intention, we lay the foundation for recognising issues users may have while executing them.

Author Keywords

Usability task identification; pattern matching; navigation sequence visualisation;

ACM Classification Keywords

H.5.1. Information Interfaces and Presentation (e.g. HCI): User Interfaces – Evaluation/methodology

I.5.3.Pattern Recognition: Clustering – Similarity measures

General Terms

Human Factors; Design; Measurement.

MobileHCI '14, September 23 – 26 2014, Toronto, ON, Canada.

http://dx.doi.org/10.1145/2628363.2628384

INTRODUCTION

Associating user sequences (e.g. clickstreams) with actual tasks (e.g. writing an email) is of high interest for different fields, such as usability evaluation or e-commerce [19]. Although results for clickstream analysis of web logs (i.e. web farming) are available, there is little knowledge about task identification and interaction sequence mining of mobile applications.

In the course of a pilot study, we have interviewed developers and product managers of seven different companies from three different branches (i.e. automation engineering, m-commerce and telecommunications) about their requirements regarding effective and useful app analytics. It turned out that knowing what users intend to achieve when they use an app (i.e. which task they have in mind), and how they actually execute tasks that have been designed by developers, can be crucial in order to improve the user experience as well as the usability of mobile applications. For the companies we have interviewed, understanding how users execute tasks in different mobile contexts (e.g. activities) is essential for reliable usability studies.

In order to find out how users execute specific tasks, why they probably do not perform them as developers intended them to do, and which of them are more prominent and therefore executed more frequently than others, companies conduct expensive, time consuming controlled experiments to get feedback from end users. Additionally, they also resort to reviews and ratings from app stores. However, both ways have their shortcomings. The results of controlled studies are based on the limited observations examiners are able to make (e.g. figuring out the exact position where users tapped). Moreover, they are limited to a rather small number of participants. Results from the reviews and ratings are based on the subjective impression of users. For example, bad reviews often do not contain enough information about the real circumstances and what actually happened, and most of the users do not give feedback at all. Therefore, a lot of information about what users like, dislike or have problems with is unreachable for the developers.

To get access to objective data from real-world situations and obtain quantitative statements, the usage of an app can be tracked. A common method, which is used by companies like Microsoft for their products, is that users willingly sub-

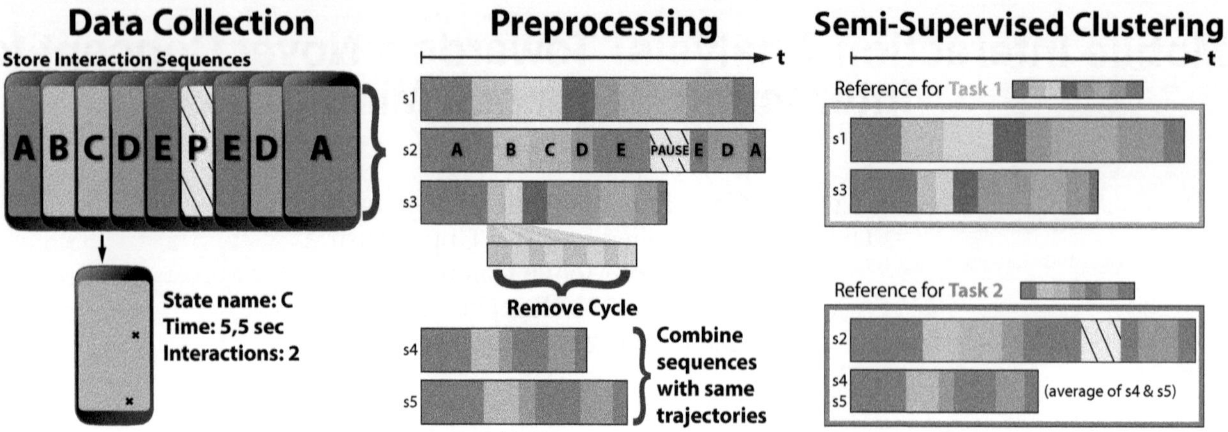

Figure 1. Illustrates the different stages of the proposed interaction sequence mining approach. First, user interaction sequences – i.e. ordered lists of UI states in mobile applications (e.g. page visits or dialogues popping up on a certain screen) triggered by user events (e.g. button clicks or long press gestures) – are collected from real users in the field. Second, the sequences are preprocessed by eliminating cycles and combining equal sequences. Finally, the sequences are grouped using a semi-supervised clustering approach and associated with reference tasks (e.g. writing an email).

mit their usage data (e.g. the Customer Experience Improvement Program for Microsoft Office). With this data available, developers can re-enact the actions of the users and can determine which task was executed.

Mapping tracked data to tasks for a large number of users is possible, but very time consuming if it needs to be done by a human. Based on logged interaction sequences, which contain information on visited states (e.g. a certain page), such as the amount of time that was spent in each state and the number of registered interactions (i.e. user events) in each state, we accomplished to automatically group interaction sequences based on their similarity (i.e. clustering) and to assign them to predefined reference tasks (i.e. classification), which is outlined in Fig. 1. Additionally, we describe in short how to visually prepare collected and clustered interaction sequences to allow designers to draw conclusions on their users' usage behaviour.

RELATED WORK

In web analytics, a lot of research has been done in the field of clickstream analysis. Web clickstream data is routinely collected to study how users browse the web or use a service. Shen et al. [19] point out that the ability to recognise and summarise user behaviour patterns from such data can be highly important for e-commerce companies in order to foresee potential user events (i.e. recommendation system) by logging how users click through a web page. Just like Zhang et al. [27], Shen et al. propose the usage of Markov Models in order to find the most probable path users will follow in accordance to previous user input, as well as the most probable user event at a certain time. Although Markov Models turn out to be very efficient for recommendation systems, we propose a different approach for interaction sequence mining, as we do not want to foresee possible future interaction sequences, but assign known interaction sequences to reference tasks to allow a comparison between the designers' perception of how users should perform a task and how users actually execute it in the field.

A different approach for clickstream analysis is presented by Ting et al. [23], who propose to use Continuous Common Subsequences in order to find unexpected browsing behaviours in clickstream data. Just like for the approach presented in this paper, expected routes have to be extracted beforehand. In contrast to the presented approach, Ting et al. transform these expected routes (i.e. common subsequences) into rules, which can be used to identify interaction sequences that do not match. Thus, this solution is only capable of finding browsing behaviours that do not match pre-defined rules. We, on the other hand, are able to identify and group interesting interaction sequences that do not completely match a specific reference task as well.

The most promising related approach is presented by Banerjee et al. [3], who try to associate user clickstreams on the web with certain tasks (i.e. buying a product on Amazon). Therefore, they propose to use a similar approach like the one presented in this paper. They record the time spent between clicks and use this information instead of the actual link trajectory for classification. As it turns out, classification solely based on time metrics is not sufficient in order to produce accurate assumptions regarding the belonging of clickstreams to a specific task. As a consequence, they manually associate hyperlinks and pages with semantic meanings (i.e. labels) and a probability beforehand. For example, it is very likely that users are in the process of buying a product, if they visit their shopping carts. In contrast to Banerjee et al., we do not need to associate a semantic meaning with a certain state or user event beforehand by introducing additional metrics.

Generally, clickstream analysis or web farming is important for predicting user behaviour such as personalizing websites, preloading content, creating recommendations or sorting search results [5, 6, 21, 10]. In contrast, we support task identification (i.e. clustering) to analyse and compare different interaction sequences collected from real users. Thus, we are able to find out which tasks users actually execute and how they differ from the developers' intention. This has been investigated by Coman et al. [8] in the context of automatically identifying different tasks of a software development session (e.g. clean, build, run). In case of Coman, task-related subsections as well as a rough approximation of their position in a development session have to be manually predefined. In contrast, the predefined tasks required for our semi-supervised clustering process can be recorded by actually using the application. Thus, it is possible to record new reference tasks on the fly without changing the application's source code.

For visualising the tracked data and the results of the analysis process, we examined visualisation techniques for finding patterns and interesting structures within sequences as well as for being able to compare several sequences. Church et al. introduced *Dotplots* which are used to find structures and compare similarities in text or source code [7]. Interesting structures can be found in form of diagonals, squares and texture within the dotplots. Wattenberg et al. [25] criticised that dotplots can get confusing when applied to strings with frequent repeated substrings, which would be a problem for our dataset as well. Wattenbergs' *Arc Diagrams* scale efficiently for strings with many repeating instances. Unfortunately for representing and comparing several sequences arc diagrams do not scale well.

Lastly, Sankey Diagrams were considered for displaying our results. As mentioned by Riehmann et al., Sankey diagrams are traditionally used for visualizing a flow of energy or material in networks and processes [18]. Riehmanns' *Interactive Sankey Diagrams* should facilitate the exploration of complex energy flows. Sankey diagrams support investigation of energy distribution, finding energy losses and the allocation of what energy is used for which purpose. These questions can easily be transferred to our field of displaying interaction sequences: interaction distribution, locating the places where users cancel an interaction sequence (i.e. task) and determining what interactions lead to the execution of a specific task. Therefore, we decided to represent the tracked data and the results of the analysis process with a Sankey based visualisation. As the presented visualisation is not focus of this paper, only an internal evaluation within our department has been performed by now.

SEQUENCE MINING

In order to extract user interaction sequences produced by real users in the field, and to assign them to predefined reference tasks, we propose a multi-stage process. The process consists of two preprocessing steps to speed up the clustering process on the one hand, and to make it more robust against errors on the other hand. Collected user interaction sequences are clustered by different similarity estimates, which are calculated between the collected sequences and the predefined reference tasks. For the calculation of these estimates, the sequence trajectories as well as the number of interactions and the amount of time spent in the different states are used. This section outlines how each part of the presented approach works.

Data Collection

User interaction sequences are collected for each session (i.e. between each start and stop of an application) and each user with the interaction logging framework presented in [13]. An interaction sequence basically consists of a sequential arrangement of states. The definition of states by annotating source code is mainly up to the developers' decision. However, in most situations, a state will be defined as a certain visual representation (e.g. page or screen), which is valid under a defined context. For example, one possible state in the Facebook app would be the *news feed* state. Although the screen appearance might change due to dynamic input (e.g. new status posts), the state will stay the same because this input is related to the same contextual information, namely status posts. Regarding data collection, each state is augmented with the time users spend actively in it, as well as the interactions (e.g. button clicks, text field input, gestures, etc.) that take place on the associated screen. External influences, such as interrupts by incoming voice calls or turning off the display, are recognised automatically and marked as *pause interval* states within interaction sequences (see Fig. 2).

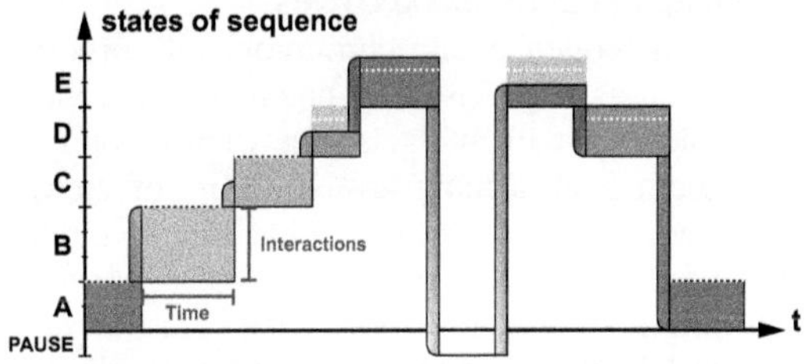

Figure 2. Illustrates a single interaction sequence. Different states are printed in different colors, their length indicates the time spent in these states, their height stands for the number of interactions that took place while the node has been active.

Preprocessing

Because interaction sequences are potentially collected by thousands of different users, the proposed solution requires certain preprocessing steps for the following reasons:

- It is very likely that common interaction sequences occur multiple times. Thus, equal interaction sequences (i.e. sequences that share the exact same trajectory) can be merged, in which case the logged user interactions and times in states are averaged to be more robust against outliers. As a result, we can assume that classification accuracy improves the more often a certain interaction sequence occurs. In addition, we are also capable of identifying obviously more important user sequences, which are probably related to a specific task and to separate them from random, rarely occurring interaction sequences.

- Interaction sequences can consist of sub-sequences that are repeated multiple times (e.g. switching back and forth between state A and B $\rightarrow$ ABABAB). We assume that repeating subsequences, which share the same trajectory, does not change the contextual meaning of a sequence. For example, no matter how often a specific setting in an app is changed, it refers to changing this specific setting (e.g. ABABAB $\equiv$ (AB)*).

Merging Sequences with Equal Trajectory

As mentioned above, merging interaction sequences that share the same trajectory (e.g. $a = b = ABC$), is done for multiple reasons. First of all, it is possible to rank all collected user sequences according to their prominence (i.e. number of occurrences). Second, collected session times and user interactions, such as button clicks, can be averaged on the basis of datasets from many different users, which will make the sequence more robust against outliers for similarity estimation and clustering. Third, it will improve the runtime performance as it tremendously reduces the number of sequences that have to be compared to reference sequences in terms of their similarity.

Based on unique hash values for the trajectories of each interaction sequence, the list of all collected sequences can be sorted. As a result, all interaction sequences with the exact same trajectories, and thus sharing the same hash value, are grouped together. The count for each unique hash value can be determined by iterating over the entire list of interaction sequences.

Extracting and Substituting Cycles

Interaction sequences are chronologically ordered chains of states, such as page visits, or changes in the view hierarchy by interactions with widgets (e.g. dialog popup). By looking at them from a more abstract point of view, interaction sequences can be interpreted as character text, where each sequence represents a single word (e.g. $MainMenu = A$). Each single state (e.g. a page visit) can be seen as a single literal in the character text. As a result, it is possible to measure the similarity between two interaction sequences based on their string similarity, which is an essential and well-researched process in biomedical engineering and other fields [24].

By looking at collected interaction sequences of an Android app for the first time, we encountered that certain interaction subsequences can occur multiple times within the same sequence. Subsequences that do not add additional semantic or contextual information to the interaction sequence (e.g. changing the same setting over and over again) and which are repeated in immediate succession, represent cycles. As string similarity methods heavily depend on the trajectory of the strings to be compared, and because they are often based on the number of edit operations to change one sequence into another, cycles inside interaction sequences can have a negative input on the result quality of the presented approach [14, 16, 20]. However, as these cycles are just recurrences of one and the same interaction subsequence, finding repeating subsequences inside an interaction sequence can be broken down to locating specific character strings embedded in character text. This can be efficiently represented with regular expressions [22].

Baeza-Yates et al. presented an algorithm for searching regular expressions in sub-linear time with suffix trees [2]. In computer science, suffix trees are compressed digital trees, containing all suffixes of a given text as keys and their positions as values [11] (see Fig. 3). Suffix trees can also be used to find all occurrences z of the patterns $P_1 ... P_n$ of a total length m as substrings [12]. Although constructing a suffix tree can be memory intense for larger texts (e.g. news paper articles), we consider them appropriate in order to find and count the occurrence of each subsequence within a given interaction sequence, because interaction sequences consist of a rather small number of variables.

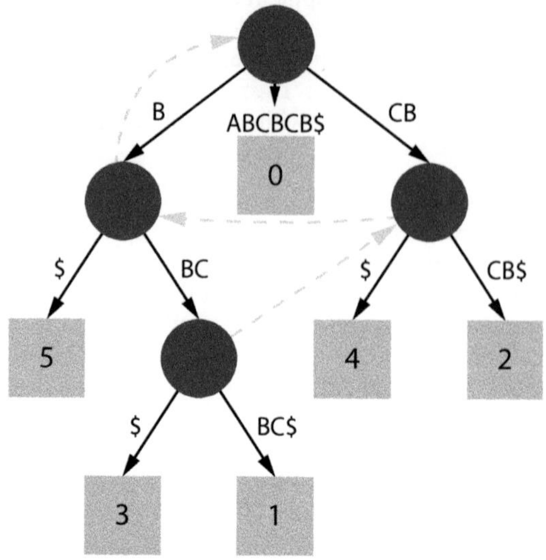

Figure 3. Simplified (i.e. compressed) suffix tree for the interaction sequence ABCBCB. Each subsequence is terminated by a terminal symbol (i.e. $). Each of the possible 6 suffixes (B$, CB$, BCB$, CBCB$, BCBCB$ and ABCBCB$) correspond to a path from the root node to a leaf, which are represented as boxes in the figure. The leaves store the actual start position of the suffix within the sequence. The dashed links are suffix links, which are used to construct the suffix tree.

By traversing the suffix tree, we can count how often a certain interaction subsequence appears inside the tree. Therefore, the algorithm counts how often a node (e.g. B, CB, BC, etc.) or subtree (e.g. BCB, CBCB, etc.) with a certain key is visited during the traversal. As a result, we can receive a list of interaction subsequences with their corresponding positions in the provided sequence, whose string length is greater than 1 and which appear more than once in the sequence.

In order to identify certain suffixes being cycled, the suffix positions, which are stored in leaves of the suffix tree, can be used. Thus, we iterate over all found suffix tree nodes and compare their positions based on the condition

$$s(i)_{idx} == s(i-1)_{idx} + len(s(i-1)) \qquad (1)$$

where $s(i)_{idx}$ is the start position of the current suffix and $len(s(i-1))$ the end position of the previous suffix within the sequence. It does not matter which of the subsequences is processed first, as the outcome will be the same for all possible situations (i.e. A(BC)*B ≡ ABCB and AB(CB)* ≡ ABCB). The information regarding node attributes, such as the number of interactions or session time, from eliminated cycles is not thrown away, but taken into account as averaged values for the regular expressions (i.e. BCBCBC ≡ (BC)*). In advance, cycle optimisation turns out to be a very promising preprocessing step, which will improve the result quality for the clustering process. To back these assumptions, we would like to refer to the results from our study as shown in Fig. 10, which demonstrates representatively for all metrics we investigated that the result quality is significantly higher if cycle optimization is applied.

Semi-Supervised Clustering of User Sequences

As outlined in the introduction of this section, clustering user interaction sequences by their contextual meaning (e.g. writing an email, buying a ticket, etc.) requires some sort of supervision to partition sequences, which share the same task, into one cluster, because it is not necessarily guaranteed that just the same classes of sequences (i.e. tasks) are grouped together. In contrast to Basu [4] and Finley et al. [9] however, the proposed approach does not require noticeable large training data sets to produce accurate results. For the presented approach, supervision can be reduced to predefining reference tasks, which partly turns the clustering problem into a classification problem [1]. These reference tasks can be created by app designers, because they think about and define how tasks are planned to be executed by users for their apps.

Similarity Estimation

In order to be able to decide which sequences should be clustered together and classified as a certain task, the similarity between these sequences and the reference tasks has to be determined. Therefore, we propose a combined similarity measure based on the three different and independent attributes (i) trajectory, (ii) time and (iii) number of interactions, which are used in the following in order to compute the similarity between reference tasks and user sequences.

String Similarity

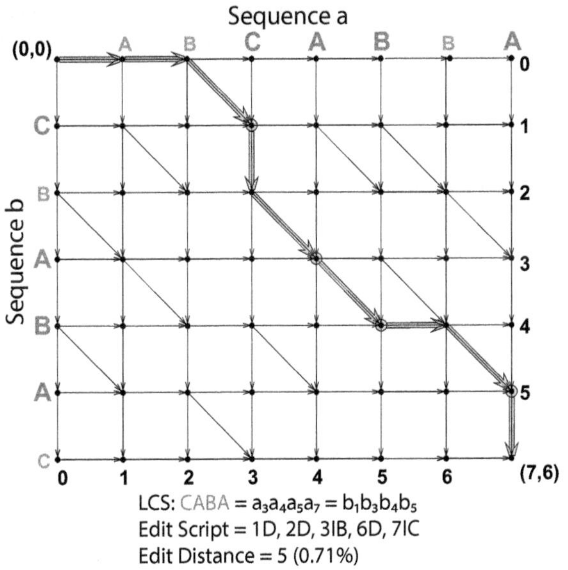

Figure 4. Edit graph illustrating the process of creating the edit script, and in the following the edit distance, for two different sequences. Source: [15]

As already mentioned, it is possible to treat interaction sequences as character text, where each state of the sequence is seen as a single literal. Finding the similarity based on the trajectory of a string is strongly related to finding DNA sequences in biomedical engineering.

One of the most common approaches there is to compare strings based on their *longest common subsequence (LCS)*. An LCS of two strings is a subsequence of maximal length that appears in both strings. The Levensthein (LV) distance (i.e. edit distance), which is defined as the number of editing steps (insert, delete or replace) required in passing from one string to the other, is a common measure for the similarity of two string based on their LCS [17].

Fig. 4 illustrates, how edit graphs can be used to calculate the similarity between two sequences based on their LCS. The edit script describes the number of edit operations required to transform one sequence (a) into another (b). The number of edit operations itself is defined as edit costs. In the graph, delete operations D are represented by horizontal steps, insert operations I are shown as vertical steps. A normalised score describing the similarity of the two paths can be described as

$$sim_{LV}(a,b) = 1 - \frac{n}{max(len_a, len_b)} = [0...1] \quad (2)$$

where n is the number of edit operations (i.e. insert, delete, replace) to change sequence a to sequence b and len_a and len_b are their lengths (i.e. total number of states). The following listing shows some simple examples for string similarities based on the edit distance:

$$sim_{LV}(ABC, ABC) = 1 - \frac{0}{max(3,3)} = 1.00 \quad (3)$$

$$sim_{LV}(ABC, ADC) = 1 - \frac{1}{max(3,3)} = 0.\overline{66} \quad (4)$$

$$sim_{LV}(ABC, AEF) = 1 - \frac{2}{max(3,3)} = 0.\overline{33} \quad (5)$$

One common problem with the Levensthein distance is that each edit operation is equally expensive. Unweighted edit costs can especially be a problem in long sequences, because mutations within a sequence can add too much noise to allow a meaningful comparison of those regions. As a result, the approach has to be modified in order to be able to obtain correct alignments in regions of low similarity between distantly related sequences. Algorithms to solve this issue have been proposed by Needleman et al. [16] and Smith et al. [20]. Both propose a solution for biological sequence comparison (i.e. protein and nucleotide sequences) based on dynamic programming. In contrast to Needleman, the algorithm proposed by Smith covers parts of the sequences and thus finds the best local alignment between two sequences instead of the best global alignment with respect to a scoring system (i.e. weight matrix) being used:

$$sim_{LV}(ABC, ABDEDFDC) = 0.37 \quad (6)$$

$$sim_{NW}(ABC, ABDEDFDC) = 0.56 \quad (7)$$

$$sim_{SW}(ABC, ABDEDFDC) = 0.\overline{66} \quad (8)$$

In contrast to the Levensthein distance (LV), Needleman-Wunsch (NW) as well as Smith-Waterman (SW) produce a much higher similarity score, as they are able to identify the subsequence $DEDFD$ as one linked delete operation. Thus, the edit costs for the whole substring are 1 instead of 5

Time Similarity

Although string similarity achieves good results per se, it can become unstable in case of shorter sequences (e.g. ABC and ABD). As all presented string similarity algorithms would return a similarity score of 0.66 for $sim(ABC, ABD)$, it is uncertain whether a single different state makes a new task out of it or not.

A different approach is presented by Banerjee et al. [3], who propose similarity estimation based on session times. As similarity measures solely based on time turn out to be too inaccurate for sequence clustering, we propose to use the similarity between sequences (a and b from different users) based on the averaged time T users spent in their LCS (with a length of n states) in addition to string similarities:

$$sim_{TIME}(a,b) = \frac{1}{n}\sum_{i=1}^{n}\frac{min(T^a_{LCS(i)}, T^b_{LCS(i)})}{max(T^a_{LCS(i)}, T^b_{LCS(i)})} \quad (9)$$

where $LCS(i)$ represents a single state in the LCS at position i and n is the number of total states in the LCS.

LCS Weight Estimation

In addition to similarity estimates, interaction sequences contain information that can be used in order to improve the reliability of the clustering process [3]. In this case, we will show how it can be used as additional, independent feature to enhance the result quality. Therefore, we propose to measure the impact or weight of the LCS of a sequence in relation to the entire sequence based on the time users spent in each state as well as the number of interactions that were executed within each state. As a consequence, it will be possible to rate the impact of an LCS. The longer the LCS, the more impact it has on the clustering process. The weight of the overlapping region of two sequences can be computed by

$$imp(a,b) = \sqrt{\frac{T^a_{LCS}}{T^a}\cdot\frac{T^b_{LCS}}{T^b}}\cdot\sqrt{\frac{I^a_{LCS}}{I^a}\cdot\frac{I^b_{LCS}}{I^b}} \quad (10)$$

where T refers to the total time, and I to the total number of interactions, users spent within a sequence (i.e. session time). T_{LCS} is the amount of time and I_{LCS} the number of interactions users spent in the LCS. As it is assumed that both sequences are not independent of each other (they share the same LCS), the geometric mean instead of the arithmetic mean is used in order to compute the average weight of both sequences.

We apply the same formula to the number of interactions to show how many interactions (e.g. button clicks) are performed in the LCS in relation to the total sequence. For example, the LCS for the two sequences $a = A_2B_5C_7D_4E_3F_5$ and $b = A_7C_5G_2H_3E_2F_2$, where the indices stand for the interactions in each state, is $ACEF$. Using the formula above, we get the following interaction weight:

$$imp(a,b) = \sqrt{\frac{17}{26}\cdot\frac{16}{21}} \approx 0.71 \quad (11)$$

Clustering and Classification

Based on the similarity and weight estimates, we compute a compound score representing the overall similarity between the collected user sequences and each predefined reference task. The single scores are treated as independent measures in the range of [0...1] for a specific feature. Therefore, we can compute the compound score by plain multiplication of the similarity measures. The pair with the highest similarity is seen as the most-likely positive match. However, it cannot be guaranteed that a most-likely match always indicates the correct cluster. For example, users do not always perform a certain task when they interact with an application. Especially, when users start using an app, a learning phase, where they explore the application without a specific aim, needs to be taken into account. Moreover, it is possible that users coincidently identify new tasks, which have not been predefined by designers.

As a consequence, a threshold is required in order to allow to sort out user interaction sequences, which cannot be associated with a cluster unambiguously. This threshold will be used in order to eliminate sequences which would have been associated with a wrong cluster otherwise (i.e. false positives). However, thresholding is a tricky task, as an optimal threshold cannot be calculated automatically without using training data (i.e. supervised clustering). If the threshold is set too low, invalid sequences (e.g. random paths) will be added to the cluster with the highest similarity. If it is set too high, valid sequences, which otherwise would have been associated with the correct cluster, will be marked as "unknown" (i.e. false negative). Thus, the overall goal of the clustering process is to maximise the number of true positive results by minimizing the false positives at the same time. Based on the experiments we conducted for threshold estimation, we achieved good results with the following target function

$$f(x) = 0.7\cdot TP - 0.25\cdot FP - 0.05\cdot FN \quad (12)$$

where TP is the number of true positives, FP the number of false positives and FN the number of false negatives. The weight for false positives is also considered being higher, because a higher number of false positives will introduce noise to clusters.

SEQUENCE VISUALISATION

For displaying the tracked interaction sequences and the results of the semi-supervised clustering, we created a visualisation which enables app developers to take a look at the different ways how the users accomplished certain tasks. It is possible to compare different sequences, all associated with a certain task, solely based on their state visits or in combination with either the time spent or the number of interactions happened on each state. To visualise how users navigate through an app, we chose a visualisation based on Sankey diagrams, which is embedded in a web application (see Fig. 5, 6 and 7). The implementation of the visualisation builds on Kunal Bhallas'[1] d3[2] implementation of Sankey diagrams with the ability of displaying loop-backs. Fig. 5 shows 26 sequences assigned to one task, where each state (e.g. A, B or C) is represented as a (rectangular) node and each sequence

[1] `https://github.com/kunalb/`

[2] `http://d3js.org/`

(e.g. ABC, ABAC etc.) as the connecting paths through several nodes. The height of each node represents how often a state was activated/visited (e.g. A was visited 40 times). The width of a path connecting two states indicates how often the state at the end of the path was activated from the state at the beginning of the path.

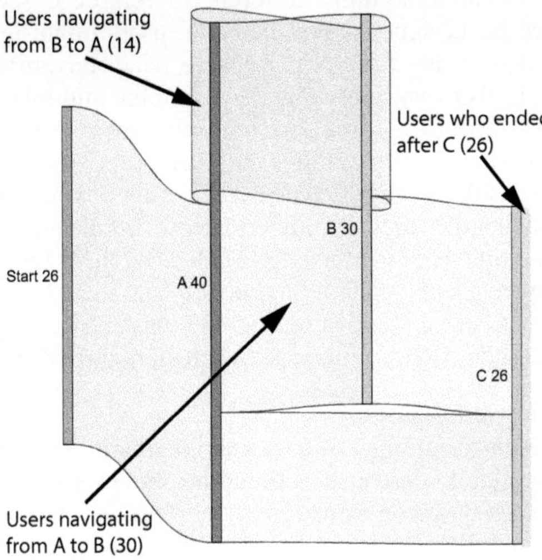

Figure 5. Visualisation of 26 sequences assigned to one task (predefined reference ABC) in different variations: AC, ABC, ABAC, ABABC.

Based on the nature of Sankey diagrams, the number of activations of a state (incoming paths, left side) has to be the same as the number of activations from a state (outgoing paths, right side). Inspired by Googles Flow Visualisation[3], we decided to add a path from the last node of the sequence leading nowhere, when a sequence ends (so called dropouts, as seen in Fig. 5 at the right side of node C).

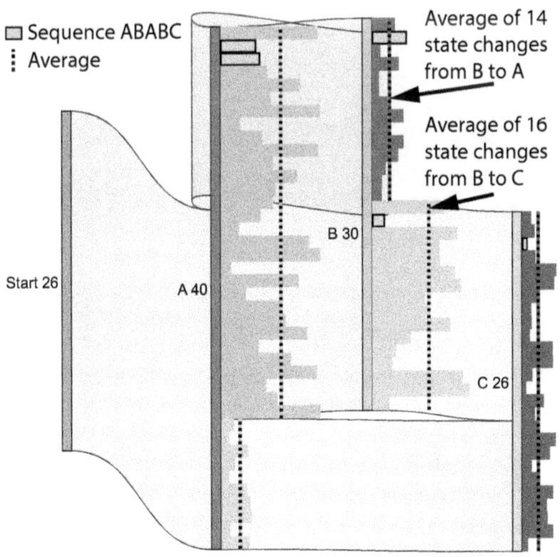

Figure 6. Visualisation of 26 sequences augmented with the time spent at each of the 96 state visits. By hovering over a state of a sequence (here ABABC), all corresponding states are highlighted. Additionally, the average times of the existing state changes are indicated by a vertical dashed line.

[3]`https://support.google.com/analytics/topic/2472754`

Additionally to the aggregated information of how often a certain node was visited and how the users navigated through the app, each single state visit is displayed as a horizontal bar next to its corresponding node. The length of the bar indicates either the number of interactions happened at this state or the time the user spent on it, depending on the viewers choice. Fig. 6 shows the same data as seen in Fig. 5 with all state visits represented as bars and one sequence (ABABC) highlighted. In this example, the bars are displayed in their chronological order.Vertical black dashed lines, where the intervals are filled with the same color as the target state, indicate the averaged current displayed values (in Fig. 6 the time spent at each state).

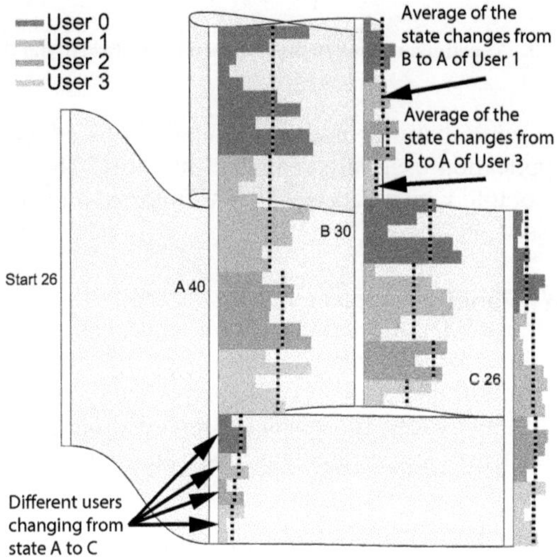

Figure 7. Visualisation of 26 sequences, grouped by their user and all executing the same task. Additionally, the average times of the existing state changes of each user are displayed as vertical dashed lines.

The viewer can change the representation from displaying common state changes (as seen in Fig. 5 and 6) to display grouped users or tasks. The size of the nodes and paths is not affected by this choice, only the arrangement of the horizontal bars. Fig. 7 again shows the same data as before, but with dissimilar users indicated by different colors of the relevant bars. The viewer has another two options when it comes to displaying the averaged values: First, as seen in Fig. 7, the average is obtained over each state change of the same user, second, it will be further separated between the different tasks (e.g. the average of User 0 changing from state A to B while performing Task 2).

EVALUATION

Participants

We conducted a study based on user interaction sequences, collected from real, unbiased users in the field, in order to find out how well the proposed clustering concept performs on user task classification. Therefore, we integrated the proposed data collection framework into an Android application for buying public transport tickets. Over a period of two weeks, we collected 500 interaction sequences from 150 arbitrarily selected, anonymous users, who were not instructed on how to use the application. The participants were notified and

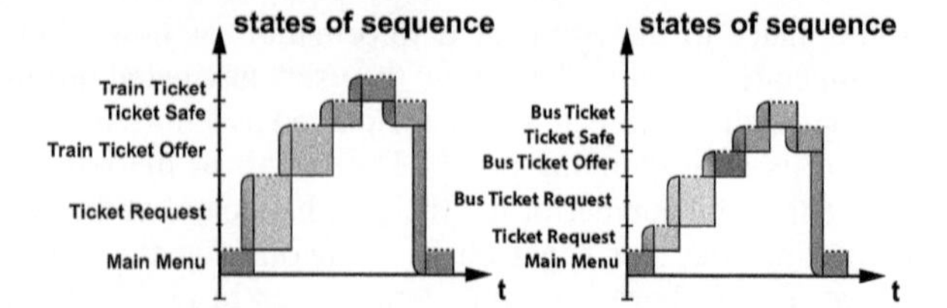

Figure 8. Predefined reference task for ordering a bus and a train ticket.

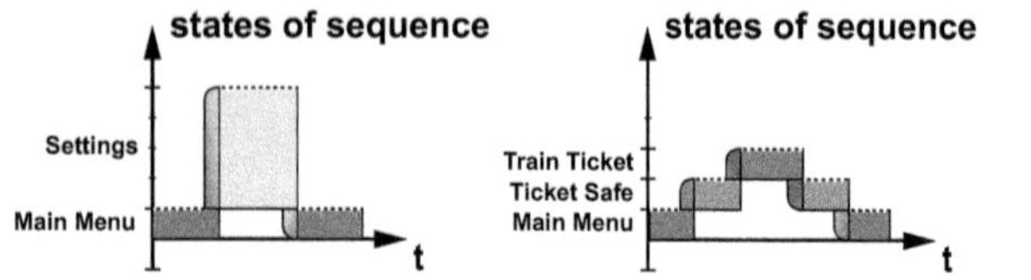

Figure 9. Predefined reference task for settings and verifying the ticket.

had to agree that user interaction data will be collected during application usage for scientific purposes. However they were not told which data exactly we collected and how it was processed.

Study Design

From these 500 collected interaction sequences, we extracted 200 unique paths by merging those sequences that share the exact same trajectories. For the experiment, we identified four different tasks, for which we recorded optimal interaction sequences each including time and number of interactions:

- **Order Train Ticket:** Users can order a train ticket. They have to select departure and destination station, number of persons (i.e. adults and children) and request an offer. Once an offer is received, the user can select either to pay the full ticket price or to get a discount based on a membership card. If the purchase order is confirmed, users get their ticket which will be displayed immediately. Alternatively, users can select to store a certain ticket request in their favourites. In this case, they can skip the ticket request procedure and will receive an offer directly.
- **Order Bus Ticket:** Users can order bus tickets for short-distance traffic in Austria's provincial capitals. Therefore, they have to select a city and the number of tickets they want to order. Additionally, they can choose between single and day tickets. After they received an offer, they can simply accept or refuse it. If users accept, they receive a short-distance traffic ticket, which will be displayed immediately.
- **Change Settings:** Users can predefine some settings for the ticket purchase process. They can for example predefine an id for memberships or select the payment service.
- **Verify Tickets:** Users can access a so-called ticket safe in order to have tickets verified by ticket inspectors. Therefore they can select any ticket (i.e. bus or train) from a list.

In order to verify clustering and classification results, we manually assigned the correct task labels (e.g. Order Bus Ticket) to all 500 interaction sequences as meta information. User sequences that we could not explicitly identify and associate with tasks (e.g. random, explorative paths) were labelled as "unknown", but were left in the test data set as noise to find out if they are sorted out accordingly by the algorithm.

Basically, user sequences – although executing a predefined task – might look quite different to reference sequences recorded by designers. For example, users might leave the application at any time (e.g. because of an incoming voice call). It is also very likely that they combine multiple tasks or that they repeat the same task multiple times. For example, they first change their settings and then order a ticket or they order a bus ticket after they ordered a train ticket. Thus, one of the main goals of this study is to show that the proposed solution is capable of dealing with such differences by ensuring that sequences that cannot be uniquely associated with a reference path are not added to a wrong cluster, or by applying preprocessing steps to increase the clustering robustness.

Results and Findings

The presented findings of the experiment are twofold. First, we were able to derive an optimal threshold for the provided test data set based on Equation 12 by repeating the clustering process for all possible thresholds in the range of 0.0 to 1.0 in steps of 0.05. Second, the accuracy for each possible combination of the proposed similarity measures was estimated for any threshold.

Threshold Determination

In order to provide accurate results for each possible combination of the proposed similarity measures, we determined the optimal threshold by exhaustively finding the optimal threshold for a manually classified subset.

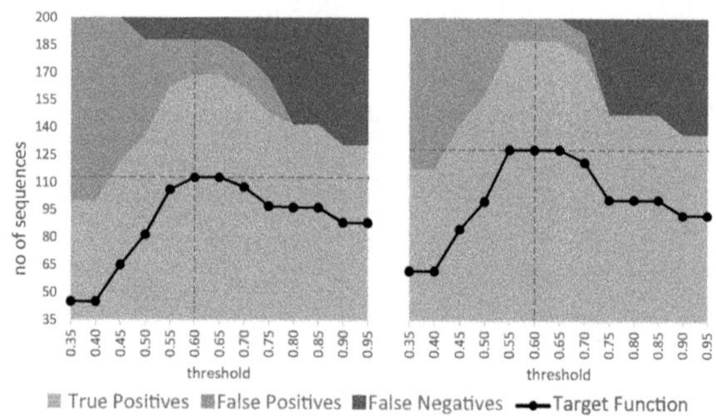

Figure 10. Clustering results with (right) and without (left) cycle optimisation based on string similarity only.

Fig. 10 shows the clustering result for the string similarity measure, where it is clearly visible that a better result (i.e. more true positives) can be achieved if cycle optimisation is used during preprocessing. In this case, the optimal threshold is 0.60, therefore Fig. 10 only shows a range around this values.

Similarity Estimation Accuracy

By determining the optimal threshold for each combination of the proposed similarity measures, we can calculate the accuracy for each of these combinations (see Table 1). In order to show how the proposed measures perform under the worst case, cycle optimisation was not used during the preprocessing. The most promising related approach by Banerjee et al. [3], who used clickstream data from ordering articles in a webshop which is very similar to our ticketing application, achieved 66.67% of correctly clustered user sequences, however 33.33% of all sequences were associated with a wrong cluster. Banerjees' combined score only consists of the product of time similarity and time weight (see Table 1, orange row).

SS = String Similarity TS = Time Similarity
LWT = Time Weight LWI = Interaction Weight

SS	TS	LWT	LWI	TP	FP	FN
√	√	√	√	94.44%	0.00%	5.56%
√	√	√		72.22%	0.00%	27.78%
√	√		√	88.89%	0.00%	11.11%
√		√	√	77.78%	11.11%	11.11%
√		√	√	89.89%	0.00%	11.11%
√		√		83.33%	0.00%	16.67%
√			√	88.89%	5.56%	5.56%
√				88.89%	5.56%	5.56%
	√	√	√	83.33%	0.00%	16.67%
	√	√		66.67%	33.33%	0.00%
	√		√	77.78%	22.22%	0.00%
	√			50.00%	0.00%	50.00%
		√	√	88.89%	5.56%	5.56%
		√		88.89%	5.56%	5.56%
			√	83.33%	5.56%	11.11%

Table 1. Shows the clustering results for each possible combination of the proposed similarity measures, based on the optimal threshold for each combination (result of combined score of Banerjee et al. in orange).

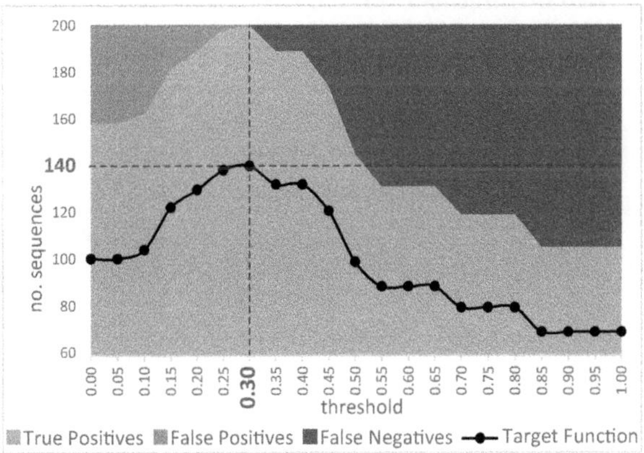

Figure 11. Clustering result by combining all four proposed similarity measures with cycle optimisation.

The best result is achieved by combining all four proposed similarity measures. In this case 94.44% of all sequences are clustered correctly. The remaining 5.56% of the sequences are labelled as "unknown" by mistake (i.e. false negatives). However, there are not any sequences that are associated with a wrong cluster (i.e. false positives). As shown in Fig. 11, by activating cycle optimisation as a preprocessing step, all user interaction sequences are clustered correctly.

CONCLUSION AND FUTURE WORK

In this paper, we presented a novel approach for user interaction sequence mining based on similarity measures that can be used in order to compare user-generated interaction sequences to predefined reference tasks. First, we showed how to preprocess collected user interaction sequences in order to increase the performance, and to make the clustering process more robust, by identifying and substituting cycles (i.e. repeated subsequences) within sequences. Second, we demonstrated how to compare collected interaction sequences with predefined reference tasks based on their trajectory (i.e. string similarity) and averaged session times. Additionally, we showed how further metrics (i.e. session time and interactions) can be used in order to calculate the weight of the longest common subsequence of interactions sequences sequence and their potential reference tasks.

In contrast to [3], we showed that it is not necessary to manually augment certain states with meta information such as category labels in order to correctly assign interaction sequences to the correct tasks.

Based on interaction sequences we collected from a ticketing application from real, unbiased users in the field, we showed that the presented approach works well for wizard type applications, where users are guided and the navigation the interaction flow (i.e. possible interaction sequences) is restricted. Based on the presented related work, which already achieved acceptable solutions in the web domain, we assume that the presented approach will also achieve valid results with other types of mobile applications (e.g. games). However, this is subject to future work, and currently work in progress.

In addition, we will further investigate thresholding in order to enhance the accuracy for applications with more degrees of freedom. Therefore, we will search for a possibility to include unsupervised feature weighting (i.e. Baysian feature weighting) such as proposed by Huang et al. [26].

Moreover, we are searching for a solution to get rid of the necessity for predefined tasks, which can probably be achieved with affinity propagation clustering.

Using the results of the clustering process, we are able to compare differences of how users execute one task. The presented visualisation supports the identification of interesting sequences (i.e. users who needed significant longer or triggered essential more interactions than the designer intended to execute a task), however still needs to be evaluated and compared with existing visualisations and analysis tools.

ACKNOWLEDGMENTS

The research presented is conducted within the Austrian project "AUToMAte – Automatic Usability Testing of Mobile Applications" funded by the Austrian Research Promotion Agency (FFG) under contract number 839094.

REFERENCES

1. Al-Harbi, S. H., and Rayward-Smith, V. J. Adapting k-means for supervised clustering. *Applied Intelligence 24*, 3 (June 2006), 219–226.

2. Baeza-Yates, R. A., and Gonnet, G. H. Fast text searching for regular expressions or automaton searching on tries. *J. ACM 43*, 6 (Nov. 1996), 915–936.
3. Banerjee, A., and Ghosh, J. Clickstream clustering using weighted longest common subsequences. In *In Proceedings of the Web Mining Workshop at the 1st SIAM Conference on Data Mining* (2001), 33–40.
4. Basu, S. *Semi-supervised Clustering: Probabilistic Models, Algorithms and Experiments*. PhD thesis, University of Texas at Austin, 2005.
5. Belkin, N. J. Helping people find what they don't know. *Commun. ACM 43*, 8 (Aug. 2000), 58–61.
6. Chi, E. H., Pirolli, P., and Pitkow, J. The scent of a site: A system for analyzing and predicting information scent, usage, and usability of a web site. In *Proceedings of the SIGCHI Conference on Human Factors in Computing Systems*, CHI '00, ACM (New York, NY, USA, 2000), 161–168.
7. Church, K. W., and Helfman, J. I. Dotplot: A program for exploring self-similarity in millions of lines for text and code. *Journal of American Statistical Association, Institute for Mathematical Statistics and Interface Foundations of North America 2*, 2 (June 1993), 153–174.
8. Coman, I., and Sillitti, A. Automated identification of tasks in development sessions. In *Program Comprehension, 2008. ICPC 2008. The 16th IEEE International Conference on* (June 2008), 212–217.
9. Finley, T., and Joachims, T. Supervised k-means clustering. Tech. rep., Department of Computer Science Cornell University, Ithaca, NY, USA, February 2008.
10. Fu, Y., Fu, H., and Au, P. An integration approach of data mining with web cache pre-fetching. In *Parallel and Distributed Processing and Applications*, J. Cao, L. Yang, M. Guo, and F. Lau, Eds., vol. 3358 of *Lecture Notes in Computer Science*. Springer Berlin Heidelberg, 2005, 59–63.
11. Giegerich, R., and Kurtz, S. From ukkonen to mccreight and weiner: A unifying view of linear-time suffix tree construction. *Algorithmica 19* (1997), 331–353.
12. Gusfield, D. *Algorithms on Strings, Trees, and Sequences: Computer Science and Computational Biology*. Cambridge University Press, New York, NY, USA, 1997, 123.
13. Lettner, F., and Holzmann, C. Automated and unsupervised user interaction logging as basis for usability evaluation of mobile applications. In *Proceedings of the 10th International Conference on Advances in Mobile Computing & Multimedia*, MoMM '12, ACM (New York, NY, USA, 2012), 118–127.
14. Levenshtein, V. Binary Codes Capable of Correcting Deletions, Insertions and Reversals. *Soviet Physics Doklady 10* (1966), 707.
15. Myers, E. W. An O(ND) difference algorithm and its variations. *Algorithmica 1* (1986), 251–266.
16. Needleman, S. B., and Wunsch, C. D. A general method applicable to the search for similarities in the amino acid sequence of two proteins. *Journal of Molecular Biology 48*, 3 (Mar. 1970), 443–453.
17. Paterson, M., and Dank, V. Longest common subsequences. In *Mathematical Foundations of Computer Science 1994*, I. Prvara, B. Rovan, and P. Ruzika, Eds., vol. 841 of *Lecture Notes in Computer Science*. Springer Berlin Heidelberg, 1994, 127–142.
18. Riehmann, P., Hanfler, M., and Froehlich, B. Interactive sankey diagrams. In *IEEE Symposium on Information Visualization. INFOVIS 2005.* (2005), 233–240.
19. Shen, Z., Wei, J., Ma, K.-L., and Sundaresan, N. Visual cluster exploration of web clickstream data. In *Proceedings of the 2012 IEEE Conference on Visual Analytics Science and Technology (VAST)*, VAST '12, IEEE Computer Society (Washington, DC, USA, 2012), 3–12.
20. Smith, T. F., and Waterman, M. S. Identification of common molecular subsequences. *Journal of molecular biology 147*, 1 (Mar. 1981), 195–197.
21. Spiliopoulou, M. Web usage mining for web site evaluation. *Commun. ACM 43*, 8 (Aug. 2000), 127–134.
22. Thompson, K. Programming techniques: Regular expression search algorithm. *Commun. ACM 11*, 6 (June 1968), 419–422.
23. Ting, I.-H., Kimble, C., and Kudenko, D. Ubb mining: Finding unexpected browsing behaviour in clickstream data to improve a web site's design. In *Proceedings of the 2005 IEEE/WIC/ACM International Conference on Web Intelligence*, WI '05, IEEE Computer Society (Washington, DC, USA, 2005), 179–185.
24. Wang, J., Feng, J., and Li, G. Trie-join: Efficient trie-based string similarity joins with edit-distance constraints. *Proc. VLDB Endow. 3*, 1-2 (Sept. 2010), 1219–1230.
25. Wattenberg, M. Arc diagrams: Visualizing structure in strings. In *Proceedings of the IEEE Symposium on Information Visualization (InfoVis'02)*, INFOVIS '02, IEEE Computer Society (Washington, DC, USA, 2002), 110–116.
26. Yun, J., Jing, L., Yu, J., and Huang, H. Unsupervised feature weighting based on local feature relatedness. In *Advances in Knowledge Discovery and Data Mining*, J. Huang, L. Cao, and J. Srivastava, Eds., vol. 6634 of *Lecture Notes in Computer Science*. Springer Berlin Heidelberg, 2011, 38–49.
27. Zhang, Z., and Nasraoui, O. Efficient hybrid web recommendations based on markov clickstream models and implicit search. In *Proceedings of the IEEE/WIC/ACM International Conference on Web Intelligence*, WI '07, IEEE Computer Society (Washington, DC, USA, 2007), 621–627.

FlexiGroups: Binding Mobile Devices for Collaborative Interactions in Medium-Sized Groups with Device Touch

Tero Jokela, Andrés Lucero
Nokia Research Center
P.O. Box 1000, FI-33721 Tampere, Finland
tero.jokela@nokia.com, lucero@acm.org

ABSTRACT
We present a touch-based method for binding mobile devices for collaborative interactions in a group of collocated users. The method is highly flexible, enabling a broad range of different group formation strategies. We report an evaluation of the method in medium-sized groups of six users. When forming a group, the participants primarily followed viral patterns where they opportunistically added other participants to the group without advance planning. The participants also suggested a number of more systematic patterns, which required the group to agree on a common strategy but then provided a clear procedure to follow. The flexibility of the method allowed the participants to adapt it to the changing needs of the situation and to recover from errors and technical problems. Overall, device binding in medium-sized groups was found to be a highly collaborative group activity and the binding methods should pay special attention to supporting groupwork and social interactions.

Author Keywords
Collocated interaction; mobile phones; user interfaces; device ecosystem binding; group association; pairing.

ACM Classification Keywords
H.5.m. Information interfaces and presentation (e.g., HCI): Miscellaneous.

INTRODUCTION
While mobile devices have traditionally been very personal devices targeted at individual use, over the last years there has been a growing interest in systems that combine several mobile devices together to create broader ecosystems of interaction [24]. Such ecosystems allow groups of collocated users to engage in rich collaborative activities and shared experiences with their devices. Potential application scenarios include presenting and collaboratively editing documents in business meetings, sharing photographs and videos within groups of friends in a café, or playing multi-player games with other family members in the living room.

But before a group of collocated users can engage in collaborative interactions with their mobile devices, they must first join their devices together into a multi-device ecosystem. This is a complex procedure with several steps. The necessary system and application software needs to be initiated on all devices. The devices must discover the other devices existing in the proximity and the devices intended to participate in the ecosystem must be identified. A communication channel then needs to be established between the devices participating in the ecosystem, in order to allow exchange of data and coordination of the interactions. Typically, short-range radio technologies, such as WLAN or Bluetooth, are used to transmit data between devices. This process of setting up the ecosystem is generally known as device binding or ecosystem binding [24] (also known as device association, pairing, or coupling [4]). As the intention is to enable spontaneous interactions, it should be possible to bind devices having no prior knowledge of each other in a fast and easy way. If the process of binding devices is too complicated or tedious, the users might lose interest in using multi-device interactions in the first place. As the users cannot see the wireless connections between the devices, they cannot be sure that they are really connecting to the other devices intended to. Therefore, the binding process should also provide sufficient cues and security, so that the users can ensure that the right devices are connected.

In this paper, we study establishing an ecosystem of mobile devices to support collaborative interactions within medium-sized groups of collocated users. While the problem of a single user pairing two devices has been extensively studied in prior research, more complex scenarios involving multiple users, especially more than four users, have received little attention in prior research. We present a touch-based group-binding method called FlexiGroups that builds on earlier research by Jokela and Lucero [13] and Lucero, et al. [16]. The method is highly flexible, enabling the users to apply a broad range of different group formation strategies. We also present a laboratory evaluation of FlexiGroups in a realistic photo sharing application context with four groups of six users. The evaluation results indicate that the method was generally found easy and intuitive to use. We analyze the different group creation strategies and patterns used by the

MobileHCI 2014, September 23–26, 2014, Toronto, ON, Canada.
COPYRIGHT © 2014 ACM 978-1-4503-3004-6/14/09…$15.00.
http://dx.doi.org/10.1145/2628363.2628376

participants during the evaluation. The participants primarily followed viral patterns where they opportunistically added other participants to the group without advance planning. The participants also suggested a number of more systematic patterns, which required the group to agree on a common strategy but then provided a clear procedure to follow. The flexibility of the method allowed the participants to adapt it to the changing needs of the situation and to recover from errors and technical problems. Overall, device binding in medium-sized groups was found to be a highly collaborative group activity and the binding methods should pay special attention to supporting groupwork and social interactions.

The rest of this paper is structured as follows. First, we provide an overview of the related work. We then give a detailed description of the FlexiGroups binding method and the evaluation procedure. Finally, we present the results of the evaluation, followed by discussion and conclusions.

RELATED WORK

The problem of ad hoc device binding has been thoroughly studied in the fields of human-computer interaction and security research. A wide range of methods for device binding has been proposed – in security research alone, over 20 different methods have been identified [20]. These methods vary in terms of device hardware requirements, amount of user involvement, and level of provided security.

The most common device-binding methods today, such as those typically used in Bluetooth and WLAN networks, are based on scanning the environment for available devices and presenting a list of the found devices to the user for selecting the other device to bind with. The connections are authenticated using short strings that the user is expected to copy or compare between devices. The authentication strings can be represented as numbers, words, graphical images, audio signals, or gestures in the user interface.

The proposed alternative methods include a variety of techniques based on synchronous user actions, for example, pressing buttons on both devices [22] or touching both devices [26] simultaneously, shaking the devices together [10], or bumping the devices together [8]. Further, device binding can be based on continuous gestures spanning from one device display to another [9]. Methods based on spatial alignment of the devices include pointing, for example, with laser light [18], touching [23], or placing the devices in close proximity of each other [15]. It is also possible to bind devices with various auxiliary devices such as tokens [1] or cameras [19]. Some of the proposed methods cover only device identification or authentication, while others combine both identification and authentication into a single user action.

Binding methods are not only means for connecting devices – they have strong social and emotional aspects. In real-life situations, people do not always pick the easiest or fastest method available, nor the one they like best. Many factors influence their choice of binding method, including the place, the social setting, the other people present, and the sensitivity of data [12, 21]. Users are willing to take security risks to comply with social norms [12].

The majority of earlier research has focused on scenarios of a single user binding two devices with each other (for example, binding a headset with a mobile device, or a mobile computer with a wireless access point). Only recently have researchers started to consider more complex scenarios involving multiple users and devices. Such multi-user scenarios differ in many respects from single-user scenarios, making the single-user device-binding methods not necessarily applicable to multi-user scenarios. In multi-user scenarios, communication between group members provides an additional source for potential errors. On the other hand, the users are typically willing to help each other and make decisions by mutual agreement, which reduces the amount of errors [14]. Methods that involve physical exchange of devices have been found to be unacceptable unless the users know each other very well, as the users are unwilling to hand in their devices to strangers [25, 5].

While numerous methods and technologies have been proposed for group association, Chong and Gellersen [2] present an interesting study on what people would spontaneously do to associate a group of devices. In their study, groups of four users were asked to suggest and rate techniques for binding together different combinations of low-fidelity acrylic prototypes of various mobile and fixed devices. Device touch based methods were found to be among the most frequently proposed methods, and were also considered popular and easy to use.

The group creation task can be divided in different ways between the members of the group [13, 14]. Leader-driven methods, which concentrate the task on a single participant, allow strong control over the group and require only one participant to be able to form a group. Peer-based methods, which distribute the work between all members, help to create a stronger sense of community and scale better to larger group sizes and distances. Further, group association can be seen as a one-step procedure of binding all devices with a single action, or as a sequence of pairwise associations [2, 24].

Finally, Chong and Gellersen [4] present a framework that sums up and categorizes the different factors that influence the usability of spontaneous device association. They identify technology, user interaction, and application context as the three most important criteria.

STUDY

Objectives

In this study, we were primarily interested in two research questions:

First, earlier studies have suggested that device-binding methods should be flexible, allowing people to adopt different group creation strategies in different situations [13, 12]. Still, many of the methods tested in earlier studies have been very specific, enforcing a detailed procedure that has to be followed exactly. We wanted to test a more flexible method that would give users more freedom to adapt it to different situations. On the other hand, giving the users more options might potentially be confusing to them and provide additional possibilities for errors.

Second, we wanted to study group binding in a medium-sized group of six users. Earlier studies on device binding have focused either on individual users, pairs, or small groups of up to four participants. As the size of the group increases, a much wider variety of different approaches and strategies becomes possible. The overall process also becomes much more parallel. We wanted to better understand the different possible approaches and their strengths and weaknesses. We were also interested in group behavior, communication, and collaboration between users during the group-formation task.

FlexiGroups

In order to study these research questions, we designed a group-binding method called FlexiGroups. The method builds on the results of an earlier comparison of three group-binding methods by Jokela and Lucero [13]. While the FlexiGroups method itself is generic and can be used in many different applications, we decided to study the group-binding method in the context of a multi-user photo sharing application to create a more realistic setting for the evaluation. The application was a simplified version of Pass-Them-Around [16]. It allowed the users to browse their own photo collections stored in their devices and also supported spatial interactions of sharing photos by throwing them from one device to another.

Figure 1 illustrates the FlexiGroups group-binding method. To create a new group, one of the persons first starts the FlexiGroups application on their device by tapping the application icon in the Application Grid (Fig. 1.a). The application starts in the Add Device view (Fig. 1.b). Visual feedback on the screen instructs the person to hold the device in portrait mode and to touch another device to add it to the group. When the person moves their device close to another device, the device detects the new device (see Fig. 2). Visual, auditory, and haptic feedback is provided to indicate that the other device has been detected and to instruct the person to hold the device still while the new device is added to the group. When the new device has been added to the group, the person can continue adding more devices by touching them following the same procedure. When the person does not want to add any more persons to the group, they should press the "Done" button to enter the Tabletop Overview view (Fig. 1.d).

Note that the person who is added to the group does not have to start the application manually from the Application Grid – their device can remain idle (Fig. 1.c). When another

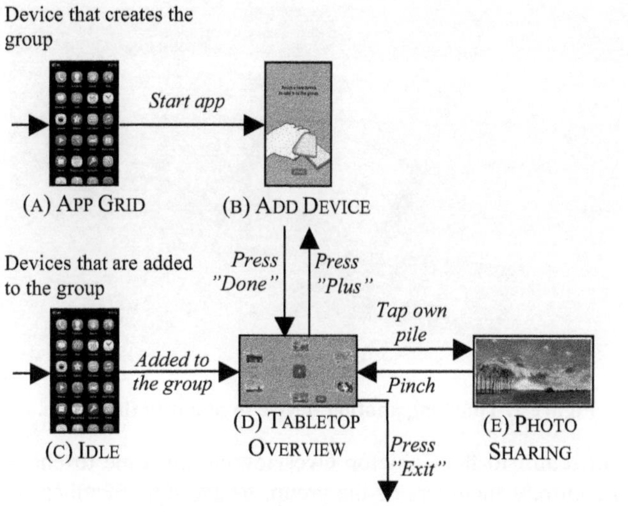

Figure 1. FlexiGroups group-binding method.

person touches the device and adds it to the group, the application is automatically launched and starts in the Tabletop Overview (Fig. 1.d). The Tabletop Overview (see Fig. 3) shows all the persons who have been added to the group. Each person is represented as a pile of photos with a textual name defined by the person next to the pile. If the person wants to add more persons to the group, they can press the "Plus" button at the center of the screen to enter the Add Device view (Fig. 1.b). The person can then add new devices by touching them in the same way as described in the previous paragraph. Any member of the group is allowed to add new devices and several persons can add new devices simultaneously.

FlexiGroups also supports defining the positions of the devices relative to each other in order to enable spatial interactions such as throwing photos between devices. This ordering phase is optional and can be omitted in applications that do not require the order of the devices to be defined. Alternatively, a similar mechanism can also be used to define other kinds of roles within the group, for example, to divide the group into two competing teams in a game application and to select captains for both teams. The ordering mechanism in FlexiGroups works as follows. The persons appear in the Tabletop Overview (see Fig. 3) in the order they are added to the group. If the order of the devices on the screen is different from the order of the devices in the real world, any member of the group can correct it by dragging the devices to the right positions on the screen. Only one person can change the order of the devices at a time. When one person is dragging a device to a new position, the other devices' screens are locked and grayed out to indicate that another person is reordering the devices.

When the order of the devices is correct on the screen, the people can enter the Photo Sharing view (Fig. 1.e) by tapping their piles of photos on the Tabletop Overview and start sharing photos by throwing them between devices. By pinching to zoom out in the Photo Sharing view, the person

Figure 2. Touching another device to add it to the group.

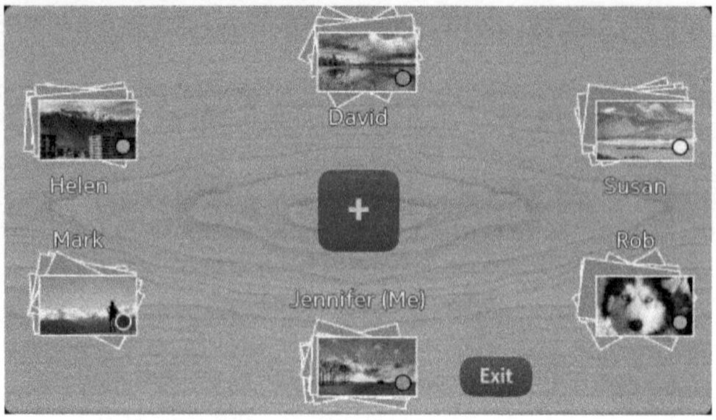

Figure 3. Tabletop Overview.

can return to the Tabletop Overview at any time to check the current members of the group, to add new members to the group, or to change the order of the devices. To leave the group, the person presses the "Exit" button in the Tabletop Overview. The group continues to run on the other devices until the last member exits the group.

Prototype Implementation

We implemented a prototype of the FlexiGroups binding method on Nokia N9[1] mobile devices running the MeeGo operating system. The prototype was built as a native C++ application on top of the Qt 4.7 software framework. QML and Qt Quick with OpenGL ES hardware acceleration were used to implement a smooth animated user interface. Device touch interactions were detected with a radio technology, which was able to detect other devices at distances closer than 20 cm (8 inches) in approximately five seconds based on wireless signal strength. While the technology generally worked reliably, there were occasionally delays in detecting the other devices in the proximity and detections of devices further away. Detailed connectivity and initialization information was then sent to the discovered device over Bluetooth. A server, which was listening to a pre-defined Bluetooth socket on the discovered device, received the information and started the FlexiGroups application. The application then established an ad hoc WLAN network and connected to the group according to the connectivity information it had received. An ad hoc WLAN network was used for communication between the devices in order to allow the application to be used anywhere independent of the available network infrastructure. All communication was handled directly between the devices without a server backend. The prototype was fully functional with real network communication, except for the security protocols, which were only simulated in the user interface.

[1] http://swipe.nokia.com/

Participants

We recruited a total of 24 participants for the evaluation by posting an advertisement on a local mailing list. The participants were recruited in groups of two to four people, as we wanted that each participant would know some of the other participants to make the situation more natural and comfortable to them. We assigned the participants into four evaluation sessions of six people each in the order they registered for the study, so that every participant knew at least one other participant, but no participant knew all the others in the same session. Six of the participants were female and 18 male. The ages of the participants varied between 25 and 41 years (M=32.8, SD=4.7). One participant was left-handed and 23 right-handed. The participants represented a variety of different professions, with six participants having a software engineering background, 13 having other technical background (for example, mechanical engineering), and five having a non-technical background (for example, teaching or photography). The participants were fairly advanced users of information technology – on a scale between 1-7 (1=novice, 7=expert), they evaluated their IT skills above average (M=5.5, SD=1.2). All participants were experienced smartphone users, but only two of them had used a Nokia N9 device before the study.

Procedure

We organized a total of four evaluation sessions. The sessions were arranged in our usability laboratory. In each session, there were six participants and a moderator present. Figure 4 shows the evaluation setup. The participants were sitting around a round table with a radius of 120 cm (48 inches). Each participant was provided with a Nokia N9 mobile device with the FlexiGroups application pre-installed. While all the devices were of the same model, we used devices of different colors to make them easier to differentiate: there was one black, one white, two cyan, and two magenta devices. The average duration of the evaluation sessions was 60 minutes.

As the participants arrived in the laboratory, the moderator guided them to their seats around the table and asked them to fill in the background information and consent forms.

The moderator then introduced the participants to collaborative multi-device applications and demonstrated the idea with the photo sharing application. The participants could try the application with their own devices and practice throwing photos to each other. The moderator explained that before the participants could share photos like this, they first had to bind their devices together into a group, and that the purpose of the evaluation was to test a method for this task. The moderator then continued by describing the detailed evaluation procedure. The moderator also told the participants that the method to be tested was based on device touch interactions and demonstrated how to touch another device. The participants could practice touching with their own devices until they felt comfortable doing it. We considered practicing touch interactions necessary as while many participants were aware of device touch as an interaction method, few had practical experience using it.

To start the actual evaluation, the moderator played a video that demonstrated the FlexiGroups group-binding method. We used instructions recorded on video to ensure that all groups received uniform guidance on how to use the method. The instructions demonstrated the operations that an individual user could do – they did not show how a group of users should use the method together. The moderator then asked the participants to set up a group using the method that was just demonstrated to them, so that they could start sharing photos between devices. The moderator observed the situation and only intervened if the participants encountered obvious technical problems with their devices that prevented them from proceeding. When the participants had successfully created a group and could throw photos between devices, the moderator asked the participants to exit the application and create a new group so that a different person would start the group creation. Overall, the participants created three or four groups during each evaluation session.

When the participants had tested the method several times, the moderator asked them to fill in two validated questionnaires: AttrakDiff [7], which measures the attractiveness of interactive products, and NASA-TLX [6], which measures the subjective workload experience when performing a task. To gain a broader understanding of the tested method, we extended the NASA-TLX with four additional scales: Learnability, Quickness, Security, and Overall Preference. After the participants had completed the questionnaires, the moderator interviewed them about their experiences with the FlexiGroups method. The interview was semi-structured and covered general feedback about the strengths and weaknesses of the tested method as well as specific topics such as different group formation strategies, device touching orders, and arrangement of the devices into the correct positions. The average duration of the interviews was 20 minutes. To close the evaluation session, the moderator thanked the participants and gave each participant a small reward to compensate them for their time.

Figure 4. Evaluation setup.

The group creation tasks were recorded with two video cameras: the first was placed on a tripod pointing towards the table at an angle (Fig. 4) and the other was mounted in the ceiling providing a top view of the table surface (Fig. 8 and Fig. 9). The interviews were recorded with a single video camera. Two researchers independently watched the video recordings and wrote notes about their observations. They also drew diagrams that recorded the sequences of participant actions in every group creation attempt. The same two researchers then collaboratively analyzed the data and built an Affinity Diagram [11] in a series of interpretation sessions. Each researcher independently studied the notes and grouped them into clusters of related items. The clusters then evolved to broader categories that were naturally revealed and were jointly revisited, discussed, and refined. In the end, the categories were processed into more general findings that form the core of the Results section. A quantitative analysis of the AttrakDiff and NASA-TLX questionnaires was done separately.

RESULTS

General

The evaluation produced overall positive results. All four evaluation groups succeeded in all of their attempts to bind their devices together and form a group. While the groups encountered some problems and made some mistakes, especially in their initial attempts to use FlexiGroups, the robustness of the method allowed them to recover and continue, and to successfully complete the group creation task. Most participants (18/24) commented that FlexiGroups was generally easy and intuitive to use and it was also easy to learn.

These qualitative results are supported by the AttrakDiff questionnaire [7] results, which are illustrated in Figure 5. The main bars indicate the means for each product dimension, while the error bars indicate standard errors. Pragmatic quality (PQ) refers to the product's ability to

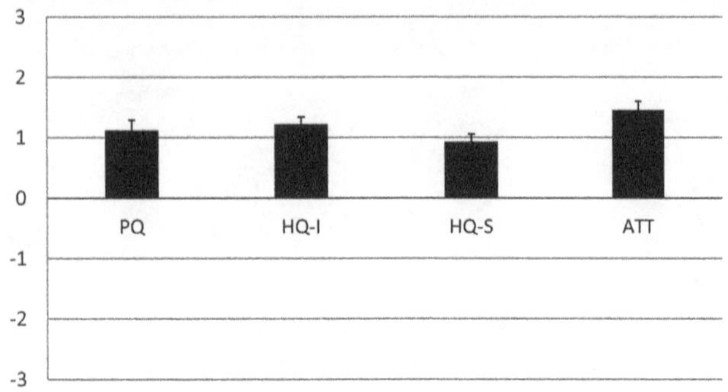

Figure 5. AttrakDiff results (higher is better).

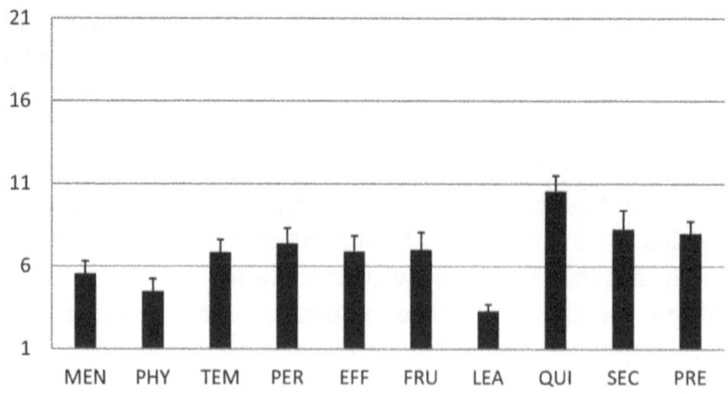

Figure 6. Extended NASA-TLX results (lower is better).

support the achievement of behavioral goals (usability). Hedonic quality refers to the users' self: stimulation (HQ-S) is the product's ability to stimulate and enable personal growth, while identification (HQ-I) is the product's ability to address the need of expressing one's self through objects one owns. Perceived attractiveness (ATT) describes a global value of the product based on the quality perception. Both pragmatic and hedonic dimensions of AttrakDiff as well as overall attractiveness show positive and well-balanced results.

The extended NASA-TLX questionnaire [6] results are illustrated in Figure 6. The main bars indicate the means for each subscale, while the error bars indicate standard errors. The original six subscales of NASA-TLX presented on the left show an overall positive trend. The four subscales that we added for the purposes of this study are shown on the right. The low Learnability (LEA) score indicates that the method was considered very easy to learn. The method was also considered relatively secure (SEC). The Overall Preference (PRE) score further confirms the generally positive attitude towards the tested method.

However, several participants (7/24) commented that the group formation should have been faster. *"[P14] I think it is a bit slow process. It should be somehow faster. It takes a long time to set up."* The relatively high subjective Quickness (QUI) score of the extended NASA-TLX results supports these qualitative comments. We measured the fastest group creation time for each group using the video recordings. The average time to set up a six-person group was 111 seconds.

We can identify three main phases in forming a group: initiating the group creation, adding the participants to the group, and arranging the participants in the correct order for spatial interactions. We will next discuss each of these phases in more detail.

Initiating the Group

Every time the FlexiGroups application is started from the application grid, a new group is created. Therefore, when the participants wanted to create a new group, they had to agree who of them would start the application, while the others had to wait until they were added to the group. Initially, this proved to be challenging for the participants as they were used to the common practice of each person first starting the application on their device. *"[P10] I found it confusing that by just starting the application, I started my own group."* In every evaluation group, several participants started the application in parallel during their first attempt to form a group. However, the visualization of the devices in the Tabletop Overview allowed the participants to quickly realize that there were several parallel groups. The participants solved the problem by agreeing that those people in the smaller groups should exit the application and be then added to the main group by the other participants. One of the participants saw it as an interesting opportunity that there could be several parallel subgroups within a larger group. *"[P21] If you are in a bar or restaurant and there are a lot of people in the table, you are not going to be talking to everyone. ... For me, it is quite natural that you have different groups."*

As the participants understood that only one of them should start the application, they quickly developed practices to agree verbally, or with gestures, who would start the application. These practices included announcing that one would start, asking for permission to start, and suggesting that another participant should start the application. However, half of the participants (12/24) proposed that it should be possible to start several groups in parallel and then merge the groups together. This would enable building a group from bottom up so that anybody could start and also would make the group creation faster. A few participants (4/24) commented that there should be a security mechanism to confirm that both groups really want to merge. Three participants also expressed more general concerns that somebody could add them to a group that they did not wish to join by touching their devices and suggested there should always be a confirmation before a device joins to a group.

Touching Patterns

FlexiGroups gave the participants a lot of freedom regarding the overall approach on how to form a group and the order in which the individual participants were added to

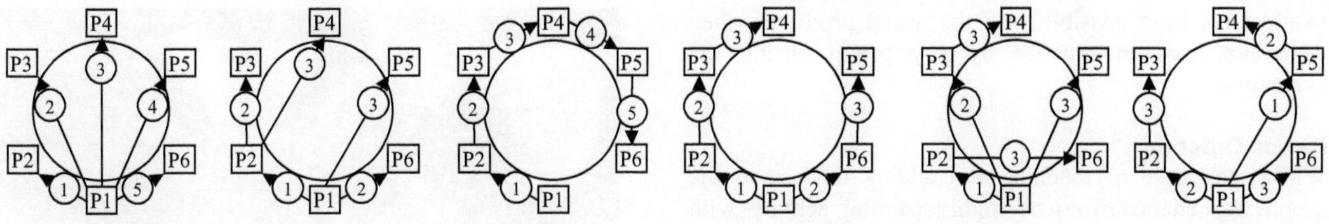

Figure 7. Different group creation patterns. Boxes P1-P6 represent the participants. Arrows show the touch actions between the participants, while the numbered circles indicate the order of the touch actions.

the group. A single participant could add all participants to the group, or several participants could participate in setting up the group. The participants could be added to the group one at a time, or multiple participants could be added in parallel. During the evaluation tasks and the interviews, the participants suggested a wide variety of different patterns for building a group. Figure 7 illustrates different patterns suggested by the participants.

Systematic Patterns

In systematic patterns, the participants followed a well-defined procedure in setting up a group.

Leader (Fig. 7.a). The participant P1 (the leader) creates a new group and adds all the other participants one after another. The leader may proceed in clockwise or counter-clockwise order around the group.

Co-Leaders (Fig. 7.b). The participant P1 (the leader) creates a new group and then selects another participant P2 as a co-leader and adds the co-leader to the group. The two co-leaders P1 and P2 then add the other participants one after another proceeding in opposite directions around the group. While similar to the Leader pattern, having several co-leaders scales better to larger groups.

Ring (Fig. 7.c). The participant P1 creates a new group and adds another participant P2 next to them. The participant P2 then adds the next participant P3, who continues by adding P4. This way the ring proceeds around the group. The ring can be formed in clockwise or counter-clockwise order.

Two-Way Ring (Fig. 7.d). The participant P1 creates a new group and adds another participant P2 next to them. P1 and P2 then continue by adding the participants next to them like in Ring but in opposite directions. The Two-Way Ring pattern is similar to Ring, but more efficient as it proceeds in both directions around the group.

Viral Pattern

While the participants suggested many systematic patterns, in practice their behavior was usually more random. *"[P14] Somebody initiated the group creation and then it started to spread around the table."* The participants opportunistically selected which device to touch next. *"[P3] It was very random. ... Going left and right. It didn't have any strict form."* This way the group membership spread like a viral infection, or fire, across the group from one participant to another. Figures 7.e and 7.f show examples of real viral patterns employed by the participants during the evaluation.

It was common to connect to one's own neighbors first and then add other participants further away if needed. Participants who were not yet members of the group also requested the participants who were already in the group to add them to the group. If some participant had problems in detecting another device, the other participants were eager to help and add the new device with their own devices. Sometimes the participants intentionally touched and "infected" another participant on the opposite side of the table (for example, touch action #1 in Fig. 7.f) to make the group membership spread faster. It was common that several participants were touching and adding new devices simultaneously (see Fig. 8).

Alternative Patterns

In addition to the main patterns described above, individual participants suggested a range of alternative approaches for group creation. Interesting alternatives include patterns where several devices were touched simultaneously to make the group creation more efficient. In one variation, the participant who creates the group puts their device at the center of the table. The other participants who want to be added to the group then put their devices next to it. In another variation, all devices are collected next to each other on the table and the participant who creates the group then touches all of them in one action. While these patterns

Figure 8. Three persons touching and adding devices in parallel.

would have been possible with the tested prototype, they were not used in practice by any group during the evaluation.

Device Ordering

While the phase of touching and adding devices to the group was characterized by highly parallel activity with several participants adding other people simultaneously (see Fig. 8), acting either independently or in small sub-teams, the phase of device ordering required the participants to more closely co-operate and coordinate their actions within the whole group. The transition from the adding phase to the ordering phase provided an important synchronization point in the group formation task.

Device ordering was done collaboratively with different participants taking different roles (see Fig. 9). While some participants actually moved devices on the screen, others checked whether the order was correct and provided suggestions on the needed changes verbally and with hand gestures. In most cases, several participants moved devices on the screen – typically two to four participants were involved. This created problems as several participants tried to move the devices simultaneously. While the screens of the other devices were grayed out and locked when one of the participants started to move a device around, there was a small delay in locking the screens, which sometimes allowed another participant to start moving until their screen was grayed out. Many participants (13/24) complained that they felt the device ordering phase was confusing. Several participants (7/24) also commented that the ordering phased was unnecessary and should be avoided. The system should have been able to define the device positions automatically instead.

Physical Device Handling

Half of the participants (12/24) made a natural and spontaneous gesture of pushing their devices forward when they wanted to be added to the group. Most commonly, a participant would move their device towards another participant asking them to touch the device and add it to the group. Alternatively, a participant could push their device towards the center of the table asking any of the other participants to add it to the group.

While the participants commonly touched each other's devices with their own devices to add them to the group, there was a high barrier of taking another participant's device into one's hands or manipulating it with one's fingers. This was true even if the participants did not use their own personal devices but devices we had given to them for the purpose of the evaluation. In all the sessions, there were only a few cases where a participant touched another participant's device with their hands. In those few cases, the reason was usually to help another participant who had technical problems with their device.

Figure 9. Ordering devices.

We encouraged the participants to keep their devices on the table as that would allow everybody to see the screens of the other participants and help create a common awareness of the group status. Keeping the devices on the table also made the proximity detection technology work faster and more reliably. Still, the participants often chose to hold their devices in their hands. In 27% of the touch actions recorded on video, both participants kept the devices in their hands, making the touch action resemble a handshake (see Fig. 8). In one of the sessions, all participants held the devices in their hands also during the reordering phase. In the other sessions, two participants liked to fiddle or toy with their devices while waiting to be added to the group.

Collaboration

We observed a high level of communication and collaboration between the participants when they were forming a group. Participants were very eager to help each other if some participant encountered problems with the application. For example, if a participant's device could not detect and add another device to the group, another participant would use their device to help and add the participant. Helping others mostly occurred spontaneously when a participant noticed that another participant could not complete some action or was doing something incorrectly. Only rarely did the participants explicitly ask for help.

A major challenge for the evaluation groups was creating and maintaining a common understanding of the overall task status as there were six persons involved and many actions were taking place in parallel. *"[P23] I cannot keep an eye on what every other person is doing."* Several techniques were used to accomplish common awareness of the task status. Verbal communication and coordination between the participants played a major role, including the participants announcing intentions to do some actions, providing feedback on other participants' actions, instructing others to take some actions, asking and confirming facts, and stating the common group status aloud. Another important technique was to observe the other participants, including both real-world actions taken by the others as well as the status information shown on the their device screens. When adding participants to the group, everybody could easily perceive the touch actions. The devices also provided audio feedback when another device was detected and added to the group. While the audio feedback was useful and could also be observed by all the participants, the participants had problems in identifying the source of the audio when several participants were touching devices in parallel. In the ordering phase, the participants had to rely more on information on the device screens, and peeking at and comparing information between other participants' screens was common. Figure 9 shows an example of a situation where all participants have placed their devices in a close formation at the center of the table to make the coordination easier.

DISCUSSION

As observed in our study and in earlier studies [13, 14], device association in large groups is a highly collaborative group activity. Considering the design of binding methods for groups, while good usability is definitely important, people as a group can help each other and are capable of overcoming and solving together most usability and technical problems they encounter. However, in larger groups, the main challenges are related to groupwork and social interactions within the group: making decisions and agreeing on a common strategy, coordinating and synchronizing actions, and keeping track of the others and the overall task status. An important consideration is also keeping everybody engaged in the process, as people easily get bored or distracted when they cannot do anything but wait for others to complete the group formation.

In the evaluation sessions, people most commonly and naturally employed Viral patterns (see Fig. 7.e and 7.f) where the group membership spread like a contagion from one person to another [24]. These required the least advance planning within the group and provided most flexibility. The Viral patterns are efficient and keep everybody involved also in large groups due to the high level of parallel activity. The possibility of forming a group bottom-up by first forming smaller groups and then merging them together into a larger group, which was suggested by some of the study participants, is interesting and should be studied further.

The participants also suggested a variety of more systematic patterns. These patterns require that the participants are aware of and agree on a common strategy to form a group. While this requires some initial planning, the systematic pattern then defines a precise sequence of actions that each participant should follow, reducing the need for coordination between the participants later. Further, the Leader pattern (see Fig. 7.a) enables the leader to have strong control over the group [13], which may be important, for example, in situations where there are unknown people present. The Co-Leaders pattern (see Fig. 7.b) provides an extension of the Leader pattern, which scales better to larger groups.

While the participants were able to successfully arrange the devices in the right order for spatial interactions in all group creation attempts, the majority of them found the ordering phase confusing. While this can be partially attributed to implementation issues, such as delays in locking the screens of the other devices when one device was used for rearranging, the ordering technique needs to be improved. Ideally, device ordering should be automatic, removing the need for manual ordering completely. However, in real-life applications this may be difficult to achieve as it may require special tracking equipment or dedicated infrastructure that may not be widely available. As suggested in an earlier study by Jokela and Lucero [13], device ordering would probably work better when done by one person. This person could be, for example, the person who creates the group. Alternatively, one of the participants could reserve the role for a longer period of time and arrange all the people in the right places. If strictly followed, the systematic patterns might enable defining the device order based on the touch order, but this may be in many cases too restrictive [13].

When designing binding methods for groups of users, it is important to consider robustness in real-life conditions. While many methods can work well in theory or with mock-ups, in reality, multi-user multi-device applications are complex distributed systems. As multiple devices are involved, there is an increased risk of technical issues: the devices may fail to detect each other, the software may crash, and the network connections may be broken. Also, all persons may not be aware of the procedure they should follow, or they may be unable to do so, for example, because they arrive late or they are occupied with other tasks such as incoming telephone calls. Therefore, the methods should not expect an exact procedure to be followed. The methods should be flexible and robust, allowing people to adapt them to the changing needs of the situation and to recover from failures.

FUTURE WORK

Our experiment, like all the other experiments with group-binding methods we are aware of, was done in a usability laboratory under ideal conditions. Also, the use case was defined by the researchers and given to the participants. In real life, various contextual and situational factors influence the group creation process. Therefore, to gain a deeper understanding of group binding in realistic situations and tasks, we believe it would be important to study group-binding methods also in more realistic settings and over extended periods of time with longitudinal field trials.

CONCLUSION

We have presented FlexiGroups, a touch-based method to bind mobile devices for collaborative interactions within a group of collocated users. The method is highly flexible, enabling a broad range of different group formation strategies. In a laboratory evaluation with four groups of six users, the method was found to be generally intuitive and easy to use and learn. When forming a group, the participants primarily followed viral patterns where they opportunistically added other participants to the group without advance planning. The participants also suggested a number of more systematic patterns, which required the group to agree on a common strategy but then provided a clear procedure to follow. The flexibility of the method allowed the participants to adapt it to the changing needs of the situation and to recover from errors and technical problems. Overall, device binding in medium-sized groups was found to be a highly collaborative group activity and the binding methods should pay special attention to supporting groupwork and social interactions.

ACKNOWLEDGMENTS

We would like to thank Arto Palin, Juha Riippi, Iiro Vidberg, Arttu Pulli, Markus Rinne, and Mikko Tolonen for implementing the software prototype.

REFERENCES

1. Ayatsuka, Y. and Rekimoto, J. tranSticks: physically manipulatable virtual connections. In *Proc. CHI '05*, 251-260.
2. Chong, M. and Gellersen, H. How groups of users associate wireless devices. In *Proc. CHI '13*, 1559-1568.
3. Chong, M. and Gellersen, H. How users associate wireless devices. In *Proc. CHI '11*, 1909-1918.
4. Chong, M. and Gellersen, H. Usability classification for spontaneous device association. *Personal and Ubiquitous Computing* 16, 1 (2012), 77-89.
5. Hang, A., von Zezschwitz, E., De Luca, A. and Hussman, H. Too much information!: user attitudes towards smartphone sharing. In *Proc. NordiCHI '12*, 284-287.
6. Hart, S. G. and Staveland, L. E. Development of NASA-TLX (Task Load Index): Results of empirical and theoretical research. In Hancock and Meshkati (eds.) *Human Mental Workload*, North Holland Press, 1988.
7. Hassenzahl, M. The Interplay of Beauty, Goodness, and Usability in Interactive Products. *Human-Computer Interaction* 19, 4 (2004), 319-349.
8. Hinckley, K. Synchronous gestures for multiple persons and computers. In *Proc. UIST '03*, 149-158.
9. Hinckley, K., Ramos, G., Guimbretiere, F., Baudisch, P. and Smith, M. Stitching: pen gestures that span multiple displays. In *Proc. AVI '04*, 23-31.
10. Holmquist, L.E., Mattern, F., Schiele, B., Alahuhta, P., Beigl, M. and Gellersen, H. Smart-Its friends: a technique for users to easily establish connections between smart artefacts. In *Proc. UbiComp '01*, 116-122.
11. Holtzblatt, K., Wendell, J. B. and Wood, S. *Rapid Contextual Design*. Morgan Kaufmann, 2004.
12. Ion, I., Langheinrich, M., Kumaraguru, P. and Čapkun, S. Influence of user perception, security needs, and social factors on device pairing method choices. In *Proc. SOUPS '10*.
13. Jokela, T. and Lucero, A. A comparative evaluation of touch-based methods to bind mobile devices for collaborative interactions. In *Proc. CHI '13*, 3355-3364.
14. Kainda, R., Flechais, I. and Roscoe, A. Two heads are better than one: security and usability of device associations in group scenarios. In *Proc. SOUPS '10*.
15. Kray, C., Rohs, M., Hook, J. and Kratz, S. Group coordination and negotiation through spatial proximity regions around mobile devices on augmented tabletops. In *Proc. TABLETOP 2008*, 1-8.
16. Lucero, A., Holopainen, J. and Jokela, T. Pass-Them-Around: collaborative use of mobile phones for photo sharing. In *Proc. CHI '11*, 1787-1796.
17. Lucero, A., Jokela, T., Palin, A., Aaltonen, V. and Nikara, J. EasyGroups: binding mobile devices for collaborative interactions. In *CHI EA '12*, 2189-2194.
18. Mayrhofer, R. and Welch, M. A human-verifiable authentication protocol using visible laser light. In *Proc. ARES '07*, 1143-1148.
19. McCune, J.M., Perrig, A. and Reiter, M.K. Seeing-is-believing: using camera phones for human-verifiable authentication. In *Proc. SOUPS '05*, 110-124.
20. Nithyanand, R., Saxena, N., Tsudik, G. and Uzun, E. Groupthink: usability of secure group association for wireless devices. In *Proc. Ubicomp '10*, 331-340.
21. Rashid, U. and Quigley, A. Interaction techniques for binding smartphones: a desirability evaluation. In *Proc. HCD '09*, 120-128.
22. Rekimoto, J. SyncTap: synchronous user operation for spontaneous network connection. *Personal and Ubiquitous Computing* 8, 2 (2004), 126-134.
23. Rekimoto, J., Ayatsuka, Y., Kohno, M. and Oba, H. Proximal interactions: a direct manipulation technique for wireless networking. In *Proc. INTERACT '03*, 511-518.
24. Terrenghi, L., Quigley, A. and Dix, A. A taxonomy for and analysis of multi-person-display ecosystems. *Personal and Ubiquitous Computing* 13, 8 (2009), 583-598.
25. Uzun, E., Saxena, N. and Kumar, A. Pairing devices for social interactions: a comparative usability evaluation. In *Proc. CHI '11*, 2315-2324.
26. Zimmerman, T. G. Personal area networks: near-field intrabody communication. *IBM Systems Journal* 35, 3-4 (1996), 609-617.

Ubi-jector: An Information-Sharing Workspace in Casual Places Using Mobile Devices

Hajin Lim[1], Hyunjin Ahn[2], Junwoo Kang[3], Bongwon Suh[4], Joonhwan Lee[5]

Human-Centered Computing Lab.[1, 4], UX Lab.[2], HCI+d Lab.[5]
Seoul National University
Seoul, Republic of Korea
{akal[1], hyunjinahn[2], bongwon[4], joonhwan[5]}@snu.ac.kr

Internet&Multimedia Engineering[3]
Konkuk University
Seoul, Republic of Korea
gaxfor@gmail.com[3]

ABSTRACT
The widespread use of mobile devices has transformed casual places into meeting places. However, in these places, it is uncommon to have shared information workspace such as a beam projector, making it inconvenient and inefficient to exchange information and to get a direct feedback. To address this challenge, we present *Ubi-jector,* a mobile system that provides a shared information space that is equally distributed to each participant's mobile device and allows group members to share documents and collaborate real-time. We first characterized the information sharing patterns and identified the limitations of the current practice in meeting places without a shared workspace, by conducting qualitative user studies. Next, we implemented Ubi-jector with the design guidelines drawn in the prior stage. Also, we performed an evaluation study that showed the possibilities of Ubi-jector to facilitate an effective information sharing and foster an active participation even in poorly-equipped environments.

Author Keywords
Co-located Interaction; shared display; information sharing; CSCW; F2F; co-located; mobile collaboration

ACM Classification Keywords
H.5.3 Group and Organization Interfaces: Computer-supported cooperative work

General Terms
Human Factors; Design

INTRODUCTION
The technology advances in mobile computing and the wide penetrations of mobile devices enable us to work and collaborate everywhere, anytime we want. These changes also enable casual places (Figure 1) such as cafés, airports, restaurants, or school lounges to be actively utilized as places for collaboration. This tendency also aligns well with the BYOD (Bring Your Own Device) mentality in organizations.

MobileHCI 2014, September 23–26, 2014, Toronto, ON, Canada.

http://dx.doi.org/10.1145/2628363.2628397

Figure 1. Meetings in casual places.

Traditionally, meeting places where face-to-face (F2F) meetings requiring spaces that are equipped with a large round table, conference systems, network connection, and information-sharing devices, such as a beam projector, and a whiteboard in order to run an effective meeting. However, in casual places where meetings are often taken place, it is very uncommon to deploy these kinds of equipment.

The main drawback in casual places is that shared information workspace is usually absent, compared with a traditional meeting room environment where shared large displays, such as a large screen TV or a beam projector are equipped. Shared information spaces play an important role in sharing information and enabling participants to communicate efficiently [4]. The lack of shared information space in casual meeting places often makes it inconvenient and inefficient to exchange information and get feedback directly with documents.

To address this issue, we proposed a mobile information-sharing system called *Ubi-jector*, which is designed to support effective team collaboration even in poorly-equipped meeting environments. The main idea of Ubi-jector is to utilize each mobile device as a shared workspace as well as a personal workspace. This system provides a shared information space that is equally distributed to each participant's mobile device and allows group members to share documents and feedback in real-time. Ubi-jector provides specialized features and usability suited for the unique characteristics of F2F group meetings in casual places. It is implemented on Android OS using peer-to-peer (P2P) protocol without requiring any extra hardware or complicated registration process.

In previous research and commercial systems, mobile devices have been situated in remote as well as on the move collaboration contexts [2,15]. Even though there are a number of attempts to use mobile devices in F2F meeting settings, they mostly remain as a tool for personal input rather than shared information workspace [21]. Because mobile devices have limitations, such as small screen and limited interaction capacity, they are rarely utilized for providing shared information workspace.

This research aims to explore the opportunity of the use of mobile devices as shared workspaces. To address the challenge, we first conducted the user study to characterize the current practices found in poorly-equipped meeting settings. Also, we developed design guidelines, which were applied to the design and implementation of Ubi-jector. Lastly, we evaluated its usability and effectiveness, followed by discussions for improvements and its applicability to wider contexts.

The contributions of this paper were as follows:

- Performing a user study for identifying the information-sharing patterns and the limitations of the current practices in poorly- equipped meeting settings.
- Development of the design guidelines to utilize mobile devices as a shared information workspace in casual meeting places.
- Design and implementation of the research prototype; 'Ubi-jector'
- System evaluation and following discussions for exploring the issues in developing mobile applications for supporting co-located information-sharing.

RELATED WORK AND MOTIVATION

In this section, we first address the important role of a shared information space in the context of collaboration. We continue with the review of prior research on co-located collaboration. Finally, we take a look at prior systems that support co-located collaboration using mobile devices.

The Role of Shared Information Space in Collaboration

To achieve a mutually shared goal of the group, information-related works in collaboration such as identifying the needed information and creating a shared understanding [17] are essential. To meet the continued need for information exchange during a group work, a shared information space has been pointed out as a crucial component of collaboration [3]. The shared information workspace is where multiple people can see the same objects at the same time to enable knowledge held by individual and their attitudes visible to others [7]. Kraut and Fussell's research confirmed that shared visual space helps collaborators to understand the current state of their task and support their conversations efficiently, which leads to faster and better task performance [7]. A shared view is also useful in supporting knowledge processing, maintaining integrity, or supporting agreement by fostering shared awareness [20].

Co-located Collaboration

Much research about co-located collaboration has been performed in a variety of contexts. For example, Mejia et al. [14] characterized the informal co-located collaboration practices in hospital work, and Huang and Mynatt [5] focused on the application of public displays in small co-located group environments, specifically the academic lab setting. Brodie and Perry [3] examined what mobile workers do when they collaborate in a face-to-face manner away from the office.

There has been a set of research to provide effective applications for supporting co-located collaboration. A number of these focused on providing interactive tabletop surfaces or large displays, which enabled users to exchange various information and share feedback. For example, Wespace[21] proposed a collaborative workspace that integrates a large display with a multi-touch table. UbiTable [19] examined the design space of tabletops to support a kiosk-style walk-up interaction for impromptu face-to-face collaboration.

The aforementioned research often focused on introducing extra hardware and software systems to existing traditional meeting room environments where all required apparatus were already equipped. In this paper, we explore collaboration in poorly-equipped meeting environments and design the system which does not need any extra hardware or software except mobile devices.

Co-located Collaboration Systems using Mobile Devices

Mobile devices have traditionally been personal devices targeted at individual use [11]. Even in collaborative uses of mobile devices, most mainly focused on the remote contexts [2, 15]. However, the recent studies have started to explore shared co-located interactions, which allow people to have "on the spot" meetings where they cooperatively execute tasks and manipulate shared information spaces through their mobile devices [12].

A set of research focused on developing mobile systems for sharing photos among co-located people; '*Pass-them-around*'[9] supported co-located photo sharing using the metaphor of passing paper photos around, and Kun et al. [8] presented the prototype that allows users to share photos with other co-present users by synchronizing the display on multiple mobile devices. In other applications, '*WaggleBee*'[16] provided an easy means of sharing mobile Web contents among co-located groups, and '*MobiComics*' [10] allowed a group of collocated persons to flexibly create and edit comic strip panels using their mobile phones.

Building on the aforementioned research, we would like to focus on the information-sharing practices of co-located groups in casual places and introduce Ubi-jector for facilitating effective exchanges of information and feedback in real-time.

UNDERSTANDING CASUAL MEETING ENVIRONMENTS

In this section, we report the results of qualitative user studies, including interviews and observations to enrich our understanding of F2F meetings in casual places. In our user research, we aimed to reexamine the current practices of casual meeting settings by characterizing the information-sharing patterns of users. Also, we identified limitations of the current practices in poorly-equipped environments.

Methods

To gain a holistic understanding of F2F meetings in casual places, we conducted a semi-structured interview. We recruited four undergraduate students and four graduate students, aged 21 to 27 years (Avg. age: 24.4; 4 females) from varied backgrounds (social science, business, engineering, etc.). We recruited several prospect participants through postings on social network sites. Among them, only those who reported that they were involved in at least two group projects during the spring semester and reported to have group meetings in casual places frequently were selected for our user study. The interviews lasted approximately for 25 to 40 minutes.

As group collaboration situation can be varied and complex due to many contextual factors, we developed the pre-set criterion (Table 1) for interviews. We tried to dismantle a complicated group meeting context into six factors by combining the contextual elements for the analysis and design of mobile collaborative application of Alarcon et al. [1] and the classification for the realization of a collaborative environment of Shah [18].

Contextual Factors	Components
Environment Context	F2F / Co-located / Poorly-equipped place (Fixed conditions in our research)
Group Context	Type/ Size/ Purpose/ Role/ Work Phase
Activity Type	Tasks/ Communication/ Interaction
Information	Info Source/ Info Type
Info-Sharing Method	Tool/ Device/ System
Etc.	Satisfaction, Pain point, Requirement

Table 1. The pre-set criterion for the interview.

Reflecting this criterion, we formulated the interview questions to look at a larger group context, focusing on the situations that got them into collaboration, what kinds of information were shared, and how they shared information. Through several pilot interviews, we elaborated the interview questions. All interviews were transcribed and analyzed according to the criterion.

In addition, we ran two sets of observational studies to confirm the current practices that we derived from the interviews and to extend the understanding of the dynamics of real meeting settings in casual places. Among the interview participants who had been engaged in projects at that moment, two of them were requested to observe their meetings. After the groups were informed of the purpose of observations, we took field notes and some representative photos of them to capture their characteristic behaviors.

Following initial interviews and observations, we used affinity diagramming [6] to cluster unique characteristics and draw information-sharing patterns.

User Study Results

By conducting the user study, we could identify the information-sharing patterns and found limitations of the current practices in poorly- equipped meeting settings.

Group Context and Activity: Why they need to have F2F meetings.

Teams (mostly 3 to 6 members) were formed because of class projects or extracurricular activities to complete required tasks and yield various types of outcomes such as reports, papers, presentations, or videos.

Study participants reported that F2F meetings were preferred when they needed to exchange various opinions and information frequently and directly. Besides F2F meetings, they frequently used online channels such as chat, e-mail, video call, shared cloud storage, and instant messenger (IM) to communicate and collaborate with one another remotely. They reported that working remotely via online channels was effective when browsing information sources or making a separate piece of document.

However, in the initial and final phase of a project, team members tend to feel the necessity to have F2F meetings. In the initial phase, they need to set the goal, brainstorm for ideas, and decide the overall direction and share the workload. In the final phase, the individual pieces of work need to be synthesized into one single outcome by putting various materials and information together. Although many options are available for remote collaboration, F2F meetings still have their own merits. More specifically, we could concede that a F2F meeting is still effective, especially when various ideas and information need to be dealt with for a shared goal.

"*We tried having a meeting through Google Hangouts to make PPT; however, it did not work well. Firstly, it took a lot of time to set up. Also, most of us were easily distracted by other tasks, for example, visiting Facebook. After all, we decided to meet at the cafe the next morning.*" (P2)

Environmental Context: Why they hold meetings in casual places.

They reported that they usually have meetings in school cafeterias, cafés, lounges, classrooms, or restaurants. The reasons why they preferred those places for meetings were their ease of use and affordability. As those casual places were always open and available to use, they did not need to check vacancy or make reservations in advance. Also, they thought it was relatively affordable than renting meeting spaces. On the other hand, limited accessibility to equipped meeting environments in school sometimes made them choose casual places for meetings.

"*To use* a *seminar room in school, we need to make a reservation in advance, only if they are not all booked up. Checking vacancy, making reservation, getting permission.... That's quite burdensome.*" (P5)

"*We usually go to school cafeteria, because it's always available to use and quite affordable. We just buy cups of coffee and start the meeting, right away. That's it.*" (P3)

Information Type: What kinds of information are shared. The types of information that were shared in the meeting varied according to each work phase. In the initial phase, web links, including news articles, blog posts, online encyclopedias, or related books, were actively shared among members to go through a pre-scanning step, to get primary ideas and to examine existing solutions. In the interim phase, a relatively formal form of documents, such as a research paper, a market report, and materials of a presentation, started to be shared. In the later phase, the divided portion of final materials, which were collected separately by each member, needed to be shared and synthesized into final deliverables.

The interesting forms of information discovered throughout the group work phases were notes and memos made individually or collectively. When taking minutes, one participant usually took the role of documenting the meeting. On the other hand, during discussions, various participants participated in taking memos and notes together, using pieces of paper as a whiteboard.

Figure 2. Taking notes and memos during meetings.

Collectively made memos and notes with rough sketches, lists, tables, and scribbles (Figure 2) tended to contain the consensus and the detailed schemes about specific tasks, even though these looked messy and not well-organized. Thus, they were regarded as very important outcomes. After meetings, the memos and notes were required to be documented and distributed to all members via e-mail or IM. However, the problem was that nobody actually wanted to volunteer to take on those tasks, so they sometimes took a picture of these papers using their own smartphones instead.

Information-Sharing Method: How they share information.
We could characterize the methods of sharing information in casual places into three patterns. The first pattern (Figure 3-1) was using a mobile device that had the largest screen (mostly laptops or tablet PCs) as a shared display on behalf of a beam projector or a large screen TV. Through one single mobile device screen, presentations and discussions were visually projected. The second pattern (Figure 3-2) was using each member's personal mobile device during a meeting after transmitting documents using shared cloud storage services (such as *Dropbox*) or e-mail. The last pattern (Figure 3-3) is that paper handouts were printed beforehand and distributed to group members.

Figure 3. Three patterns in sharing information
3-1. Using one mobile screen as a shared display
3-2. Using personal devices after transmitting documents
3-3. Using paper handouts

Each pattern had its merits and limitations. First of all, in terms of the convenience in setting up, the first measure, making use of one single mobile device as a shared display was preferred because it could be set up easily on the spot unlike other methods (e.g. sending emails or preparing printouts in advance). On the other hand, as for *archivability,* the second method (sharing files) was regarded as a better option because all materials were already shared through individual e-mail or cloud storage, therefore, there was no need to share them after meetings. In addition, the third option (paper handouts) received the most favorable remarks on making annotations freely.

Nevertheless, we could find that those information-sharing patterns had their own limitations, hindering the effective exchange of information and feedback. When participants adopted the first method, the screen size was usually not large enough to allow all members to share information and interact with it, so makeshift measures accompanied with physical rearrangement, such as leaning over to the screen or gathering behind the presenter (Figure 4), were required. Meanwhile, a risk of a personal message and a push alert being likely to be exposed to others unintentionally was also pointed out.

"*When group members are more than three or four, using a laptop or tablet as a shared screen is getting tough.*" (P2)

Figure 4. Sharing a mobile screen as a group

In the cases of adopting the second or third measures, we could observe that group members usually had difficulties in catching up with the current progress during a collective review session. For example, when one pointed out a particular table, figure or sentence in documents, some members were observed to browse each page back and forth hastily to find the page that was currently being addressed. In those cases, although the materials themselves had been distributed through each participant's personal device or handout, the shared view was absent to enable multiple people to see the same object simultaneously.

The common problems among the three patterns were identified in the turn-taking process and in the process of making simultaneous contributions.

First, the current turn-taking process to switch information resource or presenter was not smooth. Every time in switching information sources, they should switch devices, transmit files to others or print new copies. Furthermore, the roles of each member were constantly switched between the presenter (who presented the information or personal opinion) and the audience (who listened to presentations or other opinions). Due to the constant change in materials in presentation and roles, the turn-taking processes in the current practices often prolonged each meeting and made it less productive.

Also, the current measures in reflecting all members' ideas and opinions simultaneously had shortcomings. For example, pointing out, evaluating, or making comments about certain parts of a document could not be delivered and reflected upon effectively between members due to a small screen (pattern 1) or the lack of a shared view (pattern 2, 3). Also, individual memos and annotations were hardly recognized and integrated. Consequently, various interview participants pointed out that most parts of the contribution tended to be predominated by a few members.

Interestingly, these problems could be found in well-equipped meeting environments as well. However, they seemed to be more intensified in poorly-equipped meeting conditions due to the lack of sophisticated presentation and meeting equipment.

Design Guidelines

In the user study, we could identify the current information-sharing practices and their limitations found in poorly-equipped environments. In this section, we presented five design guidelines along with this user study. The design guidelines would be importantly considered and applied to the design and implementation of Ubi-jector.

A. Minimize the steps to set up the meeting

In the user study, we could find that the first pattern to share information (using a single mobile device) was most preferred because of its convenience to set up. Conversely, the second and third measures were less adopted since those required redundant efforts (transmitting or printing materials) to set up. Therefore, the system for supporting information-sharing in casual places needs to minimize the efforts to set up.

B. Support the simple turn-taking process in switching information source and presenter

We could find that the information-sharing process got harder as information sources were increasingly varied and the presenter was changed constantly. These turn-taking processes often obstructed the flow of meetings and made the durations of meetings longer. To address this issue, the turn-taking process to share scattered information from various members should be simplified.

C. Support the coexistence between individual and group works

In the user study, we could find that each member's personal mobile device was frequently used as a shared display. Also, people often had difficulties in catching up with the current progress due to the lack of a shared view among participants. These practices inform us that a shared display is essentially required in co-located collaborations. At the same time, we observed that individuals often browsed materials personally and made personal memos during a meeting. It means that both individual and group works are usually progressed simultaneously. Accordingly, the system should provide users with the workspaces both for individual and group works.

D. Make all members' contributions equally reflected and recognized simultaneously

Due to the limited capacity of one single mobile device as a shared display (Measure 1) or the absence of a shared display (Measure 2, 3), reflecting all members' ideas and opinions simultaneously was tough. Also, each member's contribution was not recognized noticeably. Consequently, it was reported that most parts of the contribution were predominated by only a few members, which hindered the productive collaboration process. To fix this issue, all members' contributions should be equally reflected and recognized simultaneously.

E. Archive materials and annotations within the flow of each meeting

Sharing materials and memos that has been discussed during a meeting is essential to proceed with further works. Thus, files of materials and memos, including collectively made ones, should be transmitted to each member's device in order to review them later. However, to transmit this information, one should take charge of organizing and distributing them through e-mail or IM after each meeting. We found that some members felt these post-sharing processes sometimes made them tired and resulted in some additional burdens. To relieve the burdens, we should lessen the steps required to transmit memos, annotations, and shared documents to other members after meetings.

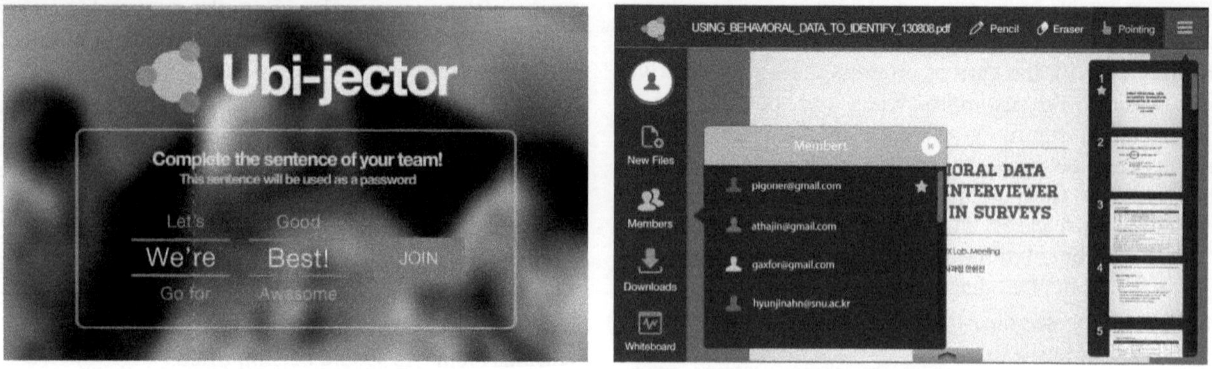

Figure 5. User Interface of Ubi-jector. (Left: Launch View / Right: Workspace View)

SYSTEM DESIGN AND IMPLEMENTATION

As we drew several design guidelines above, we could ascertain the specification and the features of Ubi-jector and implement our research prototype; Ubi-jector.

Ubi-jector:

Ubi-jector is a mobile application that provides a shared information space for supporting group works held in poorly-equipped environments. The main idea of Ubi-jector is making use of each mobile device as a public shared display instead of using one single device. Ubi-jector aims to create an effective and pleasant collaboration environment even in poorly-equipped places.

It is developed based on a P2P network model, allowing participants to share information without a central server and Internet connection. Also, making a group in Ubi-jector is very simple and quick, requiring no extra hardware and registration process.

Once members run Ubi-jector and are provided a shared view, every document is sent page by page by the presenter to the other members' mobile devices. Also, interactive annotation and pointing features are available to allow all members to actively participate in-group discussions. Lastly, the integrated archiving feature is designed to eliminate the post-sharing process of documents and memos that were presented and made during meetings.

System Architecture

Ubi-jector adopts a P2P ad hoc network model, allowing participants to be connected easily and share information promptly. For adopting a P2P model to Ubi-jector, we sought several options for P2P networking protocol enabling ad hoc, device-to-device communication without the use of an intermediary server. After inspecting several options, we decided to use the *Samsung Chord* [22], which enables us to make the prototype of Ubi-jector easily using its API. *Chord* supports the discovery of each group member using a UDP broadcast-based discovery and creates a P2P local network to share data, binary messages, and files with selected members of the network. Ubi-jector was developed on Android OS using JAVA code.

In Ubi-jector, all three canvases run at the same time: one for s shared screen, the other for private browsing, and another for a whiteboard. In the canvas for the shared screen, the presenter's page and every participant's annotation and pointing motions are processed.

One person who starts to import a document from her or his device to share is empowered as a super user in a shared space. A super user is allowed to present a document that has been converted to segmented images page by page. When a presenter turns to the next page or slide, the data, which includes the image file of each page, the total page number, the current page number, the presenter's device ID, and the current file name, are transmitted to all members. Documents are transmitted per page, instead of the whole file at once, so delay time to transfer file is minimized.

Using Ubi-jector

In this section, we describe the user interface of Ubi-jector and its features. Figure 5 shows Ubi-jector interface, which is commonly applied for both smartphone and tablet PC. The overall design consists of two main views. One is the "Launch view," and the latter is the "Workspace view." Launch view helps users to open and participate in their group's shared space easily and quickly. Workspace interface facilitates the group/individual information sharing process.

Simplified Joining Process Ubi-jector does not require making any account or user profile to use it. Instead, we implemented simple authorization methods to simplify the process for making and joining a group workspace. After connecting their devices to the same Wi-Fi or mobile AP, there is one more hurdle to ensure only group members can join in a specific shared space. When a group of people makes the same combination of text set, they can get to join in the same private channel. Two sets of picker for text completion (3*12, total 36 sets) are provided in Launch view (Figure 5), so they can pick the text set together by holding a conversation on the spot.

Easily Controllable and Switchable Presentation Area In Workspace view (Figure 5), the presentation area is where a document is presented and a whiteboard is used. Just importing a file using the "new file" button presents information to all members page by page. A member who initiates to import and present a document becomes and assumes the role of the presenter that has the right to control page turn and occupy shared view. At the same time, other members will become the audience naturally, who cannot control the shared view. In short, the shared view is controlled differently according to the role of each user. The presenter can influence how each document is showed in other members' devices by controlling not only the page turning but also the page size, which is adjustable by zooming and scrolling actions. To summarize, Ubi-jector provides easily controllable-shared space by dividing the member's roles into presenter and audience for effective presentation.

Furthermore, Ubi-jector supports the easily switchable turn-taking process. When an audience member wants to be a presenter and imports a new file, the right for controlling the shared view and the presenter status is handed over to the new presenter. It enables various types of information from multiple members to be circulated and switched smoothly.

Interactive Annotation and Pointing Although the right for page control is assigned to the presenter only, the right for making annotation and pointing is open to all members during a presentation. The toolbox containing the pencil, eraser, and pointing features works within the presentation area. Every participant is assigned with each unique color at the moment when participants join a shared space. Each annotation and pointing would be colored with their unique colors, which makes them easier to recognize and be aware of the contribution each member made. (Figure 6) Through these features, reflecting all members' ideas and opinions simultaneously is possible and each member's contribution will be recognized more prominently.

Figure 6. Interactive Annotation and Pointing

Private Browsing/Sync As we mentioned previously, a presenter controls the shared view. However, we also allowed the audience members to browse pages privately within the pages that were already presented. For example, when a presenter presented pages from 1 to 3 and now proceeded to show page 4, audience members were able to go back to page 1, 2, or 3 and browse them freely in case they needed to review them privately. Private browsing is done separately from the shared view. At the same time, the *sync* feature makes an audience quickly come back and follow up the page, which is being presented by a presenter. (Figure 7) Through this feature, we would like to support the seamless connection and transition between group and individual information processing.

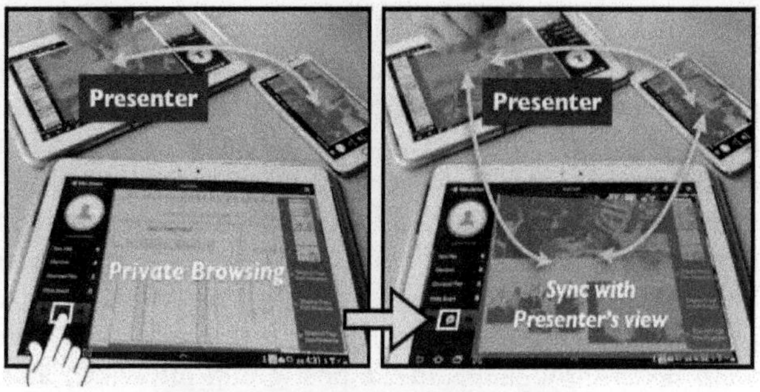

Figure 7. (Left) Private Browsing (Right) Sync with Presenter's View

Integrated Archiving of Previous Meetings When a new document is presented, the previous shared documents, including annotations, are integrated and archived in "Downloads." It would be helpful to revisit and make use of previous records of meetings. Because Ubi-jector records and archives all kinds of information being shared during a meeting, it should lessen the burden of users transmitting them later through IM or e-mail.

EVALUATION

In order to investigate the usability and effectiveness of Ubi-jector, we conducted a user study. (Figure 8) Also, we attempted to draw some lessons to improve Ubi-jector further. We recruited a total of 15 participants and divided them into five groups (three participants for each group). They were college or graduate school students from various backgrounds (music, sociology, computer science and etc.), and their average age was 25.3 years (nine females). They were recruited through social network postings. We tried to team up a group wherein participants would have known each other in advance, to minimize the possible impacts of social contextual factors such as level of closeness. Thus, we encouraged them to participate in this user study with his or her colleagues and teamed up them based on each personal intimacy.

Because we needed to mimic the meeting environments in poorly-equipped settings as similarly as possible, each group session was held in school cafeterias and lounges. There were two Android 10.1 inch tablet PCs and one Android 4.1-inch smartphone running Ubi-jector for the group session. These devices were connected to same mobile AP network. Each group was asked to conduct a group task together and complete an in-depth questionnaire. Then, we conducted post-group interviews to hear their opinion of Ubi-jector. Each group session took approximately 1 hour.

Procedure

Before the study, participants completed a short questionnaire to gather their basic information. Each study began with the short introduction session for 10 minutes to let them familiarize themselves with our system. Next, we gave them a group task, that is, to choose one of homepage design among six options. On each device, there were several PDF format files that contained several design options. We asked to assume themselves in the same team that needed to assess all options and made a decision. We encouraged them to utilize Ubi-jector as actively as possible and take both presenter and audience roles during conducting the task. After they discussed and made a decision, we asked them to fill out an in-depth questionnaire, and the following group interviews were conducted. During group sessions, their activities and uses of Ubi-jector were video-recorded, and observation notes were taken throughout. In the post-group interview, all of their comments were also recorded and transcribed.

Figure 8. Group sessions for the evaluation.

Results

In the pre-study questionnaire, 87% of the participants replied that they have had meetings in casual places very frequently. Also, 90% of the participants answered that they have known other group members very well as a friend or co-worker.

Taking the post-questionnaire responses, the first part of the questionnaire asked them to rate the difficulty level of the task and the overall satisfaction level of the task on a five-point scale (from 1 = low to 5 = high). The average rating of task difficulty was 2.2, and task satisfaction level was 3.8.

In the second parts of the questionnaire, we asked them to rate usability such as effectiveness, utility, and learnability of Ubi-jector based on 7-Likert scale (from strongly agree=7 to strongly disagree=1). The subjects evaluated the usability (5.4/7), utility (5.2/7), and applicability (5.4/7) of Ubi-jector prototype very positively.

In the third part of the questionnaire, participants evaluated each feature of Ubi-jector separately. They were given five statements describing each feature of Ubi-jector and rated the level of agreements. Most of features received high scores. Especially, "simplified joining proces" (5.8/7) and "easily controllable and switchable presentation area" (5.6/7) got the most positive responses.

In the last parts of the questionnaire (Table 2), we attempted to scrutinize the effectiveness of Ubi-jector in terms of the improvement of group communication efficiency. Using 7-point Likert scale, we estimated how much they thought this system improved their group communication effectiveness. The first two statements (d1 and d2) were designed to evaluate the effectiveness of communication compared with when they were the presenter and the audience; the other statements were about evaluating the qualities of communication (d3 and d4) and active participation (d5). At this part of questionnaire, we have got generally positive responses, too. This result showed that Ubi-jector has the possibilities that could enhance the effectiveness of information sharing and active participation in a group communication context.

Given statements	Score
D1. (When I present) the contents of information were conveyed well to other team members.	5.1/7
D2. (When I was a audience) I could get the contents of information fully.	5.1/7
D3. (Comparing previous experiences) it is more effective to share information.	5.8/7
D4. (Comparing previous experiences) it is more effective to share ideas and discuss.	5.5/7
D5. Every group member participated actively in group discussion and decision-making.	5.8/7

Table 2. Evaluation of effectiveness of group Communication

Beside these results from the in-depth questionnaire study, observations and interview also gave us powerful insights and helpful feedbacks to improve Ubi-jector further. These findings described in the Discussion section.

DISCUSSION

In this section, we first discuss the conflict patterns found and reported in the evaluation and seek possible solutions, which need to be addressed in future work. These conflicts are raised by contradicting factors and merits, so exploring each side and comparing the trade-offs needs to be conducted in developing the mobile application for supporting co-located information sharing. Also, we describe the limitation of this research and the potential extension of Ubi-jector to other environments.

Tensions between Public Space versus Personal Space

Mobile devices mainly have been used and controlled for personal purpose [9] and recognized as a private space for each individual. However, bringing a shared, public space over to a mobile device in Ubi-jector may make users feel a little awkward. In Ubi-jector, there are several considerations to address this tension between them, such as private browsing and sync features. However, especially when a presenter controls a shared view, some audience members feel uncomfortable because they feel like their territory and autonomy has been compromised.

"*I felt something uncomfortable when I saw my display was controlled by others. Maybe, as I could always do anything that I want on my own mobile device, the feeling that I could not control my device freely is a little weird.*" (P7)

Furthermore, regarding the annotation feature, many requested for private annotation space. According to Marshall and Brush's research about the relationship between personal and public annotations, only a small fraction of annotations made are directly related to those shared in discussions and personal annotations undergo dramatic changes when they are shared in public discussion [13]. Many participants said that it is somewhat uncomfortable when all of the annotations they made were shared to other members publicly because they were not ready to show them or they did not need to be shown to others.

We believe that these tensions between personal and public space found in Ubi-jector are due to the fact that Ubi-jector prototype has no clear distinction between personal and pubic space. Also, it mostly focuses on the public uses of mobile devices rather than personal uses. It was a design trade-off when we implemented Ubi-jector. As many participants pointed out, we need to consider the separation between public and personal space in our future prototype. One alternative could be providing 'dual view' (one for the presenter's view and one for private browsing). Another option would be 'invisible annotations', which can be made and used only for personal purposes.

Role and Control: Presenter versus Audience

Because of the spontaneity of F2F meetings, each member's role of members (presenter/audience) is constantly switched and various materials are shared very frequently in Ubi-jector. However, as their roles and materials are changed so frequently, they can hardly recognize their current role and status, we need to consider a clearer visual cue to show their current status and role.

On the other hands, we could find that there were clear differences in opinions according to each participant's role toward control.

"*When I was a presenter, I felt various features of controlling the shared view, such as page turning and zooming, were nice and effective. In contrast, when I became a member of the audience, I wished this system to be more flexible in terms of control.*" (P4)

This user's statement shows the different needs of users evidently; the presenter needs more hard control over the shared view, but the audience wants more flexible control. For example, some users asked us to restrict private browsing and lock all members in the presenter's shared view. Others said that the current control is so strong that it needs to be less rigid. We could not conclude which side to take at this moment, so we need to conduct further user study to address this conflict.

Screen Size: Smartphone versus Tablet PC

As each mobile device has various screen sizes, the screen size issue should have been considered very importantly in designing Ubi-jector. In our user study, we provided both a smartphone and tablet PC, so we could observe the performance and capacity differences between them. The participants who used a smartphone in the user study were more apt to try zooming and scrolling the screen than the tablet PC users. Also, they made fewer annotations on the presentation area than tablet PC users. This means that the smaller screen size of a smartphone often blocks users to use Ubi-jector freely because of its limited screen size and capability to adopt various interactions. To address this issue, we need to support users to get the optimal view of each material even in small mobile screens by allowing scrolling and zooming interactions freely. Also, offering an adjustment tool for resizing materials should be taken into account. Furthermore, we need to consider text input as an annotation method along with the current pen tool. Writing a memo using pen tool seems too uncomfortable for smartphone users, so receiving text inputs using a virtual keyboard would be a better way for making annotations.

Information Type: Text Based versus Image Based

Ubi-jector needs to be responsive for the types of information being shared, as one of study participants expressed:

"*In the case when the presented materials were filled with stuffy texts, I cannot be sure that this Ubi-jector could accommodate those kinds of documents effectively.*" (P2)

Due to the small screen sizes of mobile devices, we need to seek more effective ways of showing various types of information in mobile devices. In Ubi-jector, image-based information or PPT documents with larger and fewer texts can be presented relatively easily. However, presenting text-based documents, such as research papers, can be problematic. Thus, we need to be responsive for the characteristics of each information types, to provide more optimal presentations possible in Ubi-jector.

Study Limitations

In addition to the conflicts patterns and possible solutions in Ubi-jector, we now describe the limitations of our research. First, the situations that we created in the evaluation processes were controlled and artificial. Also, it was conducted with a limited number and range of people. Also, the amount of time spent that we observed was insufficient.

In our future research, it is required to conduct a longitudinal user study with volumes of people in real meeting settings. Furthermore, we should evaluate the effectiveness of Ubi-jector in comparison with conventional meeting environments. Finally, the current prototype is necessary to be developed further which can support varied mobile OSs and various types of information.

Extension of Ubi-jector to Other Environments

Our study demonstrated the potentiality of shared information space using mobile devices in casual places. However, we can also extend the applicability of Ubi-jector into broader scopes. Ubi-jector can be applied readily at any place and by any organization that needs to have shared information space in poorly-equipped conditions. For example, specific educational environments or industrial settings would be considered.

CONCLUSION

In this paper, we proposed a mobile system, Ubi-jector for supporting group work held in casual places where the shared information workspace is normally absent. Ubi-jector provides a shared information workspace by making use of each participant's mobile device as a shared display. Ubi-jector was designed to create effective meeting environments even in poorly-equipped conditions.

This research has its own contributions in Mobile HCI and CSCW fields because it explored the opportunity of the collaborative use of mobile devices as a shared workspace. By performing a user study, we figured out the characteristic information-sharing patterns and drew design guidelines for poorly-equipped meeting conditions. Also we implemented a mobile system, Ubi-jector that provides competitive features suited for the unique characteristics of F2F group meetings in casual places. Furthermore, we conducted an evaluation study to measure the effectiveness and usability of the prototype. The evaluation results showed that Ubi-jector has the possibilities to facilitate information sharing effectively and foster active participation. Lastly, we discussed the conflicts of contradicting factors in designing Ubi-jector and compared their trade-offs. In the future research, we would elaborate the user study further and expand the possible application of Ubi-jector to other environments.

REFERENCES

1. Alarcon, R., Guerrero, L.A., Ochoa, S.F., and Pino, J.A. Analysis and design of mobile collaborative applications using contextual elements. *Computing and Informatics 25*, 6 (2012), 469–496.
2. Ali-Hassan, H., Nevo, D., and Nevo, S. Mobile collaboration: Exploring the role of social capital. *ACM SIGMIS Database 41*, 2 (2010), 9–24.
3. Brodie, Jacqueline, and Mark Perry. Mobile collaboration at the tabletop in public spaces. In *Proc. CSCW* 2002. ACM Press (2002), 1-6.
4. Fussell, S.R., Kraut, R.E., and Siegel, J. Coordination of communication. In *Proc. CSCW 2000*, ACM Press (2000), 21–30.
5. Huang, E.M. and Mynatt, E.D. Semi-public displays for small, co-located groups. In *Proc. CHI 2003*, ACM Press (2003), 49-56.
6. Kawakita, J. *The original KJ method.* Tokyo: Kawakita Research Institute, 1991.
7. Kraut, R.E., Gergle, D., and Fussell, S.R. The use of visual information in shared visual spaces: Informing the development of virtual co-presence. In *Proc. CSCW 2002*, ACM Press (2002), 31-40.
8. Ah Kun, L. M., & Marsden, G., Co-present photo sharing on mobile devices. In *Proc. MobileHCI 2007,* ACM Press (2007), 277-284.
9. Lucero, A., Holopainen, J., and Jokela, T. Pass-them-around: collaborative use of mobile phones for photo sharing. In Proc. CHI 2011, ACM Press (2011), 1787-1796.
10. Lucero, A., Holopainen, J., and Jokela, T. MobiComics: collaborative use of mobile phones and large displays for public expression. In *Proc. MobileHCI 2012*, ACM Press(2012), 383-392.
11. Lucero, A., Keränen, J., and Korhonen, H. Collaborative use of mobile phones for brainstorming. In *Proc. MobileHCI 2010*, ACM(2010), 337-340.
12. Luyten, K., Verpoorten, K., and Coninx, K. Ad-hoc co-located collaborative work with mobile devices. In *Proc. MobileHCI 2007*, ACM(2007), 507–514.
13. Marshall, C.C. and Brush, A.J.B. Exploring the relationship between personal and public annotations. *Digital Libraries, 2004.* In *Proc. Joint ACM/IEEE Conference 2004*, IEEE (2004), 349–357.
14. Mejia, D.A., Morán, A.L., and Favela, J. Supporting Informal Co-located Collaboration in Hospital Work. *Groupware: Design, Implementation, and Use*, Springer (2007), 255–270.
15. Meyer, E.M., Wichmann, D., Büsch, H., and Boll, S. Supporting Mobile Collaboration in Spatially Distributed Workgroups with Digital Interactive Maps. *Mobile Networks and Applications 17*, 3 (2011), 365–375.
16. Reis, S. and Church, K. Insights into co-located shared mobile search. *Ext. Abstracts CHI EA 2013*, ACM Press (2013), 1401-1406.
17. Schrage, M. No more teams!: Mastering the dynamics of creative collaboration. Currency Doubleday New York, 1995.
18. Shah, C. Collaborative Information Seeking : A Literature Review. *Advances in Librarianship 32*, 2010, 3–33.
19. Shen, C., Everitt, K., and Ryall, K. UbiTable : Impromptu Face-to-Face Collaboration on Horizontal Interactive Surfaces. *UbiComp 2003: Ubiquitous Computing,* Springer (2003), 281-288
20. Sutcliffe, A. Applying small group theory to analysis and design of CSCW systems. *ACM SIGSOFT Software Engineering Notes*, ACM Press (2005), 1–6.
21. Wigdor, D., Jiang, H., Forlines, C., Borkin, M., and Shen, C. WeSpace: the design development and deployment of a walk-up and share multi-surface visual collaboration system. In *Proc. CHI 2009,* ACM Press (2009), 1237–1246.
22. Samsung Chord http://developer.samsung.com/chord.

CoSMiC: Designing a Mobile Crowd-sourced Collaborative Application to Find a Missing Child in Situ

Hyojeong Shin[1], Taiwoo Park[2], Seungwoo Kang[3,4], Bupjae Lee[5], Junehwa Song[3], Yohan Chon[6], Hojung Cha[6]

[1] Department of Electrical & Computer Engineering, Duke University

[2] Department of Media and Information, Michigan State University, [3] Department of Computer Science, KAIST

[4] Center for Mobile Software Platform, KAIST, [5] Google Korea, [6] Department of Computer Science, Yonsei University

ABSTRACT

Finding a missing child is an important problem concerning not only parents but also our society. It is essential and natural to use serendipitous clues from neighbors for finding a missing child. In this paper, we explore a new architecture of crowd collaboration to expedite this mission-critical process and propose a crowd-sourced collaborative mobile application, CoSMiC. It helps parents find their missing child quickly on the spot before he or she completely disappears. A key idea lies in constructing the location history of a child via crowd participation, thereby leading parents to their child easily and quickly. We implement a prototype application and conduct extensive user studies to assess the design of the application and investigate its potential for practical use.

Author Keywords

Crowdsourcing; Missing child; Localization; Collaborative application

ACM Classification Keywords

H.5.3 [**Information Interfaces & Presentation**]: Group and Organization Interfaces---collaborative computing, computer-supported cooperative work

INTRODUCTION

Missing children inflict huge emotional, physical and financial impacts on family and community members [10]. As mentioned by [9], the experience of having a missing child is traumatic and grievous. Also, locating missing persons and providing them with appropriate treatment has a significant cost impact upon society [10] and is, therefore, a daunting task. To minimize such impacts, it is crucial to find missing children as soon as possible; e.g., within several minutes. In most cases, however, it is very difficult for parents to find missing children immediately.

We note that finding a missing child is inherently a collaborative search task. When a child is out of the sight of a parent or guardian who accompanies the child, the parent or guardian usually asks for help from nearby people first. However, this approach is not always effective; despite the urgency of the situation, it is hard to find someone who has actually seen and recognized the child and knows his/her whereabouts. Also, it may be a burden for most strangers who do not know the child to help search actively. Ideally, the parent repeats this process of approaching and asking a number of strangers until she finds her child, but such efforts are often futile. The parent loses critical time and, hence, the possibility of finding the child; in the end, she reports her child missing to the police to get cooperation from the authorities.

This paper explores a new architecture of crowd collaboration and proposes a crowd-sourced collaborative mobile application, CoSMiC, to expedite the mission-critical process of finding a missing child. CoSMiC helps parents find a child who has gone out of sight quickly and in situ before his/her complete disappearance. Studies have shown that the possibility of finding a missing child diminishes as time passes [9] and efforts to find someone after his/her complete disappearance are not very effective [16]. It is critical to find the child as soon as possible right after the parents recognize that the child is out of their sight. In this situation, CoSMiC enables parents to get help from a number of strangers effectively even without physically approaching and asking them. While seeking neighbors' help to find a missing child may involve psychological and social issues, we focus on technical aspects in this paper.

While the recent advance in mobile computing technologies provides opportunity to build such an application, it is still challenging to realize an effective approach for CoSMiC. Quickly locating a child is a primary technical problem in developing the application. In outdoor places, adopting a GPS technology can be an easy solution. However, it is almost impossible to locate a child in indoor places with GPS. In urban areas, there are a number of large indoor places, such as shopping malls, which parents often visit with their child to eat out or spend their leisure time. Since those places are generally large, crowded, and packed with restaurants and stores, it is easy to get separated from a child and (once separated) hard to find her quickly. To deal with indoor spaces, alternative solutions can utilize existing indoor positioning techniques [3, 4, 18, 21, 25]. However, the cost of deploying related infrastructures or building databases for indoor localization can be huge, and thus

MobileHCI '14, September 23 - 26 2014, Toronto, ON, Canada

ACM 978-1-4503-3004-6/14/09$15.00.
http://dx.doi.org/10.1145/2628363.2628400

Phase	Methods	Participants
Motivational Study	Semi-structured Interview	12 adults with lost-and-found children
Application Design and Development		
Feasibility Study	Questionnaire survey and online interview	135 adults (as crowd)
	2-week human-subject test for response rate	38 adults (as crowd)
Case Study	App usage test in an amusement park	5 adults as children, 5 as parents

Table 1. Overview of studies

applicable coverage might be highly limited; it is difficult to develop a rapid solution.

CoSMiC aims to gather collective in-situ intelligence from nearby people and deliver it to parents in an urgent situation. A key idea lies in constructing the location history of a missing child via crowd participation. Such a history, a series of landmarks, can be effective to lead parents to their child more easily [9]. To collect enough observations to find the child within a short time, the application gathers information and observations on the situation, related or seemingly unrelated, from a large number of people. The information and observation from each person may not be useful within its own context. However, it can be identified as a meaningful piece of information in the context of a large collection of related observations, which can be turned into valuable location history for parents. To this end, we propose the concept of *virtual encounter* to fully harness potential participants who are willing to help parents but do not encounter their child physically.

To ensure the motivation behind our application design as well as its feasibility and usability, we conducted a set of user studies. Table 1 summaries our studies. First, a semi-structured interview with 12 parents allows us to understand parents' experiences of losing their child in detail and identify design implications for the application. Second, we design and develop a prototype application for proof of concept based on the implications. Third, through a user survey with 135 participants and a human-subject test with 38 participants, we investigate the potential of CoSMiC in terms of crowd's willingness to help parents and perception of design choices. Fourth, from a case study in a real place, we assess the effect of application and its implication for the behavior of finding missing children.

The contributions of this paper are as follows. First, we propose a novel crowd-sourced collaborative application to help parents find a missing child quickly. Second, we provide design implications for such an application that are distilled from user interviews and surveys. Third, we implement and demonstrate the proposed application and evaluate its effectiveness through a case study in a real place.

BACKGROUND AND RELATED WORK

Approaches to Prevent and Find a Missing Child

Approaches to prevent and find a missing child can be viewed from two different points; i.e., before and after a child goes missing (the left and right side of Figure 1, respectively). Firstly, it cannot be emphasized enough that the prevention of missing children is important. Government authorities or organizations, such as National Center for Missing and Exploited Children (NCMEC) in the U.S. [20], provide guides and resources for child safety and prevention of missing; e.g., "*Know the rules for child safety in amusement or theme parks*" [15]. Such guides help parents teach their children how to stay safe or prepare a description of their child to prevent them from going missing. In addition to following the guides, parents can use off-the-shelf products such as proximity alarms and baby safety harnesses [5] when they go out with their children. However, these guides or products themselves cannot be a complete solution to prevent a child from being lost. Also, once a child goes missing, other proper solutions would be necessary to find him or her.

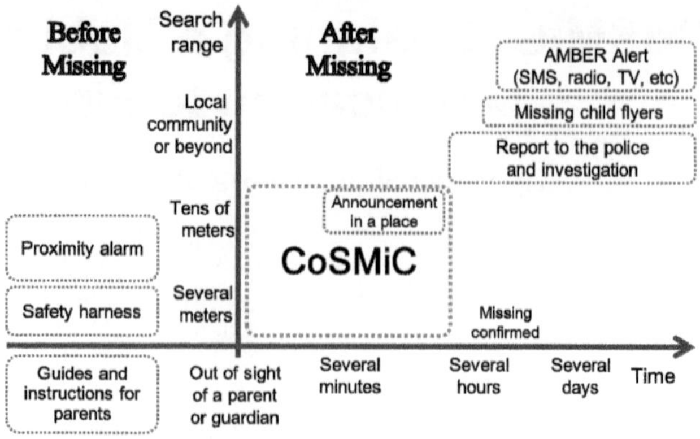

Figure 1. Approaches to prevent/find a missing child.

Secondly, efforts to find a missing child can be viewed at two points—in terms of elapsed time and search range—as shown in Figure 1; i.e., initial searches by parents or guardians mainly in the vicinity area and searches with the help of authorities, such as the police, after a missing person report is filed. Usually, when parents recognize that their child is out of their sight, they first check areas where the child was last seen and ask nearby people about their child's whereabouts. The parents repeatedly carry out the process of approaching and asking a number of people if they have seen their child.

When they fail to find their child on their own and consider their child missing, the parents contact their local law enforcement agency to report their child missing. In this stage, a guide; e.g., one provided by NCMEC [24] can help parents get firsthand advice about what to do, whom to contact, and how to assist law enforcement. Missing child flyers may be made and distributed to the public. In case of child abduction (if applicable), a child abduction alert system, such as AMBER Alert [2], can be activated and descriptions of the abduction can be distributed via a variety of channels, such as radio and television stations and SMS.

This paper explores the possibility of a meaningful solution to helping parents recover their child quickly in situ when their child goes out of sight and, thereby, prevent his or her complete disappearance. It is critical to figure out whereabouts of a missing child as soon as possible. It will be thus very helpful to support parents at the stage of initial search, when they are doing mainly by themselves (see Figure 1). CoSMiC is an attempt towards a solution in this stage. Note that a child can be lost in diverse situations, such as simple disappearance and abduction. In this paper, we focus on the former case.

Solution Design Space

To provide such a solution, we note that it is a basic and core technical problem to quickly locate a child when she is separated from her guardians. For this purpose, we can consider two alternative approaches.

The first approach is to utilize indoor positioning technologies to precisely locate a child. Indoor place sensing and learning systems can identify places with meter-level accuracy. The main idea is that two places are considered an identical place if they have relatively similar *place signatures* obtained from radio beacons (e.g., cell towers, Wi-Fi, and Bluetooth) [4] and surrounding factors (e.g., light, color, texture, and ambient noise) [3, 18]. Geometric localization systems using radio technology, such as UWB and RFID, can also be employed to pinpoint the location of objects [21, 25]. With these approaches, a child carries a tiny device that obtains place signatures, and accordingly a parent can query the location of the child in case of an emergency based on the signatures captured by the child's device. For this purpose, databases storing associated place signatures or corresponding infrastructure should be built in advance. The service coverage is significantly limited to selective space as the construction of the database. The limited coverage and its management cost can be a barrier to realizing an effective solution.

The second approach is to harness the help of the nearby crowd to avoid the cost of deploying infrastructures and databases; i.e., in-situ crowdsourcing in a localized area. With this approach, a parent provides a description of child to voluntary participants in the vicinity and asks them about his/her whereabouts. This can reduce the time and effort required by parents. However, different from most existing crowdsourcing frameworks [1, 27], which harness human intelligence to accomplish tasks that can be carried out remotely online, the problem addressed in this paper involves a strict spatiotemporal constraint on participation. Moreover, the search task and participation should be complete within a short period of time. Only people who physically encounter and recognize the child can respond to the query. Thus, the number of qualified people can be highly limited. Also, it is often ineffective to just rely on people's memory to find the child [31, 32]. It might be difficult to obtain sufficient information to locate the child quickly. A recent work studied a theoretical solution to the problem of crowd-powered package delivery which requires people to collaborate in a synchronized fashion in time and physical space [30]. However, it was not shown whether the solution can be applied to the problem of finding a missing child; even if it is possible, it would be still quite limited since it has no choice but to rely on people's physical encounter and recognition.

To address the problem, CoSMiC adopts a hybrid approach that harnesses crowdsourcing based on indoor position sensing through the use of an existing widely deployed infrastructure; i.e., Wi-Fi. As such, it avoids the cost of building and maintaining place databases while overcoming the limitation of crowd participation based on physical encounters by introducing the concept of virtual encounter.

MOTIVATIONAL STUDY

We conducted semi-structured interviews to understand parents' experiences with losing a child in detail and identify design implications for the proposed application. The interviews were conducted with 12 parents who had experiences with losing and finding their children. Since these experiences are not enjoyable, we recruited the participants personally and checked whether they were ready to share their experiences. Prior to the interview, we explained the objective of this research to the participants. All interviews were recorded, transcribed, and coded. We then iteratively clustered the codes into higher-level categories. As a result, we extracted important findings that support the motivation and provide design implications.

Children of the interviewed parents included boys and girls who were 2 to 6 years old (3 years old on average). The majority of them could walk and were immature in their communication skills. Ten of fifteen children had been lost in indoor spaces, such as department stores, or arcaded indoor places, such as markets.

Overlooking the possibility of missing their child. The interviews pointed out one important lesson: children could get lost in spite of many guardians. When a child went missing, she had usually 2–3 guardians to watch her; in one case, 6 adults were with the child. The parents overlooked the possibility of their child going missing because they thought that their child was under observation of another guardian, while in fact the child had gone missing. One interesting thought[1] was: "*Even when there were many people in the party, we lost her anyway. Everyone thought that she may be with others*" (Parent of a 4-year old girl). There is always the possibility of losing a child. We, therefore, aim to design a meaningful solution that enables in-situ local search in such a situation.

High mobility of children. The parents admitted that they did not imagine their child could disappear within a short time. It took about seven minutes on average (from two to ten) for them to notice that their child was lost. Moreover, children's walking speed was faster than expected by the parents. Many of the lost children were found at a distance of several hundred meters from the places where they became separated; one of the parents said: "*He moved about 500 meters along the road for more than 30 minutes*" (Parent of a 4-year old boy). It took around 16 minutes on average (from 10 to 60) for parents to find their child.

[1] *All the quotations were directly translated from Korean.*

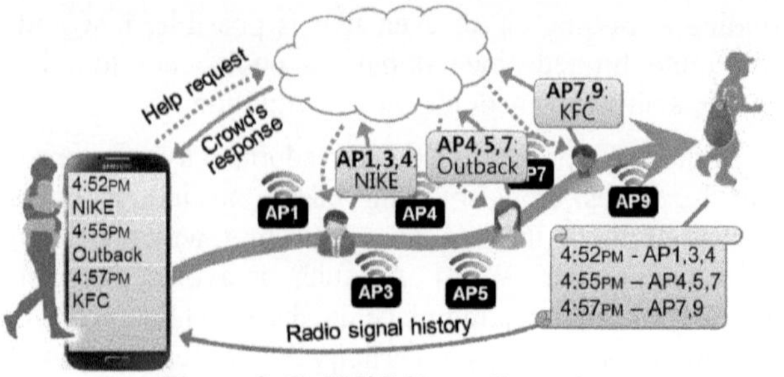

Figure 3. CoSMiC Usage Scenario.

Importance of others' help. When parents lost their child, they were usually in a panic and, therefore, were unable to think and behave rationally. In such situations, even small amounts of assistance from people nearby could be very helpful in finding the lost child. Some were lucky to find their child with guidance of other people. Also, they said that they felt relief and recovered from their panic to some extent when someone helped them.

Difficulty of getting others' help in practice. However, some parents complained that many people around them were of not much help, especially in crowded shopping malls. One said, "*People were strangers. They didn't seem interested in the situation because of their own business*" (Parent of a 4-year old girl). Even when they got some help, they usually got only rough description regarding their child, which was not much helpful.

APPLICATION USAGE SCENARIO

John is a 2-year-old toddler and he can speak some words, but is not a fluent speaker. John has a special nametag that periodically scans Wi-Fi radio channels every 5 seconds and stores the result in a log. In an emergency, the tag is able to report the log to his parents via a cellular network.

One day, the family visits a shopping mall. When they step on an elevator in the lobby to go up to children's department, John suddenly walks out of the elevator as the door closes. The parents come back to the first floor in a hurry, but John has disappeared. They quickly search the surrounding area but cannot find him. The parents run the CoSMiC application and connect to John's nametag. They receive the radio log and send it to a CoSMiC server. The server sends help requests to a number of CoSMiC application users in the area. As the users have been in the area, many (or some) of their smartphones find out that their current or recent radio observations are very similar to parts of the child's log. The applications prompt the users to input the names of the matching locations. As he is about to enter KFC, one inputs his location, "KFC", with an encouraging message. Others also respond to the parents' request quickly. The server collects the reported location information and creates an estimated location history of the child. The location history consists of names of places where John was highly likely to have passed them by and his estimated time of passing (Figure 2). The server provides this information to the parents promptly. The

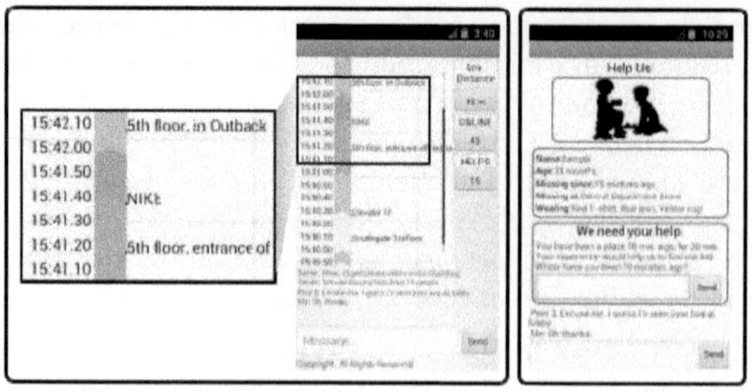

(a) Parent app (b) Crowd app

Figure 2. Screenshots of the app for (a) parent and (b) crowd.

parents reach KFC via Outback and Nike as quickly as they can. Finally, they find John wandering around.

APPLICATION DESIGN AND DEVELOPMENT

In this section, we present two key approaches in application design: landmark-based location history and virtual encounter-based crowd participation. By combining the two approaches, we aim to maximize the crowd's opportunities to participate as well as provide parents with rich information that enables them to find their child. In addition, we briefly describe the implementation of a prototype application for the proof of concept.

Virtual Encounter and Location History Construction

Landmark-based Location History of a Child

CoSMiC provides a parent with a landmark-based location history of a child. As shown in Figure 3(a), the history is presented as a series of place names (i.e., landmarks) and time stamps indicating that the child has probably passed the places at the specified times. By referring to the places, the parent can easily reach the last place in the history and thereby find the child. When compared to a way that provides only the child's current location, this strategy offers several advantages. First, it is intuitive and natural to reach a specific location by passing through landmarks on the way [8]. Second, it is still effective when searching for the child even in an unfamiliar place. Third, the history can help parents better estimate the distance and the direction of the child's movements. We describe the effectiveness of the history information later in the Case Study section.

Virtual Encounter-based Crowd's Participation

A location history of a child is instantly generated through participation of the crowd in the vicinity. To quickly and successfully construct the location history with the help of the surrounding crowd, we concentrate on two issues: (1) maximizing opportunity and (2) reducing burdens on crowds in participation. To cope with this, we propose a concept of virtual encounter and a scheme to detect it.

The notion of the virtual encounter extends that of the physical encounter, through relaxing the temporal as well as perceptual (i.e., recognition of the child) constraints of a physical encounter. A passerby is considered to have virtually encountered a lost child if she/he has visited the same place that the child had already visited or would visit later. In the example of Figure 4, a man denoted as A at

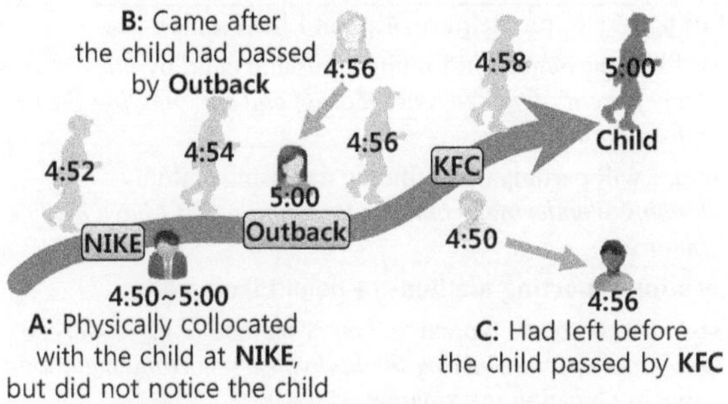

Figure 4. Virtual encounter examples.

Nike encountered a child but did not recognize her. Our application detects this event, and later asks the user the name (or meaning) of the place. The second witness (B) at Outback arrived at 5:00, after the child had passed that location. In this case, B has virtually encountered the child. The last one (C), who had been at KFC, leaves that location at 4:50, before the child was missing. Our application also regards this situation as a virtual encounter, and can ask him where he was just before 4:50.

The relaxation of the temporal dimension in virtual encounters vastly increases the number of potential contributors who can provide virtual observations of the child. The potential contributors include not only those who were at the location at the same time as the child, but all people who were there at any time. Accordingly, it expedites the collection of useful location information that leads parents to their child. As for the crowd's point of view, we ask the crowd where they are now or have been recently, instead of asking them if they have physically encountered the lost child. Asking indirect questions is highly likely to increase the number of participants who can answer the question. Upon receiving the request, people can easily report a location annotation—i.e., the name of the place—instead of an explanation of the child's whereabouts.

To detect the virtual encounter between a child and passersby, we employ Wi-Fi fingerprint-based location matching techniques [4], harnessing wireless access points (APs) widely deployed in large indoor spaces. The Wi-Fi fingerprint is a virtual landmark, which is a set of received radio signal strengths of visible APs. If a passerby's smartphone detects a Wi-Fi fingerprint highly similar to the one reported by the child, then she can contribute to constructing the location history by just reporting her location. The similarity between two sets of fingerprints is evaluated based on signal strengths of Wi-Fi APs. A collection of such encounter information from the crowd, i.e., partial and virtual observations of traces of a child, is effectively applied to construct a location history.

Other Design Considerations

In addition to maximizing the crowd's opportunity to participate, it is also important to encourage the crowd to participate. Even though it is reasonable to assume that many people have an altruistic nature to help others, the participation process should be thoughtfully designed to help people engaged [11, 13]. We discuss design choices to promote crowd participation, e.g., preferences in choosing notification and reporting methods, appropriate feedback to participants, and the issue of emotional support for parents.

Multiple Methods of Help Request and Location Report

Studies on the acceptability of notifications have shown that individuals have different acceptability regarding the urgency and intrusiveness of notifications [23]. That is, urgent messages are accepted even if the messages are presented intrusively. In addition, a recent study on mobile notification [12] argues that mobile notifications should consider "social acceptability," including the relationship between notification modalities and surrounding contexts of an individual. Referring to the studies, we designed the application to provide multiple notification methods. To help participants intuitively understand the methods, we chose three frequently used notification methods in daily smartphone usage: (1) a short (SMS-like) notification, (2) a long (ringing-like) notification, and (3) the long and most obtrusive (alarm-like) notification. Participants could freely choose and change their notification methods based on their situations or preferences.

To reflect personal preferences in reporting location information, the application also offers three alternative methods for annotation and report of location information: (1) text typing, (2) picture taking, and (3) voice recording. This is inspired by studies on ergonomics, e.g., it is known that elders prefer handwriting or voice input to an on-screen, keyboard-based text entry method [26].

Feedback and Incentives

In general, designing feedback for a crowdsourcing application is a delicate task that requires in-depth understanding of participants' motivation for and expectation from a given task [13]. In the case of voluntary tasks, such as finding a missing child, it becomes much more sensitive because the task is closely related to the crowd's intrinsic motivations, including altruism [22].

We consider three types of feedback: (1) thank-you notes from parents, (2) financial rewards, and (3) social rewards. It is expected that the crowd would accept thank-you messages well; however, it is difficult to predict their responses for the other two. A study reported that financial rewards are not very effective in motivating people to volunteer, and, at times, even diminish their motivation [11]. Fershtman and Weiss [7] showed that social rewards, such as esteem by members of a society, are effective and feasible incentive mechanisms to govern individuals' behavior. In the following section, we examine the crowd's perception of the above three methods using user surveys.

Emotional Touch

From our motivational study, many parents panicked and felt easily frustrated with the feeling of isolation, especially when they could not get help from others. It is thus important to give parents the sense of being together with others helping them find the child. The application provides a communication channel between parents and participants. The participants can send text messages to the parents for solace or provide additional information. The information in the location history can also help relieve the parents' concerns about their child's present safety, so they can keep searching for the child without being in a panic. For example, messages such as "Your child was seen at a nearby place a minute ago" imply that the child was safe at least a minute ago and is within one-minute walking distance from the reported location.

Prototype Development

The CoSMiC architecture consists of four parts: a smart-tag worn by children, an application for parents, an application for crowd, and a server. A smart-tag is a rechargeable tiny mobile device that continuously monitors ambient features, such as Wi-Fi fingerprints, on a daily basis. The tag is able to send the captured log to parents and continue to report upcoming observations. For the proof of concept, we implemented the Smart-tag as an Android application. The default setting for the period of a radio scan is fixed as 5 seconds. Note that it is impossible to track a child when the tag is detached from the child. Form-factor design and hardware development of a smart-tag, as well as optimization of radio sensing, is beyond the scope of this paper, requiring further study. The parent application provides a location history of a missing child, which is constructed by location annotations from participants. It also provides features to request the crowd's participation, send a thank-you note to participants, participate in online chatting. The crowd application provides two main features: observation of the ambient features, i.e., Wi-Fi fingerprints, and a report of location annotations (see Parent app

(b) Crowd app

Figure 2(b)). It receives a help request with Wi-Fi fingerprints from a child's tag and performs location matching for virtual encounter detection. Upon the detection, it notifies users. The CoSMiC server collects location annotations from the crowd and manages them in a place database that can be used later to generate a location history of missing child. We have implemented prototype applications of CoSMiC on the Android OS, Froyo 2.2 and ICS 4.0. The server is a standalone daemon written in Java.

FEASIBILITY STUDIES

We conducted two user studies. The first questionnaire survey explored potential crowds' perceptions of the design choices presented in the previous section. The second user study was a human-subject test on response time to requests for help to analyze temporal trends of instant responses.

Questionnaire Survey on Crowds' Perceptions

Methods

The first questionnaire explored potential crowds' willingness to participate, as well as their preferences for reporting and notification methods and feedback. Detailed questions are illustrated in Figure 5. For the questions asking willingness and admittance, we adopt the 4-point Likert scale to eliminate ambiguous responses. The responses were considered as ordinal ones. To better describe users' perceptions and to get constructive ideas, we allowed participants to write comments for each question. The survey was conducted on- and off-line with 135 Korean participants (77 females and 58 males) between 22 and 61 years old (mean age: 34.2, SD: 8.47). Ninety-nine people responded using the online survey. Eighty-six were married. Each participant was compensated with a $5 voucher after participation. A week after the survey, we conducted a quick test on the installation rate to measure the participants' willingness. We sent short messages, including a mobile link to the application, and counted how many participants installed the application.

- ✓ **Willingness to participate** (4-point Likert scale)
  - Q1. I will participate in finding a missing child by *informing his (her) parent of my current location and surrounding Wi-Fi information.*
  - Q2-3. I will participate in finding a missing child by *looking/wandering around to find him(her) if I have his/her picture.*
- ✓ **Location reporting methods** (4-point Likert scale)
  - Q4-6. I want to use typical *text entry method (e.g., on-screen keyboard)/picture-taking method/voice-recording method* to give my location information.
- ✓ **Notification methods** (4-point Likert scale)
  - Q7-9. I will allow notifications of help requests using the same way for receiving *short text messages (SMSs)/incoming calls/alarms.*
- ✓ **Feedbacks and incentives** (5-point Likert scale)
  - Q10-12. I think that it is essential to receive *words of thanks from the parents/financial rewards/social rewards* after participation.
- ✓ **Willingness to install** (4-point Likert scale)
  - Q13. Given a link to the application, I will install the application to help when a child is missing.

Figure 5. Questions for crowds' perception on participation.

	Q1	Q2	Q3	Q4	Q5	Q6	Q7	Q8	Q9	Q10*	Q11*	Q12*	Q13
Mean	3.66	3.59	2.83	3.23	3.15	2.63	3.32	2.90	2.81	3.61	2.46	3.07	1.91
SD	.62	.61	.88	.88	.94	1.07	.79	.99	1.03	1.21	1.18	1.24	.81

Table 2. Mean and standard deviations of the survey responses
*** responses from 5-point Likert scale questions.**

Results

Willingness to participate. Regarding questions Q1 to Q3, participants showed their (strong) willingness to participate in finding a missing child. The willingness to inform their location and look around was about the same (130 agreed to the two questions; all mean and SD values of the responses are shown in Table 2). However, the willingness to wander around to find the child was relatively weak, as only 89 (66%) participants agreed to Q3. Interestingly, the numbers of participants with strong willingness were different: 98 (73%), 87 (64%), and 33 (24%) participants strongly agreed with Q1, Q2, and Q3, respectively. We conjecture that this result confirms our expectation that location reporting would be relatively less burdensome and promote more participation than active search. For Q1, we further checked whether there are differences in the willingness across gender, marital status, and the number of children (Figure 6). Kruskal-Wallis test showed that there is no significant difference regarding these factors. However, we could see little differences in the detailed ratings.

Preferences for location reporting methods. As mentioned earlier, our design strategy is to provide the crowd with multiple ways to report their location. Participants mostly liked the text entry and the picture-taking method; 107 (79%), 105 (78%), and 73 (54%) participants agreed with Q4, Q5, and Q6, respectively. We also found that the strategy may help the broader population, including different age groups, to participate. As shown in Figure 7, there are differences in preferences across different age groups; the Friedman test showed a higher preference of the oldest group for voice recording method than participants in their 30s (H_3=7.90, $p<0.05$). Also, the oldest group's preferences did not show statistically significant differences, whereas other groups showed higher preferences for the text entry than the voice recording.

Preferences for notification methods. Overall, most of the participants preferred less annoying notification; 85%, 66%, and 61% of participants allowed SMS-like, ringing-like, and alarm-like notification method, respectively. From their comments, we discerned that most of the participants were afraid that the application might cause sudden disturbances in quiet places, such as a theater or workplace.

Feedback and incentives. About feedback, 57% of the participants (strongly) agreed with Q10, indicating that they would be much more encouraged to help if the parents respond with a "thanks" message. In terms of incentives, interestingly, only 15% of participants agreed with Q11 regarding a financial reward. This result is consistent with studies on volunteerism, which argued that a financial reward may hurt motivation of voluntary participants [11]. Some participants showed strong aversion to the financial reward, saying, for example:

> "*It sounds bad since it sounds like measuring the value of a kid. I do not want money.*" (22-year old woman)
>
> "*We should not profit from another's sadness.*" (53-year old man)

Regarding Q12, more than one third of participants (36%) reported that honoring the people who helped would be positive. The participants suggested many specific ways of honoring, e.g., appreciating on SNS or awarding a plaque.

Application installation rate. We asked participants whether they would like to install the application when they have a link to the application. The result was promising, as 107 agreed that they would install it. However, the actual installation rate was lower than the answers. Twenty-five participants (18.5%) installed the application within two weeks. From this result, we could see that people may be passive in installing the application in advance for uncertain future cases, whereas people in general showed willingness to help. It would be important and desirable to design incentives to encourage people to install the application, in addition to incentives to participants who give help in situ.

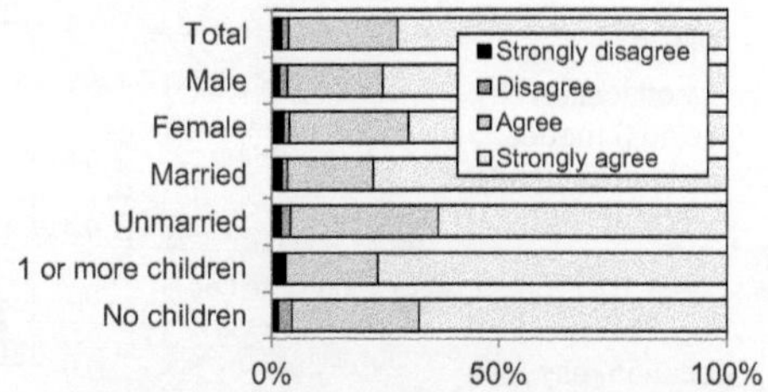

Figure 6. Willingness to participate by gender/marital status.

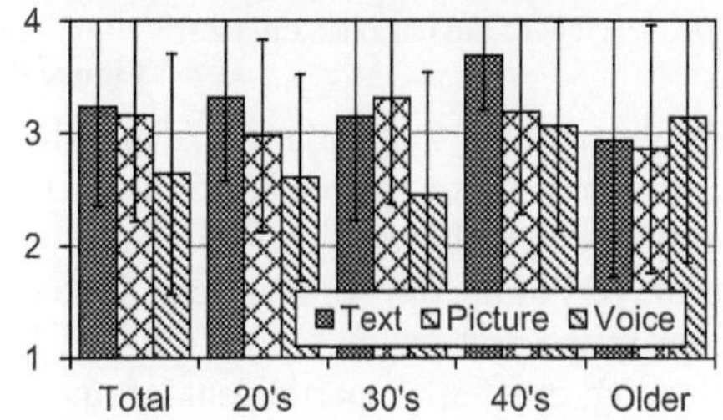

Figure 7. Preferences for input methods by age groups.

User Test on Response Time

Method

The second user study was a human-subject test on response time to help requests. The response time denotes the total time taken by a user to respond to a help request notification, which asks about the users' whereabouts. Thirty-eight participants (12 female, 26 male) were recruited from the age group of 18 to 36 years (mean age: 25.3, SD: 4.6). They were all Android users, and we installed an application to collect response times. The test was conducted for two weeks. The participants were compensated with a $30 voucher. Note that in this test the participants agreed to respond to application's requests as best as they can, and we assumed that they had good amount of willingness. Thus, the experiment aims to see the effect of situational factors such as notification methods and participants' location rather than willingness to answer.

The application is designed to give participants two virtual help requests per day at a random time (See Figure 8(a)). It gives notifications using a method randomly picked from the three notification methods as stated earlier: SMS-like, ringing-like, and alarm-like ones. When a participant clicks the notification window on her smartphone, the application shows a user interface asking her current location. After the participant submits her location, the application records the total time taken from the notification to the response. To better analyze the responding context, we tagged the response with a type of their current location. This is enabled by using the LifeMap app [6], which extracts users' location type, such as home, office, restaurants, shopping.

To avoid annoying the participants, notifications are allowed only during the daytime. We let the participants set places where they do not want to receive notifications, and

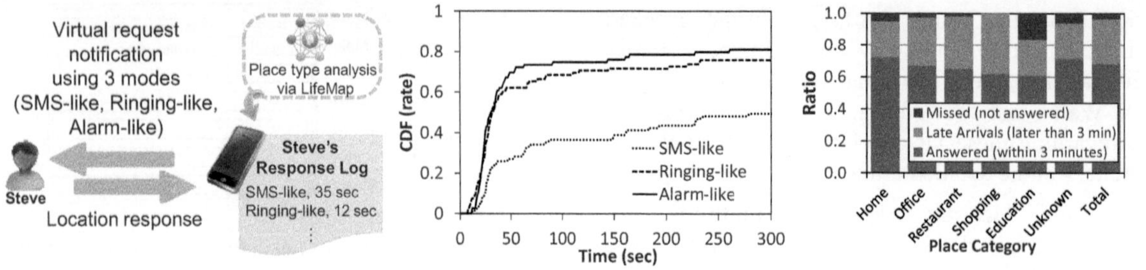

(a) Overview of the response time test (b) Trend of response time (c) Response rate regarding place type

Figure 8. Summary of response time test.

suppress the requests at those places. Also, whenever the participants do not want to receive notifications for a while, they could shut down the application for 30, 60, or 120 minutes, or the rest of the day. If a participant does not want to participate in the test anymore, we allowed him/her to stop participating; one female participant left the study after one week. To minimize the novelty effect, we only analyzed data obtained from the second week. Note that this treatment is not for ruling out the potential effect of request frequency; the actual frequency of help requests may be less than that used in this test. We analyzed the distribution of response times for notification methods and place types.

Results

A total of 438 records were issued. Among the records, 37%, 33%, and 30% of the records were from SMS-like, ringing-like, and alarm-like methods, respectively. Regarding place types, 18%, 17%, 22%, 7%, and 25% of replies were from residence, workplace, food, shop, and education, respectively. The remaining records were reported as unknown place types.

A distribution of response time is illustrated in Figure 8(b). We empirically set a time limit of meaningful responses as 3 minutes. This is because a person can move to another place from the place where the application received a request. To address this issue, the application always asks the current location of a person and checks against the current Wi-Fi fingerprint. If the fingerprint is not similar to that of help request, the location report can be dropped. The rates of responses within 3 minutes were 49%, 71% and 81% for SMS-like, ringing-like, and alarm-like methods, respectively. We could see a relatively low response rate for an SMS-like method, which was more preferred and perceived to be less intrusive. We conjecture that users pay attention more quickly to a notification by a more intrusive method and send a response.

Regarding the intrusiveness of the method, one participant commented, *"The sound sometimes embarrassed me when I was surrounded by many people. I turned off my phone immediately. If the notification had come more gently, I would have responded"*. It would be necessary to consider situations of participants as well as individual preferences in acceptability of notifications.

Response rates were slightly different across place types as shown in Figure 8(c). However, the differences were not very significant. Overall, the rate of meaningful responses was more than 60% for all place types, including restaurants and shopping malls at which people are most likely to receive help requests.

Regarding the place annotation delivered through the responses, we could find that a number of reports contained fairly useful information for guessing a location. Among 438 records, 53% of them were useful enough to identify the places in a store or room level, and 14% contained the information of building and floor. The remaining 33% contained information on the building level or beyond. From this observation, we devised the request asking the current location to explicitly describe the desirable level of information (e.g., "What is in front of you? What can you see from your current location? Which store are you in?"). Such detailed questions may help users give meaningful location information to construct a location history.

CASE STUDY

We conducted a case study to investigate the potential effectiveness of the application in finding a child. The study was carefully designed to show that the application could help parents well in realistic settings. Specifically, we intended to observe the behavior of parents finding their child in a real crowded place.

Settings

While designing the study, we noticed that it is very difficult to apply and test the application in a completely real situation in terms of a place, parents, children, and crowd. We thus simulated the event of a missing child in a real place by recruiting participants and requesting them to play the roles of parents and children. As the main goal was to investigate behaviors of parents finding a child, we focused on the parent and child roles rather than crowd roles. The study was conducted in a highly crowded indoor space, Lotte World, which is the largest indoor amusement park in Korea. Its area is about 86,000 m^2. Based on the observations from the previous study on the crowd's response to help requests and real population distribution in Lotte World, we carefully simulated crowd participation.

Ten undergraduate students, five acting as parents and five as children, were recruited on campus. The participants were given a smartphone with the CoSMiC application. The "children" moved following a designated path; two sample paths are shown in Figure 9. We let the children walk at around 0.8 meters per second. "Parents" began to find their children after 150 seconds of the departure of the children. The time was selected based on the observation from our motivational study; parents mostly thought that it took more than two minutes to notice that their child disappeared. To see a realistic use of the application in practice, we told the parents to freely use other assistive material and services, e.g., a map booklet, information desks, and staff.

To generate realistic participation of the crowd, we first investigated the population density of the park before the study. The average number of people in the park on weekdays was about 4,000. We assumed that the ratio of the crowd with the application installed is around 5%. Note that 18.5% of the participants had actually installed the test application in the previous survey, and we set the ratio in a conservative manner. We then collected 195 crowd reports with radio fingerprints and location annotation. The way of collection was intuitive; we collected one report at every place where we saw around 20 people within a radius of 10 meters. We made the report, including information such as a name of nearby store or ride, and additional spatial relationship, e.g., "in front of," "inside," and "outside." During trials to find children, the collected crowd reports were sent from the server to the parents' applications by following the response time distribution derived from the preference on the notification modality and the response times of each modality presented in the previous section. During the experiment, our staff followed the parents and observed their behavior, careful not to disturb the finding process. Exit interviews were conducted as well.

Findings

Changes in finding behavior. One intriguing finding was changes in a way to find children. Given the path of children's movements, the parents directly moved to the locations in the path. In most cases, we could observe that the parents ran to the next location with full confidence. After reaching the final location in the path, they tried to carefully look around to find their child. Parent 3 reported: *"This app changed the difficult man-finding into easy route-finding with a guidebook"*. We expect that these changes in finding behavior could reduce a burden to find missing children.

On/offline combined helps. Interestingly, the application could be better used with offline help from others. For example, parents 1, 2, and 3 tried to ask nearby people about the locations presented in the application and reduce time to move to the locations. Parent 2 asked a staff member at an information desk about the direction to the place in the path. The staff helped her figure out a shortcut to the destination. She did not follow the remaining path of the child, but rather took a shortcut to catch up with him (Route 1 in Figure 9). There was another interesting case in which participants made the best use of our application. Parent 3 (Route 2 in Figure 9) noticed that she was on the right track (0:35) and moved quickly, following the path (2:20). However, she went too far and suddenly lost her way (2:40). She got help from a nearby clerk and finally found her child (3:52). After the experiment, she commented that getting help from nearby people was very easy. Although they had not seen the child, they could tell her the locations of shops and rides.

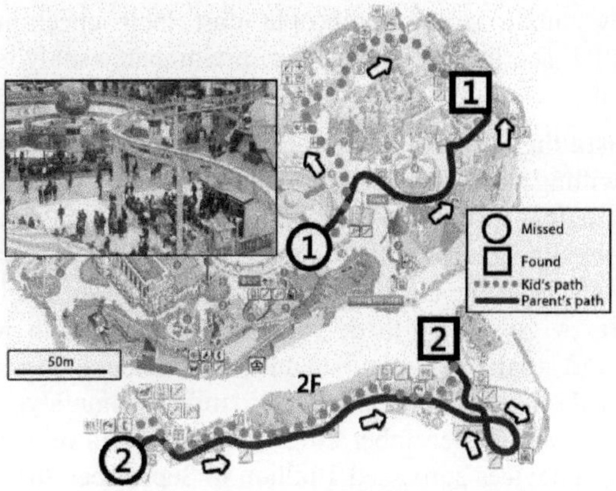

Figure 9. Sample routes on an indoor amusement park

Parent	1	2	3	4	5
Time	4:09	4:40	3:52	4:52	6:06

Table 3. Search time of amusement park case study

However, parents 4 and 5 tried to find their children only using the application and map booklets. They frequently stopped to check where the location in the path is (e.g., "Where is the Steff Hot Dog?"). We conjecture that these behaviors resulted in relatively longer search times. Refer to Table 3 for detailed results of times taken to find children.

DISCUSSION

Privacy concerns. While 130 out of 135 participants were willing to provide their location data from our user study, it is important to address privacy concerns carefully in practice. Privacy concerns regarding the use of CoSMiC largely depend on users' subjective perception and how their location data are to be used [14]. It is necessary to obtain users' consent to provide their locations selectively for the purpose of finding a missing child in some public places. Further in-depth studies are still necessary.

Quality of crowd information. Quality control of information provided by the crowd can be difficult in crowdsourcing-based systems. Even with good intent, the diverse and potentially noisy inputs might compromise the accuracy of generated location history. For example, the granularity of information for the same location could be different, e.g., Starbucks as Starbucks, cafe, and building's name. Further investigation is desirable for the automatic extraction of correct information from crowd inputs. A potential solution is to choose dominant cases that have consistent information annotated by people. The hypothesis is that the crowds of users can reliably generate more accurate and complete information than that of a single user [17]. The assistant approaches, e.g., presenting examples [17] or estimating the quality of contributed information [19], would help the crowd contributors improve the quality.

Geo-database service. Strapping a device to a child that automatically performs check-ins could be a simple solution. Geolocation services such as Foursquare, one of the largest geo-tagging services, have enormously large datasets from both geolocation and place/location mapping. Despite their scalability, these datasets have a coverage bias and include mostly public spaces as people post their check-ins for potential sharing purposes. Our preliminary study shows these datasets barely cover few locations in private areas.

Preinstalling the application. Our study found that people are willing to provide information to help parents, but encouraging people to install the application can be challenging. To enable the CoSMiC scenario in practice, the first step is to deploy the application to a large number of people. A good way to do so is to cooperate with widely deployed applications and mobile OS venders, just as on AMBER alerts. Facebook hit 945 million monthly, active mobile users in December 2013 [28], and users of activated Android devices surpassed 1 billion in September 2013 [29]. Such integration would provide a large number of potential users. In addition, prior planning by parents is necessary to get help from the CoSMiC application. Assuming pre-installed CoSMiC functionality on mobile OS, parents will need to have the child's smart tag installed and do some configurations such as authentication and device pairing.

Abduction. The current proposal might not be suitable for finding an abducted child as the first step in any abduction would be removal of the tracker. Instead, it appears better designed for cases of temporary disappearance. The significance of children's disappearance seems underestimated since such experiences often are not reported. We were astonished by things that many parents had suffered from the disappearance and recruiting interviewees was not difficult. We believe that preventing such traumatic experiences is also a meaningful social issue.

CONCLUSION

We present a crowd-sourced collaborative mobile application, CoSMiC, which instantly galvanizes the crowd to assist parents in the search for a missing child. It explores a new possibility of a crowdsourcing approach to expedite a missing-critical mission. We conducted extensive user studies and carefully designed the application to expand opportunities for crowd participation and thereby help the parents quickly find the child. We demonstrated the proof of concept of the application under a practical scenario.

ACKNOWLEDGMENTS

This work was supported by National Research Foundation of Korea (NRF) grant funded by the Korea government (No. 2011-0018120, No. 2013-027363), the IT R&D Program of MSIP/KEIT [10041313, UX-oriented Mobile SW Platform].

REFERENCES

1. Amazon mechanical turk. http://www.mturk.com/mturk
2. Amber Alert. http://www.amberalert.gov/.
3. Azizyan, M., Constandache, I. and Roy Choudhury, R., Surroundsense: mobile phone localization via ambience fingerprinting. *Proc. MobiCom 2009*, 261-272.
4. Bahl, P. and Padmanabhan, V. RADAR: An In-Building RF-based User Location and Tracking System. *Proc. INFOCOM 2000*, 775-784.
5. Child locator. http://www.mommyimhere.com/
6. Chon, Y. and Cha, H. LifeMap: Smartphone-based Context Provider for Location-based Service. *Pervasive Comput., 10*, 2 (2011). 58-67.
7. Fershtman, C. and Weiss, Y. Social rewards, externalities and stable preferences. *Public Econ., 70*, 1 (1998), 53-73.
8. Golledge, R.G. *Wayfinding behavior: Cognitive mapping and other spatial processes*. JHU Press, 1999.
9. Hanfland, K.A., et al. *Case Management for Missing Children Homicide Investigation: Executive Summary*. Olympia: Attorney General of Washington, 1997.
10. Henderson, M. and Henderson, P. *Missing people: Issues for the Australian community*. Canberra: Australian Bureau of Criminal Intelligence, 1998.
11. Heyman, J. and Ariely, D. Effort for payment a tale of two markets. *Psychol. Sci. 15*, 11 (2004), 787-793.
12. Hoggan, E. and Brewster, S.A. Crosstrainer: testing the use of multimodal interfaces in situ. *Proc. CHI 2010*, 333-342.
13. Kaufmann, N., Schulze, T. and Veit, D. More than fun and money. worker motivation in crowdsourcing – a study on mechanical turk. *Proc. AMCIS 2011*, 340.
14. Klasnja, P., Consolvo, S., Choudhury, T., Beckwith, R. and Hightower, J. Exploring Privacy Concerns about Personal Sensing. *Proc. Pervasive 2009*, 176-183.
15. Know the rules for child safety in amusement or theme parks. http://www.missingkids.com/publications/NC33
16. Lampinen, J.M., Arnal, J. and Hicks, J.L. The Effectiveness of Supermarket Posters in Helping to Find Missing Children. *Interpers. Violence, 28*, 9 (2013), 406-423.
17. Lasecki, W.S., Song, Y.C., Kautz, H. and Bigham, J.P., Real-Time Crowd Labeling for Deployable Activity Recognition. *Proc. CSCW 2013*, 1203-1212.
18. Lu, H., Pan, W., Lane, N. D., Choudhury, T. and Campbell, A. T. Soundsense: scalable sound sensing for people-centric applications on mobile phones. *Proc. MobiSys 2009*, 165-178.
19. Mashhadi A. J. and Capra, L., Quality Control for Real-Time Ubiquitous Crowdsourcing, *Proc. UbiCrowd 2011*, 5-8.
20. National Center for Missing and Exploited Children (NCMEC). http://www.missingkids.com/home
21. UbiSense. http://www.ubisense.net.
22. Unger, L.S. Altruism as a motivation to volunteer. *Econ. Psych., 12*, 1 (1991), 71-100.
23. Vastenburg, M. H., Keyson, D. V. and De Ridder, H. Considerate home notification systems: a field study of acceptability of notifications in the home. *Pers. and Ubiq. Comp., 12*, 8 (2008), 555-566.
24. When Your Child Is Missing: A Family Survival Guide. http://www.missingkids.com/en_US/publications/PDF6A.pdf
25. Wibree Technology. http://www.wibree.com.
26. Wright, P., Bartram, C., Rogers, N., Emslie, H., Evans, J., Wilson, B. and Belt, S. Text entry on handheld computers by older users. *Ergonomics, 43*, 6 (2000), 702-716.
27. Yang, J., Adamic, L.A. and Ackerman, M.S. Competing to Share Expertise: the Taskcn Knowledge Sharing Community. *Proc. ICWSM 2008*, 161-168.
28. Facebook mobile. http://www.prnewswire.com/news-releases/facebook-reports-fourth-quarter-and-full-year-2013-results-242637731.html
29. Android.https://plus.google.com/+SundarPichai/posts/NeBW7AjT1QM
30. Sadilek, A., Krumm, J., Horvitz, E. Crowdphysics: Planned and Opportunistic Crowdsourcing for Physical Tasks, *Proc. ICWSM 2013*, 536-545.
31. Lampinen, J.M., Peters, C.S., Gier, V.S. Power in numbers: The effect of target set size on prospective person memory in an analog missing child scenario. *Applied Cognitive Psychology*, 26 (2012), 702-708.
32. Sweeney, L.N., Lampinen, J.M. The effect of presenting multiple images on prospective and retrospective person memory for missing children. *Journal of Applied Research in Memory and Cognition*, 1, 4 (2012), 235–241.

Effective Multimodal Feedback for Around-Device Interfaces

Euan Freeman
Glasgow Interactive Systems Group
University of Glasgow
Glasgow, Scotland
euan.freeman@glasgow.ac.uk

ABSTRACT
Around-device interaction lets people use their phones without having to pick them up or reach out and touch them. This allows interaction when touch may not be available; for example, users could gesture to interact with their phones while cooking, avoiding touching the screen with messy hands. Well-designed feedback helps users overcome uncertainty during gesture interaction, however giving effective feedback from small devices can be a challenge and detailed visual feedback will not always be suitable. My thesis research looks at how other types of feedback may be used effectively during around-device interaction to help users.

Author Keywords
Around-device interaction; multimodal; tactile feedback.

ACM Classification Keywords
H.5.2. User Interfaces: Interaction styles.

INTRODUCTION
Gesture interfaces are being introduced to mobile phones to allow more expressive input and to let users interact when using the touchscreen is impractical. Researchers have developed a variety of sensing techniques for around-device interaction and recently Samsung included a gesture interface in their Galaxy S4 phone. As sensors continue to improve, especially in terms of power requirements, more mobile phones are likely to let users interact this way.

Providing effective feedback is important to help users overcome uncertainty during gesture interaction; however, giving effective feedback from such a small device can be challenging. Small screens limit visual feedback and mean feedback may not even be visible if users are occluding the display with their hand or gesturing from a short distance.

My research looks at how other output types can be used to give effective feedback during gesture interaction, to complement visual feedback and to help users when visual feedback is unavailable. While others have used non-visual feedback in around-device interfaces before (e.g. tactile [6] and speech [3]), research is needed to explore feedback design in greater detail and to understand what information users actually need to help them gesture and support their awareness of how the interface is responding to their actions.

Here I will discuss my thesis research, which looks at how other feedback types can be used effectively in around-device interfaces. I will outline my research goals, discuss my progress towards these goals from the first 18 months of my PhD, and talk about my plan for the remaining 18 months.

RESEARCH GOALS AND APPROACH
Multimodal feedback can address limitations with visual feedback, helping users overcome uncertainty and gesture more effectively. My thesis research aims to learn how other modalities can be used effectively in around-device interfaces. I will look at three output types in particular: tactile, audio and ambient visual. Tactile and audio feedback are commonly used in other interaction techniques, although tactile in particular has its own challenges when given in a gesture interface. Ambient visual feedback uses embedded lights (as in [7]) to illuminate space around a phone, creating visual cues which are noticeable from a distance and do not take space away from on-screen content.

I will look at what types of information users need during gesture interaction and how each modality can be used to deliver this. Each feedback type will have its own strengths and weaknesses in this context so multiple outputs may be needed to support users. I will conduct my research by creating multimodal around-device interfaces and then evaluating them in order to understand how effective feedback is. A mixture of quantitative and qualitative methods will give insight into what users like and dislike about each type of output, and what information they need to support them while gesturing. This mixed-methods approach is appropriate for this research area because user experience is important but difficult to understand through quantitative methods alone. User experience can also motivate feedback design because users may find certain feedback helpful even though it results in no performance improvement, for example.

RESEARCH STATUS
Completed Work
First I looked at designing usable and acceptable gestures for mobile phones [2]. Then I completed two studies, both focusing on tactile feedback for around-device interfaces. These studies looked at tactile feedback for selection, as this is a common around-device interaction (e.g. [1, 4, 3]).

MobileHCI 2014, September 23–26, 2014, Toronto, ON, Canada.
ACM 978-1-4503-3004-6/14/09.
http://dx.doi.org/10.1145/2628363.2634264

My first study looked at two ways of giving tactile feedback in a gesture interface: non-contact feedback using ultrasound haptics [5] and distal feedback from wearables. As well as looking at delivery, this study also compared two feedback designs. This study showed that all feedback types had similar workload (NASA-TLX) and performance (selection time and error rate), with only ultrasound feedback having significantly worse performance. Participants found tactile feedback useful because it showed system attention and supported their awareness of how the interface was responding to their gestures. Preference for feedback method and designs varied.

My second study looked at refined feedback designs, inspired by participants' suggestions from the first study. Three feedback designs were created: two which encoded selection progress tactually (using amplitude and vibrotactile roughness) and one which presented constant stimulus. The constant feedback design represented the type of tactile feedback currently available from wearables, where vibration can only simply be turned on or off. Feedback had little effect on performance but did have a significant effect on workload: dynamic feedback (those encoding selection progress) had lower workload than when no tactile feedback was given. There were no significant differences between constant feedback and no feedback, and between constant feedback and dynamic feedback. Participants also ranked all feedback types significantly higher than no tactile feedback. As before, participants said tactile feedback supported their awareness of how the interface was affected by their movements and they found rich feedback designs helpful.

These studies were a first detailed look at tactile feedback in around-device interfaces. Tactile feedback generally improves the user experience of gesturing and can lower the workload of around-device interaction. Wearables show promise as tactile displays because they can be worn in a variety of form factors and my findings show that feedback at different locations (on the wrist and on the finger) can be effective. My second study looked at refined feedback designs and found that feedback encoding selection progress reduced the workload of around-device selection. As wearable technologies grow, wearable developers should consider letting designers control more vibrotactile parameters than simply turning vibration on and off, allowing these devices to be used as rich tactile displays for other interaction modalities.

Remaining Work

In the remaining 18 months of my PhD I will look at audio and ambient visual feedback for around-device interfaces. I am currently running a study which takes a first look at ambient visual feedback in gesture interfaces. This study will look at how this new output type can be used to give feedback during gesture input in smart-home devices. Preliminary results suggest that users find ambient visual feedback helpful, especially when complemented by audio or tactile feedback. Further studies will take lessons learned and apply them to mobile phones, further exploring the design space and effectiveness of ambient visual feedback.

Further studies will also look at audio feedback design. These will focus on designing useful feedback as well as looking at the acceptability of audio feedback. Continuous audio feedback, while rich in information, could be obtrusive and annoying to nearby people so must convey useful information in an acceptable way. Finally, I will take lessons learned about each modality and create a multimodal interface which brings together these three modalities to give effective feedback.

CONCLUSION

My thesis research looks at what feedback is needed to help users when gesturing with mobile phones and how this feedback may be given. So far I have looked at how tactile feedback may be designed and presented in around-device interfaces. In the remaining eighteen months of my PhD I plan to focus more on ambient visual feedback and audio feedback, to see how these can be used to support interaction.

Attending the DC would let me engage with and get valuable feedback from other students and leading researchers in the field. As I am approaching the middle of my three-year PhD this would be an ideal time to get feedback, to help me make a stronger contribution from my research. I would particularly like to discuss how to frame my findings as the main contribution of my thesis: would a series of design recommendations be more or less useful than a taxonomy of the design space which lets others decide how to approach and extend the design of around-device feedback?

ACKNOWLEDGEMENTS

This research is funded by Nokia Research Center, Finland. Many thanks to Vuokko Lantz and Stephen Brewster for their supervision and support.

REFERENCES

1. Butler, A., Izadi, S., and Hodges, S. SideSight: Multi-touch Interaction Around Small Devices. In *Proc. UIST '08*, ACM Press (2008), 201–204.
2. Freeman, E., Brewster, S., and Lantz, V. Towards Usable and Acceptable Above-Device Interactions. In *Proc. Mobile HCI '14 Posters*, ACM Press (2014), to appear.
3. Gustafson, S., Holz, C., and Baudish, P. Imaginary Phone: Learning Imaginary Interfaces by Transferring Spatial Memory from a Familiar Device. In *Proc. UIST '11*, ACM Press (2011), 283–292.
4. Harrison, C., and Hudson, S. E. Abracadabra: Wireless, High-Precision, and Unpowered Finger Input for Very Small Mobile Devices. In *Proc. UIST '09*, ACM Press (2009), 121–124.
5. Hoshi, T., Takahashi, M., Iwamoto, T., and Shinoda, H. Noncontact Tactile Display Based on Radiation Pressure of Airborne Ultrasound. *IEEE Transactions on Haptics 3*, 3 (2010), 155–165.
6. Niikura, T., Watanabe, Y., Komuro, T., and Ishikawa, M. In-air Typing Interface: Realizing 3D operation for mobile devices. In *Proc. GCCE '12*, IEEE (2012), 223–227.
7. Qin, Q., Rohs, M., and Kratz, S. Dynamic Ambient Lighting for Mobile Devices. In *Adjunct Proc. UIST '11*, ACM Press (2011), 51–52.

Enhanced Situational Awareness and Communication for Emergency Response

Minoo Erfani Joorabchi
McGill University
3480 University Street
Montreal, Quebec, H3A 0E9
minooej@cim.mcgill.ca

ABSTRACT
It is important to recognize emergency responders' needs during emergency response to workplace incidents in order to propose solutions to facilitate responders' tasks and resolve incidents in a timely manner. To understand emergency response procedures involved in workplace incidents, we interviewed McGill Safety personnel. We identify potential areas of improvement in their procedures, which help us to shape research objectives. We then propose methods to address these objectives. We focus our investigation on a spill scenario and briefly describe our mobile solution to assist in this use context.

Author Keywords
Incidents; spills; mobile sensing; context awareness; location awareness; human and computer interaction.

ACM Classification Keywords
H.5.2. **[Information Interfaces and Presentation]:** User Interfaces.

INTRODUCTION
In this paper, we focus on workplace incidents that are harmful to health and require an emergency response. To comprehend the activities involved in such incidents, we investigated existing practices of the McGill University Safety office by interviewing their personnel and by gathering data from the University Safety website,[1] incident report forms and *myLab*, a system for safe handling and management of hazardous materials that is used by lab personnel and the McGill Safety office.

EMERGENCY RESPONSE PROCEDURES
When an incident occurs on campus, Security Services are notified and they dispatch patrollers for investigation. They decide to notify other types of first responders including health and safety, hazardous waste management, and fire prevention responders based on the patrollers' reports and incident type. To help first responders determine what equipment to bring to the incident site, Security Services usually provides situation-specific information, e.g., product name, spill volume, and location in case of a spill.

There are two main elements common to almost every workplace incident: (1) data acquisition and, (2) communication between responders. Acquiring the requisite information related to the incident is vital for the responders to deal with the situation in a timely manner during an emergency. It is important to the responders to be aware of hazardous materials and their Material Safety Data Sheets (MSDS)[2] in the affected room or adjoining rooms before entering the incident site. Although every lab is required to keep a list of hazardous materials in a binder, this is not always available at the incident site. The responders usually obtain the required information from the personnel at the lab entrance and/or by traditional telephony-based communications with an officer who creates a report from *myLab*. Consequently, lack of information makes the responders dependent on intermediaries.

RESEARCH OBJECTIVES
The first data acquisition objective we identified was that of increasing contextual awareness. This objective is motivated by several interviewees' comments regarding the need to extract information from *myLab* because it gives them a clear idea of what is in the lab and how to deal with the situation when the spill occurs. The second data acquisition objective was increasing workplace safety compliance, motivated by the comment, "One interesting aspect is to make the labs safer; what can lab personnel do to prevent a spill, or to have safer practices?"

The first communication objective we identified was to ensure that the responders understand the incident scope. This was motivated by several comments that exposed the inefficiencies of current practice, often necessitating multiple trips by responders to the incident site, first to

[1] University Safety: http://www.mcgill.ca/safety/

[2] Lab Safety: http://www.mcgill.ca/ehs/laboratory/labsafety

MobileHCI '14, Sep 23-26 2014, Toronto, ON, Canada
ACM 978-1-4503-3004-6/14/09.
http://dx.doi.org/10.1145/2628363.2634266

investigate, then to return with equipment as necessary since they don't know the incident scope, e.g., spill volume in case of a spill. Our second communication objective was to enhance communication between the responders that is motivated by a safety officer's comments who creates a report in *myLab* to provide the on site responders with the requisite information through telephony communications.

RELATED WORK

In this section, we briefly examine some prior studies involving mobile technology in the context of emergency response. Purohit et al. [1] introduce *SensorFly*, a human-steered mobile aerial sensor platform for data gathering during indoor emergency scenarios such as monitoring an indoor fire. We note that the use of smartphones provides a similar opportunity for data gathering by sensors, carried by the human responders themselves. Subbu et al. [3] introduced *LocateMe*, an Android application to locate a user by walking short distances across hallways based on the magnetic signature such as pillars, doors, and elevators collected during the walk. Fischer et al. [4] survey on tracking and navigation support for emergency responders and provides a list of systems and prototypes that are mainly focused on search and rescue operations. In general, there is a trade-off between providing high-quality location information and being easily deployable [4]. While triangulation of a responder inside a building is of possible interest, our research objectives can also be achieved by less complex and more robust approach, determining the responder's proximity to an indoor location.

PROPOSED METHODS

Our objectives can be addressed by mobile sensing [2], using the sensors built into current smartphones. To attain the data acquisition objectives, we propose to provide the first responders with instantaneous and ubiquitous access to the required information such as a list of hazardous materials at the incident site independently before entering the affected room. We believe that obtaining this information from a printed binder near the lab entrance or asking personnel in the lab is not appropriate, since the data needs to be updated regularly and incidents may occur when no one is around. Therefore one area of improvement in emergency response practices is to take advantage of location awareness as captured by an Indoor Positioning system (IPS), and use it to access the requisite information. An IPS is worthwhile by increasing context awareness based on the responder's proximity to the affected room.

To attain the communication objectives, we propose to provide them with images or video of the relevant content, transmitted by the patrollers as they arrive at the incident site. This information may be relayed to other responders as well. One possible platform designed for a similar use context is *Real-Time Emergency Response (rtER)*,[3] developed by our research group as a video-centric platform for the detection and observation of emergency situations.

EVALUATION

To evaluate the effectiveness of our proposed methods, we concentrate on one type of workplace incident, laboratory chemical spills. We will first design prototypes to explore the opportunity of leveraging the power of smartphone technology to assist the responders in accessing relevant information at the incident site, independently, and facilitating their communications. Next, we will conduct usability studies to test prototypes of our smartphone solution with McGill Safety personnel. From our initial interviews and based on the aforementioned potential areas of improvement, the main functions of our solution would be: (1) Chemical Identification: Finding chemical information such as MSDS data. (2) Lab Identification: Finding a list of materials in a room or adjoining rooms and their information such as product name, container size, and room number. (3) Video Streaming: Relaying a streaming video of the incident to the control center.

ONGOING WORK

As the next step, our proposed smartphone solution needs to be designed and implemented, then tested through usability studies before being deployed as a tool for genuine emergencies.

ACKNOWLEDGMENTS

We wish to thank the McGill University Safety office for allowing us to interview their personnel. We also thank /N SPRO[4] and McGill University for financially supporting this research.

REFERENCES

1. Purohit, A., Sun, Z., Mokaya, F., and Zhang, P. SensorFly: Controlled-mobile sensing platform for indoor emergency response applications. *In Information Processing in Sensor Networks (IPSN) 2011,* 10th International Conference (2011), 223-234.
2. Bareiss, R., Griss, M. L., Rosenberg, S., and Zhang, Y. Semantic Geotagging: A Location-Based Hypermedia Approach to Creating Situational Awareness. *Proceedings of MobiCase 2011,*100-114.
3. Subbu, K. P., Gozick, B., and Dantu, R. LocateMe: Magnetic-fields-based indoor localization using smartphones. *ACM Transactions on Intelligent Systems and Technology (TIST)*, 2013.
4. Fischer, C. and Gellersen H. Location and Navigation Support for Emergency Responders: A Survey. *IEEE Pervasive Computing*, (2010), 38–47.

[3] http://www.cim.mcgill.ca/sre/projects/rter/

[4] http://www.n-spro.com/

Email Management and Work-Home Boundaries

Marta E. Cecchinato
UCL Interaction Centre
University College London
London, WC1E 6BT
marta.cecchinato.13@ucl.ac.uk

ABSTRACT
In my PhD research I am exploring the effect of email on work-home boundaries. The ultimate goal is to design a tool that helps people manage their email better and reduces the stress associated with this activity. I argue that this will require understanding individual differences in email behaviours and how email can impact work-home boundaries.

Author Keywords
Email; work-life balance; work-home boundaries; behaviour change.

ACM Classification Keywords
H.5.m. Information interfaces and presentation (e.g., HCI): Miscellaneous.

INTRODUCTION
A benefit of mobile devices, such as smartphones and tablets, is that they enable us to be always connected, even when on the move. However, there are also costs associated with being 'always on', such as receiving work emails while at home and feeling one has to deal with them. This blurring of work-home boundaries can result in stress. How emails impact on work-home balance has not been deeply investigated in the literature, with the exception of Capra et al. [1]. In my PhD I aim to fill this gap by understanding the impact of email on work-home balance, in order to design a tool that reduces the stress of email overload.

Clark [3, p.751] proposed a work-family border theory according to which "people are border-crossers who make daily transitions between the two settings, often tailoring their focus, their goals, and their interpersonal style to fit the unique demands of each". Being able to balance these two different worlds means achieving a satisfactory relation between both, where conflict is reduced to a minimum. Within the framework of boundary theory, Nippert-Eng [7] argues that the relationship between work and family lies along an integration-segmentation continuum. She explains how the use of certain artefacts such as calendars and keys, but also particular habits, can help visualize where people position themselves on this continuum and help them find a balance. Now that mobile technologies permeate our professional and private lives resulting in an always-connected society, we can consider email as one of these artefacts. Understanding email use across work-home boundaries can help define design and best practice guidelines.

MobileHCI '14, Sep 23-26 2014, Toronto, ON, Canada
ACM 978-1-4503-3004-6/14/09.
http://dx.doi.org/10.1145/2628363.2634267

In order to lessen the effect of email overload we have argued the need for flexible tools that support both personalisation and customisation, as these processes support different behaviour change techniques [2]. Personalisation involves system-driven change and can be used, for example, to nudge people into setting appropriate goals. Customisation involves user-driven change and, in combination with appropriate information, can encourage people to reflect on their email behaviour. Haraty et al. [6] argue that customizable tools should encourage reflection, because it is an effective way to change behaviours. Cox et al. [4] also discuss how self-reflection can increase self-awareness and that the insights gained can motivate behaviour changes.

RESEARCH GOALS AND METHODS
Currently, I am only five months into my PhD and this proposal therefore contains my problem statement and research questions, framed within the relevant literature.

Goal 1: Understanding email behavioural differences and the impact of email on work-home boundaries
1. *Study 1: qualitative method* [Data collection in progress]

Capra et al. [1] suggest that emails can be considered a boundary artefact that reflects one's individual relationship between work and personal life. Their work is a pioneering study that compares email use within the same sample (university employees) across work and personal contexts. Their data was collected in 2010 and only marginally considers email use on mobile devices. Moreover, they rely only on quantitative methods (a self-report survey), asking participants identical questions about both their work and personal email accounts, using dimensions such as job role, email management, and boundaries and identities.

These limitations motivated my first study, which is aimed in general at understanding how people use email on different devices. To gain a deeper understanding of email behavioural differences among a similar professional sample, semi-structured interviews was chosen as the method. Data will be analysed using thematic analysis. Interview questions cover topics such as email management strategies, devices used to access email, physical location in which email is accessed, the concept of email overload, and the role of email in work-home boundaries.

2. *Study 2: quantitative method* [Study design in progress]

There has been little consideration in the email literature of deferral behaviour, in particular understanding what triggers an immediate response and what causes delays.

This second study is based on two unpublished experiments conducted recently within my research group. Extending Wainer, Dabbish and Kraut's email study [8] to a real-world context, two longitudinal experiments have investigated how manipulating information shown in email headers affects how people respond to emails. Both experiments were set up in the form of a competitive game than ran for 2 and 3 weeks respectively. At the end of the experiments, the two participants with the most points received a money prize. A third prize was also awarded randomly. In particular, participants, who were mainly professionals, were shown information about the urgency, utility and time cost of the email. Each day, participants received around 20 emails and were awarded points if they responded within specified times.

My second study builds on these two experiments, but focuses on understanding reasons behind deferral behaviour. Using the same game set up and the same dependent variables (number of on-time responses and response times), we will vary the four independent variables (information gap, urgency, points, cost of response). Results from this second study should give insight into what motivates people to respond immediately or defer their replies. Understanding people's prioritization strategies can shed more light on how people handle email across work-home boundaries.

Together, the first two studies in my PhD should help me identify common email strategies and provide insights into how email management tools can facilitate a satisfactory work-home balance.

Goal 2: Designing and evaluating a personalisable and customizable tool that accommodates email behavioural differences and can help change habits so that a satisfactory work-home balance can be achieved.

3. *Study 3: Email tool development and assessment* [next step]

Based on the ideas presented in our workshop paper [2] and on the data collected from the first two studies, my goal is to build a web-based tool/website that can help people reflect on their own idiosyncratic differences. I will investigate whether self-reflection facilitates changes in email behaviour that result in a more satisfactory work-home balance. To support this phase, the tool/website should provide adequate recommendations (such as suggesting what existing tool could help an individual's problem) and social engagement. This third study, both in its design phase and evaluation process will rely on behaviour change theories, such as goal-setting theory, theory of planned behaviour and nudge theory.

RESEARCH SITUATION

I started my PhD in October 2013 funded by an EPSRC DTG studentship for four years. In addition, my research is part of the Digital Epiphanies project, also funded by EPSRC (grant EP/K025392/1). By the time of the Doctoral Consortium I will have gathered and analysed data from my first two studies, which I would like to present and discuss. My primary interest is to get feedback on how to best design the tool for my third study and follow-up ones.

ACKNOWLEDGMENTS

This work is funded by an EPSRC DTG studentship.

REFERENCES

1. Capra, R., Khanova, J., & Ramdeen, S. Work and personal email use by university employees: PIM practices across domain boundaries. *Journal of the American Society for Information Science and Technology*, *64*(5), (2013), 1029-1044.
2. Cecchinato, M.E., Bird, J., & Cox, A.L. Personalised Email Tools: a solution to email overload? In *CHI Personalized Behaviour Change Technologies Workshop,* (2014).
3. Clark, S. C. Work/family border theory: A new theory of work/family balance. *Human relations*, *53*(6), (2000), 747-770.
4. Cox, A.L., Bird, J. & Fleck, R. Digital Epiphanies: How self-knowledge can change habits and our attitudes towards them. *BCS HCI 1st Workshop on Habits in Human-Computer Interaction*, (2013).
5. Dabbish, L. A., & Kraut, R. E. Email overload at work: an analysis of factors associated with email strain. In *Proc. CSCW*, (2006), 431-440.
6. Haraty, M., McGrenere, J., & Tang, C. Role of Reflection in Customization Behaviors. In *CHI Simple, Sustainable Living Workshop*, (2012).
7. Nippert-Eng, C. Calendars and keys: The classification of "home" and "work". In *Sociological Forum*, *11*(3), (1996), 563-582.
8. Wainer, J., Dabbish, L., & Kraut, R. Should I open this email?: inbox-level cues, curiosity and attention to email. In *PART 5 Proc. Human factors in computing systems,* (2011), 3439-3448.
9. Whittaker, S., & Sidner, C. Email overload: exploring personal information management of email. In *Proc. CHI* (1996), 276-283.

The Effects of Encumbrance on Mobile Interactions

Alexander Ng
Glasgow Interaction Systems Group (GIST)
School of Computing Science, University of Glasgow, Scotland
a.ng.1@research.gla.ac.uk

ABSTRACT
The popularity of touchscreen mobile devices gives users a variety of useful apps and functionality on the move. As a result, mobile devices are being used in a range of different contexts. One common scenario that has received little attention from researchers is the effects of encumbrance - carrying objects (for example, shopping bags and personal gear) and interacting with mobile devices at the same time. This is a frequent everyday situation and one that can cause interaction difficulties [3]. There is a lack of knowledge of the impact encumbrance has on interaction therefore the usability issues in these physically and mentally demanding contexts are unknown. Prior to the start of our research, there was only one related study that has examined input performance with handheld devices while multitasking with different types of objects [7]. A better understanding of the interaction problems caused by encumbrance would allow researchers to develop more effective input techniques on touchscreen mobile devices.

Author Keywords
Encumbrance; Mobile interactions; Target acquisition.

ACM Classification Keywords
H.5.2. User Interfaces: *Input devices and strategies*

THE RESEARCH GOALS AND KEY RESEARCH QUESTIONS
The main objective of our research is to understand the effects of encumbrance on interaction with touchscreen mobile phones while on the move. There are several key research questions and research goals.

Q1 - *What objects do users hold/carry when using mobile devices?*

The first research goal is to choose a small set of objects to evaluate in subsequent user studies. Since it is not feasible to assess every possible object that a user may hold during interaction, it is more practical to examine a small range of encumbrance scenarios that users frequently experience.

MobileHCI '14, Sep 23-26 2014, Toronto, ON, Canada
ACM 978-1-4503-3004-6/14/09.
http://dx.doi.org/10.1145/2628363.2634268

Q2 - *Which touch-based input technique on touchscreen mobile devices to evaluate when encumbered?*

Touchscreen interfaces provide a rich variety of finger input, from tapping (for example, typing on a soft keyboard) to multi-touch gesture input (for example, performing two finger pinching and spreading actions to scale an image). The primary focus is to examine encumbered tapping interaction since it is the fundamental input method to select icons, widgets and other touchscreen interface components. Once we have a better knowledge of tapping performance, the goal is to examine more complex multi-touch gesture interactions in encumbered contexts.

Q3 - *How to improve interactions when encumbered and on the move?*

We aim to develop novel input techniques and applications to assist the user to input more effectively in encumbered situations. The development of our input techniques will be based on the measurements collected from our user studies.

THE APPROACH TO TACKLE THE RESEARCH QUESTIONS AND RESEARCH METHODOLOGY
A series of user studies will be carried out to investigate the effects of encumbrance and mobility. The first observation-based study will be conducted to find out the objects that users frequently hold while using mobile devices. The main objective from this initial study is to define a set of common encumbrance scenarios. The second study will be conducted to measure tapping performance while walking and encumbered. The objects used to evaluate the impact of encumbrance will be based on the findings from the initial observations. We will also measure tapping performance while unencumbered and standing for baseline comparisons.

The third study will be carried out to compare walking evaluation methods in the current literature to see if these techniques are still approximate to examine encumbrance as well. Since we are measuring the effects of two physical factors (encumbrance and mobility), extra care is required when designing our experiments. The fourth study will be conducted to measure tapping performance in different one- and two- handed input postures. Users are likely to change posture (if possible) when encumbered if it becomes too challenging to input in an efficient manner. The fifth study will be carried out to evaluate our first attempt at developing an input technique (based on the results from our earlier experiments) to make tapping on touchscreens more effective while encumbered and walking.

THE KEY STUDIES CONDUCTED SO FAR AND THE RESULTS OBTAINED

Three main studies have been conducted so far to investigate the effects of encumbrance on mobile interactions. Study 1 [3] was split into two parts. In the first part, we observed users in public settings to identify the common objects that were held when mobile devices were used to allow us to define a set of encumbrance scenarios. The results showed that users carried bags and boxes the most often. In the second part of the study, we conducted a target acquisition experiment on a touchscreen mobile phone while encumbered and walking. Based on the results from the observations, two differently sized bags (held in hand) and boxes (held under the arm) were chosen as the encumbrance objects. A Vicon motion capture system was used to track body positions and hand movements to see how encumbrance and mobility affected the user's input behavior. The results showed that encumbrance caused targeting performance to significantly decrease compared to unencumbered. Target accuracy decreased to 28% when walking and holding a bag (which weighed 3kg) in the dominant hand. Also, there were significantly more hand movements and instability when the dominant side was encumbered. The preferred walking speed (PWS) dropped by 41% when the box was held under the non-dominant arm.

Study 2 [6] was conducted to examine encumbered tapping performance by using two established walking evaluation methods in the current literature. The two techniques were walking on a treadmill [1] and walking around a predefined route while following a pacesetter [2]. Similar to Study 1, a bag and a box were selected as the encumbrance objects. The results showed that encumbrance caused target accuracy to significantly decrease while selection time took significantly longer than unencumbered. Target selection performance for treadmill walking was more accurate and quicker than walking around the predefined route. However, the mean PWS recorded for treadmill walking was significantly less than walking on the ground as the participants expressed that it was difficult to judge their walking speed on the treadmill. Therefore, extra caution is required if a treadmill is used in future mobile studies if walking speed is an important factor.

Study 3 [4] was carried out to investigate the effects of encumbrance in three different input postures (two-handed index finger, one-handed preferred thumb and two-handed both thumbs). In the observations of Study 1, users were seen to interact in various input postures and we wanted to see if changing posture had an effect on performance when encumbered. A new encumbrance scenario was also evaluated - holding a bag in each hand to simulate interaction while carrying multiple objects. The results from Study 3 showed that encumbrance and walking caused targeting performance to significantly decrease in all input postures. In the one-handed preferred thumb posture, targets that were difficult to reach were severely affected but overall accuracy when encumbered was marginally higher than the other two postures despite non-significant results. Target selection using the index finger was significantly quicker than both thumb-based input postures which suggest that the advantage of an extra digit to input is reduced in encumbered contexts.

REMAINING RESEARCH EFFORTS

In the remaining period of the research, one of the main objectives is to develop input techniques to improve tapping performance on touchscreen mobile devices in encumbered situations. We will compare our technique to those methods in the current literature that have shown to improve targeting performance. We also plan to investigate the effects of encumbrance and mobility on multi-touch gesture interactions. Currently, no studies have examined how well users can perform these biomechanically complex gestures while walking and/or encumbered, yet many mobile applications require these types of onscreen actions to interact (for example, browsing a map).

LIST OF PUBLICATIONS TO DATE

Please see the following references [3,4,5,6].

REFERENCES

1. Bergstrom-Lehtovirta, J., Oulasvirta, A., and Brewster, S. The effects of walking speed on target acquisition on a touchscreen interface. *In Proc. MobileHCI 2011*, ACM (2011), 143–146.
2. Kane, S.K., Wobbrock, J.O., and Smith, I.E. Getting off the treadmill: evaluating walking user interfaces for mobile devices in public spaces. *In Proc. MobileHCI 2008*, ACM Press (2008), 109–118.
3. Ng, A., Brewster, S., and Williamson, J. The Impact of Encumbrance on Mobile Interactions. *In Proc. INTERACT 2013*, Springer-Verlag (2013), 92–109.
4. Ng, A., Brewster, S., and Williamson, J. Investigating the Effects of Encumbrance on One- and Two- Handed Interactions with Mobile Devices. *In Proc. CHI 2014*, (2014), 1981–1990.
5. Ng, A. and Brewster, S. The relationship between encumbrance and walking speed on mobile interactions. *Ext. Abstracts CHI 2013*, ACM Press (2013), 1359–1364.
6. Ng, A., Williamson, J., and Brewster, S. Comparing Evaluation Methods for Encumbrance and Walking on Interaction with Touchscreen Mobile Devices. *To appear in MobileHCI 2014*, (2014).
7. Oulasvirta, A. and Bergstrom-Lehtovirta, J. Ease of juggling: studying the effects of manual multitasking. *In Proc. CHI 2011*, ACM Press (2011), 3103–3112.

Co-Design of Cognitive Telerehabilitation Technologies

Tuck-Voon How
Institute of Biomaterials & Biomedical Engineering
University of Toronto
Toronto, Canada
tuckvoon.how@mail.utoronto.ca

ABSTRACT
Emerging mobile technologies enable new forms of interaction *in the context of our everyday life* – this has profound implications for delivering brain injury rehabilitation at a distance through technology, or *cognitive telerehabilitation*. However, a challenge lies in designing these technologies, as they require both clinical and technical expertise. This research aims to address this challenge through a co-design approach that brings together mobile technology experts and rehabilitation practitioners.

Author Keywords
Brain injury; co-design; pervasive computing; cognitive rehabilitation; contextual rehabilitation technologies.

ACM Classification Keywords
H.5.2 User interfaces, user-centered design.

INTRODUCTION
Mobile technologies in our society are advancing rapidly. Today we are witnessing significant changes in how we utilize computing technology and are moving towards a *pervasive computing* society – in which computers are increasingly a part of the medium of how people interact and collaborate in activities [1]. This has profound implications for healthcare and rehabilitation.

One intersection between technology and rehabilitation is the concept of *telerehabilitation*. By definition, telerehabilitation is the ability to conduct rehabilitative therapy, assessment, or training over a distance through the use of information and communication technology (e.g., video conferencing, phone, internet, etc.) [2]. With the changing landscape towards a pervasive computing society, the possible ways of conducting telerehabilitation are also growing. Richer modalities of human-computer interaction are grounds for more types of remote therapies and assessments. In addition, mobile forms of computing now allow for rehabilitation to be seamlessly embedded into an individual's *everyday context* [3].

MobileHCI 2014, September 23–26, 2014, Toronto, ON, Canada.
ACM 978-1-4503-3004-6/14/09.
http://dx.doi.org/10.1145/2628363.2634269

Applying pervasive computing to telerehabilitation is an emerging concept that shifts technology from just a medium of communication (e.g. videoconferencing) to an active intervener in the rehabilitation process. In contrast to desktop applications that emulate real-world scenarios, pervasive computing is done *within the context* of real-world situations, thereby enhancing "ecological validity", a known factor for rehabilitation success. Notable examples of this concept are already being applied to physical rehabilitation. For example, mobile devices are used to detect and prevent freezing-of-gait, and improve walking for Parkinson's, all in the context of a patient's everyday activities [4]. Yet, this *contextualized* approach remains largely unexplored for cognitive telerehabilitation.

BACKGROUND
Although there are unexplored opportunities, care must be taken when envisioning new healthcare technologies. Telerehabilitation technologies are driven by both technical and clinical considerations, and therefore must be grounded in both research fields. New conceptual designs cannot exceed the capabilities of emergent technologies, and also must be motivated by clinical needs and proven clinical practice. A disregard of either field will leave envisioned designs unbalanced and unsuitable for real-world use.

The challenge then lies in incorporating both fields when exploring new design opportunities and considerations for cognitive telerehabilitation. This is further complicated by the diverse needs of telerehabilitation end-users – who include recovering acquired brain-injury patients, rehabilitation clinicians, and possibly, informal caregivers. How do we develop telerehabilitation systems that make opportunistic use of emergent mobile technologies? How can we design them in such a way that incorporates clinical practice and rehabilitation values of care?

To address this challenge this research leverages Sander's *et al.* co-design approach [5]. Co-design refers to the act of facilitating joint creativity between technology designers and end-user stakeholders. This facilitation utilizes *scaffolds* that either help designers empathize with end-user considerations, or help end-users participate more actively in the technology generation process – all done through carefully designed materials, structures, or activities. Each group adds their own expertise to a shared understanding of design opportunities and considerations. Sanders envisioned that the use of co-design would create new "domains of collective creativity," which in turn would require a new set of tools and methods to promote collaboration for these domains [6]. As such, this research has two goals: (1) to increase our understanding of how we can apply pervasive computing concepts to cognitive telerehabilitation; and (2) to develop methodological tools that are aimed at facilitating co-design between mobile technology designers and cognitive rehabilitation practitioners.

RESEARCH QUESTIONS

(1) How can pervasive computing technologies be used to contextualize cognitive rehabilitation therapies and assessments for outpatient environments? (2) What qualities of our designed scaffolds best facilitate co-design between mobile technology designers and rehabilitation practitioners?

PROPOSED METHODOLOGY

This research makes use of two concepts to facilitate co-design: domain experts [7], and design cards [8]. The use of domain experts allows for representation of groups who are not always feasible to involve in all stages of research. In this case, rehabilitation clinicians will act as domain experts on behalf of their brain-injury patients, many of whom have impaired cognition during the first stages of rehabilitation. Additionally, design cards will be used to elicit a response based on the card's content. Specifically, 14 cards have been created to embody concepts from pervasive computing and the abilities of emerging mobile technologies (e.g., portable EEGs or electroencephalograms monitor brainwaves). The physical format of cards enables persistency and a re-combinational nature to ideas [8], which may facilitate the exploration process.

Participants of the study will be cognitive rehabilitation clinicians with hospital and community experience, who can represent their own views and the views of their patients. At least 9-12 participants will be recruited.

Sequentially, this research follows three steps: (1) *Initial Focus Group* – participants are introduced to pervasive computing concepts and the design cards. Each focus group will comprise of 3-4 clinicians and 1-2 design researchers. (2) *One-Week Field Kit* – each clinician is allowed time to think about how pervasive concepts could apply to their rehabilitation work and their patients. The kit consists of the design cards and a journal to log ideas. (3) *Second Focus Group* – participants will meet again to discuss their overall experience with the field kits and to collaborate together to explore possible cognitive telerehabilitation systems.

Analysis of both research questions will follow a generic inductive qualitative model approach. In which all data will be compiled as text, coded into inductively generated organizational categories, and then more substantive (i.e., interpretive) categories. Memos and affinity diagrams will facilitate the generation of these substantive ideas.

RESEARCH PROGRESS

The methods above are the first stage of a research plan to develop new contextualized, cognitive telerehabilitation system(s). The initial findings from this first stage will be presented at the MobileHCI DC. In upcoming work, these findings will be used to select at least one design idea for further iterative development (12 months). Upon completion of a working prototype, this system will be trialed with brain-injury patients, recruited from the Toronto Rehabilitation Institute, to test the feasibility of the design for use in rehabilitation practice (12 months).

CANDIDATE PUBLICATIONS

I am actively researching how mobile technologies can extend rehabilitation into the context of everyday life. My first doctoral publication explored how smartphones could support gait rehabilitation for stroke survivors [9].

MOBILE HCI DOCTORAL CONSORTIUM

My motivation for attending the DC is to receive critical feedback on my research and to dialogue with other researchers on the role that HCI can play in bridging knowledge gaps with other disciplines.

ACKNOWLEDGEMENTS

Graduate funding by CIHR-STIHR Fellowship in Health Care, Technology and Place (TGF-53911).

REFERENCES

1. Harper, R., Rodden, T., Rogers, Y. & Sellen, A. *Being human: Human-computer interaction in the year 2020.* Microsoft Research Ltd., Cambridge, England, 2008.
2. Rosen, M.J., Telerehabilitation. *NeuroRehabilitation – An Interdisciplinary Journal* 12, 1 (1999), 11-26.
3. Maitland, J., McGee-Lennon, M., and Mulvenna, M., Pervasive healthcare: from orange alerts to mindcare. *ACM SIGHIT Record* 1, 1 (2011), 38-40.
4. Bachlin, M., et al., Wearable assistant for Parkinson's disease patients with the freezing of gait symptom. *IEEE Transactions on Information Technology in Biomedicine* 14, 2 (2010), 436-446.
5. Sanders, E. B.-N., and Westerlund, B. Experiencing, exploring and experimenting in and with co-design spaces. In *Nordic Design Research Conference*, Helsinki (2011), 1-5.
6. Sanders, E. B.-N., and Stapper, P.J. Co-creation and the new landscapes of design. *CoDesign* 4, 1 (2011), 15-18.
7. Allen, M., Leung, R., McGrenere, J., and Purves, B., Involving domain experts in assistive technology research. *Univ Access Inf* Soc 7 (2008), 145-154.
8. Friedman, B., and Hendry, D. G., The envisioning cards: a toolkit for catalyzing humanistic and technical imaginations. In *Proc. CHI 2012,* ACM Press (2012) 1145-1148.
9. How, T.V., Chee, J., Wan, E., and Mihailidis, A. MyWalk: A mobile app for gait asymmetry rehabilitation in the community. In *Proc. 7th Int. Conf. on Pervasive Computing Technologies for Healthcare (PervasiveHealth),* ICST (2013), 73-77.

Adaption of Usability Evaluation Methods for Native Smartphone Applications

Ger Joyce
School of Computer Science
University of Hertfordshire
Hatfield
Hertfordshire AL10 9AB
United Kingdom
gerjoyce@outlook.com

ABSTRACT
Research has shown that traditional usability evaluation methods cannot be readily applied to the evaluation of native smartphone applications. This research investigates this issue by adapting two usability evaluation methods, applying each at different stages of the design life cycle. Both adapted methods, when combined as a framework, may help in the design of more usable native smartphone applications.

Author Keywords
Mobile; User Interface; User-centered design; Evaluation/methodology; Analytics.

ACM Classification Keywords
H.5.2 User Interfaces: User-centered design.

BACKGROUND / MOTIVATION
Being able to quickly learn, use and be satisfied with native smartphone applications is important to smartphone users [1]. Should design considerations specific to native smartphone applications not be taken into account, this could lead to difficult-to-use applications and frustrated users [2]. This issue has presented significant challenges for usability experts [3].

PROBLEM BEING ADDRESSED / RESEARCH GOALS / KEY RESEARCH QUESTIONS
To design usable applications, usability experts should have a choice of evaluation methods applicable to native smartphone applications at various stages of the design process. Yet, usability evaluation methods used prior to the release of websites and software designed for desktop monitors are not tailored for native smartphone applications built for small screens, miniature keyboards and constant changes in context of use.

In addition, usability evaluation methods used following the release of an application to users are also difficult to apply to native smartphone applications as they tend to concentrate on:

- Observing users in the lab, which may not resemble how applications are used in the field;
- Following users around, which might be uncomfortable for the user;
- Reviewing analytics data, which is designed primarily for marketing teams.

We can consider creating new pre- and post-release usability evaluation paradigms to solve these issues when evaluating native smartphone applications. However, modifying well-known, tried-and-tested usability evaluation methods for native smartphone applications would seem to be an interesting idea to adapt.

From a pre-release perspective, the applicability of a traditional Heuristic Evaluation [4] to native smartphone application usability is being investigated. This would allow User Experience teams to retain the benefits of this method, which is a relatively inexpensive, effective method of usability inspection [5].

From a post-release perspective, analytics tracking software will be investigated, then adapted to resolve the issues of observing users in the lab, following users around and reviewing analytics data aimed primarily at marketing teams.

The research questions that will address these aims are:

a) What are the main factors to be considered when conducting usability evaluations of native smartphone mobile applications prior to and following release to end users?

MobileHCI '14, Sep 23-26 2014, Toronto, ON, Canada
ACM 978-1-4503-3004-6/14/09.
http://dx.doi.org/10.1145/2628363.2634270

b) How useful are the heuristics developed as part of this research compared with other sets of heuristics when conducting usability evaluations of native smartphone mobile applications?

c) How useful is combining qualitative with quantitative (analytics) data when conducting usability evaluations of native smartphone mobile applications?

APPROACH / RESEARCH METHODOLOGY

The approach taken to address the research questions is to:

Heuristics

1. Define an initial set of heuristics based on the literature;
2. Design and develop a data collection survey website allowing HCI experts to review the initial set of heuristics;
3. Modify the heuristics, if required, based on the feedback received from the survey;
4. Empirically test the modified heuristics by measuring the frequency and severity of usability issues found using various sets of heuristics, including the heuristics defined during this research.

Analytics

1. Review currently available analytics software to investigate which might be suitable for native smartphone application tracking;
2. Design and develop a native smartphone application, then define a set of user tasks;
3. Complete a usability test of the native smartphone application, logging metrics, such as successful/ failed task completion, lostness, and time on task;
4. Empirically test the differences between the metrics collected using only analytics software against metrics tracked using analytics software adapted for native smartphone applications;
5. Combine the adapted analytics usability evaluation method with the adapted heuristics usability evaluation method to create a pre- and post-release native smartphone application usability evaluation framework.

KEY STUDIES / RESEARCH CONDUCTED / RESULTS OBTAINED / REMAINING RESEARCH EFFORTS

To date, a review of the literature of heuristic evaluation and mobile usability has been completed. From this, a set of initial native smartphone application heuristics was derived. These heuristics were reviewed and well-received by sixty HCI practitioners, educators and researchers in eighteen countries. The heuristics were updated with the feedback received and are currently being validated.

Following the completion of the heuristics phase, the second phase of the research, namely the investigation and adaption of analytics software, will commence.

PUBLICATIONS TO DATE

Publications and papers accepted for publication to date are:

- "Towards the Development of Usability Heuristics for Native Smartphone Mobile Applications" – Presented at the HCII2014 conference in Crete, Greece in June 2014;
- "Adapting Heuristics for the Mobile Panorama" – To be presented at the Interacción 2014 conference in Tenerife, Spain in September 2014.

MOTIVATION FOR ATTENDING / SPECIFIC QUESTIONS

The motivation to attend is to speak with other students about their research, as well as to discuss opportunities for collaboration. Specific questions will revolve around the methods and approaches the students used and results, if any, they have obtained.

REFERENCES

1. Rogers, Y., Sharp, H., and Preece, J. *Interaction Design: Beyond Human - Computer Interaction*. John Wiley & Sons, 2011.
2. Coursaris, C.K. and Kim, D.J. A Meta-Analytical Review of Empirical Mobile Usability Studies. *Journal of Usability Studies Vol. 6, Issue 3*, (2011), 117–171.
3. Bernhaupt, R., Mihalic, K., and Obrist, M. Usability Evaluation Methods for Mobile Applications. In J. Lumsden, ed., *Handbook of Research on User Interface Design and Evaluation for Mobile Technology:* IGI Global, 2008.
4. Nielsen, J. and Molich, R. Heuristic evaluation of user interfaces. *Proceedings of the SIGCHI conference on Human factors in computing systems*, (1990), 249–256.
5. Jeffries, R., Miller, J.R., Wharton, C., and Uyeda, K. User interface evaluation in the real world: a comparison of four techniques. *Proceedings of the SIGCHI conference on Human factors in computing systems*, (1991), 119–124.

Body-worn Sensors for Remote Implicit Communication

Jeffrey R. Blum
Shared Reality Lab
McGill University
Montreal, Canada
jeffbl@cim.mcgill.ca

PERSONAL STATUS

I am a first-year PhD student supervised by Prof. Jeremy Cooperstock in McGill's Electrical and Computer Engineering department, with approximately 40 months remaining.

RESEARCH BACKGROUND

Although there has been a great deal of work on using machine learning algorithms to categorize user activity (e.g., walking, biking) from accelerometer and other sensor data, less attention has been focused on relaying such information in real-time for remote implicit communication. Humans are very familiar with using both explicit and implicit communication with others physically near to us, for example, by using body language and modulating our voice tone and volume. Likewise, remote explicit communication has also existed for a long time in the form of phone calls, text messages, and other mechanisms for communicating explicitly over great distances. However, remote *implicit* communication between mobile users has been less explored, likely since there have been limited avenues for collecting such information and rendering it in a meaningful way while we go about our daily lives.

One effort in this direction is the Feelabuzz project [4], which connects the accelerometer in one smartphone to the vibrator in a remote phone carried by another person, providing a continuous sense of the motion between two people. However, it can be argued that the placement of the phone may not be optimal for sensing motion. Another project, CoupleVIBE, transmits unique vibration patterns from one smartphone to another when a partner arrives at an important pre-determined spot (e.g., work, home). The authors noted a variety of surprising effects from such implicit communication, and report that, "... users were adept at using context to disambiguate partially sensed cues and ignore erroneous ones. Finally, automated communication eliminated the impulse for reciprocation, keeping communication lightweight." [2]

MobileHCI 2014, September 23–26, 2014, Toronto, ON, Canada.
ACM 978-1-4503-3004-6/14/09.
http://dx.doi.org/10.1145/2628363.2634271

RESEARCH PROBLEM & QUESTIONS

Based on these and other prior works, my research attempts to leverage the fact that fitness trackers, smart watches and smartphones are all producing data about our limb and body movements, location, and physical state. These increasingly inexpensive devices are becoming smaller and lighter, and can be worn continuously on legs and arms, or in the case of a smartwatch, may already be worn on the wrist. Such commercial devices are mostly designed for gathering information, but are limited in their expressiveness beyond a screen or simple vibration. However, placement of tactile actuators directly on limbs has significant benefits for notifications, such as reaction time when responding to alerts [1]. Further, Lee at al. have demonstrated that, "wrist-mounted tactile displays are appropriate for implementing multitasking-friendly mobile user interfaces that enable easy alert perception." [3] With this in mind, I am exploring questions around three themes:

- Avoiding overload: Receiving this information on a near-continuous basis could easily be overwhelming. How do we strike the balance between annoying and truly useful, when using this data for implicit communication? What are the benefits and limits in terms of the number of sensors and actuators? How long does it take before we can gain useful information from a haptic or other signal without it being overly intrusive? How should the user be able to control what they are sending and receiving?
- Making it useful: What happens when we have a continuous sense of a remote person over a long period of time? What can we divine from such signals as they integrate into our lives? If I don't feel my partner's leg moving before a lunch date, do I even immediately realize why I know she will be late? Can we usefully switch between sensing different people, or even sense more than one at once?
- Respecting privacy: What are the privacy implications of sharing such intimate data on a continuous basis, and how can we address them through both technical and interface design methods?

RESEARCH TO DATE

Before starting my PhD, I worked on In Situ Audio Services (ISAS), a smartphone application that used spatialized audio to tell a blind person what shops, restaurants and other locations were around them while they walked down the street. This was my introduction to the problem of how to put useful information into the background while the user is occupied with other tasks, such as navigating down a street with a cane or guide dog, and piqued my interest in building a more general system linking two people together.

To date, I have developed a prototype that connects a Texas Instruments SensorTag and a Pebble smartwatch to an Android phone via Bluetooth LE. Accelerometer data is collected from the SensorTag and averaged across each of three dimensions of motion. This summary is then played back on the Pebble watch every 10 seconds as three vibration pulses, with the length of each pulse representing the amount of motion in one of the three axes. This design allows us to avoid a continuous vibration, and also lets a single vibrator represent three different axes of information. Although we have not yet run any formal user studies, anecdotal use with a few users over spans of an hour or two indicate it is possible to distinguish different types of motion. For example, a long-medium-short pulse is felt when the SensorTag is attached to the ankle, since there is considerable up-down force, some forward-back, but limited side-to-side. I have also built a PWM library for Pebble that allows the strength of the vibrations to be varied, but no comparison between the two methods has yet been run. A major flaw is that the current implementation requires that all devices be connected to the same phone, so they can only be separated by around 10-30 m. This is good enough for early testing, especially when feeling one's own motion played back, but my top priority is extending it to work over greater distances. This work is being presented as a Research Note at the upcoming GRAND 2014 conference in Ottawa.

FUTURE RESEARCH

I expect to have implemented remote communication over the Internet within the next month. This will allow the system to be used on an ongoing basis to gather feedback and discover issues that prevent it from being used continuously enough to start fading into the background of the user's daily activities. During this testing, I will be focusing on several additional goals through the remainder of 2014:

- Supporting more devices in addition to the existing SensorTags and Pebble watches. Most promising is the Tactile Labs Haptuator[1], which is already in use in our lab for other projects, and generates a much richer haptic signal than a simple vibrator. Fitness shirts with built-in heart and breath sensors are also enticing.
- Experimenting with the amount and type of feedback used, and where it occurs on the body.
- Extending the system to multiple sensors and actuators at the same time, with the ability to switch between them or change their behaviour.

Thus, I expect to have initial user trials completed later this year, and be in a good position to further refine the system and do more formal long-term studies. Although I will be keeping an eye toward privacy issues during all phases of the project, I anticipate focusing on this more heavily in 2015. I will not attempt to project specific tasks beyond 2015, as they will be guided by the results in the coming 12 months.

[1] `www.tactilelabs.com/products/haptics/haptuator/`

PUBLICATIONS

Four additional publications can be found in my CV.[2]

1. **Blum, J.R.**, Eichhorn, A., Smith, S., Cooperstock, J.R. (2014) Real-Time Emergency Response: Improved Management of Real-Time Information During Crisis Situations. J. Multimodal User Interfaces (JMUI), 8(2):161-173.
2. Listen to It Yourself! Evaluating Usability of "What's Around Me?" for the Blind. Panëels, S., Olmos, A., **Blum, J.R.** and Cooperstock, J.R. (2013) Proc. SIGCHI Conf Human Factors in Computing Systems (CHI), Paris.
3. **Blum, J.R.**, Bouchard, M. and Cooperstock, J.R. (2012) Spatialized Audio Environmental Awareness for Blind Users with a Smartphone. J. Mobile Networks and Applications. 18:295-309
4. **Blum, J.R.**, Greencorn, D., and Cooperstock, J.R. (2012) Smartphone sensor reliability for augmented reality applications. Proc Mobile and Ubiquitous Systems: Computing, Networking, and Services. Beijing, China 120:127-138
5. To, L., Thompson, B., **Blum, J.R.**, Maehara, G., Hess, R. and Cooperstock, J. R. (2011) A game platform for treatment of amblyopia. IEEE Trans. on Neural Systems and Rehab. Eng. 19(3):280-9
6. **Blum, J.R.**, Bouchard, M., and Cooperstock, J.R. (2011) What's around me? Spatialized audio augmented reality for blind users with a smartphone. Proc 8th Intl ICST Conf, MobiQuitous 2011, Copenhagen, Denmark 49-62 [best paper award]

MOTIVATION & QUESTIONS

Although I have worked in mobile computing for a very long time, I am relatively new to the fields of haptics and implicit communication. Guidance on the areas and directions most likely to be fruitful, as well as practical information on building and testing such a system, would be immensely useful in guiding my research over the next few years, especially since I am still less than a year into my program.

REFERENCES

1. Ashbrook, D. L., Clawson, J. R., Lyons, K., Starner, T. E., and Patel, N. Quickdraw: the impact of mobility and on-body placement on device access time. In *Proc 26th annual CHI conference on Human factors in computing systems - CHI '08*, ACM Press (2008), 219–222.
2. Bales, E., Li, K. A., and Griwsold, W. CoupleVIBE: Mobile Implicit Communication to Improve Awareness for (Long-Distance) Couples. In *Proc ACM conf Computer supported cooperative work - CSCW '11*, ACM Press (2011), 65.
3. Lee, S. C., and Starner, T. BuzzWear: alert perception in wearable tactile displays on the wrist. In *Proc 28th intl conference on Human factors in computing systems - CHI '10*, ACM Press (2010), 433.
4. Leichsenring, C., Tünnermann, R., and Hermann, T. feelabuzz: Direct Tactile Communication with Mobile Phones. *Intl J of Mobile Human Computer Interaction 3*, 2 (Jan. 2011), 65–74.

[2] `http://jeff.mulb.us/about/JeffBlumResume.pdf`

Urgent Mobile Tool for Hearing Impaired, Language Dysfunction and Foreigners at Emergency Situation

Naotsune Hosono
Oki Consulting Solutions Co., Ltd.
4-11-15 Shibaura,
Minato-ku, Tokyo,
108-8551 Japan
keiolab@gmail.com

Hiromitsu Inoue
Chiba Prefectural University of Health Science.
2-10-1 Wakaba, Mihama-ku,
Chiba-shi, Chiba-ken, 261-0014
Japan

Miwa Nakanishi
Keio University
3-14-1, Hiyoshi, Kohoku-ku,
Yokohama-shi, Kanagawa-ken,
223-0061, Japan

Yutaka Tomita
Fujita Health University.
1-98 Dengakugakubo,
Kutsukake-cho, Toyoake-shi,
Aichi-ken, 470-1192 Japan

MobileHCI '14, Sep 23-26, 2014, Toronto, ON, Canada
ACM 978-1-4503-3004-6/14/09.
http://dx.doi.org/10.1145/2628363.2633568

Abstract
This paper introduces a mobile application that allows deaf, language dysfunctioned, or non-native language users to report emergencies. An earlier version (booklet) was designed for hearing impaired person to be able to communicate with others without speaking. The current smart phone application allows calls to be made from a remote location. The screen transitions application follows the dialogue models used by emergency services. Users interact with the dialogues by tapping on icons or pictograms instead of using text messages. Evaluation by deaf people and a non-native speaker found that it was about three times quicker to report an emergency using this tool than it was by using text messages.

Author Keywords
Accessibility; Mobile; Human Computer Interface; Context of Use; Human Centred Design.

ACM Classification Keywords
H. INFORMATION SYSTEMS
H.1 MODELS AND PRINCIPLES
H.1.2 User/Machine Systems
Subject descriptor: Human information processing

General Terms
Design; Experimentation; Human Factors; Performance

Introduction
The development of this tool was originally motivated by the needs of a hearing impaired person who had no easy way to communicate an emergency situation to strangers.

A person being transported in an ambulance who communicates with sign language has no easy way to communicate with the paramedics. In previous research, we created a booklet with icons or pictograms that supports limited communication for those in Japan who cannot speak Japanese because of hearing impairment, language dysfunction, or some other reason [1-3]. Currently 6,000 copies of the booklet have been distributed to fire departments, hospitals, and other organizations.

Once the booklet was available, users requested that the functionality be available as a smart phone application since almost all the target users carry and use smart phones.

Previous research
In previous research, interviews with hearing impaired people, medics, nurses, therapists and emergency workers were carried out. The research outcomes were then synthesized into diagrams composed of icons and pictograms in a booklet, utilizing Multivariate analysis (MVA) [4]. For example, the presence of pain was indicated by brightly coloured animated figures. Users could simply point to the designated icons or pictograms in the booklet to communicate the situation to others.

Emergency Dialogues
We followed the human centred design process [5], with the initial requirements analysis involving observation of emergency call operators in a fire station. The observed dialogue process for these emergency situations is summarized in Figure 1. The dialogue is structured as a simple branching tree where different branches represent alternative responses such as Yes or No.

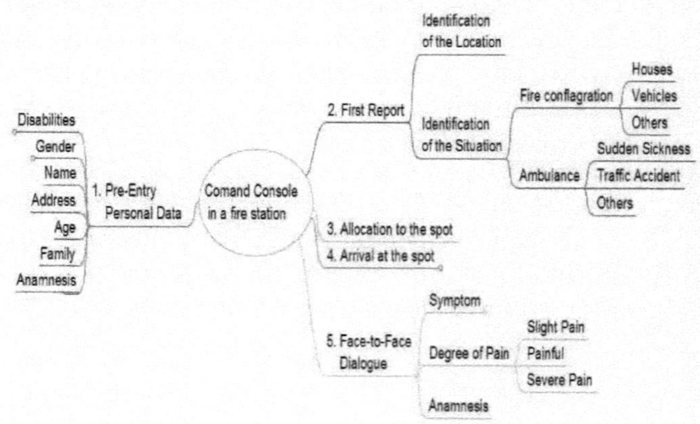

Figure 1: The Dialogue Process at Emergency Situations

Five context processes to implement
Most of the emergency calls were for fires or medical emergencies. The following five steps were selected as the basis for communicating between a person in an emergency situation and an emergency call operator (Figure 2).

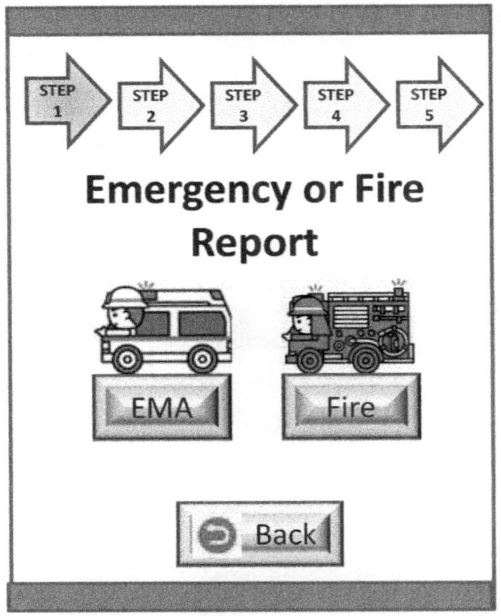

Figure 2: A screenshot of the Urgent Mobile Tool

1. Pre-Registration;
The face information of the users is registered with the system prior to the occurrence of an emergency situation.

2. Exact moment of emergency report;
The most important matter at this moment is to report promptly to the nearest fire station.

3. Dispatch of the fire engine or ambulance to the location
Users can communicate with the application while they are waiting for the emergency vehicle.

4. Approach to the reported location;
Visual and auditory alerts are available in the application to notify users that the emergency vehicle is almost there.

5. Dialogue on the spot
Once emergency workers arrive on the scene users can communicate with them using the mobile tool. Even in face to face communication, icons or pictograms are generally necessary since few emergency workers comprehend sign language.

The implementation of dialogue process

Previous research [4] discussed the issues of communicating between hearing and hearing impaired people in face to face situations. We then extended this approach to include communication between the person in trouble and the fire department. We developed a smart phone application that takes advantage of functions such as Tap to select, Flick or Swipe to move to the next page, Pinch in/out with double fingers, as well as GPS. Currently the application consists of about 20 screens on the smart phone. The application was developed using the Software Development Kit (SDK) of MIT APP Innovator. The application was implemented on the Android touch panel terminal through DeployGate.

Evaluation

The application prototype was evaluated by hearing impaired people in a usability test. The following six tasks were carried out on both a smart phone and personal computer (PC) by three hearing impaired participants and one non-native speaker.

· Task-1: Filling out the pre-entry personal data
· Task-2: Fire report by the tablet terminal.
· Task-3: Fire report by text of e-mail with PC
· Task-4: Ambulance request by text of e-mail with PC
· Task-5: Ambulance request by the tablet terminal
· Task-6: Interview with filling out questionnaires

The results were assessed in terms of effectiveness, efficiency and satisfaction [6].

Conclusion

Task performance time data was available for four participants and is reported in Table 1. These initial results suggest that reporting time is quicker using the smart phone application (taking only about one third as long for our participants). In interviews carried out after the user testing, users said that the smart phone application would reduce their anxiety in an emergency situation. Thus ease of use in this case is accompanied by improved user experience [7].

Subjects	Fire Report with Smartphone	Emergency Report with Smartphone	Fire Report with PC	Emergency Report with PC
SMZ	17.97	63.79	98.00	151.47
SZM	15.00	91.00	147.00	165.00
SZK	9.00	79.00	91.00	130.00
JMM	6.00	13.00	34.00	50.00
Average	11.99	61.70	92.50	124.12
Total Ave.	36.85		108.31	
				Unit: Second

Table 1: The Result measured by the subjects

Acknowledgements

This research is funded by the Project organized by Fire and Disaster Management Agency under Ministry of Internal Affairs and Communications (MIC) of Japan. Special thanks to Mr. M. Suzuki of AAJD, Mr. T. Yamashita of Cosmocity, Mr. T. Inaba and Mr. F. Miyajima of Kasuga Onojo Nakagawa Fire Department and Mr. M. Nishijima of Oki Consulting Solutions Co., Ltd., as well as Prof. Dr. M. Chignell of Toronto Univ.

References

1. Hosono, N., Inoue, H., Nagashima, Y., Tomita, Y.: Sensory Evaluation Method to Create Pictograms Based on Multiplex Sign Languages, ACHI2013, Nice (2013)
2. Hosono, N., Miyajima, F., Inaba, T., Nishijima, M., Suzuki, M., Miki, H., Tomita, Y.: The Urgent Communication System for Deaf and Language Dysfunction People, HCII2013, Las Vegas (2013)
3. Hosono, N., Inoue, H., Miyajima, F., Inaba, T., Nishijima, M., Nakanishi, M., Tomita, Y. : Emergency Communication Tool for Deaf, Language Dysfunction and Foreigners, AAATE2013, Faro (2013)
4. Hosono, N., Inoue, H., Nagashima, Y.: Context Analysis of Universal Communication through Local Sign Languages applying Multivariate Analysis, ICCHO2010, Vienna (2010)
5. International Organization for Standardization: ISO9241-210 (former 13407:1999), Ergonomics Human-centred design processes for interactive systems (2010)
6. International Organization for Standardization: ISO9241-11, Ergonomic requirements for office work with visual display terminals (VDTs), Guidance on usability (1998)
7. Hartson R., Pyla P.S.: The UX Book: Process and Guidelines for Ensuring a Quality User Experience, Morgan Kaufmann Publishers (2012).

JuxtaPinch: An Application for Collocated Multi-Device Photo Sharing

Heidi Selmer Nielsen
Socio-Interactive Design Center
Aalborg University
Selma Lagerlofs Vej 300, DK
DK-9220 Aalborg East
Hsn.mobil@gmail.com

Mikael B. Skov
Socio-Interactive Design Center
Aalborg University
Selma Lagerlofs Vej 300, DK
DK-9220 Aalborg East
dubois@cs.aau.dk

Marius Pallisgaard Olsen
Socio-Interactive Design Center
Aalborg University
Selma Lagerlofs Vej 300
DK-9220 Aalborg East
marius.pallisgaard@gmail.com

Jesper Kjeldskov
Socio-Interactive Design Center
Aalborg University
Selma Lagerlofs Vej 300, DK
DK-9220 Aalborg East
jesper@cs.aau.dk

MobileHCI '14, Sep 23-26 2014, Toronto, ON, Canada
ACM 978-1-4503-3004-6/14/09.
http://dx.doi.org/10.1145/2628363.2633569

Abstract
We have developed an application called JuxtaPinch that allows users to share photos on multiple devices, i.e. mobile phones and tablets, while being collocated. JuxtaPinch employs simple and intuitive interaction techniques, e.g. pinching to connect devices, and it enables flexible physical positioning of devices and supports partial photo viewing. JuxtaPinch further enables users to use their own devices and access photos stored on own devices. In the Interactivity session, audience members can explore and view photos with friends and colleagues using different devices and experience defamiliarization and playful interaction with the photos – aspects that we have uncovered during lab and field studies of JuxtaPinch.

Author Keywords
Collocated photo sharing; pinching; multi device

ACM Classification Keywords
H.5.2 Information interfaces and presentation (e.g., HCI): Miscellaneous

Introduction
Research within mobile HCI has recently begun to explore and study opportunities and challenges of user interaction across several mobile platforms. Often referred to as multi-device interaction or cross-device

Figure 1: JuxtaPinch in use where several devices are being employed.

interaction, this enables new and interesting application areas, e.g. taking and sharing photos. Collocated photo sharing plays an important role both socially and for the individual, developing people's self-image, as well as creating and strengthening relationships within social groups [7]. While online photo sharing Internet technologies, e.g. Instagram or Flickr, have gained huge success over the last years, these online photo sharing technologies lacks the richness of the social interaction that occurs when people share and view photos while being collocated. As a consequence, HCI is witnessing a growing interest in collocated sharing of photos through different kinds of mobile and pervasive technologies [2, 4], and more studies have investigated how to overcome and address some of the inherent problems when sharing photos with others on small screens on mobile devices [1, 6]. But we still lack technologies that can be used in real situations for collocated photo sharing on multiple devices.

In this paper, we present a multi-device platform application called JuxtaPinch that supports collocated photo sharing on multiple devices – both mobile phones and tablets (and different mobile operating systems). JuxtaPinch allows flexible positioning of devices next to each other and stitching their display areas together through a cross-device pinching gesture.

Motivation

With the rapidly increasing proliferation of smartphones and tablets in people's everyday lives, it is now not uncommon to have several devices at one's immediate disposal. Also, we bring and use these personal (and shared) technologies in many everyday life situations while being alone and together with other people. Research within HCI has started to explore a new class of "multi-device applications" that allow users to link individual mobile devices and use them as one joint interface. Examples of this include Pass-Them-Around by Lucero et al. [2], Junkyard Jumbotron by Borovoy & Knep [5], and Pinch by Ohta and Tanaka [4]. These all create and make use of larger screen real estate by physically placing a number of mobile devices next to each other and treating their combined display surface as joint. However, we address and provide solution for three opportunities within collocated photo sharing applications namely 1) flexible positioning of devices in relation to each other, as seen in [5], but combined with the simple interaction mechanisms for aligning and connecting devices without any external hardware [2, 4], 2) partial viewing of photos where parts of the photo can be left out and finally, 3) multi-device collocated photo sharing applications that works across different mobile operating systems.

JuxtaPinch

JuxtaPinch supports collocated photo sharing and exploration on multiple handheld and mobile devices. JuxtaPinch combines juxtapositioning, which is the act of positioning objects (i.e. devices) side-by-side, and pinching, which is the act of stitching devices together. We designed JuxtaPinch to support flexible positioning through pinching of juxtaposed devices and furthermore it supports partial viewing of photos by scaling the photo to fill all available screen real estate. The fundamental idea of JuxtaPinch is that photos from one device can be split across multiple devices (i.e. mobile phones and tablets), as illustrated in figure 1, by connecting them through the act of pinching.

Otha and Tanaka [4] argue that cross-device pinching resembles the action of stitching something together,

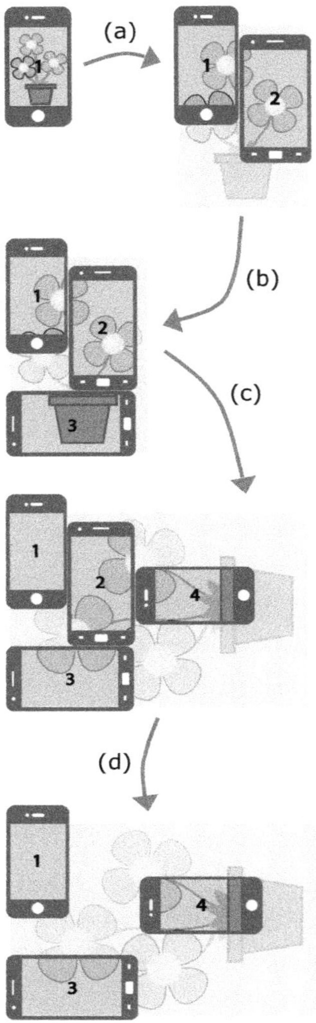

Figure 3: Scenario of use

and JuxtaPinch employs pinching as a simple technique for connecting devices. Basically, JuxtaPinch combines several screens (devices) to appear as one screen (as illustrated in the pictures in figure 1). This means that a photo shown on the system will extend over a multitude of devices. JuxtaPinch basically offers three different functionalities for exploring photos over several devices namely selecting a new photo, connecting devices, and disconnecting devices. JuxtaPinch allows the users to select photos among the photos stored in the library on the device. Users can access the gallery of their device and choose any photo from it. When a new photo has been chosen, all connected devices will disconnect such that the system provides a clean screen to build the new photo.

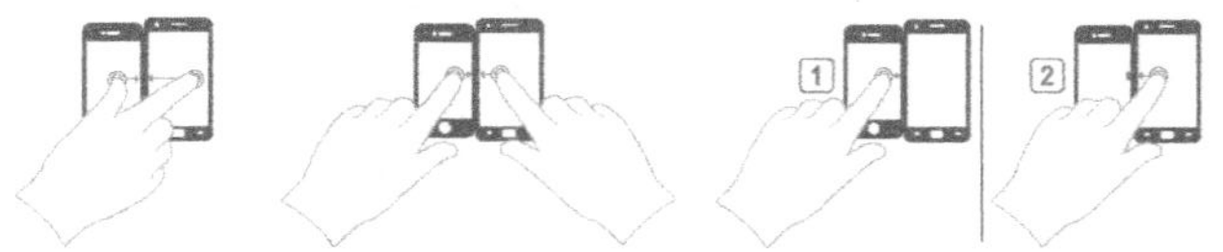

Figure 2: The implemented pinching techniques in JuxtaPinch: One-hand pinching, two-hand pinching, and two-step pinching.

We included three different but related pinching techniques to allow flexibility when connecting devices. Thus, JuxtaPinch integrates the following techniques: One-hand pinching, two-hand pinching, and two-step pinching. Inspired by Otha and Tanaka [4], we implemented one-hand pinching where users typically use their thumb and index finger on the two devices. The user then slides the fingers towards each other to connect the devices at the adjoining edges. Two-hand pinching inspired by Lucero et al [2] uses two hands. Here the users typically uses index fingers on both devices and slides them towards each other. Finally, we developed a two-step pinching technique during the testing phase of JuxtaPinch. Here the user slides his index finger to the edge of one device and then afterwards to the edge of the other device. We chose to allow all three pinching techniques because we were not interested in assessing or comparing these individual techniques, but instead interested in the use of multi-device applications enabled (for studies on pinching techniques please refer to [2, 4]).

JuxtaPinch allows users to remove and reposition devices when exploring photos. In order to reposition (or remove) a device, the user simply moves or lifts the device. Inspired by the repositioning in Otha and Tanaka [4], we utilize the accelerometer and gyroscope to detect movement as it is recognized as both tilting the device from side-to-side or top-to-bottom as well as acceleration on all axes.

In order to illustrate how JuxtaPinch can be used to explore photos while collocated, we include the following short use scenario (supported by the illustrations in figure 3). At the top left, we have a photo of a flower shown on one device. (a) Two devices are connected through pinching and the photo is shown across two devices (#1 and #2). (b) A third device is connected which now shows the lower part of the photo (the pot). (c) A fourth device is connected which makes the photo bigger (#4 is pinched together with #2) – this also rotates the photo 90 degrees. (d) Finally, device #2 is removed which creates a hole between the devices, as they are no longer positioned side-by-side. As it can be seen from the scenario, JuxtaPinch allows users to explore photos in many different ways including partial viewing where only selected parts of the photo is visible on the included devices.

Demonstration

We have presented JuxtaPinch that enables collocated photo sharing among people. JuxtaPinch allows users to share photos from one device across several devices including mobile phones and tablets.

In the demo and experience session at MobileHCI, audience members can explore and view photos with friends and colleagues using their own devices – setting up and connecting to JuxtaPinch will be simple through a website. Additionally, the researchers behind JuxtaPinch will provide additional devices – primarily tablets – to enable the audience to fully explore the application using many devices.

We have evaluated JuxtaPinch in a study with 22 participants and we found that the unification of multiple screens can change the perception of familiar photos – known as defamiliarization and the combination of several screens does not simply equal the same experience as a bigger screen. Finally, we found that partial viewing of photos encouraged playful sharing of photos where our participants would intentionally attempt to create funny situations in the photos. Our findings are further illustrated in [3].

Conclusion

We developed an application called JuxtaPinch that allows users to share photos on multiple devices, i.e. mobile phones and tablets, while being collocated. JuxtaPinch employs simple and intuitive interaction techniques, e.g. pinching to connect devices, and it enables flexible physical positioning of devices and supports partial photo viewing, and JuxtaPinch further enables users to use their own devices and access photos stored on own devices.

References

[1] Fails, J. A., Druin, A., and Guha, M. L. Content splitting & space sharing: collaboratively reading & sharing children's stories on mobile devices. In *Proceedings of the 13th International Conference on Human Computer Interaction with Mobile Devices and Services*, MobileHCI '11, ACM (New York, NY, USA, 2011), 361–370

[2] Lucero, A., Holopainen, J., and Jokela, T. Pass-them-around: collaborative use of mobile phones for photo sharing. In *Proceedings of the SIGCHI Conference on Human Factors in Computing Systems*, CHI '11, ACM (New York, NY, USA, 2011), 1787–1796

[3] Nielsen, H. S., Olsen, M. P., Skov, M. B., and Kjeldskov, J. JuxtaPinch: Exploring Multi-Device Interaction in Collocated Photo Sharing. In *Proceedings of the 16th International Conference on Human Computer Interaction with Mobile Devices and Services*, MobileHCI '14, ACM (Toronto, Canada, 2014)

[4] Ohta, T., and Tanaka, J. Pinch: An interface that relates applications on multiple touch-screen by pinching gesture. In *Advances in Computer Entertainment*, A. Nijholt, T. Romo, and D. Reidsma, Eds., vol. 7624 of *Lecture Notes in Computer Science*. Springer Berlin Heidelberg, 2012, 320–335

[5] Rick, B., and Brian, K. Junkyard jumbotron. http://jumbotron.media.mit.edu/, June 2011

[6] Stelmaszewska, H., Fields, B., and Blandford, A. The roles of time, place, value and relationships in collocated photo sharing with camera phones. In *Proceedings of the 22nd British HCI Group Annual Conference on People and Computers: Culture, Creativity, Interaction - Volume 1*, BCS-HCI '08, British Computer Society (Swinton, UK, UK, 2008), 141–150.

[7] Van House, N. A. Collocated photo sharing, story-telling, and the performance of self. *International Journal of Human-Computer Studies, 67*, 12 (Dec. 2009), 1073–1086

The Realization of New Virtual Forest Experience Environment through PDA

Kana Muramatsu
Graduate School of Frontier Sciences
The University of Tokyo
5-1-5 Kashiwanoha, Kashiwa,
Chiba 277-8563, Japan
muramatsu@nenv.k.u-tokyo.ac.jp

Akio Fujiwara
Graduate School of Agricultural and Life Sciences,
The University of Tokyo
1-1-1 Yayoi, Bunkyo-ku, Tokyo
113-8657, Japan
akio@uf.a.u-tokyo.ac.jp

Hiroki Kobayashi
Center for Spatial Information Science
The University of Tokyo
5-1-5 Kashiwanoha, Kashiwa,
Chiba 277-8563, Japan
kobayashi@csis.u-tokyo.ac.jp

Kazuhiko Nakamura
Center for Spatial Information Science
The University of Tokyo
5-1-5 Kashiwanoha, Kashiwa,
Chiba 277-8563, Japan
k_nakamura@csis.u-tokyo.ac.jp

Junya Okuno
Center for Spatial Information Science,
The University of Tokyo
5-1-5 Kashiwanoha, Kashiwa,
Chiba 277-8563, Japan
okuno@csis.u-tokyo.ac.jp

Kaoru Saito
Graduate School of Frontier Sciences
The University of Tokyo
5-1-5 Kashiwanoha, Kashiwa,
Chiba 277-8563, Japan
kaoru@nenv.k.u-tokyo.ac.jp

MobileHCI 2014, September 23-26, 2014, Toronto, ON, Canada.
ACM 978-1-4503-3004-6/14/09.
doi>10.1145/2628363.2633570

Abstract
Currently, human-computer interaction (HCI) is primarily focused on human-centric interactions; however, people experience many nonhuman-centric interactions during the course of a day. Interactions with nature, such as the experience of walking through a forest or unexpected encounter with wildlife, can imprint the beauty of nature in our memories. In this context, the present paper considers an experimental interface of such nonhuman interface for various PDA application designs through an imaginable interaction with nature. A virtual forest experience environment on PDA is made more realistic through two subsystems: "Panorama-viewer of forest" and "Remote animal sensing". The former is an application by which users can look out over the forest landscape in all directions with gyro-sensor inside PDA. The latter is a virtual system allowing users living in remote urban areas to experience interaction with wild deer in a forest virtually in real time. This novel design means that users can realize a forest experience through the PDA in their hands.

Author Keywords
Forest experience; Virtual experience; Interaction system; Remote location; HCI; PDA.

ACM Classification Keywords
H.5.2. Evaluation/methodology; Interaction styles; I.3.6. Interaction techniques

Figure 1. "Cyberforest project" monitoring the forest (natural beech forest in The University of Tokyo Chichibu Forest) every day using robot cameras [3].

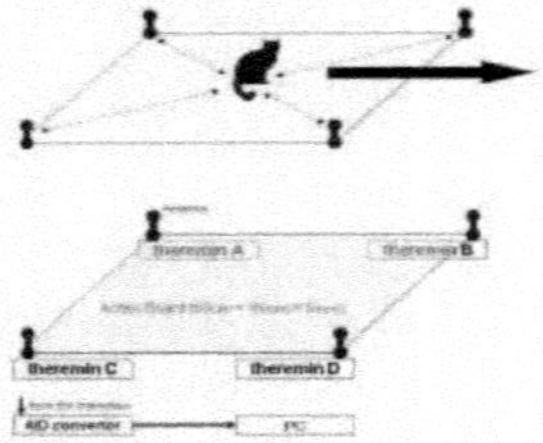

Figure 2. Diagram of Small-Scale Prototype of sensing system.@2010 H.Kobayashi[5]

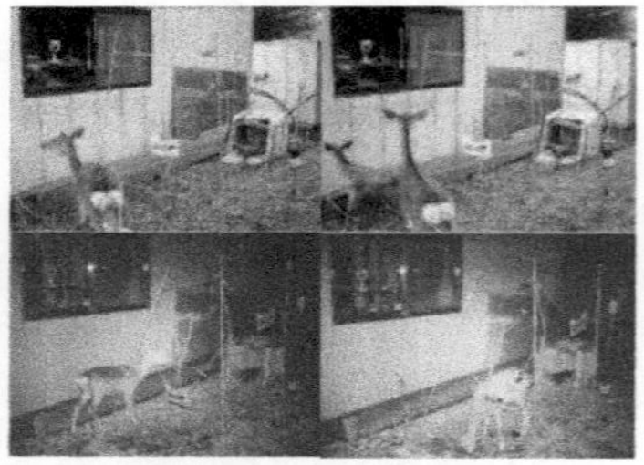

Figure 3. A result of the prototype evaluation of sensing system. Above image is of wild deer approaching the electrostatic capacitance sensor system.

Introduction and Background

Birdsong, buzzing insects, gently swaying leaves, and the trickling of water in a forest can imprint the beauty of nature in our memories (Figure 1). During significant life events, by distancing ourselves from the technologies of modern life, recalling the beauty of nature can help us slow down the pace of daily life. A reverent attitude towards nature can provide a starting point for finding a way to mental and physical well-being. Therefore, it is necessary to establish both a method and an interface by which we can achieve a feeling of belonging to nature even in the midst of city living.

In our daily lives, we unconsciously exchange and share a great deal of implicit cue information and non-verbal expression, such as the presence and mood of others, to maintain social relationships. That is, cue information helps us grasp the appropriate context during the verbalization process so that the encoded message is easily received and understood by the listener. The advent of implicit information communication opens up a new field of interaction in non-linguistic and non-verbal expression among different species, regardless of physical distance.

For instance, Lee presented a novel type of physical interaction and symbiosis between humans and pets using a wearable computer and the Internet as a new form of media [1]. Botanicalls, [2], was developed to provide a new way for plants and people to interact, in order to develop better and long-lasting relationships, regardless of the physical or genetical distance. It utilizes HCI to inform humans about the needs of the plants. Thus, HCI systems have become an inter-medium to express the telepresence of various Species in the biosphere in such a way that their non-linguistic expression is perceived and understood by each participant, which violates all the rules of linguistic science.

In previous studies on Human Computer Interaction targeting elements of nature, such as forest, it has been suggested a sensing system of small terrestrial mammals for HCI applications as Figure 2 shows (Kobayashi, 2010). This system informs urban users of the presence of approaching wildlife based on the principle of musical instrument of the theremin system (electrostatic capacitance sensor). By utilizing such a system, the information, such as presence of wildlife, can be detected and transferred to remote areas in real time. However, this system only succeeded in one-way communication (Figure 3) and, therefore, the interactive environment has not been established. For example, the users cannot interact with the wildlife. To provide a more realistic forest virtual experience environment using PDAs, this study adopted the following system.

SYSTEM DESCRIPTION

This system consists of remote, local ("Panorama-viewer of forest"), and interaction ("Remote animal sensing") systems. The remote and local systems perform a remote interaction with a wild deer in the forest to create a forest experience, a live interaction via the satellite-networked Internet.

Remote System

The environmental sound and video in the mountain forest have been recorded by a landscape monitoring system since 1995. In addition, the real-time sound and video archives have been broadcast through the University of Tokyo's Cyber Forest website ("Cyber Forest Project,") [3] every day since 2009. The real-time streaming system has been improved several times to achieve long-period stability under unmanned operating conditions. The remote system, shown on the left in Figure 1, is in an uninhabited mountain forest at

Figure 4. Gigapan EPIC pro © 2013 GigaPan System.

Figure 5. "Panorama-viewer of Forest". When the user moves the PDA, the screen image is also changed in conjunction.

Figure 6. "Galileo 30-pin" © 2013 Motrr, LLC [10].

the Cyber Forest Project site in The University of Tokyo Forests, Japan (35°56'17.28"N, 138°48'11.04"E). Networked robot camera and sensing system of small terrestrial mammals were placed to create a one way forest experience for 24 hours over 365 days. The networked robot camera consists of a weather resistant camera (Figure 1) for live streaming and GigaPan EPIC pro [6] (Figure 4) for data archiving purpose. The sensing system consists of electrostatic capacitance sensors, evenly distributed on a planar surface as shown in Figures 2 and 3. An electrostatic capacitance is an electronic musical instrument invented by Professor Lev Sergeyevich in 1919. The instrument is unique in that an electrostatic capacitance player, "living organisms" position. As regards detecting wild animals outdoors, performance conditions, or in this case conditions related to weather, vegetation, insolation, and terrain vary significantly. In situations where multiple units (Figure 3) are deployed throughout a remote area and operated for extended periods, power expenditures must be carefully controlled.

Local System "Panorama-viewer of forest"

The local system, "Panorama-viewer of forest", consists of a PDA (iPad) with built in acceleration sensor and gyro sensor. The local system receives the data from the remote system for the virtual experience forest environment as follows:

I. All direction pictures of the sample area – The university of Tokyo Chichibu Forest – were taken seamlessly using the robot camera in the remote system (Figure 5).
II. The pictures were authored using panoramic stitching software "PTGui pro [7]" and converted to equirectangular using GNU Image Manipulation Program "Gimp [8]". Then, they were uploaded to IOS application "Sphere 360 º Photography [9]". This is associated with a gyro sensor of the PDA and the omnidirectional image of the forest.
III. The unexpected arrival (encounter) of wildlife (wild deer) is detected by the sensing system of small terrestrial mammals and the user notified by slightly vibrating the interface.

Interaction System "Remote animal sensing"

To interact with "wild deer," users can move "a piece of deer-cracker (made of rock salt)" on a remotely controllable rotator in Figure 6. The system diagram image is described in Figure 7.

I. The response from the deer at the remote system occurs because its movement is captured continuously through the robot camera and sensing system in conjunction with the movement transferred to the user by the remote host with the piece of deer-cracker.
II. When the users see and confirm the movement of the wild deer, "interaction with wildlife by remote animal sensing" with slight vibration from their hands through the interface (Figure 5), they recognize that the initial input using the PDA did actually travel through the mountain forest environment. This human-computer biosphere interaction with wild deer from remote and local sites creates a forest experience remotely.

More detailed operation procedure is shown at the bottom of Figure 7.

Conclusion

The remote and local systems enable users to experience human-animal interaction. These interactions with nature, such as experiencing walking through a forest or unexpected encounter with

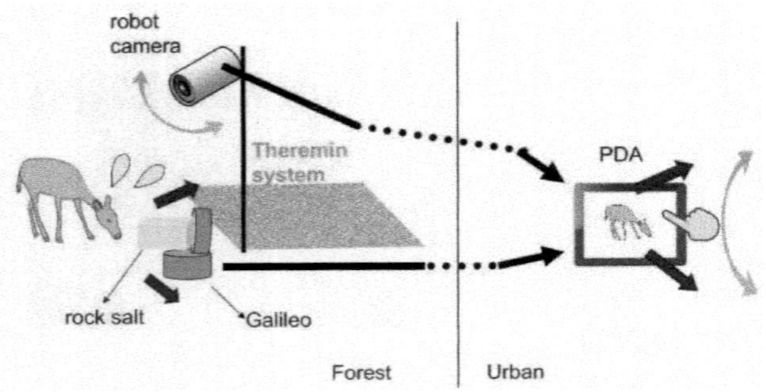

Figure 7. "Remote animal sensing". An image of the remote animal sensing system. The combination of "Galileo 30-pin[10]" (Figure 6) and the wild electrostatic capacitance sensor system(Theremin system) realized a virtual environment where users in urban areas and wild deer in the forest can communicate virtually through a PDA. (1) Galileo with a piece of deer-cracker (fixed rock salt), a favorite food of deer, was placed in the vicinity of the electrostatic capacitance sensor system. (2) Galileo moves in response to the user's action which a PDA senses. Then, deer are lured to the rock salt. By watching a picture of the deer from a surveillance camera installed in the electrostatic capacitance sensor system, which also moves in response to the movement of Galileo, users can gain a virtual experience communicating with wild deer in real time.

wildlife, can imprint the beauty of nature in our memories.

Discussion

A PDA, such as Smartphones and tablets, whose use has become widespread in recent years, is easy to carry compared with personal computers. There are, it can be seen, applications only for PDA using about 10 kinds of sensors that measure a physical quantity and touch operations. With a desktop PC, we can see visual information of remote location only passively. However, using PDA, the visual information can be changed in response to the movement of users. Thus, PDAs can make a passive media environment more active. This will greatly contribute to build an environment in which each user can experience virtual remote locations easily.

As information technology is developed, the opportunity to experience forest landscape directly is becoming rare. For this reason, some research projects have tried to show a forest landscape to distant people through the Internet (Figure 1) [3][4]. However, their video and audio data of forests on the Internet are based on the assumption that people use fixed devices like a desktop PC. Thus, the system to take advantage of PDAs has not yet been established. By utilizing PDAs' sensors to measure a physical quantity and touch operation, it is possible to link the device and users' behavior. In addition, it is evident from previous study of human-computer interaction, information is received through their movement, and they can recognize objects more intuitively. It can be considered that the use of a PDA provides urban users with the virtual experiential forest environment. Therefore, this study developed two systems for providing a virtual experience of a forest to people living in distant urban areas.

Acknowledgements

I would like to thank Ms.Shinpo and Ms.Nagahama for their support in preparing this research.

This work was supported by JSPS KAKENHI Grant Number 26700015.

References

[1]P. Lee, Cheok, et al. (2006). A mobile pet wearable computer and mixed reality system for human poultry interaction through the Internet. Pers Ubiquit Comput. 10, 5, 301-317.

[2]K. Hartman, et al., Botanicalls: The Plants Have Your Number: http://www.botanicalls.com

[3]K.Saito, et al.(2006). Design study of forest environment multimedia contents for environmental education with video data at the Tokyo university forests in Chichibu. The Bulletin of the Tokyo University Forests 116, 267-281.

[4]Cyberforest research project. http://landscape.nenv.k.u-tokyo.ac.jp/cyberforest/Welcome.html(2014.4.24)

[5]H. Kobayashi (2010). Basic Research in Human-Computer-Biosphere Interaction, a doctoral thesis, The university of Tokyo.

[6]Gigapan EPIC pro © 2013 GigaPan Systems http://gigapan.com/cms/shop/epic(2014.4.28)

[7]PTGui pro © 2000-2014 New House Internet Services B.V. http://www.ptgui.com/(2014.4.28)

[8]Gimp © 2001-2013 The GIMP Team http://www.gimp.org/(2014.4.28)

[9]Sphere - 360º Photography © 2014 Spherical, Inc. https://www.thesphere.com/(2014.4.28)

[10]Motrr Galileo 30-pin © 2013 Motrr, LLC. http://motrr.com/ (2014.5.15)

Back-of-Device Authentication with BoD Taps and BoD Shapes

Alejandro Catalá
ISSI-DSIC
Universitat Politècnica de València
acatala@dsic.upv.es

Luis A. Leiva
PRHLT Research Center
Universitat Politècnica de València
luileito@prhlt.upv.es

Work partially supported by EU FP7 program (grant 600707), GVA VALi+d program (grant APOSTD/2013/013), and MINECO (grant TIN2010-20488).

MobileHCI'14, Sep 23–26 2014, Toronto, ON, Canada
ACM 978-1-4503-3004-6/14/09.
http://dx.doi.org/10.1145/2628363.2633571

Abstract
This demonstration accompanies a paper accepted at MobileHCI'14 [1]. Back-of-device (BoD) authentication has shown to be significantly more secure than standard front-facing approaches, being *BoD Shapes* the most representative method found in the literature. With the aim of getting a better understanding and improving its usage, we developed *BoD Taps* as a novel alternative. Our experiments revealed that *BoD Taps* and *BoD Shapes* perform equally good at unlocking the device, but *BoD Taps* allows users to enter passwords about twice faster. Moreover, *BoD Taps* was perceived as being more usable and less frustrating than *BoD Shapes*. This demonstration showcases both authentication methods in action, aimed at comparing and discussing their features and potential improvements.

Author Keywords
Back of device interaction; Unlocking; Passwords

ACM Classification Keywords
H.5.2 [User Interfaces]: Input devices and strategies; K.6.5 [Security and Protection]: Authentication

References
[1] Leiva, L. A., and Catala, A. BoD Taps: An improved back-of-device authentication technique on smartphones. In *Proc. MobileHCI* (2014).

SqueezeDiary: Using Squeeze Gesture as Triggers of Diary Events

Ming Ki Chong
School of Computing & Communications
Lancaster University
Lancaster, UK
mingki@acm.org

Jon Whittle
School of Computing & Communications
Lancaster University
Lancaster, UK
j.n.whittle@lancaster.ac.uk

Umar Rashid
School of Engineering and Digital Arts
University of Kent
Canterbury, UK
U.R.Mir@kent.ac.uk

Chee Siang Ang
School of Engineering and Digital Arts
University of Kent
Canterbury, UK
C.S.Ang@kent.ac.uk

MobileHCI '14, Sep 23–26 2014, Toronto, Canada.
ACM 978-1-4503-3004-6/14/09.
http://dx.doi.org/10.1145/2628363.2633572

Abstract
The diary method has been adopted for recording participants' behaviours. However, recording diary entries can be difficult or deemed inappropriate in certain situations, like in a social group or in a meeting. In this demo we present *SqueezeDiary*, a tool that adopts squeeze gestures for users to denote triggers of diary events, and the users reflect on the triggers later when they are not busy (e.g. during lunch). Our application enables delayed reflection, where users can reflect on their recorded event instances retrospectively during their downtime.

Author Keywords
Squeeze; Temporal, Geolocation and Pressure Cues; Digital Diary

ACM Classification Keywords
H.5.m [Information interfaces and presentation (e.g., HCI)]: Miscellaneous.

Introduction
Researchers have adopted the diary method for recording participants' everyday behaviours. The methods provides the advantage of not requiring the full-time presence of the researchers, and it allows the participants to do the recording themselves, as they live through experiences of interest.

In this demo, we present *SqueezeDiary*, a new form of digital diary on mobile devices. We exploit the concept of delayed entry [3]. Users first capture snippets of information by swiftly squeezing a sensor, and then complete full diary entries at a later time. Figure 1 illustrates our SqueezeDiary demo. As the gesture of squeezing is unobtrusive and discreet, our application is particularly useful for recording diary events when the users are busy (could not provide immediate feedback) or in situations where writing diaries would be deemed socially inappropriate.

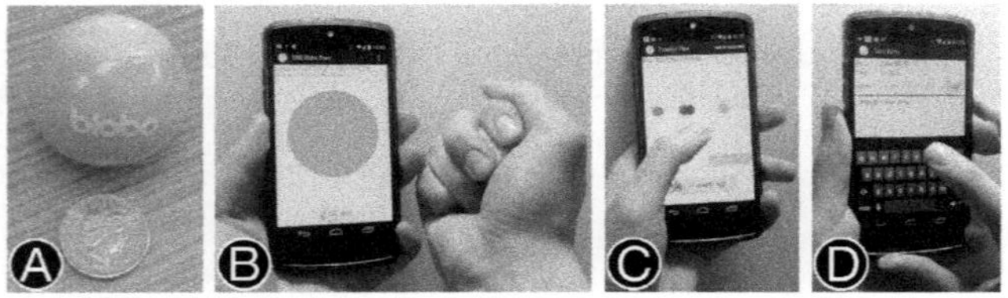

Figure 1: SqueezeDiary: Ⓐ A Blobo squeeze sensor placed next to a British one pound coin. Ⓑ A user squeezes and holds the sensor for a short duration to trigger an event instance. The instance is logged (along with location, temporal and squeeze pressure cues) on a mobile phone. Ⓒ The user reflects on the recorded instance during their downtime, and Ⓓ enters a diary description.

SqueezeDiary

SqueezeDiary is designed for recording life events/experiences that users want to keep a record of, but the feedback entry process is delayed. The users first trigger the system to record an event instance, and later enters a description for the event retrospectively. We also designed SqueezeDiary to use squeeze gestures as a trigger for recording events. We selected a small tactile ball, an off-the-self component called Blobo[1], as a squeezable interface (see Fig. 1). The device can be carried in a pocket, and users can squeeze it easily when needed, without accessing their smartphone.

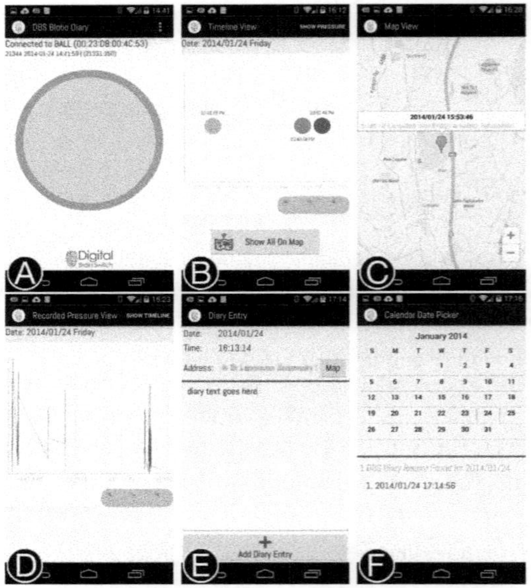

Figure 2: Screenshots of our SqueezeDiary prototype. Ⓐ *Main screen* with a blue circle indicates the Blobo sensor is connected via Bluetooth. Ⓑ *Timeline view* shows recorded events on a timeline. Ⓒ *Map view* with pins showing locations where events were recorded. Ⓓ *Pressure view* shows the intensity of recorded squeeze pressure. Ⓔ *Diary entry* interface allows users to add diary detail information for a specific event. Ⓕ *Calendar view* shows a list of diary entries for a selected day. Refer to our demo video for illustration.

We custom built our diary application on the app developed by Simm et al. [6]. The squeeze sensor interfaces with our application through Bluetooth (see Fig. 2A). A user triggers an event by simply squeezing the

[1] `http://serious-sports.org/content/blobo`

sensor for over two seconds. Upon detecting a trigger, the system records the GPS location, timestamp and the pressure levels of the squeeze event. The application provides visualisations of the recorded events on a timeline view (see Fig. 2B), on a map view (see Fig. 2C), and a graphical visualisation of recorded pressure levels (see Fig. 2D).

During users down time, they can review their recorded events and reflect by entering diary descriptions (see Fig. 2E). Our application also provides a calendar interface for users to select recorded diary entries of a particular day (see Fig. 2F).

The source code of our SqueezeDiary is available online for download as open source[2].

Conclusion and Future Extension

To the best of our knowledge, our demo application is the first to use squeeze gestures as a means for recording diary events. Our SqueezeDiary allows users to 'squeeze the moment' and reflect on it later. We have made our application open source, and we invite any interested researchers to extend or to conduct diary studies with our SqueezeDiary application.

In the future, we intend to extend SqueezeDiary with bespoke devices or alternative sensors (e.g. the Skweezee System [7]) for customising squeeze gestures for annotating different types of entries. For example, a certain type of squeeze gesture for family-related diary events and another gesture for work-related diary entries. As geolocation, temporal and pressure cues may be inadequate for users to reconstruct their memories [5], we also intend to improve memory accuracy with lifelogging technology, such as SenseCam [4], Narrative Clip [2] or Google Glass [1].

[2] `https://github.com/DigitalBrainSwitch/DBS_Blobo`

Acknowledgements

This work is part of the Digital Brain Switch project (`http://digitalbrainswitch.co.uk`) and is funded by the EPSRC (EP/K025201/1).

References

[1] Google glass. https://www.google.com/glass/start/.

[2] Narrative clip. http://getnarrative.com/.

[3] Brandt, J., Weiss, N., and Klemmer, S. R. Txt 4 l8r: Lowering the burden for diary studies under mobile conditions. In *Proc. CHI EA 2007*, ACM Press (2007), 2303–2308.

[4] Hodges, S., Williams, L., Berry, E., Izadi, S., Srinivasan, J., Butler, A., Smyth, G., Kapur, N., and Wood, K. Sensecam: A retrospective memory aid. In *Proc. UbiComp 2006*, Springer-Verlag (2006), 177–193.

[5] Kalnikaite, V., Sellen, A., Whittaker, S., and Kirk, D. Now let me see where i was: Understanding how lifelogs mediate memory. In *Proc. CHI 2010*, ACM Press (2010), 2045–2054.

[6] Simm, W., Ferrario, M. A., Gradinar, A., and Whittle, J. Prototyping 'clasp': Implications for designing digital technology for and with adults with autism. In *Proc. DIS 2014*, ACM Press (2014), 345–354.

[7] Vanderloock, K., Vanden Abeele, V., Suykens, J. A., and Geurts, L. The skweezee system: Enabling the design and the programming of squeeze interactions. In *Proc. UIST 2013*, ACM Press (2013), 521–530.

Off the Couch and out of the Hospital: Mobile Applications for Acceptance and Commitment Therapy

Marjan Verstappen
OCAD University
100 McCaul St.
Toronto
marjan.verstappen@gmail.com

Tim Bettridge
OCAD University
100 McCaul St.
Toronto
timbettridge@gmail.com

Paula Gardner
OCAD University
100 McCaul St.
Toronto
pgardner@faculty.ocadu.ca

Dora Poon
OCAD University
100 McCaul St.
Toronto
dp10jc@student.ocadu.ca

MobileHCI 2014, September 23–26, 2014, Toronto, ON, Canada.
ACM 978-1-4503-3004-6/14/09.
http://dx.doi.org/10.1145/2628363.2633573

Abstract
This paper describes the research and concept development process involved in designing a mobile app for depressed youth learning to practice mindfulness based psychotherapy entitled Acceptance and Commitment Therapy (ACT) program at Trillium Healthcare Centre in Toronto. Our process involved identifying aspects of preexisting mobile applications for mindfulness that may be discouraging for youth with depression and devising strategies to overcome these negative messages within the ACT Application. We propose to present a working prototype of mobile application at the Mobile HCI conference.

Author Keywords
Mobile Applications, User Experience, Mindfulness Therapy

ACM Classification Keywords
Methodologies, Theory and Methods, Natural Language, Prototyping.

Introduction
The ACT app is a mobile application built with participatory design [1] (uniting designers, clinicians and teen clients) to migrate the ACT therapy program

successfully to a mobile app. The app intends to augment the therapy offered in a healthcare setting. It works both as a diagnostician[1], helping users to understand thoughts and feelings, and directs users to appropriate meditation and diffusion strategies. The co-designed app embraces the manners in which these teens choose to use mobile devices, offering specific strategies they wish to access outside of the clinic. The look and feel and navigation of the app aligns with user testing, offering fun, colourful, and creative experience. Rather than tracking progress in standard ways, we provide a visualized creature that relays the user's time spent employing ACT in various areas of their life. We propose a working demonstration of the app for the Mobile HCI conference.

Our partners at Trillium Healthcare Centre, Sheri Turrell and Mary Douglas, facilitate the Acceptance and Commitment Therapy program for teens suffering from severe anxiety and depression [2]. Our research clients are a group of 15 youth who are currently undertaking, or recently graduated from the three- month ACT program at Trillium.

Designing for Mental Wellbeing

Creating the ACT app is challenging because it requires reconsiderations of where and how therapy happens. ACT requires consistent practice, such as meditation, goal settting and revision, and diffusion of unhelpful thoughts in situations where anxiety and depression occur. Success in ACT therapy comes from practice outside of therapy sessions, in contexts where stress and anxiety actually happen, such as school, or disagreements with family. Our team at OCAD University employed critical ethnographic methods [3] to capture everyday use of therapy and media devices, to ensure the app would effectively provide a therapeutic experience that augmented the clinic- experience. Our team of designers and artists developed concepts that communicate with the teen audience.

Employing interaction design methods, we used an interactive consultation process with Clinicians and client stakeholders to ideate the user experience and to sketch a user experience design for our developers and designers.

Finally, we reviewed all available mindfulness apps on the market, seeking to match their affordances and overcome their weaknesses. One competing app, Optimize [4], collects and collates 'hard' data showing how often users meditate and achieve their goals. These apps tend to discourage youth struggling with motivation, or not meeting their expressed goals and expectations. Differently, our ACT app rewards all action on the app, rather than 'success.' Instead of visualizing data 'success' and 'failure' within the app, our ACT app monitors usage and responds by changing the 'creature' on the home screen, that represents user's psychological wellbeing.

[1] Although the application is intended to compliment therapy, rather than replace it.

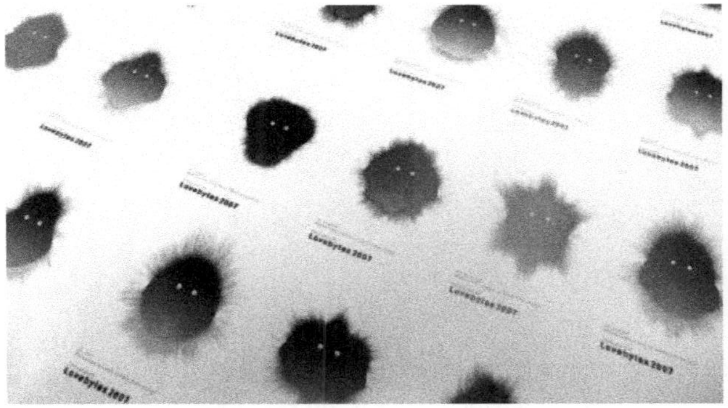

Figure 1 Creatures change shape according to user data.

Unlike many other mindfulness apps, the ACT app is tailored for youth. It is fresh, playful and positive without being patronizing. It also has sensitive diagnostic features that determine which activity within the app is best suited to the user's current mental state through a series of questions, such as,

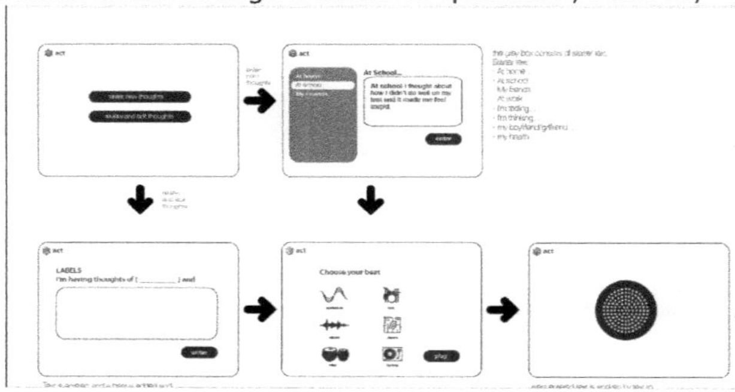

Figure 2 The diagnostic questionnaire identifies user need and directs them towards activities within the application.

"what's getting in your way?" and "are you able to do what matters?"

Through this diagnostic process, users are directed to one of three activities in the app: diffusion, goal setting, or meditation. Diffusion helps users let go of thoughts that are unhelpful ruminations. Using a combination of text-to-speech and autotune software, users can hear these thoughts read back to manners that remove their gravity, which is a diffusion technique. Meditation activities include pre-recorded meditations from the ACT program at Trillium, with options for adding different background noise. Goal setting supports users to set SMART goals and rewards them for taking action towards goals rather than simply asking if the user has achieved the goals. Users have options to receive notifications during times when they most need to work goals. Users are asked to reflect on their goals weekly with the statement "this week I've worked on ….."

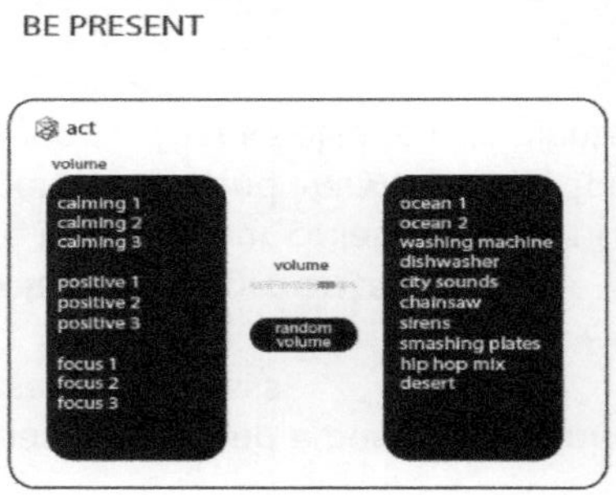

Figure 3 Guided meditations from the ACT program at Trillium with soundscape options.

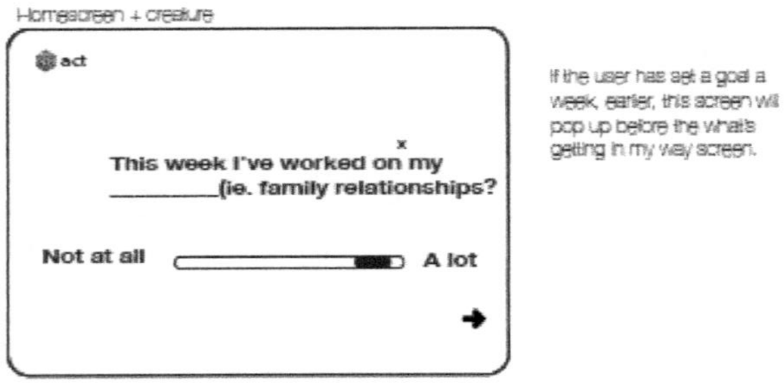

Figure 4 Sliding scale to evaluate goal activity.

Following the mindfulness philosophy of ACT psychotherapy, our ACT App does not punish users for neglecting the app. It encourages use by making interventions for episodes of anxiety and depression that are artful and fun.

For the mobile HCI conference we are proposing a demonstration of a working prototype of the ACT app. This will be presented on several Samsung tablets, and we will also have an animation of the app on an Imac screen and a poster explaining the poster and research process.

Acknowledgments

We thank all our collaborators at Trillium Healthcare; Sheri Turrell and Mary Douglas, for their feedback and support. Thanks also to our clients in the ACT program for their advice.

References

[1] J.L. Powers and J.S. Tiffany Engaging Youth in Participatory Research and Evaluation. *Journal of Public Health Management and Practice* (2006) S79–S87

[2] M.T. Greenberg and A.R. Harris Nurturing Mindfulness in Children and Youth: Current State of Research. *Child Development Perspectives* (2011), 1-6.

[3] D.S Madison *Critical Ethonography; Methods, Ethics and Performance.* Sage Publications (2012), 32.

[4] Optimisim mobile application https://itunes.apple.com/us/app/optimism/id352262677?mt=8

Wearable Haptic Gaming Using Vibrotactile Arrays

Adam Tindale
OCAD University
Toronto, ON M5T 1W1
Canada
atindale@faculty.ocadu.ca

Jessica Peter
OCAD University
Toronto, ON M5T 1W1
Canada
jp11jg@student.ocadu.ca

Michael Cumming
OCAD University
Toronto, ON M5T 1W1
Canada
mcumming@ocadu.ca

Sara Diamond
OCAD University
Toronto, ON M5T 1W1
Canada
sdiamond@ocadu.ca

Hudson Pridham
OCAD University
Toronto, ON M5T 1W1
Canada
hp12pk@student.ocadu.ca

MobileHCI 2014, September 23–26, 2014, Toronto, ON, Canada.
ACM 978-1-4503-3004-6/14/09.

http://dx.doi.org/10.1145/2628363.2633574

Abstract
In this paper we explore the design, layout and configuration of wrist-wearable, haptic gaming interfaces, which involve visual and vibrotactile spatial and temporal patterns. Our goal is to determine overall layouts and spatial and temporal resolutions on the wrist suitable for interactive tactile stimuli. Our approach is to first explore the simplest of configurative patterns that are intended to encircle the wrist, and then study their affordances. We describe various informal user studies we have employed to explore and test issues that arose.

Author Keywords
haptic gaming, vibrotactile arrays, wearable devices, multi-sensory

ACM Classification Keywords
H.5.2 [Information interfaces and presentation (e.g., HCI)]: User Interfaces.

Introduction
Tactile feedback is often used in gaming to enhance immersion. Vibrotactile arrays on wearable devices can enable a variety of information communication scenarios, the most compelling of which is when they enable users to receive information without having to look at a signifying device [9, 7]. There are many examples of projects in

Figure 1: A user playing the vibrotactile Simon Says game.

which haptic feedback is tethered to devices with screens. This project uses a wearable device that is able to offer self-sufficient gaming experiences that need not be tethered to other devices. Patterns presented to the user using these wearable devices involve both visual and tactile stimului.

We focus on simple wrist-encircling devices. We chose this type of device because of their potential for simplicity of design and manufacture, their radial symmetry and modularity, their possible suitability for wrists of various sizes and their potential as wearable devices possessing some aesthetic appeal beyond their core functionality as game interfaces.

Our demo experiences focus on an attempt to make the interactions very simple, such that they convey information in a way that presents few cognitive demands and which the user would tend to find enjoyable and engaging, even if they were not participating in a mobile game.

Related Work

Wrist-worn tactors serve many functions including: assessment of cognitive performance in the elderly [5], notification during gaming [8], discrete patterns for alerts for on-the-go users [6, 1]. A wrist-worn haptic device for swimmers is described in [4] and as assistive technology for wayfinding [2].

HandJive is a handheld device used for communication and play between people [3]. Researchers found that participants were able to successfully replicate purely haptic patterns at increasing levels of difficulty in a gameplay situation, and enjoyed improvising their own patterns. These findings suggest that haptic feedback can be incorporated as an enjoyable and meaningful way of conveying game information.

Wrist wearables must fit on wrists and must not have excessive tactor density. Matscheko notes that physiognomic studies indicate that average U.S. wrist circumferences are 18.38cm for men and 14.8cm for women. A minimum threshold distance, the minimum distance on the wrist or forearm between which people are able to discriminate tactors is 38mm [9]. This provides a limited amount of wrist 'real estate,' if the purpose is to transmit discrete symbolic messages using tactors. However, it is not clear that tactors on the wrist are suitable for transmitting discrete symbolic messages.

Various types of tactor wrist arrays can be found in the literature: a 3x3 array [1], a 3 tactor circular array [6] and a 4x1 wrist-encircling array [9].

Lee and Starner describe patterning for wrist-worn tactile displays [6]. They note that for these patterns, intensity is the most difficult parameter to distinguish and that the temporal parameter is the easiest.

Bronner notes that a sense of touch is basic to human processes of testing, expressing reality and meaning bronner1982haptic.

Chen at al. examine tactor placement on the wrist. They reason that if a mobile device is to be worn like a watch, then factors can be placed on both sides of the wrist (that is, both the dorsal and volar sides) [1].

In our research we have built prototypes that build on previous research to explore the ways that very simple tactile and visual signals can provoke rich play. Our prototypes explore the use of the whole wrist, including

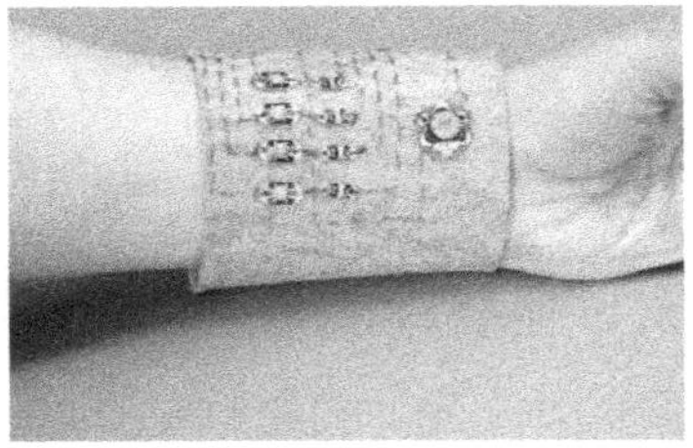

Figure 2: A wearable version of the *Simon Says* game. The wearer repeats visual patterns by pressing buttons adjacent to each LED.

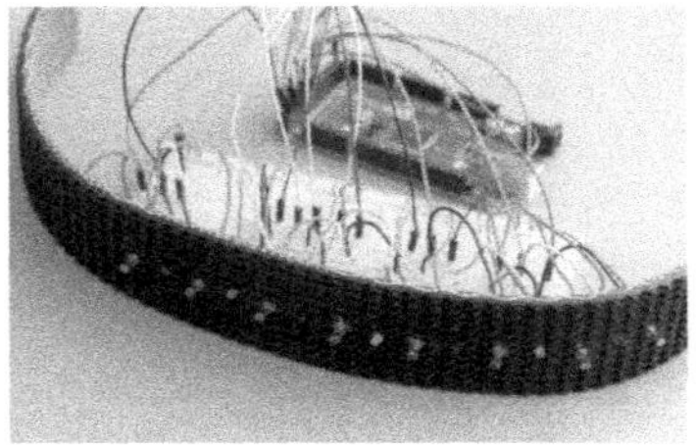

Figure 3: A prototype for a wearable that has a simple array of LEDs and vibrating motors.

Figure 4: A prototype for a wearable that has an array of buttons, LEDs and vibrating motors.

the sides, as a site of vibrotactile stimulus and information display.

Prototypes

Initial Wearable Prototype

This is a wearable version of the traditional *Simon Says* game mounted onto a flexible velcro and felt wristband (see Figure 2). The game is controlled by four push buttons each with a corresponding LED light. *Simon Says* is a memory game in which wearers repeat patterns of growing length until the player is unable to recall the whole sequence. We found that gamers bored quickly from such a game, yet we discovered that vibrotactile patterns did inspire interest, which we explored in subsequent prototypes.

Rubber vibration band version 1

This wrist band with a thick rubber band has eight vibrating motors and eight LED lights (see Figure 3). Vibrating motors and lights are arranged linearly and controlled by an Arduino Mega micro-controller board. Users were stimulated by the multiple tactors and spent time imagining other possible vibration patterns. The idea that wrist-encircling vibrotactile simulation and encoding is attractive to some users was confirmed, despite the crude prototypical nature of the device. Users also noted that they wanted an interaction channel, not afforded by a simple output-only device.

Rubber vibration band version 2

This band is similar to the first band but instead of a linear pattern, there is an array of eight buttons, eight lights, and eight vibrating motors (see Figure 4). Each row of this array has one button, one light and one vibrator that are all independent, allowing for the creation of interactive buttons games like *Simon Says*. This configuration starts to afford more possibilities for user interaction. Modal play becomes possible since many types of user notifications are possible with such an array.

Final prototype

The final interface (see Figure 5) utilizes lessons learned from the rubber band prototypes, combining visual and tactile feedback with a form factor that is able to be comfortably worn. Buttons are soft buttons activated by pressing on tactors. The final prototype lead to user sessions that increased in length. We found that users could successfully play the Simon Says game using only the vibrotactile channel.

Wearable Vibrotactile Game Interfaces

Users studies suggested that for conveyance of symbolic information wrist-encircling haptic devices have their challenges. As purely simulation that are attractive to users. They are attractive to users for pure sensory stimulation not content. *Simons Says* games can be played using tactile, in addition to visual cueing, yet this type of game quickly becomes boring for users.

Future Work

Wrist-encircling devices that employ modularity of construction, user interactivity and vibrotactile patterning appear promising areas for future exploration. We are currently developing a method of authoring the vibration sequences so that they may be more effectively created, stored, processed and shared.

One approach that does seem promising is the use of wrist devices for decorative and aesthetic purposes, as expressive devices for customized visual and vibrotactile authoring and for deployment of various signals, which are easy to distinguish between each other but which may lack

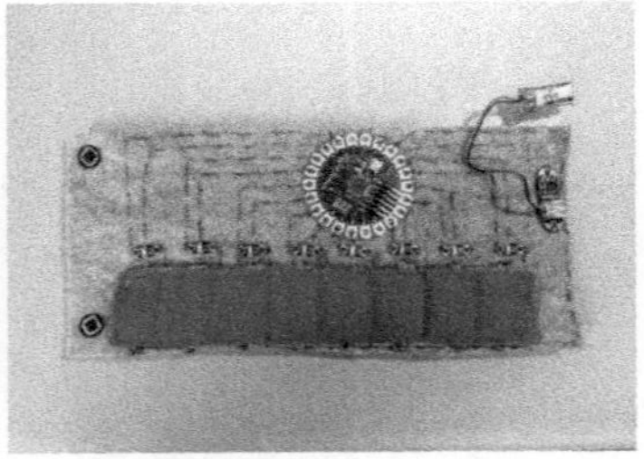

Figure 5: Final wearable prototype with 8 tactors with soft buttons and 8 LEDs.

clear self-explanatory symbolic content such as afforded, for example, by small high resolution OLED screens.

Conclusion
Vibrotactile arrays present new possibilities for information display to users through their body. We have demonstrated the use of a wearable multichannel vibrotactile and simple visual display intended for gaming in order to explore the uses and affordances in scenarios involving non-critical attention and use cases.

Acknowledgements
We would like to thank Ryan Maksymic, Boris Kourtoukov, and Steve Szigeti for their help in the development of this project. This work is generously supported by grants from the Natural Sciences and Engineering Research Council of Canada (NSERC), International Science and Technology Partnerships Canada, and OCAD University.

References
[1] Chen, H.-Y., Santos, J., Graves, M., Kim, K., and Tan, H. Z. Tactor localization at the wrist. In *Haptics: Perception, Devices and Scenarios*. Springer, 2008, 209–218.

[2] de Jesus Oliveira, V. A., and Maciel, A. Using vibrotactile communication to assist in orientation and locomotion. Tech. rep., Instituto de Informatica (INF) Universidade Federal do Rio Grande do Sul (UFRGS) Porto Alegre, Brasil, 2013.

[3] Fogg, B., Cutler, L. D., Arnold, P., and Eisbach, C. Handjive: a device for interpersonal haptic entertainment. In *Proceedings of the SIGCHI conference on Human factors in computing systems*, ACM Press/Addison–Wesley Publishing Co. (1998), 57—64.

[4] Förster, K., Bächlin, M., and Tröster, G. Non-interrupting user interfaces for electronic body-worn swim devices. In *Proceedings of the 2nd International Conference on PErvasive Technologies Related to Assistive Environments*, ACM (2009), 38.

[5] Ivorra, A., Daniels, C., and Rubinsky, B. Minimally obtrusive wearable device for continuous interactive cognitive and neurological assessment. *Physiological measurement 29*, 5 (2008), 543.

[6] Lee, S. C., and Starner, T. Buzzwear: alert perception in wearable tactile displays on the wrist. In *Proceedings of the SIGCHI conference on Human factors in computing systems*, ACM (2010), 433–442.

[7] MacLean, K. E. Putting haptics into the ambience. *Haptics, IEEE Transactions on 2*, 3 (2009), 123–135.

[8] Martins, T., Sommerer, C., Mignonneau, L., and Correia, N. Gauntlet: a wearable interface for ubiquitous gaming. In *Proceedings of the 10th international conference on Human computer interaction with mobile devices and services*, ACM (2008), 367–370.

[9] Matscheko, M., Ferscha, A., Riener, A., and Lehner, M. Tactor placement in wrist worn wearables. In *Wearable Computers (ISWC), 2010 International Symposium on*, IEEE (2010), 1–8.

MobileHCI 2014 Extended Abstracts Mobile Experience Lab: Body Editing

Stephen Surlin
Mobile Experience Lab,
OCAD University
Toronto, ON, Canada
s.m.surlin@gmail.com

Paula Gardner
Mobile Experience Lab,
OCAD University
Toronto, ON, Canada
pgardner@faculty.ocadu.ca

MobileHCI 2014, September 23-26, 2014, Toronto, ON, Canada.
ACM 978-1-4503-3004-6/14/09.

http://dx.doi.org/10.1145/2628363.2633574

Abstract
Body Editing is an interactive installation that combines depth sensing (Kinect 3D camera), biometric sensors, musical performance and abstract drawing software to create a mobile wireless interface that sonically and graphically represents the user's motion in space. The wireless nature of this gesture-controlled interface is an explicit attempt to create embodied experiences that encourages users to be more aware of their body through movement and audio/visual feedback and less focused on technological augmentation.

Author Keywords
Data Sonification; Embodiment; Movement; Gesture; Wireless; Musical; Interface;

ACM Classification Keywords
B.4.1 [Data Communications Devices]: B.4.2 [Input/Output Devices; C.5.3 Microcomputers]: D.2.2 [Design Tools and Techniques]:

Introduction
Body Editing is an interface that enables a user to make music and abstract graphical images through movement. The interface uses the Kinect 3D camera, which tracks a user's position in space to send movement data to a computer that runs both the audio and drawing software. The wireless nature of this platform makes it a very accessible interface that doesn't require the use of traditional musical MIDI interfaces (i.e. music controller keyboards), game type controllers or mouse/pointer

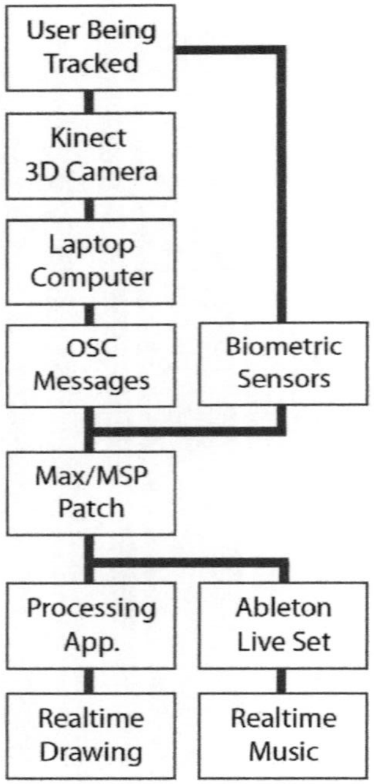

Figure 2. Body Editing process.

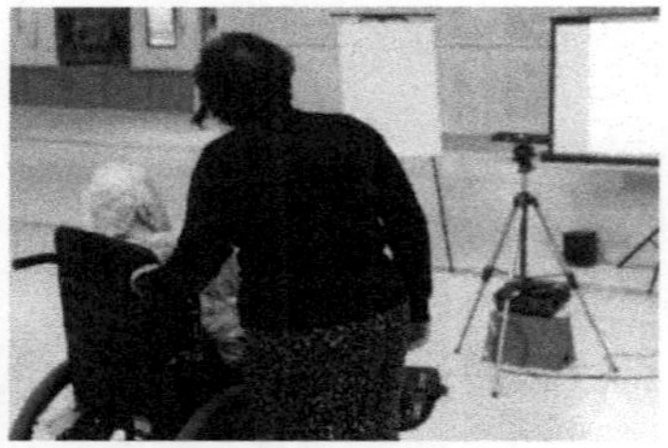

Figure 3. Baycrest demo setup, with the Kinect camera and projector visible to the right. An LED screen would save on space.

interfaces. The lack of tethering to tangible interfaces allows the user to become more embodied in their interaction with the music making and drawing software. The wireless biometric sensors, include a simple to use pulse (heart rate) sensor and an accelerometer that can track finer movements of the user.

Previous Installations of Body Editing

Body editing has been installed in various locations and institutions during recent years, including OCAD University, York University, Baycrest Elderly Care Research Centre, Hospital and Residence, and most recently, the GRAND Conference 2014 conference where Body Editing was accepted as a GRAND Experience. The proposed Body Editing experience at MobileHCI will offer the platform as an experience that provides audio visual art experience in response to both the user in the performance space and the crowd surrounding or approaching the performance space

The next sections describe the technical processes of the installation and then explain my technical requirements to create an experience at MobileHCI.

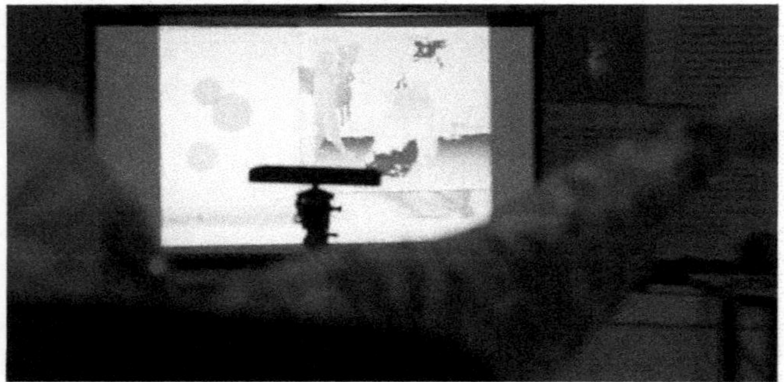

Figure 1. Example of user in wheelchair at Baycrest using Body Editing interface. Max/MSP tracking points (left of screen), Kinect 3D image (on right of screen).

Kinect Data

The Microsoft Kinect 3D camera is a depth camera that can detect a user's skeleton (a set of 16 points found around a person's body, i.e. right hand, left elbow, head, right knee, etc.). It tracks a single user at a time and uses the hand and head data to send OSC (Open Sound Control) data, in the form of spatial coordinates relative to the camera (X, Y, and Z axis) to Max/MSP (a visual coding environment). Within Max/MSP, the OSC data is translated into musical note data that is used to compose music in Ableton Live (music production software) and coordinates to create abstract line and colour drawings in a Processing application as "feedback" to the user.

Data Sonification

The X, Y and Z-axis received from the Kinect data is translated using three main criteria. The X-axis (left to right hand motion of the user) controls the note to be played, similar to the playing of a traditional piano's keyboard, where left is low notes and right is high. The Y-axis adjusts the rhythm of the note to be played; a raised hand may play a quick 16th or 32nd note, while a low hand, or one on the floor may produce a slow whole or half note. The Z-axis controls the volume or velocity of the note; when the user is near the the camera, the volume is louder and when farther away, the volume is lower. During recent demonstrations, only the left hand, right hand and head of the user is being tracked. Each of these points send the X, Y and Z coordinates to Max/MSP.

The minimum and maximum value of each parameter (effecting the sensitivity of a users movements) can be set manually, preferable for a user who has a large amount of mobility within the space visible to the Kinect camera. The min./max. values can be set automatically by detecting the users range of movement; for example, a user in a wheelchair that has limited reach from a solitary position, the min./max. values will be set so that this space can represent the entire range of notes available. This user-generated bounds system was an important feature during the Baycrest demonstration, where many of the elderly participants had very limited movement capabilities. The manually adjustable bounds and automatic user generated bounds system will be available during the MobileHCI experience.

Data Visualization

The visualization component of the Body Editing interface is created using Processing, an open-source coding environment that allows for quick and creative coding of interactive applications.

The OSC data received from Max/MSP is translated into X and Y-axis coordinates that are used to control a marker on a 2D plane. This marker (which can be made visible or invisible) acts as a magnet to several nodes that are also present on the screen. The marker represents a user's hand position, as if the participant was using their hand like a mouse on the surface of the image. As the user moves their hand in space, the nodes will move towards this point on the screen. Each of the nodes creates lines as they move. Eventually these lines build up to create a visual composition. This graphical rendering can easily be saved and printed, allowing the user to have a take away from the experience.

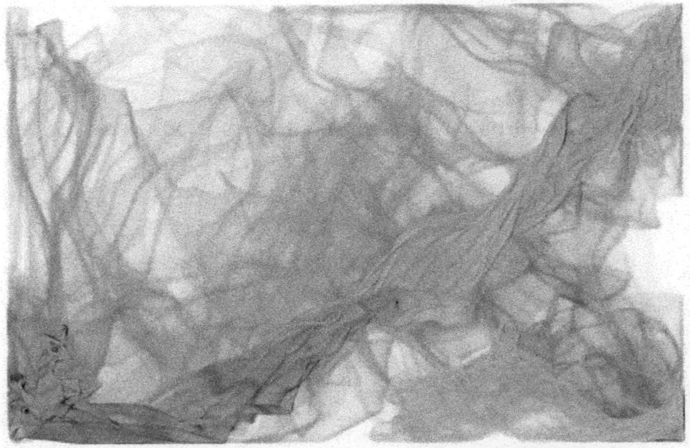

Figure 5. Example of imagery created by Body Editing interface and the Processing application.

Biometric Sensors

The pulse sensor uses a light sensor that is light pressed with the tip of the user's finger to get their pulse or heart BPM (Beats Per Minute). The BPM of the user's heart is used to set the BPM of the music. This becomes the relative measure of note lengths i.e. 8th note, 16th note, etc, making the users body more present in the interaction. The accelerometer (a sensor that detects motion) provides another way to interact with the music. This sensor can be held near the chest, in order to detect the motion of breathing – the rising and lowering of the chest. These sensors send their data to Max/MSP which is translated into MIDI (Musical Instrument Digital Interface) data to control Ableton. This data controls the BPM of the music and parameters like reverb, echo and delay of the music generated by the user's movements.

Figure 8. The accelerometer unit is displayed here. Held comfortably or placed in the pocket, fine motion can be sensed with this unit.

Figure 9. A user creating music using the Body Editing interface at the GRAND 2014 conference.

Figure 10. The user pictured in figure 9 is shown here using the pulse sensor with their thumb rather than index finger, like figure 7.

Figure 6. The wireless biometric sensors demoed at the GRAND 2014 Conference.

Figure 7. The wireless pulse sensor is shown here. The index finger is used to sense the heart's BPM (Beats Per Minute), which controls the tempo (BPM) of the music.

Results of Demonstrations

The demonstrations of Body Editing interface at OCAD U, Baycrest and the GRAND Conference 2014 revealed several trends in user response.

The ability for the interface to adapt to the users range of motion seems to be an important way to get the user engaged quickly. Since the interface will be responsive immediately, it ensures the user that it is functioning and detecting their motions.

The abstract renderings generated with the Processing application seems to distract the viewer form considering the technology and mechanics of the interface and encourages them to focus more on the effects of their body motion and their potential movement in space. These qualities may lead the user to have a more embodied experience.

Technical Needs and Specifications

Body Editing has many of the needed components already. This includes: Kinect camera, computer, sensors and etc.

For the MobileHCI experience, Body Editing will require only a television of approximately 32" LCD Screen or larger and a PA system to produce high quality stereo sound in the venue. If MobileHCI has the resources to provide a human scale rear projection setup this would be preferable. If a colour printer system was available, the user drawings could be printed out for people to take away from the experience. The experience generally requires a 10' by 10' area to allow the user to move freely within the space unobstructed.

Non-Verbal Communications in Mobile Text Chat – Emotion-Enhanced Mobile Chat

Jackson Feijó Filho
Nokia Technology Institute
Av. Torquato Tapajós, 7200 -
Col. Terra Nova. Manaus-AM
Brasil. 69093-415
jackson.feijo@indt.org.br

Thiago Valle
Nokia Technology Institute
Av. Torquato Tapajós, 7200 -
Col. Terra Nova. Manaus-AM
Brasil. 69093-415
thiago.valle@indt.org.br

Wilson Prata
PUC-Rio
Av. Torquato Tapajós, 7200 -
Col. Terra Nova. Manaus-AM
Brasil. 69093-415
Wilson.prata@indt.org.br

MobileHCI '14, Sep 23-26 2014, Toronto, ON, Canada
ACM 978-1-4503-3004-6/14/09.
http://dx.doi.org/10.1145/2628363.2633576

Abstract
Great part of human communication is carried out nonverbally. All this information is lost in mobile text messaging. This work describes an attempt to augment text chatting in mobile phones by adding automatically detected facial expression reactions, to conversations. These expressions are detected using known image processing techniques. Known related work, concerning the investigation of non-verbal communication through text messaging are considered and distinguished from the present solution. The conception and implementation of a mobile phone application with the debated feature is described and user studies are narrated. Finally, context of application, conclusions and future work are also discussed.

Author Keywords
Affective user interfaces, multimodal integration, non-verbal communication, dialogue acts.

ACM Classification Keywords
H.5.m. Information interfaces and presentation (e.g., HCI): Miscellaneous.

Figure 1. Screenshot of the application.

Introduction

Humans rely on visual cues when interacting within a social context, and in an online chatting scenario, the lack of sight due to physical remoteness interferes with the quality of social interactions. Since crucial non-verbal communication is comprised of facial gestures and expressions, text chat users are at a disadvantage when engaging in interpersonal communication. This lost information is often decisive for disambiguation. In [1], long-distance relationships and video chat technology is well debated, clearly exposing this issue. In interviews from this work, subjects have described video as a way to see their partners' facial expressions and body language.

Related Work

There has been significant work on the recognition and conveying of emotions in computer mediated communications.

Video Chat

As minutiously described in [2], the use of video chat successfully transmits consistent non-verbal elements in conversations. In this work, we will not consider video chat solutions as related work, since we are trying to intervene in online text chat scenarios. Not only structurally, video-chatting constitutes a different social ritual [1]. In addition, video-chat may often convey extra imagery such as background rooms, make-up, clothing and hair style, as opposed to transmitting only processed facial expression.

Conveying Emotion in Text Chat

Several existing approaches have been trying to derive affect from written language on a semantic basis, making use of common sense knowledge [2]. The work in [3] is an example of approaches that automatically identify emotions in texts.

The work in [4] attempts to detect deceptive chat-based communication using typing behavior and message cues. It is an example of deriving non-verbal information in chat texts with a non-semantics approach. It hypothesizes that deception influences response time, word count, lexical diversity, and the number of times a chat message is edited. It focuses on detecting deception, unlike our work, which is attempting to convey emotions.

The work in [5] distinguish itself from the others because it attempts to integrate natural language and emotions by performing the recognition of these emotions based on physiological user input. They aim at collecting additional information on the user's emotional state by recording and analyzing physiological feedback. Therefore, while interacting with the application, the user is monitored by means of bio sensors, measuring skin conductivity, heart rate, respiration and muscle activity [5]. Our work differs from these because it relies solely on low-resolution mobile phones front cameras, not requiring extra hardware. Also, it restricts the recognition of emotions to processing images of faces through mobile phones.

Emotion Enhanced Mobile Chat

Our solution attempts to intervene in mobile online text chat by detecting users' emotional reactions during the conversations. Initially, we implemented the chat application itself to be integrated with the emotion detection feature.

Face Image	Capturing Position – Front or Front-low	Smile result (0.0 – 1.0)
	Front-low	0.53
	Front-low	1
	Front	0.69
	Front	1

Table 1. Face images logged with the application, position of the phone and smile detection results.

Mobile chat application

The mobile chat application was developed using the XMPP protocol [6] (formerly and also known as Jabber) as not only it is defined in open standards but it is also widely deployed across the Internet.

Mobile Emotion Detection Software

In this work, we are trying to detect emotions only when new messages have arrived, in order to increase the probability of a facial expression to be a reaction to the most recent message. This means that real-time emotions detection performed by demanding algorithms is not necessary.

Due to the discrete nature of this detection scenario, the image processing can be executed on the server side. This is important because lower end devices, with low memory and low processing power can be used with good performance. Our system uses a commercial solution (Rekognition; Orbeus, Inc.)[7] for face and emotion detection.

System Structure

As shown in Figure 2, the user chats from the mobile, using our application. As soon as a conversation starts, the face images start being collected, converted to base64, and sent via http to the server to be processed. The server sends back a JSON feed, which is parsed to retrieve emotions status. The emotions results range from 0 to 1, providing the detected level of "happy", "surprised" and "calm". If the level one of these emotions are above a pre-determined threshold, the software automatically adds "<name-of-user> smiles" or "<name-of-user> is surprised", to the conversation thread.

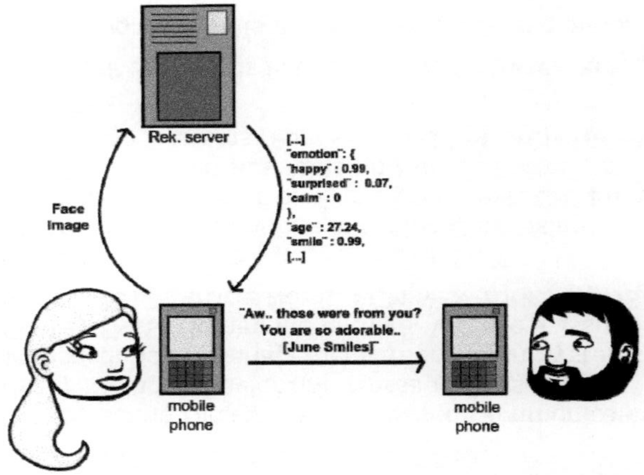

Figure 2. System structure.

Screenshot

Figure 1 is a screenshot of the application, with an on-going dialogue. It is relevant to mention that no actual face images are exchanged. This consolidates the social ritual of the text dialoguing, when people are able to have conversations unmindful facial aesthetics status. There is also a clear demonstration of when the "emotions feature" is on or off.

Interviews and Experiments

Initially, we observed that the test subjects tended to change their facial expressions for no particular reason, in order to check with their chat partners whether the emotion detection accurately worked. Because of that, we decided to implement a preliminary educational usability test phase, in order to get test subjects habituated with the software.

Question	EF	Non-EF
I became very involved in the conversation	4.6	3.7
I enjoyed using the system	4.8	3.0
It was easy to understand my partner's emotions	4.0	2.7
I emulated some of my expressions	1.2	0
I felt more connected to my chat partner	4.9	2.3
I would use this application in my everyday chat conversations.	3.8	3.2

Table 2. Comparison of the application with and without emotional feedback. Mean scores for questions about the interactive experience in chat systems with and without emotional feedback (EF and Non-EF). The possible responses ranged from 1 (disagree) to 5 (agree) (10 subjects).

We referred to some inquiries in the work by Wang [5] when developing the questionnaire. The subjects were asked to answer the questions after using both modes of chat. See Table 2. Conclusions and future work

We developed an approach to the integration of emotions to mobile text chat. The motivation is to enrich mobile text chat by conveying frequently lost non-verbal communication. This benefits users by relay information that is valuable to disambiguate dialogues. Our work is devoted to relaying emotions on mobile text chat scenarios, relying on lower end devices with front cameras.

We implemented a mobile text chat application based on the XMPP protocol, easily connectable with popular chat platforms, with the feature of detecting users' emotions automatically and transmitting them to chat partners.

During the experiments and interviews we found that people perceived their partners' reactions as an accomplishment or a reward to what they just posted. This has included some sort of pressure in the engagement of the conversation, in comparison to plain text chat. In some cases, subjects have mentioned that their partners inserted more humor then usual to the dialogue, in order to receive the automatically detected smiles. During the preliminary trials, we found that people tended to try to foresee their chat partner's reactions, creating frustration when no smiles when detected or causing great sense of accomplishment when it did.

From the interviews, which were conducted individually and in groups, we were able to observe the rise of the sense of connection that chat partners experienced with one another.

References

[1] Neustaedter,C., Greenberg,S. Intimacy in Long-Distance Relationships over Video Chat. CHI '12 Proceedings of the SIGCHI Conference on Human Factors in Computing Systems. Pages 753-762. ACM New York, NY, USA 2012

[2] Bosma, W., Andre, E. Exploiting emotions to disambiguate dialogue acts. IUI '04 Proceedings of the 9th international conference on Intelligent user interfaces. Pages 85-92. ACM New York, NY, USA 2004.

[3] Barros, L., Rodríguez, P., Ortigosa, A. Emotion Recognition in Texts for User Model Augmenting. INTERACCION '12 Proceedings of the 13th International Conference on Interacción Persona-Ordenador. Article No. 45. ACM New York, NY, USA 2012.

[4] Detecting Deceptive Chat-Based Communication Using Typing Behavior and Message Cues. ACM Transactions on Management Information Systems (TMIS) TMIS Homepage archive. Volume 4 Issue 2, August 2013. Article No. 9. ACM New York, NY, USA.

[5] Wang, H., Predinger, H., Igarashi, T. Communicating Emotions in Online Chat Using Physiological Sensors and Animated Text. CHI EA '04 CHI '04 Extended Abstracts on Human Factors in Computing Systems. Pages 1171-1174. ACM New York, NY, USA, 2004.

[6] XMPP Standards Foundation, http://www.xmpp.org

[7] Rekognition APIs and SDK, https://rekognition.com

Changed Shape of Key: An Approach to Enhance the Performance of the Soft Keyboard

Hsi-Jen Chen
Bauhaus-University Weimar
Faculty of Art and Design
7 Geschwister-Scholl-Straße
Weimar, 99423 Germany
hsi-jen.chen@uni-weimar.de

MobileHCI 2014, September 23–26, 2014, Toronto, ON, Canada.
ACM 978-1-4503-3004-6/14/09.
http://dx.doi.org/10.1145/2628363.2634213

Abstract
Text entry using a soft keyboard on small mobile devices is difficult, one reason being that there is often an offset when typing. This essay presents a soft keyboard whose key shapes have been changed in order to avoid the problem of offset. An app and a usability test prove that this soft keyboard with a changed shape of the keys can increase words per minute and reduce the error rate. Another finding is that a large space between keys is preferred.

Author Keywords
Mobile devices; text entry; touch-screens; interaction techniques

ACM Classification Keywords
H.5.2. User Interfaces: Input devices and strategies, Interaction styles, Screen design.

Introduction
Text entry on small mobile devices plays an ever increasing role given the smartphone boom, yet typing on a soft keyboard is slower and less exact than on the traditional computer keyboard. [5] Many experts believe the main reason for the inaccuracy of typing is that on a soft keyboard one does not hit the target letter, i.e. there is offset when typing. [1,4,6,7,11] One

Figure 1. App and Usability Test

variant for improving offset is to develop algorithms that dynamically resize the underlying target areas of keys. [2,10] However, in this essay I show another possibility. I changed the shape of the soft keyboard key in order to adapt the key shape to the regularly mistyped positions. An app for a usability test was programmed in order to check if the soft keyboard with a changed key shape could improve the performance of text entry on small devices. (Figure 1)

The result of the usability test shows that the keyboard performance with the changed key shape is better than that of the keyboard with the rectangular key. Another finding was that keyboards with the changed key shape appealed more to subjects, because the space between the keys on the soft keyboard with the changed shape is in parts larger than on the soft keyboard with the rectangular keys. This means a large space between the keys is preferred for soft keyboards on small mobile devices.

Related works

First I am going to identify the reason for imprecise typing on the soft keyboard. Then I will try to understand how the performance of text entry can be measured.

Inaccurate Typing on Touch-screen

The problem that one cannot precisely type a target on a touch-screen is always present with small mobile devices, e.g. smartphones. Vogel and Baudisch [11] believe that the inaccurate typing can be ascribed to the fact that on a touch-screen one does not hit the target one actually wants to hit, leading to offset when typing. Furthermore Holz and Baudisch [6] discovered that there is a permanent deviation from the target when typing on a touch-screen. Their further research showed that the actually typed positions are below the positions that one wants to type. [7] Henze et al. [3] also found a similar result in their research by analysing many data points collected by a smartphone game that was developed by them.

Referring to text entry on small mobile devices Henze et al. [4] showed how offset appears on the soft keyboard. Furthermore Azenkoti and Zhai [1] visualised in detail offset in text entry for every key of the soft keyboard under different forms of handling (right index finger, right thumb, and two thumbs). Based on these investigations I developed a new soft keyboard that is introduced in the next chapter.

Text Entry Performance

For measuring the performance of text entry, two criteria are used by default – words per minute (WPM) and the error rate. [8] The app that was used in this investigation for the usability test had an error detection function added so that the subjects did not have to correct mistakes. Hence the error rate in this investigation was calculated as follows: number of errors divided by number of key-strokes times 100.

Design

In order to solve the problem of offset various attempts have been made. [2,10] In this investigation a completely different variant is tried, namely a changed shape of each key.

Design Concept

According to the research of Azenkoti and Zhai [1] one normally wants to press the key in the middle, but actually right-handers often hit the key at the bottom

Figure 2. Different layouts and the prototype

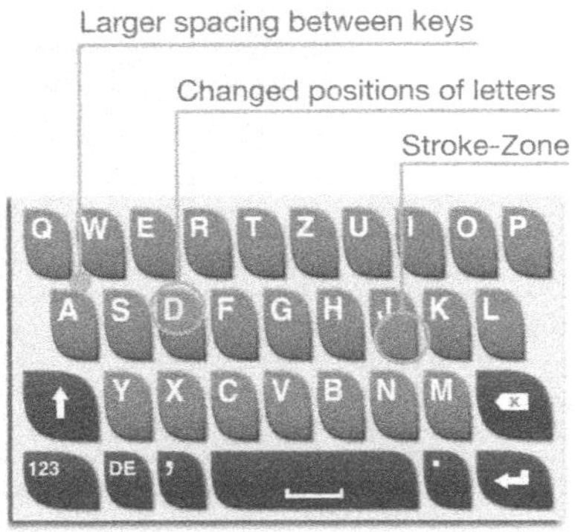

Figure 3. Soft keyboard with the changed shape of the keys

right. Consequently it can be helpful for text entry when the shape of the key fits offset by changing the shape of the keys. For this reason many different layouts of the soft keyboard with a changed key shape were developed and tried. In order to decide the final layout, I printed them out and fixed them on the wooden blocks as the prototypes. (Figure 2) With these prototypes I collected the opinions of a number of experts and users. Consequently I adjusted the details of the soft keyboard such as the size, position, shape of keys and distances between the keys. Figure 3 shows the final version of the soft keyboard.

This soft keyboard has two main aspects:

1. Changed shape of the keys: The key shape can avoid the mistakes that are caused by the offset when typing.

2. Changed positions of letters and characters: All letters are positioned on the top left so that one can still see the letters one wants to type when typing them.

App for the Usability Test
An app for the usability test is programmed in order to compare the performance of the keyboard with the changed key shape (New Keyboard) to that of the keyboard with the rectangular key (Standard Keyboard). (Figure 4)

Figure 4. New Keyboard (left) and Standard Keyboard (right).

The task for the subjects was to key in some sentences with the New Keyboard and with the Standard Keyboard. These sentences were chosen at random from 500 English sentences that were collected by MacKenzie and Soukoreff [9]. In the sentences all key-strokes occur on average with the same frequency. For text entry in the app an error detection function is added so that the error rate can be measured. Error detection function has three key aspects:

VISUAL CLUE:
The sentences which are to be keyed in are shown on the screen. If a letter is keyed in correctly, it changes color from black to red, thus providing a visual feedback. If an incorrect letter is keyed in, the user cannot proceed keying in any more letter. (Figure 5) So subjects are alerted to which letters have already been keyed in. This way missing lines when copying sentences are avoided which could lead to errors that would have nothing to do with the soft keyboard.

ERROR DETECTION:
Errors are automatically detected and an acoustic error message is provided. In doing so the subjects are forced to correct the errors straight away. When correcting they have to just key the correct letter instead of backspace followed by correct letter. In this case other errors can be avoided, e.g. mistakes that went unnoticed or a number of mistakes calling for many corrections. These types of errors are actually not related to the soft keyboard, and what I wish to measure is mistyping only.

ACOUSTIC ERROR MESSAGE:
When an error was made an acoustic error message is given in order to alert the subjects immediately to this

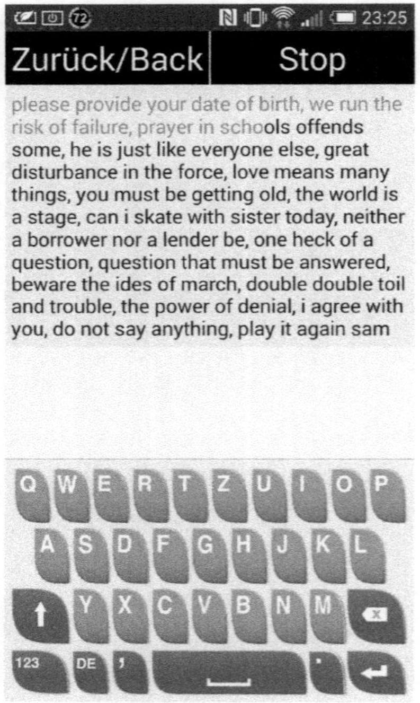

Figure 5. The correct keyed in letters are shown in red as a visual feedback.

error. In this case the problem can be avoided that subjects unintentionally make too many mistakes.

After entry the performance of each subject is shown and recorded by the app. WPM and error rate are then analysed by repeated measures ANOVA (rANOVA).

Usability test and result

Participants needed to be smartphone users with experience of keying in text on touch-screens, and they also have to be right-handed. They had to use their right index finger only for keying in sentences during the test. The smartphone used in the usability test was the HTC NEW ONE, the operating system of the smartphone was Android 4.3.

The whole usability test comprised three parts and took approx. 20 minutes. In the first part the subjects were given 5 minutes to try both types of soft keyboards and learn the rules for text entry in this app. In the second part they had 5 minutes for keying in sentences for the Standard Keyboard and also approx. 5 minutes for the New Keyboard. In between there was a short break. At the end as the third part a brief interview was conducted, in which the subjects gave their opinion on both keyboards.

28 Bauhaus University Weimar students took part in the usability test. In total 8,881 key-strokes on the New Keyboard and 8,702 key-strokes on the Standard Keyboard were counted. On average each subject keyed in 317.2 characters with the New Keyboard and 310.8 characters with the Standard Keyboard.

The result of the usability test is positive. (Table 1) The rANOVA is significant $F(1, 27) = 55.5$, $p < 0.05$. The mean of WPM of both soft keyboards differs from each other. The mean (22.3) of WPM of the New Keyboard is larger than the mean (20.8) of WPM of the Standard Keyboard. With regard to the error rate the rANOVA-Test is significant $F(1, 27) = 17.1$, $p < 0.05$. The mean (3.5%) of the error rate of the New Keyboard is lower than the mean (5.2%) of the error rate of the Standard Keyboard.

	WPM		Error Rate	
	Mean	S.D.	Mean	S.D.
New Keyboard	22.25	2.4	3.45%	2.7
Standard Keyboard	20.76	2.61	5.23%	3.78

Table 1. Result of the usability test

The feedback of the subjects is also positive. 24 subjects even said that for text entry the New Keyboard is clearly better and more comfortable than the Standard Keyboard. The main reason for this is the space between the keys. They have the impression that in comparison with the space between keys on the Standard Keyboard that on the New Keyboard is large, so that one mistypes less often.

Disscussion

The statistic analysis shows that the performance of the New Keyboard is better than that of the Standard Keyboard. Using the New Keyboard characters are keyed in faster and with fewer errors. This means the shape of the keys can improve the performance of the soft keyboard. In addition, the surface of the keys on the New Keyboard is smaller than that of the keys on the Standard Keyboard, however the height and width of each key on both keyboards is the same. (Figure 6)

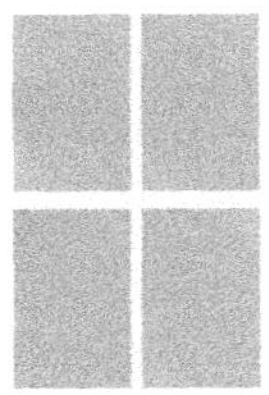

Figure 6. Key shape of the New keyboard (in orange) and key shape of the standard keyboard (in gray)

Figure 7. Zuyin keyboard layout in Taiwan

The space between the keys on the New Keyboard is only partly larger than that on the Standard Keyboard due to the change of shape, and the subjects were content with the larger spaces.

Limitations and future investigation

The keyboards tested and described in this essay are only suitable for the right-hand index finger. Therefore the result of my usability test is somewhat limited, because on the one hand the test advantages participants who use their right-hand index finger to type and disadvantages participants that use their thumb for typing, for example when using the phone with one hand one has to type with the thumb. On the other hand one incidentally uses the right-hand index finger/thumb, the left-hand index finger/thumb, or both thumbs for entry on the touch-screen. Therefore the New Keyboard for left-hand and for two thumbs should be tested in future. Besides the conditions of this experiment were not counter balanced sufficiently. Although the subjects had the time to try both keyboards before the experiment was conducted, during by the experiment they were asked to use the Standard Keyboard first and thre New Keyboard afterwards. Therefore the significant differences between the two keyboards could be due to the training effects rather than caused by the key shape. In future this factor has to be taken into account.

The soft keyboard is a cross-culture issue. The western configuration of the keyboards, e.g. QWERTY in English, QWERTZ in German, and AZERTY in French, is deeply rooted. However, this problem of the keyboard layout could be even more important in other cultures, when the configuration of the keyboard is very narrow, e.g. the Arab keyboard, the Kazhak keyboard, and the Zuyin keyboard layout in Taiwan (Figure 7) etc. That is, while typing on the smartphone, users of these non-QWERTY layouts have more difficulties. The New Keyboard can provide them an alternative to improve the efficiency of text-entry on smartphones. Besides this shape of key can be also applied to the other small mobile devices such as smart watch. (Figure 8)

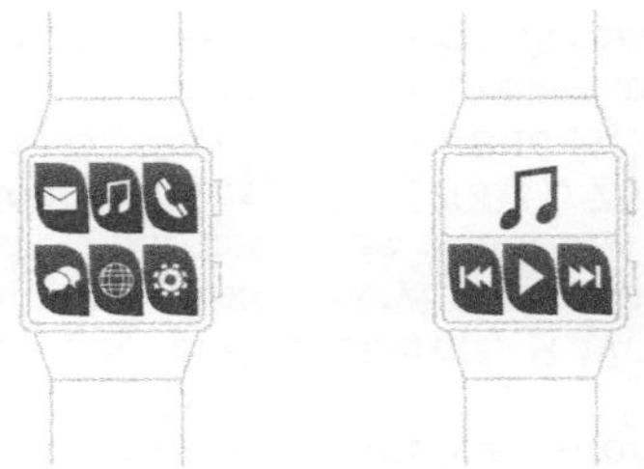

Figure 8. Advanced application, e.g. smartwatch

Conclusion

In this essay I present a new shape of the key for the soft keyboard in order to avoid offset when typing. A usability test proved that the performance of a soft keyboard can be improved by a change in the shape of the keys. The following two conclusions can be drawn:

1. This shape of the key can both increase the speed and decrease the error rate. Consequently the problem of offset is improved by this shape of the key to a certain extent.

2. This shape of the key partly enlarges the space between the keys, and according to the subjects, a large space makes for a safe and comfortable feel when entering text.

Acknowledgments

This work is a part of my doctoral dissertation and I wish to thank my two mentors, Professor Gronert and Professor Sattler of Bauhaus-Universität Weimar, all students who made suggestions and participated in the usability test, as well as Po-Chi Huang and Chih-Yuan Cho for programming the app based on my design to the keyboard and to the app. Sincere thanks also go to all researchers who contributed to this field of research.

Reference

[1] Azenkot, S. and Zhai, S. Touch behavior with different postures on soft smartphone keyboards. *Proceedings of the 14th international conference on Human-computer interaction with mobile devices and services*, ACM (2012), 251–260.

[2] Gunawardana, A., Paek, T., and Meek, C. Usability Guided Key-target Resizing for Soft Keyboards. *Proceedings of the 15th International Conference on Intelligent User Interfaces*, ACM (2010), 111–118.

[3] Henze, N., Rukzio, E., and Boll, S. 100,000,000 taps: analysis and improvement of touch performance in the large. *Proceedings of the 13th International Conference on Human Computer Interaction with Mobile Devices and Services*, ACM (2011), 133–142.

[4] Henze, N., Rukzio, E., and Boll, S. Observational and experimental investigation of typing behaviour using virtual keyboards for mobile devices. *Proceedings of the SIGCHI Conference on Human Factors in Computing Systems*, ACM (2012), 2659–2668.

[5] Hoggan, E., Brewster, S.A., and Johnston, J. Investigating the effectiveness of tactile feedback for mobile touchscreens. *Proceedings of the SIGCHI Conference on Human Factors in Computing Systems*, ACM (2008), 1573–1582.

[6] Holz, C. and Baudisch, P. The generalized perceived input point model and how to double touch accuracy by extracting fingerprints. *Proceedings of the SIGCHI Conference on Human Factors in Computing Systems*, ACM (2010), 581–590.

[7] Holz, C. and Baudisch, P. Understanding Touch. *Proceedings of the SIGCHI Conference on Human Factors in Computing Systems*, ACM (2011), 2501–2510.

[8] MacKenzie, I.S. and Soukoreff, R.W. Text Entry for Mobile Computing: Models and Methods,Theory and Practice. *Human–Computer Interaction 17*, 2-3 (2002), 147–198.

[9] MacKenzie, I.S. and Soukoreff, R.W. Phrase sets for evaluating text entry techniques. *CHI '03 Extended Abstracts on Human Factors in Computing Systems*, ACM (2003), 754–755.

[10] Rudchenko, D., Paek, T., and Badger, E. Text text revolution: a game that improves text entry on mobile touchscreen keyboards. *Proceedings of the 9th international conference on Pervasive computing*, Springer-Verlag (2011), 206–213.

[11] Vogel, D. and Baudisch, P. Shift: a technique for operating pen-based interfaces using touch. *Proceedings of the SIGCHI Conference on Human Factors in Computing Systems*, ACM (2007), 657–666.

Ergonomic Characteristics of Gestures for Front- and Back-of-Tablets Interaction with Grasping Hands

Figure 1. Hand configuration for holding the device while filling a form (left) and touch heatmaps (right).

Katrin Wolf
University of Stuttgart
katrin.wolf@acm.org

Robert Schleicher
Technical University Berlin
robert.schleicher@tu-berlin.de

Michael Rohs
Leibnitz University Hannover
michael.rohs@hci.uni-hannover.de

MobileHCI '14, Sep 23-26 2014, Toronto, ON, Canada
ACM 978-1-4503-3004-6/14/09.
http://dx.doi.org/10.1145/2628363.2634214

Abstract
The thumb and the fingers have different flexibility, and thus, gestures performed on the back of a held tablet are suggested to be different from ones performed on the touchscreen with the thumb of grasping hands. APIs for back-of-device gesture detection should consider that difference. In a user study, we recorded vectors for the four most common touch gestures. We found that drag, swipe, and press gestures are significantly differently when executed on the back versus on the front side of a held tablet. Corresponding values are provided that may be used to define gesture detection thresholds for back-of-tablet interaction.

Author Keywords
Gesture; Ergonomics; Tablet; Touch; Back-of-Device.

ACM Classification Keywords
H.5.2 [Information inter-faces and presentation]: User Interfaces - Ergonomics; Haptic I/O.

Introduction
Tablet interaction with grasping hands is, similar to one-handed phone interaction, (A) a common tablet grip that (B) constrains the gesture feasibility.(A), shown in Figure 1, has been stated by Wagner *et al.* [8]

as well as by Oulasvirta *et al.* [6]. That grip is ergonomic and allows for holding tablet stable because both hands are holding the device, which reduces the gesture feasibility at the same time. Enabling interaction on the back of the device may compensate the reduced interaction design space. The question targeted here is: How do typical touch gestures look like if executed with grasping hands on the front as well as on the back of the device?

Related work

Hoggan *et al.* [3] investigated the factors effecting touch gesture performance and ergonomics. Parameters of a rotation gesture were systematically controlled in the experiment, such as rotation angle, rotation direction, distance between fingers, and position. The study shows that within-gesture parameters, such as the angle of the fingers (given as start and final position of the two touch points) influence the gesture execution time. Wobbrock *et al.* [10] compared the performance of the index finger and the thumb for front- and back-of-phone interactions and showed that with shorter interaction times, when using the thumb on the front screen, this interaction technique has greater ergonomic values than e.g. interacting with the thumb on the rear of the phone. A comparison of front and back touch with transparent double sided touch displays, inspired by Hiraoka *et al.* [2] and Wigdor *et al.* [9], showed that touch performance on the back is lower in terms of target acquisition time, while accuracy was equal [5], as well as the position-dependent reachability [11]. However, some work on gesture ergonomics and comparison of front and back touch was done; no vector comparison for both front- and the back-of-tablet gesture interaction was done.

Method

Design. An 4x2x5x2 within design with repeated measurements experiment was designed where 18 participants, (7 female, mean Age=28, SD=3) volunteered. The dependent variables were gesture, direction, digit, hand, and device side. The independent variables were x-positions and y-positions of the changing touch points while gestures execution.

Apparatus & measurements. An application running on an ASUS Eee Pad Transformer TF101 was developed for recording the touch events. For the back-of-device conditions, the device was flipped so that the back side was facing the users, while the touchscreen allowed for recording touch events on the back. The touch events were recorded in logfiles and contained per participant five trials per device side, hand and digit for four gestures, 2 gesture orientations (horizontal, vertical) for swipe and drag; 10800 gestures in total. Handedness and demographic data were recorded by a questionnaire.

Task& procedure. The participants were asked to execute tap, press, drag, and swipe gestures with both hands and each digit per hand without getting system feedback. The drag and swipe gesture were executed in the horizontal as well as in the vertical direction. After an introduction, the participants solved the gesture execution task five times with each finger per hand. Half of the participants started with their dominant, the other half with their non-dominant hand in a standing position. All combinations were executed separately on the front and the back of the device five times each while holding the device with two hands in a standing position. After completing the tasks, the participants filled in a questionnaire.

Figure 2. Gesture vectors (grey) and median for front (orange) and back (black, see-through view) of a tablet, drawn to scale of a tablet screen of 1280x742 pixels.

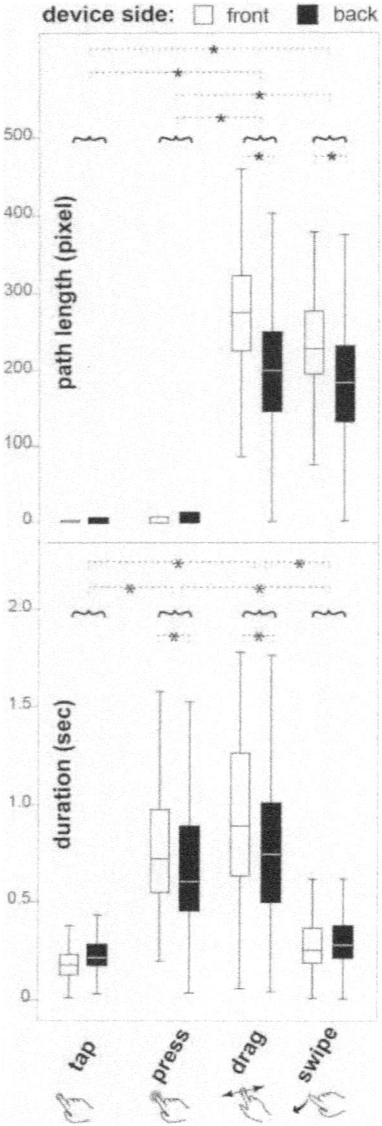

Figure 3. Boxplot of path length & duration for each gesture and significant differences* in between.

Results

For the gesture parameters (touch position, path length, and execution duration), we tested whether they are affected by gesture orientation or by the device side (front versus back of tablets) as well as whether they vary between the dominant or non-dominant hand. The individual vectors for each gesture tap, press, drag, and swipe, and typical gesture vectors using the median (see Table 1) are drawn (in orange and in black) to scale of a tablet screen of 1280x742 pixels in Figure 2. The individual gesture vectors differ a lot, which is shown by the widespread location of the whole set of gesture vectors that are drawn in gray.

Gesture position. Regarding the gesture positions, the median values for tap and press gestures were always located close to the vertical edges where that hands are places. The gesture positions differ a lot in their vertical position but less horizontally. The touch positions of the gestures when executed on the front are again slightly closer to the edge/hand palm than those performed at the back of the device.

Gesture shape. Different gesture shapes for drag and swipe gestures were observed. The vectors for horizontal gestures are slightly tilted upwards towards the middle of the screen, comparable to a fishbone pattern. Vertical gesture paths are drawn like a bow, and the imaginary middle of the circle would be inside the palm (Figure 2).

Gesture orientation. The gesture path *orientations* (horizontal, vertical) had no influence on the vector parameters (gesture path length: $F_{1,953}$=2.379, p=0.123, gesture execution duration: $F_{1,1623}$=1.545, p=0.214) in an ANOVA.

Path length in px (in mm)		Duration in s		Velocity in px/s	
left	right	left	right	left	right
Tap on the touchscreen					
1	1	0.2	0.2	5	5
Press on the touchscreen					
4	7	0.7	0.7	6	10
Vertical drag on the touchscreen					
314 (48)	(291) 45	1.0	1.1	249	251
Horizontal drag on the touchscreen					
247 (38)	221 (34)	0.8	0.7	216	233
Vertical swipe on the touchscreen					
265 (41)	285 (44)	0.3	0.2	10757	10689
Horizontal swipe on the touchscreen					
212 (32)	214 (33)	0.2	0.2	12188	15678
Tap on the back of the tablet					
4	8	0.2	0.2	20	40
Press on the back of the tablet					
17	18	0.7	0.7	24	26
Vertical drag on the back of the tablet					
213 (32)	183 (28)	0.9	0.7	2586	2569
Horizontal drag on the back of the tablet					
206 (32)	193 (30)	0.9	0.7	2632	2560
Vertical swipe on the back of the tablet					
196 (30)	203 (31)	0.3	0.3	2926	2617
Horizontal swipe on the back of the tablet					
189 (29)	174 (27)	0.3	0.2	3211	2700

Table 1. Typical gestures: medians for path length (Figure 2), gesture duration, & velocity on both device sides, both gesture orientations & with both hands.

Hand symmetry. The gesture execution is symmetric for both *hands* as shown in Figure 2. This means that the gesture vectors are flipped on an imaginary vertical line drawn in the middle of the screen. Thus, the positions (considering that they are vertically flipped) are not affected (p=0.929), and the drag as well as swipe paths do not differ in length regardless of whether they have been executed with left or right hand (p=0.885). While the gesture vectors look similar for the right or left hand, gesture execution duration differs significantly for both *hands*. Moreover, a significant interaction effect between *hand* and *gesture* was found for execution duration (p=0.003).

Front versus back of the device. The gestures differ in path length if they were executed on the front versus on the back of tablet (p>0.001). Moreover, Figure 2 shows that the gesture vectors of drag and swipe are significantly longer than tap and press, which by definition are close to zero. Swipe and tap are faster than drag and press (p>0.001). Their values are almost independent and can therefore serve as gesture classification as it is already the case in common touch gesture APIs like for iOS, Android, and mobile browsers. Interestingly, the duration and path length sometimes vary for the same gesture when executed on different device sides: drag and press are slightly, but significantly longer on the front side where the gestures are performed with the thumb. Moreover, the vectors for drag and swipe are a significantly longer when performed with the thumb on the front of the tablet compared to the gesture paths on the back side. Thus, an interaction effect was found for *gesture* device side* (Figure 3) and swipe on the back of the device has much less velocity (p>0.001) than on the front.

Discussion & conclusion

The gestures were executed close to the positions where the hands were grasping the device. These positions are in line with the interaction areas for bimanual held tablets defined for touchscreens by Odell and Chandrasekaran [4]. The parameters of the gesture paths are significantly influenced by the gesture type and the device side. The used hand influenced execution time but not the paths. The gesture orientation was neither affecting execution time nor path.

On mobile devices, gesture recognition thresholds are defined by these parameters for front- but not for back-of-device interaction. In the following section, we compare our parameters with common gesture recognition parameters of Android APIs, e.g. accessible through the getLongPressTimeout command [1].

Android versus observed parameters

- Our durations of tap (0.2s) and press (0.7s) for both, the front and the back of the device are in line with the Android thresholds (tap: <0.5s, press: >0.5s).
- Our prototypical drag performed on a tablet is 30 to 50 mm. Such values do not exist for (Android and others') gesture detection, but they help designing widgets, such as defining slider length.
- Our detected velocity for swiping on the frontscreen (avrg_front: vertical: 10723, horizontal: 13933; avrg_back: horizontal: 2956, vertical: 2772), which serves for mapping the swipe execution onto scroll friction, is within and for horizontal front swipe above the range of several Android phones (from 75 to 12000 pixels per second) and for back-of-device

within, but for touchscreen interaction above the range of the Android ASUS tablet (between 50 and 8000 pixels per seconds). We rate values above the common ranges as acceptable: users would just have no problems to scroll fast. If the maximum velocity cannot be reached, which is suggested for back-of-device interaction, the mapping should be defined correspondingly. As back-of-device swiping was up to four times smaller for back-of-tablet interactions compared to swipe velocity on the front, dividing scroll parameters by four for back-of-device interaction would be recommended.

- No thresholds are defined in existing APIs for distinguishing an unintended touch event. That event would cause Midas touch problems in back-of-device interaction. According to the presented results, touch events on the back of tablets that last longer than 1.0 sec (considering 1 SD safety distance from the press/taphold mean) without moving are unintended touch events.

In summary, gestures on the front take longer (drag, press) and are drawn over a greater distance (drag, swipe) than gestures on the back of the device. A reason for this is probably that gestures on the front are executed with the thumb is more flexible than the fingers [7]. Thus, design guidelines for touchscreen interaction cannot automatically be adapted for back-of-device interaction, and parameters that should to be defined differently for front versus back-of-device interaction are suggested.

References

[1] Android Developers Reference: developer.android.com/reference/android/view/ViewConfiguration.html, 27.7.2013.

[2] Hiraoka, S., Miyamoto, I. and Tomimatsu, K. 2003. Behind Touch: A text input method for mobile phone by the back and tactile sense interface. Proc. Interaction 2003. Information Processing Society of Japan, 131-138.

[3] Hoggan, E., Williamson, J., Oulasvirta, A., Nacenta, M., Kristensson, P.O., Lehtiö, A. 2013. Multi-touch rotation gestures: performance and ergonomics. In Proc. CHI '13, 3047-3050.

[4] Odell, D. and Chandrasekaran, V. 2012. Enabling comfortable thumb interaction in tablet computers: a Windows 8 case study. In Proc. of the Human Factors and Ergonomics Society Annual Meeting, 1907-1911.

[5] Ohtani, T., Hashida, T., Kakehi, Y., and Naemura, T. 2011. Comparison of front touch and back touch while using transparent double-sided touch display. In ACM SIGGRAPH 2011 Posters (SIGGRAPH '11).

[6] Oulasvirta, A., Reichel, A., Li, W., Zhang, Y., Bachynskyi, M., Vertanen, K., Kristensson, P.O. 2013. Improving two-thumb text entry on touchscreen devices. In Proc. CHI '13, 2765-2774.

[7] Vardy, A. 1998. Articulated Human Hand Model with Inter-Joint Dependency Constraints. *Computer Science 6752, Comp. Graphics, Project Report,* 1-13.

[8] Wagner, J., Huot, S., and Mackay, W.E. 2012. BiTouch and BiPad: designing bimanual interaction for hand-held tablets. In Proc. CHI'12, 2317-2326.

[9] Wigdor, D., Forlines, C., Baudisch, P., Barnwell, J., and Shen, C. 2007. Lucid touch: a see-through mobile device. In Proc. UIST'07, 269-278.

[10] Wobbrock, J.O., Myers, B.A., Aung, H.H. 2008. The performance of hand postures in front- and back-of-device interaction for mobile computing. International Journal of Human-Computer Studies 66 (12), 857-875.

[11] Wolf, K., Müller-Tomfelde, C., Cheng, K., and Wechsung, I. 2012. Does proprioception guide back-of-device pointing as well as vision? In EA CHI'12, 1739-1744.

Towards Usable and Acceptable Above-Device Interactions

Euan Freeman
Glasgow Interactive Systems Group
University of Glasgow
Glasgow, Scotland
euan.freeman@glasgow.ac.uk

Stephen Brewster
Glasgow Interactive Systems Group
University of Glasgow
Glasgow, Scotland
stephen.brewster@glasgow.ac.uk

Vuokko Lantz
Nokia Research Center
Espoo, Finland
vuokko.lantz@nokia.com

MobileHCI'14, September 23–26, 2014, Toronto, ON, Canada.
ACM 978-1-4503-3004-6/14/09.

http://dx.doi.org/10.1145/2628363.2634215

Abstract
Gestures above a mobile phone would let users interact with their devices quickly and easily from a distance. While both researchers and smartphone manufacturers develop new gesture sensing technologies, little is known about how best to design these gestures and interaction techniques. Our research looks at creating usable and socially acceptable above-device interaction techniques. We present an initial gesture collection, a preliminary evaluation of these gestures and some design recommendations. Our findings identify interesting areas for future research and will help designers create better gesture interfaces.

Author Keywords
Acceptability; Above-Device; Gestures; Mobile Phones

ACM Classification Keywords
H.5.2 [User Interfaces]: Interaction Styles.

Introduction
Touchscreen interaction has become the main way of interacting with mobile phones. This is often a highly engaged interaction, requiring both visual attention and precise touch input as users search the display and select what are often small targets. Users may not always be willing or able to give this much attention to their phone, for example when in a meeting and not wanting to appear rude or when

Gesture Sensing

Proximity Sensors: These sensors detect nearby objects with a range of around 5 to 30 cm. Multiple sensors can be used to detect hand [5] and finger [2] movements.

Magnetic Sensors: Magnetic field sensors, already in phones, can detect movement of magnetic objects like rings [3, 4]. Gestures, such as precise finger movements [3] for pointer control, can be sensed through materials and anywhere around the device.

Cameras: Most phones have cameras which can be used for detecting gesture interaction, for example tracking fingers [6]. Placing a lens over the camera lets phones detect simple gestures, like waving, from a distance [10].

Depth Cameras: Google's *Project Tango* [1] has a depth camera and dedicated vision processing resources. Depth cameras can detect hand orientation and pose as well as movement.

focusing on another task and not wanting to be disturbed. Touch may also be unavailable for input, for example when washing dishes or exercising and hands are wet. In these situations, gesturing with a hand in mid-air near a device would let users interact with their phones when direct touch is unavailable or inappropriate.

Gestures above a device on a table could be particularly useful as people typically keep their phones on a table or desk throughout the day when at home and at work, largely for easy access [9]. Users particularly want easy access to their notifications [9]. Above-device gestures let users dismiss unwanted interruptions while busy [7] and would let users perform less involved interactions, such as frequently checking for notifications, without having to lift their phone.

Our research looks at designing usable and acceptable above-device interactions. We gathered above-device gesture ideas from brainstorming sessions and then chose some of these gestures for further evaluation. A preliminary evaluation looked at the usability and social acceptability of these gestures. We present our findings from these studies and recommendations for creating better above-device interfaces.

Related Work

A variety of sensing technologies (discussed in the sidebar) have been used for detecting mid-air gestures near mobile phones. In this section we look at some gesture interfaces with a particular focus on the interactions they support.

Some gesture interfaces detect finger movements for cursor control, letting users interact with small devices using a larger space. *SideSight* [2] used ten proximity sensors on each side of a mobile phone to detect gestures. Users could interact on either side of the device, using the surrounding table surface for input. *Abracadabra* [3] used magnetic sensing to track finger position for controlling a cursor on a smart-watch. Users could also gesture by making circular or semi-circular paths. Finger position has also been used for mid-air typing [6], this time using a camera to sense finger movements over a virtual keyboard.

Other interfaces detect less precise hand movements and gestures. *HoverFlow* [5] used upwards facing proximity sensors to detect above-device input. Users gestured over the display, for example swiping left or right, lowering a hand, and rotating a hand. Gestures were used to navigate a colour palette. *Surround-See* [10] let users gesture from across the room, for example waving at their phone to silence it. Ketabdar *et al.* [4] used magnetic sensing to detect a small vocabulary of gestures, for example detecting gestures by a hand wearing a magnetic ring.

Some mobile phones can already detect above-device gestures. The Samsung Galaxy S4 phone can detect hand movement over the display, letting users swipe through image galleries and scroll through documents. Some Nokia Lumia phones detect hands hovering over the proximity sensor, letting users glance at their notifications without unlocking the display.

Above-Device Gestures

Despite advances in gesture sensing approaches for mobile phones, little is known about how best to design usable and acceptable above-device interactions. Our work begins to address this. We focus on above-device gestures because phones are often kept on desks and tables [9]. Gestures over phones would let users interact casually [7]. Users could also gesture when touch is inconvenient or inappropriate, for example to navigate a recipe without getting their phone messy or having to repeatedly wash their hands.

We started to explore the above-device gesture design space by brainstorming gesture ideas with participants. By taking

Brainstorming Sessions

Procedure: We first discussed scenarios where above-device gesture use may be appropriate. Then we asked participants to think of a gesture for common phone actions (listed in Table 2) while thinking aloud. There were no constraints on gesture designs and gestures could be re-used. We placed a phone in front of participants for use as a prop. After participants chose their gestures we filmed them demonstrating them. We also recorded audio for the entire session. These recordings were later analysed.

Participants: Fifteen people took part in these sessions (three female, mostly university students). Participants were recruited through email lists and were paid £6.

Gestures: We collected 175 gestures, of which 49 were unique. Three were two-hand gestures and one was performed on the table surface.

a participatory approach to gesture design we hoped to discover gestures which users would be willing to use. These sessions would also give insight into how we can design better above-device interfaces. We chose gestures from these design sessions which we evaluated further using an online survey. Our survey evaluated gestures in terms of design and social acceptability [8].

We now present the outcomes of these brainstorming sessions and our gesture evaluation. From these outcomes we create design recommendations which will help others design better gesture interfaces. Our work also contributes some usable and socially acceptable gestures for common mobile phone tasks. Finally, our findings identify interesting directions for future mobile phone gesture research.

Brainstorming Sessions

We gathered initial gesture ideas through a series of brainstorming sessions with mobile phone users. We also discussed how interfaces should react to gestures. Our procedure for these sessions is described in the sidebar. We chose two gestures for each action, inspired by the gestures proposed by our participants. Our gesture choices generally represented the most popular gestures created by participants. Figures 1 to 8 show some of these gestures.

As well as identifying suitable above-device gestures, we also analysed audio recordings and videos of participants demonstrating their own gestures. This gave insight into why people chose certain gestures and helps us understand how to create better above-device interfaces. We now discuss some key themes found from this analysis. Themes are coded (e.g. *GF* for *Gesture feedback*) for later reference.

Gesture feedback (GF)
Participants were uncertain about how well their gestures would be detected, especially those who were unfamiliar with other types of gesture interface (e.g. Kinect). Effective feedback is needed to help users overcome uncertainty and gesture confidently. Some participants said visual feedback would be ineffective because their hands gestured over the phone display. Above-device interfaces may have to give other types of feedback. Tactile feedback would not be felt (unless holding the phone) and some thought constant audio feedback may be unacceptable around other people.

Metaphorical gestures (MG)
Many gestures were based on metaphors or familiar interaction techniques. For example, some gestures imitated pointing with a cursor and others were based on a telephone metaphor with users lifting their hand to mimic lifting a phone from the receiver. Metaphors may have been chosen because the metaphor would be understood by others observing the gesture performance. If the meaning of a gesture is easily understood by other people, users may feel more comfortable using it [8]. Gestures based on metaphor may also be easier to remember.

Gesture mechanics (GM)
We observed a variety of different gesture mechanics. Some people performed swipe gestures with their entire hand, while others preferred more subtle motions with one or two fingers. Gesture "size" also varied; some participants used small, subtle hand movements over the phone only while others would perform larger versions of the same movements. Most participants gestured around 10 to 20 cm above the phone prop.

Social acceptability (SA)
One of our participants said she would be uncomfortable performing some of her gestures in public in case people saw her and thought she was gesturing at them. Cultural interpretations of gestures could also be an issue.

Survey Design

Procedure: Gestures were shown in a random order. We showed a video of each gesture along with a text description. We encouraged participants to try gestures above their own phone. Participants then rated the gesture (see below) and could give freeform comments.

Gesture Ratings: We asked participants to rate gestures in terms of: how appropriate is it for its action, how easy is it to perform, how memorable might it be, how likely would they be to use it. Ratings were on a seven-point scale.

Acceptability: We used a similar design to [8], modified after correspondence with the authors. We asked participants if they thought each gesture was appropriate to use in a variety of social situations (Table 1). Responses were yes/no checkboxes.

Participants: Forty-one people (aged 18-65, nineteen female) completed the survey.

Gesture Evaluation Survey

We evaluated our chosen gestures using an online video survey. We chose to use an online survey because it would let us reach a wider international audience and was found by Rico *et al.* [8] to be a useful method. Our survey aimed to evaluate usability aspects of our gestures as well as looking at how socially acceptable they are. Our findings could then be used to identify usable and acceptable gestures for above-device interfaces. This was also a first look at the social acceptability of above-device interaction, to see if people would be willing to interact with their phones in this way. The sidebar on the left describes our survey design.

For each gesture, we calculated an overall score as the sum of its four ratings (appropriateness, ease of use, memorability and likeliness of use). This gave a score from four to twenty-eight, where higher scores are better. We also calculated an acceptability score for each gesture as the percentage of positive responses (as in [8]). A score of 100% indicates that participants found the gesture acceptable in all situations. Table 1 shows mean acceptability scores for each social situation; these are similar to findings for device-based gestures [8].

We compared both gestures for each action to see if one was rated significantly higher, in terms of overall score and acceptability score. We used the Wilcoxon signed-rank test to compare all ratings. Acceptability scores were highly left-skewed so were compared using Wilcoxon's test rather than a t-test. Table 2 shows gesture and acceptability scores, along with results from the Wilcoxon test.

Situation	*Accept.*	*Situation*	*Accept.*
Home, alone	89%	Home, family	78%
Work, alone	86%	Work, colleagues	72%
Public, strangers	60%	Public, friends	66%

Table 1: Acceptability in social situations.

Design Recommendations

Qualitative analysis of audio and video recordings from our design sessions helped identify common themes in expectations of an above-device gesture interface. Our gesture survey provided a chance to probe some of these issues further. These recommendations arose from the outcomes of both studies and should help designers create better above-device interfaces. We refer back to themes from our brainstorming sessions when appropriate.

Give non-visual feedback during interaction
Feedback during gestures is important because it shows users that the interface is responding to their gestures and it helps them gesture effectively *(GF)*. However, above-device gestures take place over a phone so visual feedback will not always be visible. Instead, other modalities (like audio) should be used.

Make non-visual feedback distinct from notifications
Some participants suggested that they may be confused if feedback during gesture interaction was like feedback used for other mobile phone notifications *(GF)*. Gesture feedback should be distinct from other notification types. Continuous feedback which responds to input would let users know that feedback is being given for their actions.

Emphasise that gestures are directed towards a device
Some participants in our studies were concerned about people thinking they were gesturing at them rather than at a device *(SA)*. Above-device interactions should emphasise gesture target by using the device as a referent for gestures and letting users gesture in close proximity.

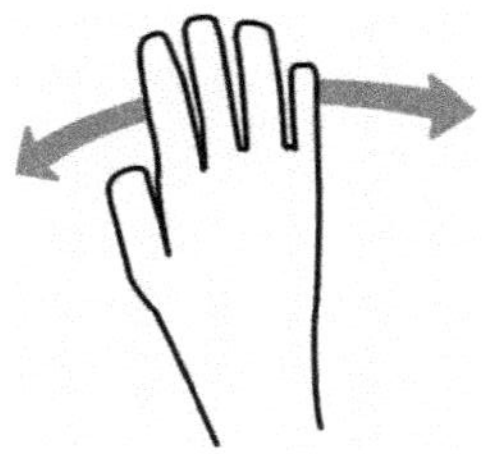

Figure 1: Swipe.

Figure 2: Point and Tap.

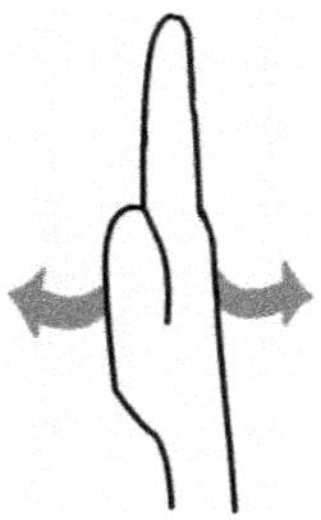

Figure 3: Flick.

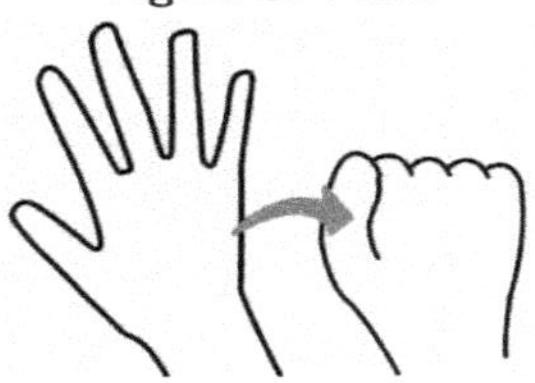

Figure 4: Scrunch.

Gesture	Median Score	Mean Acceptability
Check messages		
Swipe	21	78%
Draw Rectangle	13	70%
	Z=-4.45, p<0.001	Z=-1.55, p=0.12
Select item		
Finger Count	20	73%
Point and Tap	26	93%
	Z=-4.41, p<0.001	Z=-2.70, p=0.005
Move left / right		
Swipe	24	87%
Flick	24	84%
	Z=-0.15, p=0.88	Z=-0.60, p=0.55
Delete item		
Scrunch	23	85%
Draw X	21	79%
	Z=-0.98, p=0.33	Z=-0.86, p=0.39
Place call		
Phone Symbol	17	64%
Dial	20	74%
	Z=-2.00, p=0.04	Z=-1.84, p=0.07
Dismiss / close item		
Brush Away	20	82%
Wave Hand	20	72%
	Z=-0.51, p=0.61	Z=-1.62, p=0.11

Gesture	Median Score	Mean Acceptability
Answer call		
Swipe	19	80%
Pick Up	18	66%
	Z=-0.48, p=0.64	Z=-2.65, p=0.008
Ignore call		
Brush Away	20	79%
Wave Hand	20	77%
	Z=-0.02, p=0.99	Z=-0.36, p=0.72
Place on hold		
One Moment	20	72%
Lower Hand	19	68%
	Z=-2.04, p=0.04	Z=-0.57, p=0.57
End call		
Wave Hand	21	71%
Place Down	23	76%
	Z=-1.51, p=0.13	
Check calendar		
Thumb Out	10	59%
Draw ? Symbol	17	72%
	Z=-4.04, p<0.001	Z=-1.88, p=0.06
Accept and reject		
Thumb Up/Down	15	64%
Draw Tick/Cross	20	78%
	Z=-3.76, p<0.001	Z=-3.01, p=0.003

Table 2: Scores and results of Wilcoxon's signed-rank tests. Significantly higher scores ($p<0.05$) are highlighted.

Support flexible gesture mechanics

During our brainstorming sessions, some participants gestured with whole hand movements whereas others performed the same gestures with one or two fingers *(GM)*. Gestures also varied in size; for example, some participants swiped over a large area and others swiped with subtle movements over the display only *(GM)*. Above-device interfaces should be flexible, letting users gesture in their preferred way using either hand. Social situation may influence gesture mechanics *(SA)*. For example, users in public places may use more subtle versions of gestures than they would at home.

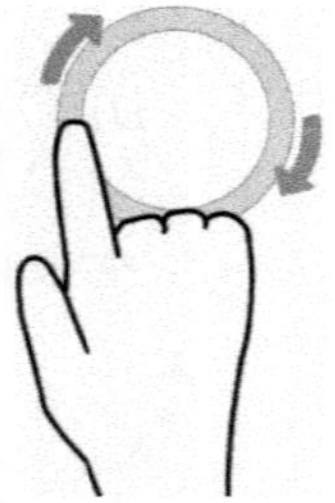

Figure 5: Dial.

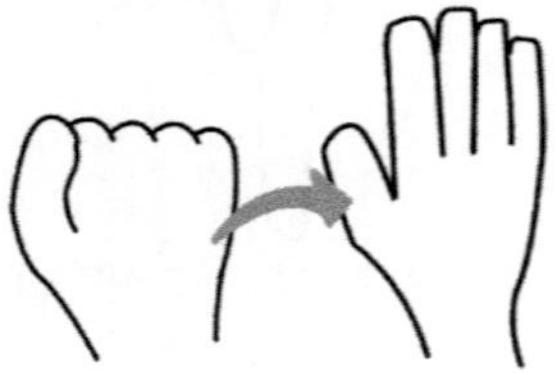

Figure 6: Brush Away.

Figure 7: One Moment.

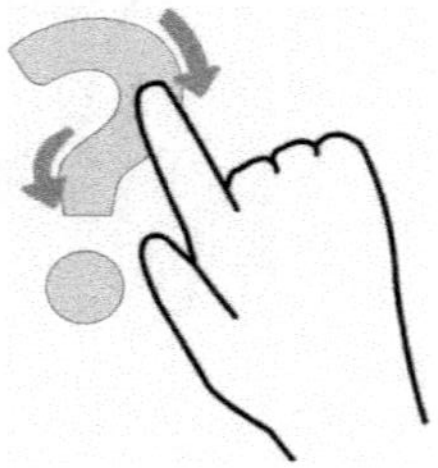

Figure 8: Draw ? Symbol.

Enable complex gestures with a simple gating gesture
Our participants proposed a variety of gestures, from basic movements with simple sensing requirements, to complex hand poses requiring more sophisticated sensors. Always-on sensing with complex sensors will affect battery. Sensors with low power consumption (e.g. the proximity sensor) could be used to detect a simple gesture which then enables more sophisticated sensors. Holding a hand over the phone or clicking fingers, for example, could start a depth camera which could track the hand in greater detail.

Use simple gestures for casual interactions
Casual interactions (such as checking for notifications) are low-effort and imprecise [7] so should be easy to perform and sense. Easily sensed gestures lower power requirements for input sensing and allow for variance in performance when gesturing imprecisely. Users may also use these gestures more often when around others so allowing variance lets users gesture discreetly, in an acceptable way *(SA)*.

Future Work

We identified the importance of giving effective feedback for gestures. Visual feedback will often be inappropriate because users will be gesturing over the display. Instead, other modalities such as audio and tactile should be used. Our research will look at how feedback can be given in the space above the device. Gesture interfaces also need to be flexible, letting users vary how they gesture and using different gesture sensing modes in different situations. We will explore these issues more in future work.

Conclusion

Our research looks at how to create usable and acceptable above-device interfaces. In this paper we presented two studies: a design study where we gathered gesture ideas and an online evaluation where we looked at some gesture ideas in greater detail. We contribute a collection of gestures for some common mobile phone tasks and an initial evaluation of these gestures. Qualitative analysis during these studies gave insight into above-device design issues. We contribute design recommendations based on these findings.

Acknowledgements

This research is funded by Nokia Research Center, Finland.

References

[1] `https://www.google.com/atap/projecttango/`

[2] Butler, A., Izadi, S., and Hodges, S. SideSight: Multi-touch Interaction Around Small Devices. In *Proc. UIST '08*, ACM (2008), 201–204.

[3] Harrison, C., and Hudson, S. E. Abracadabra: Wireless, High-Precision, and Unpowered Finger Input for Very Small Mobile Devices. In *Proc. UIST '09*, ACM (2009), 121–124.

[4] Ketabdar, H., Roshandel, M., and Yüksel, K. A. Towards Using Embedded Magnetic Field Sensor for Around Mobile Device 3D Interaction. In *Proc. MobileHCI '10*, ACM (2010), 153–156.

[5] Kratz, S., and Rohs, M. HoverFlow: Expanding the Design Space of Around-Device Interaction. In *Proc. MobileHCI '09*, ACM (2009), Article 4.

[6] Niikura, T., Watanabe, Y., Komuro, T., and Ishikawa, M. In-air Typing Interface: Realizing 3D operation for mobile devices. In *Proc. GCCE '12*, IEEE (2012), 223–227.

[7] Pohl, H., and Murray-Smith, R. Focused and Casual Interactions: Allowing Users to Vary Their Level of Engagement. In *Proc. CHI '13*, ACM (2013), 2223–2232.

[8] Rico, J., and Brewster, S. Usable gestures for mobile interfaces. In *Proc. CHI '10*, ACM (2010), 887–896.

[9] Wiese, J., Saponas, T. S., Brush, A. J. B., and Ave, F. Phoneprioception: Enabling Mobile Phones to Infer Where They Are Kept. In *Proc. CHI '13*, ACM (2013), 2157–2166.

[10] Yang, X.-d., Hasan, K., Bruce, N., and Irani, P. Surround-See: Enabling Peripheral Vision on Smartphones during Active Use. In *Proc. UIST '13*, ACM (2013), 291–300.

A Comparison of Location Search UI Patterns on Mobile Devices

Meier, Sebastian
University of Applied
Sciences Potsdam, Germany
meier@fh-potsdam.de

Heidmann, Frank
University of Applied
Sciences Potsdam, Germany
heidmann@fh-potsdam.de

Thom, Andreas
University of Applied
Sciences Potsdam, Germany
andreas.thom@fh-potsdam.de

MobileHCI '14, Sep 23-26 2014, Toronto, ON, Canada
ACM 978-1-4503-3004-6/14/09.
http://dx.doi.org/10.1145/2628363.2634216

Abstract
This poster is looking at how users utilize mobile applications that offer an interface for finding locations and how the way of interaction changes depending on the users' intent. Through the analysis of existing interfaces we identified 5 location search patterns. In a further evaluation of the existing patterns we tried to identify which patterns serve which users' demand for information. In a goal directed pilot study we were able to gain a first insight into the correlations of specific user requirements and location search patterns.

Author Keywords
Interface; Human Factors; Mobile; Design; Patterns

ACM Classification Keywords
H.1.2 Human Factors; H.5.2 User Interfaces

General Terms
Human Factors; Design

Introduction
Since the introduction of Apple's AppStore, which was soon accompanied by Google's PlayStore and other mobile app stores, navigational and location search applications (apps) have been an essential part of the apps offered. Those are apps that take the user's current position into account and use this data for

example to help users find locations. They can be categorized as Location Based Applications, or more general reactive Location Based Services (Küpper, 2005).

When we use the term location in this poster we mean a physical location like a shop or restaurant. When we are talking about a geo-referenced position, like an address we name it geo-location, place or position.

Related Work

Even though this type of interaction: finding locations via mobile devices, plays an important role in user requirements today, as a current study underlines (Gutierrez, 2013), we don't know much about how people use the variety of interfaces available within those apps. Most of the existing research in this field is focusing on the technological part of the process. For example on the optimization of location sensitive queries (Bouidghaghen, Tamine, & Boughanem, 2011) or the prediction of clicks or rather choices (Lymberopoulos, Zhao, König, Berberich, & Liu, 2011). Many of these projects are overlapping with research in the field of context aware applications. The research stronger related to HCI in this area is mostly looking at efficiency/clicks (Liu, Rau, Gao, 2010) or at specific interface elements (maps, lists, categories) (Iwata et al., 2010), but there is no research looking at the differences of the interfaces used in location search apps. To find out more about how users interact with those kinds of app interfaces we conducted a series of experiments.

Phase I – Extraction of Existing Patterns

In order to compare the existing interface elements we used the pattern methodology that is widely used in the HCI community (Borchers, 2000; Dearden & Finlay, 2006; Folmer, Welie, & Bosch, 2006; Granlund, Lafrenière, & Carr, 2001) to document and categorize those elements. For this purpose we looked at a large set of mobile apps from Apple's and Google's app store. Even though the selected apps serve various purposes e.g. social networking, navigation, location searching, to name a few, we were able to identify similar interface patterns throughout the whole set of apps. Since the number of patterns didn't increase even though we increased the number of examined apps, we will only discuss a subset of 8 apps (table 1).

We were able to extract 5 patterns from the analyzed apps. The five patterns *search slot, categories, result-list, map* and *filters* are not only used as standalone interface elements but also in combination, Google for example is using a combination of the search slot and filters.

For the apps overview (table 1) we further categorized the used elements in *first level* and *second level* elements. First level interface elements are elements that are available for interaction when opening the app or when switching to the search screen. All elements that appear later or need further interaction to appear are second level elements. Some of the apps offer direct feedback via the result-list while changing the search parameters, other require a submit action to update the results. As our focus was lying on the search patterns, we only clustered the result-views in list- and map-patterns. The reason why we saw need for looking into the result-views in addition to the search patterns were the map-views. As we state later, the map view is a mixture of a result-view and a search element at the same time.

App	Purpose	iOS / Android	First Level UI	Second Level UI	Result UI
Foursquare	Social Network, Location Finding	yes/yes	Map, Search	Category	Map, List
Yelp/Qype	Location Finding	yes/yes	Category, Search	List	Map, List
Around Me	Location Finding	yes/yes	Category, Search	List	Map, List
CityInfo	Location Finding, City Tour	yes/no	List, Search	Filter	Map, List
Urbany	Location Finding	yes/no	Category, Search	List	Map, List
Google Maps	Navigation, Location Finding	yes/yes	Map, Search	Category	Map, List
Google Local	Location Finding	yes/yes	Category, Search	List	Map, List
Facebook	Social Network, Location Finding	yes/yes	Search	List	Map, List

Table 1. Selected Applications and their main purpose as well as the first and second level interface patterns

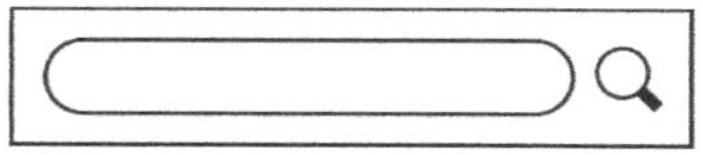

Figure 1. The Search Slot

Search Slot

The most common search interface, the search slot, prominently used by Google, is the interface element that can be found in almost every location search app. The search slot is used to enter a search term (e.g. fast food, breakfast) in order to look up a specific location or look up a place. Some apps like the Google app are using one search slot for both location and place terms. Other apps differentiate between a slot for location search terms and one for place terms. While some apps just provide an enter- and submit-functionality, other apps have auto-complete features or direct feedback results implemented. Direct feedback means that while the user is typing, the results for the incomplete search term start appearing, for example as a list.

Categories

Categories are meta-data terms under which locations are grouped (e.g. restaurants, parks, etc.). Categories can be used in an exclusive or inclusive way. The interface elements for categories are usually used in two ways. On the one hand there are apps that use categories as a first level search interface to reveal locations from a specific category (e.g. AroundMe), on the other hand there are apps that use categories as filters to narrow down a search query from a search slot. Categories were found as vertical or horizontal lists (Fig. 2 & 3). They were visualized as icons, text, or a combination of both. Beside the lists, dropdowns containing the categories were also found. Categories

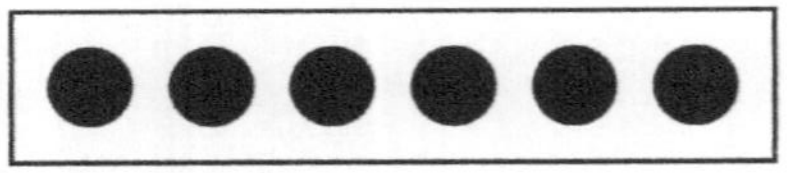

Figure 2. Horizontal icon based list of categories

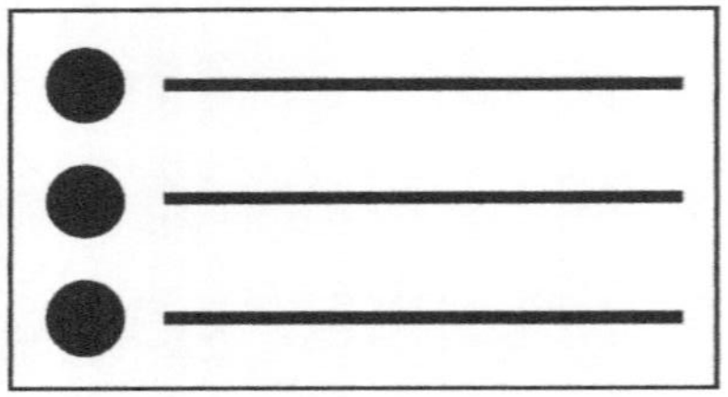

Figure 3. Vertical icon and text based list of categories

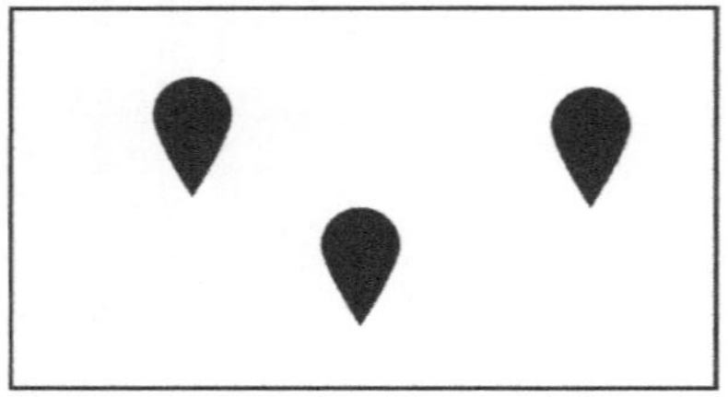

Figure 4. Map with markers

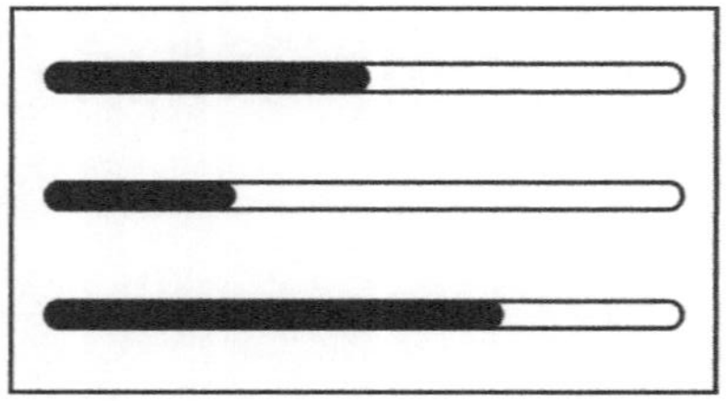

Figure 5. Filter visualization

could be subsidized under filters, as they present a predefined list of a meta data values. We have created a distinguished pattern for categories, since in contrast to the other filters, categories appear as a first level UI element in many apps.

Map

While some apps offer maps only as a result-view, other apps also offer maps as a search interface (Fig. 4). Most popular foursquare is using the map as a first level UI element, presenting a visualization of the locations available nearby. Thereby, the map serves as an interface element that can change the area on which the search query is executed. By panning the map and through that changing the boundary-box of the area in focus, the search query is modified. Beside the manipulation of the search query the map can be used to select results.

Filters

Filters are second-level search interface elements. We use this term to summarize all filter interfaces apart from categories, as they are also used as first level UI elements. Filters are meta-data elements with the purpose of refining a search query. Depending on the app those filters can be ratings, opening hours, sub-categories or price, to name a few. The modification of the search query by using a filter is, depending on the app, exclusive or inclusive. Even though we will not discuss every possible meta data value that can be presented as a filter, we want to point out that there are two classes of filters we identified. On the one hand we have *parameter filters*, those are independent from each other. On the other hand we have *sub-filters* that belong to a parent filter. The simplest examples are sub-categories.

The actual interface elements representing the filter vary throughout the apps, from sliders (Fig. 5) to dropdowns or checkbox-like-behavior. The full range of possibilities will not be discussed in this poster.

Phase II : Card Sorting

We started our experimental phase with a series of initial questionnaires with 14 tourists and locals, those gave us brief insights into what could be important in the process of finding locations. In order to construct a more solid hypothesis before we would be able to plan our study we conducted a cardsorting experiment with 10 participants. To this end we analyzed the patterns and translated them into search parameters, which could then be ranked according to the importance of finding a location. The parameters were *distance, rating, opening times, price-range, accessibility* and *weather*. Additionally, participants were asked to add parameters. Added parameters were *distance to the next public transport* and *subcategories*. Distance was ranked most important (table 2) followed by the information if the location is open and the rating.

Hypothesis

Combining the patterns we have identified in phase I, we formulate the hypothesis that *for location search tasks that are conducted on an area nearby, users will more often use a map* as a filter and search interface while in cases *when the location is further away, users will more likely use the search slot*.

Phase III : Experiment

For the experiment we developed a web-app that was connected to the Yelp/Qype API for data access. The subjects were given two tasks. The first task was to find a fastfood restaurant nearby their current position. The second task was finding a café for breakfast in a specific

Parameter	Mean	Median
Distance	1,75	1
Now Open	2,25	2
Rating	3,375	3
Price-range	4,125	4
Opening-Hours	4,125	4
Weather	6	6
Accessible	6,375	6,5

Table 2. Card sorting results (Users ranked importance from 1 = important to 7 = unimportant).

			Overall	Setup 1	Setup 2	Setup 3	Setup 4	Setup 5	Setup 6
Task 1	**Entry point**								
		Search slot	2	1	0	1	0	0	0
		Map	5	1	2	0	0	1	1
		Category	13	3	1	1	3	2	3
Task 1	**Problem solving entry**								
		Search slot	5	1	0	1	0	1	2
		Map	4	1	2	0	0	1	0
		Category	11	3	1	1	3	1	2
Task 2	**Entry point**								
		Search slot	14	5	3	1	2	1	2
		Map	3	0	0	1	1	1	0
		Category	3	0	0	0	0	1	2
Task 2	**Problem solving entry**								
		Search slot	17	5	3	1	2	3	3
		Map	0	0	0	0	0	0	0
		Category	3	0	0	1	1	0	1

Table 3. Selected Applications and their main purpose as well as the first and second level interface patterns

area further away. The app would indicate the completion of the task as soon as the participant would reach a location detail page holding the data of a location that would fit the task criteria. Every task started on a page consisting of a search slot, a map and a list of categories. From this starting point the user was just given the task, no further introduction.

To interfere with the possibility that users might just click on the UI element that comes first we made sure that throughout the experiment the elements were equally distributed vertically. This means that all possible combinations (see Fig. 7) were shown to the user. Our main focus was lying on the entry point for each task as well as on how the user would complete the task. The interaction happening in-between was logged and analyzed but will not be discussed in this poster. For logging we observed our participants as well as using logging technology on the phone.

DISCUSSION

We tested more than 25 participants. After examining the data we had to dismiss 5 sets and came down to 20 valid datasets. As we can see in the results (table 3) the entry point for the first task was in 65% of the cases the categories. In regards to the map our hypothesis has proven wrong, we have to change it to categories: *For*

Figure 7. One possible combination of the three location search interface sections.

searches on locations nearby, participants use the category interface. For the second task, the entry point is the search slot. In regards to solving the second task our second hypothesis is correct. An interesting effect that also needs more detailed observation is the fact that those participants who chose the map as an entry point for solving the second task still solved the task through the search slot in the end.

Conclusion

The study discussed above was only conducted on a small sample group, for further research this needs to be applied to a bigger sample. We only looked at two types of tasks, finding locations nearby and locations far away, in the future we would like to expand the testing on more diverse tasks. To further target the contextual and mobility factor of mobile devices, the experiment design should also be extended to include in-situ settings.

The search for locations through mobile devices is a thriving field in the area of mobile applications. We were able to identify 5 UI patterns used in apps serving this purpose. Furthermore, we conducted a pilot study revealing that categories and the search slot are important first level UI elements when conducting a search and that the map as a first level UI, in our case, doesn't lead to a successful conversion.

The results from our experiments raise the question why maps are performing worse than the other two UI elements, or rather: what are the perceptual and cognitive differences between those two elements in regards to location search?

The research conducted in this paper should provide other researchers with a starting point for looking into the behavior of users utilizing mobile apps for location search.

References

[1] Borchers, J. O. (2000). A pattern approach to interaction design (pp. 369–378). Presented at the the conference, New York, New York, USA: ACM Press.

[2] Bouidghaghen, O., Tamine, L., & Boughanem, M. (2011). Personalizing Mobile Web Search for Location Sensitive Queries. Audio, Transactions of the IRE Professional Group on, 1, 110–118.

[3] Dearden, A., & Finlay, J. (2006). Pattern languages in HCI: A critical review. Human-Computer Interaction, 21(1), 49–102.

[4] Folmer, E., Welie, M. V., & Bosch, J. (2006). Bridging patterns: An approach to bridge gaps between SE and HCI. Information and Software Technology, 48(2), 69–89.

[5] Granlund, A., Lafrenière, D., & Carr, D. A. (2001). A pattern-supported approach to the user interface design process. Presented at the Proceedings of HCI International.

[6] Gutierrez, C. (2013). 6th Annual 15miles/Neustar Localeze Local Search Usage Study Conducted by comScore, 1–18.

[7] Iwata, M., Hara, T., Shimatani, K., Mashita, T., Kiyokawa, K., Nishio, S., & Takemura, H. (2010). A Location-based Content Search System Considering Situations of Mobile Users. Procedia Computer Science, 5, 426–433.

[8] Küpper, A. (2005). Location-Based Services. John Wiley & Sons.

[9] Liu, Rau, Gao. (2010). Mobile information search for location-based information. Computers in Industry, 61(4), 8–8.

[10] Lymberopoulos, D., Zhao, P., König, C., Berberich, K., & Liu, J. (2011). Location-aware click prediction in mobile local search (pp. 413–422). Presented at the CIKM '11: Proceedings of the 20th ACM international conference on Information and knowledge management, New York, New York, USA.

GUIDES: A Graphical User Identifier Scheme Using Sketching for Mobile Web-Services

Yusuke Matsuno
Ritsumeikan University
Kusatsu, 525-8577
JAPAN
is0088vi@ed.ritsumei.ac.jp

Yu Fang
Ritsumeikan University
Kusatsu, 525-8577
JAPAN
gr0186kh@ed.ritsumei.ac.jp

Hung-Hsuan Huang
Ritsumeikan University
Kusatsu, 525-8577
JAPAN
huang@fc.ritsumei.ac.jp

Kyoji Kawagoe
Ritsumeikan University
Kusatsu, 525-8577
JAPAN
kawagoe@is.ritsumei.ac.jp

MobileHCI '14, Sep 23-26 2014, Toronto, ON, Canada
ACM 978-1-4503-3004-6/14/09.
http://dx.doi.org/10.1145/2628363.2634217

Abstract
In this paper, a novel graphical user identifier scheme for web-based mobile services. Despite a rapid progress in biological authentication technologies for user identification, the traditional text-based UserID-and-password scheme has still widely been used even for mobile web-services. In the mobile usage, a virtual keyboard is difficult to use for input texts, which causes much time to input a text. To decrease the difficulty, GUIDES (Graphical User IDEntifier using Sketching) is proposed in this paper. With GUIDES, a user can input its user identifier, called GUID (Graphical User ID) , by drawing a sketch on a mobile touchscreen device. From our experiments, it is concluded that GUIDES can enable a user input his/her User-ID more efficiently and remember it more, compared with the text-based user-id scheme.

Author Keywords
Graphical password; user authentication; login; mobile applications; web services.

ACM Classification Keywords
K.6.5. [Computing Milieux: Security and Protection].

General Terms
Security, Experimentation, Human Factors.

Introduction

Mobile users have rapidly increased owing to the progress and popularization of mobile-related technologies on CPU, memory, touch-screen, and networking devices. The users can access to many web services at any time and from any place with mobile equipment in the same way of using PCs. Most of the web services provide a user a user-customized function. For example, a web-based e-mail service is a service providing a particular user with sending and receiving e-mails only related to the user. A user of an internet shopping service can access to the user's shopping history which is only accessible to the user. In order to realize such a customized web-service, the traditional user identifier method uses a pair of user-id and password.

Although this user identifier scheme based on the user-id and password is simple and popular in PC environment, this scheme is not appropriate for a mobile user. This scheme has crucial problems, when a user manipulates a mobile device, such as 1) it is difficult for a mobile user to input his/her user-id and password via a virtual keyboard, and 2) a user frequently forgets his/her user-id and password which the user registered for a special web service. To prevent the above problems, a user stores the user-id and its password in a mobile device or writes down it on a memo. Some password management application services are available to manage a pair of user-id and password per a web service. Although they are practically useful, their usage environment may be limited in a situation when a different device necessary to be temporally used.

In this paper, a novel user-ID scheme, Graphical User IDEntifier using Sketching, called GUIDES, is proposed in order for a mobile user to input the user-id without a virtual keyboard, only by drawing a sketch on a mobile touchscreen device. In our GUIDES scheme, the sketch (Graphical User ID, GUID), drawn by a user, is transformed into a symbol sequence, followed by transforming it into an actual internal user-id used in a web service if necessary. The symbol sequence, called Symbolic-GUID, shortly Sym-GUID, plays an important role in our scheme, because the Sym-GUID is designed not only for reconstruction of the GUID from the Sym-GUID but also for used as transferable and memorable information of GUID.

In this paper, we focus only on the user-ID in the user authentication scheme that is based on the user-id and the password. Thus, both biological authentication device usage and easy-to-remember password development, such as graphical password, are out of scope of this paper.

Related Work

Although pur method proposed here is not a graphical password scheme, many graphical password schemes has been studied for the last decade [1]. Graphical password is classified as drawing-based and selection-based schemes. The typical examples in the first category are Draw-a-secret (DAS) [4], TMD [2], TMO [5], and Pass-Go [6], while the second category includes Passpoint [7]. Many graphical passwords are mainly proposed to prevent a user from dictionary attacks and shoulder-surfing attacks. None of the graphical passwords can be used as replacement of user-id.

Despite developments of the graphical passwords as

well as those of the user authentication frameworks, no user-id schemes as a replacement of text-based user-id have yet been proposed, especially appropriate for mobile users.

Requirements for graphical-based User ID
There are many schemes on text-based user-id. The typical schemes are classified into the three categories: 1) fixed-length alphanumeric strings, e.g. ABC12345 and XYZ98765, and 2) variable-length alphanumeric strings, e.g. someone123 and something99, and 3) use of e-mail address as a user-id, e.g. username@URLdomain.com. Any of the text-based user-id schemes has the following characteristics. 1) the more length it is, the more difficult to remember, 2) the id space is large enough to identify an individual user, 3) it is less necessary to hide a user-id than passwords, and 4) a keyboard is necessary to input a user-id.

From considering the above characteristics, a graphic-based user-id scheme has the following five requirements.

First, the user-id space should be large enough to register a large number of users and to enable each user identified by a user-id. If 8 alphanumeric digits are used as a text-based user-id, the space size is approximately 10^{12}. Therefore, the graphical user-id should support such a user-id space size. Second, neither a keyboard nor an additional special device is used for user-id input. It is tedious for a mobile user to log-in every time when accessing a web service using a virtual keyboard. Therefore, a friendlier user-authentication scheme, in which it is not assumed to use a keyboard, should be supported. The graphical user-id should be inputted only using the mobile touch-screen device. Third, it should be reproducible and transferable. Even if a user forgets his/her user-id, it should be transferred and provided to the user. Fourth, it should be easy to remember and to recall. As in the password, the user-id should be easy to remember and to recall without writing it on a memo for future reference. Last, an acceptable user-id candidate should be suggested when the user fails to register due to an already-registered user-id. This requirement is necessary when a user intends to register his/her preferred user-id and the user-id has already been registered by others. In this situation, it is desirable for the user to receive a suggested user-id. The last one is an important point to differentiate our scheme from graphical password schemes such as DAS.

GUIDES-I looks similar to Android pattern lock or existing grid-based graphical password schemes such as DAS, TMO, and TMD. However, there are important differences between GUIDES-I and the pattern lock scheme and grid-based graphical password schemes. First, these scheme cannon be used as the user-id, because the size of the user-id space for the scheme is much smaller than that in GUIDES-I. Moreover, these schemes cannot be extended to improve recall and remembering abilities, fundamentally. Although this password can be encoded to an alphanumeric text, currently no text distance definitions for password differentiation are used. Lastly, the user-id should be unique, while passwords can be duplicated.

GUIDES
The basic idea of GUIDES (Graphical User IDEntifier using Sketching) is to use the hand-written signature which is the smart, natural, and practical way of user

identification in a daily life. The hand-written signature is used to identify an individual or to indicate a proof of identity. Because the hand-written signature is easy for a user to remember and can easily be kept in user's memory, it is appropriate to use the signature scheme as the graphical user-id. However, a scheme using the hand-written signature as user-id, cannot meet the previously described requirements for the graphical user-id. Currently, the identification success rate of hand-written signature recognition methods is not high even in the best signature recognition method [3]. It is not practical to manage a large amount of users using the recognition methods. The model cannot transform the signature into the encoded symbolized representation of the signature. Moreover, most of the current signature recognition methods assume the use of a digitizing tablet with a pen-pressure sensor.

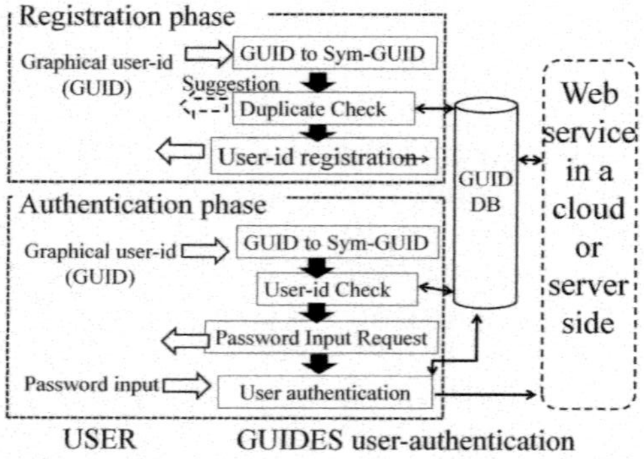

Figure 1: GUIDES architecture.

GUIDES basically uses the signature scheme for developing the graphical user-id. GUIDES provides a user to register and to write a user's signature in a restricted format. A user is assumed to know such a restricted signature format. The actual restrictions on GUIDES signatures are defined in implementing the GUIDES, which described later.

The basic architecture of GUIDES is shown in Figure 1. First, a user registers a graphical user-id GUID in the registration phase. The system transforms the GUID to its symbolic representation, Sym-GUID. The Sym-GUID is necessary to make a user-id reproducible and transferable. The Sym-GUID is checked if there is an existing Sym-GUID in the GUID DB or not. If there is one, then the system suggests another GUID, similar to the user inputted GUID. If not, the GUID is stored in DB.

In the authentication phase, after obtaining a GUID from a user, the GUID is also transformed to the Sym-GUID as it is in the registration phase. If the GUID exists in the GUID database, then the user is requested to input his/her password. After both GUID and the password are received, then the user authentication process starts.

Formally, GUIDES is described as follow. Assume that there is the GUID database $DB = \{d_i\}$, where d_i is a triplet of GUID, g_i, Sym-GUID s_i and user profile u_i for each user. s_i is obtained using a transformation function $F()$ for g_i, that is $s_i = F(g_i)$. The inverse transformation $F^{-1}(s_i)$ is an approximation of g_i. Support that a user wants to register g_q, the s_q is obtained from $F(g_q)$. The s_q is checked whether there exists an s_k or not, such that $distance(s_q, s_k) \leq \epsilon_1$, for $s_k \in DB$. If not exists, then the triplet of (g_q, s_q, u_q) are added to DB. If s_k exists, $g_{q'}$ is constructed and suggested to the user such that $\epsilon_1 < distance(s_{q'}, s_k) \leq \epsilon_2$ and $distance(s_q, s_{q'}) \leq \epsilon_3$. In the authentication phase, given the user input GUID g_q, $s_q = F(g_q)$ is obtained. Then, the s_q is checked as $distance(s_q, s_p) \leq \epsilon_1$ for $s_p \in DB$. If exists, then the obtained s_p is the user GUID, followed by password input.

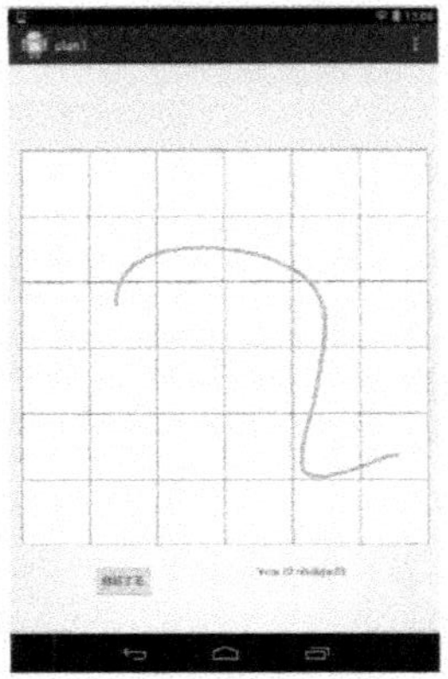

Figure 2: A GUID.

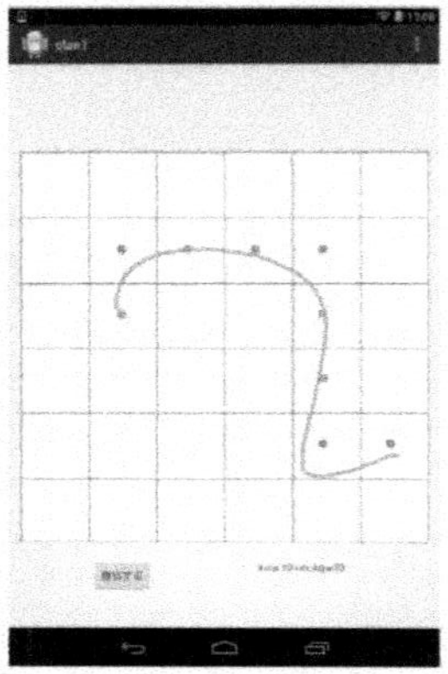

Figure 3: GUIDES-I example.

First Implementation of GUIDES (GUIDES-I)

Several versions of GUIDES are planned to develop: GUIDES-I, -II, and -III. We developed the first GUIDES (GUIDES-I) to demonstrate and to evaluate the idea and the characteristics of GUIDES. GUIDES-II is another implementation based on trajectories on discretized regions with smaller width, while GUIDES-III is the implementation based on hand-written signatures. The purpose of GUIDES-I is only to demonstrate and to evaluate the idea of GUIDES, thus the GUID and Sym-GUID formats are very simple enough to develop GUIDES-I. In GUIDES-I, a user draws a sketch on a touch-screen of a mobile device. A GUID, g_i, is represented as a trajectory, a sequence of pairs of points. GUID is transformed into a sequence of grid symbols, because the input area is decomposed into grids of n_x times n_y. As a grid symbol is assigned to each grid, the Sym-GUID s_i of g_i is easily calculated from a point in the trajectory grid regions.

An example of GUID and sym-GUID in GUIDE-I are shown in Figure 2 and 3, for $n_x = n_y = 6$. The sym-GUID in this figure is nhijkqw23" because the symbols are assigned from the left-to-right and from the-top-to-bottom of grids. The text representations can be differentiated according to the distance definition used. In GUIDES-I, the distance between texts are used, for calculating the distance between Sym-GUIDs.

In GUIDES-I, a user must draw the sketch, starting from the first grid and ending the last grid in the same grid sequence, the Sym-GUID, which were registered. Even if a sketch can include multiple crossings, it can be transformed to a Sym-GUID. The length of the sketch is fundamentally unlimited, although too large length of sketches cannot be visually distinguished. The inverse transformation function F^{-1} is represented by a polygonal line, which is constructed by connected the center of grids included in the Sym-GUID in order.

GUIDES-I meets the first three requirements described above. The user-id space size is large enough to manage the order of 10^6users in the case when the average grid sequence length is 10. GUIDES-I all provides a user with a unique function called SUGGEST for the last requirement. We will omit the details of the function due to space limitations.

Experiments and discussions

GUIDES-I was implemented on Android 4.3 devices using JAVA, Then, we conducted three experiments to evaluate GUIDES-I. The experiments include measurements of success rate, input time, and memorability. First, we checked success rate, meaning how much the GUID is correctly inputted (EX1). The success rate is defined as (Number-of-successes / Number-of-Trials). Second, the time for inputting GUID is measured (EX3). Last, we conducted the same experiment as EX1 after three days, to check the memorability. In all three experiments, the text-based user-id scheme is compared with GUIDES-I.

Ten participants were recruited to join in these experiments. Each participant first received his/her GUID which is automatically generated by our user-id generation programs, for fair comparisons. The length of the text user-id was set to 7 and the average length of GUID was 9.2. These length values were chosen to create the same user-id space. The GUIDs for ten-thousand users were generated by the GUID generation program and stored in the test user DB.

	GUIDES-I	Text-based user-id
EX1	93.3% (13.3)	96.7% (10.0)
EX2	3.56 sec. (1.08)	8.47 sec. (2.80)
EX3	83.3% (30.7)	66.7% (44.7)

Table 1: Experimental results: average (standard deviation).

Each participant input his/her GUID three times in the user authentication phase. The average success rate is calculated from results of the success rate per participant. The average input time is calculated by aggregating all the input time for authentications.

The EX1 results of the success rate are shown in the top of Table 1. Both the success rates of the text-based user-id and that of GUIDES-I are more than 90%, although the former was superior to the latter a little. Their standard deviations were also almost the same. Welch's t test was conducted, and showed that no significant difference between GUIDES-I and the text-based user-id ($p = 0.5566$, $t = -0.6$, $df = 16.69$).

The middle of Table 1 shows the EX2 results. The average time of GUIDES-I was lower than that of the text-based user-id. We also conducted Welch's t-test and obtained ($p = 0.000$, $t = -8.800$, $df = 37.48$). Thus, it was concluded that there was a significant difference between GUIDES-I and the text-based user-id in terms of user-id input time between the two schemes.

The last of Table 1 indicates that the average success rate of GUIDES-I became larger than that of the text-based user-id. We also checked Welch's t-test for the results of EX1 and the results of this experiment for both scheme. The obtained values of GUIDES-I were ($p = 0.253$, $t = 1.2$, $df = 12.30$), showing no significant difference even three days later. However, the Welch's t-test for the text-based user-id showed the significant difference occurred three days later ($p = 0.0782$, $t = 1.9641$, $df = 9.896$).

Conclusion

In this paper, we proposed a novel user-ID scheme, called GUIDES, in order for a mobile user to input the user-id without a virtual keyboard. The first GUIDES, called GUIDES-I, was implemented to demonstrate the idea of GUIDES. Our experiment results showed that GUIDES-I was superior to the conventional text-based user-id from viewpoints of input time and memorability. The remaining issues include the next implementation (GUIDES-II) and more detailed evaluations.

Acknowledgments

This work was partially supported by MEXT Prog. for the Strategic Res. Found. at Private Univ., 2013-17

References

[1] Biddle, R., Chiasson, S., and Van Oorschot, P. Graphical passwords: Learning from the first twelve years. *ACM Comput. Surv. 44*, 4 (2012), 1–41.

[2] Chiang, H.-Y., and Chiasson, S. Improving user authentication on mobile devices: A touchscreen graphical password. In *Proc. of MobileHCI'13* (2013), 251–260.

[3] Houmani, N., et al. Evaluating online signature algorithms depending on the quality of signatures. *Pattern Recognition 45*, 3 (2012), 993–1003.

[4] Jermyn, I., Mayer, A., et al. The design and analysis of graphical passwords. In *Proc. of USENIX'99* (1999).

[5] Luca, D., et al. Touch me once and i know it's you!: Implicit authentication based on touch screen patterns. In *Proc. of ACM CHI'12* (2012), 987–996.

[6] Tao, H., and Adams, C. Pass-go: A proposal to improve the usability of graphical passwords. *Int. J. Network Security 7*, 2 (2008), 273–292.

[7] Wiedenbeck, S., Waters, J., et al. Passpoints: Design and longitudinal evaluation of a graphical password system. *Int. J. of Human-Computer Studies 63*, 1 (2005), 102–127.

MuGIS - Multi-user Geographical Information System

Sebastian Schöffel
Computer Graphics & HCI
University of Kaiserslautern
67663 Kaiserslautern, Germany
schoeffel@cs.uni-kl.de

Johannes Schwank
Computer Graphics & HCI
University of Kaiserslautern
67663 Kaiserslautern, Germany
schwank@cs.uni-kl.de

Achim Ebert
Computer Graphics & HCI
University of Kaiserslautern
67663 Kaiserslautern, Germany
ebert@cs.uni-kl.de

MobileHCI'14, September 23–26, 2014, Toronto, ON, Canada.
ACM 978-1-4503-3004-6/14/09.
http://dx.doi.org/10.1145/2628363.2634219

Abstract
Collaboration between users of a system is often a crucial factor for reaching given goals in an effective and efficient way. However, in many application domains, the current systems do not sufficiently support collaborative work (sometimes they even don't support it at all). One good example is geographical information systems (GIS), that usually only follow an *one user at one time* approach. In this paper, we present the development of a scalable **M**ulti-**u**ser **G**eographical **I**nformation **S**ystem (*MuGIS*). With *MuGIS* it is now possible to integrate large display environments with mobile smart devices for remote control. The system is deployed as a client-server architecture. It uses the NASA World Wind Java framework and SOAP web services for communication. On the client side, all common mobile smart devices are supported. The underlying concept provides different user roles and multi-user identification.

Author Keywords
Geographical Information System; Mobile Devices; Collaboration; Multi-User

ACM Classification Keywords
H.5.2 [User interfaces]: Graphical user interfaces (GUI); K.4.3 [Organizational Impacts]: Computer-supported collaborative work.

Introduction & Related Work

With nowadays raising collaboration possibilities, more and more people are working together in many application domains. Today it is common to use a large scale display or a projector for showing information and collaborating. However, these systems are limited to one user input at the same time and therefore are not very appropriate for collaborative work. This is especially true when interacting with graphical representations.

On the other hand, mobile smart devices are widely used for business tasks now. One of the first projects for using mobile devices as remote controllers for PCs and appliances were the *Pittsburgh Pebbles PDA Project*[1] as well as the work of Myers [6] [7]. Also a lot of work has been done by Borchers et al. (e.g., Stanford Interactive Room [2]) to support collaborative work on large scale devices and Finke et al. [4] who are using mobile devices for interaction with large displays.

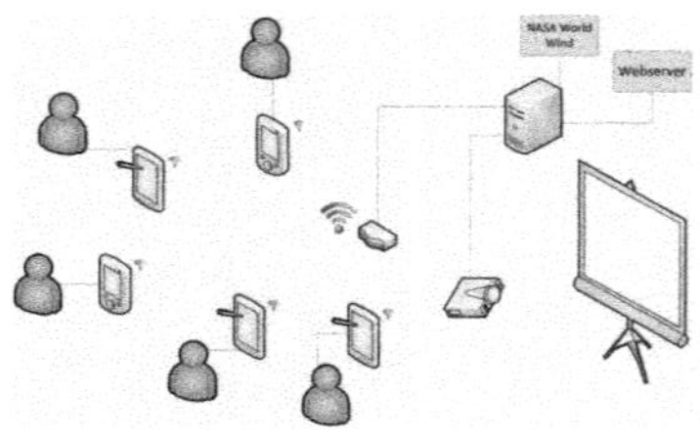

Figure 1: *MuGIS* system architecture.

Our research focuses on closing the gap between collaborative work, large display environments, and mobile smart devices for remote control. This gap is very obvious in many application domains. One prominent example is the analysis and visualization of geospatial data. Here, the present geographical information systems (GIS) [5] do not even support multiple users interacting simultaneously.

Therefore, we have designed a scalable multi-user geographical information system *(MuGIS)* for supporting collaboration when working with geospatial data. To reach this goal, we connected mobile smart devices like the Apple iPad as intuitive interaction devices with GIS. For the backend, a platform-independent, easy customizable and open-source geographical information system framework is needed. The Nasa World Wind Java SDK [8] nicely fits to these needs. Based on this SDK, a client-server architecture has been developed. The server is running on a common desktop PC presenting global information via a large scale display or a projector, while the clients are represented with common mobile devices based on iOS and Android. The communication is done via SOAP web services.

One of the main aspects of our system is the possibility for multiple users to work collaboratively with one single geographical information system. With the developed system, the following tasks can be performed:

- Users can monitor the global map with mobile devices.
- Users can navigate the global map with mobile devices.
- Users can change the visibility of layers with mobile devices.
- Users can add annotations to the global map which are being synchronized to all other clients.

In the following, we describe the system architecture and workflow concepts of *MuGIS*.

System Architecture

Figure 1 shows a general overview of *MuGIS*. It can be seen that multiple clients can access the server application via WLAN with arbitrary mobile smart devices.

The Large Display Device (LDD, e.g. high resolution projector, Digital Interactive Public Pinboards [9], Microsoft Surface) shows the global map provided by the NASA World Wind SDK. For this purpose, the server application features a webserver which receives the calls from the mobile smart devices (clients), and maps them to the methods of the underlying World Wind SDK for data manipulation. The results can directly be seen on the LDD (visual feedback). On the LDD, an overall view of the scenario is displayed (for situational awareness), while on the mobile devices it is possible (due to the very high resolution) to show desired parts of the map in full detail. The relation between the mobile devices and the LDD implements the overview+detail principle [3]. For an abstract system overview see Figure 2.

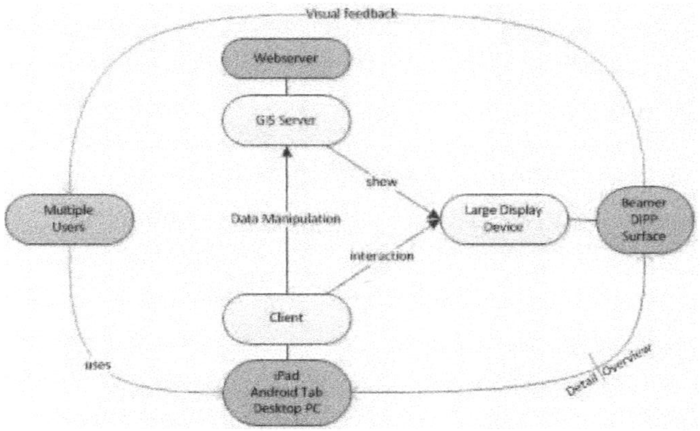

Figure 2: Abstract MuGIS system overview.

Workflow Concepts

Unfortunately, many problems can occur when multiple users work together. Therefore, a multi-user concept has been developed which enables multiple users to interact simultaneously to answer the following questions:

- Which user can perform which actions?
- Which actions can be performed simultaneously?
- Who has the priority when two users compete with each other?
- How to distinguish between actions performed by several users?

User Roles
In certain domains, an administrator is useful for managing user rights and certain critical tasks. In other domains a flat user hierarchy might be useful to get the maximum effort on a specific task, because a high parallelism is possible. While simultaneous navigation actions would lead to confusion, the parallel placing of annotations on the map is reasonable. Therefore, a mix of both approaches instead is the best approach for multi-user interaction with geographical information systems. This leads to three different user roles:

- *Viewer:* standard, read-only user.
- *Master user:* able to perform actions that should only be performed by one user at a time (e.g. moving the map).
- *Collaborative user:* closes the gap between viewer and master user, is able to create global annotations.

To ensure that only one user has master user rights at the same time, a *permission-grant-and-request concept* has been developed. Therefore, the processes *request control* and *release control* have been implemented.

- *Request control:* If a user wants to perform navigational tasks with the map or show/hide information, the following 3 steps are performed:

	Viewer	Collaborative user	Master user
Monitor map	✔	✔	✔
Monitor annotations	✔	✔	✔
Add annotations	✘	✔	✔
Navigate	✘	✘	✔
Change layers	✘	✘	✔

Figure 3: User permission concept.

1. Check if anyone else has the master user right.
2. If there is a master user, notify this user and set the own state to *waiting*.
3. If not, get the master user privileges and perform the desired map actions.

- *Release control:* The user releases his master user rights after the desired actions are performed. To assist the collaborative approach, the current master user gets notified if another user applies for these rights. The steps of the release process are simple:

  1. Release the master user rights.
  2. The user becomes a viewer or a collaborative user.
  3. The next waiting user gets the master user rights.

An overview which of the three user groups (viewer, collaborative user, master) are allowed to perform which actions is shown in Figure 3.

User Identification
To distinguish between user-created objects (e.g. placed annotations, remarks), different approaches exist. Two of them are presented in the following:

- *Labeling:*

  Users can create objects like annotations, typically having a text describing them. To mark these objects as created by a specific user, the user name can be attached to the title (e.g. *John: Berlin*). In contrast to LDDs, mobile devices have special requirements. Since screen space is limited, it can be reasonable to hide some facts if currently not enough space is available. Therefore, it can be useful to show additional information (like the user name) only if the user requests them, to keep the view on the mobile device as easy and clear as possible.

- *Color Coding:*

  According to Ware [10], colors can be used as an extremely effective code. When a user connects to the server, he gets one of twelve easy distinguishable colors assigned. All annotations the user placed on the map are displayed in the according color to distinguish which annotation belongs to which user.

MuGIS Server

For implementing the server, NASA World Wind Java SDK version 2 is used as a basis. The communication with the clients is realized via SOAP. The application is running on a Windows 7 desktop PC, but due to the platform independence of Java, OSX and Linux are also supported.

Figure 4: Screenshot of the MuGIS server application.

Figure 4 shows a screenshot of the server application with a global map showing Toronto, Canada. Two landmarks have been placed from two different users displayed with two different colors for user identification (red, green).

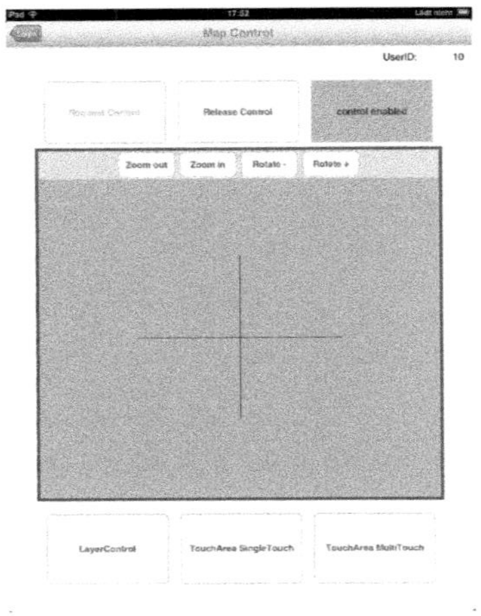

Figure 5: Screenshot of the MuGIS client control view.

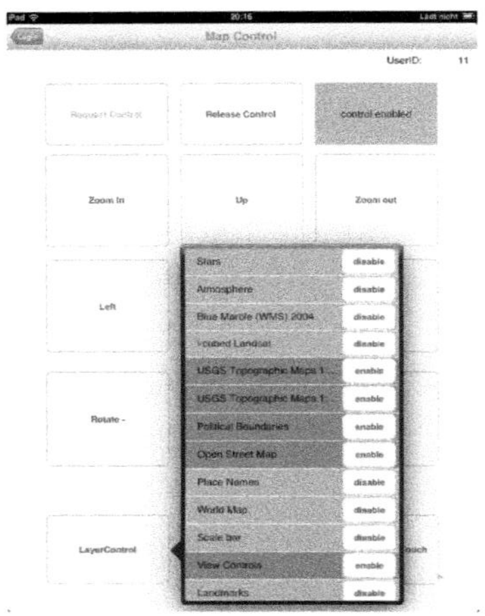

Figure 6: Screenshot of the MuGIS client layer control.

MuGIS Client

The client has been implemented for both, iOS and Android. After starting the app and successful registration on the server, the user is able to switch between the control view and the map view which are now described in detail.

- *Control View:*

  For controlling the map, different techniques are implemented to reach a wide range of user groups with different technical background. The simplest interaction is via touchable buttons, which are labeled with the corresponding action (e.g. up, zoom in). The second option implemented is a single touch area. The idea is using touch gestures instead of buttons, so that the user does not necessarily need to look at the input device to hit the desired button. The third approach is a multi-touch based interaction metaphor that also supports the OS-based default gestures for zooming and rotating. An example of the control view can be seen in figure 5.

  Another interaction possibility is the layer control (see figure 6). This enables the user to switch the visibility of different layers on the global map.

- *Map View:*

  The second key feature of the MuGIS client is the map synchronization and interaction feature. This means that on the one hand, users are able to see exactly the same map excerpt on the mobile device as on the global server map. On the other hand, they can place landmarks, which can be seen on the global map as well as on every other client map.

For synchronizing the client map with the server map, the client application requests the center coordinates and the zoom level of the global map frequently. The synchronization of the landmarks is done in a similar way, but instead of the center coordinates, the list of all landmarks is requested and compared with the local landmarks. If new landmarks are available, they got placed on the local map, or deleted respectively.

Placing landmarks on the global map is quite easy. Each collaborative user can add a landmark on his mobile device by touching the desired point on the map and providing a title (see figure 7). The landmark is automatically saved on the server, placed on the global map and delivered to all other clients.

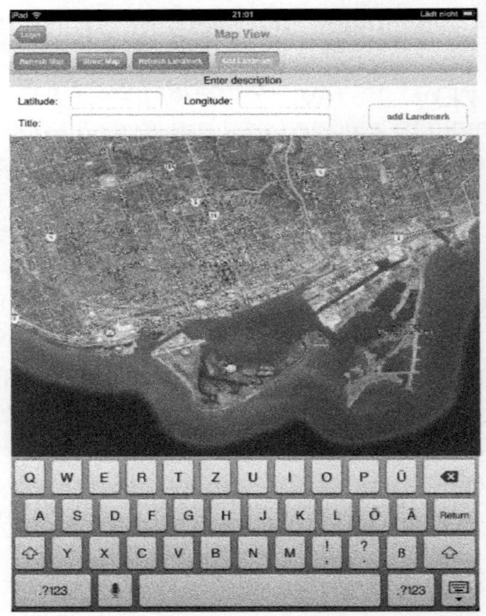

Figure 7: Screenshot of the MuGIS client map view.

Conclusion & Future Work

In this paper, we presented a scalable multi-user geographical information system, called *MuGIS*, which allows multiple users to interact simultaneously on one global geographical information system. One of the biggest advantages of our system is the platform independence as well as the open source license of the used framework. Furthermore, we designed and implemented client software for two of the most common mobile operation systems, iOS and Android.

Two important concepts for a collaborative environment have been developed, namely the user roles and the user identification. For controlling the map on the client device, we implemented and compared three different input techniques to reach a wide range of users, even for users without experience in using mobile devices.

For future work, we plan to add new features to the system (e.g. new annotation types, free hand drawing). In addition, we need to optimize the input interfaces and interaction metaphors to increase the intuitive behavior and the user satisfaction. Therefore, a combined control and map view might be helpful. To get expert user feedback, a formal user study with domain experts in geographical information systems can help for further improvements.

Acknowledgements

This project was funded by the German Federal Ministry of Education and Research (BMBF, #033W009A).

References

[1] Carnegie Mellon University - The Pittsburgh Pebbles PDA Project. http://www.pebbles.hcii.cmu.edu, 2009.

[2] Borchers, J., Ringel, M., Tyler, J., and Fox, A. Stanford interactive workspaces: A framework for physical and graphical user interface prototyping. *Wireless Commun. 9*, 6 (Dec. 2002), 64–69.

[3] Cockburn, A., Karlson, A., and Bederson, B. B. A review of overview+detail, zooming, and focus+context interfaces. *ACM Comput. Surv. 41*, 1 (Jan. 2009), 2:1–2:31.

[4] Finke, M., Kaviani, N., Wang, I., Tsao, V., Fels, S., and Lea, R. Investigating distributed user interfaces across interactive large displays and mobile devices. In *Proceedings of the International Conference on Advanced Visual Interfaces*, AVI '10, ACM (New York, NY, USA, 2010), 413–413.

[5] Goodchild, M. F. Geographic information systems. *Research Methods in Geography* (2010), 376–91.

[6] Myers, B. A. Using handhelds and pcs together. *Commun. ACM 44*, 11 (Nov. 2001), 34–41.

[7] Myers, B. A. Using handhelds for wireless remote control of PCs and appliances. *Interacting with Computers 17*, 3 (2005), 251 – 264. Special Theme - Papers from Members of the Editorial Boards.

[8] NASA. World Wind Java SDK. http://worldwind.arc.nasa.gov/java, 2013.

[9] Olech, P.-S., Cernea, D., Meyer, H., Schöffel, S., and Ebert, A. Digital interactive public pinboards for disaster and crisis management : Concept and prototype design. In *Proceedings of the 2012 International Conference on Information and Knowledge Engineering (IKE '12) at the 2012 World Congress in Computer Science, Computer Engineering, and Applied Computing (WorldComp '12)* (2012). IKE2460.

[10] Ware, C. *Information Visualization: Perception for Design*. Morgan Kaufmann Publishers Inc., San Francisco, CA, USA, 2004.

AudioTorch: Using a Smartphone as Directional Microphone in Virtual Audio Spaces

Florian Heller
RWTH Aachen University
52056 Aachen
flo@cs.rwth-aachen.de

Jan Borchers
RWTH Aachen University
52056 Aachen
borchers@cs.rwth-aachen.de

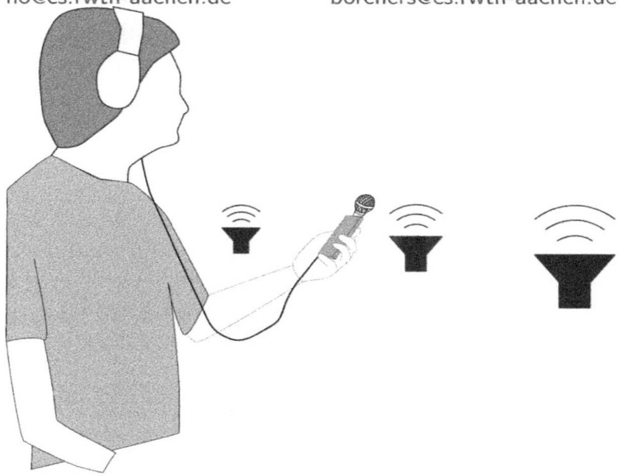

Figure 1: AudioTorch converts your mobile phone into a virtual directional microphone to experience audio augmented reality scenes.

MobileHCI'14, September 23–26, 2014, Toronto, ON, Canada.
ACM 978-1-4503-3004-6/14/09.
http://dx.doi.org/10.1145/2628363.2634220

Abstract
Mobile audio augmented reality systems can be used in a series of applications, e.g., as a navigational aid for visually impaired or as audio guide in museums. The implementation of such systems usually relies on head orientation data, requiring additional hardware in form of a digital compass in the headphones. As an alternative we propose AudioTorch, a system that turns a smartphone into a virtual directional microphone. This metaphor, where users move the device to detect virtual sound sources, allows quick orientation and easy discrimination between proximate sources, even with simplified rendering algorithms. We compare the navigation performance of head orientation measurement to AudioTorch. A lab study with 18 users showed the rate of correctly recognized sources to be significantly higher with AudioTorch than with head-tracking, while task completion times did not differ significantly. The presence in the virtual environment received similar ratings for both conditions.

Author Keywords
Virtual Audio Spaces; Mobile Devices; Audio Augmented Reality; Navigation.

ACM Classification Keywords
H.5.1. [Information Interfaces and Presentation (e.g. HCI)]: Multimedia Information Systems

Introduction

Audio augmented reality systems overlay a physical space with a virtual audio space that the users experience via headphones. This audio space contains several virtual sound sources which, through special filtering, are perceived as emerging from the physical space. These virtual sources can be part of a game [11], contain information about certain assets [1, 2, 15], or be used as a navigational aid that does not rely on the visual sense [4, 6, 10, 13]. To create a realistic experience with sources that appear to be fixed in the physical space independent of the orientation of the listener's head, this orientation has to be measured. This requires a digital compass mounted to the headphones or some other tracking technology. This additional hardware has to be available, powered, and connected to the device rendering the spatial audio. While early implementations used external hardware to render the audio [7, 14], current implementations rely on smartphones for a personal and decentralized rendering [2, 12, 13]. Since current smartphones are equipped with an internal compass, all necessary components are available in the user's hand, and by omitting the need for additional hardware, the distribution of mobile audio augmented reality systems (MAARS) is reduced to a simple download. We propose to use the smartphone as a virtual directional microphone, a metaphor that is not realistic but still results in an engaging experience. We evaluated this metaphor and compared it against the same rendering using head orientation data in a navigation task. A study with 18 participants revealed that the number of correctly detected sound sources is significantly higher with AudioTorch while the task completion time does not differ significantly. The perceived presence is rated similarly high for both conditions.

Related Work

Different aspects of interaction with virtual audio spaces have been analyzed over the last two decades, but most projects concentrate on aspects of the implementation, e.g., rendering quality or tracking latency.

Loomis [7] and Mariette [9] analyzed the paths and head orientation of people walking towards virtual sound sources. Results show that in the case of a large space, users do an initial, large head turn to get an estimate of the direction, followed by smaller movements to stay on the path towards the source.

Heller et al. [3] conducted a navigation experiment comparing head tracking to device tracking. Results indicate that using device orientation does not dramatically influence the navigation performance nor the perceived presence. During the trials, participants were not told which source of orientation was used. Measurements show that the device was aligned to the body most of the time, meaning that the participants did not take advantage of the device's mobility. By telling the users which tracking is active, we want to encourage them to move the device around to simplify navigation.

Marentakis et al. [8] evaluated pointing as an interaction technique in virtual audio spaces. While walking, participants experienced a sound coming from somewhere around them and had to point to that source. Whenever the heading of the pointing gesture was within a certain angle from the actual position of the source, a feedback sound was presented to facilitate the task. Results show that this technique is feasible to interact with virtual audio spaces, e.g., auditory menus where the items are arranged spatially around the head [5]. While our interaction is similar, we do not focus on targeting a certain sound source, but to create an auditory image of

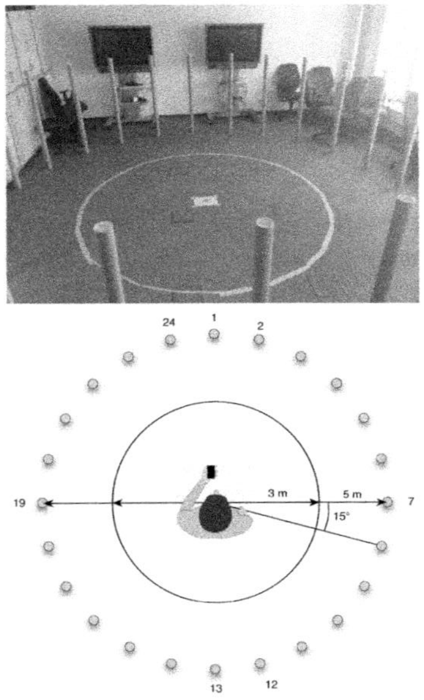

Figure 2: We placed 24 virtual sound sources, spaced by 15° in a circle of 5 m diameter. Participants had to start every trial standing in the center, facing source no. 1. They could move freely within the inner circle of 3 m diameter.

the source positions for navigation. The work presented in this paper fits in between systems focussing on realism on the one hand [9, 14], and systems that do not integrate heading information into the rendering [4, 15, 10].

Implementation

We measured the head position 34 times per second using a Ubisense[1] location tracking system with an accuracy of 5-10 cm. The head orientation was measured using an HMC6343 tilt-compensated digital compass with an update rate of 10 Hz, device orientation was measured with the on-board chip of the iPhone 4S which has an update rate of approximately 15 Hz. Both sensors have similar characteristics and the heading information was adjusted to be the same for both. This data was fed into the spatial audio rendering algorithm integrated to the OpenAL framework in iOS 5.1.1. It bases on the spherical head model and includes the following filter factors: interaural level difference, interaural time difference, head filtering, and a frequency-dependent distance filtering. To reduce the impact of front-backward confusion, we applied a low-pass filter to the sources that were behind the user's head. The filter intensity was interpolated linearly from 0dB to 36dB for sources between 90° and 180° azimuth angle. This algorithm, although less realistic than high-end systems based on head-related transfer functions (HRTF), is a good representative of spatial rendering algorithms for mobile devices.

Evaluation

We placed 24 carton tubes of 150 cm height in a circle with 5 m diameter and spaced by 15° (cf. Fig. 2). The tubes were used as physical representations of the virtual sound sources. The audio rendering algorithm used the orientation either from the head or from the device.

[1]http://www.ubisense.net

Participants started every trial standing in the center of the circle facing source no. 1 and were instructed to find the source currently audible as quickly as possible. In a real scenario, e.g., a museum or a public place, users might not be able to get close to the sources. To account for this factor, and to make sure that the experiment reveals the impact of orientation measurement, we restricted the movement to an inner circle of 3 m diameter, which forced the participants to determine the exact sound source from a distance of approximately 1 m. We used an audio sample of a male voice reciting colors at a fast pace, such that it can be considered a continuous audio source.

We used a within-subjects design with a balanced order of conditions and the order of active sound sources was randomized using Latin squares. Every participant had to navigate to all 24 sources in the *head*- and *device*-measurement condition and had to complete a 10-trial training before each condition. We measured the time between the users starting the trial by pressing the start button on the smartphone until they confirmed standing in front of the audible source by pressing a second button. Participants had to name the source that they assumed was playing. We recorded the paths the users took to walk to the sources, along with the orientation fed into the rendering algorithm. After each condition, participants had to fill out a questionnaire asking about their perceived presence in the virtual environment [16]. Answers had to be reported on a 5-point Likert scale.

Results

We recruited 18 participants (5 female) to complete the study. Their age ranged from 22 to 38 (M=28) and most had a computer science background. The rate of correctly

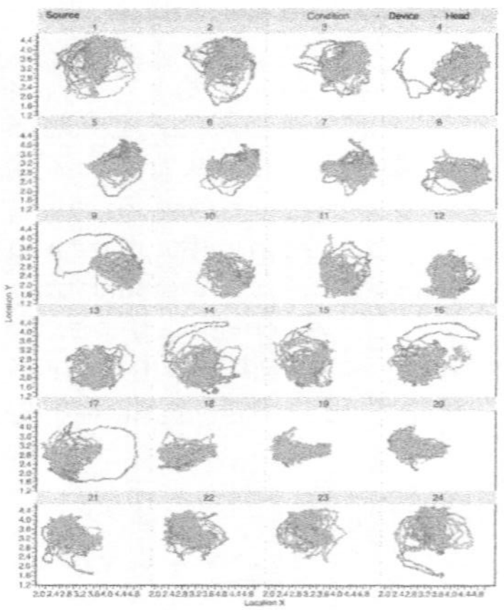

Figure 3: The recorded paths of participants localizing the audible source. There is no substantial difference between both conditions (except for one outlier in the device condition).

localized sources was higher in the *device* condition (M=0.76, SD=0.21) than in the *head* condition (M=0.5, SD=0.17). A pairwise student's-t test showed this difference to be significant ($t(18)=-4.09$, $p=0.0003$). However, nearly all errors are only off by one source from the correct result. If we consider a source to the left or to the right of the actual source as correct, then we achieve recognition rates of 98% for device tracking and 96% for head tracking. The task completion time was nearly the same in both conditions (*Head*: M=9.92, SD=4.01; *Device*: M=10.11, SD=4.11). Plotting the paths taken to the sources did not reveal substantial differences (cf. Fig 3). The cumulative distance during head-tracking trials (M=8.28 m, SD=3.28) was nearly identical to the device-tracking trials (M=8.32 m, SD=2.63). An analysis of variance showed the difference to be non-significant ($F(1)=0.0438$, $p=0.8342$).

None of the ratings of the questionnaire showed to be significantly different between the two conditions, which indicates that the perceived presence is equal. The ability to localize sounds nearly received the same overall rating for head-(M=4.0, *95% CI*=[3.7, 4.3]) and device-tracking (M=4.1, CI=[3.6, 4.5]).

Not surprisingly, the interaction with the virtual environment was perceived to be more natural using the compass on the head (M=4.2, [3.7, 4.7]) than with device tracking (M=3.9, [3.3, 4.5]), and also less distracting (head: M=4.2, [3.5, 4.9]; device: M=4.0, [3.3, 4.5]). Users felt very proficient in moving and interacting with the virtual environment at the end of the experiment in both conditions (head: M=4.3, [4.0, 4.6]; device: M=4.5, [4.2, 4.8]) and they could concentrate very well on the task rather than on the controls used to perform the task (head: M=4.7, [4.4, 5.0]; device: M=4.2, [3.8, 4.7]).

During the experiments we observed that the orientation was not necessarily used as principal cue to discriminate between two possible sources. Instead, participants used lateral movements and evaluated the changes in the audio signal. Some participants reported the head-tracking condition to be easier to adapt to, although their recognition rate was lower than in the device-tracking condition. As analyzed in [3], most of the participants held the device and head aligned with their body in both conditions.

Discussion

The recognition rate in the head tracking condition is surprisingly low. In contrast to device-tracking, using head orientation tries to reproduce an experience that we know from everyday life. We assume that this makes us very sensitive to anything unnatural, such as lag or error in the tracking data. Using the device as virtual directional microphone requires the users to develop some new technique that possibly includes compensation for the measurement error. The localization process is thus more analytical than with head-tracking. Several users reported that they stopped in front of a candidate source and then checked if the audio representation fit to that source by rotating the device or their arm. We also observed that several participants used lateral movement instead of rotation for this final check. Using optical tracking and high-end rendering hardware would probably lead to different results, however, these are not feasible for MAARS used in everyday life. Since with our setup the errors are mostly off by one source, placing the sources at approximately 1.3 m would be sufficient to ensure a correct recognition.

A technical difficulty we faced during the experiments was the drift of the magnetometers. The reported heading can differ by as much as 15° from one day to the other. We ensured that both sensors reported the same heading by recalibrating them every day before the experiments. However, this cannot be guaranteed for devices in the wild. Some participants held the device slightly rotated in front of their body, which results in the measurement being off-axis from the users perspective. Both observations support our recommendation of placing the sources further apart from each other than in our experiment.

Conclusion
From our experiment we can conclude that the AudioTorch metaphor is a suitable replacement for head tracking as it reduces the technical complexity of a mobile audio augmented reality system without negatively influencing the presence in the virtual environment nor the source recognition rate. If the exact localization of the audible source is of importance, the sources should be placed farther away from each other than the 65 cm in our experiment. Taking into account the inherent error in orientation and location measurement with wireless sensors, the distance should be more in the order of 1.3 m.

The AudioTorch metaphor is ideal for museums because it allows to distribute a next generation audio guide as a simple app. Indoor location tracking could be realized using bluetooth beacons, while outdoor location tracking can be realized using GPS. Another field is a navigation aid for visually impaired. The device could either detect certain assets through its camera or have pre-programmed locations that are augmented with an audio-source. For example, this would allow to easily differentiate between ATMs and vending machines from a distance.

Future Work
Further evaluation should analyze how the inaccuracies of GPS measurements influence the use of AudioTorch in outdoor navigation. The distance two sources should have from each other to be distinguished reliably is another interesting question. Furthermore, the effect of physical landmarks for the sound sources should be evaluated. In our study, it was clear which objects were augmented with a virtual sound source, however, in a real world application, this might not be the case. Additionally, without physical representation, the effect of tracking inaccuracies is mitigated, as long as the impression remains consistent.

This experiment was performed with the participants holding a smartphone in their hand. While this is part of the AudioTorch metaphor, further experiments could be conducted without a device in the head-tracking condition to see whether this has an influence on the recognition rate.

Since the vertical resolution of spatial hearing and spatial audio rendering is not as high as the lateral resolution, it is mostly ignored in audio augmented reality. However, with AudioTorch, searching for sound sources at different heights is possible through simple volume changes, and does not require individual HRTFs.

From an interaction perspective, it would be interesting to analyze in depth when users do notice if the orientation measurement comes from the device or the head.

Acknowledgments
We would like to thank all the participants of our study. This work was funded in part by the German B-IT Foundation.

References

[1] Bederson, B. B. Audio augmented reality: a prototype automated tour guide. In *Conference Companion of CHI '95*, ACM (1995).

[2] Heller, F., Knott, T., Weiss, M., and Borchers, J. Multi-user interaction in virtual audio spaces. In *Proc. CHI EA '09*, ACM (2009).

[3] Heller, F., Krämer, A., and Borchers, J. Simplifying Orientation Measurement for Mobile Audio Augmented Reality Applications. In *Proc. CHI '14*, ACM (2014).

[4] Holland, S., Morse, D. R., and Gedenryd, H. AudioGPS: Spatial Audio Navigation with a Minimal Attention Interface. *Personal and Ubiquitous computing 6*, 4 (Jan. 2002).

[5] Kajastila, R., and Lokki, T. Eyes-free methods for accessing large auditory menus. In *Proc. ICAD '10* (2010).

[6] Lasorsa, Y., and Lemordant, J. An Interactive Audio System for Mobiles. In *127th Convention of the Audio Engineering Society* (2009), 1–9.

[7] Loomis, J. M., Hebert, C., and Cicinelli, J. G. Active localization of virtual sounds. *The Journal of the Acoustical Society of America 88* (1990), 1757.

[8] Marentakis, G. N., and Brewster, S. A. Effects of feedback, mobility and index of difficulty on deictic spatial audio target acquisition in the horizontal plane. In *Proc. CHI '06*, ACM (2006).

[9] Mariette, N. Navigation performance effects of render method and head-turn latency in mobile audio augmented reality. In *Auditory Display*. Springer Berlin Heidelberg, 2010, 239–265.

[10] McGookin, D., Brewster, S., and Priego, P. Audio Bubbles: Employing Non-speech Audio to Support Tourist Wayfinding. In *Haptic and Audio Interaction Design*. Springer Berlin Heidelberg, 2009.

[11] Paterson, N., Naliuka, K., Jensen, S. K., Carrigy, T., Haahr, M., and Conway, F. Design, implementation and evaluation of audio for a location aware augmented reality game. In *Proc. Fun and Games '10*, ACM (2010).

[12] Sander, C., Wefers, F., and Leckschat, D. Scalable Binaural Synthesis on Mobile Devices. In *133rd Conference of the Audio Engineering Society* (2012).

[13] Stahl, C. The roaring navigator: a group guide for the zoo with shared auditory landmark display. In *Proc. MobileHCI '07*, ACM (2007).

[14] Terrenghi, L., and Zimmermann, A. Tailored audio augmented environments for museums. In *Proc. IUI '04*, ACM (2004).

[15] Wakkary, R., and Hatala, M. ec(h)o: situated play in a tangible and audio museum guide. In *Proc. DIS '06*, ACM (2006).

[16] Witmer, B. G., and Singer, M. J. Measuring Presence in Virtual Environments: A Presence Questionnaire. *Presence: Teleoper. Virtual Environ. 7*, 3 (1998), 225–240.

Wearable Remote Control of a Mobile Device: Comparing One- and Two-Handed Interaction

Jessica Speir
Carleton University
Ottawa ON K1S 5B6, Canada
jessica.speir@carleton.ca

Rufino R. Ansara
Carleton University
Ottawa ON K1S 5B6, Canada
rufino.ansara@carleton.ca

Colin Killby
Carleton University
Ottawa ON K1S 5B6, Canada
colin.killby@carleton.ca

Emily Walpole
Carleton University
Ottawa ON K1S 5B6, Canada
emily.walpole@carleton.ca

Audrey Girouard
Carleton University
Ottawa ON K1S 5B6, Canada
audrey.girouard@carleton.ca

MobileHCI '14, Sep 23-26 2014, Toronto, ON, Canada
ACM 978-1-4503-3004-6/14/09.
http://dx.doi.org/10.1145/2628363.2634221

Abstract
While wearable technologies are suitable for remotely controlling mobile devices, few studies have examined user preferences for one- or two-handed touch interaction with these wearables, especially when worn on the wrist and hand area. As these locations are recognized as socially acceptable and preferred by users, we ran a study of touch interaction to remotely control mobile devices. Our results suggest users prefer swipe gestures over touch gestures when interacting with wearables on the wrist or hand, and that users find both one- and two-handed interactions suitable for wearable remote controls.

Author Keywords
HCI; E-textiles; Wearable Computing; Conductive Fabric; Wearable Controls; Mobile Controls

ACM Classification Keywords
H.5.2 User Interfaces: Haptic I/O, Prototyping

Introduction
Electronic textiles (e-textiles) are the product of integrating textiles with electronic technologies. The term describes a variety of fabric, yarn, and thread merged with electronic components such as sensors,

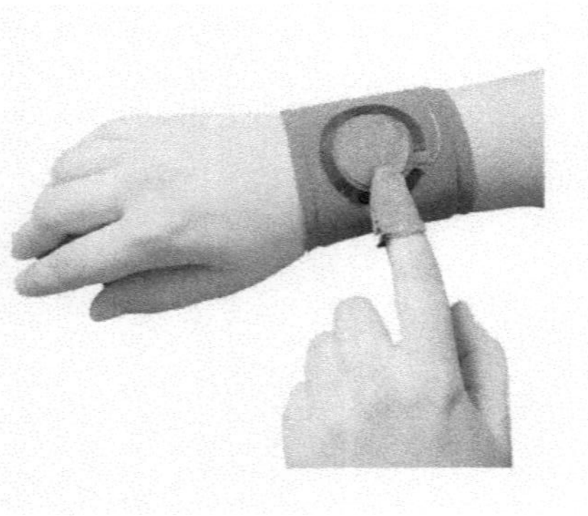

Figure 1. Final Wristband Prototype

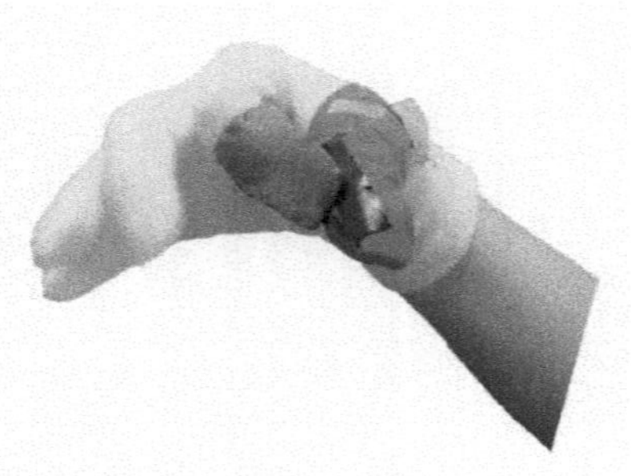

Figure 2. Final Glove Prototype

processors, and/or actuators [5]. The textile itself can contain embedded electronic components which are connected by either thread or standard wires. Many e-textiles together can produce more complex electronic devices such as those used in wearable technologies (WT) [5]. Some examples of WT include clothing for monitoring body metrics [10] and wearable solar panels for charging mobile devices [12].

One application of WT is remotely controlling mobile devices. Previous work suggest s that users prefer interacting with a small WT device on the wrist or hand [4], and that the hand and wrist are also the most socially acceptable areas for on-body interaction [8]. However, there has been little research on whether users prefer using one or two hands to interact with WT devices. It is also unclear what type of gestures users prefer to make with WT devices. In this study, we aim to investigate these aspects of wearable remote controls for mobile devices.

Music and phone applications for mobile devices are particularly suited for remote control as they allow users to perform simple tasks "eyes-free", when interaction in inhibited by sun glare [3] and environmental distractions [6], for instance. We believe the suitability of music and phone applications for remote control by WT warrants further investigation.

We conducted a study on the use of WT for remote control of mobile devices with two prototypes, a wristband and a glove (Figure 1 and Figure 2). Participants interacted with the prototypes via swipe and touch gestures, using one hand for the glove and two hands for the wristband. Both prototypes remotely controlled music and phone applications on a mobile device. We concentrated on user preference and performance of one- and two-handed gestures and the effectiveness of swipe and touch gestures. Here we present our results and discuss the lessons learned when designing for gestures and WT prototypes.

Related Work

In this section we review relevant research and identify the gaps we aim to address in our study.

Wristbands and Circular Interfaces

Wrist-mounted systems are significantly faster to access than a device stored in a pocket or on the hip [1]. Several wrist-mounted WT systems have been developed in the past decade. The GestureWrist system [9] is based on wrist-shape changes and forearm movements, and was developed for hands- and eyes-free interactions for remote control. Zeagler et al. [14] designed a jog-wheel using multilayer embroidery capable of remote control. However, little work has been done with these systems beyond the initial prototype design. Ashbrook et al. [2] modeled the error rate for buttons placed around the edge of a circular touch-screen watch, but their study did not consider eyes-free interaction. Consistent with other circular interface literature, Ashbrook et al. defined two regions of interaction, the rim and the centre of the circle [2], which influenced our design of the wristband interface in this study.

Gloves

In a survey of WT and glove devices, Sturman and Zeltzer [11] summarize the basis for most glove interactions as either finger-bend or movement detection, with none focused on swipe or touch. When users are given the choice they often prefer to use their

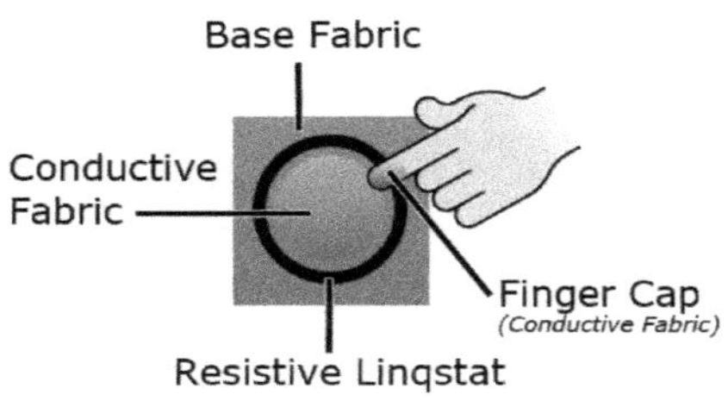

Figure 3. Fabric Potentiometer Elements

Action	Wristband Gesture	Glove Gesture
Play/ Pause	Touch and Hold - 6 O'Clock	Touch and Hold - Middle
Next Song	Touch and Hold - 3 O'Clock	Touch and Hold - Top
Previous Song	Touch and Hold - 9 O'Clock	Touch and Hold - Bottom
Increase Volume	Swipe Clockwise	Swipe Upwards
Decrease Volume	Swipe Counter Clockwise	Swipe Downwards

Table 1. Actions and gestures for the Music Application

index finger for mid-air or surface gestures [13]; this influenced the design of our prototypes.

Remote Control
Many WT devices developed can remotely control other devices (e.g. the jog-wheel [14] and GestureWrist [9]). However, these prior works rarely focused on use cases, for instance to remotely controlling music or phone applications. There is also little work on the swipe or touch gestures that can be used with the WT devices. Our study explores both of these aspects of remote control with WT.

Prototypes
We created two prototypes aimed to emulate a real product's aesthetics and functionality (Figure 1 and Figure 2). We built our wristband according to Perner-Wilson's Time-Sensing Bracelet instructions [7] for a circular potentiometer and adapted those guidelines to create the linear potentiometer on the glove (Figure 3).

Wearable Components
We were unable to obtain the resistive fabric used in the original design [7] , so we replaced it with plastic resistive Linqstat™. When users connect the Linqstat™ and the conductive fabric with the conductive finger cap, the system outputs a value that varies with the location of the touch. We used this value to determine the location of the contact and the direction of movement, if any. To build the glove, we adapted the circular potentiometer of the wristband to work as a linear potentiometer, placed along the thumb. We used the same conductive-fabric pairing and maintained the same surface area on each component as on the the index finger of the glove. The glove works on the same principle as the wristband.

Hardware and Software Applications
Our hardware consisted of a circuit that read the input values from both prototypes and transmitted them over Bluetooth® to an Android™ phone. We filtered the raw data captured from the prototypes as the Bluetooth® connection was not fast enough to stream directly. Our prototypes controlled two custom-made applications: a Music Application and a Phone Application. Both applications took the same prototype-specific gestures as input, but mapped them to different tasks.

Study Design
We conducted a within-subject factorial experiment with both applications and both prototypes. Table 1 and Table 2 list the set of gesture-action combinations for the Phone Application and Music Application.

We chose the swipe gestures to match the directionality of the actions (e.g. increase volume by swiping upwards). We chose the touch-and-hold areas on the wristband to match those of the older-model click-wheel iPods (e.g. iPod™ and iPod™ Nano 1st to 5th generation). On the glove, these touch-and-hold locations were evenly spaced along a straight line, in the same order moving down the thumb as moving clockwise on the wristband (next song, play/pause, previous song).

Participants
Seventeen participants (8 females) with a mean age of 22 participated in our one-hour user study. One participant was left-handed. Eleven participants (64.7%) had previous experience with a click-wheel iPod™. None of the users were familiar with wearable technologies. We offered the participants $10 as compensation for their time.

Action	Wristband Gesture	Glove Gesture
Answer/ Hang Up	Touch and Hold - 6 O'Clock	Touch and Hold - Middle
Increase Volume	Swipe Clockwise	Swipe Upwards
Decrease Volume	Swipe Counter Clockwise	Swipe Downwards

Table 2. Actions and gestures for the Phone Application

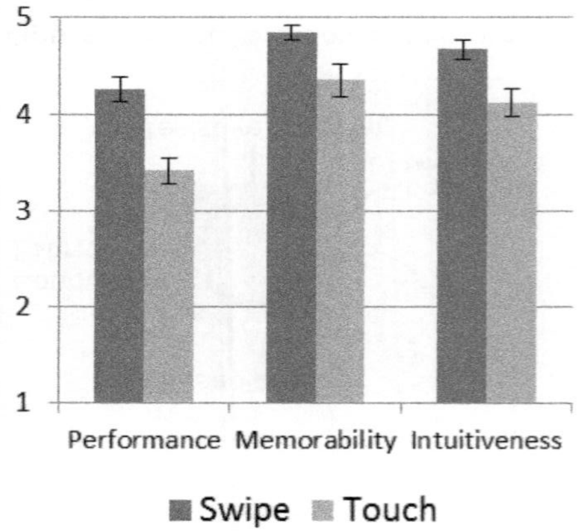

Figure 4. Mean rating for swipe and touch gestures for ease of performance, memorability, and intuitiveness. Error bars show the standard error.

Procedure

We demonstrated the gestures and actions before each participant used each application with both prototypes. We counterbalanced the order of the prototypes and the applications. The software presented all tasks in a randomized order (5 times each). The researcher told the participant which task to complete, to help participants to focus on the prototype instead of on the mobile device. At the end of the study, participants filled out a detailed survey that recorded their impressions and comments on the prototypes and the gestures.

RESULTS

Performance

The system logged the time taken in milliseconds from the start of each task until the system detected the gesture. As the study progressed, wear-and-tear on the prototypes caused erratic detection of the touch gestures on the glove. To adjust for this, we excluded any times over 8 seconds as likely caused by prototype failure. This resulted in an average of 5 cases of excluded data for each glove-touch gesture, with little-to-no missing data for the other gestures. This missing data prevented us from accurately comparing the gestures task by task, hence we compare the mean detection times for gestures by the prototype, application, and by type of gesture (swipe or touch).

We performed a 2 x 2 repeated-measures ANOVA on prototype (wristband, glove) x application (music, phone) on the average gesture-detection times. The wristband detected the gestures significantly faster (M=2974ms, SE=94) than on the glove (M=3543ms, SE=154), $F(1,16)=13.98$, $p=.002$, $\eta_p^2=.466$. There was no significant main effect of the application ($F(1, 16)=1.54$, $p=.233$) on gesture-detection time and no significant interaction effect ($F(1,16)=0.073$, $p=.790$) between the application and the prototype.

We also compared the detection times of the swipe gestures with the touch gestures. The prototypes detected the swipe gestures (M=2901ms, SE=96) significantly faster than the touch gestures (M=3592ms, SE=114), $t(16)=8.71$, $p=.000$, $r=.91$.

Subjective

Participants rated each gesture on ease of performance and memorability on 5-level Likert scales from Strongly Disagree (1) to Strongly Agree (5). Participants rated the wristband gestures (M=4.13, SE=0.14) as significantly easier to perform than the glove gestures (M=3.34, SE=0.15), $t(16)=3.82$, $p=.001$, $r=.69$. There is no significant difference between the wristband and glove in terms of memorability or intuitiveness.

Participants also rated each gesture and task combination for intuitiveness on the same 5-level Likert scale. We found no significant difference between the ratings for the music-application gestures and the phone-application gestures.

As shown in Figure 4, participants rated the swipe gestures as significantly more intuitive than the touch gestures, $t(16)=4.98$, $p=.000$, $r=.78$. Participants rated the swipe gestures significantly easier to perform than the touch gestures, $t(16)=4.98$, $p=.000$, $r=0.78$. The memorability ratings were not normally distributed, so we used the non-parametric Wilcoxon Signed-Ranks test to compare the mean ratings. The users rated the swipe gestures as significantly easier to remember than the touch gestures, $z=-25.53$, $p=.012$, $r=0.43$.

Discussion

Our results indicate that participants preferred the wristband prototype to the glove prototype and found swipe gestures easier to perform, more intuitive, and easier to remember than touch gestures. Participants were evenly split on which application, music or phone, was most suited to this type of remote control, which confirms our assumption that both are suited to eyes- and hands-free control of a mobile phone. Using the click-wheel iPod™ metaphor for the wristband did not increase the intuitiveness of those gestures over the phone-application gestures.

Wristband vs Glove

Overall, the majority of participants preferred the wristband (77%) prototype to the glove (24%). However, we are unable to attribute this preference to any particular feature of either prototype due to the technical issues we experienced with the glove. When asked specifically which prototype they would prefer for day-to-day use, the split was more even, with only 59% of participants preferring the wristband. This result, combined with participants' comments, suggests that there is no overwhelming preference for one- or two-handed interaction for remote control of a mobile device, but rather that either might be appropriate depending on the user and usage scenario.

The wristband detected gestures significantly faster than the glove, which may have been caused by the difficulties with the glove prototype near the end of the study. However, the participants also rated the wristband gestures as much easier to perform than the glove gestures. We attribute both the difference in gesture detection times and the difference in rating to the physical difficulty of performing some of the glove gestures in the smaller surface area available on the thumb compared to the wrist.

Swipe vs Touch

Participants found swipe gestures more intuitive and easier to perform and remember than touch gestures, likely because the swipe gestures relied only on direction rather than location, requiring a less precise input. We also found that clockwise/upwards movements translate well to an increase in values, whereas counter-clockwise/downwards movements translate well to a decrease in values. In contrast, mapping a right or top touch to "next" and a left or bottom touch to "previous" was not as intuitive as we expected.

Improving the Prototypes

We solicited the participants' opinions on how to improve the prototypes. Many participants wanted visual markers on the wristband to make the touch gestures easier to remember. Notably, two participants wanted the play/pause-touch gesture to be located in the centre of the wristband, rather than at the 6-o'clock position. The comments for the glove were entirely concerned with improving the reliability of the sensor.

Limitations

Some prototype limitations became evident during user testing. We created only one glove due to time and money constraints, and it did not fit tightly to the various sizes of participants' hands. Participants with smaller hands sometimes had difficulty completing the full range of gestures. On both prototypes, the shape of the fabric potentiometer was often distorted by the shape of the participant's hand or wrist. This distortion altered the values read from the circuit, which resulted in a slight shifting of gesture recognition areas between participants. Finally, towards the end of the user study wear and tear on the glove prototype caused touch gesture detection on that prototype to become erratic. This may have affected some of the data collected towards the end of the study.

Conclusion

This study explored how users perceive wearable technology and its potential as a remote control for mobile applications. We defined multiple application-appropriate gestures and determined that participants had an easier time performing swipe gestures over the touch-and-hold gestures. The majority of participants preferred the wristband prototype and rated the wristband gestures easier to perform. However, they were evenly split over which prototype they would prefer for everyday use. This indicates that users have no clear preference of one- or two-handed interactions, suggesting that both may be promising input methods.

Given the limitations of our prototype, future research includes development of more advanced prototypes and involves comparisons of user reactions to prototype rigidity and different interaction zones.

References

[1] Ashbrook, D., Clawson, J., Lyons, K., Patel, N., Starner, T., and Clara, S. Quickdraw: The Impact of Mobility and On-Body Placement on Device Access Time. *Proc. CHI*, (2008), 219–222.

[2] Ashbrook, D., Lyons, K., and Starner, T. An investigation into round touchscreen wristwatch interaction. *Proc. MobileHCI*, (2008), 311–314.

[3] Esposito, C. Wearable computers: field-test results and system design guidelines. *Interact*, (1997), 493–500.

[4] Holleis, P., Schmidt, A., Paasovaara, S., Puikkonen, A., and Häkkilä, J. Evaluating capacitive touch input on clothes. *Proc. MobileHCI*, (2008), 81.

[5] Nakad, Z., Jones, M., Martin, T., Fawaz, W. Networking in E-textiles. *Computer Communications*, (2010), 655–666.

[6] Oulasvirta, A., Tamminen, S., Roto, V., and Kuorelahti, J. Interaction in 4-Second Bursts: The Fragmented Nature of Attentional Resources in Mobile HCI. *Proc. CHI*, (2005), 919–928.

[7] Perner-Wilson, H. and Satomi, M. DIY Wearable technology. *ISEA*, (2009).

[8] Profita, H., Clawson, J., Gilliland, S., et al. Don't Mind Me Touching My Wrist: A Case Study of Interacting with On-Body Technology in Public Social Acceptability of Wearable Technology. *ISWC*, (2013), 89–96.

[9] Rekimoto, J. GestureWrist and GesturePad: unobtrusive wearable interaction devices. *Wearable Computers*, IEEE (2001), 21–27.

[10] Rest Devices. Mimo - The Smart Baby Monitor. http://mimobaby.com/.

[11] Sturman, D.J. and Zeltzer, D. A survey of glove-based input. *Computer Graphics and Applications, IEEE 14*, 1 (1994), 30–39.

[12] VanDongen, P. Wearable Solar. http://wearablesolar.nl/.

[13] Wobbrock, J.O., Morris, M.R., and Wilson, A.D. User-defined gestures for surface computing. *Proc. CHI*, (2009), 1083.

[14] Zeagler, C., Gilliland, S., Profita, H., and Starner, T. Textile Interfaces: Embroidered Jog-Wheel, Beaded Tilt Sensor, Twisted Pair Ribbon, and Sound Sequins. *ISWC,* (2012), 60–63.

Interactive Opinion Polls on Public Displays – Studying Privacy Requirements in the Wild

Matthias Baldauf
Vienna University of Technology
Wiedner Hauptstr. 76/2/2
1040 Vienna, Austria
matthias.baldauf@inso.tuwien.ac.at

Stefan Suette
FTW Telecommunications Research Center Vienna
Donau-City-Strasse 1
1220 Vienna, Austria
suette@ftw.at

Peter Fröhlich
FTW Telecommunications Research Center Vienna
Donau-City-Strasse 1
1220 Vienna, Austria
froehlich@ftw.at

Ulrich Lehner
FTW Telecommunications Research Center Vienna
Donau-City-Strasse 1
1220 Vienna, Austria
lehner@ftw.at

MobileHCI'14, Sep 23-26 2014, Toronto, ON, Canada.
ACM 978-1-4503-3004-6/14/09.
http://dx.doi.org/10.1145/2628363.2634222

Abstract

Interactive opinion polls are a promising novel use case for public urban displays. However, voicing one's opinion at such a public installation poses special privacy requirements. In this paper, we introduce our ongoing work on investigating the roles of the interaction technique and the poll question in this novel context. We present a field study comparing three different voting techniques (public touch interface, personal smartphone by scanning a QR code, from remote through a short Web address) and three types of poll questions (general, personal, local). Overall, the results show that actively casting an opinion on a timely topic is highly appreciated by passers-by. The public voting opportunity through a touch screen is clearly preferred. Offering mobile or remote voting does not significantly increase the overall participation rate. The type of poll question has an impact on the number of participants but does not influence the preferred interaction modality.

Author Keywords

Public display; public poll; mobile interaction; privacy

ACM Classification Keywords

H.5.2 [Information interfaces and presentation (e.g., HCI)]: User Interfaces.

Introduction

Nowadays, public screens have become ubiquitous in modern city landscapes and enable a plethora of interactive urban applications for passers-by. One promising use case which is recently gaining increasing interest in academia are citizen participation tools such as public opinion polls exploiting urban screens as bidirectional communication channel for identifying and discussing matters of urban governance.

While previous respective research in the field of public displays focussed on studying social phenomena around such installations, on investigating how to raise awareness for provided interactive applications or on exploring novel interaction techniques, knowledge about the privacy requirements and concerns for opinion polls on public displays is scarce. In this paper, we introduce our ongoing work on privacy aspects in the context of interactive public polls and present the results of a preliminary field study which compared the acceptance of a public voting technique and personal smartphone-mediated one and further investigated the impact of different categories of poll questions on the preferred interaction style and the participation rate.

Related Work and Research Questions

One of the earliest prototypes utilizing a large public display for citizen feedback is *Opinionizer* by Brignull and Rogers [3], an interactive shared display where passers-by could add their views using a keyboard. Two field studies showed that social embarrassment is the major deterrent preventing people from participating. Further, an easy change from being an onlooker to a participant and back again should be enabled. More recently, interactive public displays have been rediscovered as enabler for civic engagement. For example, *TexTales* [1] is an opinion forum on large public projection screen and enabled commenting of displayed photos through submitting text messages which led to active offline discussions among the participants. *Agora 2.0* [7] is another example for an interactive public display where passers-by could vote for city-related suggestions through a connected mouse. Related is the idea of Behrens [2] who investigated tangible (dis)like buttons to express opinions at related real-world locations.

Paek et al. were among the first who investigated mobile devices as remote controls for shared displays and identified polling as one promising use case promoting discussion and consensus building [5]. A first respective real-world example is *MobiLenin* by Scheible and Ojala [6]. Their system enabled guests of a restaurant to vote for video tracks to be played on a large display and included a lottery mechanism to win a voucher. Most related to the work presented in this paper is *Viewpoint* [8], a custom device providing a simple voting interface with two buttons to answer yes/no questions and a small display showing the current result. The prototype further featured voting by sending text messages, yet, this feature was not used by single participant during the trial. Overall, *Viewpoint* was very successful in engaging participants and received positive feedback.

Having studied the aforementioned literature, we identified several open questions concerning the privacy requirements of such public opinion polls and formulated the following research questions to be investigated:

1. Is a state-of-the-art mobile interaction technique such as scanning a QR code accepted for privately casting a vote through the personal smartphone?

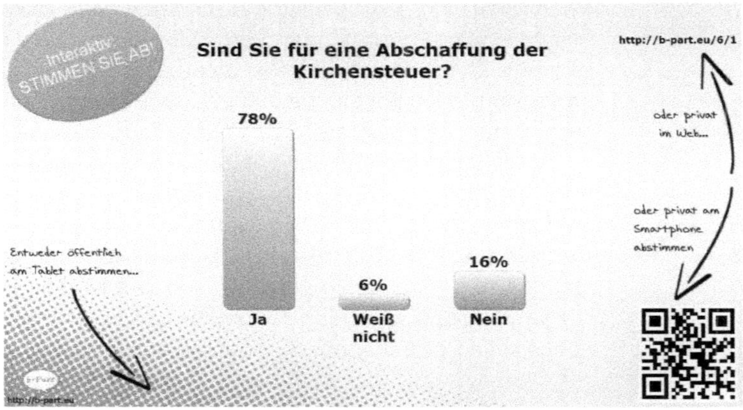

Figure 1: The screen design contained the poll question, a bar chart as well as an animated banner and short instructions on how to participate.

Figure 2: The prototype was deployed in the entrance area of a coffee house for 10 workdays.

2. Does the type of poll question (such as general or personal) influence the participants' choice of the participation technique?
3. How do participants perceive the opportunity to actively express their opinion at public locations in comparison to just seeing real-time opinion summaries?

Study Prototype
To study these research questions under real-world conditions we developed a functional study prototype based on state-of-the-art Web technologies. The Web application (run in a modern browser in full-screen mode, see Figure 1) showed a poll question in the top center and the current poll result in form of a bar chart below. Further, it contained an animated banner in the top left corner asking passers-by to participate and three short instruction texts (with arrows pointing to the respective input method) explained the three interaction techniques supported by the prototype:

- *Public touch-based voting.* A tablet computer mounted in front of the large display through a custom-made fixation showed buttons for the three available choices. Passers-by could simply cast their vote (obviously visible to nearby bystanders) by directly touching the respective button (see Figure 2).
- *Private voting on the personal device.* To enable private voting we showed a QR code on the screen. An interested passer-by who captured the code with his smartphone was forwarded to a web page where he could cast his vote by clicking the corresponding button.

- *Voting from remote.* We further included a short URL for people who notice the public poll, yet prefer to cast their vote from remote, e.g. when being back at their working place and having looked up background information. Additionally this option is suitable for smartphone users, who do not have a QR code reader app installed. The type of end-device (desktop or mobile) was logged.

To investigate the impact of different questions types, we selected 12 timely poll questions from three different categories: locally relevant as the typical question category for participative applications (e.g. *Do you wish for more shops in this area?*), personal (e.g. *Are you content with your current working situation?*), and general ones (e.g. *Do you prefer car-free city centers?*). The question on the display was switched in intervals of 15 minutes and was alternately selected from one of the three categories.

Methodology

We deployed the described prototype at a coffee shop (Figure 2) for 10 workdays. The shop is located in a business district and is visited by about 200 guests per day. In order to collect contextual data, a test assistant observed the interactions of visitors with the poll system and made notes using a prepared code sheet containing the type of interaction and the number of involved persons. In the second week, the test assistant handed out questionnaires. They contained general questions whether the participant liked the possibility to share his opinion on a current topic of interest through a public display and to see interim results, respectively, both on 5 point Likert scales. Further we wanted to know whether he had explicit privacy concerns when participating in such a poll on a public display.

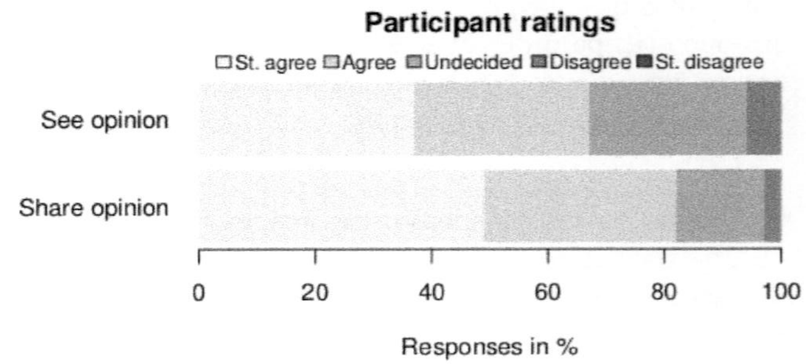

Figure 3: Participant ratings concerning the statements 'I like to share my opinion/see the opinion of others on a current topic on a public screen'.

Results

During the ten days we recorded 160 votes (participation rate about 8%) and received 30 completed questionnaires. The interviewees (12 females) were aged between 14 and 76 (mean=38.7, median=38).

Log file analysis
The analysis of the log file yielded a very clear result: we recorded only one voting through the QR code and one using the URL (on a mobile device). 99% of the votes were casted by directly touching the tablet. Concerning the type of polls, 43% of the votes were given for general questions, 33% for locally relevant ones, and 24% for personal questions.

Questionnaire
Four of 30 interviewed persons stated they have privacy concerns. Two of them explicitly mentioned the possibility of a fingerprint sensor integrated in the touch screen. The most common explanation in the group without privacy concerns was that the poll is anonymous and no private information is entered.

48% and 33% of the participants stated to fully agree and to agree, respectively, with the statement 'I like to share my opinion on a current topic on a public screen'. 15% were undecided and 3% disagreed. The second statement, 'I like to see the opinion of others on a current topic on a public screen' was answered by 36% with strongly agree, 30% with agree and 6% with disagree. 27% were undecided. For both statements, no participant fully disagreed.

Observations

In addition to well-known phenomena such as the "honeypot effect" [3] (passers-by being attracted by people already interacting with the display) and the "landing effect" [4] (people pass the display, stop late and walk back), we observed several particular social effects which partly confirm experiences from recent related studies (e.g. [9]):

Encouraging colleagues. Several times only one member of a group (such as workmates) noticed the public poll when passing by and – accepting to unveil his choice – encouraged his colleagues to vote as well.

Social deterrence. We counted less interactions with the poll screen when the table close to the screen was occupied by visitors and noticed several people who were obviously interested in the poll but turned away from the screen.

Discussions with by-standers. Often discussions about the poll topic arose, not only between persons of one group but even among visitors who obviously did not know each other before.

Waiting times. In peak times a waiting queue developed in front of the counter. While standing in the queue, several visitors used the public poll to bridge the waiting times. Due to this waiting situation, they were obviously more engaged in the interaction with the public screen.

Discussion

In this section we refer back and relate the results to our original main research questions. The results of our field study showed that even for opinion polls in a public setting a direct interaction (in our case through a touch-sensitive tablet computer) is clearly favored over the opportunity to use the personal smartphone for privately submitting a vote. Offering the QR code as a state-of-the-art mobile interaction technique did not lead to significantly more participants. While we expected the overall result, the decidedness is surprising. We avoided a native voting app which would need to be downloaded and chose a modern mobile interaction technique (plus a short URL) over old-fashioned texting (cf. [8]) and thus assumed that several participants would use their smartphones for privately casting their vote, especially in the case of personal questions. However, we saw that people who did not want by-standers to observe their voting behavior did not choose to use their smartphone (or the remote voting opportunity), but decided not to participate at all. The type of question (local, personal, general) did not have any significant impact on this behavior.

The distribution of votes to the different poll categories is explicable: we expected that personal questions would receive fewest votes due to the public setting. We assume that general questions attracted most participants since the study environment is not only visited by employees of nearby companies but also by external guests and business partners who were less interested in locally relevant topics. The responses to our questionnaire showed that the majority of the participants liked the idea of using public displays for polls in general. The slight trend that participants enjoyed more to actively express their opinion than to see the interim results is explained by participants' comments appreciating the opportunity to raise the voice and the feeling of being heard.

Conclusions and Outlook

We presented a preliminary field study which serves as a starting point to investigate privacy aspects concerning interactive public opinion polls in more depth. Our results clearly show that mobile interaction opportunities, even an advanced one like in our study, are largely ignored as private voting techniques, when direct touch interaction at the public display is provided as an alternative input method. The type of poll question (general vs. personal) has an impact on the number of participants to be expected, however, not on the preference for the direct voting technique.

As a conclusion, current mobile voting features can be neglected when realizing a public poll application which also features a direct voting technique, since they are not capable of significantly increasing the number of participants. To reach a higher participation rate also for personal questions, an open challenge is the design of novel voting techniques which are comparable to a direct touch interface in terms of simplicity and speed but still do not reveal the participant's choice when used in public.

Acknowledgments

This work has been carried out within the *JPI Urban Europe* project *b-Part* financed by FFG, Tekes and Formas. FTW GmbH is funded within the program COMET - Competence Centers for Excellent Technologies by BMVIT, BMWA, and the City of Vienna. The COMET program is managed by the FFG.

References

[1] Ananny, M., and Strohecker, C. Textales: Creating interactive forums with urban publics. In *Handbook of Research on Urban Informatics*. IGI Global, 2009.

[2] Behrens, M. Swipe "i like": location based digital narrative through embedding the "like" button in the real world. In *Proc. 5th International Conference on Communities and Technologies* (2011).

[3] Brignall, H., and Rogers, Y. Enticing people to interact with large public displays in public spaces. In *Proc. INTERACT' 03* (2003).

[4] Müller, J., Walter, R., Bailly, G., Nischt, M., and Alt, F. Looking glass: A field study on noticing interactivity of a shop window. In *Proc. CHI*, ACM (2012), 297–306.

[5] Paek, T., Agrawala, M., Basu, S., Drucker, S., Kristjansson, T., Logan, R., Toyama, K., and Wilson, A. Toward universal mobile interaction for shared displays. In *Proc. CSCW*, ACM (2004), 266–269.

[6] Scheible, J., and Ojala, T. Mobile group interaction with interactive video on large public display. In *Proc. ACM SIGGRAPH 2005 Posters* (2005).

[7] Schiavo, G., Milano, M., Saldivar, J., Nasir, T., Zancanaro, M., and Convertino, G. Agora2.0: Enhancing civic participation through a public display. In *Proc. 6th International Conference on Communities and Technologies*, ACM (2013), 46–54.

[8] Taylor, N., Marshall, J., Blum-Ross, A., Mills, J., Rogers, J., Egglestone, P., Frohlich, D. M., Wright, P., and Olivier, P. Viewpoint: Empowering communities with situated voting devices. In *Proc. CHI*, ACM (2012), 1361–1370.

[9] Valkanova, N., Walter, R., Moere, A. V., and Müller, J. Myposition: sparking civic discourse by a public interactive poll visualization. In *Proc. CSCW* (2014), 1323–1332.

Toward a Non-Intrusive, Physio-Behavioral Biometric for Smartphones

Esther Vasiete
Department of Computer Science
University of Colorado Boulder
esther.vasiete@colorado.edu

Yan Chen
Department of Computer Science
University of Colorado Boulder
yan.chen@colorado.edu

Ian Char
Department of Computer Science
University of Colorado Boulder
ian.char@colorado.edu

Tom Yeh
Department of Computer Science
University of Colorado Boulder
tom.yeh@colorado.edu

Vishal Patel
UMIACS
University of Maryland
College Park
pvishalm@umiacs.umd.edu

Larry Davis
UMIACS
University of Maryland
College Park
lsd@umiacs.umd.edu

Rama Chellappa
UMIACS
University of Maryland
College Park
rama@umiacs.umd.edu

MobileHCI '14, Sep 23–26 2014, Toronto, ON, Canada
ACM 978-1-4503-3004-6/14/09.
http://dx.doi.org/10.1145/2628363.2634223

Abstract

Biometric authentication relies on an individual's inner characteristics and traits. We propose an active authentication system on a mobile device that relies on two biometric modalities: 3D gestures and face recognition. The novelty of our approach is to combine 3D gesture and face recognition in a non-intrusive and unconstrained environment; the active authentication system is running in the background while the user is performing his/her main task.

Author Keywords

3D gesture recognition; behavioral biometric authentication; face recognition; fusion system.

ACM Classification Keywords

H.5.m. Information interfaces and presentation (e.g., HCI): Miscellaneous.

Introduction

The most common user identification techniques on mobile devices are based on passwords or on graphical puzzles. However, there are three shortcomings with these techniques. First, passwords in memory-based approaches can be forgotten, stolen, or hacked. Second, after the initial login there is no further identification procedure as long as the device remains active. An impostor could gain physical access to the device if the legitimate user leaves it unlocked and unattended. Third, the authentication mechanism is

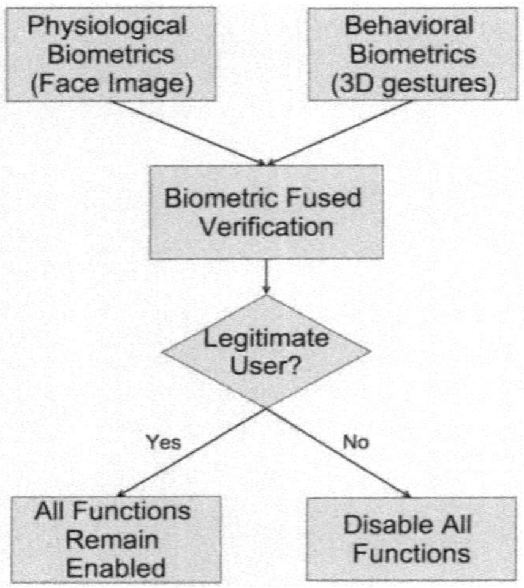

Figure 1. Proposed physio-behavioral biometric for non-intrusive active authentication.

often intrusive and disruptive; users can be momentarily forced away from their main task to enter passwords and/or perform gestures.

We propose a new approach that can address these three shortcomings (Fig. 1). Our approach is behavior-based (rather than memory-based), active (rather than login-only), and, most importantly, non-intrusive. The property of being non-intrusive is valuable from a mobile HCI perspective, as it would greatly increase the usability of the authentication procedure. On the technical side, our approach will fuse physiological and behavioral biometrics. Biometric authentication relies on an individual's personal characteristics and traits that cannot be forgotten and could be difficult to steal or mimic.

Today's smartphones come with a growing number of embedded sensors such as an accelerometer, gyroscope, digital compass, front and rear cameras, and ambient light and proximity sensors. We take advantage of the variety of available sensors to fuse two forms of biometrics: face recognition and behavioral movement dynamics. This fusion creates a unique signature that is constantly being extracted and analyzed to determine whether the current user matches the previously stored signature for the authorized user. If the current biometric measurements do not match the reference signature, the mobile device can lock itself to prevent further unauthorized use.

Other highly reliable forms of biometric authentication exist, such as fingerprint identification and retinal or iris scans, but these require the subject's participation and the use of external, often expensive, equipment. Our proposed biometric fusion authentication technique is non-intrusive (face recognition and behavioral movement analysis is performed in the background while users are performing their main tasks) and does not require any extra equipment—only the existing sensors are needed.

Related Work

Accelerometer and gyroscope sensors have been exploited extensively to capture mobile users' behavioral characteristics. In [1], a set of 43 generated features from 10-second interval accelerometer readings produced a positive authentication rate of 82.1%-92.9%. These features were independent of the user state (walking, jogging, going upstairs or downstairs). Wolff [2] also studied the accelerometer dynamics by extracting the variance in acceleration and orientation across the three dimensions (*x*, *y*, and *z*) and used a Gaussian distribution model to achieve a user classification accuracy of 83%. In [3], researchers used accelerometer and gyroscope readings during screen taps and an ensemble of machine learning classifiers to predict the letters and icons that were pressed with an accuracy of up to 80% and 90%, respectively. These findings further justify the need to increase security systems on our mobile devices.

The main drawback of 3D gesture recognition is that it is highly task-dependent and authentication is achieved by means of knowing the task context. Face recognition, on the other hand, does not require context information although it requires a partial face to be captured by the camera.

The utilization of almost real-time face recognition techniques in mobile devices is now feasible due to the increases in processing power [4, 5, 6]. To date, biometric authentication in mobile devices is used for

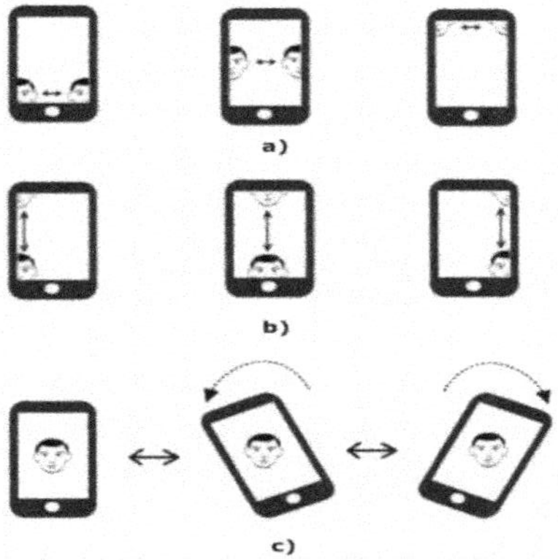

Figure 2. Enrollment task. Users are asked to scan their faces (a) horizontally, (b) vertically, and, (c) rotationally.

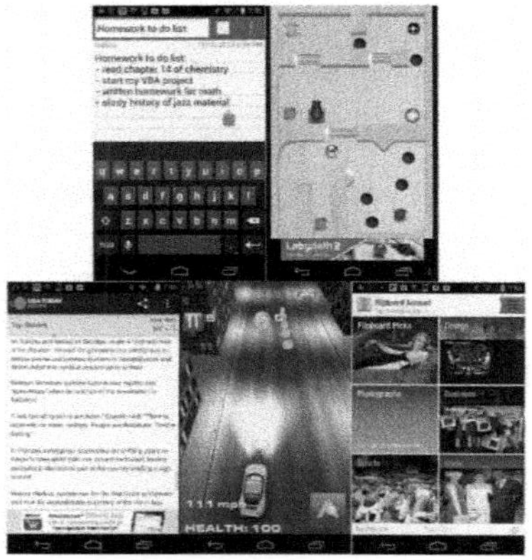

Figure 3. Snapshot from each of the five tasks performed by 30 subjects while the front-facing camera is *non-intrusively* capturing in the background.

access control (rather than a PIN or password) that corresponds to a highly constrained scenario. The combination of more than one biometric modality can increase the robustness of the authentication system. A combination of face and speech recognition in [7] outperforms either modality on its own and provides a performance gain of more than 25%. However, these existing authentication methods are still conducted intrusively during login time.

The novelty of our approach is to combine 3D gesture and face recognition in a non-intrusive and non-constrained environment—the active authentication system runs in the background while the user performs any other task (Fig. 1). Furthermore, sensor data such as proximity and ambient light will serve as inputs to the face recognition system to provide a novel way of dealing with pose and illumination variation, which still constitute the main issues in unconstrained face recognition [8, 9, 10].

Increasing Robustness

Previous work shows promises of physio-behavioral biometric data for authentication under constraint scenarios, but there are still diverse technical challenges and problems when dealing with non-intrusive authentication. Here, we outline our approach to providing robustness by combining state-of-the-art face recognition and 3D gesture recognition methods.

Face Recognition

Holistic approaches that use the whole face region as the raw data have received substantial attention among all face recognition studies in recent years [11]. Turk and Pentland [12] used principal component analysis (PCA) for face recognition by projecting face images onto a dimensionality-reduced feature space, creating the so-called Eigenfaces. Other feature spaces such as linear discriminant analysis (LDA) and independent component analysis (ICA) have also been successful. However, recent work has shown that PCA performs better than LDA and ICA when the correct distance metric is used [13, 14].

Recognition performance drastically drops when illumination and pose variations in face images are encountered. Significant work has been done to combat these issues [9, 10]. Other researchers have incorporated the extraction of key visual features to gain robustness. Instead, we propose the incorporation of sensorial features to compensate for changes in the illumination and to perform pose inference.

The accelerometer and gyroscope sensors were used in [15] to infer and compensate tilted images for face detection. We propose using the sensors that follow:

- Proximity sensors measure the proximity of an object relative to the device screen They can help infer when a user is placing a call (images will be discarded) or when the user is tapping the screen (face might be occluded by a finger).
- Light sensors measure the illumination level. Knowing the real lighting conditions makes illumination compensation technique more accurate and efficient.
- Orientation sensors measure the device's rotation around all three physical axes (x, y, z). These are used for tilt compensation in order to provide an image with an upright face to facilitate the face detection task and pose inference for view-based face recognition. Appearances can change depending on the subject's position with respect to the phone's orientation.
- Motion sensors such as the accelerometer, gyroscope, and gravity sensors will ease tracking of the

face. For instance, intensity of motion can be used to discard images too blurry due to excessive vibration.

3D Gesture Recognition

Subjects may be authenticated through gestures when using their mobiles. Motion sensors can be used to analyze each person's movements or behavior. Although hierarchical probabilistic models have been popular for human behavior modeling, they could lead to over-fitting when dealing with sensor data over long periods [16], especially in real scenarios where abnormal behavior is usually present. Recent work has used supervised or unsupervised machine learning techniques for authentication under the smartphone platform. A Gaussian mixture model is used to model pedestrians' behavioral trajectories in [17]. A user can be authenticated in [1] while walking, jogging, or climbing stairs with a phone inside a pocket. In active authentication, it is preferable to provide authentication security while the mobile device is being used. In [18], touch screen data such as pressure, size, and speed are analyzed to add an extra security layer to password patterns. Pinch and spread gestures have been found to fit a Fitts's law model on a specific resizing task [19].

Until now, behavioral authentication systems on mobile devices have been task-specific. It is important to acknowledge that 3D gestures vary greatly depending on the task (e.g., web browsing and playing a car racing game show two distinct movement dynamics). Rather than task-specific, we build models that are gesture-specific by grouping similar actions into four main classes:

1. Low-motion gestures such as carrying the phone while reading the news, checking social networks, or watching a video.
2. High-motion gestures often present when playing accelerometer games.
3. Finger-tapping. Samples can be extracted from typing, icon selection, and similar actions.
4. Swiping gestures, during scrolling, switching windows, or playing some games.

The main challenge is to extract features for each of the four classes that will retain the most within-subject variability while discriminating between-subject variability; then, a classifier will be built to provide good predictions. By aggregating time series data into samples, we compute Fourier components, moments, mean acceleration per axis, and other information.

Fused System

We acknowledge that the noisy measurements, high variance of data, and difficulties derived from an unconstrained scenario (in which the user interacts with her device with total freedom) will cause authentication accuracy to drop in any modality; however, we can expect sufficiently high authentication accuracy when combining both modalities. To accomplish this, we represent new data as a sparse linear combination of concatenated features from two or more modalities [20]. Late fusion can also be applied by combining prediction scores from both modalities into a simple score: the fused score. Any of these solutions is expected to provide higher authentication accuracy than any single modality on its own.

Preliminary Study

Our main research question is to understand to what extent behavioral biometric data collected *without* user cooperation in a non-intrusive manner can capture a user's unique characteristics for authentication. For instance, can the front-facing camera capture enough of a user's face for reliable face recognition when the

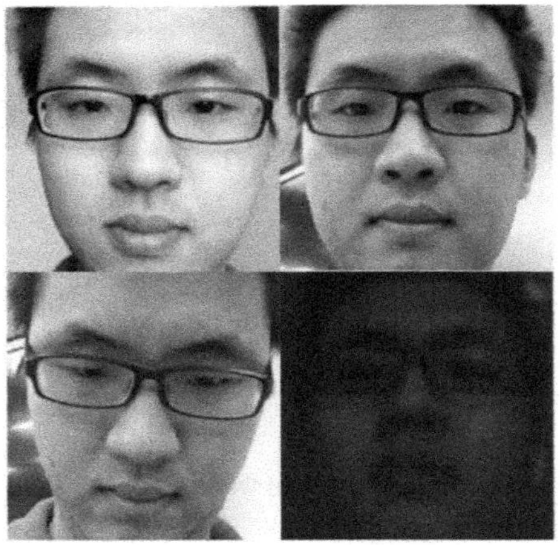

Figure 4: User appearance changes due to different pose and illumination conditions.

Figure 5. Some images extracted from the front camera. Note variation in illumination, pose, expression and face size.

user is performing a main task (e.g., playing a game) rather than when being prompted?

Data Collection
To this end, we collected a dataset of 30 subjects (20 males and 10 females). Our data collection was designed to monitor as many biometric qualities of a subject as possible while the subject performed a number of tasks (Fig. 3). We controlled for the device variation by providing each subject a Nexus 4 phone. The subjects were told to spend 5 minutes performing each of the following tasks: use a text editor application and write a response to a question that we chose, read news articles on the *USA Today* application, browse articles and pictures using *Flipboard*, play a ball balancing game called *Labyrinth*, and play a racecar game called *Crime Racing City*. Subjects performed these tasks with no further constraints (e.g., they could read whatever articles interested them and hold the phone however they wanted to). While the subjects were completing these tasks, three applications were collecting data in the background: one used the front camera to capture video of the subject's face; one recorded what was being displayed on the screen; and the last one recorded a series of sensor data. This series of sensor features included an accelerometer, a gyroscope, the device's orientation, linear acceleration, magnetic field and gravity across three dimensions, and ambient light, proximity, location, temperature, and air pressure.

In addition, we included an enrollment task that required the subjects to hold the phone at different angles from their faces (Fig. 2). This enrollment task is cooperative and intrusive, and the data can be used as a baseline as well as training data to extract face images from different views and synchronize them with the device's position using the sensor data.

Challenges
Because of the nature of the front camera recording, there are several inherent problems that arise with facial recognition. One of the problems comes from how the camera is positioned, which can cause a huge difference in the subject's appearance (see Fig. 4). Other problems include partial faces due to the closeness of the phone, partial occlusion by a finger tapping the screen, or poor lighting, especially when the user leans over the phone and blocks out light sources. Fig. 5 demonstrates some of the aforementioned scenarios.

Baseline Performance Results
So far we have experimented with Eigenfaces for face recognition and Gaussian mixture models for 3D gesture recognition. We obtained 98% face recognition accuracy when selecting face images with no or little variation in pose and illumination. This number drops significantly when no human selection is made on the face images. For instance, another experiment consisted of performing Eigenfaces (keeping 96% of the variance) on face images detected by a cascade classifier during the enrollment task and performing classification on face images detected from the remaining tasks. We used a k-nearest neighbor for classification with a k value from 1 to 100 to build the receiver-operating characteristic (ROC) in Fig. 6. These results are promising taking into account the challenges of our dataset.

We also experimented with the sensor data to explore the potential of 3D gesture recognition. By extracting only three features—acceleration on the x axis,

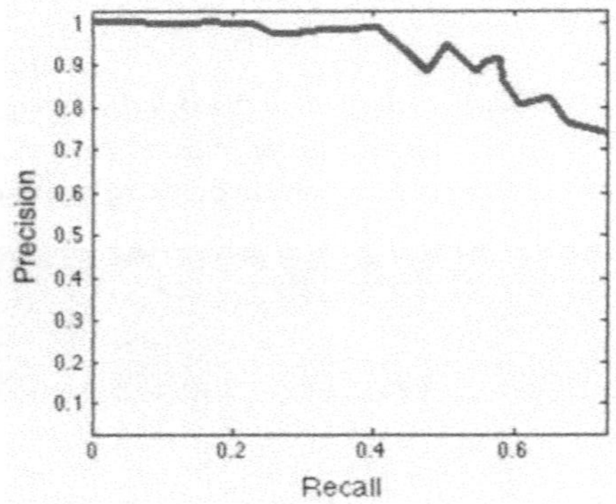

Figure 6. ROC for face recognition with Eigenfaces (face images during enrollment were used for training and face images from the remaining five tasks were used for testing).

gyroscope on the *y* axis, and orientation on the *y*—and modeling them using a Gaussian mixture model, we achieved 87% prediction accuracy when comparing the three features over the test data set for two different tasks. We aim to develop more robust models and take advantage of all the sensor data to provide features that will serve to authenticate the user under any task.

This work was supported by a DARPA grant FA8750-13-2-0279.

References

[1] Kwapisz, J.R., Weiss, G.M., and Moore, S.A. Cell phone-based biometric identification. *Biometrics*, 2010.

[2] Wolff, Matt. Behavioral Biometric Identification on Mobile Devices. *Foundations of Augmented Cognition*. Springer Berlin Heidelberg, 783-791, 2013.

[3] E. Miluzzo, A. Varshavsky, S. Balakrishnan, R. Choudhury. TapPrints: Your Finger Taps Have Fingerprints. *Proc. Mobile Systems, applications and services*, 2012.

[4] Yi-Chu Wang, Kwang-Ting Cheng. Energy-Optimized Mapping of Application to Smartphone Platform—A Case Study of Mobile Face Recognition. *ECVW*, 2011.

[5] K. Choi, K.-A. Toh, H. Byun. Realtime training on mobile devices for face recognition applications. *Pattern Recognition 44(2)*: 386-400, 2011.

[6] In-ho Choi, Kyoung-Sic Cho. Robust Facial Expression Recognition Using a Smartphone Working against Illumination Variation. *Applied Mathematics and Information Science*, No. 6, 403-408, 2012.

[7] C. McCool, S. Marcel, A. Hadid, M. Pietikainen, P. Matejka, J. Cernocky, N. Poh, J. Kittler, A. Larcher, C. Levy, D. Matrouf, J. Bonastre, P. Tresadern and T. Cootes. Bi-Modal Person Recognition on a Mobile Phone: using mobile phone data. *Proc. Multimedia and Expo Workshops*, 635-640, 2012.

[8] W. Zhao, R. Chellappa, J. Phillips, and A. Rosenfeld. Face Recognition: A Literature Survey. *ACM Computing Surveys*, 399-458, 2003.

[9] Xuan Zou; Kittler, J.; Messer, K. Illumination Invariant Face Recognition: A Survey. *Biometrics: Theory, Applications, and Systems*, 2007.

[10] Zhang, X., Gao, Y. Face recognition across pose: A review. *Pattern Recognition* 42(11): 2876-2896, 2009.

[11] R. Jafri, H. R. Arabnia. A Survey of Face Recognition Techniques. *Journal of Information Processing Systems*, Vol. 5, No. 2, 2009.

[12] M. Turk and A. Pentland. Eigenfaces for recognition. *J. Cognitive Neuroscience*, 71-86, 1991.

[13] Hyunjong Cho, Seungbin Moon. Comparison of PCA and LDA based face recognition algorithms under illumination variations. *ICROS-SICE*, 2009.

[14] K. Baek, B.A. Draper, J.R. Beveridge, K. She. PCA vs. ICA: A comparison on the FERET data set. *Joint Conference on Information Sciences*, 2002.

[15] Yang, X., You, C. W., Lu, H., Lin, M., Lane, N. D., Campbell, A. T. Visage: A Face Interpretation Engine for Smartphone Applications. *Proc. MobiCASE*, 2012.

[16] Atallah, L., Yang, G.Z. The use of pervasive sensing for behaviour profiling—a survey. *Pervasive Mob. Comput.* 5(5), 447–464, 2009.

[17] Neil Johnson, David Hogg. Representation and synthesis of behaviour using Gaussian mixtures. 20(12), 889–894, 2002.

[18] Alexander De Luca, Alina Hang, Frederik Brudy, Christian Lindner, Heinrich Hussmann. Touch me once and I know it's you! Implicit authentication based on touch screen patterns. *CHI*, 987-997, 2012.

[19] J. Tran, S. Trewin, C. Swart, B.E. John, J.C. Thomas. Exploring pinch and spread gestures on mobile devices. *MobileHCI '13*, 2013.

[20] Sumit Shekhar, Vishal M. Patel, Nasser M. Nasrabadi, Rama Chellappa. Joint Sparse Representation for Robust Multimodal Biometrics Recognition. *IEEE PAMI*. 36(1), 113-126, 2014.

A Design Framework of Branded Mobile Applications

Zhenzhen Zhao
Institut Mines-Télécom
Télécom School of Management
9 Rue Charles Fourier
91000 Evry, France
zhenzhen.zhao@it-sudparis.eu

Christine Balagué
Institut Mines-Télécom
Télécom School of Management
9 Rue Charles Fourier
91000 Evry, France
christine.balague@it-sudparis.eu

MobileHCI 2014, September 23–26, 2014, Toronto, ON, Canada.
ACM 978-1-4503-3004-6/14/09.
http://dx.doi.org/10.1145/2628363.2634224

Abstract
Mobile phone applications have received intensive attention by marketers due to the high engagement of users and its positive persuasive impact on brand. However, how can companies get on the right track of designing branded apps? Little research has been done on the identification of the elements which can be used to design branded apps strategy. Our research aims to offer a design framework of branded apps by identifying constructs from the perspective of company, user and technology respectively. By evaluating 84 mobile apps from top 11 FMCG (Fast Moving Consumer Goods) brands, we examine the usage of mobile interaction, social interaction and brand interaction in current branded apps design.

Author Keywords
Mobile application; design; brand interaction; mobile interaction; social interaction; user experience.

ACM Classification Keywords
H.4.3 **[Information systems applications]**: Communications applications.

Introduction
With the advances in mobile and wireless technologies, the past few years have witnessed end-user's increasing involvement in mobile phone applications ("apps"). This trend, not only changes and impacts on

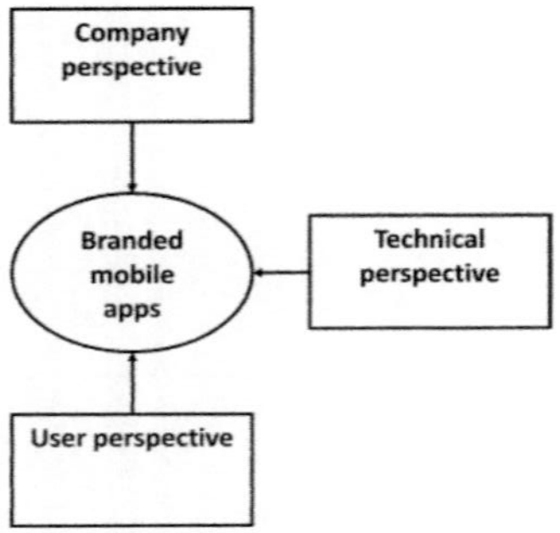

Figure 1. A design framework of branded mobile apps.

people's way of living and thinking, but also brings huge business opportunities to companies to define their mobile marketing strategies: how they market their brands and products, and how they listen to customers.

The concept of branded apps is defined in [1] as software downloadable to a mobile device which prominently displays a brand identity, often via the name of the app and the appearance of a brand logo or icon, throughout the user experience. Apps have generated intensive interest among marketers due to the high user engagement and the positive image that a brand transfers through apps [3]. It has been proved that the use of branded apps has a positive persuasive impact increasing interest in the brand [1].

In our work, we aim to offer a design framework by identifying main constructs and features in branded apps design. This framework is grounded by extensive case studies of branded apps and literature reviews in different areas of research (marketing science, human-computer interaction, computer science and social science). We further evaluate 84 apps in FMCG market, to precisely identify what mobile interaction and social features are applied, and how company markets their brands inside these apps though brand interaction.

Design Framework

A design framework of branded apps consists of three dimensions (Figure 1): From company perspective a branded app should have business value/objective, and integrate brand interaction features; from user perspective a branded app should offer good user experience which can be accepted by users, and it should bring proper social interactions and different levels of user benefits; from technical perspective a branded app should integrate smart mobile interactions. In the following sections, we further specify a set of features in each construct. Note that during the design process, companies should wisely choose the features to apply to their own business strategy.

Company Perspective

Business Objective

Business objective come first in the design process. We present five potential business objectives of branded apps. Note that one branded app often contain one or more business objectives. Also, one brand can design more than one mobile apps targeting different products and business goals.

- Communication

This goal includes communicating brand values, information and products, increasing brand image and brand awareness. Most branded apps achieve this goal as one of business objectives in apps design.

- Customer relationship management (CRM)

Branded apps can well perform as a middleware between brands and customers. The objective is to manage companies' interactions with their current and future customers. It includes brand engagement with loyal customers, user data collection, and product recommendation to current and potential clients.

- Sales

Branded apps try to make a complete new purchasing experience and interaction models for users, with a whole set of capabilities including location awareness, context sensing, and the ability to customize products.

Figure 2. Kellogg "Apple Jacks™ Race to the Bowl Rally" app. An example of brand mascots set up as player avatars.

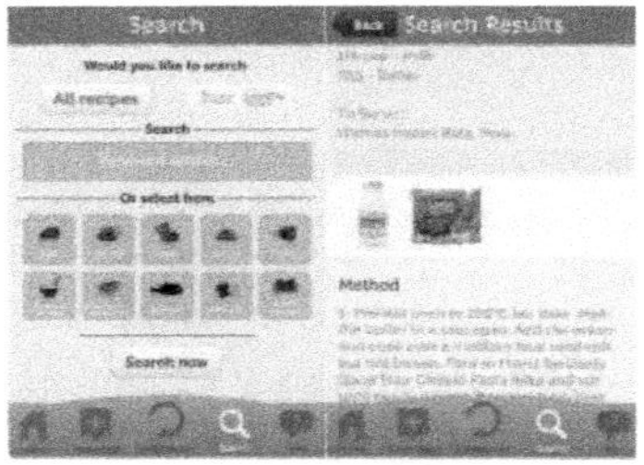

Figure 3. Heinz "Food in a minute" app. An example of product packaging displayed as product recommendation to user.

- Product innovation

Branded apps can support open innovation by allowing users to generate new ideas with products; a community is built for idea sharing and idea rating, and the most rated idea is often awarded by the brands.

- Marketing research

Branded apps can help companies to make user surveys in new ways. In the shampoo market, for instance, some companies have asked women to take and share photos with their mobiles to express what good/bad hair appearance is for them. This process provides added value information for marketers to better understand consumer behaviors.

Brand Interaction
Brand interaction indicates how companies market their brands inside apps. We classify five brand interaction elements based on our case studies: (1) brand name, (2) brand logo, (3) brand mascot, (4) product packaging and (5) brand color matching. Brand name/logo appears on most branded apps. Brand mascot is often set up as player avatars in game-like apps (Figure 2). Product packaging can be displayed as product recommendation to user (Figure 3). Some branded apps use the same color scheme as the brand logo color, this consistency is considered as an added value to brand. It's important that brand carefully choose brand interaction elements in apps design, to offer user good enough experience to remember the brand, rather than to impose it on user.

User Perspective
User perspective needs to be well considered in the design process. We classify user perspective into three categories from literature review: user benefits from marketing science, user acceptance from ICT science, and social interaction from social science.

User benefits
From marketing and brand perspective, user benefits are what consumers think the service can do for them [9]. Benefits can be further distinguished into three categories: (1) functional benefits: intrinsic advantages of service consumption. It can be interpreted as utilitarian benefits. (2) experiential benefits: relate to what it feels like to use the service. It can be interpreted as hedonic benefits [6]. (3) symbolic benefits: extrinsic advantages of service consumption, often relate to underlying needs for social approval or personal expression and outer-directed self-esteem. In [13], author proposes that designers should not only make services personally valuable with easy-to-use interfaces, but also support people's social desires for interactivity, authority, reputation, identity, and control.

User acceptance
Some research has been conducted to measure user adoption and acceptance of mobile apps. [10] finds that besides perceived usefulness and perceived ease-of-use, personal innovativeness reveals a strong predictor of mobile Internet usage behavior. [7] finds that the main motives and sought-after rewards in using mobile apps are entertainment, functionality, information, socialization, intellectual stimulation, following a trend, and learning.

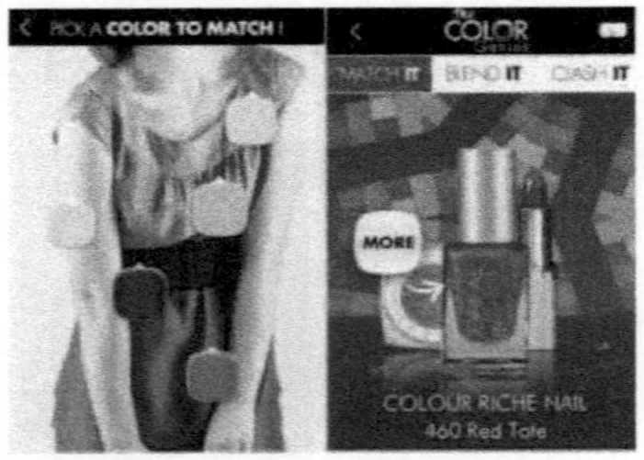

Figure 4. L'Oreal "The color genius" app. Camera feature allows users to take a photo of their outfits and to select a look as day or night, the app then proposes an on-trend combination of make-up products which suits the users' outfits.

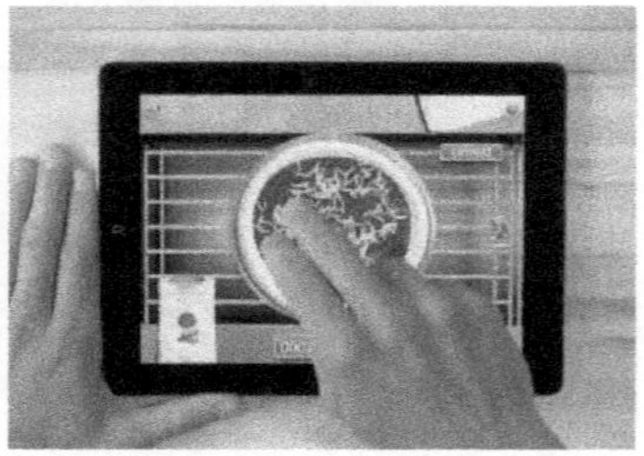

Figure 5. "Domino's Pizza Hero" app. Multi-touch gestures provide an immersing game experience by making a top quality virtual pizza by kneading dough, spreading sauce, sprinkling cheese, placing toppings as racing against the clock.

Social interaction

Social aspect is importantly mentioned in user benefit and user acceptance from above sections. From the perspective of user involvement, we classify social interaction features into two categories by taking into account the interactions among contents and interactions among users respectively.

- Interaction among contents

We classify four types of interactions among contents: (1) Content creation: User-generated-content (UGC), (2) Content personalization, (3) Content rating and content commenting, and (4) Content sharing.

- Interaction among users

The inter-connectivity among users includes the following features: (1) Follow/unfollow people. (2) Online chat: The peer-to-peer conversation with people. (3) Invite contacts from external social networks.

Technical Perspective

Another perspective to consider in the design process is the technical perspective. The company should consider technical aspects to adapt to its business goals and user perspectives.

Mobile interaction

Followed by literature review, we list up-do-date mobile interaction features which can be used in branded apps. Note that the feature chosen in app design is case by case.

- Camera-based mobile interaction [14]: allows user to snap or scan, and gives company the possibility to encourage users to take photos to interact with brand products (Figure 4), or to scan barcodes/QR-codes of products to get product information or gain credits.
- Location awareness [11]: has been widely used in branded apps, providing users with a stream of information based on their location and interests.
- Multi-touch gestures: various mobile sensors (touch sensor, tilt sensor and proximity sensor) creates rich interaction between users and mobile devices, allowing users to carry out gestures like sway, shake, swipe, pinch, spread [15] etc. These gestures have been widely used in game-like apps (Figure 5).
- Voice recognition [2]: allows mobile to recognize human voice and has been used in CRM to answer questions from clients by direct speaking.
- Augmented reality (AR) [12][5]: combines virtual data into the physical real world, allowing users to perceive virtual product in the real environment.
- Virtual mirror [4]: adjusts geometrically to reflect the viewers image in real time. This feature is used by cosmetic and apparel related brands to allow consumers to check how products really look on them.
- Mobile viral video: short and smart mobile advertising videos are used to attract people's attention, and the viral video contents can be shared through mobile social networks.
- Mobile payment: allows users to pay for a product from their mobile device, anytime and everywhere.

Exploration of 84 Branded Apps

In this section we test current branded apps on the market, to precisely indentify how features described above are used in current branded apps design. We target the apps developed by top 11 FMCG brands (referred to Interbrand annual report [8]) because

FMCG brands focus on daily products and are informal in nature comparing to other sectors. We select 84 apps in our analysis in terms of language and usability. So far we test mobile, social and brand interaction features, the business objectives, user benefits and user acceptance features need companies and users to be involved, thus will be done in the next step.

Figure 6 shows the mobile interaction features. The most used ones are mobile video (27%), camera (25%) and swipe gesture (21%). Only 10% apps enable location services, and 8% apps integrate shake/sway gesture. Augmented reality, virtual mirror and mobile payment feature are not developed among 84 apps.

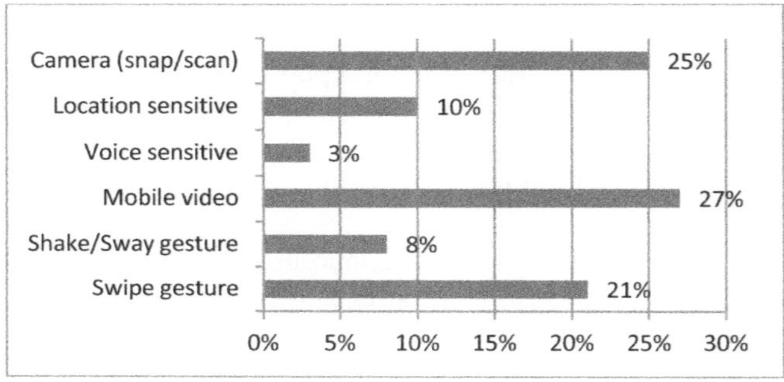

Figure 6: Mobile interaction features in 84 branded apps.

Figure 7 shows the social interaction features. 12 apps support user-generated content. Only two apps have implemented the feature "like", one app has developed the feature "comment" and one app the feature "rate". 12 apps allow users to share apps with their contacts by email, 30 apps enable users to share apps on their social networks.

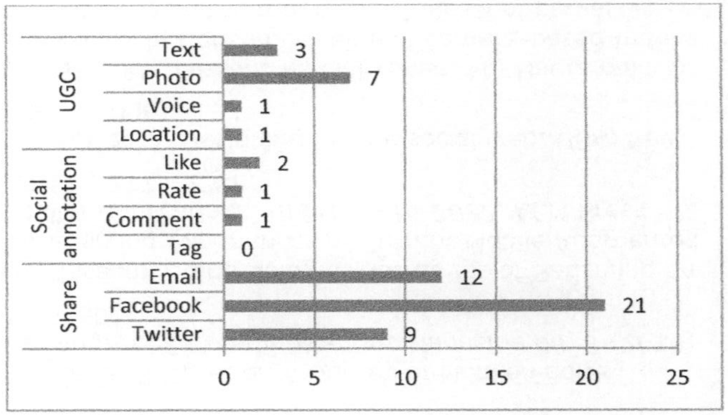

Figure 7: Social interaction features in 84 branded apps.

Figure 8 shows the brand interaction features. Brand name and brand logo are well integrated in these apps. Only in 14% apps the app color schemes are the same as corporate brand color schemes, and in 19% apps the color schemes are the same as product brand color schemes. There are 32% apps showing the product packaging, and 7% showing the product mascot.

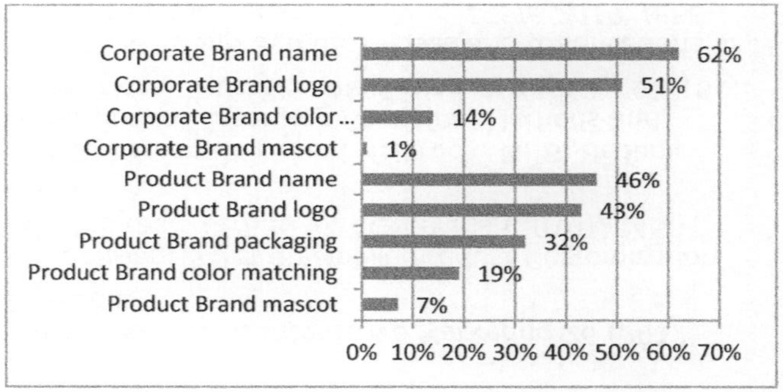

Figure 8: Brand interaction features in 84 branded apps.

Discussion and Future Work

From above analysis we can conclude that the gap between existing branded apps development and the usage trends is huge. Though massive real time content sharing (text, photo, video) becomes a main usage of mobile today, existing branded apps do not include a lot of social features. Mobile features are limitedly applied in current branded apps, though these features constitute key elements of user experience (such as location awareness, voice sensitivity, etc.)

We also underline that main branded apps are used within a communication and CRM objectives, while other strategies would have been effective, such as marketing research and open innovation.

Concerning the future work, we will further study the actual user perceptions and preferences concerning utilitarian and hedonic apps, as well as the user acceptance factors of mobile, social and brand interaction elements to understand how to build branded apps which could be positively received and accepted by users.

References

[1] Bellman, S., et al. The Effectiveness of Branded Mobile Phone Apps. *Journal of Interactive Marketing 25* (2011), 191–200.

[2] Bijani, C., Vilrokx, M. and White, B.K. Giving Voice to Enterprise Mobile Applications. *Ext. Abstracts MobileHCI 2013*, ACM Press (2013), 428-433.

[3] Calder, B. J., Malthouse, E. C. and Schaedel, U. An Experimental Study of the Relationship between Online Engagement and Advertising Effectiveness. *Journal of Interactive Marketing 23*, 4 (2009), 321–331.

[4] Cho, H. and Schwarz, N. I Like Your Product When I Like My Photo: Misattribution Using Interactive Virtual Mirrors. *Journal of Interactive Marketing 26* (2012), 235–243.

[5] Gehring, S., et al. Mobile Product Customization. *Ext. Abstracts CHI 2010*, ACM Press (2010), 3463-3468.

[6] Hirschman, E. C. and Holbrook, M. B. Hedonic Consumption: Emerging Concepts, Methods and Propositions, *Journal of Marketing 46* (1982), 92-101.

[7] Ho, H. Y. and Syu, L. Y. Uses and gratifications of mobile application users. In Proc. *ICEIE 2010*, IEEE Press (2010), 315-319.

[8] Interbrand 2013 report. http://www.interbrand.com/fr/best-global-brands/2013/Best-Global-Brands-2013.aspx#

[9] Keller, K.N. Conceptualizing, Measuring, and Managing Customer-Based Brand Equity. *Journal of Marketing 57*, 1 (1993), 1-22.

[10] Kourouthanassis, P. E., Georgiadis, C., Zamani, E. and Giaglis, G. M. Explaining the adoption of mobile Internet applications. In Proc. *ICMB-GMR 2010*, IEEE Press (2010), 148-153.

[11] Lane, N.D., et al. A Survey of Mobile Phone Sensing. *IEEE Communications Magazine 48*, 9 (2010), 140-150

[12] Olsson, T. and Salo, M. Narratives of Satisfying and Unsatisfying Experiences of Current Mobile Augmented Reality Applications. In Proc. *CHI 2012*, ACM Press (2012), 2779-2788.

[13] Porter, J. Designing for the social web. USA, New riders (2008).

[14] Salo, M., Olsson, T., Makkonen, M., Hautamaki, A. and Frank, L. Consumer value of camera-based mobile interaction with the real world. Journal of pervasive and mobile computing 9 (2013), 258-268.

[15] Tran, J.J., et al. Exploring Pinch and Spread Gestures on Mobile Devices. In Proc. MobileHCI 2013, ACM Press (2013), 151-160.

Keep an Eye on Your Photos: Automatic Image Tagging on Mobile Devices

Nina Runge, Dirk Wenig and **Rainer Malaka**
University of Bremen, tzi
Bibliotheksstr. 1
28359 Bremen, Germany
{nr, dwenig, malaka}@tzi.de

Figure 1: Prototype: Get automatic tag recommendations for your images, refuse them if they don't fit, add new ones

MobileHCI'14, Sep 23-26 2014, Toronto, ON, Canada
ACM 978-1-4503-3004-6/14/09. http://dx.doi.org/10.1145/2628363.2634225

Abstract
In this paper we present how to tag images automatically based on the image and sensor data from a mobile device. We developed a system that computes *low-level tags* using the image itself and meta data. Based on these tags and previous user tags we learn *high-level tags*. With a client-server-implementation we source out computational expensive algorithms to recommend the tags as fast as possible. We show what are the best feature extraction methods in combination with a machine learning technique to recommend good tags.

Author Keywords
Mobile Device; Recommendation; Machine Vision; Image Tagging; Automatic Tagging

ACM Classification Keywords
H.5.m [Information interfaces and presentation]: Miscellaneous.

Introduction
In this paper we present our approach to tag images automatically. Right after the users take photos, they receive appropriate tags on their mobile device and can accept or refuse them. Figure 1 shows our prototype. The differences between photo cameras and smart phones are vanishing. Because a smart phone is a constant

companion and sharing platforms are very popular, users tend to take many photos to catch every experience. The number of uploads indicates a massive photo collection on many devices. The current most popular image sharing platforms are facebook (350 million images are uploaded every day to facebook[1]), instagram (55 millionen[2]), Snapchat and Flickr (1.6 million[3]).

Many users leave the images on their mobile device or only use an automatic upload to the cloud. The mobile device is today used to present and to share the photos. With image tags it is possible to search by one single tag as well as the combination of two or more tags to find the right image. Tagging images is time consuming and boring if a user must add the same tags over and over again. Tagging images directly on the mobile device is even more exhausting than on desktop computers because of the small display and the small touch-keyboard.

Related Work

Current research for image tagging could be distinguished in two strands. 1) Research that uses the image data and machine vision to learn tags. 2) Focus on the meta data or use the co-occurrence of different tags and recommend tags if the user already adds one.

Object recognition is still an unsolved task. If a system should compute tags only based on the image data it always focuses on a limited number of tags. The google patent [2] describes how faces are automatically tagged and highlighted in an image. The described way of tagging faces is nowadays integrated in every Android-based device. Biniti et al. [3] identify lines to find buildings in the image.

Automatic image tagging is not only interesting in research but also in the industry. In the web there are some sites which offer solutions for this task, e.g. autotag.me[4] or glow[5], which was recently acquired by Yahoo[6]. However, all these approaches only use a predefined amount of tags based on image recognition.

The second strand focuses on the meta data stored by the mobile device. Lee et al. [4] use different sensor data and combine them in a Bayesian network. However, they didn't evaluate the appropriate choice of their tags. Tagsense [8] is based on sensor information of the mobile devices of all friends close to the user. If someone already assigned tags to the image, new tags could be computed based on co-occurrence [9] or [5]. This is a good idea, but the users always have to add tags. If the photo is geocoded, it allows the user to look at his images in a map view. But searching is easier by tags, so Zonetag [1] assigns tags to an image based on the GPS information, e.g. the city, zip-code.

Motivation for Tagging

There are two main reasons why people tag their documents or images: to find them easily in huge collections or to increase the visibility in a community. Some people tag images when they upload them to a photo sharing platforms or to social networks (e.g. facebook, Flickr or instagram). But usually they tag them only for the sharing purpose and not on their own device.

[1] http://goo.gl/qUCu8u
[2] www.instagram.com/press/
[3] www.flickr.com/photos/franckmichel/6855169886/
[4] autotag.me
[5] iqengines.com/glow/
[6] yahoo.com

Because we wanted to determine how people tag their images if they want to share them with others, we used public Flickr images. We counted the number of tags for 42,000 randomly selected public images from 2013. In our random sample, 90% of the images don't have any tag. Tagged photos have most of the time only 1-3 tags, maybe this seems enough for the users to describe the image. Just a few people assign more tags. It is interesting that images aren't tagged although they are public and uploaded to a sharing platform. The reason might be that the users only used the platform as a cloud or to share photos with family and friends and they aren't aware of the public status or don't care. A second reason migth be, that the users don't know, that they could increase the visibility by good image tags. The third reason could be that they are to lazy to tag the images.

We can't solve the first and second challenge. But for the case that users are only too lazy to repeatedly add the same tags, we create a user interface, that helps them to tag images easier and faster. The system produces tags automatically and learn from the users to recommend better tags for the next image. We believe that in general a tag is not good or bad, it always depends on the users opinion.

We implemented an application for Android-based devices and a server. With our prototype the user take photos, get tags and accept or refuse them and could add new tags. After users took a photo, in the background the application looks up the current GPS information. The metadata (GPS, date/time, orientation, flash and exposure) and a scaled image will be sent to the server. We only need a small image to compute the tags on the server, so we don't need a data connection with a high capacity. After the server computes the tags they are sent back to the mobile device. The application notifies the user about new tags and is automatically updated. The user can view the tags and refuse them if they are not appropriate. If the user refuses a tag, this information is send back to the server so we could update the classifiers.

Photo Tags

Before we recommend tags to the users we analyze how we could tag photos the best way. Therefore we built categories for image tags and considered how we could determine tags for every category.

Flickr and instagram offer a catalog of the most popular tags. Instagram mostly contains–let's call it–social tags, like *me, love or make-up*[7]. The most popular Flickr tags[8] are more meaningful to describe the image. To generalize these tags we used the WordNet Toolkit [7] to built categories. WordNet is a lexical database of English and offers many opportunities to find similarities between words or the categories a term belongs to.

We categorized the 142 most popular Flickr tags. We computed the most common direct hypernyms for every tag in WordNet. Most of the tags (29%) are location names, like New York or Europe. Proper names are called *entities* in the WordNet database. This is the reason why we therefor introduced the category *location name*. The other categories are: *location* (7%, beach, garden)*physical entity/object* (13%, car, water), *color* (6%, blue, red), *emotion/attribute* (5%, love, old), *living thing* (14%, couple, cat), *meta information* (10%, portrait, iphone), *time period* (8%, evening, summer) and *social event* (8%, holiday, wedding).

[7] web.stagram.com/hot/
[8] www.Flickr.com/photos/tags/

Compute Low-Level Tags

Based on our categories we distinguishe tags that could be easily computed (*low-level tags*) and those which must be learned by the system (*high-level tags*). For the *low-level tags* we identify: location name, meta information, time period and main color. We also computed some tags for social group and pysical entities, these are tags that are more or less between *low-level* and *high-level tags*. We use the raw data from the image and device sensors to determine semantics for an image. These semantics are the *low-level-tags*. Based on them we can determine the *high-level tags*.

Meta Information
If a user takes photos with the mobile device the meta data like the exposure or orientation of the image is always stored in the image header but the user usually has no access to the information. To create tags based on these information, we read the information from the device sensors and the image header and translate them into natural language. The weather at the current location is determined by requesting a webservice[9]. We use the general weather informations, e.g. clear sky or cloudy, because this is more appropriate for image tagging than degrees or air pressure.

Location Names
Often the user is not so interested in the exact location but in the district, city or country. If users look for an image of their last holiday maybe they don't know the exact position but the country or the city. Users also want to search for images with tags and not over the latitude and longitude information. For these reasons we requested the district, city and country from a webservice[10] and recommend them to the user as tags. Furthermore we requested landmarks for the image location from another webservice[11].

Time Period
Very similar to the location category is the information when the photo was taken. We have already the information on what date and time an image was taken, but these are often not the information a user is looking for. Maybe the user only remembers that she took the one particular photo some day in the summer or at a weekend. Because of that we added tags based on the time and date for the season, the weekday, for weekend or working day and the daytime.

Main Color
We determine the most dominant color in the image. We used more than 1500 color names collected from the web with the RGB-Values. Then we created a color histogram for the image. The maximum of the color histogram determines the color name.

Living Thing/Physical Entity
We used the a face detector to find people in images. Because the face detectors have a high false positive rate, especially for small image parts, we combine these detectors with a conditional probability if the faces exceed an amount of pixels in the image. Based on the image pixel information we extract the tags portrait, group or couple for the category *social setting*.

Learn High-Level Tags

Mainly the following points are important for a good learning procedure: 1) The database of labeled images, 2) The feature selection method and 3) The machine

[9] openweathermap.org
[10] geonames.org
[11] wikilocation.org

learning algorithm. Even though we could not cover every possibility for each point, we implemented the most popular approaches and evaluated the combination to find the best way to automatically compute tags for images.

Dataset
Many datasets exist for machine vision approaches. One problem is, that most of them are only appropriate for a particular task of object detection. If they are dedicated for event detection they mostly contain videos, which is not our focus at the moment. Another problem with the existing datasets is the lack of additional data, like the GPS or the date that we would like to use. We want to recommend pesonalized tags, because it might be very subjective if someone finds a tag appropriate or not. Someone who lives in California and never travels to the hills don't need tags like ski or winter.

Because of that we created our own dataset more than 300 labeled images, all taken with mobile devices, geo-coded, and date-coded. We tagged the images with 50 different tags (holiday, meeting friends, building, ocean, ...) . These tags belong to the categories: events, physical entities and locations. Every image was tagged with at least 3 Tags.

Feature Extraction
We evaluated our method against two popular approaches. If we use only the image information this task is quite similar to image retrieval. We want to find the particular image similar to the old one and transfer the tags to the new image. We use RGB-color-histogram as features. The second approach against which we test our idea is the *gist* classifier from Oliva et al. [6]. They developed this classification for natural scenes to distinguish them based on spatial structure. We use it because it gives so good examples for several scenes.

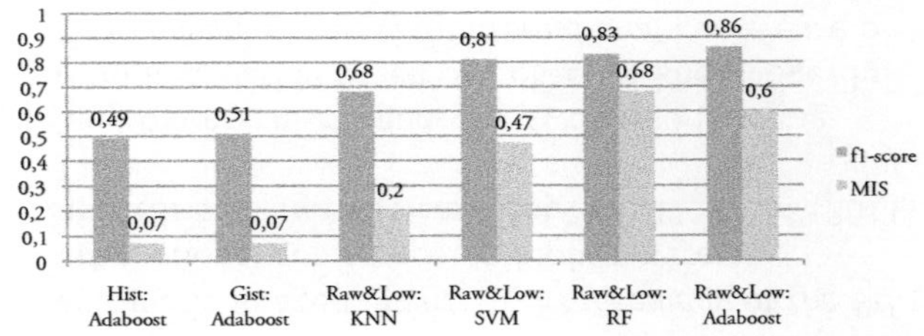

Figure 2: Best Results for the combination of Machine Learning Techniques and Features

We created a feature vector that combines the raw data (floats for latitude, longitude, face amount, etc. integers for the number of faces, the weather code, the flash, exposure etc.) and a binarization of the *low-level tags*.

Machine Learning Algorithms
We tested the most common and successful machine learning algorithms to train the different datasets and feature selections methods. We trained and tested a Support Vector Machine (SVM), Stochastic Gradient Descent, Random Forest Classifier, Adaboost and k-nearest neighbors (KNN).

Evaluation
We evaluated the machine learning algorithms and the features to determine the best way to learn *high-level tags*. It is very common to compute the $f1$-score

$$f_1 = 2 \cdot \frac{\text{precision} \cdot \text{recall}}{\text{precision} + \text{recall}}$$

This score is a good information if a classification is good or not. What is missing, however, in this score is how often one tag falls in the false category. Therefore, in multilabel classifications the *Mutual Information Score* is used.

$$mis(X,Y) = \sum_{x=1}^{X}\sum_{y=1}^{Y} P(x,y) \log \frac{P(x,y)}{P(x)P'(y)}$$

Figure 2 shows that our feature generator give the best results. For the recommendation process it is also important how fast a classifier works. Although the ensemble methods are very slow when they are trained (9-150 times slower than a SVM), they are faster to predict (only fractions of seconds) than simple methods like the KNN.

Conclusion and Future Work

In the future we want to test if we could get event better results if we combine different feature vectors in one classifier, maybe in a hierarchical way. For this purpose we plan to setup a good database for image tagging, with different users, images and tags. Furthermore, we are interested if we get better classification results if we learn the tags based on the categories they belong to. This would lead to a challenge to design an appropriate user interface to add new images, based on these categories, so the system could be trained well. We will evaluate in the how a good search interface will improve the motivation for accurate image tagging.

References

[1] Ahern, S., Davis, M., Eckles, D., King, S., Naaman, M., Nair, R., and Yang, J. Zonetag: Designing context-aware mobile media capture to increase participation. In *Proceedings of the Pervasive Image Capture and Sharing, 8th Int. Conf. on Ubiquitous Computing, California* (2006).

[2] Bambha, M., Anderson, T., Pearman, S., and Roussilhon, V. Automatic image tagging, 2010. U.S. Classification: 382/118; 345/620; 709/217.

[3] Binti Zakaria, L. Q., Lewis, P., and Hall, W. Automatic image tagging by using image content analysis. In *The International Conference on Informatics and Applications (ICIA2012)* (2012), 91101.

[4] Lee, Y.-S., and Cho, S.-B. Automatic image tagging using two-layered bayesian networks and mobile data from smart phones. In *Proceedings of the 10th International Conference on Advances in Mobile Computing; Multimedia*, MoMM '12, ACM (2012), 3946.

[5] Leong, C. W., Mihalcea, R., and Hassan, S. Text mining for automatic image tagging. In *Proceedings of the 23rd International Conference on Computational Linguistics: Posters*, COLING '10, Association for Computational Linguistics (Stroudsburg, PA, USA, 2010), 647–655.

[6] Oliva, A., and Torralba, A. Modeling the shape of the scene: A holistic representation of the spatial envelope. *Int. J. Comput. Vision 42*, 3 (May 2001), 145–175.

[7] Princeton University. About wordnet., 2010.

[8] Qin, C., Bao, X., Roy Choudhury, R., and Nelakuditi, S. TagSense: a smartphone-based approach to automatic image tagging. In *Proceedings of the 9th international conference on Mobile systems, applications, and services*, MobiSys '11, ACM (2011), 114.

[9] Sigurbjörnsson, B., and van Zwol, R. Flickr tag recommendation based on collective knowledge. In *Proceedings of the 17th international conference on World Wide Web*, WWW '08, ACM (New York, NY, USA, 2008), 327–336.

Gravity: Automatic Location Tracking System between a Car and a Pedestrian

Changhoon Oh
User Experience Lab
Seoul National University
Seoul, South Korea
yurial@snu.ac.kr

Bongwon Suh
Human Centered Computing Lab
Seoul National University
Seoul, South Korea
bongwon@snu.ac.kr

Jeongsoo Park
Music and Audio Research Group
Seoul National University
Seoul, South Korea
psprink@snu.ac.kr

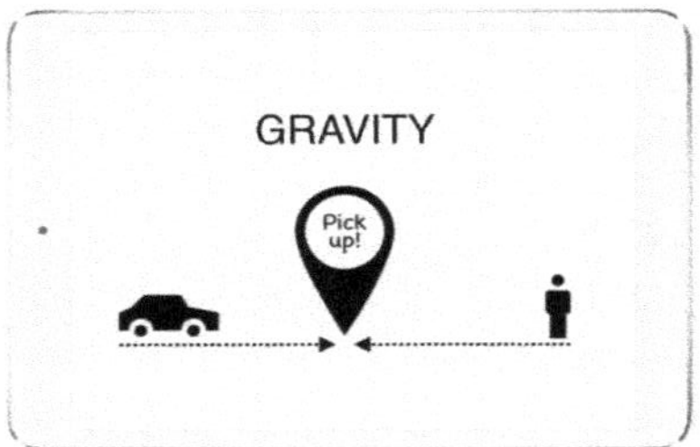

Figure 1. The concept view of "Gravity" we developed. As the name suggests, the main function of the system is to link between a car and a pedestrian in a "picking up" situation.

MobileHCI '14, Sep 23-26 2014, Toronto, ON, Canada
ACM 978-1-4503-3004-6/14/09.
http://dx.doi.org/10.1145/2628363.2634226

Abstract
The use of car navigation system is very common nowadays. Most of the car navigation services are based on turn-by-turn instructions and distance calculations. Academic research in this field has focused on evaluating basic usability. However, such products and studies have not covered users' various needs that arise in specific driving situations. For example, in a complex city space, drivers often face burdensome problems, especially when picking up pedestrians. We conducted a semistructured online survey asking specific problems, work-arounds, and their suggestions in picking-up situations. We grouped responses into several issue points based on their similarities and induced design implications for a car navigation system supporting picking-up situations. Through this user-centered design approach, we developed "Gravity—Automatic Location Tracking System between a Car and a Pedestrian" as a prototype and evaluated its usability, and we received favorable feedback.

Author Keywords
Car navigation system, user-centered design, usability

ACM Classification Keywords
H.5.2. User interfaces.

Introduction
It is very common for drivers to use car navigation systems in a car. Various types of navigation systems such as in-dash navigation systems, personal navigation devices (PNDs), and navigation apps for mobile phones have been introduced so far. In-car navigation systems allow people to move forward the way they did not know before without hesitation. Drivers can get local information about the places that they have never visited before. Like the concept "extension of man" that Marshall McLuhan suggested [9], a navigation system could be seen as a device that enables humans to overcome the limitation of their own space, expanding their mobility.

Despite their benefits, however, navigation systems on the market have rather uniform functions based on turn-by-turn instructions along with distance calculations such as "turn left a hundred meters ahead." They are insufficient to specifically provide situation-dependent information that users want in various way-finding situations. A recent study showed that there are various types of normal and natural troubles when driving with GPS [5]. To solve these different troubles that users face in real driving situations, not only basic instructions but also situation-specific solutions should be considered, which can satisfy drivers' whole user experience with the navigation systems.

To address the issues, this paper intended to develop a car navigation service that can solve specific problems in real driving situations. In particular, we aimed to deal with not a general way-finding situation where the point of interest is fixed but a "picking-up" situation where drivers and pedestrians meet on the road. Picking somebody up is a very common phenomenon, particularly in a complex city space. However, if picking someone up on the road is failed and repeated, it can lead to "phantom jams," in which small disturbances in traffic can become amplified [2]. In this regard, this situation is worth being dealt with in particular.

We have conducted a user survey with open-ended questions to find out users' distinctive behavior features in picking-up situations. Then, we induced four design implications: (1) not affecting safe driving, (2) sharing their points of interest in real time, (3) automatically tracking each other's locations, and (4) recommending spots appropriate for pulling over. We developed the prototype navigation system "Gravity," evaluated its usability, and received favorable feedback from users.

The main contribution of this paper is that we introduced a new concept of "navigation system for a specific situation where bi-directional users encounter" and developed it in practice with a user-centered design approach. We hope that other various problems that users face in real driving situations could be solved with user-centered approaches and could give both the driver and the pedestrian a better user experience.

Related Works
The research in the navigation system area has focused on basic usability. Schreiber studied that the function of a map and its aesthetic perception heavily depend on the user's situational cognitive load [11]. Another research about navigation usability revealed that when using PNDs, wrong messages can potentially reduce the credibility of those devices [6]. Jensen suggested that different output configurations—audio, visual, and audiovisual—of a GPS system affect driving behavior and performance [7]. These previous studies have significance because they have focused on the basic

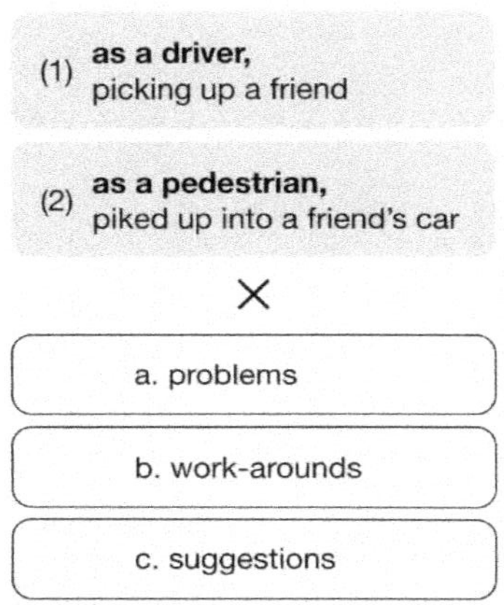

Figure 2. The structure of the user survey. We supposed two specific situations, (1) as a driver picking up a friend and (2) as a pedestrian picked up into a friend's car, and asked specific problems, work-arounds, and their suggestions in each situation.

components of navigation systems in detail. However, research about solving problems in specific situations that users face was rather insufficient.

Meanwhile, Lee developed the maps optimized for vehicular environments (MOVE) in-car navigation display, which provides situationally appropriate navigation information to the drivers [8]. Brown observed interactions among drivers, passengers, and GPS systems by recording real driving situations with a video recorder [5]. He suggested five troubles that users encounter: destinations, routes, maps and sensors, timing, and relevance and legality in detail. From Lee's research, we accept the concept of providing a situation-proper solution, and from Brown's research, we accept his approach of observing users specifically and finding out problems in detail. In this study, we use user-centered design approaches, with which we aim to apprehend the problems of picking-up situations in a complex city space. With the design guidelines obtained from a user survey, we developed a research prototype, Gravity. We also performed a user study to assess its usability.

User Survey

Using Google forms, we made a survey sheet asking about a picking-up situation where a driver and a pedestrian meet together downtown. A total of 102 participants responded to the survey (60 men [59%] and 42 women [41%]). Most of the respondents lived in the Seoul metropolitan area (80%). In order to get realistic responses from users, we supposed two specific situations: (1) as a driver picking up a friend and (2) as a pedestrian picked up into a friend's car. We asked the respondents to describe how they would behave if they were in each situation. We also asked them to provide potential problems, work-arounds, and suggestions when arranging the meeting. We collected responses and grouped them into several issues based on their similarities.

For the case of being a driver (case 1), there were three main patterns identified: (1) difference of viewpoints between the driver and the pedestrian, (2) difficulty in concentrating on safe driving, and (3) worrying about missing each other. In the case of (1), the respondents said, "When driving, I can't understand what a pedestrian says on the phone" and "There seems to be differences between driver and pedestrian, especially who has never driven a car." In the case of (2), there were opinions such as "Calling or messaging with the pedestrian continuously is very hard for my driving" and "Because I have to concentrate my driving, I can't spend my time in communicating with the friend." And in (3), the respondents said, "I'm worrying if my friend is standing where pulling over is hard or following cars are blowing horns" and "I turned left but my friend is standing in another place. I have to do a U-turn."

As work-arounds, drivers noted that they sometimes deliberately tried to be late because they thought it would be better to make a pedestrian wait than to wander, waiting for the pedestrian, while driving. Other respondents said they constantly contacted the pedestrian while driving. When asked to describe specific services that they need, some respondents said, "When contacting a pedestrian, I want to automatically track his location and guiding" and "I wish I could share my location with my friend using a smartphone in real time." Drivers need a navigation system automatically linking the car and the

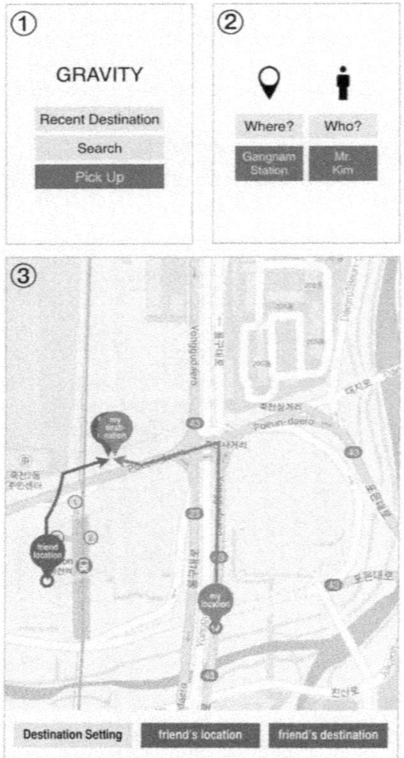

Figure 3. Key views of Gravity. ① We added a "pick up" menu separately at the first view of the system. ② After selecting the "pick up" menu, the user should set two features: (1) "where" and (2) "who." ③ On the map, the route is presented with a red line, and four main location marks are presented: (1) my location, (2) my destination, (3) friend's location, and (4) friend's destination.

pedestrian. They also suggested a "navigation system that recommends spots appropriate for pulling over."

In the case of being a pedestrian (case 2), there were two main patterns: (1) difficulty of communication with the driver and (2) uncertain waiting while not knowing the exact direction of the car. In the case of (1), the respondents said, "It is hard to understand what the driver is saying, and it makes me so confused" and "I tried but I couldn't tell the driver an appropriate spot for pulling over. I had no idea." In the case of (2), the respondents said, "I often looked around for the car because I couldn't get the exact direction of the car" and "Similar cars are passing by and it is confusing . . . I'm worried about missing my friend's car." To solve these problems, as work-arounds, respondents replied that they would communicate with the drivers constantly, waiting in front of a conspicuous place such as a gas station or convenience store. They suggested several ideas like a "navigation service that links a car and a pedestrian automatically," a "picking-up-only space," and a "push alert when the car comes close."

Design Implications

After gathering the user survey data, we conducted a repetitive ideation process. Three researchers reviewed the data and had a series of face-to-face meetings. Through these phases of analysis, we induced three main design implications for a navigation system supporting picking-up situations in a complex city space: (1) automated system without interrupting the driver's primary task (driving), (2) tracking the locations of both the car and the pedestrian in real time, and (3) sharing and setting each other's location and point of interest.

Prototype: GRAVITY

Following the design implications, we developed a prototype navigation system: Gravity—Automatic Location Tracking System between a Car and a Pedestrian. The system was developed as an iOS application, operating on an iPad (for the driver) and an iPhone (for the pedestrian). The basic components of a navigation system, such as a map and a guidance way, were implemented by using T-map API [1]. The server communication system was constructed using Parse.com service, which enabled both devices to share their locations with each other.

The main function of Gravity is "picking up." We added a "pick up" menu separately at the first view of the system (Figure 3). After selecting the "pick up" menu, the user should set two features: "where" and "who." By searching a specific location on the search bar, the user can select his or her destination. At the next view, a list of friends who were registered earlier is presented, and the user is allowed to select one of them. Then, the setting is completed (e.g., "Picking up 'Mr. Kim' nearby 'Gangnam Station'"), and the next view simply visualizes distances and estimates the time for the car driver to reach the pedestrian's destination.

After that, the main guidance is started. On the map, the route is presented with a red line, and four main location marks are presented: *my location*, *my destination*, *friend's location*, and *friend's destination*. Basically, *my location* is located in the center of the display, and the user can check the other marks by moving and zooming out the map. After the user starts driving and gets closer to the destination, both *my location* and *friend's location* are presented on the screen. The driver can select one option between the two—(*a*) set the "friend's destination" as "my

(a) driver's view

(b) pedestrian's view

(c) completion of picking up

Figure 4. User Test

destination" and (*b*) set "friend's location" as "my destination." If the driver chooses option *a*, he or she can receive a guide to the pedestrian's final destination. Of course, the pedestrian can change his or her destination freely only by touching the screen, and as it changes, the driver's destination is also altered in real time. By selecting option *b*, the driver can set up the pedestrian's real-time location as his or her destination. If the driver and the pedestrian miss each other on the way, by simply using option *b*, they can finally meet each other in a certain point. With these options, the users can come together at one spot and complete their pick-up.

User Test

We conducted a usability test of Gravity in real-driving settings. We recruited 16 participants (8 drivers and 8 pedestrians). All the tests were conducted in pairs of a driver and a pedestrian, accompanied by researchers. We provided a testing car equipped with an iPad for drivers and gave pedestrians a ride near the destination, which was set up beforehand (a nearby intersection). We asked each pair of participants to complete their picking up only using Gravity. By setting up the "pick up" menu, the test was started. Drivers drove following the directions of the system, and so did pedestrians. Once each other's location was presented on the screen, they coordinated their final location using option *a* or *b* and finally met each other at a certain spot. Except for two retrial cases due to unstable communication, all the tasks were successful. All the driving was recorded with an in-car recording system. After driving, to measure its usability, we provided the participants with a questionnaire composed of the System Usability Scale (SUS), a reliable evaluation tool developed by Brooke [4].

Result

The average SUS score of all participants is 78.91. According to the standard that Sauro (2012) suggested, the score is in the range of B+, which means that the overall satisfaction level of the system is within the highest 20% range [10]. According to another standard that Bnagor (2008) suggested, the score is in "good" range in the aspect of "adjective range" standard and "acceptable" in the "acceptability range" [3]. These results show that the participants felt that the core function of Gravity—supporting picking-up situations—is "useful," and they were satisfied to a certain degree. Calculated separately between drivers and pedestrians, the former score is 77.5, which is B+, and the latter is A−, which means that the system is slightly more useful to pedestrians than drivers in this bidirectional communication.

In the post hoc interview, the participants showed positive responses in general, such as "The concept of linking a car and a person is very good" (D3), "The core function would be very useful" (P7). In detail, there was a positive opinion about safety driving due to the navigation system ("It would be very safe because while using it, I don't need to call or message the driver" [P2]), and some participants said it could also solve uncertainty of picking-up situations ("I can check the location of my friend [driver] frequently, and I can prepare to be picked up well" [P5]). On the other hand, some participants pointed out its completion quality problem, saying, "The quality of the system is poor" (D3), and "It needs a simple UI design (P5)"; and some of them additionally suggested a specific UI component, saying, "It would be great if it shows a simple summary of the distance between me and my friend in real time, at the upper side of the view" (P5). In common with the results of the user survey, some participants expressed their need for a recommendation system showing places where it is easy to pick up based on social data ("I need some service recommending places for picking up, like avoiding bus stops" [D7]).

Conclusion and Future Work

Way finding, while driving, using GPS navigation systems, has been common in a complex city space. However, most of the systems provide a rather uniform function. In order to enhance their user experience, this research, introducing a user-centered design approach, conducted a user survey and induced design implications. Then we made a prototype, "Gravity," and evaluated its usability, and it received favorable feedback from the interview. The research could be applied and extended to other situations such as a group meeting associated with multiple users from various locations.

There are two limitations in this study: (1) the implemented system has a low degree of completion and (2) its usability was evaluated only by users' subjective satisfaction. Based on the user test results and interviews, we plan to develop the system more precisely by improving the UI structure and the design and solving unstable server problems so that it can be used in real driving situations. And as users repeatedly said, with the accumulated data, we will introduce a spot-recommending system appropriate for picking up. In the next step, we will evaluate its usability and user experience quantitatively as well as qualitatively, revealing its improvement significantly.

References

[1] T-Map Navigation. http://www.tmap.co.kr/tmap2/

[2] Massachusetts Institute of Technology. "Mathematicians Take Aim At 'Phantom' Traffic Jams: New Model Could Help Design Better Roads." ScienceDaily. ScienceDaily, 14 June 2009. <www.sciencedaily.com/releases/2009/06/090608151550.htm>.

[3] Bangor, Aaron, Philip T. Kortum, and James T. Miller. "An empirical evaluation of the system usability scale." Intl. Journal of Human–Computer Interaction 24.6 (2008): 574-594.

[4] Brooke, John. "SUS-A quick and dirty usability scale." Usability evaluation in industry 189 (1996): 194.

[5] Brown, Barry, and Eric Laurier. "The normal natural troubles of driving with GPS." Proceedings of the 2012 ACM annual conference on Human Factors in Computing Systems. ACM, 2012.

[6] Hipp, Markus, et al. "Interaction weaknesses of personal navigation devices." Proceedings of the 2nd International Conference on Automotive User Interfaces and Interactive Vehicular Applications. ACM, 2010.

[7] Jensen, Brit Susan, Mikael B. Skov, and Nissanthen Thiruravichandran. "Studying driver attention and behaviour for three configurations of GPS navigation in real traffic driving." Proceedings of the SIGCHI Conference on Human Factors in Computing Systems. ACM, 2010.

[8] Lee, Joonhwan, Jodi Forlizzi, and Scott E. Hudson. "Iterative design of MOVE: A situationally appropriate vehicle navigation system." International Journal of Human-Computer Studies 66.3 (2008): 198-215.

[9] McLuhan, Marshall. Understanding media: The extensions of man. MIT press, 1994.

[10] Sauro, Jeff, and James R. Lewis. Quantifying the user experience: Practical statistics for user research. Access Online via Elsevier, 2012.

[11] Schreiber, Julia. "Bridging the gap between useful and aesthetic maps in car navigation systems." Proceedings of the 11th International Conference on Human-Computer Interaction with Mobile Devices and Services. ACM, 2009

Shake ‘n’ Tap: A Gesture Enhanced Keyboard for Older Adults

Mark Dunlop
University of Strathclyde
26 Richmond St.
Glasgow G1 1XH, UK
mark.dunlop@strath.ac.uk

Iain Hamilton
University of Strathclyde
26 Richmond St.
Glasgow G1 1XH, UK
iain.hamilton@beakable.com

Andreas Komninos
University of Strathclyde
26 Richmond St.
Glasgow G1 1XH, UK
andreas.komninos@strath.ac.uk

Emma Nicol
University of Strathclyde
26 Richmond St.
Glasgow G1 1XH, UK
emma.nicol@strath.ac.uk

MobileHCI '14, Sep 23-26, 2014, Toronto, ON, Canada.
ACM 978-1-4503-3004-6/14/09.
http://dx.doi.org/10.1145/2628363.2634227

Abstract
The need for text entry on smartphones and other touch-screen devices is key for many tasks and also a key factor in the usability of these devices. Physical and cognitive issues associated with age can aggravate the task of text entry for older adults. Technological exclusion due to low usability can present a significant problem both for social and ongoing business-related tasks with older adults. This paper investigates a new touch-screen keyboard design for older adults that combines the familiar QWERTY keyboard layout with physical gesture. User studies with older adults showed our keyboard reduced miss-taps, but was slower to use, and raised issues for further research.

Author Keywords
Older adults; text input; gesture keyboards.

ACM Classification Keywords
H.5.2 User Interfaces: Input devices and strategies.

Introduction
The developed world has an increasingly aging population: in the UK 17% of the population was over 65 years old in 2010 with a predicted growth to 23% by 2035 [7]. As the size of the older working age population rises, an increasing number of workers will want to continue to use mobile technologies for work

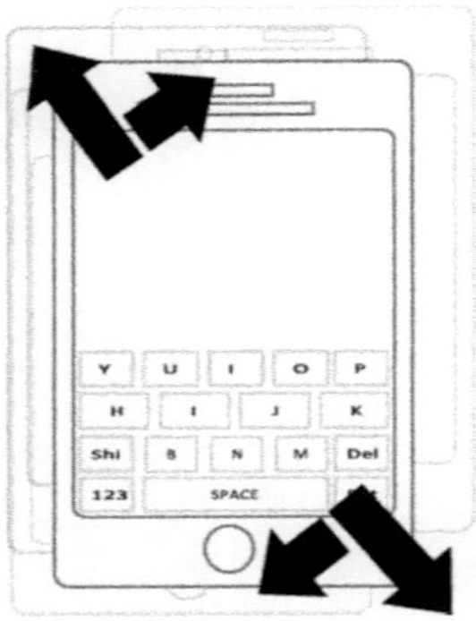

Fig. 1: Shake gesture for keyboard flipping on Shake'n'Tap

Fig. 2: Gesture keyboard input task. Shaking the device replaces the current half-keyboard with the other half.

into their 60s and beyond. Furthermore, many people will want to continue professional, social and lifestyle usage of mobiles into their late retirement as these technologies can lead to increased community involvement and personal independence. Unfortunately, however, the aging process can interfere considerably with mobile technology usage. For example, the normal aging process typically involves a decline in visual acuity together with a decline in working memory, selective attention, and motor control [1]. Even in their 40s many people can experience vision changes that affect their near focus, while from 60s onwards physical movements can be slower and less accurate [1].

Text is core to many interactions on mobiles such as emailing, social networking, instant messaging, searching etc. The majority of smartphones no longer have a physical keyboard but rely on on-screen touch keyboards. Text entry on these keyboards has been shown to be slower and more error-prone than traditional mini-physical keyboards (e.g. [2,4]), but they are popular as they permit full screen services and a larger reading area. While there have been numerous studies of text entry usage on touchscreens, to date there has been very little work studying the effects of aging on text entry, and none on modern touchscreen phones where diminutions in visual acuity, motor control and working memory are all likely to have an impact.

In this short paper we present an investigation into text entry using two touchscreen keyboards on mobile devices, one a standard QWERTY keyboard, the other involving the use of gesture. We focus on the results obtained for older users, here being defined as those users aged 50 years and over, but contrast this with younger users in the same study.

Keyboard Design

Our preliminary workshops with older adults highlighted that older users appeared more willing to adopt new keyboard layouts than younger users, largely due to their different experiences of and familiarity with QWERTY soft keyboards. We also identified a strong dislike of predictive text entry and "distracting" word suggestions. To increase the key size without the need for predictive texting and related dictionary-based models or slow multi-tapping, we designed a wide format keyboard where the standard and familiar QWERTY layout was spread across double the width of the screen (see Fig. 1). We were motivated to use gestures by previous studies on tilting text entry (e.g. [3, 10]) and research showing that older adults can perform familiar gestures more accurately than younger adults [9]. After testing various gestures we chose a simple shake gesture to swap the keyboard between halves of the QWERTY layout. Shake is a straightforward gesture to explain to participants and is instantly understandable. It has also been shown to be a gesture that comes naturally due to typical past user experience. A study by Ruiz et al showed that the shake gesture was frequently selected by participants to switch a device to its home screen, arguably due to their familiarity with "Etch-A-Sketch' [8].

As an example, input of the phrase *"batman wears a cape"* would require 19 taps on standard QWERTY, or 19 taps plus 8 side-swap shakes on our design. Although an increased number of inputs is required with our keyboard, the layout has the benefit of larger

Invalid keypresses

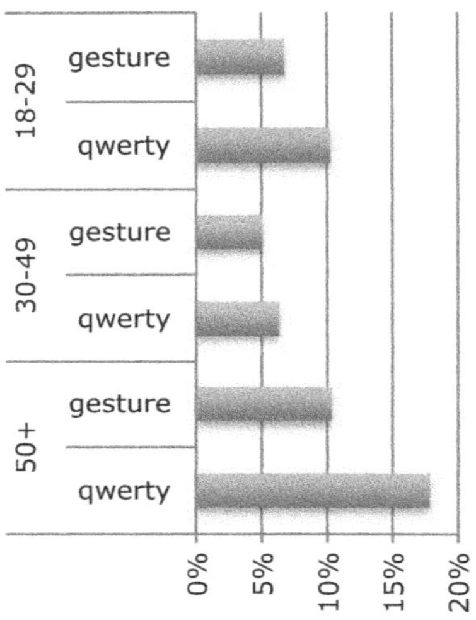

Fig. 3: Percentage of invalid keypresses

target button areas, allowing both larger fonts and less precise tapping.

Methodology

We conducted a user study to investigate use of the QWERTY and Shake'n'Tap keyboards. We initially recruited 124 participants through our standard mailing list and forum recruitment procedures for user studies. Unfortunately, this did not result in enough older adults. To compensate we liaised with our University's Centre for Lifelong Learning to increase the numbers of older participants and recruited a further 23 participants in the 50+ category, bringing the total number of participants to 136.

Our study was based around a standard text entry study methodology using the MacKenzie and Soukoreff phrase set [6] that was designed to give short memorable phrases (e.g. see Fig. 2). Participants were initially presented with a standard QWERTY layout and given some practice time until they felt comfortable. After this they moved on to enter 10 timed phrases (randomly selected from two blocks). They were then shown the Shake'n'Tap keyboard and repeated the practice and timed tasks. In line with previous text entry studies, we did not counterbalance due the ubiquity of the first input method. After each set of task phrases the participants provided subjective feedback through a series of on-screen questions (using 5 point Likert scales). The two key measures of success of a text entry method are speed and accuracy. For timed tasks, times were recorded from first key press to last key. Accuracy was calculated using Levenshtein edit-distance, removing the artificial entry constraint of forcing participants to maintain perfect accuracy [5] and allowing us to investigate both corrected and uncorrected errors in reasonably natural typing. Each key tap location was also recorded for later heat-map analysis.

Our experimental keyboard was implemented in HTML5, using standard accelerometer access for shake detection and a canvas for drawing the keyboard. We chose HTML5 to support platform portability, though all tests were conducted on iOS devices. Input was logged to a PHP/MySQL Server.

Results

Fig. 3 shows that the average number of incorrect key-presses during the input tasks was lower for Shake'n'Tap than the standard layout. The difference is statistically significant for the 18-29 and 50+ groups. This observation is also shown by the heatmap of key press errors screen coordinates (Fig. 4), where the Shake'n'Tap keyboard shows fewer off-key taps. The heatmaps highlight that often errors occur due to users inadvertently registering touches inbetween keys.

Despite the difference in incorrect key-presses, Fig. 5 shows that the accuracy of the final entered phrases is similar for all groups ($p>0.05$, paired t-tests per age group). For the 50+ group, the number of incorrect key presses was almost double using the standard QWERTY keyboard: while the final phrase accuracy was similar, the older adults made less corrections as they typed with Shake'n'Tap.Fig. 6 shows that task completion time grew with age but that the Shake'n'Tap keyboard was consistently slower - paired T-tests confirm this ($p<0.01$ for all age groups). However, the difference is less extreme for the older adults group.

18-29

Gesture

QWERTY

30-49

Gesture

QWERTY

50+

Gesture

QWERTY

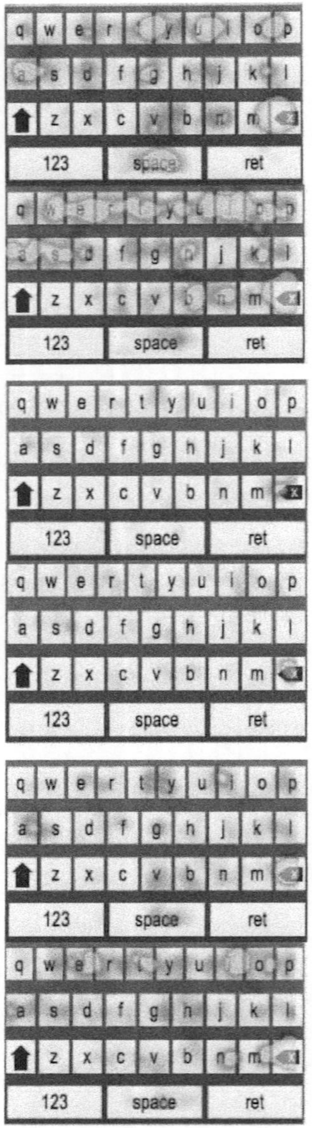

Figure 4: Invalid keypresses heatmap for the Gesture Keyboard

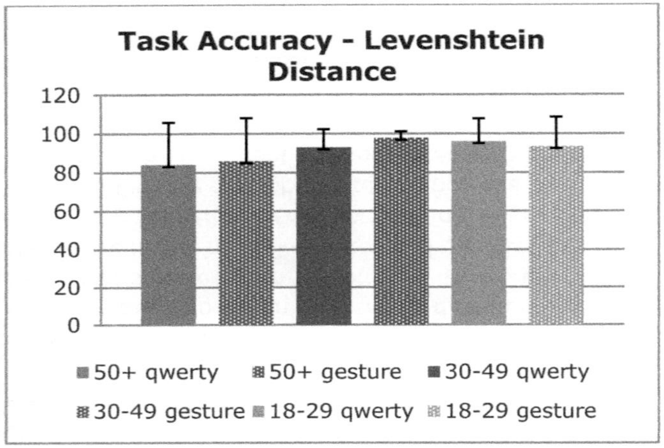

Fig. 5: Average task accuracy (Levenshtein distance)

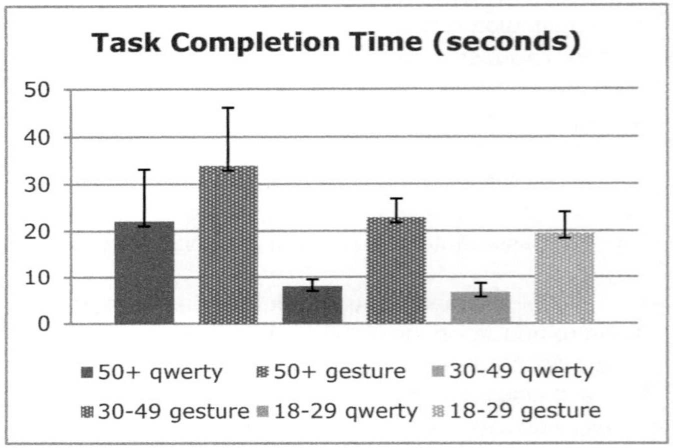

Fig. 6: Average task completion times

Participants were observed to carry out the gestures in a variety ways: a sharp shake with a forward motion; a side to side shake; a tilt of the device slowly left to right with a wrist turning action; and one participant turned the device close to 90° (which triggered the screen to auto-rotate). Those who used single finger text entry tended to perform the gesture using the same hand that they used to hold the device while entering text. For those using two thumbed text entry (2 participants) were observed to use both hands to hold the device as it the gesture was performed.

Subjective feedback is summarised in Fig. 7. Desktop touch-typists tended to state familiarity as the reason for their preferring QWERTY over Shake'n'Tap. While fewer participants favoured the Shake'n'Tap keyboard over the QWERTY keyboard, nearly all participants said that they learned to use it quickly and that towards the end of the study session they were no longer thinking about where the letters were, they just somehow "knew" which screen to be on in order to find the correct letter. A few said they were surprised by how quickly they got used to using the gesture after initial doubts and concerns when it was first demonstrated. Interestingly, the one participant who had not used a mobile phone before indicated a preference for the Shake'n'Tap keyboard, though he was certainly familiar with QWERTY on PCs and other non-mobile devices. Several participants regretted the absence of predictive texting in the application, however there were more who said they were relieved to see that they were not required to use predictive texting as they found it to be unhelpful in normal use.

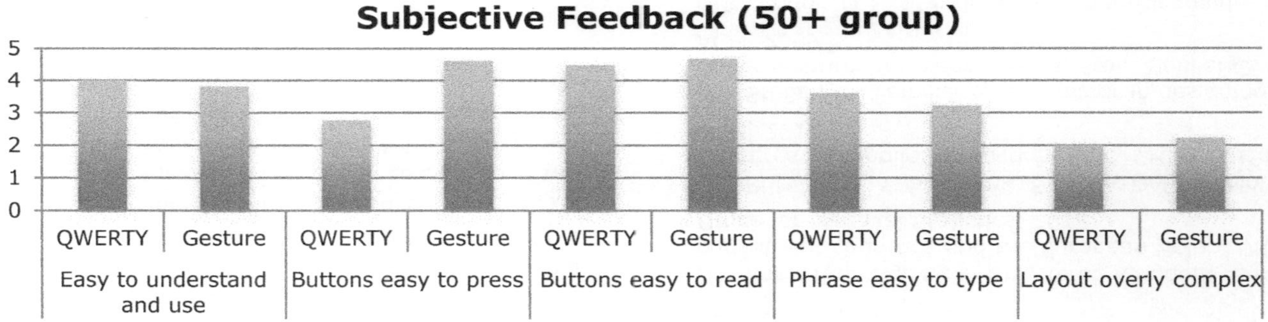

Fig. 7: Subjective feedback from the older adults (50+) group

Around half of the participants suggested making the device more sensitive to the shake gesture as they felt that the action currently required to carry out the gesture successfully was fairly vigorous.

Discussion

In this short paper we set out to design and evaluate a gesture based keyboard, that allows for larger key targets, in order to help older adults with accurate typing. In line with previous studies, our results showed that users were keen to complete input tasks accurately. With QWERTY keyboards, users were more prone to errors and the heat-maps show fewer areas of erroneous taps for the larger keyed keyboard. We also saw considerable use of the backspace key, as users strived to achieve the desired accuracy. The Shake'n'Tap keyboard succeeded in helping users type in more accurately, albeit at the expense of input speed. We expected, given the requirement for additional input due to the shake, that task times would be longer. For older adults, despite the longer task times with the Shake'n'Tap keyboards, subjective feedback did not indicate a preference for any of the two keyboard types. We did receive several comments regarding their willingness to learn to use the gesture keyboard style and confidence that their performance would increase with more practice. After refinement of the shake gesture and implementation as a full IME, we hope to conduct a further field trial that will allow users to take advantage of the Shake'n'Tap keyboard in real-life tasks, as part of longitudinal studies.

Another significant finding is the confirmation that text input is a significant problem for older adults. Our keyboard design is not optimal. However, it provides valuable insight at designing input methods for older adults. Our work shows that for this age group, multimodal interaction based on physical gestures is a viable option that deserves further exploration. Through the process of participatory design, we will, in the near future, investigate alternative designs involving physical and touch gestures as well as further investigate the speed / accuracy trade-off with this group and issues raised concerning predictive input / word suggestions.

Conclusions

Text input is core to much of our interaction on mobiles. In this study we confirmed that older adults are slower and less accurate entering text than younger adults: while many users find text entry on mobiles frustratingly inaccurate and slow, this is worse for older adults. Our study investigated the use of a double-width keyboard with a simple gesture to flick between sides of the keyboard. This provided larger target areas and was shown to result in significantly fewer mistypes by older adults. While younger users expressed a strong preference for the standard QWERTY layout, older users were more balanced between the two and found the larger keys easier to use.

Our initial design goal of avoiding predictive text and dictionary-based methods needs further investigation as this study gave contradictory feedback - some missed predictive technologies while some welcomed its absence. The studies also raised some methodological issues: there is long debate in mobile interface design as to whether laboratory based evaluation is valid. While our "quiet location" based studies gave valuable insights, issues concerning error correction strategy may be better evaluated in more natural locations. We plan to develop further prototypes in collaboration with groups of older adults with the aim of developing keyboards that can make a real difference to the input performance of an increasingly large percentage of the population.

Acknowledgments

Research was partly funded by the EPSRC under grant reference EP/K024647/1. We thank them and our participants.

REFERENCES

[1] Fisk, A. D., Rogers, W. A., Charness, N., Czaja, S. J. and Sharit, J. Designing for Older Adults: Principles and Creative Human Factors Approaches, 2nd ed. Taylor & Francis, 2009.

[2] Hoggan, E., Brewster, S. A. and Johnston, J. Investigating the effectiveness of tactile feedback for mobile touchscreens. In Proc. CHI '08, 1573-1582, ACM, 2008.

[3] Jones, E., Alexander, J., Andreou, A. and Subramanian, S., 'GesText: Accelerometer-Based Gestural Text-Entry Systems', Proc. CHI '10, 2173-2182, ACM, 2010.

[4] Lee, S. and Zhai, S. The performance of touch screen soft buttons. In Proc. CHI '09, 309-318, ACM, 2009.

[5] MacKenzie, I.S. and Soukoreff, R.W., Measuring Errors in Text Entry Tasks: An Application of the Levenshtein String Distance Statistic, CHI '01 Extended Abstracts, 319-320, ACM, 2001.

[6] MacKenzie, S. and Soukoreff, R.W., Phrase Sets for Evaluating Text Entry Techniques, Proc. CHI '03, 754-755, ACM, 2003.

[7] Population Ageing in the United Kingdom its constituent countries and the European Union. UK Office for National Statistics, 2012.

[8] Ruiz, J., Li, Y. and Lank, E., User-Defined Motion Gestures for Mobile Interaction, Proc. CHI '11, 197-206, ACM, 2011.

[9] Stößel, C., Familiarity as a factor in designing finger gestures for elderly users, Proc. MobileHCI '09, ACM, 2009.

[10] Wigdor, D.J., Chording and tilting for rapid, unambiguous text entry to mobile phones, PhD, Univ. Toronto, 2004.

Augmenting Bend Gestures with Pressure Zones on Flexible Displays

Rufino Ansara
Carleton University
Ottawa, Ontario
K1S 5B6, Canada
ransara@connect.carleton.ca

Audrey Girouard
Carleton University
Ottawa, Ontario
K1S 5B6, Canada
audrey.girouard@carleton.ca

MobileHCI '14, Sep 23-26 2014, Toronto, ON, Canada
ACM 978-1-4503-3004-6/14/09.
http://dx.doi.org/10.1145/2628363.2634228

Abstract
Flexible displays have paved the road for a new generation of interaction styles that allow users to bend and twist their devices. We hypothesize that bend gestures can be augmented with "hot-key" like pressure areas. This would allow single corner bends to have multiple functions. We created three pressure and bend interaction styles and compared them to bend-only gestures on two deformable prototypes. Users preferred the bend only prototype but still appreciated the pressure & bend prototype, particularly when it came to the lock/unlock application. We found that pressure interaction is a poor replacement for touch interaction, and present design suggestions to improve its performance.

Author Keywords
Deformable User Interface; Flexible Displays; Gestures; Mobile Device; Bimanual Interaction.

ACM Classification Keywords
H.5.2. Information interfaces and presentation: *User Interfaces – Interaction styles, user-centered design.*

Introduction
Flexible displays are an emergent technology that has inspired researchers to explore interaction techniques such as bending, twisting and crumpling [1] on

Figure 1. Press & Bend as Simultaneous Gestures

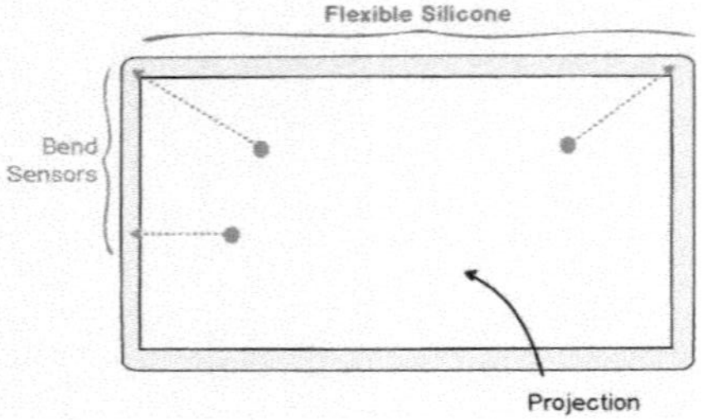

Figure 2. Bend Only Prototype

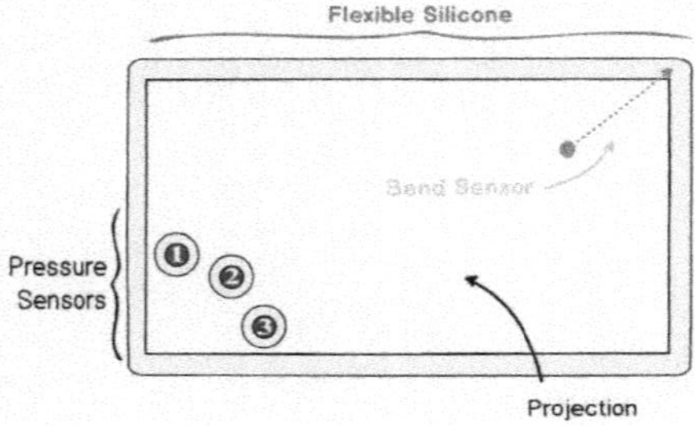

Figure 3. Bend and Pressure Prototype

multimedia devices [2,3]. We can use these gestures on a variety of applications, such as phones, music players, map navigation, e-readers [2,3].

As these applications become more complex, the number of bend gestures necessary for interaction will increase. Our research goal is to reduce the amount of bends a prototype might have to support while keeping the directionality and tangibility bend gestures provide. To achieve that, we leverage recent work that found that users can efficiently interact with the thumb of the holding hand on both rigid and flexible devices [6]. Hence, we propose that the behavior of one gesture can be modified by using three pressure zones (Figure 1). We suggest making these areas act like control keys on a keyboard, changing the behavior of a bend to match different application appropriate actions. We hypothesize that this would reduce the number of complex bend gestures the user would need to memorize. In this paper, we define new interaction styles for the press & bend prototype and compare them with the bend only gestures to determine user preference.

Related Work

We introduce bend gestures on flexible devices, before discussing pressure and touch input, and thumb interaction with touch rigid or deformable devices.

Bend Gestures on Flexible Devices

Kildal et al. discussed the development and testing of the Kinetic Device [2], a deformable user interface that focused on bending and twisting. Users found that bending to zoom and twisting to scroll to be intuitive gestures that required little learning. They also found that the gestures were more easily performed when holding the device with two hands.

PaperPhone is a flexible E Ink display that features bend gesture recognition [3]. Lahey et al. determined the effectiveness of several bend gestures through smartphone applications. They found that the directionality of actions appeared to be based on the participant's mental models. Their results also indicate that users preferred gestures that were conceptually simpler, and that they gravitated towards the different sides and corners of the display. Warren et al. [8] classified and determined which bend gestures users find the most friendly and intuitive. Their results showed a preference for the top corners and the sides. They recommended mapping frequently used functions to the top corners. The authors argued that bend gestures should be limited to two levels of magnitude; though note that this might be specific to their own prototype.

Thumb Interaction with Touch Devices

BiPad explores bimanual interaction on tablets and identifies five holds that permit simultaneous support and interaction [7]. Wagner et al.'s results suggest that participants significantly preferred bimanual taps (with the thumb) over other bimanual gestures. Riyadh explored tapping with the thumb of the holding hand on flexible tablets and found that users can efficiently interact with their thumb on both rigid and flexible devices [6]. He identifies a preference for holding the device on the center of the sides or the bottom corners (analogous with BiPad's findings). He also found that users can equally tap two or three regions for each hold. Riyadh suggests that future research explore how

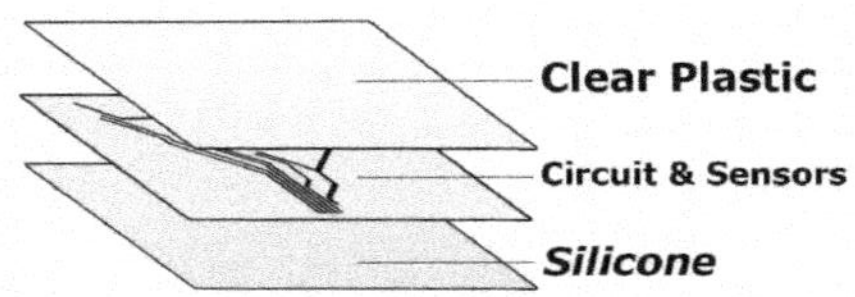

igure 4. Exploded view of our prototypes

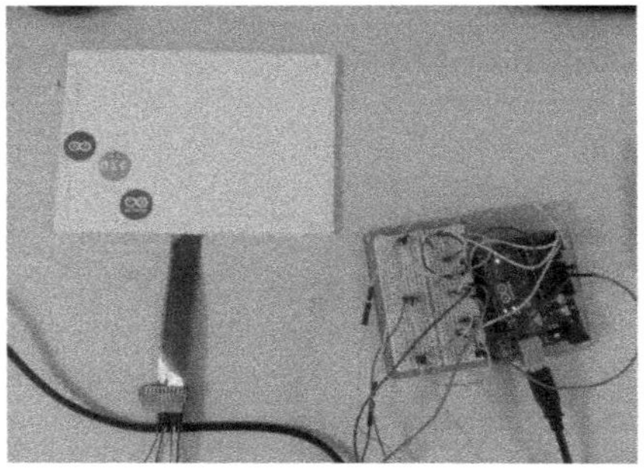

Figure 5. Bend & Pressure Prototype

the use of thumb gestures can complement bend gestures in bimanual simultaneous interactions.

McLachlan et al. demonstrated that pressure sensors can provide a useful augmentation to finger/stylus inputs on touch screens [5]. Their results suggest that users can apply, release and maintain pressure accurately when using their non-dominant hand while interacting with a touch-screen.

Prototypes

For this study, we created two flexible prototypes: bend only, pressure & bend. The bend only prototype (Figure 2) includes three bend sensors, placed on the top corners and on the left side. This placement is based both on Warren et al.'s suggested best bend locations [8], and to keep the right side interactions as similar as possible to the two prototypes.

Our second prototype (Figure 3) includes a single bend sensor located on the top right corner, and three pressure sensors located on the left bottom corner. This leverages Riyadh's findings in terms of hold position and touch targets [6]. We chose to use pressure sensors as a quick and inexpensive prototyping material, since flexible transparent touch sensors are currently difficult to find. The pressure sensors also allowed us to explore the possible benefits of using the amount of pressure as an input value. We placed static stickers to indicate their location to the user.

We built the two prototypes using a similar methodology as in Lo & Girouard [4]. Our prototypes consist of a thin film of clear plastic, a custom flexible printed circuit, and a layer of Alumilite Silicone Rubber (70A) (Figure 4). This creates a flexible, deformable prototype that naturally reverts to a flat state (Figure 5). We simulated the flexible display using a pico-projector.

Interactions Styles

We propose three interaction styles that combine bend and pressure gestures. We utilize the pressure sensors as a simulation of touch (low pressure/no pressure), and as a force input (amount of pressure exerted).

Pressure to change the behavior of bend gestures

One bend gesture is used to activate different functions according to the pressure sensor activated (at a low threshold). For example, in a physics game, applying pressure to a specific sensor while bending the right top corner up and down can raise or lower the intensity of an element (e.g. gravity, wind or air pressure). Each element would be associated with a different sensor.

Pressure to change the intensity of bend gestures

One bend gesture triggers the same action at different intensities, depending on the pressure sensor activated. For example, in a game, holding different sensors while bending can change the speed of player movement.

Varying pressure to change the behavior of bend gestures

One bend gesture triggers different actions depending on the force exerted on the pressure sensor(s). This may be particularly useful for actions that need user attention, such as unlocking/locking the device or confirming an action with significant consequences (e.g., reformatting the device, confirming credit card purchases).

Experimental Study

Our main goal was to evaluate and compare participant satisfaction between bend only and pressure & bend interactions. We ran a within-subject factorial experiment with two prototypes and three applications. Participants first interacted with the prototypes to familiarize themselves with the new interactions styles. We counterbalanced the order of the prototypes and the applications. Participants filled out a survey that recorded their impressions and comments.

Applications

We implemented three applications: lock/unlock, e-book reader and a music player. We selected them to represent typical applications a user might find on their mobile devices [2,3]., as well as implement all three interaction styles. Table 1 lists the different gestures for each action, on each prototype. The bend up/down actions were selected accordingly to the directionality of the action. We kept the bend directionality identical between prototypes.

LOCK AND UNLOCK

This application simulates a mobile device's lock screen. On the Bend & Pressure prototype, the bend is only activated if the user exerts more than a preset amount of pressure onto the sensor. Conversely, the Bend Only prototype requires two simultaneous bends for the device to lock or unlock.

ZOOM AND SCROLL

The zoom functionality allows users to zoom in and out of a small circle, simulating modifying the size of elements on their screen. The scroll functionality allows users to scroll up and down to read different sections of a short passage of text. On our bend only prototype,

Action	Pressure + Bend Prototype	Bend Only Prototype
Lock	Strong press #2, Bend up	Both top corners bend up
Unlock	Strong press #2, Bend down	Both top corners bend down
Zoom/Scroll in at speed 1,2,3	Press #1,#2 or #3, Bend Up	Small/Medium/Large Left Corner bend Up
Zoom/Scroll out at speed 1,2,3	Press #1,#2,#3, Bend down	Small/medium/large left corner bend down
Play song	Left corner up	Left corner up
Pause song	Left corner down	Left corner down
Next song	Press #2, Bend down	Right corner down
Previous song	Press #2, Bend up	Right corner up
Lower Volume	Press #3, Bend down	Left side down
Raise Volume	Press #3, Bend up	Right side up
Browse Library	Press #1, Bend down/up	Both top corners l bend down/up

Table 1. Gesture Pairing for Each Action/Prototype

the size of the bends determines the speed of the action, whereas in our bend & pressure prototype, the speed is determined by the area pressed.

MUSIC PLAYER

The music player allows the user to listen to various songs. On our bend only prototype, we mapped functionalities to a different bend gesture. For the bend and pressure prototype, the action executed by the top-left bend is determined by the pressed zone.

Participants

Twelve participants (6 males) completed the hour long usability study and received $10 as compensation.

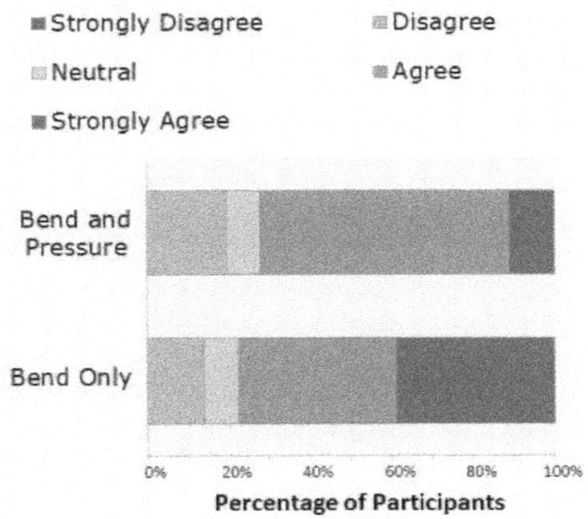

Figure 6. Average satisfaction level across applications.

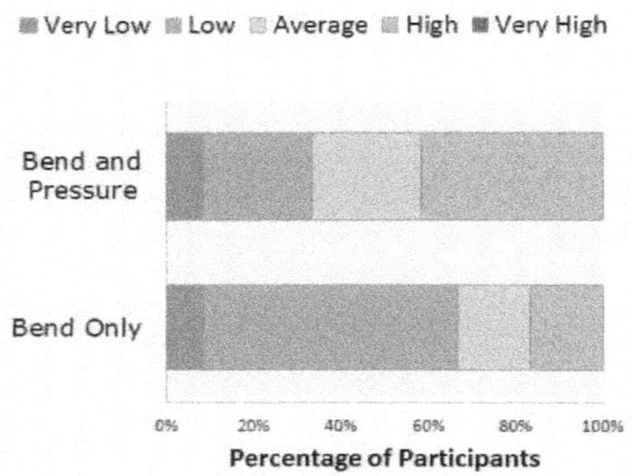

Figure 7. Frustration Levels

Results

Overall, 84% of participants preferred the "bend only" prototype, 16% preferred the "bend & pressure" prototype.

We invited participants to rate their satisfaction levels with each application on each prototype (Figure 6). 72% of participants agreed or strongly agreed to having enjoyed using the Bend + Pressure prototype, against 77% for the bend only prototype. Specifically, 84% participants agreed or strongly agreed to enjoying the lock/unlock prototype on both prototypes. Figure 7 compares the participants' frustration levels: 42% of users felt a high level of frustration (strongly agree) when using the bend & pressure prototype, versus 17% for the bend only prototype.

When asked which application the preferred using each prototype, participants scored the scroll up/down (specifically at speed 2) gesture the lowest: only 50% of participants preferred performing this gesture on the bend only prototype. In contrast, 84% of participants preferred the raise/lower volume on the bend only prototype (highest score).

Discussion

Our results show that users found the bend only prototype more enjoyable to use than the pressure and bend prototype. A large majority (84%) preferred the bend only prototype, but participants showed similar satisfaction levels (77% vs 72%). These results suggest the potential of our interaction styles.

The key difference between the two prototypes is the amount of physical actions needed to complete each task. Apart from the lock/unlock application, the bend only prototype required users to perform a single action (bend different areas of the device up or down), whereas the bend & pressure prototype required them to do two (apply pressure on an area, and bend up/down). These coupled actions took longer to complete and made users more prone to errors.

Additionally, participants seemed to regularly forget the functionality of the pressure zones. Only half of participants agreed that gestures were easy to remember on for the pressure & bend prototype, with 58% for the bend only prototype. Participants commented on how haptic and dynamic visual feedback (such as dynamic labeling of the buttons) would be an effective method of helping them remember the uses for each gesture/press.

Finally, we used pressure sensors to simulate touch due to prototyping constraints. However, the sensors only activated reliably when users squeezed the area instead of applying simple unidirectional pressure. This forced participants to locate the front and back areas of the sensors instead of simple touches on the surface. We observed that this negatively impacted their experience. Because of this, we believe that pressure sensors, specifically, force-sensing resistors, present a poor simulations of touch interactions. However, the results for lock/unlock application suggests that varying pressure can be a valid input source.

Design Recommendations

We formulate 3 recommendations based on our results. First, we suggest that pressure as a simulation of touch to augment a bend gesture be used only to replace complex bends, such as gestures that require bending multiple corners at once. Second, participants did not appreciate the pressing (squeezing) gestures as a simulation of touch. We recommend only using pressure sensors when there is a need for an extra dimension of input. Finally, when possible, provide appropriate dynamic visual feedback to all applications, such as labeling touch/pressure areas to make them easier to remember.

Limitations

Our prototypes were not optimal: there were loose areas, exposed circuits, air bubbles and weak adhesion that caused the bend and pressure sensors to output erratic values at different intervals. We also noted that bending away caused the pressure exerted on the pressure sensors to diminish, causing them to deactivate and cause erratic behavior. Interestingly, this gesture has caused "ergonomic challenges" on bend only devices [8]. Finally, we also only tested one level of flexibility, with one device size. Finally, while the simulation of display by projection is lightweight, participants observed distortion and occlusion when bending the device causing some frustration.

Conclusion

In this paper, we explored augmenting bend gestures with pressure areas to reduce the amount of bends a prototype might have to support. We introduced three new interaction styles and compared a bend & pressure and a bend only prototype to analyze user preferences and frustration levels. Furthermore, the pressure & bend prototype showed promise (72% enjoyed the applications). Because of this, we believe that exploring the combination of bend and touch gestures is still worth it. Future work includes augmenting pressures areas with resistive or capacitive touch areas to allow for reliable touch and pressure input. We also suggest exploring different sizes, and levels of thickness and flexibility to evaluate the influence of the form factor on the experience.

Acknowledgements

This work was supported and funded by the National Sciences and Engineering Research Council of Canada.

References

[1] Kildal, J., Lucero, A., and Boberg, M. Twisting Touch□: Combining Deformation and Touch as Input within the Same Interaction Cycle on Handheld Devices. *Proc. MobileHCI*, (2013), 237–246.

[2] Kildal, J., Paasovaara, S., and Aaltonen, V. Kinetic Device□: Designing Interactions with a Deformable Mobile Interface. *Proc. CHI EA*, (2012), 1871–1876.

[3] Lahey, B., Girouard, A., Burleson, W., and Vertegaal, R. PaperPhone: Understanding the Use of Bend Gestures in Mobile Devices with Flexible Electronic Paper Displays. *Proc. CHI*, ACM (2011), 1303–1312.

[4] Lo, J. and Girouard, A. Fabricating Bendy: Design and Development of Deformable Prototypes. *IEEE Pervasive Special Issue on Fabrication and Printing*, (2014, in print).

[5] McLachlan, R., Boland, D., and Brewster, S. Transient and transitional states: pressure as an auxiliary input modality for bimanual interaction. *Proc. CHI, ACM* (2014), 401–410.

[6] Riyadh, M. Exploring Tapping with Thumb Input for Flexible Tablets. *Proc. CHI, Student Research Competition*, (2014), 1–6.

[7] Wagner, J., Huot, S., and Mackay, W. Bitouch and bipad: Designing bimanual interaction for hand-held tablets. *Proc. CHI 2012*, May (2012), 2317–2326.

[8] Warren, K., Lo, J., Vadgama, V., and Girouard, A. Bending the Rules: Bend Gesture Classification for Flexible Displays. *Proc. CHI*, (2013).

A Systematic Comparison of 3 Phrase Sampling Methods for Text Entry Experiments in 10 Languages

Germán Sanchis-Trilles
PRHLT Research Center
Universitat Politècnica de València
gsanchis@prhlt.upv.es

Luis A. Leiva
PRHLT Research Center
Universitat Politècnica de València
luileito@prhlt.upv.es

Work partially supported by EU FP7 program under grant agreements 287576 (CASMACAT) and 600707 (tranScriptorium).

MobileHCI'14, Sep 23–26 2014, Toronto, ON, Canada
ACM 978-1-4503-3004-6/14/09.
http://dx.doi.org/10.1145/2628363.2634229

Abstract

Today's reference datasets for conducting text entry experiments are only available in English, which may lead to misleading results when testing text entry methods with non-native English speakers. We compared 3 automated phrase sampling methods available in the literature: RANDOM, NGRAM, and MEMREP. It was found that MEMREP performs best according to a statistical analysis and qualitative observations. This resulted in a collection of 30 datasets across 10 major languages, and we wish to share them with the community via this paper.

Author Keywords

Text Entry; Sampling; Memorability; Representativeness

ACM Classification Keywords

H.5.2 [**Information interfaces and presentation**]: *Input devices and strategies, Evaluation/Methodology*

Introduction

Text entry is perhaps the task that users perform the most on a mobile device. In fact, there is a wealth of research on text entry methods through development and evaluation. Among these two fronts, in this paper we are interested in the latter, in order to better understand and improve them both.

The most popular methodology for evaluating text entry methods, whether on a mobile device or not, is to ask participants to transcribe a predefined set of phrases (short sentences). This methodology is interesting for a number of reasons [8]. First, a transcription task eliminates noise by reducing the variability that might occur otherwise if users were allowed to enter free text. Second, if the phrases used as stimuli are always the same for all participants, this facilitates the comparison of different text entry techniques. Third, a transcription task does not require participants to create their own text, which removes additional cognitive processing time. Last, and most important, this allows results to be reproducible.

It may seem more natural to have users enter free text in order to increase the external validity of the experiment. However, it is critical to make the text entry method the only independent variable in the experiment, i.e., increasing its internal validity. Then, the question of how to present the phrases to the user still prevails. In general, copy-tasks should prefer memorable stimuli [3, 4, 7]. This is important to avoid participants consulting often the reference text, which shifts attention away from the text entry method.

In this paper, we provide 30 datasets (of 2,000 phrases each) across 10 major languages. These datasets are publicly available and are intended to be a reference source to conduct text entry experiments in languages other than English, though we included English phrase sets in order to allow others to compare their overall performance. We performed a systematic comparison of all datasets according to memorability and representativeness, two desired properties for conducting mobile text entry experiments. We conclude that MemRep is the most adequate phrase sampling method.

Related Work

For the past decade, text entry researchers have predominately used the MacKenzie and Soukoreff dataset [4], which contains 500 phrases that were manually selected according to three criteria: moderate in length, easy to remember, and representative of general English. More recently, Vertanen and Kristensson [7] released a phrase set based on genuine mobile emails. Mobile text entry method evaluations should use this dataset because it consists of memorable and representative phrases taken from actual mobile email messages. Moreover, this dataset has been carefully reviewed so that phrases are well-formed and different subsets are suitable for use in a variety of text entry evaluations.

Unfortunately, these popular datasets are only available in English. In contrast, today text is entered into mobile devices in many different languages, where text entry methods might perform very differently; c.f., English vs. Polish vs. Russian. This may lead to misleading results when testing text entry methods with non-native English speakers, as it has been shown that task performance is highly influenced by language proficiency [2, 3].

Paek and Hsu [5] devised a procedure for creating representative phrase sets by randomly sampling sets of n-grams (sequences of n words) and choosing the set with less entropy with regard to the original dataset. Being data-driven, this procedure allows to generate phrase sets in potentially any language. Finally, Leiva and Sanchis-Trilles [3] presented an automated phrase sampling method that takes into account memorability and representativeness. This method has been shown to work well for English and Spanish, though it has not been explored in other languages.

Language	Corpus	Size
Dutch	Wikipedia	1.2
	OpenSubtitles	3.7
English	Wikipedia	6.9
	OpenSubtitles	14.0
French	Wikipedia	2.5
	OpenSubtitles	3.9
German	Wikipedia	3.6
	OpenSubtitles	0.8
Italian	Wikipedia	1.8
	OpenSubtitles	2.0
Polish	Wikipedia	1.1
	OpenSubtitles	7.3
Portuguese	Wikipedia	1.0
	OpenSubtitles	4.1
Russian	Wikipedia	2.7
	OpenSubtitles	1.5
Spanish	Wikipedia	2.2
	OpenSubtitles	6.8
Swedish	Wikipedia	0.8
	OpenSubtitles	1.1

Table 1: Size of input datasets in GB. Note that the corpora are fairly large, and processing them is very costly, e.g., processing the English data required around 0.5 TB RAM using MapReduce. Hence, we hope that having these sets readily available will foster cross-lingual text entry research.

Phrase Sampling Methods

Our datasets were compiled using 3 different sampling techniques for text entry experiments: RANDOM, NGRAM, and MEMREP. To our knowledge, these techniques are the only ones within the literature that are completely automated, and can be used to build datasets that are comparable across languages and domains.

The RANDOM method relies on selecting phrases at random from the input dataset. This is the most simple form of phrase selection. If the sample obtained is sufficiently large, then representativeness is ensured. However, this method does not take into account phrase memorability.

The NGRAM method [5] focuses on a more precise measure of representativeness, as computed according to perplexity (cross-entropy). One limitation of this technique is that it does not sample complete phrases, but n-grams of fixed length. Moreover, it does not take into account the memorability of the sampled n-grams.

The MEMREP method [3] computes memorability based on a number of phrase features selected empirically. Representativeness is taken into account by weighting phrases with a probability density function over the phrase features. This method relies on having two different input datasets: one which is considered large enough to be descriptive of general language, and one from which phrases will be selected.

Datasets

Ideally, phrases for mobile text entry experiments should be sampled from publicly available email or SMS datasets. However, mainly for privacy reasons, the public release of these kind of data is rare [7]. In fact, we are not aware of any dataset composed of actual mobile messages in languages different from English. Therefore, we considered the OpenSubtitles 2011 dataset (see [6] for details) for ten major languages (Tables 1 and 2). Previous work [1] has shown that this kind of texts are likely to be memorable, a desired property for conducting text entry experiments. Phrase repetitions were removed prior to sampling.

Language	Sentences	Word count	Voc. Size	Singletons
Dutch	127.8 M	737 M	1,018.8 k	116.9 k
English	265.1 M	1,575 M	812.3 k	244.1 k
French	129.8 M	781 M	694.2 k	111.2 k
German	25.1 M	137 M	611.4 k	106.7 k
Italian	65.7 M	376 M	610.1 k	55.9 k
Polish	183.9 M	843 M	1,113.5 k	108.0 k
Portuguese	141.0 M	764 M	684.9 k	73.0 k
Russian	28.9 M	144 M	962.3 k	227.0 k
Spanish	212.1 M	1,219 M	1,153.2 k	184.0 k
Swedish	38.1 M	200 M	660.2 k	98.7 k

Table 2: Overview of the Subtitles corpus for all languages.

Since the MEMREP technique requires an additional dataset as input to model the knowledge of each language, we downloaded the latest Wikipedia articles (May 2014) for those languages having at least 1 million articles (Tables 1 and 3). This large amount of data can be considered representative enough of a language; c.f. vocabulary sizes in Tables 2 and 3. However, because MEMREP relies on some character-based features, we excluded those languages where words are ideograms, e.g., Chinese. This being done, the eventually selected languages were: Dutch, English, French, German, Italian, Polish, Portuguese, Russian, Spanish, and Swedish. We believe this language selection will comprise a big part of the languages that might be subject of study in mobile text entry experiments. The datasets are available at `http://personales.upv.es/luileito/memrep/`

Language	Sentences	Word count	Voc. Size	Singletons
Dutch	7.7 M	192 M	2.6 M	1.1 M
English	63.2 M	1,232 M	5.8 M	3.0 M
French	13.6 M	428 M	2.7 M	1.3 M
German	16.0 M	534 M	7.3 M	3.9 M
Italian	9.2 M	300 M	2.3 M	1.1 M
Polish	6.1 M	156 M	2.5 M	1.1 M
Portuguese	5.2 M	165 M	1.7 M	0.8 M
Russian	6.9 M	20 M	4.1 M	2.1 M
Spanish	10.1 M	374 M	2.6 M	1.3 M
Swedish	5.5 M	114 M	2.4 M	1.1 M

Table 3: Overview of the Wikipedia corpus for all languages.

Analysis

Table 4 provides an overview of the phrases sampled by each technique and for all languages. Three interesting observations can be appreciated. First, even though the average number of words per phrase are similar, RANDOM produces more variability (min. *SD*=3.7 in Swedish and max. *SD*=5.3 in Italian). This reveals that this method may pick very long sentences, and therefore we discourage its use for conducting mobile text entry experiments.

Second, MEMREP tends to produce short words of similar length (min. *SD*=1.5 in Swedish and max. *SD*=2.0 in Italian), whereas the other techniques do not; e.g., min. *SD*=2.7 for RANDOM and min. *SD*=2.8 for NGRAM. This suggests that both RANDOM and NGRAM tend to produce very long (but also very short) words, which overall will be harder to memorize.

Third, the 3 sampling methods produce vocabularies of similar length, around 2k and 3k words per language, although the MEMREP vocabularies are consistently 1k smaller and, more importantly, it is the only method where *all* phrases are comprised of frequent words.

Further analysis is shown in Figure 1, where we plot the density functions of memorability and representativeness, according to previous work [3]. It can be observed that both RANDOM and NGRAM present very disperse curves, which suggests that highly memorable and representative phrases are mixed along with others which are neither representative nor memorable. This dispersion should not be underestimated, since it might introduce undesired variability into a text entry experiment and thus might compromise its internal validity. On the contrary, MEMREP presents a very sharp peak, both in representativeness and in memorability. Hence, all of the selected phrases, although different, are statistically similar in their properties.

We conclude that MEMREP is the most adequate sampling method to generate phrase sets for mobile text entry experiments. Examples of the selected phrases are shown in Figure 2.

Language	Words/Phrase			Letters/Word			OOV Ratio		
	R	N	M	R	N	M	R	N	M
Dutch	5.7	4.8	5.0	4.3	4.1	4.12	6.0 %	0.8 %	0 %
English	6.0	4.8	4.0	3.8	3.8	3.55	1.4 %	0.2 %	0 %
French	5.9	4.8	5.0	4.1	4.0	3.81	3.4 %	0.7 %	0 %
German	5.5	4.7	4.0	4.8	4.7	4.39	5.7 %	1.0 %	0 %
Italian	5.8	4.8	4.0	4.6	4.5	4.15	6.3 %	1.5 %	0 %
Polish	4.6	4.7	4.0	5.0	4.9	4.18	11.9 %	2.7 %	0 %
Portuguese	5.4	4.7	4.0	4.3	4.3	4.01	6.2 %	1.1 %	0 %
Russian	5.0	4.7	4.0	4.8	4.7	4.04	11.1 %	1.9 %	0 %
Spanish	5.8	4.8	4.0	4.4	4.3	4.43	5.8 %	1.1 %	0 %
Swedish	5.4	4.7	4.0	4.2	4.2	3.85	6.7 %	1.6 %	0 %

Table 4: Overview of the 2,000 phrases selected by RANDOM (R), NGRAM (N) and MEMREP (M). OOV stands for Out-Of-Vocabulary, i.e., unique words that did not appear in the Wikipedia corpus.

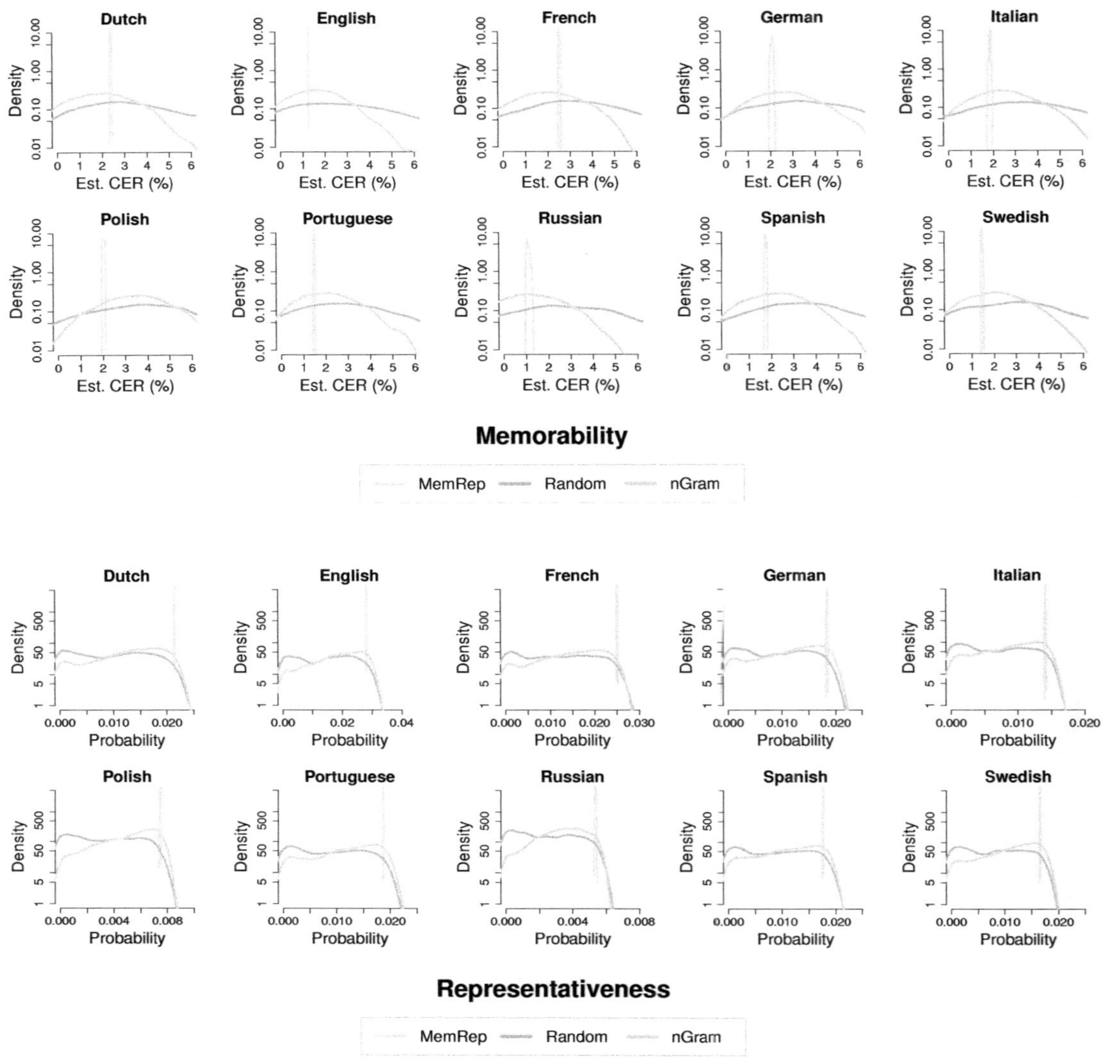

Figure 1: Dataset distributions overview. MEMREP phrases are consistently concentrated around more desirable values of memorability (low estimated character error rate, top row) and representativeness (high probability, bottom), according to [3].

Conclusion and Future Work

We have collected new datasets for conducting mobile text entry experiments in 10 major languages. All datasets are statistically comparable, however we recommend the MEMREP datasets because they are highly memorable and representative of each language. A limitation of our work is that the datasets have not undergone full human inspection. However, the statistical analysis conducted suggests that their behavior will be similar across all languages, and MEMREP has already been assessed with English and Spanish speakers [3]. Nevertheless, in future work we will test all datasets with their native speakers.

References

[1] Danescu-Niculescu-Mizil, C., Cheng, J., Kleinberg, J., and Lee, L. You had me at hello: How phrasing affects memorability. In *Proc. ACL* (2012), 892–901.

[2] Isokoski, P., and Linden, T. Effect of foreign language on text transcription performance: Finns writing English. In *Proc. NordiCHI* (2004), 109–112.

[3] Leiva, L. A., and Sanchis-Trilles, G. Representatively memorable: Sampling the right phrase set to get the text entry experiment right. In *Proc. CHI* (2014), 1709–1712.

[4] MacKenzie, I. S., and Soukoreff, R. W. Phrase sets for evaluating text entry techniques. In *Proc. CHI EA* (2003).

[5] Paek, T., and Hsu, B.-J. P. Sampling representative phrase sets for text entry experiments: a procedure and public resource. In *Proc. CHI* (2011), 2477–2480.

[6] Tiedemann, J. Parallel data, tools and interfaces in OPUS. In *LREC* (2012), 2214–2218.

[7] Vertanen, K., and Kristensson, P. O. A versatile dataset for text entry evaluations based on genuine mobile emails. In *Proc. MobileHCI* (2011), 295–298.

[8] Vertanen, K., and Kristensson, P. O. Complementing text entry evaluations with a composition task. *ACM TOCHI 21*, 2 (2014), 8:1–8:33.

Language	Method	Sample phrases
Dutch	RANDOM	oké niet huilen
	NGRAM	getuiges in een belangrijke zaak als ik jou niet afmaak
	MEMREP	grapje het is gewoon bier zo heette mijn moeder ook
English	RANDOM	and i ain't so afraid of losing something [8+] pipe it
	NGRAM	we intend to escape he can strip naked and
	MEMREP	the future seemed bright at the lemon slice
French	RANDOM	non t'es sur la liste à la réputation peu reluisante
	NGRAM	oublié de l'interroger sur depuis que vous avez conçu
	MEMREP	nous restons avec le peuple parfois je blague avec elle
German	RANDOM	jemanden mit einem 100 000 wagen [7+] 651 01 07 33 652 gt 01 07 35 210 ja i m [2+]
	NGRAM	marie die mir den kopf waren vor 100 jahren abhängig
	MEMREP	hab ich auch gehört mein antrieb ist weg
Italian	RANDOM	robin che lavora con gisborne potrebbe [2+] scusi ho sbagliato strada
	NGRAM	e tutto cosi confortevole e sta facendo un inchiesta per
	MEMREP	e' tanto grave questa sabbia si sposta

Language	Method	Sample phrases
Polish	RANDOM	ohydny dobry jest
	NGRAM	jakby pisał z myślą o że może mieć grypę
	MEMREP	teraz nie ma niczego nie są za pomocni
Portuguese	RANDOM	moradores são mais que bem vindos bebe do sapato
	NGRAM	que faça uma argumentação convencida de que é o
	MEMREP	não não matou ninguém bem pessoal acho que
Russian	RANDOM	ложись дэнни почему все так трясутся когда заходит речь [4+]
	NGRAM	подобное с другим человеком жизни и ты не хочешь
	MEMREP	не пускай их сюда он придет за мной
Spanish	RANDOM	bien lo admito es un cocodrilo centrai regreso con ustedes despues de caminar [2+]
	NGRAM	no bromearía con una cosa tu cara que ibas a
	MEMREP	así lo hacemos todos vuela como un pájaro
Swedish	RANDOM	det är miss och vivian bättre än på både violet och grace
	NGRAM	jag drömmar framträda och drömmar nej jag menade inte
	MEMREP	det finns alltså nån vi gjorde dock inget

Figure 2: Examples of the selected phrases, extracted at random from each dataset. [N+] means that the phrase contains N more words, which have been removed here for space reasons. The MEMREP datasets are available in three forms: full phrases, punctuation symbols removed, and tokenized + lowercased + no punctuation (as in this figure). The other datasets are provided for replicability and therefore are only available in tokenized + lowercased + no punctuation form.

Developing Tactile Feedback for Wearable Presentation: Observations from using a Participatory Approach

Flynn Wolf
UMBC
1000 Hilltop Circle
Baltimore MD 21250 USA
flynn.wolf@umbc.edu

Ravi Kuber
UMBC
1000 Hilltop Circle
Baltimore MD 21250 USA
rkuber@umbc.edu

MobileHCI '14, Sep 23-26 2014, Toronto, ON, Canada
ACM 978-1-4503-3004-6/14/09.
http://dx.doi.org/10.1145/2628363.2634230

Abstract
In this paper, we describe a participatory-based approach to developing tactile feedback for a head-mounted device. Three focus groups iteratively designed and evaluated tactile interaction concepts for user-generated use-case scenarios. Results showed productive design insights from the groups regarding approaches to tactile coding schemes addressing the scenario conditions, as well as method-innovations to participatory design techniques for interaction development in unfamiliar sensory modalities such as touch. The study has culminated in the development of a library of tactile icons relating to spatial concepts, which will be tested as part of future work.

Author Keywords
Participatory design; tactile; situational awareness

ACM Classification Keywords
H.5.2. User Interfaces: Haptic I/O

General Terms
Human Factors

Introduction
Tactile feedback has been widely researched for its potential to mitigate sensory overload by offering an additional sensory channel for users. The wide potential

Example Tactile Use-Case Scenarios (1-3 of 7)
1. Julia is a 22-year old, able-bodied college student. She is riding her bike, while wearing our prototype device, and receives a text message. How should that text event to be communicated to Julia by the device? 2. Julia is also expecting an important phone call while she is on her bike ride. How can that event be communicated by the device? How should the alert be different for another call from someone Julia does not consider urgent? 3. Julia's device visually detects an obstacle directly in front of her, in her direction of travel, a tree branch at head-height. How should the device alert her to this? Should this alert be different if the detected obstacle is on the ground?

Table 1. Example tactile use-cases derived from user survey responses

for using tactile stimuli to improve human users' spatial perception and decision making has been explored in rigorous real-world scenarios. In these cognitively and perceptually challenging work domains, such as aviation, industrial control, and military command and control, a user's perception, understanding, and ability to anticipate events in their environs, or situational awareness (SA), has also been the subject of active research and development [6]. A wearable tactile interface can offer considerable promise to provide this information. A review of the development of systems combining tactile feedback and situational awareness demonstrates that embedding tactile cues into control interfaces is a complicated human factors challenge, requiring care to avoid compounding common breakdowns in situational awareness. Creating these useful interactions requires research practices focused on the challenges inherent in assessing tactile feedback [1]. These challenges include eliciting detailed design ideas from users, due to the novelty of the task and the general difficulty of describing tactile feedback. A participatory design approach that accounts for the unfamiliarity of tactile signal parameters and descriptive terminology, and allows the user to work in concert with the tactile designer, could offer one method of helping overcome these barriers.

This paper therefore describes method-innovations and design conclusions from a participatory design process applied to the development of a tactile interface. This interface is intended to support the redirection of a user's attention via tactile cues to the head regarding realistic situational events such as spatial obstacles. Using a participatory approach, users were encouraged by several methods to take an active role in the tactile design process. These methods included an exercise to develop participants' shared descriptive vocabulary by associating tactile and sensory-related terminology with sample cues, and visual and tactile aids that overlaid user-generated use-case scenarios and tactile alert prototypes for an interface.

A head-mounted device was chosen for development for several reasons. Wearable head-mounted sensing devices are now entering broad use, and research on their potential as conduits for tactile alerting is limited compared to vest or belt-based approaches. Additionally, a head-mounted device supports study of attention redirection between a broad range of realistic, hands-free tasks, while providing valuable localized alerting to important situational events. As researchers have yet to focus in depth on the perceptual issues involved with presenting tactile cues to sites on the head, our studies aim to contribute to the knowledge in this area, and generally to effective participatory design approaches for unfamiliar modalities such as touch.

Related Work

Given its practical potential to augment other sensory channels and assist in maintaining spatial orientation, tactile feedback has been well-studied with regard to navigation. In their study of route navigation, Jacob et al. [1] found cognitively distracted users had better post-trial recall of their geographic environment when assisted by tactile cues in their task. Obrist et al. [5] utilized the explicitation interview technique to gather and analyze fourteen categories of user-structured vocabulary for the diachronic and synchronic structure of tactile signals presented to mechanoreceptors of the hand. Myles and Kalb [4] identified significant effects for scalp location and frequency threshold for vibration signals presented via a head-mounted tactile array. As

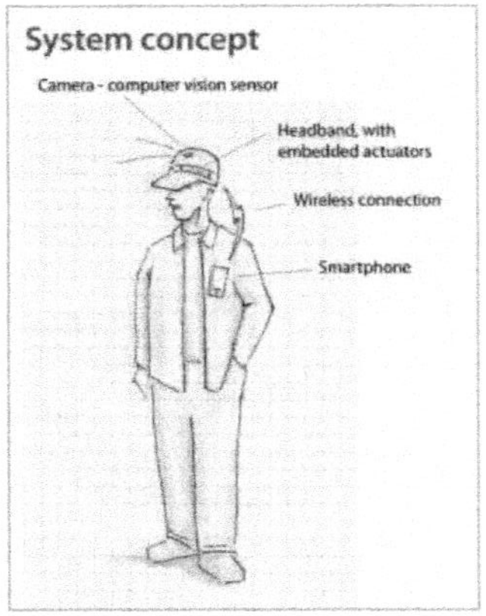

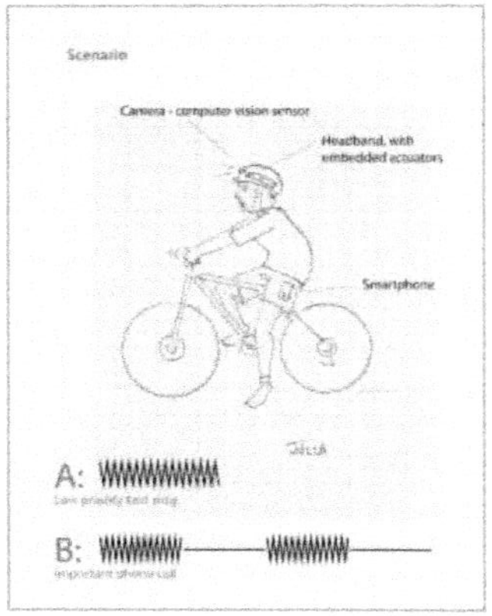

Figure 1. Visual aids presented to focus groups participants. At top, an initial system concept illustration. Beneath, a use-case scenario cartoon, with annotated waveform design concept created by a previous focus group.

research has yet to focus upon the design of cues which are most meaningful to users for head-based presentation, a study was developed to address this.

Study Design

A participatory design approach was adopted, enabling the users to play an active role in the design process. The approach was also thought to reinforce consideration for real world usage contexts, aspects of which may be unfamiliar to the developer [2]. The method would also offer a means to obtain a greater buy-in from the user community, leading to an improved sense of contribution and confidence to the conclusions and products of the process [3]. Scenarios were presented to participants as part of the approach. These were intended to focus design teams on better helping and empathizing with the situational awareness needs of potential users.

In order to inform the design of scenarios, a twenty-question survey was first developed and administered online and in-person to collect user descriptions of real-world experiences in which their situation awareness and task performance had been impaired, and how their daily use of mobile technology impacted those scenarios. The attentional and environmental factors the survey participants described were then coded and categorized, yielding seven representative use-case scenarios (Table 1). These scenarios were then used as participatory design challenges, tasking users and developers with formulating tactile signals with which to convey contextualized situational cues addressing each realistic scenario and common multitasking conditions.

Three focus groups were assembled, with each group comprised of 3-5 participants (aged 21-49), who had experience in situations where additional spatial or situational awareness of surroundings or events would have helped them. Researchers familiar with tactile interface design were also present at the focus groups to offer insights on the types of feedback developed for other systems which had proved to be useful for purposes of interaction.

Focus Group Procedures

As part of the introduction of the focus group task, participants were encouraged to assume all aspects of the project, including the possible applications and hardware and interaction design, were open to their modification and suggestions. Terms such as situation awareness and tactile feedback were also defined. Participants were then asked to comment on several example vibration signals, in order to establish a common vocabulary regarding the parameters of these signals. This vocabulary exercise was intended to allow participants to share a descriptive basis for discussion and conceptualization. In contrast with auditory terms, tactile terms are known to be difficult to naturally verbalize.

The participants were prompted to comparatively describe the signals using a worksheet with four categories of tactile signal parameters and corresponding example terms (Table 2). Participants were asked to comment and elaborate upon those terms. These procedures were also employed at the outset of the two following focus groups. The sample tactile signals were presented in the first focus group through a standard Android smartphone using Immersion's Haptic Effect Preview application, as it

Descriptive Term	Examples
Duration	Short, long, intermittent, repetitive
Amplitude	Low, mild, harsh, loud, variable
Waveform	Smooth, harsh, soothing, startling, rough, abrasive
Miscellaneous	Pleasant, unpleasant, distracting

Table 2. Tactile vocabulary worksheet

enabled the designer to develop and modify cues quickly. In successive groups, cues were then presented via the tactile actuators of the head-mounted device prototype (Fig. 2). The headset, originally described in detail in [7], presents signals up to eight sites on the user's head, controlled by software. Participants referred to the vocabulary sheet frequently, sometimes running a finger across the descriptive terms to evaluate its match with the participant's impression of the signal. The rapid uptake and use of the vocabulary was demonstrated by some participants' choice to directly reference the terms from the provided worksheet. This suggests that a longer list, explored by capturing and expanding upon participant responses in real-time, could have practical value in enriching the participants' design discussion.

The participants were then shown a simple sketch of the proposed tactile-SA system (Fig. 1), including a visual sensor mounted on the front of a hat, a headband with embedded tactors at cardinal points, and a wireless connection to a smartphone. Participants were encouraged to modify or critique the system in any way, without strict concern for engineering feasibility. Following the vocabulary exercise and introduction of the prototype illustration, the series of seven use-case design challenges were presented, depicting personas dealing with realistic spatial and situational alerts. These scenarios were generated from user surveys in the initial phase of the experiment. The scenarios were intended to progressively challenge design assumptions for tactile feedback to address realistic and increasingly rigorous situational, attentional, and environmental conditions. For example, participants would first be asked to devise a tactile alert for a basic spatial threat, such as an object in the path of a user, when the visual channel was occupied (e.g. when composing an SMS while ambulatory). This was based on the common survey observation of stumbling while walking head-down. The design problem would then be compounded with additional survey-based requirements to address simultaneous alerts, such as a non-spatial event alert, or an alert for a spatially oriented threat coming from a different direction or at a different rate of speed. This was intended to provoke discussion from the participants regarding the scope and nature of a complete tactile coding scheme, which could account for realistic issues such as complexity and de-conflicting simultaneous tactile alerts.

Sketches of each use-case scenario were used to reinforce the various conditions. Participants were also provided with drawing materials, and encouraged to sketch any concepts. Drawings produced by the participants included rudimentary waveforms, illustrations of variations in signal parameters such as amplitude or interval, and alternate hardware configurations for the head-mounted device. These suggestions were collected, coded and categorized, and then added onto the scenario drawings for subsequent focus groups. Participants in successive focus groups were asked to evaluate and iterate previously proposed design concepts for conveying information via tactile feedback (Fig. 1).

Results

A number of useful observations were made by the focus groups, with several consistent across all three, such as the need to generally maintain simplicity in a tactile coding scheme, and to reuse wherever possible familiar rhythms and patterns to limit cognitive workload when resolving cues. The groups also agreed

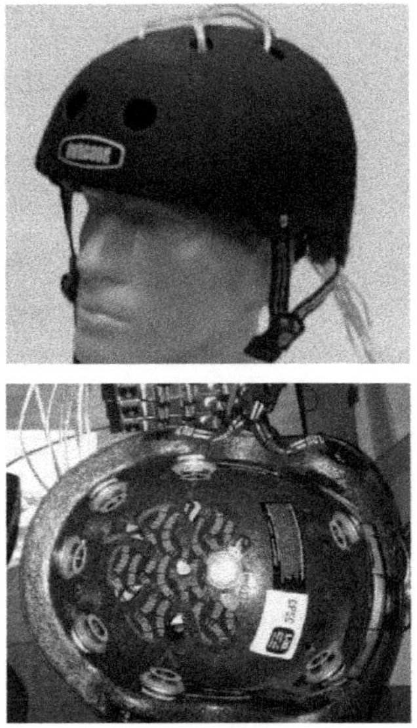

Figure 2. The outside and inside of the current head-mounted tactile device prototype [7].

that the design of a head-mounted device had to reconcile with social concerns, such as not being so noisy or visually conspicuous as to draw unwanted attention. In this regard, the inclusion of the experience and perspectives of numerous participants supported a broad and thoughtful consideration of the prototype design and the goal of collecting ideas for conveying, via the sense of touch, that which would otherwise be difficult to convey. The groups also agreed that a head-mounted system, when presenting spatial alerts, should account for the lateral and forward extension and flexion and longitudinal rotation of the head about the neck, relative to the vector of the approaching threat. The groups also differed on several conclusions. The second group prioritized the need to allow customization of tactile cues on any device, while the third group (citing their own experience with mobile technology) prioritized the need for optimal "out of the box" performance.

Beyond these comparisons, the focus groups were also able to successfully iterate concepts for applied uses of tactile feedback, the design of situational cues, and hardware layout. For example, the third focus group built upon use-case observations from the prior groups by suggesting that tactile encoding would be better served by modes for types of travel, such as pedestrian versus bicycle or automobile. This type of iteration also occurred with the descriptions of the waveforms. Sample tactile signals, based on the suggestions from the previous group for specific scenarios, were prepared and presented to the third group. Based upon these examples, the third group was able to provide more detailed suggestions regarding situationally appropriate waveforms and patterns for tactile cues.

Discussion and Design Implications

In addition to the design conclusions of the focus groups regarding the interface, several observations can be made about the tactile-specific innovations made to the participatory approach itself. For example, successfully prototyping in an unfamiliar sensory modality across consecutive focus groups was successful, but required establishing **exercises to produce common vocabulary**. Similarly, the ability of the focus groups to successfully iterate design ideas seemed dependent on providing **specific and richly contextualized detail** to subsequent focus groups. For example, annotating descriptive illustrations of the **use-case scenarios** with detailed visual and tactile descriptions allowed subsequent participants to comprehend and elaborate upon proposed tactile cues.

This was demonstrated when the participants were challenged to design a tactile alert for the head-mounted device for a scenario where two spatial threats existed, one low to the ground and one at head height. The first focus group described basic azimuth coding on one horizontal band of tactors in the direction of the obstacles, while the second group recommended additional horizontal rows of tactors around the head, which would allow relative vertical coding of alerts. Using combined use-case and design concept visual and tactile aids, the third group then iterated upon this concept by suggesting sequential signal patterns and waveform parameters that would be suitable to the scenario and the multi-row tactor layout. Similar evolutions in design occurred across the three groups for other tactile alert conditions, such as varying the waveform, amplitude, and time interval in tactile patterns to convey changing distance to an approaching spatial threat, and the number of threats detected.

Method-innovations related to participatory signal design
1. Utilize comparative introductory exercises to establish shared descriptive vocabulary for signal parameters 2. Provide examples illustrating potentially unfamiliar signal parameters 3. Provide realistic use-case scenarios to prompt thorough consideration of potential interactions of signals and user conditions 4. To support iteration between successive focus groups, produce specific, richly contextualized, multimodal prototypes for evaluation

Example tactile signals were also provided to participants. These were often referenced in later discussion, suggesting that these examples and the vocabulary of tactile terms were effective at seeding the participants' discussion with parameters for creating or modifying tactile alerts which might otherwise have been missed. The terms provided, however, were actually used as a checklist for evaluation in one case, suggesting that the direct influence on participants of the materials provided should be carefully considered in advance.

While the participants' breadth of experience yielded clear dividends to the tactile design process, the evaluation of some use-case scenarios might benefit from deliberately selecting participants that could offer a specific perspective. For example, one participant in the first focus group offered a unique insight on the spatial aspects of situational awareness and safety from a family member who uses a wheelchair. A need was identified to convey the position of pedestrians or wheel chair users in close proximity, to better indicate when it is safe to stop without injuring others.

Conclusion and Future Work

The participatory design sessions were effective at gathering unexpected solutions to challenging tactile feedback scenarios. The approach also suggested useful method-innovations for focus groups addressing unfamiliar sensory modalities or applied technologies. These insights will be applied to a follow-on study.

Existing studies, as well as focus group feedback, regarding tactile feedback have indicated that a user's body posture and concurrent physical activity can interact and interfere with their perception of tactile cues [1]. Given this, follow-on research proposes to engage users in physical activities to assess potential masking effects of biomechanical exertion on perception of tactile signals generated in these focus groups, concurrent to realistic "neck down" multi-tasking conditions.

Acknowledgements

This research is supported by the National Science Foundation – Award No. 1352924.

References

[1] Jacob, R., Winstanley, A., Togher, N., Roche, R. & Mooney, P. Pedestrian navigation using sense of touch. *Computers, Environment and Urban Systems, 36* (2012), 513–525.

[2] Kuber, R., Yu, W., & McAllister, G. Towards developing assistive haptic feedback for visually impaired internet users. In *Proc. SIGCHI 2007*, ACM Press (2007), 1525-1534.

[3] Muller, M.J. Chapter Fifty-Four: Participatory Design: The Third Space in HCI. *The Human Computer Interaction Handbook* (2nd Edition). Sears, A.L. and Jacko, J.A. (eds). 1061-1081, 2008.

[4] Myles, K., & Kalb, J.T. Vibrotactile sensitivity of the head (No. ARL-TR-4696). Army Research Lab, Human Research and Engineering Directorate (2009).

[5] Obrist, M., Seah, S.A., & Subramanian, S. Talking about tactile experiences. In *Proc. SIGCHI 2013*, ACM Press (2013), 1659-1668.

[6] Wickens, C.D. Situation awareness: Review of Mica Endsley's 1995 articles on situation awareness theory and measurement. *Human Factors, 50*(3), 397-403.

[7] Wolf, F., Feldman, P. & Kuber, R. Towards supporting situational awareness using tactile feedback. In *Proc. 3DUI 2014*, IEEE (2014), 131-132.

"People Don't Bump": Sharing Around Mobile Phones in Close Proximity

Afshan Kirmani
UCL Interaction Centre
University College London
Gower Street,
London WC1E 6BT, UK
afshankirmani@gmail.com

Rowanne Fleck
UCL Interaction Centre
University College London
Gower Street,
London WC1E 6BT, UK
r.fleck@ucl.ac.uk

MobileHCI '14, Sep 23-26 2014, Toronto, ON, Canada

ACM 978-1-4503-3004-6/14/09.

http://dx.doi.org/10.1145/2628363.2634231

Abstract
A large body of mobile phone sharing research focuses on creating new interaction techniques for sharing, and considers the usability of such applications and features whilst ignoring the context of their use, their adoption or appropriation. Therefore it is not known whether these technologies are used in practice or whether they really meet people's sharing needs. The aim of this research was to understand current real-world user sharing practices around mobile smart phones through the use of a diary study with 63 participants. We focused on close proximity sharing and discovered that new technologies to support this kind of sharing, for example bumping handsets together to exchange files, are not being widely used. More than half of all sharing via phones in this sample involved only telling, showing or passing the phone, though this often triggered further sharing. Possible explanations for this and their implications are discussed.

Author Keywords
Mobile phones; sharing; face-to-face; diary study

ACM Classification Keywords
H.5.m. Information interfaces and presentation (e.g., HCI): Miscellaneous.

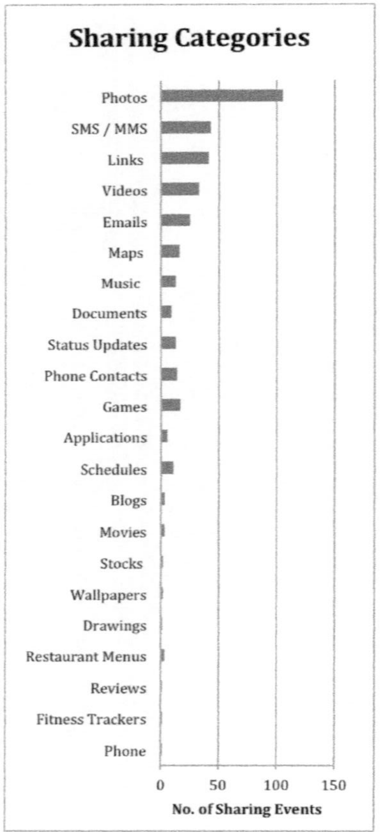

Figure 1: Categories of Sharing

(Q1) *"I showed my friends the profile pictures album of my ex-roommate who is visiting Peru soon and she lives there."* (human resource manager, aged 45).

Introduction

The mobile smart-phone now enables people to capture and share with others all sorts of media from text messages, photographs, video, web pages and more. However there is limited recent research which explores exactly how and what people are sharing with these new capabilities. A number of new interaction techniques allow people to share such content between smartphones when in f2f situations in novel and fun ways (e.g. bumping, shaking and tapping to pair devices [6,7,8]), but the focus of research in this area has been on the usability of these tools and how people interact with the technology, not whether these technologies are used in practice or really meet people's sharing needs. Therefore, the main aims of this study were to understand current sharing behaviour with mobile phones in close proximity among pairs and groups of people to understand if and how people make use of novel f2f sharing mechanisms, and to suggest ways in which technology might be better designed to support these activities.

Related work

For the purposes of this research, we take a very broad definition of the word 'share' which includes all examples of sharing, showing or sending something via or from the phone when f2f or in close proximity to people sharing, showing or sending things to. Previous research which has looked at what people share by mobile phone has found that photos are shared more than other self-generated media (i.e. video or audio) [4]. However although this research reveals f2f sharing is prevalent, it does not consider specifically sharing in f2f situations. Research which does consider specifically f2f or close proximity use of mobile phones reports on ways phones are used to enhance social situations, including ways conversations are triggered around incoming messages [9]. In addition mobile phones can be used to talk/text to someone who is close by but out of hearing (e.g. at the front of a queue) or to text someone close by you could not otherwise talk to either because it is too noisy or for privacy reasons [3,9].

Technologies for sharing in close proximity
A number of technologies and applications have been developed to support people to share media etc. between mobile phones specifically in f2f or close proximity situations. These include applications that allow one to share photos [2], applications that make use of Bluetooth [1] and applications to support the sharing of various media in large group situations like spectator events [10]. Interaction techniques developed to support the moving of information from one device to another in close proximity include holding two devices together and 'stitching interactions' between devices [7] shaking them [8] bumping them together [6] tapping to sync devices [11], picking and dropping items from one device to another through direct manipulation [12] and by pressing a button to share information [11]. However, in all cases there is at most some usability testing of these applications presented but no research that looks at if and how such technologies are adopted and used beyond the lab.

We conducted a one week diary study in order to investigate what, how, where and why people share via their mobile phone when in close proximity to others.

Methodology

Participants
Sixty-three participants (31 male, 32 female) were recruited through flyers posted around the city of

(Q2) "*I needed to talk to my group of friends but I couldn't say it out loud with people around me. So I shared it via a text message.*" (student, 22)

(Q3) "*I just played some music on my iTunes for a group of people that I'm with at the moment. It's 6pm. Someone asked me for the song and I sent him an email to give him the details of that song.*" (client service, 31).

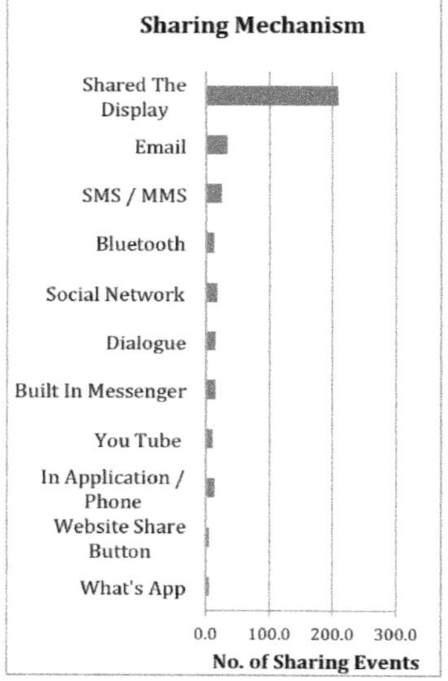

Figure 2: Sharing Mechanisms

London. All currently owned and had used a smartphone (iPhone or Android device) for over 6 months, and reported sharing via mobile phone with people in close proximity at least once a week. They were 19-60 years old (M = 27.5, SD = 6.9) from a variety of cultures (73% British, others African, Asian, Hispanic and American) and jobs. Participants were entered into a prize draw with the potential to win £50 for participating.

Procedure
Each participant was provided with our definition of 'sharing in close proximity', which included sharing of anything (e.g. photos, texts, links etc.) via mobile phone (including passing around/showing) with another person or in a group when f2f with them. Each participant was asked to send a SMS/text message to the researcher after they had shared something with a friend(s) in close proximity noting the time of day, what was shared, how, with whom, why and where they were. Three SMS's were sent to participants each day, and an email sent at the end of the day to remind/prompt participants to report any relevant sharing events.

Analyses
We found that participants often reported occasions where they had shared 'a number of photographs' or 'was texting' someone without specifying exactly how many photographs were shared or texts sent etc. Therefore we counted 'sharing events' in our analysis defined as the sharing of one or more of the same kind of media via the same mechanism in the same time and place to the same person/people. These sharing events were coded and categorized in terms of what was shared, how, whether with one other person or a group, why they shared and where they were at the time.

Findings
Over the course of the week, a total of 363 f2f sharing events were recorded (an average of 5.7 per participant) with a total of 213 events that involved sharing between pairs, and 150 to a group.

As found in previous research, the most common category of sharing via mobile phone when f2f was photographs, accounting for 30.5% of all sharing events (Figure 1). Our findings also suggest that groups shared relatively more photographs with each other (38% of all group sharing events) than pairs did (23% of all pair sharing events). We found that when in groups, 38.7% of the sharing events of photographs occurred via the display. These included photographs from participants' own photo albums, but also their own and other's photographs on the website of social networking sites (Q1). Participants also reported sharing photographs by email, dialogue (talking about the pictures aloud and looking into the phone), chat messenger like What's App, by uploading it to social networks like Facebook and Twitter and through a phone service like iPhone gallery. Similarly, videos were most often shared via the phone display followed closely by through a website like 'You Tube'. They were also shared via the share button on a website, via a link sent by text or email and in the same way as photographs.

TEXT MESSAGES
Participants also reported sharing text messages with others in close proximity. Overall, text messages accounted for 11.8% of sharing events and included

(Q4) *"I was at a party and talking about a friend's baby to a friend. I showed her the pictures and she wanted a copy of it which made me email it to her immediately"* (accountant, aged 37).

(Q5) *"I normally have a chat group with four of us girls. We met the other day for coffee and one of our friends were missing. We sent her a message immediately to let her know what she was missing. Soon after this, we began chatting as a group while sipping on some coffee"* (student, 22).

*(Q6)"I was in a meeting. As u know meetings can be boring as h***. I shared an email that had a joke to someone in the meeting room. I also shared it with another friend. "* (software engineer, 28)

using the phone's built in text messaging system (including blackberry messenger), the application 'What's App', and also by showing others the display of the phone. 46.5% of these involved people sharing with others f2f and remotely at the same time. Participants used texts to communicate things that required privacy in a public setting (Q2). They also used it to communicate with one other person when in a group either because they were bored or wanted privacy, and to communicate when in noisy places were others were unable to hear them clearly. Participants also brought messages that they received from friends remotely into f2f conversations, either to start a conversation or because the conversation was interrupted by a text message.

LINKS

11.2% of all sharing events were categorized as 'links' which included the sharing of any website address via mobile phone by any means and included news articles, music, schedules, restaurant menus, directions to places, personal website addresses and movies amongst other things. Many of these involved copying and pasting the link website address from a browser window on the mobile phone and sending this out to others through emails and text messages or by clicking 'share link' buttons on a website or social media site.

MUSIC

One way music was shared was simply by playing it – either through the phone's music player (categorized as 'in application/phone) or via external speakers (e.g. Q3). Others reported sharing music in other ways too, like via What's App and even recording on their phone a song playing in the car and sharing that.

OTHER CATEGORIES

Other things participants reported sharing were, games, schedules, maps, phone contacts, emails, documents, status updates, applications, drawings, stocks, fitness trackers, wallpapers and the phone itself (see Figure 1). These were shared in a variety of, often creative, ways.

Mechanisms for Sharing

Figure 2 shows a breakdown of sharing mechanisms used overall. We found that participants shared most often via the display of their phones, and in this way more often to groups than between pairs. Some sharing only occurred as dialog (discussing or reading out what was on the phone without showing) or playing audio through the phone. However, it was observed that this 'no transfer' sharing was often followed up with another sharing mechanism (e.g. Q3, Q4).

Also, sharing whilst in close proximity was sometimes coupled with sharing remotely. Of the 363 sharing events reported, 48 (13%) involved sharing both f2f and with remote others at the same time. This seemed to occur in a number of ways including involving f2f friends in a remote conversation by reading out incoming text messages, or vice-versa by involving remote people in conversation with f2f, for example using online group chats when one member of the friendship group was not present (e.g. Q5). Sharing with one person also often triggered participants to share the same item with others or via a social networking site (e.g. Q6).

Discussion

A number of technologies have been developed to support people sharing around mobile phones in close

(Q7) "Bluetooth is most often known to be error prone. In addition, media can only be sent to a single recipient. I'm unable to share in groups while using my mobile device" (student, 21).

proximity. However these are evaluated mainly in lab-based usability studies. With the exception of Walton [14] who looked at mobile-phone sharing in South Africa, previous research which looks at how people share in the real world is now becoming out of date and does not consider specifically f2f sharing. Given the rapid development of technology in this space, our research set out to investigate people's current f2f sharing in context. It is important to note that the sample we used in this research were relatively wealthy smart-phone users in the London area where the cost of access to mobile networks and wifi was likely less of an issue to our participants than to populations elsewhere in the world with different access to phone technology and network infrastructures. Therefore caution is needed in generalizing these findings beyond the studied population. However, we did make a number of observations we think are worthy of note.

1. People don't 'bump'. None of our participants reported using any of the fun or novel techniques available for sharing in close proximity. Our participants only made use of two sharing mechanisms that were specifically f2f: showing/telling without any file or data transfer, and very occasionally they used Bluetooth. There are a number of reasons why our participants may not have used specific f2f sharing mechanisms including that a suitable f2f or close proximity sharing mechanism may not have been available to participants in our study. Many of the mechanisms we introduced earlier are not widely known and are therefore not quickly and readily available to all parties who wished to share. However the likelihood of their use when available or adoption may be predicted by consideration of our other findings.

2. People often share when in groups or with more than one person at a time. 41% of the sharing events we recorded involved sharing with more than one other person, and sharing the display occurred proportionally more in these situations. We also observed that sharing with one person often prompted sharing to a wider audience, people often shared with those f2f and remote simultaneously and that people often shared to more than one person via networks. This might be why mechanisms like Bluetooth and others that can only be used to transfer information between two phones at a time were not helpful (Q7). In contrast, mechanisms that made use of internet or mobile phone networks allowed participants to share with people both f2f and remote at the same time. These reasons might be why much group sharing in particular, that involved file or media transfer made use of in-built messenger services, What's App, Blackberry Messenger and email which allowed sharing amongst established groups even when one or more of the group were together f2f at the time of sharing.

3. People do a lot of showing. 58% of f2f sharing events we recorded involved either showing or sharing orally without any transfer of information from one device to another or via a social network. This may even be an underestimate as such sharing could be easier to forget. It is possible that this kind of sharing was so prevalent because of a lack of an alternate suitable mechanism for sharing, it is also a quick and convenient way to exchange information or show something to someone beside you, and the screens on today's smartphones are large enough for either two people to look at side by side, or at least for the sharer to be aware of what the receiver is looking at if the phone is passed over. Also, showing on the phone enables people to share with others they do not have the contact details of already on their phone. In addition participants may not have wanted (or for legal reasons been able) to give others to keep everything they reported showing another person on their phone (for example personal photographs or their fitness app home screen). Showing something, especially something personal, does not imply the same intimacy between participants as giving. Therefore successful sharing technologies might be those that allow a stage of 'augment showing', supporting the showing of files (e.g. via projection [5] or to another's phone screen [13]) without giving.

4. Showing often leads to or precedes file transfer. This observation suggests that successful f2f sharing technologies might be those that mirror the way people currently share by allowing file transfer to follow from the 'augmented showing' described above with an added level of security or identification. The ability to share more widely to remote others and via social network sites could also be an option at this point.

References

1. Beale, R. Supporting social interaction with smart phones. *Pervasive Computing,* IEEE (2005) 35-41.
2. Clawson, J., Voida, A., Patel, N., Lyons, K. Mobiphos: A collocated–synchronous mobile photo sharing application. In *Proc. MobileHCI'08*, ACM Press (2008) 187-195.
3. Faulkner, X., Culwin, F. When fingers do the talking: a study of text messaging. *Interacting with Computers, 17, 2* (2004) 167-185.
4. Goh, D., Ang, R., Chua, A., Lee C. Why We Share: A study of motivations for mobile media sharing. *Active Media Technology*. Springer (2009) 195–206.
5. Greaves, A., Rukzio, E. View and Share: Exploring co-present viewing and sharing of pictures using personal projection. In Proc MobileHCI'09 ACM Press (2009) 281-288.
6. Hinckley, K. Synchronous gestures for multiple users and computers, In *Proc. User interface software and technology*. ACM (2003) 149-158.
7. Hinckley, K. Ramos, G., Guimbretiere, F., Baudisch, P., Smith, M. Stitching: Pen gestures that span multiple displays, In *Proc. of the working conference on Advanced visual interfaces*. ACM (2004) 23-31.
8. Holmquist, L., Mattern, F., Schiele, B., Alahuhta, P., Beigl, M., Gellersen, H. Smart-Its Friends: A technique for users to easily establish connections between smart artefacts. *Ubicomp 2001,* Springer (2001) 116-122.
9. Ito, M., Okabe, D. Technosocial situations: Emergent structurings of mobile email use. *Personal, portable, pedestrian: Mobile phones in Japanese life* (2005) 257-273.
10. Jacucci, G., Oulasvirta, A., Salovaara, A., Sarvas, R. Supporting the shared experience of spectators through mobile group media. In *Proc. Supporting Group Work,* ACM Press (2005) 207–216.
11. Okabe. Emergent Social Practices, Situations and Relations through Everyday Camera Phone Use. *Mobile Communication and Social Change* (2004) 18-19.
12. Rekimoto, J. Pick And Drop: A direct manipulation technique for multiple computer environments. In Proc. UIST 1997, ACM Press (1997) 31-39.
13. Snapchat. www.snapchat.com
14. Walton, M., Haßreiter, S., Marsden, G., Allen, S. Degrees of Sharing: Proximate Media Sharing and Messaging by Young People in Khayelitsha. In *Proc. MobileHCI 2012*, ACM Press (2012) 21–24.

Mobile Designs to Support User Experiences of Energy Conservation in Hotels

Xiying Wang
Cornell University
Ithaca, NY 14850 USA
xw282@cornell.edu

Susan R. Fussell
Cornell University
Ithaca, NY 14850 USA
srf72@cornell.edu

Abstract

In the U.S., hotels are a heavy energy-consuming sector. Yet they sometimes prioritize customer satisfaction over lower energy use. In this study, we discuss how mobile designs can help to motivate energy-saving behaviors while maintaining users' satisfaction. We conducted a diary study of 13 participants and an interview study of 20 participants to understand user experiences around energy consumption in hotel and motel rooms. We found that people unnecessarily consume energy because they are *unfamiliar* with the hotel room environment and they want to *be catered to* by the hotel. We suggest two mobile design ideas: *location-based energy conservation*, and *blending lights*, and discuss the opportunities of mobile designs to balance personal controls and automation to support user experience and satisfaction yet decrease energy use in hospitality settings.

Author Keywords

HCI; user experience; satisfaction; energy conservation;

ACM Classification Keywords

H.5.m. Information interfaces and presentation (e.g., HCI): Miscellaneous.

MobileHCI '14, Sep 23-26 2014, Toronto, ON, Canada
ACM 978-1-4503-3004-6/14/09.
http://dx.doi.org/10.1145/2628363.2634232

Introduction

In the United States, hospitality is the 3rd largest energy consumption sector [8]. Many reasons make hospitality stand out in energy consumption. First, unlike hotels in other countries, hotels in the United States do not have a smart key card system that automatically turns off the electricity after customers leave their hotel rooms. Second, hotels consider the customer's satisfaction as a top priority, and may engage in unnecessary energy use to please the customer (e.g., keeping pools or gyms open and lit even when no one is present) [7]. Third, evidence suggests hotel customers are not likely to cut their energy use even when they claim to be energy conservative [7, 12].

In addition, energy consumption in hospitality settings is different in nature from energy consumption in the home or office. On one hand, hotel customers have more limited control over energy use in hotels and motels than they do at home. For example, they cannot install energy efficient light bulbs in their hotel rooms even though they might do so at home. On the other hand, hotel customers have more control over their energy use than does the typical officer worker. For example, lighting in a shared workspace is often centrally controlled and workers cannot switch on/off the lights. Achieving a balance of different controls over energy is important for energy conservation, which affects people's experience of consuming energy.

The novelty of energy consumption in hospitality settings inspires us to rethink the user experience, particularly users' satisfaction with their energy consumption. In this study, we aim to answer the following two research questions: 1) How do hotel customers feel about consuming energy in their rooms? and 2) What are the mobile design opportunities for maintaining users' satisfaction while motivating them to save energy?

Literature review

With the discussion of *sustainable interaction design* introduced by Blevis [1], much research looks at motivations, awareness, and behaviors of energy conservation. Investigators and designers have purposed multiple methods to motivate energy-conserving behaviors or to increase awareness of energy conservation, e.g., providing energy-related information and feedback [5, 11], rewarding certain behaviors [4], showing visualizations [9], or presenting social comparisons and social supports [10]. In particular, Cialdini pointed out that hotel customers' energy-consuming behaviors are influenced by social norms such as what others consider is reasonable for energy use [3].

However, most of the research focuses on energy consumption at the personal level, looking at how awareness of energy use, change of behaviors, and motivations for energy conservation affect personal decisions, controls, daily practices, and energy saving behaviors. There is much less discussion of what degree of control an individual vs. the system (automation) should have over energy usage. For example, is it better to motivate people to turn off lights when they leave a room, or to install sensor based lights that turn off automatically when no one is present? Under what circumstances is it better to have personal control of energy use, under what circumstances it is better to have intelligent system

Interviewee #11: *"But I think I even might have left the bathroom lights on when I was sleeping, just because when you were in a new environment, I was like 'if I am going to the bathroom, I am going to get confused, or run into any furniture', so I just left the bathroom lights on there at least I could find my way to the bathroom... Ya, you are like 'just a little bit of lights'. Because I mean at home, I feel really comfortable when sitting in the dark. I don't know. It's just that something with the unfamiliar space."* (Female, hotel)

Interviewee #5: *"If I am more familiar with my room, I don't need to keep more lights on because I could see every single concern of my room. But in the hotel room, I would typically keep the hallway light on when I am awake. So it just makes me feel safe."* (Female, hotel)

control of energy use, and under what circumstances is a combination of personal and system control optimal?

Another theme tightly associated with energy conservation is persuasive technology, where researchers and designers attempt to persuade people to adapt to energy-conserving behaviors or practices [2]. However, many persuasive designs tend to highlight the experience and effectiveness of persuading users to behave sustainably according to researchers' or designers' intentions, without much discussion of the user's satisfaction with using such technology to save energy.

Our study focuses on both aspects that have been neglected from the field. First, we want to understand user experience, particularly feelings of satisfaction around energy consumption. Second, we discuss design opportunities suitable for personal control, system control, or both.

Methodology

We used a two-step research procedure. First, we conducted a diary study with 13 participants to understand people's experience around energy consumption in hospitality settings, their use of technology (e.g., personal electronics, hotel room devices) when staying at a hotel, and their opinions about several design ideas for tools to reduce energy consumption. In particular, we asked them to document how long they used each hotel room device, once per day of hotel stay ranging from one day to a week. All diaries were filled out while the participants were staying in the hotel. Second, we conducted 20 semi-structured interviews to further understand people's attitudes, feelings, behaviors, and overall experience of energy use in hotels and motels. Each interview lasted 30 to 45 minutes. All interviews were transcribed, and the diary studies and interviews were coded iteratively using the constant comparative analysis introduced by Glaser and Strauss [6].

All respondents were graduate students or working people who could pay for their own hotel stay. Of the 13 participants in the diary study, 8 were doctoral students and 5 were working in big companies. Of the semi-structured interview participants, 16 were doctoral students, and 4 were working in big companies. 8 of the 20 participants in the semi-structured interviews had also participated in the diary study.

User experience around energy consumption

We are interested in understanding user experience around energy consumption in hospitality. In particular, we attempt to find out how hotel customers use energy in a hotel room and the reason why they consume energy in such ways. We identified two major themes regarding user experience: *preparation for the unknown*, and *luxury*.

Preparation for the Unknown

Participants mentioned that they would keep one or two lights on before going to bed or during sunset time before going out, for two major reasons: unfamiliarity with the environment and safety concerns.

Unfamiliarity with the environment led to perceived risks of stumbling, falling over, or failing to find one's way in a hotel room at night. Participants mentioned that they kept lights on all night to prevent potential danger. Most (16 out of 20) interviewees mentioned that they were concerned that they would stumble into

Interviewee #6: *"My mom is very old fashion, she'd like to have fresh towel every day. So ... each person has two towels in the hotel room, so it's like 10 towels. If it I hang them up, she would throw it to the floor to signal new towels. So when I travel, I reuse my towels, but she doesn't like it, and she doesn't reuse them either...I don't think she sees the reason the hotel room has this, but for me, I do see the values of reusing the towels, to save electricity, the wash like that. And my mother is wonderful, but it's always been a tough sell for her. It's not that she doesn't believe it is a good idea, but it's just like while she's travelling, I'm expecting this, and I'm paying for this so I will have fresh towels every day." (Male, hotel)*

something at night and hurt themselves. Some were concerned that they would not be able to find their way in the dark if they woke up at night (as described by interviewee #11).

Half of the participants (10 interviewees) mentioned that they had safety concerns of staying in a hotel room but most of them did not specify a particular reason for these concerns. However, they reported that, keeping one or two lights on in the evening increased their sense of security (as described by interviewee #5).

Luxury
Luxury is often associated with personal comfort when staying in hotel rooms and people's desire to be catered to in a hotel.

Personal comfort in the hotel room—for example, pleasant room temperature, sufficient brightness, fresh air in the room, and an overall relaxing environment—were all important issues for our participants. All of the participants from the interviews and nearly half of diary studies (6 participants) discussed what they did to achieve personal comfort in a hotel room. However, achieving higher comfort levels usually came at the cost of greater energy use, e.g., keeping the air conditioning or heating on once it reached a comfortable temperature, turning on extra and unnecessary lights, opening the hotel room door to bring in fresh air while blasting the air conditioner, and turning on the TV to create a relaxing environment.

In addition, participants viewed hotels as a special place that is different from their home or office. As is mentioned by interviewee #6, hotel customers are being catered to or taken care of by the hotel staff or service. For example, hotel services change the bed sheets and towels, and clean the room for customers. Several participants in the interviews mentioned that they have the right and freedom to consume as much energy as they want, because electricity and water is already included in the price of staying in a hotel.

Mobile design ideas

In this section, we discuss two smartphone design ideas inspired from our findings about energy consumption in hospitality settings: *location-based energy conservation* and *blending lights*. Our intention is to provide the user with *ways to consume less energy while maintaining their satisfaction, and in such a way that it does not have a negative influence on the user's experience of consuming energy*. We argue that more personal control over energy use via smartphones is better under some situations, more automated controls are better in other contexts, and some situations are suitable for both types of controls.

Idea 1: Location-based Energy Conservation
This idea is inspired by the theme of *luxury*, but it can be applied in other circumstances such as *unfamiliarity*. Our design idea, location-based energy conservation smartphone application, aims to satisfy people's desires for a luxury experience while conserving energy at the same time. A key feature of this idea is GPS detection, an automatic device switch to control the electronic devices in the hotel room, and the ability to remember temperature and lighting settings. For example (see **Figure 1**), if the customer leaves the air conditioning at 70 degrees, the application triggers the automatic switch to turn on the air conditioning and set it to 70 degrees when the customer is close to the hotel. The lights are also automatically turned on. Similarly, if a

Figure 1: Location-based energy conservation app (hotel lamps and temperature are activated when a user comes back to the hotel)

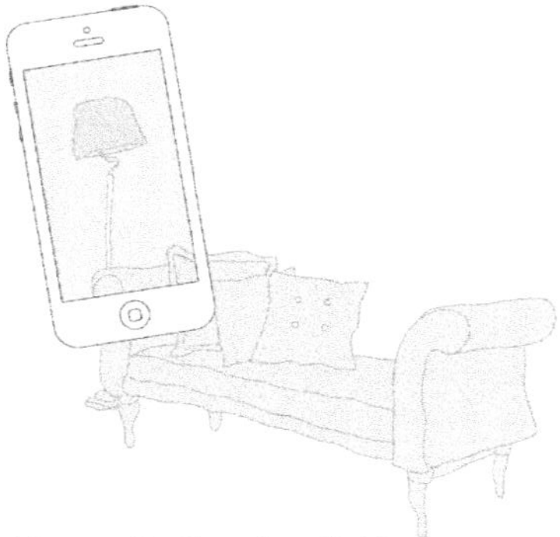

Figure 2: Blending lights

customer is leaving the hotel, the application will trigger the automatic switch to turn off the room devices. Even if the customer forgets to turn off the devices, e.g., lights, TV, or air conditioning, this application prevents them from staying on all day.

We suggest giving more controls to a smartphone system rather than a person when energy consumption is motivated by a desire for *luxury*, that is, when people's satisfaction is associated with greater energy use. People are unlikely to decrease their satisfaction and enjoyment because they feel they have already paid for or are accustomed to luxury. In such circumstances, system control over energy conservation can be effective because intelligent systems can adjust to an energy-saving environment when no one is in the room and return control to the users when they return, thereby maximizing both user satisfaction and energy conservation.

Idea 2: Blending Lights

The idea of blending light is inspired by people's comments about *unfamiliarity* and *laziness*. For example, participants were worried about stumbling in the dark and safety, especially in the evening. Lighting up the room when it is needed becomes important in these circumstances. However, after lighting the room, participants mentioned that they sometimes just left the lights on because the switches were out of reach. Thus, it is important that the light switch be easy to reach from anywhere in the room.

Blending light is the idea that a person can control the lights in a hotel room via his or her smartphone. The hotel environment and the smartphone are blending together, as in **Figure 2**. When a user puts his or her smartphone over the room environment, its camera captures the room environment and blends the environment with the smartphone. A user can simply touch the bedside reading lamp, floor lamp, and other devices figures on their smartphone, in order to turn the devices on or off. Blending light is convenient for people to use their smartphones to light up the hotel room in the evening or turn off electronic devices.

This idea provides more personal control than smartphone system control over energy use. When a user is unfamiliar with the environment and wants to create a sense of safety, consuming energy is a strategy to bring and enhance familiarity and safety. It respects their choices of energy consumption and provides an alternative way for them to use less energy. This design also takes into account participants' reports that laziness sometimes resulted in more energy consumption, e.g., leaving lights on for the whole night. Thus, providing a convenient and easy means of controlling these devices can lead to lower energy use. This design solution is not unique to the hotel setting, and it can also be applied to household contexts.

Conclusion

The goal of our study is to use smartphones to support users' satisfaction and expectation around energy consumption in hotel settings, and explore mobile design opportunities for energy conservation.

We identified two major reasons why people consume more energy than expected in hotels: (1) *preparation for the unknown*. *Unfamiliarity* and *safety concerns* are two important reasons for energy use under this theme; (2) *luxury*. People's desires for *comfort* and *being catered to in a hotel* are the major reasons for energy consumption. Inspired by these findings, we proposed two mobile design ideas, *location-based energy conservation* and *blending lights* to motivate energy conservation in U.S. hospitality settings while maintaining customers' satisfactions. We also discussed possibilities of maintaining user's satisfaction around energy conservation based on two levels of control – personal control and system control (automation). Creating more system controls over energy conservation seems to better maintain people's desires to enjoy a *luxury* environment, while giving more personal control can help to reduce *unfamiliarity*.

In future work, we plan to further evaluate these mobile designs to examine which features are effective for motivating energy conservation and supporting users' satisfaction, and to generalize our design strategies for motivating energy conservation using mobile technology to other types of settings.

Acknowledgements

We thank our participants for volunteering in our study, and all the reviewers for their useful and insightful comments.

References

[1] Blevis, E. (2007). Sustainable interaction design: invention & disposal, renewal & reuse. In *Proc. CHI*, 503-512.

[2] Brynjarsdottir, H., Håkansson, M., Pierce, J., Baumer, E., DiSalvo, C., & Sengers, P. (2012). Sustainably unpersuaded: how persuasion narrows our vision of sustainability. In *Proc. CHI*, 947-956.

[3] Cialdini, R. B., Reno, R. R., & Kallgren, C. A. (1990). A Focus theory of normative conduct: recycling the concept of norms to reduce littering in public places. *Journal of Personality and Social Psychology*, 58(6), 1015-1026.

[4] Froehlich, J., Dillahunt, T., Klasnja, P., Mankoff, J., Consolvo, S., Harrison, B., & Landay, J. A. (2009). UbiGreen: investigating a mobile tool for tracking and supporting green transportation habits. In *Proc. CHI*, 1043-1052.

[5] Froehlich, J., Findlater, L., & Landay, J. A. (2010). The design of eco-feedback technology. In *Proc. CHI*, 1999-2008.

[6] Glaser, B., & Strauss, A. (1999). *The discovery of grounded theory: strategies for qualitative research*. Aldine Transaction.

[7] Goldstein, N. J., Cialdini, R. B., & Griskevicius, V. (2008). A room with a viewpoint: using social norms to motivate environmental conservation in hotels. *Journal of Consumer Research*, 35, 472-482.

[8] International Energy Agency. (2008): 'Worldwide trends in energy use and efficiency: key insights from IEA indicator analysis', *International Energy Agency*.

[9] Mankoff, J., Fussell, S. R, Glaves, R., Grevet, C., Johnson, M., Mattews, D., Mattews, H. S., McGuire, R, Thompson, R., Shick, A., & Setlock, L. (2010). StepGreen.org: increasing energy saving behaviors via social networks. *AAAI*.

[10] Petkov, P., Goswami, S., Köbler, F., & Krcmar, H. (2012). Personalised eco-feedback as a design technique for motivating energy saving behaviour at home. In *Proc. NordiCHI*, 587-596.

[11] Pierce, J., & Paulos, E. (2012). Beyond energy monitors: interaction, energy, and emerging energy systems. In *Proc. CHI*, 665-674.

[12] Ricaurte, E., Verma, R., & Withiam, G. (2012). Hospitality sustainability report: slow, steady progress. *Cornell Hospitality Proceedings*.

Mobile-Based Tangible Interaction Techniques for Shared Displays

Ali Mazalek, Ahmed Sabbir Arif
Synaesthetic Media Lab
Ryerson University
Toronto, Ontario, Canada
{mazalek, asarif}@ryerson.ca

ABSTRACT
This tutorial explores the possibility of using touchscreen-based mobile devices as active tangibles on an interactive tabletop surface. The tutorial starts with an open discussion about various aspects of tangible interaction, including an overview of different approaches and design principles. It then guides participants through the design and development of innovative interaction techniques, where mobile phones are used as active tangibles on a shared tabletop display. The intent is to encourage the mobile HCI community to further explore the possibility of using everyday devices such as mobile phones as tangibles.

Author Keywords
Tangible interaction; mobile device; shared displays; interactive tabletops; rapid prototyping; user interface.

ACM Classification Keywords
H.5.2 User Interfaces: Input devices and strategies (e.g., mouse, touchscreen), interaction styles (e.g., commands, menus, forms, direct manipulation).

General Terms
Design; Experimentation.

INTRODUCTION
Multi-touch has become the dominant interaction technique on shared displays such as interactive tabletops [2]. Alternative techniques include interactive pens and wands [8], in-air gestures [1], and conventional pointing devices such as a mouse. A theoretically appealing but less explored approach is tangible interaction. Tangibles are physical objects that act as both control and representation for the underlying system, allowing users to create, access, and manipulate digital information [7]. Tangibles can offer a comparatively richer interaction experience by providing users with additional sensory information, such as pressure and friction. Active tangibles, which are powered objects that can be equipped with sensors and actuators/displays, can further extend the interaction and display space and provide off-screen content control and feedback.

MobileHCI '14, Sep 23-26 2014, Toronto, ON, Canada
ACM 978-1-4503-3004-6/14/09.
http://dx.doi.org/10.1145/2628363.2645668

Yet, researchers and designers are often discouraged to further explore this possibility, as they usually need to develop additional hardware as tangibles. This not only increases production cost but also requires users to learn a new technology. An obvious solution to this is to use consumer electronic devices as tangibles. Towards this, we explore the possibility of using touchscreen-based mobile devices as active tangibles. Touchscreen-based devices are rapidly becoming an integral part of our everyday life. A recent survey showed that about 68% mobile users in the U.S. own a smartphone and about 84% of the new buyers chose smartphones for their new handsets [5]. Utilizing these devices as tangibles could partly eliminate the need for developing new hardware as active tangibles. This could also reduce learning cost, as users are already familiar with basic interaction approaches used with these devices.

The purpose of this tutorial is to explore how touchscreen-based mobile devices could be used as tangibles to interact with/on a shared tabletop display in a useful manner, enabling cross-device interactions between display devices of different scales [10]. The goal is to familiarize participants with the concept of tabletop tangible interaction. We hope that this tutorial will encourage them to further explore this promising interaction paradigm.

Audience and Background
This tutorial is intended for mobile HCI enthusiasts who are interested in exploring mobile-based tangible interactions. Participants must have experience developing with Android SDK, HTML5, and JavaScript. In addition, a basic understanding of gesture recognition and touch-based interaction approaches is useful. Participants are expected to bring their own laptops for development.

STRUCTURE
The tutorial begins with an overview of the concept of tangible interaction based on recommended reading materials, provided by the organizers ahead of time. Open discussion addresses design possibilities and practices for mobile-based tangible interactions. Participants then divide into groups of four, and each group is provided with two Android mobile devices, a development toolkit containing a gesture recognizer [9], JavaScript libraries, and sample source code. They are also provided with several example scenarios, where the use of mobile devices as active tangibles may benefit users. We include three examples below.

Example 1: Viewing and Copying Images

Placing a mobile device on the interactive surface launches a marking menu [4] in close proximity to the device, with several available options. The user selects the "Display Images" option. The images from the device are displayed around the device, on the tabletop surface. The user can drag an image away from the device to a particular location of the surface to make a copy, or move the entire collection around the surface by moving the mobile device. Mobile device movements can be tracked using fiducial markers [3]. Multi-touch gestures can be used to manipulate the images on the surface, e.g. to zoom or rotate. Similar techniques can be used to view/copy other kinds of files such as documents.

Example 2: Common Music Playlist

Two users put their mobile devices on the table and select the "Show Music" option from the menu. A list of songs contained on each device is shown on the table, near the device. When the two devices are moved close together, the system displays only the common songs from the two devices' playlists. In this way, the users can enjoy listening to music they both like.

Example 3: Receiving Messages

When receiving a phone call, a user places his/her mobile phone on the table. This launches the caller's contact card, along with a marking menu with options such as "Accept", "Reject", "Hold", and "Speaker". The user selects an option to perform the corresponding task. While talking to the caller, the user may share a file with him/her. S/he does that by simply dragging the intended file from the surface to the caller's contact card.

The above scenarios are only examples and do not limit participants from designing new and innovative interaction approaches. They are encouraged to use the mobile devices' internal sensors, i.e. accelerometer, gyroscope, and compass, to design new approaches. Upon completion of the design and development activity, there is a short debriefing discussion of each group's work.

SUMMARY AND CONCLUSION

By the end of the tutorial, we expect participants to have a better understanding of the concept of tangible interaction and of how mobile devices can be used as active tangibles on shared tabletop displays. Through an open discussion, participants first learn how tangible interaction can complement and enhance mobile device interactions on tabletop displays. They are then guided through the implementation of example scenarios or their own new designs. This tutorial thus teaches them not only how to use mobile phones for tangible tabletop interaction, but also how to implement these designs quickly and efficiently using simple languages, such as HTML5 and JavaScript.

Our hope is that this tutorial will encourage the mobile HCI community to further explore the possibility of using everyday devices, such as mobile phones, as active tangibles for interacting with shared displays, and, more broadly, we hope it will encourage further exploration of interactions that cross display devices at different scales, from small mobile displays to larger shared surfaces.

ACKNOWLEDGMENTS

We would like to thank Ryerson University and the Canada Research Chairs program for supporting this tutorial.

REFERENCES

1. Arif, A. S., Stuerzlinger, W., Filho, E. J. de M., and Gordynski, A. Error behaviours in an unreliable in-air gesture recognizer. *Ext. Abstracts CHI 2014*, ACM (2014), 1603-1608.
2. Hinrichs, U. and Carpendale, S. Gestures in the wild: Studying multi-touch gesture sequences on interactive tabletop exhibits. *Proc. CHI 2011*. ACM (2011), 3023-3032.
3. Kaltenbrunner, M. reacTIVision and TUIO: A tangible tabletop toolkit. Proc. ITS 2009. ACM (2009), 9-16.
4. Kurtenbach, G. and Buxton, W. User learning and performance with marking menus. *Proc. CHI 1994*. ACM (1994), 258-264.
5. Multiplying Mobile: How Multicultural Consumers Are Leading Smartphone Adoption. Nielsen (2014). http://shar.es/MRg55
6. Steimle, J., Khalilbeigi, M., Mühlhäuser, M., and Hollan, J. D. Physical and digital media usage patterns on interactive tabletop surfaces. *Proc. ITS 2010*. ACM (2010), 167-176.
7. Ullmer, B. and Ishii, H. Emerging frameworks for tangible user interfaces. *IBM Systems Journal 39,* 3-4 (2000), 915–931.
8. Wigdor, D. and Wixon, D. *Brave NUI world: Designing natural user interfaces for touch and gesture*. Morgan Kaufmann, Burlington, MA, USA, 2011.
9. Wobbrock, J. O., Wilson, A. D., and Li, Y. Gestures without libraries, toolkits or training: A $1 recognizer for user interface prototypes. *Proc. UIST 2007*. ACM (2007), 159-168.
10. Wu, A., Mendenhall, S., Jog, J., Hoag, L.S., and Mazalek, A. A nested API structure to simplify cross-device communication. *Proc. TEI 2012*. ACM (2012), 225-232.

BIOGRAPHIES

Ali Mazalek is an Associate Professor and Canada Research Chair in Digital Media at Ryerson University, an Associate Professor at Georgia Tech, and director of the Synaesthetic Media Lab. Her research focuses on tangible and embodied interactions for creative practices in both arts and sciences. She holds a Ph.D. from the MIT Media Lab.

Ahmed Sabbir Arif is a Postdoctoral Research Fellow at Ryerson University, working under the supervision of Dr. Mazalek. His primary research interests are in the area of human-computer interaction. As a researcher he has worked on a wide-range of projects, both independently and in collaboration with academic and industrial research labs. He holds a Ph.D. in Computer Science from York University.

Wearable Computing: A Human-centered View of Key Concepts, Application Domains, and Quality Factors

Vivian Motti, Spencer Kohn, Kelly Caine
School of Computing
McAdams Hall – Clemson University
{vgenaro,skohn,caine}@clemson.edu

ABSTRACT
This tutorial presents a human-centered view of the state-of-the-art of wearable computing. Considering scientific and industrial aspects, it provides key definitions in the domain, goes through practical applications and use case scenarios, and concludes with quality factors and best design practices. An interactive component will aid participants to apply the theoretical concepts presented.

Author Keywords
Wearable devices; Wearability; Human Factors; Design.

ACM Classification Keywords
H.5.2. Information interfaces and presentation (User Interfaces): User-centered design.

INTRODUCTION
Wearable devices have evolved rapidly since the first sensors that were small enough to be carried on the body were produced. This evolution applies to hardware through the miniaturization of technologies, the improvement of batteries, as well as the creation of novel sensors. Wearable devices have been applied in many domains, from entertainment to medical and safety critical systems. Sensors can monitor the vital signs, augment human capabilities, replace sensory organs, or alert in emergencies.

Wearable computing is characterized by body-worn devices, such as clothing and accessories, which integrate computational capabilities to provide specific features to users. According to their applications, wearable devices have many form factors: armband [5], anklet [14], bracelet [2], contact lenses [10], necklace [3], glasses [7], gloves [11], jacket [6], ring [16], shoes [12], watches [1]. Wearable computing offers support and has already been applied to various scenarios: from safety critical domains, as aircraft control, healthcare, monitoring vital signs [5], for accessible communication [8], to leisure [6], gaming, and sports [12]. By employing different sensors, wearable devices support many human activities, providing a large potential for various applications when their integration is considered.

MobileHCI '14, Sep 23-26 2014, Toronto, ON, Canada
ACM 978-1-4503-3004-6/14/09.
http://dx.doi.org/10.1145/2628363.2645669

They provide solutions to users when they have situation-induced impairments and disabilities. Low-cost wearable devices can manage chronic health problems, prevent diseases, help in earlier diagnosis, and provide continuous monitoring, reducing medical expenses [4,15]. Although wearable devices have already proven successful in many scenarios, their problem space is wide and their design space is broad and largely unexplored [13]. Relevant information is scattered across sources, making it hard for interested parties to find unified support that guides them in making the right design decisions for wearable applications.

This tutorial offers an overview of the state-of-the-art in wearable computing from a human-centered perspective. It covers key concepts, applications, existing approaches, related principles, and quality factors.

BIOGRAPHIES
Vivian Motti is a postdoctoral research fellow at Clemson University, investigating human factors and privacy issues in wearable computing. She earned a BA in Biomedical Informatics, a MS in HCI at University of São Paulo (Brazil), and a PhD in Computer Science at Université catholique de Louvain (Belgium).

Spencer Kohn earned a BA in Psychology of Clemson University. He works as a research assistant in the HATlab (hatlab.org), investigating Human Factors and HCI.

Kelly Caine is an Assistant Professor in the Human-Centered Division of the School of Computing at Clemson University and Director of the Humans and Technology Lab (hatlab.org). She earned a BA at the University of South Carolina, and a MS and PhD in Engineering Psychology at Georgia Institute of Technology. She conducts research in usable privacy and security, health informatics and design for special populations.

TUTORIAL ORGANIZATION
In the tutorial, participants will learn about the state-of-the-art of wearable computing, including: form factors, devices, definitions, design principles, guidelines, quality factors and applications. Participants will interact with wearables. The tutorial includes: definitions, applications and qualities.

The main *definitions* in this field will be clarified, presenting wearability, devices available on the market (FitBit, Nike Fuel Band, Google Glass, Peeble) and academic research (Sixthsense [9]). Participants will have a comprehensive view of existing form factors (anklets, armbands, belts, shoes, rings), sensors (GPS, glucometer, altimeter), body placements (head-mounted, chest-mounted), and vital signs (heart rates, blood pressure). Wearables from industry will be presented, and analyzed. A range of *applications* will be discussed, illustrating different domains (medical scenarios, safety critical, sports, entertainment, leisure, gaming), and use case scenarios (early diagnoses, stress monitoring, diabetes treatment, smoke cessation, assistive technologies, communication, activity tracking, fitness). *Quality factors* will be described, presenting design constraints (attention level, cognitive load, modalities), novel perspectives (future trends and technologies, multimodal interaction paradigms), best practices (user centered design, iterative approaches), and design principles (comfort, aesthetics, responsiveness, privacy), potential trade-offs will also be discussed.

The tutorial integrates multidisciplinary perspectives from industry and academia, involving human, technological and medical aspects. Contents are based on literature search industry reports, infographics, and the academic experience of the authors. Two interactive sessions encourage attendees to apply the theoretical concepts presented:

Brainstorming (15'). After the theoretical concepts are presented, participants will reflect about their own experiences and preferences concerning wearables. Based on their personal opinion, they will list quality factors that can impact decisions in wearable applications and how the context information affects these factors. Comfort, for example, is a key aspect for wearable devices, however the perception of comfort differs depending on age, gender, and interests of users. The perception of qualities also varies for practitioners and users. By discussing these concepts, participants will identify not only the most relevant qualities to be incorporated during the design process, but also how the context of use can influence quality factors.

Focus Group (45'). This interactive session focuses on the implications of design decisions in specific wearable applications. In this session, first a scenario for a given application will be described (e.g., stress management, diabetes treatment, etc.); then relevant design decisions to tackle it will be defined (which biometric inputs to collect, from which body placement, how, and how often to collect them, which form factors and sensors to use). As a result, different groups of participants will report about their prototypes, decisions, and ideas (device, shape, input, output, modalities), clarifying and justifying their choices. To assess the solutions proposed, other groups of participants will be invited to analyze the decisions taken and discuss their advantages and disadvantages for different users' profiles (e.g., elderly users, children). The goal of this activity is to give participants the opportunity to engage in a more practical experience and reflect about the different challenges involved in the human-centered design of wearable applications.

ACKNOWLEDGEMENTS

This material is based upon work supported by the National Science Foundation under Grant No. 1314342.

REFERENCES

1. Atallah, L., Lo, B., King, R., & Yang, G.-Z. (2010). Sensor Placement for Activity Detection Using Wearable Accelerometers. 2010 Int. Conf. on Body Sensor Networks, 24–29. doi:10.1109/BSN.2010.23
2. Cheng et al. (2013). Towards zero-shot learning for human activity recognition using semantic attribute sequence model. In UbiComp '13, (2), 355. doi:10.1145/2493432.2493511
3. Gamboa, H., Silva, F., & Silva, H. (2010). Patient tracking system. Proc. of the 4th Int. ICST Conf. on Pervasive Computing Technologies for Healthcare, 9–10. doi:10.4108/ICST.PERVASIVEHEALTH2010.8916
4. Hoof, C. Van, & Penders, J. (2013). Addressing the healthcare cost dilemma by managing health instead of managing illness, 3–5.
5. Jalaliniya, S., & Pederson, T. (2012). A wearable kids' health monitoring system on smartphone. Proc. of NordiCHI '12, 791. doi:10.1145/2399016.2399150
6. Keng, J., Teh, S., & Cheok, A. D. (2008). Huggy Pajama : A Mobile Parent and Child Hugging Communication System, 250–257. IDC'08
7. Kim, M. Y., Yang, S., & Kim, D. (2012). Head-mounted binocular gaze detection for selective visual recognition systems. Sensors and Actuators A: Physical, 187, 29–36. doi:10.1016/j.sna.2012.08.016
8. Li , Y., et al. (2010). Automatic recognition of sign language subwords based on portable accelerometer and EMG sensors. In - ICMI-MLMI '10, 1 doi:10.1145/1891903.1891926
9. P. Mistry, P. Maes. SixthSense – A Wearable Gestural Interface. In SIGGRAPH 2009. Yokohama, Japan.
10. Pandey, J., et al. (2009). Toward an active contact lens: Integration of a wireless power harvesting IC. 2009 IEEE Biomedical Circuits and Systems Conference, 125–128. doi:10.1109/BIOCAS.2009.5372069
11. Perng, J. K., et al. (1999). Acceleration sensing glove (ASG). 3rd Int. Symposium on Wearable Computers
12. Spelmezan, D. (2012). An investigation into the use of tactile instructions in snowboarding. In MobileHCI '12, 417. doi:10.1145/2371574.2371639
13. Suhonen, K., et al. (2012). Haptically Augmented Remote Speech Communication: A Study of User Practices and Experiences, 361–369. NordiCHI'12.
14. Troshynski, E., Lee, C., & Dourish, P. (2008). Accountabilities of Presence: Reframing Location-Based Systems. CHI 2008 Proceedings, 487–496.
15. Zheng, J., et al. (2013). Emerging Wearable Medical Devices towards Personalized Healthcare. Proceedings of the 8th International Conference on Body Area Networks, 1. doi:10.4108/icst.bodynets.2013.253725.
16. Werner, J., & Hornecker, E. (2008). United-Pulse: Feeling Your Partner's Pulse. MobileHCI'08, 535–538.

Mobile Health:Beyond Consumer Apps

Jill Freyne
CSIRO, Digital Productivity and Services Flagship
GPO Box 76, Epping, 1710, NSW, Australia.
jill.freyne@csiro.au
+61 2 9372 4453

ABSTRACT

The explosion of apps for the medical and wellness sectors has been noted by many. Consumer apps, which provide innovative solutions for self management for a range of health problems have flooded the market, due to high consumer demand. More recently we have seen increased presence of truly medical applications for clinical professionals and patients of serious conditions. In the majority of cases consumer based mHealth apps allow people to do old things in new ways, such as recording health measures digitally rather than on paper. Medical apps, aimed at increasing the quality and efficiency of existing health care delivery models, provide clinical staff with convenient tools and easy to access resources and communication mechanisms. Finally, in rare and exciting cases we are seeing mHealth applications that are doing things in entirely new ways to drive real innovation in health care delivery through mobile devices. This tutorial will inform participants about the breadth of mHealth applications that are transforming the Health Services sector and put forward a strong case for HCI and efficacy research.

Author Keywords

health; wellbeing; wellness; mobile; human computer interaction; human factors.

ACM Classification Keywords

H.5.m. Information Interfaces and Presentation (e.g. HCI): Miscellaneous

General Terms

Human Factors; Design; Measurement.

INTRODUCTION

In excess of one million mobile applications are available to download, and over 110 billion download of applications were recorded in 2013. The iOS App store lists over 45,000 apps under the Medical (20,000) or Health and Fitness (25,000) categories, with Google Play quickly catching up with 33,000 health and medical apps listed. Many of the health based apps, are targeted to consumer needs in the area of health and fitness, but applications for patients with medical conditions and tools to support clinicians are emerging and becoming more popular. Many commentators have expressed concern at the lack of evidence base available in support of the use of mobile technology in Health [5, 2, 1, 6, 3]. This evidence base is needed not only to judge the quality of applications but to quantify the impact of use on productivity, patient or clinician satisfaction, safety, access to services and more. Without a strong evidence base commentators fear that widespread adoption will be challenging and slow. The HCI community, along with other research capabilities, has been challenged to assist in realising the true potential of mobile health technologies by contributing to an evidence base which will communicate the positives and highlight the negative impact of these technologies to ensure appropriate standards and safety measures are put in place [4].

As a response to this call, this tutorial will highlight the wide range of mHealth applications that go beyond trackers and behavior change tools. The tutorial will highlight real world, high impact mobile research that is relevant to the key discipline of Mobile HCI. An overview of medical and health focussed mobile applications will be provided to highlight the range of application purposes, the variety of beneficiaries and truly innovative technology available. Four key areas of mHealth applications will be discussed including *Apps for the HealthyWell*, *mHealth in Hospitals*, *Practice and Clinical Apps* and *Patient Apps* and will cover applications for health assessment, treatment and triage, behavior change, chronic illness, mental health, adolescent health, rehabilitation and age care. The tutorial will discuss the need for rigorous evaluation and efficacy analysis to generate a comprehensive evidence base, and provide examples of exemplary work in this space. Finally, the interactive component of the tutorial will focus on real articulated need for mobile apps in health services. Groups will be given case studies, from real clinicians and hospitals gathered at CSIRO and will be required to workshop design and pitch mobile solutions, and evaluation studies to validate their ideas.

The second component of the tutorial is the Interactivity session. Groups of participants will workshop new innovative mHealth applications. Case studies of medical and clinical requirements, gathered from real clinicians through projects at CSIRO, will be provided to participants and ideas for mobile technology to meet the challenges sought from participants. Groups will classify their proposed apps in terms of

MobileHCI 2014, September 23–26, 2014, Toronto, ON, Canada.
ACM 978-1-4503-3004-6/14/09.
http://dx.doi.org/10.1145/2628363.2645670

the perceived efficiency gain, doing old things in new ways or creating true innovative models. They will identify the challenges involved in large scale deployment and create an evaluation plan to evaluate the efficacy of their produce and present these to the group.

PRESENTER BIO

Jill Freyne is a Senior Research Scientist and Major Project Leader at the CSIRO, Australia's national science agency based in Sydney. Jill received her PhD from University College Dublin, where her research focused on collaborative, community based web search. Jill continued her research into human computer interaction, personalization and recommender technology as a Postdoctoral Fellow at the Clarity Center for Sensor Web technologies and at IBM Research in Cambridge, MA where she worked primarily on influence in social networking.

Since joining CSIRO Jill has worked primarily with the Preventative Health (now Food and Nutrition) and Digital Productivity and Services Flagships (http://www.csiro.au/Organisation-Structure/Flagships.aspx) where her research has focused on human computer Interaction, recommender systems and persuasive technologies to impact attitude and behaviour in health. Jill's role has primarily involved the design and evaluation of user facing online and mobile technologies. Jill has extensive experience in leading a range of projects that focus on digital health interventions and health services in the diet and lifestyle, age care and chronic disease domains. Jill has significant experience gleaned from several years leading a variety of projects with partners from the food industry, Australian Hospitals, State and Federal Health departments and Not for Profit organisations such as the Australian National Heart Foundation.

In the consumer app space, Jill has designed and evaluated several persuasive mobile applications that exploit behavioural theory in their design, and combine program information, reminders, self monitoring tools and scheduled tasks to engage users for an extended period of time to assist them in losing weight.

In the Health Services space Jill leads a user centric design project to design a ipad application for the *CSIRO Safer, Smarter Homes* project for independent living for the elderly. The work here was primarily in the assessment of user needs to inform functionality, modality and design of an application for self monitoring of health, tele-health and security within the home.

More recently Jill is leading projects which design and evaluated mobile technologies for use in hospital environments through a collaboration with a variety of Australian Hospitals in the area of predictive modelling for bed planning, and the assessments of patients from culturally and linguistically diverse backgrounds.

Jill is the author of over 60 publications published in top quality journals and conferences. Jill recently chaired the International Conference on Persuasive Technology and serves on the organising committees of international conferences such as IUI, Hypertext, Recommender Systems and SocialCom. Jill has given a wide variety of tutorials in recent years on Personalization in Health, Persuasive Technologies and Recommender Systems.

REFERENCES

1. Barton, A. J. The regulation of mobile health applications. *BMC medicine 10*, 1 (2012), 46.
2. Buijink, A. W. G., Visser, B. J., and Marshall, L. Medical apps for smartphones: lack of evidence undermines quality and safety. *Evidence Based Medicine* (2012), ebmed–2012.
3. Eng, D. S., and Lee, J. M. The promise and peril of mobile health applications for diabetes and endocrinology. *Pediatric diabetes 14*, 4 (2013), 231–238.
4. Kumar S, Nilsen W, P. M. S. M. Mobile health: revolutionizing healthcare through transdisciplinary research. *Computer 28-45* (2013).
5. Muessig, K. E., Pike, E. C., LeGrand, S., and Hightow-Weidman, L. B. Mobile phone applications for the care and prevention of hiv and other sexually transmitted diseases: a review. *Journal of medical Internet research 15*, 1 (2013).
6. Wolf, J. A., Moreau, J. F., Akilov, O., Patton, T., English, J. C., Ho, J., and Ferris, L. K. Diagnostic inaccuracy of smartphone applications for melanoma detection. *JAMA dermatology 149*, 4 (2013), 422–426.

Speech-based Interaction: Myths, Challenges, and Opportunities

Cosmin Munteanu
Institute for Communication, Culture, Information, and Technology
University of Toronto at Mississauga
cosmin@taglab.ca

Gerald Penn
Department of Computer Science
University of Toronto
gpenn@cs.toronto.edu

ABSTRACT

Human-Computer Interaction (HCI) research has for long been dedicated to better and more naturally facilitating information transfer between humans and machines. Unfortunately, humans' most natural form of communication, speech, is also one of the most difficult modalities to be understood by machines. This is largely due to speech being the highest-bandwidth communication channel we possess. As such, significant research efforts, from engineering, to linguistic, and to cognitive sciences, have been spent during the past several decades on improving machines' ability to understand speech. Yet, the MobileHCI community (and HCI in general) has been relatively timid in embracing this modality as a central focus of research. This can be attributed in part to the relatively discouraging levels of accuracy in understanding speech, in contrast with often-unfounded claims of success from industry, but also to the intrinsic difficulty of designing and especially evaluating speech and natural language interfaces.

The goal of this course is to inform the MobileHCI community of the current state of speech and natural language research, to dispel some of the myths surrounding speech-based interaction, as well as to provide an opportunity for researchers and practitioners to learn more about how speech recognition and speech synthesis work, what are their limitations, and how they could be used to enhance current interaction paradigms. Through this, we hope that MobileHCI researchers and practitioners will learn how to combine recent advances in speech processing with user-centred principles in designing more usable and useful speech-based interactive systems.

MobileHCI '14, Sep 23-26 2014, Toronto, ON, Canada
ACM 978-1-4503-3004-6/14/09.
http://dx.doi.org/10.1145/2628363.2645671

Author Keywords
Speech and Language Interaction; Automatic Speech Recognition; Natural Language Processing; Hands-free User Interfaces.

ACM Classification Keywords
H.5.2 [User interfaces]: Voice I/O, Natural language, User-centered design, and Evaluation/methodology.

OUTLINE

- How Automatic Speech Recognition (ASR) and Speech Synthesis (or Text-To-Speech – TTS) work and why these are such computationally-difficult problems
- Where are ASR and TTS used in current commercial interactive applications
- What are the usability issues surrounding speech-based interaction systems, particularly in mobile and pervasive computing
- What are the challenges in enabling speech as a modality for mobile interaction
- What is the current state-of-the-art in ASR and TTS
- What are the differences between ASR systems' accuracies and the needs of interactive applications
- What are the difficulties in evaluating the quality and usability of TTS systems
- What opportunities exist to enhance systems' interactivity by enabling speech

AUDIENCE AND FORMAT

This interactive tutorial will be beneficial to all MobileHCI researchers or practitioners without a strong expertise in ASR or TTS, who still believe in fulfilling HCI's goal of developing methods and systems that allow humans to naturally interact with the increasingly ubiquitous mobile technology, but are disappointed with the lack of success in using speech and natural language to achieve this goal.

The aim of the presentation is two-fold: present new

concepts to the audience, and foster discussions and exchange of ideas. Slides will be used to introduce the main points, while videos and audio clips will be played to illustrate various examples. After (and during) each of the main concepts of the tutorial outline is presented, time will be allocated for interaction between presenters and audience.

PROCEEDINGS

This three-hour tutorial includes opportunities for classroom participation, discussion of recent uses of ASR and TTS in commercial hands-free products, and two interactive activities.

The interactive activities will be carried out in groups of 4 to 6 participants. During these, participants will have to access various existing functions on their smartphones or tablets (such as speech-based search). Groups will be formed to ensure at least 1-2 mobile devices are present per group. The activities do not require any technical background, although familiarity with high-level HCI concepts (e.g. usability, interface design) is recommended.

Interactive activity 1

Designing the erorr-handling interaction of the smartphones' voice-based personal assistant. For this, participants will be guided to find examples of spoken utterances that are not handled properly by the search assistant (e.g. misunderstood voice input), and map these example to the components of the ASR system (language, acoustic, semantic). Once the root causes of these errors are identified, participants will engage in a short design activity, aimed at proposing design alternatives for handling such errors, in the form of redesigning the voice interaction (e.g. prompts) or as a complementary multimodal interface (speech + touch).

Interactive activity 2

Evaluating the quality of synthetic speech output. Synthesized speech (artificial voices) is an essential component in any mobile-based speech interface, yet the evaluation of such components is highly subjective. For this exercise, participants will first engage in a brief evaluation session, similar to that of the Blizzard challenges, in which several text-to-speech systems are ranked based on accuracy and naturalness. Following this, participants will be asked to identify shortcomings of the current evaluation methods, and then engage in a design exercise that will propose an alternate evaluation of synthetic speech output that better reflect the mobile user experience. No hardware will be required for this activity – the presenters' laptop will be used for the playback of the audio samples.

AUTHORS' BIOGRAPHIES

Cosmin Munteanu

http://cosmin.taglab.ca/

Cosmin is an Assistant Professor at the Institute for Communication, Culture, Information, and Technology (University of Toronto at Mississauga), and Associate Director of the Technologies for Ageing Gracefully lab. His area of expertise is at the intersection of Automatic Speech Recognition (ASR) and Human-Computer Interaction, having extensively studied the human factors of using imperfect speech recognition systems, and having designed and evaluated systems that consider humans as an important part of the ASR process. Cosmin's research interests include speech and natural language interaction for mobile devices, mixed reality systems, learning support, and technologies for older adults.

Gerald Penn

http://www.cs.toronto.edu/~gpenn/

Gerald is a Professor of Computer Science at the University of Toronto. His area of expertise is in the study of human languages, both from a mathematical and computational perspective. Gerald is one of the leading scholars in Computational Linguistics, with significant contributions to the formal study of natural languages. His publications cover many areas, from Theoretical Linguistics, to Mathematics, and to Automatic Speech Recognition, as well as Human-Computer Interaction.

People, Places & Things: A Mobile Locative Mapping Workshop

Martha Ladly, PhD
Professor
OCAD University
100 McCaul Street, Toronto, ON
M5T 1W1
mladly@faculty.ocadu.ca

Bryn A. Ludlow, MA
Graduate Research Assistant
Research & Graduate Studies
OCAD University
100 McCaul Street, Toronto, ON
M5T 1W1
bludlow@faculty.ocadu.ca

Guillermina Buzio, MFA
Graduate Research Assistant
Research & Graduate Studies
OCAD University
100 McCaul Street, Toronto, ON
M5T 1W1
guillebuzio@gmail.com

MobileHCI 2014, September 23–26, 2014, Toronto, ON, Canada.
ACM 978-1-4503-3004-6/14/09.
http://dx.doi.org/10.1145/2559206.2574795

Abstract
Personal digital technologies have become the tools of reproduction for personal narration and broad cultural critique. Mobile social media enables individuals to function as storytellers and public commentators, with practices that offer an explicit engagement between people, places, and things. Mobile technologies and mapping tools enable direct connection to place, involving local communities and public dissemination. Mobile narratives and their creators can also make a larger contribution to collective memories of place, speaking back to aspects of culture at large.

Author Keywords
Mobile design; mobile technology; mapping; GPS; social media; storytelling; narrative; location-based gaming; community; public space; public art.

ACM Classification Keywords
H.5.m. Information interfaces and presentation (e.g., HCI): Miscellaneous.

Workshop Topics

Ethnographical and field studies with mobile technologies; group interaction and mobile communities; mobile entertainment, storytelling, and location based gaming.

Workshop Overview

This practical hands-on workshop will instruct participants in current narrative practices with locative mobile media, using Google Earth mapping tools. Cultural production is about people (both contemporary and historical); places (existing situations, and their connections with the past); and things (artifacts and archives). In this workshop participants will learn how to explore people, places, and things through the creation of personal narratives, in small collaborative groups. They will then visit and locate their stories in public space at a nearby local park, connecting with their potential audiences through mobile storytelling and interactive GPS mapping on Google Earth.

Each participant will investigate a story that they want to explore in the workshop; case studies and projects involving best practices and outcomes with mobile storytelling will be reviewed; and the historical and cultural background of the local environment will create a framework for our investigations.

Workshop Introduction

This workshop focuses on narrating the moments when the disjunction between past and present is suspended through personal memories and the act of storytelling. The Italian philosopher Adriana Cavarero states: "Every human being, without even wanting to know it, is aware of being a *narratable self* — immersed in the spontaneous auto-narration of memory" [1]. The setting or context of this workshop is related to subjective narration, using digital tools to connect stories to place [2]. This notion is attentive to place, described by Cavarero as the "plural and interactive space of exhibition" which makes explicit a relational interaction and provides a place of exchange between the narrator and their community of recipients [2]. By inserting its texture, place provides a location, a context, and a local reception that brings plurality and communality into the narrative exchange.

Mobile storytelling practices allow individuals to experience stories and places differently and anew. Narrators may use these opportunities to access and re-narrate situations, and remediate surroundings. These range from serendipitous discovery of the past, to more strategic support for collective community building and social exchange. In this way, the personal narrative in mobile locative media builds relationship to the community or public narrative. Such practices allow for the collective process of sharing and co-constructing narratives in ways that annotate existing communities in new ways. Mobile media might also support the creation of new communities around playful forms of inhabiting shared physical and virtual space [Sheller (Drexel University, Philadelphia), personal communication, n.d.].

Workshop Times & Locations

This is a full day workshop, held at the Mobile Experience Lab at OCAD University, and Grange Park, Toronto, adjacent to OCAD University and the Art Gallery of Ontario (See Figure 1).

Figure 1: Historic Grange Park adjacent to the Art Gallery of Ontario and OCAD University. Photo credit: Dan Cronin (2010).

Workshop Framework

The experiments in this workshop are based on the BOPPPS learning model: bridge, objectives, pretest, participatory interaction, posttest, and summary [3].

First, we will familiarize workshop participants with readily available tools that are currently in use in a wide variety of cultural settings, prioritizing easily accessible tools such as the Google Cultural Institute and Art Project tools [4] and the Google Earth Outreach Open Data Kit [5]. We will explore these tools through a variety of case studies and informative best practice examples.

We will then apply this "toolkit" to the specific stories brought to the workshop by the participants. Working in small collaborative groups, participants will be guided to develop innovative ways to show and tell their narratives in public space. We will work in situ, creating narratives and documenting the park, returning to the lab to edit and implement documentation with Google Earth and other software tools. Participant's narratives will then be presented and discussed with the larger group (See Figure 2).

Workshop Learning Outcomes

Evocative examples, case studies, and innovative digital tools will inspire workshop attendees. They will gather insights and skills for telling stories and mapping narratives to public space; find out how to choose and use the appropriate tool/s to engage their audiences; identify culturally appropriate strategies to engage different types of audiences, e.g. children, teenagers, families, elders; and learn how to create strong links between people, social communities, and culturally significant places.

Figure 2: Locative narrative workshop participants in the field, Park Walk. Photo credit: Martha Ladly (2006).

Workshop Agenda

- Introduction to the workshop, workshop leaders, participants, and the workshop goals and activities. - Case studies, tools and best practices. Introduction to Google Earth, mapping tools and the Open Data Kit. - Participants form groups of 3-4; brainstorming session about narrative and storytelling.
- Field work: Mobile narratives created by groups via participant's smartphones and supplied cameras; workshop leaders available for tech support and questions.
- Lab work: Groups share experiences of their park experiences; edit; upload data to Google Earth; link data to maps, create interactive maps interactive for group presentations.
- Review data on Google Earth with participants; conclude workshop with a discussion about participant experiences, and gather participant feedback with a short survey.

Workshop Attendees

Students, researchers, mobile business and industry stakeholders will increase their fluency with mobile narrative concepts and GPS mapping tools. Workshop leaders will select participants based on the submission of a short (maximum 500 word) summary of their interest in the topics of the workshop. Authors must be registered for the conference. Summaries should be addressed to: bludlow@faculty.ocadu.ca

Workshop Website

http://research.ocadu.ca/mobilelab/project/people-places-and-things-a-mobile-locative-mapping-workshop

Required Software and Devices

Google Earth Outreach Open Data Kit (installed on Mobile Lab PCs); participant's mobile phones with GPS, photo and/or video recording capabilities; alternatively a digital camera with upload capabilities.

Acknowledgements

OCAD University and the Mobile Experience Lab, and the original research protocol designed by Martha Ladly and Bruce Hinds for the MDCN *Park Walk* Project.

References

[1] Cavarero, Adriana. *Relating narratives: Storytelling and selfhood*. London: Routledge, 2000.

[2] Cavarero, Adriana. *For more than one voice: Toward a philosophy of vocal expression*. Stanford University Press, 2005.

[3] BOPPPS Learning Model: http://hlwiki.slais.ubc.ca/index.php/BOPPPS_Model

[4] Google Cultural Institute and Art Project http://www.google.com/culturalinstitute/project/home

[5] Google Earth Outreach Open Data Kit http://www.google.com/intl/en/earth/outreach/tools/index.html

PID-MAD 2014: Second International Workshop on Prototyping to Support the Interaction Designing in Mobile Application Development

Shah Rukh Humayoun
Computer Graphics and HCI Group
University of Kaiserslautern
67663 Kaiserslautern, Germany
humayoun@cs.uni-kl.de

Achim Ebert
Computer Graphics and HCI Group
University of Kaiserslautern
67663 Kaiserslautern, Germany
ebert@cs.uni-kl.de

Steffen Hess
Fraunhofer IESE
Fraunhofer-Platz 1
67663 Kaiserslautern, Germany
steffen.hess@iese.fraunhofer.de

Yael Dubinsky
IBM Research – Haifa
Mount Carmel, Haifa
31905, Israel
dubinsky@il.ibm.com

MobileHCI '14, Sep 23-26 2014, Toronto, ON, Canada
ACM 978-1-4503-3004-6/14/09.
http://dx.doi.org/10.1145/2628363.2634256

Abstract
The current mobile paradigm is in many ways fundamentally different from the conventional desktop paradigm due to many factors such as multi-touch gesture interaction, usage of sensors, single-task focused model, etc. These factors mean several new challenges for the interaction designers with regard to communicating their ideas and thoughts during early design activities, which they might be unable to tackle properly using traditional prototyping techniques. Therefore, we envision that research must address the need for a change in existing prototyping techniques as well as focus on novel prototyping approaches and frameworks that would support not only the interaction design process but also the whole development process of mobile app development. In the footsteps of the first workshop, PID-MAD 2014 provides a platform to the interested communities for discussing issues and will bring together researchers and practitioners for sharing their knowledge and experience in order to tackle the upcoming challenges.

Author Keywords
Interaction Design; Prototyping; Mobile Application Development.

ACM Classification Keywords
D.2.2 [Design Tools and Techniques]: Evolutionary prototyping, H.5.2 [Information Interfaces and Presentation]: User Interfaces - Prototyping

Introduction and Motivation

Recently, we have witnessed a rapid increase in the utilization of mobile applications (commonly abbreviated as *mobile apps* or just *apps*) in people's lives for daily activities such as getting information (e.g., news, weather forecast, bus schedule), shopping, maintaining social contacts, entertainment, and much more. There is also increasing demand by users for business services to be available through these mobile apps to support them in performing their tasks more efficiently and comfortably. The growing popularity of mobile apps is due to many factors, such as availability of a great variety of smart devices (from smartphones to tablets), sensor-based functionality of smart devices [1], different mobile operating systems (e.g., Google Android, Apple iOS, Windows Phone 8, etc.), the addition of multi-touch gesture interaction, single-task focused model, and permanent mobile accessibility.

Influenced by these factors, mobile environments and apps are in many ways fundamentally different from the conventional desktop paradigm and applications. Consequently, the current mobile paradigm means several new challenges for the responsible parties (e.g., the interaction design team, the development team, the architects, etc.) in mobile app development with regard to designing usable mobile apps that will meet the users' requirements accurately and enable them to perform their tasks efficiently.

Building sketches, wireframes, mockups, and prototypes (all of these will be referred to as *prototyping techniques* in the following) is mostly part of the interaction design process. Interaction designers use these prototyping techniques as a way to communicate their ideas and thoughts to other stakeholders (e.g., developers, users, customers, etc.). As most of the existing prototyping approaches and techniques are based on the conventional desktop paradigm and are aimed at desktop applications, significant modifications are necessary to tackle the new challenges brought on by the current mobile paradigm. A major shift in adapting prototyping techniques to the current mobile paradigm has already started, for instance as a result of the availability of prototyping tools for mobile apps (e.g., Antetype[1], Axure[2], Fluid UI[3], POP[4], and iMocBuilder [2]), and was also demonstrated by the work presented at the first edition of this workshop [4] held at the MobileHCI 2013 conference. However, work still needs to be done in many different directions – such as how to build and utilize prototypes; novel approaches and techniques – to support the interaction design process of mobile application development properly.

Targeting the above concerns, we envision that research must address the need to change the conventional way of prototyping in order to make it appropriate for the current mobile paradigm. As one step in this direction, we held the first PID-MAD workshop (http://hciv.de/pidmad13) at MobileHCI 2013 [3, 4], on 27 August 2013 in Munich, Germany. The focus of the first workshop was on novel prototyping

1 Antetype Prototyping Innovation – http://www.antetype.com/

2 Axure RP – http://www.axure.com

3 https://www.fluidui.com/

4 http://popapp.in/

approaches and frameworks for supporting interaction design paradigms and processes in mobile application development in order to enable the interaction designers to communicate their ideas properly.

With PID-MAD 2014 (http://hciv.de/pidmad14/), we aim to once again provide a platform for the interested communities (i.e., interaction designers, usability engineers, HCI experts, mobile app developers, and others) to discuss issues and define novel methods and approaches for suitable mobile app prototyping, to integrate these methods and approaches into the interaction design process of mobile application development, and to make them usable in other development phases such as during implementation or user evaluation. We intend to make PID-MAD a regular event in order to provide a permanent platform for researchers and practitioners in related fields.

Workshop Topics

PID-MAD 2014 is dedicated to observations, concepts, approaches, frameworks, and practices that promote understanding, facilitating, and increasing the awareness of the role of prototyping, particularly during interaction designing phases as well as in other phases of mobile application development. Topics of interest include, but are not limited to:

- Novel techniques and frameworks for building sketches, mockups, wireframes, and prototypes suitable for the mobile environment
- Tools and environments that support building mockups/wireframes/prototypes for mobile apps
- Novel approaches for utilizing prototyping in other phases of mobile application development, e.g., in implementation or in testing
- Prototyping approaches that focus on leveraging sensor usage (e.g., using the accelerometer) in early design phases
- Prototyping of user context
- Evaluation strategies for mobile prototyping techniques
- Case studies and best practices

Workshop Goals

This workshop aims at achieving the following goals:

- Consolidating research and practices related to prototyping practices in the interaction design process from the context of the mobile environment
- Establishing a platform for bringing the interested communities (such as interaction designers, requirement engineers, developers, HCI experts, etc.) closer together to discuss how to make changes in the existing approaches and frameworks, as well as to examine novel methods for making prototyping useful not only within the interaction design process but also throughout the whole development process of mobile application development
- Growing the body of knowledge related to prototyping and interaction design for the mobile environment and identifying challenges and future avenues for research relevant to both academia and industry
- Providing a dedicated forum to the relevant communities for exchanging ideas and best practices and thus foster collaboration between industry and academia.

After The Workshop

We intend to publish the workshop results in the following ways: a) workshop introduction in the IJMHCI, b) a summary report including the results of the interactive sessions in an issue of ACM magazine, and c) a special book with the extended versions of accepted papers from PID-MAD 2013 and 2014.

Organizing Committee

Shah Rukh Humayoun is working as a postdoc research fellow in the Computer Graphics and HCI Group at the University of Kaiserslautern, Germany. His current interests lie in HCI, mobile application development, scalability issues regarding mobile user interfaces, interactive visualization and usability engineering, and human factors in software engineering. In the past, he successfully co-organized different workshops, e.g., "UsARE 2014" (at RE 2014), "PID-MAD 2013", "USARE 2012" (at ICSE '12).

Steffen Hess is leading the Usability and User Experience group at Fraunhofer IESE. His current research interests are in requirements, usability, and user experience engineering in different application domains, with special focus on interaction design, user experience prototyping, and customization of mobile business apps. He was the main organizer of the first Workshop on Integrating Mobile Devices into the Car Ecosystem and co-organizer of "PID-MAD 2013".

Achim Ebert is a professor at the University of Kaiserslautern, Germany and co-head of its Computer Graphics and HCI Group. His current research topics include information visualization, immersive scenarios, and HCI. He founded and is heading the IFIP working group 13.7 on Human-Computer Interaction and Visualization. He is also a member of the IFIP technical committee TC13 on Human-Computer Interaction (IFIP – International Federation for Information Processing).

Yael Dubinsky is affiliated with the Emerging Quality and Design Technologies Department at IBM Research - Haifa (HRL). For more than ten years, she has also been an instructor of project-based courses at Technion IIT. She has published her work at conferences and journals related to software engineering and information systems, and facilitated workshops and tutorials at leading conferences. Yael has significant experience in guiding agile implementation processes in industry and academia. Her book on Agile Software Engineering, which she co-authored with Orit Hazzan, was published by Springer in 2008.

Acknowledgment

This work has been partially supported by the German Ministry of Education and Research, grant number 01IS12053.

References

[1] Gartner. 2012. Market Insight: Ten Consumer Mobile Applications to Watch in 2012. A market research report published 2011.

[2] Humayoun, S. R., Hess, S., Kiefer, F., and Ebert, A. i2ME: A Framework for Building Interactive Mockups. *MobileHCI '13*, ACM, 6 pages, 2013.

[3] Humayoun, S. R., Hess, S., and Ebert, A. Workshop on prototyping to support the interaction designing in mobile application development (PID-MAD 2013). *MobileHCI '13*, ACM, 633-636, 2013.

[4] Humayoun, S. R., Hess, S., and Ebert, A. Report from the Workshop on Prototyping to Support the Interaction Designing in Mobile Application Development (PID-MAD 2013). SIGSOFT Software Engineering Notes 39, 1, 28-30, 2014.

Enhancing Self-Reflection with Wearable Sensors

Genovefa Kefalidou, Anya Skatova, Michael Brown, Vicky Shipp, James Pinchin
Horizon Digital Economy Research
University of Nottingham
Nottingham, NG7 2TU, UK
{Genovefa.Kefalidou, Anya.Skatova, Michael.Brown, Victoria.Shipp, James.Pinchin}@nottingham.ac.uk

Paul Kelly
Nuffield Department of Population Health
Rosemary Rue Building
Old Road Campus
University of Oxford
Headington, Oxford OX3 7LF, UK
paul.kelly@dph.ox.ac.uk

Alan Dix
HCI Centre
School of Computer Science
University of Birmingham
Birmingham
B15 2TT, UK
alan@hcibook.com

Xu Sun
Science and Engineering Building
199 Taikang East Road
University of Nottingham
Ningbo, China
xu.sun@nottingham.edu.cn

MobileHCI 2014, September 23–26, 2014, Toronto, ON, Canada.
ACM 978-1-4503-3004-6/14/09.
http://dx.doi.org/10.1145/2628363.2634257

Abstract
Advances in ubiquitous technologies have changed the way humans interact with the world around them. Technology has the power not only to inform and perform but also to further peoples' experiences of the world. It has enhanced the methodological approaches within the CHI research realm in terms of data gathering (e.g. via wearable sensors) and sharing (e.g. via self-reflection methods). While such methodologies have been mainly adopted in isolation, exploring the implications and the synergy of them has yet to be fully explored. This workshop brings together a multidisciplinary group of researchers to explore and experience the use of wearable sensors with self-reflection as a multi-method approach to conduct research and fully experience the world on-the-go.

Author Keywords
Methods; Self-reflection; Diaries; Sensors; Multi-disciplinary

ACM Classification Keywords
H.5.m. Information interfaces and presentation (e.g., HCI): Miscellaneous.

Introduction

Understanding human behaviour is vital for developing technology following a user-centred approach [10]. Exploring wearable sensors, data entry techniques and design for appropriation is not new within CHI workshop themes. Indeed, the nature of wearable computing and the available devices have been discussed in the CHI community in the context of how people interact with them and how data is captured [2, 9]. Designing for reflection on experience has also been explored and discussed within the CHI community [16]. However, the ubiquity of wearable sensors and self-reflection methods opens up new horizons for conducting research with potential impact across different disciplines and contexts. It is the synthesis, coordination and collaboration of these methods that now requires further exploration. This CHI workshop aims to build upon the existing knowledge and enhance the understanding of synthesizing self-reflection tools and sensors for creating, recording and responding to experiences 'in the wild'.

Mobile diary applications and self-reflection methods facilitate data collection in situ across different settings such as exploring and experiencing cultural sites [8], travelling [1], understanding serendipity [18], enhancing learning within classroom settings [12] or reflecting on everyday spending [15]. Such methodologies have provided a new level of individual self-awareness. For example, self-reflection methods can be highly insightful and beneficial for peoples' mental, psychological and social health [14].

Wearable sensors have been used in research to capturing data and experiences in in naturalistic settings [13]; for designing for smart cities [11]; for understanding attentional needs while on-the-go [17] and lifelogging [7]. Furthermore, sensors allow the collection of physiological data while on-the-go [19] and information about peoples' activity [4, 3]. It is acknowledged by many that sensing complex systems provides an opportunity for gaining insight as to how people and systems behave, interact and re-organise themselves in a dynamic environment. Indeed, self-report diary techniques and smart phones with sensors allow access to subjective reflections on behaviors of interest that otherwise would have been impossible to extract while on-the-go [6]. This workshop aims to explore the synergies between these methodologies, how we can synthesize them, how they influence each other, and the different environments in which they can be applied. We will address and reflect upon using these methodologies in conjunction to realize the dynamic and responsive nature of HCI.

Topics of Interest and Workshop Goals

The multidisciplinary background of the organisers includes HCI, engineering, psychology, design, social sciences, mathematics and human factors. We will invite contributions and opinions from individuals involved in a variety of different projects in which they have applied such methodologies. This workshop will revolve primarily around the following points:

- Discussion and experiences exchange from using wearable sensors and self-reflection methodologies across different settings and case studies (including pros and cons, challenges and benefits, validation and reliability issues, privacy and security issues)
- Exploring the way the synthesis of wearable technology and self-reflection enhances data

collection and user experiences in a wide variety of novel settings through scenarios development, role-playing and live field explorations.

- Identifying implications that synthesizing of technologies pose not only in the individuals but also for societies and technological advancement.

A particular focus of this workshop will be exploring refinements and extensions of these methodologies across different groups of people, themes and contexts. Validation and reliability issues will also be discussed.

Examples of Issues to be Addressed

Cross-Disciplinary Applications of Sensor and Self-Reflection Methodologies: The adoption of wearable sensor technologies and self-reflection means as data collection methods can have significant differences in perception and the behaviour that people exhibit. Furthermore, their use across different environments and settings and by people from different disciplines provides a rich mosaic of experiences of interacting with these technologies. Recent field experience by Alan Dix (Alan Walks Wales - http://alandix.com/alanwalkswales/) has been an example of how such methodologies could be adopted and 'embedded' as part of a deep experiential and personal history perspective. Living lab 'perceptions in the wild' are being transformed into a self-observatory and self-reflective journey using high-tech sensors technology and mobile phone infrastructure.

Capture, Feel, Reflect, Respond, Behave in the Wild: Exploring the opportunities and synergies of capturing *sensor data* while *self-reflecting* in the wild and vice versa, offers opportunities for understanding new norms and processes that occur within our natural and social environment. Issues regarding awareness, collaboration and performance are being raised as well as issues relating to the validity, reliability and ethics of these methodologies. Can capturing, feeling, reflecting, responding and behaving be part of one conceptual and methodological entity? They can certainly inform the way we think, experience and understand our surrounding environment as explored within projects at The University of Nottingham [15, 8, 18, 4]. The border between data collecting and 'living' the data is merging. The implications posed in synergising, designing and evaluating these methodologies will be identified and discussed with an aim to construct a framework of novel application and use.

Outcomes & Future Directions

The workshop will be used to explore and define the experiential utility of these methodological approaches when in synergy through 'hands-on' activities and role-playing. We will create a 'concept cloud' reflecting themes and issues as identified in the research field, while scenarios and role-playing will reveal tensions, advantages and potentials. 'Hands-on' experience with current technologies will offer further insight as to how people interact with these technologies when in conjunction. Based on these we will discuss and identify implications of adopting and using these methodologies together, their impact on the individuals' and on the socio-cognitive perceptions and behaviors. We will share our insights, activities and discussions via online documents hosted in a workshop-dedicated webpage, hoping to create an active community where interested parties can share insights, knowledge and best practice. This workshop builds on a prior event hosted at the University of Nottingham in June 2013. The further exploration of the interplay and the potential synergies that these methodologies provide needs to be discussed and experienced through cross-fertilisation, new collaborations and cross-insight.

References

[1] Alan Walks Wales, http://alandix.com/alanwalkswales/.

[2] Bass, L., Mann, S., Siewiorek, D. & Thompson, C., Issues in Wearable Computing: A CHI 97 Workshop, *ACM SIGCHI Bulletin*, 29, 4. (1997). 34-39.

[3] Beaudin, J., Intille, S. & Tapia, P. M., Lessons Learned Using Ubiquitous Sensors for Data Collection in Real Homes. *Ext. Abstracts CHI '04 EA*. (2006) ACM Press. 1359-1362.

[4] Brown, M., Coughlan, T., Lawson, G., Goulden, M., Mortier, R. & Houghton, R., Exploring Interpretations of Data from the Internet of Things in the Home, *Interacting with Computers, 25, 3. (2013)*. Elsevier. 204-217.

[5] Doherty, A., Kelly, P. & Foster, C., Wearable Cameras: Identifying Healthy Transportation Choices, *IEEE Pervasive Computing*, (2013). 12:44-47.

[6] Eagle, N. & Pentland, A., Reality mining: sensing complex social systems, *J. Personal and Ubiquitous Computing, 10*, (2006). 255-268.

[7] Gouveia, R. & Karapanos, E., Footprint Tracker: Supporting Diary Studies with lifelogging. In CHI '13, (2013) ACM Press. 2921-2930.

[8] Kefalidou, G., Georgiadis, M., Coles, B. A. & Anand, S., Crowdsourcing our Cultural Heritage, In C. Mills, M. Pidd & E. Ward (Eds.), *Proceedings of the Digital Humanities Congress 2012. Studies in the Digital Humanities*. Sheffield: HRI Online Publications, 2014. Available online at: <http://www.hrionline.ac.uk/openbook/chapter/dhc2012-kefalidou>

[9] Li, I., Froehlich, J., Larsen J. E., Grevet, C., Ramirez, E., Personal Informatics in the Wild: Hacking Habits for Health & Happiness. *Ext. Abstracts CHI* '13, (2013) ACM Press. 3179-3182.

[10] Maguire, M., Methods to support human-centred design, *International Journal of Human-Computer Studies*, 55, 4, (2001). 587-634.

[11] Matassa, A., Rapp, A. & Simeoni, R., Designing for smart cities: connecting and binding citizens to urban spaces through a new wearable interactive system *In Proc. Ubicomp* (2013), Springer-Verlag. 757-760.

[12] Orford, D. & Kefalidou, G. Electronic Lecturing and Teaching Aid Using Collaborative Smart Phones *In Proc.* IEEE Co-sponsored SAI (2013) IEEE, 744-750.

[13] Palen, L. & Salzman M., Voice-mail diary studies for naturalistic data capture under mobile conditions, In Proc. CSCW '02. (2002) ACM Press. 87-95.

[14] Sedikides, C., & Strube, M. J., Self-evaluation: To thine own self be good, to thine own self be sure, to thine own self be true, and to thine own self be better, In M. P. Zanna (Ed.), *Advances in Experimental Social Psychology, 29,* (1997), New York: Academic Press. 209-269.

[15] Skatova, A., Papaeconomou, P., Houghton, R. & Smillie, L. D., Do Personality Traits predict Everyday Mood and Behaviours?: A Diary Study of Daily Mood and Spending, In Proc. ISSID '13 (2013). 30.

[16] Sas, C. & Dix, A. (2009) Designing for Reflection on Experience. *Ext. Abstracts CHI* '09. (2009) ACM Press. 4741–4744.

[17] Sohn, T., Li, K., Griswold,W. & Hollan, J., A Diary Study of Mobile Information Needs, In Proc. CHI '08. (2008). ACM Press. 433-442.

[18] Sun, X., Sharples, S. & Makri, S., A User-Centred Mobile Diary Study Approach to Understanding Serendipity in Information Research. *Information Research, 16:3, (2011). paper 492.*

[19] Velloso, E., Bulling, A. & Gellersen, H. AutoBap: Automatic Coding of Body Action and Posture Units. *In Proc. ACII '13*, (2013) IEEE. 135-140.

Socio-Technical Practices and Work-Home Boundaries

Anna L Cox
UCL Interaction Centre
University College London
London, WC1E 6BT
anna.cox@ucl.ac.uk

Jon Bird
City University London
Department of Computer Science
Northampton Square
London EC1V 0HB, UK
jon.bird@city.ac.uk

Natasha Mauthner
Business School
University of Aberdeen
Aberdeen, UK
n.mauthner@abdn.ac.uk

Susan Dray
Dray & Associates, Inc.
Minneapolis, MN 55408 USA
susan.dray@dray.com

Anicia Peters
Iowa State University / Polytechnic of Namibia
Virtual Reality Applications Center
Ames, Iowa, 50014
anpeters@iastate.edu

Emily Collins
UCL Interaction Centre
University College London
London, WC1E 6BT
e.collins@ucl.ac.uk

MobileHCI 2014, September 23–26, 2014, Toronto, ON, Canada.
ACM 978-1-4503-3004-6/14/09.
http://dx.doi.org/10.1145/2628363.2634259

Abstract
Recent advances in mobile technology have had many positive effects on the ways in which people can combine work and home life. For example, having remote access enables people to work from home, or work flexible hours that fit around caring responsibilities. They also support communication with colleagues and family members, and enable digital hobbies. However, the resulting 'always-online' culture can undermine work-home boundaries and cause stress to those who feel under pressure to respond immediately to digital notifications. This workshop will explore how a socio-technical perspective, which views boundaries as being constituted by everyday socio-technical practices, can inform the design of technologies that help maintain boundaries between work and home life.

Author Keywords
Work home boundary management; HCI; work; leisure; personal informatics; wellbeing.

ACM Classification Keywords
H.5.m. Information interfaces and presentation (e.g., HCI): Miscellaneous.

Introduction

Advances in mobile and CSCW technologies have facilitated flexible working practices that give many people more choice about where and when they work. However, although these technologies can help people manage their family and work responsibilities they can also bring these different aspects of their lives into conflict. For example, devices such as laptops are often used for both business and pleasure, which can result in the 'extensification' [6] of work into non-work times and spaces [1, 2]. This blurring of the boundaries between work and personal contexts [3, 5, 14] can have negative consequences, such as stress, absenteeism, burnout and high employee turnover (4; 7,; 11; 13). Here we outline four relationships between technology and work-home boundary management (our workshop themes), that are perhaps familiar territories for HCI researchers, which illustrate the conflicting roles that technology can play:

1. Mobile technologies support flexible working

Perhaps for the first time, technology is enabling people to better balance work with non-work responsibilities. The internet is creating opportunities for people to communicate and set up work contracts, often without even meeting face to face e.g MTurk. Technologies such as Skype enable meetings to occur at times convenient to those in different time zones and without the need for travel.

2. Mobile technologies support leisure pursuits

Even for those who enjoy their work, recovery is a necessary factor in avoiding work-related strain and in feeling prepared for the next day of work [17]. In order for recovery to be successful, an individual must experience psychological detachment from work, relaxation, mastery experiences and a sense of control [16]. Research suggests active pastimes involving some mental engagement are more effective in distracting from work stresses than passive ones. Online hobbies such as taking part in citizen science projects (e.g. FoldIt) and playing digital games offer an opportunity to provide such a distraction and thereby to aid recovery from work stress.

3. Mobile technologies and work-home conflicts

Ubiquitous technologies have the potential to give rise to more demanding, faster paced work and personal lives [1]. Whilst some argue that the use of technology at work is directly causing a more demanding workplace with greater workloads and increased feelings of time pressure, [15] suggest that these negative consequences "arise from habits that develop though co-evolutionary interactions between technologies, specific design affordances of devices and software, and wider work/life and socioeconomic contexts." However our digital habits develop, they lead to work seeping into non-work times and spaces which can result in work-home conflicts [8, 12].

4. Mobile technologies facilitate reflection on work and non-work habits

Personal informatics tools provide us with the opportunity to record and reflect on data from many aspects of our lives. Location trackers enable reflection on time spent at work, on the commute, and with friends and family. They can also tell us how many emails we've sent and received (ClearContext) and how much time we've spent gaming or on social network sites (RescueTime). People often have an inaccurate perception of their habits, for example, how long they spend doing various activities and how their behaviour compares to that of other people. The resulting inaccurate comparisons can lead to increased stress levels that can impact health and well-being. Reflecting on data about how time is spent enables people to consider whether the way in which they are currently living their lives is in accordance with their own values.

A Socio-technical Perspective

Understanding the positive and negative impacts of mobile technology on work-home boundaries is important to a range of stakeholders, including families, employers, worker organizations and policymakers. HCI would appear to be in a unique position to address this research area, given its interdisciplinary focus on the relationship between people and technologies. Public and academic debates tend to address the narrow issues of 'work-life balance' and how technologies act as a barrier or facilitator to its achievement, as outlined above. However, a socio-technical perspective [9, 10] encourages a broader reflection on how boundaries, and bounded entities (e.g. work, family, technology, parent, child, worker), come to be constituted through everyday socio-technical practices. Adopting a wider perspective, this workshop will focus on how these practices are configured, and how they could be productively reconfigured to maintain boundaries between work and home.

Summary of workshop goals

Our workshop will not only involve HCI practitioners (ranging from interaction scientists to CSCW specialists) but also sociologists who adopt a broader and often critical perspective on the role of work and technology in people's lives. From a socio-technical perspective, boundaries and norms are empirically investigated in order to explore how technology, work and family are made in everyday practices. Technology is understood less in terms of how it threatens or enhances work and home life but rather in terms of how it helps *make* 'work' and 'home' in specific ways. The nature, meaning and effects of technology are understood as being achieved through the specific uses and purposes to which it is put.

The main goal of the workshop is to consider how this perspective could inform new ways of thinking about technology design by highlighting the ways in which technologies are bound with particular values and practices. In particular we will consider the potential of different technology designs to: change the nature and meaning of work and family; generate new ways of doing work and family life; constitute new norms and values around work and family; and privilege some 'goods' over others thereby benefitting some constituencies while disadvantaging others.

Importantly, a goal of the workshop is to generate 'actionable' knowledge that will not only provide HCI researchers with insights into work-life boundaries but enable them to implement design solutions. Therefore, the workshop will also critically consider each of the four specific relationships between technology and work-home boundary management outlined above, and consider how the socio-technical perspective can inform technology design.

Summary

Maintaining work-home boundaries is important for health and well-being. Understanding how technology can undermine or maintain these boundaries is an important research issue for a wide range of stakeholders. The workshop will consider how a socio-technical perspective, which emphasizes that socio-technical practices create boundaries, can inform the design of technologies that help maintain boundaries between work and home life.

References

[1] Chesley, N. (2010) Technology use and employee assessments of work effectiveness, workload, and pace of life. *Information, Communication & Society*, Vol 13 (4), pp485-514.

[2] Currie J. and Eveline J. (2011) E-technology and work-life balance for academics with children. *Higher Education*, Vol 62, pp533–550.

[3] Duxbury, L. and Smart, R. (2011), 'The "Myth of Separate Worlds": An Exploration of How Mobile Technology has Redefined Work-Life Balance', in S. Kaiser et al (eds) *Creating Balance?* Springer, pp269-284.

[4] Edwards, J. R., and Rothbard, N. P. (2000) Mechanisms Linking Work and Family: Clarifying the Relationship Between Work and Family Constructs. *Academy of Management Review*, 25, pp178–199.

[5] Gant, D. & Kiesler, S. (2001), Blurring the Boundaries: Cell Phones, Mobility, and the Line between Work and Personal Life, in B. Brown and N. Green, *Wireless World*, Springer, pp121-31.

[6] Jarvis J. and Pratt A. C. (2006) Bringing it all back home: The extensification and 'overflowing' of work. *Geoforum*, 37, pp331–339.

[7] Kreiner, G. E., Hollensbe, E. C., and Sheep, M. L. (2006) On the Edge of Identity: Boundary Dynamics at the Interface of Individual and Organizational Identities. *Human Relations*, 59, pp1315–1341.

[8] Mark, G., Gudith, D. and Klocke, U., (2008), The cost of interrupted work: more speed and stress, In *Proc. CHI 2008*, ACM, pp107-110

[9] Nansen, B., Arnold, M., Gibbs, M., Davis, H. (2010) Time, space and technology in the working-home: an unsettled nexus. *New Technology, Work and Employment* 25:2, pp136-153.

[10] Orlikowski, W. J. (2010) The Sociomateriality of Organisational Life: Considering Technology in Management Research. *Cambridge Journal of Economics*, 34, pp125–141.

[11] Parasuraman, S., & Greenhaus, J. H. (2002) Toward Reducing Some Critical Gaps in Work-Family Research. *Human Resource Management Review*, 12, pp299–312.

[12] Perlow, L.A. (1999), The time famine: Towards a Sociology of Work Time. *Administration Science Quarterly*, Vol 44 (1), pp57–81.

[13] Rice, R. W., Frone, M. R., & McFarlin, D. B. (1992) Work-Nonwork Conflict and the Perceived Quality of Life. *Journal of Organizational Behavior*, 13, pp155–168.

[14] Sadler, K., Robertson, T., Kan, M. and Hagen, P. (2006), Balancing Work, Life and Other Concerns: A Study of Mobile Technology Use by Australian Freelancers, In *Proc. of 4th Nordic Conference on Human-Computer Interaction*, ACM, pp413-416.

[15] Shabajee, P. & Preist, P. (2013) Digitally Assisted Life-(Im)Balance? Proceedings of 1st Workshop on Habits in HCI, HCI2013.

[16] Sonnentag, S. & Fritz, C. (2006). Endocrinological processes associated with job stress: Catecholamine and cortisol responses to acute and chronic stressors. In P. L. Perrewé, & D. C. Ganster (Eds.), Research in Occupational Stress and Well Being: Employee health, coping, and methodologies, pp. 1-60.

[17] Sonnentag, S. & Zijlstra, F. R. J. (2006). Job characteristics and off-job activities as predictors of need for recovery, well-being, and fatigue. Journal of Applied Psychology, 91, 330-350.

Re-imagining Commonly Used Mobile Interfaces for Older Adults

Emma Nicol, Mark Dunlop, Andreas Komninos, Marilyn McGee-Lennon,
The Mobiquitous Lab
Univ. Strathclyde, Glasgow, UK
strathclyde@olderadults.mobi

Lynne Baillie
Interactive & Trustworthy Technologies Group
Glasgow Caledonian University, UK
L.Baillie@gcu.ac.uk

Alistair Edwards
York HCI
University of York, York, UK
alistair.edwards@york.ac.uk

Parisa Eslambolchilar
Computer Science Department
Swansea University, Swansea, UK
p.eslambolchilar@swansea.ac.uk

Joy Goodman-Deane
Engineering Design Centre,
Univ. Cambridge, Cambridge, UK
jag76@cam.ac.uk

Lilit Hakobyan, Jo Lumsden
Computer Science
Aston University, Birmingham, UK
hakobyl1@aston.ac.uk

Ingrid Mulder
Industrial Design
Delft University of Technology, NL
I.J.Mulder@tudelft.nl

Patrick Rau
Human Factors & Ergonomics,
Tsinghua University, Beijing, PRC
rpl@mail.tsinghua.edu.cn

Katie Siek
Informatics and Computing
Indiana University, USA
ksiek@indiana.edu

MobileHCI 2014, September 23–26, 2014, Toronto, ON, Canada.
ACM 978-1-4503-3004-6/14/09.
http://dx.doi.org/10.1145/2628363.2634261

Abstract
Many countries have an increasingly ageing population. In recent years, mobile technologies have had a massive impact on social and working lives. As the size of the older user population rises, many people will want to continue professional, social and lifestyle usage of mobiles into 70s and beyond. Mobile technologies can lead to increased community involvement and personal independence. While mobile technologies can provide many opportunities, the ageing process can interfere with their use. This workshop brings together researchers who are re-imagining common mobile interfaces so that they are more suited to use by older adults.

Author Keywords
Older adults, mobile interface design, inclusive design

ACM Classification Keywords
H.5.2 User Interfaces.

Background and motivation
The world population is ageing, with the percentage of older people rising, e.g. adults over 65 are expected to form 39% of the UK population and 71% of the Japanese population by 2050. Mobile technologies are increasingly important in supporting independent living and social contact. In addition, many healthcare solutions are moving away from purpose-built

equipment to exploiting mainstream mobiles and tablets for supporting older adults growing older independently. Together these trends open up a wealth of opportunities and challenges to design mobile solutions that are usable by older adults.

The natural ageing processes can make smartphone interaction particularly challenging for older adults. Key recommendations by Fisk et al [6] for designing for this age group are at a complete contrast with typical smartphone touchscreen interactions where:

- Soft buttons require almost zero force to activate and have zero travel;
- Soft keyboards typically have no gap between keys (with visible gaps often being interpreted to keys);
- Surfaces that are high gloss, low friction, glass;
- and Interfaces often have reduced contrast for styling, exacerbated by sunlight and reflections.

This workshop brings together researchers from many disciplines to build a MobileHCI centered community on overcoming issues in mobile interfaces for older adults.

The HCI Design Process with older adults

Design for ageing involves understanding the diverse and unique capabilities and limitations of older adults: identifying their needs, preferences and desires for technology in their lives and involving them in the design process [13]. However, this group brings challenges to design teams, and researchers need to be sensitive to the characteristics, sensory and cognitive capabilities, and the attitudes of older people towards computers and their being included in research studies [5].

In the early work on cultural probes, Gaver et al [7] used probes with older adults to better understand their habits and interests. They found that the technique also provoked the participants to think about the roles they play and the pleasures they experience, and that probes can help to establish a rich conversation between designers and users. Recently, Vines et al [17] called for a more nuanced understanding of how control is shared between researchers and participants, for the initiators and beneficiaries to be more explicitly revealed and for there to be a more reflexive understanding of how participation takes place.

Physical mobile interaction and older adults

While older adults are, overall, still slower than younger adults when interacting with mobile interfaces, studies (e.g. [4]) have shown that, touchscreens reduce this performance gap when compared to traditional keys and mice. However, the size of on-screen buttons has a clear influence on interaction speed and accuracy (e.g. [10][14]) and dwell times are significantly longer for users with motor-control difficulties [14]. Studies on the effects of tremor in older user text entry showed that omitted letters were the most common error [11]. Encouragingly though, touch models, filters and simple re-designs, e.g. moving touch targets from the edges, can reduce error rates considerably [12].

On the display side, studies have found that age can have a significant impact on navigation and learnability [1], that older users often have difficulty in assessing the function of buttons, can have difficulty understanding mobile scroll bars [9], and that font choice can be a particular issue for this group [2].

Opportunities for novel mobile interaction

Designing interfaces that exploit the wealth of sensors and technologies in modern smartphones and personalizing interaction to different user groups gives great opportunities for better interaction. We have seen that, due to different backgrounds and experiences, older adults can actually be more open to new interaction approaches than young adults, who have more intense use of current mainstream mobile interaction. Even where there is resistance to novel interaction, studies of technology acceptance using mobiles found that tutorial training can significantly affect acceptance outcomes for older users [20].

One major opportunity is to look at how multisensory or multimodal interaction can be best harnessed for this group as a whole and to widen the range of users and range of use-locations. In homecare reminder systems, multimodal notifications have been successfully tested using visual, oral and olfactory modalities [18]. Stößel found that gestural interaction can have benefits over conventional key input for older adults [15].

Design changes that provide environmental support for declining cognitive, perceptual and psychomotor abilities can serve as a powerful intervention for maintaining and improving older adult performance [3]. Goodman et al [8] showed that a mobile navigation aid significantly outperformed a paper-based map and that older people derived substantially more benefit than younger users. In a study of the use of tablets to create and share photographs it was demonstrated that even the oldest adult group embraced opportunities to express themselves creatively through digital content production when designed for their needs [19].

Mobile health informatics (m-health) is a growing field in itself. In a study of requirements for reminder systems for tele-care [18], results suggested that developers should design for diversity, context, priorities, autonomy, shared spaces, and optimal care. The use of gaming in rehabilitation is another area of particular growth and challenges that could have considerable impact on the health and wellbeing of older adults (e.g. [16]).

Going forward

Using mobiles into older life is an increasing need in society in order to support active, socially connected independent living. Current mobile interfaces can pose considerable challenges for older adults but there is a wealth of opportunity to be had from multidisciplinary research focused around older adults. This workshop aims to bring together researchers from a wide range of disciplines to discuss and enhance activities to push this domain forward within the wider MobileHCI community.

Acknowledgements

The workshop is partly supported by the UK EPSRC Council through project reference EP/K024647/1 on designing mobile text entry for older adults.

References

[1] Balakrishnan, V. and Yeow, P.H. Texting satisfaction: Does age and gender make a difference. *Int. J. Comp. Sci. and Security 1*, 1 (2007), 85–96.

[2] Bernard, M., Liao, C.H., and Mills, M. The Effects of Font Type and Size on the Legibility and Reading Time of Online Text by Older Adults. *CHI '01 Extended Abstracts*, ACM (2001), 175–176.

[3] Charness, N. Aging and human performance. *Human Factors: The Journal of the Human Factors and Ergonomics Society 50*, 3 (2008), 548–555.

[4] Chung, M.K., Kim, D., Na, S., and Lee, D. Usability evaluation of numeric entry tasks on keypad type and age. *Int. J. Industrial Ergonomics 40*, 1 (2010), 97–105.

[5] Dickinson, A., Arnott, J., and Prior, S. Methods for human–computer interaction research with older people. *Behaviour & Information Technology 26*, 4 (2007), 343–352.

[6] Fisk, A.D., Rogers, W.A., Charness, N., Czaja, S.J., and Sharit, J. *Designing for older adults: Principles and creative human factors approaches*. CRC press, 2012.

[7] Gaver, B., Dunne, T., and Pacenti, E. Design: Cultural Probes. *interactions 6*, 1 (1999), 21–29.

[8] Goodman, J., Gray, P., Khammampad, K., and Brewster, S. Using Landmarks to Support Older People in Navigation. *Proc. MobileHCI 2004*, Springer Berlin Heidelberg (2004), 38–48.

[9] Gould, J. and Schaefer, M. User Interface Considerations for Older Users. *Proceedings of the 10th Annual SIGCSE Conference on Innovation and Technology in Computer Science Education*, ACM (2005), 408–408.

[10] Jin, Z.X., Plocher, T., and Kiff, L. Touch Screen User Interfaces for Older Adults: Button Size and Spacing. *Proceedings of the 4th International Conference on Universal Access in Human Computer Interaction: Coping with Diversity*, Springer-Verlag (2007), 933–941.

[11] Matero, J. and Colley, A. Identifying Unintentional Touches on Handheld Touch Screen Devices. *Proceedings of the Designing Interactive Systems Conference*, ACM (2012), 506–509.

[12] Nicolau, H. and Jorge, J. Elderly Text-entry Performance on Touchscreens. *Proceedings of the 14th International ACM SIGACCESS Conference on Computers and Accessibility*, ACM (2012), 127–134.

[13] Rogers, W.A. and Fisk, A.D. Toward a psychological science of advanced technology design for older adults. *The Journals of Gerontology Series B: Psychological Sciences and Social Sciences 65*, 6 (2010), 645–653.

[14] Sesto, M.E., Irwin, C.B., Chen, K.B., Chourasia, A.O., and Wiegmann, D.A. Effect of touch screen button size and spacing on touch characteristics of users with and without disabilities. *Human Factors: The Journal of the Human Factors and Ergonomics Society 54*, 3 (2012), 425–436.

[15] Stößel, C., Wandke, H., and Blessing, L. Gestural Interfaces for Elderly Users: Help or Hindrance? *Proc. 8th International Conference on Gesture in Embodied Communication and Human-Computer Interaction*, Springer-Verlag (2010), 269–280.

[16] Uzor, S., Baillie, L., and Skelton, D. Senior Designers: Empowering Seniors to Design Enjoyable Falls Rehabilitation Tools. *Proc. SIGCHI Conference*, ACM (2012), 1179–1188.

[17] Vines, J., Clarke, R., Wright, P., McCarthy, J., and Olivier, P. Configuring Participation: On How We Involve People in Design. *Proc. SIGCHI Conf. Human Factors in Computing Systems*, ACM (2013), 429–438.

[18] Warnock, D., McGee-Lennon, M., and Brewster, S. Multiple Notification Modalities and Older Users. *Proc. SIGCHI Conference*, ACM (2013), 1091–1094.

[19] Waycott, J., Vetere, F., Pedell, S., et al. Older Adults As Digital Content Producers. *Proc. SIGCHI Conference*, ACM (2013), 39–48.

[20] Wilkowska, W. and Ziefle, M. Which Factors Form Older Adults' Acceptance of Mobile Information and Communication Technologies? *Proc. 5th Symposium of the Workgroup Human-Computer Interaction and Usability Engineering of the Austrian Computer Society on HCI and Usability for e-Inclusion*, Springer-Verlag (2009), 81–101.

Workshop on Designing the Future of Mobile Healthcare Support

Sara Diamond
President and Vice-Chancellor
OCAD University, Canada
sdiamond@ocadu.ca

Derek Reilly
Faculty of Computer Science
Dalhousie University, Canada
reilly@cs.dal.ca

Bhuvaneswari Arunachalan
Visual Analytics Lab
OCAD University, Canada
barunachalan@ocadu.ca

Anne Stevens
Visual Analytics Lab
OCAD University, Canada
annestevenz@gmail.com

MobileHCI 2014, September 23–26, 2014, Toronto, ON, Canada.
ACM 978-1-4503-3004-6/14/09.
http://dx.doi.org/10.1145/2628363.2634263

Abstract
This workshop aims to discuss and develop ideas on how healthcare services, mobile technologies, and visual analytics techniques can be leveraged and contribute to new ways of mobile healthcare supportive system designs. Designing contemporary mobile support systems for healthcare support requires a clear understanding of information requirements, behaviors and basic needs of users. Design must take into account the challenges of human-device interactions in the healthcare environment; the extension of the care environment beyond the institutional setting and the engagement of patients, facility residents and families in an extended circle of care; and issues of formal and informal data sharing and privacy. This workshop invites researchers and designers working in relevant fields to discuss, compare, and demonstrate effective design approaches that can be adopted to improve the designs of mobile support systems for interactive visualization in healthcare.

Author Keywords
Mobile technologies, healthcare support, human-device interaction, interactive visualizations

ACM Classification Keywords
H.5.2 [User interfaces]: Prototyping, User-centered design

Introduction
Mobile communication, interaction, and visualization tools can provide pervasive healthcare services that operate on heterogeneous platforms and allow for effective support of patients within and outside of the institutional healthcare setting. Mobile care systems must address the specificity of workflow in care facilities or in ambulatory care; the needs of caregivers to document and share patient status, to analyze documentation relative to long term health goals and treatments, and to share information with other caregivers, including non-professionals and to engage with patients.

Evolving multimodal technologies on mobile devices such as touch, motion, speech, and sound, facilitates effective interactions depending upon application content and its context [1] [2]. As increasing number of users are accessing high-speed data services available on mobile devices for gathering information, interactive information visualizations has become increasingly possible. Designing mobile support systems for interactive visualizations requires a clear understanding of information requirements, behaviors and basic needs of users.

Design must take into account the challenges of human-device interactions in the pervasive environment of healthcare; the extension of the care environment beyond the institutional setting and the engagement of patients, facility residents and families in an extended circle of care; and issues of formal and informal data sharing and privacy. The daily needs of patients exist within the context of long term health goals and immediate needs and issues, which can be tailored for individual residents' needs, at times tied to a lead professional but are often administered or identified by multiple caregivers. Collaboration and clear communication between caregivers and professionals is essential for the delivery of effective care. Analysis and constant sharing of patient status over time is needed in order to evaluate a status change and define treatments.

Mobile care systems must address the specificity of workflow in care facilities or in ambulatory care; the needs of caregivers to document and share patient status, to analyze documentation relative to long term health goals and treatments, and to share information with other caregivers, including non-professionals and to engage with patients. We present a horizon scan of work in this growing field that points to five requirements (i) the support of data capture in multiple formats, (ii) the use of visual analytics tools to analyze records, (iii) the integration of collaborative tools that facilitate information sharing, the organization of care and the engagement of a wider circle of care, including the patient, (iv) user interaction through multi-modal inputs, and (v) design strategies that effectively integrate these elements.

Design Method
Existing design approaches adopted by HCI and mobile computing research community engage with designs in several ways [3] bringing new artefacts to life and enhancing user interaction with technologies. A common design approach that mobile system designers often choose is to port existing applications available for larger platforms and adjust the necessary details. However, such approach generally leads to unwieldy and impractical applications. The reason for designers to follow such strategies is the absence of specific methodologies for mobile, handheld and ubiquitous devices [4]. Customized user-centered design methodologies [5] [6] might be applied to this specific

design process; but, the unique features and constraints that ubiquity and pervasiveness, require new or deeply refined approaches. In this workshop, we explore different solutions for the challenges in three design stages that are sensitive and present [7]:

- *Data gathering:* Data gathering and analysis of requirements from a user centered perspective are essential in a system design process. Conducting ethnographic sessions and interviews bring designers the possibility to understand the work flow on various activities and detect problems that might be solved by a technological system. However, on pervasive and mobile systems, these methodologies provide insufficient details and guidelines on how to achieve required results and on how to apply existing techniques. For this purpose, current design methodologies include methods such as ethnography, task analysis, inquiries amongst others. Yet, using a mobile device and applications for various tasks and settings introduces new details that are hardly detectable with the simple use of such methods.
- *Prototyping:* Low-fidelity prototypes fail to show the peculiarities of mobile devices and their usage scenarios. Using paper sheets and a set of detachable cards to activate a user interface is an acceptable way to test a future desktop application. However, it is likely that such technique fails to provide a clear perspective on usage problems for a mobile device used on a multitude of locations. Furthermore, the technique per se seems difficult to apply on such conditions.
- *Usability Evaluation:* Usability evaluation out of the lab, especially on early design stages, which proved to be essential are not well-defined. The used methodology provided no insight on how to conduct any type of multiple context or setting evaluation. Following a user while he/she tests a prototype on every imagined scenario might be impossible to achieve. This practice might cause ethical, privacy, and social problems. Thus, no observation and detection of usability errors could be made. The design methodology provides no guidance on such procedures and solutions are yet to be identified.

We hope that this workshop will be a place for those designing mobile systems to find a suitable solution for the above specified challenges, share best practices and learn from each other's approaches.

The Workshop

Our participatory design activities include concept ideation, collaborative prototyping, card sorting, and scenario and concept testing — all aimed at fostering the evolution of relevant concepts and the development of prototypes. The workshop will have four main components:

- *Horizon scan*: This introductory section will contextualize designing healthcare support systems for mobile platforms in terms of developments in mobile technologies and data visualization and trends in demographics and the culture of healthcare. It will include a horizon scan of real world applications in the health care field.
- *The Pecha Kucha presentations*: Consisting of 20 slides shown for 20 seconds each (totalling six minutes forty seconds), each participant will present their own work and position on the workshop topic – Pecha Kucha style.
- *Participatory design challenges:* Working in groups, participants will apply hands-on research methods to design problems related to mobile applications in healthcare. Methods could include

persona and scenario development, body storming, paper-prototyping and ideation methods such as card sorting, game generators and design fiction.

- *Reflection and wrap-up:* Participants will be invited to reflect on the workshop methods and outcomes in relation to the work originally presented in the earlier Horizon Scan and Pecha Kucha parts of the workshop. We will also hold a discussion about possible next steps, including the potential of an edited volume focusing on design strategies for mobile healthcare.

Discussion

This workshop aims to discuss and develop ideas on how healthcare services, mobile technologies, and visual analytics techniques can be leveraged and contribute to new ways of mobile healthcare supportive system designs. We want to bring together researchers from a wide array of disciplines who have experience with studies of technology in healthcare contexts, clinical communication trials, and designing mobile technologies. Issues we want to discuss include, but are not limited to:

- Conceptual approaches for designing mobile healthcare support systems such as iterative design processes vs throwaway methodology
- User centric design including suitable methods for involving users in the design process and retaining user interest through design cycle
- Multimodal user interfaces for mobile devices
- Visualization techniques for mobile systems
- Methods of analysis and visualization of aggregated data, which provides information on design requirements on data collection and data handling (including privacy of user data)
- Interaction design models
- Natural user interface designs for mobile systems
- Methods of categorizing a system's users (such as experts, patients) for whom feature designs might be targeted
- Importance of differences of user expectations between different platforms used to inform design.
- Ways to track changes in use under different design conditions

During this workshop, we hope to move discussion of mobile supportive system methodology beyond use as a tool to collect large amounts of data. We look to established techniques and emerging practices for the ways in which mobile HCI and visual analytics research can be used to inform future healthcare system design.

References

[1] Sven Kratz, Fabian Hemmert, and Michael Rohs, Natural User Interfaces in Mobile Phone Interaction, CHI 2011

[2] B Shneiderman, C Plaisant, Designing the User Interface: Strategies for Effective Human-Computer Interaction, 4th Edition (2005)

[3] Eberts, R. E, User interface design, Book, Englewood Cliffs, NJ: Prentice Hall, 1994.

[4] Raptis, D., N. Tselios, and N. Avouris. Context-based Design of Mobile Applications for Museums: A Survey of Existing Practices. MobileHCI'05. 2005. Salzburg, Austria, ACM

[5] Beyer, H., Holtzblatt, K., 1998. Contextual Design: Customer Centered Approach to Systems Design, Academic Press, San Francisco, CA, USA.

[6] Mayhew, D.J. (1999). The Usability Engineering Lifecycle. Morgan Kaufmann, USA.

[7] Sá, M., Carriço, L., Low-Fi Prototyping for Mobile Devices. In Proceedings of CHI'06 (extended abstracts), Montréal, Canada, pp. 694-699, ACM

NARRATIVES: Geolocative Cinema Application

Solomon Nagler
Researcher, Author
NSCAD University
1649 Brunswick St.
Halifax, NS B3J 2G3 CAN
snagler@nscad.ca

Andrew Hicks
Researcher, Author
NSCAD University
1649 Brunswick St.
Halifax, NS B3J 2G3 CAN
ahicks@nscad.ca

Michael Hackett
Lead Programmer
1649 Brunswick St.
Halifax, NS B3J 2G3 CAN
michael.hackett@dal.ca

Katja Zachkarko
Graphic Designer
1649 Brunswick St.
Halifax, NS B3J 2G3 CAN
k.zachkarko@nscad.ca

Abstract
A tool for filmmakers and spectators, *Narratives* looks at how interactive technology can transform cinematic experience, augmenting the interactivity of traditional cinematic form with locative media practices that expand storytelling into traversable spaces.

MobileHCI 2014, September 23–26, 2014, Toronto, ON, Canada.
ACM 978-1-4503-3004-6/14/09.
http://dx.doi.org/10.1145/2628363.2645695

Author Keywords
Interactive Cinema; Geolocative Media; Mobile Narratives; Database Narrative

ACM Classification Keywords
Algorithms; Design; Experiementation; Human Facotrs; Measurements; Theory

Theoretical Foundation
This project explores how storytelling can be augmented through an integration of emergent mobile technologies, specifically hand-held devices. As an interactive cinema application, *Narratives* encourages filmmakers and spectators to re-evaluate the relationship between stationary cinematic reception and a mobile engagement with story; between cinematic production and the reproduction of space; between filmmaker and spectator.

Through the application, both filmmaker and spectator are ambiguously positioned; neither are fully in control over the images, their delivery, or reception. Filmmakers are asked to rethink and experiment with the foundations of cinematic authorship: genre, reception, and the possibilities of blending time-based media with the randomness of everyday life. More explicitly, they are required to relinquish their control over montage as the flow of their work comes to be

Figure 1. Login Menu

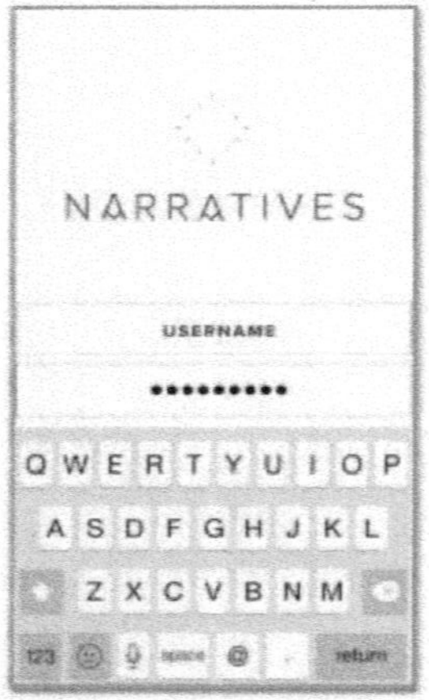

Figure 2. Gallery Menu for story selections.

dependent upon the movement of a spectator, freed from the confines of the theatre.

In turn, spectators are required to abandon themselves to the contingencies of movement through traversable space—those unpredictable occurrences that alter direction and redirect flow, these are the plot-points of *Narratives*, shaping and directing its cinematic outcome. The role of the spectator, then, (like that of the filmmaker) is at once active and passive. They assume some responsibility for the data they collect, but in contrast to how a growing number of people move (engaged in a near constant digital documentation), they are not in control of generating images; instead, as they drift and wander, they compile the fragments (offered by the filmmaker) which will form the narrative of their encounter within any given environment.

When the mobile application is in use , GPS data is collected; direction over time. After activating GPS tracking, the hand-held device is put away. The drift goes uninterrupted, freeing the participant of the growing social requirement to capture and share lived-experience as it occurs. Over the course of a few hours, or potentially days, a sort of peripatetic montage is assembled as mobile participants passively access an archive of cinematic moments, either fragmented or whole, depending upon their route and their willingness to explore. When the user concludes their journey, collected GPS data from the mobile device is interpreted by the application.

This interpreted data is translated into a list of commands. The server takes these commands and delivers video clips from a database to the mobile phone application. Drawing on a digital archive of cinematic fragments, a film specific to the user's unique directional data is compiled and displayed on the application's media player.

Narratives offers unique opportunities for filmmakers to reconfigure the production and distribution of their stories. Cinematic form is changed; elliptical stories are edited into fragments, replacing linear plot-lines with threads of narrative that are reconfigured beyond the restriction of a si ngular duration. This interactive narrative application offers a new form of montage, one which replaces dialectical progression and teleological duration with a database of still and moving images that can be assembled into an infinite set of narrative sequences.

Theory to Computer Science and Design

The Database

To date, while in a current state of development, filmmakers can upload multiple .mpeg format video files through a client web based interface and a solution stacked MAMP on a MacPro that is connected to a wireless router. This setup allows filmmakers to prototype their narrative content on an internal network, avoiding an external server system setup.

The Apache server is able to handle requests and network the information, whereas a RESTful state server is architected to interact with the database and add new records to the database using the Jason programing language. The *Narratives* application will send requests to the RESTful state server preparing an assemblage of video clips.

After internal testing, the current *Narratives* database and server setup will be moved to a public database, allowing public access and distribution.

The Mobile Application

Written in Objective-C using Xcode, the *Narratives* mobile application is designed for general spectators. Integration of the application into one's lifestyle, as well as how users can connect their uncovered narrative experiences with the user interface, have been two critical areas of focus when developing the prototype. These technologies include harnessing the mobile device's compass, accelerometer and GPS vector data. The compass and accelerometer data are primarily connected to user interface aspects, whereas GPS vector data sequences the order of video clips from an intranet MAMP RESTful state server.

When activating the *Narratives* application, the software uses a combination of the phone's GPS, cellular, and WiFi hardware to capture the user's position over time. It then transforms this data into movement vectors along the four or eight compass directions to which narrative content has been assigned. Each time the user accumulates some minimum distance of travel in a particular direction, the next segment of narrative along that axis is appended to a list of unviewed segments, which the user can later watch in the order that the segments were added.

Narratives is an application that aims to reimagine the way that users develop content for and interface with interactive art. Rather than requiring persistent clicks and navigations through embedded content[1], the aim is to create a gap between the gathering of narrative fragments and the assessment of assembled visual material. Discovered incrementally, the films generated by *Narratives* are available to participants after their journey, thereby rejecting the immediacy and simultaneity often associated with mobile phone applications such as Instagram and Twitter. The resulting film, streamed on the application's media-movie player within the application, permits participants to appreciate a the story with the same focus and attention of more traditional cinema spaces.

Figure 3: GUI representing the beginning, middle and end of a users journey through a chosen narrative.

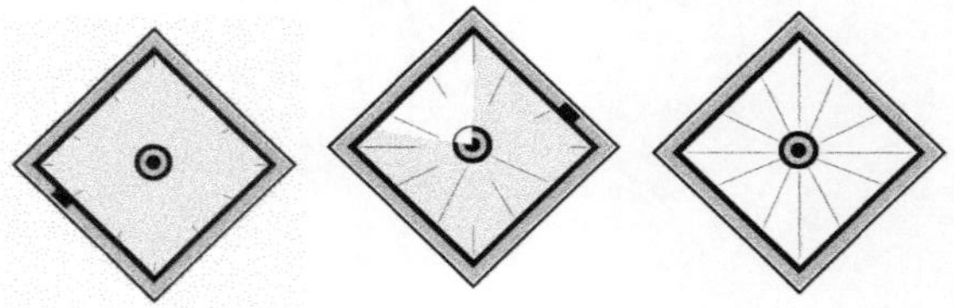

Figure 4. After video clips are accumulated, the user can view the sequence of ordered video clips.

Acknowledgements

Social Sciences and Humanities Research Council, GRAND - NCE: A&D NODE, NSCAD University.

[1] An example of this is GPS Film: Locative Based Mobile Cinema; http://www.dshessels.com/artworks/gpsfilm/about.html

The Switchboard: A Virtual Proprioceptive Training and Rehabilitation Device

Edgar Rodriguez
Programme Director –
Industrial Design
Victoria University
139 Vivian Street
Wellington 6011, NZ
Edgar.Rodriguez-Ramirez@vuw.ac.nz

Sarah Hadfield
Product Design
Swibo Limited
Victoria University
139 Vivian Street
Wellington 6011, NZ
hadfield.s.a@gmail.com

Kah Chan
Lecturer –
Media Design
Victoria University
139 Vivian Street
Wellington 6011, NZ
Kah.Chan@vuw.ac.nz

MobileHCI 2014, September 23–26, 2014, Toronto, ON, Canada.
ACM 978-1-4503-3004-6/14/09.
http://dx.doi.org/10.1145/2628363.2645696

Abstract
Swibo Limited is currently engaging in the product development of the Switchboard in order to increase motivation of patients requiring proprioceptive awareness and balance training. This paper summarises the findings made since project inception in November 2013.

Author Keywords
Virtual rehabilitation; tele-rehabilitation; exergaming

ACM Classification Keywords
I.6.8 [Simulation and Modeling]: Types of Simulation --- Gaming

General Terms
Design, Human Factors, Performance

Introduction
Switchboard is an exciting system that incorporates a newly designed balance board wirelessly connected to videogames that intelligently assist people in their rehabilitation and pre-habilitation exercises. Numerous studies have illustrated that balance boards are effective in both muscle pre-habilitation and rehabilitation [5][8], leading to their extensive use by health professionals around the world. After interviewing a number of health professionals and physical trainers, we identified the main faults of the traditional balance boards were a lack of users' motivation, poor compliance with programmes and no consistent measurement of progress. Traditional balance boards consist most commonly of a round, flat plane that is secured to a hemispherical base, on which

Figure 2: Child demonstrating engagement with Switchboard model.

Figure 1: Switchboard prototypes with secure cellphone pocket.

an individual can complete training exercises. Generally the exercise movements are prescribed by a physiotherapist and aim to increase mainly proprioceptive awareness in the ankle, knee and core regions. However, the main problem is that they lack a motivational element for regular use.

Market Validation

Videogames that require exercising to play them, or exergames, can be applied to motivate patients of different ages, including children, to complete physiotherapy exercises. A lack of motivation has been identified as a major barrier in the treatment of children with medical conditions - even during one-on-one sessions with a therapist [1]. There is evidence that computer-based games can assist in keeping users and patients motivated to complete their exercises [6]. This can be used to motivate and record performance and therapy progress. The instant feedback loops provided by a sensor-enabled rehabilitation tool empowers patients with more autonomy over their therapy: providing a challenge (a digital game) that functions as a motivator [3] to perform what are more mundane exercises. The game can also be tailored to the specific abilities of a patient, progressing in difficulty to match the patient's progress [2][7].

Product Description

To address the issues above, Swibo has created the *Switchboard*. The system takes inspiration from a traditional balance board model, recruiting mobile technology and exergames to increase the capabilities of the traditionally more basic (and inadequate) rehabilitation model. Using interactions through a smart phone tangible results of the patient's movements are represented on screen through a character avatar. Obstacles are created through a series of games that guide the player through a variety of exercises, simulating those given to the user by their health professional. With the smart phone secured to the board, the motion of tilting in a given direction or movement will prompt the avatar to dodge, jump, turn and rotate through the desired course.

After citing the need for a balance board programme, the physiotherapist can determine what data they want to collect. This can help to identify a number of issues relating to weaknesses in body stance and weight distribution, or simply collecting data on performance improvement. The data can be useful to both physiotherapists and the patient, as they can determine what they can change and improve upon. The patient acquires the board, downloads the *Switchboard* smart phone application, and places their smart phone within the board. The player can then choose their favourite game and begin playing. The accelerometer and gyroscope on the mobile device collects data on the movement of the board, which is then presented to the player in their preferred format.

In order to gauge levels of improvement, the patient initially completes series of basic balancing tests. This will help to identify any existing weaknesses and give an overall view of the patient's competence on the board. As the patient continues to use the board, data will be continuously updated to reflect change in strength, speed and accuracy. This progress can be represented through trend data. Having the ability to remotely and tangibly measure the patient's progress has the potential to be an immensely valuable resource for health professionals as the market for tele-rehabilitation, the practice of rehabilitating a patient that cannot meet with their physician, increases.

The visual feedback provided by the *Switchboard* improves the basic product in a number of ways. Firstly, it increases the patient's motivation to train. Being able to see tangible and measurable evidence of improvement helps to reassure the patient that they are making progress in the pre-habilitation and/or rehabilitation process. It also encourages the user to improve independently, as well as beat other patients' high scores. The app has an online leaderboard system, where you can connect with other players to both challenge and the view their progress. As the patient's actions are pre-determined, the programme tells the patient what activities to complete and how frequently per game, without relying on the user to remember and

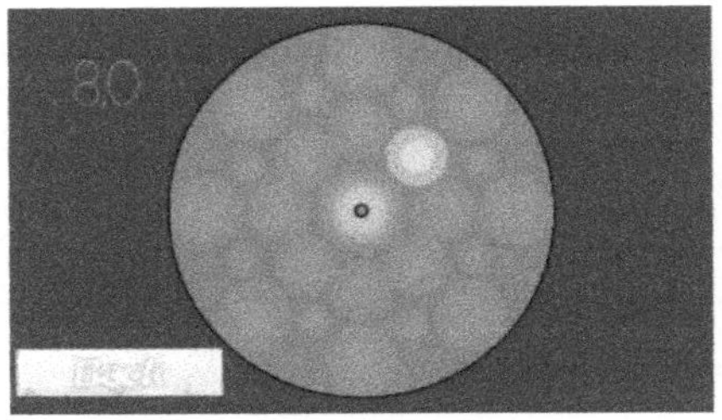

Figure 3: Initial testing game interface.

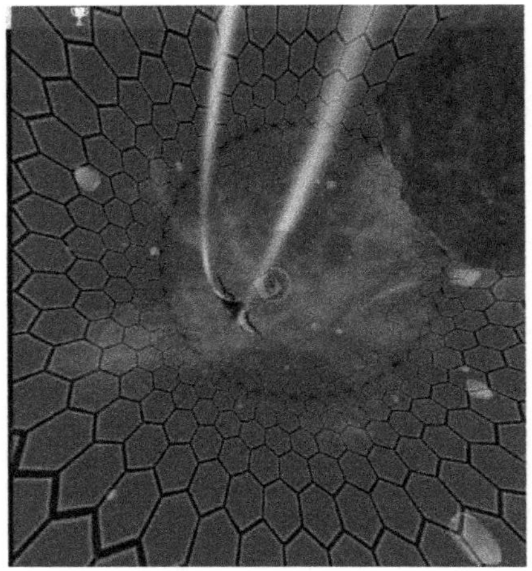

Figure 4: "Choob Racer" a virtual rehabilitative game developed for Swibo.

complete all exercises independently. The virtual rehabilitation component of the product is essential and has been proven to improve the motivation and adhesion level to treatment in similar studies [4].

Another advantage of *Switchboard* is that it gives physiotherapists the opportunity to remotely monitor their patients. Results from a patient's workout can be sent directly to their physiotherapists via an online service. Physiotherapists found one of the major reasons for slow rates of rehabilitation was the inability to comply with exercises. With the *Switchboard*, patients will be made aware of the remote monitoring and increased engagement with their physiotherapists, meaning they are more likely to comply with exercises given. The inclusion of smart phones into the system is integral to *Switchboard*'s success. By utilising the capabilities of the current generation of smart phones, we are able to record and store raw data and send it remotely to be analysed. The use of their personal smart phone introduces more of a connection between the user and their rehabilitation.

Acknowledgements

We thank all associated parties of the Futures Programme, namely Victoria University Schools of Design and Schools of Engineering and Computer Science, and Creative HQ for their ongoing support. Thank you to both the Wellington and Palmerston North based personal trainers, sports managers and physiotherapists without whom we could not have completed our research and development stage. Our greatest thanks go to VicLink, Wellington - without their support, this project would not be possible.

References

[1] Bartlett, D.J. and R.J. Palisano, *Physical therapists' perceptions of factors influencing the acquisition of motor abilities of children with cerebral palsy: Implications for clinical reasoning.* Physical Therapy, 2002. **82**(3): p. 237-284.

[2] Burke, J.K., et al., *Optimising engagement for stroke rehabilitation using serious games.* The Visual Computer, 2009. **25**(12): p. 1085-1099.

[3] Fogg, B.J., *Persuasive Technology: Using computers to change what we think and do.* 2003, San Francisco: Morgan Kaufmann Publishers.

Conclusion

As people's lives get increasingly busy, it is hard to find the time to exercise. Physiotherapists we consulted have expressed their frustration at their patients not complying with their exercises, slowing down their recovery. *Switchboard* is a product that can amplify most of the advantages that balance boards can produce. It does so by offering an extra motivation through intelligently responsive exergames. People no longer need to follow their routine exercises through arduous (and often boring) lists of tasks. They now only need to play their favourite exergame and benefit from the improved leg strength, and improved balance and proprioception that playing with *Switchboard* brings.

[4] Gil-Gomez, Jose-Antonio., et al., *Effectiveness of a Wii balance board-based system (eBaVir) for balance rehabilitation: a pilot randomized clinical trial in patients with acquired brain injury.* Journal of NeuroEngineering and Rehabilitation, 2011. **8**(30).

[5] Kiani, A. , et al., *Prevention of Soccer-Related Knee Injuries in Teenaged Girls.* Archives of Internal Medicine, 2010. **170**(1): p. 43-49.

[6] Levac, D., P. Miller, and C. Missiuna, *Usual and virtual reality video game-based physiotherapy for children and youth with acquired brain injuries.* Physical and Occupational Therapy in Pediatrics, 2012. **32**(2):p. 180-195.

[7] Sampayo-Vargas, S., et al., *The effectiveness of adaptive difficulty adjustments on students' motivation and learning in an educational computer game.* Computers & Education, 2013. **69**(452-462).

[8] Wedderkopp, N., et al., *Prevention of injuries in young female players in European team handball. A prospective intervention study.* Scandinavian Journal of Medicine & Science in Sports, 1999. **9**(1): 41-47.

Time Tremors: Developing Transmedia Gaming for Children

Conor Holler
Xenophile Media Inc.
250 Augusta Ave.
Toronto, ON M5T 2L7 Canada
conor@xenophilemedia.com

Patrick Crowe
Xenophile Media Inc.
250 Augusta Ave.
Toronto, ON M5T 2L7 Canada
patrick@xenophilemedia.com

Alex Mayhew
Xenophile Media Inc.
250 Augusta Ave.
Toronto, ON M5T 2L7 Canada
alex@xenophilemedia.com

Adam Tindale
OCAD University
100 McCaul Street
Toronto, ON M5T 1W1 Canada
atindale@faculty.ocadu.ca

Sara Diamond
OCAD University
100 McCaul Street
Toronto, ON M5T 1W1 Canada
sdiamond@ocadu.ca

MobileHCI '14, September 23-26, 2014, Toronto, ON, Canada
ACM 978-1-4503-3004-6/14/09.
http://dx.doi.org/10.1145/2628363.2645698

Abstract
Time Tremors is a transmedia experience for children aged 8-14 that crosses television, web, locative media, and mobile apps. *Time Tremors* is a collection game in which players search for objects from history supposedly scattered throughout time and space, hidden, invisible to the human eye but detectable and collectable using a variety of mobile and online broadband technologies. Extending the game into locative augmented reality and mobile play was an applied research challenge that required narrative continuity while ensuring safe play.

Author Keywords
Transmedia; COPPA; Children's Entertainment; Cross-platform; Engagement; Locative; Augmented Reality; Wearable.

ACM Classification Keywords
H.5.1 Information Interfaces and Presentation: Multimedia Information Systems,
Artificial, augmented, and virtual realities

General Terms
Transmedia, Mobile Gaming, Augmented Reality

Design Case Study

Time Tremors is a transmedia entertainment property aimed at children aged 7- 12. *Time Tremors* unfolds as players explore space, time and alternate dimensions and different media platforms to hunt, collect, trade and compete across a range of mysterious interactive relics known as Time Treasures. Time Treasures can be detected and collected using mobile apps featuring Augmented Reality and interactive TV functionality, in addition to web-based experiences. Players can upload collected Time Treasures to their personal collection point, known in game as the Celestial Atlas, which releases TV-quality story content like video and audio clips, photographs etc. *Time Tremors* balances story and game for a unique interactive entertainment experience.

Time Tremors Location-based Quests at art galleries and museums provide an enhanced experience delivered to mobile platforms that encourage loyalty, repeat visits and new visits to partnered cultural institutions and sites around the world. These new experiences also offer children and families new, site-specific ways to engage with the *Time Tremors* property in safe, controlled real-world locations. A variety of story driven prompts encourage users to crossover to different platforms directly. Exclusive content, like functional game items that – once collected – are accessible on all platforms.

Time Tremors uses Unity 3D to streamline cross-platform development. Although some custom coding is necessary for the more advanced interactions like shape recognition, augmented reality, and sub-sonic audio triggers, the vast majority of the front-end programming can be run through Unity. As well, any custom Unity programming can be added to Unity's libraries for reuse by the community and are opportunities for further monetization.

Related Work

There are few relevant competitors in the cross platform game space that offer an experience as comprehensive as *Time Tremors*. Other cross platform projects such as The 39 Clues[1] and Moshi Monsters[2] are examples of cross-platform gaming. However neither has leveraged significant television, cultural additions or game modules across multiple media platforms.

Discussion

Opportunities working with children

Children are well-documented cross-platform entertainment consumers [1, 2]. They are comfortable moving and engaging with digital experiences across multiple channels [3]. Children engage on multiple platforms and are more open to experimental modes of interaction [4]. The use of Augmented Reality and site-specific play experiences introduce new forms of digital gaming that appeal to children's sense of discovery. These experiences bridge the gap between traditional screen-based play and real world play to bring stories to life in new, more interactive ways. Children are lead users for whole family experiences. Quality family time is often dictated by the needs of the child and transmedia storytelling can tap into this trend to create story driven experiences aimed at children and the whole family. *Time Tremors* facilitates this whole family experience through the creation of themed *Time Tremors* hunts for mobile devices at partnered cultural institutions. *Time Tremors* offers children an engaging

[1] http://the39clues.scholastic.com/

[2] http://www.moshimonsters.com/welcome

way to explore the art gallery and the museum and means to involve the entire family in the play experience.

Challenges in developing for children
COPPA, or Children's Online Privacy Protection Act, protects children under the age of 13 who visit web sites and other online destinations. COPPA states that any operator of a website that is directed at children, and collects any kind of data from them, must post a notice of its information practices on its website and requires the express consent of parents. In order to maintain optimal user experience *Time Tremors* doesn't ask users to sign into the game until they want to leave. That way, users play the game first and if they like it and want to maintain their score and collected game items, they will go through the process of seeking consent.

Like COPPA consent, Parental Gates also impacts the user flow and pull audience members out of the experience. *Time Tremors* uses history questions that highlight themes and content from the property in order to maintain cohesion during the Parental Gate.

Additionally, the dangers related real world play must be reduced if children are to participate. Geolocative gaming is often not an option due to the lack of control over the play space [5]. The dangers of geolocation game play are reduced by partnering with "safe" institutions like art galleries, museums, schools etc., to create controlled environments for children to play. *Time Tremors* provides game experiences that do not rely on wireless technology and creating compelling, story driven games that take advantage of real world locations. Game mechanics like shape recognition, augmented reality and other verification games are designed to ensure that children have arrived at the correct location within the gallery and to provide challenges designed to keep users in the optimal flow.

Conclusion
Time Tremors is an example of modern, well-designed transmedia storytelling for children. It reaches children on multiple platforms and does so in a cohesive and compelling way. This drives user adherence, extends the life of the property and increases revenue potential.

Acknowledgements
This work is generously supported by the Natural Sciences and Engineering Research Council of Canada (NSERC), International Science and Technology Partnerships Canada.

References
[1] Davies, M.M. *Children, Media, and Culture*. Open University Press. Maidenhead, UK (2012)
[2] Attewell J. Mobile communications technologies for young adult learning and skills development (m-learning). *European Workshop on Mobile and Contextual Learning,* (2002), 5-8;
[3] Jacobs, Stephen, Geoffrey Long, Kathering Isbister, and Richard Rouse III. Occasionally reconcilable differences: bringing games and linear entertainment IP together, for better and for worse. *ACM SIGGRAPH symposium on Videogames*, (2006), 13-17.
[4] Enrenli, K. The impact of gamification: A recommendation of scenarios for education. *Interactive Collaborative Learning*, (2012), 1-8.
[5] Jacob, J.T.P.N., and Coelho, A.F. Issues in the development of location-based games. *International Journal of Computer Games Technology.* (2011).

CoPerformance: A Rapid Prototyping Platform for Developing Interactive Artist-audience Performances with Mobile Devices

Bohdan Anderson, Technical Director
ALSO Collective
408-196 Spadina Ave.
Toronto, ON M5T2C2 CA
bohdan@alsocollective.com

Symon Oliver, Creative Director
ALSO Collective
408-196 Spadina Ave.
Toronto, ON M5T2C2 CA
symon@alsocollective.com

Patricio Davila, Principal Investigator
OCAD University
100 McCaul St.
Toronto, ON M5T1W1 CA
pdavila@faculty.ocad.ca

MobileHCI '14, September 23-26, 2014, Toronto, ON, Canada
ACM 978-1-4503-3004-6/14/09.
http://dx.doi.org/10.1145/2628363.2645699

Abstract
How can mobile technology create new models for audience participation in live performances? CoPerformance is a research project that aims to develop a set of plug-and-play participatory performance modules. These modules will allow designers to quickly build/test interactive experiences that utilize mobile devices. CoPerformance can be deployed via web browsers or native applications. The goal of this platform is to use existing frameworks to offer designers a powerful set of tools, templates, and scripts for interactive performances; and decrease the barriers for building participatory performances.

Author Keywords
Interaction design; platforms; real-time mobile; Node.js; Socket.IO; AngularJS; performance

ACM Classification Keywords
D.2.2 Design Tools and Techniques; D.2.10 Design, J.5 Arts and Humanities; K.8.m Miscellaneous

Introduction
Enhancing live music performances has been an ongoing concern for music producers and with the advent of mobile devices the opportunities for

Web Application	Native Application
Gyroscope	Gyroscope
Accelerometer	Accelerometer
Speaker	Speaker
Touch	Touch
Unreliable	Camera
Unreliable	Compass
n/a	Flash / Light
n/a	Vibrotactile Feedback
n/a	Notifications
Unreliable	Microphone

Table 1. Shows the availability of input and output features based of the deployment method.

participation at live events have increased substantially. Many audiences have become accustomed to recording performances, sending messages during performances or using the built-in light on mobile phones to create spontaneous crowd light shows. Over the past decade HCI researchers have endeavoured to understand how this interaction might work and how it may be enhanced through the use of sensors, wireless networks and mobile computers [4, 5, 6, 7, 8]. We look to three influential projects for insights into user engagement, distributed real-time interaction, and spontaneous audience organization [9, 10, 11].

Until recently, building distributed mobile interactive performances has presented both a design and technical challenge. Existing frameworks require significant knowledge of server-side languages, and/or mobile development. The relatively recent introduction of Google's V8 Engine, HTML5, CSS3, and decreased hosting costs has changed the web considerably. Since theses changes, there has been an explosion in rich web-based applications being developed by novice developers. As web technologies progress, new frameworks offer increased utility and distributed connectivity. We are using these new frameworks to develop a series of boilerplate modules that will facilitate the design and build of distributed mobile participatory performances without the need for the expert level programming skills. In the following text we will cover our design rationale, technical documentation, and our work in progress with the musical group The Battle of Santiago. We look to three influential projects for insights into user engagement, distributed real-time interaction, and spontaneous audience organization [9, 10, 11].

Server-side JavaScript & AngularJS

Node.js represents a substantial contribution and shift in server-side development, allowing for the development of server-side JavaScript applications. Node.js is scalable, event-driven, lightweight, and efficient for real-time network applications across distributed devices [1]. Socket.IO—a Node Package—allows for real-time bidirectional communication between agents (client/server) [3]. AngularJS, is a MVW (Model View Whatever), which in short is a framework optimized for dynamic HTML that interacts between client and server fluidly [2]. We are using the above frameworks/packages to create CoPerformance.

Philosophy of Non-abstraction

CoPerformance avoids the addition of new semantic layers, and ensures that the code remains written in a syntax that is readable as conventional JavaScript. By building without abstraction, the platform remains open and familiar. Any techniques learned through the use of CoPerformance are transferrable to future projects beyond CoPerformance. Most importantly the platform will be community driven, while avoiding the pitfalls of managing proprietary knowledge and mediums.

Core Module, Sub-modules, & Communication

The Core Module is device and operating system agnostic Node.js server utilizing Socket.IO, enabling upwards of 250,000 concurrent bidirectional connections. The main role of the Core Module is to send/receive data from input/output modules and rebroadcast to all connected input/output modules.

Acting as satellites to the Core Module, sub-modules extend the input/output from the Core Module to other applications, enabling them to emit and receive data within the CoPerformance platform. Without the feed

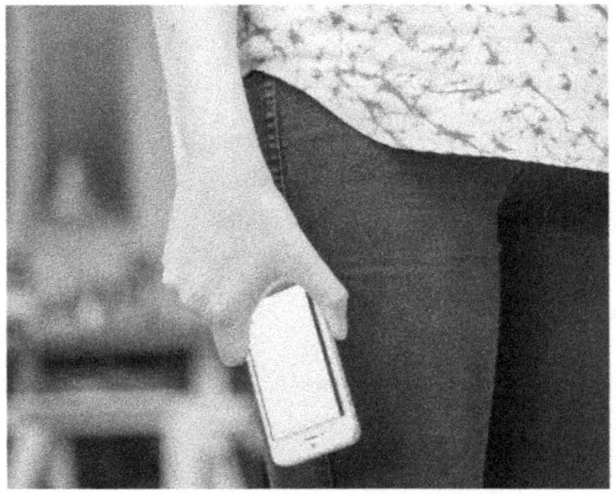

Figure 1. The tapper uses accelerometer and gyroscope data from each connected mobile device. Users tap the phone to the drumbeat of the audio performance. This gesture flashes the screen bright white on every detected tap, and sends the tapping rhythm to our main controller. The main controller renders each tap as a white band, revealing a video. Each new user connection subdivides the projected image playing behind the musicians.

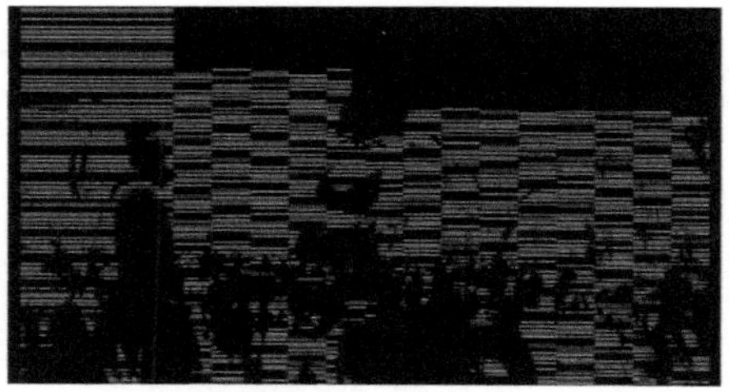

Figure 2. User feedback, as seen on the video projection behind the performers.

from the Core Module, these satellites would only perform predetermined routines. Modules cast for output, receive data from the Core Module, triggering changes in visuals, lighting, or audio. Modules for input rely heavily on the data they receive from the Core Module. These modules send and receive data to the Core Module, which in turn transmit to any connected input/output modules.

We use four low-level communication standards for input/output can be easily received and/or transmitted from a wide range of sources: Socket.IO (TCP), UDP (extends to other UDP based libraries), MIDI (facilitates bidirectional communication to audio platforms), Serial (sensors, microcontrollers, and lighting systems).

UI/UX Modules

CoPerformance introduces a set of key UI/UX templates designed and built in AngularJS. These modules will be composed of interface elements, animations, and templates written to using the best practices of web development. Users are able to customize down to the finest details, or build their own custom interface without the use of these templates. The templates speed up the prototyping of these applications and forego the need to write from scratch.

Depending on the intentions of the user, the platform can be easily deployed as a traditional Web Application, or as a Phone Gap App that allows for access to native features of mobile devices. The distinction is represented in Table 1.

Current Prototype & Future Work

Our prototype is within the testing phase, and will be tested at a live concert with 100 participants. The test will be conducted over the duration of five songs, using two styles of interactions, and three styles of passive visual feedback. The interactions will be: Tapping, and Shaking. TouchDesigner will transmit passive visuals, videos, and drumbeats to all connected mobile devices. Users are cued to interact via notifications on their mobile devices, and/or callouts from the performers. Users become a form of embodied input of the music—whereby tapping, clapping, shaking, and gyrating can become inputs into large-scale visualizations that occur with the musical performance.

References

[1] Node.js. (n.d.). Retrieved June 6, 2014, from http://nodejs.org/
[2] AngularJS — Superheroic JavaScript MVW Framework. (n.d.). Retrieved June 6, 2014, from https://angularjs.org/
[3] Socket.IO. (n.d.). Retrieved June 6, 2014, from http://Socket.IO/
[4] Barkhuus, L., & Jørgensen, T. (2008). Engaging the crowd: Studies of audience-performer interaction. In CHI '08 Extended Abstracts on Human Factors in Computing Systems (pp. 2925–2930). New York, NY, USA: ACM.
[5] Bongers, B. (2000). Physical interfaces in the electronic arts: Interaction theory and interfacing techniques for real-time performance. In Trends in Gestural Control of Music (pp. 41–70).
[6] Brown, B., O'Hara, K., Kindberg, T., & Williams, A. (2009). Crowd computer interaction. In CHI'09 Extended Abstracts on Human Factors in Computing Systems (pp. 4755–4758). New York, NY, USA: ACM.
[7] Freeman, J. (2005). Large audience participation, technology, and orchestral performance. In Proceedings of the 2005 International Computer Music Conference (pp. 757–760).
[8] Ulyate, R., & Bianciardi, D. (2001). The interactive dance club: Avoiding chaos in a multi participant environment. In Proceedings of the 2001 Conference on New Inter- faces for Musical Expression (pp. 1–3). Singapore, Singapore: National University of Singapore.
[8] [9] Levin, G., et al. (2002). Dialtones (A Telesymphony). Swiss National Exposition '02. Romandy, Switzerland.
[9] [10] Longford, M., Shea, G., King, R. (2011). Tentacles 1.0. MoMA Exhibition: Talk to Me. New York, NY, USA.
[11] Carpenter, L. (1991). Loren Carpenter Experiment. In SIGGRAPH '91. Las Vegas, NV, USA: ACM.

Phonorama: Mobile Spatial Navigation By Directional Stereophony

Michael Markert
Bauhaus-Universität Weimar
Marienstr. 5
D-99423 Weimar, Germany
michael.markert@uni-weimar.de

Jens Heitjohann
Hochschule für Musik und Theater Felix Mendelssohn Bartholdy
Grassistr. 8
D-04107 Leipzig, Germany
jens.heitjohann@hmt-leipzig.de

Jens Geelhaar
Bauhaus-Universität Weimar
Marienstr. 5
D-99423 Weimar, Germany
jens.geelhaar@uni-weimar.de

MobileHCI '14, Sep 23-26 2014, Toronto, ON, Canada
ACM 978-1-4503-3004-6/14/09.
http://dx.doi.org/10.1145/2628363.2645700

Abstract
Phonorama is a sonar-like mobile application that uses audio hotspots bound to specific geo-locations. Decreasing the distance to the audio source increases the volume. New to this known concept is the addition of direction indicators, enabling rich and immediate, immersive audio-only spatial explorations:

The direction of the audio hotspot source relative to the user's location is represented by a realtime stereo-panning (Directional Stereophony). If the audio source is left of the user, the volume on the left headphone speaker is louder than the volume on the right speaker. While the software has been created for audio guides in the context of media arts, it might be useful for all kinds of acoustic navigations, e.g. information hotspots in museums and public space, navigational aid, assistive technologies, social networking or localized advertisements.

Author Keywords
Location Based Audio; Mobile Computing; Geolocation; Navigation; Directional Audio; Distance to Volume; Direction to Pan.

ACM Classification Keywords
H.5.m. Information interfaces and presentation (HCI): Miscellaneous;
H.5.1. Multimedia Information Systems;
H.5.5. Sound and Music Computing;
J.5 Arts and Humanities.

Figure 1: Flakhelferin am Horchgerät, 1943. Bundesarchiv, Bild 101I-674-7757-18 / Zoll / CC-BY-SA

Figure 2: Demo Screenshots of Interactive Phonorama Audio Guides

Introduction
Directional audio in a technological context has so far been seen mainly during the world wars as air reconnaissance machinery. Huge listening devices with attached human listeners connected through binaural tubes are one of the first indicators of cybernetic feedback loops between man and machine utilizing acoustic spatial location techniques (see Figure 1).

The ubiquitous availability of mobile smartphones with location and position sensing technologies and navigational capabilities changes our perception of space observably [1]. Location specific audio sources are already used in some Audio-Guide applications, where a decreased distance to the audio source results in an increased volume. This concept however, doesn't give any indication of the direction of audio hotspots, thus not dealing with the navigational aspect of the system. To enable a truly cybernetic feedback system [2] that affects the movement and behavior of the user, a new mobile application concept is introduced: »Directional Stereophony«

Audio-Driven Interactivity
Audio guides usually require listening continuously from beginning to end. Common user-interactivity is often restricted to a selection of tracks and basic media control: pausing or skipping the current track. Audio-Guides communicate something relevant about an object of interest (for example in exhibitions) or about the user's current location (cities, parks, landsites, ...). They often prompt to look at something or to explore specific locations by means of our physical presence. Adding imagery and requiring visual on-screen input is potentially conflicting with this aim by occupying three important senses (visual, aural, haptic).

Immersive Audio
By introducing location specific audio hotspots and Directional Stereophony, the user may choose freely if he or she wants to interact with the application only via audio and movement in space, enabling an immersive acoustic experience. Hands- and »eyes-free«, users can now spend their full attention on the actual object of interest (see Figure 2).

Directional Stereophony enables users to walk wherever they want to, without having to interact with any visual interfaces. The interest of the user is controlling all media controls autonomously just by moving around in space. Whenever the user hears something that catches his or her attention, the interaction to locate the direction of the source is as simple and natural as facing towards somebody speaking to us: once the source direction has been determined, walking towards it increases this hotspot's volume while decreasing the volume of less interesting ones.

Technical Description
The mobile application reads GeoJSON encoded files containing standardized information about hotspots (see Figures 3 and 4).

The nearer the user gets to the inner radius, the louder the volume. Additionally, the bearing and heading influence the stereo pan in relation to the current location of the audio source. If the user's device faces towards the hotspot's center, the panning is centered (0.0). If the user turns 90° left, the panning is moved to the right ear (1.0). If the user turns 90° right, the panning is moved to the left ear (-1.0). For bearings between 90° and 270° (that is if the user turns away

```
"features": [
{
  "type": "Feature",
  "properties": {
    "identifier": 1,
    "name": "Plantagenstation
      Usungula",
    "description": "Deutsch-
      Ostafrikanische
      Ausstellung",
    "lang": "de-DE",
    "innerRadius": 20,
    "outerRadius": 45,
    "mediaFile":
     "OA_Usungula.mp3"
  },
  "geometry": {
    "type": "Point",
    "coordinates":
     [12.362066, 51.331574]
  }
},
...
```

Figure 4: GeoJSON example defining one hotspot

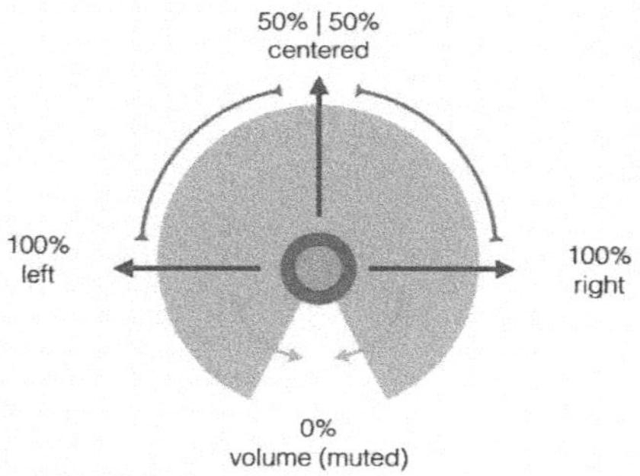

Figure 5: Directional Stereophony (Direction to Pan)

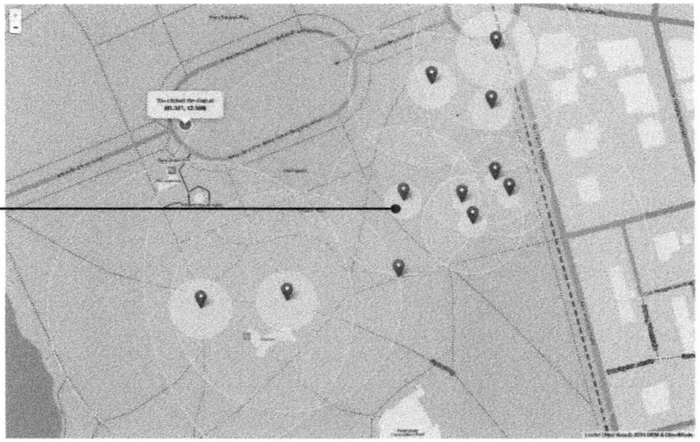

Figure 3: Graphical Representation of a GeoJSON file

from the source, facing towards the opposite direction), the volume is decreased to 0% at 180° (see Figure 5). Additionally, sounds have a very subtle delay to increase the perception of direction: Sounds that meet the right ear first, will be perceived by the left ear with a slight delay that increases the directional impression [3].

Accessory Extensions

A current limitation is that the system only knows the bearing of the user's device and not the user's head. This could be overcome by additional accessories like hats, necklaces, earrings or special earplugs with an embedded magnetometer to accurately measure the bearing of the user's head.

Conclusion

With more refined and new location and positioning technologies available in the near future (especially for indoor positioning systems like Bluetooth Low Energy iBeacons), one can expect an increased need for innovative mobile location based applications.

Spatial navigation by directional stereophony on mobile handheld devices could be a solution for immersive audio-only navigation with lots of potential useful use-cases in many disciplines, for example arts and culture (guided tours, museums, spatial explorations, radio), localized information (public transport, tourist guides), assistive tools for disabled persons, new social networks (»dropping messages«) and even commercial applications in downtown areas and shopping malls (special events or offers).

Acknowledgments

Bauhaus-Universität Weimar, BMBF, EU, ESF, Teri Rueb, Galerie für Zeitgenössische Kunst Leipzig (GfZK).

References

[1] Willis K.S., Wayfinding Situations. In Eckardt F. et al (eds.), Mediacity: Situations, Practices and Encounters, Berlin, Frank&Timme, 2008, pp. 21-40.

[2] Wiener N., Kybernetik (1948). In: Dotzler, B. ed. Norbert Wiener: futurum exaktum - ausgewählte schriften zur kybernetik und kommunikations-theorie, Wien, Springer-Verlag, 2002, pp. 15-29.

[3] Pierce J. R., Klang: Musik mit den Ohren der Physik, Heidelberg, Spektrum der Wissenschaft, 1989, pp. 135-136.

Experimenting on the Cognitive Walkthrough with Users

Wallace Lira
Vale Institute of Technology
Av. Boa Ventura da Silva, 400
C.P. 668 – 13.560-970
Belém, Brazil
wallace.lira@gmail.com

Cleidson de Souza
Vale Institute of Technology
Av. Boa Ventura da Silva, 400
C.P. 668 – 13.560-970
Belém, Brazil
cleidson.desouza@acm.org

Renato Ferreira
Universidade Federal do Pará
Rua Augusto Corrêa, 01
C.P. 479 – 66075-110
Belém, Brazil
renpina@gmail.com

Schubert R Carvalho
Vale Institute of Technology
Av. Boa Ventura da Silva, 400
C.P. 668 – 13.560-970
Belém, Brazil
schubert.carvalho@itv.org

MobileHCI 2014, September 23–26, 2014, Toronto, ON, Canada.
ACM 978-1-4503-3004-6/14/09.
http://dx.doi.org/10.1145/2628363.2628428

Abstract
This paper presents a case study aiming to investigate which variant of the Think-Aloud Protocol (i.e., the Concurrent Think-Aloud and the Retrospective Think-Aloud) better integrates with the Cognitive Walkthrough with Users. To this end we performed a case study that involved twelve users and one usability evaluator. Usability problems uncovered by each method were evaluated to help us understand the strengths and weaknesses of the studied usability testing methods. The results suggest that 1) the Cognitive Walkthrough with Users integrates equally well with both the Think-Aloud Protocol variants; 2) the Retrospective Think-Aloud find more usability problems and 3) the Concurrent Think-Aloud is slightly faster to perform and was more cost effective. However, this is only one case study, and further research is needed to verify if the results are actually statistically significant.

Author Keywords
Usability Evaluation; Cognitive Walkthrough; Think Aloud-Protocol; Mobile apps.

ACM Classification Keywords
H.5.2. [User Interfaces]: Miscellaneous

Introduction

Usability can be defined as "a fairly broad concept that basically refers to how easy it is for users to learn a system, how efficiently they can use it once they have learned it, and how pleasant it is to use" [13]. The usability of mobile applications have been of great concern to the industry. For example, Apple and Google both have published user interface guidelines regarding mobile apps [2, 4]. Due to these reasons, it is necessary to apply usability tests to evaluate the usability of mobile applications. Popular usability testing methods includes both the Think-Aloud Protocol [9] and the Cognitive Walkthrough [13].

The Think-Aloud Protocol instructs the evaluators to observe and collect feedback from a user interacting with the evaluated software. The user should speak everything he is thinking of regarding the evaluated software. This work focuses on two variants of this method: the Concurrent Think-Aloud, which instructs the user to talk while he is interacting with the software; and the Retrospective Think-Aloud that instructs the user to talk while he watches a video of his interaction with the software [9].

The Cognitive Walkthrough, on the other hand, provides a test process which includes four heuristics to be used in the inspection of each possible user action by an usability expert. There are some variants of the Cognitive Walkthrough, which were compiled in a paper by *Mahatody et. al.* [8]. The Cognitive Walkthrough with Users [5] was one of them. This usability testing method blends both the Concurrent Think-Aloud and the Cognitive Walkthrough. However, *Mahatody et. al.* [8] wonders whether the Concurrent Think-Aloud is the most appropriate usability testing method to be merged with the Cognitive Walkthrough with Users. The objective of this work is to investigate which variation of the Think-Aloud Protocol (Concurrent or Retrospective Think-Aloud) integrates best with the Cognitive Walkthrough with Users. The evaluated application is simply referred as Digital Plants, which is an app for automatic plant identification and classification using leaf images.

This work is organized as follows. The section Case Study details of its execution. The findings related to the experiment conducted can be found in the Findings section. The last section presents the conclusions and some possible future works that could follow up this research.

Case Study

This work presents a case study to investigate if there are differences in the results of the Cognitive Walkthrough with Users should the variation of the Think-Aloud Protocol (Concurrent or Retrospective Think-Aloud) integrated with it change. This was referenced as an interesting course of action [8]. Furthermore, the two variants of the Think-Aloud Protocol can achieve different results [16].

Evaluated Application

The use of leaf images for automating plant identification and classification processes has been the subject of numerous studies [1, 6, 15]. The main features extracted from leaf images are based on their shape and venation. Leaf venation will be referred as the leaf texture when describing the Digital Plants' functions even though it is possible to extract other data by analysing the leaf's texture.

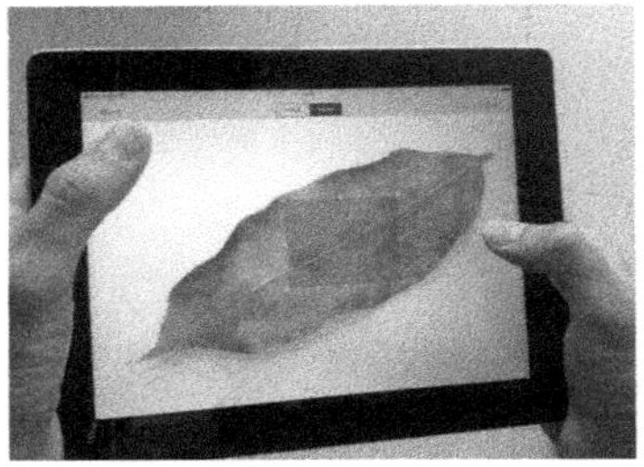

Figure 2: Leaf analysis using the Digital Plants app.

The main goal of the Digital Plants app is to automate the plant identification process. The app should also provide a plant catalogue with extensive information on them.

The app's intended use is to help botanists to identify the species of plants through a single leaf without harming the plant. Today, this process is performed manually with the help of textbooks and people without formal training but with vast experience regarding the local flora.

The Fig. 1 presents the Digital Plants functions in a mind map. There are two main modules on the tool: *Plant List* and *Leaf Analysis*. We applied principles of mobile usability [2, 12] at the development the Digital Plants app user interface. We can see an example of the tested user interface at the Fig. 2.

Participants
There were 12 users in the case study. It is widely accepted that only five users are enough to find around 85 % of the usability problems using the Think-Aloud Protocol [11]. Therefore 6 users were subjected to each variant of the Think-Aloud Protocol, which gave us enough information for comparing both usability evaluation methods. Table 1 shows the age, which mobile operating systems he had experience on, for how long he owns a mobile device with that operating systems and to what variant of the Think-Aloud Protocol he was subjected to.

The mean participant age in years is 33.25 and the standard deviation is 7.14. The mean experience with mobile operating systems in years is 1.01 while the standard deviation is 0.9. Furthermore, each of the participants are researchers working at Vale Institute of Technology. The Think-Aloud Protocol variant that each participant was subjected to was determined randomly.

Table 1: Participant characteristics.

ID	Age	Mobile OS	How many years	TA Variant
P1	29	Android	0.3	Concurrent
P2	40	IOs and Android	3	Concurrent
P3	35	-	0	Concurrent
P4	23	Android	1	Concurrent
P5	30	Android	1.4	Concurrent
P6	40	-	0	Concurrent
P7	48	-	0	Retrospective
P8	30	-	0	Retrospective
P9	24	Android	2	Retrospective
P10	32	Android	2	Retrospective
P11	37	Android	1.5	Retrospective
P12	31	Android	1	Retrospective

Usability Testing Protocol
The case study performed can be summarized by the following steps: Select Tasks, Select Participants, Perform the Traditional Cognitive Walkthrough, Perform the Think-Aloud Protocol Variant, Summarize the Usability Problems Found, Critical and Statistical Analysis.

In the first phase, we selected the tasks that were evaluated by the traditional Cognitive Walkthrough. Not every possible scenario must be evaluated, but we are recomended to select relevant ones. We selected 3 tasks: Discover where the plant with scientific name *Amelanchier Laevis* can be found; Discover to what species a real leaf belongs to through the leaf shape analysis; Discover to what species the same leaf belongs to through the leaf texture analysis.

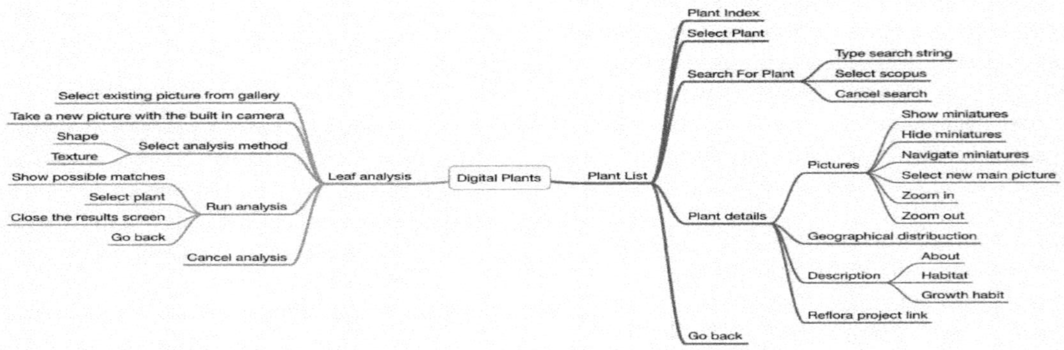

Figure 1: A mind map with the Digital Plants functions.

The participants were selected and their characteristics (as presented in Table 1) were identified. The Cognitive Walkthrough was then performed. The usability experts identified usability problems that needed further investigation during the Cognitive Walkthrough. Additionally, the assumptions about the user experiences were based on the participant characteristics presented in the Participants subsection.

The next step aims at performing both Think-Aloud Protocol variants. In this step, the participants were randomly split in two groups. One of these was subjected to the Concurrent Think-Aloud and the other one to the Retrospective Think-Aloud. All the testing sections were recorded. We restricted the analysis presented in this paper to cognitive usability problems because it is possible to find them applying the Cognitive Walkthrough, so the matter of efficiency and satisfaction will not be addressed.

Afterwards we summarized the usability problems found by the Cognitive Walkthrough and by each version of the Think-Aloud Protocol. Finally, we should perform a critical analysis of the usability problems summarized. It is important to know if the problems that the usability experts found performing the Cognitive Walkthrough were really a concern to the users.

Findings

The number of usability problems of an user interface is $N(1-(1-L)^n)$ [11]. Where **N** is the total number of usability problems in the user interface, **L** is the proportion of usability problems discovered while testing with a single user and **n** is the number of users that participated in the usability test. This formula means that around 85% of the usability problems should be found, assuming an **n** value of 6, and an **L** value of 31%.

We needed to evaluate whether the Retrospective Think-Aloud and the Concurrent Think-Aloud had similar results. This analysis turned out to reveal differences between the methods. We can observe from Fig. 3 that the Retrospective Think-Aloud found 66% more usability problems than the Concurrent Think-Aloud. The number of usability problems found performing both variants of the Think-Aloud Protocol seems to be converging to a maximum number of discoverable usability problems as the number of participants involved increases. This happens because the usability problems found by each user can also be found by the previous users, so we get diminishing returns when we increase the number of participants. This behavior is consistent with the results presented by [10].

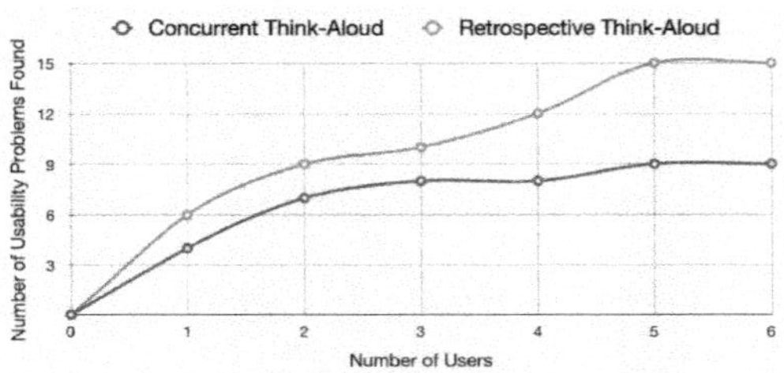

Figure 3: Number of usability problems found and the number of participants involved.

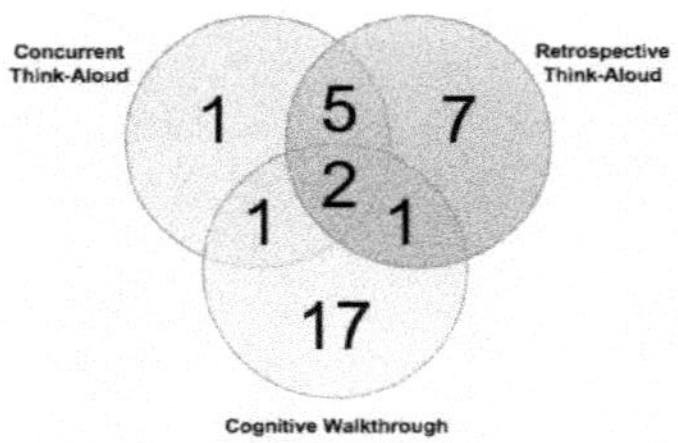

Figure 4: Venn Diagram of the number of usability problems found using each evaluation method.

We then sought to unveil whether the usability problems found by the Cognitive Walkthough, Concurrent Think-Aloud and Retrospective Think-Aloud were similar. The Fig. 4 points out that the Retrospective Think-Aloud had comparatively identified more unique usability problems compared to the Concurrent Think-Aloud.

The high number of usability problems found only by the Cognitive Walkthough method may imply that the evaluator was mistaken because the users did not judge the would-be problems a real issue. Even though this may happen, the Cognitive Walkthrough analysis can help the evaluator to improve his skills using that method because he had reliable feedback.

One of the possible reasons of the disparate result was that the participants felt generally more at ease when subjected to the Retrospective Think-Aloud as opposed to the Concurrent Think-Aloud. This may have happened because the Retrospective Think-Aloud allows the user to focus on the task at hand. However, the Concurrent Think-Aloud was 28% faster to perform with an average duration of 6.75 per user, with an associated standard deviation of 3.5, while these values for the Retrospective Think-Aloud were respectively 8.7 and 3.1. However, this data does not take into account the time that the usability evaluator took to analyse the footage of the users interaction with the application.

Finally, other metric that can be found analysing the data presented in this section is the time spent to find an usability problem. The Concurrent Think-Aloud was slightly more effective in this regard, finding 0.42 usability problems per minute. The Retrospective Think-Aloud, on the other hand, found 0.37 usability problems per minute.

Conclusions and Future Work

This paper presented a comparative analysis of how two Think-Aloud Protocol variants integrate with the Cognitive Walkthrough with Users. We found that both of these variants are equally compatible with the Cognitive Walkthrough with Users. Additionally, we found that the Retrospective Think-Aloud unveiled around 66% more usability problems compared to the Concurrent Think-Aloud. On the other hand, the Concurrent Think-Aloud was around 2 minutes faster to perform per user compared to the Retrospective Think-Aloud. Moreover, using the Concurrent Think-Aloud alowed the evaluator to find more usability problems per minute of users interaction, being slightly more cost effective compared to the Retrospective Think-Aloud.

It is important to note that the results presented in this work were obtained in only one case study. Therefore, to strenghten these conclusions we would need to run several sessions with different users and compare averages of usability issues found with each method associated with their margin of error.

Acknowledgments

We would like to thank the Vale Institute of Technology researchers for their participation in the usability tests.

References

[1] Abbasi, S., Mokhatarian, F., and Kitter, J. Reliable classification of chrysanthemum leaves through curvature scale space. *International Conference on Scale-Space Theory in Computer Vision* (1997), 284295.

[2] Apple. Apple ios human interface guidelines. `http://developer.apple.com/library/ios/documentation/UserExperience/Conceptual/MobileHIG/Introduction/Introduction.html`, 2014. Acessed: 2014-03-24.

[3] Easterbrook, S., Singer, J., Storey, M.-A., and Damian, D. Selecting empirical methods for software engineering research, 2008.

[4] Google. Google user interface guidelines. `http://developer.android.com/guide/topics/ui/index.html`, 2014. Acessed: 2014-03-24.

[5] Granollers, T., and Lores, J. Cognitive walkthrough with users: An alternative dimension for usability methods. *11th International conference on Human-computer interaction* (2005).

[6] Im C., N. H., and L., K. T. Recognizing plant species by leaf shapes - a case study of the acer family. *IEEE International Conference on Pattern Recognition* (1998), 11711173.

[7] Lewis, C., Polson, P., Wharton, C., and Rieman, J. Testing a walkthrough methodology for theory-based design of walk-up-and-use interface. In *Proceeding of ACM Computer-Human Interaction* (1990).

[8] Mahatody, T., Sagar, M., and Kolski, C. State of the art on the cognitive walkhrough method, its variants and evolutions. *International Journal of Human-Computer Interaction* (2010), 741–785.

[9] Nielsen, J. *Usability Engineering*. Academic Press, Boston, MA., 1993.

[10] Nielsen, J. Why you only need to test with 5 users, `http://www.nngroup.com/articles/why-you-only-need-to-test-with-5-users/`, March 2000.

[11] Nielsen, J. How many test users in a usability study?, `http://www.nngroup.com/articles/how-many-test-users/`, June 2012.

[12] Nielsen, J., and Budiu, R. *Mobile Usability*. Pearson Education, 2012.

[13] Nielsen, J., and Mack, R. L. *Usability Inspection Methods*. John Wiley & Sons, 1994.

[14] Polson, P., Lewis, C., Rieman, J., and Wharton, C. Cognitive walkthrough: a method for theory-based evaluation of user interface. *International Journal of Man-Machine Studies 36* (1992), 741–773.

[15] Söderkvist, O. J. O. Computer vision classification of leaves from swedish trees. Master's thesis, Linkping University, Sweden, September, 2001.

[16] van den Haak, M. J., de Jong, M. D., and Schellens, P. J. Retrospective vs. concurrent think-aloud protocols: testing the usability of an online library catalogue. *Behaviour and Information Technology 22*, 5 (September 2003), 339–351.

Logging and Visualization of Touch Interactions on Teach Pendants

Clemens Holzmann
University of Applied Sciences
Upper Austria
4232 Hagenberg, Austria
clemens.holzmann@fh-hagenberg.at

Werner Wetzlinger
University of Applied Sciences
Upper Austria
4400 Steyr, Austria
werner.wetzlinger@fh-steyr.at

Florian Lettner
University of Applied Sciences
Upper Austria
4232 Hagenberg, Austria
florian.lettner@fh-hagenberg.at

Paul Latzelsperger
KEBA AG
Gewerbepark Urfahr
4041 Linz, Austria
ltz@keba.com

Christian Grossauer
University of Applied Sciences
Upper Austria
4232 Hagenberg, Austria
christian.grossauer@fh-hagenberg.at

Christian Augdopler
KEBA AG
Gewerbepark Urfahr
4041 Linz, Austria
aug@keba.com

MobileHCI 2014, September 23–26, 2014, Toronto, ON, Canada.
ACM 978-1-4503-3004-6/14/09.

http://dx.doi.org/10.1145/2628363.2628429

Abstract
In industrial automation, there is a growing use of touch panels for controlling and programming machines. Compared to traditional panels with physical buttons, they provide higher flexibility and operating efficiency. A big challenge in the user interface design is their usability, which is directly related to the operator's safety and performance. In this paper, we present a software solution for the acquisition and visualization of user interaction data on teach pendants, which are handheld terminals for teaching robot positions. Interaction data include touch coordinates and navigation sequences, and they are visualized with a heatmap and a graph view, respectively. The design and implementation of the software is based on interviews which we conducted with companies from the automation industry. The painless integration of our software by manufacturers, together with the automated recording and visualisation of user interactions, allow for cost-efficient usability analysis of handheld terminals.

Author Keywords
Interaction logging; handheld terminal; field research; touch heatmap; navigation sequence visualization

ACM Classification Keywords
H.5.1. [Information Interfaces and Presentation (e.g. HCI)]: User Interfaces – Evaluation/methodology.

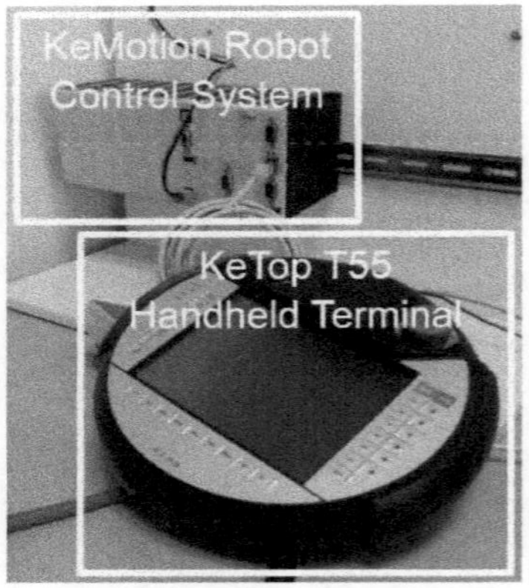

Figure 1: KeMotion robot control system with attached KeTop T55 teach pendant. The drive controllers and servo motors are not shown in this picture.

Introduction

Usability evaluation of industrial touch panels is a crucial and yet unresolved issue in automation engineering. Despite well evaluated interaction concepts and established best practices for touch-based user interfaces of mobile applications, there is just little knowledge about their industrial applicability. Therefore, an evaluation of their usability under realistic conditions, and over long periods of time, is desirable. However, in harsh factory environments, field evaluations by observing machine operators can be a difficult and expensive task.

The research challenge of this paper was to find a cost-efficient software solution which supports the usability evaluation of handheld terminals in the automation industry. We have chosen robotic teach pendants as a representative for touch-based user interfaces in industrial environments. However, the presented solution could be transferred to other stationary and mobile terminals, too.

The general idea was to log user interactions in the field, and visualize them in a way that allows to identify usability problems and potentials for improving the user interface. A requirement was that our software solution can easily be integrated in the used teach pendant terminal, and that the recorded data can be imported and visualized on a PC.

We built upon previous work presented in [2], where we used aspect-oriented programming to log user interactions in mobile applications without changing their source code, and applied it to the industrial domain. In particular, we added specific visualizations which allow to comprehend the actual workflow of machine operators. Additionally, our solution has been designed to log various different contextual data like the orientation of the device, environmental conditions (e.g. brightness and noise) or the operator's current activity (e.g. standing or walking), which can be used to relate logged interactions with the context of use in future work.

At first, we conducted several interviews with large-sized companies from the automation industry. Based on the interview results, we designed and implemented a fully functional software prototype for the KeMotion robot control system and its teach pendant, the handheld terminal KeTop T55, of the company KEBA AG[1] (see Fig. 1). The robot control system is a combination of a classic PLC (i.e. Programmable Logic Controller) and a fully-fledged robot controller. The KeTop teach pendant is used to create, execute and modify sequential robot programs via its touch panel.

The developed prototype can be seen as a first step towards an iterative design and development of control terminals in industry, where the logged an visualized interaction data from real-world device usage provides the basis for improving the user interface in subsequent development iterations. Changes to the user interface will be made by a usability expert after analyzing the interactions based on the provided visualizations (e.g. to detect navigation problems or unused functions).

Research Methodology

In order to identify the requirements related to usability evaluation in the automation industry, we conducted three semi-structured, face-to-face interviews with open questions. We interviewed a programmer as well as a product manager of one enterprise, and a product manager of another enterprise. Based on the ISO 9241-11 definition of usability, the interview guide and its questions were structured along the following five

[1] http://www.keba.com

categories: (i) General classification of the enterprise and the interview participant, (ii) context of use of control terminals (e.g. environmental noise or dirt), as well as (iii) usability metrics (e.g. time on screen), (iv) evaluation methods (e.g. A/B testing) and (v) data representations (e.g. Heatmap visualization) which would be helpful for the company to improve their mobile user interfaces, and (vi) debriefing.

The interview guide contained 25 open questions out of these categories. To every question, predefined hints in the form of examples were defined to ensure an equal level of support from the interviewer over all interviews. To follow the defined methodology, examples were only given after the unsupported question had been asked and the interviewee needed help in answering it; this should ensure comparability across the interviews.

Based on work of Mayring [3], the evaluation of the interviews was carried out in the following phases: (i) Transcription, (ii) paraphrasing, (iii) generalization of statements, (iv) identification and categorization of requirements for each interview, (v) comparison and aggregation across all interviews, (vi) consistent encoding of all requirements, and (vii) final revision.

All together, we collected 96 requirements from these interviews. Each requirement was assigned to a specific area, the most important ones are shown in Table 1.

Area of Requirement	Number
Context of use	39
Usability metrics	18
Evaluation methods	28
Data representation	11

Table 1: Most frequently mentioned areas.

Within these areas, different topics were identified. The most important topics, ranked by the number of identified requirements, were navigation path analysis (area "evaluation methods") with 15 requirements and usage intensity (area "usability metrics") with 7 requirements.

System Design and Implementation

As a consequence of the identified requirements, we put our focus on the acquisition and visualization of navigation paths and raw touch data from handheld terminals, in order to discover unexpected navigation behaviours and frequently used areas or functions, respectively. Although numerous works on automatically discovering unexpected browsing behaviours [5] or drawing general conclusions on user behaviour in daily life routines [4] have been published for web sites, this is a little investigated field with respect to mobile device usage in industrial environments.

Interaction Logging and Visualisation

In order to record interaction data, a prototype for logging on the KeTop handheld terminal has been developed. It makes use of aspect-oriented programming (AOP) [1] to cut across UI events that occur in the mobile application. The upside of this approach is that no modifications of the application source code are required. Interaction information is stored in a file for post-processing purposes. In our first prototype, only touch clicks are recorded, an extension with touch gestures is subject of future work.

In addition to raw touch clicks, navigation information such as the dwell time on a view and the navigation flow are recorded. Whenever the user opens or closes a view, the event is recorded and stored in the log file. In the post-processing phase, those navigation sequences can be visualized.

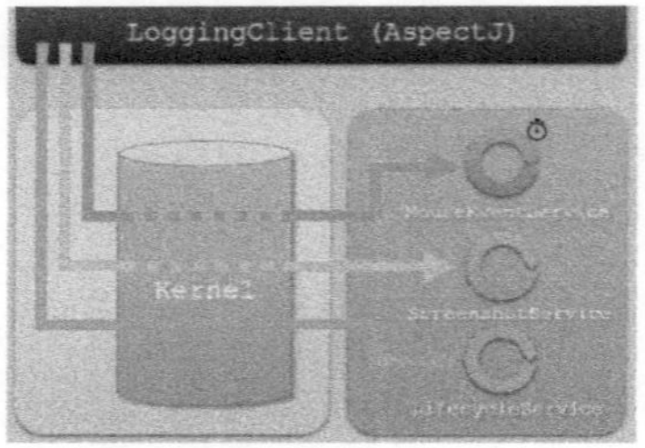

Figure 2: Events that are generated in the logging framework are routed to their respective services through the logging kernel.

Several different visualizations were implemented to represent the logged information. For the implementation, Java Swing was used. For the visualization of touch positions, we decided to use a heatmap, where touch intensities are represented with colours ranging from blue to red. For the visualization of navigation paths, we decided for a directed graph, where the nodes represent different views of the user interface and edges the number of transitions between these views.

Implementation
The client implementation of the proposed solution is based on a generic logging framework that we have previously published in [2]. This framework provides a plugin-based infrastructure that offers functionality to implement services and to send and receive interaction events. Services are plugins that can be registered with the logging kernel and fulfil a certain logging task. For AOP in Java, the AspectJ[2] extension was used.

In the course of the presented solution, the logging framework was extended with specific services in order to record touch interactions (mouse event service) and information about the user navigation (lifecycle service), as well as to take screenshots (screenshot service) while users are interacting with the KeTop terminals in the field. As shown in Fig. 2, interaction events (i.e. Java AWT events) raised by the application are caught via AOP and sent to the logging kernel.

Within the framework, the kernel is responsible for managing and distributing these events to services that have registered as listeners for them. When the user clicks on the screen of the mobile device, each service that is registered for such an event gets notified. In the following, the three services will be described in more detail.

Mouse Event Service
The core task of the service is to persist click events (`MouseClickEvent` objects) in a file so that they can be associated with the corresponding screen content later on. In order to conserve resources and to minimize file I/O operations, the mouse event service maintains a queue of click events and serializes them to a file in discrete time intervals. As a consequence, events arrive asynchronously (upon user interaction), but they are processed synchronously in given time intervals by the logging kernel.

In order to receive information about the X/Y-coordinates of a touch event (i.e. a mouse click), it is necessary to catch the event chain at the lowest possible level. For this purpose, a central listener for intercepting all of the generated AWT events was implemented.

Screenshot Service
Basically, the purpose of this service is to write raw image data to a file. Due to limited resources, screenshots may not be created for each interaction event, but only if relevant screen content changed. First of all, it is important to associate mouse click events with a certain view or mask, which is required to create touch heatmaps on top of their corresponding screenshots. For this purpose, it is necessary to know on which mask the click occurred. Since each mask has a unique name in the teach pendant application, these names can be used to associate clicks with them. Thus, the screenshot service is also responsible for associating a click events with screenshots.

With AOP, the framework kernel is able to detect whenever a new mask is opened, for example after clicking a button in the teach pendant, and raises an event

[2]http://eclipse.org/aspectj/

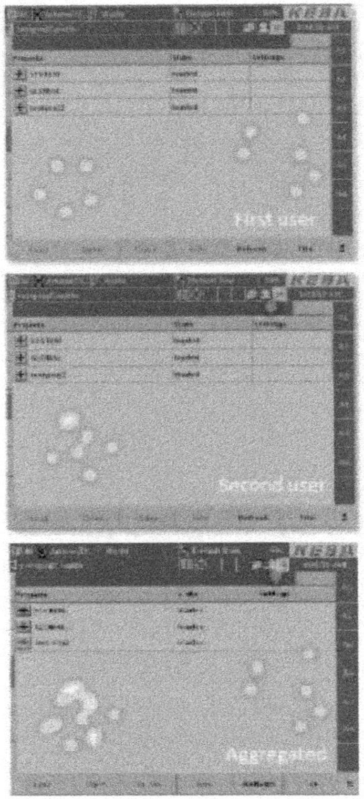

Figure 3: Shows touch interaction of two different users (first two screenshots) as well as the aggregation of both with heatmaps.

(`ScreenshotEvent` object) which is received by the screenshot service. After receiving this event, the service creates a screenshot of the current mask and stores it together with the mask name as a JPEG file on the internal flash memory of the teach pendant.

In order to associate click events with screenshots, the service also receives the mouse click events created by the kernel and assigns them to the screenshot of the current mask. Consequently, every click event will be associated with the last captured view. Typical actions to trigger a screenshot are view changes, UI interactions that potentially cause a change in the content of the view (e.g. combobox selection) or a dialogue popup, among others.

Lifecycle Service
The teach pendant uses different masks to visualize data and processes from the robot controller. Only one mask can be visible at a time, thus no multitasking is used. The lifecycle service collects information about how long the user stays on a certain mask and how they navigate through masks. The service receives events whenever a mask is opened (`MaskOpenEvent` object) or closed (`MaskCloseEvent` object) by the user as a result of navigating from one mask to another.

After changing from one mask to another, first the dwell time for the previous mask is calculated (i.e. time user spent on that mask). Moreover, the service keeps track of the transitions between these two masks, which are stored in an edge list together with the number of edge visits. As a result, it is possible to find out if transitions between different masks occur more often than others.

Industrial Application

The presented concept was implemented and applied to the actual hardware of the project partner (KEBA AG). It has also been reviewed by a focus group of the hardware manufacturer. According to their feedback, the most important requirements could successfully be met by the proposed concept.

Performance issues that we did expect due to hardware restrictions on the real KeTop terminals did not have any noticeable impact and thus, were not observed by the focus group. In general, the developed system was considered useful for identifying workflow issues in the course of the development process.

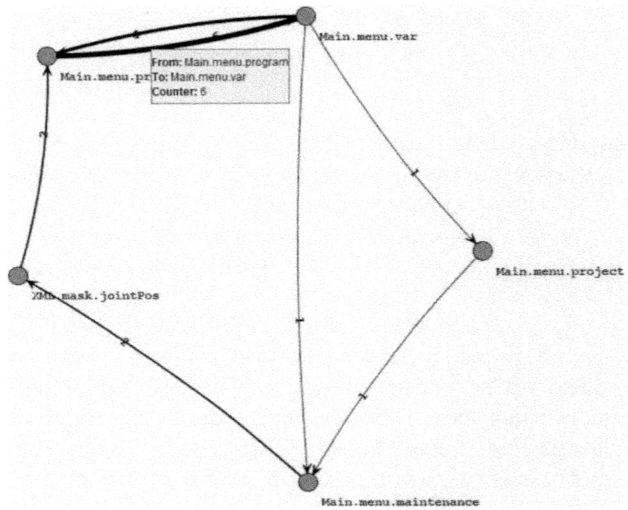

Figure 4: Graph-based view of the logged transitions (edges) between masks (nodes) on the teach pendant.

In order to provide an evaluation possibility to the focus group, a data viewer application for visualising interaction data, which can be recorded while the KeTop panels are used in daily life routines, was developed. The data viewer combines the recorded click interactions with captured screenshots in order to visualise touch interactions with a heatmap. Per default, each heatmap shows only touch clicks that where performed on that particular screen. However, there is the possibility to aggregate data by overlaying all screen masks with the same name (i.e. the same masks captured at different points in time) and creates a heatmap resulting from that compound set of data (see Fig. 3).

Based on the recorded interaction data, the data viewer application is capable of displaying the navigation path with a directed graph (see Fig. 4). It visualizes the navigation behaviour throughout a session, namely which masks the user opened on the teach pendant (each mask is a node in the graph), how often they did that (showed upon right-click on a node) and which transitions occurred (directed edges between the nodes). The number of transitions is represented by the thickness of the edges.

Discussion and Conclusions

Based on the main goal of the project and the system design requirements, we built a system that is capable of recording interaction data (touch interactions and navigation data) without interfering with the code of the monitored application. The analysis of the collected data is supported by visually representing the data in form of heatmaps and graph-based navigation paths.

The possibility to aggregate the data for each individual mask enables developers to represent a user's actions and therefore identify possible problems and differences between the designed workflow (developer) and the actually executed workflow (user/operator). Although the data is only aggregated over same masks, we observed that the nature of their possibly dynamic content might lead to visual clutter in two ways. First, blending different content, which makes it hard to distinguish them; second, mapping interaction data to potentially wrong content (mapping a touch click to an unrelated visible content).

Capturing the needed screenshots is an important aspect of the system. Because of limited processing power and the possibly CPU-intense capturing process, its frequency and execution points in time had to be considered wisely. Although no delay was noticeable when using the teach pendant in the development setting, the field usage under real circumstances still needs to be evaluated.

Acknowledgements

The research presented is conducted within the Austrian project "AUToMAte – Automatic Usability Testing of Mobile Applications" funded by the Austrian Research Promotion Agency (FFG) under contract number 839094.

References

[1] Kiczales, G., Lamping, J., Mendhekar, A., Maeda, C., Lopes, C. V., Loingtier, J.-M., and Irwin, J. Aspect-oriented programming. In *Proc. ECOOP 1997*, Springer Verlag (1997), 220–242.

[2] Lettner, F., and Holzmann, C. Automated and unsupervised user interaction logging as basis for usability evaluation of mobile applications. In *Proc. MoMM 2012*, ACM Press (2012), 118–127.

[3] Mayring, P. Qualitative content analysis. *Forum: Qualitative Social Research 1*, 2 (2000).

[4] Shen, Z., Wei, J., Ma, K.-L., and Sundaresan, N. Visual cluster exploration of web clickstream data. In *Proc. VAST 2012*, IEEE CS (2012), 3–12.

[5] Ting, I.-H., Kimble, C., and Kudenko, D. UBB mining: Finding unexpected browsing behaviour in clickstream data to improve a web site's design. In *Proc. WI 2005*, IEEE CS (2005), 179–185.

Polly: "Being There" through the Parrot and a Guide

Sven Kratz[1◇], **Don Kimber**[1◇], **Weiqing Su**[2], **Gwen Gordon**[1♠], **Don Severns**[3]

[1]FX Palo Alto Laboratory
3174 Porter Dr.
Palo Alto, CA, 95136, USA
◇lastname@fxpal.com
♠gwengordon@comcast.net

[2]University of California San Diego
San Diego, California, USA
wsu@ucsd.edu

[3]RCManchild
San Francisco, CA, USA
rcmanchild@gmail.com

MobileHCI '14, Sep 23-26 2014, Toronto, ON, Canada,
ACM 978-1-4503-3004-6/14/09
http://dx.doi.org/10.1145/2628363.2628430

Abstract
Telepresence systems usually lack mobility. Polly, a wearable telepresence device, allows users to explore remote locations or experience events remotely by means of a person that serves as a mobile "guide". We built a series of hardware prototypes and our current, most promising embodiment consists of a smartphone mounted on a stabilized gimbal that is wearable. The gimbal enables remote control of the viewing angle as well as providing active image stabilization while the guide is walking. We present qualitative findings from a series of 8 field tests using either Polly or only a mobile phone. We found that guides felt more physical comfort when using Polly vs. a phone and that Polly was accepted by other persons at the remote location. Remote participants appreciated the stabilized video and ability to control camera view. Connection and bandwidth issues appear to be the most challenging issues for Polly-like systems.

Author Keywords
telepresence; remote guiding; wearable; gimbal; user feedback

ACM Classification Keywords
H.5.m [Information interfaces and presentation (e.g., HCI)]: Miscellaneous.

Figure 1: The current Polly prototype consists of a smart phone mounted on a three-axis brushless gimbal that can be carried, placed on perches or flat surfaces, or worn by the guide at shoulder level.

Introduction

Two fundamental human traits are the curiosity to explore our environment and the need to be close to loved ones. Most people have a desire to go outside and visit interesting locations (e.g., museums, zoos or parks) and also to experience events, such as family gatherings or even rock concerts together with other people. However, not everyone is able to fulfill their wishes to explore or be able to be close to their kin. Reasons for this may be that these persons are physically immobile, sick in a hospital or simply very far away from where they would like to be.

To address this issue of mobility and presence, we have developed a wearable system called *Polly*, motivated by the metaphor of a remotely controlled parrot which could rest on someone's shoulder and look around independently of the view of the person carrying it[1]. Polly consists of a three-axis stabilization gimbal driven by silent brushless motors holding a mobile phone that provides the audio and video feed and a connection to the internet. Polly can be carried by hand, placed on "perches", rest on surfaces, or worn by way of a backpack frame with an attachment holding Polly near the shoulder of its wearer.

We implemented an application that lets the remote user control the gimbal orientation (pitch and tilt) from their location. We used Skype[2], Vidyo[3] and Google Hangouts[4] for audio and video transmission, but any suitable software with a mobile client should work with Polly.

We chose a wearable solution since mobile robots are difficult to control and lack mobility over terrain that is not adapted to their style of locomotion (e.g., staircases). The solution we believe that works best with the current level of technology is to use a human "guide" at the location a remote person wishes to visit.[5] Having a human guide who carries or wears the Polly device has the following advantages: (1) the guide is in constant communication with the remote user and can easily understand their wishes, (2) humans are extremely mobile and agile, especially in environments built by and for humans, (3) the guide can mediate conversations between the remote operator and other people encountered and (4) the social interaction between the guide and remote person may be a positive part of the overall experience.

The phone is stabilized by a gimbal, and can be worn on the shoulder for the following reasons: firstly, we thought it would be advantageous for the guide to have two free hands and, secondly, not worry about pointing the camera, but allow the remote operator to do this. Finally, we found that if the mobile phone is worn on a lanyard or mounted rigidly to the wearer, the video quality is significantly reduced while the guide is walking, due to excessive movement in the image. The brushless gimbal uses IMUs for active rotation compensation and leveling to produce a very smooth video feed, much like a steadicam rig, but much smaller in size and weight.

In the rest of this case study, we describe the design process of Polly from its initial prototype to its current shape and contribute a set of initial design observations based on several field deployments of Polly we have conducted in the San Francisco Bay Area, USA and Cleveland, OH, USA.

[1] Also motivated by the remarkably stabilized head pose of many birds. `http://www.youtube.com/watch?v=UytSN1Hw8J8`
[2] `http://www.skype.com`
[3] `http://www.vidyo.com`
[4] `http://www.google.com/hangouts/`

[5] The term *guide* is for expositional brevity. In some scenarios, the remote person may be more familiar with and knowledgable about the space being explored.

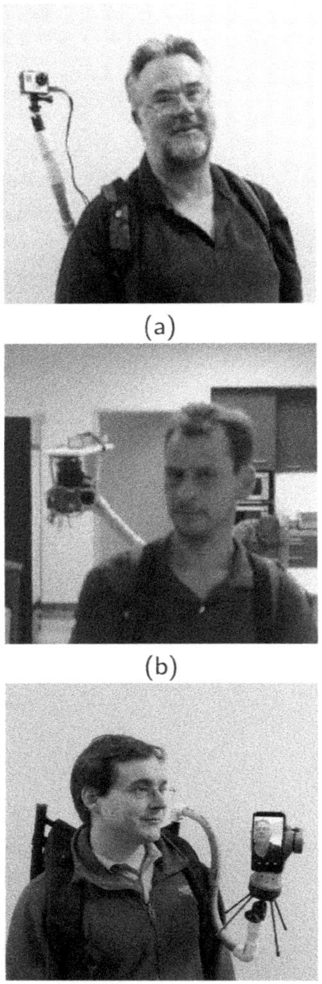

Figure 2: Polly Prototypes—
(a) first frame mounted version,
(b) first stabilized version,
(c) current prototype.

Related Work

Drugge et al. proposed a wearable telepresence system consisting of an HMD and a head-mounted camera [1]. In contrast to Polly, this does not allow the remote participant the same degree of control, as view direction cannot be changed, as is the case using Polly's gimbal. Similarly, systems such as Google Glass streaming to a hangout, or the Tele-actor system [2] do not give the remote user any direct control over view. The MH2 [4] is a shoulder-worn humanoid telepresence robot with a focus on conveying gestures and poses made by the remote participant. Polly, on the other hand is not based on embodiment by physical shape. Rather, a camera image of the remote participant, displayed via a smartphone, is used to embody him or her. *TEROOS* [3] is a shoulder-mounted wearable telepresence system, that is perhaps the wearable telepresence system with the closest resemblance to Polly, as it is also uses a gimbal that is controllable by the remote operator. There are, however, two main differences: firstly, the platform of TEROOS camera does not appear to be stabilized, which, as we found out during initial tests of Polly, makes for very low quality videos while the local operator is walking. Secondly, TEROOS follows the avatar concept, similar to MH2, and uses an abstracted form of embodiment in the shape of a decorated camera. Again, we believe that actually showing the remote operator directly may be advantageous, for example in cases where the mobile user knows the person he is interacting with personally.

Development of the Polly Prototypes

The baseline case for Polly scenarios is what people currently do when no specialized solution is available—they run a videoconferencing app on a phone, tablet or laptop and walk around carrying these devices while trying to communicate with their remote friends.

Our baseline experience consisted of using a phone in this manner, where the phone was hand held, or held by a simple strap. The videoconferencing apps we tried were Skype, Vidyo, and Google hangout. Although none of the apps clearly dominated the others in all respects, overall we had better success in terms of video quality and persistence of connections using Skype.

First frame mounted version

The first mounted prototype (Figure 2 (a)) consisted of a fixed shoulder mount frame with no stabilization gimbal, and a small daypack that could carry a tablet, some digitization hardware, and a battery. We created two versions, one using a Logitech 920C webcam, connected to a Microsoft surface running Skype. Another version used a GoPro which could record HD video onto a SD card, while simultaneously outputting analog video, which was digitized using a USB digitizer. We tried several vendors for USB digitization, including Diamond and Hauppauge. None of them worked well directly as the video input for Skype, but we found that using third party virtual camera programs such as XSplit[6] or ManyCam[7], the video from the GoPro could be input to Skype to be streamed.

First stabilized version

We found two main drawbacks to the baseline and first mounted version. One was the lack of camera direction control by the remote participant. The second was that during walking, the video was very shaky and unpleasant to watch. To address these, the next version (Figure 2 (b)) used a gimbal which provides a sort of steady cam type stabilization, and for which the camera can be pointed remotely. The gimbal used was a three axis brushless motor gimbal designed for a GoPro camera on a

[6] http://www.xsplit.com/
[7] http://www.manycam.com/

small UAV, and using the Alex Mos SimpleBGC[8] board and software. These kind of gimbals have become very popular over the past year and a half for UAV use, and are starting to be used for hand held camera stabilization. The camera direction control inputs to the gimbal are provided as PWM (pulse width modulation) signals, which output from a Pololu USB to PWM device.

As with our first frame mounted prototype, the stabilized GoPro version requires a separate device for running Skype, and because the GoPro output was analog, the video needed to be digitized with the Diamond device. (GoPro also outputs HDMI, but we could not find a good portable solution for making HDMI video available as input to Skype.) One difficulty is that wires carrying the video signal from the cameras must cross three stabilization motor axes, so its not possible to get full travel for the motors. Furthermore the PWM signals from the Pololu device needed to cross the yaw axis. We considered a modified version to address these problem with slip rings, but found problems with high frequency noise with the slip rings.

Current versions

The biggest difficulty we had with the first stabilized version was the complexity of the system requiring the camera, gimbal, multiple USB devices, and MS Surface tablet, in addition to intermediate programs such as XSplit that were necessary in addition to the basic video conferencing program. We decided the best approach for a much simpler more usable device would be an entirely self-contained unit consisting only of the gimbal and a smart phone (Figures 1 and 2 (c).) In this design, the camera, videoconferencing software, and all necessary control software is provided on the phone. The gimbal case contains a battery, and a Bluetooth 4.0 BLE to PWM device which the user never needs to be aware of. That allows a PollyControl App running on the phone to receive messages sent from the remote user, and send the necessary PWM signals to the gimbal via the BLE device. Another advantage of the current self-contained unit is modularity. Polly can be easily carried by snapping it onto a shoulder mounted rig, but can also be carried by hand, or can rest on its own "feet", all while remaining fully functional and being remotely controlled. We are also in the process of designing additional mounting options, including a "perch" which can provide power, allowing permanent operation.

User Interface and Usage Modes

We implemented several versions of user interface for the remote viewer to control Polly. The simplest consists of a wxPython based GUI with sliders for controlling pitch and yaw, which can be used in conjunction with Skype. We also implemented an Oculus Rift based interface where the viewer would see the streamed video on a head mounted display, and head orientation would control the direction of the Polly camera. Most of our usage however has been with a web based interface that allows sliders or arrow keys for controlling the view. We experimented with several usage modes for the prototypes involving stabilization gimbals. One modal distinction is between *angle mode*, in which the yaw or pitch angles are proportional to slider position, and a *speed mode* in which the sliders specify angular velocity. For low latency, the speed mode is easy to use, but when the latency is more than about a half second, it becomes difficult to control. Direct control angle mode works much better as the latency increases.

[8] `http://www.basecamelectronics.com/simplebgc/`

Test ID	Location Type	Region	Scenario	Duration (min)	Device	Software	Connectivity
T1	lab office nuilding	R1	in-office test	45	Polly	Skype	phone data connection
T2	aviation museum	R1	museum visit	60	Polly	Vidyo	location's WiFi
T3	computer store	R1	remote shopping	15	Polly	Skype	location's wiFi
T4	aviation museum	R1	museum visit	45	Polly	Skype	phone data connection
T5	warehouse club	R1	remote shopping	15	phone	Skype	phone data connection
T6	historic costume fair	R1	event visit	60	phone	Skype	phone data connection
T7	conference	R1	conference attendance	20	phone	Skype	location's WiFi
T8	hospital	R2	hospital visit	10	phone	Skype	phone data connection

Table 1: Summary of field the field tests of Polly-style remote interactions conducted so far. Region R1 is the San Francisco Bay Area in California, USA, and Region R2 is the Cleveland Metro Area in Ohio, USA.

Another modal distinction is between *heading lock* mode and *follow* mode. In heading lock mode, the camera points in a fixed direction (although this direction may be controlled by the remote operator) *independently* of how the camera is held or the orientation of the frame of the person carrying it. In follow mode, outside of a small "deadband", the camera will gradually orient so that its yaw is relative to the carrying frame. The heading lock mode is useful when the remote participant wants to look at something independently of the motion of the carrier. Follow mode is useful when the remote viewer wants to look forward (matching the forward direction of the carrier), or look sideways to carry on a discussion with the carrier.

Preliminary Evaluation of Polly

To gain further insight into Polly-style usage scenarios we conducted a total of 8 tests at different locations. Four tests were done with Polly, and four with just a smart phone running a video conferencing software. One reason for this is that we wanted to see how Polly would compare with a less sophisticated solution. Also, some situations without using Polly simply arose spontaneously. As shown in Table 1, studies were conducted at a total of 7 distinct locations, in two different regions of the USA. For video calls Skype was used on 7 and Vidyo on one occasion. The phone's internal data connection (all phones were LTE-capable) was used on 5 occasions and the remote location's publicly accessible WiFi was used on 3 occasions.

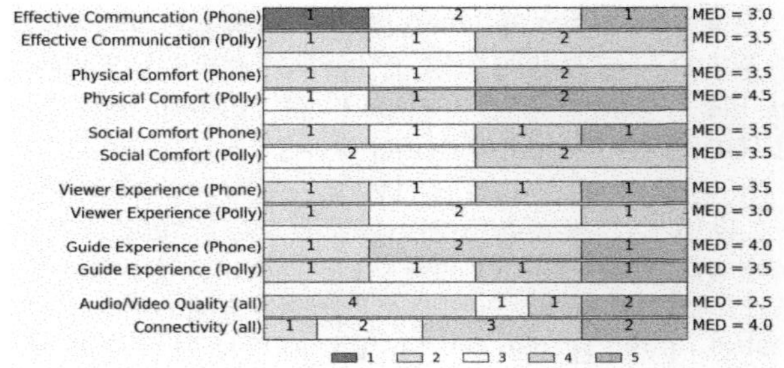

Figure 3: Qualitative feedback obtained from post-test questionnaire. Items were rated on a 5 point Likert scale.

Qualitative Feedback

After each (formal or spontaneous) test, we asked the remote participants and the Polly guide to jointly fill out an online questionnaire with the data represented in Table 1 and, in addition, free-form comments and qualitative statements on a five point Likert scale. Figure 3 shows an overview of the this feedback. Although the sample size so far is too small to do meaningful statistical analysis, Figure 3 does highlight some issues we perceived during the tests. For one, the most negatively rated aspect of the Polly-style interactions was the audio quality, with a median rating of 2.5. This is also reflected in several user comments, e.g., Don commented: "*The real number one problem is poor video quality and dropout.*". Another thing we note is that the median physical comfort rating for the guide was higher when using Polly (4.5 vs. 3.5). Dave made the following comment on this aspect: "*As my hands became more engaged with shopping, I wished I had a Polly mount with me!"*.

Other Observations
One behavior frequently observed was that the remote user would move the camera between looking forward in the direction Polly was being carried, and looking towards the person carrying Polly. The activity of moving the camera view could sometimes be tedious, but made the experience feel less passive. Having presets for forward and for eye-to-eye engagement between local and remote user might be useful. During discussions involving a few people at the Polly location, the remote viewer would often point the camera towards the person talking. This was was fairly easy with only a couple of people staying relatively fixed, but could be confusing with more people or when people moved more.

Discussion and Future Work

The single biggest difficulty we had in using and testing the system was getting a consistently high enough bandwidth connection to maintain good video and audio quality. However, we expect that over the next few years this will become less of an issue and devices like Polly will find increased use. Furthermore, the capability of recording high quality video on Polly while streaming whatever lower quality is supported by the wireless network allows for the production of a high quality video after the fact. Our earlier GoPro based prototypes had this capability, and we expect to add it to our future versions.

Our personal experience and the limited initial tests suggest several hypotheses. These include: (1) Stabilized camera motion is much more pleasing than jerky motion from unstabilized hand held or head mounted views, (2) The ability to control the camera gives a sense of engagement, even when it is not being exercised, (3) Bad audio can lead to the remote person feeling "left out" of the experience even when they feel in control of their camera view.

Based on these results, we plan to next identify specific interesting locations that provide consistent wireless network, and do more careful studies based on larger numbers of users, particularly drawn from special populations with mobility issues such as seniors, or the disabled.

Acknowledgments

Gimbal technology and design work for this project were provided by RCManChild. (`http://rcmanchild.com/`)

References

[1] Drugge, M., Nilsson, M., Parviainen, R., and Parnes, P. Experiences of using wearable computers for ambient telepresence and remote interaction. In *Proc. 2004 ACM SIGMM workshop on Effective telepresence*, ACM (2004), 2–11.

[2] Goldberg, K. Y., Song, D., Khor, Y.-N., Pescovitz, D., Levandowski, A., Himmelstein, J. C., Shih, J., Ho, A., Paulos, E., and Donath, J. S. Collaborative online teleoperation with spatial dynamic voting and a human "tele-actor". In *ICRA*, IEEE (2002), 1179–1184.

[3] Kashiwabara, T., Osawa, H., Shinozawa, K., and Imai, M. Teroos: a wearable avatar to enhance joint activities. In *Proc. 2012 ACM annual conference on Human Factors in Computing Systems*, ACM (2012), 2001–2004.

[4] Tsumaki, Y., Ono, F., and Tsukuda, T. The 20-dof miniature humanoid mh-2: A wearable communication system. In *ICRA*, IEEE (2012), 3930–3935.

UX Suite: A Touch Sensor Evaluation Platform

Justin Mockler
Synaptics, Inc.
1251 McKay Drive
San Jose, CA 95131 USA
justin.mockler@synaptics.com

MobileHCI '14, Sep 23-26 2014, Toronto, ON, Canada
ACM 978-1-4503-3004-6/14/09.
http://dx.doi.org/10.1145/2628363.2628431

Abstract
We present UX Suite, which is a set of free testing tools that can be downloaded and used to evaluate the touch sensor performance of Android devices. The tools in the application focus on evaluating touchscreen sensor quality and human performance on mobile devices. Current tests include the Fitts' test, which is one of the most widely accepted predictive models for testing the accuracy of target selection, and an accidental activation test. Additional tests will be included in the future that will measure other characteristics of the touch sensor. This paper discusses the application and a user study that was conducted to assess the application's usability. The results of this study show that users are able and willing to complete the tests in the application without a moderator. Due to the remote testing features, this will allow large, distributed user studies to be run with little oversight from researchers.

Author Keywords
Fitts' law; testing tools; mobile; Android.

ACM Classification Keywords
H.5.2. Information interfaces and presentation: User Interfaces – Benchmarking, Input devices and strategies.

Introduction

Although there are many applications for conducting Fitts' tests that can be downloaded online for researchers to utilize, no tools have been identified which are currently compatible with Android-based devices. This is in stark contrast to the large number of these devices that currently exist. As shown by previously developed applications and research on the topic, researchers and practitioners find these tools very important in order to assess performance of systems regardless of their operating system. Touchscreen performance on mobile devices is especially important due to issues like non-linearity across the surface, poor edge performance, industrial design limitations, varied usage environments, and a wide range of form factors.

We developed an application to conduct large-scale, remote user studies on Android devices for research related to touchscreen sensor quality and performance on mobile devices. Although we believe it's important to conduct in-person, synchronous user research, the large amount of data collection that this application enables will help inform more traditional user studies in the future. This tool is an additional resource to the current testing tools that have been created internally by Synaptics to assess selection on different operating systems for other input devices, such as touchpads.

Another focus of the application was to improve the process of conducting user studies, data collection, and analysis and make it as painless as possible by eliminating inefficiencies with the usability study process. The application was designed to be a platform for multiple tests that can evaluate different characteristics of touch sensors instead of solely being dedicated to conducting one type of test. Our contribution is this set of free testing tools that follows the ISO/TS 9241-411 standard for evaluation methods for the design of physical input devices [5]. The application can be downloaded for public use via the Synaptics website to assist other researchers and practitioners who want to conduct similar research.

Related Work

Bi et al. [2] derived the FFitts model, which is an expansion and also refinement of Fitts' law for finger touch input. The authors conducted their experiments on an application built for the HTC Nexus smartphone running the Android OS. Other applications such as WinFitts by the University of Oregon [4], FittsStudy [3], and The Generalized Fitts' Law Model Builder [9] only work on Windows-based devices. Similarily, Model Builder was built to work on the Apple Macintosh [11]. Movement Time Evaluator by Schedlbaur [7] was written in Java for cross-platform compatibility, but does not work on Android-based devices.

Waterson et al. [10] found that users who were conducting studies remotely were fairly good at finding usability issues related to web content displayed on the screen of the device. However, the authors found that remote studies were not comparable to an in-person study for finding usability issues with the device itself. Andreasen et al. [8] found that conducting studies with remote users synchronously was virtually equivalent to the conventional method. However, when performed asynchronously the authors found that users could identify less usability problems as the tradeoff for relieving the researchers from extensive work and enabling large data collection. Thompson et al. [6] found similar results that synchronous testing is just as effective as traditional testing. The authors also found that asynchronous testing caused the loss of "think aloud" data, user feedback, and real-time debriefing information.

Platform Capabilities

The application was built both for researchers who are performing usability studies with participants in-person as well as for participants who are remotely located and unfamiliar with the usability study process. Android was chosen as the operating system for our research platform as it is open source and is used for a variety of different devices including development boards, television set-top boxes, laptops, tablets, and mobile phones. The broad range of different form factors related to the types of devices above makes Android an ideal platform for creating a tool to simplify the challenges in evaluating device usability characteristics. Other reasons include that Android has a large market share and that the OS supports mouse, stylus, and touch inputs.

The power of the platform comes from the combination of a web-based control panel that interacts with an Android application that's installed on a device.

Web Control Panel

The control panel for the application resides on an external web server that researchers can interact with through their browser. They are able to set default values for the test that are populated to the device at launch without having to update or adjust the settings in the application manually. The values that can be automatically set include typical Fitts' test values including widths, distances, angles, and replications. Specific settings for Android devices that can be updated include orientations and error feedback. Most of the user-facing messages inside the application can be updated remotely including the description and instruction cards that are shown on the Fitts' test main page. Other optional messages that can be set include an introduction dialog as well as pre-survey and post-survey dialogs. All of these settings can be specified either across all applicable devices or customized on a device-by-device basis.

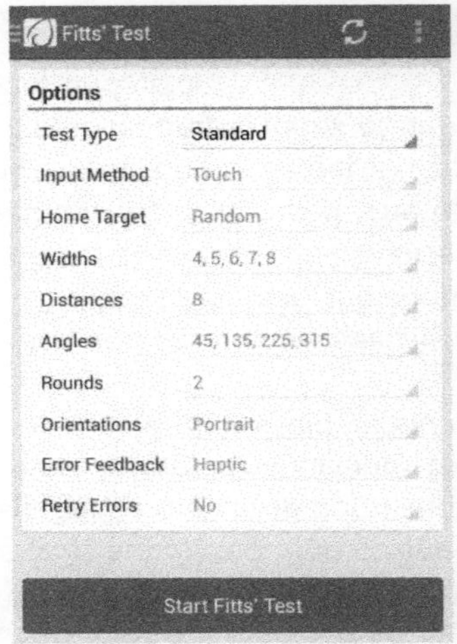

Figure 1. Screen capture of the Fitts' test settings.

Performance data from each study is automatically uploaded to the remote server at the end of each session where researchers can then manage results by downloading or clearing the data file. The result files are downloaded in a standard CSV format for easy importing and analysis in most statistical applications. The application also hooks into Google Drive to handle post-test surveys in order to ease survey creation and analysis. A randomly generated identifier is passed along to both the web-based control panel as well as Google Drive to match up performance and survey results.

Application
The application works on any Android-based device running an OS version of 4.0 (Ice Cream Sandwich) or later, which accounts for 84.3% of active devices at the time of this writing [1].

If the researcher chooses, then the previously discussed network functionality can be disabled and the tests included in the application will save the resulting data files to the internal storage of the device. The researcher can also adjust various settings within the application including the test background color, default audio level, default haptic strength, and whether results are shown to the participant at the end of the test session.

Figure 2. Screen capture of the Fitts' test in the application.

Output Data File
A small portion of the output file can be seen below in Figure 3. The file is a standard CSV file with headers dedicated to session identifiers, device information, test configuration, and the test results.

The test metadata that are included in the output file include what version of the application was used, the time the result was submitted, and a randomly generated identifier to match up performance and result data. Device information includes the manufacturer, model, and Android version.

Test configuration and results are specific to the individual test. For the Fitts' test, the configuration details include feedback types, device orientation, and what input method was being used. The test results follow the typical reporting of target XY, touch XY, target width, distance, angle, index of difficulty, movement time, and error.

Manufact	Model	OS	Rnd	Targ X	Targ Y	Touch X	Touch Y	Width	Dist	Angle	ID	MT	Err
Samsung	SGH-M919	4.2.2	1	1016	1558	1016	1554	5	48	315	3.41	1060	0
Samsung	SGH-M919	4.2.2	1	806	377	824	393	3	10	135	2.12	562	0
Samsung	SGH-M919	4.2.2	1	688	1051	715	1048	6	10	45	1.42	366	0
Samsung	SGH-M919	4.2.2	1	624	1069	641	1085	2	10	45	2.58	388	1
Samsung	SGH-M919	4.2.2	1	637	1382	633	1393	4	10	315	1.81	453	0
Samsung	SGH-M919	4.2.2	1	267	766	290	762	4	48	135	3.7	573	0
Samsung	SGH-M919	4.2.2	1	159	1140	195	1158	6	48	135	3.17	529	0
Samsung	SGH-M919	4.2.2	1	316	252	323	267	3	48	135	4.09	573	0
Samsung	SGH-M919	4.2.2	1	253	1421	276	1410	6	10	225	1.42	227	0
Samsung	SGH-M919	4.2.2	1	675	1580	668	1558	5	10	315	1.58	279	0

Figure 3. Sample output of the application with values removed related to test configuration and completion time.

User Study
An internal user study was conducted on the application to assess application usability and the self-moderated study process. All participants conducted the Fitts' test

Day	# Completed
Monday	12
Tuesday	2
Wednesday	1
Thursday	1
Friday	2

Table 1. Most participants completed the study the same day when installing the application on their own device.

within the UX Suite application. Subjective questionnaires were administered after the test through an embedded Google Drive survey within the application.

Participants were given instructions on how to download the application on their personal device. The goal of using the participant's device was that it would be familiar and potentially ease the installation and conducting of the test. One of the benefits using this approach was that a large variety of devices with different properties, including device sizes and touch sensor manufacturers, could be collected. All instructions for the user study, except how to install the application, were shown inside the application after being remotely downloaded from an internal web server.

Results

Over a five day period, eighteen internal participants completed the research study. When asked about the instructions that were included inside the app, fifteen participants (83%) said they were "very clear", two participants (11%) said "clear" and one participant (5%) answered "neutral." No participants responded that the instructions were "confusing" or "very confusing." Sixteen (89%) of the participants said completing the study without a moderator present was "very easy" while two participants (11%) answered that it was "easy." No participants responded that completing the study was "difficult," "very difficult," or "neutral." All participants (100%) said they would complete more self-moderated in the future.

Compared to a preliminary study that was conducted prior to this user study, participants completed this study much faster. The preliminary study showed that a total of five participants were able to complete the study in seven days when an unfamiliar device was dropped off at their desk. The current study showed that, utilizing personal devices, eighteen participants completed the study in five days. The results related to when participants completed this user study can be seen in Table 1.

Discussion

More than half of the user study participants completed the test on the same day the instructions were sent out via email. Of note in the results was that most participants believed that the instructions inside the application were "very clear" and that completing the study without a moderator present was "very easy." The result that showed all participants would complete more asynchronous, self-moderated studies in the future was very encouraging and has justified the continued refinement of the application and self-moderated process.

Conclusion

UX Suite allows the conducting of competitive benchmarking and evaluation of touch sensors with very little oversight while allowing researchers to focus their time on synchronous research studies that require a moderator to be present. Current plans for the application include the addition of more tests, which could include ways to evaluate linearity, edge sensitivity, and proximity performance. Since the beginning of the year, the application has been tested internally at Synaptics and some other industry partners.

Interested researchers and practitioners can download the Android and server applications by visiting http://www.synaptics.com/en/uxsuite.php, where future updates about the testing tools will be published. The hope is that the different types of tests and time-saving features implemented in these tools are valuable to others who are evaluating touchscreen sensor quality and human performance on mobile devices.

The plan in the distant future is to market the application to end-users on the Google Play store in order to do distributed data collection with those who want to participate in mobile device research, but are either located remotely or unfamiliar with the usability study process. Having access to that breadth of data from so many diverse devices will help accelerate the process of evaluating mobile devices with the goal of creating better and more accurate touch sensors in the future.

Acknowledgements

The author wishes to thank the members of the User Experience Design Team at Synaptics for providing feedback during the design and development of the application. The author would also like to thank all the Synaptics employees who participated in testing the application.

References

[1] Android Developer Dashboards. http://developer.android.com/about/dashboards/index.html

[2] Bi, X., Li, Y., and Zhai, S. FFitts law: Modeling finger touch with Fitt's law. In ACM Conference on Human Factors in Computing Systems (CHI), ACM (2013).

[3] FittsStudy. http://depts.washington.edu/aimgroup/proj/fittsstudy/

[4] Human Computer Interaction (HCI) at the University of Oregon. http://www.cs.uoregon.edu/research/hci/research/winfitts.html.

[5] ISO/TS 9241-411:2012 - Ergonomics of human-system interaction -- Part 411: Evaluation methods for the design of physical input devices. http://www.iso.org/iso/home/store/catalogue_tc/catalogue_detail.htm?csnumber=54106.

[6] Katherine E. Thompson, Evelyn P. Rozanski, and Anne R. Haake. 2004. Here, there, anywhere: remote usability testing that works. In Proceedings of the 5th conference on Information technology education (CITC5 '04).

[7] Martin J. Schedlbaur. 2007. An extensible platform for the interactive exploration of Fitts' Law and related movement time models. In CHI '07 Extended Abstracts on Human Factors in Computing Systems (CHI EA '07).

[8] Morten Siker Andreasen, Henrik Villemann Nielson, Simon Ormholt Schrøder, and Jan Stage. 2007. What happened to remote usability testing?: an empiricial study of three methods. In Proceedings of the SIGCHI Conference on Human Factors in Computing Systems (CHI '07).

[9] R. William Soukoreff and I. Scott MacKenzie. 1995. Generalized Fitts' law model builder. In Conference Companion on Human Factors in Computing Systems (CHI '95).

[10] Sarah Waterson, James A. Landay, and Tara Matthews. 2002. In the lab and out in the wild: remote usability testing for mobile devices. In CHI '02 Extended Abstracts on Human Factors in Computing Systems (CHI EA '02).

[11] Scott MacKenzie and William Buxton. 1993. A tool for the rapid evaluation of input devices using Fitts' law models. SIGCHI Bull. 25, 3 (July 1993), 58-63.

Design and Field Testing of a System for Remote Monitoring of Sea Turtle Nests

Thomas G. Zimmerman
IBM Research-Almaden
San Jose, CA 95138
tzim@us.ibm.com

Britta Muiznieks
Cape Hatteras
National Seashore
National Park Service
Britta_muiznieks@nps.gov

Eric Kaplan
Hatteras Island Ocean Center
Hatteras, NC 27943
ekaplan@hioceancenter.org

Samuel Wantman
NerdsWithoutBorders
sam@wantman.net

Lou Browning
Hatteras Island
Wildlife Rehabilitation
Frisco, NC 27936
loub@hiwr.us

Eric Frey
Cape Hatteras
National Seashore
National Park Service
eric_frey@nps.gov

MobileHCI 2014, September 23–26, 2014, Toronto, ON, Canada.
ACM 978-1-4503-3004-6/14/09.
http://dx.doi.org/10.1145/2628363.2628432

Abstract
Protective barriers are often deployed to safely guide sea turtle hatchlings to the ocean but the barriers are contentious for they impede foot and vehicle traffic of beach users. Our goal is to develop a wireless system that can detect sea turtle hatching to enable "just in time deployment" of barriers, and notify tourists so they can watch sea turtles emerge from nests, generating awareness and compassion for these endangered species. We report on the development of a sensor and data acquisition system capable of detecting nest hatching activity in the harsh environment of a beach, including sensor selection, wireless networking, low-power design, data processing and environmental packaging. Field tests confirm the suitability of a low-cost low-power three-axis accelerometer and mobile networks for detecting and remotely communicating sea turtle hatching activity.

Author Keywords
Remote monitoring; wireless; sensors; monitoring biological systems; data acquisition.

ACM Classification Keywords
C.3 [SPECIAL-PURPOSE AND APPLICATION-BASED SYSTEMS] -Microprocessor/microcomputer applications,

Figure 1. Flipper trail produced by female sea turtle crawl from the ocean to nest.

Figure 2. Black pipe contains batteries, microprocessor and phone. Wire cable runs under sand to top of turtle nest 2 meters towards ocean and about 30 cm below the sand.

Real-time and embedded systems, Signal processing systems.

Introduction

Female turtles lay their eggs on beaches, often in proximity to tourists and residents (Figure 1). When hatchlings emerge from a nest, the trough created by tire tracks on the sand and residential house lights can steer them away from the ocean.

The sea turtles on Cape Hatteras, North Carolina are protected by the National Parks Service (NPS). Current protocol is to erect the barricade from the nest to the ocean 50 days after a nest is discovered and remove it after hatching or 90 days, when the nest is determined to be not viable. The barricade is a major source of contention between the beach-goers and the NPS, as it blocks recreational vehicles and pedestrian movement. A hatching notification system could provide a win-win-win solution for the sea turtles, the NPS and the beach-enjoying public. Barricades could be erected a few days prior to hatching, minimizing their impact on residents and tourists. Hotels could help tourists schedule nighttime nest visits to see a "boil", when a hundred hatchlings emerge from their sandy nest and scurry to the ocean. Encouraging participation in this eco-tourist event can build awareness and empathy for the plight of sea turtles.

Rallying around this challenge, a team quickly formed and relationships established among an industrial research lab, ecology education non-profit, government agency and community volunteers, contributing skills in electrical engineering, computer science, wireless communication, mechanical engineering, hardware fabrication, marine biology, community relations and fund raising. This paper focuses on the initial design, selection and field-testing of components to create a system (Figure 2) capable of wirelessly monitoring *in-situ* sea turtle hatching events.

Related Work

Researchers have incorporated environmental sensors in mobile phones to monitor the environment [4][2]. Mesh networks have been used to provide wireless connectivity when mobile service is not available [1]. The ZebraNet project uses peer-to-peer networks to track wildlife [5]. Minimizing power consumption is essential for remote wireless monitoring systems and can be achieved by combining and managing multiple processing components [10].

There are surprisingly few published experiments on monitoring and detecting *in-situ* sea turtle hatching. Japanese engineers from Epson have installed mechanical tilt detectors in sea turtle nests to detect hatching [9]. In March 2013 researchers at University of Malaysia Terengganu's (UMT) Sea Turtle Research Unit (SEATRU) [8] began a project to monitor temperature, humidity and motion of sea turtle nests, powered by solar panels. However, their efforts were hampered during the rainy season by insufficient solar energy, reinforcing the need for low-power monitoring and communication. It is more common to monitor nest temperature to study temperature-dependent sex determination [6] and track sea turtles in the ocean using satellite radios attached to their shell [3].

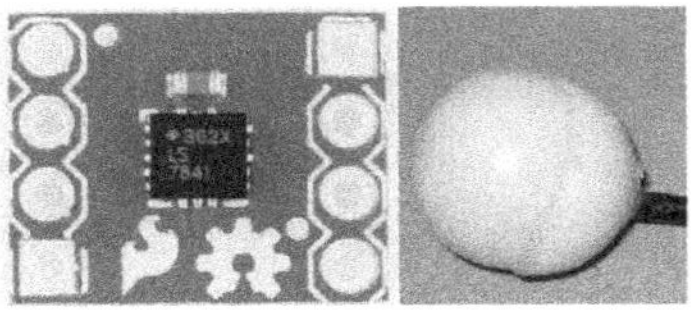

Figure 3. Accelerometer mounted on breakout board *(L)* installed in a plastic ping-pong ball filled with silicon sealer or epoxy *(R)* connected to 8-conductor cable.

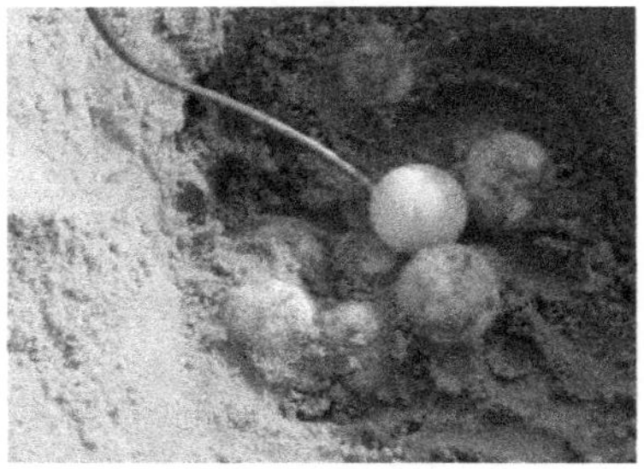

Figure 4. Egg-sensor containing an accelerometer sensor packed in a plastic ping-pong ball with silicon sealer or epoxy is installed on top of sea turtle nest.

Design Objectives

The long-term objective of our work is to produce a sea turtle nest monitoring system that can be practically deployed by field technicians and automatically communicate with a remote server that will electronically notify interested parties on nest status, including the prediction of hatching. The objective of the initial work reported here is to make and deploy a "first version" system to determine appropriate sensing technology and system components.

The project started in the middle of the 2013-hatching season so the top priority was to quickly get a working sensor in the field and collect data to get an indication of the magnitude and frequency of hatching events, to validate the suitability of the selected sensor.

Previous temperature monitoring experiments take samples every two hours, so we use this as our sampling interval. As we don't know how to predict hatching, the first system should send a summary of nest activity at the end of every sampling interval (two hours). To minimize power consumption, the data summary must fit in one text message (<160 characters), and the system must operate autonomously for at least 90 days (the maximum hatching period) in the wet, hot, salty, sandy environment of the unprotected Barrier islands.

System Components

Hatching Sensor

Sea turtles are cold-blooded so the nest temperature tracks the ambient temperature and would therefore probably not be a good indicator of hatching. Measuring respiration gasses like oxygen and carbon dioxide are difficult in a wet environment and gas sensors consume considerable power.

The hatchlings use a temporary tooth to break out of their leathery shell. The eggs are packed tightly together, over one hundred to a nest. The young hatchlings wiggle their way to the top of the nest so they can emerge en-mass. Our hypothesis is motion would be a good feature to detect hatching. Fortunately, the wide commercial use of motion sensing in tablets and phones creates a large market for small low-cost low-power multi-axis accelerometers.

We selected the ADXL362 Analog Devices Micro-power, 3-Axis, Digital Output MEMS Accelerometer (Figure 3, *left*). The sensor is inexpensive (<$15), compact (3.3 mm square), sensitive (1 mG/LSB), extremely low power (<2 uA) and includes a digital thermometer (+/- 0.5 C sensitivity). The accelerometer is surface mounted on a circuit board inside a plastic ping-pong ball (Figure 3, *right*), which is about the same shape and appearance as a sea turtle egg (Figure 4). Two versions were prepared for field-testing, one filled with silicone sealer, the other filled with epoxy. We operate the accelerometer at maximum sensitivity and gain (1 uG/LSB) and maximum filter cutoff (400 Hz) to increase the chance of detecting hatching activity.

Microprocessor

A Texas Instruments MSP430F2013 microprocessor operating in low frequency mode at 32kHz (<10 uA), programmed in C, samples the X, Y, Z acceleration and temperature 30 times a second for two hours, accumulating the absolute change in acceleration (known in physics as "jerk") into 10 bins that are logarithmically weighted, creating a jerk amplitude histogram with a dynamic range of 1:1000 (Table 1). Bin 1 contains jerk events with magnitude 1 uG, Bin 2=2 uG events, Bin

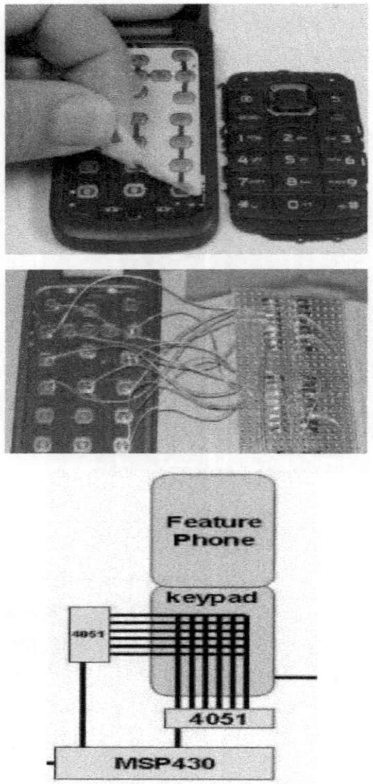

Figure 5. Plastic key overlay is removed from phone *(top)* and exposed keypads are wired to switches *4015 (middle)* controlled by microprocessor *MSP430 (bottom)* to simulate key presses.

3=4 uG events, etc. Every two hours the jerk histogram bins, average temperature and sensor orientation are sent as an SMS text message, encoded as alpha-numeric characters.

The SMS packet format, summarizing the nest activity in a 2 hour sampling interval, is as follows--time temp X Y Z b10 b9 b8 b7 b6 b5 b4 b3 b2 b1-- where *time* is the software counter, *temp* is the nest temperature, *X Y Z* is the orientation of the sensor, and *b1-b10* are the jerk amplitude histogram bins. The *time* software counter confirms that the microprocessor has been continually running during the sampling interval.

Wireless Radio
Many remote sensing research projects use smart phones or cellular modules to send data over the commercial cellular infrastructure. The former use data plans that are relatively expensive and require a development system and often software license targeted to a particular operating system. The latter are hardware modules designed for machine-to-machine (M2M) communication, a field that is experiencing rapid growth as businesses network remote devices to their electronic information infrastructure [7] [4].

To meet our goal of fast deployment we wired the microprocessor to the keypad of a conventional feature phone with CMOS switches [11] (Figure 5, *bottom*), enabling the microprocessor to operate the phone as a human would by electrically "pushing" buttons.

System Power
The phone is turned on for about 2 minutes to send an SMS text message every two hours. The rest of the time the phone is completely shut down. We found the safest and easiest way to extend the phone battery life is to plug in an external battery pack into the phones' power jack, simulating a wall transformer.

To improve charging efficiency the external battery pack is electrically connected to the phone every tenth message (about once a day), resulting in an average energy consumption of 3.4 mAhr/call, providing more than 100 days of operation with 4 "D" batteries.

System Enclosure
To survive the harsh conditions of the exposed beach we enclose the system electronics in 4" PVC pipe (Figure 6) which is bolted to a 4" PVC pipe cast in cement in a 14 liter bucket, to provide a stable base that discourages theft (Figure 7). A sensor (Cat5) cable inside the tower pipe emerges from a 2.5 cm hole drilled in the side, at the base of the pipe and travels under the sand to the turtle nest sensor 2 meters away (blue cable at base of tower in Figure 7).

Since hatching happens at least 50 days after a nest is laid, and sensors are installed when a nest is first discovered, the data collection system hardware (called "communication head") can be installed up to 50 days after the sensor is installed.

Backend Data Processing
Every two hours the deployed system sends a text message to the authors email account summarizing motion data ("jerk amplitude histogram") collected over the past two hours. Several times a day the author previews emails to confirm that the units are working and look for movement (e.g. signals in the upper bins). Every few days all of the text emails from systems in the field are exported as a text file and processed with a

Figure 6. Phone, electronics and batteries *(L)* are packed inside 4" PVC pipe with Styrofoam *(R)*. A magnet under blue tape *(R)* engages an internal reed switch that turns off the system during storage and shipping.

Figure 7. Commutation head is attached to pipe anchored in a cement bucket. A blue cable at tower base connects to the egg sensor in the sea turtle nest 2 meters away.

program written in Python to convert the text messages into a comma separated value (CSV) file that can be viewed and plotted using Excel (Figure 8).

Field Evaluation

Five egg-sensors and three communication heads were deployed between August and November 2013. Figure 8 shows two days of typical temperature data and 5 days of bin 2 movement data from a system operating in the field. As it was late in the hatching season, we shuffled the communication heads among the sensors, attempting to find a viable nest where hatching activity might occur. One instrumented nest was washed over, drowning the nest. Most of the other nests were not viable, as they were late in the season and the weather was rather cold. One of the last nests we visited had one live hatchling in the top of the nest that was lethargic and another one underneath that was coming out of the egg. An egg sensor was placed on the nest and the next day we detected a large motion in one of the two-hour sample windows. Referring to Table 1, bin 2 (B2) established a baseline in the 400-event range. Bin 1 is not shown for it is saturated (65,536) due to mechanical and electrical noise arising from the high gain and wide open filter settings in the accelerometer. For the sampling interval between 6:29 and 8:36 AM (local time) there was significant motion detected.

Corrosion was detected on the RJ11 Ethernet connector that attaches the sensor cable to the communication head and will be replaced with a larger Molex connector, similar to those used in automotive applications. Corrosion was also detected on the sensor circuit board packed with silicon sealer, so future sensor boards will be coated with epoxy.

Our first unit used black PVC pipe that became very hot in the sun. Subsequent units use white PVC pipe that also blends well with the environment. Cementing lower PVC joints prevents water entry and press-fitting upper joins with grease allows disassembly while maintaining hermetic seals. Adding a desiccant bag inside the pipe removes any residual moisture that could otherwise condense during cold nights.

Conclusion

The field trial successfully demonstrates the use of a three-axis accelerometer and wireless data collection system to remotely detect hatching events. The combination of a low-power accelerometer, low-power microprocessor, small data payload, and turning the phone on only during data transmissions, all contribute to a very low power system.

Although we got a late start and only detected hatching activity in one sampling window, the magnitude of the hatching signal was eight times the background noise (bin 5 vs. bin 2) and 1/32 of full scale (bin 5 vs. bin 10), indicating that hatching activity signals are within the sensitivity and dynamic range of the accelerometer, and demonstrating the value of having a logarithmic representation of the jerk amplitude histogram.

Placing the motion sensor on top of the nest makes for a convenient installation, with minimal disturbance to the nest, and should produce large signals, as the hatchlings must pass by the sensor as they rise to the surface of the sand on their way to the ocean.

Separating the sensor from the communication head provides deployment flexibility and convenience. Sensors are small and inexpensive and can be carried by field

Table 1. Jerk amplitude histogram bins shows hatching motion at time interval 8:36. B2=2uG B3=4uG B4=8uG B5=16uG

Time	B5	B4	B3	B2
6:29	0	0	0	454
8:36	47	111	177	710
10:42	0	0	0	560

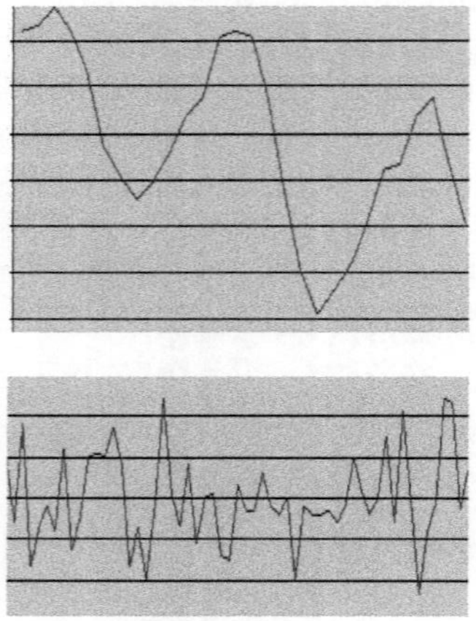

Figure 8. Two days of temperature (0.5 C/division) *(upper)* and bin 2 motion events of 2 uG magnitude (10

technicians while searching for nests. The heavier and more expensive communication head can be installed 50 days after the nest discovery, improving resource utilization.

The next phase of the project is currently underway for the 2014-nesting season. We have included a microprocessor in the egg sensor to hold calibration data, differential line drivers to speed up sensor data transfer, and replaced the phone with a General Radio Packet Service (GPRS) modem. The system is powered by 8 rechargeable NiMiH "AA" size batteries, packed in a 3" PVC pipe to operate the entire hatching season (~7 months) on a single charge. The objective of the second phase is to deploy enough systems in enough nests to gather sufficient data to develop an algorithm to predict hatching and the emergence of hatchlings.

Acknowledgements
The authors would like to thank David Hermeyer for electrical engineering support, the Superintendent and Deputy Superintendent, the field technicians who monitored the test sites, Marie Reed for procuring supplies and North Carolina State biologist Matthew Godfrey for granting us an Endangered Species Permit to conduct this research.

References

[1] Banerjee, N., Corner, M., Levine, B. Design and field experimentation of an energy-efficient architecture for DTN throwboxes. IEEE/ACM Transactions on Networking archive, Vol 18 Issue 2 (2010), 554-567

[2] Eisenman, S.B., Miluzzo, E., Lane, N.D., Peterson, R.A., Ahn, G.-S. and Campbell, A.T. The BikeNet Mobile Sensing System for Cyclist Experience Mapping. Proc. SenSys ACM Press (2007), 87-101.

[3] Godley, B., Blumenthal, J., Broderick, A., Coyne ,M., Godfrey, M., Hawkes, L., Witt,M. Satellite tracking of sea turtles: Where have we been and where do we go next? Endangered Species Research, Vol 3 (2007)

[4] Honicky, R., Brewer, E., Paulos, E., White, R. N-SMARTS: Networked Suite of Mobile Atmospheric Real-time Sensors. NSDR, Seattle, Washington (2008)

[5] Juang, P., Oki, H., Wang, Y., Martonosi, M., Peh, L. S., Rubenstein, D. Energy-efficient computing for wildlife tracking: Design tradeoffs and early experiences with ZebraNet. ACM Sigplan Notices, Vol. 37, No. 10 (2002) 96-107

[6] Morreale, S., Ruiz, G., Spotila, J., Standora, E. Temperature-dependent sex determination: current practices threaten conservation of sea turtles. Science 1982 Jun 11, 216:4551 (1982), 1245-7.

[7] Saran, C. Cisco predicts machine-to-machine traffic will increase 22-fold. Computer Weekly (2012)

[8] Sea Turtle Research Unit (SEATRU) of Universiti Malaysia Terengganu http://seatru.umt.edu.my/research-2/inest-monitoring-system/

[9] Solon, O. Wireless sensor networks aid turtle conservation in Japan. Wired.Co.UK (2013) http://www.wired.co.uk/news/archive/2013-02/06/turtle-conservation-epson

[10] Sorber, J., Banerjee, N., Corner, M., Rollins, S. Turducken: Hierarchical Power Management for Mobile Devices. MobiSys (2005), 261-274

[11] Zimmerman, T., Chang, K. Simplifying home health monitoring by incorporating a cell phone in a weight scale. PETRA, Athens, Greece (2008)

Author Index

www.ingramcontent.com/pod-product-compliance
Ingram Content Group UK Ltd.
Pitfield, Milton Keynes, MK11 3LW, UK
UKHW051418290926
15471UKWH00009B/1669

9 781450 333689